Admiralty Record®

Volume 5

PUBLISHED ADMIRALTY OPINIONS OF
THE SUPREME COURT OF THE UNITED STATES AND
THE UNITED STATES COURTS OF APPEALS ISSUED DURING
THE CALENDAR YEAR

2017

Cite as: 5 Adm. R. _____

REPORTED BY KIRK N. AURANDT, ESQ.
MEMBER OF THE BAR IN LOUISIANA AND PENNSYLVANIA

ADMIRALTY RECORD PUBLISHING COMPANY, L.L.C.
MANDEVILLE, LOUISIANA, U.S.A.

ISSN 2334-5411
ISBN 978-0-9983853-8-9

Admiralty record: published admiralty opinions of the Supreme Court of the United States and the United States Courts of Appeals issued during the calendar year ... Mandeville, Louisiana, U.S.A.: Admiralty Record Publishing Company, LLC, 2014-

KF1104 .A75
ISSN: 2334-5411

https://lccn.loc.gov/2014200303

PREFACE

Volume 5—the fifth annual edition of the *Admiralty Record*®—reports the published admiralty opinions of the Supreme Court of the United States and the United States Courts of Appeals that were issued during the calendar year 2017. The opinions reported are the original majority, concurring, and dissenting opinions of the Court, with only minor changes in formatting to better suit a dual-column presentation. The pagination found in the Court's original opinion is indicated by the number contained inside of black brackets, *see, e.g.*, **[—15—]**. The pagination found in the official Reporter is indicated by the number contained inside of black braces, *see, e.g.*, **{–15–}**. Also, where applicable, I have added parallel citations to opinions reported in this Volume and in prior Volumes of the *Admiralty Record*®.

The decision to select an opinion to appear in Volume 5 of the *Admiralty Record*® was made solely by me following an examination of those opinions that each of the above-named courts designated for publication in 2017. Every effort has been made to ensure inclusion of all 2017 federal appellate court admiralty opinions that were designated for publication; however, to the extent that a relevant admiralty opinion has been inadvertently overlooked or otherwise mistakenly omitted, the error is regretted and is solely my own. A few opinions from appeals in civil cases that technically may not have fallen under a federal district court's admiralty or maritime jurisdiction have been reported if they touched upon admiralty matters, or were otherwise deemed to be of potential interest to the admiralty practitioner. Additionally, several opinions from criminal cases involving maritime crimes and civil cases arising under the Federal Employers' Liability Act have been included.

To assist the reader in locating those opinions from 2017 involving subject matters of interest, I have prepared an Index to the opinions. I have also prepared Tables of Authority, which supply page references to the cases, statutes, and rules cited in each opinion. Prior to relying upon any of the opinions reported herein, the reader is reminded to verify the current status of any particular case as valid precedent by checking the case with a reliable citator.

Additional copies of Volume 1 (covering 2013), Volume 2 (covering 2014), Volume 3 (covering 2015), Volume 4 (covering 2016), Volume 5 (covering 2017) and succeeding-year Volumes may be ordered at www.admiraltyrecord.com. I hope that the *Admiralty Record*® will become a valuable and ready reference source for not only the admiralty practitioner, but for anyone who is interested in reading the published admiralty opinions of the federal appellate courts.

KIRK N. AURANDT, ESQ.

This page intentionally left blank

Table of Contents[1]

(Cases arranged chronologically by Court)

[1] In 2017, there were no published admiralty opinions from the United States Courts of Appeals for the Tenth and Federal Circuits.

This page intentionally left blank

Supreme Court of the United States

Supreme Court of the United States

No. 16-405

BNSF RY. CO.
vs.
TYRRELL

On Writ of Certiorari to the Supreme Court of Montana

Decided: May 30, 2017

Citation: 581 U.S. ___, 137 S.Ct. 1549, 5 Adm. R. 2 (2017).

GINSBURG, J., delivered the opinion of the Court, in which **ROBERTS, C.J.,** and **KENNEDY, THOMAS, BREYER, ALITO, KAGAN,** and **GORSUCH, J.J.,** joined. **SOTOMAYOR, J.,** filed an opinion concurring in part and dissenting in part.

[—1—] {-1553-} GINSBURG, J:

The two cases we decide today arise under the Federal Employers' Liability Act (FELA), 35 Stat. 65, as amended, 45 U. S. C. §51 *et seq.*, which makes railroads liable in money damages to their employees for on-the-job injuries. Both suits were pursued in Montana state courts although the injured workers did not reside in Montana, nor were they injured there. The defendant railroad, BNSF Railway Company (BNSF), although "doing business" in Montana when the litigation commenced, was not incorporated in Montana, nor did it maintain its principal place of business in that State. To justify the exercise of personal jurisdiction over BNSF, the Montana Supreme Court relied on §56, which provides in relevant part:

> "Under this chapter an action may be brought in a district court of the United States, in the district of the residence of the defendant, or in which the cause of action arose, or in which the defendant shall be doing business at the time of commencing such action. The jurisdiction of the courts of the United States un- **[—2—]** der this chapter shall be concurrent with that of the courts of the several States."

We hold that §56 does not address personal jurisdiction over railroads. Its first relevant sentence is a venue prescription governing proper locations for FELA suits filed in federal court. The provision's second relevant sentence, using the term "concurrent" jurisdiction, refers to subject-matter jurisdiction, not personal jurisdiction. It simply clarifies that the federal courts do not have exclusive subject-matter jurisdiction over FELA suits; state courts can hear them, too. **{-1554-}**

Montana's Supreme Court, in the alternative, relied on state law, under which personal jurisdiction could be asserted over "persons found within . . . Montana." Mont. Rule Civ. Proc. 4(b)(1) (2015). BNSF fit that bill, the court stated, because it has over 2,000 miles of railroad track and employs more than 2,000 workers in Montana. Our precedent, however, explains that the Fourteenth Amendment's Due Process Clause does not permit a State to hale an out-of-state corporation before its courts when the corporation is not "at home" in the State and the episode-in-suit occurred elsewhere. *Daimler AG* v. *Bauman*, 571 U. S. ___, ___ (2014) (slip op., at 8) (internal quotation marks omitted). We therefore reverse the judgment of the Montana Supreme Court.

I

In March 2011, respondent Robert Nelson, a North Dakota resident, brought a FELA suit against BNSF in a Montana state court to recover damages for knee injuries Nelson allegedly sustained while working for BNSF as a fuel-truck driver. 383 Mont. 417, 419, 373 P. 3d 1, 3 (2016). In May 2014, respondent Kelli Tyrrell, appointed in South Dakota as the administrator of her husband Brent Tyrrell's estate, similarly sued BNSF under FELA in a Montana state court. *Id.*, at 419–420, 373 P. 3d, at 3. **[—3—]** Brent Tyrrell, his widow alleged, had developed a fatal kidney cancer from his exposure to carcinogenic chemicals while working for BNSF. *Id.*, at 420, 373 P. 3d, at 3. Neither plaintiff alleged injuries arising from or related to work performed in Montana; indeed, neither Nelson nor Brent Tyrrell appears ever to have worked for BNSF in Montana. *Id.*, at 419–420, 373 P. 3d, at 3.

BNSF is incorporated in Delaware and has its principal place of business in Texas. *Id.*, at 419, 373 P. 3d, at 3. It operates railroad lines in 28 States. No. DV 14–699 (13th Jud. Dist., Yellowstone Cty., Mont., Oct. 7, 2014), App. to Pet. for Cert. 63a. BNSF has 2,061 miles of railroad track in Montana (about 6% of its total track mileage of 32,500), employs some 2,100 workers there (less than 5% of its total work force of 43,000), generates less than 10% of its total revenue in the State, and maintains only one of its 24 automotive facilities in Montana (4%). *Ibid.* Contending that it is not "at home" in Montana, as required for the exercise of general personal jurisdiction under *Daimler AG* v. *Bauman*, 571 U. S. ___, ___ (2014) (slip op., at 8) (internal quotation marks omitted), BNSF moved to dismiss both suits for lack of personal jurisdiction. Its motion was granted in Nelson's case and denied in Tyrrell's. 383 Mont., at 419, 373 P. 3d, at 2.

After consolidating the two cases, the Montana Supreme Court held that Montana courts could exercise general personal jurisdiction over BNSF. *Id.*, at 429, 373 P. 3d, at 9. Section 56, the court determined, authorizes state courts to exercise personal jurisdiction over railroads "doing business" in the State. *Id.*, at 426, 373 P. 3d, at 7 (internal quotation marks omitted). In addition, the court observed, Montana law provides for the exercise of general jurisdiction over "[a]ll persons found within" the State. *Id.*, at 427, 373 P. 3d, at 8 (quoting Mont. Rule Civ. Proc.4(b)(1) (2015)). In view of the railroad's many employees and miles of track in Montana, the court concluded, BNSF **[—4—]** is both "doing business" and "found within" the State, such that both FELA and Montana law authorized the exercise of personal jurisdiction. 383 Mont., at 426, 428, 373 P. 3d, at 7–8 (internal quotation marks omitted). The due process limits articulated in *Daimler*, the court added, did not control, because *Daimler* did not involve a **{–1555–}** FELA claim or a railroad defendant. 383 Mont., at 424, 373 P. 3d, at 6.

Justice McKinnon dissented. Section 56, she wrote, is a federal-court venue prescription, and also confers subject-matter jurisdiction on state courts in FELA cases, concurrent with federal courts. *Id.*, at 435–437, 373 P. 3d, at 13. But §56, she maintained, does not touch or concern personal jurisdiction. *Ibid.* Furthermore, she concluded, *Daimler* controls, rendering the Montana courts' exercise of personal jurisdiction impermissible because BNSF is not "at home" in Montana. 383 Mont., at 433–434, 373 P. 3d, at 11–12.

We granted certiorari, 580 U. S. ___ (2017), to resolve whether §56 authorizes state courts to exercise personal jurisdiction over railroads doing business in their States but not incorporated or headquartered there, and whether the Montana courts' exercise of personal jurisdiction in these cases comports with due process.

II

Nelson and Tyrrell contend that §56's first relevant sentence confers personal jurisdiction on federal courts, and that the section's second relevant sentence extends that grant of jurisdiction to state courts. Neither contention is tenable. Section 56's first relevant sentence concerns venue; its next sentence speaks to subject-matter jurisdiction.[1] **[—5—]**

A

The first sentence of §56 states that "an action may be brought in a district court of the United States," in, among other places, the district "in which the defendant shall be doing business at the time of commencing such action." In *Baltimore & Ohio R. Co.* v. *Kepner*, 314 U. S. 44 (1941), we comprehended this clause as "establish[ing] venue" for a federal-court action. *Id.*, at 52. Congress, we explained, designed §56 to expand venue beyond the limits of the 1888 Judiciary Act's general venue provision, which allowed suit

[1] Section 56's first sentence, which provides a time bar for FELA claims, is not relevant to the issue at hand. For ease of reference, we hereinafter refer to the first relevant sentence, describing where suit "may be brought," as the provision's "first" sentence, and the sentence that immediately follows, referring to "concurrent" jurisdiction, as the "second."

only "in districts of which the defendant was an inhabitant." *Id.*, at 49; see Act of Aug. 13, 1888, §1, 25 Stat. 434. Nowhere in *Kepner* or in any other decision did we intimate that §56 might affect personal jurisdiction.

Congress generally uses the expression, where suit "may be brought," to indicate the federal districts in which venue is proper. See, *e.g.*, 28 U. S. C. §1391(b) (general venue statute specifying where "[a] civil action may be brought"); J. Oakley, ALI, Fed. Judicial Code Rev. Project 253–290 (2004) (listing special venue statutes, many with similar language). See also *Kepner*, 314 U. S., at 56 (Frankfurter, J., dissenting) ("The phrasing of [§56] follows the familiar pattern generally employed by Congress in framing venue provisions.").

In contrast, Congress' typical mode of providing for the exercise of personal jurisdiction has been to authorize service of process. See, *e.g.*, 15 U. S. C. §22 (Clayton Act provision stating that "all process in [cases against a corporation arising under federal antitrust laws] may be served in the district of which [the defendant] is an inhabitant, or wherever [the defendant] may be found"); §53(a) (under Federal Trade Commission Act, "process may be served on any person, partnership, or corporation **{–1556–}** wherever it may be found"). See also *Omni Capital Int'l, Ltd.* v. *Rudolf Wolff & Co.*, 484 U. S. 97, 106–107 (1987) (discussing statutes that authorize (or fail to authorize) nation- **[—6—]** wide service of process). But cf. *Schlanger* v. *Seamans*, 401 U. S. 487, 490, n. 4 (1971) (though "Congress has provided for nationwide service of process" in 28 U. S. C. §1391(e) (1964 ed., Supp. V), that statute was meant to expand venue, not personal jurisdiction). Congress uses this terminology because, absent consent, a basis for service of a summons on the defendant is prerequisite to the exercise of personal jurisdiction. See *Omni Capital*, 484 U. S., at 104.

Nelson and Tyrrell, however, argue that §56 relates to personal jurisdiction. In their view, the 1888 Judiciary Act provision that prompted §56's enactment, 25 Stat. 434, concerned *both* personal jurisdiction and venue. According to House and Senate Reports, they contend, two cases had brought to Congress' attention the problem with the prior provision—namely, that in federal-question cases it authorized suit only in the district of the defendant's residence. Brief for Respondents 16–18. See H. R. Rep. No. 513, 61st Cong., 2d Sess., 6 (1910) (citing *Macon Grocery Co.* v. *Atlantic Coast Line R. Co.*, 215 U. S. 501 (1910); *Cound* v. *Atchison, T. & S. F. R. Co.*, 173 F. 527 (WD Tex.1909)); S. Rep. No. 432, 61st Cong., 2d Sess., 4 (1910) (same). In both cases, the courts had dismissed FELA suits for "want of jurisdiction." *Macon Grocery*, 215 U. S., at 510; *Cound*, 173 F., at 534. To avert such jurisdictional dismissals, they urge, Congress enacted §56.

Legislative history "throws little light" here. *Kepner*, 314 U. S., at 50.[2] Driving today's decision, we have long read the 1888 Judiciary Act provision to concern venue only. See *Green* v. *Chicago, B. & Q. R. Co.*, 205 U. S. 530, 532–533 (1907) (analyzing personal jurisdiction separately, **[—7—]** after concluding that venue was proper under 1888 Judiciary Act provision). See also *Lee* v. *Chesapeake & Ohio R. Co.*, 260 U. S. 653, 655 (1923) (noting that materially identical successor to 1888 Judiciary Act provision, Act of Mar. 3, 1911, §51, 36 Stat. 1101, "relates to the venue of suits"). Indeed, reading the 1888 Judiciary Act provision to authorize the exercise of personal jurisdiction would have yielded an anomalous result: In diversity cases, the provision allowed for suit "in the district of the residence of either the plaintiff or the defendant." 25 Stat. 434. Interpreting that clause to provide for jurisdiction would have allowed a plaintiff to hale a defendant into court in the plaintiff 's home district, even if the district was one with which the defendant had no affiliation, and the episode-in-suit, no connection.

[2] We note, moreover, that Nelson and Tyrrell overlooked the Senate Report's explicit reference to the first sentence of §56 as a venue provision, with no mention of personal jurisdiction. S. Rep. No. 432, 61st Cong., 2d Sess., 3 (1910).

B

The second §56 sentence in point provides that "[t]he jurisdiction of the courts of the United States under this chapter shall be concurrent with that of the courts of the several States." Nelson and Tyrrell argue that this sentence extends to state courts the first sentence's alleged conferral of personal jurisdiction on federal courts. But, as just discussed, the first sentence concerns federal-court venue and confers no personal jurisdiction on any court. **{–1557–}**

We have understood §56's second sentence to provide for the concurrent *subject-matter* jurisdiction of state and federal courts over actions under FELA. See *Second Employers' Liability Cases*, 223 U. S. 1, 55–56 (1912). As Nelson and Tyrrell acknowledge, Congress added the provision to confirm concurrent subject-matter jurisdiction after the Connecticut Supreme Court held that Congress intended to confine FELA litigation to federal courts, and that state courts had no obligation to entertain FELA claims. See Brief for Respondents 23 (citing *Hoxie* v. *New York, N. H. & H. R. Co.*, 82 Conn. 352, 73 A. 754 (1909)). **[—8—]** As Justice McKinnon recognized in her dissent from the Montana Supreme Court's decision in Nelson's and Tyrrell's cases, "[t]he phrase 'concurrent jurisdiction' is a well-known term of art long employed by Congress and courts to refer to subject-matter jurisdiction, not personal jurisdiction." 383 Mont., at 436, 373 P. 3d, at 13. See, *e.g.*, *Mims* v. *Arrow Financial Services, LLC*, 565 U. S. 368, 372 (2012) ("federal and state courts have concurrent jurisdiction over private suits arising under the [Telephone Consumer Protection Act of 1991, 47 U. S. C. §227]"); *Claflin* v. *Houseman*, 93 U. S. 130, 133–134 (1876) (State courts retain "concurrent jurisdiction" over "suits in which a bankrupt" party is involved, notwithstanding exclusive federal jurisdiction over bankruptcy matters).

C

Pointing to a quartet of cases, the Montana Supreme Court observed that this Court "consistently has interpreted [§]56 to allow state courts to hear cases brought under FELA even where the only basis for jurisdiction is the railroad doing business in the forum [S]tate." 383 Mont., at 421–423, 425–426, 373 P. 3d, at 4–7 (citing *Pope* v. *Atlantic Coast Line R. Co.*, 345 U. S. 379 (1953); *Miles* v. *Illinois Central R. Co.*, 315 U. S. 698 (1942); *Kepner*, 314 U. S. 44; *Denver & Rio Grande Western R. Co.* v. *Terte*, 284 U. S. 284 (1932)).

None of the decisions featured by the Montana Supreme Court resolved a question of personal jurisdiction. *Terte* held that a FELA plaintiff, injured in Colorado, could bring suit in Missouri state court against a railroad incorporated elsewhere. 284 U. S., at 286–287. The dispute, however, was over the Dormant Commerce Clause, not personal jurisdiction; the railroad defendants argued that the suit would unduly burden interstate commerce, and the decision rested on two Commerce Clause decisions, *Michigan Central R. Co.* v. *Mix*, 278 U. S. 492 (1929), and **[—9—]** *Hoffman* v. *Missouri ex rel. Foraker*, 274 U. S. 21 (1927), not on an interpretation of §56. See *Terte*, 284 U. S., at 285, 287. In *Kepner* and *Miles*, this Court held that a state court may not, based on inconvenience to a railroad defendant, enjoin its residents from bringing a FELA suit in another State's federal (*Kepner*) or state (*Miles*) courts. *Kepner*, 314 U. S., at 54; *Miles*, 315 U. S., at 699–700, 704. *Pope* held that 28 U. S. C. §1404(a)'s provision for transfer from one federal court to another did not bear on the question decided in *Miles*: A state court still could not enjoin a FELA action brought in another State's courts. 345 U. S., at 383–384.

Moreover, all these cases, save *Pope*, were decided before this Court's transformative decision on personal jurisdiction in *International Shoe Co.* v. *Washington*, 326 U. S. 310 (1945). **{–1558–}** See *Daimler*, 571 U. S., at ___, n. 18 (slip op., at 20, n. 18) (cautioning against reliance on cases "decided in the era dominated by" the "territorial thinking" of *Pennoyer* v. *Neff*, 95 U. S. 714 (1878)).

III

Because FELA does not authorize state courts to exercise personal jurisdiction over a railroad solely on the ground that the railroad does some business in their States, the Montana courts' assertion of personal jurisdiction over BNSF here must rest on Mont. Rule Civ. Proc. 4(b)(1), the State's provision for the exercise of personal jurisdiction over "persons found" in Montana. See *supra*, at 2–3. BNSF does not contest that it is "found within" Montana as the State's courts comprehend that rule. We therefore inquire whether the Montana courts' exercise of personal jurisdiction under Montana law comports with the Due Process Clause of the Fourteenth Amendment.

In *International Shoe*, this Court explained that a state court may exercise personal jurisdiction over an out-of-state defendant who has "certain minimum contacts with **[—10—]** [the State] such that the maintenance of the suit does not offend 'traditional notions of fair play and substantial justice.'" 326 U. S., at 316. Elaborating on this guide, we have distinguished between specific or case-linked jurisdiction and general or all-purpose jurisdiction. See, *e.g.*, *Daimler*, 571 U. S., at ___ (slip op., at 8); *Goodyear Dunlop Tires Operations, S. A.* v. *Brown*, 564 U. S. 915, 919 (2011); *Helicopteros Nacionales de Colombia, S. A.* v. *Hall*, 466 U. S. 408, 414, nn. 8, 9 (1984). Because neither Nelson nor Tyrrell alleges any injury from work in or related to Montana, only the propriety of general jurisdiction is at issue here.

Goodyear and *Daimler* clarified that "[a] court may assert general jurisdiction over foreign (sister-state or foreign-country) corporations to hear any and all claims against them when their affiliations with the State are so 'continuous and systematic' as to render them essentially at home in the forum State." *Daimler*, 571 U. S., at ___ (slip op., at 8) (quoting *Goodyear*, 564 U. S., at 919). The "paradigm" forums in which a corporate defendant is "at home," we explained, are the corporation's place of incorporation and its principal place of business. *Daimler*, 571 U. S., at ___ (slip op., at 18–19); *Goodyear*, 564 U. S., at 924. The exercise of general jurisdiction is not limited to these forums; in an "exceptional case," a corporate defendant's operations in another forum "may be so substantial and of such a nature as to render the corporation at home in that State." *Daimler*, 571 U. S., at ___, n. 19 (slip op., at 20, n. 19). We suggested that *Perkins* v. *Benguet Consol. Mining Co.*, 342 U. S. 437 (1952), exemplified such a case. *Daimler*, 571 U. S., at ___, n. 19 (slip op., at 20, n. 19). In *Perkins*, war had forced the defendant corporation's owner to temporarily relocate the enterprise from the Philippines to Ohio. 342 U. S., at 447–448. Because Ohio then became "the center of the corporation's wartime activities," *Daimler*, 571 U. S., at ___, n. 8 (slip op., at 12, n. 8), suit **[—11—]** was proper there, *Perkins*, 342 U. S., at 448.

The Montana Supreme Court distinguished *Daimler* on the ground that we did not there confront "a FELA claim or a railroad defendant." 383 Mont., at 424, 373 P. 3d, at 6. The Fourteenth Amendment due process constraint described in **{-1559-}** *Daimler*, however, applies to all state-court assertions of general jurisdiction over nonresident defendants; the constraint does not vary with the type of claim asserted or business enterprise sued.[3]

BNSF, we repeat, is not incorporated in Montana and does not maintain its principal place of business there. Nor is BNSF so heavily engaged in activity in Montana "as to render [it] essentially at home" in that State. See *Daimler*, 571 U. S., at ___ (slip op., at 8) (internal quotation marks omitted). As earlier noted, BNSF has over 2,000 miles of railroad track and more than 2,000 employees in Montana. But, as we observed in *Daimler*, "the general jurisdiction inquiry does not focus solely on the magnitude of the defendant's in-state contacts." *Id.*, at ___, n. 20 (slip op., at 21, n. 20) (internal quotation marks and

---

[3] The Montana Supreme Court also erred in asserting that "Congress drafted the FELA to make a railroad 'at home' for jurisdictional purposes wherever it is 'doing business.' " 383 Mont. 417, 425, 373 P. 3d 1, 6 (2016). As discussed, *supra*, at 5–7, in §56's first sentence, Congress dealt with venue only, not personal jurisdiction.

alterations omitted). Rather, the inquiry "calls for an appraisal of a corporation's activities in their entirety";"[a] corporation that operates in many places can scarcely be deemed at home in all of them." *Ibid.* In short, the business BNSF does in Montana is sufficient to subject the railroad to specific personal jurisdiction in that State on claims related to the business it does in Montana. But in-state business, we clarified in *Daimler* and *Goodyear*, does not suffice to permit the assertion of general jurisdiction over claims like Nelson's and Tyrrell's that are unrelated **[—12—]** to any activity occurring in Montana.[4]

IV

Nelson and Tyrrell present a further argument—that BNSF has consented to personal jurisdiction in Montana. See Brief for Respondents 50–51. The Montana Supreme Court did not address this contention, see 383 Mont., at 429, n. 3, 373 P. 3d, at 9, n. 3, so we do not reach it. See *Cutter* v. *Wilkinson*, 544 U. S. 709, 718, n. 7 (2005) ("[W]e are a court of review, not of first view.").

* * * **{-1560-}**

For the reasons stated, the judgment of the Montana Supreme Court is reversed, and the cases are remanded **[—13—]** for further proceedings not inconsistent with this opinion.

It is so ordered.

(Reporter's Note: Opinion concurring in part and dissenting in part follows on p. 8).

[4] JUSTICE SOTOMAYOR, dissenting in part, renews a debate comprehensively aired in *Daimler AG* v. *Bauman*, 571 U. S. ___ (2014). There, as again here, JUSTICE SOTOMAYOR treats the assertion of jurisdiction by the State of Washington courts in *International Shoe Co.* v. *Washington*, 326 U. S. 310 (1945), as an exercise of general, dispute-blind, jurisdiction, *post*, at 3, thereby overlooking the fundamental difference between *International Shoe* and these cases. In *International Shoe*, the defendant corporation's in-state activities had "not only been continuous and systematic, but also g[a]ve rise to the liabilities sued on." 326 U. S., at 317. The state courts there asserted jurisdiction not over claims that had nothing to do with the State; instead, they exercised adjudicatory authority to hold the defendant corporation accountable for activity pursued within the State of Washington. *Daimler*, 571 U. S., at ___, ___, n. 10 (slip op., at 7, 14, n. 10). This Court, therefore, had no occasion in *International Shoe* to "engage in a comparison between International Shoe's contacts within the State of Washington and the other States in which it operated." *Post*, at 3. In marked contrast to *International Shoe*, Nelson's and Tyrrell's claims have no relationship to anything that occurred or had its principal impact in Montana.

This Court's opinion is not limited to §56 because the Montana Supreme Court went on to address and decide the question: Do "Montana courts have personal jurisdiction over BNSF under Montana law?" 383 Mont., at 426, 373 P. 3d, at 7. See also *id.*, at 429, 373 P. 3d, at 9 ("Under Montana law, Montana courts have general personal jurisdiction over BNSF.").

[—1—] **{-1560-}** SOTOMAYOR, J, concurring in part and dissenting in part:

I concur in the Court's conclusion that the Federal Employers' Liability Act (FELA), 45 U. S. C. §51 *et seq.*, does not confer personal jurisdiction over railroads on state courts. I also agree that the Montana Supreme Court erred when it concluded that the nature of the claim here—a FELA claim against a railroad—answers the question whether the Due Process Clause allows the exercise of personal jurisdiction over BNSF. But my agreement with the majority ends there. I continue to disagree with the path the Court struck in *Daimler AG* v. *Bauman,* 571 U. S. ___ (2014), which limits general jurisdiction over a corporate defendant only to those States where it is "'essentially at home,'" *id.,* at ___ (slip op., at 8). And even if the Court insists on adhering to that standard, I dissent from its decision to apply it here in the first instance rather than remanding to the Montana Supreme Court for it to conduct what should be a fact-intensive analysis under the proper legal framework. Accordingly, I join Parts I and II of the Court's opinion, but dissent from Part III and the judgment.

The Court would do well to adhere more faithfully to the direction from *International Shoe Co.* v. *Washington,* 326 [—2—] U. S. 310 (1945), which instructed that general jurisdiction is proper when a corporation's "continuous corporate operations within a state [are] so substantial and of such a nature as to justify suit against it on causes of action arising from dealings entirely distinct from those activities." *Id.,* at 318. Under *International Shoe,* in other words, courts were to ask whether the benefits a defendant attained in the forum State warranted the burdens associated with general personal jurisdiction. See *id.,* at 317–318. The majority itself acknowledges that *International Shoe* should govern, describing the question as whether a defendant's affiliations with a State are sufficiently "'continuous and systematic'" to warrant the exercise of general jurisdiction there. *Ante,* at 10. If only its analysis today reflected that directive. Instead, the majority opinion goes on to reaffirm the restrictive "at home" test set out in *Daimler*—a test that, as I have explained, has no home in our precedents and creates serious inequities. See 571 U. S., at ___–___ (SOTOMAYOR, J., concurring in judgment) (slip op., at 8–19).

The majority's approach grants a jurisdictional windfall to large multistate or multinational corporations that operate across many jurisdictions. Under its reasoning, it is virtually inconceivable that such corporations will ever be subject to general jurisdiction in any location other than their principal places of business or of incorporation. Foreign businesses with principal places of business outside the United States may never be subject to general jurisdiction in this country even though they have continuous and systematic contacts within the United States. See *id.,* at ___–___ (slip op., at 17–18). What was once a holistic, nuanced contacts analysis backed by considerations of fairness and reasonableness has now effectively been replaced by the rote identification of a corporation's **[—3—]** principal place of business or place of incorporation.[1] The **{-1561-}** result? It is individual plaintiffs, harmed by the actions of a farflung foreign corporation, who will bear the brunt of the majority's approach and be forced to sue in distant jurisdictions with which they have no contacts or connection.

Moreover, the comparative contacts analysis invented in *Daimler* resurfaces here and proves all but dispositive. The majority makes much of the fact that BNSF's contacts in Montana are only a percentage of its contacts with other jurisdictions. *Ante,* at 3, 11. But *International Shoe,* which the majority agrees is the springboard for our

[1] As many commentators have observed, lower courts adhered to the continuous-and-systematic standard for decades before *Daimler,* and its predecessor *Goodyear Dunlop Tires Operations, S. A.* v. *Brown,* 564 U. S. 915 (2011), wrought the present sea change. See, *e.g.,* Cornett & Hoffheimer, Good-Bye Significant Contacts: General Personal Jurisdiction after *Daimler AG* v. *Bauman,* 76 Ohio St. L. J. 101 (2015); Parry, Rethinking Personal Jurisdiction after *Bauman* and *Walden,* 19 Lewis & Clark L. Rev. 607 (2015); Doernberg, Resoling *International Shoe,* 2 Tex. A&M L. Rev. 247 (2014); Feder, *Goodyear,* "Home," and the Uncertain Future of Doing Business Jurisdiction, 63 S. C. L. Rev. 671(2012).

modern personal jurisdiction jurisprudence, *ante,* at 9, applied no comparative contacts test. There the Court analyzed whether the Delaware corporation had "by its activities in the State of Washington rendered itself amenable to proceedings" in the State. 326 U. S., at 311. The Court evaluated whether the corporation had offices in the forum State, made contracts there, delivered goods there, or employed salesmen there. See *id.*, at 313. Despite acknowledging that the corporation maintained places of business in several States, *ibid.*, the Court did not engage in a comparison between International Shoe's contacts within the State of Washington and the other States in which it operated.[2] The Court noted that the corporation **[—4—]** employed 11 to 13 salesmen in Washington but did not query how that number compared to the number of salesmen in other States. *Ibid.* As well it should not have; the relative percentage of contacts is irrelevant. The focus should be on the quality and quantity of the defendant's contacts in the forum State.[3]

The majority does even *Daimler* itself a disservice, paying only lip service to the question the Court purported to reserve there—the possibility of an "exceptional case" in which general jurisdiction would be proper in a forum State that is neither a corporate defendant's place of incorporation nor its principal place of business. See 571 U. S., at ___, n. 19 (slip op., at 20, n. 19). Its opinion here could be understood to limit that exception to the exact facts of *Perkins* v. *Benguet Consol. Mining Co.*, 342 U. S. 437 (1952). See *ante*, at 10–11. That reading is so narrow as to read the exception out of existence entirely; certainly a defendant with significant contacts **{-1562-}** with more than one State falls outside its ambit. And so it is inevitable under its own reasoning that the majority would conclude that BNSF's contacts with Montana are insufficient to justify the exercise of personal jurisdiction here. This result is perverse. Despite having reserved the possibility of an "exceptional case" in *Daimler*, the majority here has re- **[—5—]** jected that possibility out of hand.

Worse, the majority reaches its conclusion only by departing from the Court's normal practice.[4] Had it remanded to the Montana Supreme Court to reevaluate the due process question under the correct legal standard, that court could have examined whether this is such an "exceptional case." Instead, with its ruling today, the Court unnecessarily sends a signal to the lower courts that the exceptional-circumstances inquiry is all form, no substance.

I respectfully concur in part and dissent in part.

---

[2] The majority responds that the language from *International Shoe* **[—4—]** informs only a specific jurisdiction case. *Ante*, at 12, n. 4. But the majority's view of *International Shoe* is overly restrictive. The terms "specific jurisdiction" and "general jurisdiction" are nowhere to be found in that opinion. And I continue to believe, as I noted in *Daimler*, that there is no material difference between the "continuous and systematic" terminology *International Shoe* used for what we now call specific jurisdiction and the "continuous" and "substantial" terminology it used for what we now call general jurisdiction. See *Daimler*, 571 U. S., at ___, n. 6 (SOTOMAYOR, J., concurring in judgment) (slip op., at 8, n. 6).

[3] Indeed, in neither *Perkins* v. *Benguet Consol. Mining Co.*, 342 U. S. 437 (1952), nor *Helicopteros Nacionales de Colombia, S. A.* v. *Hall*, 466 U. S. 408 (1984), did the Court engage in a comparative-contacts analysis.

[4] The Montana Supreme Court reached this question only by wrongly assuming that 45 U. S. C. §56 is a jurisdictional statute and that a defendant's unique status as a railroad company is dispositive of the jurisdictional question. A remand rather than an outright reversal is this Court's traditional practice where a lower court applies the incorrect legal standard; we have done it repeatedly just this Term. See, *e.g., Bethune-Hill* v. *Virginia State Bd. of Elections*, 580 U. S. ___ (2017); *Bolivarian Republic of Venezuela* v. *Helmerich & Payne Int'l Drilling Co., ante,* p. ___; *McLane Co.* v. *EEOC, ante,* p. ___; *Moore* v. *Texas, ante,* p. ___.

This page intentionally left blank

United States Court of Appeals for the First Circuit

United States Court of Appeals
for the First Circuit

No. 15-2482

MEDITERRANEAN SHIPPING CO.
VS.
BEST TIRE RECYCLING, INC.

Appeal from the United States District Court for the District of Puerto Rico

Decided: February 6, 2017

Citation: 848 F.3d 50, 5 Adm. R. 12 (1st Cir. 2017).

Before **HOWARD,** Chief Judge, **TORRUELLA,** and **KAYATTA,** Circuit Judges.

[—2—] {-51-} TORRUELLA, Circuit Judge:

The present dispute arises out of a contract for the shipment of used tires from {-52-} Puerto Rico to Vietnam. The shipment accrued demurrage charges, port storage charges, and related administrative fees, apparently because it arrived late to Vietnam. On summary judgment, the district court found that Best Tire Recycling, Inc. ("Best Tire") was the shipper, and therefore, pursuant to the bills of lading, was liable for the charges and fees to the carrier, Mediterranean Shipping Co. ("Mediterranean"). Best Tire now contends that the district court erred in holding that there were no genuine issues of material fact as to whether Best Tire was the shipper. However, Best Tire was designated as the shipper on the bills of lading, and we therefore affirm the findings of the district court.

I. *Background*

Mediterranean is an ocean common carrier that transports goods between the United States and foreign countries. Best Tire is a Puerto Rico-based corporation that collected and transported scrap tires, among other things, within Puerto Rico. In 2012, John Wayne Kwange ("John Wayne"), doing business as Armstrong Exchange and/or Armstrong International, Inc. ("Armstrong") hired Best Tire to deliver forty containers of scrap tires to the port of San Juan, Puerto Rico for $600 a container. Best Tire instructed John Wayne to contact Mediterranean, the common **[—3—]** carrier, to get booking information and then inform Best Tire of the arrangement.

On April 3, 2012, John Wayne emailed Gypsa Carrión, of Oceanic General Agency, an agent of Mediterranean, and requested price quotes to ship tires from San Juan, Puerto Rico to Haiphong, Vietnam. Best Tire was copied on this email and admits to receiving it. In this email, John Wayne designated Best Tire as the "shipper" and Phong Vuong Limited Company as the "consignee." On April 11, Ms. Carrión sent a reply email to John Wayne and Nydia Caro, Best Tire's administrative assistant, providing them with "booking numbers for the next 4 sailings" and further notifying them that Mediterranean was "creating the shipper in their system." In this email, Ms. Carrión also stated: "[Y]our trucker may start pulling out the [container] units with . . . just the [booking] number[s]."

Once Best Tire received the booking information, it subcontracted with IPM Transport to bring empty containers from the port of San Juan to Best Tire's storage facilities in Rincón, Puerto Rico, and then to transport the containers, filled with scrap tires, back to Mediterranean's cargo ship in the port of San Juan. Between April and May of 2012, all containers were delivered and Best Tire charged John Wayne $600 per delivered container. Mediterranean issued bills of lading for each of the scrap tire **[—4—]** shipments and, consistent with John Wayne's initial email, identified Best Tire as the shipper.

Best Tire admits that it received the bills of lading. Mediterranean's standard bill of lading provides that, *inter alia,* "[e]very Person defined as a Merchant is jointly and severally liable towards [Mediterranean] for all of the various undertakings, responsibilities, and liabilities of the Merchant." A "Merchant" is defined to "include[] the Shipper, Consignee, holder of th[e] Bill of Lading, the receiver of the Goods and any Person owning, entitled to or claiming the possession of the Goods or of this Bill of Lading or anyone acting on behalf of this Person." "Freight" is defined to "include[] the freight and all charges, costs and expenses whatsoever payable to [Mediterranean] in accordance with the applicable Tariff and this Bill of Lading, including storage, per diem and demurrage." Mediterranean's standard bill of lading **{-53-}** also incorporates "[t]he terms and conditions of [Mediterranean's] applicable Tariff," which include information about "demurrage, per diem, storage expenses and legal fees."

When the cargo ultimately arrived at its destination in Vietnam, the consignee refused to accept delivery, apparently because the shipment arrived late. As a result of the consignee's refusal to accept the shipment, Mediterranean had to store it. In **[—5—]** total, this stored cargo incurred demurrage charges totaling $353,083.50, port-storage charges totaling $36,780, and an administrative fee totaling $300. Moreover, Mediterranean argued "that $69,889.54 of the cost to ship the freight from Puerto Rico to Vietnam remained unpaid." Best Tire received a total of $24,000 for its services in this transaction.

The district court sitting in admiralty granted Mediterranean's motion for summary judgment, holding that Best Tire was a party to the contract of ocean carriage and as such was liable to Mediterranean for unpaid ocean freight charges, shipping container demurrage, port storage and related administrative fees.

II. *Standard of Review*

"Summary judgment is appropriate when the record shows that 'there is no genuine dispute as to any material fact and the movant is entitled to judgment as a matter of law.'" *Farmers Ins. Exch. v. RNK, Inc.*, 632 F.3d 777, 782 (1st Cir. 2011) (quoting Fed. R. Civ. P. 56(a)). "We review *de novo* the grant of a motion for summary judgment." *Id.* "[W]e may affirm the entry of summary judgment on any ground made manifest by the record, so long as the record reveals that there is no genuine issue as to any material fact and that the moving party is entitled to judgment as a matter of law." *Batista v. Cooperativa de Vivienda Jardines de San Ignacio*, 776 F.3d 38, 42 (1st Cir. 2015) (citation omitted). **[—6—]**

III. *Discussion*

"'To ascertain what contract was entered into[, courts] look primarily to the bills of lading, bearing in mind that the instrument serves both as a receipt and as a contract' and that '[o]rdinarily, the person from whom the goods are received for shipment assumes the obligation to pay the freight charges; and his obligation is ordinarily a primary one.'" *EIMSKIP v. Atlantic Fish Market, Inc.*, 417 F.3d 72, 77 (1st Cir. 2005) (quoting *Louisville & Nashville R.R. v. Cent. Iron & Coal Co.*, 265 U.S. 59, 67 (1924)).

Nevertheless, the "pattern and presumption" that the party identified as "shipper" on the bills of lading is the party that bears liability "can be overcome by statute, by contractual provisions, or by the parties' course of conduct." *Id.* (citing *Louisville & Nashville R.R.*, 265 U.S. at 67-68.).

It is uncontested that Best Tire is designated as the shipper on all of the bills of lading. Best Tire does not argue that the presumption this creates is overcome by statute or by a contractual provision. Rather, Best Tire argues that the parties' course of conduct overcomes the pattern and presumption that Best Tire bears liability. We find that it does not.

Best Tire relies heavily on our reasoning in *EIMSKIP*. In *EIMSKIP*, the district court had found Atlantic liable to **[—7—]** EIMSKIP, the common carrier, even though Atlantic was not identified as the shipper on the bills of lading; Atlantic appealed, and we affirmed. *Id.* at 76. We relied on Atlantic's conduct: it had booked the shipments with EIMSKIP, it was invoiced for the shipments, and it had orally agreed to **{-54-}** pay for them. *Id.* Mayflower, the party designated as the shipper on the bills of lading, was never invoiced for the shipments. *Id.* Best Tire sees a similarity between the conduct of John Wayne and/or Armstrong and the conduct of Atlantic, in that John Wayne was the one who contacted Mediterranean to organize the shipments and, seemingly, prepaid a number of the shipments.

The fundamental flaw in Best Tire's argument is that in *EIMSKIP*, we found that *both* Mayflower (who was identified as the shipper on the bills of lading) and Atlantic (who was not) were liable to the carrier. "Two parties may each make themselves liable to a third party for payment of the same freight on a single shipment—one by a contract reflected in part by the bill of lading and the other by explicit promises and course of conduct independent of the bill of lading." *Id.* Thus, our reasoning in *EIMSKIP* does not absolve Best Tire of liability. At most, our reasoning suggests that John Wayne and/or Armstrong could also be held liable—however, the district court was unable to serve either John Wayne or Armstrong, as they are apparently nowhere to **[—8—]** be found. In any event, Mediterranean can elect which party it will hold liable, because Best Tire is jointly and severally liable to Mediterranean—the question whether John Wayne and/or Armstrong could also be held liable is not before us.

Best Tire also relies on *Norfolk S. Ry. v. Groves*, 586 F.3d 1273 (11th Cir. 2009), for the proposition that "a party must assent to being named as a consignee on the bill of lading to be held liable as such, or at the least, be given notice that it is being named as a consignee in order that it might object or act accordingly." *Id.* at 1282. We need not decide whether Best Tire's silence can be construed as assent to being named a party on the bill of lading, because Best Tire was given notice of this fact. Best Tire had received two email messages notifying it that it would be the shipper. As Best Tire itself admits, it "could have refused being named as the shipper by replying to those messages." In addition, Best Tire received the six bills of lading on four separate occasions between April 24, 2012 and June 28, 2012. Best Tire was designated as the shipper on all these bills of lading. Yet Best Tire made no objections until August of 2013, when it received invoices for demurrage and other charges—well over a year after it had accepted the bills of lading.[1] **[—9—]**

IV. *Conclusion*

The decision of the district court is affirmed.

Affirmed.

[1] Best Tire raised two additional issues in its appeal brief: (1) because some of the shipments were marked as "freight prepaid" Mediterranean is estopped from collecting from Best Tire; **[—9—]** (2) pursuant to the doctrine of laches, Mediterranean may only collect demurrage and port charges accrued in the 180 days prior to the filing of the complaint by Mediterranean. The first of these issues is being raised for the first time on appeal. Although Best Tire did identify "laches" as one of several affirmative defenses in its complaint, these arguments were never clearly raised or argued before the district court. Both of these arguments are therefore waived. *See Nat'l Ass'n of Soc. Workers v. Hardwood*, 69 F.3d 622, 627 (1st Cir. 1995).

United States Court of Appeals
for the First Circuit

No. 16-1765

CHUNG
vs.
STUDENTCITY.COM, INC.

Appeal from the United States District Court for the District of Massachusetts

Decided: April 14, 2017

Citation: 854 F.3d 97, 5 Adm. R. 15 (1st Cir. 2017).

Before **HOWARD,** Chief Judge, **SELYA,** and **LYNCH,** Circuit Judges.

[—2—] {-99-} **SELYA,** Circuit Judge:

District courts have authority to enter summary judgment on grounds not raised by the parties. That authority, though, is far from unbridled. Here, the district court—with the acquiescence of the parties—limited pretrial discovery to specific issues. It later entered summary judgment on a completely different issue—an issue not briefed and on which discovery had not been allowed. Concluding, as we do, that the district court's shift in focus exceeded its authority, we vacate the judgment and remand for further proceedings consistent with this opinion.

I. BACKGROUND

We rehearse the facts in the light most amenable to the parties opposing summary judgment (here, the plaintiffs). *See Jones v. Secord*, 684 F.3d 1, 3 (1st Cir. 2012). StudentCity.com, Inc. (StudentCity) is a Delaware corporation that maintains its principal place of business in Massachusetts. It sells vacation packages to students, including those traveling for spring break or to celebrate graduations.

In the fall of 2007, Lisa Tam Chung and Loren Daily were high-school seniors in Grand Prairie, Texas. A StudentCity representative contacted Loren to promote the firm's wares and piqued her curiosity about booking a graduation trip. Once a critical mass of students had expressed interest about such a trip, the StudentCity representative held an informational meeting. **{-100-}** The **[—3—]** representative assured the assemblage (including several parents) that StudentCity staff attend all events and that participating students would not be permitted to go anywhere unaccompanied. She also distributed promotional materials that stated in pertinent part:

- StudentCity will provide "[o]n site staff at all scheduled events—beginning to end."
- StudentCity "staffs all scheduled events from beginning to end."
- StudentCity maintains "the largest staff-to-student ratio and our 24-hour staff is there to give you the peace of mind you need."
- StudentCity staff will be present "to assure that everyone is having a great and responsible time."

Loren's parents met with the StudentCity representative and read the written materials. Lisa relayed StudentCity's representations to her parents, who had limited English proficiency. With the blessing of both families, the girls purchased vacation packages for a June 2008 trip to Cancún, Mexico, adding an optional snorkeling excursion.

The snorkeling excursion took place on June 7, when the participants boarded the SS Sea Star, a catamaran owned and operated by Servicios Maritimos y Acua del Caribe SA de C.V. (SMA). A StudentCity staff member transported Lisa and Loren to the Sea **[—4—]** Star, a vessel approved to carry eighty passengers and three crew members for this kind of outing.[1] On the day in question, however, it carried at least 120 StudentCity

[1] StudentCity offered some evidence that the catamaran's maximum capacity was 250 passengers (though not for voyages to the coral reef). At the summary judgment stage, however, we are constrained to view disputed facts in the plaintiffs' favor. *See Houlton Citizens' Coal. v. Town of Houlton*, 175 F.3d 178, 184 (1st Cir. 1999).

travelers and no fewer than 210 persons in total. No on-duty StudentCity representative was on board.

The snorkeling trip had a tragic ending: the Sea Star hit a coral reef and began to take on water, yet the crew provided no assistance to the passengers (indeed, some crew members deserted ship). Acting on their own, Lisa and Loren donned life preservers and tried to reach safety by grabbing a rope that extended between the Sea Star and a small private vessel. Their efforts failed and they were pulled under the water. Loren suffered serious injuries, but survived; Lisa was pronounced brain dead at a local hospital and died on June 10, 2008.

Following an investigation, the harbormaster concluded that the "concentration of passengers in the boat" caused a "considerable imbalance," which most likely led to the Sea Star's collision with the coral reef. Similarly, the Mexican government attributed the accident to the catamaran's "imprudent overload" and the "negligent performance" of the captain. **[—5—]**

A civil action ensued. Although this suit originally had a wider compass, the only claim that is still velivolant is the claim for Lisa's wrongful death—a claim brought by her parents, Oahn Nguyen Chung (individually and in her capacity as administratrix of Lisa's estate) and Liem Chung.[2] As to this claim, StudentCity moved to dismiss or, in the alternative, for summary judgment. *See* Fed. R. Civ. P. 12(b)(6), 56(a). The district court denied the motion to dismiss, but reserved decision on summary **{-101-}** judgment. *See Chung v. StudentCity.com, Inc.* (*Chung I*), No. 10-10943, 2013 WL 6528516, at *2 (D. Mass. Dec. 12, 2013). It reasoned that

> [d]iscovery has not yet begun in this matter. . . . Much of the factual information plaintiffs desire is in defendant's control and can be turned over expeditiously. That information may affect the determination of whether defendant voluntarily undertook a duty to ensure the safety of trip participants, and whether defendant knew or should have known about [SMA]'s dubious prior safety record, if indeed it exists.

Id.

After limited discovery—a circumstance to which we shortly shall return—the district court granted summary judgment in favor of StudentCity. With respect to one of the issues to **[—6—]** which discovery had been allowed, the court concluded that there was "no evidence to suggest that the steps StudentCity took in selecting its snorkeling excursion vendor were unreasonable under the circumstances."[3] With respect to the other issue, the court concluded that "StudentCity voluntarily assumed a duty to generally supervise tour participants during all StudentCity-organized/scheduled events, including the June 7, 2008 snorkeling excursion." Even so, the court ruled that the negligent supervision "claim fails on causation" because "Lisa's death resulted not from inadequate supervision by StudentCity staff, but rather from the boat accident caused by the overloading of the *Sea Star* and its negligent operation by [SMA]." This timely appeal followed.

II. ANALYSIS

We review a district court's entry of summary judgment de novo. *See Gomez v. Stop & Shop Supermkt. Co.*, 670 F.3d 395, 396 (1st Cir. 2012). In conducting this appraisal, we take "all the facts in the light most flattering to the nonmoving party, resolving any evidentiary conflicts in that party's favor, and drawing all reasonable inferences therefrom to his behoof." *Id.* "We will affirm only if the record discloses no genuine issue as **[—7—]** to any material fact and the moving

[2] The remaining claims, including claims brought by and on behalf of Loren, were consigned to arbitration pursuant to the terms of StudentCity's standard customer agreement. *See Chung v. StudentCity.com, Inc.*, No. 10-10943, 2013 WL 504757, at *4 (D. Mass. Feb. 12, 2013). That ruling has not been appealed.

[3] This portion of the district court's summary judgment ruling has not been challenged on appeal, and we treat the "negligent selection" claim as foreclosed.

party is entitled to judgment as a matter of law." *Tropigas de P.R., Inc. v. Certain Underwriters at Lloyd's of London*, 637 F.3d 53, 56 (1st Cir. 2011). An issue is genuine if a reasonable factfinder could resolve it in favor of either party. *See id.* An issue is material if it holds the potential to change the outcome of the suit. *See id.*

Jurisdiction in this case is predicated on diversity of citizenship and the existence of a controversy in the requisite amount. *See* 28 U.S.C. § 1332(a). In a diversity case, state law supplies the substantive rules of decision. *See Erie R.R. Co. v. Tompkins*, 304 U.S. 64, 78 (1938); *Geshke v. Crocs, Inc.*, 740 F.3d 74, 77 (1st Cir. 2014). The parties agree that, consistent with the choice-of-law provision in the customer agreement, Massachusetts law controls here. We have said that "a federal court sitting in diversity is free, if it chooses, to forgo independent analysis and accept the parties' agreement" as to which state law applies. *Borden v. Paul Revere Life Ins. Co.*, 935 F.2d 370, 375 (1st Cir. 1991). Accordingly, we look to Massachusetts law.

Under Massachusetts law, wrongful death is a species of negligence, *see* Mass. Gen. Laws ch. 229, § 2 (imposing liability for damages against "[a] person who . . . by his negligence causes the death of a person"), and as such demands **{-102-}** proof of four elements: "that the defendant owed the plaintiff a duty of **[—8—]** reasonable care, that the defendant breached this duty, that damage resulted, and that there was a causal relation between the breach of the duty and the damage," *Jupin v. Kask*, 849 N.E.2d 829, 834-35 (Mass. 2006).

The existence vel non of a duty presents "a question of law to be resolved by the judge." *Cottam v. CVS Pharmacy*, 764 N.E.2d 814, 819 (Mass. 2002). Massachusetts courts recognize that a duty may be voluntarily assumed and, if it is, "must be performed with due care." *Id.* at 821 (quoting *Mullins v. Pine Manor Coll.*, 449 N.E.2d 331, 336 (Mass. 1983)). Causation, by contrast, generally presents a question of fact within "the special province of the jury." *Jupin*, 849 N.E.2d at 835. It is thus apparent that duty and causation are separate and distinct elements of negligence and negligence-like actions.

Here, the plaintiffs' principal argument is that the district court erred in premising its summary judgment decision on the perceived absence of causation—an issue that was neither argued by StudentCity nor open to discovery. StudentCity demurs: it asserts that the issue of causation was squarely raised at summary judgment. The record, though, belies this assertion. We start there.

StudentCity posits that its motion papers made clear that neither it nor its agents were **[—9—]**

> part of the *Sea Star's* crew, and had no responsibility for boarding passengers, determining where passengers were to be positioned, navigating the vessel, providing safety equipment on the vessel, controlling or limiting the number of passengers, or otherwise instructing the passengers or the StudentCity participants on the *Sea Star's* rules and regulations.

In context, however, it is pellucid that these arguments were advanced not in connection with any issue of causation, but to support StudentCity's lack-of-duty theory. Its summary judgment briefing does not in any way, shape, or form link these arguments to causation. Instead, the arguments—to use StudentCity's own term—related to its "responsibility," and "responsibility" is synonymous with "duty." *See* Responsibility, *Oxford English Dictionary* (3d ed. 2010), http://www.oed.com/view/Entry/163862 (defining responsibility as "[t]he state or fact of being in charge of or of having a duty towards a person or thing").

Nor is StudentCity's assertion made more plausible by either of two additional statements in its summary judgment papers. It notes that, in its motion, it alleged that "[t]our operators such as StudentCity are simply not liable for the alleged negligence of third-party service suppliers, . . . regardless of the theory advanced." This broad statement is of no help to StudentCity, though, because it ignores the district court's holding that, in this instance, StudentCity voluntarily assumed a duty to supervise. Once assumed, that duty had to be performed with due care. *See Cottam*, 764 N.E.2d at 821. **[—10—]**

StudentCity also points to a sentence in the memorandum accompanying its summary judgment motion, to the effect that "StudentCity owed no such duty [the breach of] which was the proximate cause of Lisa Tam Chung's death." This statement plainly went to duty, not causation, as a basis for summary judgment. Consequently, we conclude, without serious question, that StudentCity never raised causation as a ground for summary judgment. **{-103-}**

Because causation was not placed in issue, we deem the district court's decision to base its ruling on that ground to be "a species of sua sponte summary judgment." *Berkovitz v. Home Box Office, Inc.*, 89 F.3d 24, 28 (1st Cir. 1996). While a district court may in rare circumstances enter summary judgment on a ground not raised by any party, *see* Fed. R. Civ. P. 56(f)(2), that power should be exercised sparingly and "with great circumspection," *Stella v. Town of Tewksbury*, 4 F.3d 53, 55 (1st Cir. 1993). The "spontaneous nature" of the district court's action, though, does not affect our de novo standard of review. *Berkovitz*, 89 F.3d at 30; *accord John G. Alden, Inc. of Mass. v. John G. Alden Ins. Agency of Fla., Inc.*, 389 F.3d 21, 24 (1st Cir. 2004).

When considering the boundaries of a district court's authority to grant summary judgment sua sponte, we have regularly imposed two constraints: first, discovery must be "sufficiently advanced" to afford the parties "a reasonable opportunity to glean **[—11—]** the material facts"; and second, the "targeted party" must have been given "notice and a chance to present its evidence on the essential elements of the claim or defense." *Berkovitz*, 89 F.3d at 29; *accord Block Island Fishing, Inc. v. Rogers*, 844 F.3d 358, 363, 4 Adm. R. 47, 51 (1st Cir. 2016); *Wells Real Estate Inv. Trust II, Inc. v. Chardon/Hato Rey P'ship*, S.E., 615 F.3d 45, 51 (1st Cir. 2010). These conditions afford important protections: access to discovery ensures that a litigant has an opportunity to learn the relevant facts, and notice that an issue is in play ensures that a litigant has an opportunity to put his best foot forward. Both safeguards are applicable where, as here, the district court grants summary judgment on a ground not previously raised. *See Block Island Fishing*, 844 F.3d at 363, 4 Adm. R. at 51.

In applying these tenets, discovery is deemed to be sufficiently advanced once it has "proceeded to the point where the parties underst[an]d the material facts." *Sanchez v. Triple-S Mgmt., Corp.*, 492 F.3d 1, 7 (1st Cir. 2007) (quoting *Penobscot Indian Nation v. Key Bank of Me.*, 112 F.3d 538, 562 (1st Cir. 1997)). This means, at a minimum, that there must be a reasonable opportunity to conduct discovery on a particular issue. Here, the plaintiffs were not given the chance to conduct any discovery at all on the causation issue. The district court's order reserving decision on the summary judgment motion, fairly read, contemplated discovery on only two factual issues: the existence of a duty to **[—12—]** supervise (that is "whether defendant voluntarily undertook a duty to ensure the safety of trip participants") and whether StudentCity breached its duty to investigate SMA (that is, "whether defendant knew or should have known about [SMA]'s dubious prior safety record"). *Chung I*, 2013 WL 6528516, at *2.

Subsequent proceedings and communications drove home the circumscribed scope of the permitted discovery. When the parties expressed uncertainty about the reach of the court's order, the plaintiffs sought to confirm (by an e-mail to the court clerk) "that the fact discovery deadline . . . only relates to the facts related to the summary judgment issue of whether the defendant had a duty to protect the decedent and the deadline does not relate to all fact discovery on all issues in the event the motion for summary judgment is denied." The clerk responded that discovery was so limited and that "if the motion is denied, I will set up another hearing for the parties to come in and talk to the Judge." StudentCity's counsel was copied on both parts of this e-mail exchange.

StudentCity's own objections to the plaintiffs' discovery requests support our **{-104-}** conclusion that discovery was limited and excluded causation. In framing these objections, StudentCity insisted that discovery was limited to "whether [it] represented to Lisa Chung that it would be providing supervision on the snorkeling excursion, the scope of that allegedly-assumed **[—13—]** duty, whether that duty was breached, and whether StudentCity negligently selected [SMA]." Causation was not mentioned—a fact that undercuts StudentCity's assertion (at oral argument in this court) that the plaintiffs could have deposed its employees freely to seek information on the cause of Lisa's death. That assertion is also undercut by the fact that, during discovery, StudentCity objected to providing "the name and contact information of all employees of [StudentCity] responsible for supervision and student safety on the date of the subject accident."[4]

Later, the district court, acting on a motion to compel, issued an order that confirmed the circumscribed nature of the permitted discovery:

> In its previous order the court allowed the parties to conduct discovery limited to certain issues raised by defendant's motion for summary judgment. They include (1) representations made to the plaintiffs, both, participants and their parents, concerning the safety of participants; (2) investigations defendant undertook of the entities engaged for particular activities and of any brokers or agents who assisted the selection of such entities; (3) defendant's knowledge of the qualifications of the owners and crew of the vessel in issue; and (4) any other information that bears on defendant's duty, if any, to ensure participants' safety and how they performed that duty. **[—14—]**

Chung v. StudentCity.com, Inc., No. 10-10943, 2014 WL 644439, at *1 (D. Mass. Feb. 19, 2014). The purport of this order was quite clear.[5] And if any doubt lingered about the limited scope of the permitted discovery, that doubt was erased when the parties (after the discovery period ended) filed their supplemental briefing. Most telling was StudentCity's supplemental brief, which declared:

> the only issues are (1) whether StudentCity negligently selected the *Sea Star* and thus could be held liable to the plaintiffs on a negligent selection theory or (2) whether StudentCity voluntarily assumed a duty where one would not otherwise exist to ensure Lisa Chung's safety on board the *Sea Star*.

The district court's summary judgment order overlooks the restricted nature of the parties' opportunity to develop the facts. It incorrectly states that "[d]iscovery is now complete." It makes no mention of the limitation theretofore imposed on discovery. The order, which turned on an issue not argued by the parties and as to which no discovery had been allowed, was beyond the district court's authority. "When a court charts a procedural route, lawyers and litigants are entitled to rely on it." *Berkovitz*, 89 F.3d at 30. **[—15—] {-105-}**

To compound the error, the plaintiffs had no notice that causation was an issue ripe for decision at this stage of the case. It is common ground that, as a precondition to the entry of summary judgment, the targeted party must be "on notice that she had to come forward with all of her evidence." *Celotex Corp. v. Catrett*, 477 U.S. 317, 326 (1986). In this context, adequate notice has two components: "the summary judgment target is

[4] Even though StudentCity proceeded to furnish this information, it restated its belief "that this request . . . exceeds the scope of the Court's . . . order in that it is not limited to whether StudentCity assumed a duty to supervise the June 7, 2008 snorkeling excursion."

[5] StudentCity argues that the phrase "how they performed that duty" imports some ambiguity into the order. Given the context, we do not think that a reasonably prudent lawyer would have believed that this oblique reference, without more, opened the door for unlimited discovery. *Cf. Benitez-Garcia v. Gonzalez-Vega*, 468 F.3d 1, 4 (1st Cir. 2006) (explaining that failure to honor discovery orders may expose attorneys to sanctions).

entitled to know both the grounds that the district court will consider and the point at which her obligation to bring forth evidence supporting the elements of her claim accrues." *Rogan v. Menino*, 175 F.3d 75, 79 (1st Cir. 1999). Here, the plaintiffs were not seasonably apprised that the court would consider the causation issue, nor were they put on notice to adduce evidence supporting their view of that issue.

In *Block Island Fishing*, we suggested, albeit without deciding, that it may be necessary to show prejudice when seeking to vacate a sua sponte summary judgment. *See* 844 F.3d at 364 & n.1, 4 Adm. R. at 52 & n.1. Here, the plaintiffs have satisfied any such burden. For one thing, there is every reason to believe that discovery directed at causation would have shed light on whether StudentCity's acts or omissions contributed to Lisa's death. For another thing, even on this underdeveloped record, the district court's conclusion (that no reasonable jury could find that a breach of StudentCity's voluntarily assumed duty to supervise caused Lisa's death) is far **[—16—]** from ironclad. The district court stated, without any elaboration, that "Lisa's death resulted not from inadequate supervision by StudentCity staff, but rather from the boat accident caused by the overloading of the *Sea Star* and its negligent operation by [SMA]." As we explain below, the facts do not necessarily support that leap in logic.

The plaintiffs' flagship claim is that StudentCity's failure to supervise the snorkeling excursion, *in combination with the shipowner's negligence*, caused Lisa's death. The district court's reasoning seems to give insufficient weight to the venerable rule that more than one tortfeasor can be held responsible for a single incident. *See Shantigar Found. v. Bear Mtn. Builders*, 804 N.E.2d 324, 332 (Mass. 2004) ("Under our current system of joint and several liability, a plaintiff injured by more than one tortfeasor may sue any or all of them for her full damages.").

On the meager record before us, numerous potential jury questions loom. For example, would an on-duty StudentCity representative, if on board at the commencement of the voyage, have thought that the boat was overcrowded and confronted its captain and crew?[6] Would that representative have prevented the **[—17—]** passengers from congregating on one side of the vessel, and thus avoided its tragic imbalance? Would StudentCity supervision have effected a more efficient emergency exit for Lisa, particularly in view of the fact that some Sea Star crew members deserted ship?

The answers to these (and other) questions of fact are not certain. What is certain, though, is that none of these questions was properly before the district court at summary judgment.

To say more would be to paint the lily. The record reflects that the district court granted summary judgment for StudentCity on an issue—causation—as to which no **{-106-}** discovery had been allowed and no notice had been afforded. That was error, and manifestly not harmless. The summary judgment ruling, therefore, must be set aside.

III. CONCLUSION

We need go no further. For the reasons elucidated above, we vacate the judgment of the district court and remand for further proceedings consistent with this opinion.

Vacated and Remanded. **Costs shall be taxed in favor of the plaintiffs.**

---

[6] In this regard, we note that StudentCity admitted, through the deposition of its director of operations, *see* Fed. R. Civ. P. 30(b), that its employees should step in to quell "obvious" **[—17—]** dangers. At an event not run by StudentCity, this might include alerting the managers of the gathering to the danger.

United States Court of Appeals
for the First Circuit

No. 16-2103

GOETHEL
vs.
UNITED STATES DEP'T OF COMMERCE

Appeal from the United States District Court for the District of New Hampshire

Decided: April 14, 2017

Citation: 854 F.3d 106, 5 Adm. R. 21 (1st Cir. 2017).

Before **KAYATTA,** Circuit Judge, **SOUTER,** Associate Justice,* and **STAHL,** Circuit Judge.

* Hon. David H. Souter, Associate Justice (Ret.) of the Supreme Court of the United States, sitting by designation.

[—3—] {-108-} **STAHL,** Circuit Judge:

This case arrives on the court's deck from regulations promulgated by the National Marine Fisheries Service (NMFS), which require that on certain commercial fishing trips, fishermen must be accompanied on their vessels by at-sea monitors to ensure compliance with catch quotas, and that the industry must foot the bill for these unwelcome guests. David Goethel, a New Hampshire fisherman joined in these proceedings by a group of commercial fishermen subject to this "industry funding" requirement, brought suit in federal district court in New Hampshire, claiming that the industry funding requirement violates several pertinent statutes and is also unconstitutional.

The district court granted summary judgment in favor of the government, reasoning that Goethel's suit was not filed within the applicable statute of limitations and that Goethel's statutory and constitutional challenges would have failed even if timely. On appeal, Goethel renews the bulk of his constitutional and statutory arguments, and urges this court to find that his suit was not time-barred. Because we agree with the district court that Goethel's suit was not timely, we AFFIRM the grant of summary judgment in favor of the government, and do not reach the question of whether the industry funding requirement contravenes the edicts of the relevant statutes or the Constitution. **[—4—]**

I. Facts & Background

A. The Regulations

The Magnuson-Stevens Fishery Conservation and Management Act (MSA), 16 U.S.C. §§ 1801-1884, was passed by Congress in 1976 in "[r]espon[se] to depletion of the nation's fish stocks due to overfishing." *Associated Fisheries of Me., Inc. v. Daley*, 127 F.3d 104, 107 (1st Cir. 1997). The stated goals of the MSA were, *inter alia*, to "conserve and manage the fishery resources found off the coasts of the United States" and "to promote domestic commercial and recreational fishing under sound conservation and management principles." 16 U.S.C. § 1801(b)(1),(3). The MSA tasked the Department of Commerce[1] with regulating commercial fishing throughout the Exclusive Economic Zone of the United States, which extends 200 nautical miles from the seaward boundary of each coastal state. *Id.* § 1802(11); *see also* Pres. Proc. No. 5030, Exclusive Economic Zone of the United States, 48 Fed. Reg. 10,605 (Mar. 10, 1983) (defining the geographic scope of the **[—5—]** Exclusive Economic Zone of the United States and the **{-109-}** sovereign rights exercised therein under international law).

Pursuant to the MSA, eight regional Fishery Management Councils (FMCs) were established and charged with preparing, and, if circumstances warranted, amending, regional Fishery Management Plans (FMPs), which set certain standards for the fishing industry within the given FMC's regional purview. The MSA was amended in 2007 to

[1] The Department of Commerce in turn delegated this role to the National Oceanic and Atmospheric Administration ("NOAA"), which regulates the fisheries through its sub-agency, the National Marine Fisheries Service ("NMFS"). For simplicity's sake, these entities (all of which are named as defendants-appellees along with their respective chiefs in their official capacities) are referred to throughout this opinion as the "government."

include a requirement that each FMP include "measures to ensure accountability" with respect to catch limits. *See* 16 U.S.C. § 1853(a)(15). In an effort to effectuate this requirement, the regional FMP at issue in this case, the Northeast Multispecies FMP, was amended by the New England Council (the relevant FMC) to include a requirement that commercial fishermen within the purview of the Northeast Multispecies FMP must, on occasion, be accompanied by at-sea monitors (ASMs) who would collect certain data related to the particular fishing trip and the vessel's catch. *See generally* Northeast (NE) Multispecies Fishery, Amendment 16, 75 Fed. Reg. 18,262 (Apr. 9, 2010). The amendment that added this monitoring requirement was known as "Amendment 16," and was published on April 9, 2010, following a period of public comment. Goethel was a council member at the time of the enactment of Amendment 16 and voted against the proposal.

The at-sea monitors are human employees of private, third-party contractors who accompany the fishermen on board their **[—6—]** vessels during certain fishing trips, observe their activities to ensure compliance with fishing limits, and file reports upon their return to port. While catch quotas had previously been imposed, and overall catch hauls recorded upon a fisherman's return to port, at-sea monitors were intended to verify the specific geographic areas in which a boat fished, and also to monitor fish discards at sea. *See* 75 Fed. Reg. at 18,342. While not every fishing journey is monitored, costs for the monitors when a particular fishing trip is selected for such monitoring are estimated at $700-$800 per trip. *See Goethel v. Pritzker*, No. 15-CV-497-JL, 2016 WL 4076831, at *1 (D.N.H. July 29, 2016). Application of the at-sea monitoring program depends on whether a particular fishmerman is a member of a "sector," an association of "vessels that have voluntarily signed a contract and agree[d] to certain fishing restrictions," most notably catch restrictions and management requirements compiled in a sector operations plan. *See Lovgren v. Locke*, 701 F.3d 5, 15-16 (1st Cir. 2012) (citing Northeast (NE) Multispecies Fishery, Amendment 13, 69 Fed. Reg. 22,906, 22,945 (Apr. 27, 2004)). The sector program is voluntary and those vessels that choose not to join a sector are still able to fish from the "common pool" allocation of fish under a separate program that tracks number of days spent at sea, rather than using catch limits, and that does not require at-sea monitoring. *See generally* 50 C.F.R. § 648.82 (discussing days-at-sea restrictions for **[—7—]** members of the common pool). The relevant sectors in this case are comprised of those fishing for groundfish.[2]

As is the case with many government regulations, Amendment 16 requires compliance without offering to pay or reimburse the regulated entity for the cost of compliance. To the contrary, Amendment 16 itself requires that the sector fishermen bear the costs of the at-sea monitors. *See* Northeast (NE) Multispecies Fisheries, Amendment 16, 75 Fed. Reg. 18,262, 18,342 (April 9, 2010) ("Beginning in fishing year 2010, a sector must develop, implement, **{-110-}** and pay for, to the extent not funded by NMFS, an independent third-party dockside/roving and at-sea/electronic monitoring program that is satisfactory to, and approved by, NMFS . . . ."). Notwithstanding this clear requirement, the government paid the ASM costs throughout the first several years of the program's existence. *See, e.g.*, Standardized Bycatch Reporting Methodology Omnibus Amendment, 80 Fed. Reg. 37,182, 37,185 (June 30, 2015) ("To date, we have been able to provide sufficient funding for the groundfish sector at-sea monitoring program such that industry did not have to pay for at-sea monitoring.").

However, a 2011 ruling by the D.C. Circuit required NMFS to fund a separate reporting program, *see Oceana v. Locke*, 670 **[—8—]** F.3d 1238 (D.C. Cir. 2011), which in turn depleted the funds that the agency had available for the at-sea monitoring program in the Northeast. Beginning in 2015, responding to funding shortfalls caused by the requirements of the D.C. Circuit ruling, NMFS took a series of steps to inform the

[2] "Groundfish" is a generic term for various bottom-dwelling fish species including, most notably, cod, haddock, halibut, and flounder. *Goethel*, 2016 WL 4076831, at *2 n.4.

sectors that it could no longer fund the at-sea monitoring costs, and the sectors themselves and their constituent fishermen would soon be on the hook for these costs, as envisioned by Amendment 16. Because of the importance of the various dates in 2015 for purposes of the statute of limitations, we explain the relevant communications between the agency and the regulated sectors below.

- **March 9, 2015**: NMFS published a Proposed Rule to approve seventeen sector operations plans for fishing years 2015 and 2016. While noting that the agency had been able to pay the costs of ASM coverage during the years 2012 to 2014, the agency explained that this would change: "Due to funding changes . . . we expect that sector vessels will be responsible for paying at-sea costs associated with the ASM program before the end of the 2015 fishing year." Proposed Rule, 2015 and 2016 Sector Operations Plans for Northeast Multispecies Fishery, 80 Fed. Reg. 12,380, 12,385 (Mar. 9, 2015).

- **May 1, 2015**: NMFS published a final rule that reiterated the same language from the March 9th proposed rule, namely, that the agency "expect[ed] that sector vessels will be responsible for paying the at-sea portion of costs associated with the sector ASM program before the end of the 2015 fishing year." Final Rule, 2015 and 2016 Sector Operations Plans for Northeast Multispecies Fishery, 80 Fed. Reg. 25,143, 25,148 (May 1, 2015). The notice also added that "funding for our portion of ASM costs is expected to expire before the end of the 2015 fishing year" but "we have begun working on an implementation plan to **[—9—]** help ensure a seamless transition when the industry assumes responsibility for at-sea costs in 2015." *Id.* at 25,149.

- **November 10, 2015**: NOAA Northeast Fisheries Science Center announced that "federal funds in the major at-sea monitoring contracts for northeast groundfish sectors will be expended by December 31, 2015," and that "[t]ransition of monitor sea-day costs to industry will therefore be effective January 1, 2016." This announcement was sent to the relevant sectors in an email, but was not published in the Federal Register. The email, titled "Update: Federal Funding for At-Sea Monitoring Ends December 31, 2015," stated, in pertinent part:

  > Based on the data we have on actual fishing effort, we have determined **{–111–}** that federal funds in the major at-sea monitoring contracts for northeast groundfish sectors will be expended by December 31, 2015. Transition of monitor sea-day costs to industry will therefore be effective January 1, 2016.

Although the November 10th email notification purported to establish a date certain when industry funding would kick in (January 1, 2016), the government was ultimately able to continue paying ASM costs through mid-February 2016. Additionally, on June 23, 2016, a NOAA email notification informed the Northeast Sector that the agency would fully fund the shore-based monitoring program and would "use remaining funds to offset some of industry's costs of the groundfish at-sea monitoring program."

B. The Parties

Plaintiff-appellant David Goethel is a New Hampshire-based commercial fishermen and sector member who is subject to the **[—10—]** various provisions of the Northeast Multispecies FMP, including the industry funding requirement for the at-sea monitoring program. Plaintiff-appellant XIII Northeast Fishery Sector, Inc. ("Sector 13"), one of the approved groundfish sectors, is a corporation organized under Section 501(c)(5) of the U.S. Internal Revenue Code, and consists of thirty-two fishermen and twenty active boats. The members of Sector 13 are also subject to the Northeast Multispecies FMP, including the at-sea monitoring program. Goethel and Sector 13 presented evidence that the industry funding requirement for the at-sea monitoring program would impose draconian costs on the Sector and its members, including citing a NOAA report which concluded that "nearly 60% of the fleet could see negative returns to owner when full 2015 ASM costs are factored in." Plaintiffs-appellants are concerned that the industry funding requirement will essentially render the groundfish industry no longer viable from a commercial standpoint.

The defendants-appellees are the U.S. Department of Commerce, the NOAA, and the NMFS, as well as their respective directors in their official capacities.

C. The Lawsuit

Goethel filed his suit on December 9, 2015. As discussed in greater detail below, Goethel argues that because his complaint was filed within thirty days of the November 10th email notification, it was therefore timely under the MSA's thirty-day **[—11—]** statute of limitations. In his complaint and subsequent briefing to the district court, Goethel advanced a multitude of alleged statutory and constitutional violations, falling into one of three categories: an allegation that the industry funding requirement is unlawful, a challenge to the at-sea monitoring requirement in general, and a facial attack on the entire Magnuson-Stevens framework. We briefly describe these claims below.

First, Goethel alleged that the industry funding requirement was unlawful because the agency acted in excess of its statutory authority under the MSA and failed to follow proper procedures, resulting in agency action that was arbitrary, capricious, and an abuse of discretion, in violation of the requirements of the Administrative Procedure Act (APA), 5 U.S.C. § 706(2)(A).[3] In addition to alleging a violation of the APA, Goethel cast his net even further, alleging that the industry funding requirement was an improper tax in violation of the Appropriations Clause, U.S. Const. art. I, § 9, cl. 7, the Anti- **{-112-}** Deficiency Act (ADA)[4], 31 U.S.C. § 1341, and the Miscellaneous **[—12—]** Receipts Act (MRS)[5], 31 U.S.C. § 3302, and also constituted the imposition of improper user fees in violation of the Independent Offices Appropriations Act (IOAA)[6], 31 U.S.C. § 9701. He also alleged that the industry funding requirement violated the interstate commerce clause, U.S. Const. art. I, § 8, cl. 3, by requiring that the fishermen enter the market for at-sea monitors and purchase those services. Finally, he alleged two procedural violations: that the agency failed to prepare a Regulatory Flexibility Analysis, as required by the Regulatory Flexibility Act (RFA), 5 U.S.C. §§ 601-612, and that it failed to assess the impact of its regulatory actions on the environment, as required by the National Environmental Policy Act (NEPA), 42 U.S.C. §§ 4321–4370e. All of these arguments are preserved on appeal, with the exception of the alleged NEPA violation, which is not raised in Goethel's opening brief.

---

[3] With some exceptions not relevant to the present case, the MSA generally incorporates the APA's judicial review provisions. *See* 16 U.S.C. § 1855(f)(1)(B).

[4] In relevant part, the ADA prohibits federal officers from "mak[ing] or authoriz[ing] an expenditure or obligation exceeding an amount available in an appropriation or fund for the expenditure or obligation" and from "involv[ing] [the United States] in a contract or obligation for the payment of money before an **[—12—]** appropriation is made unless authorized by law." 31 U.S.C. § 1341(a)(1)(A)-(B).

[5] This statute provides that "an official or agent of the Government receiving money for the Government from any source shall deposit the money in the Treasury as soon as practicable without deduction for any charge or claim." 31 U.S.C. § 3302(b).

[6] The IOAA permits an agency to "prescribe regulations establishing the charge for a service or thing of value provided by the agency," 31 U.S.C. § 9701(b), in effect recouping fees from those who receive services provided by the agency.

Second, Goethel challenged the at-sea monitoring program itself (as distinct from the requirement that the sectors pay for **[—13—]** it) on constitutional grounds. The sheer volume of constitutional claims that Goethel made initially suggests that he was, in a manner of speaking, on a fishing expedition. Specifically, he alleged that the at-sea monitoring requirement violates the First Amendment by "compelling fishermen to join sectors"[7]; violates the Port Preference Clause[8] by discriminating between the various States, leading fishing vessels to prefer one state's port over another; and violates the Fourth Amendment's prohibition on unreasonable searches and seizures. Not content to leave any part of the kitchen sink unused, Goethel also alleged that the at-sea monitoring program violates the Third Amendment's prohibition on the quartering of soldiers during peacetime because fishermen were compelled to accommodate federally-mandated monitors on multi-day fishing voyages.[9] Of these **{-113-}** arguments, only the Fourth Amendment claim is preserved in this appeal. **[—14—]**

Third, Goethel alleged that the entire MSA regulatory framework was unconstitutional. First, he alleged that the regional FMCs are improperly constituted, in violation of the Appointments Clause, U.S. Const. art. II, § 2, cl. 2, because members of the councils are "inferior officers" whose appointments could thus only be vested "in the President alone, in the Courts of Law, or in the Heads of Departments." Goethel argues that because the governors of the various coastal states are involved in nominating individuals to the councils, and because state executive officials are not among the permissible entities in which Congress can vest the appointment power for inferior officers, the councils are constitutionally infirm and actions taken by those councils, including the Northeast Multispecies FMP, are void. Second, Goethel argues that the MSA conscripts state officers by requiring that they participate in the councils, in turn violating the Tenth Amendment anti-commandeering doctrine. *See Printz v. United States*, 521 U.S. 898, 935 (1997) ("The Federal Government **[—15—]** may neither issue directives requiring the States to address particular problems, nor command the States' officers, or those of their political subdivisions, to administer or enforce a federal regulatory program."). The alleged violations of the Appointments Clause and the Tenth Amendment are preserved in this appeal.

D. The District Court Ruling

After the parties cross-moved for summary judgment, the district court, in an order dated July 29, 2016, rejected Goethel's various challenges and granted summary judgment in favor of the government. First, the court found that the claims were not timely because "the plaintiffs [sic] 30–day window to challenge the industry funding component of ASM closed, at the latest, in June 2015, well before this suit

---

[7] This argument was abandoned by the plaintiffs during an early phase of the proceedings below, was not addressed by the district court in its opinion, and is not raised on appeal.

[8] *See* U.S. Const. art. I, § 9, cl. 6 ("No Preference shall be given by any Regulation of Commerce or Revenue to the Ports of one State over those of another; nor shall Vessels bound to, or from, one State, be obliged to enter, clear, or pay Duties in another."). Goethel likewise abandoned this argument prior to summary judgment, and does not raise it on appeal.

[9] *See* U.S. Const. Amend. III ("No Soldier shall, in time of peace be quartered in any house, without the consent of the Owner, nor in time of war, but in a manner to be prescribed by law."). The Third Amendment was a response to the Quartering Acts of 1765 and 1774, in which Parliament authorized British military commanders to requisition private homes as barracks, *see Englblom* [—14—] *v. Carey*, 677 F.2d 957, 967 (2d Cir. 1982) (Kaufman, J., concurring in part and dissenting in part), and its application to private contractors engaged in on-board monitoring of the fishing industry is a dubious proposition to say the least. However, as with the Port Preference Clause and First Amendment claims, the plaintiffs conceded their Third Amendment argument before summary judgment, thus depriving this court of the rare opportunity to opine on the scope and application of the Third Amendment. *See Goethel*, 2016 WL 4076831, at *9 n.13 ("Earlier in this litigation, plaintiffs also argued that industry funding of ASM also violated the Third Amendment's prohibition against quartering of soldiers. They no longer advance that claim.").

was filed." *Goethel*, 2016 WL 4076831, at *4. The district court rejected Goethel's argument that the November 10th email notification was a separately reviewable "action" under the MSA, but also declined the government's invitation to find that the statute of limitations began to run in 2012 when the regulations implementing Amendment 16 took effect, which would have meant Goethel's claims were time-barred by a matter of years. *See id.* at *3-4.

Second, the court, after concluding that Goethel's suit was time-barred, proceeded to analyze Goethel's statutory and constitutional claims, and found that they would have failed on **[—16—]** the merits even if his suit had been filed within the MSA's thirty-day statute of limitations.

This timely appeal followed.

II. Analysis

The district court determined that Goethel's complaint was barred by the MSA's statute of limitations, a finding that we review de novo. *See Santana-Castro v. Toledo-Dávila*, 579 F.3d 109, 113 (1st Cir. 2009). The MSA includes provisions that govern judicial review. Specifically, parties may challenge "regulations promulgated **{-114-}** by" NMFS, 16 U.S.C. § 1855(f)(1), and they may also seek review of "actions that are taken by the Secretary under regulations which implement a fishery management plan, including but not limited to actions that establish the date of closure of a fishery to commercial or recreational fishing," *id.* § 1855(f)(2). Furthermore, as relevant (and ultimately dispositive) to this case, judicial review is only available if a complaint "is filed within 30 days after the date on which the regulations are promulgated or the action is published in the Federal Register, as applicable." *Id.* § 1855(f)(1).

As an initial matter, we address an argument that Goethel spends much time advancing in both his opening and reply briefs: that he is entitled to pre-enforcement review under the APA, in lieu of violating the statute and then bringing his statutory and constitutional arguments as a defense to an enforcement action. **[—17—]** The thirty-day statute of limitations embodied in the MSA, Goethel argues, does not apply to pre-enforcement review. Not so. Of course pre-enforcement review is available as a general matter under the MSA, but, as the district court noted below, "plaintiffs cite no authority which permits the court to waive the statute of limitations applicable to pre-enforcement review" of agency action under the MSA. *Goethel*, 2016 WL 4076831, at *4 n.4.

On appeal, Goethel renews this same argument, but fails to cite any authority for the proposition that the thirty-day statute of limitations in the MSA can be deep-sixed simply by the fact that the party seeking judicial review is making a pre-enforcement challenge to the statute in question. Indeed, the courts that have encountered this question appear to have uniformly concluded that the thirty-day statute of limitations cannot be sidestepped when a party is challenging a regulation promulgated pursuant to NMFS authority under the MSA. *See, e.g., Turtle Island Restoration Network v. U.S. Dep't of Commerce*, 438 F.3d 937, 939 (9th Cir. 2006) (concluding that although the appellant's claims were "framed . . . in terms of violations of the APA [and environmental statutes]," they were "in actuality . . . challenge[s] to the reopening of the [swordfish] Fishery" and thus subject to the MSA's thirty-day statute of limitations); *N.C. Fisheries Ass'n, Inc. v. Evans*, 172 F. Supp. 2d 792, 798–99 (E.D. Va. 2001) (holding that challenges to regulations arising from an **[—18—]** FMP amendment must be filed within the thirty-day statute of limitations period from the promulgation of the amendment itself); *F/V Robert Michael, Inc. v. Kantor*, 961 F. Supp. 11, 15 (D. Me. 1997) (concluding that lobstermens' challenge to the Department of Commerce's denial of permits, on the grounds that such a denial violated the MSA, was time-barred because "[p]laintiffs' quarrel lies with the regulation itself" and that regulation had been promulgated long before the plaintiffs sought review); *Stinson Canning Co. v. Mosbacher*, 731 F. Supp. 32, 34–35 (D. Me. 1990) ("Plainly, Congress intended pre-enforcement review since it provided that a petition for such review must be filed thirty days from promulgation."). We agree with these cases and hold that Goethel's pre-enforcement challenge only can proceed if it was filed within thirty days of the "action" in question as required by § 1855(f)(1).

Goethel's case, therefore, hinges on whether the November 10th email is a separately reviewable "action" for purposes of the thirty-day statute of limitations, since any of the other pertinent dates—the 2010 promulgation of Amendment 16 which included by its own terms a requirement of industry funding, and the March 9th and May 1st, 2015, proposed **{–115–}** and final rules announcing the expected exhaustion of government contributions to the at-sea monitoring program—would fall well outside the thirty-day window. Goethel argues that it was on November 10th, **[—19—]** for the first time, that the government established a "date certain" when industry funding would finally take effect, and therefore this date should be treated as the relevant "action."

In support of this argument, he cites to *Bennett v. Spear*, 520 U.S. 154 (1997), where the Supreme Court explained that agency actions are reviewable under Section 704 of the APA when they (1) "mark the 'consummation' of the agency's decision-making process" and (2) are events "by which 'rights or obligations have been determined,' or from which 'legal consequences will flow.'" *Id.* at 177-78. Here, Goethel argues, the November 10th date was both the "consummation of the agency's decision-making process" by setting a date on which money would no longer be expended by the agency, and also when "obligations" had been "determined," namely who would pay the monitoring costs. Goethel also argued to the district court, and argues again on appeal, that prior to having a date certain on which industry funding actually would kick in, a potential suit would have been dismissed as unripe. *See Goethel*, 2016 WL 4076831, at *4 n.6 (rejecting Goethel's ripeness argument as "necessarily speculative," but also observing that it was "inconceivable that a suit filed within 30 days of the Rule's publication in May 2016 [sic] would have been found unripe").

We are not convinced by Goethel's argument. First, the language of § 1855(f) itself requires that for judicial review to be available, a complaint must be "filed within 30 days after the **[—20—]** date on which the regulations are *promulgated* or the action is *published in the Federal Register*, as applicable." 16 U.S.C. § 1855(f)(1) (emphasis added). Goethel does not argue that the November 10th email is a stand-alone "regulation," which, although not defined in the MSA, generally "refers to legally binding obligations placed upon a council and/or the agency which have the force and effect of law and, as such, are analogous to substantive rules issued by an administrative agency which are subject to APA review." *Tutein v. Daley*, 43 F. Supp. 2d 113, 121 (D. Mass. 1999) (citing *Chrysler Corp. v. Brown*, 441 U.S. 281, 301–302 (1979)). Nor was the November 10th email published in the Federal Register.

Second, to the extent that the language of the statute allowing for review within thirty days of the time when "the action is published in the Federal Register, as applicable," envisions a category of "actions" for which publication is *not applicable*,[10] **[—21—]** we disagree that the November 10th email

[10] In briefing and at oral argument, Goethel emphasized that insulating all non-published agency actions from review might create incentives for agencies to announce changes in particular regulatory programs that do shift certain legal obligations for regulated parties, and avoid legal challenges by refraining from publishing such decisions. While documents "having general applicability and legal effect" are generally "required to be filed for public inspection with the Office of the Federal Register and published in the Federal Register," 1 C.F.R. § 5.2(c), we do share Goethel's concern that a bright-line rule requiring publication in order for judicial review to be available under the MSA might preclude judicial review in cases where an unpublished action taken by an agency does, in fact, lead to a change in the legal position of regulated parties. Because we find that NOAA's November 10th email had no such effect, we save for a later day whether, under **[—21—]** certain circumstances, unpublished agency actions could still be subject to judicial review under the MSA.

{-116-} would qualify. Agency "action" for purposes of administrative law generally "includes the whole or a part of an agency rule, order, license, sanction, relief, or the equivalent or denial thereof, or failure to act." 5 U.S.C. § 551(13). Goethel's argument, that the email notification was the equivalent of an agency "order," clearly fails, as the APA defines an order as resulting from agency adjudication, *see id.* § 551(7), and there is no suggestion that the November 10th email was the product of an agency adjudication. Rather, the email was one of several updates sent to regulated parties throughout 2015, a routine effort to keep the sectors abreast of developments pursuant to a final rule which had been published in May of 2015.[11] In short, the November 10th notification does not have the significance that Goethel seeks to [—22—] assign to it, and we conclude that it is not a separately reviewable agency "action" for purposes of § 1855(f)(1).[12]

We agree with the district court that the most recent "action" that could have plausibly been challenged was the May 2015 final rule, and for that reason we agree with the district court that the "plaintiffs [sic] 30–day window to challenge the industry funding component of ASM closed, at the latest, in June 2015, well before this suit was filed." *Goethel*, 2016 WL 4076831, at *4. Therefore, the suit is time-barred.

III. Conclusion

Because we find that Goethel's suit was not filed within the MSA's thirty-day statute of limitations, we need go no further, and we take no position on the district court's statutory and constitutional rulings. However, given NOAA's own study which indicated that the groundfish sector could face serious difficulties as a result of the industry funding requirement, we note that this may be a situation where further clarification from Congress would be helpful for the regulated fisheries and the [—23—] agency itself as it balances the competing goals of conservation and the economic vitality of the fishery.

While the concurring opinion suggests that this is inappropriate, we note that it is not uncommon in this and other circuits to include language in opinions that flags potential issues for Congress to consider, should it choose to do so.[13] *See, e.g.*, {-117-} *Sony BMG Music Entm't v. Tenenbaum*, 660 F.3d 487, 490 (1st Cir. 2011) (commenting, in the context of a copyright infringement suit, that the case "raises concerns about application of the Copyright Act which Congress may wish to examine"); *Slayton v. Am. Express Co.*, 604 F.3d 758, 772 (2d Cir. 2010) (noting, while not deciding the issue, that "Congress may wish to give further direction on how to resolve [a] tension" in the Private Securities Litigation Reform Act); *Holender v. Mut. Indus. N. Inc.*, 527 F.3d 352, 357 (3d Cir. 2008) (observing, in a dispute over the scope of the Age Discrimination in Employment Act, that

---

[11] While we need not reach this issue given that the November 10th email does not meet the basic requirements for reviewable agency "action," we think, as a factual matter, that the sectors' obligation to pay was certainly consummated, at the latest, with publication of the May 2015 final rule. Therefore, *Bennett v. Spear*, which observed that for agency action to be "final," it must "mark the 'consummation' of the agency's decision-making process," 520 U.S. at 178 (internal citation omitted), is of no help to Goethel in this case because the November 10th email had no such effect.

[12] Goethel and Sector 13 were subject to the applicable regulations at the time NMFS promulgated Amendment 16, and at the time that the government announced, in the May 2015 final rule, that the industry funding requirement would kick in at the beginning of the 2016 calendar year. Therefore, we need not consider what other rights, if any, a party who became subject to the regulations for the first time more than thirty days after the May 2015 final rule would have, nor do we take any position on how the MSA's thirty-day statute of limitations would apply to a claim by such a party.

[13] Indeed, beginning in 1995 with the Long Range Plan for the Federal Courts, the Judicial Conference and Congress have collaborated on the Project to Provide Congress with Appellate Opinions Bearing on Technical Matters of Statutory Construction, and we have occasionally sent opinions to Congress that we believe may warrant additional clarification via legislation, precisely because, as the concurring opinion suggests, the judiciary lacks expertise on the policy trade-offs faced by Congress.

"Congress may wish to revisit this regulatory regime if it proves unworkable"); *Elsenety v. Health Care Fin. Admin.*, 85 F. App'x 405, 410 (6th Cir. 2003) (acknowledging that the statutory framework in question **[—24—]** created a "harsh rule" and that "[a]t some point in the future, Congress may wish to reexamine" the statute); *Cefalu v. Vill. of Elk Grove*, 211 F.3d 416, 428 (7th Cir. 2000) (suggesting that certain in-trial evidence presentations are likely reimbursable under statute governing fees for exemplification, but noting that "[g]iven the costs associated with some of these" practices, "this is an area that Congress may wish to revisit and supply further guidance"); *see also United States v. Godin*, 534 F.3d 51, 65 (1st Cir. 2008) (Lynch, J., concurring) (noting that "Congress may wish to clarify in new legislation the scope of the enhanced penalties" under an aggravated identity theft statute); *Schafer v. Am. Cyanamid Co.*, 20 F.3d 1, 7 (1st Cir. 1994) (Stahl, J., concurring) (agreeing with the majority's interpretation of the National Childhood Vaccine Injury Act, but "respectfully suggest[ing] that this is an issue which Congress may wish to revisit."); *Olson v. Gen. Dynamics Corp.*, 960 F.2d 1418, 1425 (9th Cir. 1991) (Reinhardt, J., concurring) ("The proliferation of ERISA [Employee Retirement Income Security Act] preemption cases, in my view, raises a question as to whether ERISA is having an effect that is substantially contrary to that intended by those who favored its adoption. This is a matter which Congress may wish to examine carefully."); *United States v. Collins*, CR No. 03-51 S, 2016 WL 6477031, at *3 n.1 (D.R.I. Nov. 2, 2016) (suggesting that "Congress may wish to consider amending the enumerated offenses clause of **[—25—]** [the Armed Career Criminal Act] to include those crimes, such as murder, which previously were understood to fall squarely within the residual clause.").

Because Goethel's claim is untimely, however, we **AFFIRM** the grant of summary judgment in favor of the government.

–Concurring Opinion Follows–

(Reporter's Note: Concurring opinion follows on p. 30).

[—26—] KAYATTA, Circuit Judge, concurring:

I join in the panel's opinion with the exception of its call on Congress to provide further clarification. The nicely reasoned conclusion that the petition is untimely means that we lack jurisdiction to consider the merits of the appeal. *See Norbird Fisheries, Inc. v. Nat'l Marine Fisheries Serv.*, 112 F.3d 414, 416 (9th Cir. 1997). My colleagues nevertheless call on Congress to provide "further clarification" not concerning the matter of our jurisdiction, but rather concerning "the industry funding requirement" in light of the "competing goals" at stake. To the extent my colleagues imply that the statute is unclear, or that the "competing goals" at stake trigger some sort of express statement preference in these circumstances, I respectfully disagree. The default norm, manifest without express statement in literally hundreds of regulations, is that the government does not reimburse regulated entities for the cost of complying with **{–118–}** properly enacted regulations, at least short of a taking. If this statute needs clarification on this point, then so too do hundreds of others. Additionally, given that we have no jurisdiction to hear the merits of this appeal, nor any expertise on the policy trade-offs made by Congress in deciding how best to protect our fisheries from overfishing, and who should pay for that protection, I think it prudent to be more parsimonious with our advice. *See* Stephen Breyer, *Active Liberty: Interpreting Our Democratic* **[—27—]** *Constitution* 5 (2005) ("The judge, compared to the legislator, lacks relevant expertise.").

United States Court of Appeals for the First Circuit

No. 15-2105

UNITED STATES vs. BUENO-BELTRÁN

Appeal from the United States District Court for the District of Puerto Rico

Decided: May 15, 2017

Citation: 857 F.3d 65, 5 Adm. R. 31 (1st Cir. 2017).

Before **HOWARD,** Chief Judge, **TORRUELLA,** and **THOMPSON,** Circuit Judges.

[—2—] {–66–} PER CURIAM:

Defendant-Appellant Eduardo Bueno-Beltrán appeals from the district court's revocation of his supervised release and imposition of a 24-month term of imprisonment. Because the district court did not **{–67–}** abuse its discretion when it admitted hearsay evidence or err in finding that Bueno violated his supervised release terms, we affirm.[1]

In 2014, Bueno, a citizen of the Dominican Republic, pled guilty to conspiracy to bring unauthorized aliens into the United States without going through an authorized port of entry, in violation of 8 U.S.C. § 1324(a)(1)(A)(i) and (v). He was sentenced to one year of imprisonment and three years of supervised release. Bueno was deported shortly thereafter. During Bueno's period of supervised release, U.S. Coast Guard personnel interdicted his boat off the coast of the Dominican Republic. Bueno and two other Dominican citizens were aboard the vessel, which was allegedly en route to Puerto Rico. The officers attested that as they approached the boat, the three men began throwing bales overboard, and that when the officers boarded the boat, Bueno identified himself as its captain. Nine bales recovered from the water surrounding the boat field-tested positive for cocaine. **[—3—]** Bueno was subsequently arrested and indicted for importing and conspiracy to import and possess, with intent to distribute, controlled substances on board a vessel subject to United States jurisdiction. *See United States v. Bueno-Beltrán*, No. 15-cr-00189-GAG (D.P.R. filed Mar. 18, 2015).

After being notified of the new charges against Bueno and holding a hearing, the district court revoked Bueno's supervised release, finding four separate violations: 1) committing another federal, state, or local crime; 2) possessing, using, distributing or administering any controlled substance; 3) associating with any person engaged in criminal activity; and 4) returning to the United States after removal. The court imposed a 24-month term of imprisonment, to be served consecutively with any sentence that he would receive in the then-pending drug-importation case.

On appeal, Bueno challenges the district court's admission of hearsay evidence in the form of two Coast Guard officers' statements detailing what transpired when they approached and boarded Bueno's vessel.[2] Bueno contends that admitting these statements violated his Sixth Amendment right to **[—4—]** confront the witnesses against him. *See Crawford v. Washington*, 541 U.S. 36, 68-69 (2004).

We note at the outset that although "the Sixth Amendment forbids the introduction of an out-of-court testimonial statement unless the witness is unavailable and the defendant has previously had an opportunity to cross-examine her . . . [this prohibition] does not apply to supervised release revocation proceedings." *United States v. Rondeau*, 430 F.3d 44, 47 (1st Cir. 2005) (internal citation

[1] Bueno also challenges his initial three-year term of supervised release, which was imposed in 2014. However, this claim is not properly before this Court, as it is untimely. *See* Fed. R. App. P. 4(b)(1)(A); *Perez-Perez v. Popular Leasing Rental, Inc.*, 993 F.2d 281, 282 (1st Cir. 1993).

[2] During the revocation hearing, Bueno also made a Confrontation Clause challenge to the admissibility of the field-test results, offered in the form of photos showing two separate tests conducted on the bales. However, he makes only a cursory reference to this argument on appeal and it is thus waived. *See United States v. Zannino*, 895 F.2d 1, 17 (1st Cir. 1990).

omitted). We also note that the Federal Rules of Evidence do not apply to revocation proceedings, *see* Fed. R. Evid. 1101(d)(3), and revocation proceedings "should be flexible enough to consider evidence including letter affidavits, and other material that would not be admissible in an adversary **{-68-}** criminal trial." *See Rondeau*, 430 F.3d at 47 (quoting *Morrissey v. Brewer*, 408 U.S. 471, 489 (1972)). Nonetheless, criminal defendants still have limited confrontation rights under Fed. R. Crim. P. 32.1(b)(2)(C), which confers the right to "question any adverse witness unless the court determines that the interest of justice does not require the witness to appear." *Rondeau*, 430 F.3d at 48 (quoting Fed. R. Crim. P. 32.1(b)(2)(C)). This requires the court to balance the defendant's right to confront the witnesses with the government's good cause for denying confrontation. *Id.* A court should consider "the reliability of the hearsay testimony and the government's reason for declining to produce the **[—5—]** declarant." *Id.* We review a district court's decision to admit hearsay evidence under this rule for abuse of discretion. *Id.*

We conclude that the court did conduct this balancing test and acted within its discretion in finding that the hearsay testimony was reliable. First, the court noted that the details elucidated in the officers' statements were "clearly, clearly, well defined." *See United States v. Marino*, 833 F.3d 1, 6 (1st Cir. 2016) (finding hearsay evidence reliable when it was "packed with details"). Second, the statements were corroborated by photographs depicting Bueno at the stern of the boat, the bales recovered in the water around the boat, and images of the field-test results. *See Rondeau*, 430 F.3d at 48 (identifying corroboration as another indicator of reliability). As for cause, the fact that the officers were based in Miami, Florida, while the revocation hearing was held in San Juan, Puerto Rico, provided sufficient reason for the court to excuse their absence. *See Marino*, 833 F.3d at 5 ("'[C]oncern . . . with the difficulty and expense of procuring witnesses from perhaps thousands of miles away' is a paradigmatic example of the type of situation that might call for the admission of hearsay evidence at a revocation proceeding." (quoting *Gagnon v. Scarpelli*, 411 U.S. 778, 782 n.5 (1973))). Thus, the district court did not abuse its discretion in admitting this hearsay testimony. **[—6—]**

Bueno also challenges the court's reliance on the field tests conducted on the bales, on the grounds that the tests were not "sufficiently reliable" to indicate that the substance was cocaine. In the main, the substance of his argument is that the field tests "cannot be used as prima facie evidence that [he] violated the terms of his supervised release." We review this challenge—which was not raised below—for plain error. *See United States v. Millan-Isaac*, 749 F.3d 57, 66 (1st Cir. 2014).

We spy no error, plain or otherwise, in the district court's consideration of the field test results to support the finding that Bueno violated the terms of his supervised release. Such violations need only be proven by a preponderance of the evidence. *See* 18 U.S.C. § 3583(e)(3); *United States v. Oquendo-Rivera*, 586 F.3d 63, 66 (1st Cir. 2009). We review the evidence in the light most favorable to the government, remembering again that the Rules of Evidence do not apply, and that the hearing is in front of a judge, not a jury, while also noting that credibility is largely a matter for the finder of fact. *Oguendo-Rivera*, 586 F.3d at 67. Here, the government presented evidence of two separate field tests conducted on the bales, both indicating that the substance was cocaine. The experienced judge observed that, while such tests are not inherently admissible in a full-blown criminal trial, they are "very, very reliable." Indeed, several Courts of Appeals have held that positive field test results, **[—7—]** coupled with other evidence, have been sufficient to prove that a substance is a narcotic. *See, e.g.,* **{-69-}** *United States v. Thompson*, 633 Fed. App'x 534, 537 (2d Cir. 2015); *United States v. Crane*, 599 Fed. App'x 383, 384 (11th Cir. 2015); *United States v. Ching Tang Lo*, 447 F.3d 1212, 1222-23 (9th Cir. 2006). We see no reason to chart a different course in this type of proceeding. When considered with the statements indicating that the boat's occupants threw the bales overboard upon the Coast Guard's approach, the district court's reliance, in part, on these field tests was not an error.

For the foregoing reasons, the district court's revocation of Bueno's supervised release and imposition of a 24-month sentence are ***affirmed***.

United States Court of Appeals
for the First Circuit

No. 16-1551

UNITED STATES
vs.
DÍAZ-ROSADO

Appeal from the United States District Court for the District of Puerto Rico

Decided: May 16, 2017

Citation: 857 F.3d 89, 5 Adm. R. 34 (1st Cir. 2017).

Before **TORRUELLA, LIPEZ,** and **BARRON,** Circuit Judges.

[—2—] {-91-} BARRON, Circuit Judge:

On August 15, 2013, José Díaz-Rosado ("Díaz") was indicted in the United States District Court for the Southern District of Florida for his role in planning and organizing a maritime smuggling operation involving over 1,000 kilograms of cocaine. Five days later, Díaz was indicted again—this time, in the United States District Court for the District of Puerto Rico—for his role in planning and organizing a maritime smuggling operation involving over 1,000 kilograms of cocaine. Díaz contends that the Double Jeopardy Clause of the United States Constitution bars his prosecution on the Puerto Rico charges because the Florida charges already encompass the conduct for which he was indicted in Puerto Rico. For the reasons set forth below, we reject this challenge and affirm the decision of the District Court to deny Díaz's motion to dismiss the Puerto Rico indictment on double jeopardy grounds.

I.

Because Díaz's double jeopardy challenge to the Puerto Rico indictment hinges in part on the procedural history of the Florida case, we first need to describe the two indictments and their subsequent travel in some detail. We will then be well **[—3—]** positioned to explain why we are unpersuaded that the Puerto Rico indictment must be dismissed on double jeopardy grounds.

A.

On August 6, 2012, federal agents intercepted a vessel carrying approximately 1,032 kilograms of cocaine off the coast of Guayama, Puerto Rico.[1] The vessel was registered to Díaz, who had rented a dock for it in Fajardo, Puerto Rico. The government later determined that Díaz also hired the vessel's two-man crew: Jorge Suárez-Albelo and Joel Perpiña-Quiles. Although Díaz was not on board at the time of its seizure, he and another individual were responsible for following behind the vessel in a separate boat.

Roughly five months later, on December 30, 2012, federal authorities intercepted a second vessel off the coast of St. Croix, United States Virgin Islands—this one carrying approximately 1,157 kilograms of cocaine. This vessel had a different two-man crew: José De León and Wilson Concepción. Díaz had purchased this second vessel. He also had directed an associate—who later became a confidential source of the Broward County, Florida, Sherriff's Office—to purchase two outboard motors for it. **{-92-}**

The December seizure formed the basis for a one-count indictment filed against Díaz in the United States District Court **[—4—]** for the Southern District of Florida on August 15, 2013. Díaz was charged with one count of conspiracy to possess with intent to distribute five kilograms or more of cocaine, in violation of 21 U.S.C. §§ 846 and 841(b)(1)(A)(ii). Díaz pleaded guilty several months later.

During sentencing, the Florida district court relied on both the August and December seizures as evidence that Díaz was responsible for trafficking 2,189 kilograms of cocaine. The Florida district court also applied a four-level sentencing enhancement under § 3B1.1(a) of the United States Sentencing Guidelines for acting as the organizer or leader of a criminal activity involving five or more participants,

[1] We recite these uncontested facts as laid out in the Magistrate Judge's report and recommendation, the pre-sentence report accompanying Díaz's Florida guilty plea, and the prosecutor's statements at Díaz's change-of-plea hearing.

and a two-level sentencing enhancement under § 3C1.1 of the Guidelines for obstruction of justice for encouraging the confidential source to lie to government investigators. Díaz was initially sentenced to life in prison.

Five days after Díaz was indicted in Florida, the government filed a two-count indictment against him in the United States District Court for the District of Puerto Rico. Based on the August seizure, the Puerto Rico indictment charged Díaz with one count of conspiracy to import more than five kilograms of cocaine into the United States, in violation of 21 U.S.C. §§ 952, 960, and 963, and one count of conspiracy to possess with intent **[—5—]** to distribute five kilograms or more of cocaine, in violation of 21 U.S.C. §§ 846 and 841(b)(1)(A)(ii).

Díaz moved to dismiss the Puerto Rico indictment the same day he entered his plea of guilty in the Florida case. Díaz contended that the conduct charged in the Puerto Rico indictment—in particular, Díaz's participation in the events leading up to the August seizure—had already been charged in the Florida case and thus that dismissal of the Puerto Rico indictment was required by the Fifth Amendment's Double Jeopardy Clause.

The District Court did not rule on that motion right away. Instead, the District Court held that motion in abeyance pending the resolution of the Florida proceedings.

With the Puerto Rico case on hold, Díaz pursued an appeal of his sentence in the Florida proceedings to the Eleventh Circuit. In that appeal, he contended, among other things, that the Florida district court erred in applying the four-level leadership enhancement, and in failing to apply a two-level downward adjustment for acceptance of responsibility, pursuant to § 3E1.1 of the Guidelines. *United States v. Díaz-Rosado*, 615 Fed. Appx. 569, 572 (11th Cir. 2015).

On June 25, 2015, the Eleventh Circuit vacated and remanded the sentence. *Id.* at 569. That court concluded, first, that "no evidence was provided to support [Díaz's] leadership role with respect to the four crewmen"—Suárez, Perpiña, De León, and **[—6—]** Concepción—and second, that the confidential source could not be "considered a participant." *Id.* at 579. On this basis, the Eleventh Circuit then remanded the case to the Florida district court for reconsideration of its decision to apply the leadership enhancement, directing the district court also to reconsider its decision not to apply the downward adjustment for acceptance of responsibility. *Id.* at 581. Upon remand, Díaz was sentenced on February 18, 2016 to 240 months of imprisonment.[2] **{–93–}**

B.

Several days later, the proceedings in the federal district court in Puerto Rico resumed. The District Court referred the motion to dismiss the indictment to a magistrate judge. The Magistrate Judge issued a report and recommendation recommending **[—7—]** that the District Court deny Díaz's motion to dismiss on April 5, 2016.

The Magistrate Judge found as follows. With respect to Count One of the Puerto Rico indictment, the Magistrate Judge first noted that the offense charged therein was not an offense charged in the Florida case. Accordingly, citing *United States v. Ortiz-Alarcon*, 917 F.2d 651, 652 (1st Cir. 1990), the Magistrate Judge denied Díaz's motion to dismiss Count One. The Magistrate Judge explained that the elements of the statute

[2] The Eleventh Circuit upheld the Florida district court in two other respects. First, *Díaz-Rosado* held that the District Court did not plainly err in finding that there was a factual basis for the plea. 615 Fed. Appx. at 573-74. Second, *Díaz-Rosado* held that the Florida district court adequately explained the charges against Díaz and thus did not plainly err during the plea colloquy. *Id.* at 574-75. On remand, the parties agreed that Díaz was eligible for a two-level downward adjustment pursuant to the so-called "safety-valve" provisions laid out in 18 U.S.C. § 3553(f), and §§ 2D1.1(b)(17) and 5C1.2 of the Guidelines. In sentencing Díaz a second time, the Florida district court did not apply the four-level leadership enhancement, nor did it apply the two-level downward adjustment for acceptance of responsibility.

Díaz was charged with violating in that count, 18 U.S.C. § 952, are different from the elements of the statute Díaz was charged with violating in the one-count Florida case and therefore his prosecution on Count One in the Puerto Rico case presented no double jeopardy problem.

With respect to Count Two of the Puerto Rico indictment, the Magistrate Judge held that the conspiracy for which Díaz was charged in the Puerto Rico indictment was a separate one from the conspiracy for which he was charged in the Florida district court. Applying the five-factor test we laid out in *United States v. Laguna-Estela*, 394 F.3d 54, 56 (1st Cir. 2005), the Magistrate Judge concluded that three of the *Laguna-Estela* factors—the time of the activities, the persons involved, and the evidence that would be adduced at trial—favored the government.

First, as to timing, the Magistrate Judge noted that the conspiracy charged in Puerto Rico "ended in September 2012," and **[—8—]** therefore "covers a different time period than the conspiracy alleged in the Florida indictment, which began in October 2012." Second, as to personnel, the Magistrate Judge emphasized that the August conspiracy—the one charged in Puerto Rico—involved Suárez and Perpiña, whereas the December conspiracy—the one charged in Florida—involved De León and Concepción. Finally, as to evidence, the Magistrate Judge noted that there "were two different drug shipments, involving different time periods and persons," which "supports a finding that distinct evidence would have to be adduced in order to establish each of the two conspiracies." "What is more," the Magistrate Judge held, "because none of the individuals in the December 2012 conspiracy (apart from Díaz) were involved in the alleged August 2012 conspiracy, the government may prove an agreement—the essential component of a conspiracy—between Díaz and the individuals in the August 2012 voyage without resorting to proof of an agreement between Díaz and the individuals involved in the December 2012 voyage."

The Magistrate Judge, however, held that the remaining two *Laguna-Estela* factors—the places involved and the fact that the two statutory provisions under which Díaz was charged were the same—did weigh in favor of Díaz. The Magistrate **{-94-}** Judge noted that "either the 'Dominican Republic or Puerto Rico' were the 'final destination' for the shipments" charged in both indictments. (citation omitted). And, the Magistrate Judge also **[—9—]** noted that Count Two of the Puerto Rico indictment and the one count of the Florida indictment both "alleged violations of the same statutory provisions," thus tipping the fifth *Laguna-Estela* factor in Díaz's direction. But, after weighing these five factors, the Magistrate Judge ultimately concluded that the conspiracies charged in the two indictments were separate ones insofar as the conduct charged in the two indictments involved distinct time periods, personnel, and evidence, and recommended that the District Court deny Díaz's motion to dismiss Count Two of the Puerto Rico indictment on double jeopardy grounds.

The Magistrate Judge's report and recommendation informed Díaz that he had fourteen days to file objections. The report and recommendation also notified Díaz that "[f]ailure to file timely and specific objections . . . [would constitute] a waiver of the right to appellate review." Díaz, however, did not file any objections to the report and recommendation. Accordingly, on April 26, 2016, the District Court adopted the Magistrate Judge's report and recommendation that Díaz's motion to dismiss be denied and directed that the parties proceed with trial preparation.

Díaz then filed this timely interlocutory appeal. We agree with the parties that we have jurisdiction to hear the appeal pursuant to the Supreme Court's decision in *Abney v. United States*, 431 U.S. 651, 661-62 (1977), which made clear that a "double **[—10—]** jeopardy challenge to [an] indictment must be reviewable" before the defendant is to stand trial on that indictment. *United States v. Toribio-Lugo*, 376 F.3d 33, 37 (1st Cir. 2004) (noting that, while ordinarily a "defendant cannot pursue an immediate appeal from an interlocutory order in a criminal case," defendants may nevertheless "immediate[ly] appeal[] from denials of a motion to dismiss" if the appeal is "premised on colorable double jeopardy grounds").

II.

As this case comes to us, it appears that Díaz waived his right to bring the challenge he now advances by failing to file objections to the Magistrate Judge's report and recommendation. *See United States v. Lugo Guerrero*, 524 F.3d 5, 14 (1st Cir. 2008) (holding that the defendant "waived his right to . . . appeal because he failed to object to the recommendation of the magistrate's report"); *see also Thomas v. Arn*, 474 U.S. 140, 142 (1985) ("The question presented is whether a court of appeals may exercise its supervisory powers to establish a rule that the failure to file objections to the magistrate's report waives the right to appeal the district court's judgment. We hold that it may."); *Davet v. Maccarone*, 973 F.2d 22, 31 (1st Cir. 1992) ("Failure to raise objections to the Report and Recommendation **[—11—]** waives the party's right to review in the district court and those claims not preserved by such objection are precluded on appeal.").

Díaz contends that his double jeopardy claim is exempt from the ordinary application of these waiver rules because his guilty plea in the Florida case does not now foreclose him from bringing this double jeopardy challenge. It is by no means clear, however, that, under *United States v. Broce*, 488 U.S. 563, 571 (1989), Díaz's failure to object to the Magistrate Judge's report and recommendation did not thereby waive his right to bring this challenge. *See id.* (holding that "when [the defendants] **{-95-}** pleaded guilty to two charges of conspiracy on the explicit premise of two agreements which started at different times and embraced separate objectives, they conceded guilt to two separate offenses," and therefore could not subsequently "challenge the theory of the indictments and . . . attempt to show the existence of only one conspiracy"); *see also United States v. Stefanidakis*, 678 F.3d 99-100 (1st Cir. 2012). Nevertheless, even assuming that Díaz has not waived his right to bring this challenge, we conclude, as we now explain, that this interlocutory appeal fails on the merits.

A.

Díaz purports to challenge both counts of the Puerto Rico indictment on double jeopardy grounds. But, as Díaz does not dispute the District Court's conclusion that Count One of the Puerto Rico indictment did not present a double jeopardy problem **[—12—]** because it charged an offense that was not charged in the Florida case, we affirm and proceed to consider his challenge regarding Count Two of the Puerto Rico indictment.[3]

The government contends that we review the District Court's ruling under *Laguna-Estela* for abuse of discretion. *See Toribio-Lugo*, 375 F.3d at 38 ("The baseline standard of review applicable to a denial of a motion to dismiss on double jeopardy grounds following the declaration of a mistrial is abuse of discretion."). *Laguna-Estela* itself, however, seems to have applied a clear-error standard of review, 394 F.3d at 57. That case notwithstanding, we held in *United States v. Fornia-Castillo*, 408 F.3d 52, 68 (1st Cir. 2005)—decided several months afterwards—that "[t]he availability of double jeopardy protection is a constitutional question reviewable de novo." Here, because our conclusion holds irrespective of the standard of review, rather than choose among the various standards, we apply the more defendant-friendly standard of de novo review that Díaz contends is applicable. For even on de novo review, we disagree with Díaz that the District Court's denial of Díaz's motion to dismiss must be reversed under *Laguna-Estela*. **[—13—]**

Díaz first contends that there is a substantial overlap between the evidence at issue in the Florida case and the evidence that would be adduced at trial here, given the "obvious relatedness of the conduct." For that

[3] Because the District Court adopted the unobjected-to Magistrate Judge's report and recommendation, our references to the District Court's reasoning and conclusions encompass the Magistrate Judge's report and recommendation.

reason, he argues, the fourth *Laguna-Estela* factor—whether "the same evidence [would] be used to prove the two conspiracies," 394 F.3d at 57—favors him, rather than the government, as the District Court concluded. But, Díaz points to no specific facts in the record before the District Court that suggest that the District Court incorrectly applied or weighed this fourth *Laguna-Estela* factor. And while Díaz also argues that unidentified "principal players" in the two seizures at issue were the same—and thus that the second, personnel-based *Laguna-Estela* factor also favors him—that assertion, without more, is insufficient to meet his burden of "presenting evidence to establish a prima facie non-frivolous double jeopardy claim," *Laguna-Estela*, 394 F.3d at 56 (quoting *United States v. Booth*, 673 F.2d 27, 30-31 (1st Cir. 1982)), even if we assume that Díaz preserved this argument below.[4] Accordingly, Díaz provides no **[—14—]** basis **{-96-}** on which the District Court's ruling may be reversed under the framework we established in *Laguna-Estela*.

B.

Díaz does make a number of other arguments in support of his contention that the District Court erroneously denied his motion to dismiss. None have merit.

Díaz argues that, during the sentencing phase of the Florida proceedings, the government itself relied on evidence from the August seizure (the one charged in the Puerto Rico indictment) to demonstrate his responsibility for the December seizure (the one charged in the Florida case), thus making clear that Díaz participated in only one "overarching conspiracy." But, assuming favorably to Díaz that our review is de novo, we disagree.

The Supreme Court has explicitly rejected the argument "that double jeopardy principles bar a later prosecution or punishment for criminal activity where that activity has been considered at sentencing for a separate crime." *Witte v. United States*, 515 U.S. 389, 398 (1995). Thus, the fact that the government presented evidence to the Florida district court concerning the seizure for which Díaz was charged in this case does not suffice to show that the crimes charged in the two cases are the same for double jeopardy purposes.

Díaz also contends that the motion to dismiss must be granted based on two aspects of the record that he identifies for **[—15—]** the first time on appeal. Specifically, he contends that: (1) the Florida and Puerto Rico indictments were coordinated, and therefore represented the culmination of a "joint investigation" between law enforcement authorities in Florida and Puerto Rico and (2) the government opposed Díaz's request that his defense in the Florida case be handled by a former federal prosecutor in Puerto Rico because the Puerto Rico case and the Florida case were "essentially the same." But, Díaz made no reference to these facts in his motion to dismiss before the Magistrate Judge, and he did not object before the District Court to the Magistrate Judge's report and recommendation. Thus, our review is, at best, for plain error. *See United States v. Catalán-Roman*, 585 F.3d 453, 472 (1st Cir. 2009), *as amended* (Dec. 23, 2009) (holding that a double jeopardy claim not raised below is subject to plain error review). Díaz must therefore show that "(1) that an error occurred (2) which was clear or obvious and which not only (3) affected the defendant's substantial rights, but also (4) seriously impaired the fairness, integrity, or public reputation of judicial proceedings." *Stefanidakis*, 678 F.3d at 99 (quoting *United States v. Duarte*, 246 F.3d 56, 60 (1st Cir. 2001)).

We are, however, hard pressed to see how, taking Díaz's characterization of the record as true, the fact that the two prosecutions were similar enough to be handled by the same team of prosecutors in and of itself shows that the two conspiracies at **[—16—]** issue here are, in fact, one conspiracy under the Double

---

[4] Below, Díaz stated the following: "The facts of the Puerto Rico case occur right in the middle of the time frame of the conspiracy of the Southern District case, refer to the same alleged conduct . . . and occurred in Puerto Rico. The facts coincide in place, time, geographic area and factual description." He thus made no reference to any high-level individuals common to both conspiracies.

Jeopardy Clause. And Díaz offers no basis on which to conclude that the District Court's contrary ruling, notwithstanding these facts, was an error, let alone a clear or obvious one. Thus, we reject this challenge, too.

Finally, Díaz points to the Eleventh Circuit's decision vacating and remanding **{–97–}** his sentence in the Florida case as one that requires us to dismiss the indictment on double jeopardy grounds. But the Eleventh Circuit was plainly not, in so ruling, passing on whether the Puerto Rico and Florida cases involved the same conspiracy or different ones. As we have already noted, the Eleventh Circuit merely overruled the Florida district court's decision to apply a four-level leadership enhancement to Díaz for the conspiracy charged in that case (whatever its scope), and instructed the lower court to reconsider its decision not to apply a two-level downward adjustment for acceptance of responsibility. *Díaz-Rosado*, 615 Fed. Appx. at 571 (finding "no merit in [Díaz's] challenge to his conviction," and "revers[ing] his sentence and remand[ing] for resentencing"). For this reason, Díaz's final challenge must also be rejected.

III.

We ***affirm*** the judgment of the District Court.

United States Court of Appeals
for the First Circuit

No. 15-2171

SANTOS-RODRÍGUEZ
vs.
SEASTAR SOLUTIONS

Appeal from the United States District Court for the District of Puerto Rico

Decided: June 8, 2017

Citation: 858 F.3d 695, 5 Adm. R. 40 (1st Cir. 2017).

Before TORRUELLA, THOMPSON, and BARRON, Circuit Judges.

[—3—] **{-696-}** TORRUELLA, Circuit Judge:

Plaintiff Bernardino Santos-Rodríguez ("Santos") was injured in a boating accident when a corroded rod end that was part of the boat's steering mechanism failed. Santos and several relatives sued Defendant Seastar Solutions ("Seastar"), the manufacturer of the boat's steering mechanism, alleging a design defect and a failure to warn. Santos appeals from the district court's grant of summary judgment in favor of Seastar. We affirm.

I. BACKGROUND

A. Factual Background

1. The Boating Accident

On June 25, 2010, Santos was riding in a twin-engine boat in a bay near Guayama, Puerto Rico. Raúl Viera-Torres ("Viera") owned the boat, which was equipped with a hydraulic steering system manufactured in 2002 by Seastar (then known as Teleflex Canada Ltd.). The rod connecting the steering system to the right motor had a ball-joint at the end, which broke while the boat was in motion, resulting in a loss of steering and ejecting Santos from the boat. Santos sustained extensive injuries, resulting in paraplegia. None of the other plaintiffs, all relatives of Santos, were in the boat. Subsequent examination revealed that the rod end failed because of corrosion. **[—4—]**

2. The Instruction Manual and the Boat's Maintenance

The steering system's instruction manual (the "Manual") informed owners that "[b]i-annual inspection [of the steering system] by a qualified marine mechanic is required" and instructed them to "[c]heck fittings and seal locations for leaks or damage and service as necessary." The Manual did not include a specific warning about corrosion of the rod end.

The boat's owner, Viera, acquired it second-hand. He did not perform maintenance on the boat, did not keep a maintenance log or request maintenance documentation from the previous owner, and did not read the Manual or any of the warnings affixed to the steering system. Viera hired third-party mechanics to maintain the boat, but none of those mechanics ever brought the corroded rod end to Viera's attention. **{-697-}**

B. Procedural History

On June 14, 2012, Santos and four relatives filed the operative complaint, claiming diversity jurisdiction and, in the alternative, maritime jurisdiction. On March 13, 2015, the district court granted summary judgment to Seastar. It first ruled that federal maritime law, rather than the substantive law of Puerto Rico, applied to the plaintiffs' claims. The district court then determined that the plaintiffs' expert did not identify a specific design defect in his expert report. In doing so, the district court ruled that the expert's deposition testimony that **[—5—]** Seastar had used a type of stainless steel that was prone to corrosion in marine environments was inadmissible because it was not raised in the expert's report. The district court also ruled that Santos could not show causation on his failure-to-warn claim because there was no evidence that Viera or any person maintaining the boat had ever looked at the Manual or the steering system's warning labels. Finally, the district court dismissed claims by Santos's relatives, which were contingent on Santos's claims. The district court denied the plaintiffs' motion to alter or amend the judgment on September 8, 2015.

The plaintiffs timely appealed both orders.

II. ANALYSIS

"We review orders for summary judgment *de novo*, assessing the record in the light most favorable to the nonmovant and resolving all reasonable inferences in that party's favor." *Bingham v. Supervalu, Inc.*, 806 F.3d 5, 9 (1st Cir. 2015). Summary judgment is appropriate if "there is no genuine dispute as to any material fact and the movant is entitled to judgment as a matter of law." Fed. R. Civ. P. 56(a).

The plaintiffs claim that the district court erred by applying federal maritime law, rather than the substantive law of Puerto Rico. We need not address this choice-of-law issue, however, because even under the law of Puerto Rico, the plaintiffs **[—6—]** have not created a triable issue of fact on their claims for either a design defect or a failure to warn.

A. Santos Cannot Prove That Any Failure to Warn Caused His Injuries

Under Puerto Rico law,

> [a] plaintiff alleging failure to warn must prove[:] "(1) the manufacturer knew, or should have known of the risk inherent in the product; (2) there were no warnings or instructions, or those provided were inadequate; (3) the absence of warnings made the product inherently dangerous; [and] (4) the absence of adequate warnings or instructions was the proximate cause of plaintiff's injury."

Cruz-Vargas v. R.J. Reynolds Tobacco Co., 348 F.3d 271, 276 (1st Cir. 2003) (quoting *Aponte Rivera v. Sears Roebuck*, 44 P.R. Offic. Trans. 6, 144 D.P.R. 830 (1998)). The district court ruled that Santos had not shown causation because it was uncontested that Viera did not read the Manual, and there was no evidence that Santos himself, the mechanics who maintained the boat, or the boat's previous owner ever read the Manual or that anyone communicated the warnings in the Manual to Viera.

Here on appeal, the plaintiffs briefly summarize evidence that the Manual did not include any warnings about corrosion of the rod end and their expert's conclusion that the rod end was corroded and that this "caused loss of control of the steering of the boat," leading to the accident and Santos's injuries. They then assert, without citation, that "[u]nder Puerto Rico law, this is sufficient to raise a genuine issue of material **[—7—]** fact." This argument does not address the district court's conclusion that "no evidence has been brought **{-698-}** [to] the court's attention from which the trier of fact could reasonably infer that the omission of additional warnings caused Santos's damages." Unless someone read the Manual, no warnings in it could have prevented Santos's injuries. Thus, even assuming that the Manual did not contain "adequate warnings or instructions," that cannot be "the proximate cause of [Santos's] injury." *Cruz-Vargas*, 348 F.3d at 276; *see Ramírez v. Plough, Inc.*, 863 P.2d 167, 177 (Cal. 1993)[1] ("Plaintiff's mother, who administered the [drug] to plaintiff, neither read nor obtained translation of the product labeling. Thus, there is no conceivable causal connection between the representations or omissions that accompanied the product and plaintiff's injury."); *Massok v. Keller Indus., Inc.*, 147 F. App'x 651, 660 (9th Cir. 2005) (applying California law) ("[The plaintiff] admits that he did not read the warnings and so the sufficiency of [the manufacturer's] warnings is therefore irrelevant. [The plaintiff's] claim based on failure to warn is without merit."). **[—8—]**

[1] "[T]he Supreme Court of Puerto Rico has consistently relied upon California Supreme Court precedent when considering issues raised by the doctrine of strict product liability." *Acosta-Mestre v. Hilton Int'l of P.R., Inc.*, 156 F.3d 49, 55 (1st Cir. 1998) (citing *Collazo–Santiago v. Toyota Motor Corp.*, 149 F.3d 23, 25 (1st Cir. 1998)).

B. Santos Cannot Prove That Any Design Defect in the Steering Rod Caused His Injuries

To prove a products liability claim under Puerto Rico law, Santos must show that: "(1) [Seastar's] equipment has a defect, in any of its modalities; (2) the defect existed when the product left [Seastar's] control; (3) [Seastar] is in the business of selling this type of product; (4) the defect was the adequate cause of [Santos's injuries]; and (5) [Viera] use[d] the product in a manner that was reasonable and foreseeable by [Seastar]." *Rodríguez-Méndez v. Laser Eye Surgery Mgmt. of P.R., Inc.*, 195 D.P.R. 769, translation at 23-24 (June 15, 2016).[2] In *Rodríguez-Méndez*, the plaintiff developed an eye issue after he received laser eye surgery, and he sued the manufacturer of the surgical equipment for selling a defective product. *Id.* at 3. After discovery, the manufacturer moved for summary judgment, arguing, among other things, that the plaintiff had not identified a specific defect in the surgical equipment. *Id.* at 5. The court of first instance denied summary judgment, but the Puerto Rico Supreme Court reversed and ordered dismissal. *Id.* at 25. It determined that the plaintiff's reliance on the presence of metal particles in his eye was insufficient "to establish that [the surgical] equipment suffer[ed] from a manufacturing defect [or] **[—9—]** was defectively designed." *Id.* at 24. Rather, the plaintiff's evidence established only "that it is not normal to fin[d] metal particles in one's eye," and that showing was "deficient and insufficient" to survive summary judgment. *Id.* at 23.

Here, the plaintiffs' expert reported that the rod end was corroded and that this corrosion "was the main cause for the failure of the subject hydraulic steering cylinder rod end." No admissible evidence shows that the corrosion was because of some defect in the product's design. In fact, the plaintiffs' expert report focuses almost exclusively on whether the Manual included adequate warnings; it does not address whether the product was properly designed.[3]

The plaintiffs assert that the rod end "failed to perform as safely as an ordinary consumer would expect" and that their **{-699-}** expert "reported that the product's design was subject to corrosiveness." Their expert report, however, stated only that Seastar was "required to warn against all foreseeable hazards . . . associated with the subject hydraulic steering cylinder rod end's **[—10—]** interchangeability, corrosiveness, preventive maintenance, and the risks associated with its failure." It does *not* say that the rod end's design made it particularly susceptible to corrosion.

The plaintiffs' real argument is that the rod end failed, and that this is sufficient evidence of a design defect. This is precisely the type of showing rejected in *Rodríguez-Méndez*, where the plaintiffs' only evidence was that something was wrong—he had metal in his eye. 195 D.P.R. 769, translation at 23. Here, the plaintiffs' only showing is that something was wrong—the rod end failed.[4] Thus, the plaintiffs did not present evidence that

[2] All citations are to the certified translation filed by Seastar at Docket No. 69, Exhibit A.

[3] At his deposition, the plaintiffs' expert testified that Seastar used a type of stainless steel that "is not a good selection for [a] marine environment," rather than a less-corrosive type of stainless steel. But the district court ruled that that testimony was inadmissible because it constituted a new theory not addressed in the plaintiffs' expert report. On appeal, the plaintiffs "rely . . . simply on the expert report, and do without the deposition testimony."

[4] The plaintiffs cite to *Pérez-Trujillo v. Volvo Car Corp. (Sweden)*, 137 F.3d 50, 55 (1st Cir. 1998), for the proposition that "the malfunction itself is circumstantial evidence of a defective condition." This fails, first, because it is contrary to *Rodríguez*. Second, *Pérez-Trujillo* was a manufacturing defects case, in which the defendant argued that its product could not have malfunctioned in the way described. But an eyewitness directly observed the product malfunction—an airbag deploying under normal driving conditions—and the Court stated that "*direct observation of* the malfunction itself is circumstantial evidence of a defective condition." *Id.* (emphasis added).

Seastar's design of the rod end was defective.[5]
[—11—]

C. The Plaintiffs' Derivative Claims Cannot Survive

As Santos's four family members admit, their claims under Article 1802 of the Puerto Rico Civil Code—Puerto Rico's general tort statute—are derivative of Santos's claims, and so if his "claim fails, so too do[] the relative[s'] derivative claim[s]." *González Figueroa v. J.C. Penney P.R., Inc.*, 568 F.3d 313, 320 (1st Cir. 2009). Because the district court properly granted summary judgment on Santos's underlying claims, his relatives' derivative claims cannot succeed.

III. CONCLUSION

For the foregoing reasons, we affirm the district court's judgment. The parties shall bear their own costs.

Affirmed.

---

[5] The plaintiffs also assert that because Santos was an invitee, he was not responsible for the boat's maintenance. Thus, they reason, if "the accident was attributable to the owner's negligence in maintenance, and not to its design," it was Seastar's burden to cross-claim against Viera. The plaintiffs cite no authority for the proposition that Seastar could be liable for Viera's negligence after he purchased the steering system, and *Rodríguez-Méndez* forecloses this possibility. 195 D.P.R. 769, translation at 24 (holding that the manufacturer would not be liable if the doctor "departed from the reasonable use of the surgical machinery or did not give the require[d] maintenance").

United States Court of Appeals
for the First Circuit

No. 16-1320

UNITED STATES
vs.
ORTIZ-CARRASCO

Appeal from the United States District Court for the District of Puerto Rico

Decided: July 10, 2017

Citation: 863 F.3d 1, 5 Adm. R. 44 (1st Cir. 2017).

Before **HOWARD,** Chief Judge, **SELYA,** Circuit Judge, and **McCONNELL,** District Judge.*

* Of the District of Rhode Island, sitting by designation.

[—2—] {-1-} **SELYA,** Circuit Judge:

Much of our law traces its origins to pre-Revolutionary times. The jurisprudence {-2-} of the federal sentencing guidelines, though, is relatively young. Thus, we frequently encounter new questions of guideline interpretation. Defendant-appellant Raúl Ortiz-Carrasco attempts to serve up just such a question: whether a guideline provision that affords an enhancement for death occurring during the commission of an offense, *see* USSG §2L1.1(b)(7)(D), should be construed as including, sub silentio, a proximate cause requirement?

This question has splintered our sister circuits, but this court has not yet grappled with it. Although it might be tempting to stick our oar into these murky waters, we recently have warned that "courts should not rush to decide unsettled issues when the exigencies of a particular case do not require such definitive measures." *Privitera v. Curran (In re Curran),* 855 F.3d 19, 22 (1st Cir. 2017). We heed this warning today and, given the district court's supportable factfinding, hold that, regardless of whether or to what extent section 2L1.1(b)(7)(D) incorporates a causation requirement, the district court did not err in applying the enhancement. Accordingly, we affirm the sentence imposed.

I. BACKGROUND

We glean the facts from the unchallenged portions of the presentence investigation report (PSI Report) and the transcripts **[—3—]** of the multiple sentencing hearings. *See United States v. Cintrón-Echautegui,* 604 F.3d 1, 2 (1st Cir. 2010); *United States v. Dietz,* 950 F.2d 50, 51 (1st Cir. 1991). In June of 2014, the defendant and a confederate, Rando Bautista-Caraballo (Bautista), became part of a plot to smuggle migrants from the Dominican Republic into the United States. On June 22, the defendant navigated a yola (a small boat, commonly used for fishing) to the shores of the Dominican Republic. Once there, he joined forces with Bautista and took 20 undocumented Haitian migrants aboard. The yola then set out for Mona Island, Puerto Rico; Bautista and the defendant alternated as helmsmen.

With 22 persons aboard, the yola was severely overloaded and—to make a bad situation worse—it carried no life jackets or other safety equipment. The conditions of the voyage portended significant risks: the vessel would be traveling into the night in rough seas, with waves up to a foot and swells up to six feet. Heedless of these dangers, Bautista and the defendant pressed onward.

A Coast Guard helicopter spotted the yola mid-way through the voyage (when the craft was 12 nautical miles from the Dominican Republic and approximately 23 nautical miles from Mona Island). Noticing the helicopter, Bautista and the defendant reversed course and headed back toward the Dominican Republic. The helicopter, later supplanted by a Border Patrol airplane, kept **[—4—]** the yola under aerial surveillance until a Coast Guard cutter arrived. By then, it was nearly dark and the yola was stopped (with its engine off).

The Coast Guard sent out a boarding party. As the Coast Guard launch neared the yola, someone aboard the yola cried out that the boat was taking on water. Several of the passengers leaped to their feet, and the yola capsized. The two smugglers and 19 of the migrants were rescued, but the remaining migrant (Georges Yvon) drowned.

The government did not take this botched alien-smuggling operation lightly. Following some preliminary skirmishing (not relevant here), the defendant waived indictment and pleaded guilty to an information that charged him with unlawfully attempting to bring aliens into the United States at a place other than a designated point of entry. *See* 8 U.S.C. § 1324(a)(1)(A)(i). The final version of the **{-3-}** PSI Report recommended a ten-level enhancement because a person had perished during the commission of the offense of conviction. *See* USSG §2L1.1(b)(7)(D) (authorizing such an enhancement "[i]f any person died" during the commission of the offense). The defendant's total offense level (26), combined with his criminal history category (II), yielded a guideline sentencing range (GSR) of 70-87 months.

A series of sentencing hearings followed, primarily directed to the appropriateness of the ten-level enhancement. At **[—5—]** the first two hearings, the court took testimony from a Coast Guard officer, the defendant, and Bautista, and reviewed videotapes and photographs.[1] The government argued that the language of section 2L1.1(b)(7)(D) should be taken literally and, therefore, applied to the offense of conviction. The defendant argued that section 2L1.1(b)(7)(D) required a showing of causation, that the government had not proven that he caused Yvon's death, and as a result, that the enhancement was inappropriate in his case.

Prior to the third (and final) sentencing hearing, the district court filed a closely reasoned rescript, in which it concluded that the ten-level enhancement applied. The court found that, regardless of whether section 2L1.1(b)(7)(D) demanded a showing of causation, the enhancement fit the defendant's case.

When the district court convened the final sentencing hearing, the defendant sought reconsideration of the earlier ruling. Upon reconsideration, the court again ruled that the defendant was subject to the enhancement. The court then adopted the recommended GSR and imposed a downwardly variant sentence of 57 months' imprisonment. This timely appeal followed. **[—6—]**

II. ANALYSIS

This is a rifle-shot appeal: the defendant challenges only the application of the ten-level enhancement. Inasmuch as this challenge was preserved below, we review the sentencing court's "interpretation and application of the sentencing guidelines" de novo, the court's "factfinding for clear error," and its "judgment calls for abuse of discretion." *United States v. Ruiz-Huertas*, 792 F.3d 223, 226 (1st Cir.), *cert. denied*, 136 S. Ct. 258 (2015). In conducting this tamisage, we keep in mind that facts found by a sentencing court must be supported by a preponderance of the evidence. *See United States v. Cordero*, 42 F.3d 697, 702 (1st Cir. 1994).

As postured by the parties, this appeal revolves around the due interpretation of section 2L1.1(b)(7)(D). The courts of appeals have expressed widely divergent views about the type of causal connection, if any, that is necessary to trigger an enhancement under section 2L1.1(b)(7)(D). *See United States v. De La Cruz-García*, 842 F.3d 1, 2, 4 Adm. R. 36, 36-37 (1st Cir. 2016) (noting circuit split and collecting cases). To illustrate:

- The Tenth Circuit is at one end of the gamut. It has observed that the text of section 2L1.1(b)(7)(D) "contains no causation requirement" and, thus, courts "have no license to **[—7—]** impose one." *United States v. Cardena-Garcia*, 362 F.3d 663, 666 (10th Cir. 2004).[2] **{-4-}**

[1] Bautista pleaded guilty to a similar charge, and two of the three sentencing hearings involved both the defendant and Bautista. The two men were sentenced separately, though, and Bautista is not a party to this appeal. Consequently, we eschew any further reference to his sentencing.

[2] The court, however, added a caveat. It went on to say that when death is not an element of the underlying offense and section 2L1.1(b)(7)(D) is applied merely as a relevant conduct enhancement, it "might" be appropriate to consider whether the death was "reasonably foreseeable" and the

- The Fifth Circuit is at a mid-way point along the gamut. It acknowledges that the text of section 2L1.1(b)(7)(D) is bereft of any explicit causation requirement, but it reads that guideline provision in conjunction with USSG §1B1.3(a)(3), thereby implying a causation requirement. *See United States v. Ramos-Delgado*, 763 F.3d 398, 401-02 (5th Cir. 2014).[3] Consequently, the Fifth Circuit has concluded that section 2L1.1(b)(7)(D) requires at least but-for causation. *See id.*

- The Eighth Circuit is at the other end of the gamut. It has adopted a standard that bears a family resemblance to a proximate cause standard. Under the Eighth Circuit's formulation, the inquiry focuses on whether the death was **[—8—]** "causally connected to the dangerous conditions created by [the defendant's] unlawful conduct." *United States v. Flores-Flores*, 356 F.3d 861, 863 (8th Cir. 2004).

- The Eleventh Circuit is in somewhat the same place. It has embraced a standard reminiscent of the Eighth Circuit's standard, but which goes a step further. The inquiry focuses on foreseeability, that is, whether it was "reasonably foreseeable . . . that [the defendant's] actions or the actions of any other member of [his criminal] operation could create the sort of dangerous circumstances" likely to result in death. *United States v. Zaldivar*, 615 F.3d 1346, 1350-51 (11th Cir. 2010).

Against this chiaroscuro backdrop, the government, presumably because of uncertainty about exactly where the Tenth Circuit stands, *see supra* note 2, exhorts us to follow the Fifth Circuit's lead and adopt a but-for standard. For his part, the defendant exhorts us to read section 2L1.1(b)(7)(D) more grudgingly and incorporate a "proximate cause" standard, which—in context—appears to be an argument in favor of adoption of the Eighth Circuit's "causally connected" standard.[4] **[—9—]**

This compendium of dueling decisions and the parties' conflicting views present an interesting question—a question that this court has not yet answered. Such a question would pique the interests of a legal scholar, but judges—unlike academicians—are not at liberty to scratch every intellectual itch. As we explain below, the enhancement is appropriate in this case under any of the myriad interpretations of section 2L1.1(b)(7)(D); and where, as here, the question that the parties present can safely be left for another day, a court should not hurry to answer it. **{-5-}**

We need not tarry over the Tenth Circuit's rule, even if we take as a given that court's express statement that no showing of causation is required. In that court's view, the enhancement is proper so long as a death occurred during the commission of the offense. *See Cardena-Garcia*, 362 F.3d at 666. In this instance, the defendant does not dispute that Yvon died during the commission of the offense.

We turn next to the government's proposed but-for standard. An action is a but-for cause of a harm if "'the harm would not have occurred' in the absence of . . . the defendant's conduct." *Burrage v. United States*, 134 S. Ct. 881, 887-88 (2014) (quoting *Univ. of Tex. Sw. Med. Ctr. v. Nassar*, 133 S. Ct. 2517, 2525 (2013)). But-for cause is "*the minimum* requirement for a finding of causation." *Id.* at 888 (citation omitted). **[—10—]**

---

defendant's "conduct was a contributing factor." *Cardena-Garcia*, 362 F.3d at 666.

[3] USSG §1B1.3(a)(3) describes the "Relevant Conduct" that a sentencing court may consider when calculating a defendant's GSR. Such conduct in this context includes a defendant's "acts and omissions," USSG §1B1.3(a)(1)(A), as well as "all harm that resulted from [those] acts and omissions," *id.* §1B1.3(a)(3). The Fifth Circuit has reasoned that the phrase "'resulted from' imposes a requirement of actual or but-for causation" in connection with section 2L1.1(b)(7)(D). *Ramos-Delgado*, 763 F.3d at 401.

[4] To the extent that the defendant is attempting to advocate for the adoption of some other standard, that attempt is underdeveloped and, thus, not properly before us. *See United States v. Zannino*, 895 F.2d 1, 17 (1st Cir. 1990) (explaining that "issues adverted to in a perfunctory manner, unaccompanied by some effort at developed argumentation, are deemed waived").

It is nose-on-the-face plain that the defendant's actions were, at the very least, a but-for cause of Yvon's demise. Had the defendant not embarked on a voyage in an overloaded yola, traveling in rough seas and in the dark of night without a soupcon of safety equipment aboard, Yvon would not have drowned. No more is exigible to satisfy the minimalistic requirements needed to establish but-for causation.

In an ill-conceived effort to blunt the force of this reasoning, the defendant tries to shift the blame to the Coast Guard. He protests that the yola began taking on water because the Coast Guard launch came too close to it; that the migrants stood up only because the Coast Guard ordered them to raise their hands; and that Yvon might not have drowned had the Coast Guard brought along extra life jackets. These protests ring hollow. Say, for example, that a student neglects his studies, ignores required readings, declines to take advantage of available tutorials, and subsequently flunks the course. The student's indolence is a but-for cause of his failing mark, and that causal connection is not dissolved simply because the instructor posed hard questions on the final examination or refused to grade on a curve.

So it is here. The defendant's conduct would remain a but-for cause of Yvon's death even if the sentencing court had found—which it did not—that the Coast Guard's actions **[—11—]** contributed to the occurrence. *See Burrage*, 134 S. Ct. at 888 (explaining that an act can be a but-for cause even "if the . . . act combine[d] with other factors to produce the result" as long as "the other factors alone would not have done so").

The defendant fares no better under the Eighth Circuit's "causally connected" standard. The sentencing court, analogizing this case to *Flores-Flores*, 356 F.3d at 862-63, found as a matter of fact that such a causal connection existed. In *Flores-Flores*, the defendant accepted money to transport eleven undocumented aliens from one state to another by van. *See id.* at 862. The van was overcrowded (there were not enough seats to go around), so eight of the aliens had to sit on the floor without seatbelts. *See id.* Partway through their non-stop 2,000-mile trek, the defendant turned the steering wheel over to one of the passengers. *See id.* When that driver fell asleep at the wheel, the van crashed and two passengers died. *See id.* The district court applied the section 2L1.1(b)(7)(D) sentencing enhancement,[5] **{–6–}** and the Eighth Circuit affirmed, holding that the deaths were "causally connected **[—12—]** to the dangerous conditions created by [the defendant's] unlawful conduct." *Id.* at 863. The fact that the defendant transported more passengers than the van could safely carry "created a substantial risk of death or serious bodily injury" within the meaning of the guidelines. *Id.*

Though the defendant's reckless actions occurred at sea and not on land, his case is much the same as *Flores-Flores*. The defendant overloaded the yola with more people than it safely could carry, set out late in the day in rough seas, and provided nothing in the way of safety equipment. Any one of these conditions would have been hazardous; the combination was lethal. We hold, therefore, that the district court did not err at all—let alone clearly err—in finding a causal connection between the defendant's actions and Yvon's death.

Nor did the district court err when it found reasonably foreseeable that the defendant's actions "could create the sort of dangerous circumstances" likely to result in death. *Zaldivar*, 615 F.3d at 1351; *see De La Cruz-García*, 842 F.3d at 3, 4 Adm. R. at 37. It requires little imagination to foresee that setting out on a small and overloaded boat in stormy seas and with night approaching is an

[5] The Eighth Circuit opinion refers to section 2L1.1(b)(6)(4) rather than section 2L1.1(b)(7)(D). *See Flores-Flores*, 356 F.3d at 862. But this is because the Eighth Circuit was dealing with an earlier edition of the Guidelines Manual, and former section 2L1.1(b)(6)(4) was renumbered as section 2L1.1(b)(7)(D) without any substantive change in later editions of the Guidelines Manual (including the November 2015 edition, which was in effect when the defendant was sentenced). Since nothing turns on this renumbering, *Flores-Flores* is on-point authority with respect to the question before us.

invitation to disaster. Here, the defendant accepted just such an invitation, and he certainly could have foreseen the sort of calamity that eventually transpired. The court below recognized that the defendant had turned a blind eye to obvious danger and, **[—13—]** thus, found it reasonably foreseeable that the yola would "capsize in the middle of the sea, with unpredictable weather conditions, and in the dark of night." Similarly, the court found reasonably foreseeable that the passengers would panic, render the yola unstable, and wind up getting hurt without the customary safety equipment. Last—but not least—the court concluded that it must have been foreseeable to the defendant that the Coast Guard would try to prevent the yola from reaching the United States, especially since the defendant knew that his conduct was illegal.

In the end, we take no view of whether or to what extent section 2L1.1(b)(7)(D) requires a showing of causation. We have that luxury because, in the case at hand, all roads lead to Rome. Regardless of what level of causation, if any, section 2L1.1(b)(7)(D) is construed to require, the defendant was subject to the ten-level enhancement.

III. CONCLUSION

We need go no further. For the reasons elucidated above, the defendant's sentence is

Affirmed.

United States Court of Appeals for the First Circuit

No. 16-1589

IRONSHORE SPECIALTY INS. CO.
VS.
UNITED STATES

Appeal from the United States District Court for the District of Massachusetts

Decided: September 15, 2017

Citation: 871 F.3d 131, 5 Adm. R. 49 (1st Cir. 2017).

Before **BARRON, STAHL,** and **LIPEZ,** Circuit Judges.

[—3—] {-133-} LIPEZ, Circuit Judge:

This appeal arises out of an incident on the South Boston Waterfront, where a large military transport vessel, the FISHER, unexpectedly spilled over 11,000 gallons of fuel next to Boston Harbor. **{-134-}** Ironshore Specialty Insurance Company ("Ironshore"), the entity that paid the cleanup costs, appeals from a district court order dismissing claims it brought against American Overseas Marine Company, LLC ("AMSEA") and the United States under the Oil Pollution Act of 1990 ("OPA"), 33 U.S.C. §§ 2701-2761, general admiralty and maritime law. After carefully considering the parties' arguments and the relevant law, we affirm in part and reverse in part.

I.

The FISHER is a large, medium speed, "roll on, roll off" transport vessel and vehicle cargo ship. The Military Sealift Command, a division of the United States Navy, owns the FISHER. The vessel is deployed principally to carry military vehicles and containerized cargo for the Department of Defense.

In 2010, the Military Sealift Command entered into a contract with AMSEA, in which AMSEA agreed to crew, maintain, and make routine repairs to the FISHER. In June 2014, pursuant to that contract, the FISHER entered a Boston graving dock owned by Boston Ship Repair ("BSR"), with whom AMSEA had subcontracted to **[—4—]** perform routine maintenance.[1] No aspect of the maintenance related to fueling the FISHER, and only AMSEA crew members were permitted to conduct fuel transfers. On July 9, while the FISHER was propped up on blocks within the graving dock, an oil spill occurred as a result of the allegedly negligent conduct of AMSEA crew members. More than 11,000 gallons of diesel fuel poured out of the vessel and into the graving dock. To prevent the fuel from escaping into Boston Harbor—and to minimize damages to the FISHER and BSR's graving dock—BSR quickly acted to contain and remove the fuel.

BSR incurred nearly $3,000,000 in costs associated with cleaning up the FISHER's fuel spill, which Ironshore reimbursed as BSR's pollution policy insurer. As BSR's subrogee, Ironshore filed this action in the United States District Court for the District of Massachusetts against AMSEA and the United States to recover the money it paid to reimburse BSR's cleanup costs. Ironshore's three-count complaint sought (1) cleanup costs and damages under the OPA; (2) a declaratory judgment finding AMSEA and the United States to be strictly liable parties under the OPA; and (3) damages sounding in general admiralty and maritime law as a result of AMSEA's and the United States' alleged negligence. **[—5—]**

The United States and AMSEA each filed a motion to dismiss Ironshore's OPA claims under Federal Rule of Civil Procedure 12(b)(6). AMSEA also asked the district court to dismiss Ironshore's negligence claims against it. The district court granted both parties' motions to dismiss in full. The district court went further, however, and also dismissed sua sponte Ironshore's negligence claim against the United States, concluding that the OPA foreclosed the option of bringing any negligence claim relating to oil spills under general admiralty and maritime law.

[1] A "graving dock" is "a permanent structure on land with gates that allow vessels to enter and that then can be closed to drain out the water. In other words, it is a drydock." *Vasquez v. GMD Shipyard Corp.*, 582 F.3d 293, 298 (2d Cir. 2009) (quoting *San Francisco Drydock, Inc. v. Dalton*, 131 F.3d 776, 777 (9th Cir. 1997)).

Ironshore timely appealed, asserting that (1) the district court inappropriately considered documents outside the pleadings when it decided the defendants' motions to dismiss; and (2) it erroneously dismissed **{-135-}** each of Ironshore's OPA and negligence claims.

II.

We review a district court's grant of dismissal under Rule 12(b)(6) de novo, treating as true all well-pleaded facts in the complaint. *Isla Nena Air Servs., Inc. v. Cessna Aircraft Co.*, 449 F.3d 85, 87 (1st Cir. 2006).

A. Documents Outside the Pleadings

Ironshore argues that, as a threshold matter, the district court committed reversible error when it relied upon materials outside the pleadings in granting AMSEA's and the United States' 12(b)(6) motions to dismiss. Specifically, Ironshore challenges the district court's decision to consider the Military **[—6—]** Sealift Command's contract with AMSEA. Ironshore did not include or append this contract to its complaint. Rather, AMSEA and the United States provided excerpts of the contract to the district court alongside their respective motions to dismiss, and the United States appended the full contract to its reply to Ironshore's opposition to its motion to dismiss.[2] Ironshore asserts that, by relying on the contract in its disposition of the defendants' motions, the district court inappropriately converted the Rule 12(b)(6) motions to dismiss into Rule 56 summary judgment motions that "could not be properly resolved until the completion of discovery." We disagree.[3]

"Ordinarily[] . . . any consideration of documents not attached to the complaint, or not expressly incorporated therein, is forbidden, unless the proceeding is properly converted into one for summary judgment under Rule 56." *Watterson v. Page*, 987 F.2d 1, 3 (1st Cir. 1993). We have recognized, however, that when **[—7—]** considering 12(b)(6) motions to dismiss, "courts have made narrow exceptions for documents the authenticity of which are not disputed by the parties; for official public records; for documents central to plaintiffs' claim; or for documents sufficiently referred to in the complaint." *Id.* Moreover, "[u]nder First Circuit precedent, when 'a complaint's factual allegations are expressly linked to—and admittedly dependent upon—a document (the authenticity of which is not challenged),' then the court can review it upon a motion to dismiss." *Diva's Inc. v. City of Bangor*, 411 F.3d 30, 38 (1st Cir. 2005) (alteration in original) (quoting *Alternative Energy, Inc. v. St. Paul Fire & Marine Ins. Co.*, 267 F.3d 30, 34 (1st Cir. 2001)).

Although Ironshore's complaint does not explicitly reference the contract between the Military Sealift Command and AMSEA or the relationship between the two parties, the complaint alleges that the United States was the owner of the FISHER and that AMSEA was "[a]t all times material [to the dispute] the operator" of the FISHER. It further alleges that AMSEA and the United States are "responsible parties," subject to strict liability under **{-136-}** the OPA. Because the OPA indisputably exempts public vessels from liability, 33 U.S.C. § 2702(c)(2), Ironshore's OPA claims hinge upon the question of whether the FISHER qualifies as a public vessel. That question, in turn, requires an examination of the contractual relationship between the Military **[—8—]** Sealift Command and AMSEA. Ironshore has not preserved any challenge to the authenticity of the contract, and, as we explain below, the contract answers the determinative OPA question.[4] Hence, the district court did not

[2] AMSEA also submitted a number of other documents outside the pleadings along with its motion to dismiss, but the district court only relied upon one document outside the pleadings—the contract between the Military Sealift Command and AMSEA—in its memorandum of decision.

[3] Ironshore has also argued that even if it may have been appropriate to convert the defendants' Rule 12(b)(6) motions to dismiss into Rule 56 motions for summary judgment, the district court failed to provide Ironshore reasonable opportunity to present any additional material pertinent to such a summary judgment motion as required under Rule 12(d). Because we find no such conversion occurred, we need not address this grievance.

[4] In the district court, Ironshore urged the court to exclude the contract from consideration when

commit a reversible error by considering the contract between AMSEA and the Military Sealift Command when it decided the defendants' motions to dismiss.

B. Oil Pollution Act Claims

In 1989, the oil tanker Exxon Valdez ran aground in the Prince William Sound on the Alaska coast, causing the largest oil spill at that point in U.S. history. Congress enacted the OPA in response.[5] *See Metlife Capital Corp. v. M/V EMILY S.*, 132 F.3d 818, 820 (1st Cir. 1997). Before passage of the OPA, the Clean Water Act "provided liability limitations for federal pollution removal costs associated with oil spills." *Id.* The OPA altered the Clean Water Act framework by "impos[ing] strict liability for pollution removal costs and damages on the 'responsible party' for **[—9—]** a vessel . . . from which oil is discharged." *Id.* at 820-21 (citing 33 U.S.C. § 2702(a)). In turn, the OPA limits the total dollar amount for which a responsible party can be held liable, so long as that party has not committed acts of gross negligence or willful misconduct. *Id.* at 821. Finally, the statute "consolidated previously established oil pollution funds into the Oil Spill Liability Trust Fund[,] . . . which pays claims brought under the OPA after they have first been presented to the responsible party, if the responsible party is entitled to a defense, or the liability limit under the statute has been reached." *Id.*

In the context of oil spills occurring from a ship, the OPA defines a "responsible party," in part, as "any person owning, operating, or demise chartering the vessel." 33 U.S.C. § 2701(32)(A). But there is a caveat. The OPA explicitly states that the statute "does not apply to any discharge . . . from a public vessel." *Id.* at § 2702(c)(2). Furthermore, in spelling out which vessels fall under the purview of the OPA, the statute defines the term "vessel" as "every description of watercraft or other artificial contrivance used, or capable of being used, as a means of transportation on water, *other than a public vessel.*" *Id.* at §2701(37) (emphasis added). The statute defines a "public vessel" as "a vessel owned or bareboat chartered and operated by **[—10—]** the United States[] . . . except when the vessel is engaged in commerce." *Id.* at § 2701(29).

Ironshore seeks to recover costs that it incurred when it reimbursed its insured, BSR, for cleaning up the diesel spill. All parties agree that the OPA applies to diesel spills occurring in graving docks such as the one owned by BSR, and no party **{-137-}** argues that the FISHER was engaged in commerce when it discharged its fuel. AMSEA and the United States both assert that the FISHER is exempt from the OPA because it was both owned and operated by the United States at the time of the spill and, hence, qualifies as a public vessel under the act. Ironshore responds that while the United States was the owner of the FISHER at the time of the spill, AMSEA was its sole operator. Because AMSEA crew operated the ship rather than government employees, Ironshore argues, the FISHER does not qualify as a "public vessel" under the OPA, and Ironshore can recover from both parties under the statute.

Although the OPA states that vessels "owned and . . . operated by the United States" are public vessels, the statute provides no definition of the word "operated." Nor are we aware of any federal court, aside from the district court in this case, that has been required to interpret the precise definition of "public vessel" under the OPA. But the OPA is not the only federal statute that employs the term "public vessel." Congress enacted the Public Vessels Act in 1925, waiving the United States' **[—11—]** sovereign immunity and allowing parties to sue the government for damages arising from the negligent operation of public vessels. *See Canadian*

---

ruling on the motions to dismiss, noting that the motions included only excerpts of the contract and that Ironshore—a nonparty—had never seen the entire document. After the government subsequently provided the full document, Ironshore did not challenge the full document either by seeking leave to file a written objection or at the hearing on the motions to dismiss. In these circumstances, we deem waived any challenge to the contract's authenticity.

[5] Although we refer to the OPA's rules regarding "oil spills," the statute applies equally to diesel fuel spills, such as the spill occurring on the FISHER. 33 U.S.C. § 2701(23).

Aviator, Ltd. v. United States, 324 U.S. 215, 218-19 (1945). Unlike the OPA, the Public Vessels Act has provided a substantial body of case law interpreting the term "public vessels."

In 1966, the Third Circuit faced an analogous set of facts to those we face here in the case of *In re United States*, 367 F.2d 505 (3d Cir. 1966). There, the court had to decide whether a military transport tanker owned by the U.S. Navy's Military Sea Transportation Service and crewed by a private contractor constituted a "public vessel" under the Public Vessels Act. *Id.* at 507-08. The Third Circuit did not consider it a difficult question, stating, "we would have thought it too clear for serious argument that a ship owned by the United States and used as directed by the Navy for the transportation of military supplies is 'a public vessel of the United States.'" *Id.* at 509. The court flatly rejected claimants' argument that only ships crewed by public employees constitute "public vessels" under the Public Vessels Act, concluding that "government ownership and use as directed by the government exclusively for a public purpose suffice without more to make a ship a public vessel." *Id.* (citing *Smith v. United States*, 346 F.2d 449, 454 (4th Cir. 1965)). **[—12—]**

Likewise, the Second Circuit held in 1985 that a government-chartered vessel operated by a private contractor constituted a "public vessel" under the Public Vessels Act because "Congress understood the term 'public vessel' in the [Public Vessels Act] to include a vessel . . . used solely in public service." *Blanco v. United States*, 775 F.2d 53, 59 (2d Cir. 1985). Courts have continued to apply the same meaning to "public vessels" under the Public Vessels Act since the passage of the OPA. *See, e.g., Taghadomi v. United States*, 401 F.3d 1080, 1083 n.3 (9th Cir. 2005); *Favorite v. Marine Pers. & Provisioning, Inc.*, 955 F.2d 382, 385 (5th Cir. 1992).

It is a familiar principle of statutory construction that "[s]tatutes which relate to the same subject matter should be considered together so that they will harmonize with each other and be consistent with their general objective scope." *United States v. Gray*, 780 F.3d 458, 467 (1st Cir. 2015) (quoting *Rathbun v. Autozone, Inc.*, 361 F.3d 62, 68 (1st Cir. 2004)). Moreover, the canon of *in pari materia* advises that Congress generally intends specific words to carry consistent meaning when used in **{-138-}** the same context. *Erlenbaugh v. United States*, 409 U.S. 239, 243 (1972). When Congress opted to exempt "public vessels" from OPA liability, it did so against a backdrop of federal law that had consistently interpreted the term "public vessels" to include government owned ships crewed by private contractors acting on **[—13—]** behalf of the government. We harbor no doubt that Congress intended the OPA term "public vessels" to be interpreted in the same manner as "public vessels" under the Public Vessels Act. In the context of the OPA, we therefore adopt the sound consensus of our sister circuits, holding that if a vessel functioning in a public capacity is owned (or bareboat chartered) by the United States, but crewed by a private contractor, such a vessel constitutes a "public vessel" so long as the private contractor is acting under the operational control of the United States and except when the vessel is engaged in commerce.[6] *See In re United States*, 775 F.2d

---

[6] Ironshore insists that the term "public vessel" should be interpreted more narrowly under the OPA than its interpretation under the Public Vessels Act because the OPA is a "strict liability statute," while the Public Vessels Act requires a higher burden of proof associated with standard negligence. Ironshore, however, points to no authority—and we can find none—for its alternative interpretation. Instead, relevant legislative history indicates that Congress intended for the term "public vessel" to sweep quite broadly. In its final report on the OPA, the House Committee on Merchant Marine and Fisheries—the committee with principal jurisdiction over the bill—noted that a "'Public Vessel' is a subclass of vessel that performs governmental functions for federal, state, or local units of government." H.R. Rep. No. 101-242, pt. 2, at 54 (1989). The only carve-out that the committee report envisioned was for government-owned vessels engaging in "commercial service," which the report defined as "all types of trade or business involving the transportation of goods or persons but exclud[ing] those vessels performing service as combatant-vessels." *Id.* This carve-out for government owned vessels "engaged in commerce" also appears in the enacted statute. *See* 33 U.S.C. § 2701(29).

at 53 ("[G]overnment ownership and use as directed **[—14—]** by the government exclusively for a public purpose suffice without more to make a ship a public vessel.").

Applying this principle to the FISHER gives us little pause. Although AMSEA agreed in its contract with the Military Sealift Command to "provide personnel, operational and technical support ashore and afloat, equipment, tools, provisions, and supplies to operate, maintain, and repair the [FISHER]," the contract clearly established that at all times the FISHER would be controlled by the U.S. military. A section of the contract titled "Operational Control" stipulated that the vessel would "operate in the worldwide service under the ultimate operational control" of one of five military commands.[7] Moreover, a separate section stated that the "Military Sealift Command Headquarters" would exercise "Administrative Control" of the ship.

As part of its day-to-day operations, AMSEA was "responsible for performing scheduled and unscheduled maintenance and repairs, as necessary, on a 24 hour a day basis." It held authority to subcontract for certain maintenance and repair work outside its own crew's capabilities, though any subcontract exceeding $100,000—and any changes altering a subcontract by **[—15—]** more than $50,000—had to be approved in advance by the government. Furthermore, **{-139-}** AMSEA was required to incorporate specific provisions into any subcontract it executed, including the subcontract to use BSR's graving dock. Finally, at all times AMSEA's civilian "Master" of the ship was under an obligation to follow both a Navy standard operating manual and any additional definitive instructions from the United States Navy.

The strict hierarchical relationship between the Military Sealift Command and AMSEA establishes, as the district court concluded, that AMSEA crewed the FISHER under the operational control of the United States. AMSEA did not lease the FISHER from the United States, nor was it permitted to use the vessel for its private gain. Rather, all of AMSEA's work on the FISHER benefited the Military Sealift Command and the United States directly. Under the OPA, the United States both owned and operated the FISHER.

Because the FISHER is a military vessel owned and operated by the United States, it qualifies as a public vessel under the OPA. 33 U.S.C. § 2701(29). As such, it is exempt from OPA liability. *Id.* at § 2702(c)(2). Hence, the district court properly dismissed Ironshore's OPA claims against the United States and AMSEA. **[—16—]**

C. Negligence Claims

Ironshore's remaining claims sound in negligence against the United States and AMSEA under general admiralty and maritime law. We address each party in turn.

1. Claims against the United States

The district court dismissed all of Ironshore's remaining negligence claims brought under general maritime and admiralty law, concluding that the OPA supplants and preempts all such claims. For this principle, the district court quoted our decision in *South Port Marine, LLC v. Gulf Oil Ltd. P'ship*, 234 F.3d 58 (1st Cir. 2000), where we noted that "Congress intended the enactment of the OPA to supplant the existing general admiralty and maritime law." *Id.* at 65. However, the district court interpreted the holding of *South Port Marine* too broadly.

In *South Port Marine*, a private marina filed suit under the OPA against a petroleum company to recover damages incurred after an oil spill allegedly caused by the petroleum company's employee. *Id.* at 60-61. The district court determined that punitive damages were unavailable under the OPA. *Id.* at 61. We affirmed the district court, concluding that when Congress supplanted general admiralty and maritime law by passing the OPA—a

[7] These commands, specifically, were the United States Fleet Forces Command, the United States Transportation Command, the Commander of the United States Pacific Fleet, the Commander of the United States Naval Forces Europe-Africa, and the Commander of the United States Naval Forces Central Command.

statute that provides no punitive damages—it sought to eliminate punitive damages entirely in any case where OPA liability applied. *Id.* at 65-66. **[—17—]**

Although we acknowledged in *South Port Marine* that the OPA supplants general admiralty and maritime law when the OPA is triggered, we said nothing about the statute's effect on general admiralty and maritime law outside the OPA context. Put simply, *South Port Marine* was silent regarding the OPA's effect on the ability of parties to sue for negligence under general admiralty and maritime law when a public vessel is the genesis of an oil spill.

Fortunately, the statute itself is not silent. In a subsection of its savings provision titled "Admiralty and Maritime Law," the OPA states: "Except as otherwise provided in this Act, this Act does not affect . . . admiralty and maritime law." 33 U.S.C. § 2751(e). Hence, because public vessels lie outside the sweep of OPA liability, any preexisting admiralty and maritime law that applied to public vessels before the OPA's passage survives its enactment. The district court erroneously **{-140-}** dismissed Ironshore's negligence claims against the United States when it did so sua sponte.

The United States argued in its brief that even though Ironshore's general admiralty and maritime negligence claims against the United States are not foreclosed by the OPA, Ironshore has either abandoned or waived those claims because it alluded only to Massachusetts state law claims in its opposition to AMSEA's motion to dismiss. This argument is misguided. In responding to **[—18—]** pretrial motions, Ironshore never had to assert its general admiralty and maritime law claims against the United States, because the United States had not moved to dismiss them. Rather, as noted above, the district court dismissed those claims sua sponte. Ironshore has since vigorously asserted its general admiralty and maritime claims against the United States in its briefing before us. We do not view those claims as abandoned or waived.

2. Claims against AMSEA

Because we are reinstating Ironshore's negligence claims against the United States, its claims against AMSEA, cannot survive. In order to explain this conclusion, we must briefly address the principle of sovereign immunity.

The United States, as sovereign, cannot be subject to a suit unless it waives its sovereign immunity. *See Thames Shipyard & Repair Co. v. United States*, 350 F.3d 247, 253 (1st Cir. 2003). The provisions of such a waiver define its scope. *Id.* Ironshore has filed its negligence claims against the United States pursuant to the Suits in Admiralty Act, which includes an explicit sovereign immunity waiver for certain admiralty and maritime claims.[8] But **[—19—]** the strings attached to this sovereign immunity waiver prove fatal to Ironshore's negligence claims against AMSEA.

The Suits in Admiralty Act states that "[i]f a remedy is provided by this chapter, *it shall be exclusive of any other action* arising out of the same subject matter against the . . . agent of the United States . . . whose act or omission gave rise to the claim." 46 U.S.C. § 30904 (emphasis added); *see also Ali v. Rogers*, 780 F.3d 1229, 1233, 3 Adm. R. 540, 542 (9th Cir. 2015). Ironshore argues that AMSEA should not be considered an agent of the United States for purposes of the Suits in Admiralty Act's exclusivity provision because record evidence indicates it was "acting entirely on its own behalf."

This argument is misguided. In cases filed pursuant to the Public Vessels Act, other circuits have held that a private contractor crewing a ship that qualifies as a public vessel is necessarily an "agent of the United States" for purposes of the Suits in Admiralty Act's exclusivity provision. *See Favorite Marine v. Marine Pers. & Provisioning, Inc.*, 955 F.2d 382, 388 (5th Cir. 1992) ("As a matter of legal

---

[8] Under the Suits in Admiralty Act the United States waives its sovereign immunity "[i]n a case in which, if a vessel were privately owned or operated . . . a civil action in admiralty could be maintained." 46 U.S.C. § 30903(a); *see also Thames Shipyard & Repair Co.*, 350 F.3d at 253.

definition, 'agent' of the United States is an appropriate characterization of such a contract operator of a public vessel." (quoting *In re United States*, 367 F.2d 505, 509-10 (3d Cir. 1966)); *see also id.* ("[T]he general statement of an agency concept . . . include[s] any instrumentality through and by which the public vessels are operated." (quoting *In* **[—20—]** *re United States*, 367 F.2d at 510) (second alteration in original)). Having already decided that the concept of a "public vessel" has the same meaning under the OPA and the Public Vessels Act **{-141-}** (*see supra* Section II.B.), we conclude that contractors crewing a ship deemed a "public vessel" for purposes of the OPA are—as a matter of legal definition—agents of the United States for purposes of the Suits in Admiralty Act's exclusivity provision. Hence, AMSEA crewed the FISHER as an agent of the United States. As such, the Suits in Admiralty Act's exclusivity provision prevents Ironshore from advancing any claims against it.

III.

We *affirm* the district court's dismissal of Ironshore's OPA claims against the United States, but we *reverse* the district court's dismissal of Ironshore's general admiralty and maritime negligence claims brought against the United States pursuant to the Suits in Admiralty Act and *remand* those claims to the district court for further proceedings consistent with this opinion. We affirm the district court's dismissal of all of Ironshore's claims against AMSEA. Each party shall bear its own costs.

So ordered.

United States Court of Appeals
for the First Circuit

No. 16-1917

SHARP
VS.
HYLAS YACHTS, LLC

Appeal from the United States District Court for the District of Massachusetts

Decided: September 22, 2017

Citation: 872 F.3d 31, 5 Adm. R. 56 (1st Cir. 2017).

Before **LYNCH**, **KAYATTA**, and **BARRON**, Circuit Judges.

[—3—] {-36-} **KAYATTA**, Circuit Judge:

Following an eleven-day jury trial and verdict, the district court entered judgment against Hylas Yachts, LLC and in favor of plaintiffs Nelson Sharp and his LLC, Destiny Yachts, in the amount of $663,774 plus interest and costs, on account of numerous defects in a brand-new yacht that Hylas custom built and sold to plaintiffs. Both sides appeal. For the following reasons, neither side persuades us to upset the judgment.

I. Background

To frame the principal issues raised on this appeal (Hylas's challenges to the verdict and plaintiffs' challenge to the judgment as a matter of law entered on one of its claims), we summarize the relevant evidence as a reasonable factfinder might have viewed it most favorably to plaintiffs. *See Atl. & Gulf Stevedores, Inc. v. Ellerman Lines, Ltd.*, 369 U.S. 355, 364 (1962); *Acevedo-Garcia v. Monroig*, 351 F.3d 547, 565 (1st Cir. 2003).

Our summary begins in June of 2009, when Sharp and Hylas signed a contract for the purchase and sale of a new seventy-foot yacht, to be named "Destiny," for $1.99 million. A semiretired mechanical engineer with a background in hydraulics, Sharp had owned a boat before—two years prior, he had purchased a fifty-four-foot sailboat from another company—but never a vessel as big as the one he planned to buy from Hylas, a luxury yacht seller in Marblehead, Massachusetts. **[—4—]**

The purchase agreement between Sharp and Hylas included detailed provisions devoted to the yacht's commissioning, the delivery and closing, and assorted warranties. The agreement provided that the yacht would be commissioned in Ft. Lauderdale, Florida, and commissioning would "include all work necessary to install all equipment . . . and place same in good and proper operating condition." The agreement also included a warranty provision in which Hylas guaranteed that the yacht delivered to Sharp would be "of excellent quality, of good workmanship and materials, seaworthy and suitable for its intended use of extended ocean cruising." Hylas agreed "for a period of three (3) years after Delivery, to either fix any warranty defects by the factory or reimburse [Sharp] for the cost incurred in fixing it." And Hylas agreed to indemnify Sharp from claims brought by Hylas's subcontractors and suppliers, and to pay attorneys' fees incurred by Sharp in handling such claims.

To build the yacht, Hylas contracted with a number of vendors who supplied, installed, and serviced certain components of the yacht. GMT Composites, Inc. supplied the boom (a "long spar used to extend the foot of the sail") and all boom-related components, including the boom-furling system, part of the gooseneck assembly, the mandrel, and the pawl assembly. Forespar Products Corp., another vendor, supplied the mast, the plates **[—5—]** connecting the mast to the gooseneck assembly, and other parts of the gooseneck assembly.

Sharp made a substantial down payment to Hylas on July 12, 2010, from his personal bank account. The remaining balance was paid at closing from a bank account held by Destiny Yachts, LLC, a limited **{-37-}** liability company Sharp set up. When Sharp closed on and took possession of the yacht on December 4, 2010, he did so on Destiny Yachts' behalf as its sole member. From that point forward, Destiny Yachts owned Destiny in full.

After taking possession of the yacht, Sharp sailed from Ft. Lauderdale toward St. Thomas in the Caribbean on December 4. About four or five hours into the maiden journey, Sharp noticed a hydraulic fitting leaking. He turned the boat around and a Hylas employee in Ft. Lauderdale met him the following morning and tightened the fitting. Within a day and a half of Sharp's second departure from Ft. Lauderdale, though, the fitting began to leak again. A more "massive failure" occurred a few days later when the boom came loose, the furling motor connections and hydraulic lines broke, and hydraulic oil spilled on Destiny's deck. When Destiny arrived in St. Thomas, Hylas and GMT arranged for a local rigging company called Island Rigging to repair the boom and the hydraulics.

Between January 4, 2011, and February 26, 2011, Destiny sailed through the Caribbean to Grenada. The yacht had numerous **[—6—]** other problems during its journey, including hydraulic system malfunctions, malfunctions of the electronic throttle, a broken generator, failing battery chargers, and toilet malfunctions. Sharp corresponded repeatedly with Hylas and GMT, expressing his dissatisfaction with the services Hylas was rendering and frustration with the continuing problems his crew was experiencing. Sharp later recalled spending several weeks in Grenada trying to repair the hydraulic system, which continued to fail, and the charging system, which by this point "was almost non-existent." When Sharp could not get these systems repaired, he decided to return to Ft. Lauderdale so that Hylas could effect repairs before Destiny would continue on to the Mediterranean.

On April 7, 2011, the yacht left Grenada for Ft. Lauderdale. During the trip, the clevis pin fell out of the boom, causing the boom to completely fall off the mast. Sharp eventually put in at Ft. Lauderdale to undergo repairs. Hylas sent the hydraulic system manufacturer to replace the controls for the hydraulic system, and sent the charging system manufacturers to replace the charging system. A GMT technician repaired the damage done when the boom fell.

Problems continued to arise. They included boom-fitting, mandrel, foot-track, and hydraulic oil issues. Destiny eventually docked in Newport, Rhode Island, where it underwent eight days of repairs. Graham Robertson, who joined the crew as **[—7—]** Destiny's captain in June 2011, recalled that GMT performed all of the repairs; nobody from Hylas was involved.

On June 23, 2011, Destiny left Rhode Island for the Mediterranean. Sharp received an email from Hylas's vice president, Kyle Jachney, the day before the yacht departed, stating that Jachney planned to come see the yacht and conduct sea trials. Destiny departed before Jachney made it, however. While the yacht was sailing across the Atlantic, Robertson noticed that in addition to emerging problems with the mandrel foot track and the sail feeder, the bolts in the boom fitting connecting the boom to the mast appeared to be loosening. Destiny could not be sailed, and had to travel using a motor to get to the Azores for repairs; nobody there could fix it, so it made its way unrepaired to Palma de Mallorca.

On June 27, 2011, Sharp forwarded to Jachney an email he had received from Robertson describing all of these problems, and Sharp asked Jachney to "provide your insights and suggested course of action." **{-38-}** Roughly two weeks later, Sharp, who had at this point made his way to Palma de Mallorca to tend to Destiny, emailed Jachney again to state that he had received no response to his email request, and that he and Destiny's crew were going to "proceed[] to the best of [their] ability to effect a fix that will still salvage part of the Summer in the Mediterranean." Sharp indicated that he would be forced to conduct repair work and he **[—8—]** expected Hylas to reimburse him for the work and the value of the lost use of the yacht. He also reminded Jachney that Hylas did not ever provide Destiny's hydraulic system schematics despite Sharp's request for them in early May 2011.

Taking the advice of mechanics who said some of the parts connecting the boom and mast were undersized, Sharp had the mast connection rebuilt and increased the size of the clevis. Still, subsequent emails he sent to Jachney and David Schwartz, the president of GMT, alerted Hylas and GMT that Destiny continued to experience problems with loosening screws and bolts in the boom along with continual hydraulic leaks.

On July 31, 2011, Destiny left Palma de Mallorca and experienced more problems, this time with the pawl (the component used to raise and lower the sail). After stopping for more repairs in Sardinia, Destiny resumed its journey through the Mediterranean on August 5, 2011.

On October 13, 2011, plaintiffs sued Hylas, alleging breach of contract, breach of warranties, negligence, misrepresentation, and violations of Massachusetts General Laws chapter 93A. Hylas impleaded GMT and Forespar, and GMT leveled fourth-party contract claims against plaintiffs based on a bill it issued that was allegedly never paid.

As Destiny headed back across the Atlantic in November 2011, more screws in the boom-to-mast connection broke or loosened. **[—9—]** Robertson noticed that bolts in the gooseneck were shearing; he instructed the crew to check them twice a day, and at least one bolt required tightening at each check. The pawl assembly again had problems, as did the bolts in the gooseneck assembly, so the yacht sailed the last few days into the Carribean under reduced sail. After the yacht made its way to Newport, Rhode Island from Ft. Lauderdale in June 2012, Sharp eventually had the boom replaced in early September 2012. No further significant problems ensued.

The case went to trial in July 2015. Plaintiffs claimed damages of $1,019,066, consisting of $320,000 in lost charter revenue, $364,514 in depreciation during the 8-1/2 months when Destiny could not be used, $140,789 to replace the gooseneck and boom, and assorted lesser amounts for other repairs, travel, lost time, and marina and diversion expenses.

The jury signed a special verdict form in which they found that Hylas's breach of contract and breaches of implied and express warranties rendered it liable to Sharp in the amount of $663,774. The jury also found that GMT breached its contract with Hylas and breached an express warranty and implied warranties of merchantability and workman-like conduct, and that at least one of these breaches proximately caused harm to Hylas. But the jury found that Hylas was entitled to no damages from GMT, the liability findings notwithstanding. The jury found against Hylas on all of its contract claims against Forespar, and found that plaintiffs **[—10—]** did not breach a contract with GMT or become unjustly enriched by failing to pay an unpaid bill. A few months later, the magistrate judge found against plaintiffs on their chapter 93A claims. Hylas's post-trial motions were denied, and Hylas and plaintiffs both appealed. **{-39-}**

II. Discussion

Hylas complains that the jury verdict holding it liable to Sharp for a substantial sum was necessarily inconsistent with the jury's verdict that GMT, the boom supplier, breached contractual commitments and warranties given to Hylas, yet owed Hylas no damages. Hylas also argues that the district court improperly dismissed its indemnification claim against GMT, and that the verdict was tainted by erroneous instructions, improperly admitted evidence, and a failure to hold Sharp accountable for the spoliation of evidence. Plaintiffs, in turn, press on cross appeal the contention that they were entitled as a matter of law to multiple damages and attorneys' fees under Massachusetts state law. Mass. Gen. Laws ch. 93A, § 11. As we will explain, none of these arguments persuade us.

A. Damages evidence

Hylas claims that the trial court abused its discretion in allowing plaintiffs to put into evidence and claim as damages the $320,000 in alleged lost charter revenues and the roughly $536,000 in depreciation, crew salaries and expenses, fuel costs, **[—11—]** marina charges, and Sharp's own time and expense. In maritime law, such amounts are sometimes referred to as "demurrage" or "detention damages." Hylas's argument is that Destiny was a pleasure craft owned for personal use, not a commercial charter, hence detention damages are not recoverable in this breach of contract action.

Hylas rests this argument on the Supreme Court's decision in *The Conqueror*, 166 U.S. 110 (1897), a case in which the Court found that the owner of a pleasure yacht could not recover damages for loss of pleasure use. *Id.* at 133. The Court observed that "the loss of profits or of the use of a vessel pending repairs, or other detention, arising from a collision or other maritime tort, and commonly spoken of as 'demurrage,' is a proper element of damage," but only "when profits have actually been, or may be reasonably supposed to have been, lost, and the amount of such profits is proven with reasonable certainty." *Id.* at 125. With no evidence that the yacht owner had any interest in engaging the vessel in "profitable commerce," the Court found that such proof was lacking. *Id.* at 133.

The Conqueror arose under markedly different circumstances: It disposed of an action alleging a maritime tort under admiralty law, not contract claims possibly governed by Massachusetts law. Hylas does not expressly argue that federal maritime law applies, nor do plaintiffs argue that it does not. **[—12—]** Notably, however, the parties did not object to the district court's instruction to the jury that plaintiffs are not entitled to any damages based on "any loss of use . . . for recreational purposes," because "[m]ere inconvenience arising from an inability to use the vessel for purposes of pleasure is not recoverable." They also agreed to the district court's instruction that lost profits and lost charter revenues could be recovered if proven "with a reasonable degree of certainty." These instructions suggest that the parties implicitly agreed to the application of *The Conqueror*'s framework in this case. We therefore assume, without deciding, that *The Conqueror* applies fully to plaintiffs' claims; hence, Sharp cannot recover damages for lost pleasure use of a pleasure vessel.

Observing that plaintiffs did not produce brochures, hire a broker, or otherwise make any effort to charter Destiny at any point during the several months they claimed losses prior to filing suit, Hylas argues that it was inappropriate for the jury to consider evidence of the damages plaintiffs allegedly incurred in lost profits **{-40-}** and use of Destiny pending repairs.[1] *The* **[—13—]** *Conqueror*'s holding, however, is not so broad. While it does provide that the owner of a pleasure craft may not recover based on the loss of pleasure use that occurs when a vessel needs repairs, it does not purport to bar the owner of a multipurpose vessel from recovering damages attributable to lost business use. *See Oswalt v. Resolute Indus., Inc.*, 642 F.3d 856, 864–65 (9th Cir. 2011) (distinguishing *The Conqueror* and affirming an award of business-related and nonspeculative loss-of-use damages). *The Conqueror* did not reach so broadly because the record was devoid of any testimony "tending to show that [the vessel owner] bought [the vessel] for hire, or would have leased [the vessel] if he had been able to do so." 166 U.S. at 133–34. Circuit courts have, in turn, adopted a rule allowing owners of multipurpose vessels to recover detention and demurrage damages where owners can show with "reasonable certainty" that those damages arose from lost business use rather than lost pleasure use. *See, e.g., Cent. St. Transit & Leasing Corp. v. Jones Boat Yard, Inc.*, 206 F.3d 1373, 1376–77 (11th Cir. 2000); *Oswalt*, 642 F.3d at 864–65.

According to Hylas, the "reasonable certainty" standard can only mean that "to be awarded damages for lost profits, a recreational vessel must have a history of income. Absent such history, these damages are too speculative and cannot be awarded."

---

[1] Specifically, Hylas takes issue with Trial Exhibit 38, a summary of Sharp's calculations of the damages he sought against Hylas, which was admitted over objection during Sharp's testimony at trial. Because we find that it was not an abuse of discretion for the magistrate judge to allow Sharp's testimony and evidence concerning detention and demurrage damages, we need not address plaintiffs' argument that Hylas failed to preserve its objection by not repeating its objection at the time Exhibit 38 was finally **[—13—]** entered into evidence and by stipulating to the admission of another exhibit containing a copy of the contents of Exhibit 38.

[—14—] But no court has crafted so strict a rule. Instead, courts have consistently observed that "what constitutes 'reasonable certainty' is of necessity a fact-intensive inquiry in which the issue of evidentiary sufficiency can only be determined on a case-by-case basis." *Yarmouth Sea Prods., Ltd. v. Scully*, 131 F.3d 389, 395 (4th Cir. 1997). Although courts typically require a showing that the vessel "has been engaged, or was capable of being engaged in a profitable commerce," *Delta S.S. Lines, Inc. v. Avondale Shipyards, Inc.*, 747 F.2d 995, 1001 (5th Cir. 1984) (internal quotation marks omitted), we have previously stated:

> The burden of proof imposed on a vessel owner claiming demurrage is not excessive:
>
> "It is not necessary for him to show by direct evidence that he would have employed his vessel . . . . It suffices if he shows a state of facts from which a court or jury can find that there was an opportunity to do so, and that he would have availed himself of it."

Trans-Asiatic Oil Ltd., S.A. v. Apex Oil Co., 804 F.2d 773, 782 (1st Cir. 1986) (quoting *Skou v. United States*, 478 F.2d 343, 346 (5th Cir. 1973)); *see also Jackson v. Innes*, 121 N.E. 489, 491 (Mass. 1919) (citing *The Conqueror* for the proposition that a defendant "cannot avoid liability" for "the loss of the use of [a] boat during [a] period of detention" merely because "no income was derived from it," and observing that "evidence of the fair market rental value for the use of the boat was admissible on the question of damages"). [—15—]

Hylas's fallback argument is that the evidence was insufficient to warrant {-41-} treating Destiny as other than a pleasure craft for the noncommercial use of Sharp and his friends and family. Hylas notes that the evidence shows that the insurance policy on Destiny covered only Sharp's private use of the yacht, and that Sharp did not take a business deduction on the yacht when he filed his taxes the year he made the purchase. But the record also includes Sharp's testimony that he formed Destiny Yachts LLC—prior to closing on and taking possession of Destiny—"because [he] was going to charter the yacht," so he "wanted to put it into, essentially, a corporate shell." Sharp explained that seventy-foot yachts like Destiny are very expensive to maintain, and he did not plan to live his life at sea, so he intended from the start to charter the yacht during the extensive amount of time each year that he himself would be unavailable to sail. The record also included undisputed evidence that Destiny was eventually regularly chartered at a rate of $20,000 per week after all repairs were completed. The fact that this occurred after suit was filed is a talking point for Hylas's attorney, but not a bar to a jury concluding that Sharp would have "availed himself" of the opportunity to charter Destiny sooner if it were not for the yacht's constant need of repairs. *Trans-Asiatic Oil*, 804 F.2d at 782. [—16—]

All in all, the trial court had before it a mixed record, with some evidence supporting the conclusion that Sharp would have chartered the yacht but for its troubles, and other evidence pointing to the contrary. This is why we have jurors. And in this case, the duly empaneled jurors were properly instructed that plaintiffs had to prove their lost profits to a "reasonable degree of certainty." On such a record, the trial court certainly did not abuse its discretion in allowing plaintiffs to offer their evidence of damages for the jury's evaluation.

B. Spoliation of evidence

In June of 2012, plaintiffs notified Hylas that they planned on replacing the boom in September. Seven weeks later, Hylas requested to conduct a sea trial of Destiny. The following week, Hylas conducted an inspection of Destiny, and voiced no concerns regarding the vessel's seaworthiness. On August 31, the magistrate judge ordered plaintiffs to turn over the yacht to Hylas for a sea trial. When plaintiffs did so the following week, the yacht was unsafe to sail. Before Hylas could reschedule a sea trial, plaintiffs replaced the boom. Hylas claimed that by replacing the boom, plaintiffs had effectively and in bad faith destroyed evidence. It moved for sanctions, seeking dismissal or at least an instruction to the jury that they were "entitled in [their] deliberations to draw a negative inference form [sic] the fact that the Plaintiffs have precluded by their conduct the **[—17—]** Defendants from adequately and fairly testing the components while the Yacht is under sail."

In response to Hylas's request for dismissal, the district court held a two-day evidentiary hearing on spoliation. The court ultimately concluded that "the vessel was delivered for the sea trials in a conditions [sic] in which it was dangerous to sail." For that reason, the district court ordered plaintiffs to "pay the defendants' reasonable expenses in arranging to be present at the sea trial." The district court declined, however, to dismiss plaintiffs' claims against Hylas. Later, the district court also declined to give an adverse-inference instruction to the jury concerning spoliation of evidence. On appeal, Hylas challenges the district court's refusal to grant its requests,[2] which we review for **{-42-}** abuse of discretion. *See Booker v. Mass. Dep't of Pub. Health*, 612 F.3d 34, 46 (1st Cir. 2010).

Neither an adverse-inference instruction nor dismissal was required. Although it is true that "an adverse inference **[—18—]** instruction may be allowed when a party fails to produce [evidence] that exists or should exist and is within [the party's] control," *Astro-Med, Inc. v. Nihon Kohden Am., Inc.*, 591 F.3d 1, 20 (1st Cir. 2009), such an instruction "usually makes sense only where the evidence permits a finding of bad faith destruction." *United States v. Laurent*, 607 F.3d 895, 902 (1st Cir. 2010). The record in this case supports a contrary conclusion: Three months in advance, plaintiffs proactively informed Hylas that they intended to replace the boom in early September. As best the briefs reflect, Hylas never insisted that the replacement be put off until after sea trials were completed. Plaintiffs sent scores of pictures and measurements to Hylas to allow Hylas to prepare for trial. Moreover, the record contained evidence from which the district court could have concluded that during the two years that passed from the time the yacht was commissioned to the date the boom was replaced, Hylas had a number of other opportunities to examine the boom, inspect the yacht, and conduct sea trials. Aside from Hylas's vague reference to the generalized prejudice it suffered from being "precluded from presenting a valid defense" to plaintiffs' claims, Hylas is unable to explain what it thinks it might have discovered upon inspection of the boom that it could not learn from the materials and information plaintiffs provided, or why the time it was given to make accommodations in light of the impending boom replacement was insufficient. In sum, the **[—19—]** district court did not abuse its discretion in concluding, in effect, that "no adverse-inference instruction would make sense here." *Laurent*, 607 F.3d at 903.

If an adverse-inference instruction was not required, sanctioning the plaintiffs with dismissal was also not required. "The intended goals behind excluding evidence, or at the extreme, dismissing a complaint, are to rectify any prejudice the non-offending party may have suffered as a result of the loss of evidence and to deter any future conduct, particularly deliberate conduct, leading to such loss of evidence." *Collazo-Santiago v. Toyota Motor Corp.*, 149 F.3d 23, 29 (1st Cir. 1998). "While a district court has broad discretion in choosing an appropriate sanction for spoliation, 'the applicable sanction should be molded to serve the prophylactic, punitive, and remedial rationales underlying the spoliation doctrine.'" *Silvestri v. General Motors Corp.*, 271 F.3d 583, 590 (4th Cir. 2001) (quoting *West v. Goodyear Tire & Rubber Co.*, 167 F.3d 776, 779 (2d Cir. 1999)). We have also counseled that, in light of our "prefer[ence] that adjudications be driven by the merits of a case," *McKeague v. One World*

---

[2] In a heading in its opening brief, Hylas frames its argument as asserting that it was an abuse of discretion not to impose "*any* sanction . . . based on spoliation of evidence." (Emphasis added). But beyond this general statement, Hylas does not advance any further argument that the district court should have imposed some sanction other than dismissal. Any such argument is therefore waived. *See Vallejo Piedrahita v. Mukasey*, 524 F.3d 142, 144 (1st Cir. 2008) ("It is well settled that issues adverted to on appeal in a perfunctory manner, unaccompanied by some developed argumentation, are deemed to have been abandoned."(internal quotation marks omitted)).

Techs., Inc., 858 F.3d 703, 707 (1st Cir. 2017), dismissal should be granted only in extreme cases. *Collazo-Santiago*, 149 F.3d at 28 (citing *Benjamin v. Aroostook Med. Ctr., Inc.*, 57 F.3d 101, 107 (1st Cir. 1995)). Here, where Hylas cannot identify the prejudice it allegedly suffered and where the evidence **{-43-}** fails to **[—20—]** compel a finding that plaintiffs acted in bad faith, the district court was not required to do more than it did.

C. Implied indemnity

In its first amended third-party complaint, Hylas sought indemnification against GMT under Massachusetts law. Although Hylas conceded that it did not have an express indemnification agreement with GMT, Hylas claimed that it nevertheless had an indemnity relationship with GMT under an implied contract theory or a tort theory. *See Araujo v. Woods Hole Martha's Vineyard, Nantucket Steamship Auth.*, 693 F.2d 1, 2 (1st Cir. 1982) (describing the three ways an indemnity relationship may arise). By "implied contractual indemnity," Hylas means that, in addition to its warranty obligations, GMT was responsible for "mak[ing] good *any* loss or damage incurred by [Hylas] while acting at [GMT's] request for [its] benefit"; in other words, for reimbursing Hylas for any and all damages incurred by Sharp in connection with the boom. Although the claim survived a summary judgment motion from GMT prior to trial, it eventually fell to a motion for judgment as a matter of law. The district court found that the record was devoid of evidence that showed the contractual relationship between Hylas and GMT to be of the type that can give rise to implied indemnity. It also found that "common law" indemnification could not be shown because common law indemnification exists under Massachusetts law only in tort actions. **[—21—]**

Hylas contends that the district court erred in dismissing the indemnity claim, arguing that the record included enough evidence to withstand summary adjudication on the question whether Hylas had an implied contractual indemnity relationship with GMT.[3] Pointing to evidence that GMT conducted repairs, gave advice, offered redesigns, and interacted directly with plaintiffs and third-party repairers of GMT components, Hylas argues that GMT was far more than just a boom vendor that contracted with Hylas as its vendee. Rather, says Hylas, this evidence, along with the warranties GMT provided to Hylas on the boom and the service and support GMT provided "above and beyond its claimed contractual obligations," shows that GMT built a "special relationship" with Hylas whereby Hylas would not be liable to others for any boom-related damages. We review the district court's decision granting GMT's motion for judgment as a matter of law de novo, viewing the evidence and the reasonable inferences that can be drawn therefrom in the light most favorable to Hylas. *See Delgado v. Pawtucket Police Dep't*, 668 F.3d 42, 50 (1st Cir. 2012).

In contending that it had a "special relationship" with GMT, Hylas misunderstands the way a relationship between parties can override the absence of an express indemnity agreement to create an indemnification obligation under Massachusetts law. **[—22—]** Contrary to Hylas's contention, merely going "above and beyond" what is required under a contract does not create a "special relationship" that implies indemnity. Rather, for a relationship to generate an obligation to indemnify, the relationship must be "generally recognized" as special. *Fireside Motors, Inc. v. Nissan Motor Corp.*, 479 N.E.2d 1386, 1391 (Mass. 1985). Hylas does not contend that its relationship with GMT is generally recognized as one that establishes **{-44-}** indemnity. Instead, it argues that a plethora of evidence adduced at trial demonstrated that GMT was more involved with repairs than the contract demanded, working directly with plaintiffs, assuming primary control over everything related to the boom, and demonstrating its willingness to be more than merely a vendor who relinquished its handiwork to its vendee. Hylas essentially contends that "'special factors' surround[ed] the contractual rela-

[3] Hylas does not challenge the district court's finding that common law indemnity could not be shown.

tionship which indicate[d] an intention by one party to indemnify [the other] in [this] particular situation." *Fall River Housing Auth. v. H.V. Collins Co.*, 604 N.E.2d 1310, 1313 (Mass. 1992) (quoting *Decker v. Black & Decker Mfg. Co.*, 449 N.E.2d 641, 644 (Mass. 1983)); *see also Fireside Motors*, 479 N.E.2d at 1391 (recognizing that a right to indemnification may be implied "when there are unique special factors demonstrating that the parties intended that the putative indemnitor bear the ultimate liability" (internal quotation marks omitted)); *E. Amanti & Sons,* **[—23—]** *Inc. v. R.C. Griffin, Inc.*, 758 N.E.2d 153, 162–63 (Mass. App. Ct. 2001).

The nature of the relationship between the parties may be relevant to whether there exist "special factors" that would imply indemnity, but Massachusetts courts "infer[] the existence of indemnity agreements only when the terms of the contract themselves contemplate[] such indemnification." *Larkin v. Ralph O. Porter, Inc.*, 539 N.E.2d 529, 532 (Mass. 1989); *see also Decker*, 449 N.E.2d at 643 (distinguishing between an "implied contract of indemnity" and a tort-based "obligation implied from the relationship of the parties"). On the few occasions when the Supreme Judicial Court of Massachusetts has found an implied contractual right to indemnification, it has done so where the natural reading of the contract itself established an indemnity relationship between the parties. *See Larkin*, 539 N.E.2d at 532 (collecting cases); *Monadnock Display Fireworks, Inc. v. Town of Andover*, 445 N.E.2d 1053, 1056–57 (Mass. 1983) (finding town responsible for indemnifying a fireworks company for damages arising from town's failure to furnish police for crowd control it had promised to provide); *Great Atl. & Pac. Tea Co. v. Yanofsky*, 403 N.E.2d 370, 374 (Mass. 1980) (inferring, from "express agreement" to make all outside repairs, existence of agreement to indemnify for damages from failure to repair). **[—24—]**

The district court correctly found that no reasonable juror could infer the existence of an indemnity relationship from the contract between Hylas and GMT. Although Article IV of the contract set forth a warranty "that the Boom delivered to [Hylas] shall be free of all defects of workmanship and engineering, to the extent that such engineering is provided by [GMT], for one year from the date of delivery," this was the "sole warranty" GMT gave to Hylas, and it was "strictly limited" by express terms. GMT warranted that it would repair components that turned out to be defective, but Hylas would be responsible for "transportation to and from the repair facility and for all costs associated with removing and installing the equipment in the boat." GMT made "no warranty . . . as to the duration of any delay necessary for repairs," and expressly disclaimed responsibility "for any damage to the original purchaser or any others for loss of time, inconvenience, loss or damage to personal property, injury to persons, loss of revenue or any other damages consequential or otherwise." Nothing about these warranties, or any other aspect of the contract between GMT and Hylas, signals that the parties contemplated indemnification. **{-45-}**[4] **[—25—]**

As a last resort, Hylas falls back on the argument that judgment as a matter of law was inappropriate because the doctrine of implied indemnity, at least in Massachusetts, is not well defined, as at least one district court has noted: "Massachusetts law on the issue of implied contractual indemnification can perhaps best be described as unsettled." *Steffen v. Viking Corp.*, 441 F. Supp. 2d 245, 251 (D. Mass. 2006). According to Hylas, the fact that the law of implied indemnity may not be fully settled in Massachusetts should prevent a court from being able to grant judgment as a matter of law on the issue. This argument confuses the summary judgment requirement that the material facts be indisputable with a nonexistent requirement that the relevant law be clear and firmly entrenched. In the absence of evidence

[4] GMT and Hylas each devote considerable attention to the question whether the evidence did or did not show that they had forged an ordinary vendor–vendee relationship. But even if GMT was contractually obligated to do more than a typical vendor, which the evidence arguably shows here, that would not be the same as having an indemnification obligation.

tending to support the existence of the "special factors" from which Massachusetts courts have inferred a right to indemnification, the district court was correct to grant judgment as a matter of law in favor of GMT.

D. Jury instructions

In its tenth instruction, the court admonished the jury that if they found "that the boom, mast, or related components were defective, or that repairs performed by GMT were not performed properly, by virtue of the contract, those problems are attributable to Hylas." Out of context, this instruction could have been read in a rather nonsensical manner as indicating that **[—26—]** Hylas could not recover from GMT even if GMT breached its obligations owed to Hylas. And Hylas objected on these grounds.

In context, though, the instruction was clearly directed at explaining that, as between plaintiffs and Hylas, Hylas could not escape liability by passing the buck to its supplier, GMT. The trial court first described plaintiffs' breach-of-contract claim against Hylas; then it described Hylas's waiver defense against plaintiffs' breach-of-contract claim. Next, the court instructed the jury on plaintiffs' breach-of-express-warranties claim against Hylas, plaintiffs' claim that Hylas violated the implied warranty of merchantability, and plaintiffs' claim that Hylas violated the implied warranty of fitness for a particular purpose. The court instructed the jury that plaintiffs' breach-of-warranty claims could not succeed if the jury found plaintiffs did not give reasonable notice.

Only after these instructions concerning plaintiffs' claims against Hylas were given did the court turn its attention to Instruction 10, explaining to the jury the law that governed Hylas's claims against GMT. When it did, the court repeated the elements of a breach-of-contract claim, and reminded the jury of the elements of express- and implied-warranty claims, this time with reference to GMT's potential liability to Hylas. The court explained that Hylas could succeed on its claim of breach of contract against GMT if the jury found by a preponderance of the **[—27—]** evidence that "Hylas performed its obligations under the contract," GMT "breached or violated the contract," and "Hylas suffered damages as a result of the breach of the contract." The jury heard as well that Hylas would have an "entitlement to recover" from GMT if **{-46-}** the jury found GMT breached certain warranties.

But, says Hylas, counsel for Forespar in closing pointed to Instruction 10 as meaning that problems with the boom, mast, or related components would be attributable to Hylas, rather than Forespar. Hylas argues that that argument by Forespar spun the instruction in a manner that would cause the jurors to conclude that no damages should be awarded against GMT. As we have just noted, though, the judge expressly told the jurors that Hylas would be entitled to recover damages from GMT if the requisite findings were made. Pointing out that Hylas—rather than Forespar—would be liable to plaintiffs for problems with the boom is not inconsistent with that instruction.

"[A] single instruction to a jury may not be judged in artificial isolation, but must be viewed in the context of the overall charge." *Cupp v. Naughten*, 414 U.S. 141, 146–47 (1973); *see McDonald v. Town of Brookline*, 863 F.3d 57, 65 (1st Cir. 2017) ("[O]ur role is to evaluate whether the jury instructions as a whole adequately explained the law or whether they tended to confuse or mislead the jury on controlling issues . . . ."). **[—28—]** Viewing the instructions as a whole in this case, we see no reason to think that the jurors transplanted a portion of the plaintiffs-versus-Hylas instructions into the Hylas-versus-GMT instructions in a manner that would have made the latter instructions nonsensical.[5]

E. Verdict inconsistency

Finally, we arrive at Hylas's central argument on appeal: that a new trial should be ordered because the jury's verdict was inconsistent.

---

[5] A fortiori, Hylas's identified but unpreserved objection to Instruction 11 (like 10, but referencing the Island Rigging repairs) fails.

The jury returned a special verdict in which it found that Hylas (1) breached an express warranty to plaintiffs; (2) breached an implied warranty of merchantability to plaintiffs; (3) breached an implied warranty of fitness for a particular purpose to plaintiffs; and (4) breached its contract with plaintiffs. Answering "yes" to the question whether "any of the breaches" they found caused plaintiffs harm, the jury determined that plaintiffs were entitled to $663,774 from Hylas. Next, the jury also found that GMT (1) breached an express warranty to Hylas; (2) breached an implied warranty of merchantability to Hylas; (3) breached an implied warranty of workmanlike product; and (4) breached its contract with Hylas. Although the jury found **[—29—]** that GMT proximately caused harm to Hylas, it ultimately concluded that Hylas was not entitled to any damages from GMT.

Hylas does not dispute that the evidence in the record was sufficient to show that Hylas breached its contract with plaintiffs and breached the warranties expressly and impliedly provided therein. Rather, Hylas contends that because the weight of the evidence adduced by plaintiffs at trial concerned the defective boom GMT provided and the damage caused each time the boom collapsed, fell off the mast, or otherwise malfunctioned, the jury's verdict awarding substantial damages to plaintiffs from Hylas cannot be reconciled with the decision to award no damages to Hylas from GMT, the manufacturer and servicer of the boom.

We are "substantial[ly] reluctan[t] to consider inconsistency in civil jury verdicts a basis for new trials." **{-47-}** *McIsaac v. Didriksen Fishing Corp.*, 809 F.2d 129, 133 (1st Cir. 1987) (quoting *Merchant v. Ruhle*, 740 F.2d 86, 91 (1st Cir. 1984)); *see also Climent-García v. Autoridad de Transporte Marítimo y Las Islas Municipio*, 754 F.3d 17, 20 (1st Cir. 2014) ("The tide runs strongly against a litigant seeking to overturn a jury verdict."). "When a party claims that jury verdicts are inconsistent, we 'attempt to reconcile the jury's findings, by exegesis if necessary.' This exercise involves determining whether the jury could have, consistent with its instructions, rendered the challenged verdicts." *Davignon v. Hodgson*, 524 F.3d 91, 109 (1st **[—30—]** Cir. 2008) (citation omitted) (quoting *Acevedo-Diaz v. Aponte*, 1 F.3d 62, 74 n.15 (1st Cir. 1993)).

It is true that plaintiffs presented a substantial amount of evidence and testimony concerning the defective design, manufacture, and installation of the boom provided by GMT, and the failure of subsequent repairs (rendered by GMT) to fully resolve the problem. But Hylas would have us conclude, from the sheer volume of evidence demonstrating that boom failures resulted in harm to the plaintiffs, that the jury could not consistently find Hylas responsible for over $600,000 in damages to plaintiffs while also finding that GMT owed Hylas nothing. For several reasons, we disagree.

The jury was asked whether any of the breaches by GMT were a "proximate (substantial) cause of any harm suffered by Hylas," to which they responded, "Yes." Hylas places a lot of weight in this answer. But all it means is that the jury concluded that GMT's breaches were *a* cause of *at least some* of Hylas's harm. The evidence, in turn, supported a finding that GMT fixed or paid for fixing many problems with the boom. So, if it was these problems that constituted GMT's breach causing harm to Hylas, the jury may have concluded that any resulting loss to Hylas or to the plaintiffs had already been remedied. To the extent that there were alleged problems with the boom that GMT did not remedy, the jury could have found those problems were caused by something other **[—31—]** than a GMT warranty breach (e.g., interfacing components, shoddy outside repair work, or improper use[6]). Or the jury may not

[6] For example, the jury heard evidence that Hylas changed hydraulics systems and added a pressure intensifier to Destiny without informing GMT. They also heard testimony that "if . . . hooked up to the boom hydraulics, [an intensifier] could put excess pressure above what [GMT] would assume onto [its] system," and that the intensifier was indeed attached to the boom. On another occasion, heard the jury, the boom fell off the mast not because GMT failed to properly service it, but because Island Rigging (acting on Hylas's behalf) failed to properly set screws during a repair. And

have included other boom costs in plaintiffs' damage award.

There was, after all, evidence that the boom was but one of many components of the yacht that suffered multiple failures of great enough magnitude to require repair and prevent chartering. For example, the jury heard testimony that the hydraulics—which were used to operate "just about everything required to run the boat"—failed "three, four times a week" when plaintiffs first took possession of Destiny, and that Hylas's failure to provide installation drawings or operation manuals (as required by its contract with plaintiffs) made repair work impossible in some situations. Sharp also testified that during some of the most significant incidents of equipment failure, including a "[c]ouple in particular" in which repairs to the hydraulic systems were needed, "there were big delays in . . . communication" after he reached out to Hylas for support. **{-48-}** In addition, evidence was **[—32—]** presented that after Island Rigging made repairs in St. Thomas, Destiny experienced failures of its electronic throttle, generator, battery chargers, and toilets. And the jury heard testimony that the mast, too, had problems that required repair. Sharp and Robertson both testified that a GMT technician who was sent twice to conduct repairs on Destiny had expressed confusion about "why he was there," because the required repairs were not his expertise. Virtually every time Destiny was forced to stop to fix mechanical failures, repairs were required for, and made to, more than just the GMT boom. It is thus not necessarily true that the damages associated with repairs were for boom failures.

Furthermore, even if the jury did award damages for some of the expenses associated with repairing and replacing the boom, they could have found that the damages arose from Hylas's breaches of contract and warranty, not GMT's. To explain why, we must briefly revisit the warranties GMT and Hylas gave.

As we mentioned above, GMT warranted to Hylas that "the Boom delivered to [Hylas] shall be free of all defects of workmanship and engineering, to the extent that such engineering is provided by [GMT], for one year from the date of delivery." GMT promised to pay to repair defectively manufactured components it provided, but expressly stated that Hylas would be responsible for "transportation to and from the repair facility and for all costs associated with removing and installing the equipment in the **[—33—]** boat." GMT made "no warranty . . . as to the duration of any delay necessary for repairs," and expressly disclaimed responsibility "for any damage to the original purchaser or any others for loss of time, inconvenience, loss or damage to personal property, injury to persons, loss of revenue or any other damages consequential or otherwise."

Hylas, by contrast, more broadly warranted that the yacht would "be of excellent quality, of good workmanship and materials, seaworthy and suitable for its intended use of extended ocean cruising," and guaranteed for three years "to either fix any warranty defects by the factory or reimburse the Buyer for the cost incurred in fixing it." Hylas also agreed that "[a]ny defects by the factory for issues that apply to the deck and hull for a period of ten (10) years shall be the responsibility of [Hylas]."

An even more obvious and relevant difference between these warranties is that GMT's warranty to Hylas does not cover consequential damages, including all detention or demurrage damages, which were enough by themselves to account for the entire damage award. Therefore, plaintiffs could have suffered damages of a consequential type that were attributable to Hylas, and for which GMT bore no responsibility. Hylas's principal rejoinder to this point is that the detention damages were caused by problems with the boom, so GMT should owe Hylas damages for the cost of repair or replacement of the boom. As we have explained, this is **[—34—]** not clearly correct. But even if the boom problems caused some of the detention damages, it may well have been that those boom problems were the ones for which GMT paid, or were caused

evidence was offered indicating that user error caused at least some of the boom problems.

by someone other than GMT in using or repairing the yacht. Perhaps the jury found that GMT did, in fact, breach its contract and warranty to Hylas because the boom it provided was faulty, but did not breach the contract's requirement that GMT pay for repairs. After all, the jury heard evidence that all but one of the repairs GMT performed were done at no charge to plaintiffs or Hylas, and the one time GMT charged plaintiffs directly **{-49-}** for the repair, no money ever changed hands. The jury then may have found the additional costs associated with boom repairs were for transportation, removal or installation, delay, loss of time, inconvenience, and loss of revenue—items expressly excluded from GMT's warranty to Hylas, but potentially included in Hylas's warranty to plaintiffs, to pay for whatever "cost[s]" plaintiffs "incurred" to fix the yacht.

"An appellate court confronted with a claim of inconsistent special verdicts 'must affirm if there is a view of the case that makes the jury's answers to the interrogatories consistent.'" *Kavanaugh v. Greenlee Tool Co.*, 944 F.2d 7, 9 (1st Cir. 1991) (quoting *Mashpee Tribe v. New Seabury Corp.*, 592 F.2d 575, 590 (1st Cir. 1979), *cert. denied*, 444 U.S. 866 (1979)). For **[—35—]** the foregoing reasons, there is such a view here. Hylas's verdict-inconsistency claim therefore fails.[7]

F. Chapter 93A claim

We turn now to plaintiffs' appeal. In their complaint, plaintiffs alleged that Hylas violated Massachusetts General Laws chapter 93A by willfully or knowingly breaching its warranties to the plaintiffs. The parties reserved the chapter 93A claims for post-trial disposition by the court. After trial concluded and the jury found in favor of plaintiffs on their breach-of-contract and warranty claims, the parties submitted proposed findings of fact and rulings of law to the district court. The district court found in favor of Hylas.

On appeal, plaintiffs argue that because the jury found Hylas breached its warranties to plaintiffs, the district court was required to find a chapter 93A violation occurred as well. In plaintiffs' estimation, a breach of warranty under Massachusetts law is a per se chapter 93A violation. Plaintiffs alternatively argue that even if chapter 93A liability is not the per se rule anytime a breach of warranty has been found, Hylas's breaches of warranty were nonetheless deceptive and unfair in contravention of chapter 93A. Plaintiffs therefore ask that we reverse the district **[—36—]** court and remand for the district court to consider whether chapter 93A's damages multiplier should apply and to calculate an award of attorneys' fees. We review the district court's legal conclusions de novo, but we conduct that review based on the facts as found by the district court except where those factual findings are clearly erroneous. *McDermott v. Marcus, Errico, Emmer & Brooks, P.C.*, 775 F.3d 109, 115 (1st Cir. 2014).

Chapter 93A prohibits "unfair methods of competition and unfair or deceptive acts or practices in the conduct of any trade or commerce." Mass. Gen. Laws ch. 93A, § 2(a). It provides that a court should be "guided by the interpretations given by the Federal Trade Commission and the Federal Courts to section 5(a)(1) of the Federal Trade Commission Act [FTCA]," *id.* § 2(b), and that the Massachusetts Attorney General may implement "rules and regulations interpreting the provisions" of Chapter 93A, section 2(a) so long as those rules and regulations are not "inconsistent with the rules, regulations and decisions of the Federal Trade Commission and the Federal Courts interpreting the provisions of [the FTCA]," *id.* § 2(c).

Although "whether or not particular conduct violates Chapter 93A is generally determined on a case-by-case basis," *McDermott*, 775 F.3d at 117 (citing **{-50-}** *Kattar v. Demoulas*, 739 N.E.2d 246, 257 (Mass. 2000)), Massachusetts courts have identified a few situations in which violation of some other law constitutes a per **[—37—]** se violation of chapter 93A. For example, as identified in *McDermott*, the Supreme Judicial

[7] Finding no error by the district court, we also reject Hylas's argument that the district court abused its discretion by refusing to order a new trial.

Court of Massachusetts has recognized that a violation of the state unfair claims settlement act, Mass. Gen. Laws ch. 176D, is itself a violation of chapter 93A pursuant to chapter 93A, section 9(1). *Id.*; *see Polaroid Corp. v. Travelers Indem. Co.*, 610 N.E.2d 912, 917 (Mass. 1993). Likewise, a violation of the state home improvement contractor's law, Mass. Gen. Laws ch. 142A, has been found to be a violation of chapter 93A not based on a standalone provision of chapter 93A so providing, but based on language in the home improvement contractor's law itself providing that "[v]iolations of any of the provisions of this chapter shall constitute an unfair or deceptive act under the provisions of chapter [93A]," Mass. Gen. Laws ch.142A, § 17.

Plaintiffs insist that this is another such situation, and urge us to follow a regulation promulgated by the Massachusetts Attorney General providing that "[i]t shall be an unfair and deceptive act or practice to fail to perform or fulfill any promises or obligations arising under a warranty." 940 Mass. Code of Regs. § 3.08(2). But, as we explained in *McDermott*, "the Attorney General is not empowered to issue regulations rendering certain statutory violations 'per se' Chapter 93A violations." 775 F.3d at 120; *see also Klairmont v. Gainsboro Rest., Inc.*, 987 N.E.2d 1247, 1255, 1257 (Mass. 2013) (finding a chapter 93A violation, but holding that a knowing violation of building codes **[—38—]** was not a per se violation of chapter 93A because the Attorney General's regulation at issue covered more than just unfair and deceptive conduct in trade or commerce). We agree with the district court that the Massachusetts Attorney General's regulation does not require us to find that any and all breaches of warranty are necessarily violations of chapter 93A.

Seizing on our statement in *McDermott* that there are two "alternative paths to per se Chapter 93A liability: the text of Chapter 93A itself, or the text of an independent statute," *McDermott*, 775 F.3d at 122, plaintiffs offer another theory: that breach of warranty is a per se chapter 93A violation because under the Magnuson-Moss Warranty Act (MMWA), 15 U.S.C. § 2310(d)(1), it is unfair and deceptive for a "supplier, warrantor, or service contractor" to fail to comply with an obligation to a "consumer" under a written warranty. *See also* 15 U.S.C. § 2310(b) (stating that it is an unfair practice to violate any prohibition listed in this chapter, including § 2310(d)(1)). This argument, however, comes far too late for us to pay it any mind: Plaintiffs did not sue under the MMWA, nor did they argue to the district court that the breaches of warranty they proved at trial satisfy the elements of an MMWA claim; plaintiffs gave neither Hylas nor the district court the opportunity to consider this theory, and the district court accordingly made no related findings of fact or conclusions of law. The raise-or-waive rule bars plaintiffs from advancing **[—39—]** this belated argument on appeal. *See Tutor Perini Corp. v. Banc of Am. Sec. LLC*, 842 F.3d 71, 84–85 (1st Cir. 2016).[8] **{-51-}**

With neither chapter 93A itself nor the Massachusetts Attorney General's regulations requiring us to find per se liability under chapter 93A, plaintiffs are left arguing that the district court was required, under the facts of this case, to find that Hylas's breaches of warranty were unfair or deceptive under chapter 93A. They do so on two bases: that the district court's findings of fact were clearly erroneous, and that its conclusions of law were incorrect. We disagree.

The district court found that Hylas failed to deliver a yacht "in completely sound condition

[8] In their reply brief and at oral argument, plaintiffs attempted to explain why this is a case in which we should find the raise-or-waive rule does not apply. *See Lang v. Wal-Mart Stores E., L.P.*, 813 F.3d 447, 455 (1st Cir. 2016) (rejecting an argument that the raise-or-waive rule does not apply). In essence, their argument—that they "could not reasonably anticipate that the trial judge would conclude that dishonoring express and implied warranties causing $663,774 of damage 'did not in fact produce unfairness or deception'"—is that a party that does not know ahead of time that the court will reject its argument should be forgiven for failing to raise a different one. A litigant choosing not to make an argument based on an errant assumption that a different argument will succeed is not the type of "extraordinary circumstance" that allows one to circumvent the raise-or-waive rule. If it were, there would be no raise-or-waive rule.

with all systems and equipment operating safely and properly," in violation of its warranties to plaintiffs. But it also found that "Hylas'[s] failure to do so was due in large part to its inability to conduct sufficient sea **[—40—]** trials, which was motivated by nothing more than a desire to please its customer." In so finding, the district court was referring to the fact that the contract anticipated that Hylas would conduct all sea trials before Sharp finally accepted the yacht and paid all balances due. As things played out, Hylas forewent completing at least some sea trials it would have otherwise conducted had Sharp not wanted to set sail as soon as possible. The court explained that

> Sharp's request to close on the sale of the Yacht came suddenly and unexpectedly and Hylas expected to be able to conduct further sea trials after closing. However, the Yacht left without adequate notice before Hylas had the opportunity to conduct further sea trials.

The district court also found that "[e]ach time Sharp or his crew encountered problems with the Yacht, Hylas attempted to resolve the problem." Plaintiffs argue that these factual findings were clearly erroneous because the court "ignored" (1) evidence that Jachney did not believe plaintiffs prematurely departing from port caused problems; (2) extensive evidence showing that plaintiffs repeatedly sought repairs for numerous failures over many months; (3) evidence showing Hylas did not reimburse plaintiffs for the cost of replacing the boom, despite the contract between the parties requiring Hylas to reimburse Sharp for costs incurred in fixing the yacht; and (4) Hylas's failure to respond to plaintiffs' demand letter, sent prior to commencing suit. **[—41—]**

The district court, however, did not ignore this evidence. The court expressly found that plaintiffs "served on Hylas a demand for relief under Chapter 93A, Section 9," and that "Hylas made no substantive response and no offer of settlement." It noted that Sharp incurred the cost of replacing the boom, and it agreed with the jury that Hylas failed to live up to its express warranty to reimburse plaintiffs for costs associated with fixing the yacht. It listed the numerous occasions on which Destiny needed to be repaired, and observed that Hylas's repairs were "ineffectual." And although the record included an email from Jachney stating that "[t]he timing . . . as far as shaking the yacht down I do not think was an issue," other evidence in the record supports the district court's determination that Hylas intended to do more extensive testing before plaintiffs took possession of the yacht: The district **{–52–}** court considered an email from Jachney two days before closing disclosing his intention to take the yacht out for a test sail and Jachney testified that Sharp's request to close on the yacht in early December 2010 came suddenly and did not provide adequate time to finish testing. The email plaintiffs cite also sheds no contrary light on the district court's conclusion concerning Destiny's abrupt departure from Newport in June 2011, when Jachney again emailed Sharp stating that he intended to participate in sea trials before Destiny departed Newport. **[—42—]**

In light of these factual findings, we cannot say that the district court erred as a matter of law in finding that "Hylas'[s] actions constituted a breach of contract and breach of express and implied warranties," but that the breaches of warranties in this case "did not in fact produce unfairness or deception." While it is true that "[g]enerally, a breach of warranty constitutes a violation of [chapter 93A]," *Maillet v. ATF-Davidson Co.*, 552 N.E.2d 95, 100 (Mass. 1990), neither the Massachusetts legislature nor the Supreme Judicial Court has gone so far as to find that all breaches of warranties are inherently deceptive or unfair. *See Evans v. Lorillard Tobacco Co.*, 990 N.E.2d 997, 1038 n.25 (Mass. 2013) ("[W]e decline, as we did in *Maillet*, to decide whether liability should be 'imposed automatically under [Mass. Gen. Laws ch. 93A] whenever a defendant has violated the warranty of merchantability,' even where there is no finding of negligence."). Where, as here, the district court finds (without clearly erring) that the defendant made genuine but ultimately ineffectual efforts to live up to its contractual obligations, the mere breach of express and implied warranties is not sufficient to mandate a finding of liability under chapter 93A.

III. Conclusion

For the foregoing reasons, we *affirm*.

United States Court of Appeals
for the First Circuit

No. 16-1342

UNITED STATES
vs.
CORTEZ-VERGARA

Appeal from the United States District Court for the District of Puerto Rico

Decided: October 17, 2017

Citation: 873 F.3d 390, 5 Adm. R. 71 (1st Cir. 2017).

Before **HOWARD**, Chief Judge, **SELYA** and **BARRON**, Circuit Judges.

[—2—] {-392-} **HOWARD**, Chief Judge:

After pleading guilty to maritime drug and conspiracy offenses, Freddy Cortez-Vergara was sentenced to a bottom-of-the-range guidelines sentence of 108 months' incarceration. He now challenges his sentence on the ground that the sentencing court erred by not granting him a minor role adjustment under U.S.S.G. §3B1.2(b). Finding Cortez's argument meritless, we affirm.

I.

Because Cortez pled guilty, we draw the facts from the change-of-plea and sentencing hearing transcripts and the Presentence Investigation Report's ("PSR") uncontested portions. *See United States v. Rossignol*, 780 F.3d 475, 476 (1st Cir. 2016).

Prior to his arrest, Cortez worked as a fisherman in Ecuador. Cortez met with a man named "Abraham," another local fisherman, who offered Cortez $2,000 to join the crew of one of Abraham's vessels on a trip to Guatemala. Cortez and two other crew members set out from Ecuador in January 2015 on Abraham's thirty-foot boat. One of the two men served as the boat's captain, the other was the boat's mariner, and Cortez helped steer the boat.

The crew voyaged approximately 200 nautical miles to rendezvous at sea with Abraham, who was aboard another vessel. Abraham supplied the crew with cocaine bales and fuel containers. The three-person crew then continued for approximately 400 miles before the Coast Guard intercepted the boat about 291 miles south **[—3—]** of the Guatemala-El Salvador border. Shortly before the Coast Guard boarded the vessel, Cortez and his confederates realized that they were being tracked and started throwing the cocaine bales and excess fuel tanks overboard. When it apprehended the crew, the Coast Guard determined that the vessel was without nationality and thus subject to United States jurisdiction. 46 U.S.C. § 70502(c)(1)(A). About 433 kilograms of cocaine were recovered from the scene.

Cortez and the two other men were brought to Puerto Rico, where, in February 2015, a grand jury indicted them on two counts. The first count alleged that the three men conspired to possess with the intent to distribute a controlled substance on board a vessel subject to the jurisdiction of the United States, in violation of 46 U.S.C. §§ 70503(a)(1), 70504(b)(1) and 70506(a) and (b). The second count alleged that the men possessed, and aided and abetted the possession, with the intent to distribute a controlled substance on board a vessel subject to the jurisdiction of the United States, in violation of 46 U.S.C. §§ 70503(a)(1), 70504(b)(1) and 70506(a) and (b). Cortez entered an unconditional guilty plea in October 2016.

At sentencing, Cortez contested the PSR's recommendation that he be denied a two-level downward minor role adjustment under U.S.S.G. §3B1.2(b). Cortez claimed that he played a minor role because he "was only a small part of" an "overall very large **[—4—]** conspiracy." Agreeing with the PSR's recommendation, the district court denied Cortez's request on the ground that Cortez was responsible for transporting 433 kilograms of cocaine across the ocean. The court sentenced Cortez to a bottom-of-the-range guidelines sentence of 108 months. After being sentenced, Cortez seasonably filed this appeal.

II.

We apply an abuse of discretion standard of review to procedural challenges to sentences. *United States v. Coleman*, 854 F.3d 81, 84-85 (1st Cir. 2017). Within this framework, we review the district **{-393-}** court's conclusions of law de novo and its findings of fact for clear error. *Rossignol*, 780 F.3d at 477. And because "[r]ole in-the-offense determinations are notoriously fact-specific," "absent a mistake of law," we will only reverse the district court's decision if it is clearly erroneous. *United States v. Perez*, 819 F.3d 541, 545-46, 4 Adm. R. 20, 21 (1st Cir. 2016) (internal citations omitted). Because a district court's choice between multiple permissible inferences cannot be clearly erroneous, we will "rarely reverse[] a district court's decision regarding whether to apply a minor role adjustment." *United States v. Bravo*, 489 F.3d 1, 11 (1st Cir. 2007) (citing *United States v. Tom*, 330 F.3d 83, 95 (1st Cir. 2003)).

A defendant seeking a minor role adjustment under U.S.S.G. §3B1.2(b) must demonstrate by a preponderance of the **[—5—]** evidence that: (1) they are less culpable than their coconspirators or accomplices; and (2) they are less culpable than "most of those who have perpetrated similar crimes." *United States v. Mateo-Espejo*, 426 F.3d 508, 512 (1st Cir. 2005). Overcoming an adverse minor role decision is a difficult burden for a defendant to meet on appeal, for the district court's determination is, as noted, "invariably fact-specific and, thus, appellate review of such a determination is respectful." *United States v. Meléndez-Rivera*, 782 F.3d 26, 28 (1st Cir. 2015).

"[A] defendant need not be the key figure in a conspiracy in order to be denied a mitigating role-in-the-offense adjustment." *See id.* at 29. In *Meléndez-Rivera*, we rejected a drug-smuggler's argument that he played a minor role simply because he characterized himself "as an 'expendable cog' in the venture" and because he was not the conspiracy's leader. *Id.* Similarly, we upheld the denial of a minor role adjustment where the defendant's sole role was hauling a single shipment of thirty kilograms of cocaine by truck. *United States v. Vargas*, 560 F.3d 45, 50 (1st Cir. 2009).

Moreover, in *United States v. Perez*, we recently rejected a defendant's argument that he was a minor participant in a nautical narcotics-smuggling scheme because he merely assisted in transporting drugs across the sea. 819 F.3d at 545-46, 4 Adm. R. at 21-22. Similar to Cortez, the defendant in *Perez* also protested that "he played **[—6—]** a bit part" compared to the drugs' owners and U.S. distributors. We rejected those claims because "[w]hen two persons undertake to transport by themselves a large quantity of drugs in a long and hazardous voyage at sea, it is not clear error for a sentencing court to regard each as a principal and refuse to grant any mitigating role adjustment." *Id.* at 546, 4 Adm. R. at 22.

Perez controls this case. Like the defendant in *Perez*, Cortez asserts that he is entitled to a minor role adjustment because he only assisted in transporting the drugs across the sea. Here, Cortez helped steer the vessel and he was one of just three crew members who, by themselves, and otherwise unsupervised, moved a large quantity of drugs hundreds of miles over the Eastern Pacific Ocean. Accordingly, the district court's determination that Cortez was not less culpable than his codefendants or the average seafaring drug smuggler falls far short of clear error. Therefore, the district court did not abuse its discretion when it declined to assign to Cortez a two-level downward minor role adjustment under U.S.S.G. §3B1.2(b).

III.

For the foregoing reasons, we ***AFFIRM*** Cortez's sentence.

United States Court of Appeals
for the First Circuit

No. 16-2356

UNITED STATES
vs.
PEAKE

Appeal from the United States District Court for the District of Puerto Rico

Decided: October 23, 2017

Citation: 874 F.3d 65, 5 Adm. R. 73 (1st Cir. 2017).

Before **HOWARD,** Chief Judge, **SELYA** and **LIPEZ,** Circuit Judges.

[—2—] **{-67-}** **SELYA,** Circuit Judge:

Defendant-appellant Frank Peake, smarting under the double sting of his conviction for antitrust conspiracy and this court's affirmance of that conviction, asked the district court to wipe the slate clean and grant him a new trial based on freshly discovered evidence. The district court demurred. Peake appeals. After careful consideration, we affirm the judgment below.

I. BACKGROUND

We sketch the facts, mindful that the reader who hungers for more exegetic detail may consult our earlier opinion affirming the underlying conviction and the district court's thoughtful rescript denying the appellant's motion for a new trial. *See United States v. Peake* (*Peake I*), 804 F.3d 81, 3 Adm. R. 83 (1st Cir. 2015), *cert. denied*, 137 S. Ct. 36 (2016); *United States v. Peake* (*Peake II*), No. 11-cr-512, 2016 WL 8234673 (D.P.R. Oct. 18, 2016).

The government's case against the appellant had its roots in "one of the largest antitrust conspiracies" in United States history. *Peake I*, 804 F.3d at 84, 3 Adm. R. at 83. Between 2002 and 2008, Sea Star Line (Sea Star) and Horizon Lines (Horizon), both leading freight carriers, agreed to fix rates and surcharges for Puerto Rico-bound cargo in a multi-pronged effort to maintain market share and to squelch competition.[1] *See id.* at 85, 3 Adm. R. at 83. In 2003, the appellant **[—3—]** became Sea Star's chief operating officer and, later, its president. During his tenure, Sea Star reaped over half-a-billion dollars in total revenue. *See id.* at 99-100, 3 Adm. R. at 96.

While the appellant joined the conspiracy in 2005, we fast-forward to November of 2011, at which time, a federal grand jury indicted the appellant on a charge of conspiracy to violate section one of the Sherman Act, which proscribes "agreements in restraint of trade or commerce 'among the several [s]tates.'" *Id.* at 86, 3 Adm. R. at 84 (quoting 15 U.S.C. § 1). During the appellant's nine-day trial in 2013, the government introduced testimony from three cooperating witnesses: Gabriel Serra (a Horizon senior vice president), Greg Glova (a mid-level Horizon executive who reported to Serra), and Peter Baci (a Sea Star executive who reported to the appellant). These three witnesses consistently described the conspiracy's modus operandi and hierarchical structure. Pertinently, Baci and Glova would resolve day-to-day issues relating to pricing and market-share allocation, while the appellant and Serra would settle any lingering disputes. For instance, Serra testified that when Walgreens, a significant importer of consumer goods to Puerto Rico, decided to deal exclusively with Horizon rather than splitting shipping contracts between Horizon and Sea Star, Serra and the appellant agreed that Horizon "would compensate" Sea Star for its lost **{-68-}** revenue "by shifting cargo to Sea Star vessels" and paying Sea Star to carry **[—4—]** Horizon cargo. *Id.* at 85, 3 Adm. R. at 83. This trio of witnesses also described meetings that the appellant had with Horizon officials regarding the conspiracy, including a 2006 summit meeting in Orlando at which the appellant and Serra resolved price-fixing and market-allocation issues.

The government's case included a trove of incriminating e-mails linking the appellant to the conspiracy. Among these e-mails was one sent by the appellant to a Horizon executive

[1] Although not relevant here, a third company, Crowley Lines, was part of the conspiracy.

discussing prices quoted to a customer and expressing the appellant's desire to "avoid a price war." *Id.*, 3 Adm. R. at 84. In other e-mails, the appellant consulted with Horizon officials before sending proposals to potential customers so that the two companies would maintain balanced market shares.

All in all, an "overwhelming amount" of evidence, including travel and telephone records, corroborated the appellant's leading role in orchestrating the conspiracy. *Id.* at 94, 3 Adm. R. at 91. Indeed, the evidence showed that the appellant and Serra had more than 300 conversations, using their personal telephones, between 2003 and 2008.

In addition, Ron Reynolds, a United States Department of Agriculture (USDA) agent, testified about the conspiracy's impact on federal food assistance programs. Gabriel Lafitte, the purchasing director for nearly 200 Burger King restaurants in **[—5—]** Puerto Rico, testified about the conspiracy's impact on the chain's island-wide costs and prices.

The appellant did not offer any witnesses at trial. Nor did he spend much time attacking the existence of the charged conspiracy. Instead, his counsel argued that the government had failed to prove that the appellant knowingly participated in the conspiracy. In this vein, counsel made much of the fact that William Stallings, a former Sea Star executive cooperating with the government, had recorded conversations with conspiracy participants for two months, but had never recorded any statements by the appellant.

The jury rejected the appellant's defense and found him guilty. The district court sentenced him to sixty months' imprisonment, and we affirmed the conviction and sentence. *See id.* at 85, 100, 3 Adm. R. at 84, 97.

Long after the jury had rendered its verdict, the appellant learned that Stallings (whom neither party had called as a witness) had filed a qui tam action pursuant to the False Claims Act (FCA), 31 U.S.C. §§ 3729-3733, on January 15, 2013. In his complaint, Stallings alleged that Sea Star and Horizon had collogued to defraud the government. Stallings's qui tam action was unsealed and settled approximately thirteen months later.[2] Sea **[—6—]** Star agreed to pay the government $1,900,000 and Horizon agreed to pay the government $1,500,000. For his part, Stallings received over half-a-million dollars as a whistleblower. *See id.* § 3730(d).

On April 18, 2014, the appellant moved for a new trial in his criminal case pursuant to Federal Rule of Criminal Procedure 33. He argued that the government's failure to inform him of Stallings's qui tam action offended the due process guarantees memorialized in *Brady v. Maryland*, 373 U.S. 83 (1963). The district court denied the motion without an evidentiary hearing. *See Peake II*, 2016 WL 8234673, at *11. The **{-69-}** court reasoned that, in light of the "massive amount of independently incriminating evidence" introduced against the appellant at trial, there was no reason to believe that earlier disclosure of the qui tam action would have changed the outcome. *Id.* This timely appeal followed.

II. ANALYSIS

In this venue, the appellant advances two assignments of error. First, he renews his contention that the government's nondisclosure of Stallings's qui tam action demanded a new trial, and he therefore faults the district court for denying his Rule 33 motion. Second, he contends for the first time that relief under Rule 33 is warranted because Puerto Rico should not be treated **[—7—]** like a state for the purposes of the Sherman Act. We address these contentions one by one.

A. The Nondisclosure Claim.

Rule 33 authorizes the district court, on motion of a criminal defendant, to "grant a new trial if the interest of justice so requires."

[2] The FCA authorizes private plaintiffs to initiate, on the government's behalf, suits that allege fraud in government **[—6—]** programs. *See* 31 U.S.C. § 3730(b); *see also United States ex rel. Winkelman v. CVS Caremark Corp.*, 827 F.3d 201, 203 (1st Cir. 2016). The statute directs that such complaints be filed under seal. *See* 31 U.S.C. § 3730(b)(2).

Fed. R. Crim. P. 33(a). When, as now, a Rule 33 motion is made more than fourteen days after the verdict, it must be "grounded on newly discovered evidence." Fed. R. Crim. P. 33(b). Under ordinary circumstances, a defendant seeking such relief must satisfy four conditions: he must show that the specified evidence "was unknown or unavailable to him at the time of trial"; that the failure to discover such evidence was not the result of his "lack of diligence"; that "the evidence is material" and not "merely cumulative or impeaching"; and that "the evidence is such that its introduction would probably result in an acquittal upon a retrial of the case." *United States v. Maldonado-Rivera*, 489 F.3d 60, 66 (1st Cir. 2007) (citing *United States v. Wright*, 625 F.2d 1017, 1019 (1st Cir. 1980)).

This formulation is somewhat different if a movant colorably asserts that the government violated *Brady*. Under *Brady*, the government offends due process if it causes prejudice to the defendant by "either willfully or inadvertently" suppressing "exculpatory or impeaching" evidence in its custody or control that is "favorable to the accused." *United States v. Connolly*, **[—8—]** 504 F.3d 206, 212 (1st Cir. 2007) (citing *Strickler v. Greene*, 527 U.S. 263, 281-82 (1999)). A defendant who seeks to premise his motion for a new trial on a *Brady* violation must satisfy the first (unavailability) and second (due diligence) elements of the conventional test. *See id.* at 212-13. But the third and fourth elements (materiality and prejudice, respectively) are merged and "replaced with the unitary requirement" that the defendant need demonstrate only "'a reasonable probability that, had the evidence been disclosed to the defense'" in a timely manner, "'the result of the proceeding would have been different.'" *Id.* at 213 (quoting *United States v. Bagley*, 473 U.S. 667, 682 (1985) (opinion of Blackmun, J.)); *see Kyles v. Whitley*, 514 U.S. 419, 434 (1995).

This alteration in the Rule 33 framework eases a defendant's burden in two significant ways. For one thing, instead of having to demonstrate "*actual* probability that the result would have differed," the defendant need only point to "something sufficient to 'undermine[] confidence in the outcome of the trial.'" *United States v. Mathur*, 624 F.3d 498, 504 (1st Cir. 2010) (emphasis and alteration in original) (quoting *Kyles*, 514 U.S. at 434). For another thing, while impeachment evidence is ordinarily insufficient to show materiality in the Rule 33 context, *see Connolly*, 504 F.3d at 213, **{-70-}** impeachment evidence that is undisclosed in violation of *Brady* may "suffice[] to undermine **[—9—]** confidence in the outcome of the trial" and, if so, warrant a new trial, *Mathur*, 624 F.3d at 504 (internal quotation marks omitted).

In applying these principles, we do not write on a pristine page. Rather, our review of a decision denying a Rule 33 motion must take into account that the district court "has a special sense of the ebb and flow of the . . . trial." *Id.* (internal quotation marks omitted). Consequently, we afford substantial deference to the district court's views regarding the likely impact of belatedly disclosed evidence and review its denial of a Rule 33 motion solely for abuse of discretion. *See id.*; *Connolly*, 504 F.3d at 211.

Here, the district court conducted a searching appraisal of the record and found no hint of cognizable prejudice stemming from the government's failure to disclose Stallings's filing of the qui tam action. *See Peake II*, 2016 WL 8234673, at *11. We explain briefly why this determination was well within the encincture of the district court's discretion.

It is uncontroverted that, at the time of trial, the appellant was unaware of Stallings's plan to file a qui tam action. Nor does the government suggest that the appellant's lack of awareness stemmed from any failure of diligence on his part. But even assuming that the government knew about such evidence and had **[—10—]** custody of it,[3] the

[3] We note that the appellant, in an apparent effort to prove that the information about Stallings's initiation of suit was within the government's custody and control, attached to his reply brief a series of 2012 e-mails between Stallings and the lead prosecutor. This proffer does not gain him any traction. After all, "evidentiary

appellant's claim founders on the district court's finding that he failed to show cognizable prejudice.

The appellant insists that, had he been aware of the qui tam action, he would have called Stallings to testify and would have elicited testimony regarding three data points: that a different Sea Star executive (Leonard Shapiro) consummated Sea Star's conspiratorial agreement with Horizon in 2002; that Baci (the appellant's subordinate) played a central role in the conspiracy; and that the appellant was not a participant in any of the seventeen conversations that Stallings recorded while acting under the government's auspices. None of these data points, though, had anything to do with the qui tam action. Moreover, none of them was controversial. The government never disputed that it was Shapiro who forged the fifty-fifty arrangement with Horizon in 2002 (indeed, the government itself introduced trial testimony to that effect). So, too, Baci testified at the trial **[—11—]** as a government witness and made clear that he managed the day-to-day details touching upon Sea Star's anticompetitive arrangement with Horizon. Last—but far from least—the government produced Stallings's seventeen recordings in discovery, and the appellant's counsel harped upon the appellant's absence from the recordings in his opening statement.

The short of it is that the appellant—who could have called Stallings as a trial witness but chose not to do so—fails to **{-71-}** offer any coherent explanation as to why the existence of the qui tam action would have led him to reevaluate this decision. Put another way, the appellant has not articulated "any plausible strategic option" that the failure to reveal the existence of the qui tam action either "hampered or foreclosed." *Mathur*, 624 F.3d at 506. For aught that appears, knowledge of the qui tam action would not have benefited the defense in any meaningful way.

The appellant resists the district court's conclusion to this effect, mustering a litany of other possible uses that he might have made of the qui tam action (had he known about it). These are, however, shots in the dark—and none of them comes close to hitting the mark.

To begin, the appellant submits that he would have introduced the qui tam complaint into evidence. The complaint would have been useful, he suggests in hindsight, because of what it does not say (that is, it hardly refers to the appellant). But **[—12—]** this is whistling past the graveyard: the qui tam complaint contains two highly incriminating references to the appellant, which would have buttressed the government's theory that he was a moving force in the conspiracy.[4] Thus, introduction of the qui tam complaint into evidence would have tended to weaken, not strengthen, the appellant's lack-of-knowledge defense.

Next, the appellant argues that timely disclosure of the qui tam action would have enabled him to impeach Stallings regarding the latter's financial incentive to cooperate with the government. One flaw in this argument is that neither side called Stallings as a trial witness, so any such impeachment evidence would have been inadmissible. *See United States v. Silva*, 71 F.3d 667, 670-71 (7th Cir. 1995). And even assuming that Stallings had testified, any impeachment value arising out of the filing of his qui tam action would have been miniscule compared to the impeachment evidence that the appellant already had available (such as evidence of

matters not first presented to the district court are . . . not properly before us." *United States v. Kobrosky*, 711 F.2d 449, 457 (1st Cir. 1983).

Relatedly, the appellant invites us to remand this matter to the district court so that he may explore what the government knew about Stallings's decision to file the qui tam action and when the government knew it. Since we have assumed, arguendo, that the government had custody and control over the information about Stallings's decision, remand would serve no useful purpose.

[4] The qui tam complaint alleges that any pricing matters that were not resolved between Baci and Glova "would be bumped up the chain of command to be addressed and resolved by" the appellant and Serra. Similarly, the complaint describes the 2006 Orlando meeting, during which Baci, Glova, Serra, and the appellant discussed implementation of the companies' anticompetitive marketshare agreement.

Stallings's hip-deep involvement in the conspiracy and his avoidance of potentially significant prison time through his cooperation with the government). **[—13—]**

Sounding a similar note, the appellant contends that he could have used the qui tam action to impeach Reynolds (the USDA agent) who testified for the government. Evidence of the qui tam action would have been useful to prove Reynolds's bias, the appellant insists, inasmuch as the appellant's conviction would have tended to increase the likelihood of a substantial recovery by the government in the qui tam action.

This contention borders on the frivolous. Reynolds's testimony was offered solely to prove that the conspiracy affected interstate commerce. *See Peake I*, 804 F.3d at 92, 96-97, 3 Adm. R. at 90, 94 (discussing Sherman Act's interstate commerce requirement). Accordingly, Reynolds's testimony was brief and limited to a narrow point: the impact that the conspiracy had on federal food assistance programs. Seen in this light, the impeachment value of the qui tam action vis-á-vis Reynolds would have been slim to none.

Grasping at straws, the appellant argues that knowing about the qui tam action would have propped up his unsuccessful motion to transfer the criminal case to the Middle District of Florida. This argument is hopeless. In the first place, **{-72-}** the appellant never advanced this argument below and, as a general rule, "legal theories not raised squarely in the lower court cannot be broached for the first time on appeal." *Teamsters, Chauffeurs, Warehousemen & Helpers Union, Local No. 59 v. Superline Transp. Co.*, 953 F.2d 17, 21 (1st Cir. 1992). In the second place, the **[—14—]** propriety of venue is not material either to guilt or punishment. *Cf. United States v. Lanoue*, 137 F.3d 656, 661 (1st Cir. 1998) (noting that "[v]enue is not an element of the offense"). Consequently, information that is material only to a venue decision does not implicate *Brady*.

To say more on the prejudice point would be supererogatory. Common sense teaches that an undisclosed piece of evidence often looms larger in the eyes of a hopeful defendant than its actual dimensions warrant. In the *Brady* context, though, prejudice cannot be viewed in a funhouse mirror. Instead, it is a fact-specific phenomenon that must be gauged objectively in light of the circumstances of a particular case. It is not enough that a defendant thinks (or professes to think) that somehow, some way, his theory of defense would have prevailed had he been given timely access to the allegedly withheld information.

To sum up, we conclude that the district court's finding that the appellant suffered no cognizable prejudice from the delayed disclosure is fully supportable. The government's failure to disclose the qui tam action is "manifestly insufficient to place the trial record in 'such a different light as to undermine confidence in the verdict.'" *Mathur*, 624 F.3d at 505 (quoting *Kyles*, 514 U.S. at 435).

A loose end remains. The appellant argues, in the alternative, that the district court should have convened an **[—15—]** evidentiary hearing on his Rule 33 motion. This argument contains more cry than wool.

We previously have explained that "evidentiary hearings on new trial motions in criminal cases are the exception rather than the rule." *Connolly*, 504 F.3d at 220. Where, as here, the trial court supportably concludes that a Rule 33 motion "is conclusively refuted . . . by the files and records of the case," such a hearing would be futile. *Id.* at 219-20 (internal quotation marks omitted). Given its intricate web of findings, we discern no abuse of discretion in the district court's declination to hold an evidentiary hearing on the appellant's Rule 33 motion.

B. <u>The Status Claim</u>.

The appellant has one last arrow in his quiver. He complains that his conviction is invalid due to Puerto Rico's status. This plaint builds on the uncontroversial premise that the statute of conviction (the Sherman Act) outlaws conspiracies "in restraint of trade or commerce among the several [s]tates." 15 U.S.C. § 1. While acknowledging our case law holding that such a proscription applies to commerce between Puerto Rico and one or more states, *see, e.g., Córdova & Simonpietri Ins. Agency Inc. v. Chase Manhattan Bank N.A.*, 649 F.2d 36, 38 (1st Cir. 1981), he exhorts us to reconsider this holding in light of the decision in *Puerto Rico v. Sanchez Valle*, 136 S. Ct. 1863, 1868 (2016) **[—16—]** (concluding that Puerto Rico is not a separate sovereign for the purpose of the Double Jeopardy Clause).

Even without dwelling on the fact that this claim is foreclosed because it was not raised below, *see Superline Transp.*, 953 F.2d at 21, it is without force. Under Rule 33, a new trial motion filed more than fourteen days after the verdict—like this one—must draw its essence from "newly discovered evidence." Fed. R. Crim. P. 33(b). It is nose-on-the-face plain that a **{–73–}** change in the law does not amount to newly discovered evidence within the purview of Rule 33. *See United States v. King*, 735 F.3d 1098, 1108-09 (9th Cir. 2013).

In all events, the appellant's claim is misdirected. The record in this case makes pellucid that the conspiracy in which the appellant participated involved more than commerce between a state and Puerto Rico. As we noted in affirming the appellant's conviction, the trial evidence showed that "the commerce affected by the conspiracy was not only between a state and Puerto Rico, but also among the states." *Peake I*, 804 F.3d at 86, 3 Adm. R. at 84.

III. CONCLUSION

We need go no further. For the reasons elucidated above, the judgment of the district court is

Affirmed.

United States Court of Appeals for the First Circuit

No. 15-2120

UNITED STATES vs. CARBAJAL-VÁLDEZ

Appeal from the United States District Court for the District of Puerto Rico

Decided: November 3, 2017

Citation: 874 F.3d 778, 5 Adm. R. 79 (1st Cir. 2017).

Before **LYNCH, SELYA,** and **STAHL,** Circuit Judges.

[—2—] {-780-} SELYA, Circuit Judge:

In this appeal, defendant-appellant Juan Francisco Emilio Carbajal-Váldez advances two claims of error. First, he contends that the district court erred in imposing a sentencing enhancement based largely on his admission that he captained the cocaine-laden boat used in the smuggling attempt. Second, he contends that the government breached a plea agreement between the parties both in responding to the district court about the prospective enhancement and in supporting the **{-781-}** resultant sentence on appeal. Concluding, as we do, that these contentions are unpersuasive, we affirm.

I. BACKGROUND

Because this appeal follows a guilty plea, "we draw the facts from the plea colloquy, the uncontested portions of the presentence investigation report, and the sentencing transcript." *United States v. Nuñez*, 852 F.3d 141, 143 (1st Cir. 2017). After accepting an offer of $50,000 to transport drugs from Venezuela to Puerto Rico, the appellant embarked on an ill-fated voyage with two fellow seamen and a large quantity of cocaine. Just before midnight on March 16, 2015, a Puerto Rico Police Department maritime patrol boat spied their vessel operating without navigation lights off the coast of Puerto Rico. When the police stopped the vessel and boarded it, they saw a number of sacks containing white brick-shaped objects in plain view. A field test, conducted while at sea, revealed these bricks to be cocaine. In **[—3—]** total, the police recovered approximately 1,434 kilograms of cocaine.

The police seized the boat and arrested the three men on board: the appellant, José Miguel Váldez-Vázquez, and Ramón Pache. The government alleges (and the appellant does not dispute) that at the moment of interdiction, the appellant identified himself as the captain of the craft.

The authorities proceeded to file criminal complaints against all three seafarers, charging that they possessed and conspired to possess with intent to distribute five kilograms or more of cocaine. *See* 21 U.S.C. §§ 841(a)(1), 846. In short order, a federal grand jury indicted the trio on the same charges. At first, the appellant resisted the indictment, maintaining his innocence. His codefendants adopted a similar stance.

After defense counsel met with the prosecutor and obtained discovery, the appellant and his codefendants decided to change their pleas and entered into substantially identical plea agreements with the government. During a joint change-of-plea hearing, each man pleaded guilty to a single count of conspiring to possess five or more kilograms of cocaine with intent to distribute. The appellant's plea agreement (the Agreement) contemplated a base offense level of 38, premised largely on drug quantity. It also contemplated a three-level reduction for acceptance of responsibility, *see* USSG §3E1.1(a), and left open **[—4—]** the possibility of a further two-level reduction if the appellant proved to satisfy the requirements for the so-called safety valve, *see id.* §2D1.1(b)(17). Both sides pledged not to seek any further adjustments or departures, up or down.

The Agreement took no position as to the appropriate criminal history category and, thus, did not forecast a specific guideline sentencing range. The government, though, agreed that when the guideline range was established, it would recommend a within-the-range sentence. The Agreement made pellucid that any such recommendation would not be binding on the sentencing court.

Once the district court had accepted all three guilty pleas, the probation office prepared a separate presentence investigation report (PSI Report) for each defendant. When those reports were compiled, the probation office recommended a sentencing enhancement for the appellant that it did not recommend for either of his codefendants: a two-level enhancement as captain of the boat under USSG §2D1.1(b)(3)(C). This enhancement was appropriate, the probation office stated, because the appellant had been identified as the master of the vessel and had admitted to the probation officer that his job **{-782-}** had been to get the boat, bring it to the loading port, and "steer the vessel and transport the drugs to [Puerto Rico]."

Neither the appellant nor the government objected in writing to any of the findings or recommendations contained in the **[—5—]** PSI Report. At the disposition hearing, the district court—rejecting the exhortations of both the appellant and the government—adopted the guideline calculations limned in the PSI Report. These calculations included the captain enhancement, which ratcheted up the appellant's adjusted offense level and produced a higher guideline range. The court then imposed a 168-month term of immurement.[1]

Earlier the same day, the district court held separate sentencing hearings for each of the appellant's codefendants. The court did not tag either of them with the captain enhancement. In the absence of that enhancement, the court sentenced each man to 135 months' imprisonment.

This timely appeal ensued. The waiver-of-appeal clause contained in the Agreement offers no impediment: that clause is contingent upon the district court imposing a sentence within the sentence recommendation provisions of the Agreement, and the appellant's sentence—increased by the captain enhancement—did not trigger that contingency. **[—6—]**

II. ANALYSIS

Generally speaking, appellate review of a federal criminal sentence is imbued with a "frank recognition of the substantial discretion vested in a sentencing court." *United States v. Flores-Machicote*, 706 F.3d 16, 20 (1st Cir. 2013). More specifically, though, such review is bifurcated: a reviewing court must first determine whether a challenged sentence is procedurally sound and then must determine whether it is substantively reasonable. *See United States v. Ruiz-Huertas*, 792 F.3d 223, 226 (1st Cir. 2015). In evaluating the procedural integrity of a sentence, we afford de novo review to the district court's interpretation and application of the sentencing guidelines, appraise its factfinding for clear error, and evaluate its judgment calls under an abuse-of-discretion rubric. *See id.*

The usual standards of appellate review are altered when a party fails to preserve claims of sentencing error in the district court. In that event, appellate review is solely for plain error. *See United States v. Rodríguez-Milián*, 820 F.3d 26, 34 (1st Cir.), *cert. denied*, 137 S. Ct. 138 (2016). This rigorous standard requires an appellant to show "(1) that an error occurred (2) which was clear or obvious and which not only (3) affected the defendant's substantial rights, but also (4) seriously impaired the fairness, integrity, or public reputation of judicial **[—7—]** proceedings." *United States v. Duarte*, 246 F.3d 56, 60 (1st Cir. 2001).

Against this backdrop, we turn to the case at hand. The appellant presses two separate claims of procedural error. We address them sequentially.

[1] The guideline sentencing range recommended by the probation office (168-210 months) included offense-level reductions for both acceptance of responsibility and the safety valve. The sentence imposed by the district court was at the bottom of this range. Had the court not applied the enhancement, the guideline range would have been 135-168 months.

A. Imposition of the Enhancement.

The appellant's principal challenge is to the district court's imposition of the captain enhancement under USSG §2D1.1(b)(3)(C). This challenge takes dead aim at the factual finding that the appellant acted as the captain of the cocaine-laden ship. One problem, however, is **{–783–}** that the PSI Report contained such a finding and recommended the concomitant enhancement, but the appellant did not seasonably object to these statements. Such an omission normally would constitute a waiver or, at least, a forfeiture, thus paving the way for plain error review. *See United States v. Turbides-Leonardo*, 468 F.3d 34, 38 (1st Cir. 2006); *see also* Fed. R. Crim. P. 32(f) (requiring objections to presentence report within 14 days); D.P.R.R. 132(b)(3)(A) (similar).

Here, however, there is a potentially countervailing consideration. At the disposition hearing, defense counsel disputed both the effect of the appellant's characterization of himself as the captain and the application of the enhancement. Neither the government nor the district court questioned the timeliness of these objections, and a colorable argument can be **[—8—]** made that the objections sufficed to preserve the claim of error. *See, e.g., United States v. Perkins*, 89 F.3d 303, 306-07 (6th Cir. 1996).

In all events, courts should not rush to untangle knotty legal questions when there is no real need to do so. So it is here: because the standard of review is not decisive with respect to this issue, we assume, favorably to the appellant, that his objections were preserved.

The claim of error turns, of course, on the supportability of the sentencing court's factual finding. That finding is reviewed for clear error. *See Ruiz-Huertas*, 792 F.3d at 226. Clear error is not an appellant-friendly standard; it is "satisfied only if, 'upon whole-record-review, an inquiring court form[s] a strong, unyielding belief that a mistake has been made.'" *Nuñez*, 852 F.3d at 144 (alteration in original) (quoting *United States v. Cintrón-Echautegui*, 604 F.3d 1, 6 (1st Cir. 2010)). The government bears the burden of proving sentence-enhancing factors by a preponderance of the evidence. *See id.* Raw facts contained in unchallenged portions of a presentence report are ordinarily "considered reliable evidence for sentencing purposes." *United States v. Morrillo*, 8 F.3d 864, 872 (1st Cir. 1993); *see United States v. Fernandez-Cabrera*, 625 F.3d 48, 54 (1st Cir. 2010); *United States v. Garcia*, 954 F.2d 12, 18 (1st Cir. 1992). **[—9—]**

Here, the sentencing court found that the captain enhancement applied. The court, though, did not spell out its subsidiary findings. Such inattention to subsidiary findings invites confusion. The better practice is for a sentencing court to make reasonably specific findings as to why an enhancement is appropriate. *See, e.g., United States v. McDowell*, 918 F.2d 1004, 1012 (1st Cir. 1990).

Nevertheless, we are reluctant to exalt form over substance. Notwithstanding our preference for explicit findings, we have recognized that the absence of such findings is not always fatal. *See United States v. Van*, 87 F.3d 1, 3 (1st Cir. 1996). A reviewing court may uphold a sentencing court's conclusion if it seems apparent that the sentencing court adopted, albeit implicitly, relevant findings contained in a presentence investigation report and those findings provide a sufficient basis for the conclusion. *See United States v. Schultz*, 970 F.2d 960, 963 n.7 (1st Cir. 1992); *McDowell*, 918 F.2d at 1011-12. The key is whether the sentencing record, taken as a whole, reliably shows that the relevant factual questions were "implicitly resolved" by the sentencing court. *Van*, 87 F.3d at 3.

In the case at hand, the district court stated at the disposition hearing that it agreed with the probation officer concerning the enhancement. This statement, coupled with the court's explanation that the captain enhancement was applied **[—10—]** because the appellant "acted as the captain aboard **{–784–}** the vessel which carried controlled substances," makes manifest that the court impliedly adopted the findings contained in the PSI Report. Consequently, the question reduces to the sufficiency of those findings.

The PSI Report, fairly read, offers enough information to eliminate any guesswork about what facts the sentencing court envisioned as the basis for the captain enhancement. To begin, the PSI Report captures the appellant's admission that it was his role to procure the boat in Maracaibo, Venezuela, and take it to another port (where the drugs were brought on board). He then received instructions to undertake the voyage to Piñones, Puerto Rico. During that voyage, he steered the vessel (although at least one of his codefendants helped with the steering). We think that these facts justified the sentencing court's decision to apply the enhancement to this defendant and not to his codefendants.

To cinch the matter, defense counsel acknowledged during the disposition hearing that, at the time of interdiction, the appellant admitted that he was the captain. Counsel indicated that he had confirmed the veracity of this admission with the appellant. Consistent with this self-identification, the PSI Report denominated the appellant as the "master of the vessel." That designation, in turn, became part of the predicate that undergirded the captain enhancement. **[—11—]**

Faced with these data points, the appellant never denied that he had identified himself as the captain. Instead, he argued in the district court that "the title doesn't make . . . the description of the specifics of this case." Before us, the appellant makes essentially the same argument, suggesting that the captain enhancement should not depend on the title alone, but on the functions that he performed. Although this suggestion possesses a patina of plausibility, it fails on the facts.

The sentencing guidelines do not define the word "captain." Since undefined terms in the guidelines should customarily be given their plain and ordinary meaning, *see Chapman v. United States*, 500 U.S. 453, 461-62 (1991); *United States v. Brewster*, 1 F.3d 51, 54 (1st Cir. 1993), the sentencing court was entitled to give the appellant's "captaincy" admission some weight. Here, moreover, the appellant's self-identification, considered alongside his actual conduct in procuring the vessel, taking it to the loading point, receiving the itinerary, and steering the boat, furnished an adequate predicate for the court below to apply the captain enhancement. *See United States v. Guerrero*, 114 F.3d 332, 346 (1st Cir. 1997) (upholding pilot enhancement under USSG §2D1.1(b)(3)(C); *cf. United States v. Trinidad*, 839 F.3d 112, 115-16, 4 Adm. R. 25, 26-27 (1st Cir. 2016) (upholding navigator enhancement under USSG §2D1.1(b)(3)(C) where defendant had relied on GPS to keep the boat on course for some part of voyage). **[—12—]**

To sum up, this is not a case in which we are left "to fend for ourselves" in order to understand the basis on which the district court concluded that the captain enhancement was appropriate. *McDowell*, 918 F.2d at 1012. The PSI Report and the transcript of the disposition hearing, taken together, furnish clear guidance as to the basis on which the court rested the enhancement. Because that basis was plausible, "we cannot say that [the sentencing court's] conclusions were unfounded or clearly erroneous." *United States v. Ruiz*, 905 F.2d 499, 508 (1st Cir. 1990) (quoting **{-785-}** *United States v. Jimenez-Otero*, 898 F.2d 813, 815 (1st Cir. 1990)).[2]

B. Alleged Breach of Plea Agreement.

This brings us to the appellant's claim that the government breached the Agreement. Since the appellant failed to raise this claim

[2] The appellant argues in his reply brief that applying the enhancement resulted in an unwarranted sentencing disparity between himself and his codefendants. This argument is doubly flawed. In the first place, "issues raised for the first time in an appellant's reply brief are generally deemed waived." *United States v. Torres*, 162 F.3d 6, 11 (1st Cir. 1998). In the second place, the "general rule of thumb is that a defendant is not entitled to a lighter sentence merely because his co-defendants received lighter sentences." *United States v. Reyes-Santiago*, 804 F.3d 453, 467 (1st Cir. 2015). Here, only the appellant declared himself to be the boat's captain and only the appellant received the captain enhancement. Because there is no basis for an "apples to apples" comparison among the three defendants, the claim of an unwarranted sentencing disparity founders on the merits. *Id.*

below, our review is for plain error. *See United States v. Almonte-Nuñez*, 771 F.3d 84, 89 (1st Cir. 2014). **[—13—]**

A defendant who enters into a plea agreement and thereafter pleads guilty to a criminal charge waives an array of important rights. The government, of course, is expected to carry out its side of the bargain. Consequently, courts long have held prosecutors to "meticulous standards of both promise and performance." *Correale v. United States*, 479 F.2d 944, 947 (1st Cir. 1973); *see Santobello v. New York*, 404 U.S. 257, 262 (1971). They must do more than merely pay "lip service" to the covenants undertaken in plea agreements. *Almonte-Nuñez*, 771 F.3d at 89.

Withal, a prosecutor's duty to observe and carry out the undertakings memorialized in a plea agreement does not exist in a vacuum. A prosecutor has a corollary duty: a "concurrent and equally solemn obligation" to provide relevant information to the sentencing court. *Id.* at 90. These twin obligations must necessarily coexist, with the result that "prosecutors must manage them so as to give substance to both." *United States v. Saxena*, 229 F.3d 1, 6 (1st Cir. 2000).

In this instance, the appellant zeros in on certain statements made by the prosecutor during the disposition hearing. Specifically, the appellant calumnizes the prosecutor for responding affirmatively to the court's inquiry about whether the appellant had identified himself as the captain of the boat and for conceding that the probation officer, given his findings and conclusions, had correctly calculated the guideline range. These **[—14—]** statements, the appellant asserts, worked a breach of the Agreement.

This assertion will not wash. We repeatedly have held that actions such as merely responding in factual terms to the sentencing court's questions or acknowledging the correctness of admittedly accurate guideline calculations do not amount to a breach of a plea agreement. *See, e.g., United States v. Marín-Echeverri*, 846 F.3d 473, 479 (1st Cir. 2017); *Almonte-Nuñez*, 771 F.3d at 90.

The appellant attempts to skirt these precedents by arguing that the government "unnecessarily prompted" the discussion about the appellant's role as captain. This argument rings hollow. The PSI Report recommended application of the captain enhancement, which put the issue squarely in play—so much so that the appellant's own counsel began the disposition hearing by asserting that "all three persons indicted in this case all were captains." **{-786-}**[3] When the district court turned to the government for a response to defense counsel's argument, the prosecutor acknowledged that the appellant had identified himself **[—15—]** as the captain. That was a fact—and the prosecutor's duty of candor to the court left him no choice but to acknowledge it.

So, too, the prosecutor had no legitimate alternative but to confirm that, given the probation officer's proposed findings and conclusions, the guideline calculations limned in the PSI Report were correct. In the spirit of the Agreement, the prosecutor immediately followed this statement by asking the court to impose the same sentence on the appellant that it had imposed on his codefendants. The prosecutor also offered a number of reasons why the lower sentence contemplated by the Agreement should be imposed. Taken in their entirety, the prosecutor's statements with respect to the enhancement did not cross the border into forbidden terrain. *See Almonte-Nuñez*, 771 F.3d at 90. Though the court chose to take a different path, that was not within the prosecutor's control.

We have recognized before, and today reaffirm, that the government's dual obligations at sentencing are in tension and, therefore, must be balanced carefully. *See Saxena*, 229 F.3d at 5-6. In this case, though,

[3] Before us, the appellant's newly appointed counsel renews the claim that all three defendants were peas in a pod. The record does not validate that claim. Only the appellant identified himself as the boat's captain, and an examination of the presentence reports for all three defendants supports a reasonable inference that the appellant was the leader of the crew. Indeed, one of his codefendants, Váldez-Vázquez, also identified the appellant as the boat's captain.

the government has carried out the required "legal funambulism." *Id.* at 6. Accordingly, we hold that the prosecutor's statements at sentencing did not breach the Agreement.

The appellant has one more shot in his sling: he suggests that the government breached the Agreement by defending the **[—16—]** sentence on appeal. For two reasons, this shot sails well wide of the mark.

First, the government does not waive anywhere in the Agreement the right to defend, on appeal, whatever sentence the district court lawfully may impose. The absence of such a restriction is significant because plea agreements are interpreted with the aid of contract-law principles, *see United States v. Atwood*, 963 F.2d 476, 479 (1st Cir. 1992), and the Agreement itself provides that "[t]he United States has made no promises or representations except as set forth in writing in this plea agreement and den[ies] the existence of any other term and conditions not stated herein." The appellant—like the government—is bound by the terms of the plea agreement. *See United States v. Tilley*, 964 F.2d 66, 70 (1st Cir. 1992). And in view of the language quoted above, there is simply no basis for extending the government's obligations in the manner suggested by the appellant.

As an appellee, the government is tasked, in effect, with defending the district court's judgment when a criminal defendant appeals.[4] In our view, the **{-787-}** government normally should be free, on appeal, to support a ruling of the district court even **[—17—]** though a plea agreement precluded it below from arguing the position that underpins the ruling. *See United States v. Colón*, 220 F.3d 48, 51-52 (2d Cir. 2000). Consequently, the government was free to argue in this court—as it has done—in support of the imposition of the captain enhancement. It has not violated the Agreement by doing so.

[4] Of course, there are narrow exceptions to this rule, such as when the government is obligated to confess error in the judgment. *See, e.g., Berger v. United States*, 295 U.S. 78, 88 (1935); *United States v. Leahy*, 668 F.3d 18, 21 (1st Cir. 2012). No such exception pertains here.

III. CONCLUSION

We need go no further. For the reasons elucidated above, the sentence is

Affirmed.

United States Court of Appeals
for the First Circuit

No. 16-2467

MAINE UNIFORM RENTAL, INC.
vs.
NOVA STAR M/V

Appeal from the United States District Court for the District of Maine

Decided: November 7, 2017

Citation: 875 F.3d 38, 5 Adm. R. 85 (1st Cir. 2017).

Before **HOWARD,** Chief Judge, **TORRUELLA** and **BARRON,** Circuit Judges.

[—3—] {-40-} TORRUELLA, Circuit Judge:

We have before us an appeal from the district court's judgment limiting the in rem maritime lien claim of Plaintiff-Appellant Maine Uniform Rental, Inc., d/b/a Pratt Abbott Uniform & Linen ("Pratt Abbott" or "Appellant") on the arrested ship, the M/V NOVA STAR ("NOVA STAR"). **{-41-}** Pratt Abbott's claim arises from its agreement (the "Agreement") with the ship's charterer, Nova Star Cruises Limited ("Nova Star Cruises"), to rent linens and other related items for the ship's ferry service. Given this case's maritime and admiralty nature,[1] and the need to interpret the Federal Maritime Lien Act[2] (FMLA) to reach a resolution, this case was properly before the district court. 28 U.S.C. § 1331. This Court has appellate jurisdiction of that district court's final decisions, 28 U.S.C. § 1291, and the case is now properly before us.

We are asked to extend the reach of a maritime lien claim to encompass a pre-established purchase cost of items rented by a charterer pursuant to a temporary rental and service contract. **[—4—]** After review of the record and the parties' arguments, we refrain from doing so and affirm the judgment of the district court.

I. BACKGROUND

A. Setting Sail (The Facts)

Given that neither party claims to challenge the court's factual findings, we draw the facts from the district court's findings, filling in undisputed facts from the record as necessary to the analysis.

In 2013, Singapore Technologies Marine Ltd. ("ST Marine"), owner of the NOVA STAR, and Quest Navigation, Inc. ("Quest") entered into a joint venture to operate a ferry service between Yarmouth, Nova Scotia, and Portland, Maine. Together, ST Marine and Quest incorporated Nova Star Cruises in Nova Scotia to operate the ferry service, and Nova Star Cruises chartered the NOVA STAR. The plan was to turn the NOVA STAR into a floating hotel that cruised between Yarmouth and Portland.

Appellant is a Maine corporation in the business of supplying linens, uniforms, mats, rugs, towels, and related items to large customers, such as hotels, restaurants, medical establishments, and auto dealerships. The relationship between Nova Star Cruises and Pratt Abbott began when Nova Star Cruises reached out to Pratt Abbott asking if it would be interested in **[—5—]** supplying linens[3] for the NOVA STAR. While the general practice in the hotel industry is to have customers purchase their own goods with the supplier processing (wash, dry, fold, press, etc.) and returning them, Pratt Abbott offered Nova Star Cruises the option of renting the linens to reduce its upfront expenses. Nova Star Cruises opted for the rental option. In April 2014, Nova Star Cruises entered into the Agreement with Pratt Abbott, agreeing to rent linens over a five-year period. The Agreement included a clause that stated:

[1] 28 U.S.C. § 1333.

[2] 46 U.S.C. §§ 31301-31343. Section 31343 provides that "[t]he district courts of the United States shall have jurisdiction over a civil action in Admiralty to declare that a vessel is not subject to a lien claimed under [the Maritime Lien Act], or that the vessel is not subject to the notice of claim of lien, or both, regardless of the amount in controversy or the citizenship of the parties."

[3] As did the district court, we use this term to encompass everything that Pratt Abbott supplied to the NOVA STAR for use under the Agreement, including towels, linens, carts, napkins, etc.

> If the contract is terminated prior to the expiration date, [Nova Star Cruises] agrees to promptly purchase all merchandise that has been ordered for or put into service for [Nova Star Cruises] at [Pratt Abbott's] then current published replacement rate schedule (this agreed sale of all merchandise is in recognition of the substantial investment of **{-42-}** [Pratt Abbott] including, but not limited to merchandise, equipment, labor, energy, transportation and future planning).

Before finalizing the Agreement, Nova Star Cruises paid Pratt Abbott a deposit of $51,536.45 and filled out a credit application through Pratt Abbott. On this application, Nova Star Cruises provided its bank account information at the Bank of Nova Scotia.

Pratt Abbott purchased specific items in large quantities to meet Nova Star Cruises's needs pursuant to the **[—6—]** contract, such as special linen carts that could maneuver around tight spaces on the vessel, bed sheets, table linens, and napkins. Some of these linen products, such as the table cloths, were uniquely shaped to meet the needs of the NOVA STAR. Pratt Abbott also purchased new equipment that it would not have purchased otherwise in order to meet the needs of the rental contract. Under the contract, Pratt Abbott maintained ownership of all these linens and specialty items.

At the end of the 2015 ferry season, Nova Star Cruises asked that Pratt Abbott leave specific items onboard the NOVA STAR. Pratt Abbott did so and sent Nova Star Cruises an invoice for the cost of the items. That same year, Nova Star Cruises terminated the ferry service after just two seasons. Upon realizing that the Agreement was, in effect, terminated, Pratt Abbott demanded that Nova Star Cruises purchase the inventory of linens pursuant to the Agreement and pay past-due invoices. The unpaid invoices totaled $16,187.50 for the last completed rental service and regular cleaning ($12,558.21), the items that Nova Star Cruises requested remain on the ship ($3,223.29), and the specialty items that were cleaned and returned to the ship prior to its arrest ($406). Nova Star Cruises ignored Pratt Abbott's requests for payment. The inventory of linens that Pratt Abbott had purchased for use on the NOVA STAR remains in Pratt Abbott's warehouse in Westbrook, Maine. **[—7—]** The total replacement cost of the stored inventory under the Agreement is $178,023.02.[4]

B. Steering the Course (Procedural History)

A number of creditors asserted maritime liens against the NOVA STAR in the U.S. District Court for the District of Maine, and the district court issued several warrants for the ship's arrest. On November 17, 2015, Pratt Abbott filed a motion to intervene, asserting its own maritime lien against the arrested vessel for the replacement cost of the stored inventory and the balance of unpaid invoices. A week later, Pratt Abbott also filed a verified complaint against the vessel and Nova Star Cruises for the same amount, alleging breach of contract, unjust enrichment, and quantum meruit. In its in rem action, Appellant initially claimed a lien in the amount of $262,001.50, but this claim has since been reduced to $194,510.12 ($16,187.50 for the unpaid invoices, and $178,023.02 for its stored inventory). On **[—8—]** November 30, 2015, the district court granted ST Marine's motion to substitute the vessel for a bond. **{-43-}**

The district court held a one-witness bench trial on Pratt Abbott's maritime lien claim on August 24, 2016. At the conclusion, the district court found that the supplies and services that Pratt Abbott had provided to the

---

[4] Pratt Abbott alleges that the district court found the "cost" of the stored inventory, and therefore its "value," to be $178,023.02. But Pratt Abbott ignores the qualifier in the district court's finding. The district court found the "replacement cost" of the inventory "under the contract" to be this amount. This did not reflect the cost to Pratt Abbott of the stored inventory, but rather the "replacement cost," or purchase price in the event of contractual breach, established by Pratt Abbott's replacement rate schedule. Our reference to the "replacement cost" throughout this opinion reflects the established purchase price of the stored inventory in the Agreement.

NOVA STAR under the Agreement, allowing the ship to operate as a mobile hotel, constituted "necessaries"[5] under maritime law. However, the court found that the lien did not extend to the period after the arrest, when the rental items were no longer being used by the NOVA STAR. Additionally, the court found that only the rental and cleaning services provided by Pratt Abbott before the service ceased at the end of the 2015 season, the specialized items that Nova Star Cruises requested remain with the ship, and the specialty items that were cleaned and returned to the ship had been provided or "delivered" for purposes of the maritime lien requirement. *See Cianbro Corp. v. George H. Dean, Inc.*, 596 F.3d 10, 14-15 (1st Cir. 2010); *see also Piedmont & George's Creek Coal Co. v. Seaboard Fisheries Co.*, 254 U.S. 1, 6-7 (1920). The district court denied Pratt Abbott's claim for the replacement cost of the inventory remaining in its Maine warehouse, stating that those physical items **[—9—]** had not been furnished to the ship. The district court entered judgment for Pratt Abbott on September 7, 2016, for the unpaid invoice amount of $16,187.50. *Me. Unif. Rental, Inc. v. M/V Nova Star*, No. 2:15-cv-442-DBH (D. Me. Sept. 7, 2016). This appeal ensued.

II. DISCUSSION

A. Rules of Engagement (Standard of Review)

As this appeal arises following a bench trial, we review "the [district] court's factual determinations for clear error and its legal conclusions de novo." *Ne. Drilling, Inc. v. Inner Space Servs., Inc.*, 243 F.3d 25, 37 (1st Cir. 2001); *accord Commercial Union Ins. Co. v. Seven Provinces Ins. Co.*, 217 F.3d 33, 40 (1st Cir. 2000). We adopt the district court's findings of fact "unless we are left with the definite and firm conviction that a mistake has been committed." *Vinick v. United States*, 205 F.3d 1, 6 (1st Cir. 2000) (citation and internal quotation marks omitted).

Pratt Abbott claims to agree with all of the district court's factual findings and appeals only the legal conclusions, yet asserts facts in its brief beyond those found below. In light of Pratt Abbott's pronouncement that it does not dispute the district court's factual findings and appeals only the court's legal conclusions, we review the legal conclusions only, and do so *de novo*. **[—10—]**

B. Navigating the Waters (Analysis)

Appellant argues that the district court erred when it refused to grant Appellant's maritime lien claim in its entirety. The purpose of a maritime lien is two-fold: first, to allow ships to continue to function for their intended purpose, and second, to hold the ship—rather than its owner—liable for its debts. *Equilease Corp. v. M/V Sampson*, 793 F.2d 598, 602 (5th Cir. 1986) (en banc) ("The maritime lien concept thus somewhat personifies a vessel as an entity with potential liabilities independent and apart from the personal liability of its owner."). "The overarching goal is keeping the channels of maritime commerce open-by ensuring that people who service vessels have an efficient way of demanding reimbursement for their labor and are thus willing to perform the services necessary to keep vessels in operation." *Mullane v. Chambers*, 438 F.3d 132, 138 (1st Cir. 2006); *see* **{-44-}** *Atl. & Gulf Stevedores, Inc. v. M/V Grand Loyalty*, 608 F.2d 197, 201 (5th Cir. 1979) ("[I]t was the intent of the Congress to make it easier and more certain for stevedores and others to protect their interests by making maritime liens available where traditional services are routinely rendered.").

However, as such liens are believed to "encumber commerce," *People's Ferry Co. v. Beers*, 61 U.S. (20 How.) 393, 401 (1857); *Cianbro*, 596 F.3d at 14 ("Because a maritime lien is deemed **[—11—]** to encumber commerce, it is disfavored in the law . . . ." (internal quotation marks and citation omitted)), the requirements for the allowance of a maritime lien are construed *stricti juris*. *Tramp Oil & Marine, Ltd. v. M/V "Mermaid I"*, 805 F.2d 42, 46 (1st Cir. 1986). As advised by the Supreme Court, such liens must not be extended by "construction, analogy, or

5 46 U.S.C. § 31301(4).

inference." *Osaka Shosen Kaisha v. Pac. Exp. Lumber Co.*, 260 U.S. 490, 497 (1923).

To establish a maritime lien on a vessel, a claimant must show that it provided "necessaries" to the vessel[6] at the order of the vessel's owner or a person authorized by the owner, including a "charterer." *Cianbro*, 596 F.3d at 14 (quoting 46 U.S.C. § 31341). Thus, although the in rem claim asserted by Pratt Abbott bears no particular relation to the NOVA STAR *qua* a ship, and arises as a result of a default purchase provision in the Agreement, Appellant may still be entitled to a maritime lien by showing that it provided items that were "necessary" to the ship's intended purpose. 46 U.S.C. § 31342; *see Equilease*, 793 F.2d at 602.

1. The rental and cleaning services of the inventory were "necessaries"

"'[N]ecessaries' includes repairs, supplies, towage, and the use of a dry dock or marine railway," 46 U.S.C. § 31301(4), as **[—12—]** well as "most goods or services that are useful to the vessel, keep her out of danger and enable her to perform her particular function." *Trico Marine Operators, Inc. v. Falcon Drilling Co.*, 116 F.3d 159, 162 (5th Cir. 1997) (quoting *Equilease*, 793 F.2d at 603); *see Farrell Ocean Servs., Inc. v. United States*, 681 F.2d 91, 92-93 (1st Cir. 1982). "It is the present, apparent want of the vessel . . . which makes it a necessary." *Equilease*, 793 F.2d at 603 (quoting 2 *Benedict on Admiralty* § 34 (7th ed. 1984)).

Consistent with the FMLA's goal of affording financial protection to those who provide vessels with required services and provisions, courts have broadly interpreted what constitutes "necessaries" under the Act. *See Farrell Ocean Servs.*, 681 F.2d at 92 (interpreting Section 971, from which Section 31301 was derived, and finding "'other necessaries' [as used in Section 971] should be interpreted broadly in order to encourage the provision of services that will keep ships active . . . ."); *see, e.g., Trico Marine Operators*, 116 F.3d at 162 (transportation of drinking water, food, drilling equipment, and supplies constituted "necessaries"); *Port Ship Serv., Inc. v. Int'l Ship Mgmt. & Agencies Serv., Inc.*, 800 F.2d 1418, 1421 (5th Cir. 1986) (water taxi service to and from vessel may give rise to a maritime lien); *Equilease*, 793 F.2d at 600 (finding that insurance is a "necessary" to keep a vessel in commerce, giving rise to a maritime lien); **[—13—]** *Sec. Pac. Bank of Wash. v. September Morn*, 754 F. Supp. 813, 814-15 (W.D. Wash. 1990) (services to secure, prepare, and file documents in connection with marine mortgages were "necessary"). *But see, e.g.,* **{-45-}** *Bradford Marine, Inc. v. M/V Sea Falcon*, 64 F.3d 585, 589-90 (11th Cir. 1995) (attorney's fees incurred by vessel repair company were not necessaries); *James Creek Marina v. Vessel My Girls*, 964 F. Supp. 20, 23 (D.D.C. 1997) (attorney's fees to enforce lien were not "necessaries"). To determine whether Pratt Abbott's services constituted "necessaries," we examine its role in enabling the vessel to continue in its intended function. *See Farrell Ocean Servs.*, 681 F.2d at 92-93.

As the district court correctly noted, the Agreement specified two types of services that Pratt Abbott performed for Nova Star Cruises: the delivery and cleaning of the rental items, and the rental—or use—of the physical items themselves. The details of both of these services were laid out in the Agreement. The very first line of the Agreement states that the contract is for all of Nova Star Cruises's "rental requirements." The first page of the Agreement further states that the rental rates shall be increased at each anniversary of the Agreement and that merchandise worn out through normal wear will be replaced at no charge to Nova Star Cruises. The addendum to the contract lists the items to be rented, the rental rates, and the quantity of each **[—14—]** item being rented. The Agreement also describes the delivery and cleaning services of the items that Appellant agreed to perform, stating that the rental items "will be furnished, cleaned and maintained exclusively by [Pratt Abbott]." Thomas Gridley, General Manager of Pratt Abbott, testified at trial that this delivery and cleaning service included the processing of the linens being taken on and off the ship, including "soil counting, washing,

[6] 46 U.S.C. § 31342(a).

drying, folding, pressing, packaging, staging, [and] shipping."

Having described the service performed by Pratt Abbott, we next look to the NOVA STAR's intended purpose to determine whether these services were "necessaries." *Trico Marine Operators*, 116 F.3d at 162. The intended function of the NOVA STAR was to operate a ferry service between Yarmouth, Nova Scotia, and Portland, Maine, serving as the functional equivalent of a mobile hotel. Hotels, by their very nature, require clean linens, whether those linens are purchased by the hotel itself or rented and serviced by an outside contractor. For the operation of this hotel, Pratt Abbott supplied the NOVA STAR with two changes of linen to be placed on board the ship for each roundtrip service to and from Nova Scotia. Upon the ship's return to Portland, Pratt Abbott off-loaded the soiled linens and restocked the ship with two full sets of linens in preparation for the next ferry service. The ship operated seven days a week, with the inventory used by **[—15—]** the ship set up to be laundered and processed every two to three days.

There is little dispute that the rental items and services provided pursuant to the Agreement, both on the ship and at the processing facility, enabled the ship to serve as a hotel and were necessary to keep the ship's business afloat. *See Dampskibsselskabet Dannebrog v. Signal Oil & Gas Co. of Cal.*, 310 U.S. 268, 280-281 (1940). The district court found as much and neither party has challenged this conclusion. Based upon our review, we agree with the district court that the two services that Pratt Abbott provided under the contract constituted "necessaries" during the time of the ship's operation.

2. After termination of the Agreement, the rental and cleaning services were no longer "necessaries"

In addressing the rental services, including the delivery and retrieval of the rental items from the ship, the district court found that **{-46-}**

> Pratt Abbott cannot assert a maritime lien for rental services that it did not actually provide to the vessel. The lien extends to the period during which the rental items were actually necessaries but does not include the period after the arrest, when the rental items were no longer being used by the Nova Star.

Me Unif. Rental, 2016 WL 4681097, at *4. In light of this conclusion, the district court limited the maritime lien that it awarded to Appellant to the rental services rendered prior to the **[—16—]** ship's arrest. Inherent in its finding was that, after the ship's arrest, the rental items were no longer "necessaries" to the continued operation of the vessel.

Pratt Abbott postures that the district court conflated a claim for future rental charges with one for contract-supported replacement cost, and therefore denied a claim that Pratt Abbott did not assert. We disagree. Pratt Abbott asserted a maritime lien claim for the total replacement cost of the inventory in its warehouse, as well as the balance of unpaid invoices (for the rental and cleaning services already provided). In its motion to intervene, Pratt Abbott alleged that "[n]either Nova Star Cruises nor M/V Nova Star has fully paid for the linen rental and cleaning and merchandise," and included the cost of those services in the amount of the total asserted maritime lien. In its verified complaint, Pratt Abbott alleged that the financial benefit conferred on the NOVA STAR for unpaid services was $262,001.50. Given these claims, the district court properly tailored its legal conclusions to address whether a maritime lien is proper, and the amount thereof, for both of the "necessaries" that were purportedly furnished.

Once ferry operations ceased at the end of the 2015 season and the Agreement was terminated, the rental items ceased to be "necessaries" for the NOVA STAR's intended purpose. *See* **[—17—]** *Itel Containers Int'l. Corp. v. Atlanttrafik Express Serv. Ltd.*, 781 F. Supp. 975, 986 (S.D.N.Y. 1991) ("Plaintiffs' rental charges, however, must be limited to the time period during which the [rental items] were actually 'necessaries.'"), *rev'd on* *other grounds*, 982 F.2d 765 (2d Cir. 1992); *see, e.g., Patricia Hayes & Assocs., Inc. v. M/V BIG RED BOAT, II*, No. 00-cv-6925, 2002 WL 1163555, at *8 (S.D.N.Y. May 31, 2002) (amusement games not necessary for vessel's care and preservation after its arrest, and therefore accrual of lien for lease payments for games terminated at ship's arrest). Even before the ship's arrest, Nova Star Cruises had ceased the ship's function as a mobile hotel and the rental items in inventory were no longer being used. Thus, Pratt Abbott cannot assert a lien for the use of these rental items, or the rental delivery, retrieval, and cleaning services beyond the date that the 2015 ferry season concluded.

3. "Delivery" of the rental and cleaning services

We are left to determine whether the rental items and cleaning services, which were "necessaries" only during the vessel's ferry operations, were "provided" or "delivered" to the ship during that time for purposes of a maritime lien. Herein lies the heart of this dispute.

Appellant challenges the district court's findings that the items that remained in Pratt Abbott's inventory had not been **[—18—]** provided or "delivered" to the ship in a manner sufficient to establish a maritime lien. In rejecting this portion of Pratt Abbott's claim, the district court relied on the fact that, pursuant to the Agreement, Pratt Abbott continued to own the items in the warehouse. The district court reasoned that any previous movement of the items to and from the vessel was simply the rental and cleaning services for which the parties **{-47-}** contracted, and not a "delivery" sufficient to establish a maritime lien for the replacement cost of the items. While Pratt Abbott may have had a breach of contract claim against Nova Star Cruises[7] for failing to purchase this inventory in accordance with the terms of the Agreement, the district court found this to be distinct from a maritime claim in rem for items that had been "delivered" to the vessel.

Pratt Abbott argues that the district court construed the term "delivered" too narrowly, contrary to precedent and public policy. Even though the linens were not onboard the ship at the time of its arrest and were not delivered that very day, they remained "necessaries" that had been "delivered" to the NOVA STAR on a consistent, rotating basis, allowing the ship to serve its **[—19—]** purpose. In furthering its public policy argument, Appellant avers that the district court's narrow interpretation runs afoul of FMLA's goal of protecting those who provide required provisions to vessels.

To establish that the "necessaries" have been provided or furnished to a vessel, the "necessaries" must be either physically delivered or "constructively dispatched to the vessel by the handing over of the supplies to the owner or the owner's authorized agent for use on a designated vessel." *Cianbro*, 596 F.3d at 14; *see Piedmont*, 254 U.S. at 6-10 (finding no maritime lien when coal delivered by a coal company was not directly delivered to any vessel, the company had no direct dealings with the officers of any vessel, and there were no invoices to the fleet or any vessel). Appellant urges this court to broadly interpret the term "delivered," as both the linens onboard at the time of arrest and the linens stored for future voyages were, at one point, physically delivered to the vessel. Appellant cites to the Fifth Circuit's decision in *Equilease* to support the notion that this Court should view "delivery" through a broad lens. 793 F.2d at 603 ("We find no persuasive reason to read the term 'furnishing' so narrowly as [to require a physical delivery to the vessel].").

We do not find the holding in *Equilease* to support the requested extension of the scope of maritime liens as asserted in **[—20—]** this case. The issue before the *Equilease* Court was whether an intangible item, insurance for the ship, could be "furnished" when no physical item had actually been delivered. *Id.* Here, there is no question that the entire stock of physical inventory had, at some point, been

[7] On June 15, 2016, Pratt Abbott filed a notice of dismissal of its in personam action against Nova Star Cruises, but preserved its in rem action against the vessel.

physically placed aboard the NOVA STAR. Furthermore, whereas the vessel insurance policies in *Equilease* were owned by the vessel charterer and insured the vessels, *id.* at 600, Pratt Abbott maintained ownership and full control of all of the inventory in question. During the period in which the rental items were "necessaries," Nova Star Cruises contracted for the use—not ownership—of the inventory stored at the Westbrook warehouse. As acknowledged at oral argument, Pratt Abbott remained free to do with the specific items in its inventory, each bedsheet, towel, napkin, or cart, as it pleased so long as it fulfilled its service obligations to the charterer.

Continued ownership, in itself, does not prevent a finding that rental items have been provided or "delivered" to a vessel. *See Itel Containers*, 781 F. Supp. at 982-84. Nonetheless, when necessary items have been rented or leased to a vessel's authorized agent, courts have consistently found that it is the *use* of the necessary item—not the necessary item itself—that has **{-48-}** been furnished to the vessel, and have limited maritime liens to the accrued rental value, depreciation, cost of necessary **[—21—]** repairs, and replacement value of unrecoverable inventory. *Id.* at 986-87; *see S.C. State Ports Auth. v. M/V Tyson Lykes*, 67 F.3d 59, 61 (4th Cir. 1995) (finding lien for dockage and wharfage while loading and unloading containers); *see also Total Safety US, Inc. v. Con-Dive, LLC*, No. H-08-2782, 2009 WL 3673051, at *1 (S.D. Tex. Nov. 4, 2009) (finding maritime lien for the rental value of "required safety equipment"); *Silver Star Enters., Inc. v. Saramacca M/V*, Civ. A. No. 92-1297, 1994 WL 794721, at *1-3 (E.D. La. July 20, 1994) (finding maritime lien for full rental charges of containers used exclusively aboard the vessel and prorated rental charges for containers used occasionally), *rev'd on other grounds*, 82 F.3d 666 (5th Cir. 1996); *Redcliffe Ams. Ltd v. M/V Tyson Lykes*, 806 F. Supp. 69, 72-73 (D.S.C. 1992) (finding leased containers had been "furnished" to vessels in amount of unpaid monthly rental charges, plus repair and replacement charges), *rev'd on other grounds*, 996 F.2d 47 (4th Cir. 1993); *Clubb Oil Tools, Inc. v. M/V George Vergottis*, 460 F. Supp. 835, 837 (S.D. Tex. 1978) (finding maritime lien for rental expense, as well as costs for recovery, testing, repairing, and replacing damaged oil piping).

We have found no cases that extend this lien to include the replacement cost of inventory retained by the plaintiff after termination of a rental agreement, and Pratt Abbott cites none. **[—22—]** In light of the doctrine of *stricti juris* noted above, we find it unwise to extend the application of maritime liens to encompass Appellant's asserted claim. We find that the limitations noted in the preceding paragraph apply in this case.

Pratt Abbott attempts to characterize the Agreement as a "five-year lease back with charterer responsible for paying over time for the linens Pratt Abbott purchased." This characterization is contrary to the uncontested facts found by the district court and the plain language of the Agreement. As previously noted, the Agreement made it clear that this contract was a rental and servicing agreement. On these specific facts, even had Nova Star Cruises ultimately purchased the inventory according to the Agreement's default purchase clause, the obligation to purchase was triggered only in the event that the charterer breached the contract, at which time the linens were no longer "necessaries." Therefore, in this situation, no maritime lien would result from this default purchase clause.

4. Exclusive Use

Appellant further argues that, because the inventory in its Westbrook warehouse was purchased and earmarked for exclusive use on the NOVA STAR, and Pratt Abbott relied on the credit of the vessel in supplying these necessaries, the rental items themselves were provided to the vessel and created an enforceable maritime **[—23—]** lien. Pratt Abbott cites a host of cases[8] from varying

[8] *Dampskibsselskabet Dannebrog*, 310 U.S. 268; *Piedmont*, 254 U.S. 1; *In re Container Applications Int'l, Inc.*, 233 F.3d 1361 (11th Cir. 2000); *Rascal Survey U.S.A., Inc. v. M/V Count Fleet*, 231 F.3d 183 (5th Cir. 2000); *Silver Star Enters., Inc.*, 82 F.3d 666; *Redcliffe Ams. Ltd.*, 996 F.2d 47; *Bankers*

federal circuits and the Supreme Court to support the proposition that setting aside necessaries for exclusive use by a specific vessel, unlike delivering them to a fleet of vessels for later distribution, creates an actionable in rem claim against that ship. **{-49-}**

We need not address the merits of Appellant's argument as it is simply unsupported by the record. In its uncontested factual findings, the district court found that, in order to meet the Nova Star Cruises's needs under the contract, Pratt Abbott purchased certain specialty items in large quantities such as specialty linen carts, flat twin sheets, table napkins, and table cloths. The district court further found that, in order to meet the rental contract, Pratt Abbott purchased new equipment that it would not normally have purchased. Noticeably absent from the district court's findings is Appellant's proclamation that the inventory was purchased and earmarked exclusively for the vessel. After the district court issued its findings of fact and conclusions of law, Pratt Abbott filed a motion for additional **[—24—]** findings, requesting that the district court make the following additional findings:

> 1. The [inventory] supplied by Pratt Abbott for the vessel and consisting of the specialty items in large quantities . . . were purchased exclusively for the vessel.
>
> . . .
>
> 4. This linen inventory was not used for any other customer, remains segregated, and was needed to meet the vessel's service requirements . . . .

ST Marine objected to the adoption of the additional findings, and the district court denied the motion. Given that the Appellant has conceded agreement to the court's factual findings, it cannot now assert facts outside of the record on appeal.

Tr. Co. v. Hudson River Day Line, 93 F.2d 457 (2d Cir. 1937).

We agree with the district court that the items in inventory were not "delivered" to the ship in such a manner as to create a maritime lien for their replacement cost. The use of the rental items in inventory was part of the rental and cleaning service provided under the rental contract, and the district court properly awarded a lien for the amount owed for past services at the time of termination ($12,558.21). The district court also properly awarded a maritime lien for unrecoverable items remaining aboard the ship, including the items that Nova Star Cruises requested ($3,223.29), as well as the specialty items that were cleaned and returned to the ship ($406). **[—25—]**

III. CONCLUSION

For the reasons stated above, the district court properly limited the maritime lien to the amount of $16,187.50. The district court correctly concluded that the inventory remaining in Pratt Abbott's warehouse in Westbrook, Maine, was not "delivered" in a manner as to create a maritime lien for its replacement cost according to the default provision of the rental contract. Accordingly, the judgment of the district court is affirmed.

Affirmed.

United States Court of Appeals for the Second Circuit

United States Court of Appeals
for the Second Circuit

No. 16-607

MANHATTAN BY SAIL, INC.
vs.
TAGLE

Appeal from the United States District Court for the Southern District of New York

Decided: October 5, 2017

Citation: 873 F.3d 177, 5 Adm. R. 94 (2d Cir. 2017).

Before **LEVAL, SACK,** and **RAGGI,** Circuit Judges.

[—2—] {-179-} LEVAL, Circuit Judge:

Charis Tagle, who was injured while a passenger on the sailing vessel Shearwater Classic Schooner (the "Shearwater"), appeals from the judgment of the United States District Court for the Southern District of New York (Valerie Caproni, *J.*) entered after a nonjury trial, which exonerated the vessel owners, Manhattan by Sail, Inc. and Shearwater Holdings, Ltd., from liability for the injury. Tagle was injured when a deckhand unclipped a weighted halyard from the forestaysail at the bow of the vessel and lost hold of it, so that it swung free and struck her in the head. The shipowners offered no evidence explaining why he lost hold of it. The district court ruled that the passenger failed to show negligence or entitlement to application of the doctrine of res ipsa loquitur because a seaman's loss of control of a line *can* occur without negligence. This was error. The passenger made a showing of **[—3—]** negligence, which the shipowners failed to rebut. The judgment is vacated, and the matter remanded with directions to enter a finding of negligence.

BACKGROUND

1. <u>The Accident at Issue</u>

On April 30, 2011, Charis Tagle purchased passage aboard the Shearwater, a sightseeing vessel which takes passengers on excursions in New York Harbor. Tagle boarded the ship, and a crewmember directed her to sit on a wooden hatch next to the forestaysail mast. The forestaysail mast is positioned between the main mast (near the center of the ship) and the bow.

The Shearwater cast off under engine power into the lower Hudson River. David Zimmerman, the captain, ordered the crew to raise the forestaysail. The forestaysail is raised by means of a halyard, which runs from the base of the forestaysail mast vertically up the mast to a wooden block (or pulley) near the top of the mast, through the block, and from there forward to the bow, where it is attached to a grommet at the top corner of the triangular forestaysail by means of a one-pound stainless steel clip, called a pelican clip. The sail is raised by pulling downward on the end of the halyard at the bottom of the mast, so that the other end of the halyard (the end attached to **[—4—]** the sail at the bow) pulls the top of the sail upward toward the pulley near the top of the mast. When the pelican clip at the forward end of the halyard is clipped to the sail, the forward part of the halyard is immobilized. On the other hand, if the clip is detached from the sail when the halyard is extended forward from the mast toward the bow, the halyard will be pulled by gravity toward the base of the mast from which it hangs and, unless held secure, will swing as a pendulum.

When Zimmerman ordered that the forestaysail be raised, Christopher Biggins, a deckhand, detached the halyard from the sail. In his testimony at trial, Biggins could not remember why he unclipped the halyard. Tugged by gravitational force toward the mast, the freed halyard pulled loose from Biggins's grip and swung back towards **{-180-}** the mast where Tagle was seated. The clip at the end of the halyard struck Tagle and cut her forehead. Although Biggins knew immediately after losing control of the halyard that it had struck and injured a passenger, he testified at trial that he could not recall why he lost control of it. The captain testified that Biggins reported at the time that "while he was hooking up the halyard to the forestaysail, it slipped out of his hands and swung like a pendulum . . . ." A-63–64. **[—5—]**

2. <u>The Instant Action</u>

Tagle filed suit in New York state court, alleging that the negligence of the crew caused her injury. The owners of the Shearwater then filed this petition in admiralty seeking exoneration from liability, pursuant to the Limitation of Liability Act, 46 U.S.C. § 30501, *et seq.* Tagle's state court lawsuit was stayed pending resolution of the district court's action. The district court conducted a bench trial on the question whether Tagle's injury resulted from negligence.

In summation, Tagle contended she had established that the Shearwater's crew breached their duty of care, and argued for application of res ipsa loquitur. The court rejected her arguments. It reasoned that "sailors do, even when exercising ordinary care, sometimes lose control of a line—whether due to wind or an unexpected wave or wake." A-145 n.5. Because this was not "the sort of accident that [can] occur *only* because of someone's negligence," the court rejected the application of res ipsa loquitur, A-145 (emphasis added), and found that Tagle failed to prove negligence. The court accordingly granted the owners exoneration from liability. **[—6—]**

DISCUSSION

1. <u>Res Ipsa Loquitur</u>

On appeal, Tagle argues, *inter alia*, that the district court misapplied the doctrine of res ipsa loquitur. We agree. That phrase means, "The thing speaks for itself." The doctrine enables a plaintiff to prevail in a certain type of circumstance in proving negligence even though the plaintiff cannot show exactly who or what caused her injury. Under that doctrine, a fact-finder may infer negligence merely from the happening of the event that caused the harm if: (1) the event is of a type that ordinarily would not occur in the absence of negligence; (2) it is caused by an agency or instrumentality under the exclusive control of the party charged with negligence; and (3) it is not due to any voluntary action or contribution on the part of injured party. *Sojak v. Hudson Waterways Corp.*, 590 F.2d 53, 55 (2d Cir. 1978) (per curiam); *Savard v. Marine Contracting Inc.*, 471 F.2d 536, 542–43 (2d Cir. 1972).

The district court at first correctly formulated the question as whether this was "the kind of event that does not *ordinarily* occur in the absence of someone's negligence?" A-144 (emphasis added). The court then answered that question in the negative, however, on the basis of an incorrect **[—7—]** reformulation of the test. The court found that nothing in the record contradicted the "common sense notion that a deckhand exercising due care *can* lose control of a line." A-145 (emphasis added). This was not, in the district court's view, "the sort of accident that could occur *only* because of someone's negligence." *Id.* (emphasis added). The court therefore rejected the application of the doctrine.

This was error. Res ipsa loquitur is not limited to accidents that could occur *only* because of negligence. For res ipsa loquitur to apply, a claimant must show that the event is of a type that *ordinarily* does not occur in the absence of negligence. **{-181-}** An injured claimant is not required to "eliminate with certainty all other possible causes or inferences, which would mean that the plaintiff must prove a civil case beyond a reasonable doubt." W. Page Keeton, *et al.*, Prosser and Keeton on the Law of Torts § 39, at 248 (5th ed. 1984) (hereinafter Prosser & Keeton); *see also Johnson v. United States*, 333 U.S. 46, 49 (1948) ("No act need be explicable only in terms of negligence in order for the rule of res ipsa loquitur to be invoked.").

Tagle's evidence satisfied her burden of making a prima facie showing of entitlement to res ipsa loquitur. Moreover, the shipowners failed to rebut **[—8—]** her evidence. An extended halyard that is permitted to swing freely from the top of the mast represents an obvious danger, especially when it has a one pound clip attached to the swinging end. It is a seaman's job to keep such lines secure to prevent them from swinging dangerously. Roy Scott, Tagle's marine expert, testified that an unsecured halyard would "fall back to the base of the pendulum" (that being the base of the forestaysail mast where Tagle was seated), Docket No. 75, at 44, and "swing indiscriminately," *id.* at 47, risking "really bad things." A-34. The shipowners offered no evidence to rebut those propositions, and they are not debatable.[1] Scott added that "if for some reason [the halyard] did have to be detached" from the forestaysail, it was his opinion that the crew "should have done it without passengers on board." Docket No. 75, at 50. While no doubt things can happen at sea that could cause an extended halyard to slip out of a seaman's grasp without negligence, Tagle's evidence was sufficient to show that this does not *ordinarily* happen without negligence. **[—9—]**

The sufficiency of Tagle's evidence is established by Supreme Court precedent in *Johnson v. United States*, 333 U.S. 46 (1948). In *Johnson*, the claimant was standing on the main deck of a ship, rounding in two blocks. Another sailor was standing on a deck above claimant, holding one of the blocks. *Id.* at 47. For some unknown reason, the block above the claimant was permitted to fall, and it struck the claimant on the head. *Id.* at 48. The Supreme Court held that res ipsa loquitur applied. The Court concluded that "[a] man who is careful does not ordinarily drop a block on a man working below him." *Id.* The Court recognized that "[s]ome external force might conceivably compel" the sailor to drop the block, but on the record presented, the sailor "alone remain[ed] implicated, since . . . either he or [the claimant] was the cause of the accident and it appears that [the claimant] was not responsible." *Id.*

The same is true here. A deckhand who *carefully* exercises the *skills* required for the seaman's job will not ordinarily lose hold of an extended weighted halyard—all the more so when passengers are seated in the halyard's swing-path. Waves and wind, and the consequent shifting and rolling of the deck, are the normal conditions of the sea, in which seamen **[—10—]** must work protecting the safety of passengers and crew. While it is no doubt true that sudden unexpected turbulence can be of such force that a seamen's loss of control of a line could be deemed non-negligent, there was no evidence in the record of any such abnormal circumstance that caused the halyard to **{-182-}** slip from Biggins's grasp. As *Johnson* made clear, the mere possibility that "some external force"—here, perhaps an unusual wave or gust—"might conceivably compel" a seamen to let go of a dangerous halyard is not sufficient reason to reject the application of res ipsa loquitur if this would ordinarily not happen in the absence of negligence, and there was no evidence of any such unusual external force.

The district court reasoned that the facts of *Johnson* were "very different than those here." A-145 n.5. In the district court's view, the distinguishing factor was that, in *Johnson*, "[t]here was no evidence that blocks are regularly dropped due to the movement of the ocean," while in our case, there was testimony "that the risk from lines on a sailing vessel cannot be totally eliminated." *Id.* This reasoning fails. It essentially repeats the district court's misapplication of the res ipsa loquitur rule. The issue was not whether the risks resulting from a seamen's failure to hold onto a halyard could "be **[—11—]** totally eliminated" by the exercise of due care and skill. Rather, the question was whether such a harm does not *ordinarily* occur in the absence of due care and skill.

There was nothing in the record to suggest that Biggins's error was caused by some extraordinary force or turbulence to let the halyard slip out of his hands. While Tagle's expert described New York Harbor as an area of "an immense confusion of wakes, waves, boats, [and] vessels," A-28, there was no evidence of any turbulence on the particular day, much less at the particular time, that might have caused Biggins to lose control of the halyard, and Biggins made no such claim.

Relying on *Irwin v. United States*, 236 F.2d 774 (2d Cir. 1956), the shipowners argue that

[1] This aspect of Scott's testimony was comparable (depending on a slightly different application of the law of gravity) to testimony that a workman on a scaffolding high above a street where pedestrians are walking risks causing serious injury if he allows a one pound weight to fall out of his hands and drop toward the street.

courts refuse to apply res ipsa loquitur to cases in which sea conditions can cause an accident. The argument does not describe *Irwin* correctly. The claimant, Irwin, was in a lifeboat being lowered from a ship when a "freak swell" of the sea hit the lifeboat, causing him to be tossed violently from one side of the boat to the other. *Irwin v. United States*, 111 F. Supp. 912, 915 (E.D.N.Y. 1953). In rejecting Irwin's claim to res ipsa loquitur, this court reasoned that, because the accident was shown to have been **[—12—]** "caused by an unpredictable 'freak swell' of the sea," the defendant did "not have control of the agency causing the accident." *Irwin*, 236 F.2d at 776. There was no comparable evidence here. Not only did the shipowners fail to offer evidence that Biggins's loss of control was attributable to any abnormal lurch; they did not even offer evidence of the general presence at the same time of extra-ordinary turbulence. Their position depended on sheer speculation. Had there been evidence in this case that a freak wave had caused Biggins to lose his balance and drop the halyard, *Johnson* might arguably be distinguishable, and *Irwin* might control. But there was no such evidence here.

Nor was this a circumstance where it would be arguably unreasonable to impose on the defendant the obligation to put forth evidence of an asserted non-negligent cause of the accident, such as might arise if the ship's crew had been unaware of the claimant's injury at the time, and thus had no reason to focus on, or remember, the conditions. Here, it was instantly known by Biggins and the captain that, when Biggins lost control of the halyard, it struck Tagle in the head and caused an injury. The captain immediately made a log entry noting the event. If some external force outside of the ordinary **[—13—]** had caused Biggins to let go of the halyard, Biggins and the captain had every reason to note, record, and remember it. But Biggins testified that he did not know why he lost control of **{–183–}** the halyard. He did not identify any non-ordinary condition to explain the mishap. The ship's log reflects no explanation for Biggins's losing control of the halyard, and the captain testified that Biggins had acknowledged that the line "*slipped out of his hands*." A-63–64. The absence of any evidence of unusual circumstances powerfully supports the proposition that there were none and that Biggins's loss of control of the line was due to his negligence and nothing else. Tagle's evidence was thus sufficient to support the application of res ipsa loquitur.

2. <u>Negligence</u>

Tagle's evidence was, furthermore, sufficient to prove negligence regardless of whether the res ipsa loquitur doctrine applied.[2] We recognize that the doctrine permits, but does not require, a fact-finder to draw an **[—14—]** inference of negligence. *Johnson*, 333 U.S. at 48 (citing *Sweeney v. Erving*, 228 U.S. 233, 240 (1913)). Res ipsa loquitur is most commonly applied in circumstances where, unlike this case, it is not known exactly who or what caused the accident. *See Kambat v. St. Francis Hosp.*, 678 N.E.2d 456, 458 (N.Y. 1997) ("Where the actual or specific cause of an accident is unknown, under the doctrine of res ipsa loquitur a jury may in certain circumstances infer negligence merely from the happening of an event and the defendant's relation to it." (citations omitted)). Here, it was established beyond doubt that the accident was caused by Biggins's loss of control of the halyard. The only question was whether his failure should be deemed negligent.

To prevail on this claim of negligence, Tagle was required to prove, by a preponderance of the evidence, that (1) the ship's crew owed her a duty of care, (2) that duty was breached, and (3) the breach proximately caused her injuries. *Pasternack v. Lab. Corp. of America Holdings*, 807 F.3d 14, 19 (2d Cir. 2015); *see also Withhart v. Otto*

[2] If our judgment were based solely on the district court's incorrect application of the res ipsa doctrine, we would have directed the district court to reconsider whether Biggs was negligent, giving Tagle the benefit of res ipsa loquitur. Because our judgment is that Tagle has proved negligence regardless of the applicability of res ipsa loquitur, we have reached a different judgment—that the district court must rule in favor of Tagle as to Biggins's negligence as the cause of her injury. Accordingly, our discussion of the standards for res ipsa loquitur is dictum and not a holding of this case.

Candies, L.L.C., 431 F.3d 840, 842 (5th Cir. 2005) ("The elements of a maritime negligence cause of action are essentially the same as land-based negligence under the common law."). **[—15—]**

Tagle's evidence established these three elements, and the shipowners offered no evidence to place any of them in doubt. As to duty, it was established without doubt or contradictory evidence that an extended, weighted halyard slipping out of a seaman's grasp would represent a danger to a passenger seated at the base of the mast. To avoid such danger, a "seaman must act with the care, skill, and ability expected of a reasonable seaman in like circumstances." *Gaylor v. Canal Barge Co., Inc.*, No. 14-2398, 2015 WL 5321756, at *2 (E.D. La. 2015) (citing *Gautreaux v. Scurlock Marine, Inc.*, 107 F.3d 331, 339 (5th Cir. 1997) (en banc)); *see Barlow v. Liberty Mar. Corp.*, 746 F.3d 518, 527 n.15, 2 Adm. R. 48, 54 n.15 (2d Cir. 2014) (observing that a seaman is charged with the duty to act with the care and skill required of a "reasonably prudent *seaman*, not that of a reasonably prudent *person*" (emphasis in original)). Those who are held out as competent to perform duties requiring training **{–184–}** and skills must possess those skills and employ them in their actions. *See* 3 Lindahl, *Modern Tort Law: Liability and Litigation* § 26:122 (2d ed. 2017); Prosser & Keeton § 32, at 185 ("[Those] who undertake any work calling for special skill, are required not only to exercise reasonable care in what they do, but also to possess a standard minimum of special knowledge and ability."). A seaman **[—16—]** who has detached a halyard that is stretched forward from the mast to the bow of the ship is required to exercise the care and skill necessary to prevent it from pulling loose.

That Biggins breached his duty is evident from his contemporaneous description of the mishap as having occurred because "the line slipped out of his hands." A-63–64. The circumstantial evidence overwhelmingly supported the conclusion that Biggins's failure to keep control of the halyard was attributable to nothing other than his failure to use due care and skill. The possibility of causes other than negligence was supported by nothing other than conjecture. Because the shipowners had no evidence supporting an inference of any cause other than negligence, no issue of material fact that might contradict or undermine the inference of negligence was presented to the fact-finder. In similar circumstances we reversed the trial judge's findings that two vessels were not responsible for a collision. *See Otal Invs. Ltd. v. M.V. Clary*, 494 F.3d 40, 62 (2d Cir. 2007) (reversing district court's findings, after a bench trial, that only one ship was responsible for an accident, and instead "conclud[ing] all three vessels committed violations of [regulations] that caused the collision"). **[—17—]**

In the absence of evidence of any cause, other than negligence, to explain why Biggins let the halyard slip dangerously out of his grasp, the only inference having a basis in the evidence was that Biggins failed to use the care and skill required of the seaman to avoid an obvious danger to a passenger.

We recognize that Biggins testified that he "didn't intentionally drop" the halyard, that his practice is to handle lines "as carefully as possible," and that this is what he was doing "immediately prior to the incident." A-78. That he did not act intentionally in no way rebutted the inference that he acted negligently. There was no evidence whatsoever to support the suggestion that a careful, competent seaman would have lost hold of a weighted halyard, absent some extra-ordinary cause, and, as we have repeatedly said, there was no evidence of any such extra-ordinary cause. And as we have already noted, the evidence included no reason to doubt that, had there been a cause other than negligence for Biggins's loss of control, Biggins would have reported it. One who drives a car onto the sidewalk injuring pedestrians does not successfully contradict the logical inference of lack of due care or due skill merely by asserting that he was driving carefully. **[—18—]**

We recognize that it is unusual for an appellate court to direct a verdict of negligence. What is unusual in this case, however, is the absence of any evidence by the person who caused the accident of a justifying cause in circumstances where he would have had to have been aware of any such cause at the time of the injury. It is no doubt a tribute to Biggins's honestly that he did not fabricate a justifying cause for his loss of control of the halyard. Nonetheless, without evidence of a justifying cause, the only inference reasonably supported by the evidence is of negligence.

In short, the evidence adduced at trial gives no reasonable support to any other conclusion than that Biggins, in a circumstance that posed an obvious danger to Tagle, failed to exercise the combination of **{–185–}** skill and care that is required of a seaman, and that his failure was the cause of Tagle's injury. **[—19—]**

CONCLUSION

For the reasons stated above, the district court's judgment is VACATED, and the case is REMANDED with instructions that the court enter a finding of negligence as the cause of Tagle's injury.[3]

[3] Under the Limitation of Liability Act, 46 U.S.C. § 30501, *et seq.*, "[w]hether a vessel owner is entitled to limit its liability requires a two-step analysis." *Otal Invests. Ltd. v. M/V CLARY*, 673 F.3d 108, 115 (2d Cir. 2012). First, the court must determine whether acts of negligence caused the accident which caused plaintiff's injuries. *Id.* "Second, the court must determine whether the ship owner had knowledge or privity of those same acts of negligence." *Id.* (internal quotation marks and alterations omitted). The district court concluded that the shipowners were not negligent, and dismissed on that ground. The court therefore did not rule on the issue of privity. As we conclude that negligence was established, the case is remanded for a determination on the issue of privity.

United States Court of Appeals
for the Second Circuit

No. 16-1092

IN RE BUCHANAN MARINE, L.P.

Appeal from the United States District Court for the Northern District of New York

Decided: October 27, 2017

Citation: 874 F.3d 356, 5 Adm. R. 100 (2d Cir. 2017).

Before **KEARSE, CABRANES,** and **CHIN,** Circuit Judges.

[—3—] {-360-} CHIN, Circuit Judge:

In this case, claimant-appellant Wayne Volk worked at a quarried rock processing facility on the Hudson River, inspecting and maintaining barges used to transport rock down the river. In the accident that led to these proceedings, Volk was inspecting a moored barge when he slipped on some loose stone and fell, injuring himself. **{-361-}** He asserted claims against the barge company as his employer, the owner of the barge, and the operator of the rock processing facility, under the Jones Act, 46 U.S.C. §§ 30101-30106, the Longshore and Harbor Workers' Compensation Act (the "LHWCA"), 33 U.S.C. §§ 901-950, general maritime law, and New York state law.

The principal question presented is whether Volk was a "seaman" within the meaning of the Jones Act. The district court (Sharpe, *J.*) held that Volk **[—4—]** was not a seaman and dismissed his claims under the Jones Act. It also dismissed Volk's remaining claims.

We affirm the dismissal of Volk's Jones Act claims because we agree with the district court that Volk does not qualify as a "seaman" within the meaning of the Jones Act. We hold, however, that the district court erred in dismissing certain of Volk's remaining claims against the owner of the barge and the operator of the rock processing facility. We therefore affirm in part and vacate in part and remand for the district court to conduct further proceedings consistent with our rulings below.

BACKGROUND

I. *The Facts*

The facts are largely undisputed and are summarized in the light most favorable to Volk, against whom summary judgment was granted.

Volk worked for petitioner-counter-defendant-appellee Buchanan Marine, L.P. ("Buchanan") at the Clinton Point quarried rock processing facility on the Hudson River, in Dutchess County, New York, as a "barge maintainer" **[—5—]** from 1999 until his accident on May 19, 2011.[1] At the Clinton Point facility, claimant-counter-claimant-appellee Tilcon New York, Inc. ("Tilcon") processes quarried rock for use in, *e.g.*, construction work, and loads the rock onto barges supplied by Buchanan. Buchanan then transports the loaded barges, using its tugboats, down the Hudson River to Tilcon's customers.[2]

The loading process has three steps. First, before an empty barge is loaded, and while it is tied to the dock, it is inspected by a Buchanan barge maintainer. The barge maintainer checks the barge for damage and excess water and repairs any damage so that the barge is in acceptable condition for loading. Second, the barge is moved to the loading facility by Tilcon, where it is loaded with quarried rock. Third, after the barge is loaded, it is moved back to the dock by Tilcon, where a Buchanan barge maintainer conducts a final inspection. During the first and third steps of the loading process, the barge is in the water and secured to the dock, either tied directly to the dock or to barges already tied to the dock. Moored barges may be three or four barges deep, with the closest **[—6—]** barge

---

[1] Volk also used other phrases throughout the proceedings to describe his position, such as "[w]elder, pumper, [and] boat checker." App'x 982.

[2] Buchanan's barges are "dumb" barges, meaning they have no independent means of propulsion and, therefore, a tugboat is required to transport them.

tied to the dock and the outward barges tied to one another. When a barge was tied to other barges—rather than tied directly to the dock—barge maintainers would climb over the barges to get to the one they needed to inspect.

When Volk was inspecting a barge, he would walk along the perimeter of the barge on the "margin decks," which ran the length of the barge. App'x at 185. The margin decks were "so narrow [that] they were difficult to walk on or stand on," *id.*, lacked guard or hand rails, and were often **{-362-}** wet and soiled with excess gravel that spilt over from the loading process. When a barge required repairs, Volk would sometimes stand on a pontoon work boat—a flat floatable device powered by a motor—on the barge's water side to do the work.

Volk was not assigned to any specific barge; rather, he worked on all Buchanan barges that arrived for loading at the Tilcon facility. Volk was not a crewmember of any of Buchanan's tugboats that transported the barges down the Hudson River. He worked an hourly shift, went home at the end of each work day, and did not take meals or sleep on any barge. He was a member of the International Union of Operating Engineers, which represents equipment operators. He did not belong to a maritime union or hold a maritime license. **[—7—]**

On May 19, 2011, Volk was walking along the margin decks of Barge B-252 (the "Barge"), which had been loaded with stone, when he slipped on excess wet stone and injured his right arm and shoulder on the side of the Barge. He filled out an incident report with his dock supervisor, Timothy Conn, the same day. The next day, Conn drove Volk to the local medical clinic, where Volk was diagnosed with a sprained arm and prescribed pain medication. Later that day, Volk saw a chiropractor, who advised him that he could not work. Volk has not worked since the accident and has been receiving workers' compensation benefits under the LHWCA.

II. *The Proceedings Below*

On October 16, 2012, Volk and his wife Karen Volk commenced a personal injury action against Buchanan and Tilcon in New York State Supreme Court, Ulster County. On April 15, 2013, A.P. Franz, Jr., the owner of the Barge, and Buchanan, as bareboat charterer of the Barge,[3] commenced this action in the **[—8—]** district court pursuant to the Limitation of Liability Act of 1851, 46 U.S.C. §§ 30501-30512, seeking exoneration from or limitation of liability.[4] In accordance with Rule F of the Supplemental Rules for Admiralty or Maritime Claims and Asset Forfeiture Actions of the Federal Rules of Civil Procedure, the court approved a $47,420.77 security bond, representing Franz and Buchanan's interest in the Barge, directed issuance of notice to all persons asserting claims affected by the limitation proceeding, ordered that any claim related to the incident be filed with the court within a specified time period, and enjoined the filing or prosecution of any suits related to the incident.[5] **{-363-}**

[3] A "bareboat charter" is a "charter under which the shipowner surrenders possession and control of the vessel to the charterer, who then succeeds to many of the shipowner's rights and obligations," typically including the provision of "personnel, insurance, and other materials necessary to operate the vessel." Black's Law Dictionary 284 (10th ed. 2009). Thus, the "bareboat charterer"—also called a "bareboat charterparty," among other things, *see id.*—is the non-owner operator of a vessel. Here, Franz had bareboat chartered the Barge along with his fleet of other barges and **[—8—]** tugboats to Buchanan. Pursuant to the bareboat charter, Franz transferred exclusive control to Buchanan to use, operate, command, and navigate his fleet of barges and tugboats.

[4] The Limitation of Liability Act limits the owner of a vessel's liability for maritime accidents to "the value of the vessel and pending freight." 46 U.S.C. § 30505(b). The statute thus alters the usual rules of vicarious liability. *See In re City of N.Y.*, 522 F.3d 279, 283 (2d Cir. 2008).

[5] "Typically, 'once the [vessel] owner files a petition for limitation, all other claims and proceedings against the owner related to the matter in question shall cease.'" *In re Petition of Germain*, 824 F.3d 258, 264, 4 Adm. R. 92, 95 (2d Cir. 2016) (quoting *Tandon v. Captain's Cove*

Tilcon and the Volks answered the complaint and asserted counterclaims. Tilcon asserted claims against Franz and Buchanan for **[—9—]** indemnification or contribution. The Volks asserted claims against Franz, Buchanan, and Tilcon under the Jones Act, the LHWCA, general maritime law, and New York state law.

The Volks filed a motion to dismiss on August 16, 2013. The district court denied the motion on March 28, 2014. The parties thereafter cross-moved for summary judgment. On March 10, 2016, the district court granted the motions of Franz, Buchanan, and Tilcon, denied the Volks' cross-motion, and granted Franz and Buchanan's complaint for exoneration from liability. The court exonerated Franz, Buchanan, and Tilcon from liability for Volk's injury, except for Buchanan's liability for workers' compensation. The court concluded that Volk's Jones Act claims fail because he is not a "seaman" under the Jones Act. The court also concluded that all of Volks' remaining claims under the LHWCA, general maritime law, and state law fail.

This appeal followed.

DISCUSSION

"We review *de novo* a district court's grant of summary judgment to determine whether the district court properly concluded that there was no genuine dispute as to any material fact, such that the moving party was entitled **[—10—]** to judgment as a matter of law." *Myers v. Patterson*, 819 F.3d 625, 632 (2d Cir. 2016).

I. *Overview*

Maritime workers injured in the course of their employment may proceed, depending on their status and the status of the responsible party, on four possible theories or sets of theories: the Jones Act, the LHWCA, general maritime law, and state law. *See generally* *O'Hara v. Weeks Marine, Inc.*, 294 F.3d 55, 61-62 (2d Cir. 2012).

Marina of Bridgeport, Inc., 752 F.3d 239, 244, 2 Adm. R. 57, 60 (2d Cir. 2014)) (alterations omitted).

The Jones Act confers a cause of action in negligence to any "seaman injured in the course of employment." 46 U.S.C. § 30104. Prior to the passage of the Jones Act, general maritime law entitled seamen only to "maintenance and cure" from their employer, and to damages "from the vessel's owner for [any] injuries received . . . in consequence of the unseaworthiness of the ship." *Chandris, Inc. v. Latsis*, 515 U.S. 347, 354 (1995) (internal quotation marks omitted). Suits to recover for injuries caused by their employers' negligence, however, were barred. *Id.* The Jones Act changed this by creating "an express right of action in tort." *O'Hara*, 294 F.3d at 61-62. **[—11—]**

The LHWCA is a workers' compensation system, which provides scheduled compensation for injury to a broad range of land-based maritime workers. *Chandris*, 515 U.S. at 355. It covers "any person engaged in maritime employment, including any longshoreman or other person engaged in longshoring operations, and any harbor-worker including a ship repairman, shipbuilder, and ship-breaker," 33 U.S.C. § 902(3), but does not include "a master or member of a crew of any vessel," *id.* § 902(3)(G).[6] The scheduled no-fault compensation structure is the *exclusive* remedy for injured workers against their employers. *Id.* § 905(a).

The LHWCA does not, however, affect an employee's right to sue the owner or charterer of the vessel on which he or she was injured for negligence. *Id.* § 933(a); *see also* **{-364-}** *Gravatt v. City of N.Y.*, 226 F.3d 108, 115 (2d Cir. 2000) (noting that, under LHWCA, employee "may sue negligent third parties in tort, notwithstanding his entitlement to no-fault compensation provided by the employer"). Pursuant to § 905(b), a claimant retains the right to bring an action for damages "caused by the negligence of a vessel,

[6] A longshoreman is "[a] maritime laborer who works on the wharves in a port; esp., a person who loads and unloads ships." Black's Law Dictionary 1085 (10th ed. 2009).

. . . against such vessel as a **[—12—]** third party." 33 U.S.C. § 905(b). A claimant is not required to elect between statutory compensation from the employer and an action for damages against another, as he "can both accept compensation and file a civil action against a third party tortfeasor." Thomas J. Schoenbaum, 1 Adm. & Mar. Law § 7-10 (5th ed. 2016). A cause of action under § 905(b) against the vessel owner is for negligence in maritime tort, *id.*, and "[t]he remedy provided in this subsection shall be exclusive of all other remedies against the vessel except remedies available under this chapter," 33 U.S.C. § 905(b).

In some cases, the vessel owner is also the employer, and a different analysis will be required. *Gravatt*, 226 F.3d at 118-20; 33 U.S.C. § 905(b). In these dual-capacity situations, "[i]nsofar as the employer-vessel is negligent in its stevedore-employer capacity, it is immune from suit under section 905(a), [but,] insofar as it is negligent in its vessel capacity, it will be liable under section 905(b) in the same manner as a third party." *Gravatt*, 226 F.3d at 120.[7] *See generally* Schoenbaum § 7-10.

In short, "[t]he Jones Act allows seamen to recover for negligence against their employers; the LHWCA authorizes maritime workers *other than* **[—13—]** seamen to recover for negligence, but only against parties *other than* their employers." *O'Hara*, 294 F.3d at 62. The two remedies are mutually exclusive. *Chandris*, 515 U.S. at 355-56 ("[T]he Jones Act and the LHWCA are mutually exclusive compensation regimes.").

The Jones Act does not define "seaman," but, as noted above, the LHWCA excludes from coverage "a master or member of a crew of any vessel." 33 U.S.C. § 902(3)(G). Thus, courts have recognized that a worker is a seaman if he or she is "a master or member of a crew of any vessel." *Id.*; *see O'Hara*, 294 F.3d at 62 ("It is . . . 'odd but true that the key requirement for Jones Act coverage now appears in another statute.'" (quoting *Chandris*, 515 U.S. at 356)). We discuss the elements of "seaman" status more fully below.

Maritime workers may also have common law remedies available to them, including, as noted, general maritime remedies for "maintenance and cure" and "unseaworthiness." *Chandris*, 515 U.S. at 354 (internal quotation marks omitted). The Jones Act—unlike the LHWCA—does not eliminate pre-existing common law causes of action. *See Miles v. Apex Marine Corp.*, 498 U.S. 19, 29 (1990) ("The Jones Act evinces no general hostility to recovery under maritime law."); *see also Atl. Sounding Co. v. Townsend,* 557 U.S. 404, 429 (2009) (Alito, J., **[—14—]** dissenting). And while the LHWCA eliminates common law claims against the employer, it permits harbor workers to sue third-party vessel owners for negligence under federal common law standards that establish certain duties of care. *See O'Hara*, 294 F.3d at 64-65.

In *Scindia Steam Navigation Company v. De Los Santos*, 451 U.S. 156 (1981), the Supreme Court set forth standards to **{-365-}** guide judicial determinations of liability under the LHWCA and general maritime law. It identified three duties of care. First, as we have noted, the "turnover duty" imposes on the vessel owner a duty to "exercise ordinary care under the circumstances to have the ship . . . in such condition that an . . . experienced stevedore will be able by the exercise of reasonable care to carry on its cargo operations with reasonable safety" and "a duty to warn stevedores . . . of hazards of which the [owner] know[s] or should know and which are unknown or would not be obvious to the stevedore." *O'Hara*, 294 F.3d at 65 (citing *Scindia*, 451 U.S. at 167). Second, the active control duty imposes liability on an owner "if it actively involves itself in [the vessel's] operations and negligently injures" the employee. *Id.* (internal quotation marks omitted). Third, the duty to intervene requires the vessel owner to "intervene if it acquires actual knowledge that (1) a condition of the vessel or **[—15—]** its equipment poses an unreasonable risk of harm and (2) the stevedore . . . is not exercising reasonable care

[7] A "stevedore" is a "person or company that hires longshore and harbor workers to load and unload ships." Black's Law Dictionary 1640 (10th ed. 2009).

to protect its employees from that risk." *Id.* (internal quotation marks omitted).

Finally, in some circumstances, maritime workers may assert claims under state law. *Id.* at 68 (discussing claims under New York Labor Law §§ 200 and 241(6)).

II. *Jones Act Claims*

The district court dismissed Volk's Jones Act claims because it concluded that Volk did not qualify as a "seaman" within the meaning of the Jones Act. We agree.

A. Applicable Law

Congress enacted the Jones Act in 1920 to provide "heightened legal protections to seamen because of their exposure to the perils of the sea." *O'Hara*, 294 F.3d at 61 (internal quotation marks and alterations omitted). It "gives seamen an express right of action in tort because of their status as 'wards of the admiralty' who 'are by the peculiarity of their lives liable to sudden sickness from change of climate, exposure to perils, and exhausting labour.'" *Id.* at 61-62 (quoting *Chandris*, 515 U.S. at 354-55). "[T]o qualify as a seaman under the Jones **[—16—]** Act, a maritime employee must have a substantial employment-related connection to a vessel in navigation," *Chandris*, 515 U.S. at 373 (emphasis omitted), or "to an identifiable group of such vessels," *id.* at 368.

To have an "employment-related connection" to a vessel, "the worker's duties must contribute to the function of the vessel or to the accomplishment of its mission." *O'Hara*, 294 F.3d at 63 (internal quotation marks omitted). This standard is liberal: "[t]he putative seaman need not aid in the navigation or contribute to the transportation of the vessel, but a seaman must be doing the ship's work." *Id.* (internal quotation marks omitted); *see also Harbor Tug & Barge Co. v. Papai*, 520 U.S. 548, 554 (1997) (noting this prong focuses on whether the worker "contributed to the function of the vessel or the accomplishment of its mission"). Moreover, "the worker's connection to the vessel must be 'substantial in both its duration and its nature.'" *O'Hara*, 294 F.3d at 63 (quoting *Tonnesen v. Yonkers Contracting Co.*, 82 F.3d 30, 32 n.2 (2d Cir. 1996)). This inquiry "focuses on whether the [worker] derives his livelihood from sea-based activities." *Id.* (internal quotation marks omitted). "Land-based maritime workers do not become seamen because they happen to be working on board a vessel when they are injured, and seamen do not lose Jones Act **[—17—]** protection when the course of their service **{-366-}** to a vessel takes them ashore." *Chandris*, 515 U.S. at 361.

Nevertheless, the "recognized [] distinction between land-based and sea-based maritime workers" does not mean "that a maritime employee must work *only* on board a vessel to qualify as a seaman under the Jones Act." *Id.* at 363. Rather, "the ultimate inquiry" is whether, in light of the totality of the circumstances, "the worker in question is a member of the vessel's crew or simply a land-based employee who happens to be working on the vessel at a given time." *Id.* at 370; *see also Harbor Tug & Barge Co.*, 520 U.S. at 555 ("For the substantial connection requirement to serve its purpose, the inquiry into the nature of the employee's connection to the vessel must concentrate on whether the employee's duties take him to sea."). "Whether [a worker] qualifies as a seaman 'is a mixed question of law and fact.'" *O'Hara*, 294 F.3d at 63-64 (quoting *Harbor Tug & Barge Co.*, 520 U.S. at 554).

The Supreme Court has emphasized that it is important "to focus upon the essence of what it means to be a seaman and to eschew the temptation to create detailed tests to effectuate the congressional purpose." *Chandris*, 515 U.S. at 369. "The Jones Act remedy is reserved for sea-based maritime employees **[—18—]** whose work regularly exposes them to 'the special hazards and disadvantages to which they who go down to sea in ships are subjected.'" *Id.* at 370 (quoting *Seas Shipping Co. v. Sieracki*, 328 U.S. 85, 104 (1946) (Stone, C.J., dissenting)). The key is whether the individual "'had a sufficient relation to the navigation of vessels and the perils attendant thereon.'" *Id.* (quoting

Wallace v. Oceaneering Int'l, 727 F.2d 427, 435 (5th Cir. 1984)).

B. Application

In weighing "the total circumstances" of Volk's employment, we conclude as a matter of law that Volk does not qualify as a seaman under the Jones Act. *See id.* As a reasonable factfinder could only conclude, his work on the barges did not regularly expose him to the special hazards and disadvantages of the sea. *See id.* at 369-70.

Volk did not "derive[] his livelihood from sea-based activities." *O'Hara*, 294 F.3d at 64 (internal quotation marks omitted). Volk never operated a barge and only worked aboard the barges when they were secured to the dock. *See Harbor Tug & Barge Co.*, 520 U.S. at 555 ("For the substantial connection requirement to serve its purpose, the inquiry into the nature of the employee's connection to the vessel must concentrate on whether the employee's duties take **[—19—]** him to sea."). The barges Volk worked on were moved to the loading dock by Tilcon workboats and Tilcon employees, and transported down the Hudson River by Buchanan tugboats.[8] Volk was not a crew member of and did not serve on the Buchanan tugboats.[9] Indeed, **{-367-}** Volk reported to the dock foreman, not a ship's officer, and it was the dock foreman who brought him to the medical clinic after his accident. Volk belonged to a union that represents equipment operators. He did not belong to a maritime union and did not hold a maritime license or other "seaman's papers." *O'Hara*, 294 F.3d at 64. Finally, Volk never spent the night aboard a barge; he worked an hourly shift and went home every night after his shift ended. In contrast, a traditional Jones Act seaman normally **[—20—]** serves for voyages or tours of duty. *See, e.g., Aguilar v. Standard Oil Co.*, 318 U.S. 724, 731-32 (1943) (voyages); *Sellers v. Dixilyn Corp.*, 433 F.2d 446, 447-48 (5th Cir. 1970) (tours of duty).

In *O'Hara*, we concluded that a dock worker who was injured while repairing the Staten Island pier aboard a barge was not a "seaman" as a matter of law because he had, at most, "a transitory or sporadic connection" to the barges "in their capacity as vessels in navigation." 294 F.3d at 64 (emphasis omitted). Key to our holding was that the dock worker (1) belonged to a dock workers union rather than a maritime union, (2) lacked a maritime license, (3) never spent the night aboard a barge, and (4) never operated a barge or assisted in its navigation and only worked aboard the barges when they were fully secured to the pier that the dock worker was employed to repair. *Id.* We emphasized that, although the worker "spent more than half his working hours . . . aboard the barges, . . . he spent all of that time performing tasks related to the repair of the Staten Island pier while the barges were secured to the pier." *Id.* This case is not substantially different from *O'Hara*.

Volk seeks to rely on the Fifth Circuit's decision in *Naquin v. Elevating Boats, LLC*, 744 F.3d 927, 2 Adm. R. 200 (5th Cir. 2014), *cert. denied* 135 S. Ct. 1397 (2015). **[—21—]** There, a shipyard worker "spent approximately 70 percent of his total time working aboard" so-called "lift-boats" that "were moored, jacked up or docked in [the] shipyard

---

[8] Volk would occasionally ride on the Tilcon workboats from the pier, where he performed his work on the barges, to the loading dock. The distance was "[p]robably" a "couple hundred yards," App'x 1012, and Volk did not perform any inspection or repair work while on the Tilcon workboats. *See Casser v. McAllister Towing & Transp. Co.*, 10 Civ. 1554 (JSR), 2010 WL 5065424, at *3 (S.D.N.Y. Dec. 7, 2010) (rejecting argument that once a person steps onto a vessel he is a seaman because "if this argument were accepted, then there would be no distinction between a longshoreman and a seaman").

[9] Volk argues for the first time on appeal that he was a crew member of the small pontoon work boat that he used to approach a moored barge from the water side to make repairs to the barge. Even if this argument were not waived, *see Green v. United States*, 13 F.3d 577, 586 (2d Cir. 1994) ("[I]t is a well-established general rule that an appellate court will not consider an issue raised for the first time on appeal."), it does not change our analysis as the pontoon work boat, like the Buchanan barges, was unmanned, had no crew members, and was only used, on occasion, as a work platform by Volk and his fellow workers.

canal." *Id.* at 930, 2 Adm. R. at 200. His duties included "inspecting [the lift-boats] for repairs, cleaning them, painting them, replacing defective or damaged parts, performing engine repairs, going on test runs, securing equipment, and operating the vessels' marine cranes and jack-up legs." *Id.*, 2 Adm. R. at 200. The worker was occasionally "dispatched . . . to repair a vessel or fill in as a vessel crane operator while the vessel was operating in open water." *Id.* at 931, 2 Adm. R. at 200. The Fifth Circuit affirmed the jury verdict in favor of the shipyard worker awarding Jones Act damages, finding that the shipyard worker was exposed to the perils of a maritime work environment such that he was a seaman. *Id.* at 935, 2 Adm. R. at 204.

The Fifth Circuit's decision is not controlling on us, and it is in any event distinguishable. The shipyard worker there clearly had a more substantial connection to seafaring vessels than Volk does. For example, the shipyard worker operated "the vessels' marine cranes and jack-up legs" and worked aboard the vessels in open water, even if only "occasionally." *Id.* at 930, 2 Adm. R. at 200. Volk did none of these things; Volk worked on barges that were moored, directly or indirectly, to the Tilcon dock and did not operate the Tilcon workboats or **[—22—]** Buchanan tugboats that transported the **{–368–}** barges. *See Schultz v. Louisiana Dock Co.*, 94 F. Supp. 2d 746, 750 (E.D. La. 2000) ("Plaintiff's duties were limited to inspecting and repairing barges moored at the facility. He did not go to sea or face the perils of the sea in the manner associated with seaman status. Plaintiff ate meals ashore and went home every night. He admitted that with respect to the vessels used to transport him around the facility he did not serve as a deckhand.").

In sum, none of Volk's work was of a seagoing nature. Volk's duties were limited to inspecting and repairing barges that were secured to the dock at the Clinton Point facility. Volk did not go to sea and he was not exposed to the "perils of the sea" in the manner associated with seaman status. *See Denson v. Ingram Barge Co.*, 5:07-cv-00084-R, 2009 WL 1033817, at *3 (W.D. Ky. Apr. 16, 2009) ("The hazards Denson states he faced do not rise to the level of the special hazards and disadvantages faced by seamen; they are hazards that longshoremen commonly encounter. Therefore, Denson was an intended beneficiary of the LHWCA."). Accordingly, considering the total circumstances of Volk's employment, we conclude as a matter of law that Volk does not qualify **[—23—]** as a "seaman" within the meaning of the Jones Act, and we affirm the dismissal of his Jones Act claims.

III. *Other Claims*

Volk also asserted claims under the LHWCA, general maritime law, and New York law against all three appellees: Buchanan, Franz, and Tilcon. The district court dismissed all these claims. We conclude that the district court should have permitted certain of these claims to proceed.

A. Buchanan

The district court correctly dismissed all the remaining claims against Buchanan. Buchanan is Volk's employer and ordinarily would be immune from suit under 33 U.S.C. § 905(a). As bareboat charterer of the Barge, however, Buchanan is a dual capacity employer-vessel owner. *See Reed v. S.S. Yaka*, 373 U.S. 410, 412 (1963) ("It has long been recognized in the law of admiralty that for many, if not most, purposes the bareboat charterer is to be treated as the owner."). Therefore, if Buchanan were negligent in its vessel capacity in relation to Volk's injury, Buchanan would be liable under 33 U.S.C. § 905(b) in the same manner as a third party. *Gravatt*, 226 F.3d at 119. The district court ruled that Buchanan was not acting in a capacity as vessel owner in **[—24—]** relation to Volk's injury, and therefore is liable exclusively for Volk's workers' compensation payments under the LHWCA. *See* 33 U.S.C. § 905(a) (stating that employer is liable exclusively for scheduled no-fault compensation). Volk does not challenge that ruling on appeal. Because the statutory, no-fault compensation payments under the LHWCA are Volk's exclusive remedy as to Buchanan, his general maritime law and state law claims against Buchanan were properly dismissed. *See id.*

B. Franz

As vessel owner, Franz was subject to suit for negligence under the LHWCA. 33 U.S.C. § 905(b). Although the district court correctly noted that Franz was not an employer or bareboat charterer of the Barge and therefore was only responsible for his "turnover duty," *see O'hara*, 294 F.3d at 65, the district court did not properly analyze the LHWCA claims. While he could not be responsible for the presence of excess stone, Franz arguably had a duty, as owner, to address the condition of the Barge before turning it over to Buchanan. **{-369-}**

As the district court itself recognized, Volk's negligence claim could have been based on the condition of the vessel, not just the presence of excess stone on the margin deck. *See* Special App'x at 27 ("The alleged negligence which **[—25—]** caused W. Volk's injury could plausibly originate from one of two sources. *The first is where the stones reached the margin deck of the B-252 from a barge weeper, which is a drainage hole on the side of a barge.* The second is where the stones could have been overloaded by Tilcon and spilled onto the margin deck." (citation omitted and emphasis added)). On remand, the district court shall consider whether there is a viable claim under § 905(b) of the LHWCA against Franz as owner based on the condition of the vessel. *See Gravatt*, 226 F.3d at 115 ("[T]he employee may sue negligent third parties in tort."); *see also Pellegrino v. A.H. Bull S.S. Co.*, 309 F. Supp. 839, 842 (S.D.N.Y. 1969) ("The shipowner owes an absolute and non-delegable duty to . . . longshoremen properly aboard its vessel to provide a seaworthy ship."). As that statute is the sole basis under which Volk can recover against Franz, 33 U.S.C. § 905(b), the general maritime and state law claims otherwise must be dismissed. *See Norfolk Shipbuilding & Drydock Corp. v. Garris*, 532 U.S. 811, 818 (2001) (noting that the LHWCA preempts all other claims against a vessel owner).

C. Tilcon

The district court correctly held that Tilcon, the operator of the rock processing facility, has no LHWCA liability because it did not employ Volk or **[—26—]** own the Barge. *See* 33 U.S.C. § 905. The district court also correctly held that the general maritime claims asserted against Tilcon fail because Tilcon is not an owner of the Barge and because Volk is not a seaman. Tilcon had no duty to provide a seaworthy vessel or to provide maintenance and cure because it did not own the Barge. *See Oxley v. City of New York*, 923 F.2d 22, 24-25 (2d Cir. 1991) (noting that a vessel owner has a duty to supply a seaworthy vessel); *Lewis v. Lewis & Clark Marine, Inc.*, 531 U.S. 438, 441 (2001) ("A claim for maintenance and cure concerns the vessel owner's obligation to provide food, lodging, and medical services to a seaman injured while serving the ship."). Further, Volk is not entitled to maintenance and cure because he is not a seaman. *See* 1B-IV Benedict on Admiralty § 44 (2015) ("Longshoremen, of course, have never been entitled to maintenance and cure.").

The district court erred, however, in dismissing Volk's New York state law claims against Tilcon for negligence, gross negligence, and violations of N.Y. Labor Law § 200. The district court determined that these claims failed because the alleged hazard—the presence of excess stone on the margin deck of the Barge—was open and obvious. The district court's holding in this regard was based on an error of law. New York law utilizes a comparative negligence **[—27—]** scheme, meaning the doctrines of contributory negligence and assumption of risk are not complete defenses as a matter of law. *See Integrated Waste Servs., Inc. v. Akzo Nobel Salt, Inc.,* 113 F.3d 296, 300 (2d Cir. 1997) ("[W]hen New York, by statute, adopted comparative negligence, it abolished not only contributory negligence as a complete defense, but also assumption of risk. Under the statute, liability is split between plaintiffs and defendants based on the relative culpability and causal significance of their conduct." (citing N.Y. C.P.L.R. § 1411)); *see also Payne v. United States*, 359 F.3d 132, 138 (2d Cir.

2004) ("[U]nder New York law the open and obvious nature of a dangerous condition . . . does not absolve **{-370-}** the landowner of its general duty of care."). Even assuming the condition was open and obvious, a factual question exists as to the relative fault of the parties.

Accordingly, the district court's grant of summary judgment to Tilcon on these state law claims was error.

CONCLUSION

To summarize, we conclude as follows:

1. The district court correctly dismissed: (a) the Jones Act claims against all three appellees; (b) the LHWCA, general maritime law, and state law **[—28—]** claims against Buchanan; and (c) the LHWCA and general maritime claims against Tilcon; and

2. The district court erred in dismissing: (a) the LHWCA claim against Franz to the extent it is based on the alleged breach of Franz's duty, as owner, to turn over a reasonably safe vessel; and (b) the state law claims against Tilcon for negligence, gross negligence, and violation of N.Y. Labor Law § 200.

Accordingly, the case is **AFFIRMED IN PART, VACATED IN PART,** and **REMANDED** for such further proceedings as may be appropriate.

United States Court of Appeals for the Third Circuit

United States Court of Appeals
for the Third Circuit

No. 15-3353

IN RE VEHICLE CARRIER SERVS. ANTITRUST LITIG.

Appeal from the United States District Court for the District of New Jersey

Decided: January 18, 2017

Citation: 846 F.3d 71, 5 Adm. R. 110 (3d Cir. 2017).

Before **AMBRO, SHWARTZ,** and **FUENTES,** Circuit Judges.

[—12—] {-77-} SHWARTZ, Circuit Judge:

Ocean common carriers transport cargo between foreign countries and the United States. In this case, Plaintiffs[1] used the services of such carriers to transport vehicles. Some plaintiffs made arrangements with and received vehicles directly from the carriers (direct purchaser plaintiffs or "DPPs"), while other plaintiffs obtained the benefit of the carrier services by ultimately receiving vehicles transported from abroad (indirect purchaser plaintiffs or "IPPs"). Plaintiffs allege that Defendants, who are ocean common carriers, entered into agreements to fix prices and reduce capacity in violation of federal antitrust laws and various state laws. Because the ocean common carriers allegedly engaged in acts prohibited by the Shipping Act of **[—13—]** 1984, 46 U.S.C. § 40101 *et seq.* (the "Shipping Act" or the "Act"), and the Act both precludes private plaintiffs from seeking relief under the federal antitrust laws for such conduct and preempts the state law claims under circumstances like those presented here, the District Court correctly **{-78-}** dismissed the complaints. We will therefore affirm.

I[2]

Defendants transport vehicles from their country of origin to the country where they will be sold, including the United States, at which point the vehicles are delivered to dealers and individuals, such as Auto Dealer IPPs, Truck Center IPPs, and End-Payor IPPs. The vehicle manufacturers and DPPs purchase vehicle carrier services from Defendants, and the costs of these services are passed on to IPPs.

In September 2012, law enforcement raided Defendants' offices in connection with antitrust investigations, and several Defendants thereafter pleaded guilty to antitrust violations based on price-fixing, allocating customers, and rigging bids for vehicle carrier services to and from the United States and elsewhere.

Plaintiffs filed complaints with jury demands alleging that Defendants entered into "secret" agreements in connection with Defendants' carriage of vehicles. These **[—14—]** agreements included: (1) price increase coordination agreements; (2) agreements not to compete, including coordination of responses to price reduction requests and allocation of customers and routes; and (3) agreements to restrict capacity by means of agreed-upon fleet reductions. Plaintiffs claim they suffered economic injuries as a result of these agreements and seek relief under the Clayton Act for violations of the Sherman Act. IPPs also assert state antitrust, consumer fraud, and unjust enrichment claims.

Defendants moved to dismiss the complaints pursuant to Fed. R. Civ. P. 12(b)(6), claiming they are immune from antitrust liability under the Shipping Act and that the state law claims are preempted. The District Court agreed and dismissed the complaints with prejudice.

---

[1] The plaintiffs fall into two categories: Direct Purchase Plaintiffs ("DPPs") and Indirect Purchase Plaintiffs ("IPPs"). The latter category consists of Auto Dealer IPPs, End-Payor IPPs, and Truck Center IPPs.

[2] Because this appeal arises from an order dismissing the complaints pursuant to Fed. R. Civ. P. 12(b)(6), the facts are derived from the complaints and are accepted as true. *Connelly v. Lane Constr. Corp.*, 809 F.3d 780, 786 (3d Cir. 2016).

While the motions to dismiss were pending, IPPs informed the District Court that they reached a putative class action settlement in principle with two groups of defendants, "K" Line and MOL Defendants (the "Settling Defendants"), but no motions to approve any settlement were filed. After the Court dismissed the complaints, IPPs filed a motion for reconsideration under Fed. R. Civ. P. 59(e) and 60(b) and Local Civil Rule 7.1(i) alleging that, before the cases were dismissed, they had notified the Court that they agreed in principle to settle and requested that it retain jurisdiction to approve a class settlement.

The District Court denied IPPs' motion for reconsideration because it had determined that the Federal Maritime Commission ("FMC") was the appropriate forum to **[—15—]** hear the dispute[3] and because IPPs "did not identif[y] an intervening change in the controlling law, alert[ ] the Court to the availability of new evidence that was not available when the Court issued its Opinion, or allege[ ] that the Opinion was the result of a clear error of fact or law or will result in manifest injustice." Joint App. 62-63.

Plaintiffs appeal the order dismissing the complaints and IPPs also appeal **{-79-}** the order denying reconsideration.[4] **[—16—]**

II

To resolve this appeal, we must first examine the Shipping Act of 1984. Broadly, the Shipping Act establishes a uniform federal framework for regulating entities, such as ocean common carriers,[5] and attempts to place U.S.-flag **[—17—]** vessels on a level economic playing field with their foreign counterparts. The Act sets forth four specific purposes:

> (1) establish a nondiscriminatory regulatory process for the common carriage of goods by water in the foreign commerce of the United States with a minimum of government intervention and regulatory costs;
> (2) provide an efficient and economic transportation system in the ocean commerce of the United States that is, insofar as possible, in harmony with,

---

[3] While IPPs' motion for reconsideration was pending, Plaintiffs filed complaints with the FMC.

[4] The District Court had jurisdiction pursuant to 28 U.S.C. §§ 1331 and 1337, and we have jurisdiction pursuant to 28 U.S.C. § 1291. We exercise plenary review of a district court's order granting a motion to dismiss under Rule 12(b)(6), *Burtch v. Milberg Factors, Inc.*, 662 F.3d 212, 220 (3d Cir. 2011), and apply the same standard as the District Court. *See Santomenno ex rel. John Hancock Tr. v. John Hancock Life Ins. Co.*, 768 F.3d 284, 290 (3d Cir. 2014). Under this standard, we must determine whether the complaints "contain sufficient factual matter, accepted as true, to 'state a claim to relief that is plausible on its face,'" *Ashcroft v. Iqbal*, 556 U.S. 662, 678 (2009) (quoting *Bell Atl. Corp. v. Twombly*, 550 U.S. 544, 570 (2007)), "but we disregard rote recitals of the elements of a cause of action, legal conclusions, and mere conclusory statements." *James v. City of Wilkes-Barre*, 700 F.3d 675, 679 (3d Cir. 2012). Our review of the District Court's order denying IPPs' motion to reconsider is "plenary where the denial was based on the 'interpretation and application of a legal precept.' Otherwise, we review such denials for abuse of discretion." *United* **[—16—]** *States v. Smith*, 445 F.3d 713, 716 (3d Cir. 2006) (citations omitted).

[5] Under the Shipping Act, the "term 'ocean common carrier' means a vessel-operating common carrier." 46 U.S.C. § 40102. Under the Act, a

> "common carrier"—(A) means a person that—(i) holds itself out to the general public to provide transportation by water of passengers or cargo between the United States and a foreign country for compensation; (ii) assumes responsibility for the transportation from the port or point of receipt to the port or point of destination; and (iii) uses, for all or part of that transportation, a vessel operating on the high seas or the Great Lakes between a port in the United States and a port in a foreign country; but (B) does not include a carrier engaged in ocean transportation by ferry boat, ocean tramp, or chemical parcel-tanker, or by vessel when primarily engaged in the carriage of perishable agricultural commodities—(i) if the carrier and the owner of those commodities are wholly-owned, directly or indirectly, by a person primarily engaged in the marketing and distribution of those commodities; and (ii) only **[—17—]** with respect to the carriage of those commodities.

Id.

and responsive to, international shipping practices;
(3) encourage the development of an economically sound and efficient liner fleet of vessels of the United States capable of meeting national security needs; and
(4) promote the growth and development of United States exports through competitive and efficient ocean transportation and by placing a greater reliance on the marketplace.

46 U.S.C. § 40101. Taken together, these purposes show that the Act seeks to promote economically sound, evenhanded, and efficient ocean commerce that responds to international shipping practices. *See also* **{-80-}** *Waterfront Comm'n of N.Y. Harbor v. Elizabeth-Newark Shipping, Inc.*, 164 F.3d 177, 185 (3d Cir. 1998) ("The primary purpose of the Shipping **[—18—]** Act . . . is to eliminate discriminatory treatment of shippers and carriers.").

One way the Act sought to achieve these goals was to broaden the provisions of the prior law that provided very limited antitrust immunity.[6] The House Committee on Merchant Marine and Fisheries, which reported on the bill, noted "[t]he perception . . . that the threat of U.S. antitrust prosecution weighs much more heavily on U.S. operators than their foreign-flag competition" and recognized "the need to foster a regulatory environment in which U.S.-flag liner operators are not placed at a competitive disadvantage vis-a-vis their foreign-flag competitors." Report of the House Committee on Merchant Marine and Fisheries, H.R. Rep. No. 98-53(I), 98th Cong., 1st Sess., at 9, 10.[7] To address this **[—19—]** disadvantage, the Shipping Act "exempt[ed] from the antitrust laws those agreements and activities subject to regulation by the" FMC. H.R. Rep. No. 98-53(I), at 3. Such agreements include those that:

(1) discuss, fix, or regulate transportation rates, including through rates, cargo space accommodations, and other conditions of service;
(2) pool or apportion traffic, revenues, earnings, or losses;
(3) allot ports or regulate the number and character of voyages between ports;
(4) regulate the volume or character of cargo or passenger traffic to be carried;
(5) engage in an exclusive, preferential, or cooperative working arrangement between themselves or with a marine terminal operator;
(6) control, regulate, or prevent competition in international ocean transportation; or
(7) discuss and agree on any matter related to a service contract.

Id. § 40301.

The Act provides federal antitrust immunity for agreements filed with the FMC that address these topics.[8] **[—20—]** The FMC reviews each filed agreement and can seek information about it. 46 U.S.C. § 40304. If the FMC takes no action on such an agreement, that agreement becomes effective,[9] and,

[6] The Shipping Act of 1916, 46 U.S.C. § 801 *et seq.*, provided antitrust immunity for rate-making agreements approved by the FMC. *See, e.g., Carnation Co. v. Pac. Westbound Conf.*, 383 U.S. 213, 216-18 & n.1 (1966) (noting that the Shipping Act of 1916 included only a limited antitrust exemption and holding that the implementation of rate-making agreements not approved by the FMC was subject to the antitrust laws); *Nat'l Ass'n of Recycling Indus., Inc. v. Am. Mail Line, Ltd.*, 720 F.2d 618, 618 (9th Cir. 1983) (stating that the Shipping Act of 1916 immunized collective rate-making activity provided that the rate-making was authorized by agreements which the FMC approved and all rates were filed with the FMC).

[7] H.R. Rep. No. 98-53 relates to the proposed Shipping Act of 1983, S. 504, H.R. 1878, 98th Cong., 1st Sess., which was not passed but was considered by the same Congress that passed the Shipping Act of 1984. The proposed Shipping Act **[—19—]** of 1983 is the same in all relevant respects as the Shipping Act of 1984.

[8] 46 U.S.C. § 40302 provides that a "true copy of every agreement referred to in section 40301(1) or (b) of this title shall be filed with the [FMC]. If the agreement is oral, a **[—20—]** complete memorandum specifying in detail the substance of the agreement shall be filed."

[9] Under the Shipping Act, an agreement is effective:

pursuant to **{-81-}** § 40307(a), the federal antitrust laws, such as the Sherman Act and the Clayton Act, "do not apply to [such] an agreement." 46 U.S.C. §§ 40102, 40307(a). Thus, activities described in § 40301 that are undertaken pursuant to agreements filed with the FMC are immune from federal antitrust laws.

The Act also provides immunity from private antitrust suits based on conduct prohibited by the Act. For example, the Act prohibits conduct undertaken pursuant to agreements **[—21—]** that are not effective or have been rejected. Specifically, § 41102(b) provides:

> Operating contrary to agreement.—A person may not operate under an agreement required to be filed under section 40302 or 40305 of this title if—
>
> (1) the agreement has not become effective under section 40304 of this title or has been rejected, disapproved, or canceled; or
>
> (2) the operation is not in accordance with the terms of the agreement or any modifications to the agreement made by the Federal Maritime Commission.

46 U.S.C. § 41102(b). If an agreement has not been filed, it cannot become effective and thus operating under such an unfiled agreement is prohibited. *See* 46 C.F.R. § 535.901 ("Any person operating under an agreement . . . that has not been filed and that has not become effective pursuant to the Act . . . is in violation of the Act . . . ."). A party injured by activities occurring under such an unfiled, and hence not effective, agreement may not obtain Clayton Act relief. *Id.* § 40307(d) (stating that "[a] person may not recover damages under section 4 of the Clayton Act (15 U.S.C. 15), or obtain injunctive relief under section 16 of that Act (15 U.S.C. 26), for conduct prohibited by" the Shipping Act); *see also* H.R. Rep. No. 98-53(I), at 12 ("The antitrust exposure for these so-called 'secret' agreements is limited to injunctive and criminal prosecution by the Attorney General, and does not carry with it any private right of action otherwise available under the antitrust laws."). **[—22—]**

Although the Act bars private federal antitrust lawsuits based on such prohibited conduct, it does provide an avenue for relief before the FMC. *A & E Pac. Constr. Co. v. Saipan Stevedore Co.*, 888 F.2d 68, 71 (9th Cir. 1989). Either on a complaint filed by a private party, 46 U.S.C. § 41301(a), or its own motion, the FMC may investigate alleged violations of the Shipping Act, *id.* § 41302. In such proceedings, the parties may engage in discovery, *id.* § 41303, and request hearings before the FMC, *id.* § 41304. If a plaintiff shows the Act has been violated, the FMC may assess penalties, *id.* § 41109(a), award damages of up to double the amount of the actual injury, grant attorneys' fees, *id.* § 41305, and provide a means to obtain equitable relief, *id.* § 41307.[10] *A & E Pac. Constr. Co.*, 888 F.2d at 71 (noting that "while no private party may sue for damages or for injunctive relief under the antitrust laws for conduct falling within the purview of the [Shipping] Act, the FMC is empowered to order reparations, including double damages, to impose sanctions and penalties for prohibited conduct, and to **{-82-}** file suit in federal district court against the offending party" (citations omitted)); *see also Fed. Mar. Comm'n v. S.C. State Ports Auth.*, 535 U.S. 743, 759 (2002) ("[T]he similarities between FMC proceedings and civil litigation are overwhelming."). Congress gave the FMC this broad authority to, among other things, "provide a deterrent effect which has

---

(1) on the 45th day after filing, or on the 30th day after notice of the filing is published in the Federal Register, whichever is later; or

(2) if additional information or documents are requested under subsection (d)—(A) on the 45th day after the Commission receives all the additional information and documents; or (B) if the request is not fully complied with, on the 45th day after the Commission receives the information and documents submitted and a statement of the reasons for noncompliance with the request.

46 U.S.C. § 40304.

[10] After filing a complaint, a private party may also file a complaint in a district court for injunctive relief, *id.* § 41306, and seek enforcement of FMC orders in a district court, *id.* § 41309.

previously been available only by invoking the antitrust laws," H.R. Rep. No. 98-53(I), at 4, and "end the uncertainty and delay that surrounds U.S. Government regulation of ocean liner shipping, by providing **[—23—]** a predictable legal regime and streamlined regulatory process administered and enforced by a single independent Federal agency (the [FMC]) to better serve the needs of U.S. foreign commerce," Report of the Senate Committee on Commerce, Science, and Transportation, S. Rep. No. 98-3, 98th Cong., 1st Sess. at 1.[11] *See also* H.R. Rep. No. 98-53(I), at 12 ("[T]he remedies and sanctions provided in the Shipping Act . . . will be the exclusive remedies and sanctions for violation of the Act."); *Seawinds Ltd. v. Nedlloyd Lines, B.V.*, 80 B.R. 181, 184, 185 (N.D. Cal. 1987) (stating that, "[b]y removing the courts from this regulatory process, Congress removed the potential for continuing regulatory uncertainty" under the antitrust laws), *aff'd*, 846 F.2d 586 (9th Cir. 1988).

Thus, the Shipping Act's text, scheme, and legislative history demonstrate Congress's intent to create a comprehensive, predictable federal framework to ensure efficient and nondiscriminatory international shipping practices.

III

Mindful of this framework, we will first address whether the Shipping Act bars Plaintiffs' Clayton Act claims. There is no dispute that operating under unfiled price fixing and/or market allocation agreements is prohibited under §§ 40301 and 40302 of the Shipping Act. **[—24—]**

Plaintiffs assert, however, that the Shipping Act does not prohibit a carrier from operating under unfiled agreements to restrict capacity. For support, they point to a statement by an FMC Commissioner made at a trade symposium during which he said that agreements to restrict capacity "would be outside of the Shipping Act purview." DPP Appellants' Br. 24. Plaintiffs assert that we should treat this comment as the agency's interpretation of a statute it administers. This argument fails for several reasons. First, the Commissioner stated that "[m]y remarks today reflect my personal views and thoughts and are not offered as the official position of the United States or the Federal Maritime Commission." Joint App. 39-40. Second, and relatedly, *Chevron* deference only applies to agency action, and by his own statements the Commissioner acknowledged that he was not speaking or acting for the agency. Thus, *Chevron* deference is not applicable. *See Chevron U.S.A. Inc. v. Nat. Res. Def. Council, Inc.*, 467 U.S. 837 (1984); Br. for Fed. Mar. Comm'n and United States as Amici Curiae 16 n.22.

Moreover, the Commissioner's statement is undermined by the Act itself. Sections 40301(a)(3) and (4) require parties to file agreements that restrict capacity. For example, § 40301(a)(4) requires carriers to file agreements that "regulate the volume or character of cargo or passenger traffic to be carried." Relatedly, § 40301(a)(3) requires **{-83-}** carriers to file agreements that "regulate the number and character of voyages between ports." Entering agreements concerning these activities without filing them is prohibited.

Plaintiffs allege they were injured by acts taken pursuant to these unfiled, and thus prohibited, agreements and seek damages under the Clayton Act. The Shipping Act, **[—25—]** however, bars them from obtaining Clayton Act relief. *Id.* § 40307(d); *see Seawinds*, 80 B.R. at 183 ("The Shipping Act of 1984 expressly bars private antitrust suits based on conduct prohibited by the Act."). As explained above, the Shipping Act specifically provides that operating under an unfiled, and hence ineffective, agreement is a prohibited act, *id.* § 41102(b), and those injured by such a prohibited act cannot obtain Clayton Act relief, *id.* § 40307(d).

Plaintiffs nonetheless argue that Clayton Act immunity set forth in § 40307(a) must be read in light of § 40307(d) and suggest that the two provisions cover the same subjects.

[11] Like H. Rep. 98-53 discussed above, *supra* note 7, S. Rep. No. 98-3 relates to the proposed but not passed Shipping Act of 1983, which is the same as the Shipping Act of 1984 in all relevant respects.

They are mistaken. In § 40307(a), Congress granted immunity from antitrust prosecution for conduct permitted by the Shipping Act, while in § 40307(d) Congress provided immunity from private Clayton Act liability for conduct prohibited by the Shipping Act. Plaintiffs' reading destroys this carefully drawn delineation.

For all of these reasons, Plaintiffs cannot obtain Clayton Act relief, and the District Court correctly dismissed Plaintiffs' Clayton Act claims.[12] **[—26—]**

IV

We next examine whether the District Court correctly concluded that IPPs' state law antitrust, consumer protection, and unjust enrichment claims are preempted.

A

The preemption doctrine is based on the Supremacy Clause, which provides that "the Laws of the United States . . . shall be the supreme Law of the Land . . . any Thing in the Constitution or Laws of any State to the Contrary notwithstanding." U.S. Const. art. VI, cl. 2. Congress thus **[—27—]** has the power to preempt state law. *Arizona v. United States*, 132 S. Ct. 2492, 2500 (2012) (citation omitted). **{-84-}**

Preemption is an affirmative defense, *In re Asbestos Prods. Liab. Litig. (No. VI)*, 822 F.3d 125, 133 n.6 (3d Cir. 2016), and so we examine only the defense asserted before us, *see Oneok, Inc. v. Learjet, Inc.*, 135 S. Ct. 1591, 1595, 1602 (2015). Defendants argue that IPPs' state law claims are subject to conflict preemption.[13] There are two types of conflict preemption: (1) where "compliance with both federal and state duties is simply impossible," and (2) where "compliance with both laws is possible, yet state law poses an obstacle to the full achievement of federal purposes." *MD Mall Assocs. v. CSX Transp., Inc.*, 715 F.3d 479, 495 (3d Cir. 2013). Defendants rely on "obstacle" conflict preemption. Thus, we will examine whether IPPs' state law claims pose an obstacle to achieving Congress's goals under the Shipping Act.

B

1

We recognize that "all preemption cases 'start with the assumption that the historic police powers of the States were not to be superseded by [a] [f]ederal [a]ct unless that was the **[—28—]** clear and manifest purpose of Congress.'" *Sikkelee v. Precision Airmotive Corp.*, 822 F.3d 680, 687 (3d Cir. 2016) (quoting *Wyeth v. Levine*, 555 U.S. 555, 565 (2009)), *cert. denied sub nom. Avco Corp. v.*

---

12 Plaintiffs alternatively argue that the complaints should not be dismissed with respect to contracts for the shipping of "new[ly] assembled motor vehicles." 46 U.S.C. § 40502. They raised this argument for the first time during oral argument before the District Court, and when the District Court confronted them with the fact that this was a new argument, they agreed not to "make those arguments." Defs. App. 141. Despite this statement, Plaintiffs argue that they did not waive the argument because it is currently pending before the District Court in a different case. Raising the **[—26—]** argument in another case does not cure their failure to raise the argument here, and this failure waives the argument. *Brenner v. Local 514, United Bhd. of Carpenters & Joiners of Am.*, 927 F.2d 1283, 1298 (3d Cir. 1991).

Even if the argument were not waived, it would not change the outcome. Section 40502 provides that the requirement to file a service contract with the FMC does not apply to contracts regarding "new[ly] assembled motor vehicles." 46 U.S.C. § 40502(b) ("Each service contract entered into under this section by an individual ocean common carrier or an agreement shall be filed confidentially with the Federal Maritime Commission. . . . [This provision] does not apply to contracts regarding . . . new assembled motor vehicles."). This exemption from filing service contracts for newly assembled motor vehicles, however, does not relieve Defendants from their obligation to file the other agreements referred to in § 40301(a) or (b) with the FMC.

13 Although the Shipping Act contains no express preemption clause or savings clause, that does not "'bar[ ] the ordinary working of conflict pre-emption principles.'" *Buckman Co. v. Plaintiffs' Legal Comm.*, 531 U.S. 341, 352 (2001) (quoting *Geier v. Am. Honda Motor Co.*, 529 U.S. 861, 869 (2000)).

Sikkelee, --- S. Ct. ----, 2016 WL 4944476 (Nov. 28, 2016).[14] From this assumption, we presume claims based on laws embodying state police powers are not preempted. This "presumption against preemption," however, does not apply here because our case concerns the regulation of international maritime commerce, an area uniquely in the federal domain. *United States v. Locke*, 529 U.S. 89, 108 (2000) ("The state laws now in question bear upon national and international maritime commerce, and in this area there is no beginning assumption that concurrent regulation by the State is a valid exercise of its police powers."); *see also Farina v. Nokia Inc.*, 625 F.3d 97, 116 (3d Cir. 2010) ("The presumption applies with particular force in fields within the police powers of the state, but does not apply where state regulation has traditionally been absent." (citation omitted)).[15] **[—29—]**

2

As there is no presumption against preemption in this case dealing with maritime conduct, we will determine whether the Shipping Act preempts IPPs' state law claims. This requires us to consider Congress's intent. *Mabey Bridge & Shore, Inc. v. Schoch*, 666 F.3d 862, 868 (3d Cir. 2012); *see also Wyeth*, 555 U.S. at 565. To do so, we consider the language, structure, and purpose of the **{-85-}** statute, as well as legislative history where appropriate. *See Sikkelee*, 822 F.3d at 687; *Bruesewitz v. Wyeth, Inc.*, 561 F.3d 233, 243-44 (3d Cir. 2009).

As noted previously, one purpose of the Act is to "establish a nondiscriminatory regulatory process for the common carriage of goods by water in the foreign commerce of the United States with a minimum of government intervention and regulatory costs." 46 U.S.C. § 40101(1). A second purpose is to ensure that U.S.-flag ships are on a level playing field with foreign vessels. *See, e.g., id.* § 40101(2) (stating that a purpose of the Act is to provide an efficient system of ocean transportation that is "in harmony with, and responsive to, international shipping practices").

To those ends, the Act granted ocean common carriers certain antitrust immunities. Section 40307(a) expressly immunizes agreements filed with the FMC from the federal criminal and civil antitrust laws, and § 40307(d) bars recovery of damages and injunctions under the Clayton Act for conduct prohibited by the Act. Through these provisions, Congress sought to limit the application of the antitrust laws to enable U.S.-flag carriers to compete against their foreign counterparts who may not be subject to similar restrictions. **[—30—]** *See* H.R. Rep. No. 98-53(I), at 9, 10 (noting "[t]he perception . . . that the threat of U.S. antitrust prosecution weighs much more heavily on U.S. operators than their foreign-flag competition" and recognizing a "need to foster a regulatory environment in which U.S.-flag liner operators are not placed at a competitive disadvantage vis-a-vis their foreign-flag competitors"); S. Rep. No. 98-3, at 7 (noting trading partners' "blocking statutes" and stating that "[c]lear antitrust immunity . . . marks a major step in revitalizing our maritime industry because it removes a major handicap created by uneven enforcement"); *see also* S. Rep. No. 98-3, at 1 (recommending the bill "in order to . . . harmonize U.S. shipping practices with those of our major trading partners, especially by reaffirming antitrust immunity for certain carrier and conference activities"). To allow state antitrust claims to proceed would interfere with this goal. *See Am. Ass'n of Cruise Passengers, Inc. v. Carnival Cruise Lines, Inc.*, 911 F.2d 786, 792 (D.C. Cir. 1990) ("Congress was concerned about a carrier being subject to 'parallel jurisdiction,' i.e., remedies and sanctions for the same conduct made unlawful by both the Shipping Act and the antitrust laws." (emphasis and citation omitted)); H.R. Rep.

---

[14] This assumption is invoked "because respect for the States as 'independent sovereigns in our federal system' leads us to assume that 'Congress does not cavalierly pre-empt state-law causes of action.'" *Wyeth*, 555 U.S. at 565 n.3 (quoting *Medtronic, Inc. v. Lohr*, 518 U.S. 470, 485 (1996)).

[15] Even if the presumption did apply, the text, purposes, scheme, and legislative history of the Shipping Act embody a "clear and manifest" congressional intention to preempt the state laws in question. *See Farina*, 625 F.3d at 117 (citation omitted).

No. 98-53(I), at 12 (reflecting Congress's intent "that violations of this Act not result in the creation of parallel jurisdiction over persons or matters which are subject to the Shipping Act"). Put simply, to subject the carriers to potential state antitrust liability would essentially undo Congress's work in expanding antitrust immunity and undermine its efforts to assist U.S.-flag ships avoid a competitive disadvantage. *See* H.R. Rep. No. 98-53(I), at 25 (noting that the Act would meet the objective to keep ocean liners "free of . . . threatened penalties under changing **[—31—]** interpretations of the antitrust laws"). Thus, we hold that the Shipping Act preempts IPPs' state law antitrust claims.

IPPs' consumer protection and unjust enrichment claims are also preempted. While these state laws reflect the exercise of traditional police powers, applying them here would allow the States to impose rules in an area Congress has historically regulated: maritime commerce. *Locke*, 529 U.S. at 108. It would also thwart Congress's goal of ensuring uniform regulation of ocean common **{-86-}** carriers' business practices.[16] *See* 46 U.S.C. § 40101(1)-(2); Report of the Senate Committee on Commerce, Science, and Transportation, S. Rep. No. 98-3, 98th Cong., 1st Sess. at 1 (supporting the bill to end, among other things, "the uncertainty and delay that surrounds U.S. Government regulation of ocean liner shipping, by providing a predictable legal regime and streamlined regulatory process administered and enforced by a single independent Federal agency (the [FMC])").

To achieve these goals, Congress prohibited certain activities. Among other things, the Shipping Act makes certain unfair devices unlawful, such as operating under unfiled and ineffective agreements on specific matters, *id.* § 41102(b), failing to establish just and reasonable regulations **[—32—]** and practices regarding receiving, handling, storing, or delivering property, *id.* § 41102(c), unreasonably refusing to deal or negotiate, *id.* §§ 41104(10), 41105, and allocating shippers in an unauthorized manner among specific carriers who were parties to an agreement, *id.* § 41105.

In addition to prohibiting such acts, Congress created specific enforcement mechanisms for persons and entities injured by these illegal practices. It empowered the FMC to investigate and punish illegal conduct pursuant to a uniform regime. By granting the FMC this authority, Congress has put in place a regulator familiar with complex foreign commerce issues confronting ocean common carriers. This expertise enables the FMC to make informed decisions about whether conduct violates the Act and warrants punishment.[17] *See Farina*, 625 F.3d at 126; 46 U.S.C. §§ 41109, 41305. **[—33—]**

[16] This is not to say that all conduct in which ocean common carriers engage is never subject to state law. *See, e.g., Pasha Auto Warehousing, Inc. v. Phila. Reg'l Port Auth.*, No. CIV. A. 96-6779, 1998 WL 188848, at *6-9 (E.D. Pa. Apr. 21, 1998) (concluding that the FMC did not have exclusive or primary jurisdiction over declaratory relief action concerning lease agreements).

[17] At least where the subject matter is technical and the history and background are complex and extensive, we give some deference to an agency's explanation of how state law affects the federal scheme. *See Farina*, 625 F.3d at 126-27. The weight accorded to "the agency's explanation of state law's impact on the federal scheme depends on its thoroughness, consistency, and pervasiveness." *Wyeth*, 555 U.S. at 577 (citing *United States v. Mead Corp.*, 533 U.S. 218, 234-35 (2001), and *Skidmore v. Swift & Co.*, 323 U.S. 134, 140 (1944)). Here, the FMC and United States, as amici, assert that IPPs' state law antitrust claims are not preempted (but appear to take no position with respect to IPPs' other state law claims). We decline to defer to their views on preemption in this case. First, they discuss field preemption but, as stated above, that is not the preemption defense asserted before us. Second, to the extent amici seek to draw a **[—33—]** distinction between filed and unfiled agreements, we need not address that distinction because only unfiled agreements are at issue here. Finally, the FMC's and United States' position on conflict preemption is not "persuasive[ ]." *See Wyeth*, 555 U.S. at 577. We recognize, as they assert, that the Shipping Act and its legislative history are silent regarding state law claims. However, the position that the Shipping Act contemplates state law antitrust enforcement is inconsistent with the conclusion that the Shipping Act bars Clayton Act claims (with which amici agree); it also overlooks the purposes of the Act as set forth in the statute and legislative history as

Moreover, Congress provided a means for private parties injured by the illegal acts of such carriers to seek relief ranging from double damages and attorneys' fees to injunctions. Allowing state laws to impose different standards would upset this **{-87-}** carefully crafted scheme.[18] *See* **[—34—]** *Farina*, 625 F.3d at 123 ("Allowing state law to impose a different standard permits a re-balancing of those considerations."); *cf. Buckman Co. v. Plaintiff's Legal Comm.*, 531 U.S. 341, 348 (2001) ("The balance sought by the Administration can be skewed by allowing fraud-on-the-FDA claims under state tort law."). Further, allowing juries to decide liability, as IPPs seek, would conflict with the scheme that vests the FMC with decision-making power. *See Farina*, 625 F.3d at 125 ("Allowing juries to impose liability on cell phone companies for claims like Farina's would conflict with the FCC's regulations."). For these reasons, permitting IPPs to pursue their state law claims that Defendants allegedly had secret agreements to coordinate price increases, not to compete, and to restrict capacity would interfere with Congress's goal of uniform regulation of common carriers' international maritime activity. *See* 46 U.S.C. § 40101(1)-(2).

Accordingly, we hold that the Shipping Act preempts IPPs' state law consumer protection and unjust enrichment claims because allowing them to proceed would pose an obstacle to achieving Congress's objectives in passing the Act. **[—35—]**

V

IPPs' challenge to the District Court's order denying their request that it reconsider the dismissal order also fails. A judgment may be altered under Rule 59(e) if the party seeking reconsideration shows at least one of the following: "(1) an intervening change in the controlling law; (2) the availability of new evidence that was not available when the court granted the motion . . . ; or (3) the need to correct a clear error of law or fact or to prevent manifest injustice." *Howard Hess Dental Labs. Inc. v. Dentsply Int'l, Inc.*, 602 F.3d 237, 251 (3d Cir. 2010) (citation and internal quotation marks omitted). Similarly, Rule 60(b) provides, in relevant part, relief from a judgment for: (1) "mistake, inadvertence, surprise, or excusable neglect," Fed. R. Civ. P. 60(b)(1); (2) a "judgment [that] is void," Fed. R. Civ. P. 60(b)(4); or (3) "any other reason that justifies relief," Fed. R. Civ. P. 60(b)(6).

IPPs asked the District Court to reconsider its dismissal order and "retain jurisdiction over claims asserted against K Line and MOL [Defendants] for the limited purpose" of approving class action settlements. Joint App. 60. However, IPPs did not submit a motion for preliminary and final approval of any settlement or a motion to stay the matter before the District Court dismissed Plaintiffs' claims. Furthermore, IPPs did not identify an intervening change in the controlling law, present new evidence, allege that the District Court's opinion was the result of a **{-88-}** clear error of fact or law, or point to any extraordinary circumstance that would warrant granting relief. Because IPPs failed to meet any of the grounds for reconsideration, the District Court did not **[—36—]**

---

well as the comprehensive scheme for enforcement of Shipping Act violations before the FMC.

[18] We have observed that situations in which the federal government "is required to strike a balance between competing statutory objectives lend themselves to a finding of conflict preemption." *Farina*, 625 F.3d at 123; *see also Buckman*, 531 U.S. at 348 ("The conflict stems from the fact that the federal statutory scheme amply empowers the FDA to punish and deter fraud against the [FDA], and that this authority is used by the [FDA] to achieve a somewhat delicate balance of statutory objectives. The balance sought by the [FDA] can be skewed by allowing fraud-on-the-FDA claims under state tort law."); *City of Burbank v. Lockheed Air Terminal Inc.*, 411 U.S. 624, 638-39 (1973) ("The Federal Aviation Act requires a delicate balance between safety and efficiency, and the protection of persons on the ground. . . . **[—34—]** The interdependence of these factors requires a uniform and exclusive system of federal regulation if the congressional objectives underlying the Federal Aviation Act are to be fulfilled." (citation omitted)). This case presents such a situation.

abuse its discretion in denying their motions for reconsideration.[19]

VI

For the foregoing reasons, we will affirm.

[19] IPPs argue that the District Court "erred in concluding that it lacked subject matter jurisdiction to effectuate settlements with the two largest defendants." IPP Appellants' Br. 44. The Court did not deny IPPs' motions for reconsideration on the basis of a lack of subject matter jurisdiction. Indeed, it was aware that it possessed subject matter jurisdiction over the dispute and exercised its discretion not to entertain the request to approve the settlements because it had determined that the FMC provided a forum to resolve Plaintiffs' dispute.

United States Court of Appeals
for the Third Circuit

No. 16-1772

IN RE CHRISTOPHER COLUMBUS, LLC

Appeal from the United States District Court for the Eastern District of Pennsylvania

Decided: September 25, 2017

Citation: 872 F.3d 130, 5 Adm. R. 120 (3d Cir. 2017).

Before **HARDIMAN** and **KRAUSE**, Circuit Judges, and **STENGEL**, Chief District Judge.*

* The Honorable Lawrence F. Stengel, United States District Court for the Eastern District of Pennsylvania, sitting by designation.

[—3—] {–131–} STENGEL, Chief District Judge:

Christopher Columbus, LLC appeals the District Court's dismissal of its limitation action, brought pursuant to the Limitation of Vessel Owner's Liability Act, 46 U.S.C. § 30511. Christopher Columbus filed this action after Appellee Michael Bocchino filed a negligence lawsuit against it in the Philadelphia Court of Common Pleas. Both of these actions arise out of a drunken brawl which erupted among passengers who were enjoying a cruise on the Delaware River onboard the vessel Ben Franklin Yacht. Following a hearing on the issue of subject-matter jurisdiction in the limitation action, the District Court found that maritime jurisdiction was lacking and dismissed the limitation action. For the reasons that follow, we find there is maritime jurisdiction over the dispute, and we will therefore vacate the District Court's dismissal of the limitation action.

I <u>Background</u>

Christopher Columbus owns and operates the passenger vessel "Ben Franklin Yacht," which provides cruise services **[—4—]** on the Delaware River.[1] The Ben Franklin Yacht, which is over eighty feet long and has three passenger decks, departs from and docks at Pier 24, located at 401 North Columbus Boulevard in Philadelphia, Pennsylvania. Pier 24 is located just north of the Ben Franklin Bridge and is adjacent to the main shipping channel of the Delaware River.

Bocchino was a patron on a cruise on the Ben Franklin Yacht on May 3, 2013. Bocchino was apparently "assaulted on the vessel and/or in the parking lot near the **{–132–}** dock where the Ben Franklin Yacht was moored by 'unknown patrons of the cruise and/or agents, servant[s], workmen and/or employees'" of Christopher Columbus. App. 47a. Bocchino filed a complaint against the Ben Franklin Yacht and others in the Court of Common Pleas for Philadelphia County, alleging claims for negligence, negligent infliction of emotional distress, assault, and punitive damages. Christopher Columbus then filed its Complaint for Exoneration From or Limitation of Liability in federal court ("the limitation action"). Bocchino and three additional passengers on the May 3, 2013 cruise asserted claims in the limitation action, alleging that (1) while passengers for hire on the Ben Franklin Yacht, they were assaulted and injured by fellow passengers,[2] and (2) the vessel's crewmembers caused these injuries by providing **[—5—]** inadequate security and overserving alcohol to passengers. The claimants asserted that the assaults began while they were still onboard the vessel and while the vessel was in the process of berthing at Pier 24.

While cross-motions for summary judgment were pending, the District Court *sua sponte* ordered argument and invited briefing on the issue of subject-matter jurisdiction. After hearing oral argument, the District Court determined that the test for maritime jurisdiction had not been met and dismissed the limitation action for lack of subject-matter jurisdiction. For the reasons discussed below, we will reverse.

[1] The Ben Franklin Yacht is documented by the United States Coast Guard to carry paying passengers on cruises.

[2] Bocchino claimed to have been assaulted while aboard the vessel and in the parking lot on the pier, while the other three claimants alleged that they were assaulted on the vessel.

II Jurisdiction and Standard of Review

We have jurisdiction over this appeal under 28 U.S.C. § 1291. We review de novo a district court's determination of its own admiralty jurisdiction.[3] *Hargus v. Ferocious & **[—6—]** Impetuous, LLC*, 840 F.3d 133, 135, 4 Adm. R. 155, 156 (3d Cir. 2016) (citing *Maher Terminals, LLC v. Port Auth. of N.Y. & N.J.*, 805 F.3d 98, 104, 3 Adm. R. 164, 165-66 (3d Cir. 2015) and *Sinclair v. Soniform, Inc.*, 935 F.2d 599, 601 (3d Cir. 1991)). **{-133-}**

[3] This appeal comes to us in a somewhat unusual posture for a determination of admiralty jurisdiction. It is more often the case that the question of whether admiralty jurisdiction applies to a particular dispute is raised at the outset, and is therefore answered on the basis of the allegations in the pleadings. *See, e.g., Maher Terminals, LLC v. Port Auth. of N.Y. & N.J.*, 805 F.3d 98, 104, 3 Adm. R. 164, 165-66 (3d Cir. 2015). At the initial stages of litigation in this case, both sides agreed that there was subject-matter jurisdiction. It was only later, after the District Court had been presented with the parties' summary judgment motions and their competing sets of disputed facts taken from a developed evidentiary record, that the District Court questioned whether there was admiralty jurisdiction in this case. The nature of the "attack" on jurisdiction was, therefore, factual rather than facial. *See, e.g., Constitution Party of Pa. v.* **[—6—]** *Aichele*, 757 F.3d 347, 358 (3d Cir. 2014) (distinguishing facial attacks on jurisdiction from factual attacks). Thus, while the issue did not arise in the context of a motion to dismiss, it is akin to a factual attack which "is an argument that there is no subject matter jurisdiction because the facts of the case—and here the District Court may look beyond the pleadings to ascertain the facts—do not support the asserted jurisdiction." *Id.* Accordingly, when assessing our subject-matter jurisdiction over Christopher Columbus's limitation action, we rely on the undisputed facts drawn from the summary judgment record. *See id.* (discussing "the standard of review applicable to a factual attack, in which a court may weigh and 'consider evidence outside the pleadings.'") (quoting *Gould Elecs. Inc. v. United States*, 220 F.3d 169, 176 (3d Cir. 2000)); *see also Hartig Drug Co. Inc. v. Senju Pharm. Co.*, 836 F.3d 261, 268 (3d Cir. 2016) (explaining that a factual attack on subject-matter jurisdiction "strips the plaintiff of the protections and factual deference provided under 12(b)(6) review.") (citing *Davis v. Wells Fargo*, 824 F.3d 333, 348–50 (3d Cir. 2016)).

III Discussion

Christopher Columbus raises three principal arguments on appeal, but we address only the first:[4] whether the District **[—7—]** Court erred in finding that the alleged incident aboard the Ben Franklin Yacht had insufficient potential to disrupt maritime commerce, and that therefore admiralty jurisdiction pursuant to 28 U.S.C. § 1333(1) was lacking. Appellee Michael Bocchino did not file a cross-appeal, so we do not address his contention that the District Court erred in dismissing his summary judgment motion as moot.[5] **[—8—]**

[4] Because we find that the test for admiralty jurisdiction pursuant to 28 U.S.C. § 1333(1) is satisfied, we need not address Christopher Columbus's second and third issues on appeal: that the District Court erred in finding that the **[—7—]** Extension of Admiralty Jurisdiction Act, 46 U.S.C. § 30101(a), did not confer an independent basis for jurisdiction; and that the District Court erred in finding that the Limitation of Vessel Owner's Liability Act, 46 U.S.C. § 30501, *et seq.*, did not confer an independent basis for jurisdiction.

[5] Bocchino asserts that the entirety of the District Court's Dismissal Order is now before us for review because Christopher Columbus did not limit its Notice of Appeal to the portion of the Order dismissing the case for lack of subject-matter jurisdiction. He therefore urges us to consider whether his motion for summary judgment should have been granted, instead of being denied as moot, in light of what he contends are undisputed facts showing that he is entitled to summary judgment in the limitation action, so that he may then proceed in state court with his negligence action.

We have previously said that "an appellee may, without taking a cross-appeal, support the judgment as entered through any matter appearing in the record, though his argument may attack the lower court's reasoning or bring forth a matter overlooked or ignored by the court." *EF Operating Corp. v. Am. Bldgs.*, 993 F.2d 1046, 1048 (3d Cir. 1993) (citations omitted). **[—8—]**

Here, Bocchino does not seek to support the District Court's decision to dismiss for lack of subject-matter jurisdiction, or its denial of the summary judgment motions as moot, through alternative grounds. Instead, he seeks to have his summary judgment motion granted on the merits, so that the limitation action can be dismissed and the case can be remanded to state court for a jury

Under the United States Constitution, the federal courts have the power to hear "all Cases of admiralty and maritime Jurisdiction." U.S. Const. art. III, § 2, cl. 1. Congress codified that jurisdiction at 28 U.S.C. § 1333(1), which provides that federal district courts have original jurisdiction over "[a]ny civil case of admiralty or maritime jurisdiction." 28 U.S.C. § 1333(1). As noted in our recent decision in *Hargus v. Ferocious & Impetuous, LLC*, "[t]he fundamental interest **[—9—]** giving rise to maritime jurisdiction is 'the protection of maritime commerce.'" 840 F.3d at 136, 4 Adm. R. at 156 (quoting *Sisson v. Ruby*, 497 U.S. 358, 367 (1990) (citation omitted)).

With respect to maritime tort claims, the test for determining admiralty jurisdiction concerns both the incident's location and its connection with maritime activity: **{-134-}**

> When a party seeks to invoke federal admiralty jurisdiction over a tort claim, the claim "must satisfy conditions both of location and of connection with maritime activity." *Jerome B. Grubart, Inc. v. Great Lakes Dredge & Dock Co.*, 513 U.S. 527, 534 (1995)). The location aspect is satisfied if "the tort occurred on navigable water" or the "injury suffered on land was caused by a vessel on navigable water." *Id.* The connection aspect is a conjunctive two-part inquiry. First, we "must 'assess the general features of the type of incident involved' to determine whether the incident has 'a potentially disruptive impact on maritime commerce.'" *Id.* (quoting *Sisson v. Ruby*, 497 U.S. 358, 363, 364 n.2 (1990)). Second, we "must determine whether 'the general character' of the 'activity giving rise to the incident' shows a 'substantial relationship to traditional maritime activity.'" *Id.* (quoting *Sisson*, 497 U.S. at 364 n.2, 365). Federal admiralty jurisdiction is only proper when the location test and both prongs of the connection test are satisfied. *Id.*

Hargus, 840 F.3d at 136, 4 Adm. R. at 156. **[—10—]**

As Bocchino concedes, the location aspect of the jurisdictional test is satisfied because the alleged tort occurred on the Delaware River. Bocchino also concedes that the second part of the connection test is satisfied, because carrying passengers for hire on a vessel on navigable waters is substantially related to traditional maritime activity. Thus, our analysis of whether there is admiralty jurisdiction in this case is focused on the first part of the connection test: an assessment of the general features of the incident, and whether such an incident has the potential to disrupt maritime commerce.

The United States Supreme Court has instructed courts to "assess the general features of the type of incident involved to determine whether such an incident is likely to disrupt commercial activity." *Sisson*, 497 U.S. at 363. Such an assessment "turns . . . on a description of the incident at an intermediate level of possible generality." *Jerome B. Grubart, Inc. v. Great Lakes Dredge & Dock Co.*, 513 U.S. 527, 538 (1995). As discussed in our decision in *Hargus*, *Sisson* and *Grubart* provide illustrative examples of how the specific factual details of an incident may be distilled into a description of the general character of that incident.

In *Sisson*, a fire started in the washer/dryer area of a pleasure yacht docked at a marina on Lake Michigan, which

---

trial. In other words, he asks that, if we reverse the District Court on the issue of subject-matter jurisdiction, we decide the merits of his summary judgment motion in his favor. Seeking this form of relief, in light of the procedural history of this case, requires a cross-appeal. *See EF Operating Corp.*, 993 F.2d at 1048–49 (reasoning that "[a] grant of summary judgment and a dismissal for lack of personal jurisdiction . . . are wholly different forms of relief. The latter is a dismissal without prejudice, whereas the former is a ruling on the merits which if affirmed would have preclusive effect" and holding that a cross-appeal was required) (citation omitted). Accordingly, because Bocchino did not file a cross-appeal, we will not consider in the first instance his argument that summary judgment should have been entered in his favor, and leave it to the District Court to address the merits of that motion on remand.

destroyed the yacht and damaged several other vessels as well as the marina. 497 U.S. at 360. For connection test purposes, the Court described the incident as "a fire that began on a noncommercial vessel at a marina located on a navigable **[—11—]** waterway."[6] *Id.* at 362. In *Grubart*, the Court considered an incident where "flooding [of basements in downtown Chicago allegedly] resulted from events several months earlier, when . . . Great Lakes Dredge and Dock Company had used a crane, sitting on a barge in the river next to a bridge, to drive piles into the riverbed above the tunnel." *Grubart*, 513 U.S. at 529. There, the Court described the incident as "damage by a vessel in navigable water to an underwater structure." *Id.* at 539. **{-135-}**

Our own maritime tort jurisprudence is also instructive when crafting "general features" descriptions for purposes of applying the connection test to a particular set of facts. For example, in *Neely v. Club Med Management Services, Inc.*, we considered a scenario where a scuba-diving instructor and vessel crewmember was injured after being hit by a dive boat's propellers while she was out with resort patrons. 63 F.3d 166, 170 (3d Cir. 1995) (en banc). The description we chose for purposes of determining jurisdiction was "damage by a vessel in navigable water to [a seaman]." *Id.* at 179 (alteration in original). Most recently, in *Hargus*, we were presented with a case where the captain of the vessel One Love threw an empty insulated coffee cup from the beach that hit a passenger standing on the One Love, which at the time was anchored in knee-deep water approximately twenty-five feet away. *Hargus*, 840 F.3d at 134–35, 4 Adm. R. at 155. We described that activity as "throwing a small inert object from land at an individual onboard an anchored vessel." *Id.* at 137, 4 Adm. R. at 157. **[—12—]**

In formulating a general features description in this case, we are mindful of the Supreme Court's caution to avoid descriptions that are "too general" such that they cannot be useful in comparing cases, or descriptions that are overly specific such that they would ignore an incident's capacity to have an effect on maritime commerce. *See Grubart*, 513 U.S. at 538–39 (discussing the incident in *Sisson* and observing that "[t]o speak of the incident as 'fire' would have been too general to differentiate cases; at the other extreme, to have described the fire as damaging nothing but pleasure boats and their tie-up facilities would have ignored, among other things, the capacity of pleasure boats to endanger commercial shipping that happened to be nearby."). Rather, we must look at the facts of this case and formulate a description that will enable us to determine "whether the incident could be seen within a class of incidents that posed more than a fanciful risk to commercial shipping." *Id.* at 539. Applying these principles, we hold that the incident at issue here is best described as "an altercation between passengers on a boat in the process of docking."[7] **[—13—]** Describing the incident this way captures the general nature of the tort and its attendant circumstances without being too generic or too specific.[8] *Grubart*, 513 U.S. at 538–39. **[—14—]** **{-136-}**

---

[6] In a subsequent case, the Court referred to the incident in *Sisson* as "the burning of docked boats at a marina on navigable waters." *Grubart*, 513 U.S. at 533–34.

[7] Taking the disputed and undisputed facts into account, the District Court concluded that "the fight, if one occurred, erupted toward the end of the cruise." App. 9a–10a. The degree to which the Ben Franklin Yacht had completed docking was unclear as a result of conflicting deposition testimony from crewmembers and the claimants. The District Court specifically noted the following factual disputes: whether the vessel was docking or docked when the altercation occurred; the magnitude of the altercation and the total number of passengers involved, which was allegedly as many as forty to forty-five passengers; whether and when members of the crew became involved in resolving the altercation; and whether passengers left the vessel on their own or with the assistance of **[—13—]** the vessel's employees and crew. Thus, although it is not possible to ascertain the location of the vessel relative to the pier on the summary judgment record before us, such a precise determination is unnecessary to resolve the question of subject matter jurisdiction. For purposes of crafting a general features description to which the connection test may be applied, we need only state that the vessel was "in the process of docking" while the altercation was occurring.

[8] After reviewing and comparing the witnesses' recollections and setting forth the parties' respective versions of the disputed facts based on

Having crafted our description of the general features of the incident in this case, we must now "ascertain 'whether the incident could be seen within a class of incidents that posed more than a fanciful risk to commercial shipping.'" *Hargus*, 840 F.3d at 136, 4 Adm. R. at 156 (quoting *Grubart*, 513 U.S. at 539). We turn to the first prong of the connection test, which "requires us to assess the 'potential' disruptive effects that the type of incident involved could have on maritime commerce, not whether the particular incident at hand actually disrupted maritime commerce." *Id.* at 136, 4 Adm. R. at 156 (quoting *Grubart*, 513 U.S. at 538–39). A brief review of our discussion in *Hargus* illustrates the type of factors to consider when assessing an incident's potential to disrupt maritime commerce.

In *Hargus*, we discussed *Tandon v. Captain's Cove Marina of Bridgeport, Inc.*, a Second Circuit case which involved an injury to passengers that did not have the potential to disrupt maritime commerce. *Hargus*, 840 F.3d at 137, 4 Adm. R. at 157 (citing *Tandon*, 752 F.3d 239, 249, 2 Adm. R. 57, 64 (2d Cir. 2014)). The Second Circuit described the general features of the incident as "a physical altercation among recreational visitors on and around a permanent dock surrounded by navigable water." *Tandon*, 752 F.3d at 249, 2 Adm. R. at 64. The court found that the incident did not have the potential to disrupt maritime commerce because it "threaten[ed] only its participants," could not "create any obstruction to the free passage of commercial ships along navigable waterways" or "lead to a disruption in the course of the waterway itself," and could not "immediately damage nearby commercial vessels." *Id.*, 2 Adm. R. at 64-65. In addition, because the incident did not occur at sea, it "could not 'distract the crew from their duties, endangering the safety of the vessel and risking collision with others on the same waterway,'" nor could it "force the vessel 'to divert from its course to obtain medical **[—15—]** care for the injured person,'" who "was not 'employed in maritime commerce.'" *Hargus*, 840 F.3d at 137, 4 Adm. R. at 157 (quoting *Tandon*, 752 F.3d at 250, 2 Adm. R. at 65). The Second Circuit was careful to note that "the class of incidents we consider here includes only fights on permanent docks . . . . This type of incident does not pose the same risks to maritime commerce as a fistfight occurring on a vessel on navigable water." *Tandon*, 752 F.3d at 250, 2 Adm. R. at 65. This was so, in part because "[a] fight on a vessel may distract the crew from their duties, endangering the safety of the vessel and risking collision with others on the same waterway." *Id.*, 2 Adm. R. at 65.

Similar assessments in this case lead us to conclude that an altercation between passengers on a boat in the process of docking has the potential to disrupt maritime commerce. Although the record is unclear about the location of the vessel when the fight broke out, how many people were involved in the fight, and the crew's involvement, if any, in stopping the fight, there are numerous scenarios that could result from a passenger altercation, each of which poses more than a fanciful risk to maritime commerce. First, this type of incident has the potential to distract the captain or crew during the docking procedure, which could have resulted **{–137–}** in the vessel crashing into or in some way colliding with the pier, causing damage to the vessel or to the pier. Depending on the degree of damage to the pier, it could be rendered unusable. Second, a mishap during docking also has the potential to cause injuries to passengers or the crew, the latter of which could leave the vessel unable to dock at

---

the summary judgment record, the District Court concluded that the incident "should be described as something like a physical altercation among recreational passengers on board a vessel that is in the immediate process of docking." App. 23a. We respectfully disagree with the District Court's formulation of a general features description, as it is too specific in the following three ways: first, a verbal altercation arising at an inopportune time could be as distracting to the crew as a physical altercation; second, the fact that the passengers are "recreational" is not a determinative factor for admiralty jurisdiction, so long as the activity underlying the incident has a "substantial relationship to a 'traditional maritime activity,'" *Sisson*, 497 U.S. at 365; and third, the "immediacy" of the Ben Franklin Yacht's docking at the time the altercation started is not clear from the record. For these reasons, we have chosen the slightly more generalized description set forth above.

the pier. Such injuries could require a rescue of those on board, which might then lead to a Coast Guard investigation. Finally, if the crew was sufficiently sidetracked by the altercation and unable to execute the docking maneuver, the vessel could be forced back out on the **[—16—]** waterway with a veritable riot among the passengers. That would certainly be distracting to the captain and crew, and also pose a risk to nearby vessels. Any of these outcomes were possible, and all have the potential to disrupt maritime commerce.

Bocchino's argument to the contrary is not persuasive. He asserts that, due to the nature of the finger pier where the Ben Franklin Yacht docks, the vessel was not in open waters during the altercation, and thus could not encounter other vessels or block their navigation, cause a disruption on the waterway, or cause any immediate damage to other vessels while docking because it was in an isolated location. This argument has two flaws. First, it depends in part on the overly-specific "general features" description Bocchino proposes, which characterizes Pier 24 as an "isolated location." Bocchino Br. 18 n.4. Second, it focuses on what did not actually happen to the Ben Franklin Yacht as a result of the altercation taking place while the vessel was in the process of docking, rather than what *could* have happened. As previously stated, the connection test requires us to "assess the 'potential' disruptive effects that the type of incident involved *could* have on maritime commerce, not whether the particular incident at hand *actually* disrupted maritime commerce." *Hargus*, 840 F.3d at 136, 4 Adm. R. at 156 (emphases added) (citing *Grubart*, 513 U.S. at 538–39); *see also Tandon*, 752 F.3d at 252 n.8, 2 Adm. R. at 67 n.8 (noting that, to the extent that the parties arguing in favor of maritime jurisdiction rested their argument "on specific aspects of the incident that actually occurred, [that argument] clearly fails, because our analysis looks only to the general type of incident at issue rather than particular facts about that incident.") (citing *Grubart*, 513 U.S. at 538). Had the altercation distracted the crew or required their intervention during the docking **[—17—]** process—two very real possibilities—any damage to the vessel or the pier that may have resulted could easily have caused a disruption to maritime commerce.[9] Hence, our conclusion that the first prong of the connection test is met. As the other aspects of the location and connection tests are satisfied, we therefore hold that admiralty jurisdiction is appropriate in this case.

* * *

For the reasons stated, we will reverse the judgment of the District Court and vacate its dismissal of the limitation action. This case is remanded for further proceedings consistent with this opinion.

---

[9] We respectfully disagree with the District Court's assessment that, based on its view that the Ben Franklin Yacht was in the immediate process of docking when the altercation started, the risk of disrupting maritime commerce was merely fanciful. The general features of this type of incident, which are what we must consider for purposes of determining jurisdiction, demonstrate that there is a potential for an altercation between passengers on a boat in the process of docking to disrupt maritime commerce, and that the potential for disruption to maritime commerce is more than fanciful.

United States Court of Appeals
for the Third Circuit

No. 16-2602

IN RE ASBESTOS PRODS. LIAB. LITIG. (NO. VI)

Appeal from the United States District Court for the Eastern District of Pennsylvania

Decided: October 3, 2017

Citation: 873 F.3d 232, 5 Adm. R. 126 (3d Cir. 2017).

Before **VANASKIE**, **SHWARTZ**, and **RESTREPO**, Circuit Judges.

[—4—] {–234–} **VANASKIE**, Circuit Judge:

These asbestos cases involve the availability of the "bare-metal defense" under maritime law. The defense's basic idea is that a manufacturer who delivers a product "bare metal"—that is without the insulation or other material that must be added for the product's proper operation—is not generally liable for injuries caused by asbestos in later-added materials. A classic scenario would be if an engine manufacturer ships an engine without a gasket, the buyer adds a gasket containing asbestos, and the asbestos causes injury to a worker. May the manufacturer be held liable? Some courts **[—5—]** say no—never. Others rely on a more fact-specific standard and ask whether the facts of the case made it foreseeable that hazardous asbestos materials would be used. Neither this Court nor the Supreme Court has confronted the issue.

In that void, we survey bedrock principles of maritime law and conclude that they permit a manufacturer of even a bare-metal product to be held liable for asbestos-related injuries when circumstances indicate the injury was a reasonably foreseeable result of the manufacturer's actions—at least in the context of a negligence claim. The District Court had instead applied the bright line rule approach and entered summary judgment against the plaintiffs. We will vacate the entry of summary judgment on the plaintiffs' negligence claims, affirm the entry of summary judgment on the plaintiffs' product liability claims (which we conclude were abandoned on appeal), and will remand, for further proceedings.

I.

Appellants Roberta G. Devries and Shirley McAfee are the widows of deceased husbands who served in the United States Navy. Each couple filed a Complaint in Pennsylvania state court alleging that the husband contracted cancer caused by exposure to asbestos. Devries alleges that on the *U.S.S. Turner* from 1957-60, her husband was exposed to asbestos-containing insulation and components that were added onto the ship's engines, pumps, boilers, blowers, generators, switchboards, steam traps, and other devices. McAfee alleges her husband was similarly exposed through his service on two ships and in the Philadelphia Naval Shipyard.

Devries and McAfee named a number of defendants, of which Appellee manufacturers ("Manufacturers") are a **[—6—]** subset.[1] The Manufacturers each made their products "bare metal," in that if they manufactured an engine, they shipped it without any asbestos-containing insulation materials that would later be added.

Devries and McAfee's Complaints each allege claims of negligence and strict liability. The Manufacturers removed to the Eastern District of Pennsylvania and invoked **{–235–}** the bare-metal defense in support of their respective summary judgment motions, arguing that because they shipped their products bare metal, they could not be held liable for the sailors' injuries. The District Court agreed and granted the Manufacturers summary judgment motions.

Devries and McAfee each appealed separately, raising an issue as to whether the District Court's decision addressed their negligence claims. We summarily remanded with instructions that the District Court address the negligence issue and also consider

[1] The Appellee-Manufacturers are Air & Liquid Systems Corp., CBS Corp., Foster Wheeler LLC, General Electric Co., IMO Industries Inc., Warren Pumps LLC, and Ingersoll Rand Co.

a split in authority as to whether a bright-line rule or a fact-specific standard governed the bare-metal defense's availability. *In re Asbestos Prods. Liab. Litig.*, No. 15-2667, Order (3d Cir. May 12, 2017) (McAfee); *In re Asbestos Prods. Liab. Litig.*, No. 15-1278, Order (3d. Cir. Feb. 5, 2016) (Devries).

On remand, the District Court applied the bright-line-rule version of the bare-metal defense, and clarified that summary judgment had been entered in favor of the **[—7—]** Manufacturers on both the strict liability and negligence claims. The Court reasoned that the rule approach was best because, according to the Court's view of the precedents, maritime law favors uniformity and the rule approach was the majority view.

Devries and McAfee appealed for a second time. We consolidated their appeals and ordered coordinated briefing.

II.

The District Court had federal-officer jurisdiction under 28 U.S.C. § 1442(a)(1), and maritime jurisdiction under 28 U.S.C. § 1333(1). We have jurisdiction under 28 U.S.C. § 1291. We review the District Court's grant of summary judgment *de novo. Faush v. Tues. Morning, Inc.*, 808 F.3d 208, 215 (3d Cir. 2015).

III.

The key question in this case is the bare-metal defense's availability: When, if ever, should a manufacturer of a product that does not contain asbestos be held liable for an asbestos-related injury most directly caused by parts added on to the manufacturer's product? Neither the Third Circuit nor the Supreme Court has addressed the question, and the courts from other jurisdictions that have are split. Some courts apply a bright-line rule, holding that a manufacturer of a bare-metal product is never liable for injuries caused by later-added asbestos-containing materials. *See, e.g.*, *Lindstrom v. A-C Prod. Liab. Tr.*, 424 F.3d 488, 492, 494-97 (6th Cir. 2005); *Cabasug v. Crane Co.*, 989 F. Supp. 2d 1027, 1038-43 (D. Haw. 2013). Others apply a more fact-specific standard, stating, for example, that a bare-metal manufacturer may be **[—8—]** held liable if the plaintiff's injury was a reasonably foreseeable result of the manufacturer's conduct. *See, e.g.*, *Quirin v. Lorillard Tobacco Co.*, 17 F. Supp. 3d 760, 768-70 (N.D. Ill. 2014) (determining whether the addition of asbestos material was "foreseeable" by asking whether addition of asbestos-containing materials was "inevitable," and whether those added materials were "necess[ary]" or "essential" to the manufacturer's product); *Chicano v. Gen. Elec. Co.*, 2004 WL 2250990, at *6 (E.D. Pa. Oct. 5, 2004) (asking if the addition of asbestos-containing materials was "foreseeable").[2] **{-236-}**

In addressing this question, we (1) examine the doctrinal roots of the bare-metal defense, and (2) address how **[—9—]** it should be applied in Devries and McAfee's negligence actions.

A.

The doctrinal root of the bare-metal defense has proved to be a particularly vexing question. Some courts have rooted the defense in causation: When if ever can it be said that a bare-metal manufacturer *causes* an asbestos-related injury? *See, e.g.*, *Thurmon v. Ga. Pac.*,

---

[2] Illustrative of the unsettled status of this issue, we recently certified to the Pennsylvania Supreme Court the question of whether under Pennsylvania law a manufacturer of a product can assert the bare metal defense in the context of a negligent failure to warn claim arising out of exposure to asbestos. *See In re Asbestos Products Liability Lit. (No. VI), Crane Co.,* No. 16-3704 (3d Cir. Sept. 27, 2017) (Petition for Certification of Question of State Law).

Whether, under Pennsylvania law, a manufacturer has a duty to warn about the asbestos-related hazards of component parts it has neither manufactured nor supplied.

If such a duty exists, what is the appropriate legal test to determine whether the company is in fact liable for failing to warn about the risks of asbestos?

Id. at 11.

LLC, 650 F. App'x 752, 756 (11th Cir. 2016) ("the 'bare metal defense' is, essentially, a causation argument"). Others locate the defense in duty: Can a manufacturer's *duty* to act with reasonable care with respect to reasonably foreseeable risks and plaintiffs, be said to extend to asbestos-related injuries? *See, e.g.*, *Quirin*, 17 F. Supp. 3d at 767-70 (reviewing the issue as one of "legal duty"). The question is more than academic. If the elemental root is duty, the defense should be expected to operate differently in strict liability as compared to negligence, because a defendant's duty of course differs between the two types of actions. *See Chesher v. 3M Co.*, 234 F. Supp. 3d, 693, 700-03 (D.S.C. 2017) (holding that the defense should apply in a weaker fashion in a negligence action, as compared to strict liability). The opposite might be true too—the defense should operate in similar fashion in both negligence and strict liability if it is rooted in causation, because the proximate cause inquiry cuts across the two types of actions. *See, e.g.*, *Lindstrom*, 424 F.3d at 492 (suggesting the defense applies similarly under "both negligence and strict liability theories").

We find that both approaches are correct: the defense is rooted in both duty *and* cause because its keystone is the concept of foreseeability. When parties debate the bare-metal defense, they debate when and whether a manufacturer could **[—10—]** reasonably foresee that its actions or omissions would cause the plaintiff's asbestos-related injuries. The bright-line rule approach says it is never reasonably foreseeable, and the fact-specific standard approach says it sometimes is. This debate over foreseeability sounds in both duty and cause, because foreseeability is a concept embedded in each element. *See Gibbs v. Ernst*, 647 A.2d 882, 891 (Pa. 1994) (highlighting "the common law notion of foreseeability as found in the concepts of duty and proximate cause"). In the duty element in a negligence action, foreseeability limits a defendant's liability to only the risks and plaintiffs that are reasonably foreseeable. *See* Restatement (Third) of Torts: Phys. & Emot. Harm § 7, cmt. j (2010 Am. Law Inst.) (acknowledging "widespread use" of foreseeability as an aspect of the duty of reasonable care, despite the Restatement's disagreement with such an approach). And in proximate cause, foreseeability limits a defendant's liability to only the injuries that are a reasonably foreseeable result of the defendant's actions. *Id.* § 29, cmt. j (discussing foreseeability as an aspect of proximate cause in both negligence and strict-liability **{-237-}** actions).[3] Thus, the bare- **[—11—]** metal defense is nothing more than the concept of foreseeability, as embedded in the duty of reasonable care in a negligence action and the proximate cause standard in a negligence or strict-liability action, as applied to the facts of a certain subset of asbestos cases.

This dual-elemental home for the defense does not, however, totally explain when or whether the defense's application should differ from strict-liability to negligence. It might be that the defense could apply the same in both types of actions, because of the shared proximate-cause element. Or the differences in the two actions' duty elements might mean the defense is more forceful in one action than the other. *See, e.g.*, *Chesher*, 234 F. Supp. 3d at 700-03 (holding that the defense is weaker in negligence and stronger in strict liability, because in strict liability the manufacturer's duty is limited to the product, but with negligence the duty extends further); *Bell v. Foster Wheeler Energy Corp.*, No. 15-6394, 2016 WL 5780104, at *5-7 (E.D. La. Oct. 4, 2016) (same). And of course the facts of a given case could be the most important variable.

We need not settle these doctrinal distinctions today, because Devries and

[3] Instead of starting from subject-specific asbestos cases, we begin our focus with the ordinary and traditional principles of maritime and tort law, as exemplified in the most reliable treatises and restatements. *Cf. M&G Polymers USA, LLC v. Tackett*, 135 S. Ct. 926, 929-30 (2015) (abrogating a circuit's labor-law-specific rule for contract interpretation, and calling on lower courts in labor-law cases to still adhere to "ordinary" and "traditional" principles of contract law); *Paroline v. United States*, 134 S. Ct. 1710, 1719-20 (2014) (citing, as authority for the federal common law of proximate **[—11—]** cause, the Restatement (Third) of Torts, Prosser and Keeton's treatise on torts, and LaFave's treatise on criminal law).

McAfee waived their strict liability claim in this appeal. As a general matter, an appellant waives an argument in support of reversal if it is not raised in the opening brief. *McCray v. Fidelity Nat'l Title Ins. Co.*, 682 F.3d 229, 241 (3d Cir. 2012). Here, in this appeal Devries and McAfee focused the entirety of their briefing on their negligence claims, yet attempted to also incorporate their strict-liability **[—12—]** claim through a footnote: "By concentrating on [negligence] issues in this brief, Appellants do not waive any issues argued in their original briefs as to Defendants' liability under [the strict liability claims]." (Appellants' Br. at 2 n. 1). This attempt to shoehorn in an argument outside the briefs is insufficient to raise an issue on appeal. *See John Wyeth & Brother Ltd. v. CIGNA Int'l Corp.,* 119 F.3d 1070, 1076 n. 6 (3d Cir. 1997) (stating that "arguments raised in passing (such as, in a footnote), but not squarely argued, are considered waived"); *see also Skretvedt v. E.I. DuPont De Nemours*, 372 F.3d 193, 202-04 (3d Cir. 2004) (declining to consider arguments not properly raised and therefore waived). In particular, it fails to give fair notice of the claims being contested on appeal. Thus, Devries's and McAfee's waiver of their strict-liability arguments means that we will affirm the District Court's decision to that extent, and need not fully explore the precise contours of the defense's distinctions in strict liability and negligence, beyond the unifying principle of foreseeability.

B.

For the negligence claims, rooting the bare-metal defense in foreseeability does not on its own resolve the issue, because the split in authority can be characterized as a debate over what a bare-metal manufacturer could reasonably foresee—no asbestos-related injuries, *see, e.g.,* **{-238-}** *Lindstrom*, 424 F.3d at 492, 494-97, or some, *see, e.g., Quirin*, 17 F. Supp. 3d at 769-70. **[—13—]**

These two choices raise familiar tradeoffs between rules and standards.[4] A rule is a legal directive that attempts to capture a background principle into an easy-to-apply form that is predictable and efficient. A speed limit is a good example: its goal is road safety, but because liability turns on speed rather than the amorphous definition of "safety" itself, it is easier for drivers, police, and insurers to shape their conduct accordingly. Rules have downsides though too, in that they necessarily result in errors of over- and under-inclusion. In the case of the speed limit, it furthers the policy of road safety, but does so imperfectly: speedy drivers get punished even if they speed safely, and slow drivers go free even if they amble along haphazardly.

A standard, on the other hand, collapses the background principle into the actual legal directive, resulting in better accuracy and "fit" with the underlying purpose, and fewer errors of over- and under-inclusion. Another road-safety example would be a reckless-driving prohibition that simply prohibits driving that is "reckless." Such a prohibition is less predictable and efficient than the speed limit, in that it is harder to predict what a decisionmaker will find to be "reckless" than whether he or she will agree that 76 miles per hour exceeds a **[—14—]** 70 m.p.h. speed limit. But liability better tracks the actual goal of road safety, because almost all "reckless" drivers are unsafe.

The point is there are tradeoffs, and courts face those tradeoffs in choosing an approach to the bare-metal defense. The rule-based approach is efficient and predictable—bare-metal manufacturers are simply not liable—but the downside is some deserving sailor-plaintiffs will not receive their due. On the other hand, the standard-based approach is bound to be less predictable and less efficient, because the standard's fact-centered nature will push more cases into discovery, *see, e.g., Quirin,* 17 F. Supp. 3d at 771-72 (denying defendant's motion to dismiss after applying the standard), but the most-deserving sailor-

[4] For a review of the characteristics and tradeoffs of rules and standards, *see* Bryan A. Garner et al., *The Law of Judicial Precedent* 78 (2016) (noting that "*rules* and *standards* . . . denote different levels of specificity for norms" and "judicial holding[s]"); Kathleen M. Sullivan, *The Supreme Court, 1991 Term—Foreword: The Justices of Rules and Standards,* 106 Harv. L. Rev. 22, 58-59 (1992).

plaintiffs are less likely to be denied compensation.

Thankfully, we do not weigh these tradeoffs in a vacuum. Maritime law is undergirded by established principles, at least four of which are implicated here. First and perhaps foremost, maritime law is deeply concerned with the protection of sailors, due to a historic and "special solicitude for the welfare of those men who undertook to venture upon hazardous and unpredictable sea voyages." *Moragne v. States Marine Lines, Inc.*, 398 U.S. 375, 387 (1970). This "special solicitude" developed "unknown to the common law," and so maritime law is at times more lenient toward a sailor than a state's common law may be to a similarly-situated plaintiff. *Id.* This divergence is acceptable if not appropriate because the "humane and liberal character of" maritime law counsels that it is better "to give than to withhold the remedy" wherever "established and inflexible rules" do not require otherwise. *Id.* (quoting *The Sea Gull*, 21 F. Cas. 909, 910 (C.C. Md. 1865)). For example, in *Moragne v. States Marine Lines*, the Supreme Court made it permissible for maritime plaintiffs to bring wrongful death actions even though the **{-239-}** common law **[—15—]** disapproved of such actions. 398 U.S. at 381-88, 408-09. In arriving at that holding, the Court explicitly referenced and discussed maritime law's special solicitude for sailor safety and how that solicitude permitted maritime law to have more sailor-friendly rules than the common law. *Id.* at 386-88.[5]

Here, maritime law's special solicitude for sailors' safety similarly favors the adoption of the standard-like approach to the bare-metal defense. A standard will permit a greater number of deserving sailors to receive compensation, and compensation that is closer to what they deserve. Given that results for sailor-victims will differ under a rule as compared to a standard, and since no "established" or "inflexible" rule prohibits the more forgiving standard, the "humane and liberal character" of maritime law counsels that we follow the standard. Even if certain states' common laws would call for a more stringent rule, maritime law's more liberal attitude permits us to diverge from that path.

Second, maritime law is built on "traditions of simplicity and practicality," *Kermarec v. Compagnie Generale Transatlantique*, 358 U.S. 625, 631 (1959), but that principle cuts in both directions and does not provide much guidance. On one hand, "simplicity" might be seen as favoring the rule-based approach, because simplicity is related to predictability, and it is easier to predict how a rule will apply than a standard. **[—16—]** On the other hand, "simplicity" could also be seen as favoring a foreseeability-based standard, because simplicity is related to familiarity, and foreseeability is such a familiar and key part of tort law. *See id.* at 631-32 (choosing to adopt a familiar standard over a "foreign" and "alien" rule while invoking maritime law's "traditions of simplicity and practicality").

The third and fourth principles implicated in this case are also not particularly helpful. Maritime law has a "fundamental interest" in "the protection of maritime commerce," *Exxon Corp. v. Cent. Gulf Lines, Inc.*, 500 U.S. 603, 608 (1991) (quoting *Sisson v. Ruby*, 497 U.S. 358, 367 (1990)), and seeks out "uniform rules to govern conduct and liability," *Foremost Ins. Co. v. Richardson*, 457 U.S. 668, 674-75 (1982). Here, the parties all argue these two principles encourage the Court to side with whatever side is winning in the split in authority. The idea is that the sooner one side wins out over the other, the sooner the split in authority is ended and the goals of seamless commerce and uniformity of rules will be achieved. The rub, however, is determining which view is the majority. The bright-line rule could be said to be in the lead because it has on its side the Sixth Circuit, the only court of appeals to weigh in. *Lindstrom*, 424 F.3d at 492, 494-97. The standard could similarly be said to be the majority view because the courts that have confronted the question most recently have generally favored the standard, and have done so after a much

[5] *Moragne*'s holding was based most directly on principles other than the special solicitude for sailor safety, but the special solicitude was still crucial to the Court's decision because it explained why the Court's ruling was appropriate even though it likely diverged from the common law. *Moragne*, 398 U.S. at 386-88.

more thorough analysis than that found in the Sixth Circuit's opinion in *Lindstrom*, which was decided much earlier in the debate over the bare-metal defense. *Compare Chesher*, 234 F. Supp. 3d at 696-712 (analyzing in painstaking detail the split in authority and adopting a version of the standard); *Bell*, 2016 WL 5780104, at *3-7 (same), *with* **{–240–}** *Lindstrom*, 424 F.3d at 494-97 (not mentioning the split in **[—17—]** authority). We need not decide which approach is winning in terms of wins and losses—it is enough that the score is too close for us to say that the goals of seamless commerce and rule-uniformity push in one way or the other.

In sum, the special solicitude for the safety and protection of sailors is dispositive, because it counsels us to follow the standard-based approach, and none of the other principles weigh heavily in either direction. The standard-based approach is the one we will therefore follow: foreseeability is the touchstone of the bare-metal defense; a manufacturer of a bare-metal product may be held liable for a plaintiff's injuries suffered from later-added asbestos-containing materials if the facts show the plaintiff's injuries were a reasonably foreseeable result of the manufacturer's failure to provide a reasonable and adequate warning; and although cases will necessarily be fact-specific, already-decided precedents show, for example, that a bare-metal manufacturer may be subject to liability if it reasonably could have known, at the time it placed its product into the stream of commerce, that

(1) asbestos is hazardous,[6] and

(2) its product will be used with an asbestos-containing part,[7] because **[—18—]**

(a) the product was originally equipped with an asbestos containing part that could reasonably be expected to be replaced over the product's lifetime,[8]

(b) the manufacturer specifically directed that the product be used with an asbestos-containing part,[9] or

(c) the product required an asbestos-containing part to function properly.[10]

These may or may not be the only facts on which liability can arise. The finer contours of the defense, and how it should be applied to various sets of facts, must be decided on a case-by-case basis.

IV.

Finally, the Manufacturers advanced two alternative arguments in support of an affirmance on the negligence claims. They argued (1) insufficient evidence had been presented as to causation and was fatal to Devries and McAfee's claims, and (2) the government-contractor defense should insulate the Manufacturers from liability. These arguments were also presented below, but the District Court **[—19—]** declined to rule on them because its bare-metal-defense holding was sufficient to enter summary judgment in favor of the Manufacturers. The Manufacturers urge us to address them now, on the grounds that we may affirm a judgment for any reason supported by the record. *Brightwell v. Lehman*, 637 F.3d 187, 191 (3d Cir. 2011). Addressing alternative grounds for affirmance, however, is a matter left to our discretion. *See Gov't of the V.I. v. Walker*, 261 F.3d 370, 376-77 (3d Cir. 2001) (declining to reach arguments raised before but not decided by the lower court, and instead remanding). Given that we are without the benefit of the District Court's well-regarded expertise, and the parties' briefing and oral argument was appropriately focused on the bare-metal defense, we will leave the insufficient-evidence and contractor- **{–241–}** defense arguments to be dealt with on remand.

[6] *See Bell*, 2016 WL 5780104, at *5.

[7] *See id.*

[8] *See Chesher*, 234 F. Supp. 3d at 714; *Quirin*, 17 F. Supp. 3d at 769-71.

[9] *See Bell*, 2016 WL 5780104, at *5, 7.

[10] *See Chesher*, 234 F. Supp. 3d at 714; *Quirin*, 17 F. Supp. 3d at 769-70.

V.

In conclusion, maritime law's special solicitude for the safety and protection of sailors counsels us to adopt a standard-based approach to the bare-metal defense that permits a plaintiff to recover, at least in negligence, from a manufacturer of a bare-metal product when the facts show the plaintiff's injuries were a reasonably foreseeable result of the manufacturer's conduct. We will affirm the decision of the District Court with respect to Devries and McAfee's strict liability claims, and remand for further proceedings on their negligence claims consistent with this Opinion.

United States Court of Appeals
for the Third Circuit

No. 16-1967

TROTTER
vs.
7R HOLDINGS, LLC

Appeal from the District Court of the Virgin Islands

Decided: October 12, 2017

Citation: 873 F.3d 435, 5 Adm. R. 133 (3d Cir. 2017).

Before **GREENAWAY, JR., SHWARTZ,** and **FUENTES,** Circuit Judges.

[—2—] {-438-} GREENAWAY, JR., Circuit Judge:

In this appeal, we must determine whether the District Court properly exercised its power to dismiss a case pursuant to the *forum non conveniens* doctrine when it dismissed **[—3—]** Appellant's claims under the Jones Act, 46 U.S.C. § 30104 (2012), and general maritime laws for unseaworthiness, negligence, and maintenance and cure. We shall affirm the District Court in two steps. First, we hold that the general presumption that "[t]he possibility of a change in substantive law should ordinarily not be given conclusive or even substantial weight in the *forum non conveniens* inquiry," *Piper Aircraft Co. v. Reyno*, 454 U.S. 235, 247 (1981), applies to these claims (a) because the remedy provided by the alternative forum is not clearly inadequate and (b) because the Jones Act does not contain a special venue provision. Second, we hold that the District Court did not abuse its discretion in exercising its *forum non conveniens* power (a) because the District Court correctly determined that an adequate alternative forum existed and (b) because the District Court reasonably balanced the relevant private and public interest factors.

I.

This case arises from the following facts. Luis A. Rubi ("Rubi"), a U.S. citizen, serves as the Director of 7R Holdings, LLC, a limited liability company with its principal place of business in Puerto Rico. 7R Holdings holds 7R Charters Limited.[1] 7R Charters owned M/Y Olga, a yacht registered in the British Virgin Islands ("BVI"). Bernard Calot captains M/Y Olga. In a series of conversations over email and the telephone, Captain Calot, while in Puerto Rico, hired Michelle Trotter ("Trotter"), while in Florida, to work as a chef on M/Y Olga. On December 19, 2012, Trotter boarded M/Y Olga in **[—4—]** St. Thomas, U.S. Virgin Islands ("USVI"). On December 24, 2012, M/Y Olga traveled to Scrub Island, BVI, and let down its anchor. Trotter allegedly sustained an injury while descending stairs that connected M/Y Olga to Scrub Island's dock. Shortly after the accident, Trotter received treatment for her alleged injuries at a BVI hospital and then flew back to Florida.

Trotter sued Rubi, 7R Holdings, and M/Y Olga ("Appellees") in the District Court of the Virgin Islands pursuant to the Jones Act and general maritime laws for the personal injury that she claims that she sustained on Scrub Island. Appellees moved to dismiss Trotter's complaint for *forum non conveniens*.

The District Court granted the motion. The District Court, relying on *Eurofins Pharma U.S. Holdings v. BioAlliance Pharma SA*, 623 F.3d 147 (3d Cir. 2010), divided its decision into two parts. First, it found that the alternative forum, the BVI, qualified as an adequate alternative forum. Second, it held that the balance of the public and private interests overcame Trotter's choice of forum.

On appeal, Trotter raises two issues. First, Trotter argues that, as a matter of law, we should vacate the District Court's decision because the District Court failed to perform a choice of law analysis before dismissing Trotter's complaint pursuant to *forum non conveniens*. Second, Trotter asserts **{-439-}** that we should vacate the District Court's decision because the District Court abused its discretion by granting the motion to dismiss pursuant to *forum non conveniens*. Appellees insist that these arguments lack merit. We agree and will affirm. **[—5—]**

[1] The record does not provide information on 7R Charters's principal place of business but the District Court stated, without citation, that it is a British Virgin Islands corporation.

II.[2]

In resolving this case, we must address two issues. First, did the District Court err in failing to determine whether U.S. law applies before deciding *forum non conveniens*? Second, did the District Court abuse its discretion in dismissing Trotter's claims for *forum non conveniens*? We review the first question de novo, *Maniscalco v. Brother Int'l (USA) Corp.*, 709 F.3d 202, 206 (3d Cir. 2013), and the second question for abuse of discretion, *Kisano Trade & Invest Ltd. v. Lemster*, 737 F.3d 869, 872 (3d Cir. 2013).

A.

The District Court did not err in failing to determine whether U.S. law applies before dismissing the case for *forum non conveniens*. This conclusion rests on the Supreme Court's *forum non conveniens* jurisprudence.

The Supreme Court, "in one form of words or another, has repeatedly recognized the existence of the power to decline jurisdiction in exceptional circumstances." *Gulf Oil Corp. v. Gilbert*, 330 U.S. 501, 504 (1947). One example of this power is the principle of *forum non conveniens*. "The principle of forum non conveniens is simply that a court may resist imposition upon its jurisdiction even when jurisdiction is authorized by the letter of a general venue statute." *Id.* at 507. A court may exercise this power when litigating the case in the **[—6—]** chosen forum would either oppress a defendant "out of all proportion to plaintiff's convenience" or cause the court "administrative and legal problems." *Piper Aircraft Co.*, 454 U.S. at 241 (internal quotation marks omitted).

In deciding whether a venue would oppress a defendant, courts may consider "private interests," such as access to proof, availability of process, and other practical issues. *Gulf Oil*, 330 U.S. at 508. In determining whether a venue would cause administrative or legal problems, courts may consider "public interests," such as the burdens on the courts and local juries. *Id.* at 508–09. "[T]he combination and weight of factors requisite to given results are difficult to forecast or state . . . ." *Id.* at 508. As a result, "The forum non conveniens determination is committed to the sound discretion of the trial court" and "[i]t may be reversed only when there has been a clear abuse of discretion." *Piper Aircraft Co.*, 454 U.S. at 257. "[W]here the court has considered all relevant public and private interest factors, and where its balancing of these factors is reasonable, its decision deserves substantial deference." *Id.*

In *Piper Aircraft Co.*, a case involving wrongful-death actions, the Supreme Court held that "[t]he possibility of a change in substantive law should *ordinarily* not be given conclusive or even substantial weight in the *forum non conveniens* inquiry." *Id.* at 247 (emphasis added). The Supreme Court came to this conclusion because privileging this factor **{-440-}** would prevent the doctrine from serving private and public interests. It would undermine the private interests because "[i]f substantial weight were given to the possibility of an unfavorable change in law . . ., dismissal might be barred even where trial in the chosen forum was plainly inconvenient." *Id.* at 249. It would harm the public interests because "[i]f the possibility of a change in law were given **[—7—]** substantial weight . . . [c]hoice-of-law analysis would become extremely important, and the courts would frequently be required to interpret the law of foreign jurisdictions." *Id.* at 251.

In at least two situations, however, the Supreme Court has concluded that choice of law questions must receive substantial or conclusive weight in *forum non conveniens* decisions. First, "if the remedy provided by the alternative forum is so clearly inadequate or unsatisfactory that it is no remedy at all, the unfavorable change in law may be given substantial weight." *Id.* at 254. Second, a "plaintiff's choice of a forum cannot be defeated on the basis of *forum non conveniens*" when "the special venue act under which those cases are brought [is] believed to require

[2] Trotter invoked the District Court's jurisdiction under 28 U.S.C. § 1331. Trotter filed a timely notice of appeal on April 17, 2016. This Court has appellate jurisdiction pursuant to 28 U.S.C. § 1291.

it." *Gulf Oil*, 330 U.S. at 505. Special venue acts "specifically provide[] where venue may be had in any suit on a cause of action arising under that statute." *Id.* at 506.

The Supreme Court has found that at least two special venue acts prohibited courts from dismissing cases for *forum non conveniens*. In the first case, *Baltimore & O. R. Co. v. Kepner*, the Court held that Congress gave "[a] privilege of venue" to sue pursuant to the Federal Employers' Liability Act and that "this right of action cannot be frustrated for reasons of convenience or expense." 314 U.S. 44, 54 (1941). In the second case, *United States v. National City Lines*, the Court concluded, "In the face of th[e Clayton Act's] history we cannot say that room was left for judicial discretion to apply the doctrine of forum non conveniens so as to deprive the plaintiff of the choice given by the section." 334 U.S. 573, 588 (1948). Congress subsequently superseded these Supreme Court decisions by enacting the domestic-transfer statute, 28 U.S.C. § 1404(a) (2012), which allows a district court to **[—8—]** "transfer any civil action to any other district or division where it might have been brought" for "the convenience of parties and witnesses, in the interest of justice." *Id.*; *see United States v. Nat'l City Lines, Inc.*, 337 U.S. 78 (1949) (recognizing that § 1404(a) allows for the transfer of Clayton Act suits); *Ex parte Collett*, 337 U.S. 55 (1949) (recognizing that § 1404(a) allows for the transfer of Federal Employers' Liability Act suits).

Trotter does not recognize *Piper Aircraft Co.*'s general presumption against giving choice of law "substantial weight in the *forum non conveniens* inquiry," 454 U.S. at 247, or the two exceptions to this rule. We, however, do recognize this rule and its exceptions. As a result, we address whether either of the two exceptions apply here. We answer these questions, even though Trotter did not raise them in her written or oral communications to us, because they are antecedent legal issues that we must resolve before deciding the case as a whole. *See Haybarger v. Lawrence Cty. Adult Probation & Parole*, 667 F.3d 408, 412–13 (3d Cir. 2012).

We conclude that the first exception does not apply because the District Court correctly held that the alternative forum would recognize Trotter's negligence claims. As a result, this is not a case **{-441-}** where "the remedy provided by the alternative forum is so clearly inadequate or unsatisfactory that it is no remedy at all." *Piper Aircraft Co.*, 454 U.S. at 254.

We hold that the second exception—the special venue provision exception—does not apply either. When Congress passed the Jones Act, it sought "to provide liberal recovery for injured workers," *Kernan v. Am. Dredging Co.*, 355 U.S. 426, 432 (1958), and included a "special venue provision" that "provided a more generous choice of forum than would have been available at that time under the general venue statute," **[—9—]** *Pure Oil Co. v. Suarez*, 384 U.S. 202, 204–05 (1966). The special venue provision, as originally enacted, read as follows: "Jurisdiction in such actions shall be under the court of the district in which the defendant employer resides or in which his principal office is located." The Merchant Marine Act, Pub. L. No. 66-261, § 20, 41 Stat. 988 (1920).[3] The contemporaneous general venue statute, by contrast, omitted any reference to the location of "his principal office" and instead only allowed plaintiffs to sue a defendant "in the district where he resides." Act March 3, 1911, c. 231, § 52, 36 Stat. 1101 (1913).

Congress amended the Jones Act in 2008 by striking the special venue provision in its entirety. Because of this amendment, we conclude that *Piper Aircraft Co.*'s general presumption—that choice of law decisions are not entitled to substantial weight in the *forum non conveniens* analyses—controls, and the special-venue exception does not apply to the Jones Act.

[3] Jurisdiction means venue in this context. *Pan. R. Co. v. Johnson*, 264 U.S. 375, 384–85 (1924) ("[T]he provision is not intended to affect the general jurisdiction of the District Courts as defined in section 24, but only to prescribe the venue for actions brought under the new act of which it is a part.").

The Amendment's legislative history does not question this conclusion. In passing this amendment, the House of Representatives Committee on the Judiciary published a report that explained that it did not intend to change the substantive law: "This subsection is being repealed to make clearer that the prior law regarding venue, including the holding of *Pure Oil Co. v. Suarez*, 384 U.S. 202 (1966) and the cases following it, **[—10—]** remains in effect, so that the action may be brought wherever the seaman's employer does business." H.R. Rep. 110–437, 5 (2007). *Pure Oil Co.* held that 28 U.S.C. § 1391 expanded the Jones Act's "reside[nce]" requirement and the availability of venue from the defendant's place of incorporation and place of principal office to the place of incorporation, the place of license, and the place where the corporation does business. 384 U.S. at 203–05, 206. It observed that the Jones Act contained a "special venue provision." *Id.* at 204. This case, as cited in the legislative history, did not concern *forum non conveniens* at all, but instead focused on the proper scope of venue under the Jones Act. Thus, neither *Pure Oil Co.* nor the legislative history undermines our conclusion.

Our sister courts of appeals' decisions do not give us pause. Of the five circuits to consider the question, three concluded that the Jones Act, as originally enacted, contained a special venue provision that prohibited *forum non conveniens* dismissal. *See, e.g.*, *Vasquez v. YII Shipping Co.*, 692 F.3d 1192, 1197 (11th Cir. 2012) ("Under the federal maritime choice-of-law test, applicable to Jones Act seafarers in federal district court, a case should not be dismissed on grounds of forum non conveniens **{-442-}** if federal maritime law applies to the case . . . ."); *Loya v. Starwood Hotels & Resorts Worldwide, Inc.*, 583 F.3d 656, 662 (9th Cir. 2009) ("[I]n Jones Act cases . . . a court must first make a choice of law determination before dismissing for *forum non conveniens.*"); *Needham v. Phillips Petroleum Co. of Nor.*, 719 F.2d 1481, 1483 (10th Cir. 1983) ("In order to apply the doctrine of *forum non conveniens*, the trial court must conduct a choice of law analysis in order to determine whether American or foreign law governs. If American law is applicable to the case, the *forum non conveniens* doctrine is inapplicable."). *But see Camejo v.* **[—11—]** *Ocean Drilling & Expl.*, 838 F.2d 1374, 1379 (5th Cir. 1988) ("We therefore, expressly disapprove of and overrule our Jones Act and general maritime caselaw that utilizes a modified forum non conveniens analysis."); *Cruz v. Mar. Co. of Phil.*, 702 F.2d 47, 48 (2d Cir. 1983) ("To summarize, when the Jones Act is applicable[,] federal law is involved and the district court must exercise its power to adjudicate, absent some exceptional circumstances such as the application of the abstention doctrine or, as here, the equitable principle of forum non conveniens."). In *DeMateos v. Texaco, Inc.*, 562 F.2d 895 (3d Cir. 1977), we indicated our support for the majority rule, but both Congress's repeal of the Jones Act's special venue provision and *Piper Aircraft Co.* call this majority rule into question. *See id.* (describing *DeMateos*'s interpretation as "dictum"). The absence of a special venue provision in the Jones Act demonstrates that there is no special-venue exception to the normal *forum non conveniens* approach and therefore no choice of law inquiry is required.

B.

Having found that neither exception to the general presumption against giving choice of law questions substantial weight in *forum non conveniens* decisions applies, we review the District Court's decision for abuse of discretion. *Kisano Trade & Invest Ltd.*, 737 F.3d at 872.

Here, the District Court did not abuse its discretion. "[W]hen considering a motion to dismiss on *forum non conveniens* grounds, a district court must first determine whether an adequate alternate forum can entertain the case." *Eurofins Pharma US Holdings*, 623 F.3d at 160 (alteration in original). After finding that an adequate alternative forum exists, the district court must "determine[] the amount of **[—12—]** deference due to the plaintiff's choice of forum" and "balance the relevant private and public interest factors." *Id.*

The private interest factors include: "access to sources of proof; availability of compulsory process for attendance of unwilling . . . witnesses;" "the cost of obtaining attendance of willing . . . witnesses; possibility of view of premises, if view would be appropriate to the action; and all other practical problems that make trial of a case easy, expeditious and inexpensive." *Gulf Oil Corp.*, 330 U.S. at 508.

The public interest factors include: the possibility of turning courts into "congested centers;" the likelihood that the case will burden a jury composed of people with "no relation to the litigation;" the probability that the case will "touch the affairs of many persons" in the community; and the chances that the court will be "at home with the . . . law that must govern the case." *Id.* at 508–09.

In articulating these factors, the Supreme Court repeatedly emphasized the district court's discretion in selecting and reviewing factors. "Wisely, it has not been attempted to catalogue the circumstances which will justify or require either **{-443-}** grant or denial of remedy" and that "the combination and weight of factors requisite to given results are difficult to forecast or state." *Id.* at 508. As a result, this list of factors is both over and under inclusive: "This list of considerations to be balanced is by no means exhaustive, and some factors may not be relevant in the context of a particular case." *Van Cauwenberghe v. Biard*, 486 U.S. 517, 528–29 (1988). "The moving defendant must show that an adequate alternative forum exists as to all defendants and, if so, that the private and public interest factors weigh heavily on the side of **[—13—]** dismissal." *Lacey v. Cessna Aircraft Co.*, 862 F.2d 38, 44 (3d Cir. 1988).

1.

In this case, the District Court found that the BVI could serve as an adequate alternative forum (a) because the BVI's judicial process resembled the USVI's legal procedures; (b) because the Defendants "have stipulated that they will submit themselves to the jurisdiction of the BVI courts;"[4] and (c) because the BVI's law would recognize Trotter's negligence claim. *Trotter v. 7R Holdings, LLC*, No. CV 2014-99, 2016 WL 1271025, at *2–3 (D.V.I. Mar. 30, 2016).

Trotter appeals two facets of this conclusion. First, she argues that the BVI could not serve as an adequate alternative forum because "it has no jurisdiction over *any* of the Defendants." Appellant's Br. at 25. Trotter asserts this contention despite her acknowledgement, and the District Court's finding, that the Appellees have "stipulated that they will submit themselves to the jurisdiction of the BVI courts." *Trotter*, 2016 WL 1271025, at *2. Trotter asks us to question this finding on the grounds that "[a] statement by counsel in a brief is not binding on the party or enforceable in any court." Appellant's Br. at 26. We reject this argument and side with the District Court because "one cannot casually cast aside representations, oral or written, in the course of litigation" and because "a reviewing court may properly consider the **[—14—]** representations made in the appellate brief to be binding as a form of judicial estoppel." *EF Operating Corp. v. Am. Bldgs.*, 993 F.2d 1046, 1050 (3d Cir. 1993).

Second, she claims that the BVI is not an adequate alternative forum because "Defendants have not established that BVI law provides *any* theory for Plaintiff to recover against Defendants." Appellant's Br. at 25. Trotter rests this claim on the observation that U.S. law provides a more favorable liability standard than the common law. She notes that "the Jones Act and unseaworthiness causes of action allow a condition on the dock to be imputed to Defendants even though they do not control the area where the seaman is injured" and that "a seaman injured in the service of the ship, even on shore leave, is entitled to maintenance and cure without any fault on the part of the vessel." *Id.* at 28.

---

[4] At Oral Argument, Appellees' counsel consented to service on behalf of all of his clients. Oral Arg. Recording at 24:00–25:30, http://www2.ca3.uscourts.gov/oralargument/audio/16-1967Trotterv.7RHoldingsLLC.mp3.

We find this argument unpersuasive. In *Piper Aircraft Co.*, the Supreme Court held that a district court properly dismissed a claim under *forum non conveniens* and held that "there is no danger that [the plaintiffs] will be deprived of any remedy" even though the plaintiffs "may not be able to rely on a strict liability theory." 454 U.S. at 255. Trotter's argument mirrors the argument rejected by *Piper Aircraft Co.* because, in both cases, the plaintiffs claimed that **{-444-}** U.S.—but not the foreign—law would allow them to recover without proving the defendants' negligence or fault. Because Trotter makes an argument that resembles the argument rejected by the Supreme Court in *Piper Aircraft Co.*, we affirm the District Court on this issue. **[—15—]**

2.

The District Court held that, although Trotter's choice should receive "great deference" because she is a U.S. citizen, the "balance of the public and private factors clearly favors an alternate forum." *Trotter*, 2016 WL 1271025, at *4 (citing *Windt v. Qwest Commc'ns Int'l, Inc.*, 529 F.3d 183, 190 (3d Cir. 2008)). Private factors counseled in favor of dismissal, the District Court found, (a) because no fact witness resided in the USVI; (b) because the accident occurred on either a vessel owned by a BVI corporation or on a piece of land in the BVI; and (c) because litigating the case in the USVI would cause the parties to "incur significant expenses." *Id.* at *5–6. Public factors supported dismissal, the District Court held, because it would be unfair to subject the citizens of the USVI to deciding a dispute that hinged on foreign evidence and foreign law and because the other factors came out as neutral.

Trotter appeals this decision by arguing that the District Court should have weighed these factors differently and should have considered additional factors. In making this argument, though, Trotter provides no persuasive case law. Indeed, the two cases that she claims most support her position differ from the instant case in important respects.

In the first case, *Lacey v. Cessna Aircraft Co.*, Graeme Lacey suffered injuries in a plane crash in Canada and sued three of the plane's manufacturers in the Western District of Pennsylvania. 932 F.2d 170, 172 (3d Cir. 1991).[5] The **[—16—]** manufacturers successfully moved to dismiss the case pursuant to the court's *forum non conveniens* power. *Id.* In granting the motion, the district court recognized the potential difficulty in compelling U.S. witnesses to appear in Canada and conditioned its dismissal "on defendants making all relevant witnesses and documents in their control available to plaintiff in the alternative forum for discovery and trial, at defendants' expense." *Lacey v. Cessna Aircraft Co.*, 736 F. Supp. 662, 664 (W.D. Pa. 1990). On appeal, we reversed in four steps. First, we observed that relevant evidence related to the plane's exhaust system, a product that a Pennsylvania-based defendant allegedly manufactured. *Lacey*, 932 F.2d at 173. Second, we noted that the Pennsylvania-based defendant "now represents that *no* documents relating to or personnel familiar with the company's prior aircraft exhaust business are under its control." *Id.* Third, because Lacey's claims depended on evidence related to the exhaust system and because no defendant controlled this evidence, we concluded that the court's conditional dismissal, which compelled defendants to produce all relevant witnesses and documents in the Canadian court, could not "ensure [Lacey's] access to sources of proof." *Id.* Fourth, the inadequacy of the conditional dismissal mattered because **{-445-}** Canada's procedural laws prevented Lacey from obtaining evidence within the control of non-parties in the United States. *Id.* at 173–74. **[—17—]**

---

[5] We do not address *Lacey*'s predecessor, *Lacey v. Cessna Aircraft Co.*, 862 F.2d 38 (3d Cir. 1988), at length. In the prior case, we reversed the district court because it had granted the defendants' *forum non conveniens* motion even though the **[—16—]** defendants "submitted no evidence to support their contentions, except for a copy of a pleading filed in the British Columbia litigation." *Lacey*, 862 F.2d at 44. Here, the Appellees submitted affidavits to bolster their claims. As a result, *Lacey*'s predecessor provides little guidance and requires minimal attention.

Unlike in *Lacey*, the relevant evidence in the case at bar rests in the alternative forum. To prove her claims, Trotter may require documents from BVI companies, witnesses from the scene of her accident in the BVI, and access to the relevant dock in the BVI. Thus, our reasoning in *Lacey* does not apply here.

In the second case, *Lony v. E.I. Du Pont de Nemours & Co.*, Adolf Lony, a German sole proprietorship, bought cellophane from Du Pont, a Delaware corporation, and sold it to Haribo, a German corporation. 886 F.2d 628, 630 (3d Cir. 1989).[6] During the transaction, Du Pont told Lony that the cellophane did not contain a specific toxic chemical. *Id.* When it received the cellophane, Haribo discovered that it contained the specific toxic chemical and canceled its contract with Lony. *Id.* Lony claimed that it suffered a loss and sued Du Pont in the United States District Court for the District of Delaware. *Id.* at 631. Du Pont successfully moved for *forum non conveniens* and Lony appealed. *Id.* We reversed, *inter alia*, because the District Court abused its discretion in weighing the private and public interests. *Id.* at 643–44. It specifically abused its discretion in weighing the private interests, we held, because it regarded the private interest factors as standing in "equipoise or tipped to the defendant" but incorrectly **[—18—]** concluded that this balance "favors dismissal." *Id.* at 640. It abused its discretion in considering the public interest factors, we found, because it erroneously assumed that only foreign law would apply to Lony's claims in a U.S. court. *Id.* at 642–43.

Neither of these issues applies to the case at bar. With regard to the private interest factors, *Lony*'s analysis does not extend to this case because the District Court did not regard the private interest factors as standing in equipoise. Instead, it held that two of the "factor[s] counsel[ed] in favor of dismissal" and that one "factor strongly favor[ed] the case being heard in the BVI." *Trotter*, 2016 WL 1271025, at *6. With respect to the public interest factors, *Lony*'s holding does not apply because the District Court did not assume that foreign law applied. Rather, the District Court "[wa]s uncertain whether United States law or BVI law would apply" and, as a result, "refrain[ed] from attributing much weight to this particular factor." *Id.* at *7. Because the District Court reasonably balanced the private and public interest factors, we will affirm the District Court on this issue.

III.

For the foregoing reasons, we will affirm the District Court's order of dismissal.

---

[6] We need not dwell on *Lony*'s progeny, *Lony v. E.I. Du Pont de Nemours & Co.*, 935 F.2d 604 (3d Cir. 1991). In the subsequent case, we reversed the district court because of its "failure to consider the extent of merits activity already completed and underway in Delaware." *Lony*, 935 F.2d at 613. Here, the District Court did not allow any discovery, let alone the six months of discovery at issue in *Lony*'s progeny. As a result, *Lony*'s progeny merits little discussion.

United States Court of Appeals
for the Third Circuit

No. 16-3553

JOYCE
VS.
MAERSK LINE LTD

Appeal from the United States District Court for the District of New Jersey

Decided: December 4, 2017

Citation: 876 F.3d 502, 5 Adm. R. 140 (3d Cir. 2017) (en banc).

Before **SMITH**, Chief Judge, **McKEE**, **AMBRO**, **CHAGARES**, **JORDAN**, **HARDIMAN**, **GREENAWAY, JR.**, **VANASKIE**, **SHWARTZ**, **KRAUSE**, **RESTREPO**, and **ROTH**, Circuit Judges.

[—2—] {-503-} **JORDAN**, Circuit Judge:

Today we stop swimming against the tide of opinion on an important question of maritime law. Following the lead of several of our sister circuits, we now hold that a union contract freely entered by a seafarer—a contract that includes rates of maintenance, cure, and unearned wages—will not be reviewed piecemeal by courts unless there is evidence of **[—3—]** unfairness in the collective bargaining process. In so holding, we overrule our decision in *Barnes v. Andover Co., L.P.*, 900 F.2d 630 (3d Cir. 1990).

I. Background

The facts of this case are not in dispute. James Joyce was a member of the Seafarers International Union. He signed "Articles of Agreement" with the shipping company Maersk Line Limited and agreed to serve as a bosun aboard the MAERSK OHIO for a three-month period, from September 18, 2012 until December 18, 2012. **{-504-}** The Union and Maersk had reached a collective bargaining agreement that governed the terms of all unionized seafarers' employment with Maersk. The collective bargaining agreement was incorporated by reference into the Articles of Agreement between Joyce and Maersk.

Not long after the MAERSK OHIO departed as scheduled from the Port of Newark, New Jersey, Joyce fell ill. He was examined onboard and diagnosed with kidney stones. That diagnosis was later confirmed at a hospital in Spain, and he was declared unfit for duty and repatriated to the United States.

The collective bargaining agreement provided that, if a seafarer was medically discharged prior to the conclusion of his contract, he was entitled to unearned wages for the remaining period of the contract. Overtime was not included in the definition of unearned wages. Joyce accordingly received only base pay as unearned wages for the time left on his contract after he was medically discharged. **[—4—]**

Dissatisfied, Joyce filed a putative class action in the United States District Court for the District of New Jersey. He alleged that the "portions of the [collective bargaining agreement] governing unearned wages ... violated general maritime law[.]" *Joyce v. Maersk Line, Ltd.*, No. 13-5566, 2016 WL 3566726, at *1 (D.N.J. June 30, 2016). More particularly, he claimed that he was owed overtime pay.[1] *Id.* at *2. The District Court disagreed and granted summary judgment to Maersk on the ground that, as a matter of law, given the collective bargaining agreement, Joyce was not entitled to overtime. *Id.* at *6-7. In doing so, the Court distinguished our decision in *Barnes*. *Id.* We

[1] It may seem odd to assert that overtime pay is owed for overtime not worked, but there is precedent for Joyce's assertion that overtime a seafarer expected to work but was unable to because of illness or injury is pay that should be included in unearned wages. *See Padilla v. Maersk Line, Ltd.*, 721 F.3d 77, 82, 1 Adm. R. 34, 36 (2d Cir. 2013) (recognizing that, where "much of [a seafarer's] income was derived from overtime compensation," an injured seafarer could recover overtime as unearned wages because he "was entitled to recover in full the compensation that he would have earned 'but for' his injury"); *Lamont v. United States*, 613 F. Supp. 588, 593 (S.D.N.Y. 1985) (holding that where the "apparent custom and practice" of seafarers was to work a substantial amount of overtime, an injured seafarer was "entitled to recover, in full, the compensation that he would have earned but for his illness or injury").

had said in that case that the specifics of what is covered by a seafarer's right to "maintenance"—traditionally, the right to food and lodging expenses—could be modified by a court, even if **[—5—]** those specifics were established in a collective bargaining agreement. *Barnes*, 900 F.2d at 640.

Joyce now asks us to overturn the District Court's ruling on unearned wages.[2] Because seafarers were entitled at common law to both maintenance and unearned wages, he argues that our holding in *Barnes* should extend to unearned wages set by a collective bargaining agreement, making the union contract subject to change by court order to conform with traditional maritime law. His appeal presents an opportunity for us to reconsider our holding in *Barnes*.[3] **{-505-}**

II. Standard of Review

Because the District Court granted Maersk's motion for summary judgment, we review its determination *de novo*, applying the same standard that it applied. *Shelton v. Bledsoe*, 775 F.3d 554, 559 (3d Cir. 2015). A "court shall grant summary judgment if the movant shows that there is no genuine dispute as to any material fact and the movant is entitled to judgment as a matter of law." Fed. R. Civ. P. **[—6—]** 56(a). There are no factual disputes at all in this case. Instead, we are faced with a pure question of law: whether, on the agreed facts, Maersk was entitled to judgment based on the collective bargaining agreement. Our review is thus plenary. *See McCann v. Newman Irrevocable Tr.*, 458 F.3d 281, 286 (3d Cir. 2006) (explaining that we exercise plenary review over questions of law).

III. Discussion[4]

A. *Review of* Barnes v. Andover Co., L.P., *900 F.2d 630 (3d Cir. 1990)*

Joyce's argument relies heavily on our holding in *Barnes*, so we turn to it first. The question in that case was whether a seafarer was bound by the maintenance rate set in a collective bargaining agreement between the shipowner and the seafarers' union. *Barnes*, 900 F.2d at 631. We began our analysis by recognizing the deeply rooted duty at common law for a shipowner to pay a seafarer's maintenance. *Id.* at 633. "Maintenance is the living allowance for a seaman while he is ashore recovering from injury or illness." *Id.* It derives from medieval maritime laws and has long been recognized by American courts. *Id.* The right to "cure," which is payment for "medical expenses incurred in treating the seaman's injury or illness[,]" has the same origin. *Id.*

The duty to pay maintenance and cure arose from what was viewed as the "peculiarity" of seafarers' lives. *Id.* **[—7—]** Justice Story explained the views of society at the time: "[seamen] are generally poor and friendless, and acquire habits of gross indulgence, carelessness, and improvidence." *Id.* (quoting *Harden v. Gordon*, 11 F. Cas. 480, 483 (C.C.D. Me. 1823) (No. 6,047)). Thus, "[i]f some provision be not made for them in sickness at the expense of the ship, they must often in foreign ports suffer the accumulated evils of disease, and poverty, and sometimes perish from the want of suitable nourishment." *Id.* (quoting *Harden*, 11 F. Cas. at 483). By imposing the duty on shipowners to pay for maintenance and cure, "the interest of the owner will be immediately connected with that of the seamen." *Id.* (quoting *Harden*, 11 F. Cas. at 483). That arrangement benefitted both seafarers and owners—the former had the benefit of someone "watch[ing] over their health with vigilance and fidelity," and the latter had employees who were "urge[d] ... to encounter hazards in the ship's service." *Id.* (quoting *Harden*, 11 F. Cas. at 483).

[2] Joyce had also brought suit based on the Shipowners' Liability Convention and the daily per diem maintenance rate under the collective bargaining agreement. Although the District Court ruled against him on those claims too, he does not appeal those rulings here.

[3] We thank Professor Martin J. Davies of Tulane University Law School for his insightful amicus brief discussing *Barnes* and the questions of maritime law before us.

[4] The District Court had jurisdiction under 28 U.S.C. § 1333. We have appellate jurisdiction pursuant to 28 U.S.C. § 1291.

Those duties remain in maritime law. Indeed, in *Barnes* we observed that, besides being long entrenched in maritime law, the responsibility to pay maintenance and cure has been "construed liberally" and "consistently expanded" by the courts. *Id.* The scope of that responsibility extends "beyond injuries sustained on board ship or during working hours" and is in force "until the seaman has reached the point of maximum cure." *Id.* at 633-34. The right to maintenance and cure exists "regardless of ... fault" by the seafarer. **{-506-}** *Id.* at 633. Only in cases of willful misconduct has a seafarer been held to be outside the scope of the right. *Id.*

With that background, we directed our attention to the central question in *Barnes*, namely whether a contract that **[—8—]** established a maintenance rate was binding on a union member. *Id.* at 631. The contract at issue established a rate of maintenance of $8 per day. *Id.* at 632. We held that it was "inconsistent ... with the traditional doctrine of maintenance" to say that the rate in a union contract "is binding on a seaman who can show higher daily expenses." *Id.* at 640. We therefore analyzed the $8 per day rate and determined it to be inadequate. *See id.* at 644 (concluding that the maintenance award should include "expenses actually incurred or paid in connection with ... permanent lodging," including "gas and electric bills" and "home insurance" but not "automobile expenses and toiletries").

In reaching that conclusion, we acknowledged that we were departing from the reasoning of three other United States Courts of Appeals—the First, Sixth, and Ninth Circuits—which had faced the same question but decided the matter differently. *Id.* at 635. Those other courts had determined that the "contractual rate should be binding so long as the collective bargaining process ha[d] been fair and the rate of maintenance ha[d] been subject to real negotiation." *Id.* (citing *Gardiner v. Sea-Land Serv., Inc.*, 786 F.2d 943, 949 (9th Cir. 1986)). They recognized that federal labor laws did not directly preempt maritime law on maintenance, but they saw the policy behind national labor laws as sufficiently weighty and clear to prevent courts from modifying a bargained-for rate of maintenance in a union contract. *Id.*

Barnes explicitly rejected that reasoning.[5] Although we indicated "sympath[y] with an approach that would **[—9—]** encourage the use and reliability of collective bargaining agreements," we believed it was not well-founded in law. *Id.* at 640. We declared that we "kn[e]w of no basis for permitting such contracts to override a common law maritime right of a seaman that has not been preempted by the labor laws." *Id.* Therefore, we said, "unless Congress determines that the circumstances giving rise to the need for maintenance have changed and that collective bargaining is now a more appropriate way to deal with the issue of the ill or injured seaman, the common law remedy must remain in full force." *Id.*

We placed a caveat on our holding, however, noting that unions and shipowners could "agree on what they believe is a realistic rate of maintenance with the expectation that the parties would voluntarily abide by that rate and thereby avoid litigation." *Id.* Somewhat incongruously, though, we then immediately approved the frustration of such expectations by saying that the plaintiff in *Barnes* had "met his common law burden of producing evidence ... that the $8 rate was insufficient to provide him with food and lodging." *Id.* Hence, the bargained-for rate was set aside. *Id.*

B. *Joyce's Argument*

Joyce argues that *Barnes* allows us to hold that he is entitled to overtime pay in his unearned wages. His logic proceeds in three steps. First, he says that the seafarer's right to unearned wages dates back almost a thousand years and should be treated exactly like the right to maintenance. Second, he claims that overtime pay **{-507-}** has consistently been a part of the common law right to unearned wages. Third, Joyce connects the first two steps to *Barnes*: an unearned **[—10—]** wage rate set in a

[5] We did agree, however, that the union contract was not directly preempted. *See Barnes*, 900 F.2d at 637-39.

collective bargaining agreement can be set aside when there is evidence that it is insufficient, as was the maintenance rate in *Barnes*.

We do not take issue here with Joyce's first assertion. There is ample evidence that, at common law, seafarers were and still are entitled to unearned wages. *See Vaughan v. Atkinson*, 369 U.S. 527, 535 n.2 (1962) (Stewart, J., dissenting) (collecting cases for the proposition that "[t]he earliest codifications of the law of the sea provided for medical treatment and wages for mariners injured or falling ill in the ship's service."); *see also Flores v. Carnival Cruise Lines*, 47 F.3d 1120, 1122 (11th Cir. 1995) (recognizing that unearned wages were historically part of the relief sought in an action for cure and maintenance). There is less of an historical anchor, though, for the second step in Joyce's argument, that the common law right to unearned wages includes overtime. Nonetheless, that proposition is sound. Wage rates for ancient mariners were typically set by contract in an agreement then known as the shipping articles, and the general rule was that "[t]he stipulation in the shipping articles [was] conclusive as to wages[,] and no more [could] be recovered on any special promise to pay for severe or extra labor or exposure in the course of duty[.]" 1 Theophilus Parsons, *A Treatise on Maritime Law* 447-48 (1859) (footnote omitted). A seafarer's right to his "full wages," *The R.R. Springer*, 4 F. 671, 672 (S.D. Ohio 1880), therefore meant recovery only of the amount stipulated in the articles. Gradually, however, that recovery broadened to encompass "the full amount reasonably expected by the parties to be paid during the voyage." *Lamont v. United States*, 613 F. Supp. 588, 593 (S.D.N.Y. 1985). Modern courts have therefore included tips, *Flores*, 47 F.3d at 1122-25, and accumulated **[—11—]** time off, *Lipscomb v. Foss Mar. Co.*, 83 F.3d 1106, 1109-11 (9th Cir. 1996), as part of the unearned wage remedy under general maritime law. Thus, today, as long as the parties' "reasonable expectation includes 'overtime,'" *Lamont*, 613 F. Supp. at 593, and such wages are "not speculative," *Padilla v. Maersk Line, Ltd.*, 721 F.3d 77, 82-83, 1 Adm. R. 34, 36 (2d Cir. 2013), they are recoverable. *See id.* at 82, 1 Adm. R. at 36 (awarding payment for overtime as part of unearned wages for seafarers who fell ill because "it was the custom and practice for seafarers ... to derive substantial income from overtime compensation and that, consequently, such compensation was a common expectation of both the seamen and of [the shipowner]"); *see also Shaw v. Ohio River Co.*, 526 F.2d 193, 199 (3d Cir. 1975) (noting that accumulated leave time is a component of wages).

There is undeniable wisdom to an approach that looks to the expectations of the parties when delimiting the unearned wage remedy of a seafarer. When overtime is a "common expectation" and the seafarer's entitlement to it is "essentially undisputed," *Padilla*, 721 F.3d at 82, 1 Adm. R. at 36, overtime can be considered merely "wages the seaman would have earned" absent injury, *Barnes*, 900 F.2d at 634 n.2.

If we were to follow *Barnes*, then, Joyce would likely be correct on the third point of his argument as well; we would be hard-pressed to say that courts have no power to modify unearned wage rates established by collective bargaining agreements.[6] But **{-508-}** every other circuit court to **[—12—]** address the conflict between collectively bargained-for rights and seafarers' rights at common law has seen the issue differently than we did. Joyce's claim thus hinges on the continuing validity of *Barnes*.

---

[6] The District Court concluded that *Barnes* was not binding because it viewed that precedent as being cabined to maintenance. *See Joyce*, 2016 WL 3566726, at *6 ("The **[—12—]** Court agrees with Defendant that *Barnes* does not govern Plaintiff's claim with respect to unearned wages."). That is not an unreasonable position, and we agree with Amicus Curiae that "the right to unpaid wages is different in some respects from the right to maintenance and cure." (Amicus Curiae Br. at 6.) We are not persuaded, however, that those differences would necessitate limiting *Barnes* (and our holding today) to maintenance. We therefore think that Joyce has the better of that particular argument and that, if we were not to overrule *Barnes*, its logic would militate strongly in his favor.

C. *Reconsidering* Barnes

"It is the tradition of this court that the holding of a panel in a precedential opinion is binding on subsequent panels." Third Circuit I.O.P. 9.1. "We adhere strictly to that tradition[]" and will only depart "on a rare occasion." *In re Grossman's Inc.*, 607 F.3d 114, 117 (3d Cir. 2010) (en banc). Consideration by the entire court en banc is therefore required to overrule a prior panel's precedent, Third Circuit I.O.P. 9.1, and "[w]e do not overturn our precedents lightly." *Al-Sharif v. U.S. Citizenship & Immigration Servs.*, 734 F.3d 207, 212 (3d Cir. 2013) (en banc). We also recognize, however, that "*stare decisis* 'is not an inexorable command.'" *Id.* (quoting *Payne v. Tennessee*, 501 U.S. 808, 828 (1991)). **[—13—]**

In general, "we decide cases before us based on our own examination of the issue, not on the views of other jurisdictions." *In re Grossman's*, 607 F.3d at 121. But, when we find that our reasoning has been met by "universal disapproval" by other jurisdictions, those contrary views may "impel us to consider whether the reasoning applied by our colleagues elsewhere is persuasive." *Id.* That was the case in *In re Grossman's*, where we reevaluated a test established for stays in bankruptcy cases. *Id.* at 119-20. The decision we were considering then had been called "one of the most criticized and least followed precedents" in the bankruptcy realm, *id.* at 120 (quoting *Firearms Imp. & Exp. Corp. v. United Capital Ins. Co. (In re Firearms Imp. & Exp. Corp.)*, 131 B.R. 1009, 1015 (Bankr. S.D. Fla. 1991)), and had been "uniformly" rejected by other courts. *Id.*

Barnes has not been met with the same vocal rejection, but, when it was decided, three other courts of appeals had already reached the opposite conclusion, holding that the rate of maintenance in a freely bargained-for union contract was binding on the seafarers who signed it. *Al-Zawkari v. Am. Steamship Co.*, 871 F.2d 585, 588 (6th Cir. 1989); *Macedo v. F/V Paul & Michelle*, 868 F.2d 519, 522 (1st Cir. 1989); *Gardiner*, 786 F.2d at 949-50. As already noted, the Court in *Barnes* recognized those decisions but rejected their reasoning. *See Barnes*, 900 F.2d at 632 ("[W]e will depart from the position of the First, Sixth and Ninth Circuits."). In the twenty-seven years since, every other circuit to consider the question has, in turn, rejected *Barnes* and adopted the majority position. *Ammar v. United States*, 342 F.3d 133, 146 (2d Cir. 2003); *Frederick v. Kirby Tankships, Inc.*, 205 F.3d 1277, 1291 (11th Cir. 2000); *Baldassaro v. United States*, 64 F.3d 206, 212 (5th Cir. 1995). And three circuits have **[—14—]** extended their holdings to cover not just maintenance but also unearned wage rates established in collective bargaining agreements. *See Padilla*, 721 F.3d at 82, 1 Adm. R. at 35 ("[W]hile the entitlement to unearned wages arises under general maritime law, rates for unearned wages may **{-509-}** be defined and modified in collective bargaining agreements[.]" (citing *Ammar*, 342 F.3d at 146-47)); *Cabrera Espinal v. Royal Caribbean Cruises, Ltd.*, 253 F.3d 629, 631 (11th Cir. 2001) ("[T]he remedies provided for in maritime law [including wages] may be altered although not abrogated by collective bargaining agreements." (citing *Frederick*, 205 F.3d at 1291)); *Lipscomb*, 83 F.3d at 1108 ("[T]he method for calculating the amount of maintenance, cure, and wages may be determined by the collective bargaining process[.]" (citing *Gardiner*, 786 F.2d at 949)). Our opinion in *Barnes* leaves us standing alone and suggests that a reevaluation of that decision is in order.

Barnes rested on the idea that common law protections for seafarers arose from the "traditional doctrine[s]" of maintenance and cure, and that there was "no basis" in the law to allow union contracts "to override [those] common law maritime right[s]" when they had not been expressly "preempted by the labor laws." *Barnes*, 900 F.2d at 640. But, as recognized by the Ninth Circuit, this country's "national labor policy is built on the premise that employees can bargain most effectively for improvements in wages, hours, and working conditions by pooling their economic strength and acting through freely chosen labor organizations." *Gardiner*, 786 F.2d at 948. Those policies favor honoring holistic contracts between "labor and management ...

that will effectively regulate every aspect of their ... relationship ... from the most crucial to the most minute[.]" *Id.* at 948-49 (quotations and citations omitted). **[—15—]**

We now agree that the "broad labor policies which undergird federal labor law, as well as the nature of the collective bargaining process, require adherence" to the terms of a collective bargaining agreement, including rates established for maintenance and unearned wages. *Frederick*, 205 F.3d at 1291. For that conclusion, we do not rely on the doctrine of preemption; rather, we recognize, as have our sister circuits, that "the need for judicial intervention to protect seamen has been substantially lessened[,]" *Ammar*, 342 F.3d at 146, and thus the common law basis for requiring courts to disregard the freely negotiated agreements of private parties and to refuse to enforce the terms of the collective bargaining agreement also carries substantially less force, *see Gardiner*, 786 F.2d at 948. Although maritime remedies cannot be abrogated, courts should not "lightly embrace the repudiation of contractual obligations enumerated in a collective bargaining agreement," *id.*, and Congress has clearly expressed that it is generally the role of private labor agreements, not courts, to "regulate all aspects of the complicated relationship" between employer and employee, *id.* at 949 (quoting *United Steelworkers of Am. v. Warrior & Gulf Nav. Co.*, 363 U.S. 574, 580 (1960)). That is not only the better outcome for shipping companies, which can plan with certainty what their responsibilities will be, but it is also better for seafarers, whose collective bargaining strength can negotiate more favorable employment terms and conditions. We are persuaded that piecemeal judicial review of "one of many elements ... over which the parties negotiate" discourages that back-and-forth process. *Id.* (citation omitted). Put differently, "[t]he adequacy of the maintenance [or overtime] rate should not be examined in isolation by the court because the determination of its adequacy in relation to **[—16—]** the whole scheme of benefits has already been made by the union and the seamen who voted for the contract." *Baldassaro*, 64 F.3d at 213 (quoting *Gardiner*, 786 F.2d at 949); *see also Gardiner*, 786 F.2d at 949 ("[T]he nature of the 'give and take' process of collective bargaining suggest[s] that acceptance **{-510-}** of a particular package of benefits should be binding on the union members.").

With our course change today, we remove ourselves from "engaging in overt legislation of particular dollar figures" in union contracts, and instead "enforce privately negotiated contractual rates[.]" *Al-Zawkari*, 871 F.2d at 588. The majority position we adopt accepts the "modern reality" of unionized seafarers who negotiate for comprehensive contracts. *Ammar*, 342 F.3d at 146. At the start of this century, the Second Circuit recognized that the days when wary and "friendless" seafarers needed the protection of the common law had largely passed. *Id.* "[T]oday, 'most seamen are union members with a union-negotiated package of compensation and benefits of which the right to maintenance [and unearned wages] is a small component[.]'" *Id.* (quoting T. Schoenbaum, *Admiralty and Maritime Law* § 6-32, at 361 (2d ed. 1994)); *cf. Macedo*, 868 F.2d at 522 (recognizing that collective bargaining agreements are "highly approved generally" and that enforcing their limitations on maintenance is "quite different" from enforcing limitations negotiated by "an individual seaman"). Unionization has produced a "well-organized work force with sophisticated leaders who constantly press for better working conditions" and the need for judicially fashioned protection has "substantially lessened." *Ammar*, 342 F.3d at 146. Negotiated union contracts strike a balance by "encompassing a wide range of issues for which some provisions will result in greater **[—17—]** protection ... while others will result in less." *Cabrera Espinal*, 253 F.3d at 631 (citing *Frederick*, 205 F.3d at 1291). Enforcing union contracts as written respects the priorities that modern seafarers have expressed through arms-length and well-informed negotiations.[7] **[—18—]**

[7] In considering the preemption question in *Barnes*, we recognized the modern reality that seafarers are "neither friendless nor improvident." 900 F.2d at 636. Yet we rejected the idea that collective bargaining agreements could replace common law rights. Our opinion was rooted in the understanding that "the Supreme Court has shown

The scope of our decision today makes the holding in *Barnes* untenable, so that unearned wages and maintenance are alike subject to modification by union contracts. *See, e.g.*, *Lipscomb*, 83 F.3d at 1108 ("[T]he method for calculating the amount of maintenance, cure, and wages may be determined by the collective bargaining process[.]"). That is logical given the shared common law origins of maintenance, cure, and unearned wages. *See Cabrera Espinal*, 253 F.3d at 631 ("General maritime law guarantees seamen: '(1) maintenance, which is a living allowance; (2) cure, which covers nursing and medical expenses; and (3) wages.'" (quoting Herbert R. Baer, *Admiralty Law of the Su* **{-511-}** *preme Court* 6 (3d ed. 1979))).[8] Our holding thus overrules *Barnes* and extends that reversal to the case before us.

But we also adopt a backstop protection for seafarers, as prescribed by our sister circuits. Consistent with principles of contract law, a seafarer with a basis to allege that an entire collective bargaining agreement is, or the process whereby it was entered into was, "unfair or inadequate" may bring that complaint to court. *Gardiner*, 786 F.2d at 949. The Second Circuit implicitly made that point when it upheld a maintenance figure set in a union contract where there was no allegation "that [the] agreement was not a legitimately negotiated agreement, or that [the seafarer's] interests were not adequately represented in the negotiation process, or that the agreement as a whole is unfair." *Ammar*, 342 F.3d at 146. Other circuit courts have also stressed that protection. *See* **[—19—]** *Frederick*, 205 F.3d at 1291 ("[A]s in *Baldassaro*[*v. United States*] and *Gardiner*[*v. Sea-Land Service, Inc.*], [the plaintiff] makes no allegations that the [collective bargaining agreement] as a whole is unfair or that the union did not adequately represent him."); *Baldassaro*, 64 F.3d at 213 ("As in *Gardiner*, there is no allegation in this case that the [collective bargaining agreement] as a whole is unfair or that this seaman was not adequately represented by the Union."). Joyce has not challenged the negotiation process or the contract in its entirety, so that backstop is not at issue here.

We note a significant further limitation on our ruling: maintenance, cure, and unearned wages are so deeply rooted in common law that, absent congressional action, they cannot be completely abrogated by contract. *See, e.g.*, *De Zon v. Am. President Lines, Ltd.*, 318 U.S. 660, 667 (1943) (recognizing that "no private agreement is competent to abrogate" the shipowner's duty to pay maintenance and cure); *Al-Zawkari*, 871 F.2d at 588 ("While the duty to provide maintenance cannot be *entirely* abrogated, as an implied contractual provision, the right to maintenance can be modified and defined by contract."); *Gardiner*, 786 F.2d at 948 ("Although the right to maintenance is presumed to exist because of its establishment at common law, its rate may be subject to the negotiation process."). We would look askance, then, at any collective bargaining agreement that purported to eliminate those rights. We need not wrestle with that limitation today, however, because we are satisfied that defining unearned wages without including overtime was, "in relation to the whole scheme of benefits[,]" *Gardiner*, 786 F.2d at 949, not a **[—20—]** complete abrogation of Joyce's common law right to

no inclination to depart from its long-established solicitude for seamen." *Id.* at 637. Just a few months later, however, the Supreme Court did place some bounds on that solicitude and acknowledged that when Congress "speak[s] directly" to maritime remedies, courts are limited in their ability "to supplement Congress' answer" by pointing to the special status of seamen. *Miles v. Apex Marine Corp.*, 498 U.S. 19, 31 (1990) (internal quotation marks omitted); *see id.* at 27 ("We no longer live in an era when seamen and their loved ones must look primarily to the courts as a source of substantive legal protection .... In this era, an admiralty court should look primarily to these legislative enactments for policy guidance."). So, while the Court has since reiterated that seafarers remain "wards of admiralty," *Atl. Sounding Co., Inc. v. Townsend*, 557 U.S. 404, 417 (2009), our departure from *Barnes* in favor of enforcement of the labor laws is consistent with the pronouncements of the Court as well as those of the courts of appeals. It also reflects an appreciation of the problems inherent in deciding piecemeal the terms of freely entered collective bargaining agreements.

[8] We recognized in *Barnes* that "[t]he right to unearned wages ... has the same historical basis as maintenance and cure." 900 F.2d at 634 n.2.

wages.[9] *Cf. Barnes*, 900 F.2d at 645 (Lifland, J., dissenting) ("Collective bargaining has not abrogated the right when it clearly recognizes the right and places a dollar value on [it] ... in the context of ... bargaining over wages, hours and other terms and conditions of employment which results in a myriad of benefits appropriate to the maritime environment.").[10] **[—21—] {-512-}**

IV. Conclusion

It is the rare case in which we overrule our own precedent. But when our Court is in disagreement with every other circuit to consider a question, it can be wise to reconsider our prior reasoning. Having done so here, we overrule *Barnes v. Andover* and will enforce the rate of unearned wages set forth in the collective bargaining agreement between Joyce and Maersk. Consequently, we will affirm.[11]

---

[9] We urge courts who are faced with the question of whether a right has been abrogated to consider the agreement holistically. A contract that limits the common law rights to maintenance, cure, and unearned wages is most likely to withstand scrutiny if it expressly recognizes those rights and indicates how the rates have been bargained for in the negotiation.

[10] We also emphasize that, consistent with our reasoning, our holding only applies to unionized seafarers. The collective bargaining process is such a benefit to unionized seafarers and shipowners that it warrants enforcing collective bargaining agreements that modify traditional maritime rights of maintenance, cure, and unearned wages. This rationale does not apply to modify those traditional rights of a non-unionized employee. The disparate treatment of unionized and non-unionized seafarers is not inequitable, *but cf. Gardiner*, 786 F.2d at 951 (Fletcher, J., dissenting) ("[U]nion seamen and non-union seamen working for the same employer might receive different maintenance rates."); rather, it reflects the different choices of free agents who are then differently situated.

[11] "We may affirm the district court on any ground supported by the record." *Tourscher v. McCullough*, 184 F.3d 236, 240 (3d Cir. 1999).

This page intentionally left blank

United States Court of Appeals for the Fourth Circuit

United States Court of Appeals
for the Fourth Circuit

No. 15-2525

METRO MACH. CORP.
vs.
DIRECTOR, OFFICE OF WORKERS' COMPENSATION PROGRAMS

On Petition for Review of an Order of the Benefits Review Board

Decided: January 20, 2017

Citation: 846 F.3d 680, 5 Adm. R. 150 (4th Cir. 2017).

Before **TRAXLER, FLOYD,** and **THACKER,** Circuit Judges.

[—2—] {-683-} **TRAXLER,** Circuit Judge:

Metro Machine Corporation and Signal Mutual Indemnity Association, Limited, petition for review of an order of the Benefits Review Board affirming decisions of an ALJ granting a claim for medical benefits under the Longshore and Harbor Workers' Compensation Act ("the Act"), *see* 33 U.S.C. § 907. Finding no reversible error, we deny the petition.

I.

Before setting out the facts underlying this appeal, we will begin with a brief discussion of some of the relevant legal concepts.

The Act "creates a comprehensive federal scheme to compensate workers injured or killed while employed upon the navigable waters of the United States." *Estate of Cowart v. Nicklos Drilling Co.*, 505 U.S. 469, 470-71 (1992). The Act requires employers to furnish medical care to employees who suffer an "injury" within the meaning of the Act. 33 U.S.C. § 907. As is relevant here, "injury" is defined as an

> accidental injury or death arising out of and in the course of employment, and such occupational disease or infection as arises naturally out of such employment or as naturally or unavoidably results from such accidental injury.

33 U.S.C. § 902(2). "Arising 'out of' *and* 'in the course of' employment are separate elements: the former refers to injury causation; the latter refers to the time, place, and **[—3—]** circumstances of the injury." *U.S. Indus./Fed. Sheet Metal, Inc. v. Director, OWCP*, 455 U.S. 608, 615 (1982) ("*U.S. Industries*"). "Through what has come to be known as the aggravation rule, the courts have extended [§ 902(2)'s)] definition such that, if an employment injury aggravates, accelerates, or combines with a previous infirmity, the entire disability is compensable." *Newport News Shipbuilding & Dry Dock Co. v. Fishel*, 694 F.2d 327, 329 (4th Cir. 1982).

Because Congress recognized that the elements of § 902(2) "would be difficult to **{-684-}** prove," *Director, OWCP v. Greenwich Collieries*, 512 U.S. 267, 280 (1994), Congress provided the § 20(a) presumption, the proper interpretation of which is a central issue in this appeal. The statute describing the presumption provides, "In any proceeding for the enforcement of a claim for compensation under this Act it shall be presumed, in the absence of substantial evidence to the contrary . . . [t]hat the claim comes within the provisions of this Act." 33 U.S.C. § 920(a).

The parties agree that to invoke the presumption, an employee must allege a prima facie case that "(1) an injury or death (2) . . . arose out of and in the course of (3) his maritime employment." *Universal Maritime Corp. v. Moore*, 126 F.3d 256, 262 (4th Cir. 1997). To establish this prima facie case, a claimant must show "(1) that he suffered physical harm **[—4—]** and (2) that a workplace accident or workplace conditions *could have* caused, aggravated, or accelerated the harm." *Bath Iron Works Corp. v. Fields*, 599 F.3d 47, 53 (1st Cir. 2010) (emphasis added). Once the prima facie case is established, the burden of production shifts to the employer, who must produce evidence that could justify a reasonable factfinder in concluding that the claimant either did not suffer physical harm or that no workplace accident or workplace conditions caused, aggravated, or accelerated the harm. *See id.*; *accord Moore*, 126 F.3d at 262-63. If the employer satisfies this burden, the presumption falls out of the case, and the factfinder is left to find the necessary facts without considering the presumption. *See Moore*, 126 F.3d at 262-63.

II.

We now turn to the facts before us. John Stephenson ("Claimant") worked for Metro Machine Corporation as a pipefitter in Virginia from August 1983 until August 2011. He has a long history of breathing problems. He suffered from asthma until he was approximately eight years old, and he began smoking when he was 16. He has received treatment for bronchitis caused by his smoking since the early 1980s. And he received treatment for a productive cough and wheezing in 1985 and 1986. Additionally, he regularly suffered from bronchitis during winters, and his bronchitis was treated with antibiotics. **[—5—]** He has been taking steroids for his wheezing and coughing since 1986. He was diagnosed with chronic obstructive pulmonary disease[1] ("COPD") in 1996 and emphysema in 2001.

On February 18, 2008, Claimant was working in the superstructure of a vessel. During his workday, which lasted more than eight hours, he inhaled fumes from welding and burning and the application of epoxy paint ("the exposure"); inhaling these fumes caused him breathing problems. After Claimant finished his shift and went home, the problems continued all night, prompting him to go to the emergency room the next morning. At the hospital, he was diagnosed with "[e]xacerbation of chronic obstructive pulmonary disease." S.J.A. 1. He was admitted and remained hospitalized for eight days, during which time he was prescribed steroids, inhalers, empiric antibiotics, and albuterol to treat his COPD. Upon discharge, he was prescribed a nebulizer and oxygen concentrator, which he had not used prior to the hospitalization. **{-685-}**

Metro paid Claimant compensation for temporary total disability from February 19, 2008, through August 3, 2008, and later for temporary partial disability from September 16, 2009, through September 29, 2009. When he returned to work, he was **[—6—]** restricted from going aboard the ship and limited in the amount of weight he could lift.

Claimant voluntarily retired in 2011. Since his retirement, he has begun using his oxygen concentrator more frequently. He has continued taking the same medications he took when he was hospitalized, but he has increased his dosages. He reports that his coughing has improved over time although his shortness of breath has worsened.

In October 2011, Claimant was treated for a fracture at the T7 vertebra by Dr. Alireza Jamali. Dr. Jamali stated in an office note that the fracture was "most likely due to excessive coughing." S.J.A. 8. In February 2012, Dr. Jamali wrote that Claimant "required a long-term intake of the steroid for management of his respiratory condition," which "contributed to osteoporosis and pathological fracture of T7." S.J.A. 15. Dr. Jamali opined that the fracture was "directly due to long-term steroid intake" from the management of Claimant's respiratory condition. S.J.A. 15.

Asserting that his injuries were the result of the exposure, Claimant requested that Metro pay for his medical treatment. Metro refused and filed a notice of controversion on March 15, 2012, asserting that the treatment he had requested was not related to the exposure. On March 30, 2012, Claimant filed a claim for compensation, Form LS-203, under the Act. In **[—7—]** the spaces on the form calling for the date of the injury and a description of the accident, he answered "2/18/2008" and "exposure to fumes," and in the space calling for identification of the part of body affected, he answered, "Lungs." J.A. 11.

On May 15, 2012, a claims examiner held an informal conference. Memoranda memorializing the conference indicate that Claimant had sought medical benefits for both

[1] COPD is "any disorder characterized by persistent or recurring obstruction of bronchial air flow, such as chronic bronchitis, asthma, or pulmonary emphysema." *Dorland's Illustrated Medical Dictionary* 530 (32nd ed. 2012).

his ongoing COPD and his fractured vertebra. The claims examiner recommended payment of benefits for both conditions.

The ALJ held a hearing regarding the claim on September 25, 2013. The parties stipulated that Claimant injured his pulmonary organs on February 18, 2008; that the injury arose out of and in the course of Claimant's employment with Metro; and that the Act applies to the claim.

The medical evidence introduced at the hearing included the May 2013 deposition of Claimant's long-time treating physician, Dr. Ignacio Ripoll, who was board-certified in pulmonary medicine and had been a practicing pulmonary specialist for approximately 30 years. The evidence also included three letters Dr. Ripoll had written before the deposition concerning the possible causal relationship between the exposure and Claimant's worsening COPD. The letters evidenced Dr. Ripoll's changing views regarding the existence of such a causal relationship. **[—8—]**

The ALJ summarized the contents of the three letters:

> In a letter dated January 10, 2012, Dr. Ripoll wrote that Claimant suffers from severe COPD with a grade IV impairment using the AMA guides. Dr. Ripoll listed the dates and results of several pulmonary function tests beginning in June of 2008, noting that at that time Claimant's COPD was severe and deteriorating at a rate of three percent per year. Dr. Ripoll noted that Claimant had more symptoms after the 2008 exposure than prior to it and therefore found with a reasonable degree of medical certainty **{-686-}** that the exposure worsened his pulmonary condition, which has declined since that time.
>
> After receiving pulmonary function testing results dating back to January of 1986, Dr. Ripoll wrote a follow-up letter dated July 16, 2012. Dr. Ripoll opined that the historical data cast doubt on the role of fume exposures respecting Claimant's declining respiratory function. Dr. Ripoll stated that the data indicated that the exposure caused an acute pulmonary event, but did not affect the rate of progression of the underlying disease. Dr. Ripoll included the caveat that the November 2001 and January 2007 results could be artificially low due to some acute condition at those times and additional testing after the January 2007 values could indicate whether Claimant's lung function improved to a stable baseline.
>
> A November 28, 2012 letter included a graph of Claimant's FEV1 [one-second forced expiratory volume results] from 1986 until 2011. Dr. Ripoll noted that the slope of Claimant's FEV1 decline changed after Claimant's exposure to fumes in 2008. Dr. Ripoll found that the rate of deterioration increased following the inhalation injury and thus concluded that it was highly likely that the February 2008 inhalation injury caused the rapid deterioration in lung function seen after that time.

J.A. 193-94 (citations omitted).

Finally, in his 2013 deposition, Dr. Ripoll described Claimant's lung disease as "chronic obstructive lung disease or **[—9—]** chronic bronchitis, chronic inflammation." J.A. 43. He testified that Claimant's lungs had been irreparably damaged by his many years of smoking, and that his lung function would continue to deteriorate despite any medications he might take. Nevertheless, he testified that he continued to believe, to a reasonable degree of medical certainty, that the data showed a significant acceleration in the progression of the lung disease after the 2008 exposure.

Following the hearing, the ALJ found that Claimant established a prima facie case by showing a harm—the worsening of his COPD—and a work incident that could have caused or aggravated that harm. Therefore, he found Claimant entitled to the § 20(a) presumption that the worsening of his COPD was compensable.

The ALJ observed that Metro sought to show that any aggravation of Claimant's COPD caused by the exposure was only temporary. In support of this position, Metro submitted the opinion of Dr. Ripoll, along with treatment records. Given the contradictory and uncertain opinions that Dr. Ripoll had issued, however, the ALJ concluded that Dr. Ripoll's opinions were "entitled to little weight" and "insufficient to rebut the presumption. J.A. 205. Noting that no other evidence tended to show that any exacerbation of Claimant's COPD caused by the exposure was only temporary, the ALJ concluded that Metro had **[—10—]** not rebutted the § 20(a) presumption. He thus awarded Claimant past and future medical benefits for his work-related COPD.

Despite prevailing regarding the COPD, Claimant moved for reconsideration, contending that the ALJ had failed to address a part of his claim that the parties had addressed at the hearing, namely, his claim that he was entitled to medical treatment for his vertebra fracture. The ALJ granted the motion and proceeded to consider the compensability of the fracture. The ALJ rejected an argument by Metro that the § 20(a) presumption did not apply since the fracture was not specifically identified on Claimant's Form LS-203 that he had filed in March 2012. The ALJ further found that Claimant established a prima **{-687-}** facie case linking his fracture to excessive coughing from, and the steroids he was prescribed for, his work-related COPD. Regarding Metro's attempt to rebut the prima facie case, the ALJ concluded that the fact that Claimant, prior to the exposure, had had respiratory problems and took steroids did not constitute evidence that the primary injury did not cause, aggravate, or hasten his fracture. Finding that Metro had not rebutted the presumption that the fracture was compensable, the ALJ awarded Claimant medical benefits for the fracture.

Metro appealed the decisions concerning the compensability of the COPD and fracture to the Board, which affirmed. The Board held that substantial evidence supported the ALJ's finding **[—11—]** that Claimant established a prima facie case regarding his COPD and thus that the ALJ properly invoked the § 20(a) presumption. The Board rejected an argument by Metro that Claimant needed to present *medical* evidence directly linking his COPD to the exposure to establish his prima facie case. The Board also concluded that the ALJ properly found that Metro failed to rebut the presumption on the basis that Dr. Ripoll's opinion was equivocal.

Regarding the vertebra fracture, the Board rejected an argument by Metro that the § 20(a) presumption does not apply to "secondary injuries," such as the fracture. The Board also rejected the argument that the presumption should not have applied because the fracture was outside the scope of Claimant's claim. The Board noted that Claimant had raised the claim for medical benefits regarding his fracture before both the district director and the ALJ, and Metro had not contended that it was surprised by the issue or that any late notice prejudiced its ability to defend against the claim.

Metro now petitions for review of the Board's decision.

III.

Metro advances various arguments in support of its petition for review. We review the Board's decisions for errors of law and to determine whether the Board adhered to its standard of review. *See Newport News Shipbuilding & Dry Dock Co. v. Harris*, **[—12—]** 934 F.2d 548, 550 (4th Cir. 1991). The Board's standard of review requires that the ALJ's findings of fact be considered "conclusive if supported by substantial evidence in the record considered as a whole." *Newport News Shipbuilding & Dry Dock Co. v. Director, OWCP*, 131 F.3d 1079, 1080 (4th Cir. 1997) (per curiam) (internal quotation marks omitted). And importantly, the Act "must be liberally construed in conformance with its [remedial] purpose." *Northeast Marine Term. Co. v. Caputo*, 432 U.S. 249, 268 (1977) (internal quotation marks omitted).

In this appeal, the Director of the Office of Workers' Compensation Programs of the Department of Labor (the "Director"), is a respondent. We afford deference to the Director's views concerning the construction of the Act because he has policy-making authority with regard to the Act. *See Director, OWCP v. Newport News Shipbuilding & Dry Dock Co.*, 8 F.3d 175, 179 (4th Cir. 1993). When, as here, the Director is advancing his position in litigation, his position is "entitled to respect . . . to the extent that it has the power to persuade." *West Virginia CWP Fund v. Stacy*, 671 F.3d 378, 388 (4th Cir. 2011) (internal quotation marks and alteration omitted). We accord no deference to the Board's legal interpretation of the Act since the Board does not serve in a policy-making role. *See* **{-688-}** *Newport News Shipbuilding & Dry Dock Co. v. Stilley*, 243 F.3d 179, 181 (4th Cir. 2001). **[—13—]**

A.

Regarding Claimant's COPD, Metro contends that the ALJ erred in relying on Dr. Ripoll's opinions to find that Claimant had established a prima facie case. Metro argues that if Dr. Ripoll's opinions were too contradictory to rebut Claimant's prima facie case, they must also have been too contradictory to establish Claimant's prima facie case in the first place.

This issue is easily disposed of because the ALJ did not rely on Dr. Ripoll's opinions as a basis for finding that Claimant established his prima facie case. The ALJ found that "Claimant has demonstrated and [Metro] has agreed that a work related injury occurred February 18, 2008 when Claimant was exposed to welding and epoxy fumes, leading to an aggravation of his preexisting COPD." J.A. 203. Indeed, substantial evidence supported the ALJ's finding that Claimant established a prima facie case.[2] Claimant offered evidence that the day after the exposure, he was diagnosed with "[e]xacerbation of [COPD]" and hospitalized for eight days as a result. S.J.A. 1. The evidence showed that his COPD continued to worsen after that **[—14—]** point as well, and his lung function never returned to its pre-exposure level. This evidence was easily sufficient to satisfy Claimant's "fairly light burden," *Bis Salamis, Inc. v. Director, OWCP*, 819 F.3d 116, 127, 4 Adm. R. 209, 216 (5th Cir. 2016), to produce evidence raising the possibility that the exposure had permanently aggravated his COPD. *Cf. Moore*, 126 F.3d at 262 (holding that ALJ properly invoked presumption regarding claim for back problems when claimant testified that he experienced back pain immediately after the accident even though other evidence cast significant doubt on the credibility of that testimony and claimant had acknowledged that he had suffered back pain as a result of another prior injury); *Champion v. S&M Traylor Bros.*, 690 F.2d 285, 295 (D.C. Cir. 1982) (holding that because "claim [wa]s supported by far more than enough evidence to remove it from the category of 'mere fancy,'" the presumption was invoked). And, regardless of Dr. Ripoll's changing opinions regarding whether he could say to a reasonable degree of medical certainty that the exposure did permanently worsen Claimant's condition, he never opined that it was not possible that the exposure had that effect.

Metro also suggests that the ALJ improperly required Metro, in order to rebut the presumption, to actually *prove by a preponderance of the evidence* that the exposure did not aggravate his lung condition. Again, Metro misstates what the **[—15—]** ALJ did. The ALJ applied the proper standard, requiring Metro to proffer evidence that *could allow a reasonable factfinder to infer* that Claimant's lung condition was not permanently aggravated by the exposure. *See Moore*, 126 F.3d at 262-63. And the ALJ rightly concluded that Dr. Ripoll's July 2012 opinion that there was no permanent

[2] Metro argues that it did not agree that the exposure aggravated his COPD but only stipulated that "Claimant injured his pulmonary organs on February 18, 2008 at [Metro's] place of business." J.A. 191. We need not address the effect of this stipulation in light of our conclusion that substantial evidence supported the ALJ's finding that Claimant established a prima facie case independent of any stipulation.

aggravation from the exposure could not support such a reasonable inference since Dr. Ripoll had abandoned that opinion.

For all of these reasons, we conclude that substantial evidence supports the **{-689-}** ALJ's order awarding Claimant medical benefits for his work-related COPD, and the Board was therefore correct to affirm.

B.

Metro also argues that the Board erred in affirming the ALJ's decision granting Claimant medical benefits for his vertebra fracture.

1.

Some of Metro's arguments regarding the fracture relate to the differences, if any, between how the Act treats primary injuries—meaning compensable injuries that arise out of, and occur in the course of, employment—and secondary injuries—meaning other injuries that develop later as the result of primary injuries. We will begin by addressing those arguments. **[—16—]**

Metro does not deny that a secondary injury can qualify as an "injury" within the meaning of 33 U.S.C. § 902(2), but Metro maintains that because the fracture was a secondary injury, it was compensable only if it "naturally or unavoidably result[ed]" from a primary injury. Metro also argues that because the fracture was a secondary injury and was not identified in Claimant's March 2012 claim form, the § 20(a) presumption should not have applied concerning the fracture's compensability regardless of whether Claimant established a prima facie case.

In questions of statutory interpretation, we begin with the language of the statute. *See Dean v. United States*, 556 U.S. 568, 572 (2009). If the statutory language is clear and unambiguous, "we are duty bound to give effect to that language." *United States v. Ivester*, 75 F.3d 182, 184 (4th Cir. 1996).

As we have discussed, the Act defines "injury," in relevant part, as an

> accidental injury or death arising out of and in the course of employment, and such occupational disease or infection as arises naturally out of such employment or as naturally or unavoidably results from such accidental injury.

33 U.S.C. § 902(2). There is no question that "the composition of [§ 902(2)] is awkward." *Cyr v. Crescent Wharf & Warehouse Co.*, 211 F.2d 454, 456 (9th Cir. 1954). At the same time, it is apparent—and Metro does not dispute—that Congress included **[—17—]** in the definition of "injury" both "accidental injury . . . arising out of and in the course of employment"—primary injuries—and injuries that "naturally or unavoidably result[] from such accidental injury"—secondary injuries. *See, e.g., Jones v. Director, OWCP*, 977 F.2d 1106, 1110-12 (7th Cir. 1992); Cyr, 211 F.2d at 456.

2.

It is at this point in the analysis that the views of the various participants in this appeal diverge. Metro contends that because the vertebra fracture was not a primary injury, the ALJ erred in applying the § 20(a) presumption in determining its compensability. Relying on two split-panel decisions of the Fifth Circuit, Metro maintains that the presumption applies only to questions of whether alleged primary injuries are compensable and does not apply to questions of whether alleged secondary injuries are compensable. *See Insurance Co. of State of Pa. v. Director, OWCP*, 713 F.3d 779, 784-86, 1 Adm. R. 246, 248–50 (5th Cir. 2013); *Amerada Hess Corp. v. Director, OWCP*, 543 F.3d 755, 761-63 (5th Cir. 2008). Claimant and the Director argue that these two decisions that Metro relies on were wrongly decided to the extent they conclude that the presumption does not apply to claims concerning secondary injuries. And the Director notes that one judge on each panel expressed **{-690-}** disagreement with the majority's analysis. *See Amerada Hess*, 543 F.3d at 765 (Reavley, J., **[—18—]** concurring) (concluding that the presumption should have applied to the secondary injury if the claimant had established a prima facie case, but concurring in the majority's result because the claimant failed to establish his prima facie case); *see also Insurance Co. of the State of Pa.*, 713 F.3d at 786, 1 Adm. R. at 251 (Graves, J., concurring) (noting that although the panel was bound to follow circuit precedent, he agreed with Judge Reavley that "the *Amerada Hess* majority erred in finding that the presumption created by § 20(a) of the [Act] is inapplicable to a 'secondary' injury or an injury not expressly listed on the original claim form").

We agree with the Claimant and the Director that the presumption applies to claims regardless of whether they concern secondary injuries. By its terms, the § 20(a) presumption is that the "*claim* comes within the provisions of th[e] Act." 33 U.S.C. § 920(a) (emphasis added). As we have explained, the Act allows claims regarding primary injuries, secondary injuries, or both. Section 20(a) does not distinguish between claims concerning primary injuries and those concerning secondary injuries, and in fact § 20(a) makes no reference to injuries at **[—19—]** all. Accordingly, we agree with the Director that the presumption unambiguously applies to all types of claims.[3]

Metro contends that *U.S. Industries* supports its argument that the presumption does not apply to secondary injuries, but we respectfully disagree with Metro's understanding of that decision. In *U.S. Industries*, the claim at issue asserted that the employee suffered an injury at work on November 19, 1975, when he was lifting duct work and felt a sharp pain in his neck. *See* 455 U.S. at 610, 612. The ALJ denied the claim, finding that the alleged accident actually had not occurred and that the employee and his co-worker had testified falsely regarding its occurrence. *See id.* at 610. A divided panel of the Board affirmed. The Court of Appeals vacated, however, on the basis that the employee could be found to have suffered an "injury" when he awoke in pain the day after the alleged accident; the Court of Appeals reasoned that an injury need not occur during work hours and need not be traceable to a specific work incident. *See id.* at 611. The Court of Appeals thus held that **[—20—]** if the claimant did suffer such an injury, the § 20(a) presumption would apply to it. *See id.* at 611-12.

The Supreme Court granted certiorari and reversed, holding that the Court of Appeals had committed two errors. The first error concerned the scope of the employee's claim. The Court reasoned that the only claim the employee had made was that he was injured at work on November 19 in an accident the ALJ found had not actually occurred. *See id.* at 612. Because the employee had not claimed that any injury occurred on November *20*, there could be no presumption that applied to any November 20 injury. *See id.* at 612-13. The Court noted that despite the existence of very liberal rules allowing the amendments of pleadings and variances between pleading and proof, such variances cannot be so **{-691-}** great that they prejudice an employer's ability to defend against a claim. *See id.* at 613 n.7. In the case before the Court, the assertion of a November 20 injury was not supported by the claim form the claimant had filed "or by the evidentiary record." *Id.*

The Court also reasoned that the Court of Appeals erred in determining that the attack of pain claimant suffered on the morning of November 20 could qualify as an "injury" within the meaning of the Act. *See id.* at 615. That is so because for an injury to have occurred "in the course of employment," it "must have arisen during the employment," and thus a prima facie claim **[—21—]** for compensation must allege an injury that arose while the claimant was working. *Id.* However, the only such injury that the claimant had asserted in his claim was the November 19

[3] Additionally, we know of no reason why Congress would have put the initial burden on the claimant to produce evidence actually proving the causation link and other elements in secondary-injury cases while relieving claimants of that burden in other cases. *See Director, OWCP v. Greenwich Collieries*, 512 U.S. 267, 280 (1994) (noting that purpose of the § 920(a) presumption is "Congress' recognition that claims such as those involved here would be difficult to prove").

injury that the ALJ had found did not actually occur. *See id.* at 615-16.

Metro argues that the attack of pain on the morning of November 20 in *U.S. Industries* was in essence a secondary injury and that that status as a secondary injury was the reason that the Supreme Court did not apply the § 20(a) presumption. We conclude this is a misreading of *U.S. Industries*. As the Director explains, *U.S. Industries* does not suggest that the § 20(a) presumption does not apply to claims of secondary injuries. Rather, the case merely stands for two propositions: (1) the presumption applies only to claims of injuries that are actually made, (2) a claim must include a primary injury, which, by definition, must arise during work.

In the present case, because the ALJ properly found that Claimant suffered a compensable primary injury—the exacerbation of his COPD—*U.S. Industries* poses no obstacle for him so long as his claim included the fracture. Metro does not appear to challenge the conclusions of the ALJ and the Board that Claimant's claim evolved to include the fracture even though the claim form he originally filed in 2012 had only explicitly mentioned his lung injury. And, *U.S. Industries* **[—22—]** specifically recognized that those making claims under the Act need not even make claims on claim forms and that "an informal substitute . . . may be acceptable if it identifies the claimant, indicates that a compensable injury has occurred, and conveys the idea that compensation is expected." *Id.* at 613 n.7 (internal quotation marks and alterations omitted). The Court also recognized that "considerable liberality is usually shown in allowing amendment of pleadings" and in allowing "variance between pleading and proof," so long as the amendment or variance is not so significant that the defendant's ability to defend itself is prejudiced. *Id.* (internal quotation marks and alterations omitted). On these facts, the ALJ and Board properly treated Claimant's claim to include the fracture. As the Board determined, Metro was not prejudiced by Claimant's failure to identify the fracture as part of his claimed injuries on his original claim form. Even if Metro had not previously been aware that Claimant sought medical benefits for the fracture, at the informal conference on May 15, 2012—16 months before the ALJ hearing—the Claimant expressly sought such benefits, as he did before the ALJ. The ALJ therefore correctly treated Claimant's claim as including the fracture and rightly concluded that the § 20 presumption would apply regarding the **[—23—]** compensability of the fracture if Claimant established a prima facie case.[4] **{-692-}**

3.

Metro alternatively argues that, even assuming that the § 20(a) presumption can apply to secondary injuries, the ALJ erred by treating the fracture claim as if it were a primary-injury claim and thus failed to apply the "naturally or unavoidably results" standard. In this regard, we will discuss Claimant's attempt to establish his prima facie case separately from Metro's attempt to rebut the presumption.

a.

The ALJ noted that:

> [Metro argued that because] the T7 fracture was not included on the initial claim form, [the § 20(a) presumption does not apply and] Claimant must demonstrate that the fracture naturally or unavoidably arose from the original lung injury. In support, [Metro] cited

[4] The Fifth Circuit's decisions in *Insurance Company of the State of Pennsylvania* and *Amerada Hess* holding that the § 20(a) presumption was not properly applied to the secondary injures seem to be primarily based on the courts' conclusions that the claims before them did *not* include the secondary injuries at issue, *see Amerada Hess Corp. v. Director, OWCP*, 543 F.3d 755, 761-62 (5th Cir. 2008); *Insurance Co. of State of Pa. v. Director, OWCP*, 713 F.3d 779, 785, 1 Adm. R. 246, 249–50 (5th Cir. 2013), a circumstance that would distinguish the present case. To the extent that the Fifth Circuit decisions may also suggest that even a secondary injury that was included in the claimant's claim could not receive the benefit of the § 20(a) presumption, their reasons for adopting that position are simply not clear.

> two Fifth Circuit cases. This case is **[—24—]** governed by the law of the . . . Fourth Circuit[, which] has not articulated such a standard.

J.A. 215 n.1. The ALJ found that Claimant established his prima facie case by producing evidence that "the workplace exposure accident could have caused, aggravated, or accelerated the [fracture]." J.A. 214. Other than in his description of Metro's argument, the ALJ made no reference to the "naturally or unavoidably results" standard in his analysis. We therefore are inclined to agree with Metro that the ALJ erred in failing to recognize that the "naturally or unavoidably results" standard applied.

Because that standard applied, the ALJ should have recognized that the compensability of the fracture depended on the fracture (or its aggravation or hastening) *naturally or unavoidably* resulting from the primary injury. Consequently, for Claimant to establish his prima facie case, the ALJ should have required him to produce evidence that the primary injury could have *naturally or unavoidably* caused, aggravated, or accelerated the fracture. Nevertheless, on the particular facts of this case, the ALJ's failure to consider naturalness or avoidability made no difference.[5] **[—25—]**

The ALJ reasoned that Claimant demonstrated that the exposure permanently aggravated his COPD and that "features of the COPD, namely steroid treatment and excessive coughing," could have caused, aggravated, or accelerated the fracture. J.A. 214. Considering the exacerbation of Claimant's COPD—and resulting hospitalization—following the exposure, substantial evidence supported the ALJ's finding.

Because the fracture was not a primary injury, the ALJ should have gone the next step and considered whether Claimant **{-693-}** produced evidence that the fracture (or its aggravation or hastening) could have *naturally or unavoidably* resulted from the primary injury, but this extra step would have posed no hurdle for Claimant on these facts. Regardless of any possible argument concerning whether the fracture or its aggravation or hastening naturally resulted, "naturally or unavoidably results" is a disjunctive requirement. *See Jones v. Director, OWCP*, 977 F.2d 1106, 1111 (7th Cir. 1992). Thus, Claimant could establish his prima facie case simply by showing that the fracture or its aggravation or hastening could have *unavoidably* resulted from **[—26—]** the exacerbation of his COPD.[6] But Metro has never suggested any way that Claimant could have avoided any effect that the exacerbation of his COPD had on his fracture. Accordingly, were we to remand for reconsideration in light of the "naturally or unavoidably results" standard, the ALJ would certainly conclude, for the same reasons that he found Claimant proved that the fracture or its aggravation or hastening *could have resulted*, that it also *could have unavoidably resulted*. We will not engage in such a futile exercise. *See George Hyman Constr. Co. v. Brooks*, 963 F.2d 1532, 1539 (D.C. Cir. 1992).

b.

Metro also maintains that even if the ALJ correctly invoked the § 20(a) presumption regarding the fracture, substantial evidence did not support the ALJ's finding that Metro failed to rebut the presumption. We disagree. Again, the ALJ, apparently not recognizing that he should be applying the "naturally or unavoidably results" standard, considered only whether Metro offered evidence sufficient

[5] We note that the primary injury was part of the causal chain linking the exposure to the secondary injury, so the fact that the ALJ considered whether Claimant produced evidence of whether the *exposure* could have caused, aggravated, or
(Continued) **[—25—]** accelerated the fracture instead of whether the *primary injury* could have caused, aggravated or accelerated the fracture is of no moment. And Metro makes no complaint regarding this distinction.

[6] We offer no opinion regarding whether the "naturally" prong would have posed any obstacle to Claimant on these facts. *See Jones v. Director, OWCP*, 977 F.2d 1106, 1110-14 (7th Cir. 1992) (discussing "naturally or unavoidably results" standard).

to support a reasonable inference that the fracture was not caused, aggravated, or accelerated by the exposure. **[—27—]**

Metro argues that the ALJ erred in concluding that the evidence that Claimant used steroids for 22 years prior to the exposure was not sufficient to support a reasonable inference that the fracture would have occurred regardless of whether the exposure occurred. We agree with the ALJ, though, that any such inference would not be reasonable, but instead would be based on mere speculation. There is no evidence whatsoever that any medical professional believed that the aggravation of Claimant's lung condition, his increased steroid use, or his increased cough did not hasten, aggravate, or cause the fracture. At best, Metro produced evidence that gave rise to a reasonable inference that *it was possible* that the fracture was not hastened, aggravated, or caused by the exposure. That was not enough to rebut the presumption.

And for the same reasons that we discussed regarding Claimant's establishment of his prima facie case, no purpose would be served by vacating and remanding for application of the "naturally or unavoidably results" standard as it pertains to Metro's attempt to rebut the presumption. Because Metro has not suggested any way that Claimant could have avoided the fracture (or its hastening or aggravation) once the exposure occurred, the ALJ would certainly find again on remand that Metro did not rebut the presumption. **[—28—]**

IV.

In sum, because we conclude that the only error the ALJ committed was in failing to apply the "naturally or unavoidably **{-694-}** results" standard to the fracture claim and because remand for application of that standard would be a futile exercise, given that there was no issue presented regarding avoidability, we deny Metro's petition for review of the Board's order affirming the ALJ's decision.

PETITION DENIED

United States Court of Appeals
for the Fourth Circuit

No. 15-1041

CERES MARINE TERMINALS, INC.
vs.
DIRECTOR, OFFICE OF WORKERS' COMPENSATION PROGRAMS

On Petition for Review of an Order of the Benefits Review Board

Decided: March 24, 2016
Amended: January 27, 2017

Citation: 848 F.3d 115, 5 Adm. R. 160 (4th Cir. 2016).

Before **GREGORY, DUNCAN,** and **FLOYD,** Circuit Judges.

[—3—] {–117–} **GREGORY,** Circuit Judge:

This case arises from a horribly tragic work-related accident. Samuel P. Jackson, an employee of Ceres Marine Terminals, Inc. ("CMT"), was operating a forklift when he accidently struck and killed his coworker, Paula Bellamy. After this event, Jackson, who was diagnosed with post-traumatic stress disorder ("PTSD"), filed a claim with the Director of the Office of Workers' Compensation Programs (the "Director") for disability benefits under the Longshore and Harbor Workers' Compensation Act ("LHWCA" or the "Act"), 33 U.S.C. § 901. The Administrative Law Judge ("ALJ") reviewing the claim determined that Jackson was entitled to benefits and the Benefits Review Board (the "Board") affirmed.

CMT now petitions for review of the Board's decision, arguing that a person bringing a claim under the LHWCA is required to satisfy the "zone of danger" test outlined by the Supreme Court's decision in *Consolidated Rail Corp. v. Gottshall*, 512 U.S. 532 (1994). "Under this test, a worker within the zone of danger of physical impact will be able to recover for emotional injury caused by fear of physical injury to himself, whereas a worker outside the zone will not." 512 U.S. at 556. Had the Board adopted such a test, CMT asserts, Jackson would have been precluded from any recovery under the LHWCA because he was not in the zone of danger and thus did not **[—4—]** suffer a compensable injury. In addition, CMT contends that the ALJ erred in failing to give the report of an independent medical examiner, appointed pursuant to 33 U.S.C. § 907(e), dispositive weight. We disagree on both points and therefore deny the petition.

I.

A.

On March 28, 2011, Jackson, employed by CMT as a longshoreman, was operating a forklift on a pier in Portsmouth, Virginia, when he accidently struck and killed Bellamy. At the time, Jackson was transporting barrels of container pins when he veered the forklift to his left to avoid being struck by a hustler truck that was backing up and carrying a forty foot container. When he veered, he hit Bellamy, a spotter, who had her back towards him. Jackson did not see Bellamy, and did not realize he had hit her **{–118–}** until another spotter "hollered at [him] to let [him] know that [he] had just ran over . . . somebody." J.A. 61. Jackson immediately got off his forklift to help extricate Bellamy who was almost completely pinned underneath the forklift. Another forklift driver drove over and, with his machine, raised the back end of Jackson's forklift. Jackson and others worked to free Bellamy from under his forklift. **[—5—]**

Once they were able to lift the forklift, it was apparent that Bellamy's condition was dire: Jackson testified that "[Bellamy] was bleeding from her mouth. Her arm was burned and pretty mangled, hanging off." J.A. 63. Jackson further testified that Bellamy's leg was wrapped around the axle of the forklift. For about ten minutes, Bellamy's condition was in full view until emergency vehicles arrived. By this time, approximately one hundred people gathered at the scene, including ambulance and fire truck personnel and CMT employees. During the entire time that the first responders worked to save Bellamy, Jackson stood ten to fifteen feet away, with a clear view of her.

After the ambulance left for the hospital, Jackson spent the rest of the day reporting the accident to the Portsmouth Police Department, Virginia International Terminals Police Department, the Occupational Safety and Health Administration, and CMT officials. Jackson testified that after his conversation with Gregory Concepcion, the superintendent for CMT, he sought medical attention.

B.

Jackson saw several medical professionals for mental health treatment after the March 2011 accident. Jackson visited Dr. Margaret Stiles, his primary care physician, on March 29, 2011, one day after the incident. Dr. Stiles noted that Jackson **[—6—]** was "acutely extremely upset, stressed," and diagnosed and treated him for PTSD. J.A. 351, 354, 360. At and around this time, Dr. Stiles recommended that Jackson not return to work because of his condition. On April 6, 2011, Dr. Stiles referred Jackson to Gregory Griffin, a licensed clinical social worker, for counseling. Griffin recommended brief supportive crisis-debriefing counseling and that Jackson not return to work for four to six weeks. Griffin diagnosed Jackson with an adjustment reaction with depressed mood.

After Jackson's family noticed "dramatic changes" in his behavior, they collectively "persuade[d]" Jackson to see Dr. Norbert Newfield. J.A. 286-87. Dr. Newfield, a clinical psychologist, first evaluated Jackson on July 11, 2011. Dr. Newfield found that Jackson suffered from PTSD with significant levels of anxiety and depression resulting from the work-related accident. Over the course of his treatment—from mid-2011 through 2013—Dr. Newfield usually saw Jackson on a weekly basis, sometimes twice a week. On February 20, 2012, almost a year after the accident, Dr. Newfield noted that Jackson was still experiencing extremely bad nightmares and levels of guilt, shame, and grief that prevented him from **[—7—]** returning to work. Dr. Newfield monitored Jackson for suicide as well.[1]

Dr. Patrick Thrasher, a psychiatrist retained by CMT, conducted an independent **{-119-}** medical examination of Jackson on September 14, 2011, and reviewed Jackson's medical records. Dr. Thrasher diagnosed Jackson with PTSD and major depression, and he concluded that these diagnoses were causally related to the work accident. Dr. Thrasher stated that the severity of Jackson's depression and PTSD rendered him incapable of returning to work. Dr. Thrasher further stated that with aggressive psychiatric treatment and psychotherapy, Jackson might be able to return to work within six to twelve months. After reviewing updated medical records, Dr. Thrasher, on February 12, 2012, noted that Jackson was undermedicated, and recommended a more aggressive psychotropic treatment targeting Jackson's depressive symptoms and sleep disturbance.

Based on Dr. Thrasher's recommendation that Jackson was undermedicated, CMT requested, pursuant to 33 U.S.C. § 907(e), an independent medical examination to determine if Jackson was **[—8—]** receiving proper medical care. In light of this request, the Office of Workers' Compensation Programs referred Jackson to psychiatrist Dr. Paul Mansheim for an independent medical examination. Dr. Mansheim evaluated Jackson on November 15, 2012, and reviewed Jackson's medical records, as well as the results of a standardized personality assessment inventory test. In his December 8, 2012 report, Dr. Mansheim stated that the diagnoses suggested by the personality assessment inventory test were extremely broad and suggested PTSD, schizophrenia, and major depressive disorder. Dr. Mansheim,

[1] Dr. Newfield referred Jackson to a psychiatrist, Dr. Deborah Giorgi-Guarnieri. Dr. Giorgi-Guarnieri began treating Jackson on November 14, 2011. Dr. Giorgi-Guarnieri's notes indicate that she treated Jackson every two to four weeks. Dr. Giorgi-Guarnieri recorded that Jackson had been battling depression and anxiety and suffered from flashbacks and nightmares. Dr. Giorgi-Guarnieri continued to see Jackson for medication management.

however, "rule[d] out the [PTSD] diagnosis" because Jackson "did not experience a threat to himself" and "was never in danger" during the accident. J.A. 154. Dr. Mansheim further opined that Jackson demonstrated "significant evidence of malingering, attempting to appear more ill than is actually the case." J.A. 155. Dr. Mansheim concluded that Jackson was able to work as a longshoremen.

After reviewing Dr. Mansheim's report, CMT—who had voluntarily paid Jackson temporary total disability benefits—terminated its payments on December 17, 2012.

C.

Jackson filed a claim for disability benefits under the LHWCA, alleging that he suffered from PTSD as a result of the **[—9—]** work-related incident.[2] CMT disputed the claim, arguing that Jackson was not entitled to compensation under the LHWCA for a psychological injury because he did not sustain a physical injury or was placed in immediate risk of physical injury by the incident. In other words, Jackson was not in the zone of danger. CMT further contended that the ALJ should give dispositive weight to Dr. Manshiem's conclusion that Jackson did not suffer from PTSD.

In his November 13, 2013 decision, the ALJ rejected CMT's "contention that a claimant cannot recover for psychological injury unless he sustains a physical injury or is placed in immediate risk of harm." **{-120-}** J.A. 44. The ALJ held that "[l]ongshore case law has established that a claimant can obtain benefits for a work-related psychological injury," and declined "to carve out a negligence law based exception whereby claimants are not entitled to benefits if they are emotionally harmed **[—10—]** without being physically harmed or threatened with physical harm." *Id.* Addressing the medical evidence, the ALJ first refused, as contrary to Board precedent, to accord dispositive weight to Dr. Manshiem's opinion. After weighing the evidence, the ALJ found that Jackson suffered from PTSD which was causally related to the March 28, 2011, work incident. The ALJ concluded that, because Jackson "is suffering from work-accident related PTSD," he was entitled to temporary total disability benefits and medical benefits under the LHWCA. *Id.* at 50.

CMT appealed, raising the same arguments to the Board. In its November 25, 2014 opinion, the Board rejected CMT's contention that the zone-of-danger test precluded Jackson from recovery in this case. The zone-of-danger test, the Board held, is a "tort concept which does not apply to the workers' compensation provisions of the Longshore Act." J.A. 10. The Board stated that CMT's "argument fails to acknowledge the critical distinction, [as recognized in *Consolidated Rail*], between tort actions, which rely on common law fault and negligence principles, and worker's compensation claims, which are not governed by those principles." *Id.* It is well established, the Board concluded, "that a work-related psychological impairment, with or without an underlying physical harm, may be compensable under the Act." *Id.* at 9-10. **[—11—]**

In addition, the Board rejected CMT's contention that Dr. Mansheim's opinion should be given dispositive weight, holding that Dr. Mansheim's opinion "should be weighed along with the other medical opinions in the record." *Id.* at 12. Because the ALJ properly weighed the evidence, the Board affirmed the ALJ's finding that Jackson sustained a compensable work-related injury.

[2] In addition to filing a claim under the LHWCA, Jackson filed a claim with the Virginia Workers' Compensation Commission. The commission denied Jackson's claim for medical benefits and compensation, holding that Jackson was not in the zone of danger. *See Jackson v. Ceres Marine Terminals, Inc.*, 769 S.E.2d 276, 277 (Va. Ct. App. 2015). The Court of Appeals of Virginia reversed, declining to adopt a zone of danger test under Virginia law. The court held that "psychological injury must be causally related to either a physical injury or an obvious sudden shock or fright arising in the course of employment, without a specific requirement that the claimant be placed at risk of harm." *Id.* at 280. The court remanded the case back to the commission to apply the correct legal standard. That case is currently pending.

II.

CMT has petitioned this Court for review, and we possess jurisdiction pursuant to 33 U.S.C. § 921(c). In reviewing the Board's decision, we must determine "whether the Board observed its statutorily-mandated standard for reviewing the ALJ's factual findings." *Newport News Shipbldg. & Dry Dock Co. v. Stallings*, 250 F.3d 868, 871 (4th Cir. 2001) (internal quotations and citations omitted). We are also guided by the principle that an ALJ's factual findings "shall be conclusive if supported by substantial evidence in the record considered as a whole." 33 U.S.C. § 921(b)(3). Substantial evidence requires "more than a scintilla but less than a preponderance." *Norfolk Shipbldg. & Drydock Co. v. Faulk*, 228 F.3d 378, 380–81 (4th Cir. 2000). Further, an ALJ's findings "may not be disregarded on the basis that other inferences might have been more reasonable. Deference must be given the fact-finder's . . . credibility **[—12—]** assessments, and . . . the scope of review of ALJ findings is limited." *Newport News Shipbldg. & Dry Dock Co. v. Tann*, 841 F.2d 540, 543 (4th Cir. 1988). In reviewing legal issues, the Board's "adjudicatory interpretation of the LHWCA is entitled to no special deference, and is subject to our independent review. However, a reasonable interpretation of the LHWCA by the Director should be respected." *Stallings*, 250 F.3d at 871 (internal quotations and citations omitted).

III.

The LHWCA was enacted to create a federal workers' compensation statute **{–121–}** for longshoremen and harbor workers, in light of the Supreme Court's decision that state workers' compensation statutes constitutionally could not apply to injured maritime workers. *See Nogueira v. N.Y., New Haven & Hartford R. Co.*, 281 U.S. 128 (1930). The LHWCA, like most workers' compensation legislation, represents a compromise between employer and employee. "Consistent with the central bargain of workers' compensation regimes—limited liability for employers; certain, prompt recovery for employees—the LHWCA requires that employers pay benefits voluntarily, without formal administrative proceedings." *Roberts v. Sea-Land Servs., Inc.*, 132 S. Ct. 1350, 1354 (2012). **[—13—]**

In other words, the LHWCA strikes a balance between the competing interests of injured workers and their employers in which the certainty of benefits is exchanged for tort immunity. *See Morrison-Knudsen Constr. Co. v. Dir., OWCP*, 461 U.S. 624, 636 (1983); *Potomac Elec. Power Co. v. Dir., OWCP*, 449 U.S. 268, 281-82 & n.24 (1980). The LHWCA, therefore, "imposes liability without fault and precludes the assertion of various common-law defenses . . . ." *Potomac Elec. Power Co.*, 449 U.S. at 281; *see also* 33 U.S.C. § 904(b) ("Compensation shall be payable irrespective of fault as a cause for the injury.").

To be entitled to benefits under the LHWCA, a claimant must have sustained an injury within the meaning of the Act. *See* 33 U.S.C. § 903(a) ("Compensation shall be payable under this [Act] in respect of disability . . . of an employee, but only if the disability . . . results from an injury."); *see also Metro. Stevedore Co. v. Rambo*, 515 U.S. 291, 294 (1995) (stating that the LHWCA "is a comprehensive scheme to provide compensation in respect of disability or death of an employee . . . if the disability or death results from an injury occurring upon the navigable waters of the United States"). Section 902(2) of the LHWCA provides,

> The term "injury" means accidental injury or death arising out of and in the course of employment, and such occupational disease or infection as arises naturally out of such employment or as naturally or unavoidably **[—14—]** results from such accidental injury, and includes an injury caused by the willful act of a third person directed against an employee because of his employment.

33 U.S.C. § 902(2).

Injuries are presumed to be work related under 33 U.S.C. § 920 after the claimant establishes a prima facie case that the injury not only was caused by the employment, but that it also arose during employment. *See U.S.*

Indus. Fed. Sheet Metal, Inc. v. Dir., OWCP, 455 U.S. 608, 615 (1982) ("Not only must the injury have been caused by the employment, it also must have arisen during the employment."). "Once the presumption is invoked, the burden shifts to the employer to rebut it through facts—not mere speculation—that the harm was not work related." *Conoco, Inc. v. Dir., OWCP*, 194 F.3d 684, 687-88 (5th Cir. 1999). "If the ALJ finds that the employer rebutted the presumption, then the ALJ must weigh all of the evidence to determine whether the harm was caused by the claimant's employment." *Ramsey Scarlett & Co. v. Dir., OWCP*, 806 F.3d 327, 331, 3 Adm. R. 426, 427 (5th Cir. 2015).

IV.

In its petition for review, CMT makes two primary arguments. First, CMT argues **{-122-}** that Jackson did not suffer a compensable injury within the meaning of the LHWCA because he **[—15—]** was not in the zone of danger; that is, only those who suffer a physical injury or were within the zone of danger of physical impact can recover for a work-related psychological injury. Because Jackson was outside of the zone of danger, CMT asserts, he did not suffer any compensable injury under the LHWCA. Second, CMT contends that the ALJ committed error by failing to give Dr. Mansheim's opinion dispositive weight. The Director maintains, on the other hand, that it is well established that psychological injuries—with or without physical injury or the threat of physical injury—are compensable under the LHWCA. The Director further contends that Dr. Mansheim's opinion was not entitled to dispositive weight and is not binding on the factfinder. For the reasons explained below, we agree with the Director on both issues.

A.

CMT does not dispute that Jackson can recover for a psychological injury under the LHWCA. Rather, CMT contends that Jackson cannot, under the LHWCA, recover for a psychological injury *unless* he sustains a physical injury or was placed in immediate risk of physical harm. In support of this argument, CMT relies exclusively on the zone-of-danger test set forth by the Supreme Court in *Consolidated Rail*—a case that did not involve the statute at issue in this case. CMT's contention is not only inconsistent with the statute's text, the structure of **[—16—]** the statute, and precedent but is also contradicted by the very reasoning of the case on which it relies so heavily—*Consolidated Rail*.

The LHWCA plainly does not encompass such a limitation by its express terms. The LHWCA does not distinguish between psychological and physical injuries—the statute simply says "injury." *See* 33 U.S.C. § 902(2) (defining "injury," without limitation, as any "accidental injury or death arising out of and in the course of employment"). Nowhere in the statute is there a requirement that psychological injuries be accompanied by actual or threatened physical harm. To be sure, Congress could have easily written the statute to contain such a requirement, but it did not. We therefore refuse to "amend [the] statute under the guise of statutory interpretation, a task we are not at liberty to perform." *Newport News Shipbldg. & Dry Dock Co. v. Hall*, 674 F.2d 248, 251 (4th Cir. 1982). For good reason. The zone-of-danger test is, after all, a "well-established common-law concept of negligence." *Consolidated Rail*, 512 U.S. at 555 (quotations and alterations omitted). The rules of the common law for tort actions, however, generally do not apply to cases arising under LHWCA—a "no-fault workers **[—17—]** compensation scheme."[3] *See Newport News Shipbldg. and Dry Dock Co. v. Brown*, 376 F.3d 245, 249 (4th Cir. 2004).

Further, courts interpreting § 902(2) of the LHWCA have held that claimants can recover for a work-related psychological injury, and have never mandated actual or threatened physical harm to be a prerequisite for coverage. *See, e.g., Pedroza v. Dir., OWCP*, 624 F.3d 926, 931 (9th Cir. 2009) ("It is well

[3] We recognize that, under certain limited circumstances, the longshore worker may seek damages in a statutory negligence action from the owner of the vessel on which he was injured under 33 U.S.C. § 905(b). This case does not present such circumstances.

settled that a psychological impairment, which is work related, is presumed to be compensable under the Act. Therefore, to receive the benefit of this § 920(a) presumption, the claimant must prove not only that he has a psychological **{–123–}** impairment, but that an accident occurred, or working conditions existed, which could have caused the impairment." (citation omitted)); *Dir., OWCP v. Potomac Elec. Power Co.*, 607 F.2d 1378, 1385 (D.C. Cir. 1979); *Am. Nat'l Red Cross v. Hagen*, 327 F.2d 559, 561 (7th Cir. 1964). Nor has the Board endorsed such a limitation. *See, e.g.*, J.A. at 9-10 ("[I]t is well established that a work-related psychological impairment, with or without an underlying physical harm, may be compensable under the Act."). **[—18—]**

Moreover, CMT's reliance on *Consolidated Rail* is wholly misplaced. In *Consolidated Rail*, a case in which a railroad worker experienced severe psychiatric problems after witnessing the death of a fellow worker while on the job and was required to continue working within sight of the coworker's body, the Supreme Court held that claims for negligent infliction of emotional distress are cognizable under the Federal Employers' Liability Act ("FELA"). 512 U.S. at 550. But to curtail what it believed might otherwise be "unpredictable and nearly infinite liability for defendants," *id.* at 552, the Court adopted the zone-of-danger test developed as common law in many jurisdictions. *Id.* at 554-55. The Court expressly stated that FELA was not a workers' compensation statute and emphasized that the basis of an employer's liability under FELA is its negligence, which turns on common-law principles. Unlike the statute at issue here, FELA "does not make the employer the insurer of the safety of his employees while they are on duty. The basis of his liability is his negligence, not the fact that injuries occur." *Id.* at 543 (quoting *Ellis v. Union Pac. R. Co.*, 329 U.S. 649, 653 (1947)). Thus, by its terms, *Consolidated Rail* is inapposite to a claim for workers' compensation benefits under the LHWCA. **[—19—]**

Because we are not free to engraft on the statute a requirement that Congress did not place there, we decline to adopt the zone-of-danger test.

B.

CMT next contends that the ALJ erred in failing to give the report of Dr. Mansheim, an independent medical examiner appointed pursuant to 33 U.S.C. § 907(e), dispositive weight. We disagree, as there is nothing in the plain language of the statute that indicates that Congress intended to give the opinion of an independent medical examiner dispositive weight or to make the examiner's opinion binding on the parties.

Section 7(e) provides in part,

> In the event that medical questions are raised in any case, the Secretary shall have the power to cause the employee to be examined by a physician employed or selected by the Secretary and to obtain from such physician a report containing his estimate of the employee's physical impairment and such other information as may be appropriate. *Any party who is dissatisfied with such report may request a review or reexamination of the employee by one or more different physicians employed or selected by the Secretary.* The Secretary shall order such review or reexamination unless he finds that it is clearly unwarranted.

33 U.S.C. § 907(e) (emphasis added). Were we to read the statute as CMT does, we would nullify the second clause of § 907(e), which provides the opportunity for further review by another physician if a party is dissatisfied with the **[—20—]** independent medical examiner's opinion. We therefore decline CMT's invitation to do so, as the second clause clearly indicates that the independent medical examiner's opinion is not **{–124–}** binding on the ALJ or the parties. Rather, the independent medical examiner's opinion must be weighed along with the other medical opinions of record, as the Board has repeatedly held. *See Cotton v. Newport News Shipbldg. & Dry Dock Co.*, 23 B.R.B.S. 380, 387 (1990); *Shell v. Teledyne Movible Offshore, Inc.*, 14 B.R.B.S. 585 (1984).

Our interpretation of this provision is not only consistent with other circuits but is also consistent with the position advanced by CMT in a separate case. In *Ceres Marine Terminal v. Hinton*, 243 F.3d 222 (5th Cir. 2001), CMT argued, "an opinion of a Department of Labor IME is entitled to great weight. This is not to say that the Department of Labor IME's opinion is dispositive." *Compare* Br. of Pet., *Ceres Marine Terminal v. Hinton*, 243 F.3d 222 (5th Cir. 2001) (No. 00-60171), 2000 WL 34004373, at *46, *with* CMT's Br. at 40 ("Dr. Mansheim's opinion should have been dispositive. . . . Indeed, isn't the whole purpose of a section 7(e) evaluation to resolve the case?"). The Fifth Circuit rejected CMT's argument, holding that the ALJ's conclusions—after weighing all the medical evidence, including the independent medical examiner's report—must only **[—21—]** be "supported by substantial evidence in the record as a whole." *Hinton*, 243 F.3d at 225.

CMT further argued in *Hinton* that if the ALJ "is going to reject the Department of Labor IME's opinion, the [ALJ] needs a very good reason for doing so." Br. of Pet., *Hinton*, 2000 WL 34004373 at *46. Here, CMT should take solace in the fact that the ALJ provided several "good reason[s]" in giving less weight to Dr. Mansheim's opinion. One reason, among many, was Dr. Mansheim's unsubstantiated statement that the traumatic event experienced by Jackson—the prime actor in this incident—would not meet the criteria for PTSD because, if Jackson qualified, then more than half the population would meet the diagnosis, as that population has seen an image of a mangled body. The ALJ concluded that "Dr. Manshiem's estimates on population experience raise concerns that his report is not well-reasoned and well-documented." J.A. 49. Indeed.

Because the statute clearly does not contemplate an ALJ giving dispositive weight to an independent medical examiner's opinion, we decline to "amend [the] statute under the guise of statutory interpretation." *Hall*, 674 F.2d at 251.

C.

In weighing the evidence as a whole, the ALJ found the opinions of Jackson's treating psychologist, Dr. Newfield, and CMT's expert psychiatrist, Dr. Thrasher, credible; both **[—22—]** physicians diagnosed Jackson with PTSD and concluded that this diagnosis was causally related to the work accident. The ALJ further found that those opinions outweighed Dr. Mansheim's opinion that Jackson did not meet the criteria for a diagnosis of PTSD. CMT's arguments on appeal, in effect, seek a reweighing of the evidence, which we are not empowered to do. Thus, the ALJ's conclusion that Jackson suffered a work-related psychological injury is amply supported by substantial evidence when the record is considered as a whole.

V.

For the foregoing reasons, CMT's petition must be denied.

PETITION FOR REVIEW DENIED

(Reporter's note: This case was originally issued as an unpublished opinion on March 24, 2016, and was later designated for publication on January 27, 2017).

United States Court of Appeals for the Fourth Circuit

No. 16-1530

SAWYER
vs.
FOSTER WHEELER LLC

On Appeal from the United States District Court for the District of Maryland at Baltimore

Decided: June 22, 2017

Citation: 860 F.3d 249, 5 Adm. R. 167 (4th Cir. 2017).

Before **NIEMEYER, KING,** and **DUNCAN,** Circuit Judges.

[—4—] {-251-} NIEMEYER, Circuit Judge:

In this appeal, we are presented with the single issue of whether a government contractor was entitled to remove a state tort action to federal court under 28 U.S.C. § 1442(a)(1) based on the contractor's assertion that it had a colorable federal defense of government-contractor immunity.

Joseph Morris worked as shipbuilder at the Bethlehem Steel Sparrows Point Shipyard, beginning in 1948 and continuing into the 1970s. He died of mesothelioma in 2015. Morris' family and the personal representative of his estate commenced this **{-252-}** action against Foster Wheeler LLC and other defendants in a Maryland state court, alleging that Morris' death was caused by exposure to asbestos while assembling boilers at the Shipyard and that the defendants failed to warn him of the dangers of asbestos, which was a component of the boilers.

Foster Wheeler, a manufacturer of the boilers that Morris and other Shipyard employees assembled for use aboard U.S. Navy vessels, removed this action to federal court pursuant to 28 U.S.C. § 1442(a)(1), claiming that it manufactured the boilers under a contract with the Navy and therefore possessed a colorable federal defense of government-contractor immunity. The district court, however, granted the plaintiffs' motion to remand the case to state court, concluding that Foster Wheeler did not make a sufficient showing that it had a colorable federal defense and that, in any event, the conduct for which it was sued was not causally connected to official authority.

On appeal, we conclude that the district court applied the wrong standard for determining removability under § 1442(a)(1), and, because we conclude that Foster **[—5—]** Wheeler met the statute's requirements, we reverse. But because the court left open the question of whether Foster Wheeler's removal was timely noticed, we remand the case to the district court to make that determination in the first instance.

I

In June 2015, Morris' surviving spouse, his children, and the representative of his estate commenced this action against Foster Wheeler and other defendants in the Circuit Court for Baltimore City, Maryland, alleging—in claims for strict liability, breach of warranty, and negligence, among others—that the defendants had failed to warn Morris of the dangers of asbestos. They asserted that Morris was exposed to asbestos while working in the boiler shop at the Sparrows Point Shipyard from 1948 through the 1970s and that his exposure caused the mesothelioma that killed him in 2015. In response to interrogatories, the plaintiffs explained in more detail that Morris and other Shipyard employees assembled boilers containing asbestos at the Shipyard that had been manufactured offsite, including ones manufactured by Foster Wheeler.

Foster Wheeler filed a notice of removal pursuant to 28 U.S.C. § 1446, claiming authority for removal under § 1442(a)(1), which provides for removal by federal officials and their agents in specified circumstances. In its notice, Foster Wheeler stated that, during the relevant time period, it manufactured boilers for the U.S. Navy under the Navy's strict specifications; that its boilers were sent in pieces to the Sparrows Point Shipyard for assembly; that Morris and his fellow employees assembled the boilers at the Shipyard; and that the boilers contained asbestos. It asserted, moreover, that "in the

[—6—] manufacture and sale of boilers and auxiliary equipment for the Navy, including all aspects of warnings associated with that equipment, [it] was acting under an officer or agency of the United States" and therefore had a colorable defense of government-contractor immunity, entitling it to remove the case to federal court to have that defense heard there.

In support of its notice, Foster Wheeler submitted an affidavit from J. Thomas Schroppe, a former Foster Wheeler employee who, from 1962 to 1999, rose through the ranks of Foster Wheeler as an engineer and eventually became president of its subsidiary Boiler Corporation. Schroppe, who stated that he was "personally involved" in the Navy's procurement {–253–} contracts for boilers "at all the various stages of development," described "the contract process from the perspective of Foster Wheeler as the vendor, as well as the levels of interaction between Foster Wheeler and the Navy." He stated that Foster Wheeler designed boilers to match highly detailed ship specifications and military specifications provided by the Navy, and that "deviations from these specs were not acceptable." He also spoke to the "intense direction and control" that the Navy exercised "over all written documentation to be delivered with its naval boilers," explaining:

> The Navy required that every piece of equipment be supplied with a defined number of copies of one or more technical manuals. Navy personnel participated intimately in the preparation of this kind of information and exercised specific direction and control over its contents. These manuals included safety information related to the operation of naval boilers and economizers only to the extent directed by the Navy.
>
> Furthermore, the Navy had precise specifications, practices and procedures that governed the content of any communication affixed to machinery supplied by Foster Wheeler to the Navy. Foster Wheeler would not be permitted, under the specifications, associated regulations and procedures, [—7—] and especially under actual practice as it evolved in the field, to affix any type of warning or caution statement to a piece of equipment intended for installation onto a Navy vessel, beyond those required by the Navy.

The plaintiffs filed a motion to remand the case to state court, arguing that Foster Wheeler's notice of removal was untimely because it was filed more than 30 days after Foster Wheeler learned that it had a possible federal defense and that, in any event, it failed to meet the substantive requirements of § 1442(a)(1). With respect to those requirements, the plaintiffs argued that Foster Wheeler's evidence of the Navy's control over the design of its boilers and warning labels did not establish a federal defense to their particular theory of liability. As the plaintiffs summarized:

> The liability asserted by Plaintiffs against Foster Wheeler is based on a failure to warn . . . relating to the erection of boilers. The boilers were not constructed upon U.S. Naval Ships, but at an off-ship boiler shop, under the direction of Foster Wheeler personnel, and only later transported and installed upon U.S. Naval ships. Navy specifications in no way restricted Foster Wheeler's ability to warn individuals constructing the boilers of the presence of asbestos and their need to take proper precautions.

They therefore claimed that Foster Wheeler failed to meet any of the three requirements for removal under § 1442(a)(1)—it did not act under the direction of a federal officer; it did not possess a colorable federal defense; and it did not engage in government-directed conduct causally related to the plaintiffs' claims.

In response to the plaintiffs' motion to remand, Foster Wheeler submitted a 2006 affidavit from Lawrence Stilwell Betts, a retired Navy Captain and medical consultant, which had been given in connection with a different action. Based on contemporary medical literature, Betts stated that "the Navy was well aware of the health hazards associated with the use of asbestos from the early 1920s" and that the Navy's information **[—8—]** "with respect to the specification and use of asbestos, and the health hazards associated with its use aboard Navy vessels, far exceeded any information that possibly could have been provided by a boiler manufacturer." **{-254-}**

The district court granted the plaintiffs' motion to remand. First, it acknowledged that the timeliness of Foster Wheeler's notice of removal was "a close question," but it assumed the removal's timeliness because of its conclusion that Foster Wheeler failed to meet the substantive requirements of § 1442(a)(1). As to those requirements, the court stated that, while Foster Wheeler had shown through affidavits "that the Navy provided Foster Wheeler with detailed specifications governing warnings and written information that accompanied Foster Wheeler boilers," there was no "evidence to show that the Navy exercised any discretion over Foster Wheeler's ability to warn its workers in the Shipyard's boiler shop." Furthermore, the court explained, "Foster Wheeler [did] not claim that it proposed any type of warning to the Navy concerning asbestos exposure in the Shipyard's boiler shop, much less that the Navy considered and rejected such a warning." Reasoning from those observations, the court concluded that Foster Wheeler lacked a colorable federal defense of government-contractor immunity with respect to the plaintiffs' theory of liability and that, "[f]or similar reasons," there was "no causal connection between the plaintiffs' claims" and the aspects of Foster Wheeler's conduct that conformed to government direction. **[—9—]**

Foster Wheeler filed this appeal from the district court's remand order dated April 20, 2016, as authorized by 28 U.S.C. § 1447(d).[1]

II

Section 1442, commonly referred to as the "federal officer removal statute," authorizes the removal to federal court of any "civil action or criminal prosecution" commenced in a state court against

> any officer (or any person acting under that officer) of the United States or of any agency thereof, in an official or individual capacity, for or relating to any act under color of such office.

28 U.S.C. § 1442(a)(1). Thus, a private defendant, such as a government contractor, who seeks to remove a case under § 1442(a)(1), must show: (1) that it "act[ed] under" a federal officer, *see, e.g., Watson v. Philip Morris Cos.*, 551 U.S. 142, 147 (2007); *Ripley v. Foster Wheeler LLC*, 841 F.3d 207, 209 (4th Cir. 2016); (2) that it has "a colorable federal defense," *Jefferson County v. Acker*, 527 U.S. 423, 431 (1999); and (3) that the charged conduct was carried out for on in relation to the asserted official authority, 28 U.S.C. § 1442(a)(1). In imposing these requirements, the statute aims "to protect the **[—10—]** Federal Government from . . . interference with its 'operations,'" *Watson*, 551 U.S. at 150 (quoting *Willingham v. Morgan*, 395 U.S. 402, 406 (1969)), primarily by providing "a federal forum for a federal defense," *Ripley*, 841 F.3d at 210.

With the statute's requirements in hand, we address whether Foster Wheeler satisfied each of them. **{-255-}**

[1] The parties subsequently filed a series of motions related to the record on appeal. The plaintiffs moved to strike the affidavit of retired Navy Rear Admiral Benjamin Lehman, who apparently died in April 2013, and moved to supplement the record with his obituary. Lehman's affidavit contained information about the Navy's control over Foster Wheeler's design and labeling of its boilers. Foster Wheeler contested the plaintiffs' motions, and additionally sought to supplement the record with Navy "Mil Specs" that covered warnings affixed to ship boilers. Because we think that this case can readily be decided without use of the affidavit that the plaintiffs seek to strike and without any of the material that either party wishes to add to the record, we find it unnecessary to expand the record at this stage of the proceedings.

A

First, there can be no question that Foster Wheeler was a "person acting under" the Navy when it constructed the boilers with asbestos that allegedly harmed Morris. When a private entity is involved, the Supreme Court has interpreted the phrase "acting under" to contemplate a relationship where the government exerts some "subjection, guidance, or control," *Watson*, 551 U.S. at 151 (quoting *Webster's New International Dictionary* 2765 (2d ed. 1953)), and where the private entity engages in an effort "to assist, or to help carry out, the duties or tasks of the federal superior," *id.* at 152 (emphasis omitted). In *Watson*, the Court distinguished relationships where private entities are merely subject to federal regulation—holding that mere regulation of private entities cannot justify removal under the statute—from the relationships where the private entity contracts with the government to fulfill a government need. As the Court explained:

> The assistance that private contractors provide federal officers goes beyond simple compliance with the law and helps officers fulfill other basic governmental tasks. . . . Moreover, at least arguably, [a contractor] perform[s] a job that, in the absence of a contract with a private firm, the Government itself would have had to perform. **[—11—]**

Id. at 153–54. In addition, the Court stated that the phrase "acting under" is "broad" and is to be "liberally construed" in favor of the entity seeking removal. *Id.* at 147.

Accordingly, courts have unhesitatingly treated the "acting under" requirement as satisfied where a contractor seeks to remove a case involving injuries arising from equipment that it *manufactured for the government. See Hurley v. CBS Corp.*, 648 Fed. Appx. 299, 303 (4th Cir. 2016) (per curiam) ("GE is a 'person acting under' a federal officer because it was acting under a valid government contract at all times relevant to the litigation"); *Papp v. Fore-Kast Sales Co.*, 842 F.3d 805, 813 (3d Cir. 2016) ("Papp's allegations are directed at actions Boeing took while working under a federal contract to produce an item the government needed, to wit, a military aircraft, and that the government otherwise would have been forced to produce on its own").

In this case, the record shows that during Morris' tenure as an employee at the Sparrows Point Shipyard, Foster Wheeler manufactured boilers under contracts with the U.S. Navy for use on its vessels. Given the Supreme Court's direction that we construe the statute liberally and the holdings of courts that have followed that direction, Foster Wheeler's status as a Navy contractor readily satisfies the requirement that it have acted under the Navy, as used in § 1442(a)(1).

B

Second, we conclude that Foster Wheeler has asserted a colorable federal defense—the defense of government-contractor immunity—to the plaintiffs' claims. **[—12—]**

The Supreme Court first articulated the government-contractor immunity defense in *Boyle v. United Technologies Corp.*, 487 U.S. 500 (1988), to prevent the imposition of state tort liability "for design defects in military equipment" when three requirements are met:

> (1) the United States approved reasonably precise specifications; (2) the equipment conformed to those specifications; and (3) the supplier warned the United States about the dangers in the use of **{–256–}** the equipment that were known to the supplier but not to the United States.

Id. at 512.

As the district court recognized, the defense in *Boyle* can apply not only to a "design defect" claim, but also to a claim like that asserted here—one based on Foster Wheeler's alleged *failure to warn* Morris about the dangers of asbestos. As we explained in *Ripley*, imposing failure-to-warn liability on a contractor could produce the same conflict with federal policy that the Supreme Court sought to prevent in *Boyle. See* 841 F.3d at 211; *see also In re Joint*

E. & S. Dist. N.Y. Asbestos Litig., 897 F.2d 626, 629 (2d Cir. 1990) ("When a federal contract and state tort law give contrary messages as to the nature and content of required product warnings, they cause the sort of conflict *Boyle* found so detrimental to the federal interest in regulating the liabilities of military contractors").

The courts applying *Boyle* to failure-to-warn cases have articulated three criteria necessary to establish the immunity defense, holding that it is established when "(1) the government exercised its discretion and approved certain warnings; (2) the contractor provided the warnings required by the government; [and] (3) the contractor warned the **[—13—]** government about dangers in the equipment's use that were known to the contractor but not to the government." *Oliver v. Oshkosh Truck Corp.*, 96 F.3d 992, 1003–04 (7th Cir. 1996); *see also, e.g.*, *Jowers v. Lincoln Electric Co.*, 617 F.3d 346, 352 (5th Cir. 2010); *Tate v. Boeing Helicopters*, 55 F.3d 1150, 1157 (6th Cir. 1995). Under this formulation, which we also now adopt, the government need not prohibit the contractor from providing additional warnings; the defense applies so long as the government dictated or approved the warnings that the contractor actually provided. *See, e.g.*, *Tate*, 555 F.3d at 1157 ("Government *discretion* is required, not dictation or prohibition of warnings"). Where "the government chooses its own warnings," rather than merely approves of a contractor's, it has "certainly" exercised the requisite discretion to support a colorable defense for the contractor. *Oliver*, 96 F.3d at 1004; *see also Tate*, 55 F.3d at 1157.

In this case, Foster Wheeler satisfied all three of the criteria for showing a colorable government-contractor defense in failure-to-warn cases. *First*, Foster Wheeler showed that the Navy "exercised intense direction and control over all written documentation to be delivered with its naval boilers," including those manufactured by Foster Wheeler. Thomas Schroppe's affidavit states that "Foster Wheeler would not be permitted, under the specifications, associated regulations and procedures, and especially under actual practice as it evolved in the field, to affix any type of warning or caution statement to a piece of equipment intended for installation onto a Navy vessel beyond those required by the Navy." *Second*, Foster Wheeler actually gave the warnings that were required by the Navy. Schroppe's affidavit describes a rigorous inspection process and indicates that the Navy would notice and penalize any deviation. And *third*, Foster **[—14—]** Wheeler credibly demonstrated, with Lawrence Betts' affidavit, that the Navy's knowledge of asbestos-related hazards exceeded Foster Wheeler's during the relevant time period. Indeed, several other courts have cited the same affidavit as supporting a finding that the government contractor did not withhold risk-related information of which the military was unaware. *See, e.g.*, *Hagen v. Benjamin Foster Co.*, 739 F. Supp. 2d 770, 784 (E.D. Pa. 2010) (asbestos MDL action). Thus, Foster Wheeler has made at least a colorable showing that the government exercised **{-257-}** discretion in requiring Foster Wheeler to provide certain notices and warnings, having full knowledge of the dangers involved. And the fact that the government did not prohibit Foster Wheeler from giving additional warnings—and may not even have considered requiring additional warnings—does not undermine the colorability of the immunity defense. *See Oliver*, 96 F.3d at 1004 n.8; *Tate*, 55 F.3d at 1157.

The district court, in concluding that Foster Wheeler did not demonstrate a colorable federal defense as to the plaintiffs' negligence claim, applied a different standard that does not follow the established criteria. It found that, even though the Navy "provided Foster Wheeler with detailed specifications governing warnings and written information that accompanied Foster Wheeler boilers," the fact that the Navy did not consider *additional* warnings to employees was fatal to Foster Wheeler's defense. Specifically, the court explained that, because the warnings that Foster Wheeler could have given employees in the workplace were not prohibited by the Navy, and because Foster Wheeler did not propose and the Navy did not reject the giving of such warning, the defense does not apply, as it "does not shield defendants where the government might **[—15—]** have exercised its discretion and final authority but did not." (Internal quotation marks and citation omitted). The district court's clear implication is that, unless the government explicitly regulated all possible warnings, Foster Wheeler could not have a colorable federal defense of immunity. But this reasoning overlooks the fact that, in specifying some warnings in response to the known dangers of asbestos, the government necessarily exercised discretion in not requiring additional warnings. *See Oliver*, 96 F.3d at 1004; *Tate*, 55 F.3d at 1157. It is this exercise of governmental discretion that, under the reasoning of *Boyle*, supports a defense for federal contractors who execute it.

Moreover, the district court failed to recognize, even on the terms of its own analysis, that removal need not be justified as to all claims asserted in the plaintiffs' complaint; rather, the defense need only apply to one claim to remove the case. *See* 28 U.S.C. § 1442(a) (allowing removal of "[a] civil action . . . commenced in a State court . . . for or relating to *any act* under color of [federal] office" (emphasis added)); *Bennett v. MIS Corp.*, 607 F.3d 1076, 1084 n.7 (6th Cir. 2010) (affirming denial of remand and noting that "§ 1442 authorizes removal of the entire case even if only one of the controversies it raises involves a federal officer or agency" (quoting Charles Alan Wright et al., *Federal Practice and Procedure* § 3726, at 275 (4th ed. 2009))). In this case, the plaintiffs included, among others, a products-liability claim based on faulty warning *with respect to the boilers* themselves, which the district court treated as distinct from other warnings (or the lack thereof) given to employees. *See, e.g., May v. Air & Liquid Sys. Corp.*, 139 A.3d 984, 988 (Md. 2015) (noting that under Maryland law a failure-to-warn claim may be brought under either a negligence or strict liability theory); *Phipps v.* **[—16—]** *General Motors Corp.*, 363 A.2d 955, 958 (Md. 1976) (noting that a strict liability claim focuses "not on the conduct of the manufacturer but rather on the product itself"). As the district court conceded, the warnings with respect to the boilers themselves were comprehensively mandated by the Navy, and it therefore follows that the plaintiffs' products-liability claim, even under the district court's analysis, is subject to a colorable government-contractor defense, thereby supporting removal.

C

Addressing the third requirement, we conclude that Foster Wheeler has established **{-258-}** a sufficient connection between the charged conduct and asserted official authority. While the statute requires that the act in question be "for or relating to" the federal office, 28 U.S.C. § 1442(a)(1), the district court applied a requirement for a *strict causal connection* between the two.

Before 2011, the contractor had to establish that the suit against it was "*for* a[n] act under color of office," *Acker*, 527 U.S. at 431 (alterations in original) (quoting 28 U.S.C. § 1442(a)(3) (1994)), which the Supreme Court then characterized as a "causal connection between the charged conduct and the asserted official authority," *id.* (internal quotation marks omitted). But even then, the Court rejected "narrow, grudging interpretation[s] of the statute, recognizing that one of the most important reasons for removal is to have the validity of the defense of official immunity tried in a federal court." *Id.* (internal quotation marks omitted). The Court explained, "Just as requiring a clearly sustainable defense rather than a colorable defense would defeat the purpose of **[—17—]** the removal statute, so would demanding an airtight case on the merits in order to show the required causal connection." *Id.* at 432 (internal quotation marks and citation omitted).

But in 2011, Congress amended § 1442(a)(1) to cover actions "for *or relating to* any act under color of [federal] office," adding the words "or relating to." Removal Clarification Act of 2011, Pub. L. No. 112-51, 125 Stat. 545. This new language "broaden[ed] the universe of acts" that enable federal removal, H.R. Rep. 112-17, 6, 2011 U.S.C.C.A.N. 420, 425, such that there need be only "'a *connection or association* between the act in question and the federal office.'" *Papp*, 842 F.3d at 813 (emphasis added) (quoting *In re Commonwealth's Motion to*

Appoint Counsel Against or Directed to Defender Assoc., 790 F.3d 457, 471 (3d Cir. 2015)).

Foster Wheeler has amply shown a sufficient "connection or association" in this case. As Foster Wheeler explains, the Navy dictated the content of warnings on Foster Wheeler's boilers, and Foster Wheeler complied with the Navy's requirements. That relationship was sufficient to connect the plaintiffs' claims, which fault warnings that were not specified by the Navy, to the warnings that the Navy specified and with which Foster Wheeler complied. These claims undoubtedly "relat[e] to" all warnings, given or not, that the Navy determined in its discretion.

The district court imposed a stricter standard of causation than that recognized by the statute. It concluded that "[b]ecause no federal officer provided any direction regarding whether to warn Foster Wheeler's workers in the shipyard's boiler shop about asbestos, Foster Wheeler has not established the necessary causal nexus between their **[—18—]** actions and the plaintiffs' claims." In demanding a showing of a specific government direction, however, the district court went beyond what § 1442(a)(1) requires, which is only that the charged conduct *relate to* an act under color of federal office.

The record in this case shows that the Navy was aware of the dangers of asbestos; that it required the use of asbestos in boilers for which it contracted with Foster Wheeler to manufacture; that it provided for a comprehensive set of warnings, but not all possible warnings; and that Foster Wheeler complied with the Navy's requirements. Foster Wheeler's alleged failure to give warnings to Shipyard employees is therefore clearly related to Foster Wheeler's performance of its contract with the Navy.

* * * **{-259-}**

In sum, Foster Wheeler in this case satisfied all three of § 1442(a)(1)'s requirements. It plausibly asserted that it was acting under the Navy when it manufactured boilers; that it possessed a colorable government-contractor defense to the plaintiffs' claims that it allegedly failed to give some warnings in connection with its manufacture of those boilers; and that the plaintiffs' claims are related to Foster Wheeler's government-directed conduct. Accordingly, we reverse the district court's conclusion that Foster Wheeler did not meet the substantive requirements of § 1442(a)(1). Permitting Foster Wheeler to remove this case serves the overarching policy of giving government contractors a federal forum in which to present their federal immunity defense and thereby avoiding possible state court hostility to the defense that could undermine federal interests. **[—19—]**

Because the district court addressed only the substantive requirements of § 1442(a)(1) before remanding the case to state court, it never addressed the question of whether Foster Wheeler's notice of removal was timely. Accordingly, in view of our conclusions, we remand this case to the district court to allow it, in the first instance, to determine the timeliness of Foster Wheeler's removal.

REVERSED AND REMANDED

United States Court of Appeals
for the Fourth Circuit

No. 16-2211

FAWZY
vs.
WAUQUIEZ BOATS SNC

On Appeal from the United States District Court for the District of Maryland at Baltimore

Decided: October 12, 2017

Citation: 873 F.3d 451, 5 Adm. R. 174 (4th Cir. 2017).

Before **NIEMEYER, KING,** and **HARRIS,** Circuit Judges.

[—3—] {-452-} **NIEMEYER,** Circuit Judge:

Dr. Amr Fawzy commenced this action against Wauquiez Boats SNC, a French partnership, alleging that a yacht that he purchased from Wauquiez Boats in 2011 was defective. Invoking the admiralty and maritime jurisdiction of the district court, as conferred by 28 U.S.C. § 1333, he asserted claims for "breach of a maritime contract" and for "products liability under the general maritime law." In response to a motion filed by Wauquiez Boats, the district court dismissed the complaint under Federal Rule of Civil Procedure 12(b)(1) for failing adequately to demonstrate admiralty and maritime jurisdiction, denied Wauquiez Boats' request for sanctions, and closed the case.

Unbeknownst to the district court, Fawzy filed an amended complaint under Federal Rule of Civil Procedure 15 roughly an hour before the district court filed its order dismissing the case. Instead of bringing the amended complaint to the attention of the court, however, Fawzy appealed the district court's order dismissing his original complaint, contending that the district court erred in finding a lack of admiralty and maritime jurisdiction.

Because the amended complaint remains the operative complaint in the district court and stands unaddressed by Wauquiez Boats or the court, we conclude that the district court's order dismissing the original complaint and denying sanctions was not a final decision under 28 U.S.C. § 1291. We therefore dismiss Fawzy's appeal, as well as Wauquiez Boats' cross-appeal requesting sanctions, for lack of appellate jurisdiction. **[—4—]**

I

In June 2011, Dr. Fawzy purchased a 55-foot sailing vessel from Wauquiez Boats in northern France for approximately **{-453-}** $1.13 million. After taking possession of the vessel in Port Camargue, France, and while sailing it across the Atlantic Ocean on course to his home in Scituate, Massachusetts, Fawzy began to experience difficulties operating the vessel. He alleged in his complaint that "numerous problems" arose "pertaining to the main sail, the foresail, and other components of the Vessel, many of which only became apparent while the Vessel was underway with Plaintiff on board, which resulted in great danger to Plaintiff's life." Fawzy also alleged that these problems persisted over the next two years despite his efforts to have Wauquiez Boats resolve them.

Fawzy commenced this action on October 6, 2016, coordinating the filing of his complaint with the United States Sailboat Show in Annapolis, Maryland, where Wauquiez Boats was showing a new 48-foot sailing vessel.[1] On the day after he filed his complaint, he obtained a writ of maritime attachment under Supplemental Admiralty Rule B on that vessel for the purposes of obtaining jurisdiction over Wauquiez Boats and securing a judgment for damages claimed in the amount of over $1.44 million. The proceedings in the district court thereafter moved quickly. On October 11, 2016, Wauquiez Boats filed a motion to dismiss the action for, among other things, a lack of **[—5—]** admiralty and maritime jurisdiction. The motion also requested sanctions, claiming that the attachment was wrongful, malicious, and especially injurious to Wauquiez Boats' effort to sell the new vessel at the boat show. The next day, October

[1] Fawzy also commenced an action in France in 2013, "seeking return of the purchase price of the Vessel and other, related expenses caused by the repetitive but unsuccessful attempts to repair or replace the defective components," which remains pending.

12, the district court conducted a hearing on Wauquiez Boats' motion, and on October 14, at 2:22 p.m., the court filed a memorandum and order: (1) dismissing the case for lack of admiralty or maritime jurisdiction; (2) vacating the attachment; (3) releasing Wauquiez Boats' vessel; (4) denying Wauquiez Boats' request for sanctions; and (5) directing the clerk of court to "close this case."

Unbeknownst to the district court—and calling to mind the script of a Greek tragedy—Fawzy had filed an amended complaint pursuant to Federal Rule of Civil Procedure 15(a)(1) at 1:16 p.m., a little more than an hour *before* the district court closed the case. The amended complaint added claims for negligent design of the vessel, failure to warn, intentional misrepresentation, and intentional infliction of emotional distress, and it added eight paragraphs alleging new facts. The amended complaint also increased Fawzy's damages claim to $1,573,500. Fawzy took no steps following the district court's order of dismissal to advise the court that he had previously filed an amended complaint. Rather, a few days later, on October 19, 2016, he filed this appeal, challenging the district court's ruling dismissing this case for a lack of admiralty and maritime jurisdiction. Wauquiez Boats then filed a cross-appeal, challenging the district court's order refusing to award sanctions for Fawzy's allegedly malicious attachment of its vessel.

By order dated August 28, 2017, we directed counsel for the parties to file simultaneous supplemental briefs addressing our subject matter jurisdiction. In his **[—6—]** supplemental brief, Fawzy contended that, despite the fact that his amended complaint rendered his original complaint a nullity and that the district court never addressed his amended complaint, we nonetheless have appellate jurisdiction. He argued that the district court's "subsequent dismissal of the initial Verified Complaint **{-454-}** was [simply] in error" such that we could review it as we would any other error. He argued further that after the district court dismissed the case, he could not file a Rule 60 motion to preserve the court's error for appeal because the error was "substantive" and not simply a "clerical mistake or a mistake arising from oversight or omission," quoting Federal Rule of Civil Procedure 60(a). In its supplemental brief, Wauquiez Boats likewise contended that we have appellate jurisdiction because the district court intended to render a final decision on all claims before it, whether or not they were specifically raised in the original complaint. It asserted that the amended complaint, which the district court never addressed, "[did] not contain any new causes of action that would deny appellate court jurisdiction in this matter" and that, in any event, any new allegations were discussed during the oral argument on its motion to dismiss the original complaint. Wauquiez Boats also argued that Fawzy failed to preserve his ability to rely on the amended complaint because he "did not alert the district court of the oversight prior to filing his appeal," making the original complaint the operative one and the district court's order dismissing it a final, appealable decision.

II

At the outset, we address our jurisdiction, as we must. **[—7—]**

Section 1291 of Title 28 confers jurisdiction over appeals from "all *final decisions* of the district courts of the United States" (emphasis added), subject to a limited number of exceptions not applicable here.[2] A final decision is one that "ends the litigation on the merits and leaves nothing for the court to do but execute the judgment." *Catlin v. United*

[2] These exceptions include, for example, appeals from the entry of injunctions, *see* 28 U.S.C. § 1292(a)(1); from orders variously certified as final, *see id.* § 1292(b); Fed. R. Civ. P. 54(b); and from certain collateral orders, *see Mohawk Industries, Inc. v. Carpenter,* 558 U.S. 100, 103 (2009); *Cohen v. Beneficial Indus. Loan Corp.*, 337 U.S. 541, 546 (1949), including orders dissolving a maritime attachment, *see Swift Co. & Packers v. Compania Colombiana Dell Caribe, S.A.*, 339 U.S. 684, 688–89 (1950). Neither party argues, however, that any of these exceptions apply, and they expressly declined to invoke the collateral order doctrine with respect to the district court's order dissolving the maritime attachment, pressing only our review of the district court's Rule 12(b)(1) dismissal order and its denial of sanctions.

States, 324 U.S. 229, 233 (1945); *see also United States ex rel. Lutz v. United States*, 853 F.3d 131, 136 (4th Cir. 2017). The question thus presented at the outset is whether the district court's order dismissing Fawzy's original complaint was a final decision that left nothing further to be done in the case.

In response to the complaint invoking admiralty and maritime jurisdiction under § 1333, Wauquiez Boats filed a motion to dismiss on the ground that the complaint failed adequately to demonstrate admiralty and maritime jurisdiction. Following a hearing on the motion, the district court dismissed the action, relying on *Flota Maritima Browning de Cuba, Sociadad Anonima v. Snobl*, 363 F.2d 733 (4th Cir. 1966) (holding that a contract for the sale of a ship is not a maritime contract), and *East River S.S. Corp. v. Transamerica Delaval, Inc.*, 476 U.S. 858 (1986) (holding that no products-liability claim **[—8—]** lies in admiralty when the only injury claimed is economic loss), and closed the case, thereby purporting to enter a "final decision." That decision **{-455-}** would, in the ordinary course, be appealable under § 1291.

The twist in this appeal, however, comes from the fact that one hour before the district court filed its order of dismissal, Fawzy filed an amended complaint under Rule 15, of which the court was neither forewarned nor had knowledge when it purported to issue its "final decision." But the effect of the amended complaint's filing was fatal to our jurisdiction.

Fawzy filed his amended complaint as a matter of right under Rule 15, which requires, in the circumstances here, no prior approval by the court or the opposing party. Rule 15 provides in relevant part that "[a] party may amend its pleadings once as a matter of course within . . . 21 days after service of a motion under Rule 12(b)." Fed. R. Civ. P. 15(a)(1)(B). In this case, Fawzy filed his amended complaint on October 14, 2016, only three days after Wauquiez Boats filed its Rule 12(b)(1) motion. Thus, the conditions for amending a complaint as of right under Rule 15 were satisfied.

Because a properly filed amended complaint supersedes the original one and becomes the operative complaint in the case, it renders the original complaint "of no effect." *Young v. City of Mt. Ranier*, 238 F.3d 567, 573 (4th Cir. 2001). Accordingly, when Fawzy filed his amended complaint as a matter of right at 1:16 p.m. on October 14, 2016, his filing rendered his original complaint "of no effect." As a consequence, when the district court subsequently dismissed the original complaint at 2:22 p.m. on the same day, it ruled on a mooted complaint, not the operative one. Indeed, the court never **[—9—]** addressed the operative amended complaint before Fawzy filed this appeal. Moreover, Wauquiez Boats never filed any motion or other response to the amended complaint, which yet stands unattended, boldly if not lonely. Because the district court's order dismissing the original complaint left the operative complaint unaddressed, the order was not a final order, but rather an interlocutory one, and we have no appellate jurisdiction to review it. *See* 28 U.S.C. § 1291. For the same reason, we also lack jurisdiction to review Wauquiez Boats' cross-appeal, taken from the district court's order denying its motion for sanctions.

Fawzy's argument that we should nonetheless address the district court's failure to address his amended complaint as a reviewable error simply ignores the final decision doctrine, which he does not even discuss in his supplemental brief.

Wauquiez Boats' argument that we have jurisdiction because the amended complaint added no new causes of action or facts fares no better. First, the amended complaint did indeed add several new causes of action that Fawzy contends fall within the admiralty and maritime jurisdiction of the court, including claims for negligent design of the vessel, failure to warn, intentional misrepresentation, and intentional infliction of emotional distress. Moreover, a number of paragraphs were added to the amended complaint alleging facts not included in the original complaint. While Wauquiez Boats argues that the additional allegations were discussed with the court at the hearing on the motion to dismiss the original complaint, that argument does not lead to a conclusion that the district court somehow addressed and dismissed the amended complaint before it was even filed or that the court intended to assess the sufficiency of the new allegations in its **[—10—]** ruling. Indeed, at the hearing, Fawzy made no request to amend his complaint and the court never indicated that Fawzy had somehow made such a request. Finally, Wauquiez Boats argues that we have jurisdiction because, by failing to notify the district court timely of its error, Fawzy cannot rely on the amended complaint, **{-456-}** making the district court's ruling on the original complaint a final decision. But, as we have already noted, the amended complaint was properly filed under Rule 15(a), and Fawzy's failure to notify the district court of its filing did not change the amended complaint's status as the operative one.

Accordingly, we conclude that the district court erroneously, albeit unwittingly, closed the case without having addressed the amended complaint and therefore that Fawzy's appeal and Wauquiez Boats' cross-appeal were taken from an interlocutory order. We thus dismiss their appeals for lack of appellate jurisdiction.

IT IS SO ORDERED.

This page intentionally left blank

United States Court of Appeals for the Fifth Circuit

United States Court of Appeals
for the Fifth Circuit

No. 15-30599

IN RE DEEPWATER HORIZON

LAKE EUGENIE LAND & DEV., INC.
vs.
BP EXPLORATION & PROD., INC.

Appeal from the United States District Court for the Eastern District of Louisiana

Decided: January 6, 2017
Revised: January 9, 2017

Citation: 845 F.3d 634, 5 Adm. R. 180 (5th Cir. 2017).

Before **BENAVIDES, DENNIS,** and **SOUTHWICK,** Circuit Judges.

[—1—] {-636-} DENNIS, Circuit Judge: **[—2—]**

Woodbridge Baric Pre-Settlement Funding, L.L.C. (Woodbridge Baric), appeals the district court's order that it pay $20,000 in restitution to the Deepwater Horizon Court-Supervised Settlement Program. In 2012 Woodbridge Baric loaned Jarrod Burrle $24,000. Woodbridge Baric and Burrle agreed that Burrle would not be required to repay the loan if his economic loss claims in connection with the Deepwater Horizon oil spill fail unless he had misrepresented his claim to Woodbridge Baric, in which case Burrle agreed to indemnify Woodbridge Baric and hold it harmless. In 2013, the settlement program paid over $50,000 on one of Burrle's claims, and Burrle's attorneys paid Woodbridge Baric $20,000 of those funds in partial repayment of the loan. Subsequently, Louis Freeh, appointed by the district court as a special master to investigate misconduct in the administration of the settlement program, determined that Burrle's claim was fraudulent and moved the court to order Burrle and others, including Woodbridge Baric, to make restitution for the funds paid in connection with that claim. The district court granted the motion as to Woodbridge Baric, finding that Woodbridge Baric would be unjustly enriched if allowed to retain the $20,000 from Burrle. For the following reasons, we reverse the district court's judgment against Woodbridge Baric.

I

In 2010, Burrle filed claims for compensation, including a claim for lost income from commercial fishing, with the Gulf Coast Claims Facility, which was tasked with processing claims related to the Deepwater Horizon oil spill. In early 2012, Burrle entered into three separate "pre-settlement funding contracts" with Woodbridge Baric.[1] Under these contracts, Woodbridge Baric **[—3—]** agreed to loan Burrle a total of $24,000, referred to as an "advance," at a specified interest rate.[2] Each of the three contracts provided that "[i]n the event [Burrle does] not recover any money from the 'lawsuit/claim,' [Burrle] shall not be obligated to repay the advance to [Woodbridge Baric]." The contracts also **{-637-}** provided that if Burrle's representations to Woodbridge Baric regarding his claims were false, he would be required to indemnify Woodbridge Baric for its losses and expenses, including the principal amount of the loan.[3]

---

[1] In an October 2001 opinion, the Office of the Attorney General of the State of Louisiana opined that pre-settlement funding contracts constitute a consumer loan as defined in the Louisiana Consumer Credit Law. La. Atty. Gen. Op. No. 2001-160, 2001 La. **[—3—]** AG LEXIS 489. The special master does not dispute that Woodbridge Baric's pre-settlement funding contracts with Burrle were consumer loan agreements.

[2] The contracts purported to "assign[ ] an interest" in Burrle's claims to Woodbridge Baric. However, as the special master points out, the Deepwater Horizon settlement agreement prohibits the assignment of rights or claims arising out of the Deepwater Horizon incident and declares any such assignment "void, invalid, and of no force and effect."

[3] Specifically, the pre-settlement funding contracts provided, in relevant part:

> **5. Representations and Warranties**: To induce "Woodbridge Baric" to pay "Me" [Burrle] the Advance and to take an assignment and or right of first distribution of my "Lawsuit/Claims," "I" hereby make the following representations and warranties under penalty of perjury . . . "I" understand that "Woodbridge Baric" is relying on the below representations and warranties to pay me the Advance. In the event any of my representations and warranties below are

In December 2012, the district court approved the Deepwater Horizon Economic and Property Damages Settlement Agreement in a class action concerning the Deepwater Horizon oil spill. In accordance with the settlement agreement, the district court established the Deepwater Horizon Court-Supervised Settlement Program to implement and administer the settlement agreement, including the processing of individual claims for compensation. **[—4—]** Shortly after the settlement program began operations, Burrle refiled his claims for compensation with the program.

In 2013, the settlement program approved Burrle's commercial fishing claim and paid him $50,015.87. Following receipt of the claim payment, Burrle's attorneys paid Woodbridge Baric $20,000 on Burrle's behalf as a partial repayment of its loan. Several months later, the district court appointed the special master, directing him to investigate claims submitted to the settlement program and initiate legal action to "clawback" funds paid on fraudulent claims. After investigating Burrle's claims, the special master determined that they were fraudulent. The special master then filed a motion asking the district court to require Burrle and third parties who benefitted from the settlement program's payment on Burrle's commercial fishing claim to return that payment.

The district court ultimately granted the special master's motion, finding that Burrle submitted fraudulent documents and made false statements in connection with his claim. In addition to ordering Burrle to repay all funds paid on his claim to the settlement program, the district court ordered Burrle's lawyers and Woodbridge Baric to repay the funds they received in connection with his claim. As to Woodbridge Baric, the district court determined that it would be unjustly enriched if allowed to retain the funds, reasoning that Woodbridge Baric's right to Burrle's repayment of the loan was contingent upon the success of Burrle's claims, which ultimately failed. Thus, the district court entered judgment against Woodbridge Baric in the amount of $20,000.00. Woodbridge Baric appeals.

II

As an initial matter, the parties disagree on the relevant standard of review on appeal. The special master argues that the district court's judgment **[—5—]** was a decision to grant relief from a judgment under Federal Rule of Civil Procedure 60(b), which is reviewed for abuse of discretion. Woodbridge Baric responds that the district court's entry of a final judgment against it was essentially a grant of **{-638-}** summary judgment, and thus review is de novo. However, we need not decide the nature of the district court's ruling. Even if characterized as a decision to grant relief from a judgment under Rule 60(b), this court reviews de novo any question of law underlying the district court's decision. *See Frazar v. Ladd*, 457 F.3d 432, 435 (5th Cir. 2006). Because the parties' respective arguments pertain only to questions of law, we will review the district court's determinations as to those questions de novo. *See id.*

"It is a long-standing legal principle that a person who has conferred a benefit upon another in compliance with a judgment, or whose property has been taken thereunder, is entitled to restitution if the judgment is reversed or set aside, unless restitution would be inequitable." *Mohamed v. Kerr*, 91 F.3d 1124, 1126 (8th Cir. 1996) (citations, alteration, and internal quotation marks omitted); *accord United States v. Morgan*, 307 U.S. 183 (1939); *Atlantic Coast Line R. Co. v. Florida*, 295 U.S. 301, 309 (1935); RESTATEMENT (THIRD) OF RESTITUTION & UNJUST ENRICHMENT § 18 ("A transfer or taking of property, in compliance with or otherwise in consequence of a judgment that

---

> untrue, "I" agree to indemnify and hold harmless "WOODBRIDGE BARIC" against all losses, expenses [and] costs (including the Advanced Amount . . .).

As part of his representations and warranties under the contracts, Burrle guaranteed that any information he provided to Woodbridge Baric relating to his claim or to Woodbridge Baric's decision to provide him with funding was "accurate and complete in all respects."

is subsequently reversed or avoided, gives the disadvantaged party a claim in restitution as necessary to avoid unjust enrichment."). Thus, it is well established that when a prior judgment is invalidated, the district court has inherent equitable power to enforce restitution of what has been done in compliance with its prior judgment. *See, e.g.*, *Baltimore & O. R. Co. v. United States*, 279 U.S. 781, 786 (1929); *Morgan*, 307 U.S. at 198.

The court's power being equitable in nature, restitution pursuant to this power is a matter of equity rather than a matter of right. *Atlantic Coast Line*, **[—6—]** 295 U.S. at 310; *Mohamed*, 91 F.3d at 1126. To prevail, a party seeking restitution "must show that the money was received in such circumstances that the possessor will give offense to equity and good conscience if permitted to retain it." *Id.* at 309. "The question no longer is whether the law would put [the possessor] in possession of the money if the transaction were a new one. The question is whether the law will take it out of his possession after he has been able to collect it." *Id.* at 310.

Relevant to the instant case, it is a generally recognized rule of equity that a third party who receives funds in good faith from a judgment creditor in satisfaction of a debt is not liable to repay those funds in restitution. *See, e.g.*, *Mohamed*, 91 F.3d at 1126 ("[E]quity will not compel restitution from a third party who receives monies, in good faith, from the initial judgment creditor in payment of a debt."); *see also Equilease Corp. v. Hentz*, 634 F.2d 850, 853 (5th Cir. 1981) (applying Florida law and stating, "[I]t is patently unfair to require an innocent payee who has received and used the money to satisfy a debt to repay the money"); RESTATEMENT § 67(1)(a) (a bona fide payee who "accepts the funds in satisfaction or reduction of the payee's valid claim as creditor" is not liable to repay the funds). Relying on this rule, Woodbridge Baric argues that it is a bona fide payee who received funds from Burrle in partial satisfaction of a valid claim. In this regard, Woodbridge Baric notes that it made a $24,000 loan to Burrle and that it is undisputed that it had no knowledge of the fraudulent nature of Burrle's settlement program claim. Woodbridge Baric also highlights that it was not a party to Burrle's litigation before the settlement program, notwithstanding its expectation **{-639-}** of receiving a share of the proceeds of his claims.

The district court concluded that Woodbridge Baric was not entitled to retain the funds because its right to Burrle's repayment of the loan was **[—7—]** contingent upon the successful settlement of Burrle's claims. Because Burrle's fraudulent claim ultimately failed, the district court determined that Woodbridge Baric would be unjustly enriched if allowed to retain the funds. In so concluding, the district court relied on an exception, recognized by some courts, to the rule that bona fide third-party payees are not liable in restitution. Under this exception, an attorney who receives a share of a judgment pursuant to a contingency-fee agreement does not take the money as a bona fide payee. *E.g.*, *Mohamed*, 91 F.3d at 1127; *Cox v. Cox*, 780 N.E.2d 951, 962 (Mass. App. Ct. 2002); *see also* RESTATEMENT § 18 cmt. g. This exception rests on the premise that by conditioning his or her fees on success in litigation, the attorney assumes the risk of non-recovery. *E.g.*, *Mohamed*, 91 F.3d at 1127; RESTATEMENT § 18 cmt. g. Because the initial judgment creditor ultimately collects nothing after the judgment is reversed, the attorney is also entitled to nothing pursuant to the terms of the fee agreement and is therefore liable to repay the funds in restitution. *Mohamed*, 91 F.3d at 1127. Many authorities have therefore likened an attorney with a contingency fee agreement to a real party in interest or assignee *pro tanto* of the client's judgment and thus view the attorney as standing in the client's shoes. *See e.g.*, *Mohamed*, 91 F.3d at 1127; *Excel Corp. v. Jimenez*, 7 P.3d 1118, 1126 (Kan. 2000); *Abrahami v. UPC Const. Co.*, 670 N.Y.S.2d 457, 468 (N.Y. App. Div. 1998).

While the logic of this exception could arguably extend to non-attorneys, so far, all of the cases that discuss this exception have involved attorneys. *See, e.g.*, *Mohamed*, 91 F.3d at 1127; *Cox*, 780 N.E.2d at 962; *Excel Corp.*, 7 P.3d at 1126; *Abrahami*, 670 N.Y.S.2d at 468; *Ehsani v. McCullough Family P'ship*,

159 P.3d 407, 411 (Wash. 2007) (en banc). This is not surprising considering that attorneys are far more likely than anyone else to condition their rights to payment upon the results of litigation. But we need not decide whether this **[—8—]** exception applies beyond the context of attorneys' contingency fees because, even assuming this exception could apply to non-attorneys, it would have no application in this case.

Woodbridge Baric's right to Burrle's repayment of the principal amount of its loan did not depend solely on the success of Burrle's claims: Woodbridge Baric's contracts with Burrle expressly required Burrle to indemnify and hold Woodbridge Baric harmless for the loss of the principal amount of the loan if his representations to Woodbridge Baric regarding his claims were not accurate and complete in all respects. Although Woodbridge Baric assumed some of the risks associated with non-recovery in its contracts with Burrle, it specifically disclaimed the risk that Burrle had asserted fraudulent claims and withheld that information from it.[4] Accordingly, Woodbridge **{-640-}** Baric was entitled to Burrle's full repayment of the principal under their contracts. Where, as here, a "bona fide creditor is entitled to payment regardless of the judgment's validity, that creditor is not unjustly enriched by retention of the payment after the judgment's reversal." *Cox*, 780 N.E.2d at 962. In other **[—9—]** words, because Burrle's payment to Woodbridge Baric discharged an unconditional, bona fide obligation, Woodbridge Baric is not liable in restitution to the settlement program. *See id.*

Treating an attorney with a contingency fee agreement as standing in his or her client's shoes is only warranted to the extent the attorney's claim against the client rests solely upon the now-failed contingency. *See Mohamed*, 91 F.3d at 1127 (remanding for determination of the portion of proceeds retained by attorney that represented payment of a contingent fee); *Abrahami*, 670 N.Y.S.2d at 468 (holding that law firm was liable for restitution of contingency fee but not of other, non-contingent fees following vacatur of judgment); *cf. Ehsani*, 159 P.3d at 411 ("[T]here is no unjust enrichment vis-à-vis the judgment debtor where a party receives only that to which he is entitled under the terms of a valid, preexisting agreement with the judgment creditor."). Consider an attorney with a fee-for-service arrangement under which the client is to pay the attorney $1,000, regardless of the result of litigation. In this scenario, if an initially favorable judgment is subsequently overturned or nullified, the attorney would not be liable to repay the fee in restitution. *See, e.g.*, *Mohamed*, 91 F.3d at 1126; *see also* Restatement § 67(1)(a). Now assume that the fee agreement also provides that in the event the attorney obtains a favorable result in litigation, the client must pay the attorney a total of $1,500. If the initially favorable judgment is subsequently invalidated, must the attorney forfeit not only the $500 that were contingent upon success in litigation but also the $1,000 he would have been entitled to regardless of the outcome? We see no basis in precedent or in equity for requiring such an odd result. *Cf. Ehsani*, 159

[4] We need not decide whether an attorney would be able to assert bona fide payee status under similar circumstances, as that case is not before us. We note, however, that, unlike lenders, attorneys have both a legal and an ethical duty to reasonably investigate the facts prior to filing pleadings with the court. *See, e.g.*, *Callahan v. Schoppe*, 864 F.2d 44, 46 (5th Cir. 1989) ("Rule 11 of the Federal Rules of Civil Procedure imposes a duty of reasonable investigation into the facts and the law prior to filing a document with a court."); Mod. Rules Prof. Cond. § 3.1 ("A lawyer shall not bring or defend a proceeding, or assert or controvert an issue therein, unless there is a basis in law and fact for doing so that is not frivolous."); *In re Zohdy*, 892 So.2d 1277 (La. 2005) (lawyer who sought to intervene in chemical products liability class action violated rules of professional conduct by failing to investigate whether his clients were exposed to chemical). Courts may wish to consider an attorney's disregard for these duties in determining whether the attorney's acceptance of payment pursuant to his client's fraudulent claim was in good faith. *Cf. Excel Corp. v. Jimenez*, 7 P.3d 1118, 1126 (Kan. 2000) (an attorney's status as an officer of the court "places him on a different legal footing," and the court could not approve the retention of an attorney's fees where the client was guilty of fraudulent conduct in procuring the judgment).

P.3d at 411; *Abrahami*, 670 N.Y.S.2d at 468; *Cox*, 780 N.E.2d at 958 n.12, 962 & n.19 ("[An] attorney is not liable in restitution to the judgment debtor upon reversal of the judgment **[—10—]** unless the judgment debtor . . . proves either that the payment did not discharge an unconditional, bona fide obligation the client had to the attorney or that, although the payment did discharge such an obligation, other circumstances exist that make the attorney's retention of the payment unjust," such as "breach of some duty, a violation of trust, bad faith, or fraud").

Because Woodbridge Baric's claim for the repayment of the loan was not purely contingent upon the success of Burrle's claims for compensation, the failure of this contingency did not extinguish Woodbridge Baric's claim and does not prevent Woodbridge Baric from asserting its valid interest in defense of its right to retain the **{–641–}** funds as a bona fide payee. *See Abrahami*, 670 N.Y.S.2d at 468; *see also Cox*, 780 N.E.2d at 962. While the special master argues that Burrle did not purport to pay Woodbridge Baric under the warranty provisions of their agreements, Burrle nonetheless paid Woodbridge Baric in partial satisfaction of a valid debt.[5] At bottom, Woodbridge Baric was simply not unjustly enriched by its good faith acceptance of the funds from Burrle in partial repayment of his debt. *See Mohamed*, 91 F.3d at 1126-27; *see also* RESTATEMENT §§ 18 cmt. g, 67(1)(a) & (c).

III

For these reasons, the judgment of the district court is REVERSED.

[5] At oral argument, the special master argued for the first time that Burrle may be able to defend himself from Woodbridge Baric's claim against him by asserting that the interest rate the parties had agreed upon was usurious under Louisiana law. This argument is forfeited. *See Whitehead v. Food Max of Miss., Inc.*, 163 F.3d 265, 270 (5th Cir. 1998) ("Needless to say, we do not generally consider points raised for the first time at oral argument."). In any case, as discussed above, Woodbridge Baric had loaned Burrle $24,000 but received only $20,000 in partial repayment of Burrle's debt. The special master has not established that a credit provider's usurious interest rate relieves the consumer from the obligation to repay the *principal* under Louisiana state law. *Cf.* LA. REV. STAT. § 9:3552(A)(1)(a) (providing that a credit provider's violation of the provisions of this chapter, including by charging an excessive interest rate, entitles the consumer to a refund of all loan finance charges but not a refund of the principal).

United States Court of Appeals
for the Fifth Circuit

No. 16-30137

COASTAL CONSERVATION ASS'N
VS.
UNITED STATES DEP'T OF COMMERCE

Appeal from the United States District Court for the Eastern District of Louisiana

Decided: January 17, 2017
Revised: January 26, 2017

Citation: 846 F.3d 99, 5 Adm. R. 185 (5th Cir. 2017).

Before **STEWART**, Chief Judge, **SMITH** and **DENNIS**, Circuit Judges.

[—1—] {–103–} DENNIS, Circuit Judge:

Several private anglers and the Coastal Conservation Association, a group representing private anglers (collectively, CCA), appeal the district **[—2—]** court's summary judgment dismissal of their lawsuit, which challenged Amendment 40 to the Reef Fish Fishery Management Plan and the Final Rule implementing that amendment. Because we find that Amendment 40 is consistent with its organic statute and was properly devised and implemented, we AFFIRM the judgment of the district court.

I

This dispute centers on the management of the red snapper fishery in the Gulf of Mexico. This fishery is regulated pursuant to the Magnuson-Stevens Act, 16 U.S.C. § 1801 *et seq.* (the MSA or the Act). The MSA was passed by Congress in 1976 in order to "take immediate action to conserve and manage the fishery resources found off the coasts of the United States" and "promote domestic commercial and recreational fishing under sound conservation and management principles." *Id.* at § 1801(b)(1), (3). To accomplish these goals, the MSA established eight Regional Fishery Management Councils, each tasked with preparing fishery management plans (FMPs) to address conservation and management of fisheries under their control. The Councils are empowered to draft FMPs that are "necessary and appropriate for the conservation and management of the fishery, to prevent overfishing and rebuild overfished stocks, and to protect, restore, and promote the long-term health and stability of the fishery." *Id.* at § 1853(a)(1)(A).

The Gulf Council is one such regional council, with authority to manage fisheries in the federal waters of the Gulf of Mexico off the coasts of Texas, Louisiana, Mississippi, Alabama, and Florida. The Act requires the Councils to form their fishery management plans through a process of notice-and-comment rulemaking. FMPs are proposed by the Regional Councils, with final regulations promulgated by the Secretary of Commerce through the National Marine Fishery Service (NMFS). Once the Secretary, through the NMFS, **[—3—]** reviews the plans and publishes the final regulations in the Federal Register, they have the full force of law. *Id.* at § 1854.

Every FMP must be consistent with ten National Standards, codified at 16 U.S.C. § 1851(a). Two of these standards are relevant to the instant litigation:

> (2) Conservation and management measures shall be based upon the best scientific information available.
>
> (8) Conservation and management measures shall, consistent with the conservation requirements of this chapter (including the prevention of overfishing and rebuilding of overfished stocks), take into account the importance of fishery resources to **{–104–}** fishing communities by utilizing economic and social data that meet the requirements of paragraph (2), in order to (A) provide for the sustained participation of such communities, and (B) to the extent practicable, minimize adverse economic impacts on such communities.

Id. at § 1851(a).

In addition to the National Standards, the management of Gulf of Mexico red snapper is addressed specifically in Section 407 of the Act. Section 407, which was added to the Act in 1996, requires that any FMP for the red snapper fishery adopted by the Gulf Council must "establish separate quotas for recreational fishing (which, for the purposes of this subsection shall include charter fishing [i.e., fishing from chartered vessels]) and commercial fishing that, when reached, result in a prohibition on the retention of fish caught during recreational fishing and commercial fishing, respectively, for the remainder of the fishing year." *Id.* at § 1883(d)(1).

Red snapper stock is managed under the Reef Fish FMP, first implemented by the Secretary in 1984. In 1990, in response to observed declines in the adult population of red snapper, the Council implemented Amendment 1 to the Reef Fish FMP with the goal of rebuilding the adult red **[—4—]** snapper population by 2000.[1] The Gulf Council manages the recreational sector using several imprecise measures, including length of season. *Guindon v. Pritzker*, 31 F. Supp. 3d 169, 178 (D.D.C. 2014). The recreational sector exceeded its quota in every year from 1991-2005, from 2007-2009, and from 2011-2013.[2] The Gulf Council has largely responded to these violations by shortening the fishing season. 79 Fed. Reg. 27,768, 27,768-69 (May 15, 2014) (Emergency Rule To Revise the Recreational Accountability Measures and Revise the 2014 Recreational Fishing Season for Red Snapper in the Gulf of Mexico). The season in 2014 was only nine days long. *Id.* at 27,770.

NMFS is responsible for ensuring that the entire recreational Gulf harvest does not exceed the recreational quota, taking into account harvest in both federal and state waters. *See* 50 C.F.R. § 622.8(a). While the Gulf Council has shortened the fishing season in federal waters, the Gulf states have responded by loosening restrictions in state waters: in 2014, while the season in federal waters was nine days long, Mississippi and Alabama waters were open for 21 days, Florida for 52 days, Louisiana for 286 days, and Texas for 365 days. Only private anglers with boats can take advantage of the state seasons; federal regulations require federally permitted charter boats to comply with the federal regulations, which "are more restrictive than state regulations . . . regardless of where the fish are harvested." 50 C.F.R. § 622.20(a)(1). And while there has been a moratorium on the issuance of new charter vessel permits for Gulf reef fish since 2003, "there is no limit to the number of anglers fishing from private recreational vessels that target reef fish species." 80 Fed. Reg. 3541, 3,542 (January 23, 2015) (Notice of Proposed Amendment 40). **[—5—]**

In 2013, the Gulf Council and NMFS proposed Amendment 40 as a means to address problems that had arisen with the red snapper fishery. In the notice of proposed rulemaking, the Secretary explained, **{-105-}** "Establishing separate components [for charter and private anglers] is . . . intended to provide a basis for flexible management that can be tailored to the needs of each component, thereby reducing the likelihood for recreational quota overruns which could negatively impact the rebuilding of the red snapper stock." *Id.* The Secretary also described how the privileged position of private anglers—in particular, the access to state waters during state seasons and the lack of a limit on private vessels targeting red snapper—had adversely affected the charter industry, explaining that "[b]y establishing separate sectors, NMFS intends to stabilize the Federal for-hire component's participation in the sector." *Id.*

The Final Rule, issued in 2015, contains measures to establish two components within the recreational sector for Gulf of Mexico red snapper: a federal charter component and a private angling component. 80 Fed. Reg.

---

[1] This target date was ultimately extended to 2032. *Coastal Conservation Ass'n v. Gutierrez*, 512 F. Supp. 2d 896, 899 (S.D. Tex. 2007).

[2] The Charter Fisherman's Association notes in its brief that "2006 and 2010 were unusual years, because 2006 followed Hurricanes Katrina and Rita and 2010 was the year of the Deepwater Horizon oil spill."

22,422 (April 22, 2015) (Final Rule Implementing Amendment 40). The Final Rule allocates the red snapper recreational quota between these two components and establishes separate red snapper season closure provisions for the two components. *Id.* Each component's season will begin on June 1 and the season length will be projected from each component's annual catch target. *Id.* at 22,423. The separate component quotas and associated management measures are only effective for the 2015, 2016, and 2017 fishing years, after which they sunset unless the Gulf Council takes further action. *Id.* The Final Rule reiterated NMFS's finding that Amendment 40 will provide a basis for increased flexibility in future management of the recreational sector, and reduce the likelihood of recreational quota overruns, which could negatively impact the rebuilding of the red snapper stock. *Id.* at 22,422. **[—6—]**

The CCA filed this action against the Secretary of Commerce, the Director of NOAA, and the Director of NMFS (collectively, the Secretary) challenging Amendment 40 and the Final Rule in late April, 2015. The Charter Fisherman's Association (the CFA), which represents charter fishing businesses, intervened as a defendant. The parties filed cross-motions for summary judgment; on January 5, 2016, the district court granted the defendants' and intervenor-defendants' motions. This appeal followed.

II

We review a grant of summary judgment de novo, applying the same standard as the district court. *Louisiana Crawfish Producers Ass'n-W. v. Rowan*, 463 F.3d 352, 355 (5th Cir. 2006). On appeal, the CCA argues that: (1) the MSA prohibits the Gulf Council from regulating charter fishing separately from other recreational fishermen; (2) the Gulf Council and the NMFS failed to adequately "assess, specify, and analyze" the likely economic and social effects of Amendment 40; and (3) the selection of data ranges used to calculate quota allocations was arbitrary and capricious. We address each argument in turn.

A. Subquotas within the Recreational Sector

In reviewing an agency's construction of a statute that it is tasked with administering, this court follows the two-step framework set out by the Supreme Court in *Chevron, U.S.A., Inc. v. Natural Resources Defense Council, Inc.*, 467 U.S. 837 (1984). "First, always, is the question whether Congress has directly spoken to the precise question at issue. If the intent of Congress is clear, that is the end of the matter; for the court, as well as the agency, **{-106-}** must give effect to the unambiguously expressed intent of Congress." *Id.* at 842-43. However, "if the statute is silent or ambiguous with respect to the specific issue, the question for the court is whether the agency's answer is based on a permissible construction of the statute." *Id.* at 843. The agency's view "governs **[—7—]** if it is a reasonable interpretation of the statute—not necessarily the only possible interpretation, nor even the interpretation deemed *most* reasonable by the courts." *Entergy Corp. v. Riverkeeper, Inc.*, 556 U.S. 208, 218 (2009) (emphasis in original).

The CCA argues that Amendment 40's establishment of two components within the recreational sector for Gulf of Mexico red snapper—a federal charter component and private angling component—conflicts with the unambiguously expressed intent of Congress in adopting Section 407. Specifically, the CCA argues that "[t]he words of 16 U.S.C. § 1883(d) on their face prohibit a separate charter fishing quota," and that "[t]he plain meaning of 16 U.S.C. § 1883(d) is also shown by two canons of statutory interpretation." We find neither of these arguments persuasive.

As to the former, the CCA begins from a false premise: Amendment 40 does not in fact create a "separate" charter fishing quota. Rather, it creates a *sub*-quota for charter fishing within the recreational sector. *See* 80 Fed. Reg. 22,422, 22,422 ("This final rule contains measures to establish two components *within the recreational sector* for Gulf of Mexico . . . red snapper (a Federal charter vessel/headboat (for-hire) component and private angling component)." (emphasis added)). This is not a mere semantic distinction: Amendment 40 requires that all recreational landing—whether by private or charter anglers—cease when the total sector quota of 5.390 million pounds is reached. *See* 80 Fed. Reg. 22,422, 22,430. There is no language within Section 407 that prohibits the subdivision of the recreational or commercial fishing quotas. *See* 16 U.S.C. § 1883(d)(1).

The CCA's argument that two canons of statutory interpretation demonstrate that Section 407 prohibits the establishment of sub-quotas is equally unconvincing. First, the CCA argues that the canon of *expressio unius est exclusio alterius* militates in favor of its position. This canon holds that **[—8—]** "expressing one item of a commonly associated group or series excludes another left unmentioned." *United States v. Vonn*, 535 U.S. 55, 65 (2002). The CCA argues that this canon supports its argument because "Congress' mandate in 16 U.S.C. § 1883(d) for two quotas prohibits NMFS from creating a third quota," and "Congress' mandate that the recreational fishing quota 'shall include charter fishing' implies exclusion of authority to create a separate charter fishing quota." However, as previously discussed, Amendment 40 does not create a separate quota for charter fishing; the sub-quotas for private and charter anglers are included within the recreational fishing quota. 80 Fed. Reg. 22,422, 22,430. And the *exclusio unius* canon cannot be used to read Section 407 as prohibiting the creation of sub-quotas. As the Supreme Court has explained, the canon does not apply "unless it is fair to suppose that Congress considered the unnamed possibility and meant to say no to it." *Marx v. Gen. Revenue Corp.*, 133 S. Ct. 1166, 1175 (2013) (quoting *Barnhart v. Peabody Coal Co.*, 537 U.S. 149, 169 (2003)). Nothing in the text or the legislative history of Section 407 suggests that it would be fair to suppose that Congress considered the possibility that the Gulf Council would opt to **{-107-}** subdivide the recreational sector and meant to prohibit it from doing so. *See* 16 U.S.C. § 1883(d)(1); S. Rep. No. 104-276, 104th Cong., 2nd Sess. (May 23, 1996).

The CCA next argues that the canon that a specific statute prevails over an inconsistent general statute supports its position. "The general/specific canon is perhaps most frequently applied to statutes in which a general permission or prohibition is contradicted by a specific prohibition or permission. To eliminate the contradiction, the specific provision is construed as an exception to the general one." *RadLAX Gateway Hotel, LLC v. Amalgamated Bank*, 132 S. Ct. 2065, 2071 (2012). The CCA argues that, because the specific language of Section 407 "conflicts" with the general **[—9—]** authorization in 16 U.S.C. § 1853(b)(3)(A) for NMFS to establish regulatory quotas for fishery sectors, the later-enacted, specific language should apply. However, we perceive no conflict between the two provisions. In promulgating Amendment 40, the Secretary heeded Section 407's instruction and "establish[ed] separate quotas for recreational fishing (which, for the purposes of this subsection shall include charter fishing) and commercial fishing." 16 U.S.C. § 1883(d)(1). The fact that charter fishing is included within the recreational fishing sector as one of two distinct components is immaterial.

The CCA does not challenge the district court's finding that, viewing Section 407 as ambiguous on the issue of sub-quotas, the interpretation of Section 407(d) to allow sub-quotas is permissible under step two of *Chevron*. Nor does the CCA challenge the district court's finding that the Secretary had a "rational basis for [its] decision to subdivide the recreational quota." Those challenges are therefore forfeited. *See Cinel v. Connick*, 15 F.3d 1338, 1345 (5th Cir. 1994) ("An appellant abandons all issues not raised and argued in its initial brief on appeal.").

Amendment 40 does not create a separate quota for charter fishing; it subdivides the recreational sector into private and charter components. The directive to "establish separate quotas for recreational fishing (which, for the purposes of this subsection shall include charter fishing) and commercial fishing" does not unambiguously prohibit the Secretary from creating sub-quotas within the recreational sector. Even assuming, arguendo, that a prohibition on sub-quotas is a reasonable interpretation of the section, it could not be said that "Congress has directly spoken to the precise question at issue." *Chevron*, 467 U.S. at 842. Because Section 407 does not clearly prohibit the creation of sub-quotas, we affirm the district court's grant of summary judgment to the Secretary on this issue. **[—10—]**

B. Economic and Social Impact Analysis

In reviewing an FMP or an amendment to an FMP, this court's task "is not to review *de novo* whether the amendment complies with [the ten National Standards] but to determine whether the Secretary's conclusion that the standards have been satisfied is rational and supported by the record." *C & W Fish Co. v. Fox*, 931 F.2d 1556, 1562 (D.C. Cir. 1991); *see also Alaska Factory Trawler Ass'n v. Baldridge*, 831 F.2d 1456, 1460 (9th Cir. 1987); *Maine v. Kreps*, 563 F.2d 1043, 1050-51 (1st Cir. 1977). However, when a challenge to an FMP is based on the Secretary's interpretation of the MSA, we apply the *Chevron* analysis. 467 U.S. at 843. The CCA argues that the Secretary failed to perform her duties under National Standards 8 and 2 to use the best available economic and social data **{–108–}** to minimize adverse economic impacts of Amendment 40 and under 16 U.S.C. § 1853(a)(9) to assess, specify, and analyze the economic and social impacts of Amendment 40 and to include these findings in a Fishery Impact Statement (FIS).

No federal appellate court has yet interpreted the requirements of § 1853(a)(9). However, the two district courts that have considered challenges brought under § 1853(a)(9) agree that "[t]he FIS requirement is . . . procedural, not substantive," and that it is satisfied where NMFS produces the required assessments, without respect to their conclusions. *City of New Bedford v. Locke*, No. CIV.A. 10-10789-RWZ, 2011 WL 2636863, at *6 (D. Mass. June 30, 2011), *aff'd sub nom. Lovgren v. Locke*, 701 F.3d 5 (1st Cir. 2012); *accord Coastal Conservation Ass'n v. Blank*, No. 2:09-CV-641-FTM-29, 2011 WL 4530544, at *7 (M.D. Fla. Sept. 29, 2011) ("The issue before the Court in the Section 1853(a)(9) challenge . . . is not whether the conclusions on how [the proposed FMP amendment] will likely affect the recreational fishing sector are correct. Rather, the issue is whether the [NMFS] arrived at the answer only after complying with the obligation to assess, specify, and analyze how [the **[—11—]** amendment] would likely affect the recreational fishing sector."). We agree with this interpretation of § 1853(a)(9).

National Standard 8 requires the NMFS to "take into account the importance of fishery resources to fishing communities by utilizing economic and social data." 16 U.S.C. § 1851(a)(8). The First Circuit has noted that "the required analysis of alternatives and impacts is subject to a rule of reason, for study could go on forever." *Little Bay Lobster Co. v. Evans*, 352 F.3d 462, 470 (1st Cir. 2003). "About the best a court can do is to ask whether the Secretary has examined the impacts of, and alternatives to, the plan [s]he ultimately adopts and whether a challenged failure to carry the analysis further is clearly unreasonable, taking account of the usual considerations (e.g., whether information is available and whether the further analysis is likely to be determinative)." *Id.* In addition, the First Circuit has observed that "[t]he plain language of [National Standard] 8 and its advisory guidelines make clear that these obligations are subordinate to the MSA's overarching conservation goals." *Lovgren*, 701 F.3d at 35. Indeed, the guidelines specifically state, "Deliberations regarding the importance of fishery resources to affected fishing communities . . . must not compromise the achievement of conservation requirements and goals of the FMP." 50 C.F.R. § 600.345(b)(1).

National Standard 2 states that "conservation and management measures shall be based upon the best scientific information available." 16 U.S.C. § 1851(a)(2). According to the advisory guidelines, "best scientific information" under National Standard 2 "includes, but is not limited to, information of a biological, ecological, economic, or social nature." 50 C.F.R. § 600.315(b)(1). However, "[t]he fact that scientific information concerning a fishery is incomplete does not prevent the preparation and implementation of an FMP." *Id.* at

§ 600.315(e)(2). Our sister circuits have given great latitude to the Secretary in determining what is the best information available. *See* **[—12—]** *Gen. Category Scallop Fishermen v. Sec'y, U.S. Dep't of Commerce*, 635 F.3d 106, 115 (3d Cir. 2011); *Washington Crab Producers, Inc. v. Mosbacher*, 924 F.2d 1438, 1448-1449 (9th Cir. 1990).

The CCA first asserts that 16 U.S.C. § 1853(a)(9) and National Standard 8 impose an affirmative duty to collect and generate only quantitative, rather than qualitative, predictions of economic and **{–109–}** social effects. In support it points to Merriam-Webster's definition of data as "factual information (as measurements or statistics)" and argues that "it is clear that Amendment 40 and the documents supporting it did not contain a single piece of economic or social 'data'" so defined.

The CCA cites no law that supports its interpretation of § 1853(a)(9) and National Standard 8. It is not at all clear that Congress intended to limit the analysis of economic and social impacts to quantitative data, and it is evident that the Secretary has long interpreted "data" in National Standard 8 to mean both qualitative and quantitative data. The advisory guidelines are unambiguous on this point: "Qualitative and quantitative data may be used, including information provided by fishermen, dealers, processors, and fisheries organizations and associations." 50 C.F.R. § 600.345(c)(2). The Secretary's interpretation of "data" is reasonable. *See Chevron*, 467 U.S. at 843. Indeed, in *ConocoPhillips Co. v. United States Environmental Protection Agency*, 612 F.3d 822, 841 (5th Cir. 2010), we upheld the EPA's reliance on qualitative data against a similar challenge.

The CCA next argues that the Secretary should have acquired or produced quantitative data. This argument is also unpersuasive. National Standard 2 states that "conservation and management measures shall be based upon the best scientific information *available*." *Id.* at § 1851(a)(2) (emphasis added). The Secretary stated in the preamble to the Final Rule that the additional quantitative economic analysis that the CCA demanded was not **[—13—]** "available" within the meaning of National Standard 2. 80 Fed. Reg. 22,422, 22,426. As the Secretary explained in the FIS and in her brief on appeal:

> [T]he economic impacts of Amendment 40 on private-vessel anglers depends on such difficult-to-predict factors as how the Gulf States will choose to regulate the red snapper harvest in their waters, as well as the decisions of private-vessel anglers regarding whether to fish in State waters for red snapper or in State or federal waters for other fish species once the red snapper quota for the private-vessel component is met.

The National Standards do not require analysis of unpredictable, and thus unavailable, data. *See Little Bay Lobster*, 352 F.3d at 470. Significantly, the CCA does not identify any available information that the Secretary ignored. As several of our sister circuits have held, "[i]f no one proposed anything better, then what is available is the best." *Massachusetts ex rel. Div. of Marine Fisheries v. Daley*, 170 F.3d 23, 30 (1st Cir. 1999); *see also Nw. Envt'l Def. Ctr. v. Brennen*, 958 F.2d 930, 936 (9th Cir. 1992) (rejecting a "best scientific information available" claim because the challenger "has not pointed to any scientific evidence inconsistent with the Secretary's decision"); *Midwater Trawlers Coop. v. Dep't of Commerce*, 393 F.3d 994, 1004 (9th Cir. 2004) (affirming regulation based on best scientific evidence available when "no new information" contradicted the agency's data).

Nor is the Secretary required to "acquire or produce" the CCA's preferred quantitative data. As previously discussed, the advisory guidelines specify that "[t]he fact that scientific information concerning a fishery is incomplete does not prevent the preparation and implementation of an FMP." 50 C.F.R. § 600.315(e)(2). The Act does not unambiguously require the Secretary to produce quantitative data, and we view her interpretation of the statute's requirements as reasonable. *See Chevron*, 467 U.S. at 843. It follows from this reasonable interpretation that the Secretary is not obligated to produce **{–110–}** further data when she possesses some, albeit incomplete, scientific information. *See,* **[—14—]** *e.g., Ecology Ctr., Inc. v. U.S. Forest Serv.*, 451 F.3d 1183, 1194 n.4 (10th Cir. 2006) (citing *Recreational Fishing Alliance v. Evans*, 172 F.Supp.2d 35, 44 (D.D.C. 2001)) ("An agency is not required to collect additional evidence under the Magnuson-Stevens Fishery Conservation and Management Act."); *Washington Crab Producers, Inc. v. Mosbacher*, 924 F.2d 1438, 1448-1449 (9th Cir. 1990) ("[t]here simply is no requirement that the Secretary do what the appellants insist" when it comes to developing and analyzing the effects of an FMP).

Furthermore, the FIS prepared by the Gulf Council was based on significant background data, both quantitative and qualitative. The quantitative data includes, for example, a ranking of communities based upon the number of charter permits and charter permits divided by population; species-specific harvest data for headboats (boats renting individual seats to recreational anglers), linked to specific communities through the homeport identified for each vessel; a ranking of communities based on the number of federal for-hire permits; estimates of the number of red snapper target trips for shore, charter, and private/rental boat anglers; and estimates of the average red snapper target effort and the associated business activity.

After considering this data, the Council gave its analysis of the conservation, economic, and social impacts of the Amendment and its alternatives. Discussing the social effects of the establishment of private and charter components within the recreational section, the Council concluded:

> Indirect social benefits for the private angling component would be expected to result from management measures accounting for their specific needs and characteristics, including regional preferences for access to fishing opportunities. For the federal for-hire component, indirect social benefits would primarily result from mitigating the trend of decreasing access to red snapper by the federal for-hire component. For-hire operators, their angler passengers, and the communities where these vessels are **[—15—]** homeported would then be expected to benefit as a result of increased stability of access to red snapper.

With respect to the economic effects of the subdivision, the Council noted that the change "could potentially result in a more predictable season length, better business planning, and improvements to the economic performance of for-hire businesses," while admitting that "the establishment of separate components and allocations to each component would limit the private angling component to harvesting the proportion of the recreational red snapper quota allocated to them."

Although the Council's analysis does not offer quantitative predictions of the effects that Amendment 40 might have on the fishing community, the Council used the best available data to reasonably "assess, specify, and analyze" the likely economic and social effects of Amendment 40. 16 U.S.C. §§ 1851(a)(2), 1851(a)(8), 1853(a)(9). We therefore conclude that the "basic obligation to assess the impacts of, and alternatives to, the adopted plan as a whole was achieved." *See Little Bay Lobster Co.*, 352 F.3d at 470.

C. Allocations

Finally, the CCA argues that the Secretary's decision to base allocations on the average of two sets of catch data, one covering 2006-2013 and one covering 1986-2013, was arbitrary and capricious. We may set aside an agency action only if it is "arbitrary, capricious, an abuse of discretion, or otherwise not in accordance **{–111–}** with law." 5 U.S.C. § 706(2)(A); *Buffalo Marine Services, Inc.*, 663 F.3d at 753. "Under this highly deferential standard of review, a reviewing court has the least latitude in finding grounds for reversal." *Louisiana Crawfish Producers*, 463 F.3d at 355 (quoting *Sabine River Auth.*, 951 F.2d at 678). When determining whether an agency action was arbitrary or capricious, our task "is to ensure that the agency 'considered the relevant factors and articulated a rational connection between the facts found and the **[—16—]** choice made.'" *Sierra Club v. U.S. Fish & Wildlife Serv.*, 245 F.3d 434, 444 (5th Cir. 2001) (quoting *Baltimore Gas & Elec. Co. v. Natural Resources Defense Council, Inc.*, 462 U.S. 87, 105 (1983)).

Amendment 40 established the allocation between the federal charter and private angling components. The Secretary determined that a fair and equitable allocation between the charter and private-vessel components would result from using both historic harvest information, spanning the period from 1986 to 2013, as well as more recent harvest information. 80 Fed. Reg. 22,422, 22,429. The CCA argues that "[t]here is simply no rational basis for relying on 1986 data to make a resource allocation decision for 2015-2017," and that the use of catch history dating back to 1986 did not capture the "dramatic shift of recreational fishing away from charter boats and toward private angling," which it deems the "most dominant" change in the fishery.

Before coming to its decision, the Council considered eight alternative sets of harvest data, covering different spans of time. These alternatives were discussed at length in the FIS, as well as in the preamble to the proposed rule. *See* 80 Fed. Reg. 3,541, 3,543. The Secretary explained:

> The Council selected the alternative that combined the longest time period of available landings (1986-2013) with landings from a more recent range of years (2006-2013). Averages from each of the two time periods were then equally weighted to determine the allocation. The Council selected this allocation because it reflects both historical changes in the recreational sector as well as current conditions. It is also an approach used by the Council in setting allocations for other species (e.g., the jurisdictional apportionment of black grouper and yellowtail snapper resources between the Gulf and South Atlantic Councils).

Id. In the FIS, the Gulf Council explained these "historical changes," which include the shortening of the fishing season in federal waters, restricting the ability of charter anglers to fish, and the loosening of restrictions in state waters, increasing the ability of private anglers to fish. The Council described **[—17—]** how the changes affected the more recent landing data. The Council justified the selection of the mixed data set by explaining that it would "balance the history of the recreational sector with more current conditions."

The record demonstrates that the Secretary considered the relevant factors and provided a rational justification for her decision to include older data in making its allocations. As a result, we find the CCA has failed to carry its burden to show that this decision was arbitrary and capricious. *See Sierra Club*, 245 F.3d at 444.

IV

For the foregoing reasons, we AFFIRM the judgment of the district court.

United States Court of Appeals
for the Fifth Circuit

No. 16-30058

ZERINGUE
vs.
CRANE CO.

Appeal from the United States District Court for the Eastern District of Louisiana

Decided: January 20, 2017

Citation: 846 F.3d 785, 5 Adm. R. 193 (5th Cir. 2017).

Before **CLEMENT, PRADO,** and **OWEN,** Circuit Judges.

[—1—] {-788-} OWEN, Circuit Judge:

Howard Zeringue sued Crane Co. (Crane) and twenty other defendants in state court, asserting strict liability, negligence, and failure to warn claims to recover for injuries allegedly caused by asbestos exposure. Crane removed the case to federal court pursuant to the federal-officer removal statute. After the district court remanded the case to state court, Crane appealed. We reverse and remand.

I

Zeringue asserts that he was first **exposed** to asbestos in 1952 while deployed with the United States Navy, in which he served in various capacities as an active duty sailor aboard three Navy vessels until 1956. He alleges that **[—2—]** he was then exposed to asbestos at two other jobs, including one in which he sold insurance in Avondale Shipyard near ships that contained asbestos, but he does not provide the time period during which this exposure allegedly occurred. At no point does Zeringue specify which defendants allegedly exposed Zeringue during which jobs nor which specific objects contained asbestos at these various jobsites. Instead, Zeringue maintains that "[a]t all times relevant" thirteen of the twenty-one defendants, including Crane, "designed, evaluated, manufactured, packaged, furnished, stored, handled, transported, installed, distributed, sold and/or supplied asbestos-containing products to Plaintiff's jobsites where he was exposed."

Crane removed the case to the Eastern District of Louisiana pursuant to the federal-officer removal statute, 28 U.S.C. § 1442(a)(1). Crane's involvement in this litigation stems from contracts it obtained to manufacture and provide parts, predominately valves, for the Navy. In its removal petition, Crane asserted that "any product that [Zeringue] alleges Crane Co. manufactured for or supplied to the Navy (and any product literature, labeling, or warnings that accompanied that product) would be subject to Navy specifications and requirements" and that, accordingly, "[f]ederal officers exercised their discretion regarding whether (1) asbestos was used in the product, and (2) whether a warning would accompany the product." To bolster this claim, Crane provided affidavits and sample military specifications. Crane maintains that this evidence establishes that all products provided to the Navy required compliance with Navy specifications, some of which required asbestos use, and could not be installed on Navy ships unless the Navy Machinery Inspectors first determined that the products did in fact comply with the detailed specifications.

Zeringue moved to remand the case to state court. The district court determined that although Crane had "allege[d] all of the elements **[—3—]** for . . . federal officer removal" and had provided evidence that permitted a "plausibl[e] assum[ption] that any equipment that Crane built for the Navy was indeed subject to detailed specifications," Crane had not established that the **{-789-}** "government exercised *its* discretion, with respect to the specific design and warning problems that are implicated by Zeringue's claims." Based on this deficiency, the district court granted Zeringue's motion. Crane appealed.

II

We review a district court's decision on a motion to remand de novo.[1] We have recently observed with regard to 28 U.S.C. § 1442 that "[a]lthough the principle of limited federal court jurisdiction ordinarily compels us to resolve any doubts about removal in favor of remand, . . . courts have not applied that tiebreaker when it comes to the federal officer removal statute in light of its broad reach."[2]

Section 1442 permits, in pertinent part, "any person acting under [an officer] of the United States or of any agency thereof"[3] to remove a state suit to federal court if any of the plaintiff's claims[4] are "for or relating to any act under color of such office."[5] We have interpreted this part of the statute to require a defendant to show (1) that it is a person within the meaning of the statute, (2) that it has "a colorable federal defense," (3) that it "acted pursuant to a federal officer's directions," and (4) "that a causal nexus exists between [its] actions under color of federal office and the plaintiff's claims."[6] **[—4—]**

A

Although Crane is a corporation, "the Supreme Court has long recognized that the removal statute also applies to private persons and corporate entities 'who lawfully assist the federal officer in the performance of his official duty.'"[7] Crane is a "person" for purposes of § 1442.

B

Section 1442 "is a pure jurisdictional statute" in which "the raising of a federal question in the officer's removal petition . . . constitutes the federal law under which the action against the federal officer arises for [Article] III purposes."[8] It permits a federal *defense*, which is generally statutorily impotent to establish subject matter jurisdiction,[9] to serve as the federal question that endues the court with jurisdiction.[10] As with a federal claim that creates federal question jurisdiction,[11] a federal defense fulfilling this same function does not need to be "clearly sustainable," as § 1442 does not require a federal official, **{–790–}** or a person acting under an official, to "win his case before he can have it removed," but rather the defense needs only to be "colorable."[12] Although neither we nor the Supreme Court has defined "colorable" in the context of § 1442, the Supreme Court has clarified that a non-colorable federal claim, for the purposes of federal question jurisdiction, is a claim that is "'immaterial and made solely for the purpose of obtaining jurisdiction' or is **[—5—]** 'wholly insubstantial and frivolous.'"[13] Because § 1442 allows the assertion of a colorable federal defense to serve the function typically reserved for the assertion of a colorable federal claim, it follows that a non-colorable federal defense is a defense that is

---

1 *Savoie v. Huntington Ingalls, Inc.*, 817 F.3d 457, 462, 4 Adm. R. 225, 227 (5th Cir. 2016).

2 *Id.*, 4 Adm. R. at 227 (citing *Watson v. Philip Morris Cos.*, 551 U.S. 142, 147 (2007); *Acuna v. Brown & Root Inc.*, 200 F.3d 335, 339 (5th Cir. 2000)).

3 28 U.S.C. § 1442(a)(1).

4 *Savoie*, 817 F.3d at 463, 4 Adm. R. at 228 ("[R]emoval of the entire case is appropriate so long as a single claim satisfies the federal officer removal statute.").

5 § 1442(a)(1).

6 *Bartel v. Alcoa S.S. Co.*, 805 F.3d 169, 172, 3 Adm. R. 422, 422 (5th Cir. 2015) (internal quotation marks omitted) (quoting *Winters v. Diamond Shamrock Chem. Co.*, 149 F.3d 387, 398-400 (5th Cir. 1998)).

7 *Savoie*, 817 F.3d at 461, 4 Adm. R. at 227 (quoting *Watson*, 551 U.S. at 151).

8 *Mesa v. California*, 489 U.S. 121, 136 (1989).

9 *See New Orleans & Gulf Coast Ry. Co. v. Barrois*, 533 F.3d 321, 328-29 (5th Cir. 2008).

10 *Mesa*, 489 U.S. at 129, 136-37.

11 *Arbaugh v. Y & H Corp.*, 546 U.S. 500, 513 n.10 (2006).

12 *Jefferson Cty. v. Acker*, 527 U.S. 423, 431, 432 (1999) (internal quotation marks omitted) (quoting *Willingham v. Morgan*, 395 U.S. 402, 407 (1969)).

13 *Arbaugh*, 546 U.S. at 513 n.10 (quoting *Bell v. Hood*, 327 U.S. 678, 682-83 (1946)); *see also Colorado v. Symes*, 286 U.S. 510, 519 (1932) (holding that federal-officer removal requires that a claim be "not without foundation and . . . made in good faith").

immaterial and made solely for the purpose of obtaining jurisdiction or that is wholly insubstantial and frivolous.

Crane asserts government-contractor immunity, originally articulated in *Boyle v. United Technologies Corp.*,[14] as its federal defense. This defense is an extension of the immunity afforded to the federal government for the performance of discretionary actions pursuant to 28 U.S.C. § 2680(a).[15] The logic is that because a contractor will pass any added costs from litigation risk exposure to the government, "[i]t makes little sense to insulate the Government against financial liability for the judgment that a particular feature of military equipment is necessary when the Government produces the equipment itself, but not when it contracts for the production."[16] Accordingly, government contractors are also immune from suit for design defects if "(1) the United States approved reasonably precise specifications; (2) the equipment conformed to those specifications; and (3) the supplier warned the United States about the dangers in the use of the equipment that were known to the supplier but not to the United States."[17]

The first two conditions ensure that the government exercised *its* discretion, as required by the statutory source from which government- **[—6—]** contractor immunity derives, by considering "the design feature in question,"[18] which the government can do by "evaluat[ing] th[at] design feature."[19] The government contractor can then prove that it conformed to the government specifications by showing "[a]cceptance and use of an item following its production."[20] **{-791-}**

The gravamen of Crane's claim of government-contractor immunity is that "any product that [Zeringue] alleges Crane Co. manufactured for or supplied to the Navy (and any product literature, labeling, or warnings that accompanied that product) would be subject to Navy specifications and requirements," with which Crane would have complied. To support this claim, Crane supplied sample military specifications and three affidavits. These documents establish that Crane's claim to government-contractor immunity is colorable.

Two of Crane's provided military specifications, one from 1938 and one from 1978, required asbestos in the packing used in certain valves. Crane also provided a military specification from 1966 that required asbestos use for pipe covering, insulation, and millboard. Although Zeringue correctly recognizes that these specifications do not cover the specific period during which he served upon Navy vessels, he admitted in his briefing before the district court that "it is a bit of a stretch to even conclude that Crane Co.'s affiants" (and, logically, Crane itself) "have personal knowledge of the products and warnings at issue in this case, as allegations regarding specific products simply were not made **[—7—]** [in the petition for damages]." Certainly, a specific contract that establishes that the government required asbestos for the parts with which Zeringue came into contact would be ideal, but to require that level of specificity to establish a *colorable* federal defense would equate to requiring Crane to "win his case before he can have it removed," a requirement which we cannot impose.[21]

---

14 487 U.S. 500 (1988).

15 28 U.S.C. § 2680(a) (providing the government with immunity against "[a]ny claim . . . based upon the exercise or performance or the failure to exercise or perform a discretionary function or duty on the part of a federal agency or an employee of the Government, whether or not the discretion involved be abused").

16 *Boyle*, 487 U.S. at 512.

17 *Id.*

18 *Id.*

19 *Kerstetter v. Pac. Sci. Co.*, 210 F.3d 431, 435 (5th Cir. 2000).

20 *Miller v. Diamond Shamrock Co.*, 275 F.3d 414, 420 (5th Cir. 2001); *see also Kerstetter*, 210 F.3d at 435-36 ("Extensive government involvement in the design, review, development and testing of a product, as well as extensive acceptance and use of the product following production, is evidence that the product line generally conformed with the government-approved specifications.").

21 *See Jefferson Cty. v. Acker*, 527 U.S. 423, 431, 432 (1999) (internal quotation marks omitted)

The three submitted affidavits bolster Crane's defense. Anthony Pantaleoni, Crane's Vice-President of Environment, Health and Safety, stipulated that "[a]ll equipment supplied by Crane Co. to the Navy was built in accordance with [military] specifications" and that the military specifications "governed all aspects of a piece of equipment . . . including materials." Retired Rear Admiral David Sargent, whose assignments in the Navy primarily involved the operation and maintenance of Navy ships, echoed these claims, noting that the uniformity necessary "to ensure commonality across systems" meant that "[e]quipment could not have been installed aboard Navy vessels unless it was first determined by the Navy to be in conformity with all applicable Navy specifications."

The final affidavit is from Dr. Samuel Forman, a former Navy physician tasked with investigating the Navy's "historical handling and knowledge of various industrial hygiene issues, including asbestos disease." Dr. Forman's affidavit supports Crane's assertion that the Navy knew as much or more than Crane did about the dangers of asbestos exposure. Specifically, Dr. Forman stated that the Navy's knowledge of asbestos dangers "has been quite complete when compared to available knowledge over time, and at least by the early 1940s, the Navy had become a leader in the field of occupational medicine relating to, among other things, asbestos dust inhalation exposure." Dr. **[—8—]** Forman's affidavit demonstrates that by at least 1939, the Navy had learned that exposure to asbestos dust for prolonged periods could result in "an industrial disease of the lungs." **{-792-}**

These sample military specifications and affidavits are not definitive proof that Zeringue's asbestos exposure resulted from the Navy's—not Crane's—discretionary decision, nor are they definitive proof that Crane did not need to supply the Navy with information regarding the dangers of asbestos because of the Navy's existing knowledge. But definitive proof is not necessary for removal, and the military specifications and affidavits do suffice as a not-insubstantial and non-frivolous basis upon which Crane may assert government-contractor immunity.

C

Section 1442 also requires a government contractor seeking removal to establish that it was "acting under" an officer of the United States or an agency when the acts giving rise to the complaint occurred.[22] Although the words "acting under" are undoubtedly broad, the Supreme Court has clarified that they "must refer to . . . a relationship that involves 'acting in a certain capacity, considered in relation to one holding a superior position or office.'"[23] This relationship "typically involves 'subjection, guidance, or control,'"[24] but, at a minimum, it "must involve an effort to assist, or to help carry out, the duties or tasks of the federal superior."[25]

Direct oversight of the specific acts that give rise to a plaintiff's complaint is not required to satisfy this part of § 1442. In *Wilde v. Huntington Ingalls, Inc.*, an unpublished decision, this court held that, based on a **[—9—]** government contractor's averment that "when it allegedly exposed [the plaintiff] to asbestos, it was producing ships pursuant to the direction of the United States Maritime Commission," the contractor was acting under a federal officer.[26] The court noted that the mere fact that "the federal government would have had to build those ships had [the defendant] not done so" satisfied this requirement.[27] This reasoning is persuasive.

Crane's provision of parts in an effort to assist the Navy's construction of vessels

(quoting *Willingham v. Morgan*, 395 U.S. 402, 407 (1969)).

[22] *Watson v. Philip Morris Cos.*, 551 U.S. 142, 147 (2007).

[23] *Id.* at 151 (quoting 18 OXFORD ENGLISH DICTIONARY 948 (2d ed. 1989)).

[24] *Id.* (quoting WEBSTER'S NEW INTERNATIONAL DICTIONARY 2765 (2d ed. 1953)).

[25] *Id.* at 152.

[26] 616 F. App'x 710, 713 (5th Cir. 2015) (per curiam).

[27] *Id.*

satisfies the "acting under" requirement. The military specifications and affidavits that Crane provided suggest that the Navy exercised a significant degree of guidance and control over Crane. These affidavits, as noted above, state that "[a]ll equipment supplied by Crane Co. to the Navy was built in accordance with [military] specifications," which "governed all aspects of a piece of equipment . . . including materials," and "[e]quipment could not have been installed aboard Navy vessels unless it was first determined by the Navy to be in conformity with all applicable Navy specifications." Even absent this significant degree of oversight, the Navy directed Crane to build parts, and, had Crane not done so, the Navy would have had to build those parts instead. In accordance with our duty to avoid "a narrow, grudging interpretation of § 1442(a)(1),"[28] we conclude that the facts in the record before us are sufficient to establish that Crane was "acting under" the Navy. **{-793-}**

D

Before 2011, § 1442 allowed the removal of a state suit against a federal officer, or a person acting under a federal officer, only when the state suit was "for any act under color of such office."[29] In 2011 Congress extended § 1442 to **[—10—]** allow the removal of a state suit "for *or relating to* any act under color of such office."[30] The plain meaning of the added language broadens the scope of the statute as "the ordinary meaning of [relating to] is a broad one—'to stand in some relation; to have bearing or concern; to pertain; refer; to bring into association with or connection with.'"[31]

This element of § 1442, both before and after the 2011 amendment, requires the removing party to establish "a nexus, a 'causal connection' between the charged conduct and asserted official authority."[32] This causal nexus requirement ensures that removal "only arises when 'a federal interest in the matter' exists."[33] Even before the 2011 amendment, the causal connection did not need to be "airtight," because such a requirement would "defeat the purpose of the removal statute."[34] This reasoning led the Supreme Court to remark in *Willingham v. Morgan* that "it [is] *sufficient*" for a federal officer in a civil suit to establish the requisite causal connection by showing that the officer's "relationship to [the plaintiff] derived solely from [the officer's] official duties."[35] This court, in rejecting the argument that negligent acts are not within a person's official authority, clarified that an act is within an officer's authority, and within the scope of § 1442, "so long as he does not depart from the course of his duty so that it becomes his personal act."[36] The 2011 amendment expanded the breadth of acts sufficient to establish a causal nexus **[—11—]** even further. It remains, however, that the causal nexus inquiry "must . . . be tailored to fit the facts of each case."[37]

Despite the relatively broad reach of the causal nexus requirement, Zeringue contends that Crane has not established the existence of a causal nexus because "the causal connection must depend upon a showing of precise federal direction," which Zeringue argues Crane has not established. However, the plain language of § 1442 cannot bear Zeringue's construction.

Crane has established the requisite causal nexus between the charged conduct and its official authority. Crane's relationship with

---

[28] *Willingham v. Morgan*, 395 U.S. 402, 407 (1969).

[29] Act of June 25, 1948, ch. 646, 62 Stat. 938 (codified at 28 U.S.C. § 1442).

[30] Removal Clarification Act of 2011, Pub. L. No. 112-51, § 2(b)(2), 125 Stat. 545 (codified at 28 U.S.C. § 1442) (emphasis added); *see also In re Commonwealth's Motion to Appoint Counsel*, 790 F.3d 457, 467 (3d Cir. 2015).

[31] *Morales v. Trans World Airlines, Inc.*, 504 U.S. 374, 383 (1992) (quoting Black's Law Dictionary 1158 (5th ed. 1979)).

[32] *Jefferson Cty. v. Acker*, 527 U.S. 423, 431 (1999) (quoting *Willingham*, 395 U.S. at 409).

[33] *Winters v. Diamond Shamrock Chem. Co.*, 149 F.3d 387, 398 (5th Cir. 1998) (quoting *Willingham*, 395 U.S. at 406).

[34] *Acker*, 527 U.S. at 432.

[35] 395 U.S. at 409 (emphasis added).

[36] *Allman v. Hanley*, 302 F.2d 559, 561 (5th Cir. 1962).

[37] *Willingham*, 395 U.S. at 408.

Zeringue derives solely from its official authority to provide parts to the **{-794-}** Navy, and that official authority *relates to* Crane's allegedly improper actions, namely its use of asbestos in those parts. Although the court cannot attenuate the causal nexus requirement "to the point of irrelevance,"[38] the plain import of the phrase "relating to" is that *some* attenuation is permissible, attenuation which is irreconcilable with Zeringue's proposed requirement of precise federal direction.

Moreover, were we to require the level of precision requested by Zeringue, we also would unduly undermine the purpose of § 1442 by impermissibly requiring defendants seeking removal, like Crane, to establish more than a colorable claim that a purported design defect was the result of a federal officer's discretion. Requiring "precise federal direction" to show a causal nexus, as Zeringue urges us to do, would not only render the "colorable" federal defense requirement a nullity, as the causal nexus requirement would hold the removing party to a heightened burden, but also would be contrary to **[—12—]** the Supreme Court's admonishment that "the test for removal should be broader, not narrower, than the test for official immunity."[39]

Our recent holding in *Bartel v. Alcoa Steamship Co.*[40] is not to the contrary. In *Bartel*, the Navy—not the contractors—*supplied* ships that contained asbestos to the defendants.[41] The defendants argued that there was a causal nexus between their authority to operate the ships, derived simply from the Navy providing the ships, and the charged conduct of failing "to warn of the dangers of asbestos, to train their crews in using asbestos-containing products, and to adopt procedures for the safe installation and removal of asbestos."[42] The charged conduct was private conduct that implicated no federal interest. Because the very purpose of the causal nexus requirement is to ensure that removal "only arises when 'a federal interest in the matter' exists,"[43] an extension of § 1442 to allow those defendants to remove would have stretched the causal nexus requirement to the point of irrelevance.

Conversely, if we were to decline to extend the protection of § 1442 to this case, in which the Navy directed Crane to provide parts, we would render irrelevant Congress's decision to allow the removal of suits for acts "relating to" any act taken under official authority. Again, we will not follow such "a narrow, grudging interpretation of § 1442(a)(1)."[44] Crane has established a casual nexus. **[—13—]**

III

Crane has established the right to remove the suit pursuant to § 1442. Because "removal of the entire case is appropriate so long as a single claim satisfies the federal officer removal statute," we do not determine whether Crane independently established the right to remove Zeringue's failure to warn claim.[45]

* * * **{-795-}**

For the foregoing reasons, we REVERSE the judgment of the district court and REMAND for proceedings consistent with this opinion.

---

[38] *Wilde v. Huntington Ingalls, Inc.*, 616 F. App'x 710, 713 (5th Cir. 2015) (per curiam).

[39] *Willingham*, 395 U.S. at 404.

[40] 805 F.3d 169, 3 Adm. R. 422 (5th Cir. 2015).

[41] *Id.* at 172, 174, 3 Adm. R. at 423, 424.

[42] *Id.* at 171, 172, 3 Adm. R. at 422, 423.

[43] *Winters v. Diamond Shamrock Chem. Co.*, 149 F.3d 387, 398 (5th Cir. 1998) (quoting *Willingham*, 395 U.S. at 406).

[44] *Willingham*, 395 U.S. at 407.

[45] *Savoie v. Huntington Ingalls, Inc.*, 817 F.3d 457, 463, 4 Adm. R. 225, 228 (5th Cir. 2016).

United States Court of Appeals for the Fifth Circuit

No. 16-30258

**CLAIMANT ID 100250022
vs.
BP EXPLORATION & PROD., INC.**

Appeal from the United States District Court for the Eastern District of Louisiana

Decided: January 25, 2017

Citation: 847 F.3d 167, 5 Adm. R. 199 (5th Cir. 2017).

Before **JOLLY, HIGGINBOTHAM,** and **PRADO,** Circuit Judges.

[—1—] {-168-} PER CURIAM:

Alabama Coastal Radiology, P.C. ("ACR"), filed a claim under the Business Economic Loss ("BEL") Framework of the Deepwater Horizon Economic Loss and Property Damage Settlement Agreement. The Court Supervised Settlement Program ("CSSP") denied the claim, and an Appeal Panel affirmed the CSSP's denial. ACR requested that the district court grant review of the CSSP's decision, but ACR's request was denied. ACR now appeals the district court's denial of discretionary review. We AFFIRM.

I.

This case relates to the Deepwater Horizon Economic Loss and Property Damage Settlement Agreement ("Settlement Agreement"), which was reached **[—2—]** in the wake of the 2010 Deepwater Horizon oil spill incident.[1] As a result of its obligations under the Settlement Agreement, BP has distributed millions of dollars in damages to affected entities. *In re Deepwater Horizon*, 910 F. Supp. 2d 891, 903-04 (E.D. La. 2012), *aff'd*, 739 F.3d 790, 2 Adm. R. 140 (5th Cir. 2014).

ACR attempted to obtain compensation as a Multi-Facility Business under the BEL Framework of the Settlement Agreement. ACR is a group of sixteen radiologists. Infirmary Health Services ("IHS"), a separate entity from ACR, owns several hospitals where ACR provides radiology services. In each hospital, the ACR radiologists interpret imaging scans taken by the hospital; the scans are reviewed in a designated location referred to as a "reading room." According to ACR's certified public accountant, ACR does not have a physical office and outsources all of its administrative tasks. IHS contracted with ACR to provide the radiology services; IHS owns the "reading room" space and all of the equipment ACR uses to carry out its imaging scan review services.

ACR submitted a BEL claim under the Multi-Facility Business Framework for a reading room located inside Infirmary 65, a hospital situated in Mobile, Alabama. The Settlement Agreement allows for business claims that "include separate specialized frameworks addressing Business Economic Loss Claims by **MULTI-FACILITY BUSINESSES**." Exhibit 5 of the Agreement defines "multi-facility business" as "[a] business entity that, during the period April 1, 2010 through December 31, 2010, maintained **Facilities** in more than one location and had at least one **Facility** within the Gulf Coast Areas." A "Facility" is then defined as "[a] separate and distinct physical location of a **Multi-Facility Business** at which it performs or manages its operations." Policy 467, enacted by the CSSP, expands upon the definition of **[—3—]** "Facility" and provides that an entity must satisfy three elements to be classified as a "Facility" under the Agreement: It must be (1) "[a] separate and distinct physical structure or premises"; (2) "[o]wned, leased or operated by the Business Entity"; and (3) "[a]t which the Business Entity performs and/or manages its operations." Under the "Overall Criterion" section of Policy 467, the CSSP explains **{-169-}** that "[a]n Entity does not 'perform' or 'manage' operations at a location unless it can identify the expenses and revenues, if any, associated with the operations at that location separately from the expenses and revenues of

[1] *See In re Deepwater Horizon*, 910 F. Supp. 2d 891 (E.D. La. 2012), *aff'd*, 739 F.3d 790, 2 Adm. R. 140 (5th Cir. 2014) (describing the oil spill and development of the Settlement Agreement).

other locations owned, leased or operated by the Entity."

The CSSP denied ACR's claim. It explained in its denial notice that ACR had failed to meet all three elements of the definition of "Facility." ACR then requested a denial summary from the CSSP for additional explanation. It received the following summary:

> [ACR] only has a contract to provide radiology services at the facilities. The Claimant's Attorney also explained that the Claimant does not have an office space at the facilities for which they pay rent or lease expenses. . . . According to Policy 467, this Claimant does not have the option of filing a separate claim for operations performed at one of the hospitals. The claim should be closed, as the Claimant has filed a separate claim for a location that is not a facility.

ACR requested re-review of the denial after submitting a statement from its CPA and photographs of the reading room. The CSSP denied the claim again after re-review, and again after ACR requested reconsideration of the post-re-review denial notice. ACR appealed to an Appeal Panel. The Appeal Panel affirmed the denial of ACR's claim, explaining that "Claimant does not pay rent or lease expenses on the reading room . . . [and] [t]here is not evidence that Claimant pays for janitorial services, electricity, or other items a tenant normally has." The Panel also announced that its decision "[would] stand as the Settlement Program's final determination on this claim." **[—4—]**

Pursuant to the procedure for appeals to federal court arising out of the application of the Settlement Agreement, ACR appealed to Judge Barbier of the Eastern District of Louisiana. *See In re Deepwater Horizon*, 785 F.3d 1003, 1007, 3 Adm. R. 325, 325 (5th Cir. 2015) ("A party may then appeal the Appeal Panel's determination to the district court of Judge Barbier in the Eastern District of Louisiana, which has discretion to hear such appeals."). The district court denied discretionary review of the decision by the Appeal Panel. ACR timely appealed.

II.

The standard of review that we apply to the district court's denial of discretionary review is abuse of discretion. *Holmes Motors, Inc. v. BP Exploration & Prod., Inc.*, 829 F.3d 313, 315, 4 Adm. R. 263, 263 (5th Cir. 2016) (citing *In re Deepwater Horizon*, 785 F.3d at 1011, 3 Adm. R. at 329). Our unpublished decisions addressing actions pursuant to the Settlement Agreement have expounded upon our abuse of discretion inquiry, "ask[ing] 'whether the decision not reviewed by the district court actually contradicted or misapplied the Settlement Agreement, or had the clear potential to contradict or misapply the Settlement Agreement.'" *Id.*, 4 Adm. R. at 263 (citing series of cases). In the event that we find a contradiction or misapplication of the Settlement Agreement, we will agree that the district court abused its discretion. *Id.*, 4 Adm. R. at 263.

III.

ACR argues that the Infirmary 65 reading room constitutes a "Facility" of ACR because ACR has a contract with IHS to use the location as a "separate and distinct office space under ACR's exclusive use and control." BP counters that the reading room is a "Facility" of IHS, and thus that it cannot also be a "Facility" of ACR. The focus of the Settlement Agreement BEL Framework, BP explains, is upon remedying actual economic loss caused by the oil **{–170–}** spill. Further, BP argues that the costs of maintaining the equipment and reading **[—5—]** room space are those of IHS, not ACR. Thus, BP contends, "Infirmary 65 is an IHS 'facility.'"

In reaching our decision that the district court did not abuse its discretion in denying discretionary review of the Appeal Panel decision in the instant case, we need not examine whether the CSSP was actually correct in refusing to classify Infirmary 65's reading room as a "Facility" of ACR. Rather, we look to whether the Appeal Panel decision contradicts or misapplies the Settlement

Agreement, and we find that it does not. The Appeal Panel explains in its decision that not only does ACR "not pay rent or lease expenses on the reading room," there is also "no evidence that [ACR] pays for janitorial services, electricity, or other items" that normally accompany a lease-like relationship. The Appeal Panel further observed that the "only service provided" in the reading room "is the contracted for radiology service." It concluded that the provision of the radiology service is not sufficient to meet the three-part definition of a "Facility."

The Appeal Panel's conclusion hardly contradicts or misapplies the Settlement Agreement. The Agreement's Multi-Facility Business Framework functions as a subpart of the larger BEL Framework, which operates to compensate for business economic losses. Furthermore, the definition of "Facility" as it is found in Policy 467 contains language with which the Appeal Panel's decision is consistent. In particular, the "Overall Criterion" provision explains that a business must be able to identify the "expenses and revenues, if any, associated with the operations at that location" in order to establish that it "performs" or "manages" operations there. ACR argues that the "if any" language contemplates situations in which a location may constitute a "Facility" within the meaning of the Agreement notwithstanding a lack of rental and lease expenses associated with the location. **[—6—]**

Even if we were to agree with ACR's interpretation of the "Overall Criterion" provision and Policy 467 as a whole, the CSSP's finding is not incongruent with the language of the Settlement Agreement and the Multi-Facility Business Framework's function within the BEL Framework. Thus, the CSSP and the Appeal Panel did not contradict or misapply the Settlement Agreement.

IV.

In sum, because the district court's denial of discretionary review does not result in a contradiction or misapplication of the Settlement Agreement, we hold that it is not an abuse of discretion and AFFIRM.

United States Court of Appeals
for the Fifth Circuit

No. 16-30102

CLAIMANT ID 100212278
VS.
BP EXPLORATION & PROD., INC.

Appeal from the United States District Court for the Eastern District of Louisiana

Decided: February 9, 2017

Citation: 848 F.3d 407, 5 Adm. R. 202 (5th Cir. 2017).

Before **REAVLEY, ELROD,** and **GRAVES,** Circuit Judges.

[—1—] {-408-} PER CURIAM:

The appellant is a company that filed Business Economic Loss claims under the Deepwater Horizon Economic and Property Damages Settlement Agreement on behalf of five of its stores. Each claim was denied by the Court Supervised Settlement Program, and each denial was affirmed by an Appeal Panel. The company sought review by the district court, which the district court denied in every case. In this consolidated appeal, the company challenges the district court's denial of discretionary review in each case. Because the district court did not abuse its discretion, we AFFIRM. **[—2—]**

I.

This case involves BP's obligations under the Deepwater Horizon Economic and Property Damages Settlement Agreement. The appellant, which describes itself in its briefing as an automotive parts provider, sought to obtain compensation under the Settlement Agreement as a tourism business.[1] Designation as a tourism business **{-409-}** would have relieved the appellant of the need to demonstrate loss causation. However, the Court Supervised Settlement Program (CSSP) and the Appeal Panel determined that the stores were not tourism businesses and denied the claims for failure to satisfy the causation requirement.

Exhibit 2 to the Settlement Agreement defines tourism as follows:

> **Tourism** means businesses which provide services such as attracting, transporting, accommodating or catering to the needs or wants of persons traveling to, or staying in, places outside their home community. Therefore, if you are in one of the following businesses or work for such a business, you are in the Tourism Industry.

Exhibit 2 then lists forty-one North American Industry Classification System codes (NAICS codes) identifying various categories of businesses that qualify as tourism businesses.

The appellant claimed that it fell under NAICS code 452990 (All Other General Merchandise Stores), which is listed in Exhibit 2. It also argued, in the alternative, that it was a business "accommodating or catering to the needs **[—3—]** or wants of persons traveling to, or staying in, places outside their home community." It claimed to be a tourism business on these grounds.

Under the Settlement Agreement, the appropriate NAICS code for a claimant is to be determined based on review of: "(a) the NAICS code shown on an Entity Claimant's 2010 tax return, (b) 2010 business permits or license(s), and/or (c) other evidence of the Entity's activities necessary for the Settlement Program to determine the appropriate NAICS code." Claims Administrator Final Policy 480 v.2 clarifies that the "appropriate" NAICS Code for an entity shall be the one that "most

[1] Under the Settlement Agreement, claims are initially submitted to the Court Supervised Settlement Program, which is overseen and managed by the Claims Administrator. *In re Deepwater Horizon*, 785 F.3d 986, 989, 3 Adm. R. 341, 341 (5th Cir. 2015). A decision by the Court Supervised Settlement Program may be appealed to an Appeal Panel. *Id.*, 3 Adm. R. at 341. Although the Settlement Agreement does not establish a right of automatic appeal to the district court, the district court that authorized the settlement has retained the discretionary right to review decisions by Appeal Panels. *Id.* at 989–90, 3 Adm. R. at 341.

accurately describes [its] primary business activities" during the relevant time frame.

Claims Administrator Final Policy 289 v.2 further discusses the designation of a claimant as a tourism business. It states the Claims Administrator's finding that Exhibit 2's list of NAICS codes is illustrative, not exhaustive. Based on this finding, it states that a claimant without one of the NAICS codes listed in Exhibit 2 may be considered a tourism business "if the Claims Administrator determines in his discretion" and "based on the totality of the circumstances" that it "provide[s] services such as attracting, transporting, accommodating or catering to the needs or wants of persons traveling to, or staying in, places outside their home community." Finally, Policy 289 v.2 provides that when a claimant submits separate claims for separate facilities, as in this case, the Claims Administrator "will evaluate each facility separately to determine whether it meets the definition of Tourism . . ., notwithstanding what NAICS code may have been assigned to the Entity as a whole."

The CSSP determined that the stores were not tourism businesses and that the appropriate NAICS code for each of the stores was 441310 (Automotive Parts and Accessories Stores), a code not listed in Exhibit 2. The Appeal Panel affirmed the CSSP determination for each store. In the first of its opinions, **[—4—]** the Appeal Panel noted that the store in question advertised itself as an auto-parts store and that it did not fit the NAICS definition of "All Other General Merchandise Stores" because its auto parts line of products predominated **{-410-}** over other product lines. It also explained that the store had not established with concrete evidence that it was engaged in the business of "accommodating or catering to the needs or wants of persons traveling to, or staying in, places outside their home community." According to the Appeal Panel, the claimant's observation that its website included a list of products that drivers should inspect and consider replacing before a long trip was insufficient to qualify it for designation as a tourist business. This was particularly true since the store was not located in a tourist area and the possibility of occasional tourists stopping by the store for auto parts was "far too incidental." Based on this same reasoning, the Appeal Panel went on to affirm the denial of each store's claim. The stores appealed the decisions of the Appeal Panel to the district court, which denied discretionary review. The stores then appealed to this court.

II.

We review the district court's denial of discretionary review for abuse of discretion. *Holmes Motors, Inc. v. BP Exploration & Prod.*, 829 F.3d 313, 315, 4 Adm. R. 263, 263 (5th Cir. 2016). We generally assess whether the district court abused its discretion by looking to "whether the decision not reviewed by the district court actually contradicted or misapplied the Settlement Agreement, or had the clear potential to contradict or misapply the Settlement Agreement." *Id.*, 4 Adm. R. at 263. However, we have been careful to note that it is "wrong to suggest that the district court must grant review of *all* claims that raise a question about the proper interpretation of the Settlement Agreement." *Id.* at 316, 4 Adm. R. at 264; *see also In re Deepwater Horizon*, 785 F.3d 986, 999, 3 Adm. R. 341, 350 (5th Cir. 2015) ("We do not intend any part of this opinion to turn the district court's discretionary review into a **[—5—]** mandatory review. To do so would frustrate the clear purpose of the Settlement Agreement to curtail litigation."). It is not an abuse of discretion to deny a request for review that "involve[s] no pressing question of how the Settlement Agreement should be interpreted or implemented, but simply raise[s] the correctness of a discretionary administrative decision in the facts of a single claimant's case." *In re Deepwater Horizon*, 641 F. App'x 405, 410 (5th Cir. 2016). It may be an abuse of discretion to deny a request for review that raises a recurring issue on which the Appeal Panels are split if "the resolution of the question will substantially impact the administration of the Agreement." *In re Deepwater Horizon*, 632 F. App'x 199, 203–04 (5th Cir. 2015).

III.

The appellant has not attempted to show on appeal that the district court abused its discretion or that its request for review raised an important, recurring issue on which the Appeal Panels are split. Instead, it argues for *de novo* review and repeats substantially the same arguments it made before the CSSP and Appeal Panel. According to the appellant, the district court's denial of its request for review constitutes an interpretation of the Settlement Agreement, which is a question of contract law subject to *de novo* review. However, the appellant does not challenge the Appeal Panel's interpretation of the Settlement Agreement.[2] Rather, it disputes the Appeal Panel's factual **[—6—]** determination **{-411-}** that its stores were not tourism businesses within the meaning of the Settlement Agreement. We do not review *de novo* whether this determination was correct. *Claimant ID 100250022 v. BP Exploration & Prod.*, No. 16-30258, slip op. at 5, 5 Adm. R. 199, 200 (5th Cir. Jan. 25, 2017). Instead, we ask whether it constitutes an abuse of discretion. *Id.*, 5 Adm. R. at 200.

The stores' evidence that they were engaged in "accommodating or catering to the needs or wants of persons traveling to, or staying in, places outside their home community" does not demonstrate that the Appeal Panel abused its discretion in determining otherwise. They rely on two pieces of evidence. First, the appellant's website displays a list of automotive products that drivers should consider replacing before long trips. Second, the stores carry storage and cargo equipment primarily used by vacationers. BP contends that the Appeal Panel correctly determined there was insufficient concrete evidence to show that any of the specific stores in question qualified as a tourism business. In particular, none of the stores offers evidence regarding its actual sales of cargo equipment or sales of products on the website's list and none offers evidence of sales to non-local customers as contemplated by the Settlement Agreement. The Appeal Panel expressly considered the possibility that although the stores were not located in tourist areas, they might incidentally serve some tourists while pursuing their primary business as sellers of automotive parts and accessories. Notwithstanding this possibility, it determined that the totality of the circumstances did not show the stores to be tourism businesses. The stores have not shown that this was an abuse of discretion.

The stores' alternative argument that they should have been classified under NAICS code 452990 (All Other General Merchandise Stores) rather than NAICS code 441310 (Automotive Parts and Accessories Stores) also fails to show an abuse of discretion. The appellant does not dispute that its stores **[—7—]** advertised themselves as auto-parts stores. The Appeal Panel determined that the stores did not fit the NAICS definition of "All Other General Merchandise Stores" because their auto parts line of products predominated over other product lines. Moreover, the Settlement Agreement directs that "the NAICS code shown on an Entity Claimant's 2010 tax return" should be considered in determining the appropriate NAICS code, and the appellant used code 441310 on its 2010 tax return.[3] The appellant itself has stated on appeal that it is an automotive parts provider. Thus, it was not an abuse of discretion to

[2] BP has raised one question of interpretation in an alternative argument that we need not reach. It argues that, even if the stores were engaged in "accommodating or catering to the needs or wants of [tourists]," that is not sufficient to make them tourism businesses. According to BP, the NAICS codes listed in Exhibit 2 constitute an exhaustive list of tourism businesses, and Policy 289 v.2 impermissibly modified the terms of the Settlement Agreement by interpreting the list to be merely illustrative of a larger category of businesses "accommodating or catering to the needs or wants of [tourists]." Because the Appeal Panel determined that the stores were not businesses accommodating or catering to the needs or wants of tourists and did not abuse its discretion in doing so, we need not determine whether Exhibit 2's list of NAICS codes is exhaustive.

[3] The appellant notes that this factor is not conclusive under Policy 480 v.2 but does not explain why any of its stores ought to have a different NAICS code than the one on the company's tax return.

Apache well. Robert {-341-} Jackson was the crane operator. LePretre testified that he knew LDI owned the barge and that it was used at the well site with Apache's consent.

On the second day of the flow-back operation, Savoie and Delahoussaye were again unsuccessful, even with use of the crane. Savoie informed LePretre that he needed a coiled tubing unit, so they terminated the operation until one could be obtained. Savoie began "rigging down" and directed Jackson to lower the crane. Instead, Savoie reported the crane came toward him and "knocked [—4—] [him] off balance." He clutched the crane to avoid falling backward but eventually lost his grip, which caused him to fall approximately eight feet onto the deck of the barge. His accident resulted in "a crush type injury to the right lower extremity."

Later that year, LDI made a formal demand that STS defend and indemnify LDI against any claims Savoie may bring. STS rejected the demand. LDI then filed a Vessel Owner Limitation Action for exoneration from liability on the basis of admiralty jurisdiction under 46 U.S.C. §§ 30501–30512. Savoie answered the complaint, alleging he was injured by LDI's negligence and through no fault of his own. LDI then filed a third-party complaint against STS and its affiliates. Jackson intervened in the Vessel Owner Limitation Action, seeking protection under the MSC and the insurance policy issued by Zurich. STS ultimately settled with Savoie, and the district court severed the indemnity claims from the personal-injury case.

LDI and Jackson filed a motion for summary judgment to "enforce their contractual right to defense and indemnity." LDI and Jackson argued the MSC obligated STS to indemnify LDI and Jackson against Savoie's claims. In response, STS filed a cross-motion for summary judgment, arguing that the MSC "must be construed under Louisiana law and that the indemnity provision contained therein is void and unenforceable under the Louisiana Oilfield Indemnity Act." The district court granted the motion submitted by LDI and Jackson and denied the cross-motion submitted by STS.

Thereafter, the parties filed a joint motion to dismiss the claims not resolved by summary judgment and for entry of final judgment on the others. The parties reserved the right to appeal "the limited issue of whether Defendants were contractually obligated to defend and indemnify [—5—] Plaintiffs . . . ." The court granted the motion and entered final judgment on March 10, 2016. STS filed a timely notice of appeal.

DISCUSSION

We review *de novo* the district court's grant of summary judgment. *James v. State Farm Mut. Auto. Ins. Co.*, 743 F.3d 65, 68 (5th Cir. 2014). Summary judgment is proper "if the movant shows that there is no genuine dispute as to any material fact and the movant is entitled to judgment as a matter of law." FED. R. CIV. P. 56(a). A genuine dispute exists if a reasonable jury could find in favor of the nonmoving party. *Anderson v. Liberty Lobby, Inc.*, 477 U.S. 242, 248 (1986). All facts and evidence are viewed in the light most favorable to the non-movant. *James*, 743 F.3d at 68.

The issue here is whether maritime or state law should be applied to {-342-} determine the validity of the MSC's indemnity clause. The MSC contains a choice-of-law provision:

> This contract shall be construed and enforced in accordance with the general maritime law of the United States whenever any performance is contemplated in, on or above navigable waters, whether onshore or offshore. In the event that maritime law is held inapplicable, the law of the state in which the work is performed shall apply.

The district court correctly analyzed the conflict as being one between Louisiana state law and general maritime principles. The Louisiana Oilfield Indemnity Act provides

canal." *Producers Drilling Co. v. Gray*, 361 F.2d 432, 437 (5th Cir. 1966). Neither party disputes that the POGO qualifies as a vessel, so we do not engage in any analysis of the barge's classification.

that indemnity clauses in "agreements pertaining to wells for oil, gas, or water" are void as violations of public policy. LA. REV. STAT. § 9:2780. Maritime law "does not bar enforcement of [those] provisions." *Hoda v. Rowan Cos.,* 419 F.3d 379, 380 (5th Cir. 2005). There are, though, no **[—6—]** "clean lines between maritime and nonmaritime contracts." *See Norfolk S. Ry. Co. v. Kirby*, 125 S. Ct. 385, 393 (2004).

We articulated the legal framework for deciding cases like this in *Davis & Sons, Inc. v. Gulf Oil Corp.*, 919 F.2d 313 (5th Cir. 1990). Distinguishing between maritime and nonmaritime contracts "turns on a minute parsing of the facts," but we are bound by the *Davis* approach—however inexact it may be. *Hoda*, 419 F.3d at 380–81. In *Davis*, the parties entered a Master Service Agreement under which Gulf Oil would issue work orders directing Davis to perform specific tasks related to its natural-gas and crude-oil wells. *Davis*, 919 F.2d at 314. The agreement contained an indemnity clause requiring Davis to indemnify Gulf Oil against any claims that may arise out of their relationship. *Id.* Under the work order at issue, Davis supplied land-based barges to perform routine maintenance on the wells. *Id.* The work platforms around the wells did not provide adequate workspace, so most of the work was done on the barge itself. *Id.*

On the day of the accident in *Davis*, the barge employee supervising the operation drowned. *Id.* His representatives sued both Davis and Gulf Oil, and the parties settled. *Id.* at 315. Davis sought a declaratory judgment that Louisiana law governed the contract and that the indemnity provision was therefore void. *Id.* Gulf Oil argued that maritime law applied to validate the indemnity provision. *Id.* The district court applied Louisiana law. *Id.*

On appeal, we held that when a contract involves two parts—"a blanket contract followed by later work orders"—the two must be interpreted together to determine whether maritime or state law applies. *Id.* We then articulated a two-part analysis. *Id.* at 316. First, we determine the nature of the contract by reference to its historical treatment. *Id.* If the historical treatment is unclear, we must consider six factors: **[—7—]**

> 1) [W]hat does the specific work order in effect at the time of injury provide? 2) [W]hat work did the crew assigned under the work order actually do? 3) [W]as the crew assigned to work aboard a vessel in navigable waters[?] 4) [T]o what extent did the work being done relate to the mission of that vessel? 5) [W]hat was the principal work of the injured worker? and 6) [W]hat work was the injured worker actually doing at the time of injury?

Id.; *see also Hoda*, 419 F.3d at 381. In *Davis*, the work being performed was not historically maritime in nature. *Davis*, 919 F.2d at 316. Nonetheless, an analysis of the factors revealed "[t]he work done by the crew of Barge 11171 was inextricably intertwined with maritime activities since **{–343–}** it required the use of a vessel and its crew." *Id.* at 317.

Applying *Davis*, we find no clarity to the historical treatment of contracts like this because this court has not previously considered flow-back operations. We have found contracts for the provision of wireline services to be nonmaritime. *See, e.g., Domingue v. Ocean Drilling & Expl. Co.*, 923 F.2d 393, 397–98 (5th Cir. 1991); *Thurmond v. Delta Well Surveyors*, 836 F.2d 952, 956 (5th Cir. 1988). Wireline services include providing maintenance for partially drilled oil and gas wells and gathering "geophysical data relevant to production." *Domingue*, 923 F.2d at 394 n.3. On the other hand, contracts for casing services are maritime in nature. *See, e.g., Demette v. Falcon Drilling Co.*, 280 F.3d 492, 500 (5th Cir. 2002), *overruled on other grounds by Grand Isle Shipyard, Inc. v. Seacor Marine, LLC*, 589 F.3d 778, 787 (5th Cir. 2009) (en banc); *Campbell v. Sonat Offshore Drilling, Inc.*, 979 F.2d 1115, 1123–24 (5th Cir. 1992). Casing is "the welding together and hammering of pipe into the subsurface of the earth to create a permanent construction." *Campbell*, 979 F.2d at 1118 n.2. One distinction between the two is that wireline services often do not require the use of a vessel; casing services do. *Compare* **[—8—]** *Thurmond*, 836 F.2d at 956, *with Campbell*, 979 F.2d at 1123. Whether that distinction was sufficient to cause the different outcomes is unclear.

We now examine flow-back operations to see if they are comparable either to wireline operations or to casing services. When providing flow-back services, employees use whatever equipment is necessary to clear the well for the resumption of production. The services themselves may be performed exclusively on the well platform or may, as here, require a vessel to be alongside the well. The district court was likely correct that "flow back services have little to do with traditional maritime activity or commerce." Even if flowback services in the main are not maritime, this is not a sufficient answer under *Davis*. Because the historical treatment is unclear, we cannot rely on a generic view of the work; instead, we must consider the circumstances surrounding the injury. *See Devon Louisiana Corp. v. Petra Consultants, Inc.*, 247 F. App'x 539, 544 (5th Cir. 2007) (unpublished).

Under *Davis*. no single factor is dispositive. We find that four of the six factors—one, two, four, and six—indicate this contract is maritime in nature. The first factor concerns the specific work order in effect at the time of the injury. *Davis*, 919 F.2d at 316. Neither party can produce a written document to establish what the parties contemplated when this particular agreement arose. The MSC references vessels by requiring insurance coverage when the "contractor uses any vessels in connection with its work for Company or Company Group." While this factor concerns the specific work order and not the MSC, the language of the MSC indicates the parties at least contemplated the use of a vessel during the operations for which Apache would employ STS. Imposing a maritime obligation would not cause unfair surprise.

The second factor examines the work the crew assigned under the work order actually performed. *Id.* The STS crew performed a flow-back operation, **[—9—]** which is not primarily maritime. In fact, however, Savoie and Delahoussaye relied on the crane barge to execute the flow-back operation, and Savoie was injured as a result of its use. The district court noted that the operation "could not have been completed without the use of a crane barge . . . ." We agree. STS claims the barge was ancillary to the flow-back operation, but the presence of the barge was a necessary predicate **{-344-}** to Savoie's using the hydraulic gate valve.

The fourth factor concerns the extent to which the work being done related to the mission of the vessel. *Id.* The barge was sent to Apache's well site to serve STS in the execution of its flow-back job. STS notes that the barge was forced to move away from the well during the flow-back process to avoid safety concerns raised by having an ignition source near a gas well. Despite its physical location at the time of the operation, though, the barge was still tasked with assisting STS in its execution of the flow-back operation.

The sixth factor concerns what the injured worker was doing at the time of his injury. *Id.* Savoie, at the time of injury, was preparing to disconnect the hydraulic gate valve from the crane. During "rigging down," Savoie clutched the crane itself and fell onto the deck of the barge when he lost his grip. Thus, Savoie was injured by equipment affixed to the vessel itself.

Only the third and fifth factors militate against applying maritime law. The third factor concerns whether the crew was assigned to work aboard a vessel in navigable waters. *Id.* Neither Savoie nor Delahoussaye was assigned to work aboard the crane barge. Still, Savoie made use of the barge by loading and unloading equipment from its deck, conducting safety meetings on board the vessel,[4] and using the crane to install large

---

[4] STS states neither Savoie nor Delahoussaye boarded the barge. Delahoussaye testified that no one from STS went onto the barge "during the actual flow back services" but made no representations as to whether he had boarded the barge at other times. The district **[—10—]** court found that STS personnel had, at minimum, conducted safety meetings alongside the barge's crew.

equipment on the platform. **[—10—]** The fifth factor concerns the principal work of the injured person. *Id.* At the time of his injury, Savoie was principally employed to perform the flow-back operation at issue; he was not commissioned to be a seaman. Yet Savoie need not be a sailor to give this work order a "peculiarly salty flavor." *See Thurmond*, 836 F.2d at 953, 956.

Some of the cases that have applied *Davis* assist us in our analysis. The gravamen of our inquiry is not whether the contract required use of a vessel but whether the *execution* of the contract required a vessel. *Demette*, 280 F.3d at 500–01. STS correctly notes that "incidental or preparatory use of a vessel" is not sufficient to render a contract maritime in nature. On the other hand, when the work is "inextricably intertwined with maritime activities," the contract will be maritime. *Davis*, 919 F.2d at 317.

We find useful similarities between this case and *Campbell*, where a worker performing casing services was injured when transferring from one vessel to another. *See Campbell*, 979 F.2d at 1122–23. First, neither this operation nor the operation in *Campbell* was intrinsically maritime; both may have been performed on a fixed surface instead of a vessel. Second, a vessel at some point became necessary to execute the operations in both cases. Also, both Savoie and the injured worker in *Campbell* suffered their injuries while transferring to a vessel that had been used during the operation. Finally, and most importantly, the vessel's equipment was used to accomplish the relevant task both here and in *Campbell*. Given the similarities, Savoie's work, like the work in *Campbell*, was "inextricably intertwined with maritime activities . . . ." *See id.* at 1123 (quoting *Davis*, 919 F.2d at 317). **[—11—]**

We also find similarities between this case and *Hoda*, where a worker was injured while working aboard a vessel. *See* **{-345-}** *Hoda*, 419 F.3d at 380. His primary job under that work order was to tighten the nuts on a blowout preventer on the wellhead. *Id.* at 381. The operation was performed using a crane aboard the vessel because there was no well platform. *Id.* In this case, Apache had a fixed well platform from which the flow-back operation could have been executed. Regardless, the existence of the fixed platform is immaterial because the use of a vessel eventually became necessary to manipulate the heavy equipment used during the operation. Like the injured worker in *Hoda*, Savoie would "have had nothing to do" had LDI not provided the crane barge. *See id.* Savoie's work depended on the barge's direct involvement, which strongly indicates a maritime contract. *See id.* at 383.

Devon, an unpublished case from this court, is also analogous. There, the worker was injured aboard a vessel during inclement weather. *Devon*, 247 F. App'x at 541–42. At the time of his injury, he was working to repair an offshore well, and the operation required use of welding equipment. *Id.* Prior to the operation, the workers failed to secure a "hot work" permit, which precluded performance of welding operations on the well platform. *Id.* at 541. Thus, the welding equipment remained on the vessel, and the procedures were performed on the vessel itself. *Id.* On appeal, we decided the contract was maritime in nature because the work at issue required the vessel's direct involvement. *Id.* at 544–45. We noted that, but for the employees' failure to secure a permit, the work could have been performed on a fixed platform. *Id.* at 545. It was fair to say, then, that the operation in fact required a vessel. *Id.* This case is similar. Although Apache had a fixed production platform from which the work could have been done, Savoie relied on the crane barge to **[—12—]** perform the job when he realized he could not manipulate the heavy equipment alone. This should thus be seen as a maritime operation.

STS relies on *Thurmond* and *Domingue* to support its position. In *Thurmond*, decided before *Davis*, Gulf Oil contracted with P & S Well Services for a barge bearing equipment for the performance of wireline services. *Thurmond*, 836 F.2d at 953. Thurmond, a member of the barge's crew, was injured when he "stepped off the barge and on the wellhead[.]" *Id.* We held the contract to be nonmaritime, noting that Thurmond was "not engaged in the performance of a maritime obligation" at the time of his injury. *Id.* at 955. We also found significant that the parties' contract did not address the use of a vessel. *Id.* In *Domingue*, also concerning wireline services, the injured worker tripped over a piece of equipment the vessel's crew had placed on the well platform. *Domingue*, 923 F.2d at 394. We held that the vessel was "incidental . . . [to] the execution of [the] particular service contract." *Id.* at 397.

Thurmond and *Domingue* have been distinguished by this court under circumstances similar to this case. *See, e.g.*, *Campbell*, 979 F.2d at 1122; *Davis*, 919 F.2d at 316. Neither wireline nor flow-back services are themselves maritime activities. The flow-back services in this case, though, could not have been completed without a vessel that was more than ancillary to the operation. Also, Savoie was not injured as a result of the flow-back operation but because of Jackson's operation of the crane, which was affixed to the vessel. Both workers in *Thurmond* and *Domingue* were on the well platform at the time of injury, but Savoie clutched the crane and fell onto the deck of the barge.

Further, unlike the contract in *Thurmond*, the MSC contemplated the use of a vessel, showing that both Apache and STS recognized a vessel could be necessary to **{-346-}** the performance of its future work orders. The contract does not mention the crane barge specifically, but the MSC was a blanket **[—13—]** agreement that did not create present obligations. Instead, it required STS to accommodate Apache's work orders at unspecified future dates. In addition, "the *Davis* factors must be applied to the facts as they actually occurred" and not "as the parties intended them" to occur. *See Devon*, 247 F. App'x at 545. Even if the parties did not expect a vessel would be used during the flow-back operation, one was.

STS also relies on one of our recent nonprecedential decisions, *Riverside Construction Company, Inc. v. Entergy Mississippi, Inc.*, 626 F. App'x 443 (5th Cir. 2015). We analyzed a repair contract for Entergy's Dolphin Fender System located on a fuel dock in the Mississippi River. *Id.* at 444. Entergy removed the suit to federal court, arguing the contract was maritime because it "contemplated that [the] work would be performed from a floating barge . . . ." *Id.* at 445. We found that federal law did not apply and that removal was improper because the barge, which remained tethered to a bank during the operation, was merely used as a platform from which the work could be done—making it "auxiliary to the actual purpose of the contract[.]" *Id.* at 446.

Riverside is not factually analogous. No evidence exists to suggest the barge in this case remained tethered to a bank during the operation. Instead, it was close enough to the well platform—"located on navigable waters in West Lake Verret"—to permit the crane to access the wellhead.

STS also argues there is no basis for applying federal law to claims arising in Louisiana territorial waters, especially considering that state law applies to claims arising on the Outer Continental Shelf. The Outer Continental Shelf Lands Act extends the law of the adjacent state to the "subsoil and seabed" off its coast. 43 U.S.C. § 1333(a)(1). The adjacent state's law, though, is incorporated into federal law and "does not supplant admiralty and maritime law." ROBERT FORCE & MARTIN J. NORRIS, THE LAW OF **[—14—]** MARITIME PERSONAL INJURIES § 3:15 (2016). Accordingly, once we determine the contract is maritime, state law is irrelevant even on the Outer Continental Shelf. The policy of applying the law of the situs may seem appealing, but doing so would disrupt the "twin aims of maritime law": "achieving uniformity in the exercise of admiralty jurisdiction and providing special solicitude to seamen." *Miles v. Melrose*, 882 F.2d 976, 987 (5th Cir. 1989).

Finally, STS argues that "LDI's maritime tort is irrelevant to STS's contract." STS implies that Savoie's injury as a result of the barge is maritime, while the contract governing Apache's relationship with STS is not. In support, it notes that the personal injury lawsuit has been severed from this action, leaving us no tort issues to decide. As a result, it argues that LDI and Jackson are "attempt[ing] to cloud the nature and character of the [MSC] by emphasizing LDI's own maritime tort against Mr. Savoie." Peeling the maritime tort away from an ostensibly non-maritime contract is imaginative enough, but it is inconsistent with our prior treatment of analogous situations. The fact that Savoie brought an action in tort has no effect on our interpretation of the choice-of-law provision or our analysis of the relevant facts. The tort suit also has no bearing on the application of the indemnity provision, which is the direct subject of this appeal. In fact, the tort suit only bears passing relevance because LDI and Jackson would not be seeking indemnification otherwise. We recognize the basic distinction between tort and contract claims, but that distinction **{–347–}** is immaterial here because our outcome holds regardless of the doctrinal lens through which the facts are viewed.

Our holding is confined to the facts before us. *See Hoda*, 419 F.3d at 383. **[—15—]**

* * *

We conclude that the oral work order is the relevant contract and that it is a maritime contract. The district court did not err by determining maritime law applies. AFFIRMED.***

******(Reporter's Note: On July 7, 2017, the U.S. Fifth Circuit ordered that this case be reheard en banc, with oral argument, on a date thereafter to be fixed.)******

(Reporter's Note: Concurring opinion follows on p. 213).

[—16—] {-347-} DAVIS, Circuit Judge, joined by **SOUTHWICK,** Circuit Judge, specially concurring:

I concur in Judge Southwick's careful opinion which faithfully follows our precedent in *Davis & Sons*[1] and its progeny. I write separately to urge the court to take this case en banc and simplify the test for determining whether a contract is a maritime contract.

The multi-factor test in *Davis & Sons*, as set out in the majority opinion,[2] has been criticized by a number of judges of this court: in *Hoda v. Rowan Cos.*,[3] Judge Jones began the opinion by stating:

> This appeal requires us to sort once more through the authorities distinguishing maritime and non-maritime contracts in the offshore exploration and production industry. As is typical, the final result turns on a minute parsing of the facts. Whether this is the soundest jurisprudential approach may be doubted, inasmuch as it creates uncertainty, spawns litigation, and hinders the rational calculation of costs and risks by companies participating in this industry. Nevertheless, we are bound by the approach this court has followed for more than two decades. **[—17—]**

In *Thurmond*,[4] Judge Garwood concurred in the opinion holding that a contract to provide wireline services that required use of a vessel was not a maritime contract. In his concurring opinion, however, he stated, "I am generally in agreement with Judge Wisdom's persuasive opinion, but am troubled by the tension, or perhaps outright inconsistency, between many of our opinions in this area."[5] And later,

> However, it seems to me that it may be desirable to consider this issue en banc, in order that we may take a more consistent approach to the question of whether and in what circumstances activities in connection with mineral development in state territorial waters are maritime (or perhaps "maritime and local").[6]

Professor David W. Robertson, in his article, pointed out some of the flaws in the **{-348-}** *Davis & Sons* test:[7]

> The "historical treatment" reference does no more than remind courts and counsel to look for close analogies in the jurisprudence. This is what courts must always do when there is no clear governing general rule or principle. The six factors are too pointillistic: they have led Fifth Circuit panels down such odd lines of thought as "whether drilling mud services are more akin to wireline work [which has sometimes been viewed as quintessentially nonmaritime] or to casing services [which can be maritime if done on a vessel-type drilling rig.]"[8] **[—18—]**

---

1 *Davis & Sons, Inc. v. Gulf Oil Corp.*, 919 F.2d 313 (5th Cir. 1990).

2 The six factors are:

> (1) [W]hat does the specific work order in effect at the time of the injury provide? (2) [W]hat work did the crew assigned under the work order actually do? (3) [W]as the crew assigned to work aboard a vessel in navigable waters? (4) [T]o what extent did the work being done relate to the mission of that vessel? (5) [W]hat was the principal work of the injured worker? and (6)[W]hat work was the injured worker actually doing at the time of injury?
>
> *Id.* at 316.

3 419 F.3d 379 (5th Cir. 2005) (concerning an indemnity claim on a contract to install a blowout preventer from a jack-up drilling rig).

4 *Thurmond v. Delta Well Surveyors*, 836 F.2d 952 (5th Cir. 1988).

5 *Id.* at 957 (Garwood, J., concurring).

6 *Id.* (citing *Kossick v. United Fruit Co.*, 365 U.S. 731, 738 (1960)).

7 For a more detailed criticism of the *Davis & Sons* test, *see* David W. Robertson, *The Outer Continental Shelf Lands Act's Provisions on Jurisdiction, Remedies, and Choice of Law: Correcting the Fifth Circuit's Mistakes*, 38 J. MAR. L. & COM. 487, 540-45 (2007).

8 *Id.* at 545 (alteration in Robertson).

One problem with the multi-factor test in *Davis & Sons* is the lack of guidance about what weight to give each factor. A number of our cases seem to give the most weight to the *Davis & Sons* prong that requires examination of the precise work to be performed, e.g., wireline service, welding, casing service, or drilling. Most of our cases hold that a contract to provide any of these services on a vessel on navigable waters is a maritime contract, but panels have held that contracts to provide wireline services are non-maritime in nature whether the contractor contemplates that the services are to be performed from a vessel or not.[9] On the other hand, we have held that contracts to perform casing services are maritime because of the nature of casing work.[10]

A 2004 Supreme Court case, *Norfolk Southern Railway Co. v. Kirby*,[11] supports my view that the en banc court should abandon the *Davis & Sons* test. In *Kirby*, the Court was called upon to determine whether a bill of lading for a shipment of goods by sea from Australia to Charleston, South Carolina, **[—19—]** then by rail to Huntsville, Alabama was a maritime contract.[12] The goods were damaged in a train wreck during the land leg of the trip and the question was whether the suit to recover damages for property that was damaged on this leg of the trip fell within admiralty jurisdiction.[13] The Court concluded that both the land and water portions of the **{-349-}** bills of lading constituted maritime contracts because their primary objective was to accomplish the transportation of goods by sea from Australia to the eastern coast of the United States.[14] Although the facts of this case are not closely analogous to those in today's case, the Court provided important guidance to assist us in determining whether a contract is a maritime contract:

> To ascertain whether a contract is a maritime one, we cannot look to whether a ship or other vessel was involved in the dispute, as we would in a putative maritime tort case. . . . Nor can we simply look to the place of the contract's formation or performance. Instead, the answer "depends upon . . . the nature and character of the contract," and the true criterion is whether it has "reference to maritime service or maritime transactions."[15]

And further "the fundamental interest giving rise to maritime jurisdiction is the protection of maritime commerce."[16]

---

[9] *See Hollier v. Union Tex. Petroleum Corp.*, 972 F.2d 662, 665 (5th Cir. 1992) (holding that a contract for well testing on fixed platforms on the OCS is non-maritime); *Domingue v. Ocean Drilling & Expl. Co.*, 923 F.2d 393, 397-98 (5th Cir. 1991) (holding that a contract to provide wireline services to a jack-up rig operating on the OCS off the coast of Louisiana is nonmaritime); *Thurmond*, 836 F.2d at 956-57 (holding that a contract to provide wireline services to a fixed platform in Louisiana state waters is non-maritime).

[10] *See Demette v. Falcon Drilling Co.*, 280 F.3d 492, 501 (5th Cir. 2002) (finding that because casing work "is an integral part of drilling," which is a "the primary purpose of the vessel" a contract for casing services is maritime); *Campbell v. Sonat Offshore Drilling, Inc.*, 979 F.2d 1115, 1121 (5th Cir. 1992) (holding that a contract to provide casing services is maritime); *Corbitt v. Diamond M. Drilling Co.*, 654 F.2d 329, 332 (5th Cir. 1981) (finding that circuit precedent compels the conclusion that a contract for casing services is maritime); *see also* Kenneth G. Engerrand, *Primer of Remedies on the Outer Continental Shelf*, 4 LOY. MAR. L.J. 19, 61-63 (2005) (noting that historically, some services contracts are considered maritime in nature, including drilling and workover, casing, catering, repair, and well-site supervision, while other services contracts are traditionally non-maritime in nature, including wireline work, testing and completion operations).

[11] 543 U.S. 14 (2004).

[12] *Id.* at 18-19.

[13] *Id.* at 21-22.

[14] *Id.* at 24.

[15] *Id.* (second alteration in original) (quoting *N. Pac. S.S. Co v. Hall Bros. Marine Ry. & Shipbuilding Co.*, 249 U.S. 119, 125 (1919) (citing *Ins. Co v. Dunham*, 78 U.S. 1, 16 (1870))); *see also Exxon Corp. v. Cent. Gulf Lines, Inc.*, 500 U.S. 603, 611 (1991) ("[T]he trend in modern admiralty case law . . . is to focus the jurisdictional inquiry upon whether the nature of the transaction was maritime.").

[16] *Id.* at 25 (emphasis removed) (internal quotation marks omitted) (quoting *Exxon*, 500 U.S. at 608 (quoting *Sisson v. Ruby*, 497 U.S. 358, 367 (1990), in turn quoting *Foremost Ins. Co. v. Richardson*, 457 U.S. 668, 674 (1982))).

Thus, in determining whether a contract being sued upon is a maritime contract, we should use contract principles rather than tort principles: We look **[—20—]** to "the nature and character of the contract," "whether it has 'reference to maritime service or maritime transaction.'"[17] The Court called for a conceptual approach to the inquiry and the focus of the inquiry is the protection of maritime commerce.[18]

The six-prong test in *Davis & Sons* for determining whether the contract being sued upon is a maritime contract includes two prongs that are appropriate in a contract case: (1) what does the work order provide and (2) was the work to be performed on navigable water. The remaining factors are more appropriate in analyzing whether maritime tort jurisdiction can be exercised. In *Grand Isle Shipyard*, the en banc court encountered a similar question.[19]

In that case, another action to recover indemnity under a contract, we were faced with identifying the "situs of the controversy" under the Outer Continental Shelf Lands Act ("OCSLA").[20] If the situs was the Outer Continental Shelf ("OCS"), state law (Louisiana) applied and the indemnity agreement was unenforceable because of the Louisiana Oilfield Indemnity Act.[21] We overruled a number of our cases applying tort principles that held that the situs of the controversy for purposes of the OCSLA was the place of injury.[22] In **{-350-}** *Grand Isle Shipyard*, the injury occurred on a vessel and the appellant argued that this was the situs of the controversy.[23] We disagreed **[—21—]** and concluded that we should apply contract principles and determine where the majority of the work was to be performed under the contract.[24] Because most of the work contemplated under the contract was on stationary platforms on the OCS, we concluded that this location was the focus of the contract and the situs of the controversy.[25] This resulted in the application of state law as required under OCSLA.[26]

The same reasoning applies here. This is a suit on a contract for indemnity. We look to the blanket contract and the verbal work order for the nature and character of the contract; that is, what was the work STS was engaged to do on the well in West Lake Verret in the state of Louisiana. The answer is clear: they were engaged to work downhole from a stationary platform to dislodge downhole obstructions and get the gas well back on production. The contract did not call for any work on a vessel.

As it turned out, an unexpected problem developed that required a vessel equipped with a crane to complete the job. Apache engaged another party, LDI, to provide the vessel and crew for this work.

Considering all of the above, what is an appropriate test for determining whether a contract to provide oilfield services is maritime or non-maritime? Based on the Supreme Court's opinion in *Kirby*, our opinion in *Grand Isle Shipyard,* and the weight of our decisions in this area, I would substitute the following test for determining whether a contract for services to facilitate the drilling or production of oil and gas on state waters or the OCS is a maritime contract. **[—22—]**

So long as a contract's primary purpose is to provide services to promote or assist in oil or gas drilling or production on navigable waters aboard a vessel, it is a maritime contract. Its character as a maritime contract is not defeated simply because the contract

---

17 *Id.* at 24-25.

18 *Id.* at 25.

19 *Grand Isle Shipyard, Inc. v. Seacor Marine, LLC*, 589 F.3d 778 (5th Cir. 2009) (en banc).

20 *Id.* at 781.

21 *Id.*

22 *Id.* at 787-88 (overruling *Diamond Offshore Co. v. A&B Builders, Inc.*, 302 F.3d 531, 546 (5th Cir. 2002); *Demette*, 280 F.3d at 500; *Hodgen v. Forest Oil Corp.*, 87 F.3d 1512, 1527 (5th Cir. 1996); *Smith v. Penrod Drilling Corp.*, 960 F.2d 456, 459 (5th Cir. 1992); and *Hollier*, 972 F.2d at 664).

23 *Id.* at 781-82.

24 *Id.* at 787.

25 *Id.* at 787-88; *see also* Robert Force & Martin J. Norris, The Law of Maritime Personal Injuries § 13:9 (2016) (discussing cases applying the rule emanating from *Grand Isle Shipyard*).

26 *Id.* at 789.

calls for incidental or insubstantial work unrelated to the use of a vessel.[27]

Under this test, a contract or work order to provide specialized services to promote the drilling and production of an oil or gas well from a vessel should be considered a maritime contract. If such a contract also provides for work on land or platforms that is incidental to the work on vessels or insubstantial in relation to the vessel-related work, this does not defeat the character of the contract as a maritime contract. Under this test and consistent with most of our cases, specialized services to promote drilling or production of oil or gas to be performed solely from a stationary platform should not be considered a maritime contract.

Our cases have consistently held that oil and gas drilling on navigable waters from a vessel is considered maritime commerce.[28] It follows that other services performed on a vessel in navigable waters to **{–351–}** facilitate the drilling and production of oil and gas constitutes maritime commerce. Determining whether the contract is maritime should not depend on the nature of the particular oilfield services contracted for.

Applying this test to today's case, the verbal Apache work order called for STS to perform downhole work from a stationary platform to clear an obstruction in a gas well and get it back on production. This downhole work **[—23—]** on a stationary platform has no maritime or "salty" flavor that would qualify it as a maritime contract.

The fact that during the course of performing the work from the platform, a problem was encountered that required Apache to engage a vessel with a crane to assist in the job, does not alter the nature of Apache's contract with STS even though the STS crew performed incidental work to assist in connecting the vessel's crane to a load to be lifted.

CONCLUSION

It is time to abandon the *Davis & Sons* test for determining whether or not a contract is a maritime contract. The test relies more on tort principles than contract principles to decide a contract case. It is too flexible to allow parties or their attorneys to predict whether a court will decide if a contract is maritime or non-maritime or for judges to decide the cases consistently. The Supreme Court's decision in *Kirby* reinforces this conclusion. Just as important, the above test will allow all parties to the contract to more accurately allocate risks and determine their insurance needs more reliably.***

******(Reporter's Note: On July 7, 2017, the U.S. Fifth Circuit ordered that this case be reheard en banc, with oral argument, on a date thereafter to be fixed.)******

---

[27] Professor Robertson recommends a similar test, *see* Robertson, *supra* note 7 at 548.

[28] *Theriot v. Bay Drilling Corp.*, 783 F.2d 527, 538-39 (5th Cir. 1986) ("Oil and gas drilling on navigable waters aboard a vessel is recognized to be maritime commerce."); *Pippen v. Shell Oil Co.*, 661 F.2d 378, 384 (5th Cir. 1981) ("[O]ffshore drilling the discovery, recovery, and sale of oil and natural gas from the sea bottom is maritime commerce . . . .").

United States Court of Appeals for the Fifth Circuit

No. 16-30216

RICHARD
vs.
ANADARKO PETROLEUM CORP.

Appeal from the United States District Court for the Western District of Louisiana

Decided: March 2, 2017

Citation: 850 F.3d 701, 5 Adm. R. 217 (5th Cir. 2017).

Before ELROD, SOUTHWICK, and GRAVES, Circuit Judges.

[—2—] {-704-} GRAVES, Circuit Judge:

This appeal presents, at its core, an insurance coverage dispute. Offshore Energy Services ("OES"), the appellee, indemnified three other companies for tort claims filed against them by an OES employee. OES considered itself contractually obligated to indemnify the other companies under an agreement with an oil and gas project's principal operator.[1]

Liberty Mutual, OES's insurer, denied OES's claim for reimbursement of the funds OES spent defending against, and ultimately settling, the tort suit. Liberty Mutual now appeals two aspects of the proceedings below.

First, Liberty Mutual contends the district court erred by permitting OES and Anadarko Petroleum Corporation ("Anadarko"), the drilling project's principal, to equitably reform their master services contract (the "MSC").

Second, Liberty Mutual asserts the district court interpreted the OES-Liberty Mutual insurance policy erroneously when it concluded the policy obligated Liberty Mutual to reimburse OES for all of the attorney's fees OES incurred in connection with the tort suit, rather than a pro-rata portion of those fees.

We AFFIRM the district court's ruling permitting reformation of the MSC. We MODIFY the district court's judgment awarding attorney's fees; Liberty Mutual **{-705-}** owes $168,695.96, which represents its pro-rata share of OES's attorney's fees.

FACTUAL BACKGROUND AND PROCEDURAL HISTORY

I. Origins of the insurance coverage dispute

This appeal is rooted in Raylin Richard's personal injury lawsuit against Anadarko, Dolphin Drilling Ltd. ("Dolphin Drilling"), and Smith International **[—3—]** Inc. ("Smith International"). Richard worked as a casing supervisor for OES. Anadarko and OES had a longstanding master services contract (the "MSC"), under which OES provided casing and other services on Anadarko projects. One such project brought Richard onto a drill ship called the Belford Dolphin, where, in June 2009, he suffered an injury. Richard filed tort claims against Anadarko and other companies working on Anadarko's project, including Dolphin Drilling and Smith International.

OES, as Richard's employer, ultimately shouldered the financial burden of defending against Richard's claims and secured a full release by paying a $2.5 million settlement. OES assumed this burden pursuant to a two-part chain of contractual indemnifications. First, Anadarko's contractors, Dolphin Drilling and Smith International, turned to Anadarko for indemnification. Second, Anadarko, in turn, sought indemnity from OES for its own exposure, as well as Dolphin Drilling and Smith International's.

The MSC, which established the general terms under which OES and Anadarko would conduct business within a number of different projects, contains provisions imposing reciprocal indemnity obligations for claims relating to employees' work-related accidents. The parties vigorously dispute the scope of these indemnity obligations.

The dispute concerns paragraphs 14(a)–(b), which obligate OES and Anadarko to

[1] We follow the parties and district court in referring to this as a "knock for knock" indemnity arrangement.

indemnify each other's "indemnitees," and paragraphs 2(c)–(d), which define the relevant "indemnitees" as "[Anadarko or OES, respectively,] its Affiliates, its joint owners and venturers, if any, and its and their directors, agents, representatives, employees and insurers and its subcontractors and their employees."

Liberty Mutual, OES's insurer, denied coverage for OES's expenditures related to Dolphin Drilling and Smith International. **[—4—]**

II. Rulings related to coverage

A. Dismissal of Anadarko and Dolphin Drilling's third-party claims

After Liberty Mutual denied coverage, Anadarko and Dolphin Drilling both filed third-party complaints impleading OES and Liberty Mutual. The district court dismissed Anadarko and Dolphin Drilling's third-party claims against Liberty Mutual with prejudice. This did not, however, resolve the related issue of whether Liberty Mutual owed OES coverage for the amounts OES spent indemnifying Anadarko, Dolphin Drilling, and Smith International.

B. Summary judgment on OES's cross-claim

OES cross-claimed against Liberty Mutual seeking coverage for its indemnification of Dolphin Drilling, Smith International, and Anadarko. The district court granted summary judgment in Liberty Mutual's favor, concluding that Dolphin Drilling and Smith International were Anadarko's "contractors," which the MSC's indemnity provisions did not cover, rather than "subcontractors," which the MSC's indemnity provisions would cover.

The court found that it "[could] not answer the . . . question" of whether to reform **{–706–}** the MSC "at [that] time," but contemplated that OES and Anadarko might renew their request for reformation of the MSC in subsequent motions.

C. Reconsideration of summary judgment

On March 24, 2015, the district court granted Anadarko, Dolphin Drilling, Smith International, and OES's motions for reconsideration of the initial summary judgment ruling.[2] While the district court declined to revisit its prior construction of the MSC, the court permitted Anadarko and OES to reform the MSC to reflect a mutually-intended "knock for knock indemnity scheme that would require, under the circumstances of Mr. Richard's injury, OES to indemnify Anadarko, Smith, and Dolphin." **[—5—]**

D. Denial of Liberty Mutual's subsequent challenge to the MSC's reformation

After OES filed an amended cross-claim reflecting the reformed indemnity provision, Liberty Mutual filed a new motion for summary judgment. Liberty Mutual essentially argued that reformation should not have been granted. The district court denied the motion on October 28, 2015.

E. Interpretation of the OES-Liberty Mutual insurance policy

The parties' focus then turned to the language of the OES-Liberty Mutual insurance policy. In a one-day bench trial, the parties contested Liberty Mutual's obligation to reimburse OES for the settlement funds and attorney's fees OES spent in connection with the Richard suit.

With respect to the settlement funds, the court found Liberty Mutual owed OES $900,000, representing the policy's $1 million limit less a $100,000 deductible. With respect to attorney's fees, the court awarded the full $468,599.90 OES spent defending itself, Dolphin Drilling, and Smith International.

---

[2] Anadarko filed one motion, while Dolphin, Smith, and OES jointly filed the second.

F. Denial of Liberty Mutual's post-trial motions

The district court denied Liberty Mutual's motion for a new trial or to alter or amend the judgment on February 25, 2016. Liberty Mutual timely noticed this appeal on March 8, 2016.

JURISDICTION

The district court had jurisdiction over this case pursuant to 28 U.S.C. § 1333(1). This court has jurisdiction to review the district court's final judgment pursuant to 28 U.S.C. § 1291.

STANDARD OF REVIEW

With respect to the ruling permitting reformation of the MSC, because "the district court considered the merits of the [reconsideration] motion," this court "review[s] the reformation issue under the familiar summary-judgment **[—6—]** standard of *de novo*." *See Am. Elec. Power Co. Inc. v. Affiliated FM Ins. Co.*, 556 F.3d 282, 287 (5th Cir. 2009). We review for clear error the district court's finding regarding whether the contracting parties made a mutual mistake such that the contract fails to reflect their shared intent. *See Ill. Cent. Gulf R.R. Co. v. R.R. Land*, 988 F.2d 1397, 1402 (5th Cir. 1993) ("We freely review conclusions of law; but, because the reformation issue turns on a determination of the parties' intent, we review for clear error.") (applying Louisiana law); *see also Motors Ins. Co. v. Bud's Boat Rental, Inc.*, 917 F.2d 199, 204 (5th Cir. 1990) (holding, in the context of maritime contract reformation, **{–707–}** that "[d]etermination of intent is a question of fact for the district court, which this court can reverse only if clearly erroneous"); *Teche Realty & Inv. Co. v. Morrow*, 673 So.2d 1145, 1148 (La. Ct. App. 1996) ("A determination of mutual error is essentially a question of fact, and a trial court's finding with reference to the presence or absence of mutual error should not be disturbed unless it is clearly wrong.").

This court reviews "*de novo* the interpretation of a[n] [insurance] contract, including any questions about whether the contract is ambiguous." *Pioneer Expl., L.L.C. v. Steadfast Ins. Co.*, 767 F.3d 503, 511–12 (5th Cir. 2014).

Conflicts-of-law questions also receive *de novo* review. *Hartford Underwriters Ins. Co. v. Found. Health Servs. Inc.*, 524 F.3d 588, 592 (5th Cir. 2008) ("This Court reviews questions of law, including conflicts of law questions, *de novo* . . . .").

ANALYSIS

I. Reformation of the OES-Anadarko Master Services Contract

The first issue presented in this appeal concerns whether the district court erred by permitting OES and Anadarko to reform the MSC. We hold that the district court correctly permitted reformation. Federal maritime law permitted the introduction of parol evidence to demonstrate a mutual mistake **[—7—]** warranting reformation, Liberty Mutual's third-party interest in the MSC's indemnity provisions did not block reformation, and the record contains sufficient evidence to support reformation.

A. Application of federal maritime law

The district court correctly concluded that the MSC "is a maritime contract subject to federal maritime law."[3]

[3] The MSC's "Purpose and Scope" paragraph describes, among other planned work, "casing." In the tort claim underlying this insurance coverage dispute, Raylin Richard, an OES casing supervisor, was struck and injured by a falling joint of casing. "'Casing' is an activity performed during the drilling for oil . . . involv[ing] the 'welding together and hammering of pipe into the subsurface of the earth to create a permanent construction.'" *Demette v. Falcon Drilling Co.*, 280 F.3d 492, 494–95 (5th Cir. 2002) (quoting *Campbell v. Sonat Offshore Drilling, Inc.*, 979 F.2d 1115, 1118 n.2 (5th Cir. 1992)), *overruled on other grounds by Grand Isle Shipyard, Inc. v. Seacor Marine, LLC*, 589 F.3d 778 (5th Cir. 2009). "This court has held that indemnity provisions in contracts to provide offshore casing services are maritime." *Id.* at 500.

"[C]ourt[s] in maritime cases *must* apply general federal maritime choice of law rules." *Great Lakes Reinsurance (UK) PLC v. Durham Auctions, Inc.*, 585 F.3d 236, 241 (5th Cir. 2009) (quoting *Albany Ins. Co. v. Anh Thi Kieu*, 927 F.2d 882, 890 (5th Cir. 1991)). "Under federal maritime choice of law rules, contractual choice of law provisions are generally recognized as valid and enforceable." *Id.* at 242. The MSC includes a choice-of-law provision selecting general maritime law, or, if maritime law does not apply, Texas law.

While the parties agree that we should begin with federal maritime principles, they dispute whether federal maritime principles alone suffice to resolve the reformation issue. Liberty Mutual contends that in this case, maritime law principles conclusively foreclose reformation. OES argues the district court correctly consulted state law regarding "the specific issue of reformation of a contract when a third party (here, Liberty Mutual) may be adversely affected." We hold that the district court correctly referenced state **[—8—]** law to determine whether Liberty Mutual's interest **{–708–}** in the indemnities provided by the MSC foreclosed reformation.

B. Maritime parol evidence rule

The district court's reformation ruling did not disturb its prior conclusion that the express language of the MSC provided no indemnity coverage for Dolphin Drilling and Smith International. Liberty Mutual contends this should have ended the court's inquiry. We disagree.

The district court properly considered evidence that OES and Anadarko committed a mutual mistake by failing to write such coverage into the MSC. Mutual mistakes by contracting parties can warrant contract reformation. *See Wilcox v. Wild Well Control, Inc.*, 794 F.3d 531, 541, 3 Adm. R. 394, 399 (5th Cir. 2015) ("Reformation is an equitable remedy used to correct errors or mistakes in contracts.") (quoting *Am. Elec.*, 556 F.3d at 287). "To reform an instrument, 'there must be clear proof of the antecedent agreement as well as the error in committing it to writing.'" *Fruge v. Amerisure Mut. Ins. Co.*, 663 F.3d 743, 748 (5th Cir. 2011) (applying Louisiana law) (quoting *First State Bank & Trust Co. of E. Baton Rouge Parish v. Seven Gables Inc.*, 501 So.2d 280, 285 (La. Ct. App. 1986)).

The question of whether a court may consider parol evidence relating to a contract turns largely on whether the evidence is offered to (1) interpret the contract's terms or (2) demonstrate the contracting parties' mutual mistake in failing to accurately record an antecedent agreement in writing. Parol evidence may not be considered in the course of interpreting unambiguous contractual language, *see Har-Win, Inc. v. Consolidated Grain & Barge Co.*, 794 F.2d 985, 988 (5th Cir. 1986), but a court may evaluate parol evidence to determine whether a mutual mistake occurred, *see Travelers Indem. Co. v. Calvert Fire Ins. Co.*, 798 F.2d 826, 835 (5th Cir. 1986), *aff'd in part and rev'd in part on other grounds on reh'g*, 836 F.2d 850 (5th Cir. 1988). Courts must guard against **[—9—]** parties' "attempts to make an end-run around the parol-evidence rule," which forecloses the use of parol evidence to interpret unambiguous terms, "by framing [their] argument[s] as a request for reformation." *Am. Elec.*, 556 F.3d at 288.

Har-Win demonstrates the maritime parol evidence rule's bar against parol evidence offered to interpret unambiguous contractual terms. In that case, we concluded that the contracts at issue were complete and unambiguously called for an unconditional sale. *Har-Win*, 794 F.2d at 987. We therefore held that the lower court properly excluded parol evidence offered to show that the buyer's obligations were conditional. *Id. Har-Win*, however, made no mention of mutual mistake.

In maritime cases, "[e]quity will reform an instrument to reflect the true intent of the parties where there has been a mutual mistake . . . [and] [p]arol evidence is admissible to prove the mutual mistake." *Travelers Indem. Co.*, 798 F.2d at 835. Accordingly, the district court did not violate the maritime parol evidence rule when, after interpreting the unreformed MSC, it considered parol evidence for the purpose of determining whether the contracting parties committed a mutual drafting error warranting reformation. We perceive no clear error in the district court's conclusion that a mutual error occurred.

C. Reformation affecting interested third parties

The district court recognized that reformation might be proper if OES and Anadarko proved a mutual mistake, but also noted that federal maritime law lacked a **{–709–}** clear rule of decision on "the specific issue of reformation of a contract when a third party (here, Liberty Mutual) may be adversely affected." To fill the gap, the district court conducted a choice-of-law analysis comparing Louisiana and Texas state law.

The district court's reference to state law was proper—this Court has stated that "state law may occasionally be utilized to fill the gaps in an **[—10—]** incomplete and less than perfect maritime system," *see J. Ray McDermott & Co. v. Vessel Morning Star*, 457 F.2d 815, 818 (5th Cir. 1972) (en banc); *see also Motors Ins. Co.*, 917 F.2d at 203 (applying federal admiralty law to a maritime contract's *interpretation*, but analyzing its *reformation* under Louisiana state law due to the absence of "a well-established federal maritime rule of decision"). Finding no conflict between Texas and Louisiana state law on the issue of reformation, the district court used the law of its forum (i.e., Louisiana law).

1. *Choice of law*

This court reviews a district court's choice-of-law determinations *de novo*. *See Sims v. Kia Motors of Am., Inc.*, 839 F.3d 393, 398 (5th Cir. 2016). "[C]ourt[s] in maritime cases *must* apply general federal maritime choice of law rules." *Great Lakes Reinsurance*, 585 at 241 (quoting *Kieu*, 927 F.2d at 890). "Under federal maritime choice of law rules, contractual choice of law provisions are generally recognized as valid and enforceable." *Id.* at 242.

Where "general maritime law is not applicable," the MSC selects Texas law. Although the MSC's choice of law provision would typically lead to the application of Texas reformation principles, we perceive no error in the district court's decision to rely primarily upon Louisiana law given the apparent absence of conflict between the two jurisdictions. *See Am. Elec.*, 556 F.3d at 285 (applying Louisiana law to a dispute involving contractual interpretation and a reformation request after perceiving no conflict between Texas and Louisiana law); *see also Pioneer Expl.*, 767 F.3d at 512 (applying Louisiana law to a dispute involving contractual interpretation due to the absence of conflict with Texas law). We likewise look to Louisiana law.

2. *Louisiana reformation principles*

The district court correctly noted that, under Louisiana law, "[t]he fact that a third party may be affected by reformation of the contract does not, **[—11—]** itself, bar reformation." In *Samuels v. State Farm Mut. Auto. Ins. Co.*, for example, the Supreme Court of Louisiana affirmed reformation of an individual's contract with an excess insurer, Evanston Insurance Company, due to the contracting parties' mutual mistake despite the fact that the reformation would negatively affect State Farm, the primary insurer. *See* 939 So.2d 1235, 1239, 1241 (La. 2006).

The *Samuels* court observed that "[the] third party insurance company [i.e., State Farm] . . . did not even rely on [the contracting parties'] error in issuing its own policy." *Id.* at 1241. Similarly, the district court in this case found that "Liberty Mutual unequivocally did not study, review, or rely on the language of the OES-Anadarko Contract prior to issuing [its insurance] Policy to OES."

Liberty Mutual does not directly dispute the district court's finding that it did not review or rely on the unreformed MSC. Rather, Liberty Mutual argues that because it "assumed obligations based on the original contract language," it should receive protection from the "prejudic[ial]" effects of reformation even though it did not specifically rely on the unreformed **{–710–}** MSC. Appellant's Reply Br. at 14. We disagree.

a. *American Electric* and *Wilcox*

Liberty Mutual's argument against reformation invokes two of this court's recent opinions, *Am. Elec. Power Co. Inc. v. Affiliated FM Ins. Co.*, 556 F.3d 282 (5th Cir. 2009) and *Wilcox v. Wild Well Control, Inc.*, 794 F.3d 531, 3 Adm. R. 394 (5th Cir. 2015). Both are distinguishable.

In *American Electric*, we held that a district court did not err when it declined to reform an insurance policy (the "Chubb Policy") between Central & Southwest Corporation ("CSW") and Chubb Insurance Group ("Chubb"). *Am. Elec.*, 556 F.3d at 284–85. The district court's ruling benefitted Affiliated FM Insurance Company ("Affliliated"), whose policy insuring CSW's purchaser, **[—12—]** American Electric Power Company ("AEP"), obligated Affiliated to pay for whatever past losses at CSW the Chubb Policy would have covered. *Id.*

AEP sought coverage for past losses at "two of CSW's subsidiary limited liability companies ('LLCs')." *Id.* at 284. Affiliated declined coverage, asserting that the Chubb Policy only expressly covered CSW and its subsidiary corporations (i.e., not the unincorporated subsidiary LLCs). *Id.* at 285. Both CSW and Chubb filed affidavits stating that they intended for the Chubb Policy's references to subsidiary "corporations" to encompass CSW's subsidiary LLCs. *Id.*

We distinguished *Samuels*, where a third party's interest did not block contractual reformation, from the reformation AEP sought on two grounds. First, we observed that "*Samuels* involved a third party who did not assume or rely on the original contract in any manner." *Id.* at 288 (citing *Samuels*, 939 So.2d at 1240–41). In *American Electric*, by contrast, "Affiliated assumed the coverage obligations set forth under the unambiguous terms of the Chubb Policy," and we perceived "no indication that Affiliated knew or should have known of an informal understanding between Chubb and CSW regarding the meaning of 'corporation.'" *Id.* Reforming the Chubb Policy under such circumstances, we reasoned, "would be contrary to basic norms of fairness and notice." *Id.* (citing *Lewis v. Saucer*, 653 So.2d 1254, 1259 (La. Ct. App. 1995)).

Second, we concluded that Chubb and CSW's "broader-than-usual" intended meaning for the word "corporation" did not constitute "the type of 'error' that reformation is intended to remedy." *Id.* We contrasted the "broader-than-usual" intended definition with the "clerical mistake" at issue in *Samuels*, which involved "the inclusion of an unintended and inaccurate [insurance] policy number." *Id.* (citing *Samuels*, 939 So.2d at 1241). We discerned "a significant difference between an obvious clerical error and [an] alleged 'hidden meaning' in a contract assumed by an unwitting third party." **[—13—]** *Id.* "Equity may counsel relief for the former," we reasoned, "but it does not for the latter." *Id.*

In *Wilcox*, we affirmed a district court's refusal to reform a contract that defined the term "Owner" as meaning one specific company, Superior Energy Services, L.L.C. ("Superior"). *See Wilcox*, 794 F.3d at 541–42, 3 Adm. R. at 399–401. Relying on *American Electric*, we rejected an invitation to reform the contractual definition to encompass "all companies affiliated with Superior." *Id.*, 3 Adm. R. at 400. We emphasized *American Electric*'s admonition against permitting parties "to use parol evidence to show 'the original parties had a broader-than-usual meaning in mind when they [purposefully] included the word.'" *Id.* at 542, 3 Adm. R. at 400 (quoting *Am. Elec.*, 556 F.3d at 288).

b. Analysis

In both *American Electric* and *Wilcox*, we affirmed district court rulings denying **{-711-}** reformation where parties sought to expand express contractual terms beyond the terms' usual meaning. *See Am. Elec.*, 556 F.3d at 288; *Wilcox*, 794 F.3d at 542, 3 Adm. R. at 401. In *American Electric*, the relevant term, "corporation," was also a legal term of art carrying a generally accepted meaning narrower than the contracting parties' purported private understanding. *See Am. Elec.*, 556 F.3d at 286–87. In *Wilcox*, the contract defined the relevant term, "Owner," as a single business entity, "Superior Energy Services, L.L.C," without any indication that the definition might encompass other entities such as Superior's subsidiaries. *Wilcox*, 794 F.3d 531 F.3d at 541–42, 3 Adm. R. at 400. Under such circumstances, expanding the contracts' express terms would run "contrary to basic norms of fairness and notice" upon which third parties rely. *See Am. Elec.*, 556 F.3d at 288.

In this case, by contrast, we are persuaded that the reformation causes Liberty Mutual no unfair surprise. Like the district court, we consider the unreformed MSC's indemnity provisions strongly suggestive of OES and **[—14—]** Anadarko's mutual intention to provide for the "knock for knock" indemnity arrangement common in their industry. That intention is further evidenced by the parties' conduct after signing the MSC.[4] Specifically, less than a year after signing the MSC, OES made indemnifications under similar circumstances and successfully submitted a claim to its prior insurer, Zurich Insurance Company. *Richard v. Anadarko Petroleum Corp.*, No. 6:11-CV-0083, 2015 WL 1357013, at *9, *11 (W.D. La. Mar. 24, 2015). On the strength of such evidence, the district court permitted reformation to ensure the MSC's indemnity provisions would fully reflect OES and Anadarko's intended "knock for knock" indemnity arrangement.

Liberty Mutual does not stand on equal footing with the third parties whose interests blocked reformation in *American Electric* and *Wilcox*. Those third parties faced springing "hidden meaning[s]," such as the notions that contracting parties meant for the unambiguous word "corporation" to also encompass unincorporated entities, *see Am. Elec.*, 556 F.3d at 288, or meant for a specific reference to a single business entity to also encompass all of that entity's affiliates, *see Wilcox*, 794 F.3d at 541–42, 3 Adm. R. at 400. In this case, Liberty Mutual cannot fairly complain of such surprise.

The district court found, and Liberty Mutual has not disputed, that "Liberty Mutual unequivocally did not study, review, or rely on the language of the [MSC] prior to issuing [its] Policy to OES." *Richard*, 2015 WL 1357013, at *11. In the course of procuring the insurance policy, OES also provided Liberty Mutual with a "Loss History" reflecting OES's prior indemnification **[—15—]** claims, including a claim involving a contractor under circumstances similar to this case. *Id.* With the unreformed MSC and OES's "Loss History" in hand, Liberty Mutual had reason to perceive OES and Anadarko's shared, ultimately mistaken interpretation of the MSC indemnity provisions' scope.

D. <u>Sufficiency of the evidence for reformation</u>

Moving beyond the question of whether reformation was permissible, Liberty **{–712–}** Mutual also contends that OES failed to present sufficient evidence to warrant reformation. We disagree.

"The party seeking reformation bears the burden of establishing mutual error in the contract's creation." *Wilcox*, 794 F.3d at 541, 3 Adm. R. at 400 (citing *Am. Elec.*, 556 F.3d at 287). "Ordinarily the party must only show mistake by a preponderance of the evidence; but when a party seeks to reform a provision 'to provide coverage for a substantially different and greater risk than expressly covered, the party must demonstrate a mutual error by clear-and-convincing evidence.'" *Id.*, 3 Adm. R. at 400 (quoting *Am. Elec.*, 556 F.3d at 287 n.4).

The district court found that OES and Anadarko met the higher clear-and-convincing evidence burden. In light of the record, and in particular the evidence discussed above, we agree.

[4] Louisiana law permits courts to consider evidence of the contracting parties' post-contract conduct when evaluating the parties' antecedent agreement. *See Wilson v. Levy*, 101 So.2d 214, 217 (La. 1958) (considering contracting parties' post-sale conduct in the course of determining the intended boundaries of a land sale); *see also Agurs v. Holt*, 95 So.2d 644, 648 (La. 1957) (same); *Succession of Jones v. Jones*, 486 So.2d 1124, 1129 (La. Ct. App. 1986) (same).

E. Whether the district court had authority to reform the MSC while exercising admiralty jurisdiction

Liberty Mutual suggests, in a footnote, that "a court exercising admiralty jurisdiction" may not be able to "consider a reformation claim." Appellant's Original Br. at 35 n.103. We disagree.

This court has repeatedly indicated federal courts exercising admiralty jurisdiction may reform maritime contracts. *E.g., Motors Ins. Co.*, 917 F.2d at 203 ("The Fifth Circuit has previously applied Louisiana law to reform a maritime hull and indemnity policy."). **[—16—]**

II. Interpretation of the OES-Liberty Mutual insurance policy

The second issue presented by this appeal concerns whether the district court erred when it interpreted the OES-Liberty Mutual insurance policy to require reimbursement of all the attorneys' fees OES incurred in connection with the Richard suit. We hold that the district court did err; the insurance policy only obligates Liberty Mutual to pay a pro-rata share of the attorney's fees.

A. Relevant policy provisions and endorsements

The insurance policy sets forth general terms in sections titled "Common Policy Conditions," and "Commercial General Liability Coverage Form." The policy also includes a list of declarations and "endorsements" that make specific modifications. Liberty Mutual contends that the district court erred in its handling of two endorsements, Endorsement 3 and Endorsement 34.

Both endorsements reference a portion of the policy labeled "Supplementary Payments – Coverages A and B." The Supplementary Payments section generally outlines Liberty Mutual's obligations to pay costs borne by the insured (i.e., OES) and the insured's indemnitees.

Endorsement 3 purports to amend Supplementary Payments ¶1 to reflect a "pro-rata" formula for determining Liberty Mutual's payment obligations. Endorsement 34 states that the text it provides "replace[s] . . . Supplementary Payments – Coverages A and B."

As the district court stated, "[t]he difference between the two endorsements is that if Endorsement 3 is applied, the fees owed are $168,695.96, and if Endorsement 34 is applied the fees are $468,599.90." *Richard v. Anadarko Petroleum Corp.*, No. 6:11-CV-0083, 2015 WL 8785038, at *2 (W.D. La. Dec. 15, 2015). **[—17—]**

B. Interpretive dispute

The district court concluded that the policy and its endorsements reasonably **{–713–}** permitted the following two alternative interpretations:

1. "The replacement Supplementary Payments provision in Endorsement 34 is modified by the pro-rata formula in Endorsement 3 such that the pro-rate formula applies; or

2. Endorsement 3 amends paragraph 1 of the Supplementary Payments provision but Endorsement 34 completely replaces that provision such that the pro-rata formula does not apply."

Richard, 2015 WL 8785038, at *2.

Invoking the principle that ambiguous insurance policy provisions should generally be construed against the insurer, the district court adopted the second interpretation and awarded all the legal fees OES incurred. *Richard*, 2015 WL 8785038, at *3.

C. Discussion

We conclude that the district court's second alternative interpretation is not reasonable under Louisiana principles of contract interpretation. Only the district court's first alternative interpretation adequately gives effect to all of the policy's provisions.

"Under Louisiana law, insurance policies are contracts between the parties and 'should be construed by using the general rules of interpretation of contracts set forth in the Louisiana Civil Code.'" *Pioneer Expl.*, 767 F.3d at 512 (quoting *Cadwallader v. Allstate Ins. Co.*, 848 So.2d 577, 580 (La. 2003)). "When interpreting a contract, the court must discern the parties' common intent." *Id.* "The parties' intent as reflected by the words in the policy determine[s] the extent of coverage." *Id.* (quoting *La. Ins. Guar. Ass'n v. Interstate Fire & Cas. Co.*, 630 So.2d 759, 763 (La. 1994)) (alteration in original). **[—18—]**

"Where the terms of the contract are clear and explicit and do not lead to absurd consequences, no further interpretation may be made in search of the intent of the parties." *Id.* (citing La. Civ. Code art. 2046). "'[W]ords of a contract must be given their generally prevailing meaning,' but '[w]ords of art and technical terms must be given their technical meaning when the contract involves a technical matter.'" *Id.* (quoting La. Civ. Code art. 2047) (alterations in original). "Each provision in [the] contract must be interpreted in light of the other provisions so that each is given the meaning suggested by the contract as a whole." La. Civ. Code art. 2050.

"An insurance policy should not be interpreted in an unreasonable or a strained manner so as to enlarge or restrict its provisions beyond what is reasonably contemplated by its terms or so as to achieve an absurd conclusion." *Pioneer Expl.*, 767 F.3d at 512 (quoting *Reynolds v. Select Props., Ltd.*, 634 So.2d 1180, 1183 (La. 1994)). "If the policy wording at issue is clear and unambiguously expresses the parties' intent, the insurance contract must be enforced as written." *Id.* (quoting *Cadwallader*, 848 So.2d at 580).

"If the insurance contract terms are ambiguous, these ambiguities are generally strictly construed against the insurer and in favor of coverage." *Id.* (citing *La. Ins. Guar. Ass'n*, 630 So.2d at 764). "This rule of strict construction 'applies only if the ambiguous policy provision is susceptible to two or more reasonable interpretations; for the rule of strict construction to apply, the insurance policy must be not only susceptible to two or more interpretations, but each of the alternative interpretations must be reasonable.'" *Id.* (quoting *Cadwallader*, 848 So.2d at 580). **{-714-}**

The district court's second policy interpretation, under which Endorsement 34 entirely nullifies Endorsement 3, is unreasonable in light of Louisiana's interpretive command that policy provisions be read in light of one another "so that each is given the meaning suggested by the contract as a **[—19—]** whole." *See* La. Civ. Code art. 2050. Because only one reasonable interpretation exists, the district court erred by construing the policy against the insurer, Liberty Mutual. *Pioneer Expl.*, 767 F.3d at 512.

CONCLUSION

For the foregoing reasons, we AFFIRM the district court's ruling permitting reformation of the MSC.[5] We MODIFY the district court's judgment awarding attorney's fees; the policy entitles OES to attorney's fees totaling $168,695.96.

---

[5] Because we affirm the district court's ruling permitting reformation, we do not reach OES's alternative argument that the unreformed MSC provided the coverage OES and Anadarko seek.

United States Court of Appeals
for the Fifth Circuit

No. 16-30353

IN RE LOUISIANA CRAWFISH PRODUCERS

Appeal from the United States District Court for the Western District of Louisiana

Decided: March 28, 2017

Citation: 852 F.3d 456, 5 Adm. R. 226 (5th Cir. 2017).

Before **REAVLEY, ELROD,** and **GRAVES,** Circuit Judges.

[—1—] {-459-} ELROD, Circuit Judge:

The Louisiana Crawfish Producers Association-West and some of its commercial crawfishermen members sued a number of oil and gas companies and their insurers, claiming the companies' dredging activities caused damage to the fisheries the fishermen used. The district court granted summary judgment in favor of two of the companies, Florida Gas Transmission Co. and Southern Natural Gas Co., finding that Plaintiffs did not create a genuine issue **[—2—]** of material fact as to whether the two companies' activities constituted "dredging" so as to support maritime tort claims. Plaintiffs moved the district court to reconsider its grant of summary judgment and submitted new evidence for its review. The district court denied Plaintiffs' motion for reconsideration as to both companies. Plaintiffs appeal both the district court's order granting summary judgment as well as the denial of their motion for reconsideration. We AFFIRM the district court's grant of summary judgment and denial of the motion for reconsideration with respect to Florida Gas Transmission Co. With respect to Southern Natural Gas Co., we REVERSE the district court's denial of Plaintiffs' Rule 59(e) motion and VACATE its grant of summary judgment.

I.

Plaintiffs-Appellants are the Louisiana Crawfish Producers Association-West and over eighty individual crawfishermen who operate in the Atchafalaya Basin in Louisiana (collectively, Plaintiffs).[1] They sued **{-460-}** several companies, two of which are relevant to this appeal—Florida Gas Transmission Co. (Florida Gas) and Southern Natural Gas Co. (Southern Natural). Plaintiffs alleged that the companies' past canal dredging activities created spoil banks that damaged the Atchafalaya Basin fisheries Plaintiffs utilized.

After this case was removed from state court to the United States District Court for the Western District of Louisiana, various defendant companies filed a motion to dismiss, arguing that Plaintiffs failed to state a cause of action for maritime tort. The district court held that Plaintiffs had **[—3—]** stated a maritime tort claim against Florida Gas, Southern Natural, and Dow Chemical Co. (Dow)[2] by alleging that these defendants engaged in dredging activities.[3] The district court dismissed Plaintiffs' claims against all other defendant companies because Plaintiffs failed to allege these companies had engaged in dredging activities. Plaintiffs appealed the dismissal of these defendants, but we affirmed. *In re Louisiana Crawfish Producers*, 772 F.3d 1026, 2 Adm. R. 375 (5th Cir. 2014). Our decision left Florida Gas, Southern Natural, and Dow, along with their insurers, as the remaining defendants.

---

[1] Crawfish, also known as crayfish, crawdads, freshwater lobsters, mountain lobsters, mudbugs, or yabbies, are freshwater crustaceans resembling small lobsters. While there are over 500 species of crawfish in the world, the Southeastern United States is home to around 330 of them. Wikipedia, *Crayfish*, https://en.wikipedia.org/wiki/Crayfish (last visited March 21, 2017). In 1983, the state of Louisiana designated the Louisiana crawfish, *Procambarus clarkii*, as its Official Crustacean, becoming the first state to bestow such an honor on a species of crustaceans. Wikipedia, List of U.S. State Crustaceans, https://en.wikipedia.org/wiki/List_of_U.S._state_crustaceans (last visited March 21, 2017).

[2] Dow remains a defendant in the district court but is not a party to this appeal.

[3] Specifically, the district court found that with respect to Southern Natural, Florida Gas, and Dow, Plaintiffs' allegation of dredging on navigable waters bears a sufficient relationship to traditional maritime activity to state a claim for a maritime tort under *Jerome B. Grubart, Inc. v. Great Lakes Dredge & Dock Co.*, 513 U.S. 527 (1995).

Following our decision in *Louisiana Crawfish*, the remaining defendants and Plaintiffs conferred and prepared a case management order to establish litigation deadlines. At the time the parties created the case management order, Southern Natural's Rule 30(b)(6) deposition had not yet occurred. The parties agreed upon a proposed case management order, which stated, in pertinent part:

> 3. Dispositive Motions:
>
> a. Any party having dispositive motion(s) concerning legal issues and not requiring additional fact discovery shall file their motion(s) by July 31, 2015.
>
> b. Oppositions to dispositive motions filed on or before July 31, 2015 shall be filed by August 31, 2015.
>
> c. Any reply briefs shall be filed by September 15, 2015.
>
> d. Within thirty (30) days from receipt of the transcript of the Southern Natural Gas Company deposition in this matter, Plaintiffs shall file any dipositive motions or supplemental oppositions necessitated by factual information learned during the deposition. **[—4—]**

Southern Natural advised Plaintiffs that its earliest available deposition date was September 22, 2015. This date fell after the case management order's August 31 deadline for Plaintiffs to oppose dispositive motions. Plaintiffs nevertheless agreed to hold Southern Natural's deposition on September 22, 2015, anticipating they would be allowed to supplement their opposition to any dispositive motions with information learned at the deposition. **{-461-}**

On July 31, 2015, in accordance with the case management order, Florida Gas, Southern Natural, and Dow filed a joint motion seeking reconsideration of the district court's earlier denial of their motion to dismiss or, alternatively, seeking summary judgment and dismissal of Plaintiffs' claims. Plaintiffs timely submitted their opposition to the motion in accordance with the deadlines set forth in the case management order. Plaintiffs attached to their opposition evidence pertaining to Florida Gas and Dow, but they did not attach any evidence pertaining to Southern Natural.[4]

While the motion was pending before the district court, Southern Natural's corporate representative was deposed on September 22, 2015. During the deposition, Southern Natural's corporate representative testified that Southern Natural engaged in dredging in connection with the subject spoil banks.[5] At the end of the deposition, Southern Natural's corporate representative reserved his right to read and sign the deposition transcript. At **[—5—]** Plaintiffs' request, the court reporter provided an uncertified copy of the transcript to Plaintiffs on October 26, 2016. However, because Southern Natural's corporate representative had not yet signed the transcript, an official transcript was not yet available. After the deposition took place, Plaintiffs also forwarded requests for admissions to all defendants, ahead of the agreed-upon discovery cutoff date. In its response, Southern Natural admitted to using dredge vessels in the construction of the canal at issue.[6]

---

[4] Plaintiffs did note in their opposition brief that they would be deposing Southern Natural in the coming months, and stated that they "reserved the right to supplement this opposition after the deposition of Southern Natural Gas which is set to take place in late September, 2015."

[5] Specifically, Southern Natural's corporate representative testified:

> Q: Let's talk about the Section 28 line. Do you know how that line was actually constructed?
>
> A: I know that the line was permitted to be constructed by virtue of Southern Natural digging a flotation canal for waterborne equipment to lay the pipeline, and we know that was done in accordance with the permit.

[6] Plaintiffs' first request for admission asked Southern Natural to "Admit or deny that the canals in which Southern Natural Gas' 'South Section 28 Pipeline' . . . [is/was] situated were dredged by dredging vessels." In response, Southern Natural admitted that Southern Natural "constructed the South Section 28 Pipeline . . . in accordance with

On November 12, 2015, while Plaintiffs were still awaiting the official deposition transcript, the district court granted summary judgment in favor of Florida Gas and Southern Natural,[7] finding that Plaintiffs did not provide evidence that created a genuine issue of material fact as to whether either of these defendants had engaged **{-462-}** in dredging activities. The certified transcript of the Southern Natural deposition was finally provided to Plaintiffs on November 17, 2015—five days after the district court's ruling.

Plaintiffs moved the district court to reconsider its grant of summary judgment under Federal Rule of Civil Procedure 59(e). In their brief in support of this motion, Plaintiffs argued that the district court's ruling as it pertained **[—6—]** to Southern Natural was procedurally erroneous because Plaintiffs did not have an opportunity to supplement their opposition to the defendants' motion under the terms of the case management order. Plaintiffs also attached additional evidence to their brief which they argued supported their claims against both Florida Gas and Southern Natural. This new evidence included Southern Natural's deposition testimony, exhibits offered at Southern Natural's deposition, and Southern Natural's responses to requests for admissions.

The district court denied Plaintiffs' motion for reconsideration as to both Florida Gas and Southern Natural. Plaintiffs now appeal the district court's original order granting summary judgment as well as the district court's order denying reconsideration.

II.

We review grants of summary judgment *de novo*, applying the same standard as the district court. *Templet v. Hyrdochem Inc.*, 367 F.3d 473, 477 (5th Cir. 2004). "The court shall grant summary judgment if the movant shows that there is no genuine dispute as to any material fact and the movant is entitled to judgment as a matter of law." Fed. R. Civ. P. 56(a). "[W]here the nonmovant bears the burden of proof at trial, the movant may merely point to an absence of evidence, thus shifting to the non-movant the burden of demonstrating by competent summary judgment proof that there is an issue of material fact warranting trial. Only when 'there is sufficient evidence favoring the nonmoving party for a jury to return a verdict for that party' is a full trial on the merits warranted." *Lindsey v. Sears Roebuck & Co.*, 16 F.3d 616, 618 (5th Cir. 1994) (quoting *Anderson v. Liberty Lobby, Inc.*, 477 U.S. 242, 249 (1986)) (citations omitted). All reasonable inferences must be viewed in the light most favorable to the party opposing summary judgment, and any doubt must be resolved in favor of the non-moving party. *Matsushita Elec. Indus. Co.* **[—7—]** *v. Zenith Radio Corp.*, 475 U.S. 574, 587 (1986); *Hillman v. Loga*, 697 F.3d 299, 302 (5th Cir. 2012).

Typically, we review a district court's decision on a Rule 59 motion to reconsider for abuse of discretion. *Templet*, 367 F.3d at 477. However, this depends on whether the district court considered materials attached to the motion for reconsideration which were not previously provided to the court when it granted summary judgment. *Id.* (citing *Ford Motor Credit Co. v. Bright*, 34 F.3d 322, 324 (5th Cir. 1994)). "If the materials were considered by the district court, and the district court still grants summary judgment, the appropriate appellate standard of review is *de novo*." *Id.* "However, if the district court

---

the permits issued by United States Army Corps of Engineers . . . ."

[7] The district court denied the defendants' motion to reconsider the order denying their motion to dismiss, holding that dredging of a navigation canal, conducted from a vessel on navigable waters, shows a substantial connection to traditional maritime activity sufficient to support a maritime tort claim. (citing *Sisson v. Ruby*, 497 U.S. 358, 367 (1990) (in addition to "navigation," traditional maritime activities include "at least . . . any other activities traditionally undertaken by vessels, commercial or noncommercial"); *Grubart*, 513 U.S. at 539-40 (dredge and dock company's bridge repair and maintenance work from a vessel on a navigable waterway was substantially related to traditional maritime activity); *In re The V-14813*, 65 F.2d 789, 790 (5th Cir. 1933) ("There are many cases holding that a dredge . . . employed on navigable waters, is subject to maritime jurisdiction . . . .")). The parties do not contest this holding.

refuses to consider the materials, the reviewing court applies the abuse of discretion standard." *Id.* Under an abuse of discretion standard of review, "the district court's decision and decision-making process need only be reasonable." *Id.*

III.

We first address the district court's grant of summary judgment and subsequent **{-463-}** denial of Plaintiffs' motion for reconsideration with respect to Florida Gas. Florida Gas contends that it did not perform any dredging, but rather that its activities were limited to placing a pipeline into an already existing canal. Under our precedent, merely placing pipeline—"pipeline construction and repair"—is insufficient to support a maritime tort claim. *See Louisiana Crawfish*, 772 F.3d at 1029–30, 2 Adm. R. at 376–77. The issue before us on appeal is whether Plaintiffs met their summary judgment burden of demonstrating that a genuine issue of material fact exists as to whether Florida Gas engaged in dredging.

In opposition to Florida Gas's summary judgment motion, Plaintiffs submitted Florida Gas's United States Army Corps of Engineers permit and permit application. Plaintiffs attached additional evidence to their motion for **[—8—]** reconsideration, which included Southern Natural's corporate deposition testimony, a photograph purporting to show the canal in which Florida Gas's pipeline is placed, and a document entitled "Memorandum and Files." Because the district court considered this additional evidence in denying the motion for reconsideration as to Florida Gas, this evidence became part of the summary judgment record. *Templet*, 367 F.3d at 477–79. Therefore, we review *de novo* whether summary judgment was appropriate.[8] *Id.* at 477. We hold that the district court did not err in granting summary judgment in favor of Florida Gas and in subsequently denying Plaintiffs' motion for reconsideration as to Florida Gas.

As a threshold matter, Plaintiffs argue that the district court erred by shifting the summary judgment burden to them because Florida Gas did not submit any evidence in support of its motion for summary judgment. However, Plaintiffs—not Florida Gas—bear the burden to present evidence creating a genuine issue of material fact to defeat summary judgment. *Lindsey*, 16 F.3d at 618 ("[W]here the non-movant bears the burden of proof at trial, the movant may merely point to an absence of evidence, thus shifting to the non-movant the burden of demonstrating by competent summary judgment proof that there is an issue of material fact warranting trial."); *Little v. Liquid Air Corp.*, 37 F.3d 1069, 1075, 1076 n.16 (5th Cir. 1994) (en banc) (noting that the party moving for summary judgment may simply assert the "absence of facts supporting the elements of the plaintiffs' theory of recovery" and need not "negate the existence of facts"); *see also* 10A Charles Alan Wright & Arthur R. Miller, Federal Practice and Procedure § 2727.1 (4th ed. 2016). Plaintiffs bear **[—9—]** the burden of proving their maritime tort claims at trial and therefore bear the burden of demonstrating that Florida Gas dredged the canals in question.

In its summary judgment motion, Florida Gas "point[ed] to" the lack of record evidence that it participated in dredging activities; therefore, Plaintiffs bore the burden of "demonstrating by competent summary judgment proof" that there is a genuine issue of material fact as to whether Florida Gas dredged. *See Lindsey*, 16 F.3d at 618. The evidence submitted by Plaintiffs—either initially in opposition to summary judgment or later attached to their motion for reconsideration—was not sufficient to satisfy this burden.

Plaintiffs argue that Florida Gas's Army Corps of Engineers permit application creates a genuine issue of fact because "[e]very company that dredged canals in the Atchafalaya during this time period was required to obtain a permit like **{-464-}** these." But Florida Gas's application makes no reference to dredging; rather, it only provides for the pipeline to be dropped into an

[8] Both Plaintiffs and Florida Gas agree that the district court considered Plaintiffs' new evidence as to Florida Gas and that the *de novo* standard of review applies.

open, forty-foot-wide canal. Indeed, this application supports Florida Gas's theory that it was seeking permission to drop a pipeline into an *existing* canal—not seeking to dredge a canal.

Likewise, Florida Gas's permit itself does not create a fact issue as to whether Florida Gas dredged the canal in question. The only mention of dredging in Florida Gas's permit is in a list of boilerplate conditions that are not tied to any specific location. These conditions do not show that Florida Gas requested permission to dredge, that it received permission to dredge, or, most critically, that it actually dredged. There is nothing in Florida Gas's permit that defeats summary judgment.[9] **[—10—]**

Plaintiffs contend that Southern Natural's corporate deposition testimony also creates a genuine issue of material fact as to Florida Gas's dredging. Specifically, Plaintiffs argue that Southern Natural's corporate representative testified that if a forty-foot wide canal remained in existence today, that *could* be an indication that the canal had been dredged. Plaintiffs' reliance on this testimony is misplaced because the testimony does not specifically address Florida Gas's pipelines nor does it address whether Florida Gas had conducted any dredging. Further, Plaintiffs have not cited to anything in the record that indicates that Southern Natural's representative had any knowledge of Florida Gas's pipeline construction history.

Plaintiffs also submitted a photograph that they contend shows "an approximately forty-foot wide canal with adjacent spoil banks still in existence today in the fishery, in which FLORIDA's pipeline rests, today." Plaintiffs contend that because this canal exists, Florida Gas, "or someone on its behalf . . . dredged a canal." However, as the district court noted, the photograph is of such poor quality that it is extremely difficult to determine what it depicts. Further, even if the photograph proves the existence of a canal, this does not serve as evidence that Florida Gas dredged the canal. Indeed, Florida Gas has agreed all along that a canal exists; it only contends it did not dredge it.

The final piece of evidence offered by Plaintiffs to defeat summary judgment with respect to Florida Gas is a document entitled "Memorandum for the Files." In this document, a Southern Natural employee purportedly writes that he consulted with an employee from Florida Gas to inquire about the credentials of a dredging contractor Florida Gas had used. Plaintiffs argue **[—11—]** that given the proximity in time between when the memo was produced and when Florida Gas constructed its pipeline at issue in this case, "there is certainly a logical inference to be made that the memo refers to FLORIDA's pipelines at issue in this case." However, as the district court correctly recognized, this document cannot defeat summary judgment as to Florida Gas because the document does **{-465-}** not reference a specific Florida Gas project and there is nothing on the face of the document that connects it to any of the pipelines at issue.[10]

---

9 Plaintiffs also argue that there are "vicinity maps" in Florida Gas's permit that demonstrate there were no pre-existing canals at the time Florida Gas's permit was issued. Plaintiffs argue that if Florida Gas laid its pipeline into an existing canal, the canal would have been depicted on these maps. However, the maps themselves are unclear and it is difficult to discern what they are depicting. Plaintiffs do not offer testimony or other record **[—10—]** evidence to support their assertion that "there are no pre-existing canals depicted" on the maps, much less that Florida Gas dredged canals. Such conjecture, unsupported by competent summary judgment evidence, cannot create a fact issue to defeat summary judgment.

10 In its opinion granting summary judgment, the district court also addressed the deposition testimony of Florida Gas's corporate representative, Dennis Alters. Alters testified that after reviewing Florida Gas's "construction notes . . . foot by foot," there was no mention of any dredging activity. The district court accepted Alters's testimony as "uncontradicted and unimpeached." Plaintiffs argue that because Alters "could only speculate on how the canals came into existence" and did not testify as to what actually happened, Florida Gas "never established that there was no genuine issue of fact as to whether it engaged in dredging." Again, it is Plaintiffs' burden to produce evidence that Florida Gas dredged, not Florida Gas's burden to prove they did not. Despite Alters's testimony, however, Plaintiffs could have

In sum, none of Plaintiffs' evidence creates a genuine issue of material fact as to whether Florida Gas participated in dredging activities. *Little*, 37 F.3d at 1075. Accordingly, we affirm the district court's grant of summary judgment in favor of Florida Gas. Having done so, we also affirm the denial of Plaintiffs' motion for reconsideration as to Florida Gas.

IV.

We turn next to the district court's grant of summary judgment in favor of Southern Natural and its subsequent denial of Plaintiffs' motion for reconsideration as it pertained to Southern Natural. The district court granted summary judgment in favor of Southern Natural because Plaintiffs did not **[—12—]** submit any evidence relating to Southern Natural's dredging activity in opposition to the summary judgment motion. The district court's initial grant of summary judgment in favor of Southern Natural was proper[11]—Southern Natural pointed "to an absence of evidence" supporting Plaintiffs' claims, thus shifting to Plaintiffs "the burden of demonstrating by competent summary judgment proof that there is an issue of material fact warranting trial," a burden Plaintiffs did not satisfy. *Lindsey*, 16 F.3d at 618.

However, we must also determine whether the district court's denial of reconsideration as to Southern Natural was proper in light of the evidence Plaintiffs submitted along with their motion for the district court to reconsider Southern Natural's dismissal. Unlike the district court's review of Plaintiffs' new evidence pertaining to Florida Gas, the district court likely did not consider Plaintiffs' new evidence pertaining to Southern Natural;[12] **{-466-}** therefore, we review the district court's denial of Plaintiffs' Rule 59(e) motion as to Southern Natural for abuse of discretion. *See Luig v. N. Bay Enters, Inc.*, 817 F.3d 901, 905–06 (5th Cir. 2016) (applying the abuse of discretion standard where "[t]he district court likely did not consider [movant's] newly presented **[—13—]** evidence when denying the [Rule] 59(e) motion"). We hold that the district court abused its discretion in denying Plaintiffs' motion for reconsideration as to Southern Natural.

The district court declined to reconsider its grant of summary judgment in favor of Southern Natural despite Plaintiffs providing three types of new evidence upon reconsideration: (1) Southern Natural's deposition transcript; (2) documentary evidence offered during Southern Natural's deposition; and (3) Southern Natural's responses to requests for admission. There are several factors the district court should have considered when determining whether to grant Plaintiffs' motion for reconsideration in light of Plaintiffs' new evidence: (1) the probative value of the evidence; (2) the reason

---

defeated summary judgment as to Florida Gas had they produced evidence that created a genuine issue of material fact as to whether Florida Gas dredged. *See Matsushita Elec. Indus. Co.*, 475 U.S. at 587; *Hillman*, 697 F.3d at 302 ("Doubts are to be resolved in favor of the nonmoving party, and any reasonable inferences are to be drawn in favor of that party." (quoting *Gowesky v. Singing River Hosp. Sys.*, 321 F.3d 503, 507 (5th Cir. 2003)). Plaintiffs have failed to do so, and thus summary judgment as to Florida Gas is appropriate.

[11] Plaintiffs argue that the district court erred in "converting" Southern Natural's motion from a motion to dismiss under Federal Rule of Civil Procedure 12(b)(6) to a motion for summary judgment under Rule 56. However, Southern Natural moved the district court to reconsider its prior dismissal of Southern Natural's motion to dismiss or, alternatively, to grant summary judgment in Southern Natural's favor. To the extent that Plaintiffs argue they did not have adequate notice that the district court could grant summary judgment, the title of the defendants' motion made it clear that Southern Natural and the other defendants were seeking summary judgment.

[12] Plaintiffs contend that the district court considered Southern Natural's responses to Plaintiffs' requests for admissions wherein Southern Natural admitted to dredging. Plaintiffs argue that the district court's opinion "acknowledges the substance and contents" of Southern Natural's responses and therefore the district court "considered" them so as to trigger our *de novo* review. *See Templet*, 367 F.3d at 477. While the district court may have acknowledged the new evidence, it did not consider that evidence under the summary judgment standard, and therefore *de novo* review is inappropriate here.

for Plaintiffs' default; (3) whether the evidence was available to Plaintiffs at the time of the summary judgment motion; and (4) potential prejudice to Southern Natural. *See Luig*, 817 F.3d at 906 (citing *Templet*, 367 F.3d at 478). These factors "are simply illustrative and not exhaustive." *Templet*, 367 F.3d at 482. The district court concluded that all of the additional evidence that Plaintiffs asked the court to consider was "plainly available or easily discovered before summary judgment." We disagree with the district court's analysis, particularly as it pertains to Southern Natural's deposition transcript and responses to requests for admissions.[13] **[—14—]**

Southern Natural's deposition transcript and responses to requests for admissions are clearly probative. The district court granted summary judgment as to Southern Natural because Plaintiffs failed to present evidence that Southern Natural engaged in any dredging activities. In both its deposition and its responses to requests for admissions, Southern Natural candidly admitted that it dredged the canal in question.[14] If the district court would have considered the contents of Southern Natural's **{-467-}** deposition or its admissions, Plaintiffs would have defeated summary judgment as to Southern Natural.[15]

Plaintiffs' reasons for their default also support granting their motion for reconsideration. First, as to Southern Natural's deposition transcript, Plaintiffs had not yet received an official copy of the transcript at the time the district court granted the motion for summary judgment. In evaluating Plaintiffs' motion for reconsideration, the district court faulted Plaintiffs for failing to seek an extension of time to file supplemental briefing after Southern Natural's deposition took place and while Plaintiffs were waiting for an official copy of the transcript. However, no extension of time should have been necessary—Plaintiffs were justified in relying on the deadlines set forth in the **[—15—]** case management order. The case management order allowed Plaintiffs thirty days from the time they received Southern Natural's deposition transcript to file any dispositive motions *or any supplemental oppositions* with the court. However, the district court entered its order granting summary judgment on November 12, 2015—five days *before* Plaintiffs received the official deposition transcript. Plaintiffs submitted their motion for reconsideration along with the new evidence on November 25, 2015—a mere eight days after Plaintiffs received the official transcript and well within the thirty-day timeframe established by the case management order.[16] Contrary to the

[13] In addition to Southern Natural's deposition transcript and responses to requests for admission, Plaintiffs also offered the documentary evidence from Southern Natural's deposition as "new" evidence. Plaintiffs candidly acknowledge in their brief that "all of the deposition exhibits were in [their] possession at the time they originally opposed the summary judgment." Because this evidence was available to Plaintiffs at the time of the summary judgment motion and because Plaintiffs have not presented a satisfactory reason for not coming forward with this evidence at the time their opposition was filed, we conclude the district court did not abuse its discretion in not reconsidering its grant of summary judgment in light of this particular evidence. *See Luig*, 817 F.3d at 906. Further, it is unnecessary to address the deposition exhibits in more detail because we conclude that the district court abused its discretion when it did not reconsider its grant of summary judgment **[—14—]** as to Southern Natural in light of Southern Natural's deposition transcript and responses to request for admissions, which were sufficient to defeat summary judgment.

[14] Notably, Southern Natural does not dispute that it admitted to dredging the canal at issue in its deposition and its responses to requests for admissions. Rather, Southern Natural only contends that the district court did not abuse its discretion in denying Plaintiffs Rule 59(e) motion because Plaintiffs did not present this key evidence to the court in a timely manner.

[15] As we have noted above, the parties do not dispute the district court's holding that dredging of a navigation canal, conducted from a vessel on navigable waters, has a substantial connection to maritime activity sufficient to support a maritime tort claim. *See Grubart*, 513 U.S. at 539. Therefore, Plaintiffs' evidence that Southern Natural dredged would have been sufficient to support their maritime tort claim and defeat summary judgment.

[16] To the extent Southern Natural argues that the thirty-day time period should run from the time that Plaintiffs received the unofficial deposition transcript, this does not change our analysis. Plaintiffs received the unofficial, unsigned draft of

district court's conclusion, Plaintiffs were not required to request an extension of time in order to submit the deposition transcript to the district court.

Second, as to Southern Natural's responses to requests for admissions, the district court faulted Plaintiffs for "failing to immediately move to supplement their opposition when they received [Southern Natural's] responses" three days before the district court's ruling. But the district court failed to recognize that Plaintiffs, relying on the terms of the case management order, had no reason to believe the district court would grant the defendants' motion while Plaintiffs were still awaiting Southern Natural's official deposition transcript.[17] Plaintiffs therefore had no reason to "immediately" **[—16—]** bring Southern Natural's responses to the district court's attention, but rather were justified in waiting for the **{-468-}** transcript so that they could file a single supplemental opposition brief that would include both Southern Natural's deposition transcript and Southern Natural's responses. *See Luig*, 817 F.3d at 907 ("Although the [the movant] likely had access to the evidence presented in the [Rule] 59(e) motion at the time it filed its summary judgment motion, [the movant's] failure to present the evidence was excusable because the district court did not give [the movant] the opportunity to present this evidence before effectively granting summary judgment . . . .").

The third factor—whether the evidence was available to Plaintiffs at the time of the summary judgment motion—also favors Plaintiffs. Southern Natural contends that the case management order limits Plaintiffs' rights to file supplemental materials to those materials that include "factual information learned during the deposition." Southern Natural argues that none of the information Plaintiffs learned at the deposition or from Southern Natural's admissions was new—Plaintiffs had all of the deposition exhibits in their possession for several years before the summary judgment motion and these documents contained evidence that Southern Natural dredged.

We disagree. While it may be true that Plaintiffs had much of the relevant documentary evidence in their possession before Southern Natural moved for summary judgment, the admission made by Southern Natural that the company dredged the pipeline in question was indeed "information learned" by Plaintiffs. An admission by a party carries considerably more weight than inferences drawn from documentary evidence purporting to support a certain fact. Indeed, an admission by a party "is conclusively **[—17—]** established" as fact in the case. Fed. R. Civ. P. 36(b); *see also In re Carney*, 258 F.3d 415, 420 (5th Cir. 2001) ("Rule 36 admissions . . . are conclusive as to the matters admitted, they cannot be overcome at the summary judgement stage . . . ."); 8B Charles Alan Wright & Arthur R. Miller, Federal Practice and Procedure § 2264 (3d ed. 2017) (noting that a Rule 36 admission, "deliberately drafted by counsel for the express purpose of limiting and defining the facts in issue, is traditionally regarded as conclusive"). Plaintiffs did not have Southern Natural's admission before Southern Natural responded to Plaintiffs' requests for admissions and the Southern Natural deposition took place. We therefore conclude that Southern Natural's candid admission that it dredged the pipeline in question is new evidence that was not available to Plaintiffs at the time of the summary judgment motion.

---

the deposition transcript on October 26, 2015. Therefore, Plaintiffs still satisfied the thirty-day requirement when they filed their motion for reconsideration, along with the new evidence, on November 25, 2015.

[17] Plaintiffs were justified in believing that the district court was aware of the case management order and that the district court would abide by the deadlines agreed to by the parties. The case management order was signed by Magistrate Judge Hanna and entered into the case docket. However, in its opinion denying Plaintiffs' motion for reconsideration, the district court noted that "it was unaware" of the case management order. While we do not fault the district court for overlooking the case management order docket entry in this complicated, drawn-out case, the district court should have corrected this oversight upon **[—16—]** Plaintiffs' motion for reconsideration. Plaintiffs should not be punished as a result of the district court's oversight.

Finally, Southern Natural will not be unfairly prejudiced by the district court's consideration of Southern Natural's own admissions and deposition testimony. This is not situation in which Southern Natural was unaware that the evidence at issue existed—the contents of both the deposition testimony and admissions were always known to Southern Natural and within its control. Further, had the district court utilized the case management order, this evidence would have been properly in front of the district court before it granted summary judgment in Southern Natural's favor. *See Luig*, 817 F.3d at 907 (holding that there was no prejudice where, had the district court allowed the moving party the proper opportunity to respond, "the evidence would have been properly in front of the district court").

There are "two important judicial imperatives" relating to a motion for reconsideration: "(1) the need to bring litigation to an end; and (2) the need to render just decisions on the basis of *all* the facts." *Templet,* 367 F.3d at 479 (emphasis added). **{-469-}** Plaintiffs presented new, conclusive evidence in their motion for reconsideration pertaining to Southern Natural that they were **[—18—]** justified in not presenting earlier. The district court's failure to reconsider its grant of summary judgment as to Southern Natural in light of this new evidence amounted to an abuse of discretion. *See Luig*, 817 F.3d at 907.

V.

Accordingly, we AFFIRM the district court's grant of summary judgment and denial of the motion for reconsideration with respect to Florida Gas. With respect to Southern Natural, we REVERSE the district court's denial of Plaintiffs' Rule 59(e) motion and VACATE its grant of summary judgment. We REMAND for further proceedings consistent with this opinion.

United States Court of Appeals for the Fifth Circuit

No. 16-30481

MCBRIDE
vs.
ESTIS WELL SERVICE, L.L.C.

Appeal from the United States District Court for the Western District of Louisiana

Decided: April 10, 2017

Citation: 853 F.3d 777, 5 Adm. R.235 (5th Cir. 2017).

Before **SMITH** and **HAYNES**, Circuit Judges, and **JUNELL**, District Judge.*

* District Judge of the Western District of Texas, sitting by designation.

[—1—] {-779-} **HAYNES**, Circuit Judge:

This consolidated Jones Act and general maritime law case arises out of an accident on a barge in the navigable waterways of Louisiana. The owner of **[—2—]** the barge, Defendant Estis Well Services, L.L.C., appeals from the district court's judgment in favor of plaintiffs Virgie Ann Romero McBride, individually and on behalf of the minor **{-780-}** child I.M.S., and Saul C. Touchet.[1] For the reasons explained below, we AFFIRM.

I. Background

This is the second time this case has come before our court. The first appeal was interlocutory, and we held in an en banc opinion that McBride[2] and Touchet could not recover punitive damages on their Jones Act and general maritime law claims. *See McBride v. Estis Well Service, L.L.C.*, 768 F.3d 382, 2 Adm. R. 320 (5th Cir. 2014) (en banc). The accident in this case and the subsequent claims filed against Estis were previously described in the en banc opinion as follows:

> These consolidated cases arise out of an accident aboard Estis Rig 23, a barge supporting a truck-mounted drilling rig operating in Bayou Sorrell, a navigable waterway in the State of Louisiana. The truck right toppled over, and one crew member, Skye Sonnier, was fatally pinned between the derrick and mud tank, and three others, Saul Touchet, Brian Suire, and Joshua Bourque, have alleged injuries. At the time of the incident, Estis Well Service, L.L.C. ("Estis") owned and operated Rig 23, and employed Sonnier, Touchet, Suire, and Bourque (collectively, the "crew members").
>
> Haleigh McBride, individually, on behalf of Sonnier's minor child, and as administratrix of Sonnier's estate, filed suit against Estis, stating causes of action for **[—3—]** unseaworthiness under general maritime law and negligence under the Jones Act and seeking compensatory as well as punitive damages under both claims. The other crew members filed separate actions against Estis alleging the same causes of action and also requesting compensatory and punitive damages. Upon the crew members' motion, the cases were consolidated into a single action.

Id. at 384, 2 Adm. R. at 320 (footnote omitted).

After we affirmed the district court's judgment dismissing the punitive damages claims, the case went back to the district court, culminating in a week-long bench trial. Prior to trial, Estis conceded liability under both the Jones Act and general maritime law

[1] McBride and Touchet cross-appeal asking this court to reconsider its prior en banc decision in this case holding that punitive damages are not available to the cross-appellants on their Jones Act and general maritime law claims. *See McBride v. Estis Well Service, L.L.C.*, 768 F.3d 382, 2 Adm. R. 320 (5th Cir. 2014) (en banc). As McBride and Touchet both concede, consideration of this claim is foreclosed by our prior en banc decision.

[2] The original named plaintiff, individually and on behalf of I.M.S., was the minor child's biological mother, Haleigh Janee McBride. I.M.S. was subsequently adopted by her maternal grandparents, and Virgie McBride was substituted as the named plaintiff.

claims, but continued to dispute damages and the right to maintenance and cure. The district court made findings of fact and conclusions of law on the record, and it awarded damages to McBride and both damages and cure to Touchet. On McBride's claims, the district court ordered Estis to pay damages for, among other things, loss of past support, loss of future support, and survival damages for pre-death fear and conscious pain and suffering. On Touchet's claims, the district court ordered Estis to pay damages for, among other things, future lost earnings / loss of earning capacity and future medical expenses, and to additionally pay cure until Touchet reaches maximum medical improvement. Estis appeals the district court's judgment on these specific awards. **{–781–}**

II. Standard of Review

When reviewing a judgment from a bench trial, this court reviews the findings of facts for clear error and the legal issues de novo. *Lehmann v. GE Glob. Ins. Holding Corp.*, 524 F.3d 621, 624 (5th Cir. 2008). "Under the clearly erroneous standard, we will reverse only if we have a definite and firm conviction that a mistake has been committed." *Canal Barge Co. v. Torco Oil* **[—4—]** *Co.*, 220 F.3d 370, 375 (5th Cir. 2000). "If the district court made a legal error that affected its factual findings, 'remand is the proper course unless the record permits only one resolution of the factual issue.'" *Ball v. LeBlanc*, 792 F.3d 584, 596 (5th Cir. 2015) (quoting *Pullman-Standard v. Swint*, 456 U.S. 273, 292 (1982)).

III. Discussion

A. McBride's Damages Award

Estis challenges the district court's award of damages to McBride for both pre-death conscious pain and suffering and loss of past and future support. We address each of Estis's arguments in turn.

i. Pre-Death Fear and Conscious Pain and Suffering

Under the Jones Act, a plaintiff can recover damages for pre-death pain and suffering. *De Centeno v. Gulf Fleet Crews, Inc.*, 798 F.2d 138, 141 (5th Cir. 1986). Compensable pain and suffering includes a victim's "emotional injury caused by *fear of physical injury to himself*." *Naquin v. Elevating Boats, L.L.C.*, 744 F.3d 927, 939, 2 Adm. R. 200, 207 (5th Cir. 2014) (quoting *Consol. Rail Corp. v. Gottshall*, 512 U.S. 532, 556 (1994)). However, for a plaintiff to recover for a decedent's pain and suffering, he "must prove, by a preponderance of the evidence, that the decedent was conscious after realizing his danger." *Snyder v. Whittaker Corp.*, 839 F.2d 1085, 1092 (5th Cir. 1988).

Estis argues that the district court erroneously awarded damages for Sonnier's pre-death fear and conscious pain and suffering because objective evidence shows that Sonnier was not conscious after impact and thus did not suffer. The district court awarded a total of $400,000 for pre-death fear and conscious pain and suffering, without further delineating between pre-injury and post-injury survival damages. As a threshold matter, Estis does not challenge the district court's finding of pre-death fear and thus fails to **[—5—]** challenge one of the predicate injuries supporting the damages award. Nevertheless, even if he had challenged the finding of pre-death fear, there is sufficient evidence to support the district court's finding. Eyewitness testimony showed that Sonnier was aware of the danger and running for his life immediately prior to impact, and photographs from the scene showed that his body was positioned in such a way that his left arm was raised in a defensive posture to protect himself.

As to pre-death conscious pain and suffering, the pathologist who performed the autopsy on Sonnier testified that Sonnier could have been conscious and aware for up to five minutes after impact, but was more likely than not conscious for one to two minutes after impact. Moreover, witness testimony claimed that Sonnier was alive and gurgling blood shortly after impact, and the district court appears to have found this testimony credible. Estis's attempt to undermine the credibility of the eyewitness testimony based on prior inconsistent statements is unavailing.

See In re Port Arthur Towing Co., 42 F.3d 312, 318 (5th Cir. 1995) ("[W]eighing conflicting evidence and inference and determining the relative credibility of witnesses to resolve factual disputes is the [factfinder's] province." **{–782–}** (alteration in original) (quoting *Turnage v. Gen. Elec. Co.*, 953 F.2d 206, 207 (5th Cir. 1992))). We therefore hold that the district court's finding that Sonnier was conscious after impact, the only finding challenged relative to this award, was not clearly erroneous.

ii. Loss of Past and Future Support

Estis next argues that the district court erroneously awarded damages for loss of past and future support. The district court found that damages for loss of support were appropriate because the totality of the facts, including testimony from the child's mother and Sonnier's father, showed that Sonnier consistently supported his daughter to the extent he was able to do so. The **[—6—]** district court then relied on expert testimony to determine the amount awarded.

Estis contends that the amount awarded was too speculative and not supported by competent evidence. However, the district court found the methodology used by both experts to be reliable and generally accepted in the fields of vocational rehabilitation and economics, and Estis does not directly challenge this finding or point to evidence that otherwise discredits it. Although Estis asserts that the district court failed to consider Sonnier's earnings at the time of his death, the record clearly shows otherwise. Moreover, the district court limited its consideration of Sonnier's lost future earnings to a potential career path related to Sonnier's prior work experience, while explicitly rejecting more optimistic scenarios as too speculative.

Estis's remaining argument is that an award of damages for loss of support should be limited to the amount awarded in Sonnier's rescinded child support obligation. Estis points to no evidence that Sonnier's support for the child was limited to a terminated child support obligation, and likewise cites no case law, and we are unaware of any, showing that damages for loss of support must be limited to child support obligations.[3] To the contrary, the district court found that Sonnier was a devoted father who was committed to supporting the child to the extent he was able to do so and, except while incarcerated, provided the primary means of support for the child. Estis has not shown that this finding was clearly erroneous. Accordingly, we affirm the judgment as to McBride. **[—7—]**

B. Touchet's Damages and Cure Awards

In challenging the damages and cure awards to Touchet, Estis argues that the district court erred by awarding cure payments for future medical expenses and damages for loss of future wages. We address each argument in turn.

i. Future Medical Expenses

The district court ordered Estis to pay future cure until Touchet reaches maximum medical improvement and $55,185 in future medical expenses beyond Touchet's maximum medical improvement. Estis argues that the $55,185 award for future medical expenses was erroneous because it requires Estis to pay future cure payments for an indefinite period of time. It also seems to argue that the cure payments are erroneous as a matter of law to the extent they continue beyond Touchet's maximum medical improvement. We conclude that **{–783–}** this determination was not reversible error.

"Maintenance and cure is an obligation imposed upon a shipowner to provide for a seaman who becomes ill or injured during his service to the ship." *Boudreaux v. United States*, 280 F.3d 461, 468 (5th Cir. 2002). Maintenance entitles an injured seaman to

---

[3] *See Sea-Land Servs., Inc. v. Gaudet*, 414 U.S. 573, 584–85 (1974) ("Recovery for loss of support . . . includes *all* the financial contributions that the decedent would have made to his dependents had he lived (emphasis added)), *superseded by statute on other grounds*, Longshore and Harbor Workers' Compensation Act Amendments of 1972, Pub. L. No. 92-576, 86 Stat. 1263, *as recognized in Miles v. Apex Marine Corp.*, 498 U.S. 19 (1990).

food and lodging, and cure entitles an injured seaman to reimbursement for medical expenses and proper treatment and care. *Id.* "The maintenance and cure duty terminates only when maximum [medical improvement] has been reached, *i.e.,* 'where it is probable that further treatment will result in no betterment in the claimant's condition.'" *Id.* (quoting *Rashidi v. Am. President Lines*, 96 F.3d 124, 128 (5th Cir. 1996)). When supported by a physician's testimony, it is appropriate for a district court to award future maintenance and cure until the plaintiff reaches maximum medical improvement. *See Lirette v. K & B Boat Rentals, Inc.*, 579 F.2d 968, **[—8—]** 969–70 (5th Cir. 1978). Moreover, a plaintiff can be awarded both cure and tort damages for future medical expenses, so long as no duplication will occur, because the cure obligation is independent of tort law. *Boudreaux*, 280 F.3d at 468–69; *see also Pallis v. United States*, 369 F. App'x 538, 545–46 (5th Cir. 2010)[4] ("It is clear from *Boudreaux* that an award of future medical expenses is not duplicative of cure because the former sounds in tort while the latter is a contractual remedy.").

A review of the record reveals that, contrary to Estis's assertion, the $55,185 award for future medical expenses was not a lump sum future cure payment but rather a damages award for Estis's tort liability. The district court made it clear that cure payments would cease once Touchet reached maximum medical improvement, and medical treatments thereafter would be compensated from the $55,185 award for future medical expenses. Indeed, each time the district court ordered cure payments it explicitly ordered Estis to pay cure, whereas the judgment awarding future medical expenses makes no mention of cure payments.

The future cure payments that the district court did award, however, were limited to paying for a surgical plan of care and continued psychological treatments until Touchet reaches maximum medical improvement. Moreover, the award was appropriately supported by the testimony of Estis's treating physicians. Far from being erroneous, the award for future cure "amounts to little if anything more than a declaration of [Estis's] undoubted duty to pay maintenance [and cure] until [Touchet] attains maximum possible cure, a duty which existed independent of and regardless of the judgment." *See Lirette*, 579 F.2d at 970. **[—9—]**

ii. Future Lost Earnings

Estis argues that the award of damages for lost earnings was clearly erroneous because a video of Touchet actively engaged in crabbing work proves that he was not permanently disabled from offshore work. Touchet's treating physicians testified that Touchet's activities on the video were consistent with his condition but that he was more likely than not permanently disabled from oilfield work. Based on this testimony, the district court found that Touchet was permanently disabled. This factual finding was not clearly erroneous. Accordingly, we affirm the district court's judgment awarding future **{-784-}** cure payments, future medical expenses, and future lost earnings to Touchet.

AFFIRMED.

---

[4] Although *Pallis* is not "controlling precedent," it "may be [cited as] persuasive authority." *Ballard v. Burton*, 444 F.3d 391, 401 n.7 (5th Cir. 2006) (citing 5TH CIR. R. 47.5.4).

United States Court of Appeals for the Fifth Circuit

No. 16-30558

HALLE
VS.
GALLIANO MARINE SERV., L.L.C.

Appeal from the United States District Court for the Eastern District of Louisiana

Decided: April 19, 2017

Citation: 855 F.3d 290, 5 Adm. R. 239 (5th Cir. 2017).

Before **PRADO, HIGGINSON,** and **COSTA,** Circuit Judges.

[—1—] {-292-} PRADO, Circuit Judge:

Plaintiff–Appellant Kyle Halle sued Galliano Marine Service, LLC[1] and C-Innovation, LLC (collectively, "the Defendants") under the Fair Labor Standards Act ("the FLSA" or "the Act") to recover unpaid wages for overtime worked during his employment at C-Innovation. The district court granted summary judgment against Halle because it concluded that Halle qualified as a "seaman" under the FLSA and was thus exempt from the Act's overtime **[—2—]** provisions. Halle appealed. We REVERSE and REMAND this case for further proceedings.

I. FACTUAL AND PROCEDURAL BACKGROUND

On October 30, 2015, Kyle Halle sued the Defendants under the FLSA for unpaid overtime.[2] The Defendants in this case run a remotely operated vehicle ("ROV") business for offshore applications and employed Halle from May 12, 2009, to October 12, 2015, as an ROV Technician and ROV Supervisor.

ROVs are unoccupied mechanical devices used, among other things, to fix, service, and repair offshore, underwater drilling rigs. They are generally used to perform tasks that otherwise could not be performed by human divers because of depth or water conditions. Technicians like Halle navigate and control ROVs aboard an ROV Support Vessel, to which the ROVs remain tethered while in use. ROV Support Vessels serve as "a means of transporting their attached ROVs over water" and are specially outfitted for this purpose. The ROV's "handling system, wench, A-frame, hydraulic power unit[,] vans, and control system" are all welded to the support vessel.

The technicians who steer the ROVs work inside a windowless shipping container converted into an ROV command center located on the support vessel. From there, the ROV Technicians steer and control the ROVs using a video feed and joysticks. Although the ROV command center is located on the support vessel, technicians are not mixed with the support vessel's crew, cannot see whether any navigational issues are affecting the support vessel, and, according to Halle, are considered by the crew to be "passengers" or "third parties." According to Halle, ROV Technicians are subject to a chain of command separate and apart from that of the support vessel. Halle in **[—3—]** particular always reported to C-Innovation's Operations Coordinator and Operations Manager, both of whom are land-based.

Halle's particular duties were dedicated only to ROVs. According to Halle, he took no part in upkeep of the support vessel—he never performed maintenance work like sanding, painting, or chipping the ROV Support Vessel. Rather, the only maintenance work he performed was to the ROVs **{-293-}** themselves. Halle also never steered the support vessel but, in his role as ROV Supervisor, did occasionally relay GPS coordinates from C-Innovation's customers to the support vessel captain either by radio or by pointing to a location on a chart. This process apparently never took more than a few seconds. Despite his knowledge of the support vessel's final destination, Halle had "nothing to do with determining the ROV Support Vessel's path to the intended target, steering, anchoring, making any navigational

[1] Galliano Marine Service is the company responsible for Halle's payroll checks, W-2s, and other payroll documents.

[2] Halle sued on behalf of himself and others who are similarly situated.

decisions[,] or taking any navigational actions."

Halle sued the Defendants on October 30, 2015, for failing to pay him for overtime as purportedly required by the FLSA. The Defendants moved for summary judgment on January 25, 2016, arguing that Halle was exempt from the FLSA's overtime provisions because he qualifies as a "seaman" under the Act. On February 25, 2016, the district court granted the Defendants' motion and dismissed Halle's claim with prejudice. Thereafter, Halle filed a motion for reconsideration, which was denied on April 18, 2016. Halle now appeals.

II. DISCUSSION

"We review a grant of summary judgment de novo, applying the same standard that the district court applied." *Smith v. Reg'l Transit Auth.*, 827 F.3d 412, 417 (5th Cir. 2016). Summary judgment is proper where "the movant shows that there is no genuine dispute as to any material fact and the movant is entitled to judgment as a matter of law." Fed. R. Civ. P. 56(a). In reviewing **[—4—]** a motion for summary judgment, factual inferences are viewed in the light most favorable to the nonmoving party. *Smith*, 827 F.3d at 417.

The FLSA requires employers to provide overtime pay to any employee who works more than forty hours per week unless an exemption from this protection applies. 29 U.S.C. §§ 207, 213; *Coffin v. Blessey Marine Servs., Inc.*, 771 F.3d 276, 279, 2 Adm. R. 367, 368 (5th Cir. 2014). It is the "employer [who] bears the burden to establish a claimed exemption." *Songer v. Dillon Res., Inc.*, 618 F.3d 467, 471 (5th Cir. 2010). This case involves the "seaman" exemption to the FLSA's overtime provision, 29 U.S.C. § 213(b)(6), and presents an issue of first impression: whether ROV Technicians are seamen under the FLSA.

An employee is a seaman when the following criteria are met: "(1) the employee is subject to the authority, direction, and control of the master; and (2) the employee's service is primarily offered to aid the vessel as a means of transportation, provided that the employee does not perform a substantial amount of different work." *Coffin*, 771 F.3d at 281, 2 Adm. R. at 370 (citing 29 C.F.R. § 783.31). Per Department of Labor ("DOL") regulations,[3] "work other than seaman work becomes substantial if it occupies more than 20 percent of the time worked by the employee during the workweek."[4] *Id.* at 279–80, 2 Adm. R. at 369 (citing 29 C.F.R. § 783.37). This Court must "evaluate an employee's duties based upon the character of the work he actually performs and not on what it is called or the place where it is performed." *Id.* at 280, 2 Adm. R. at 369 (citing 29 C.F.R. § 783.33). Because "what each employee actually does" determines how the FLSA applies to him, "application of the **{-294-}** seaman exemption generally depends on the facts in each case." *Id.*, 2 Adm. R. at 369. **[—5—]**

A. The FLSA and Jones Act

We first reiterate a concept long-recognized by this Court: the definition of "seaman" in the Jones Act[5] is not equivalent to that in the FLSA. *Petroleum Treaters*, 876 at 520. The two acts are "separate and independent of each other." *Id.* While the Jones Act interprets seaman "broadly to maximize the scope of the remedial coverage," the exemptions under the FLSA "have been drawn narrowly . . . to minimize the number of employees who lose the Act's protections." *Id.* at 522–23. *Compare Barrett v. Chevron, U.S.A., Inc.*, 781 F.2d 1067, 1070 (5th Cir. 1986) (describing the "expansive interpretation" given to the word "seaman" in the Jones Act), *with Brennan v. Greene's Propane Gas Serv., Inc.*, 479 F.2d 1027, 1032 (5th Cir. 1973) (noting how

[3] Although not binding, this Court has stated repeatedly that these regulations are "entitled to great weight." *Coffin*, 771 F.3d at 279, 2 Adm. R. at 369; *accord Dole v. Petroleum Treaters, Inc.*, 876 F.2d 518, 521 (5th Cir. 1989).

[4] As this Court has recognized, however, strict application of the twenty percent rule is not necessary. *Coffin*, 771 F.3d at 284 n.5, 2 Adm. R. at 373 n.5.

[5] The Jones Act is a maritime statute that "provides a cause of action in negligence for 'any seaman' injured 'in the course of his employment.'" *Chandris, Inc. v. Latsis*, 515 U.S. 347, 354 (1995) (quoting 46 U.S.C. § 30104).

exemptions to the FLSA are construed narrowly against the employer). Given these differences, it is error for a court to resolve an FLSA case by resorting to legal standards, such as the definition of a "seaman" or an "appurtenance," from Jones Act caselaw.

B. Application

As explained above, the test for whether someone is employed as a seaman involves two prongs. *See Coffin*, 771 F.3d at 281, 2 Adm. R. at 370. The first prong asks whether the employee performs as "master or subject to the authority, direction, and control of the master aboard a vessel." 29 C.F.R. § 783.31. Here, the district court seemingly equated the ROVs with "vessels" and concluded that Halle's "direct[ion]" and "command" of the ROVs satisfied this element. But there is no evidence to suggest that the ROVs are vessels. The only "vessel" in this case is the ROV Support Vessel. And according to Halle's sworn declaration, he was not subject to the support vessel's chain of command and **[—6—]** did not report to the support vessel's captain. Contrarily, another employee submitted an affidavit attesting that Halle did report to the captain. This competing testimonial evidence precludes summary judgment as to prong one.

The second prong asks whether the "employee's service is primarily offered to aid the vessel as a means of transportation." *Coffin*, 771 F.3d at 281, 2 Adm. R. at 370 (citing 29 C.F.R. § 783.31). Because we find it dispositive in this case, the second prong will be the focus of our analysis. This inquiry concentrates on the duties of an employee. *See* 29 C.F.R. § 783.31; *Coffin*, 771 F.3d at 280, 2 Adm. R. at 369. In accordance with DOL regulations, this Court focuses on whether the employee's duties "primarily . . . aid in the operation of [the] vessel as a means of transportation." 29 C.F.R. § 783.31. We have intimated that the critical issue in analyzing this prong is determining whether the "primary purpose" of the particular individual's work is safe navigation of the ship. *Compare Owens v. SeaRiver Mar., Inc.*, 272 F.3d 698, 703–04 (5th Cir. 2001) (concluding that when the primary purpose of a tankerman's job is "get[ting] cargo on or off the barge," he is not a seaman), *with Coffin*, 771 F.3d at 283–84, 2 Adm. R. at 371–73 (finding that vessel-based tankermen responsible for constant monitoring of barges to ensure safe navigation were seamen).

This Court's decision in *Walling v. W. D. Haden Co.*, 153 F.2d 196 (5th Cir. 1946), is particularly instructive. In *W. D. Haden*, employees engaged in dredging shell deposits **{–295–}** were stationed on a dredge boat for months at a time. *Id.* at 197. In order to harvest shells from the ocean floor, dredgemen operated machinery attached to the dredge boat that would "cut[] up the shell deposit from the reef[,] suck[] it up[,] and deliver[] it upon a barge tied alongside the dredge." *Id.* Other than the actual labor of dredging, dredgemen also stood watch and managed anchor cables and barge lines while on duty. *Id.* at 199. Even though the Court recognized the dredgemen were involved in some work of the "nautical kind," it found that the "dominant employment [was] clearly **[—7—]** the industrial one, the production of shells." *Id.* In reaching its conclusion that the dredgemen were not seamen under the FLSA, this Court characterized the maritime work done by these employees as "incidental and occasional" because it took up only a "small fraction of the work time." *Id.*; *see also McKie v. Diamond Marine Co.*, 104 F. Supp. 275, 276–77 (S.D. Tex. 1952).

Halle's work here is similar to that of the dredgemen in *W. D. Haden*. Like the dredgemen, who lived on the dredge boat and operated machinery attached to the boat to do industrial work, Halle lives on the ROV Support Vessel and operates the attached ROVs in the water to complete industrial tasks. Although Halle occasionally communicates GPS coordinates to the captain of the support vessel, he does not otherwise help ensure that the support vessel navigates safely or even in any particular manner from point A to point B. ROV Technicians do not control the "path to the intended target, steer[], anchor[], mak[e] any navigational decisions or tak[e] any navigational actions." In fact, they apparently cannot even "see if there [are] navigational issues affecting the ROV Support Vessel."

The Defendants argue that because the ROVs are attached to the ROV Support Vessel, any navigation, maintenance, service, and repair of those vehicles is essentially done to the vessel itself. But no case law affirmatively supports this position. If anything, *W. D. Haden* seems to contradict this argument. Like the dredge machinery in *W. D. Haden*, which was located on the dredge boat, the ROVs are located on the support vessel. Although certain components of the ROV system are structurally welded to the vessel, the ROVs themselves appear to only be connected temporarily by tethers. This seems analogous to dredging operations where a dredge boat, which carries the dredging machinery, is towed by a tug or vessel. *See W. D. Haden*, 153 F.2d at 197; *McKie*, 104 F. Supp. at 276. Thus, because this Court has not done so in comparable situations, we decline to now equate maintenance, repair, or **[—8—]** navigation of superficially attached machinery (here, the ROVs) with maintenance, repair, or navigation of the support vessel. *Cf. Marshall v. Woods Hole Oceanographic Inst.*, 458 F. Supp. 709, 711, 716, 719 (D. Mass. 1978) (holding that scientific crew members engaged in oceanographic research aboard a vessel—whose mission was scientific and which was specially designed and outfitted with equipment to support that mission—were not employed as seamen because they did not perform duties relevant to maintenance and navigation of the ship itself).

In its order denying Halle's request for reconsideration, the district court relied primarily on *Coffin* to reaffirm its conclusion that Halle is a seaman. In *Coffin*, tankermen were responsible for both loading and unloading barges while the tug boat was docked as well as performing other barge duties while the vessel was in motion. 771 F.3d at 278 & n.3, 2 Adm. R. at 368 & n.3. Although this Court had previously concluded in *Owens* that loading and unloading barges was generally not seaman work, it noted that the duties of the vessel-based tankermen **{-296-}** in *Coffin* were distinct. *Id.* at 280–82, 2 Adm. R. at 369–72. Unlike the tankermen in the earlier *Owens* case, the tankermen in *Coffin* spent a significant portion of their time on the vessel performing loading and unloading duties during transit—i.e., inspecting and maintaining the barges to make "the captain's job [of navigating the ship] easier." *Id.* at 283–84, 2 Adm. R. at 371–72. We concluded that because the tankermen spent such a substantial portion of their time performing these duties aboard the ship to ensure the ship's safe navigation, the tankermen were seamen under the FLSA. *Id.* at 284–85, 2 Adm. R. at 372–74.

But the facts in this case are acutely distinct from those in *Coffin*. It is true that both the tankermen in *Coffin* and the ROV Technicians in this case live and work on a vessel. But the similarities end there. While the tankermen in *Coffin* were members of the ship's crew and answered to the captain, the ROV Technicians here have a completely separate command structure. Unlike **[—9—]** the tankermen in *Coffin*, who spent a significant portion of their work time performing tasks that helped the captain safely navigate the ship and attached barges, the ROV Technicians do not assist with nearly any part of navigation. The only role the ROV Technicians seem to have in navigation is the occasional communication of coordinates to the captain of the support vessel.

While giving coordinates alone can perhaps be characterized as contributing to navigation, the question this Court must then answer is what proportion of Halle's time is spent on that seaman's work. *See Coffin*, 771 F.3d at 279–80, 2 Adm. R. at 369 (recognizing that an employee is not a seaman if his nonseaman's work becomes substantial—i.e., it occupies more than approximately 20% of the employee's time). Based on the description of Halle's work responsibilities, it seems that transmitting the coordinates, and even the entire process of calculating those coordinates, does not take up a demonstrable majority of his work time. ROV Technicians control ROVs remotely to provide "emergency backup for underwater drilling operations[,] . . . turn subsea valves, disconnect and realign underwater lines, inspect underwater structures, and place marking beacons on the sea floor." They are also responsible for maintaining and servicing the ROVs themselves. Even assuming that it takes an ROV Technician several hours every few days to calculate coordinates[6] and then a few additional minutes to communicate that information to the captain of the support vessel, this does not clearly account for 80% of the estimated eighty-four plus hours worked weekly by ROV Technicians. Accordingly, the district court erred in granting the Defendant's motion for summary judgment as it has not been established as a matter of law that the seaman exemption applies. **[—10—]**

III. CONCLUSION

For the foregoing reasons, we REVERSE the district court's summary judgment and REMAND this case for further proceedings.

---

[6] To be clear, nothing in the record suggests that Halle was actually responsible for calculating the GPS coordinates for the ROV Support Vessel's next destination; rather, it seems that he simply passed along the coordinates from C-Innovation to the support vessel captain.

United States Court of Appeals
for the Fifth Circuit

No. 16-40059

DAVIS
VS.
DYNAMIC OFFSHORE RESOURCES, L.L.C.

Appeal from the United States District Court for the Southern District of Texas

Decided: May 12, 2017

Citation: 865 F.3d 235, 5 Adm. R. 244 (5th Cir. 2017).

Before **JONES, CLEMENT,** and **ELROD,** Circuit Judges.

[—1—] {–235–} CLEMENT, Circuit Judge:

Dynamic Offshore Resources LLC ("Dynamic") owns and operates offshore platforms in the Gulf of Mexico. Thomas Davis, a crane mechanic employed by Gulf Crane Services, was allegedly injured during a personnel-basket transfer to Dynamic's 86A platform. No Dynamic employees were present at the 86A platform. Independent contractors employed the lead operator, the crane operator, and all other workers on the platform. Davis brought suit against Dynamic for negligence and gross negligence. The district court granted summary judgment to Dynamic, holding that it was not vicariously liable for the alleged negligence of its independent contractors. **[—2—]** Davis appeals the district court's grant of summary judgment to Dynamic. We AFFIRM.

I

On March 26, 2013, a Gulf Crane employee told Davis that a winch on a crane on Dynamic's 86B platform had not passed inspection and needed to be replaced. A new winch was located at the 86A platform. When Davis arrived by boat at the 86A platform, an equipment transfer basket lowered the winch into the boat. Another worker was lowered into the boat via personnel-basket transfer and informed **{–236–}** Davis that they were going to change the winch at the 86B platform.

Davis decided to delay replacing the winch because of safety concerns related to wind. Davis's "stop work authority" authorized him to stop work "at all times." He needed to inform Dynamic's foreman, who was on another platform, of his decision to delay the work. Instead of contacting the foreman by radio from the boat, Davis asked the crane operator to transport him to the 86A platform via personnel basket so he could call the foreman privately from the phone located on the platform.

As Davis was being lifted, the personnel basket suddenly dropped six to eight feet. Davis testified at his deposition that the drop occurred because the crane operator swung the personnel basket *into* the wind when he should have swung it *with* the wind. After the drop, the crane operator continued the transfer until Davis was on the 86A platform. Davis testified that he immediately "felt pain in [his] shoulder, [his] back, [his] knees" after the drop.

II

This court reviews *de novo* an order granting summary judgment, "applying the same standard as the district court." *Vela v. City of Houston*, 276 F.3d 659, 666 (5th Cir. 2001). Summary judgment is appropriate "if the movant **[—3—]** shows that there is no genuine dispute as to any material fact and the movant is entitled to judgment as a matter of law.'" Fed. R. Civ. P. 56(a).

III

"It is well established that a principal is not liable for the activities of an independent contractor committed in the course of performing its duties under the contract." *Bartholomew v. CNG Producing Co.*, 832 F.2d 326, 329 (5th Cir. 1987). Louisiana law recognizes two exceptions to this general rule: (1) "a principal may not escape liability arising out of ultrahazardous activities which are contracted out to an independent contractor"; and (2) "a principal is liable for the acts of an independent contractor if he exercises operational control over those acts or expressly or impliedly authorizes an unsafe practice." *Id.* There are two issues on appeal: (1) whether personnel-basket transfers are ultrahazardous activity; and (2) whether Dynamic authorized an unsafe working condition.

First, personnel-basket transfers are not ultrahazardous activity because they "require substandard conduct to cause injury." *Ainsworth v. Shell Offshore, Inc.*, 829 F.2d 548, 550 (5th Cir. 1987). Evidence that the transfer was made in high winds is irrelevant to whether personnel-basket transfers are ultrahazardous. "Whether an activity qualifies as ultrahazardous under the Louisiana doctrine is a question of law." *Hawkins v. Evans Cooperage Co.*, 766 F.2d 904, 907 (5th Cir. 1985). Louisiana law considers only whether an activity is *per se* ultrahazardous, not whether an activity in *specific* conditions is ultrahazardous. *See, e.g., id.*; *O'Neal v. Int'l Paper Co.*, 715 F.2d 199, 201–02 (5th Cir. 1983). Davis's counsel conceded at oral argument that a personnel basket transfer is not "in and of itself" ultrahazardous. We agree. *See, e.g., Newman v. KMJ Servs., Inc.*, No. 04-2518, 2006 WL 3469563, at *2 (E.D. La. Nov. 30, 2006) (holding that personnel-basket transfers are not ultrahazardous). **[—4—]**

Second, we hold that Dynamic did not authorize an unsafe working condition. If "work is done in an unsafe manner, the [principal] will be liable if he has expressly or impliedly authorized the *particular manner* which will render the work unsafe, and not otherwise." **{–237–}** *Ewell v. Petro Processors of La., Inc.*, 364 So.2d 604, 606–07 (La. App. 1st Cir. 1978) (emphasis added). Davis presented evidence that, on the day of the accident, Dynamic's foreman ordered Davis to replace the crane winch on Dynamic's 86B platform. But Davis does not present any evidence that Dynamic ordered him to make a personnel-basket transfer to the 86A platform in high winds. To the contrary, it is undisputed that Davis *requested* a personnel-basket transfer to the 86A platform. Davis admitted at his deposition that he could have exercised his stop work authority if he "felt it too unsafe to do that transition from the platform to the boat to the 86A [platform]." Dynamic was "entitled to rely on the expertise of its independent contractor" in operating the personnel-basket transfers. *Hawkins*, 766 F.2d at 908. Dynamic did not have the duty to supervise to ensure that its "independent contractor performs its obligations in a reasonably safe manner." *Id.* Even accepting Davis's evidence as true and viewing it in the light most favorable to him, Dynamic did not *authorize*—either expressly or impliedly—an unsafe working condition that caused injury to Davis.

IV

We AFFIRM the judgment of the district court.

United States Court of Appeals
for the Fifth Circuit

No. 16-30717

IN RE DEEPWATER HORIZON

Appeal from the United States District Court for the Eastern District of Louisiana

Decided: May 12, 2017

Citation: 857 F.3d 246, 5 Adm. R. 246 (5th Cir. 2017).

Before **DAVIS, CLEMENT,** and **COSTA,** Circuit Judges.

[—2—] {-248-} DAVIS, Circuit Judge:

Appellant Crystal Seafood Company, Inc. appeals a district court order holding Crystal and two of its officers (the Trans) jointly and severally liable for a $1,034,228.42 payment that Crystal received pursuant to the BP settlement.[1] For the reasons set out below, we AFFIRM. **{-249-}**

I.

In 2013, the district court appointed a Special Master to examine and investigate suspicious past or pending claims submitted to the Deepwater Horizon Economic Claims Center ("DHECC"). The district court further ordered the Special Master to initiate legal action to "clawback" any already paid fraudulent claims.

In 2015, the Special Master and the Claims Administrator filed a joint clawback motion seeking to recoup $1,034,228.42 that the DHECC paid to Crystal Seafood Company, Inc. In order to obtain this $1,034,228.42, Crystal was required to and did swear, *inter alia*, that it did not constitute a "failed business" under the terms of the settlement agreement. The Special Master and the Claims Administrator alleged that this misstatement constituted fraud, and sought to have the district court order Crystal and any individuals who benefitted from Crystal's misstatement to remit the full $1,034,228.42 to the DHECC. **[—3—]**

On May 24, 2016, the district court granted the clawback motion without a hearing, holding that there is no genuine dispute of material fact that Crystal was a failed business under the terms of the settlement agreement and that Crystal's sworn statement to the contrary constituted fraud. The district court then went on to pierce Crystal's corporate veil and hold two of Crystal's officers, Loc "Victor" Tran and Christopher Tran, jointly and severally liable with Crystal for the $1,034,228.42 owed.

Crystal—and only Crystal—now appeals.

II.

Pursuant to the settlement agreement, we review the district court's grant of a clawback motion without a hearing as a grant of summary judgment. We review a district court's grant of summary judgment *de novo*, viewing all facts and drawing all inferences in a light most favorable to the non-moving party.[2] Summary judgment is proper when there is "no genuine dispute as to any material fact and the movant is entitled to judgment as a matter of law."[3]

III.

We treat a DHECC clawback motion as a common law fraud claim brought under general maritime law. To prove common law fraud, the Special Master and the Claims Administrator must establish: (1) that the claimant knowingly or recklessly (2) made a material misrepresentation (3) that he intended to be acted upon, and was in fact acted upon, to the detriment of the DHECC.[4]

Crystal alleges that there is, at a minimum, a genuine dispute of material fact as to the first and second elements. We address each below. **[—4—]**

---

1 For a brief history of the events leading up to the BP settlement, *see generally In re Deepwater Horizon*, 732 F.3d 326, 329, 1 Adm. R. 287, 287 (5th Cir. 2013).

2 *Burell v. Prudential Ins. Co. of Am.*, 820 F.3d 132, 136 (5th Cir. 2016).

3 Fed. R. Civ. P. 56(a).

4 *See In re Deepwater Horizon*, 643 F. App'x 377, 381 (5th Cir. 2016) (unpublished).

A.

We first consider whether Crystal made a material misrepresentation.

The settlement agreement defines a failed business as, *inter alia*, a business that subsequent to May 1, 2010, but prior to December 31, 2011: (1) ceased operations and wound down, or (2) initiated or completed a liquidation of substantially all of its assets. **{-250-}**

Crystal is a shrimp processor. It buys shrimp, processes them, and sells them for redistribution.

In terms of operations, it is undisputed that Crystal processed the last of its shrimp approximately one year before the oil spill, in April or May 2009. It is also undisputed that Crystal sold the last of its frozen inventory approximately three months after the oil spill, in August 2010.

In terms of liquidation, it is undisputed that Crystal submitted profit and loss statements to the DHECC—under oath—illustrating that Crystal stopped taking a depreciation expense[5] on its processing equipment the month of the oil spill, in May 2010. It is also undisputed that Crystal submitted tax returns to both the DHECC and the Internal Revenue Service ("IRS")—under oath—representing that Crystal "disposed" of all of its assets on or before December 31, 2010.

Based upon this information, the district court held that Crystal was a failed business and was therefore ineligible for the $1,034,228.42 that it received. This finding was, again, based upon Crystal's own sworn statements. Crystal took a depreciation expense in every month prior to May 2010—therefore, the district court held that Crystal initiated a liquidation of substantially all of its assets subsequent to May 1, 2010. Crystal "disposed" of **[—5—]** all of its assets on or before December 31, 2010—therefore, the district court held that Crystal completed a liquidation of substantially all of its assets prior to December 31, 2011.

Crystal attacks its own 2010 tax returns on two grounds. First, it provides the affidavit of Victor Tran. Tran attests that Crystal "continues to own . . . well more than a million dollars" worth of processing equipment and implies that Crystal's 2010 tax returns were in error. It is, nonetheless, well-established that a non-movant "cannot create a genuine issue of fact sufficient to survive summary judgment simply by contradicting his or her own previous sworn statement . . . without explaining the contradiction or attempting to resolve the disparity."[6] Tran's implicit assertion that Crystal's 2010 tax returns were in error—without further explanation—does not raise a genuine dispute of material fact.[7]

Second, Crystal asserts that its new lawyer, who was retained after the district court granted the now-contested clawback motion, has learned that Crystal's accountant made some mistakes on Crystal's 2010 tax returns. Specifically, some of the equipment listed as "disposed," Crystal continues to own. Crystal did not raise this **{-251-}** argument in the district court. We therefore decline to address it, "keeping with our precedent that arguments not raised **[—6—]** before the

[5] 26 U.S.C. § 167(a) allows corporations such as Crystal to reduce their taxable income a reasonable allowance for the exhaustion, wear and tear, and obsolescence of property used in the trade or business.

[6] *Cleveland v. Policy Mgmt. Sys. Corp.*, 526 U.S. 795, 806 (1999); *see also S.W.S. Erectors, Inc. v. Infax, Inc.*, 72 F.3d 489, 495 (5th Cir. 1996) (same).

[7] Because Victor Tran's affidavit does not raise a genuine dispute of material fact pursuant to *Cleveland*, we need not address the district court's reliance on *Scott v. Harris*, 550 U.S. 372, 380 (2007) (holding that "[w]hen opposing parties tell two different stories, one of which is blatantly contradicted by the record, so that no reasonable jury could believe it, a court should not adopt that version of the facts for purposes of ruling on a motion for summary judgment"), and *Bartucci v. Jackson*, No. 04-2977, 2006 WL 2631925, at *5 (E.D. La. Sept. 13, 2006) (noting that "while many courts have accepted a plaintiff's own affidavit, deposition, or verified pleadings to defeat summary judgment, a number of courts have rejected this proof when the plaintiff's statements are self-serving and conclusory").

district court are waived and cannot be raised for the first time on appeal."[8]

Crystal materially misrepresented itself as an ongoing business when it filed its claim in 2012. With respect to that point, there is no genuine dispute of material fact.

B.

In order to satisfy the scienter element of common law fraud, the Special Master and the Claims Administrator must establish that Crystal knew or should have known that it was a failed business when it filed its claim in 2012. "While the term recklessness is not self-defining, the common law has generally understood it in the sphere of civil liability as conduct violating an objective standard: action entailing an unjustifiably high risk of harm that is either known or so obvious that it should be known."[9] "A person's state of mind is rarely susceptible of proof by direct evidence, so specific intent to defraud may be, and most often is, inferred from the totality of the circumstances, including indirect and circumstantial evidence."[10] That inference, pursuant to our precedent, can be drawn not only as a matter of fact, but also as a matter of law.

For example, in *Brown v. Parker Drilling Offshore Corp.*, we inferred that Brown intentionally concealed prior back problems on a pre-employment medical questionnaire, even though Brown argued that he did not believe that his prior back problems constituted what the questionnaire described as "back trouble."[11] The evidence established that Brown well-understood that his prior back problems constituted "back trouble."[12] In fact, one of Brown's previous **[—7—]** employers—not Parker Drilling—had fired him for failing to disclose his prior "back trouble" on a pre-employment medical questionnaire.[13] We therefore held that Brown intentionally concealed his prior back problems "as a matter of law."[14]

Similarly, in *Meche v. Doucet*, we inferred that Meche intentionally concealed prior spinal injuries on a pre-employment medical questionnaire, even though Meche argued that he did not consider "his pre-existing condition to be a matter of importance."[15] Meche had "sustained three prior work-related low back and neck" injuries, for which he "received disability payments and sued his former employers."[16] We therefore held that "Meche intentionally concealed his prior [spinal] injuries as a matter of law."[17]

Crystal argues that we should view this appeal through the lens of "a small family business with unsophisticated owners trying to maneuver a complex claims process **{–252–}** to save their livelihood." However, like in *Meche*, "the record does not establish [that either Victor or Christopher Tran] lacked the literacy skills necessary to read and review" the forms and documents that Crystal submitted to the DHECC.[18]

Ultimately, it is undisputed that Crystal: (1) processed the last of its shrimp approximately one year before the oil spill, in April or May 2009; (2) sold the last of its frozen inventory approximately three months after the oil spill, in August 2010; (3) stopped taking a depreciation expense the month of the oil spill, in May 2010; and (4) submitted tax returns to both the DHECC and the IRS representing that it "disposed" of all of its assets on or before **[—8—]** December 31, 2010. Guided by this mountain of circumstantial evidence, we, like the district court, conclude that the Special Master and the Claims Administrator have proven scienter as a matter of law. Crystal either knew or should have known that it was a failed business when it filed its claim in 2012.

---

[8] *LeMaire v. La. Dep't of Transp. & Dev.*, 480 F.3d 383, 387 (5th Cir. 2007).

[9] *Safeco Ins. Co. of Am. v. Burr*, 551 U.S. 47, 68 (2007) (internal quotations omitted).

[10] *United States v. Philip Morris USA Inc.*, 566 F.3d 1095, 1118 (D.C. Cir. 2009).

[11] 410 F.3d 166, 172–75 (5th Cir. 2005).

[12] *See id.* at 172–173.

[13] *See ibid.*

[14] *Id.* at 174.

[15] 777 F.3d 237, 241, 3 Adm. R. 264, 265 (5th Cir.), *cert. denied*, 136 S. Ct. 111 (2015).

[16] *Id.* at 247, 3 Adm. R. at 269.

[17] *Id.* at 248, 3 Adm. R. at 270.

[18] *See ibid.*, 3 Adm. R. at 270.

IV.

Lastly, Crystal argues that the district court erred in holding Victor and Christopher Tran personally liable. Because the Trans have not sought to appeal the judgment of the district court, and because Crystal has not identified a genuine obstacle preventing the Trans from filing their own appeal, we hold that Crystal lacks standing to champion the rights of the Trans.

"The doctrine of standing asks whether a litigant is entitled to have a federal court resolve his grievance."[19] "Whether a party has standing to appeal 'involves both constitutional limitations on federal-court jurisdiction and prudential limitations on its exercise.'"[20] Constitutionally, the right to lodge an appeal in federal court is reserved to those who have "suffered an injury in fact, thus giving [them] a sufficiently concrete interest in the outcome of the issue in dispute."[21] This "flows from Article III's case-or-controversy requirement," and we assume that Crystal has suffered such an injury for purposes of this appeal.[22]

Prudentially, the right to lodge an appeal in federal court is generally reserved to those who seek to protect their "own legal rights and interests."[23] **[—9—]** However, this prudential limitation, unlike its constitutional counterpart, is not absolute. An appellant can protect the rights and interests of a third-party so long as it can make two showings. First, the appellant must establish that it and the third party have "a close relation,"[24] such that "their interests coincide."[25] The whole purpose **{–253–}** behind this "'close relation' factor is to ensure that the [appellant] will act as an effective advocate for the" party whose interests it seeks to represent.[26] Second, the appellant must identify a "genuine obstacle"[27] preventing the third party from "protect[ing] his or her own interests."[28] Relevant here, "[a] simple lack of motivation does not constitute a 'genuine obstacle' to asserting an interest" on appeal.[29]

The Trans apparently "do not wish" to contest the judgment of the court below.[30] Even nonparties—to the extent that the Trans are nonparties[31]—can intervene after a judgment has been rendered, so long as intervention does not prejudice the rights of the existing parties or substantially interfere with the orderly processes of the district court.[32] What is more, Crystal has failed to **[—10—]** even brief standing, which it has the burden to establish,[33] and which we lack the

---

[19] *Kowalski v. Tesmer*, 543 U.S. 125, 128 (2004).

[20] *Rohm & Hass Tex., Inc. v. Ortiz Bros. Insulation*, 32 F.3d 205, 208 (5th Cir. 1994) (quoting *Warth v. Seldin*, 422 U.S. 490, 498 (1975)).

[21] *Powers v. Ohio*, 499 U.S. 400, 411 (1991) (internal quotations omitted).

[22] *See Kowalsi*, 543 U.S. at 129 ("Instead, we shall assume the attorneys have satisfied Article III and address the alternative threshold question whether they have standing to raise the rights of others.").

[23] *See ibid.* (quoting *Warth*, 422 U.S. at 499).

[24] *Powers*, 499 U.S. at 411.

[25] *Wauchope v. U.S. Dep't of State*, 985 F.2d 1407, 1411 (9th Cir. 1993); *see also Powers*, 499 U.S. at 414 (discussing the "congruence of interests"); *Harris v. Evans*, 20 F.3d 1118, 1123 (11th Cir. 1994) (same).

[26] *Lepelletier v. F.D.I.C.*, 164 F.3d 37, 43 (D.C. Cir. 1999) (some internal quotations omitted) (citing *Singleton v. Wulff*, 428 U.S. 106, 114–15 (1976)).

[27] *Singleton*, 428 U.S. at 116.

[28] *Powers*, 499 U.S. at 411.

[29] *Viceroy Gold Corp. v. Aubry*, 75 F.3d 482, 489 (9th Cir. 1996).

[30] *Singleton*, 428 U.S. at 114.

[31] To the extent that Victor and Christopher Tran are nonparties, they may be able to challenge any attempt to enforce this portion of the district court's order. *See Taylor v. Sturgell*, 553 U.S. 880, 884 (2008) ("[O]ne is not bound by a judgment *in personam* in a litigation in which he is not designated as a party or to which he has not been made a party by service of process.").

[32] *Stallworth v. Monsanto Co.*, 558 F.2d 257, 266 (5th Cir. 1977) (internal quotations omitted); *see also* Fed. R. Civ. P. 24; *Baker v. Wade*, 769 F.2d 289, 296–97 (5th Cir. 1985) (en banc) (noting that a nonparty can only intervene if it "had no notice of the action" in the district court and the other parties do not oppose its intervention on appeal), *abrogated on other grounds by Lawrence v. Texas*, 539 U.S. 558 (2003).

[33] *Amato v. Wilentz*, 952 F.2d 742, 750 (3d Cir. 1991) (noting that the party claiming third party

right to infer.[34] For all of these reasons, we hold that Crystal lacks standing to champion the rights of the Trans.

V.

The judgment of the district court is AFFIRMED.

standing has the burden to "establish . . . third party standing"); *cf. also Sierra Club v. Babbitt*, 995 F.2d 571, 575 (5th Cir. 1993) ("Where standing to appeal is at issue, appellants must demonstrate some injury from the judgment below.").

[34] *See FW/PBS, Inc. v. City of Dallas*, 493 U.S. 215, 231 (1990) ("It is a long-settled principle that standing cannot be inferred argumentatively from averments in the pleadings, but rather must affirmatively appear in the record.").

United States Court of Appeals for the Fifth Circuit

No. 15-30811

KOCH
vs.
UNITED STATES

Appeal from the United States District Court for the Eastern District of Louisiana

Decided: May 12, 2017

Citation: 857 F.3d 267, 5 Adm. R. 251 (5th Cir. 2017).

Before **JONES, DENNIS,** and **PRADO,** Circuit Judges.

[—1—] {-269-} DENNIS, Circuit Judge:

Plaintiff Ricky Koch fell and suffered personal injuries while aboard the *S.S. Altair*, a public vessel owned by the United States and operated by its agents. Koch, a 54 year-old foreman and employee of Economy Iron Works, was inspecting the vessel in connection with his employer's bidding on repair work on the vessel. Koch and his wife, Susan Koch, brought this action in federal district court against the Government under the third-party liability provision of the Longshore and Harborworkers' Compensation Act (LHWCA), **[—2—] {-270-}** 33 U.S.C. § 905(b).[1] Following a bench trial, the district court determined that negligence attributable to the Government—failure to provide adequate lighting of a stairwell—was the factual and legal cause of Koch's fall, resulting harm, and permanent disability and awarded the Kochs $2.83 million in damages. The Government filed a timely notice of appeal. *See* FED. R. APP. P. 4(a)(1)(B). This court has jurisdiction under 28 U.S.C. § 1291.

I

A

The Government contends that, prior to his February 2, 2012 accident, Koch had become disabled by his painful chronic osteoarthritis in both his knees, as well as the degenerative disc disease in his cervical spine and carpal tunnel syndrome. Although Koch's preexisting conditions are undisputed, the district court rejected the Government's argument that Koch had been disabled by them prior to his accident. We affirm this factual finding by the district court as not clearly erroneous for the reasons set forth in detail later in this opinion. At this point, in the interest of chronological clarity, we set forth briefly the evidence of Koch's developing osteoarthritic knee and spinal diseases prior to his accident, as follows:

In 2002, Dr. Richard Corales diagnosed Koch as suffering from degenerative disc disease. In 2004, Koch was diagnosed with multiple joint arthritis by Dr. Terry Habig who referred him to a rheumatologist. In 2005, Dr. Merlin Wilson, a rheumatologist, diagnosed Koch with generalized osteoarthritis and concluded that he needed total knee replacement. In **[—3—]** December 2007, Koch saw Dr. Miranne, who recorded that Koch had a history of "progressive lower back pain for many years" and documented, inter alia, carpal tunnel syndrome. In January 2008, Dr. Lucien Miranne performed cervical spine fusion surgery of Koch's C3-4 and C4-5. In January 2009, Koch was seen by Dr. Lockwood Ochsner, who said he considered doing bilateral total knee replacement. In January 2012, Dr. Wilson saw Koch again and noted that he needed total knee replacement surgery "in the worst way."

B

On February 2, 2012, Koch boarded the *S.S. Altair*, a public vessel in reserve status owned by the United States Maritime Administration. Along with six other contractor representatives, Koch participated in a "walkthrough" of the vessel in order to submit a bid for his company on areas of the

[1] The district court had jurisdiction under its admiralty jurisdiction. 28 U.S.C. § 1333. The applicable waiver of sovereign immunity is the Public Vessels Act, 46 U.S.C. §§ 31101–31113.

vessel in need of repair. The chief engineer of the *Altair* directed the walkthrough. The contractor group eventually arrived at a stairwell leading down to the winch room, a small compartment that housed the vessel's eductor system. The chief engineer flipped the light switch at the top of the stairwell, but the fluorescent lights did not fully illuminate the area. The engineer led the contractor group down the stairwell, which became progressively darker. While some contractors used flashlights to help illuminate their descent, Koch held on to the handrails with both hands. However, he missed the last step in the dark and fell backwards, striking his head, neck, and shoulders on the bulkhead. He sat down while the other contractors inspected the winch room. Koch then continued with the group's walkthrough of the *Altair*. However, Koch did not complete a second walkthrough of another vessel, but **{-271-}** instead returned to his office. After filling **[—4—]** out an accident report, Koch remained in the office for the rest of the day. A colleague drove him home, where his wife found him immobile on a recliner.

Essentially incapacitated and experiencing severe pain in his knees, neck, and back, Koch remained at home, unable to return to work. When his symptoms did not improve after a few days of rest, he went to an urgent care clinic. The doctor at the clinic instructed Koch to follow up with a specialist; Koch saw Dr. Simon Finger, an orthopedic surgeon. Dr. Finger noted Koch's history of osteoarthritis in his knees but concluded that the February 2, 2012 shipboard fall exacerbated his preexisting osteoarthritic conditions and caused the urgent necessity for surgical bilateral knee replacements.

Prior to performing a knee replacement, however, Dr. Finger instructed Koch to see a neurosurgeon for his neck symptoms that had manifested after the fall. Koch saw Dr. Lucien Miranne, a neurosurgeon who had previously performed an anterior cervical discectomy and fusion at his C3-4 and C4-5 vertebrae in his neck in January 2008. Dr. Miranne concluded that Koch herniated his C6-7 disc as a result of the February 2, 2012 fall and aggravated his cervical spondylosis in his C5-6 discs. Dr. Miranne recommended and performed an anterior cervical discectomy and fusion at C5-6 and C6-7 on Koch on August 17, 2012.

Following this cervical spine surgery, Koch had post-surgical complications, including carpal tunnel problems in his hands. Although Koch had mild carpal tunnel prior to the fall, Dr. Miranne noted that the carpal tunnel condition was worsened by Koch's neck problems associated with his C6 and C7 nerve roots. On April 30, 2013, Dr. Miranne performed a right carpal tunnel release on Koch. **[—5—]**

Koch's symptoms, including severe pain in his neck, shoulders, arms, and hands, worsened after the August 17, 2012 surgery. Dr. Miranne concluded that because of Koch's persisting pain and discomfort, additional surgery was required, consisting of a posterior approach cervical fusion.[2] Dr. Miranne explained that he had not used the posterior approach in the first place because it is more painful and usually requires longer hospitalization than the anterior approach. Dr. Miranne recommended that Koch first have and recover from the knee replacements before undergoing the posterior cervical surgery. On July 14, 2014, Dr. Finger performed a right total knee replacement. At the time of trial, Koch was scheduled to have the left knee replacement as soon as he had fully recovered from the first knee replacement. Dr. Miranne also recommended that Koch undergo a left carpal tunnel release.

C

In May 2013, the Kochs filed suit against the Government for damages for past and future medical care, lost wages, and pain and suffering. They alleged that the Government was liable due to its negligence in failing to provide a safe work place and adequate lighting on the vessel. Following a three-day bench trial, the district court determined that the Government's negligence in failing to

[2] Dr. Miranne testified that posterior approach cervical fusion surgery requires removing bone or portions of a herniated disc to relieve Koch's neck and arm pain and the use of mass screws and rods to hold the vertebrae in place and provide stability.

provide adequate lighting above the stairwell was the factual and legal cause of Koch's accidental fall, his injuries, the exacerbation of his preexisting conditions, and his disability. **{-272-}** *Koch v. United States*, No. CIV. A. 13-205, 2015 WL 4129312 (E.D. La. July 7, 2015). **[—6—]**

Koch's supervisor, Robert Barbalich, Jr. of Economy Iron Works, testified that he knew of Koch's health issues prior to the accident, but that they never impacted his ability to work as a foreman and that he did not have mobility issues on the job. Barbalich expected Koch to work for another five to ten years before retiring. Dr. Miranne testified that Koch had returned to work without restrictions following the successful 2008 anterior cervical discectomy and fusion. Dr. Wilson, a rheumatologist, testified that when he saw Koch in January 2012 Koch said that he had worked continuously and was able to perform all of his job duties and daily living activities. Koch testified that prior to the fall he had no plans to have knee replacement surgery and had no limitations or restrictions on account of his knees or neck. Susan Koch testified that prior to the accident Koch was very active at home; he replaced the kitchen cabinets, vaulted the ceiling in their bedroom, mowed the lawn regularly, and tended to their garden. After the accident, Koch could no longer sleep in a normal bed and the couple can no longer enjoy an active social life. She testified that the stress of working full time and caring for her husband had taken its toll on her and their relationship. Koch's treating surgeons, Drs. Miranne and Finger, testified that Koch's fall caused his injuries, exacerbation of preexisting conditions, and disability and that all of his subsequent surgeries were necessitated by that accident. Dr. Finger testified that more likely than not Koch will need revision surgeries to both knees within the next fifteen to thirty years. Dr. Miranne testified that even if Koch had successful knee replacements with Dr. Finger and a successful posterior approach cervical fusion surgery, it is more likely than not that he will never be able to **[—7—]** return to any type of gainful employment due to the injuries sustained in his fall.

The district court award of damages to the Kochs of $2.83 million, including $1.3 million for Koch's pain and suffering. In its findings of fact, the district court stated:

> Prior to February 2, 2012, and despite multiple pre-existing injuries, Mr. Koch was an active, convivial man who enjoyed going to work. Although he frequently experienced pain while working, particularly in his knees, Mr. Koch performed his work activities with vigor and without restriction since at least 2010. . . . Mr. Koch was equally active at home. He mowed the lawn. He fixed the plumbing. He updated the kitchen cabinets. He removed the bedroom ceiling and reinstalled it. He even undertook to modify the drainage system in his home, which involved digging up the bulkhead, replacing existing pipe, and placing gravel rocks on top of the drain pipe.

Id. at *3–4. The district court found that "[a]s a result of the injuries he sustained on February 2, 2012 and the treatment he has received and will receive for those injuries, Mr. Koch will never work again." *Id.* at *3 (footnote omitted).

II

On appeal, the Government argues that: (1) the district court applied the wrong legal standard applicable to cases in which the injured plaintiff had a diagnosed preexisting medical condition; (2) the district court erred in holding that the accident was the sole cause of Koch's damages; and (3) the district court abused its discretion in limiting the testimony of the Government's expert witness, Dr. William Hagemann, an orthopedic surgeon. **[—8—]**

A

We review de novo the legal determinations of the district court after a **{-273-}** bench trial. *Seal v. Knorpp*, 957 F.2d 1230, 1234 (5th Cir. 1992). In determining that the Kochs are entitled to recover for all of Koch's harm and disability, without any discount or reduction because of Koch's preexisting osteoarthritic knee and degenerative spinal conditions, the district court applied the principles set forth in *Maurer v. United States*, 668 F.2d 98, 99–100 (2d Cir. 1997):

> It is a settled principle of tort law that when a defendant's wrongful act causes injury, he is fully liable for the resulting damage even though the injured plaintiff had a preexisting condition that made the consequences of the wrongful act more severe than they would have been for a normal victim. The defendant takes the plaintiff as he finds him. *See, e. g., Evans v. S. J. Groves & Sons Co.*, 315 F.2d 335, 347–48 (2d Cir. 1963) (Friendly, J.); *United States Fidelity & Guaranty Co. v. United States*, 152 F.2d 46, 49 (2d Cir. 1945) (L. Hand, J.); *The Jefferson Myers*, 45 F.2d 162 (2d Cir. 1930) (per curiam). A plaintiff's recovery for damages caused by a defendant's wrongful act may not be proportionately reduced because of a preexisting weakness or susceptibility to injury such as an osteoarthritic condition or a weakness caused by a previous injury. *See, e.g., United States Fidelity & Guaranty Co. v. United States, supra* (congenital spine defect); *Buchalski v. Universal Marine Corp.*, 393 F. Supp. 246, 248 (W.D. Wash. 1975) (preexisting weakness of lower back from prior injury that had stabilized at a nondisabling level).
>
> However, there are two exceptions to the general rule. First, when a plaintiff is incapacitated or disabled prior to an accident, the defendant is liable only for the additional harm or aggravation that he caused. *Evans v. S. J. Groves & Sons Co., supra*, 315 F.2d at 347. Second, when a plaintiff has a preexisting condition that would inevitably worsen, a defendant causing subsequent injury is entitled to have the plaintiff's damages **[—9—]** discounted to reflect the proportion of damages that would have been suffered even in the absence of the subsequent injury, but the burden of proof in such cases is upon the defendant to prove the extent of the damages that the preexisting condition would inevitably have caused. *Id.* at 348.

Applying the foregoing principles, the district court concluded that, because the defendant's negligent failure to safely illumine the stairwell was the factual and legal cause of Koch's accidental fall and its disabling consequences, the Government is fully liable for his resulting harm and disability, even though Koch's preexisting conditions made the consequences of the Government's negligence more severe than they would have been for an ordinary victim. The district court found that neither of the exceptions to this general rule articulated in *Maurer* applies in the present case. The court found that the first exception does not apply because Koch was not disabled or incapacitated *before* the accident[3]; and that the second exception does not apply here because the Government did not carry its burden to prove the extent, if any, of the damages that the preexisting conditions would *inevitably* have caused even in the absence of the accident.[4] We see no error in the district court's application of the well-settled principles set forth in *Maurer*. **{-274-}**

The Government contends, however, that *Maurer* is inapplicable because it is an "eggshell skull" plaintiff case, and that the "eggshell skull" concept applies only if the plaintiff's preexisting condition was completely latent and had not manifested itself prior to the plaintiff's accident caused by the defendant. This argument is not meritorious. *Maurer* itself involved a plaintiff **[—10—]** who suffered from already manifested "preexisting degenerative back condition (osteoarthritis)" and an unspecified injury in a prior accident. 668 F.2d at 99. Moreover, the Government cites no authority for limiting the "thin skull" or "eggshell skull" rule—described often as the "defendant takes the victim as found" rule—to cases involving only latent or unmanifested preexisting conditions. This court and district courts

[3] *See Koch v. United States*, 2015 WL 4129312, *3–4.

[4] *Id.* at *6 ("The evidence presented at trial does not establish that any of the injuries of which Mr. Koch complains were inevitable.").

within our circuit have expressed approval and acceptance of the "thin skull," "eggshell skull," or "defendant takes the victim as found" rule without limiting its application to latent or unmanifested preexisting conditions. *See Dahlen v. Gulf Crews, Inc.*, 281 F.3d 487, 495 (5th Cir. 2002); *Dunn v. Denk*, 54 F.3d 248 (5th Cir. 1995); *Cutchall v. Cal Dive Int'l, Inc.*, No. CV 12-1291, 2013 WL 12107569, at *1 (E.D. La. Apr. 2, 2013); *Johnson v. Cenac Towing, Inc.*, 599 F. Supp. 2d 721, 730 (E.D. La. 2009); *Laakso v. Mitsui & Co. USA*, No. CIV. A. 88-2450, 1989 WL 149186, 1990 A.M.C. 635, 645 (E.D. La. Dec. 6, 1989); *Curtis v. Shivers*, 674 F. Supp. 1237, 1239 (E.D. La. 1987).[5] **[—11—]**

Indeed, we have found no reported case so limiting the rule. Further, although we are not bound by the major torts treatises or the American Law Institute's Restatement of Torts, it is significant that none of them recognizes such a limitation on the rule. *See, e.g.*, W. PAGE KEETON ET. AL., PROSSER AND KEETON ON TORTS § 43, at 291–92 (5th ed. 1984); DAN B. DOBBS ET. AL., THE LAW OF TORTS § 206, at 711–13 (2d ed. 2011); RESTATEMENT (THIRD) OF TORTS § 31 (AM. LAW INST. 2010). For example, the Restatement (Third) of Torts, § 31 provides that:

> When an actor's tortious conduct causes harm to a person that, because of a preexisting physical or mental condition or other characteristics of the person, is of a greater magnitude or different type than might reasonably be expected, the actor is nevertheless subject to liability for all such harm to the person.

Section 31's Reporter's Note further states: **{-275-}**

> Every United States jurisdiction adheres to the thin-skull rule; more precisely, extensive research has failed to identify a single United States case disavowing the rule . . . . The essence of this rule prevents a defendant from seeking to avoid or reduce liability because some characteristic of the plaintiff, however unusual, combines with the tortious conduct of the defendant to produce physical or emotional harm that is greater than might be expected, unusual, or unforeseeable.

Id.

For these reasons, we conclude that the district court did not apply the wrong legal standard in this case with regard to Koch's preexisting medical conditions. **[—12—]**

B

The Government argues that the totality of the medical evidence demonstrates that Koch's preexisting conditions of spinal degenerative disease and osteoarthritic disease of his knees had caused him to become disabled prior to his fall on the *Altair* so that the district court's findings of facts to the

---

[5] *Henderson v. United States*, 328 F.2d 502 (5th Cir. 1964), the case relied upon by the Government, is inapposite. In that case, the plaintiff, a civilian, was injured when a Government agent negligently backed a truck into him on June 18, 1961. The district court found that plaintiff's preexisting osteoarthritic lumbar condition was aggravated as a consequence of the negligence of the Government but that he suffered little or no pain immediately. Although he did experience some pain beginning in early July, his pain did not become severe and disabling until he suffered a second injury to his back on September 12, 1961, without fault or negligence on the part of the Government. Because the Government was in no way responsible for plaintiff's second, more serious back injury the district court awarded him only $5,000 for his June 18 injury. This court affirmed, stating as a general rule that where there is a subsequent injury, if the subsequent event is attributable to a distinct intervening cause, the wrongdoer is held to be liable only for the original injury. As the district court, after weighing the evidence as a whole, apparently concluded that the aggravation caused by the negligence of the Government in June 1961 was not a contributing factor to the injuries occurring in September 1961, the Court of Appeals concluded that it could not say that the district court's findings and conclusion were clearly erroneous. *Id.* at 505. *Henderson*'s facts are clearly distinguishable from the present case, because here there **[—11—]** was a single accident that resulted in totally disabling harm; there was no second accident or intervening injury.

contrary are clearly erroneous and should be vacated.[6]

Because a finding of disability *vel non* is a finding of fact, the standard governing appellate review of a district court's finding of disability or lack thereof is that set forth in Federal Rule of Civil Procedure 52(a): "Findings of fact, whether based on oral or other evidence, must not be set aside unless clearly erroneous, and the reviewing court must give due regard to the trial court's opportunity to judge the witnesses' credibility." The question before us, then, is whether the district court's failure to find that Koch was disabled prior to his accident was clearly erroneous.

The general principles governing the exercise of our power to overturn factual findings of a district court may be derived from the Supreme Court's cases and our own cases. "The foremost of these principles . . . is that "[a] finding is 'clearly erroneous' when although there is evidence to support it, the **[—13—]** reviewing court on the entire evidence is left with the definite and firm conviction that a mistake has been committed." *Anderson v. City of Bessemer City*, 470 U.S. 564, 573 (1985) (quoting *United States v. U.S. Gypsum Co.*, 333 U.S. 364, 395 (1948)). "This standard plainly does not entitle a reviewing court to reverse the finding of the trier of fact simply because it is convinced that it would have decided the case differently. The reviewing court oversteps the bounds of its duty under Rule 52(a) if it undertakes to duplicate the role of the lower court." *Id.*

Thus "[i]f the district court's account of the evidence is plausible in light of the record viewed in its entirety, the court of appeals may not reverse it even though convinced that had it been sitting as the trier of fact, it would have weighed the evidence differently. Where there are two **{–276–}** permissible views of the evidence, the factfinder's choice between them cannot be clearly erroneous." *Id.* at 573–574 (citing *United States v. Yellow Cab Co.*, 338 U.S. 338, 342 (1949)). Similarly, "when a trial judge's finding is based on his decision to credit the testimony of one of two or more witnesses, each of whom has told a coherent and facially plausible story that is not contradicted by extrinsic evidence, that finding, if not internally inconsistent, can virtually never be clear error." *Id.* at 575–76.

Applying the foregoing principles in a review of the entire record in this case does not leave us with "a definite and firm conviction that a mistake has been committed," *see id.* at 573, and so we cannot characterize as clearly erroneous the district court's finding that Koch had not been disabled by his deteriorating spinal condition and his osteoarthritic knee condition prior to his accidental fall aboard the *Altair*. In making its determination, the district court credited the testimony of Koch, his wife, and his supervisor, all of whom **[—14—]** bore witness to the fact that, prior to his accident aboard the *Altair*, Koch was not disabled but was active in his job as foreman, in doing maintenance and repairs at home, and socially. The district court also credited the testimony of Koch's treating physicians, Dr. Miranne, a neurosurgeon, and Dr. Finger, an orthopedic surgeon, who testified that Koch had not been disabled by his preexisting spinal and knee conditions prior to his accident. Dr. Miranne testified that Koch had recovered from a cervical operation he performed on him in 2008, that he had some intermittent symptomatology but was doing well and had returned to work up until his accident. Dr. Miranne concluded from his examinations, MRI readings, and surgery that Koch had sustained a herniated disc at C6-7

[6] The Government's brief initially states that that the district court erred in holding that the accident was the "sole cause" of Koch's damages. Such an argument is meritless because the district court clearly did not find that Koch's accident was the "sole cause" of his resulting harm and disability. Rather, the district court found that the combination of his accident with its exacerbation of his preexisting conditions was the cause in fact and legal cause of his harm and disability. The somewhat more persuasive argument that the Government makes is that Koch had been rendered disabled by his preexisting conditions before his 2012 accident. This argument, too, is meritless, but it requires that we consider all of the evidence to determine whether the district court clearly erred in finding Koch was not disabled by his preexisting conditions prior to his accident.

in his fall aboard the *Altair*, which aggravated the effects of his preexisting spinal disease and caused it to become totally disabling. Dr. Finger concluded from his examinations that Koch's fall had aggravated his preexisting osteoarthritic knee conditions, painfully causing him to urgently need bilateral surgical knee replacements.[7] Dr. Miranne and Dr. Finger testified that all of the surgeries performed and planned by them, with Koch's consent, subsequent to Koch's fall were necessitated by that accident.

In contrast with Dr. Miranne's findings, Dr. Hagemann, the Government's expert orthopedic surgeon, saw no signs or changes between Koch's MRI films taken before and after the 2012 accident. The radiologist **[—15—]** who made the films filed a report to the same effect. Based on these readings, Dr. Hagemann thought it was unlikely that Koch had received a herniated disc or had been seriously harmed by the 2012 accident. However, Dr. Hagemann had examined Koch but once, on September 2, 2014, which was after the pretrial surgeries performed by Drs. Miranne and Finger and long after the accident. No one except Dr. Miranne and Dr. Finger had performed surgery on him. The district court resolved the conflict in the evidence in favor of the testimony of the treating physicians, Drs. Miranne and Finger. Considering all of the circumstances and reasons stated, we cannot say that the district court's determination was unreasonable or clearly erroneous. *See* **{-277-}** *id.* at 574 ("Where there are two permissible views of the evidence, the factfinder's choice between them cannot be clearly erroneous.").

C

Finally, the Government asserts that the district court erred by unfairly limiting the testimony of its expert, Dr. Hagemann, and by crediting the testimony of Koch's treating physicians over that of Dr. Hagemann because of that limitation. Dr. Hagemann examined Koch once on September 2, 2014, reviewed some of Koch's medical records, and prepared a pretrial expert report expressing his opinion that Koch did not sustain a herniated disc or any serious injury in his accident. Before his pretrial report, Dr. Hagemann had not yet personally reviewed the MRI films but based his opinion on the radiologist's reports of them. By the time of the trial, however, Dr. Hagemann had reviewed the films himself, and at trial the Government sought to have him testify, in addition to his opinion based on the radiologist's readings, that his opinion that Koch had suffered no new disc herniation or other serious injury in the accident was based on his own comparison of Koch's MRI films before and after the **[—16—]** accident. The district court sustained the Kochs' counsel's objection to the enhanced testimony on the grounds that it was an improper attempt to amend Dr. Hagemann's pretrial report after the discovery deadline had passed and would improperly allow Dr. Hagemann to testify as to other doctors' reports not included in his own report. The Government moved to make a proffer of the evidence, and the court stated that it would permit the proffer at the end of the trial. The Government did not make the proffer, however.

We review the evidentiary rulings of the district court under the deferential abuse-of-discretion standard. *Kelly v. Boeing Petroleum Servs., Inc.*, 61 F.3d 350, 356 (5th Cir. 1995). "District courts enjoy wide latitude in determining the admissibility of expert testimony, and 'the discretion of the trial judge and his or her decision will not be disturbed on appeal unless 'manifestly erroneous.'" *Watkins v. Telsmith, Inc.*, 121 F.3d 984, 988 (5th Cir. 1997) (quoting *Eiland* v. *Westinghouse Elec.*, 58 F.3d 176, 180 (5th Cir. 1995)). Even if an abuse of discretion is found, the harmless error doctrine applies unless a substantial right of the complaining party was affected. *See Compaq Comput. Corp. v. Ergonome Inc.*, 387 F.3d 403, 408 (5th Cir. 2004).

[7] Although the record indicates other doctors had previously diagnosed Koch's preexisting osteoarthritic knee condition and advised him to undergo bilateral knee replacement, Koch testified that he had not planned to have those operations until his 2012 accident; and Dr. Finger stated without contradiction that a physician does not recommend such surgery if the patient chooses to function and to live with his knee pains.

Having scoured the record, we are satisfied that the district court did not abuse its discretion in ruling to exclude the additional testimony by Dr. Hagemann about his review of the MRI films, particularly in light of the court's offer to allow the Government to make a proffer of it at the end of the trial. But even if we were to assume, *arguendo*, that the district court erred in its exclusion-with-proffer ruling and did so to the point of abuse of discretion, we would still not reverse the district court's judgment because, under the circumstances, such an error clearly appears to have been be harmless. It was plain that even without Dr. Hagemann's excluded testimony on the subject **[—17—]** that he and the radiologist, based on their reading of Koch's MRI films, differed from Dr. Miranne's findings that Koch sustained a herniated disc at C6-7 and suffered disabling exacerbating trauma as a result of his accident. But Dr. Miranne's opinion as the treating neuro-surgeon who had, inter alia, performed two surgeries on Koch's cervical spine, was based on many other factors as well as his reading of the MRI films. For these reasons and the others expressed herein the district court's decision **{–278–}** to credit Dr. Miranne's testimony over Dr. Hagemann's was not unreasonable or clear error.

For these reasons, the judgment of the district court is AFFIRMED.

United States Court of Appeals for the Fifth Circuit

No. 15-30377

IN RE DEEPWATER HORIZON

LAKE EUGENIE LAND & DEV., INC.
VS.
BP EXPLORATION & PROD., INC.

Appeal from the United States District Court for the Eastern District of Louisiana

Decided: May 22, 2017

Citation: 858 F.3d 298, 5 Adm. R. 259 (5th Cir. 2017).

Before **DAVIS, CLEMENT,** and **COSTA,** Circuit Judges.

[—1—] {-300-} DAVIS, Circuit Judge:

This appeal addresses the computation of economic losses arising out of the BP oil spill and based on the BP Settlement Agreement. In an attempt to adhere to our decision in *In re Deepwater Horizon* ("*Deepwater Horizon I*"), 732 **[—2—]** F.3d 326, 1 Adm. R. 287 (5th Cir. 2013), the district court has approved a policy adopted by the Claims Administrator known as Policy 495. Policy 495 consists of five methodologies pursuant to which the Claims Administrator is to calculate claimant compensation: one Annual Variable Margin Methodology ("AVMM") and four Industry-Specific Methodologies ("ISMs"). Class Counsel challenges all five. Because the AVMM is consistent with the text of the Settlement Agreement, but the four ISMs are not, we **{-301-}** AFFIRM as to the AVMM, REVERSE as to the ISMs, and REMAND for proceedings consistent with this opinion.[1]

I.

The Settlement Agreement seeks to reimburse claimants for economic losses related to the BP oil spill. Losses that bear a temporal relationship to the spill are said to be related to the spill. Somewhat simplified, and more than somewhat condensed, the claims process works as follows: The Claims Administrator compares a claimant's financial performance prior to and after the spill. If the former is greater than the latter, BP is liable for the difference. Causation is, in all other respects, presumed.

The Settlement Agreement grants each claimant the right to choose his or her Compensation Period, so long as it consists of three or more consecutive months between May and December 2010. The Compensation Period constitutes the post-spill period, which is then subtracted from the same pre-spill period,[2] in order to deduce the damages owed.

We first addressed damages in the context of this litigation in *Deepwater Horizon I*. The question in *Deepwater Horizon I* was whether the Settlement **[—3—]** Agreement requires the Claims Administrator to match all unmatched profit and loss statements. Before discussing our holding in *Deepwater Horizon I*, an explanation of the terms "matched" and "unmatched" is in order.

In a matched profit and loss statement, costs follow revenue, which is registered when generated or received. The two appear as part of the same month, and provide a clear picture of net income.

In an unmatched profit and loss statement, costs do not follow revenue. Revenue is registered when generated or received, and costs are registered at least one month earlier when incurred. Unmatched profit and loss statements can, pursuant to the Settlement Agreement, make it appear as if a claimant has suffered damages that he, in fact, did not suffer. Here's how.

Assume that Claimant A is a used car dealer, who chose a Compensation Period of August to October 2010. Assume that during the Compensation Period, Claimant A sold two cars. Assume that both of those cars were sold in September. Assume that the sale generated a combined $50,000 in revenue.

[1] We have jurisdiction to decide this appeal pursuant to the collateral order doctrine. *See Deepwater Horizon I*, 732 F.3d at 332 n.3, 1 Adm. R. at 289 n.3.

[2] Financial performance in the pre-spill period will, subject to the claimant's choice, be restricted to 2009; 2008 and 2009; or 2007, 2008, and 2009.

And assume that Claimant A paid $40,000 for those two cars in June.

If the costs follow the revenue, *i.e.*, if the claimant's profit and loss statements are matched, the Claims Administrator should conclude that Claimant A generated $10,000 in profits during the Compensation Period. His profit and loss statements, from August to October 2010, should list $50,000 in revenue and $40,000 in costs. The fact that the costs were incurred outside of the Compensation Period in June does not matter, because the costs follow the revenue, which was both generated and received during the Compensation Period in September. Claimant A generated $10,000 in net profits from August to October 2010.

Now assume that Claimant A's financial performance in August to October 2009 mirrored that of August to October 2010. But assume that Claimant A submitted his 2009 profit and loss statements unmatched. **{-302-}** If the **[—4—]** costs do not follow the revenue, the $40,000 that Claimant A incurred in June will not be considered, because June falls outside of the Compensation Period. Claimant A will thus appear to have generated $50,000 in net profits from August to October 2009, and $10,000 in net profits from August to October 2010. And after subtracting the latter from the former, Claimant A will be entitled to 40,000 in damages related to the spill.

In *Deepwater Horizon I*, we sought to determine whether the Settlement Agreement supports this result, or whether the Claims Administrator should be required to match all unmatched profit and loss statements. We noted that

> In interpreting a settlement, surely some weight has to be given to what damages recoverable in civil litigation actually are. If clear words in a settlement require the use of randomly associated numbers for calculating damages, even if there is little likelihood that, after subtracting one of those numbers from the other, the remainder will in fact show anything relevant to damages, then so be it. We do not perceive such clarity here.[3]

Finding the text of the Settlement Agreement ambiguous, we remanded to the district court with instructions to review relevant extrinsic evidence to ensure that the Settlement Agreement was being implemented in a manner consistent with intent of the parties at the time of the Settlement Agreement's ratification.

On remand, the district court held that the parties did not discuss the issue of "matching" prior to signing the Settlement Agreement, but "did discuss and were in agreement that similarly situated claimants must be treated alike." In order to treat similarly situated claimants alike, the district court held that the Settlement Agreement should be interpreted to mandate the **[—5—]** matching of all unmatched profit and loss statements, and ordered the Claims Administrator to craft a policy to that end.

The resultant policy is Policy 495. Policy 495 consists of five methodologies, and effectively divides claimants into two categories: those engaged in construction, education, agriculture, and professional services are subject to ISMs, and those engaged in everything else are subject to an AVMM. Class Counsel objects to all five methodologies. We review the AVMM separately, and the four ISMs together.

II.

A.

The AVMM requires the Claims Administrator to match all unmatched profit and loss statements. This means that prior to calculating damages, the Claims Administrator must ensure that costs are registered in the same month as corresponding revenue, regardless of when those costs were incurred. In *Deepwater Horizon I*, we held that the Settlement Agreement is ambiguous as to matching. Where a contractual provision "is ambiguous,

[3] 732 F.3d at 339, 1 Adm. R. at 296.

such that its construction turns on a consideration of extrinsic evidence, . . . we review the district court's interpretation for clear error."[4]

Class Counsel has not presented evidence sufficient for us to find that the district court's approval of the AVMM constituted clear error, and we now hold that it did not. The Settlement Agreement is a **{-303-}** maritime contract,[5] pursuant to which all ambiguities are to be resolved "consistent with the intent of the parties."[6] The parties intended for all "similarly situated claimants [to] be treated alike." Matching unmatched profit and loss statements promotes **[—6—]** this goal. Error is clear when it leaves us with a "definite and firm conviction that a mistake has been committed."[7] Because we hold no such conviction, the district court's approval of the AVMM is affirmed.

B.

The ISMs also require matching, but go a significant step farther, requiring the Claims Administrator to move, smooth, or otherwise reallocate revenue for claimants engaged in construction, education, agriculture, and professional services. Claimants in these four industries tend to be paid in lump sums, which are capable of generating damages awards that do not comport with tort principles. Thus, BP argues that the ISMs are necessary in order to ensure that the Claims Administrator can "process claims in accordance with economic reality,"[8] quoting our opinion in *Deepwater Horizon I.*

An example is, once again, helpful. Assume that Claimant A is a farmer, who chose a Compensation Period of August to October 2010. Assume that in 2009, Claimant A sold all of his crops on October 31st, generating $200,000 in net profits. And assume that in 2010, Claimant A sold all of his crops on November 1st, generating $200,000 in net profits again.

Claimant A did not suffer economic losses pursuant to tort principles. His net profits, after all, did not decline from 2009 to 2010.

Claimant A did, however, suffer economic losses pursuant to the Settlement Agreement. The Settlement Agreement precludes the Claims Administrator from considering the 2010 transaction, because it took place in November, outside of the Compensation Period. Thus, BP owes Claimant A **[—7—]** $200,000. $200,000 in net profits in 2009 minus $0 in net profits in 2010 equals $200,000 in damages for Claimant A.

BP argues that the parties did not intend for Claimant A to collect $200,000. And the relevant ISM would preclude this result. The relevant ISM would spread revenue across the crop season, ensuring that damages are awarded to those who have suffered real losses. This may well be a fairer alternative. But it cannot be implemented, because it is inconsistent with the plain text of the Settlement Agreement.[9]

"The interpretation of an unambiguous contract[ual provision] is a question of law, subject to de novo review."[10] "De novo [review warrants] here, as it ordinarily does, a fresh, independent determination of the matter at stake."[11] **{-304-}**

The Settlement Agreement grants each claimant the right to choose his or her

4 *See Alford v. Kuhlman Elec. Corp.*, 716 F.3d 909, 912 (5th Cir. 2013).

5 *Holmes Motors, Inc. v. BP Expl. & Prod., Inc.*, 829 F.3d 313, 315, 4 Adm. R. 263, 264 (5th Cir. 2016); *see also Guidry v. Halliburton Geophysical Servs., Inc.*, 976 F.2d 938, 940 (5th Cir. 1992) ("A settlement agreement is a contract.").

6 *See Norfolk S. Ry. Co. v. Kirby*, 543 U.S. 14, 31 (2004).

7 *United States v. U.S. Gypsum Co.*, 333 U.S. 364, 395 (1948).

8 732 F.3d at 339, 1 Adm. R. at 296.

9 *See Luv N' Care, Ltd. v. Groupo Rimar*, 844 F.3d 442, 447 (5th Cir. 2016) ("Contractual intent is determined by the words of the contract.").

10 *Alford*, 716 F.3d at 912.

11 *Doe v. United States*, 821 F.2d 694, 697—98 (D.C. Cir. 1987) (en banc) (internal quotations omitted); *see also Goodman v. United States*, 518 F.2d 505, 509 (5th Cir. 1975) ("The phrase 'de novo' means 'the court should make an independent determination of the issues.'").

Compensation Period, consisting of three or more consecutive months between May and December 2010. If the Claims Administrator is permitted to remove revenue from the Compensation Period, and spread it throughout the non-compensation months, the claimant's choice no longer matters. June is the same as December, and November is the same as July.

This is not the agreement that the parties entered into. And we decline to re-write the Settlement Agreement under the guise of contractual interpretation. When we said, in *Deepwater Horizon I*, that the Claims Administrator should "process claims in accordance with economic reality," we **[—8—]** assumed that doing so would comport with the text of the Settlement Agreement. That assumption has proven to be wrong in light of the moving, smoothing, and otherwise reallocation of revenue inherent in the ISMs.

The Settlement Agreement grants claimants the right to choose their own Compensation Period. Because the ISMs infringe upon that right, the district court's approval of the ISMs was in error and is reversed.

III.

The district court's approval of the ISMs was in error because the ISMs require the Claims Administrator to move, smooth, or otherwise reallocate revenue in violation of the Settlement Agreement. However, the ISMs, as stated, also require the Claims Administrator to match all unmatched profit and loss statements.

Having the Claims Administrator match all unmatched profit and loss statements helps ensure that all similarly situated claimants are treated alike, and is consistent with the text of the Settlement Agreement. Thus, we hold that all claimants—including those engaged in construction, agriculture, education, and professional services—shall, on remand, be subject to the AVMM.

IV.

For the reasons set out above, we AFFIRM as to the AVMM, REVERSE as to the ISMs, and REMAND for further proceedings consistent with this opinion.

United States Court of Appeals for the Fifth Circuit

No. 15-30435

BORCIK
vs.
CROSBY TUGS, L.L.C.

Appeal from the United States District Court for the Eastern District of Louisiana

Decided: June 1, 2017

Citation: 858 F.3d 936, 5 Adm. R. 263 (5th Cir. 2017).

Before **REAVLEY, JOLLY,** and **ELROD,** Circuit Judges.

[—1—] {-937-} PER CURIAM:

Eric Borcik brought this whistleblower suit against Crosby Tugs, alleging that Crosby had fired him in retaliation for reporting environmental violations. Under Louisiana law, Borcik can only recover if he reported the violation in "good faith." La. Stat. Ann. § 30:2027. The case was tried to a jury, which was instructed that "good faith" meant that "the plaintiff had an honest belief that an environmental violation occurred and that he did not report it either to seek an unfair advantage or to try to harm his employer or another employee." The jury found via special interrogatory that Borcik did not report the violation in good faith, resulting in a defense verdict. Borcik appealed, **[—2—]** arguing that the district court erred by failing to instruct the jury correctly on the definition of "good faith."

On appeal, we determined that we were not in a position to make an *Erie* guess as to the meaning of "good faith" and certified the following question to the Louisiana Supreme Court:

> What is the meaning of "good faith" as that term is used in the Louisiana Environmental Quality Act, Louisiana Revised Statutes 30:2027?

Borcik v. Crosby Tugs, L.L.C., 656 F. App'x 681, 685 (5th Cir. 2016). The Louisiana Supreme Court accepted the question and answered it as follows:

> The term "good faith," as used in R.S. 30:2027, means an employee is acting with an honest belief that a violation of an environmental law, rule, or regulation occurred.

Borcik v. Crosby Tugs, L.L.C., 2016-1372, --- So. 3d ---, 2017 WL 1716226 (La. 5/3/17).

Based on the definition of the term provided by the Louisiana Supreme Court, the district court erred by instructing the jury that "good faith" required more than "an honest belief that a violation of an environmental law, rule, or regulation occurred."

Accordingly, we remand for such orders and further proceedings as the district court, in its discretion, deems necessary and appropriate.

REMANDED.

United States Court of Appeals
for the Fifth Circuit

No. 16-31049

LEE
vs.
OFFSHORE LOGISTICAL & TRANSP, L.L.C.

Appeal from the United States District Court for the Eastern District of Louisiana

Decided: June 9, 2017
Revised: July 5, 2017

Citation: 859 F.3d 353, 5 Adm. R. 264 (5th Cir. 2017).

Before REAVLEY, HAYNES, and COSTA, Circuit Judges.

[—1—] **{-354-}** HAYNES, Circuit Judge:

Elwood Lee ("Lee") appeals the summary judgment entered against him in favor of Offshore Logistical & Transports LLC ("Offshore") on his Jones Act and maritime claims for negligence and unseaworthiness arising out of an alleged injury Lee suffered. As explained below, we VACATE and REMAND for reconsideration in light of the current Federal Rule of Civil Procedure 56.

We give only a brief discussion of the facts, because this appeal turns on the procedural ruling of the district court. Lee claims that he was employed by Offshore on its vessel, the M/V BALTY. He states that he fell while walking on the decks of the vessel. Offshore filed a motion for summary judgment **[—2—]** challenging various aspects of Lee's proof. Ultimately, the district court concluded that Lee failed to bring forward evidence that would support a finding of causation between Offshore's acts or omissions and Lee's injuries. In so doing, the district court discounted as inadmissible the signed but unsworn report of Captain James P. Jamison which Lee filed in the record. The district court did not make a finding that the report could not be placed in admissible form.

In discounting Captain Jamison's opinions, the district court relied on a prior version of Federal Rule of Civil Procedure 56 and cases thereunder, specifically old Rule 56(e) regarding affidavits. In 2010, Rule 56 was amended to clarify and streamline the procedures regarding summary judgment motions and to make clear the process for supporting assertions of fact and objecting thereto. *See* FED. R. CIV. P. 56, advisory committee's note to 2010 amendment ("Subdivision (c) is new. It establishes a common procedure for several aspects of summary-judgment motions . . . ."). Rule 56(c)(1) was amended to state as follows: **{-355-}**

> **(1)** ***Supporting Factual Positions.*** A party asserting that a fact cannot be or is genuinely disputed must support the assertion by:
>
>> **(A)** citing to particular parts of materials in the record, including depositions, documents, electronically stored information, affidavits or declarations, stipulations (including those made for purposes of the motion only), admissions, interrogatory answers, or other materials . . . .

FED. R. CIV. P. 56(c)(1)(A).

"Although the substance or content of the evidence submitted to support or dispute a fact on summary judgment must be admissible . . . , the material may be presented in a form that would not, in itself, be admissible at trial." 11 **[—3—]** MOORE'S FEDERAL PRACTICE – CIVIL ¶ 56.91 (2017); *see also Fraternal Order of Police, Lodge 1 v. City of Camden*, 842 F.3d 231, 238 (3d Cir. 2016) (holding that a "proponent need only 'explain the admissible form that is anticipated'" (quoting FED. R. CIV. P. 56, advisory committee's note to 2010 amendment)); *Humphreys & Partners Architects, L.P. v. Lessard Design, Inc.*, 790 F.3d 532, 538 (4th Cir. 2015) (recognizing that a "court may consider . . . the content or substance of otherwise inadmissible materials where the 'the party submitting the evidence show[s] that it will be possible to put the information . . . into an admissible form.'" (alteration in original) (quoting 11 JAMES WM. MOORE ET AL,

MOORE'S FEDERAL PRACTICE – CIVIL ¶ 56.91[2] (3d ed. 2015))); *Jones v. UPS Ground Freight*, 683 F.3d 1283, 1293–94 (11th Cir. 2012) (determining that a district court may consider a statement "if the statement could be reduced to admissible evidence at trial or reduced to admissible form." (citation omitted)).

Thus, the rule expressly contemplates that affidavits are only one way to "support" a fact; "documents . . . declarations, [and] other materials" are also supportive of facts. FED. R. CIV. P. 56(c)(1)(A). To avoid the use of materials that lack authenticity or violate other evidentiary rules, the new rule allows a party to object "that the material cited to support or dispute a fact cannot be presented in a form that would be admissible as evidence." FED. R. CIV. P. 56(c)(2); *see also* advisory committee's note to 2010 amendment ("The objection functions much as an objection at trial, adjusted for the pretrial setting. The burden is on the proponent to show that the material is admissible as presented or to explain the admissible form that is anticipated."). The district court dismissed Captain Jamison's report solely because it was not sworn without considering Lee's argument that Captain Jamison would testify to those opinions at trial and without determining whether such opinions, as testified to at trial, would be admissible. **[—4—]**

Before the district court, Offshore made other arguments and contentions about Captain Jamison's report that were not addressed by that court. However, no alternate ground for affirmance was briefed before our court, and, on this record, we decline to rule upon these points in the first instance. *Cf. Hernandez v. Velasquez*, 522 F.3d 556, 560 (5th Cir. 2008) (holding that a court of appeals "*may* affirm a grant of summary judgment on any grounds supported by the record and presented to the court below" (emphasis added)); *see also Burleson v. Tex. Dep't of Criminal Justice*, 393 F.3d 577, 583–84 (5th Cir. 2004) (indicating that we cannot make a certain evidentiary evaluation for the first time on appeal). We VACATE and REMAND for consideration of the summary judgment evidence under current Rule 56 including whether the particular material to which objection is lodged **{-356-}** can or cannot "be presented in a form that would be admissible at trial."

VACATED and REMANDED.

United States Court of Appeals
for the Fifth Circuit

No. 16-30459

IN RE SETTOON TOWING, L.L.C.

Appeal from the United States District Court for the Eastern District of Louisiana

Decided: June 9, 2017

Citation: 859 F.3d 340, 5 Adm. R. 266 (5th Cir. 2017).

Before **SMITH, CLEMENT,** and **SOUTHWICK,** Circuit Judges.

[—1—] {-342-} SOUTHWICK, Circuit Judge:

One flotilla of barges encountered another on the lower Mississippi River. Both followed the usual protocol of entering an agreement by radio for how one was to overtake and pass the other. A collision nonetheless resulted, causing an oil spill that closed a portion of the river for two days. Cleanup was immediately undertaken. Who ultimately pays and how much are what this suit is about. **[—2—]**

The litigation is governed by the federal Oil Pollution Act, or OPA. No one contests that Settoon Towing was properly charged by the Coast Guard with the initial cleanup and remediation, thus initially paying all expenses under the strict-liability statutory scheme. The district court, though, found both Settoon and Marquette Transportation to be negligent. Our principal issue is whether Settoon can receive contribution under the OPA from Marquette for its payment of purely economic damages, *i.e.*, for the cleanup costs. A hoary bit of maritime law has traditionally said, "no." We conclude that the OPA clearly says, "yes." Marquette's arguments to the contrary try to make the statutory question seem a whole lot harder than it really is.

The district court allowed contribution and determined the percentage of fault of each party. We AFFIRM.

FACTUAL AND PROCEDURAL BACKGROUND

On February 22, 2014, the M/V HANNAH C. SETTOON, towing two crude oil **{-343-}** tank barges, and the M/V LINDSAY ANN ERICKSON, towing twenty-one loaded grain barges, were both heading downstream on the lower Mississippi River. The LINDSAY began to stop just after it passed the College Point[1] bend near Convent, Louisiana. It was preparing to "top around" with the help of a towboat in order to drop off three of her barges and then head back upriver. At approximately 2:58 p.m., as the HANNAH was in the same bend and about 3,500 feet behind the LINDSAY, the vessels communicated by radio and entered into what the parties call a "one whistle overtaking **[—3—]** agreement."

According to the agreement, the HANNAH would pass the LINDSAY on her stern while the LINDSAY would hold steady. Once the HANNAH was clear, the LINDSAY would begin her top around. The width of the river at the location of the overtaking and passing is about 3,000 feet.

Consistent with the agreement, the HANNAH increased her speed and maneuvered in order to remain midway between the LINDSAY and the west bank of the Mississippi River. For approximately three and a half minutes, the LINDSAY held her position in the river. At 3:07 p.m., before the HANNAH had passed the LINDSAY, the HANNAH by radio seemingly released the LINDSAY from the agreement. The LINDSAY acknowledged. At some point prior to the HANNAH completely passing the LINDSAY, the LINDSAY began reversing into the river to start her top-around. At 3:09 p.m., her stern collided with the portside bow of a crude-oil barge towed by the HANNAH. Approximately 750 barrels of light crude oil were discharged

[1] So named due to the College of Jefferson which opened there on the east bank of the river in 1834. Since 1931, the Roman Catholic order of Jesuits has used the former college's 1842 main building and other structures for retreats. OLIVER P. CARRIERE, A SKETCH OF THE HISTORY OF JEFFERSON COLLEGE AND MANRESA HOUSE OF RETREATS, CONVENT, LOUISIANA 8–9, 21 (1974).

into the Mississippi River. As a result, a 70-mile stretch of the river was closed to vessels for approximately 48 hours for cleanup and recovery.

Settoon was named the strictly liable "Responsible Party" by the United States Coast Guard pursuant to the OPA. That phrase is a term of art central to this appeal and will be much discussed later. Settoon carried out its statutory responsibilities related to cleanup, remediation, and third-party claims for damages. Settoon subsequently filed Limitation of Liability proceedings pursuant to 46 U.S.C. §§ 30501–30512 in the Eastern District of Louisiana. Marquette also filed a claim. Settoon brought a counterclaim against Marquette seeking contribution under the OPA, the general maritime law, or both.

At the conclusion of a four-day bench trial on the issue of liability, the **[—4—]** district court determined both parties were at fault and apportioned 65% of the fault for the collision to Marquette and 35% to Settoon. The district court also considered a question for which, surprisingly, there is little authority: Is a Responsible Party entitled to contribution for purely economic damages from a third party found to be partially liable? The district court answered that such contribution is permitted. Marquette timely filed its notice of appeal.

DISCUSSION

Marquette claims the district court erred in two ways: (A) the OPA does not allow a Responsible Party to obtain contribution from a partially liable third party, and even if it does, (B) the district court erred in its allocation of relative fault. Because the first issue raises legal questions **{-344-}** of statutory interpretation, our review is *de novo*. *Sobranes Recovery Pool I, LLC v. Todd & Hughes Constr. Corp.*, 509 F.3d 216, 220 (5th Cir. 2007). As for the second issue, a trial court's finding on apportionment of relative fault in a maritime collision is reviewed under a clearly erroneous standard. *See Tokio Marine & Fire Ins. Co. v. FLORA MV*, 235 F.3d 963, 970 (5th Cir. 2001).

Our approach is first to discuss some basics about the relevant statute. Then, with that background, we analyze the two issues before us.

I. The Oil Pollution Act of 1990

The enactment that controls this litigation was a legislative response to the grounding of the oil tanker *Exxon Valdez* and the spilling of over eleven million gallons of crude oil into the waters of Prince William Sound, Alaska. *See* 2 THOMAS J. SCHOENBAUM, ADMIRALTY & MAR. LAW § 18-4 (5th ed. 2016). The OPA is Congress's effort "to streamline federal law so as to provide quick and efficient cleanup of oil spills, compensate victims of such spills, and **[—5—]** internalize the costs of spills within the petroleum industry." *Rice v. Harken Expl. Co.*, 250 F.3d 264, 266 (5th Cir. 2001). The OPA is codified at 33 U.S.C. §§ 2701–2762.

The OPA facilitates prompt cleanup and compensation by first requiring the President to "designate the source or sources of the discharge," who is called the "responsible party." 33 U.S.C. § 2714(a). In 1991, the President delegated that duty to the Coast Guard.[2] The "responsible party" in the case of a vessel is "any person owning, operating, or demise chartering the vessel." 33 U.S.C. § 2701(32)(A). The OPA makes the responsible party "strictly liable for cleanup costs and damages and first in line to pay any claims for removal costs or damages that may arise under OPA." *United States v. Am. Commercial Lines, L.L.C.*, 759 F.3d 420, 422 n.2, 2 Adm. R. 283, 283 n.2 (5th Cir. 2014). "Notwithstanding any other provision or rule of law . . . each responsible party . . . is liable for the removal

---

[2] "The functions vested in the President by Section 1014 of OPA [33 U.S.C. § 2714], respecting designation of sources of discharges or threats, notification to responsible parties, . . . the advertisement of designation, and notification of claims procedures, are delegated to the Secretary of the Department in which the Coast Guard is operating." Exec. Order No. 12,777, 56 Fed. Reg. 54,757, 54,768 (Oct. 18, 1991). The imprecision in identifying a Department is because the Coast Guard is within the Department of Homeland Security except when it is transferred to the Department of the Navy during wartime. *See* 14 U.S.C. § 3.

costs and damages specified in subsection (b) that result from such incident." 33 U.S.C. § 2702(a). There are three absolute defenses, but they are not relevant in this case.[3]

Well before the enactment of the OPA, it was clear that general maritime law did not permit recovery of purely economic losses. *See Robins Dry Dock & Repair Co. v. Flint*, 275 U.S. 303, 307–09 (1927). Since our decision in **[—6—]** *Louisiana ex rel. Guste v. M/V TESTBANK*, 752 F.2d 1019, 1022 (5th Cir. 1985) (en banc), this circuit "has consistently applied the rule limiting recovery in maritime cases to plaintiffs who sustain physical damage to a proprietary interest." *In re Bertucci Contracting Co.*, 712 F.3d 245, 246–47, 1 Adm. R. 225, 225 (5th Cir. 2013). Under the OPA, though, recovery of economic losses is allowed without physical damage to a proprietary **{-345-}** interest. *See* 33 U.S.C. § 2702(b)(2)(E). The only restriction on such recovery is that the loss must be "due to the injury, destruction, or loss of real property, personal property, or natural resources[.]" *Id.*

Marquette's statutory argument is that the right to contribution Settoon claims here for reimbursement of a percentage of all its costs from a jointly negligent party does not arise under the OPA. Instead, it argues that any contribution it owes is based on general maritime law and therefore is subject to the *Robins Dry Dock* bar to purely economic damages. If general maritime law is the sole source for the right to contribution, the total damages of about $4,265,000 would need to be reduced by the $1,450,000 in damages for purely economic-loss claims.

II. Marquette's Issues on Appeal

A. Does the OPA Allow Contribution for Purely Economic Damages?

Our task is to discern the meaning of a statute. If the statute's language is unambiguous, we apply the plain language absent some resulting absurdity. *Hartford Underwriters Ins. Co. v. Union Planters Bank, N.A.*, 530 U.S. 1, 6 (2000). Yet we do not look at language in isolation, as it is important to examine the statute "as a whole and [be] mindful of the linguistic choices made by Congress." *Whatley v. Resolution Tr. Corp.*, 32 F.3d 905, 909 (5th Cir. 1994). During this interpretive process, "plain statutory language is the most **[—7—]** instructive and reliable indicator of Congressional intent." *Martinez v. Mukasey*, 519 F.3d 532, 543 (5th Cir. 2008). Our power "to say what the law is," *Marbury v. Madison*, 5 U.S. (1 Cranch) 137, 177 (1803), is constrained by our mandate to "respect the role of the Legislature, and take care not to undo what it has done," *King v. Burwell*, 135 S. Ct. 2480, 2496 (2015).

One clear requirement of the OPA is that liability and damages are determined in a three-step process. First, the injured party must present its claim for damages to the designated Responsible Party. 33 U.S.C. § 2713(a). The Coast Guard identified Settoon as the Responsible Party, and that is not challenged. Second, if the Responsible Party rejects the claim or refuses to settle it within 90 days, the injured party has a statutory cause of action to sue the Responsible Party for its damages or to seek recovery from the government-created Oil Spill Liability Trust Fund. *Id.* § 2713(c). Third, once the Responsible Party pays compensation, it may seek partial or complete repayment from others by means of contribution or subrogation. *Id.* § 2709 (contribution); § 2715 (subrogation).

Six categories of damages are detailed in Section 2702(b)(2). One of them, Subsection (E), expressly allows for recovery of purely economic losses from the Responsible Party. *Id.* § 2702(b)(2)(E). Claimants must first directly assert claims against Settoon,[4] the

[3] The absolute defenses from liability, which the Responsible Party need establish by a preponderance of the evidence, are these: "(1) an act of God; (2) an act of war; or (3) an act or omission of a third party," with certain exceptions. *See* 33 U.S.C. § 2703(a).

[4] "The text of OPA implies its mandatory and exclusive nature. . . . Section 2713(a) uses the absolute words 'all' and 'shall,' directing the course of action for 'all claims' and mandating that they 'shall' be presented first to the responsible party." *Gabarick v. Laurin Mar. (Am.) Inc.*, 623 F. Supp. 2d 741, 745 (E.D. La. 2009).

Responsible Party, and purely economic loss damages may be claimed. Our question, though, is whether a Responsible Party, after suffering purely economic losses, may seek an apportioned contribution for those losses from some other tortfeasor. We will examine two sections of the OPA as we consider this issue. **[—8—] {-346-}**

We begin with the first section of the OPA after the definitions are out of the way, which is Section 1002 or, as codified, 33 U.S.C. § 2702. Entitled "Elements of liability," it details the obligation of the Responsible Party for the cleanup and identifies which costs of the federal and state governments it must reimburse and the damages for which it must compensate. 33 U.S.C. §§ 2702(a), (b). Marquette argues that a particularly relevant subsection is Section 2702(d), entitled "Liability of third parties." What Marquette finds especially attractive is that it applies only when the entity the Coast Guard designated as the Responsible Party was in fact not at fault at all and others were solely responsible for the discharge of oil. In such a case, liability will shift and the other party or parties will become the equivalent of the Responsible Party under the OPA and thus obligated to pay all costs:

> (d) Liability of third parties
>
> (1) In general
>
> (A) Third party treated as responsible party
>
> Except as provided in subparagraph (B), in any case in which a responsible party establishes that a discharge or threat of a discharge and the resulting removal costs and damages were caused solely by an act or omission of one or more third parties described in section 2703(a)(3) of this title (or solely by such an act or omission in combination with an act of God or an act of war), the third party or parties shall be treated as the responsible party or parties for purposes of determining liability under this subchapter.
>
> (B) Subrogation of responsible party
>
> If the responsible party alleges that the discharge or threat of a discharge was caused solely by an act or omission of a third party, the responsible party—
>
> (i) in accordance with section 2713 of this title, shall pay removal costs and damages to any claimant; and **[—9—]**
>
> (ii) shall be entitled by subrogation to all rights of the United States Government and the claimant to recover removal costs or damages from the third party or the Fund paid under this subsection.

Id. § 2702(d).

This section is inapplicable to our issue because Settoon's principal argument is not that it should be subrogated to the United States and any claimants in order to be reimbursed for all its payments. Instead, it seeks contribution toward what it paid based on the percentage of fault allocated to Marquette. A later section of the OPA addresses that concept. That later section's austerity of language is the opening for Marquette's argument:

> A person may bring a civil action for contribution against any other person who is liable or potentially liable under this Act or another law. The action shall be brought in accordance with section 2717 of this title.

Id. § 2709 (entitled "Contribution"). Marquette argues that the OPA itself does not establish a right to contribution but merely acknowledges it remains available under general maritime law with all that body of law's restrictions including, most relevant, no recovery for purely economic damages.

In Marquette's view, the OPA works like this. There is an initial designation by the Coast Guard of a Responsible Party. That party bears all initial costs. Because time is of the essence after a spill, the designation is straightforward—"the source or sources of the discharge" will be tagged. *Id.* § 2714(a). Here, Settoon's barge was carrying the oil that discharged. Thus, Settoon was in charge of the cleanup. Only later will the sorting out occur regarding who was actually at fault. When that time **{-347-}** comes, the initially designated Responsible Party will be entitled to subrogation if it can show that another party was solely at fault. As to contribution, Marquette contends a Responsible Party will have no rights under the OPA but will be able to recover **[—10—]** apportioned shares of the costs from others who are liable under other laws, namely, general maritime law. That means a Responsible Party must bear the entirety of what it paid for purely economic damages, though it may recover the allocated portions of payments it made for damages recognized under general maritime law.

We disagree with Marquette's key conclusion. Under the principle that we should apply the plain meaning of statutory language while considering its context in the overall enactment, we hold it to be plain that both subrogation and contribution are available "under this Act." That is what Sections 2702 and 2709 say. Marquette's argument would wholly eliminate contribution *under the Act* and restrict a Responsible Party to seek reimbursement for cleanup expenses only from a later-designated solely-at-fault entity.

Marquette insists the language is not that plain, and it cites allegedly supportive caselaw. It uses a Ninth Circuit decision that examined, under Section 2702(d)(1)(A), the shifting of fault from the initially designated Responsible Party to another participant in the accident; the court emphasized that no such shift occurs unless the other is solely at fault. *See Unocal Corp. v. United States*, 222 F.3d 528, 534 (9th Cir. 2000). In that case, though, the Responsible Party sued two other parties claiming they were solely responsible for the oil spill. *Id.* at 533. After a trial, a jury concluded that the two third parties were indeed liable and were the sole causes of the spill. *Id.* Fault was apportioned between the third parties, 80% and 20%, respectively. *Id.* The appellate court affirmed the jury's verdict. *Id.* at 536. That decision is a simple application of the OPA's rules on subrogation. We see nothing in the decision that even addresses how contribution works when the originally designated Responsible Party is partly but not entirely at fault.

Marquette also refers us to one of our unpublished decisions in which we, **[—11—]** like the *Unocal* court, applied Section 2702(d)(1)(A). *See Gabarick v. Laurin Mar. (Am.), Inc.*, 406 F. App'x 883, 888 (5th Cir. 2010). In the course of doing so, we explained the next section of the OPA, which is entitled "Defenses to liability." *See* 33 U.S.C. § 2703. That section elaborates that a Responsible Party has a complete defense to any liability if it can show someone else was solely at fault. *Gabarick*, 406 F. App'x at 888 (citing 33 U.S.C. § 2703(a)(3)). Marquette's continuing point is that the only contribution Settoon is entitled to "under this Act" is under Section 2702 when another is solely liable, which would mean Section 2709 adds nothing significant to the concept. Our continuing response is that Marquette is looking at one section in isolation.

We hold, therefore, that contribution is available under the OPA. That is not to say what the scope of contribution may be. The OPA does not define that term. When a common legal term is used but not specifically defined in a statute, we give that term its general legal meaning. *See Bradley v. United States*, 410 U.S. 605, 609 (1973). An apt definition for contribution is this: "One tortfeasor's right to collect from joint tortfeasors when, and to the extent that, the tortfeasor has paid more than his or her proportionate share . . . ." Black's Law Dictionary (10th ed. 2014). The related but distinct legal concept, "subrogation," is defined as a "substitution of one party for **{-348-}** another whose debt the party pays . . . ." *Id.*

If any limitation is to be placed on the types of damages for which contribution may be recovered under the OPA, the limit must be in the statute. We do not perceive any limitation from the manner in which the separate concept of subrogation is explained.

Perhaps, though, the word "liable" can do the work. The OPA explains that "'liable' or 'liability' shall be construed to be the standard of liability which obtains under section 1321 of this title," which is a section of the Clean Water Act ("CWA") entitled "Oil and hazardous **[—12—]** substance liability." 33 U.S.C. § 2701(17); *see also id.* § 1321.

We thus examine how the CWA treats liability for oil pollution. As with the OPA, it provides (with certain exceptions) that the "owner or operator of any vessel from which oil or a hazardous substance is discharged" is initially liable for all the costs of removal of the pollution. *Id.* § 1321(f)(1). Also as under the OPA, if a discharge of oil "was caused solely by an act or omission of a third party," the third party is liable "for the full amount of such removal costs" which may be recovered by the initially responsible party through subrogation. *Id.* § 1321(g). In addition, in a subsection entitled "Rights against third parties who caused or contributed to discharge," the CWA provides that "liabilities established by this section shall in no way affect any rights which (1) the owner or operator of a vessel or of an onshore facility or an offshore facility may have against any third party whose acts may in any way have caused or contributed to such discharge," nor does the section affect (2) the rights of the United States against such third parties. *Id.* § 1321(h).

We ask the same question of the CWA as we have of the OPA—does it create or just preserve a right of contribution? This court has already answered the question as to the CWA in a non-precedential opinion, where we held that Section 1321(h) does not create a right to contribution. *See Tetra Tech., Inc. v. Kansas City S. Ry. Co.*, 122 F. App'x 99, 102 (5th Cir. 2005). We agree with that conclusion in light of the CWA's plain language—"liabilities established by this section shall in no way affect" any rights a vessel owner "may have" to contribution. *See* 33 U.S.C. § 1321(h). Section 1321(h) has been described as preserving the right of contribution without serving as its source. *Keller Transp., Inc. v. Wagner Enters., LLC*, 873 F. Supp. 2d 1342, 1352 (D. Mont. 2012). We perforce agree with that characterization in light of the CWA's clear statutory language. **[—13—]**

Where are we? We know that liability under the OPA is determined under the same standard as for the CWA. The latter Act relies on other law to determine if a Responsible Party may seek contribution from another who was partially but not entirely responsible for the discharge. The OPA, though, has no similar reliance solely on other law to create a right to contribution. Instead, Section 2709 is solely about contribution, from title through content. It must contemplate that one tortfeasor may sue another for less than complete reimbursement, else the section is a nullity.

Most importantly for us, Section 2709 is premised on there being liability for contribution *under the Act* when it says "a civil action for contribution [may be brought] against any other person who is liable or potentially liable under this Act . . . ." 33 U.S.C. § 2709. Yes, we elided the "or another law" that ends the sentence, but that is only to show that the section recognizes contribution among joint tortfeasors can arise under the Act. To interpret otherwise is to make superfluous the premise that contribution at times **{-349-}** arises under the Act. "The rule against superfluities complements the principle that courts are to interpret the words of a statute in context." *Hibbs v. Winn*, 542 U.S. 88, 101 (2004). This basic interpretive rule has been summarized as meaning that no provision of a statute should be "inoperative or superfluous, void or insignificant . . . ." 2A N. SINGER, SUTHERLAND STATUTES AND STATUTORY CONSTRUCTION § 46.6 (7th ed. 2016).

Section 2709 identifies the set of parties who may be called on for contribution under the OPA by referring to those who are "potentially liable." That phrase also is not statutorily defined. Certainly if the party designated by the Coast Guard as responsible brought a civil action against another party and proved that the latter was solely the cause of a discharge, then that second party's potential liability would be shown to have arisen under the Act. We **[—14—]** have already discussed that eventuality: the initially designated Responsible Party would be entitled to recover all its relevant costs through the Section 2702(d)(1)(B) right to be subrogated to the United States.

Our factual situation is different. This record does not support that Marquette was solely the cause of this accident. Marquette, though, was "potentially liable" even if "liable" means the entity responsible for the entire incident. Any tortfeasor allegedly contributing to the cause of the discharge is "potentially liable" under the Act until there are fact-findings that either confirm or reject complete liability. Factual determinations must be made, be appealed, and become final. Until then, there is a legal potential that any entity who had some role in causing the pollution is liable. Giving that broad meaning to "potentially liable" is logical considering the expansive reach of the OPA and the financial impact on strictly liable Responsible Parties of paying for damages that they did not factually cause.

We find support for this interpretation from another strict-liability enactment, the Comprehensive Environmental Response, Compensation and Liability Act ("CERCLA"). *See* 42 U.S.C. §§ 9601–9675. One of its sections provides that "[a]ny person may seek contribution from any other person who is liable or potentially liable under section 9607(a) of this title[.]" *Id.* § 9613(f)(1). Though not as expansive as Section 2709, which allows for contribution to reach those "liable" or "potentially liable" under the Act or any other law, actions brought under CERCLA's contribution provision are "intended to provide a liable party under CERCLA with a cause of action to mitigate the harsh effects of joint and several liability. . . ." *Elementis Chromium L.P. v. Coastal States Petrol. Co.*, 450 F.3d 607, 612 (5th Cir. 2006).

We have interpreted "potentially liable" in CERCLA to include all who are sued under the Act: **[—15—]**

> The terms "liable or potentially liable" . . . are not defined in the statute. However, after examining the text and the structure of CERCLA, we think that the most sensible reading of the statute demands that, even before any determination of actual liability, a party may be "potentially liable" simply by being sued under the statute. The courts may eventually clear a CERCLA defendant or third-party defendant from liability; but until it does, such a defendant is at least *potentially* liable.

OHM Remediation Servs. v. Evans Cooperage Co., 116 F.3d 1574, 1582 (5th Cir. 1997) (citations omitted). Attaching the "potentially liable" label to all who are sued under CERCLA "allows parties to bring contribution actions after settlements, stipulations, or judicial determination of liability, within the three-year limitations **{–350–}** period." *Id.* at 1583. A similar three-year limitations period applies under the OPA. 33 U.S.C. § 2717(f)(3).

Even if it is correct to say that no provision in the OPA explicitly uses the word "liable" in relation to anyone other than the entity solely responsible for the damage, the phrase "potentially liable" completes the statutory scheme. The entity from whose vessel the oil was discharged must immediately turn to the cleanup without concerning itself with ultimate financial responsibility. Once done, that party may through contribution or subrogation seek payment from all others who were partially or completely at fault.

We examine some of Marquette's counters to this analysis. For example, Marquette discusses a Louisiana federal district court opinion holding that general maritime law and not the OPA governs the Section 2709 contribution action of a Responsible Party against a joint-fault third party. *Gabarick v. Laurin Mar. (Am.) Inc.*, No. 08-4007, 2010 WL 147216, at *2 (E.D. La. Jan. 11, 2010), *rev'd and remanded*, 406 F. App'x 883 (5th Cir. 2010). In that case, a third party alleged to be at fault for an oil spill sought summary judgment against the Responsible Party for all claims that fell under the OPA. *Id.* at *1. **[—16—]** The district court granted summary judgment for the third party on the grounds that evidence precluded finding the third party solely liable under Section 2702(d)(1)(A) of the OPA. *Id.* at *2. The court also concluded that the Responsible Party was "not precluded from seeking contribution under any law other than the OPA." *Id.*

We reversed because we held there was insufficient factual development to assign fault at that stage in the case. *Gabarick*, 406 F. App'x at 890. We did not discuss the part of the district court's analysis on which Marquette wishes to rely. The district court in *Gabarick* never mentioned Section 2709, which specifically deals with contribution as opposed to subrogation. We have mentioned, analyzed, and held Section 2709 to be dispositive.

Marquette also relies on two out-of-circuit district court decisions. The first involved a catastrophic oil spill in the Chicago Sanitary Ship Canal. *See United States v. Egan Marine Corp.*, 808 F. Supp. 2d 1065, 1071 (N.D. Ill. 2011). The Responsible Party sought contribution against a third party whose alleged negligence in loading oil on its barge "was the sole or partial cause of the explosion and spill." *Id.* at 1072. In resolving the third party's summary-judgment motion, the district court also focused its analysis only on Section 2702(d)(1)(A), which is the provision that governs when a third party is determined to be solely at fault. *Id.* at 1080. Because the Responsible Party failed to create a genuine issue of material fact that the third party "solely caused the oil spill," the court determined that "the OPA does not provide grounds for contribution." *Id.* at 1082. The court interpreted the OPA as providing contribution only when another entity is solely responsible, but the court never tried to explain why there would be one OPA section on subrogation and another on contribution. Respectfully, we disagree with *Egan*.

Marquette refers us to one more district court decision. *See Nat'l* **[—17—]** *Shipping Co. of Saudi Arabia (NSCSA) v. Moran Mid-Atl. Corp.*, 924 F. Supp. 1436, 1439 (E.D. Va. 1996), *aff'd sub nom. Nat'l Shipping Co. of Saudi Arabia v. Moran Trade Corp. of Delaware*, 122 F.3d 1062 (4th Cir. 1997). Highlighted is language that general maritime law controlled contribution. *Id.* at 1450. The reason, though, was that the third party from whom contribution was being sought had a defense to liability under the OPA, namely, that it was in a **{-351-}** contractual relation with the Responsible Party. *Id.* at 1446 n.4 (citing 33 U.S.C. § 2703(a)(3)); *see also id.* at 1450. Thus contribution was limited to that under the "other law" portion of Section 2709. *Id.* at 1450.

Through this caselaw, Marquette argues its liability arises only under general maritime law, leaving any contribution obligation subject to the *Robins Dry Dock* rule. "The short answer is that Congress did not write the statute that way." *United States v. Naftalin*, 441 U.S. 768, 773 (1979). Relevant to our interpretive task, a member of this panel while serving as a judge on the Eastern District of Louisiana wrote that, based on reading the statute as a whole, the "OPA establishes an entirely new, federal cause of action for oil spills." *Tanguis v. M/V WESTCHESTER*, 153 F. Supp. 2d 859, 867 (E.D. La. 2001) (Clement, J.). The OPA's "new scheme includes new remedies, which, in many respects, preempt traditional maritime remedies." *Id.*

Another particularly well-experienced district judge explained the expansion of recovery under the OPA beyond general maritime law:

> Congress intended OPA to allow a broader class of claimants to recover economic losses than allowed under general maritime law. Consistent with this intention, Subsection (E) does not require the plaintiff to be the owner of the property or natural resources injured, destroyed, or lost in order to recover under that Section. Thus, the *Robins Dry Dock* rule does not apply to a claim pursued under Subsection (E) of OPA.

In re: Oil Spill by Oil Rig "Deepwater Horizon" in Gulf of Mexico, on Apr. 20, **[—18—]** *2010*, 902 F. Supp. 2d 808, 815–16 (E.D. La. 2012) (Barbier, J.) (citation omitted).

We also conclude that limiting Section 2709 liability to contribution only under general maritime law is inconsistent with the OPA's savings clause for admiralty and maritime law. One section provides: "*Except as otherwise provided in this Act*, this Act does not affect—(1) admiralty and maritime law; or (2) the jurisdiction of the district courts of the United States with respect to civil actions under admiralty and maritime jurisdiction . . . ." 33 U.S.C. § 2751(e) (emphasis added). The emphasized language shows that the admiralty claims that are preserved are those that are not addressed in the OPA. *See Moran*, 924 F. Supp. at 1447. The contribution that is being sought in this case is addressed in the OPA. Marquette's view of the interplay between Section 2709 and Section 2751 would transform the "savings clause" into a supremacy clause by advancing general maritime law over the express provisions of the OPA. In another context, we rejected a similar argument, saying that "courts cannot, without any textual warrant, expand the operation of savings clauses to modify the scope of displacement under OPA." *Am. Commercial Lines,* 759 F.3d at 426, 2 Adm. R. at 286–87.

The OPA provides a procedure for submission, consideration, and payment of costs and damages associated with an oil spill. Responsible parties are also afforded a few absolute defenses from liability. *See* 33 U.S.C. § 2703(a). If no defense applies, "the responsible party will always bear first-level liability, but will be able to recover over against third parties either through contribution according to principles of comparative fault or by invoking a hold harmless or indemnification agreement, if applicable." *See* 2 THOMAS J. SCHOENBAUM, ADMIRALTY & MAR. LAW § 18-3 n.26 (5th ed. 2016).

We often resolve statutory interpretation questions based solely on the **[—19—]** language of the statute: "Where the statute **{-352-}** is so lucid, we need not look to the legislative history for further guidance." *Phillips v. Marine Concrete Structures, Inc.*, 895 F.2d 1033, 1035 (5th Cir. 1990). We have noted some interpretive hurdles here, though, and look to the legislative history as either strengthening or weakening the analysis.

The legislative history recognizes OPA's comprehensive nature and identifies the significance of contribution in the overall remedial scheme. The Conference Report discussed the House's suggested contribution provision, subject to certain presentment requirements. *See* H.R. REP. No. 101-653, at 110–11 (1990) (Conf. Rep.), *as reprinted in* 1990 U.S.C.C.A.N. 779, 789. Perhaps most important for our purposes, the language of the contribution provision was "changed to allow actions for contribution against any person who is liable or *may be liable* under any law." *Id.* (emphasis added). That the OPA itself would largely control liability was also clear:

> Liability under this Act is established notwithstanding any other provision or rule of the law. This means that the liability provisions of this Act would govern compensation for removal costs and damages notwithstanding any limitations under existing statutes such as the act of March 3, 1851 (46 U.S.C. 183), or under existing requirements that physical damage to the proprietary interest of the claimant be shown.

H.R. REP. NO. 101-653, at 103, *as reprinted in* 1990 U.S.C.C.A.N. 779, 781. As to Section 2702(b)(2)(E), a "claimant need not be the owner of the damaged property or resources to recover for lost profits or income. For example, a fisherman may recover lost income due to damaged fisheries resources, even though the fisherman does not own those resources." *Id.*

Numerous other courts and legal scholars agree that the OPA nullifies the *Robins Dry Dock* limitation. A maritime law professor put it this way: "Congress plainly intended . . . to overrule *Robins* [*Dry Dock*] legislatively with **[—20—]** respect to claims for lost profits and impairment of earning capacity resulting from oil spills." Robert Force et al., *Deepwater Horizon: Removal Costs, Civil Damages, Crimes, Civil Penalties, and State Remedies in Oil Spill Cases*, 85 TUL. L. REV. 889, 930–31 (2011) (citing S. REP. NO. 101-94, at 14–15

(1989), *as reprinted in* 1990 U.S.C.C.A.N. 722, 736).[5]

We conclude that the most reasonable interpretation of the language of the OPA, as confirmed by the Act's legislative history, grants to an OPA Responsible Party the right to receive contribution from other entities who were partially at fault for a discharge of oil. Specifically, a Responsible Party may recover from a jointly liable third party any damages it paid to claimants, including those arising out of purely economic losses.

B. Was the Apportionment of Fault Clearly Erroneous?

Even though contribution is allowed, that does not mean the allocation of comparative fault made by the district court is correct. Marquette argues it was improper to assign it 65% of the fault. It provides an extensive list of cases where an overtaking or give-way vessel, here the HANNAH owned by Settoon, was assigned more fault. Marquette argues that when two vessels commit an equal number of statutory faults, and one is obligated to give-way, the greater share of fault should **{-353-}** be placed on the burdened or give-way vessel, barring exceptional circumstances.

Marquette contends that a decision by the Ninth Circuit supports its argument that only in rare circumstances should the overtaken or privileged vessel be responsible for the majority of fault under a comparative-fault **[—21—]** regime. *See Crowley Marine Servs., Inc. v. Maritrans, Inc.*, 530 F.3d 1169, 1175 (9th Cir. 2008). In *Crowley*, the court took notice of the unusual facts of the case when it affirmed the district court's assessment of fault, which assigned greater liability to the overtaken vessel. *Id.* Those unusual facts included: (1) the overtaken vessel's Captain's history of alcoholism and serious medical problems; (2) the vessel owner's knowledge of these problems; and (3) "the coordinated maneuvers of the two vessels[.]" *Id.* Based on this allocation of fault, Marquette requests we reverse and reapportion fault 65% to Settoon.

These or related arguments needed to be, and were, presented to the district court. They have little role on appeal, as our review of a district court's apportionment of fault applies the deferential standard of clear error. *See Tokio Marine*, 235 F.3d at 970. This is particularly important in a bench trial where the district court's opportunity to judge the witnesses' credibility weighs strongly. *See Canal Barge Co. v. Torco Oil Co.*, 220 F.3d 370, 375 (5th Cir. 2000). "Where both parties to a collision are in violation of statutes designed to prevent collisions, the court may apportion fault between the parties, unless either party proves that its statutory violation was not a substantial contributing cause of the collision." *Stolt Achievement, Ltd. v. Dredge B.E. LINDHOLM*, 447 F.3d 360, 364 (5th Cir. 2006).

Nothing in Marquette's argument on apportionment convinces us the district court clearly erred. While the court did not provide a detailed explanation for its apportionment of fault, it made the requisite allocation of fault based on the facts before it. "[E]ven if we might have given different weight to different pieces of evidence than did the district court, this is not a reason to disturb that court's findings of relative responsibility, absent a showing of clear error." *Tokio Marine*, 235 F.3d at 971.

AFFIRMED.

[5] *See generally* David W. Robertson, *The Oil Pollution Act's Provisions on Damages for Economic Loss,* 30 MISS. C. L. REV. 157, 167 n.41 (2011) (collecting cases and commentary).

United States Court of Appeals
for the Fifth Circuit

No. 15-30377

IN RE DEEPWATER HORIZON

LAKE EUGENIE LAND & DEV., INC.
VS.
BP EXPLORATION & PROD., INC.

Appeal from the United States District Court for the Eastern District of Louisiana

Decided: June 21, 2017

Citation: 869 F.3d 351, 5 Adm. R. 276 (5th Cir. 2017).

Before **DAVIS, CLEMENT,** and **COSTA,** Circuit Judges.

[—1—] {-352-} PER CURIAM:

In its Petition for Panel Rehearing, BP asserts that the panel opinion rests upon an argument that was never raised. Specifically, BP asserts that Class Counsel never argued that Policy 495's Industry-Specific Methodologies **[—2—]** ("ISMs") are inconsistent with the text of the BP Settlement Agreement. That is simply inaccurate. In fact, Class Counsel explicitly argued that Policy 495 "Departs from the Terms of the Settlement Agreement" in its opening brief.[1]

The Petition for Panel Rehearing is DENIED.

---

[1] *See* Brief of Appellants at 23.

United States Court of Appeals
for the Fifth Circuit

No. 16-30456

INTERNATIONAL MARINE, L.L.C.
VS.
TESLA OFFSHORE, L.L.C.

Appeal from the United States District Court for the Eastern District of Louisiana

Decided: June 21, 2017
Revised: July 11, 2017

Citation: 860 F.3d 754, 5 Adm. R. 277 (5th Cir. 2017).

Before **SMITH, ELROD,** and **HAYNES,** Circuit Judges.

[—1—] {-756-} **HAYNES,** Circuit Judge: **[—2—]**

International Marine, L.L.C., International Offshore Services, L.L.C. (collectively "International"), and Tesla Offshore, L.L.C. ("Tesla"), appeal the district court's grant of summary judgment dismissing their indemnity and insurance claims.[1] For the reasons explained below, we AFFIRM in part and VACATE and REMAND in part.

I. Background

This case involves an allision in the Gulf of Mexico causing significant damage to a submerged mooring line for the M/V NAUTILUS (the "NAUTILUS"), a mobile offshore drilling unit used by Shell Offshore, Inc. ("Shell"), to conduct drilling operations. The principal dispute before **{-757-}** this court concerns whether third parties are contractually obligated to pay for that damage.

Tesla, an offshore survey company, was tasked with performing an archaeological sonar survey in the Gulf of Mexico. To perform this survey, Tesla required two vessels: a larger vessel, called the "tow vessel," and a smaller vessel, called the "chase vessel." Tesla contracted with International to provide and operate the tow vessel, called the M/V INTERNATIONAL THUNDER (the "THUNDER"). As to the chase vessel, Tesla initially contracted with Integrity Fishers, Inc. ("Integrity"), but after Integrity's vessel developed mechanical issues, Integrity substituted a different chase vessel owned and operated by Sea Eagle Fisheries, Inc. ("Sea Eagle"), called the F/V LADY JOANNA (the "JOANNA").[2] **[—3—]**

The THUNDER traveled along a survey grid while towing a "towfish," owned by Tesla. The towfish was attached to a cable, nearly two miles long, and was towed close to the bottom of the ocean, where it emitted sonar signals and transmitted the echo of those signals to Tesla equipment on the chase vessel. Tesla personnel, rather than the crew of the chase vessel, operated the Tesla equipment. At the time of the allision, the chase vessel was the JOANNA. According to Tesla's party chief aboard the JOANNA, the Tesla tracking equipment was "our responsibility," whereas the crew of the JOANNA was responsible for "driving the vessel and staying within . . . a radius of a tow fish." The Tesla equipment automatically relayed the sonar signals to the THUNDER, which allowed the Tesla survey team to monitor the towfish and maintain the proper towfish position above the ocean bottom and in relation to the survey grid.

The precipitating incident for this litigation was an allision between the towfish cable and a submerged mooring line for the NAUTILUS. Prior to the allision, the towfish had experienced technical problems, forcing Tesla to reel it onto the THUNDER for repairs. The THUNDER and the JOANNA temporarily went off the grid toward the south until the

---

[1] International attempted to amend its complaint to include claims against the insurers, but the district court denied this amendment as "futile" in its summary judgment decision. This opinion refers to the claims described in International's proposed amended complaint and Tesla's claims against the insurers collectively as the "insurance claims." On remand, the district court should reconsider the motion to amend.

[2] The parties dispute whether Integrity was also an owner of the JOANNA. Integrity admitted that Charles V. Rodriguez, Sr., is president of both Integrity and Sea Eagle, and **[—3—]** evidence suggests that Integrity has an insurable interest in the JOANNA. Nevertheless, because we affirm the dismissal of the indemnity claim, we need not resolve this dispute.

towfish was repaired and redeployed, at which point the THUNDER turned north, back toward the grid, followed by the JOANNA. According to International, this turn toward the north put both vessels on a course that brought them closer to the NAUTILUS. The JOANNA's captain informed Tesla's party chief, who was occupied with the Tesla equipment, that the THUNDER was getting too close to the NAUTILUS. The party chief then radioed the THUNDER to warn of the danger, but his warning was met with assurances that everything was okay. The party chief testified that about thirty to forty-five minutes later the towfish **[—4—]** cable allided with the mooring line of the NAUTILUS. The JOANNA was over the towfish and the Tesla equipment was sending sonar signals to the THUNDER immediately prior to the allision.

Shell, which was using the NAUTILUS for drilling operations when the allision occurred, sued Tesla and International for negligence.[3] In the *Shell v. Tesla* negligence litigation, a jury awarded damages to Shell and determined that Tesla was 75% at fault and International was 25% at fault. In the present action before this court, Tesla and International claim they are entitled to indemnity from Integrity and Sea Eagle because the allision related **{-758-}** to the operation of the JOANNA. Tesla and International additionally claim that they are entitled to insurance coverage because they were added as additional insureds on Integrity's and Sea Eagle's insurance policies with Atlantic Specialty Insurance Company/One Beacon Insurance Company ("One Beacon") and New York Marine & General Insurance Company ("NY MAGIC").[4]

The contractual relationships between Tesla, Integrity, and Sea Eagle were set out in two master service agreements ("MSAs"). The parties agree that the MSAs were identical in all relevant respects, and this litigation focuses on two articles, Article 9 and Article 11. Article 9 provides, in relevant part, that the indemnitors (here, Integrity or Sea Eagle) are liable to Tesla and **[—5—]** its contractors for damage to third party property "arising out of or related in any way to the operation of any vessel owned . . . by [Integrity or Sea Eagle] . . . to perform work under this agreement except to the extent such loss, harm, infringement, destruction, or damages is caused by [Tesla's or its contractor's] gross negligence or willful misconduct." This obligation is owed "regardless of cause including who may be at fault or otherwise responsible under any contract, statute, rule or theory of law." Article 11 requires, in relevant part, that Sea Eagle and Integrity provide insurance coverage for "third party claims arising out of or connected with the performance of Service hereunder," and name Tesla and its contractors as additional insureds. The insurance obligations purchased under the MSAs were required to be "independent of the indemnity obligations contained in the contract/agreement and [to] apply regardless of whether the indemnity provisions contained in the contract/agreement are enforceable."

The insurers filed three motions to dismiss. The district court, however, never explicitly decided these motions. While they were still pending, Integrity and Sea Eagle filed motions for summary judgment. Tesla and International responded with their own cross-motions for summary judgment. The district

[3] This litigation is referred to as *Shell v. Tesla*.

[4] This indemnity and insurance lawsuit took a circuitous route before reaching its present iteration. In response to Shell's lawsuit, Tesla and International impleaded Sea Eagle for indemnity. Upon discovering that Integrity may have had an ownership interest in the JOANNA, International subsequently filed a separate indemnity lawsuit against Integrity—which was the initiating suit for the present action before this court. The district court concluded that the Sea Eagle indemnity claim in *Shell v. Tesla* was related to the International lawsuit, and thus decided to consolidate the Sea Eagle indemnity claim with the International lawsuit. *Shell v. Tesla* continued as a trial on International and Tesla's fault for the allision with the NAUTILUS, while the International lawsuit was used to settle any indemnity and insurance claims. Thus, the district court dismissed the claims against Sea Eagle from *Shell v. Tesla* and permitted them to be reasserted here, which International did via a second amended complaint and Tesla did via a third-party demand. Tesla then impleaded Sea Eagle's and Integrity's insurers, One Beacon and NY MAGIC.

court granted Integrity's and Sea Eagle's motions and denied Tesla's and International's motions, concluding that "Shell's claims for damages based on the M/V NAUTILUS incident did not arise out of, and are not related to, the operation of the F/V LADY JOANNA." Furthermore, because it found that there was no indemnity obligation, the district court also concluded that the insurers did not have any obligations to Tesla or International, and it dismissed all claims against the insurers. Tesla and International timely appealed.[5] **[—6—] {-759-}**

II. Standard of Review

We review a grant of summary judgment de novo. *Int'l Marine, L.L.C. v. Delta Towing, L.L.C.*, 704 F.3d 350, 354, 1 Adm. R. 188, 190 (5th Cir. 2013). "Summary judgment is appropriate when 'there is no genuine dispute as to any material fact and the movant is entitled to judgment as a matter of law.'" *Id.*, 1 Adm. R. at 190 (quoting FED. R. CIV. P. 56(a)). The interpretation of a maritime contract is a question of law. *Id.*, 1 Adm. R. at 190.

III. Discussion

A. Indemnity Claims

Tesla and International make two principal arguments: the JOANNA's operation was "related to" the damages sustained by the NAUTILUS because (1) the JOANNA's job was to position itself above the towfish, thereby enabling the onboard Tesla equipment to relay a sonar signal to the THUNDER for proper navigation; and (2) the JOANNA and the THUNDER were involved in a joint sonar survey operation in which the JOANNA played an essential role. We conclude that the summary judgment evidence supports only one finding: the operation of the JOANNA was independent of the negligent conduct found to have caused damage to the NAUTILUS. Accordingly, we affirm the district court's judgment and hold that neither Sea Eagle nor Integrity owe indemnity under the MSAs.

Under federal maritime law, an indemnity contract covers losses within the contemplation of the parties but not those which are "neither expressly within its terms nor of such a character that it can be reasonably inferred that **[—7—]** the parties intended to include them within the indemnity coverage." *Corbitt v. Diamond M. Drilling Co.*, 654 F.2d 329, 333 (5th Cir. 1981). We look to the contract as a whole and can only look beyond the contract if there is an ambiguity. *Fontenot v. Mesa Petroleum Co.*, 791 F.2d 1207, 1214 (5th Cir. 1986). "[W]e have broadly construed language identical or similar to the 'arising in connection herewith' language in [the agreement at issue] to unambiguously encompass all activities reasonably incident or anticipated by the principal activity of the contract." *Id.* Though broad, however, such an undertaking is not limitless. *Marathon Pipe Line Co. v. M/V Sea Level II*, 806 F.2d 585, 591 (5th Cir. 1986) (rejecting a construction that would "read the 'occurring in connection with' language to cover a limitless number of unforeseeable casualties that might have occurred during the pendency of the construction work on [the company's] pipeline"). When one party's negligent contractual performance causes third party property damage independent of the alleged indemnitor's contractual performance, indemnity is usually not required absent a clear indication that the parties agreed to such an unusual undertaking. *See id.*

In *Marathon*, we examined whether the damage in question was related to the services performed by the alleged indemnitor, Oceanonics, under its contract. *Id.* at 590–91.

[5] In February 2016, prior to the district court's summary judgment order, Tesla, International, Integrity, and Sea Eagle reached a partial settlement, but expressly reserved **[—6—]** the indemnity and the insurance claims. As part of that agreement, Integrity and Sea Eagle were given a guarantee that no uninsured judgment would be collected against them. In Tesla's impleader and third-party complaint, it alleged that NY MAGIC issued a "Bumbershoot Policy" adding the JOANNA and providing coverage for contractual liability. Because of this agreement, although Integrity and Sea Eagle remain parties to this lawsuit, the only parties making an active defense of the district court's order are One Beacon and NY MAGIC.

We explained that the contract could not "be read in a vacuum to apply to any situation for which a colorable argument could be made that loss of property was somehow related to Oceanonics' services under the contract." *Id.* at 591. Instead, we held that "since Oceanonics did not contract to place [the vessel in question's] **{–760–}** anchors, the . . . indemnity provision created no obligation on Oceanonics' part to indemnify [the plaintiff]." *Id.*

Here, as in *Marathon*, Tesla and International's negligence, as well as the resulting damage to the NAUTILUS, was independent of the operation of the JOANNA. The principal activity of the contract between Tesla and **[—8—]** Integrity/Sea Eagle was for Integrity/Sea Eagle to operate the JOANNA as a chase vessel—i.e., to navigate the JOANNA so that it remained above the towfish. The MSAs are clear that the NAUTILUS's damage must relate to or arise out of the operation of the JOANNA before an indemnity obligation arises. Nothing about the JOANNA's successful operation as a chase vessel, however, related to Tesla's decisions to redeploy the towfish near the NAUTILUS and take the route back toward the grid that caused an allision with a submerged mooring line. The undisputed evidence shows that Tesla and International were solely responsible for deploying the towfish, positioning the towfish, releasing the appropriate amount of towline dragging the towfish, and choosing the direction in which the towfish would travel. The JOANNA's job was simply to follow the THUNDER and stay above the towfish, wherever it may go, which it performed successfully. Tesla's equipment would then relay the position of the towfish. The JOANNA's "involvement in such an effort—[the sonar survey]—did not cause the accident and did not contribute to [Tesla's and International's] decision to dr[ive] the [towfish] across [the NAUTILUS's mooring line]." *Id.* at 592.

Indemnity is not owed merely because Tesla and International were negligent during the survey, in the absence of the requisite connection to the JOANNA's operation. *See id.* at 591. Although the JOANNA was still in operation carrying out the joint sonar survey and in position over the towfish at the time of the allision, its indisputably successful operation had no bearing on the decision to redeploy the towfish near the NAUTILUS and cross the NAUTILUS's mooring line.[6] Because **{–761–}** the summary judgment evidence **[—9—]** supports only the conclusion

---

[6] In *Marathon*, we observed that "potential liability" under the indemnity provision was limited to "accidents that might occur during [the contractor's] performance of contract services." *Marathon*, 806 F.2d at 591. This statement did not mean that every accident occurring during the contractor's performance of contract services would trigger the indemnity provision. It merely meant that the potential for liability was possible only during **[—9—]** the contractor's performance of services under the contract. There are instances in which accidents occurring during a contractor's performance are nevertheless independent of that performance. This case is one example: a joint sonar survey was underway and Integrity/Sea Eagle successfully performed its obligations under the contract by positioning the JOANNA above the towfish while another contractor negligently performed its own obligations by running the towfish into a submerged mooring line, and the JOANNA had no additional relationship to the resulting damages. Under such circumstances, no indemnity is owed unless the contract indicates that Integrity/Sea Eagle "agreed to such an unusual undertaking." *Id.* In another example, if the THUNDER itself had negligently allided with the NAUTILUS while the joint sonar survey was still underway and the JOANNA was still in operation positioned above the towfish, this negligent act would be independent of the JOANNA's operation. Imposing an indemnity obligation merely because of the JOANNA's involvement in the ongoing joint sonar survey would create "an unusual and surprising obligation." *See id.* (quoting *Corbitt*, 654 F.2d at 333).

By contrast, if the JOANNA developed a technical issue impairing its performance—even if caused by the installation of Tesla's equipment or the conduct of Tesla's onboard crew—and third party damages arose from that technical failure, then those damages might arise out of or relate to the JOANNA's operation. Similarly, if, during the sonar survey, a third party boarded the JOANNA to refuel it or to repair Tesla equipment, and either the third party's equipment were damaged or personnel were injured, then those damages might arise out of or relate to the JOANNA's operation. *See Fontenot*, 791 F.2d at 1214.

that the JOANNA's operation made no contribution to the negligent act causing the NAUTILUS's damages, indemnity is not owed under the MSAs. *See id.* at 592; *cf. Fontenot*, 791 F.2d at 1216 ("[T]he Mesa-Rowandrill contract contemplated the operation of a heliport aboard the [drilling rig] and . . . Fontenot's injuries occurred 'in connection []with' the operation of that heliport." (third alteration in original)).

To be clear, we continue to subscribe to the general rule articulated in *Fontenot* that indemnity agreements containing language such as "arising out of" should be read broadly. *See Fontenot*, 791 F.2d at 1214. It is only when the alleged indemnitor's contractual performance is *completely independent* of another party's negligent act that caused damage that we apply a limitation to this general rule. *See Marathon*, 806 F.2d at 591.

In *Marathon*, we also concluded that a gratuitous warning by the alleged indemnitor to the plaintiff of potential danger did not give rise to indemnity liability that would not otherwise exist. *Id.* at 590. Similarly here, the warning **[—10—]** from the JOANNA's captain to Tesla's party chief that the THUNDER was moving too close to the NAUTILUS was, as the district court correctly concluded, a gratuitous act that has no effect on the outcome of this litigation. *See id.*

B. Insurance Claims

The district court concluded that because the indemnity claims failed, the insurance claims also failed. Although similarities in the contractual obligations for indemnity and insurance under the MSAs may suggest that indemnity and insurance claims rise and fall together in this litigation, such a parallel is not always the case. The scope of insurance coverage is determined by the language of the insurance policy obtained,[7] which may yield a different result than the indemnity provision in the original contract. *See Six Flags, Inc. v. Westchester Surplus Lines Ins. Co.*, 565 F.3d 948, 954 (5th Cir. 2009) ("The language of the policy is the starting point for determining [the parties'] intent."); *Elliott v. Cont'l Cas. Co.*, 949 So.2d 1247, 1254 (La. 2007) ("The parties' intent, as reflected by the words of the policy, determine the extent of coverage."); *see also Int'l Offshore Servs., L.L.C. v. Linear Controls Operating, Inc.*, 647 F. App'x 327, 329 (5th Cir. 2016) ("Even assuming *arguendo* that the MSC required Linear to secure [insurance] coverage, that would not determine whether Linear actually secured the coverage in this Policy. We must look to **[—11—]** the Policy's language . . . ."); *Holden v. U.S. United Ocean Servs., L.L.C.*, 582 F. App'x 271, 273 (5th Cir. 2014) (in a case involving both an indemnity obligation and an obligation to add a party as a named insured, court analyzed each possible ground for liability separately: "We **{–762–}** discern two possible ways in which there could be coverage . . . (1) if [the indemnitor] were liable via its indemnity, . . . or (2) if the [] claims against the indemnitee were covered by the policy pursuant to [its] status as an additional insured under the policy.").[8]

Here, none of the insurance policies are in the record nor is there any other evidence from which the policy language can be definitively discerned. Summary judgment cannot be granted on the insurance claims without first reviewing the insurance policies

[7] Following the Supreme Court's decision in *Wilburn Boat Co. v. Fireman's Fund Insurance Co.*, 348 U.S. 310 (1955), we have held that "the interpretation of a contract of marine insurance is—in the absence of a specific and controlling federal rule—to be determined by reference to appropriate state law." *Ingersoll-Rand Fin. Corp. v. Emp'rs Ins. of Wasau*, 771 F.2d 910, 912 (5th Cir. 1985); *see also Wilburn*, 348 U.S. at 313 ("In the field of maritime contracts as in that of maritime torts, the National Government has left much regulatory power in the States."); *Albany Ins. Co. v. Kieu*, 927 F.2d 882, 886 (5th Cir. 1991) ("State law, therefore, governs the interpretation of marine insurance policies unless an available federal maritime rule controls the disputed issue."). Under Louisiana law, insurance contracts are subject to general rules of contract interpretation under the civil code. *Bernard v. Ellis*, 111 So. 3d 995, 1002 (La. 2007).

[8] Although *International Offshore Services* and *Holden* are not "controlling precedent," they "may be [cited as] persuasive authority." *Ballard v. Burton*, 444 F.3d 391, 401 n.7 (5th Cir. 2006) (citing 5TH CIR. R. 47.5.4).

and determining their scope. It is possible that Tesla and International were added as additional insureds on a policy that provides more coverage than that set forth in the MSAs. On this record, however, we cannot make that determination. Accordingly, we vacate the district court's judgment as to Tesla's and International's insurance claims and remand those claims for appropriate disposition.

For the foregoing reasons, we AFFIRM the summary judgment dismissing the indemnity claims, VACATE the dismissal of the insurance claims, and REMAND the case to the district court for further proceedings consistent with this opinion.

United States Court of Appeals for the Fifth Circuit

No. 16-30217

IN RE LARRY DOIRON, INC.

Appeal from the United States District Court for the Western District of Louisiana

Decided: July 7, 2017

Citation: 869 F.3d 353, 5 Adm. R. 283 (5th Cir. 2017).

ON PETITION FOR REHEARING EN BANC
(Opinion February 23, 2017, 5 Cir., 2017, 849 F.3d 602, 5 Adm. R. 206)

Before **STEWART,** Chief Judge, **JOLLY, JONES, SMITH, DENNIS, CLEMENT, PRADO, OWEN, ELROD, SOUTHWICK, HAYNES, GRAVES, HIGGINSON,** and **COSTA,** Circuit Judges.

[—1—] {-354-} BY THE COURT:

A member of the court having requested a poll on the petition for rehearing en banc, and a majority of the circuit judges in regular active service and not disqualified having voted in favor, **[—2—]**

IT IS ORDERED that this cause shall be reheard by the court en banc with oral argument on a date hereafter to be fixed. The Clerk will specify a briefing schedule for the filing of supplemental briefs.

United States Court of Appeals for the Fifth Circuit

No. 16-30547

IN RE DEEPWATER HORIZON

LAKE EUGENIE LAND & DEV., INC.
vs.
BP EXPLORATION & PROD., INC.

Appeal from the United States District Court for the Eastern District of Louisiana

Decided: July 19, 2017

Citation: 864 F.3d 360, 5 Adm. R. 284 (5th Cir. 2017).

Before **STEWART**, Chief Judge, and **JONES** and **OWEN**, Circuit Judges.

[—1—] {-362-} OWEN, Circuit Judge:

This is an appeal from the denial of civil claims under the Settlement Program that was established following the *Deepwater Horizon* oil spill. Kevin S. Smith, Solomon J. Fleischman, and John C. Kelly (Claimants) are officers **[—2—]** and the sole owners of an architectural firm that received a Business and Economic Loss (BEL) award under the Settlement Program. The Claimants also submitted Individual Economic Loss (IEL) claims for lost wages as employees of the firm. We agree with the district court that the Settlement Program does not contemplate the requested compensation, and we affirm the district court's judgment.

I

In the aftermath of the *Deepwater Horizon* oil spill, BP Exploration & Production, Inc., BP America Production Co., and BP, PLC negotiated with representatives of a proposed class action. The accord that was reached resulted in the Economic and Property Damages Settlement Agreement (Settlement Agreement or Agreement), which the district court approved.[1] The Settlement Agreement designates an Economic and Property Damages Class, consisting of varying individuals and entities within certain geographic areas who suffered damages in varying categories. One damage category is the Economic Damage Category, which compensates the "[l]oss of income, earnings or profits suffered by Natural Persons or Entities as a result of the Deepwater Horizon Incident."

The Agreement divides the Economic Damage Category into Business Economic Loss (BEL) claims and Individual Economic Loss (IEL) claims. Business claimants file BEL claims for lost business profits, and individuals file IEL claims for lost employment earnings. Both BEL and IEL claimants must be within the class and satisfy certain causation requirements.

Claimants are owners and employees of the architectural firm, Fleischman & Garcia, located within a geographic area covered by the **[—3—]** Settlement. They are the sole owners of the firm. Fleischman, the firm's chief executive officer and chairman, submitted a BEL claim for lost profits on behalf of the firm, and each Claimant also submitted separate IEL claims for lost wages. The Court-Supervised Settlement Program (CSSP), which administers the Agreement, awarded the firm a substantial amount. The CSSP later denied each Claimant's IEL claim, stating:

> Our records reflect that you submitted an Economic Loss claim for your business in addition to this Individual Economic Loss claim. You cannot recover employment losses from a job at a business for which you have submitted an Economic Loss Claim.

The Claimants appealed to the internal Appeal Panel established by the Agreement, which also denied relief. The Claimants then requested discretionary review by the district court, pursuant to the Settlement Agreement. The district court denied the request for

[1] *In re Oil Spill by the Oil Rig "Deepwater Horizon" in Gulf of Mex., on Apr. 20, 2010*, 910 F. Supp. 2d 891, 964 (E.D. La. 2012), *aff'd sub nom. In re Deepwater Horizon*, 739 F.3d 790, 2 Adm. R. 140 (5th Cir. 2014).

review, and the Claimants appealed to this court, which consolidated the appeals.[2] **{-363-}**

This court, in an unpublished per curiam opinion, concluded that the district court had abused its discretion by denying review.[3] We noted that "the issues in this case have and will come up repeatedly" and that Appeal Panels had reached "varying conclusions" on the question.[4] Because we determined that the "question of contract interpretation presented in these appeals would be best addressed first by the district court charged with administering the Agreement,"[5] we vacated and remanded the case.[6]

On remand, the district court affirmed the decisions of the Appeal Panels to deny Claimants' IEL claims. Claimants again appealed. **[—4—]**

II

Resolution of this appeal turns on the Settlement Agreement's provisions. "The interpretation of a settlement agreement is a question of contract law that this Court reviews de novo."[7] The Agreement provides that it "shall be interpreted in accordance with General Maritime Law."[8]

Claimants argue that nothing in the Settlement Agreement bars the CSSP from compensating a business's owners and officers through IEL claims after their business has received compensation through a BEL claim. We disagree.

The Settlement Agreement calculates the value of BEL claims by comparing the "actual profit of a business during a defined post-spill period in 2010 to the profit that the claimant might have expected to earn" during the period. The calculation compares "Variable Profit" in a post-spill compensation period with that of an earlier benchmark period. Variable profit "reflects the claimant's revenue less its variable costs." Then, the formula applies a growth factor to account for lost growth potentially due to the spill.

This method excludes from the calculation all "fixed" costs, which the framework assumes do not change between the post-spill period and the benchmark period. Excluding fixed costs is favorable to business claimants because, even if claimants reduced these costs in the post-spill period, the Settlement Agreement awards the claimants for lost profit as if the cost reduction had not occurred.

The Settlement Agreement specifically addresses "Owner/Officer Compensation." The Agreement provides a separate methodology for determining which payroll expenses are fixed or variable, but the Agreement **[—5—]** excludes "Owner/Officer Compensation" from that methodology. Instead, the CSSP treats "Owner/Officer Compensation" as a fixed cost, and the parties do not argue otherwise.

By treating owner/officer compensation as a fixed cost, the Agreement's framework does not recognize any reduction in owner compensation as cost savings for the business claimant. Accordingly, the calculation awards any reduced owner compensation to the business claimant through a BEL claim. For this reason, the district court found that the BEL framework "inherently" compensates the business claimant for reduced owner/officer compensation, and the owners of the firm benefit from this compensation. **{-364-}**

Claimants ask that the CSSP compensate not only their business through a BEL claim, but also the Claimant's themselves as employees through an IEL claim. The Settlement Agreement, when read as a whole,[9] does not allow this double compensation. The BEL framework, by compensating the business for the owners' lost

[2] *In re Deepwater Horizon*, 632 F. App'x 199, 201-02 (5th Cir. 2015) (per curiam).

[3] *Id.* at 204.

[4] *Id.* at 203-04.

[5] *Id.* at 204.

[6] *Id.*

[7] *In re Deepwater Horizon*, 785 F.3d 1003, 1011, 3 Adm. R. 325, 329 (5th Cir. 2015).

[8] *Id.* at 1011 n.6, 3 Adm. R. at 329 n.6.

[9] *Holmes Motors, Inc. v. BP Expl. & Prod., Inc.*, 829 F.3d 313, 315, 4 Adm. R. 263, 264 (5th Cir. 2016).

wages through the fixed-cost designation of their wages, precludes compensating those same owners for the same wages through an IEL claim.

As an alternative contention, Claimants assert that the CSSP should devise a formula for determining the extent to which a business owner's IEL claim overlaps with the business's BEL claim compensation and then simply offset the IEL claim by the amount already awarded through the BEL claim. The Agreement does not provide for such a calculation or set off, and we are not empowered to judicially amend that agreement.

Claimants' final argument, that our interpretation of the Settlement Agreement violates their due process rights, is waived because they did not **[—6—]** raise it on their previous appeal to this court.[10] We nevertheless consider the merits of the argument and conclude that there has been no violation of the due process clause.

* * *

For the foregoing reasons, we AFFIRM the judgment of the district court.

---

[10] *See Ward v. Santa Fe Indep. Sch. Dist.*, 393 F.3d 599, 607 (5th Cir. 2004) ("We have held that a party cannot raise an issue on appeal that could have been raised in an earlier appeal in the same case.").

United States Court of Appeals
for the Fifth Circuit

No. 15-30975

GIC SERVS., L.L.C.
vs.
FREIGHTPLUS USA, INC.

Appeal from the United States District Court for the Eastern District of Louisiana

Decided: August 8, 2017
Revised: August 15, 2017

Citation: 866 F.3d 649, 5 Adm. R. 287 (5th Cir. 2017).

Before **ELROD, SOUTHWICK,** and **GRAVES,** Circuit Judges.

[—1—] {-653-} ELROD, Circuit Judge:

This case is about a tugboat and its voyage across the Atlantic from Houston to Nigeria. Though the tugboat arrived safely in port, the parties dispute whether it was discharged at the correct port. The party that arranged for the tugboat's transport wanted it discharged at Lagos, Nigeria; the ocean carrier believed Warri, Nigeria to be the correct port of discharge, claiming it was told so by an intermediary. Despite the parties' efforts to secure discharge **[—2—]** at Lagos, the ocean carrier was unable to do so and continued on to Warri. And there the tugboat remained. Predictably, litigation ensued. After a bench trial, the district court entered judgment, allocating the liabilities and associated damages among the parties. On appeal, the **{-654-}** ocean carrier and the intermediary challenge various aspects of the judgment. We AFFIRM in part and REVERSE in part.

I.

The plaintiff in this case, GIC Services, L.L.C. (GIC), contracted with Freightplus USA, Inc. (Freightplus), the defendant/third-party plaintiff, to arrange for the transport of a tugboat—the REBEL—to Nigeria.[1] Freightplus does not own vessels capable of transporting the REBEL, so Freightplus contracted with Yacht Path International, Inc. (Yacht Path)[2]—a broker specializing in the transportation of large water craft—who in turn contracted with Industrial Maritime Carriers, L.L.C. (IMC) as the "vessel-operating common carrier." In the end, GIC agreed to pay Freightplus $111,000 for its services, Freightplus agreed to pay Yacht Path $85,000, and Yacht Path agreed to pay IMC $70,000. While GIC paid the amount it owed to Freightplus, and Freightplus paid the amount owed to Yacht Path, Yacht Path did not remit the amount owed to IMC.

In the course of making these arrangements, representatives from Yacht Path spoke with representatives of IMC via telephone and communicated information for IMC's bill of lading,[3] including the desired port of discharge. **[—3—]** Exactly *what* was communicated by Yacht Path is in dispute: IMC claims that Yacht Path said that Warri was the port of discharge, while Freightplus claims that Yacht Path identified Lagos as the port of discharge. IMC then issued a "booking note," which purported to specify the terms of its agreement with Yacht Path. This "booking note," which was sent to Yacht Path, lists Warri as the port of discharge. Yacht Path issued its own booking note and bill of lading, both of which list Lagos as the port of discharge. In late December, Freightplus issued a "house bill of lading," identifying Lagos as the port of discharge. The next day, IMC issued a "non-negotiable" bill of lading and a cargo manifest, both of which listed Warri as the port of discharge.[4] IMC asserts that its nonnegotiable bill of lading and cargo manifest were both sent to Yacht Path. At no time prior to the REBEL's departure from

[1] The REBEL is not owned by GIC, but is owned jointly by GIC Oil and Gas Services, Ltd. (the parent company of GIC) and another entity.

[2] Yacht Path is now in bankruptcy and is not a party to this appeal.

[3] A bill of lading "records that a carrier has received goods from the party that wishes to ship them, states the terms of carriage, and serves as evidence of the contract for carriage." *Kawasaki Kisen Kaisha Ltd. v. Regal-Beloit Corp.*, 561 U.S. 89, 94 (2010) (quotation marks omitted).

[4] This bill of lading was not a final bill of lading. It is marked "non-negotiable," and so it could not have been used to claim the cargo at the port of discharge.

Houston did anyone notice or acknowledge the discrepancy as to the port of discharge.

The REBEL departed Houston in late December. In early January, while the REBEL was en route to Nigeria, communications occurred between Mr. Branting of IMC and Mr. Cummings of Yacht Path through which it became clear that there was confusion over the REBEL's port of discharge. In mid-January, representatives from Yacht Path, Freightplus, and GIC attempted to find a way to discharge the REBEL at Lagos. However, the district court found that a late-night e-mail on January 16 from a Yacht Path representative was the first occasion in which "anyone at Yacht Path or IMC discussed the need for changing the REBEL's destination" from Warri to Lagos. Despite efforts **{-655-}** to rectify the situation, IMC was unable to discharge the REBEL at Lagos. While various parties blame an inability to contact GIC's agent in Nigeria at the eleventh hour, the district court found that "manifest and customs documents" **[—4—]** listing Warri as the port of discharge also contributed to IMC's inability to discharge the REBEL at Lagos.

The ocean carrier proceeded on to Warri and discharged the REBEL there. Though GIC initially sought to obtain the REBEL's release, it was informed that the REBEL could not be released because IMC had not been paid its freight. And so, the REBEL remained in Warri in the custody of a company called Julius Berger.

GIC sued Freightplus, and Freightplus in turn brought a third-party action against IMC. IMC counter-claimed against Freightplus and the REBEL *in rem* to recover its unpaid freight. After a two-day bench trial, the district court concluded that Freightplus was liable to GIC for $1,860,985 in damages incurred as a result of the REBEL's discharge in Warri. The district court then determined that IMC was 30 percent at fault for GIC's damages and so the court required IMC to pay 30 percent of the judgment, as well as 30 percent of Freightplus's attorneys' fees. Finally, the district court concluded that IMC was entitled to recover $70,309.12, plus pre-judgment interest, from Freightplus—the amount of IMC's unpaid freight. The district court subsequently amended its judgment to remove IMC's obligation to pay 30 percent of Freightplus's attorneys' fees.[5] Freightplus and IMC both timely appealed.

After briefing in this court was completed, Freightplus filed a "Motion for Partial Dismissal of Appeal." In this motion, Freightplus represented that it and GIC have "reached a settlement" as to that part of the Second Amended Judgment "relat[ing] to GIC Services and Freightplus." Freightplus thus **[—5—]** requested that we allow it to "dismiss its appeal." A few days later, GIC filed a "Notice of Satisfaction of Judgment" in the district court, indicating that "GIC and Freightplus entered into a settlement agreement, resolving all claims between them," that "Freightplus has fulfilled the terms of the settlement agreement" and so "[t]he judgment [ ] in favor of GIC and against Freightplus is satisfied[.]" We granted Freightplus's motion and dismissed its appeal "as to those aspects of the Second Amended Judgment in favor of GIC Services, L.L.C. and against Freightplus USA, Incorporated ONLY."[6]

II.

The parties raise a host of challenges to the judgment. IMC challenges: (1) the requirement that it indemnify Freightplus for a portion of the damages award; (2) the amount of damages awarded GIC; (3) the allocation of

[5] This was the second time the district court amended its judgment. On the first occasion, the district court did so to substitute the fixed-dollar amounts of pre-judgment interest in the original judgment with percentage figures. The Second Amended Judgment also adjusted the amount Freightplus owed to GIC to $1,811,385, plus pre-judgment interest.

[6] This dismissal includes Freightplus's argument regarding whether the Carriage of Goods by Sea Act, 46 U.S.C. § 1300 *et seq.* limits Freightplus's liability to $500—along with the attendant issue of unreasonable deviation. Likewise, the issue of Freightplus's liability to GIC, including the underlying finding that Freightplus is liable to GIC based on a theory of estoppel, is no longer in this appeal.

damages between itself and Freightplus; and (4) the determination that it may not exercise a lien against the REBEL *in rem* to recover its unpaid freight. Like IMC, Freightplus objects to the allocation of damages between itself and IMC. It also challenges the district **{-656-}** court's refusal to award it attorneys' fees and the requirement that it reimburse IMC for its unpaid freight.[7] We address each of these in turn. **[—6—]**

A.

We first consider whether IMC is liable to Freightplus under a theory of tort indemnification for a portion of the judgment awarded to GIC.

Once a prominent feature of maritime law, maritime tort indemnification is now available only in limited situations. *Hardy v. Gulf Oil Corp.*, 949 F.2d 826, 833 (5th Cir. 1992). One of these situations arises from a "special relationship" between two entities. *Cities Serv. Co. v. Lee-Vac, Ltd.*, 761 F.2d 238, 240 (5th Cir. 1985) (citing *Fed. Marine Terminals, Inc. v. Burnside Shipping Co.*, 394 U.S. 404 (1969)); *see also LCI Shipholdings, Inc. v. Muller Weingarten AG*, 153 F. App'x 929, 931 (5th Cir. 2005). Under this theory, an entity will owe indemnity when its negligence is the cause of a loss to its counterpart.

The parties agree with the district court[8] that a "special relationship" exists between a "non-vessel operating common carrier" (NVOCC)[9] and a "vessel-operating common carrier" (VOCC).[10] They disagree, however, with the district court's conclusion that: (1) Freightplus was operating as an NVOCC; and (2) IMC was negligent and its negligence caused Freightplus's injury.

While we are not aware of a decision of ours recognizing maritime tort liability based on the relationship between a NVOCC and a VOCC, two of our sister circuits appear to have done so. *See SPM Corp. v. M/V Ming Moon*, 22 **[—7—]** F.3d 523, 526–27 (3d Cir. 1994); *Ins. Co. of N. Am. v. M/V Ocean Lynx*, 901 F.2d 934, 937, 941 (11th Cir. 1990). Seeing no reason to depart from these decisions, and given the parties' agreement on this question, we conclude that the NVOCC/VOCC relationship may give rise to a claim for maritime tort indemnity to the extent articulated in this opinion.

1.

The first question is whether Freightplus was operating as an NVOCC. "Non-vessel operating common carrier" is a term defined by statute. *See* 46 U.S.C. § 40102(16). As such, we review the interpretation of that term *de novo*. *See* **{-657-}** *AEL Asia Express (H.K.) Ltd. v. Am. Bankers Ins. Co. of Fla.*, 5 F. App'x 106, 107 (4th Cir. 2001). To the extent this question involves factual issues, "[m]ixed questions of law and fact are also reviewed *de novo*." *Trinity Indus., Inc. v. United States*, 757 F.3d 400, 407, 2 Adm. R. 265, 268 (5th Cir. 2014); *see also Prima U.S. Inc. v. Panalpina, Inc.*, 223 F.3d 126, 129 (2d Cir. 2000) (reviewing *de novo* whether party

---

[7] In its brief, Freightplus argues that GIC lacks standing to recover damages because GIC is not the real party in interest under Federal Rule of Civil Procedure 17(a)(1). IMC did not develop this argument in its own briefing, and it cannot prevail on this argument in any event as there is no indication it ever voiced this objection. *See* Fed. R. Civ. P. 17 (a)(3) ("The court may not dismiss an action for failure to prosecute in the name of the real party in interest until, after an objection, a reasonable time has been allowed for the real party in interest to ratify, join, or be substituted into the action."); *see In re Signal Int'l, LLC*, 579 F.3d 478, 487–88 (5th Cir. 2009).

[8] In denying IMC's motion to dismiss, the district court also decided that Freightplus was entitled to indemnity based on a separate theory—one dependent on the "difference in character of duty owed to GIC." Neither party, however, mentions this latter theory in their briefs, and it is not mentioned in the district court's order either.

[9] A "non-vessel-operating common carrier" is "a common carrier that—(A) does not operate the vessels by which the ocean transportation is provided; and (B) is a shipper in its relationship with an ocean common carrier." *See* 46 U.S.C. § 40102(16).

[10] A "vessel-operating common carrier" is an ocean common carrier. 46 U.S.C. § 40102(17). A common carrier operates the vessel carrying the cargo. *See* 46 U.S.C. § 40102(6).

was an ocean freight forwarder as a mixed question of law and fact).

In the modern shipping industry, the shipment of goods by vessel from the United States often involves a chain of multiple entities, each with defined roles. One of these is the "non-vessel operating common carrier." NVOCCs operate as intermediaries between the shipper—the entity "seek[ing] to export cargo"—and the ocean common carrier—the entity that "physically carr[ies] the cargo on [its] vessel[ ]." *Landstar Exp. Am., Inc. v. Fed. Maritime Comm'n*, 569 F.3d 493, 494 (D.C. Cir. 2009). Under the Shipping Act of 1984, 46 U.S.C. § 40101 *et seq.*, an NVOCC is defined as "a common carrier that (A) does not operate the vessels by which the ocean transportation is provided; and (B) is a shipper in its relationship with an ocean common carrier." 46 U.S.C. § 40102(16). Typically, the NVOCC's role is to "consolidate cargo from numerous shippers into larger groups for shipment by an ocean carrier." *Prima*, 223 F.3d at 129; *see also Ins. Co. of N. Am. v. S/S Am. Argosy*, 732 F.2d **[—8—]** 299, 300–01 (2d Cir. 1984); *All Pac. Trading, Inc. v. Vessel M/V Hanjin Yosu*, 7 F.3d 1427, 1429–30 (9th Cir. 1993).

An NVOCC is therefore something of a hybrid: it is a common carrier[11] vis-à-vis the shipper, but it is itself a shipper vis-à-vis the ocean common carrier. *Ins. Co. of N. Am.*, 732 F.2d at 301; *All Pac. Trading*, 7 F.3d at 1429–30. In its role as common carrier, an NVOCC issues a bill of lading to each shipper, which memorializes the terms of their agreement. *Prima*, 223 F.3d at 129; *see also Landstar*, 569 F.3d at 495. Because of an NVOCC's role as a common carrier and the issuance of a bill of lading, the NVOCC is liable to the shipper if "anything happens to the [cargo] during the voyage." *Prima*, 223 F.3d at 129; *see also Landstar*, 569 F.3d at 495. Further, in its role as a shipper, an NVOCC receives a bill of lading from each VOCC. *Landstar*, 569 F.3d at 495; *All Pac.*, 7 F.3d at 1430. Typically, "NVOCCs receive compensation only from the shipper." *Landstar*, 569 F.3d at 495; *see also Nat'l Customs Brokers & Forwarders Ass'n of Am., Inc. v. United States*, 883 F.2d 93, 101 (D.C. Cir. 1989) ("The NVOCC is compensated only by the shipper."). **[—9—]**

The parties dispute whether Freightplus was operating as an NVOCC. Yet while both parties discuss the statutory definition of an NVOCC, neither party addresses the statutory definition of the term "shipper," which appears within the definition **{-658-}** of NVOCC. *See* 46 U.S.C. § 40102(16) (NVOCC is a "*shipper* in its relationship with an ocean common carrier" (emphasis added)); *id.* § 40102(22) (defining "shipper"). Because the parties have not disputed whether Freightplus falls within the definition of "shipper," we do not reach this issue and instead decide whether Freightplus is an NVOCC based on the arguments presented to us.

We conclude that Freightplus qualifies as an NVOCC because it shares those characteristics typically associated with an NVOCC. First, Freightplus issued a bill of lading, which listed Freightplus as the "carrier"—the role an NVOCC plays vis-à-vis the ultimate shipper. *Cf. Prima*, 223 F.3d at 129 (NVOCC issues bill of lading to each shipper); *Landstar*, 569 F.3d at 495 (same). Second, the parties agree that Freightplus was paid exclusively by GIC, also an indicator

---

[11] Common Carrier means:

"a person that—(i) holds itself out to the general public to provide transportation by water of passengers or cargo between the United States and a foreign country for compensation; (ii) assumes responsibility for the transportation from the port or point of receipt to the port or point of destination; and (iii) uses, for all or part of that transportation, a vessel operating on the high seas or the Great Lakes between a port in the United States and a port in a foreign country; but (B) does not include a carrier engaged in ocean transportation by ferry boat, ocean tramp, or chemical parcel-tanker, or by vessel when primarily engaged in the carriage of perishable agricultural commodities—(i) if the carrier and the owner of those commodities are wholly-owned, directly or indirectly, by a person primarily engaged in the marketing and distribution of those commodities; and (ii) only with respect to the carriage of those commodities.

46 U.S.C. § 40102(6).

that Freightplus was acting as an NVOCC.[12] *See Landstar*, 569 F.3d at 495; *Nat'l Customs Brokers*, 883 F.2d at 101.

IMC argues that Freightplus was not operating as an NVOCC because it is not a "shipper" vis-à-vis IMC as required by Section 40102. *See* 46 U.S.C. § 40102(16). It asserts two bases for this argument: First, it argues that Freightplus is not a "shipper" because it is "not listed as a shipper on IMC's booking note, IMC's bill[ ] of lading, or [its] cargo manifest." Second, and relatedly, it argues that Freightplus cannot be considered an NVOCC because it did not "receive a bill of lading" from IMC, the VOCC. **[—10—]**

To begin with, the validity of these arguments depends in large part on whether Freightplus was a "shipper" within the meaning of Section 40102(22)—which, as noted, IMC has not addressed in its brief. Moreover, while it is true that Freightplus is not listed as "shipper" on the relevant documents and that it did not receive a bill of lading from IMC, an entity's status as an NVOCC (and as a shipper) depends on its function, not the labels ascribed to it by third parties. *See AEL Asia*, 5 F. App'x at 111 ("When dealing with NVOCCs, an intermediary's *conduct*, and not what it [is] label[ed], will be determinative of its status." (emphasis added) (quotation marks omitted)); *see* 46 U.S.C. § 40102(16), (22) (definitions of "shipper" and NVOCC). And here, it is clear that Freightplus possesses the characteristics typical of an NVOCC.

IMC argues that Freightplus was "at most a freight forwarder." But an examination of the services typically performed by a freight forwarder undermines, rather than strengthens, IMC's argument. Unlike an NVOCC, a freight forwarder (1) does not issue a bill of lading, *Prima*, 223 F.3d at 129; and (2) "receives compensation for its services both from its customer . . . and from the ocean carrier." *Nat'l Customs Brokers*, 883 F.2d at 95; *Landstar*, 569 F.3d at 495. Neither is true of Freightplus. That Freightplus's conduct differs from that typical of a VOCC confirms our conclusion that it operated as an NVOCC.

2.

We next address the validity of the district court's finding that IMC acted negligently. In the maritime context, as in any other, "[q]uestion[s] of fault, including determinations of negligence and causation, are factual issues, and may not be set aside on appeal unless clearly erroneous." **{-659-}** *In re Omega Protein, Inc.*, 548 F.3d 361, 367 (5th Cir. 2008) (citing *In re Mid-South Towing*, 418 F.3d 526, 531 (5th Cir. 2005)). Where the "district court's account of the evidence is plausible in light of the record viewed in its entirety," we will "not reverse . . . even though convinced that had [we] been sitting as the trier of fact, [we] would **[—11—]** have weighed the evidence differently." *Id.* In this context, "'[f]indings based on the credibility of witnesses demand even greater deference.'" *Id.* (quoting *Tokio Marine & Fire Ins. Co., Ltd. v. FLORA MV*, 235 F.3d 963, 970 (5th Cir. 2001)).

To establish maritime negligence, "a plaintiff must 'demonstrate that there was [1] a duty owed by the defendant to the plaintiff, [2] breach of that duty, [3] injury sustained by the plaintiff, and [4] a causal connection between the defendant's conduct and the plaintiff's injury.'" *Canal Barge Co. v. Torco Oil Co.*, 220 F.3d 370, 376 (5th Cir. 2000) (quoting *In re Cooper/T. Smith*, 929 F.2d 1073, 1077 (5th Cir. 1991) (alteration omitted)). The district court concluded that IMC was negligent because its agent (Intermarine) had notice that Lagos was the correct port of discharge for two weeks before the REBEL arrived there but did not "take steps to ensure proper delivery at Lagos."[13]

IMC raises a single objection to the finding of negligence. Specifically, IMC argues that it was contractually bound to deliver the REBEL to Warri, and so it cannot be found negligent for delivering cargo to the contractually agreed-upon port. Imposing liability under

[12] There is no dispute that Freightplus is licensed to operate as an NVOCC, but it is also licensed as a "freight forwarder."

[13] The district court also faulted IMC for its "lack of due care" in failing to preserve the shipping instructions it received from Yacht Path.

these circumstances, IMC argues, would place it in a cross-current between: (1) complying with its contractual obligations, but then facing tort-indemnity liability for refusing to change the port of discharge; or (2) avoiding tort-indemnity liability by changing the port of discharge, but then facing breach-of-contract liability for doing so.

This argument, however, sails right into the headwinds of the district court's findings. Despite IMC's repeated insistence to the contrary, the district court *did* find that IMC erroneously listed Warri as the port of discharge on its various documents. In its opinion, the district court noted IMC's argument that **[—12—]** "it was told by Yacht Path that the REBEL's final destination was Warri and therefore fully performed its contractual duties."[14] But the district court concluded that "this argument *is unsupported*," and that IMC had "mistakenly record[ed] the REBEL's port of discharge as Warri," based on the fact that IMC did not produce any evidence that Yacht Path informed IMC that Warri was to be the port of discharge.

We cannot overturn this determination absent clear error. IMC admits that it is unable to produce any documentation showing that Yacht Path identified Warri as the port of discharge. It contends, however, that "there is ample evidence in the record to prove that IMC followed its instructions when it designated Warri as the discharge port." IMC points to the testimony of Mr. Branting and Mr. Jackson, whose testimonies support IMC's account. IMC also points to the fact that its bill of lading, cargo manifest, and booking note identify Warri as the port of discharge, and to an e-mail from Mr. Cummings at Yacht Path, which indicates that "[t]he small tug"—presumably the REBEL—"is booked with my client *at Warri*." **{-660-}**

But the record also contains evidence pointing the other way. For example, the deposition of Mr. Cummings—IMC's point of contact at Yacht Path—was introduced at trial, and he testified to identifying Lagos as the port of discharge in his communications with IMC. We owe particular deference where "credibility of witnesses" is at issue. *See Omega Protein*, 548 F.3d at 367. Moreover, while the designation of Warri on IMC's documents and the e-mail from Mr. Cummings is evidence—perhaps even strong evidence—that Yacht Path did identify Warri as the port of discharge, there is evidence cutting the **[—13—]** other way, including the Yacht Path booking note—issued five days before Mr. Cummings's e-mail—which designates Lagos as the port of discharge. The existence of conflicting evidence is precisely the context in which we defer to the district court's factual findings. *See id.* (we will not reverse factual findings "even though convinced that had [we] been sitting as the trier of fact, [we] would have weighed the evidence differently").

It follows from this conclusion that IMC's objection to the district court's negligence finding must be rejected. Simply put, if IMC did not contract to deliver the REBEL to Warri, then holding IMC liable for doing so does not place it in the catch-22 it posits.[15] IMC offers no other objection to the district court's finding.

Accordingly, because the district court correctly determined that Freightplus was operating as an NVOCC and because its conclusion that IMC was negligent is not clearly erroneous, we uphold its determination that IMC is liable to Freightplus.[16]

---

[14] This statement is found in the district court's "Conclusions of Law," rather than its "Findings of Fact." However, as the district court's opinion notes: "To the extent that any conclusion of law constitutes a finding of fact, the Court adopts it as such."

[15] We note that IMC would not likely have found itself in such a dilemma if it had discharged the REBEL at Lagos. After all, all parties were striving to secure the REBEL's discharge at Lagos once the error was discovered.

[16] Freightplus argues alternatively that it is entitled to full indemnity because IMC was "actively" negligent, while it was, at most, "passively" negligent. This argument is foreclosed by our precedent, which has long since dispensed with the active/passive negligence distinction. *See Loose v. Offshore Nav., Inc.*, 670 F.2d 493, 500–02 (5th Cir. 1982) ("[T]he concepts of active and

B.

We next address the amount of damages awarded. The district court determined that Freightplus was liable to GIC in the amount of $1,811,385. **[—14—]** IMC argues that the district court erred in calculating these damages in two respects: First, it objects to the district court's reliance on a particular trial exhibit. Second, it argues that the district court did not account for GIC's failure to mitigate its damages.

We "review[ ] challenges to evidence admitted or excluded for abuse of discretion." *EMJ Corp. v. Hudson Specialty Ins. Co.*, 833 F.3d 544, 551 (5th Cir. 2016). We will reverse only if "the abuse of . . . discretion is *clearly* shown from the record," *U.S. Bank Nat'l Ass'n v. Verizon Commc'ns, Inc.*, 761 F.3d 409, 430 (5th Cir. 2014), *as revised* (Sept. 2, 2014), and "if substantial prejudice resulted from the error," *EMJ Corp.*, 833 F.3d at 551 (quotation marks omitted). "Resolution of preliminary factual questions concerning the admissibility of evidence are reviewed for clear error." **{-661-}** *Meadaa v. K.A.P. Enters., L.L.C.*, 756 F.3d 875, 880 (5th Cir. 2014). Further, we review the district court's determination of damages under a clearly erroneous standard. *Fed. Sav. & Loan Ins. Corp. v. Tex. Real Estate Counselors, Inc.*, 955 F.2d 261, 268 (5th Cir. 1992); *see also Neal v. United States*, 562 F.2d 338, 341 (5th Cir. 1977). This deferential standard of review extends to determining whether a party failed to mitigate its damages. *Marathon Pipe Line Co. v. M/V Sea Level II*, 806 F.2d 585, 592 (5th Cir. 1986). "The burden rests with the wrongdoer to show that the victim of tortious conduct failed to mitigate damages" by demonstrating "(1) that the injured party's conduct after the accident was unreasonable and (2) that the unreasonable conduct had the consequence of aggravating the harm." *Id.*

1.

For the bulk of the damages awarded, the district court relied solely on Trial Exhibit 101—an invoice sent from Visfi Nigeria Ltd. to GIC Oil and Gas Services Ltd., detailing the costs for "storing, securing, and releasing the REBEL in Warri." IMC argues that the district court was wrong to do so **[—15—]** because: (1) the invoice was never authenticated and so it was never properly admitted into evidence; and (2) it is not the "best evidence" of damages. By contrast, the district court found that IMC stipulated to the authentication of Exhibit 101.

Prior to trial, IMC objected to the admission of Exhibit 101 "under Federal Rule of Evidence 901 and 902 because it has not been properly authenticated." The district court deferred on this objection because "[Exhibit 101] [could] be authenticated at trial by witness testimony." At the same time, and as was enshrined in the final pre-trial order, GIC indicated that it intended to call "[a]ny witness needed to authenticate any documents that cannot be agreed to by stipulation."

At trial, GIC sought to introduce the testimony of Mr. Godwin Ebolo, the director of GIC Oil and Gas Services, as an authenticating witness. Though initially objecting, both Freightplus and IMC agreed to stipulate "[t]o the extent [Mr. Ebolo was called] specifically for a Rule 901 authentication . . . ." The relevant colloquy went as follows:

> MR. BOONE [GIC counsel]: Your Honor, I'd like to call Mr. Godwin Ebolo as my authentication federal witness.
>
> MR. WALTERS [Freightplus counsel]: Your Honor, we would object to this witness testifying. He was not listed in the pretrial order. *To the extent that he's called*

passive negligence have no place in a liability system that considers the facts of each case and assesses and apportions damages among joint tortfeasors according to the degree of responsibility of each party."); *Seal Offshore, Inc. v. Am. Standard, Inc.*, 736 F.2d 1078, 1082 (5th Cir. 1984) ("The concept of active and passive negligence is of no aid . . . because as a footing for [implying] indemnification it is at best a redundancy within a system of comparative fault."); *Hardy*, 949 F.2d at 834 n.13 ("The Court [has] abandoned the active/passive distinction . . . .").

specifically for a Rule 901 authentication, we will stipulate, and I think - -

MR. WAGUESPACK [IMC counsel]: *We'll stipulate as well, Your Honor.*

MR. BOONE: All right. And that's all he was going to testify to, nothing substantive, just to authenticate those documents that Freightplus and IMC both objected to, which are the three contracts and the agency agreement.

THE COURT: All right. So do we have a stipulation?

MR. WALTERS: Yes. As far as Freightplus, yes.

MR. WAGUESPACK: As far as IMC as well. **[—16—]**

THE COURT: Okay. Well, sir, you can go home. Oh, you still want to call him?

MR. WALTERS: He's been excused.

MR. BOONE: Oh, wait.

MR. WALTERS: We stipulated to authentication. There's no - - if that's the only purpose he would be testifying.

MR BOONE: Yeah. He's testifying for authentication.

MR. WALTERS: We've stipulated to authentication.

MR. BOONE: Oh, you have? **{-662-}**

MR. WALTERS: Yes.

IMC contends that its counsel was not stipulating to the authentication of Exhibit 101 since GIC's counsel specifically limited the stipulation to "the three contracts and the agency agreement." However, as the district court found in denying IMC's Rule 59 motion on this issue, the qualifying language from GIC's counsel came *after* counsel for both Freightplus and IMC had "proffered a blanket Rule 901 authentication stipulation for Godwin Ebolo's testimony." Moreover, neither Freightplus's nor IMC's counsel attempted to limit the scope of their unqualified statements agreeing to a stipulation or to confirm that they intended their stipulation to be limited to the particular documents mentioned by GIC's counsel.

We recognize, as did the district court, that "each side could have been more exact in what they were attempting to convey," and that it is possible that Freightplus and IMC did not intend to offer a blanket stipulation on authentication. At the same time, our role is not to determine how we might have come out on this issue in the first instance. *See United States v. Mata*, 624 F.3d 170, 173 (5th Cir. 2010), *as revised* (Nov. 15, 2010) ("A court of appeals may not reverse a district court's finding of fact based only on its belief that, had it been sitting as the trier of fact, it would have weighed the evidence differently and reached a different conclusion."). Instead, we can only reverse **[—17—]** the district court's finding if "viewing the evidence in its entirety, [we are] left with the *definite and firm conviction* that a mistake has been committed." *Bertucci Contracting Corp. v. M/V ANTWERPEN*, 465 F.3d 254, 258–59 (5th Cir. 2006) (emphasis added). As is the case here, "[w]here there are two permissible views of the evidence, the fact finder's choice between them cannot be clearly erroneous." *O'Malley v. U.S. Fid. & Guar. Co.*, 776 F.2d 494, 497 (5th Cir. 1985) (quoting *United States v. Yellow Cab Co.*, 338 U.S. 338, 342 (1949)). Accordingly, we hold that the district court did not clearly err in finding that Freightplus and IMC offered a blanket stipulation on authentication.[17]

---

[17] In any event, we conclude that the district court did not abuse its discretion in relying on Exhibit 101 even if there was not a blanket stipulation as to authenticity. After the May 12 colloquy, the parties agreed that GIC's authenticating witness was excused; he was no longer available to testify regarding authenticity. Moreover, the record appears to show that, as a factual matter, Exhibit 101 was admitted into evidence and was in the district court's possession after trial. Accordingly, given that GIC's authenticating witness was no longer available and that Exhibit 101 appears to have been in evidence, we conclude that the district court did not abuse its

IMC claims that, even if Exhibit 101 was properly admitted, the damages award is still clearly erroneous because other evidence in the record—namely, a "provisional" invoice from Julius Berger (the company holding the REBEL in Warri)—is much stronger evidence of "the actual amount of storage fees that must be paid in order to obtain the release of the REBEL . . . ."[18] That invoice calculates total charges at $151,169.08, while Exhibit 101 calculates them at $1,460,200.

We disagree. By arguing that the district court should have given greater **{-663-}** weight to Exhibit 117 than to Exhibit 101, IMC is effectively asking us to **[—18—]** reweigh the evidence. Again, we will not reverse the district court's factual findings "even though convinced that had [we] been sitting as the trier of fact, [we] would have weighed the evidence differently." *Omega Protein*, 548 F.3d at 367.

2.

IMC next argues that the district court did not account for GIC's alleged failure to mitigate its damages. IMC argues that this mitigation could have occurred if GIC would have "post[ed] a bond as security for IMC's freight claim in order to obtain release of the REBEL from storage."

The district court had before it testimony from Ms. Sogie Ebolo—the managing director of GIC—who testified that she made an effort to secure a bond for the REBEL but was unable to do so because she was told by her attorney that IMC would not accept a bond issued from Nigeria and because bond companies in the United States would not issue a bond for property located in foreign territory. IMC counters with Mr. Jackson's (IMC's corporate representative) testimony "that IMC was never asked about the possibility of accepting a Nigerian bond." At most, then, IMC has shown merely that there is conflicting testimony on this issue. But where "there are two permissible views of the evidence, the factfinder's choice between them cannot be clearly erroneous," and "[f]indings based on the credibility of witnesses demand even greater deference." *Omega Protein*, 548 F.3d at 367 (quotation marks omitted).

C.

We now address the district court's allocation of the damages between Freightplus and IMC. The judgment requires IMC to reimburse Freightplus for 30 percent of the damages award. Both Freightplus and IMC challenge this determination. Freightplus contends that because it was entitled to indemnity, the district court should have required IMC to reimburse it for 100 percent of **[—19—]** the judgment.[19] For its part, IMC claims that because Freightplus is a majority at fault, it is not entitled to any recovery.

1.

Ever since the Supreme Court's decision in *United States v. Reliable Transfer Co.*, 421 U.S. 397 (1975), we have steadily cabined the availability of tort indemnity and "eliminated virtually every variety of tort indemnity once available under maritime law." *Hardy*, 949 F.2d at 833 ("This Circuit recognized . . . that comparative fault displaces the traditional concept of tort [indemnity]."). In its place, we

discretion in relying on Exhibit 101, regardless of whether Freightplus or IMC offered a blanket stipulation on authenticity.

[18] IMC also argues that newly discovered evidence that it presented after trial supports its argument. This "new evidence" was presented to the district court in a Rule 60(b) motion, and the district court denied that motion, concluding that IMC had not met the stringent requirements for Rule 60(b) relief. IMC has not argued to us that the district court's Rule 60(b) ruling is incorrect, and so we will not consider IMC's new evidence.

[19] Freightplus argues in the alternative that the district court erred in concluding that it was negligent. While the district court did not find Freightplus "negligent" *per se*, it did find that the limitation of liability in the Carriage of Goods by Sea Act, 46 U.S.C. § 1300, *et seq.*, did not apply because Freightplus had effected an unreasonable deviation. The validity of that issue, however, is not before us. As noted, this court previously entered an order "dismiss[ing] . . . those aspects of the Second Amended Judgment in favor of [GIC] and against [Freightplus] ONLY." The unreasonable deviation issue was the basis for the judgment against Freightplus and in GIC's favor.

have adopted a "comparative fault" system where "damages in most cases should be allocated according to the respective fault of the liable tortfeasors." *Id.* ("A comparative fault system . . . apportions fault among joint tortfeasors in accordance with a precise determination, not merely equal or all-or-none." (quoting *Loose*, 670 F.2d at 501)). Full indemnity is now reserved for **{-664-}** those circumstances "where proportionate degrees of fault cannot be measured and determined on a rational basis," or where the party claiming indemnity is one "on which the law imposes responsibility even though [it] committed no negligent acts"—*i.e.*, was not at fault. *Id.*

Our cases have consistently held that partial fault is incompatible with full indemnity. In *Seal Offshore*, we reviewed a decision in which a third-party defendant was required to pay full indemnification based on an "implied indemnity theory" in maritime law, even though both parties were found at fault. 736 F.2d at 1080, 1082. Recognizing that our precedent "establish[ed] **[—20—]** that comparative fault principles apply in maritime cases involving both negligence and strict liability," we reversed the award of full indemnity because damages "must be apportioned according to the relative fault" of the defendant and third-party defendant. *Id.* at 1082. Likewise, in *Loose*, we reversed an award of full indemnification where, as in *Seal Offshore*, the indemnitee was found partially at fault. *See Loose*, 670 F.2d at 500–02 (reversing indemnitee award and instructing district court to "instruct the jury to assess the relative degree of responsibility of each party for the plaintiff's injuries"); *cf. Marathon Pipe Line Co. v. Drilling Rig ROWAN/ODESSA*, 761 F.2d 229, 236 (5th Cir. 1985) (upholding award of full indemnity where the "[a]ctual fault" rested with the indemnitor and so the indemnitor "may, therefore, seek full indemnity").

Our decision in *Sea-Land Service, Inc. v. Crescent Towing & Salvage Co.*, 42 F.3d 960 (5th Cir. 1995) is also informative. There, a defendant sued a thirdparty defendant "for indemnification" for a judgment against it. *Id.* at 962. The district court concluded that both were partially at fault and assessed damages accordingly, but also awarded attorneys' fees to the defendant. *Id.* The parties disputed the availability of the attorneys' fees award, with the outcome turning on whether the award was based on a theory of indemnity (where attorneys' fees may be awarded) or contribution (where they may not). *Id.* at 963. We held that "[the defendant's] partial fault preclude[d] full indemnification," and so it was "entitled to contribution (or partial indemnity) . . . and no more." *Id.* ("Indemnification was not awarded and [would not be] appropriate in th[e] case because both [parties] were found to be at fault.").[20] On this basis, we disallowed attorneys' fees. *Id.* **[—21—]**

These precedents scuttle Freightplus's claim for full indemnity. Freightplus was undeniably found to be partially at fault, and that decision is no longer being challenged by Freightplus. Moreover, while both parties contest the district court's findings of fault, neither party has suggested that the "proportionate degrees of fault" in this case "cannot be measured and determined on a rational basis." *Hardy*, 949 F.2d at 833. Under our case law, Freightplus may not recover full indemnity from IMC, but may (at most) recover partial indemnity.

2.

Just as we reject Freightplus's argument for full indemnity, we also reject IMC's argument that Freightplus is **{-665-}** barred from even *partial* indemnity because it was found to be a majority at fault.[21] In essence,

[20] Scholarly sources also agree that "[t]ort indemnity is . . . limited to cases where a non-negligent or vicariously liable tortfeasor is entitled to indemnity from a person who is guilty of actual fault." 1 Thomas J. Schoenbaum, *Admiralty & Maritime Law* § 5-19, at 340 **[—21—]** (5th ed. 2011); *see also* 2 Thomas J. Schoenbaum, *Admiralty & Maritime Law* § 10-39, at 177 (3d ed. 2001) ("Indemnity is properly allowed only when the one seeking indemnity is not guilty of any fault or breach of duty."); 2 *Benedict on Admiralty* 1-67–71 (Matthew Bender 2013).

[21] In its third-party complaint, Freightplus specified that it was seeking contribution from IMC. Though its later pleadings focus on the indemnity issue, Freightplus still indicated that it was seeking contribution.

IMC is urging us to adopt a modified comparative fault rule, where damages are divvied out proportionate to fault *except* where the party claiming indemnification is more than 50 percent at fault.

We reject this argument for the same reasons just discussed. While our cases have precluded *full* indemnity where the party seeking indemnification is partially at fault, we have consistently permitted partially at-fault parties to obtain partial recovery proportionate to the fault of the other parties. *See Loose*, 670 F.2d at 495, 501–02; *Seal Offshore*, 736 F.2d at 1082. Thus, while a partially at-fault indemnitee is not entitled to full indemnification, it may be "entitled to a contribution (*or partial indemnity*)." *Sea-Land*, 42 F.3d at 963 **[—22—]** (emphasis added). We are not aware of any authority (and IMC has cited none) indicating that the comparative fault approach we have adopted does not apply when the party seeking indemnity was more at fault than the indemnifying party. To the contrary, the "comparative fault system . . . apportions fault among joint tortfeasors in accordance with a *precise determination*, not merely equally or all-or-none." *Hardy*, 949 F.2d at 833 (emphasis added). We see no basis for charting a new course here.

The district court assigned 70 percent of the fault to Freightplus and 30 percent to IMC, and neither party has challenged the specific percentages chosen. We therefore uphold the district court's requirement that IMC indemnify Freightplus for 30 percent of the judgment in GIC's favor.

D.

Under the original judgment, the district court required IMC to pay 30 percent of Freightplus's attorneys' fees. However, in response to IMC's Rule 59 motion, the district court amended its judgment to exclude this liability. Freightplus has appealed the district court's exclusion of the attorneys' fees award. The availability of attorneys' fees—as opposed to the amount awarded—is a question of law that we review *de novo*. *See Hester v. Graham, Bright & Smith, P.C.*, 289 F. App'x 35, 44 (5th Cir. 2008) ("Because the issue of which party is entitled to attorneys' fees is a legal issue, this court reviews this award of attorneys' fees *de novo*."); *see also Sea-Land*, 42 F.3d at 963 (reviewing availability of attorneys' fees without deference).

In *Odd Bergs Tankrederi A/S v. S/T Gulfspray*, 650 F.2d 652 (5th Cir. 1981), we observed that "courts have generally denied a right to contribution for attorney's fees and expenses incurred in defense of the action brought by the injured party," but have allowed recovery of attorneys' fees in the indemnification context. *Id.* at 653–54. The rationale for this distinction is that in the indemnity context, the indemnitee's liability "is normally the result of **[—23—]** the act of the indemnitor, who bears the ultimate responsibility for the entire loss." *Id.* at 654. Attorneys' fees are recoverable by the indemnitee in these circumstances because "the indemnitee is required to defend [the] action by an injured party *because of the wrongdoing of the indemnitor*." *Id.* at 654 (emphasis added). By contrast, where the party seeking attorneys' fees is defending against charges of its *own* wrongdoing, "incurring expenses [on attorneys' fees] . . . would be necessary even if there were no other tortfeasors," **{-666-}** and so they are "not recoverable in contribution from the other negligent parties." *Id.* at 653, 655; *id.* at 654 (recovery of attorneys' fees not allowed where party "would incur the same legal expenses whether or not other parties were partly at fault for the loss").

We applied these principles in *Sea-Land*. There, a defendant found liable sought indemnification from a third party. *Sea-Land*, 42 F.3d at 962. The district court allocated damages according to the parties' fault, but also awarded attorneys' fees. *Id.* The party awarded attorneys' fees claimed that *Odd Bergs*'s rule did not apply because it "[was] not claiming recovery under a *contribution* theory" but was rather seeking indemnification. *Id.* at 963 (emphasis added). We rejected this argument, holding instead that indemnification "[was] not appropriate in [that] case because [both parties] were found to be at fault," and so the defendant was only "entitled to a contribution (or partial indemnity). . . and no more." *Id.*

There is no doubt that Freightplus's claim against IMC was litigated under a theory of indemnity. The critical question, however, is not whether the theory of recovery is one of "indemnity" or "contribution"; it is whether the justifications articulated in *Odd Bergs* and *Sea-Land* for allowing recovery of attorneys' fees in the typical indemnity context, and not in the contribution context, are present. Here, they are not. Freightplus was not held liable to GIC as a faultless party; the district court held Freightplus liable to GIC because of **[—24—]** Freightplus's "failure to ensure an accurate bill of lading," and GIC's detrimental reliance on Freightplus's misrepresentations. Thus, Freightplus's liability flows from *its own* conduct, and so the attorneys' fees expended in that defense "would be necessary even if" IMC were not involved. *Odd Bergs*, 650 F.2d at 653. Freightplus's claim to attorneys' fees is unmoored from the justifications for allowing attorneys' fee awards in the indemnity context.

We therefore agree with the district court's determination that Freightplus is not entitled to recover attorneys' fees from IMC.[22]

E.

GIC agreed to pay Freightplus $111,000 for its services. Of this amount, Freightplus agreed to pay Yacht Path $85,000, and Yacht Path agreed to remit $70,000 to IMC. Though GIC paid the amount it owed to Freightplus, and Freightplus paid the amount it owed to Yacht Path, Yacht Path did not remit the monies owed to IMC. The district court held that Freightplus was liable to IMC for the unpaid freight and so awarded IMC $70,309.12, plus pre-judgment interest. We review pure questions of law and mixed questions of law and fact *de novo*. *Trinity Indus.*, 757 F.3d at 407, 2 Adm. R. at 268.

The district court relied on a variety of factors to conclude that Freightplus, rather than GIC, is liable for IMC's freight. Critically, Freightplus **[—25—]** does not argue on appeal that GIC is liable for IMC's freight; **{-667-}** Freightplus's argument is instead that IMC *released* it from liability for freight.[23]

In *Strachan Shipping Co. v. Dresser Indus., Inc.*, 701 F.2d 483 (5th Cir. 1983)[24] a shipper remitted payment to a freight forwarder, but the freight forwarder did not remit the funds intended for the carrier. *Id.* at 484–85. The district court found that the carrier had "extended credit" to the freight forwarder, thus relieving the shipper of freight liability. *Id.* at 489. In reversing, we held that the relevant question for determining whether a carrier has released the shipper from freight liability is "not whether the carrier extended credit to the forwarder, but whether the carrier[ ] intended to release [the shipper] from its obligations and look solely to the

---

[22] Freightplus cites the Eleventh Circuit's decision in *Insurance Co. of N. Am. v. M/V Ocean Lynx*, 901 F.2d 934 (11th Cir. 1990) as establishing that "sole fault or liability on the part of the indemnitor is not a prerequisite to an award of attorneys' fees." *Ocean Lynx* does not support this rule because it does not appear that the indemnitee's liability in that case resulted from any "fault" or wrongdoing on its part. *See Ocean Lynx*, 901 F.2d at 941; *see also SPM Corp. v. M/V Ming Moon*, 22 F.3d 523, 526–27 (3d Cir. 1994) (awarding indemnity where there was "no allegation that the [NVOCC] did anything wrong" and its "liability arose entirely from its contractual relationship with [the shipper] and was trigger by the [ocean carrier's] negligence").

[23] Freightplus does argue that because it is not listed as a "merchant" on IMC's nonnegotiable bill of lading, it cannot be liable for IMC's freight. However, Freightplus does not develop this argument beyond a conclusory sentence, and so we do not consider it. *United States v. Bates*, 850 F.3d 807, 811 n.2 (5th Cir. 2017) ("Because he has failed to adequately develop this insufficiency argument, it is waived. 'Failure of an appellant to properly argue or present issues in an appellate brief renders those issues abandoned.'" (quoting *United States v. Beaumont*, 972 F.2d 553, 563 (5th Cir. 1992))). In any event, we find this argument questionable at best because the IMC non-negotiable bill of lading does not include space for a "merchant" to be listed.

[24] The district court distinguished *Strachan* in the process of concluding that GIC was not liable for IMC's freight, relying on the fact that the shipper in *Strachan* was liable under a credit agreement. *Strachan*, 701 F.2d at 485–86.

forwarder for payment." *Id.* Whether such an intent for release exists "necessarily depends upon the course of dealings of the particular parties, and must be judged from the totality of the circumstances."[25] *Id.*

Applying this approach, we concluded that the carrier did not intend to release the shipper. While the carrier "initially directed its collection efforts to" **[—26—]** the freight forwarder, this fact was "not conclusive." *Id.* We also observed that the designation "freight prepaid" on the bill of lading issued by the carrier to the freight forwarder "indicat[ed] that [the carrier] did not intend to relieve [the shipper] of its obligation[s]." *Id.*

Relying on *Strachan*, Freightplus points to several factors as showing that IMC intended to release it from liability. First, Freightplus argues that IMC's practice of "providing service [to Yacht Path] without contemporaneous receipt of payment is an extension of credit" indicative of an intent to seek freight payment exclusively from Yacht Path. Second, the fact that IMC sought to recover its freight from Yacht Path in the latter's bankruptcy proceeding is, Freightplus argues, also evidence of this intent. Third, Freightplus points to the fact that IMC's non-negotiable bill of lading is marked freight "prepaid," and argues further that IMC is estopped from recovering its freight from Freightplus.

Strachan addressed how to determine whether the primary shipper—as opposed to an intermediary—has been released from freight liability by an ocean carrier. While Freightplus is not a shipper in this sense, both parties operate under the assumption that *Strachan*'s framework also applies to determine whether an ocean carrier has released an intermediary from freight liability. We see no reason why **{–668–}** *Strachan*'s approach for deciding whether an ocean carrier has released an entity from liability should not apply when it is an intermediary, rather than the primary shipper, being sued for unpaid freight.

We conclude that IMC did not release Freightplus from liability for its freight. First, even assuming that IMC's alleged practice of providing service to Yacht Path in other transactions without "contemporaneous receipt of payment" is an extension of credit in the relevant sense (Freightplus cites no authority indicating that it is), our decision in *Strachan* rejected the argument **[—27—]** that an extension of credit is itself a sufficient indication of a carrier's intent to release a shipper from freight liability. *Strachan*, 701 F.2d at 489. There must be some indication that the extension of credit was intended to serve as a release of liability. There is no logical reason to conclude that IMC intended to look to Yacht Path alone simply because IMC previously provided services to Yacht Path without contemporaneous payment. *See Strachan*, 701 F.2d at 489–90 (finding no intent to release from liability despite extension of credit).

We also reject Freightplus's second argument. In *Strachan*, we held that a shipper was *not* relieved of freight liability to a carrier even though the carrier had "initially directed its collection efforts to" the freight forwarder. *Id.* at 489. Here also, the fact that IMC sought payment for freight from Yacht Path in the bankruptcy proceeding is not sufficient to show an intent on IMC's part to release Freightplus. *Id.*

Last, we cannot divine an intent to release Freightplus from liability solely because of the "freight prepaid" designation on IMC's draft bill of lading. Apart from simply stating the fact that IMC's draft bill of lading listed freight as prepaid, Freightplus provides no explanation for why this indicates an intention by IMC to release Freightplus from liability. In *Strachan*, we did not accept the simple fact of a "freight prepaid" designation as establishing an intent to release, and we

---

[25] This rule has been adopted by multiple other circuits. *See Hawkspere Shipping Co., Ltd. v. Intamex, S.A.*, 330 F.3d 225, 238 (4th Cir. 2003) ("The shipper's duty to pay freight is not discharged, absent evidence that the [ocean] carrier has actually released the shipper from its duty to pay . . . ."); *Nat'l Shipping Co. of Saudi Arabia v. Omni Lines, Inc.*, 106 F.3d 1544, 1545–47 (11th Cir. 1997); *Oak Harbor Freight Lines, Inc. v. Sears Roebuck & Co.*, 513 F.3d 949, 959 (9th Cir. 2008).

will not do so here.[26] *Strachan*, 701 F.2d at 489.

As we observed in *Strachan*, "there is no economically rational motive for the carrier" to release entities from liability: "[t]he more parties that are liable, the greater the assurance for the carrier that he will be paid." 701 F.2d at 490. Given this reality, we are loath to find release absent a clear indication **[—28—]** of the carrier's intent. Accordingly, because Freightplus has not demonstrated that IMC intended to release it from liability for the unpaid freight, we affirm the district court's judgment in this regard.

F.

While holding that Freightplus was liable to IMC for its unpaid freight, the district court also determined that IMC could not recover its freight from GIC by bringing an *in rem* action against the REBEL. Relying on out-of-circuit precedent and "principles of equity," the district court concluded that such recovery would impermissibly subject GIC to double payment—the first payment being its payment of $111,000 to Freightplus. We review legal issues and mixed-questions of law and fact *de novo* and any underlying factual finding for clear error. *See Trinity Indus.*, 757 F.3d at 407, 2 Adm. R. at 268.

"Under United States law, it has been settled for over a century that we presume a maritime lien exists in favor of a shipowner on cargo for charges incurred **{–669–}** during the course of its carriage." *Arochem Corp. v. Wilomi, Inc.*, 962 F.2d 496, 499 (5th Cir. 1992); *see The Bird of Paradise*, 72 U.S. 545, 554 (1866)); *see also* 2 Benedict on Admiralty § 44 (Matthew/Bender 2013) ("[M]aritime law permits an action *in rem* against the cargo itself . . . ."). Under this well-established principle, IMC obtained a maritime lien against the REBEL *in rem*. The district court recognized these principles but concluded that IMC could not exercise a maritime lien against the REBEL *in rem* by relying on a "well-reasoned consensus" that a shipper is relieved of liability for freight where the shipper has (1) remitted payment for freight to an intermediary and (2) where the ocean carrier's bill of lading is marked freight prepaid.

We disagree. As already discussed, we articulated the standard for determining whether a shipper has been released from freight liability by the ocean carrier in *Strachan*. *See* 701 F.2d at 489–90. There we held that this **[—29—]** inquiry must focus on the ocean carrier's intent, which is determined from the "totality of the circumstances." *Id.* at 489.

The district court did not follow the course set by *Strachan*, though recognizing that *Strachan* was "contrary" to the rule is applied. In *Strachan*, we rejected the argument that a "freight prepaid" designation on a bill of lading is necessarily sufficient. 701 F.2d at 489. Likewise, we made clear that the *carrier's* intent is paramount, and so we cannot discern anything about IMC's intent from GIC's act of remitting payment to an intermediary. *Cf. Strachan*, 701 F.2d at 489. In short, neither of the district court's reasons evidence an intent *by IMC* to release its maritime lien against the REBEL.

We recognize that *Strachan* involved an action for freight against the shipper itself, whereas here IMC seeks to recover against the REBEL *in rem*. In both situations, however, the relevant question is whether the ocean carrier took action to release a source liable for unpaid freight from liability. We see no reason to apply a different standard for discerning a carrier's intent to release in the context of an *in personam* action than an *in rem* action.[27] We therefore conclude that the

[26] *See also Nat'l Shipping Co.*, 106 F.3d at 1547 (finding fact issue as to intent to release on facts nearly identical to *Strachan*); *Hawksphere*, 330 F.3d at 238 (adopting *Strachan*'s rule).

[27] We do not suggest that *in personam* and *in rem* actions are to be treated identically in all respects or that standards applicable to one type of action are necessarily applicable to the other. Instead, we merely recognize that when it comes to discerning whether the carrier effected a release of liability—whether in the context of an *in personam* or *in rem* action—courts should look to whether the carrier intended such a release and should assess

district court erred in barring IMC's maritime lien against the REBEL *in rem*.[28]

On appeal, GIC does not defend the district court's rationale. It instead argues that the REBEL is not subject to a maritime lien because "there must exist privity of contract" between the cargo owner and the ocean carrier in **[—30—]** order for a maritime lien to attach. For this, GIC relies on our decision in *Lykes Lines Ltd. v. M/V Bbc Sealand*, 398 F.3d 319 (5th Cir. 2005).

GIC misreads *Lykes*. That decision acknowledged that "maritime law recognizes a lien arising as a matter of law in favor of the vessel owner against the cargo for charges including unpaid freight." *Lykes*, 398 F.3d at 323. An exception to this rule applies "when cargo is shipped *under a charter*," in which case "[the] lien only extends to cargo that is owned by the charterer." *Id.* (emphasis added). A "charter" **{-670-}** is a maritime term for the contract arising between the shipowner and the party leasing the ship to transport cargo. *See* BLACK'S LAW DICTIONARY 285 (10th ed. 2009) ("charter" and "charterparty"). But not all contracts for maritime transportation are charters. A charter "is a specialized form of contract for the hire *of an entire ship*." 2 Schoenbaum, *Admiralty & Maritime Law*, § 11-1 (West 2001) (emphasis added). These are contracts securing "private carriage," as distinct from carriage by a "common carrier" who "is available to carry cargo for all who agree to pay its charges." 8 Benedict on Admiralty § 18.01 (Matthew/Bender 2013).

The REBEL was not shipped under a charter, and no party has argued that it was. While Yacht Path arranged for the REBEL to be shipped upon IMC's vessel, it did not "hire [the] entire ship" or otherwise secure private carriage for the REBEL. 2 Schoenbaum, *Admiralty & Maritime Law*, § 11-1; 8 Benedict on Admiralty § 18.01. Mr. Cummings of Yacht Path confirmed that the REBEL was not shipped under a charter. *Lykes* has no bearing here.

Accordingly, we hold that the district court erred in barring IMC from proceeding against the REBEL *in rem*.[29] **[—31—]**

III.

We have come at long last to the end of our own voyage through the assorted issues raised by this appeal and, save for one issue, we drop anchor at the same destination as the district court. Accordingly, we REVERSE the district court's judgment disallowing IMC's *in rem* action against the REBEL and AFFIRM the judgment in all other respects.

(Reporter's Note: Dissenting opinion in part follows on p. 302).

---

this intent based on the totality of the circumstances.

[28] It is true that a maritime lien can be waived. *See* 2 Benedict on Admiralty § 44 (Mathew Bender 2013). GIC has made no argument to this effect.

[29] Because we conclude that IMC has a right to exercise its maritime lien against the REBEL *in rem*, we need not address the issue of IMC's contractual lien against the REBEL.

[—32—] **{-670-}** SOUTHWICK, Circuit Judge, dissenting in part:

My disagreement with the majority concerns its analysis of the issue of authentication of the invoice from Visifi Nigeria Limited. I do not believe there was a stipulation. Accordingly, the exhibit on which most of the damage award is based was never properly admitted into evidence.

There were two documents that allegedly provided evidence of the REBEL's storage costs. One was the Visifi invoice. The other was an invoice from Julius Berger Services, the party storing the REBEL. The two documents are quite different. The Visifi invoice lists "demurrage" fees at $1,400 per day, totaling over $1 million by the end of January 2015. The Julius Berger invoice lists "Tug storage" at $220 per day, totaling $120,120 as of March 25, 2015. The Visifi invoice lists security fees, a national inland waterway fee, impoundment fees, and overhauling fees, totaling over $400,000. The Julius Berger invoice lists stevedoring fees, mooring fees, labor and documentation fees, and taxes, totaling approximately $17,000. The Visifi invoice provides a Lagos, Nigeria address. The Julius Berger invoice provides a Warri, Nigeria address. The Visifi invoice lists a grand total of $1,460,200 as of the end of January 2015. The Julius Berger invoice lists a grand total of $151,169.08 as of April 13, 2015. The parties dispute whether these documents complement one another or offer alternative calculations of storage-related costs.

The Julius Berger invoice was admitted without objection in the district court. Before trial, GIC submitted the Julius Berger invoice to the court as "a true and correct copy of its damages reflected in and to supplement [the Visifi invoice]." During **{-671-}** trial, GIC's witness testified regarding the "demurrage" charges it was incurring from Julius Berger. At the end of trial, GIC moved to enter the Julius Berger invoice into evidence without objection, informing the court that the invoice reflects "[t]he storage charges." **[—33—]**

Freightplus and IMC consistently objected to the introduction of the Visifi invoice in the district court, and that document was never discussed at trial. Two months before trial, the parties objected to the Visifi invoice because they alleged it was not produced during the discovery period, was not relevant, and was not properly authenticated. The district court overruled most of the objections, but it deferred on authentication because the document could "be authenticated at trial by witness testimony."

In a proposed pretrial order filed the week before trial, GIC listed the exhibits it planned to introduce at trial. The list included the Visifi invoice and four other exhibits that Freightplus and IMC objected to on grounds of authentication: "Shell Petroleum Contract and all related documents, P.O. No: 4510244867," "ZED Energy Contract and all related documents, ZED 1021012 PO No. ZED/GIC/13/VOL.11/09," "Shell Petroleum Contract and all related documents PO No. 4510330438: $1,047,000.00," and the "GIC Agency Authorization from GIC Oil and Gas Services, Ltd." The proposed pretrial order also listed Godwin Ebolo as a GIC witness, saying this about his proposed testimony:

> Mr. Ebolo will give testimony in his capacity as managing director of GIC Oil and Gas Services, LTD regarding the relationship between the two entities. His testimony is also necessary to authenticate Shell Petroleum Contract and all related documents, P.O. No: 4510244867, ZED Energy Contract and all related documents, ZED 1021012 PO No. ZED/GIC/13/VOL.11/09, Shell Petroleum Contract and all related documents PO No. 4510330438: $1,047,000.00, and GIC Agency Authorization from GIC Oil and Gas Services, Ltd.

GIC did not explain in the proposed pretrial order how it would authenticate the Visifi invoice. It did, however, note that it would call "[a]ny witness needed to authenticate any documents that cannot be agreed to by stipulation." **[—34—]**

The final pretrial order continued to list the Visifi invoice, the three contracts, and the agency agreement as GIC exhibits. It also noted the objections filed by Freightplus and IMC. The final pretrial order did not list Godwin Ebolo as a GIC witness, but it continued to state GIC would call "[a]ny witness needed to authenticate any documents that cannot be agreed to by stipulation."

At trial, GIC called Godwin Ebolo to testify. The following exchange took place:

> [GIC]: Your Honor, I'd like to call Mr. Godwin Ebolo as my authentication federal witness.
>
> [Freightplus]: Your Honor, we would object to this witness testifying. He was not listed in the pretrial order. To the extent that he's called specifically for a Rule 901 authentication, we will stipulate, and I think—
>
> [IMC]: We'll stipulate as well, Your Honor.
>
> [GIC]: All right. And that's all he was going to testify to, nothing substantive, just to authenticate those documents that Freightplus and IMC both objected to, which are the three contracts and the agency agreement.
>
> THE COURT: All right. So do we have a stipulation?
>
> [Freightplus]: Yes. As far as Freightplus, yes.
>
> [IMC]: As far as IMC as well. **{-672-}**
>
> THE COURT: Okay. Well, sir, you can go home. Oh, you still want to call him?
>
> [Freightplus]: He's been excused.
>
> [GIC]: Oh, wait. **[—35—]**
>
> [Freightplus]: We stipulated to authentication. There's no—if that's the only purpose he would be testifying.
>
> [GIC]: Yeah. He's testifying for authentication.
>
> [Freightplus]: We've stipulated to authentication.
>
> [GIC]: Oh, you have?
>
> [Freightplus]: Yes.
>
> [GIC]: Oh, all right. I'm sorry. I heard you wrong.
>
> [Freightplus]: No.
>
> [GIC]: Okay.
>
> THE COURT: So you can go home.

Whether this stipulation extended to the Visifi invoice, or just "the three contracts and the agency agreement," is the central dispute.

After trial, the district court awarded over $1.8 million to GIC based almost entirely on the Visifi invoice, which it relied on instead of the Julius Berger invoice. Both Freightplus and IMC filed Rule 59(e) motions in which they objected to the district court's use of the Visifi invoice. They argued the invoice was not properly authenticated and did not accurately represent the REBEL's storage charges, which were detailed in admitted invoices provided by Julius Berger—the entity actually storing the REBEL.

The district court denied the Rule 59(e) motions. Pointing to the portion of the trial transcript reproduced above, the court concluded that "counsel for both Freightplus and IMC apparently proffered a blanket Rule 901 authentication stipulation for Godwin Ebolo's testimony before GIC's counsel then responded regarding the documents to be authenticated." The court explained that it "fairly took the intent of counsel for Freightplus and IMC to **[—36—]** be to stipulate as to authentication generally." The court also rejected the argument that it was clear and manifest error to find the Visifi document "a more credible foundation for determining GIC's damages" than the Julius Berger invoice.

IMC later filed a Rule 60(b) motion notifying the court of new evidence demonstrating that the Visifi invoice did not accurately reflect storage charges for the REBEL. This new evidence was a document just like the original Julius Berger invoice but updated to reflect current charges. The total demanded in the invoice for release of the REBEL was just over $186,000. IMC argued this document demonstrated that the Julius Berger invoice represented accurate storage-related costs and suggested that GIC knew the invoice represented accurate costs because Julius Berger was demanding payment from GIC. The district court denied the motion.

Freightplus has settled with GIC, but IMC continues to argue that the district court erred in awarding damages to GIC based on the Visifi invoice. Whether the invoice was ever authenticated is the issue.

"Authentication is a condition precedent to the admission of evidence and is satisfied when a party presents evidence sufficient 'to support a finding that the item is what the proponent claims.'" *United States v. Barnes*, 803 F.3d 209, 217 (5th Cir. 2015) (quoting FED. R. EVID. 901(a)). We review challenges to evidentiary rulings for abuse of discretion. *See EMJ Corp. v. Hudson Specialty Ins. Co.*, 833 F.3d 544, 551 (5th Cir. 2016). "We only reverse if 'substantial prejudice' resulted from the error." *Id.* "Resolution of preliminary factual questions concerning the admissibility of evidence are reviewed for clear error." *Meadaa v. K.A.P. Enters., L.L.C.*, 756 F.3d 875, 880 (5th Cir. 2014). "[A] finding is clearly erroneous 'when although there is evidence to support it, the **{-673-}** reviewing court on the entire evidence is left with the definite and firm conviction that a mistake has been committed.'" *Fed. Sav. & Loan Ins. Corp.* **[—37—]** *v. Texas Real Estate Counselors, Inc.*, 955 F.2d 261, 265 (5th Cir. 1992) (quoting *United States v. United States Gypsum Co.*, 333 U.S. 364, 395 (1948)).

I find clear error. GIC, the party introducing the authentication witness, clearly defined the scope of the stipulation to include "the three contracts and the agency agreement." The scope of the stipulation must have made sense to the parties, because the proposed pretrial order that listed Godwin Ebolo as a witness stated he would authenticate three contracts and one agency agreement. The stipulation at trial did not mention the Visifi invoice.

The majority characterizes the transcript as showing that Freightplus and IMC offered to stipulate before GIC interjected with "qualifying language." There is no indication, however, that the parties offered a "blanket stipulation." Looking at the context, the transcript makes clear that before Freightplus could complete its sentence, IMC jumped in to say it would also stipulate, and GIC immediately responded, "All right. And that's all he was going to testify to, nothing substantive, just to authenticate those documents that Freightplus and IMC both objected to, *which are the three contracts and the agency agreement.*" Only then—*after* GIC's statement—did the district court ask the parties, "So do we have a stipulation?" At that point, what was explicitly before the court as an explanation of the stipulation, to which no one objected, is that it applied to the three contracts and the agency agreement, not the Visifi invoice.

The Visifi invoice is especially problematic because GIC wholly failed to explain it in the district court, yet it alone supports the majority of the damages awarded to GIC. As already noted, GIC introduced the Julius Berger invoice to the court before trial as "a true and correct copy of its damages reflected in and to supplement" the Visifi invoice. At trial, GIC's witness testified about "demurrage" charges from Julius Berger, not Visifi. At the end of the trial, it was GIC who moved to introduce the Julius Berger invoice into evidence **[—38—]** without objection, explaining to the court that the Julius Berger invoice reflected "[t]he storage charges." There is no dispute that Julius Berger stored the REBEL. GIC provided no information at all about the Visifi invoice. Its relevance remains obscure, to say the least, though the district court found it relevant. As IMC points out, "there is no explanation anywhere in the record of who Visifi Nigeria Limited is, why they are providing the document, and from where the information contained within the document is obtained."

In light of both the district court's and my colleagues' contrary view, there must be reasonable doubt about what the stipulation covered despite my sense there is none. Consequently, instead of simply holding that the Visifi invoice never was authenticated and it is too late now, I would reverse and remand to the district court for a hearing on the Visifi invoice that would allow it to be authenticated if that can be done, and also a new decision as to its relevance once someone explains what Visifi is.

I respectfully dissent on that issue.

United States Court of Appeals
for the Fifth Circuit

No. 16-30984

STEMCOR USA INC.
VS.
CIA SIDERURGICA DO PARA COSIPAR

Appeal from the United States District Court for the Eastern District of Louisiana

Decided: September 1, 2017

Citation: 870 F.3d 370, 5 Adm. R. 306 (5th Cir. 2017).

Before HIGGINBOTHAM, GRAVES, and HIGGINSON, Circuit Judges.

[—2—] {-372-} HIGGINSON, Circuit Judge:

This case is a dispute between two creditors, each of which attached the same pig iron owned by America Metals Trading L.L.P. ("AMT"). Plaintiff-Appellant Daewoo International Corp. ("Daewoo") sued AMT in the Eastern District of Louisiana, seeking an order compelling AMT to arbitrate and an attachment of the pig iron. Daewoo invoked both maritime attachment and the Louisiana non-resident attachment statute, which allows attachments in aid of any "action for a money judgment." La. Code Civ. Proc. art. 3542. Citing both types of attachment, the district court granted Daewoo its attachment. Following Daewoo's attachment, Intervenor-Appellee Thyssenkrupp Mannex GMBH ("TKM") attached the same pig iron in Louisiana state court. TKM then intervened in the federal suit, arguing that Daewoo's attachment should be vacated because (1) maritime jurisdiction was improper and (2) **{-373-}** Louisiana non-resident attachment was inapplicable.

The district court agreed with TKM and vacated Daewoo's attachment. Specifically, the district court found that because Daewoo's underlying suit sought to compel arbitration, it was not an "action for a money judgment" and therefore Daewoo could not receive a non-resident attachment writ. Daewoo appeals only the district court's conclusion that its Louisiana non-resident attachment writ was invalid. We VACATE and REMAND.

I

Daewoo is a South Korean trading company. In May 2012, Daewoo entered into a series of contracts with AMT for the purchase of pig iron, to be delivered in New Orleans. The sale contracts contained arbitration clauses. Although Daewoo made payments under the contracts, AMT never shipped the pig iron. TKM is a German company. Between June 2010 and February 2011, **[—3—]** TKM entered into six contracts to purchase pig iron from AMT. AMT never delivered. In response to the breach of contract, TKM and AMT negotiated a settlement, which required AMT to make quarterly payments to TKM. AMT did not pay.

On December 14, 2012, Daewoo filed suit in the Eastern District of Louisiana, seeking attachment of AMT's pig iron on board the M/V Clipper Kasashio, and asserting maritime jurisdiction. The district court issued the attachment. On December 21, Daewoo amended its complaint to seek a writ of attachment under the Louisiana non-resident attachment statute. The writ was granted. On December 22, the U.S. Marshals Service served Daewoo's writ on the cargo, which was then anchored in Kenner Bend.

On December 28, 2012, TKM filed suit in Jefferson Parish state court seeking a writ of attachment over the same pig iron that Daewoo attached on December 22. TKM's state court writ of attachment was served on the cargo on December 29, 2012. TKM then moved to intervene in Daewoo's federal suit. TKM sought a federal writ of attachment over the pig iron, which was granted and served on the cargo on January 11.

That same day, all of the parties moved in federal court to sell the pig iron. The court approved the sale. The parties agreed that the proceeds of the sale would serve as substitute res, subject to TKM's jurisdictional attack on the federal attachments.

On May 9, 2016, TKM moved to vacate Daewoo's attachment.[1] The district court agreed with TKM and vacated Daewoo's writ on August 4, 2016. With Daewoo's federal writ vacated, the first valid remaining writ was TKM's state court writ. Accordingly, the district court ordered that the proceeds from **[—4—]** the pig-iron sale be transferred to the Jefferson Parish state court. On August 10, Daewoo moved to stay the district court's order, arguing that "[i]n the event that Daewoo's appeal is successful it would be difficult to retrieve the funds from the state court, assuming the state court has not already dispersed the funds, and would create serious issues of federal-state comity." The district court denied the stay request because it was filed after the district court had sent the money to the Jefferson Parish state court. **{-374-}**

II

The district court found federal subject matter jurisdiction under the Convention on the Recognition and Enforcement of Foreign Arbitral Awards (the "Convention"). We agree.

For a federal court to have jurisdiction under the Convention two requirements must be met: (1) there must be an arbitration agreement or award that falls under the Convention, and (2) the dispute must relate to that arbitration agreement. These requirements flow from the text of two sections of the Convention. The explicit jurisdictional provision is Section 203, which gives federal courts jurisdiction over all "action[s] or proceeding[s] falling under the Convention." 9 U.S.C. § 203. "An arbitration agreement or arbitral award arising out of a legal relationship, whether contractual or not, which is considered as commercial, including a transaction, contract, or agreement described in section 2 of this title, falls under the Convention." 9 U.S.C. § 202. Accordingly, the first step for determining jurisdiction is deciding whether the "arbitration agreement or award . . . falls under the Convention." *Id.*

The next step, derived from Section 203, is to ask whether the "action or proceeding"—as opposed to the arbitration agreement or award—falls under the Convention. The Convention's removal statute offers guidance on what "falling under" means because "[g]enerally, the removal jurisdiction of the **[—5—]** federal district courts extends to cases over which they have original jurisdiction." *Francisco v. Stolt Achievement MT*, 293 F.3d 270, 272 (5th Cir. 2002). Section 205 of the Convention allows for removal whenever "the subject matter of an action or proceeding pending in a State court relates to an arbitration agreement or award falling under the Convention." 9 U.S.C. § 205. We have read "relates to" to mean "has some connection, has some relation, [or] has some reference" to. *Acosta v. Master Maint. & Constr. Inc.*, 452 F.3d 373, 378–79 (5th Cir. 2006). And reading "falling under" to mean "relates to" makes sense grammatically. "Fall" means "to come within the limits, scope, or jurisdiction of something." Merriam-Webster's Collegiate Dictionary 418 (10th ed. 2002). Accordingly, the second step of the jurisdictional question is asking whether the "action or proceeding" "relates to" a covered arbitration agreement or award. *See Fred Parks, Inc. v. Total Compagnie*, 981 F.2d 1255, 1992 WL 386999, at *1–2 (5th Cir. 1992) (unpublished) (treating the question of original and removal jurisdiction under the Convention as identical).

This two-step jurisdictional inquiry is consistent with case law interpreting the Convention. *See, e.g., BP Expl. Libya Ltd. v. ExxonMobil Libya Ltd.*, 689 F.3d 481, 487 & n.4 (5th Cir. 2012) (finding jurisdiction where there was a covered arbitration agreement and the suit sought appointment of arbitrators); *Borden, Inc. v. Meiji Milk Prods. Co.*, 919 F.2d 822, 826 (2d Cir. 1990) (holding that jurisdiction over preliminary injunction in aid of covered arbitration was proper because the remedy sought did not try to "bypass arbitration"); *Sunkyong Eng'g & Const. Co. v. Born, Inc.*, 149 F.3d 1174, 1998 WL 413537, at *5 (5th Cir. 1998) (unpublished) ("The FAA grants the United States district courts original federal question jurisdiction over arbitral awards and

[1] TKM successfully moved to vacate a number of parties' attachments. Only Daewoo appealed.

agreements to arbitrate that fall within the Convention."); *Venconsul N.V. v. Tim Int'l. N.V.*, 03Civ.5387(LTS)(MHD), 2003 WL 21804833, at *3 (S.D.N.Y. Aug. 6, 2003) ("*Borden* has been interpreted as recognizing a court's power to **[—6—]** entertain requests for provisional remedies in aid of arbitration even where the request for remedies **{-375-}** does not accompany a motion to compel arbitration or to confirm an award.").

Both jurisdictional requirements are met here. First, Daewoo's arbitration agreements with AMT are covered by the Convention. For an arbitration agreement to be covered by the Convention, four requirements must be met: (1) there must be an agreement in writing to arbitrate the dispute; (2) the agreement must provide for arbitration in the territory of a Convention signatory; (3) the agreement to arbitrate must arise out of a commercial legal relationship; and (4) at least one party to the agreement must not be an American citizen. *See Freudensprung v. Offshore Tech. Servs., Inc.*, 379 F.3d 327, 339 (5th Cir. 2004); *Sunkyong*, 149 F.3d 1174, 1998 WL 413537, at *5; *Sedco, Inc. v. Petroleos Mexicanos Mexican Nat'l Oil Co. (Pemex)*, 767 F.2d 1140, 1144–45 (5th Cir. 1985). All four requirements are met here:

- There is an agreement in writing to arbitrate Daewoo and AMT's dispute.
- That agreement provides for arbitration in New York, and the United States is a signatory to the Convention.
- The agreement arises out of a commercial relationship between Daewoo and AMT.
- Both Daewoo and AMT are not American citizens.

Second, this suit is related to the AMT arbitration agreements because Daewoo seeks an attachment to facilitate the arbitration provided for in the AMT agreements. *See Borden*, 919 F.2d at 826 ("[T]he desire for speedy decisions in arbitration is entirely consistent with a desire to make as effective as possible recovery upon awards, after they have been made, which is what provisional remedies do." (internal quotation marks and citation omitted)). Our decision in *E.A.S.T., Inc. of Stamford v. M/V Alaia*, 876 F.2d 1168 (5th Cir. 1989), strongly counsels towards recognizing subject matter jurisdiction **[—7—]** based on the Convention to issue provisional remedies in aid of arbitration.[2] The court in **{-376-}** *E.A.S.T.*, albeit in the context of a maritime attachment, found that the "the

[2] At one point at least, there was significant contrary authority on this issue. *See, e.g., Simula, Inc. v. Autoliv, Inc.*, 175 F.3d 716, 726 (9th Cir. 1999) ("Because the district court correctly concluded that all of Simula's claims were arbitrable and the ICC arbitral tribunal is authorized to grant the equivalent of an injunction *pendente lite*, it would have been inappropriate for the district court to grant preliminary injunctive relief."); *I.T.A.D. Assocs., Inc. v. Podar Bros.*, 636 F.2d 75, 77 (4th Cir. 1981) ("[T]he attachment obtained by I.T.A.D. and the superseding bond posted by Podar are contrary to the parties' agreement to arbitrate and the Convention[.]"); *McCreary Tire & Rubber Co. v. CEAT S.p.A.*, 501 F.2d 1032, 1038 (3d Cir. 1974) (finding that the Convention does not allow a court to issue provisional remedies). However, it appears that the courts that read jurisdiction under the Convention restrictively have retreated from their views and now, at least in most circumstances, recognize subject matter jurisdiction to grant provisional remedies in aid of arbitration. *See Aggarao v. MOL Ship Mgmt. Co.*, 675 F.3d 355, 377 n.19 (4th Cir. 2012) ("Because the Supreme Court has rejected the *McCreary* premise, *Podar Bros.* has been effectively overruled by the Court on the jurisdictional point and is not controlling precedent with respect to [the] injunction request [in aid of arbitration]."); *Toyo Tire Holdings Of Americas Inc. v. Cont'l Tire N. Am., Inc.*, 609 F.3d 975, 980 (9th Cir. 2010) ("In contrast to *Simula*, [plaintiff] seeks an injunction to preserve the status quo until the arbitral panel can consider and rule upon Toyo's application for interim relief pending the arbitration panel's final decision. Allowing a district court to grant this type of relief is not contrary to the 'emphatic federal policy in favor of arbitral dispute resolution' of primary concern in *Simula*. To the contrary, in cases such as this, judicial interim relief may be necessary to preserve the meaningfulness of the arbitral process." (internal citation omitted)); *Rhone Mediterranee Compagnia Francese Di Assicurazioni E Riassicurazoni v. Lauro*, 712 F.2d 50, 55 (3d Cir. 1983) (allowing district court to maintain jurisdiction pending arbitration).

arrest of a vessel prior to arbitration is not inconsistent with the Convention." *Id.* at 1173. And the court noted that the Convention "does not expressly forbid pre-arbitration attachment" and that pre-arbitration attachment "may 'serve[] . . . as a security device in aid of arbitration.'" *Id.* (alteration in original) (quoting *Atlas Chartering Servs., Inc. v. World Trade Grp., Inc.*, 453 F. Supp. 861, 863 (S.D.N.Y. 1978)).

Indeed, *E.A.S.T.*'s reasoning mirrors the reasoning of courts that have found subject matter jurisdiction under the Convention to order state-law provisional remedies. Like the court in *E.A.S.T.*, those courts reason that "nothing in the Convention divests federal courts of jurisdiction to issue **[—8—]** provisional remedies . . . such as an attachment, when appropriate in international arbitrations." *Bahrain Telecomms. Co. v. Discoverytel, Inc.*, 476 F. Supp. 2d 176, 181 (D. Conn. 2007); *see also China Nat'l Metal Prods. Imp./Exp. Co. v. Apex Dig., Inc.*, 155 F. Supp. 2d 1174, 1180 (C.D. Cal. 2001) ("Rather than conflicting with the parties' agreement to arbitrate, provisional remedies such as attachment reinforce arbitration agreements by ensuring that assets from which an arbitration award would be satisfied are secured while arbitration is pending."). *E.A.S.T.* therefore strongly suggests that this court recognizes jurisdiction under the Convention to issue state-law preliminary remedies in aid of arbitration.[3]

Applying *E.A.S.T.* and the cases that follow it, the Convention grants jurisdiction over Daewoo's request for an attachment. Like the plaintiff in **[—9—]** *E.A.S.T.*, Daewoo sought to attach the pig iron in order to facilitate arbitration and increase its chance of recovering on any award. Because Daewoo sought attachment to bring about a covered arbitration—that is, because Daewoo's suit related to a covered arbitration agreement—this court has subject matter jurisdiction.[4] **{-377-}**

III

The parties dispute whether Louisiana's non-resident attachment statute allows for attachment in aid of arbitration. The district court held that it does not. With great respect for the district court, and cognizant of the lack of instructional case law and limited briefing on this issue below, we decline to adopt a categorical approach to this question. Louisiana's non-resident attachment statute

---

[3] And there are compelling reasons against reading jurisdiction under Section 203 as narrowly limited to the three remedies expressly allowed by the Convention (compelling arbitration and appointing arbitrators in Section 206 and confirming awards in Section 207). Namely,

> [n]othing in § 206 or § 207 limits the subject matter jurisdiction of federal courts. These sections merely identify the remedies that federal courts may grant, and do not speak in jurisdictional terms or refer in any way to the jurisdiction of the district courts. . . . To grant the remedies provided in those sections, the Court must first determine that it has jurisdiction . . . .
>
> Treating §§ 206 and 207 as jurisdictional provisions confuses the subject matter jurisdiction of federal courts with their remedial authority. Although jurisdiction is a word of many . . . meanings, there is a difference between the two. The nature of the relief available after jurisdiction attaches is, of course, different from the question whether there is jurisdiction to adjudicate the controversy . . . . The breadth or narrowness of the relief which may be granted under federal law . . . is a distinct question from whether the court has jurisdiction over the parties and the subject matter. Any error in granting or designing relief does not go to the jurisdiction of the court.

CRT Capital Grp. v. SLS Capital, S.A., 63 F. Supp. 3d 367, 374–75 (S.D.N.Y. 2014) (internal quotations marks, citations, and alterations omitted). Simply put, the question of what remedies are available in a Convention suit is distinct from the question of jurisdiction.

[4] We asked the parties to brief whether this court has personal jurisdiction under quasi in rem principles. We are satisfied that we have personal jurisdiction. *See Republic Nat'l Bank of Miami v. United States*, 506 U.S. 80, 88–89 (1992); *Nassau Realty Co., Inc. v. Brown*, 332 So. 2d 206, 210 (La. 1976).

allows for attachment in aid of suits to confirm monetary arbitration awards. Moreover, because Louisiana law allows for attachment in aid of yet-to-be-brought actions, non-resident attachment may be available in aid of arbitration when an eventual confirmation suit is contemplated.

As always, statutory interpretation begins with "the plain language and structure of the statute." *Coserv Ltd. Liab. Corp. v. Sw. Bell Tel. Co.*, 350 F.3d 482, 486 (5th Cir. 2003); *see also Arabie v. CITGO Petroleum Corp.*, 89 So. 3d 307, 312 (La. 2012) ("[A]ccording to the general rules of statutory interpretation, our interpretation of any statutory provision begins with the language of the statute itself."). Louisiana's attachment statute provides that "[a] writ of attachment may be obtained in any action for a money judgment, whether against a resident or a nonresident, regardless of the nature, character, or origin of the claim, whether it is for a certain or uncertain **[—10—]** amount, and whether it is liquidated or unliquidated." La. Code Civ. Proc. art. 3542. A "money judgment" is a "[a] judgment for damages subject to immediate execution, as distinguished from equitable or injunctive relief." Black's Law Dictionary 972 (10th ed. 2014). Accordingly, an "action for a money judgment" is a civil or criminal judicial proceeding seeking monetary damages.

Louisiana case law supports this interpretation. In *de Lavergne v. de Lavergne*, 244 So. 2d 698 (La. App. 4th Cir. 1971), a Louisiana court of appeals was asked to decide whether a suit for alimony was an "action for a money judgment" within the meaning of Article 3542. The court concluded that it was, reasoning:

> A proceeding for alimony is a suit for judgment ordering the payment of money just as any other suit which has for its object the recovery of money in damages or in enforcement of any obligation to pay a sum of money whether liquidated or not. The difference is that in a judgment ordering the payment of a sum of money as alimony or for child support in addition to the ordinary remedies available to the judgment creditor for execution, there is the additional remedy of a contempt proceeding and the imposition of a penalty for noncompliance with the court's order. We must reject the argument of appellants that the additional remedy makes the action something other than one for a money judgment.

Id. at 704. The *de Lavergne* court's analysis aligns with the plain meaning of Article 3542. That is, the *de Lavergne* court first asked whether a suit for alimony sought an order compelling the payment of money. *Id.* Noting, however, that an alimony suit allowed for more than just a payment of money—because an alimony proceeding allowed "the additional remedy of a contempt proceeding and the imposition of a penalty for noncompliance with the court's order"—the court asked whether the additional remedy converted alimony into "something other" than an action "for a money judgment." *Id.* **[—11—]** The court concluded that it did not because the additional contempt remedy was intended to make the money judgment more effective. *Id.*

And other sections of Louisiana law that refer to money judgments have similarly been interpreted to refer to judicial proceedings **{-378-}** seeking judgments of money damages. *See Flowers v. S. Reg'l Physician Servs. Inc.*, 247 F.3d 229, 233 n.4 (5th Cir. 2001) ("[A]s a matter of statutory interpretation, in determining the meaning of a particular statutory provision, it is helpful to consider the interpretation of other statutory provisions that employ the same or similar language."). For example, Civil Code Article 3501 sets forth the prescriptive period for "money judgments": "A money judgment rendered by a trial court of this state is prescribed by the lapse of ten years . . . ." Courts interpreting Article 3501 have found that orders for "the payment of a sum of money" are money judgments, *see, e.g.*, *Eikert v. Beebe*, 188 So. 3d 1129, 1131 (La. App. 2d Cir. 2016), but that orders directing a party to take an action are not money judgments, *see, e.g.*, *Liquidator of Clinton & P.H.R. Co. v. Whitaker*, 22 La. Ann. 209, 209 (1870) ("The judgment directs the liquidator to discharge a duty attached to his office. It is not a money judgment."); *Williams v. Perry*, 436 So. 2d 1268, 1269 (La. App. 1st Cir. 1983) (judgment of partition is not a money judgment). Courts interpreting Code of Civil Procedure Article 2291 have similarly defined "money judgment." Article 2291 provides "[a] judgment for the payment of money may be executed by a writ of fieri facias directing the seizure and sale of property of the judgment debtor." The Article has been interpreted to distinguish between orders for the payment of money and orders directing a party to take an action. *See, e.g.*, *Madere v. Madere*, 660 So. 2d 1205, 1205 (La. 1995) (order of partition "did not create" a money judgment); *Lindy Invs., III, L.P. v. Shakertown Corp.*, 631 F. Supp. 2d 815, 821 & n.13 (E.D. La. 2008) (suit seeking declaration that condition precedent for payment was met was not a suit for money judgment). **[—12—]**

Based on this definition of "action for a money judgment," we agree with the district court that a suit to compel arbitration (like this suit) is not directly an action for a money judgment. A motion to compel arbitration seeks an order requiring a party to take an action—namely, to arbitrate the dispute. Accordingly, a suit seeking to compel arbitration is not an "action for a money judgment," and Daewoo's suit seeking to compel arbitration cannot underlie a Louisiana non-resident attachment writ.

However, that Daewoo's action does not directly seek a money judgment does not end the inquiry. Louisiana law provides that, in limited circumstances, an attachment may issue before the suit underlying the attachment is filed. Article 3502 of the Louisiana Code of Civil Procedure provides:

> A writ of attachment . . . may issue before the petition[5] is filed, if the plaintiff obtains leave of court and furnishes the affidavit and security provided in Article 3501. In such a case the petition shall be filed on the first judicial day after the issuance of the writ of attachment . . . unless for good cause shown the court grants a longer delay.

Article 3502 allows for the possibility of attachments in suits like this one. In Louisiana, arbitral awards are convertible into money judgments in confirmation proceedings. *See, e.g.*, *Matherne v. TWH Holdings, L.L.C.*, 136 So. 3d 854, 860 (La. App. 1st Cir. 2013) ("A confirmed arbitration award is considered to be a valid and final judgment for purposes of res judicata."); La. Stat. § 9:4212 ("Upon the granting of an order confirming, modifying, or correcting **{-379-}** an award, judgment may be entered in conformity therewith in the court wherein the order was granted."); La. Stat. § 9:4214 (noting that when **[—13—]** an award is converted to a judgment, "[t]he judgment so entered shall have the same force and effect, in all respects, as, and be subject to all the provisions of law relating to, a judgment in an action, and it may be enforced as if it had been rendered in an action in the court in which it is entered"). Thus, as TKM's counsel conceded, an action to confirm a money award is an action for a money judgment. And because a confirmation suit can be an action for a money judgment, Section 3502 allows for attachments to be issued before the contemplated underlying confirmation suit is brought.[6]

---

[5] A petition is equivalent to a complaint under federal law. *See* La. Code Civ. Proc. art. 891.

[6] Reading Louisiana law to allow for pre-suit attachment in aid of arbitration makes sense of the statutory scheme as a whole because other provisions of Louisiana law assume that some state-law preliminary remedies are available to aid arbitration. Louisiana has adopted the UNCITRAL Model Law on interim measures in arbitration, which provides, "[i]t is not incompatible with an arbitration agreement for a party to request, before or during arbitral proceedings, from a court an interim measure of protection and for a court to grant the measure." La. Stat. § 9:4249. Moreover, the UNCITRAL Model Law indicates that attachment is one of the interim remedies that may aid an arbitration. It would be strange for Louisiana to have adopted the UNCITRAL Model Law without allowing for state law interim remedies in aid of arbitration. *See Food & Drug Admin. v. Brown & Williamson Tobacco Corp.*, 529 U.S. 120, 121 (2000) ("In determining whether Congress has specifically addressed the question at

Put into context, Section 3502 allows for attachments to issue in aid of arbitration so long as the party seeking the attachment (1) complies with the requirements of Section 3502 and (2) shows good cause for a pre-petition attachment, which will usually require showing that arbitration is likely to result in a confirmation suit and also showing a need for an immediate attachment (which may include an inquiry into the imminence of the arbitration or confirmation suit).

Thus, the critical question is not whether Daewoo's suit to compel arbitration is an action for a money judgment (it is not); instead, we must **[—14—]** further ask (1) whether Daewoo followed the requirements of Section 3502 to seek an attachment in aid of its yet to be filed confirmation suit and (2) whether Daewoo's confirmation suit would be an action for a money judgment. First, TKM's counsel conceded at oral argument that Daewoo followed the procedural requirements of Section 3502. And TKM does not argue that Daewoo failed to follow any Section 3502 conditions imposed by the district court (for example, by filing its follow-on confirmation proceeding too late). Second, from the outset, Daewoo was clear that it would be pursuing a money award in arbitration and that it needed a pre-confirmation suit attachment to secure any eventual arbitral award because AMT was hemorrhaging assets. That is, Daewoo consistently maintained that it needed an attachment so that it could return to Louisiana and collect on its successful arbitration award.

Accordingly, because Section 3502 allows Daewoo to seek a Section 3542 attachment before commencing its confirmation proceeding, and Daewoo followed Section 3502's requirements, Daewoo's attachment was valid. We therefore VACATE the district **{–380–}** court's order dissolving Daewoo's attachment and REMAND for any necessary further proceedings consistent with this opinion.

---

issue, the court should not confine itself to examining a particular statutory provision in isolation. Rather, it must place the provision in context, interpreting the statute to create a symmetrical and coherent regulatory scheme."); *Green v. La. Underwriters Ins. Co.*, 571 So. 2d 610, 616 (La. 1990) ("If two statutes can be reconciled by a fair and reasonable interpretation, we must read the statutes so as to give effect to each.").

(Reporter's Note: Concurring opinion follows *on p. 313).*

[—15—] {-380-} GRAVES, Circuit Judge, specially concurring:

I write separately because I would conclude that the underlying action seeking to compel arbitration here is clearly an "action for a money judgment" under Louisiana's non-resident attachment statute. See La. Code Civ. Proc. art. 3542. As the majority acknowledges, Daewoo has made it clear from the outset that it would be pursuing a money judgment. The "nature, character, or origin of the claim" just happens to be arbitration. La. Code Civ. Proc. art. 3542. Nevertheless, I concur with the conclusion ultimately reached by the majority.

United States Court of Appeals
for the Fifth Circuit

No. 16-30561

UNITED STATES
vs.
MOSS

Appeal from the United States District Court for the Eastern District of Louisiana

Decided: September 27, 2017
Revised: September 29, 2017

Citation: 872 F.3d 304, 5 Adm. R. 314 (5th Cir. 2017).

Before **JONES, CLEMENT,** and **ELROD,** Circuit Judges.

[—1—] {-305-} JONES, Circuit Judge:

A fatal welding accident occurred on an offshore oil platform in the Gulf of Mexico in November 2012. Three years after that incident, the government indicted the owner and operator of the platform and several oil platform contractors, charging criminal violations of the Outer Continental Shelf Lands Act (OCSLA), 43 U.S.C. §§ 1331, *et seq*., and the Clean Water Act, 33 U.S.C. §§ 1251 *et seq*., as well as involuntary manslaughter. 18 U.S.C. § 1112. The defendants moved to dismiss. The district court left all of the charges in place except for the OCSLA charges against the contractor defendants, appellees **[—2—]** Grand Isle Shipyards, Inc. (GIS), Don Moss, Christopher Srubar, and Curtis Dantin, which it dismissed for failure to state an offense. Fed. R. Crim. Pro. 12. The government timely appealed. Because the OCSLA regulations do not apply to these appellees, the judgment of the district court is **AFFIRMED**.

BACKGROUND

1. *OCSLA and Regulatory Enforcement*

Congress enacted OCSLA in 1953, granting the Department of the Interior authority to promulgate and enforce safety and environmental regulations on "any holder of a lease or permit under [OCSLA]." 43 U.S.C. § 1348(b). For over 60 years, the federal government did not regulate or prosecute oilfield contractors, as opposed to lessees, permittees, or well operators, under OCSLA.[1] **{-306-}**

A month after the 2010 Deepwater Horizon spill, however, the Secretary of the Department of the Interior reorganized the Minerals Management System (MMS), tasked with enforcing OCSLA, into three agencies: the Office of Natural Resources Revenues (ONRR), the Bureau of Ocean Energy Management (BOEM), and the Bureau of Safety and Environmental Enforcement (BSEE). *See* Secretarial Order 3299 (May 19, 2010). The newly-created BSEE started aggressively enforcing OSCLA and its regulations against a series of contractors. BSEE announced in a 2011 press release about enforcement actions, "[t]his is the first time the Department of the Interior has issued INCs [incidents of non-compliance] directly to a contractor that was not **[—3—]** the well's operator."[2] In 2012, just months before the incident that gave rise to this case, BSEE issued an internal "Interim Policy Document" opining that contractors may be liable for civil penalties under OCSLA, although this document made no mention of criminal liability. *See* Bureau of Safety and Environmental Enforcement, IPD No. 12-07, Issuance of an Incident of Non Compliance (INC) to Contractors (Aug. 15, 2012).

2. *The West Delta 32 Lease Block Incident and Indictment*

In summer 2010, Black Elk Energy Offshore Operations, LLC obtained a federal oil and gas lease covering a portion of the Gulf of Mexico known as the West Delta 32 Lease Block, and operated a three-platform

[1] The government conceded there are no reported cases of a successful prosecution of a contractor under OCSLA, and the only evidence of such a prosecution cited by the government is a New York Times article about a contractor's entering a guilty plea in 1988.

[2] *See* BSEE, "BSEE Issues Violations Following Investigation Into Deepwater Horizon," https://www.bsee.gov/newsroom/latest-news/statements-and-releases/pressreleases/bsee-issues-violations-following, accessed June 22, 2017.

production facility there. Black Elk contracted with Appellee GIS and Wood Group PSN, Inc. to provide platform workers. Wood Group also furnished a "Person-in-Charge" for the platform, Appellee Srubar. Srubar and Wood Group were responsible for conducting safety inspections and issuing safety permits for "hot work," such as welding and grinding, that emits sparks.

In September 2012, Black Elk interrupted its oil and gas production on West Delta 32 to commission construction projects on the platforms that could not be performed during production. Compass Engineering and Consulting, LLC[3] drew up the construction plans, and Compass hired Appellee Moss as an **[—4—]** independent contractor and onsite inspector to coordinate and manage the work on the West Delta 32 platform projects.

One project involved installing a divert valve on the Lease Automatic Custody Transfer (LACT) unit.[4] During this work, someone discovered that the prefabricated piping necessary to upgrade the LACT unit was missing. A Black Elk manager decided the piping should be rebuilt. To do that, the crew was required to perform "hot work" and weld the sump line piping, some of which lay within 20 feet of the Wet Oil Tank. On November 16, Wood Group issued a hot work permit to the GIS crew.

A fatal explosion occurred that morning, killing three men, injuring others, and discharging **{–307–}** pollutants into the Gulf of Mexico. The cause of the explosion is disputed, but the government contends the contractors were criminally liable because they failed to obtain proper authorization to weld, failed to conduct appropriate pre-work inspections, and failed to ensure the construction area was safe for hot work as required by OCSLA safety regulations.

Criminal indictments were issued three years later against Black Elk, as the lessee-operator, and the contractor appellees. The second superseding indictment charged the contractor-appellees with eight counts of violations of 43 U.S.C. § 1350(c) for knowing and willful violations of OCSLA's enabling regulations. The indictment charged Black Elk, GIS, Wood Group, Srubar, and Dantin with five separate counts for failing to perform pre-work inspections on each of the five days before the incident, in violation of 30 C.F.R. §§ 250.113(c)(1)(ii) and 250.146(c). It charged all of the defendants with a **[—5—]** single count for failing to perform a pre-work inspection on the actual day of the incident. It also charged Black Elk, GIS, Moss, and Dantin with failing to render the hydrocarbons in the sump-line piping and oil tanks inert before welding on the day of the explosion under 30 C.F.R. §§ 250.113(c)(3) and 250.146(c). Finally, the indictment charged those four parties with failing to obtain written authorization from the Person-in-Charge before welding the sump-line piping on the day of the explosion under 30 C.F.R. §§ 250.113(c)(1)(i) and 250.146(c).

Notably, the indictment also charged Black Elk and GIS with three counts of involuntary manslaughter, 18 U.S.C. § 1112, and all of the defendants were charged with one count of violating the Clean Water Act, 33 U.S.C. §§ 1251 *et seq.*, by negligently discharging oil into the Gulf of Mexico. The district court did not dismiss those counts and they remain pending.

3. District Court Proceedings

The defendants filed several motions to dismiss the charges against them. The district court issued a written order dismissing the OCSLA charges against Wood Group, GIS, Moss, and Dantin, and a second written order dismissing the OCSLA charges against Srubar days later. The district court analyzed each of the regulatory provisions cited in the indictment and concluded that none of the OCSLA regulations apply to oilfield contractors. Central to this analysis, the court pointed out that each of the three specific **[—6—]** provisions of OCSLA regulations

[3] Neither Wood Group nor Compass is a party to this appeal.

[4] A LACT unit measures the net volume, as well as the quality, of liquid hydrocarbons, and provides for the automatic measurement, sampling, and transfer of oil from the lease location into a pipeline.

underlying the charged criminal violations[5] imposes requirements addressed to "You." **{-308-}**

Under the OCSLA regulations, "You" is a defined term:

> *You* means a lessee, the owner or holder of operating rights, a designated operator or agent of the lessee(s), a pipeline right-of-way holder, or a State lessee granted a right-of-use and easement.

30 C.F.R. § 250.105.[6] The district court held this definition does not include contractors, subcontractors or service providers. Finding that only Black Elk is the owner, lessee, or holder of operating rights, and that no other regulatory provision brought contractors within the ambit of "You," the district court dismissed the OCSLA counts against the appellees. The government timely appealed. **[—7—]**

STANDARD OF REVIEW

The district court's interpretation of a federal statute is reviewed de novo, *United States v. Kaluza*, 780 F.3d 647, 653, 3 Adm. R. 287, 290 (5th Cir. 2015), as is the district court's interpretation of a regulation. *Anthony v. United States*, 520 F.3d 374, 377 (5th Cir. 2008). "In reviewing a challenge to an indictment alleging that it fails to state an offense, the court is required to take the allegations of the indictment as true and to determine whether an offense has been stated." *United States v. Crow*, 164 F.3d 229, 234 (5th Cir. 1999).

"This court interprets regulations in the same manner as statutes, looking first to the regulation's plain language." *United States v. Fafalios*, 817 F.3d 155, 159 (5th Cir. 2016). "[W]here, as here, a regulatory violation carries criminal penalties, the regulation 'must be strictly construed and cannot be enlarged by analogy or expanded beyond the plain meaning of the words used.'" *United States v. CITGO Petroleum Corp.*, 801 F.3d 477, 482 (5th Cir. 2015) (quoting *United States v. Clark*, 412 F.2d 885, 890 (5th Cir. 1969)). *See also Diamond Roofing Co. v. OSHRC*, 528 F.2d 645, 649 (5th Cir. 1976) ("If a violation of a regulation subjects private parties to criminal or civil sanctions, a regulation cannot be construed to mean what an agency intended but did not adequately express.").

DISCUSSION

On appeal, the government relies on four main arguments. First, the government contends that a plain reading of OCSLA subjects any person, including contractors and their employees, to criminal penalties for violating the regulations promulgated under the statute. 43 U.S.C. § 1350(c). Second, OCSLA regulations govern the appellees'

---

[5] In relevant part, those provisions read:

> 30 C.F.R. § 250.113(c)(1)(i): "(c) If you cannot weld in one of the designated safe-welding areas that you listed in your safe welding plan, you must meet the following requirements: (1) You may not begin welding until: (i) The welding supervisor or designated person in charge advises in writing that it is safe to weld."
>
> 30 C.F.R. § 250.113(c)(1)(ii): "If you cannot weld in one of the designated safe welding areas that you listed in your safe welding plan, you must meet the following requirements: (1) You may not begin welding until: . . . (ii) You and the designated person in charge inspect the work area and areas below it for potential fire and explosion hazards."
>
> 30 C.F.R. § 250.113(c)(3): "(c) If you cannot weld in one of the designated safe-welding areas that you listed in your safe welding plan, you must meet the following requirements: . . . (3) You may not weld piping, containers, tanks, or other vessels that have contained a flammable substance unless you have rendered the contents inert and the designated person in charge has determined it is safe to weld. This does not apply to approved hot taps."

[6] The Department of the Interior rewrote the OCSLA regulations in the second-person in 1999 as part of a "plain English" rendering by BSEE's predecessor MMS that described regulated parties as "You." *See* 63 Fed. Reg. 7335, 7336 (Feb. 13, 1998).

conduct because they were the "person[s] actually performing the activit[ies]," and are thus "jointly and severally responsible" under 30 C.F.R. § 250.146(c). Third, courts have upheld both civil and criminal penalties imposed under similar statutory and **[—8—]** regulatory schemes. Fourth, OCSLA's regulations support civil and criminal penalties for any person "responsible for a violation" of the regulations. 30 C.F.R. § 250.1402. We discuss each argument in turn.

I.

"Any person who knowingly and willfully" violates "any regulation or order issued under the authority of this subchapter designed to protect health, safety, or the environment . . ." may be subject to criminal penalties under OCSLA. 43 U.S.C. § 1350(c). Because OCSLA defines a "person" to include "a natural person, an association, a State, a political subdivision of a State, or a private, public, or municipal **{–309–}** corporation," 43 U.S.C. § 1331(d), the government contends any contractor, subcontractor, or individual is a "person" under this penalty provision. Further, the government argues, this plain reading is reinforced by 43 U.S.C. § 1350(d), which extends criminal liability for regulatory violations to corporations and "any officer or agent of such corporation . . . who . . . authorized, ordered, or carried out the proscribed activity."

The appellees respond that OCSLA, read as a whole, precludes the government from criminally prosecuting those who are not holders of OCS leases or permits. They argue that 43 U.S.C. § 1348 identifies who has authority to enforce safety and environmental regulations promulgated under OCSLA: "The Secretary, the Secretary of the Department in which the Coast Guard is operating, and the Secretary of the Army . . . ." 43 U.S.C. § 1348(a). The following section, 1348(b), then identifies who must comply with those regulations: "It shall be the duty of *any holder of a lease or permit* under this subchapter . . ." to comply with regulations governing workplace safety and health for their own employees and those of any "*contractor or subcontractor*." 43 U.S.C. § 1348(b) (emphases added). Because section 1348(b) specifically imposes a duty on lessees and permittees, and equally specifically references **[—9—]** but does not impose its regulatory duties on contractors and subcontractors, the latter parties are textually excluded from those duties. It necessarily follows that 43 U.S.C. § 1350(c) cannot impose criminal penalties on contractors because they are not the "persons" given a duty to comply.[7] Section 1350(c) instead places criminal exposure squarely on the lessees and permittees not only for their own misfeasance but for that of the contractors and subcontractors they hire. The appellees additionally contend that any regulations that would hold them criminally liable exceed Congress's explicit grant of statutory authority.[8]

There is much to be said for appellees' argument given the government's failure ever before to seek criminal penalties against a contractor or individual employees in the sixty-plus year history of the OCSLA. The government's past inaction speaks volumes about the scope of its regulatory authority, particularly when measured against its breathless defense of the policy importance of these indictments. To resolve this appeal, however, we need not decide whether OCSLA's criminal liability provision could

---

[7] That section 1348(b) excludes contractors and subcontractors from direct regulatory control under OCSLA is reinforced in the provision's drafting history. When enacting the provision that became section 1348 in 1977, Congress rejected language that would have extended the safety and environmental duties it imposed on lessees and permit holders to render them liable "jointly with any employer or subcontractor . . . ." OCSLA Amendments of 1977, H.R. 1614, 95th Cong. § 22(b) (1977); OCSLA Amendments of 1977, S.9. 95th Cong. § 22(b) (1977).

[8] *Accord Island Operating Co. v. Jewell*, No. 6:16-CV-00145, 2016 WL 7436665 (W.D. La. Dec. 23, 2016) ("[A] party who is neither a lease-holder nor a permit-holder . . . is not identified in Section 1348 as having a duty related to environmental and safety standards, and, thus . . . cannot be subject to a penalty or fine. Consequently, the statute's plain language, when read in context, is clear, and does not embrace contractors."), *appeal filed*, No. 17-30440 (5th Cir. May 27, 2017).

extend to contractors, subcontractors and their employees. If OCSLA regulations in force at the time of the incident do not apply to the appellees, they cannot be held criminally liable even if the statute authorizes regulations that could foist **[—10—]** criminal liability upon them. Consequently, we assume *arguendo*, without deciding, that section 1350(c) may expose **{-310-}** contractors and subcontractors to criminal liability, and move on to the issue of whether the regulations can support this criminal indictment.

II.

In its quest to penalize the contractors, the government first runs up against the regulatory definition of "You," which does not include contractors. *See* 30 C.F.R. § 250.105. The government barely mentions this provision in its briefing. Instead, the government points to § 250.146(c):

> Whenever the regulations in 30 CFR parts 250 through 282 and 30 CFR parts 550 through 582 require the lessee to meet a requirement or perform an action, the lessee, operator (if one has been designated), and the person actually performing the activity to which the requirement applies are jointly and severally responsible for complying with the regulation.

30 C.F.R. § 250.146(c). The government's essential argument is that because the appellees were the "person[s] actually performing the activity to which the [welding] requirement[s] appl[y]," they are "jointly and severally responsible for complying with the regulation." *Id.* Thus, their knowing and willful failure to comply with provisions of 30 C.F.R. § 250.113 would be a criminal violation under OCSLA's criminal enforcement provision. 43 U.S.C. § 1350(c).

It is a hornbook principle of interpretation that when "two provisions operate *in pari materia*," they "should not be read in isolation," but must be construed together. *United States v. Onick*, 889 F.2d 1425, 1433 (5th Cir. 1989). *See also RadLAX Gateway Hotel, LLC v. Amalgamated Bank*, 132 S. Ct. 2065, 2071 (2012) (referencing "the cardinal rule that, if possible, effect shall be given to every clause and part of a statute") (internal quotation omitted). As part of the same regulatory framework, sections 250.105 and 250.146(c) must be read together. Section 250.105 unambiguously defines "You" to mean "a lessee, the **[—11—]** owner or holder of operating rights, a designated operator or agent of the lessee(s), a pipeline right-of-way holder, or a State lessee granted a right-of-use and easement." 30 C.F.R. § 250.105. This definition excludes contractors and the appellees charged here. Moreover, all of the welding regulations that form the basis of the criminal indictment reference only "you"—the group of responsible parties defined in section 250.105. *See* 30 C.F.R. § 250.113, *supra* n.5.

The government's reliance on § 250.146(c) circumvents the plain language of this definition of "You." Further, taken in context, § 250.146(c) is directed to the same parties encompassed by the definition of "You." Section 250.146 begins with the question, "Who is responsible for fulfilling *leasehold obligations*?" and is followed by the statement that the government relies upon: "the lessee, operator (if one has been designated), and the person actually performing the activity. . . are jointly and severally responsible for complying with the regulation." 30 C.F.R. § 250.146(c) (emphasis added). This provision dictates the obligations of leaseholders and designated operators rather than the criminal liability of contractors. Its text refers to those parties who are "jointly and severally responsible," a term of art reserved for civil rather than criminal liability. *See Joint and Several Liability*, Bryan A. Garner, *Garner's Dictionary of Legal Usage* 493 (3d ed. 2011) (referring to joint and several liability exclusively in terms of civil law); *Honeycutt v. United States*, 137 S. Ct. 1626, 1631 (2017) (describing joint and several liability as a **[—12—]** "creature of tort **{-311-}** law"). The government cites no cases demonstrating support for joint and several *criminal* liability.[9]

[9] After oral argument in this court, the government cited several cases purporting to evidence the possibility of joint and several criminal liability, but all of them relate to criminal

Section 250.146(c) therefore provides that even when someone besides the lessee or operator is "the person actually performing the activity," the lessee and designated operator remain "jointly and severally responsible for complying with the regulation." *Id.* Indeed, when the regulation that became § 250.146(c) was first proposed, the agency explained it did not intend to expand regulatory liability to contractors, but to hold operators responsible for their contractors' actions:

> We would emphasize in Sec. 250.15(d) [now Sec. 250.146(c)] that, in addition to the lessee and the operator, all persons who conduct lease activities on behalf of the lessee or operator must also comply with our regulations. *The operator is responsible for the* **[—13—]** *performance of its contractors. [BSEE] will hold the operator accountable for the contractors' performance.*

63 Fed. Reg. 7335 (Feb.13, 1998) (emphasis added).

The government disputes the district court's reasoning that this agency explanation can be read to exclude contractor liability through the interpretive canon *expressio unius est exclusio alterius,* because a preamble cannot effect "a partial repeal . . . by implication" of a "formally enacted" rule. *United States v. Vonn*, 535 U.S. 55, 65, 122 S. Ct. 1043, 1050 (2002). We do not misapply the preamble, but we take it as a formal agency recognition of its authority that is fully consistent with both the limited definition of "You" in § 250.105 and the description of "leasehold obligations" in § 250.146(c): lessees cannot escape responsibility for regulatory compliance by hiring out work to contractors.

Moreover, the drafting history of the definition of "You" undermines the government's recently coined interpretation. In 1998, BSEE proposed to rephrase Part 250 in plain English, replacing the term "lessee" with "You." A comment submitted during rulemaking sought to define "You" to include "any person an MMS order or decision may adversely impact." Postlease Operations Safety, 64 Fed. Reg. 72756, 72758 (Dec. 28, 1999). As the appellees note, this proposed language would have extended the definition of "You" to contractors. Because complex, overlapping cross-indemnity provisions are an inherent **{-312-}** feature throughout the oil and gas industry, actions taken against lessees could adversely impact multiple layers of contractors and subcontractors that might have been swept into this broader proposed definition of "You." But BSEE rejected this comment and its proposed language in favor of a definition limited to lessee/permittee/designated operator responsibility. *Id.*

Until very recently, public statements by the regulating agencies confirmed that the regulations do not apply to contractors. In March 2011, BSEE promulgated a new "Safety and Environmental Management Systems" **[—14—]** rule designed to respond to the Deepwater Horizon incident and spill. The agency conducted a public workshop for oil and gas companies and advertised in bold,

---

conspiracy, RICO, forfeiture, or restitution. Not one of those cases implies, as the government does here, that criminal liability may be imposed jointly and severally. *See, e.g., United States v. Edwards*, 303 F.3d 606, 643 (5th Cir. 2002) (those in a RICO enterprise are jointly and several liable for the proceeds of the enterprise); *United States v. Quiroz-Hernandez*, 48 F.3d 858, 868 (5th Cir. 1995) (Co-conspirators may "be liable for the substantive offenses committed by other members of the conspiracy in furtherance of the common plan."); *United States v. Lindell*, 881 F.2d 1313, 1322 (5th Cir. 1989) (holding that marijuana possession "may be joint among several defendants."). Even more significant, the instant case concerns criminal negligence, not conspiracy or RICO charges. A conspiracy by nature is an agreement to violate the law, or "an agreement between two or more people to behave in a matter that will automatically constitute an offense by at least one of them," *Garner's Dictionary of Legal Usage* 175. Joint and several liability means that "the liability of two or more obligors may be enforced against them all by a joint action or against any of them by an individual action." *Id.* at 493. Joint and several liability may be imposed without culpability of some of the liable parties, whereas criminal liability requires individual culpability on the part of each person charged. Forfeiture and restitution concepts are relevant only as adjuncts to the individual criminal liability of defendants.

fully capitalized, underlined text that "30 CFR 250.105 defines '**YOU**' . . . This definition **DOES NOT** include a **CONTRACTOR**." Further, when publishing the final rule, BSEE stated that it "does not regulate contractors; we regulate operators." 75 Fed. Reg. 63610, 63616 (Oct. 15, 2010). The government asserts that these statements were issued in connection with different rules applicable only to leaseholders and operators, but we are unpersuaded. The new rule pertains as much to safety and the environment as the regulations these appellees are charged with violating.

The consistency of over sixty years' prior administrative practice in eschewing direct regulatory control over contractors, subcontractors and individual employees supports the district court's conclusion that these regulations do not apply to nor do they potentially criminalize the appellees' conduct.

III.

In further defense of its expansive reading of § 250.146(c), the government argues that this court has upheld criminal and civil penalties before where regulations created duties and "violators" of the regulations were sanctioned. The government cites two cases for this proposition. *See United States v. Ho*, 311 F.3d 589 (5th Cir. 2002) (upholding criminal liability under Clean Air Act regulations); *Floyd S. Pike Elec. Contractor, Inc. v. Occupational Safety & Health Review Comm'n (Pike)*, 576 F.2d 72 (5th Cir. 1978) (upholding civil liability and $800 fine for violating OSHA regulations).

No one disputes that many statutes authorize implementing regulations and then impose criminal liability on entities or individuals for violating the regulations. It is not the principle, but its specific application that is at issue here. The general principle does not answer the question of whether under **[—15—]** these OCSLA regulations criminal liability extends to these appellees. The question before us is whether the regulations that are specifically directed at lessees and permittees also extend penalties to contractors and individuals.

The virtually non-existent past enforcement of OCSLA regulations against contractors confirms that the regulations were never intended to apply to the appellees. The government marshals only two pieces of evidence that OCSLA's regulations might have been enforced against contractors: a 1988 guilty plea by a contractor reported in the New York Times, and a 1981 memorandum from the Department of the Interior that hypothetically mentions assessing civil penalties against "diving contractors." *See* Dep't of the Interior, No. M-36942, 1981 WL 29228, Opinion Letter on Refunds and Credits Under the Outer Continental Shelf Lands Act (Dec. 15, 1981). The Solicitor's Office memorandum concerned royalty payments to lessees, not criminal liability for contractors. **{–313–}**

As the BSEE itself acknowledged, it had not issued civil incidents of noncompliance against contractors before 2011. *See supra* n.2. On the contrary, past civil enforcement actions squarely placed on lessees and operators the duty to ensure contractors' compliance with leasehold obligations. *See ATP Oil and Gas Corp.*, 178 IBLA 88, 97 (Aug. 5, 2009) ("[OCS] lessees and operators are responsible for ensuring safe and workmanlike operations and conditions . . . and that includes contractors working on their behalf . . . ."); *Seneca Resources Corp.*, 167 IBLA 1 (Sept. 15, 2005) (Seneca, as leaseholder, liable for contractor's safety violations); *Petro Ventures, Inc.*, 167 IBLA 315 (Dec. 30, 2005) (same).

The government also cites *Fruge ex rel. Fruge v. Parker Drilling Co.*, 337 F.3d 558 (5th Cir. 2003) to suggest that § 250.146(c) can impose liability on contractors, but it has misread that case. In *Fruge*, a worker filed a personal injury lawsuit against an offshore platform owner and contractors hired by the **[—16—]** owner and contended that §§ 250.146(a) and (c) imposed strict civil liability upon the defendants. *Fruge* rejected the plaintiff's arguments and ruled that there was no implied private cause of action for the plaintiff.

The plaintiff did argue that section 250.146(c) "charges that the lessee, the operator, and the person actually performing the activity 'are jointly and severally responsible' for complying with the offshore [Interior] regulations."). *Fruge,* 337 F.3d at 561. But the court did not incorporate that logic into its holding. Instead, in characterizing § 250.146(c), this court noted MMS's then-official position that "both lessee and the designated operator are required to bear the non-monetary obligations under the lease as well as any obligations under the regulations." *Id.* at 565 n.4. This characterization is consistent with the regulation's definition of "You," which imposes obligations on lessees and designated operators but not contractors. The *Fruge* opinion did not find civil contractor liability.

Finally, "[t]he government has pointed to no precedent for criminal liability . . . in circumstances like those presented here." *United States v. Brennan,* 183 F.3d 139, 150 (2d Cir. 1999).

IV.

The government argues that the regulations, reviewed in a broader context, may result in criminal liability for anyone who fails to comply with them. The regulations define a "person" as "a natural person, an association . . . a State, a political subdivision of a State, or a private, public, or municipal corporation." 30 C.F.R. § 250.105. They define a "violator" as "a person responsible for a violation," and a violation includes "failure to comply with . . . any regulations issued under the OCSLA." 30 C.F.R. § 250.1402. That subpart "explains [the agency's] civil penalty procedures whenever a lessee, operator or other person engaged in oil, gas, sulphur or other minerals operations in the [outer continental shelf] has a violation." 30 C.F.R. **[—17—]** § 250.1400. Thus, the government contends that penalties cannot be limited to lessees and designated operators or even the definition of "You," but extend to any person responsible for a violation. Contractors are persons; contractors can therefore be violators, the government argues, consequently, contractors can be criminally liable.[10]

This argument ignores the rule that a general provision in a comprehensive **{-314-}** regulatory scheme must yield to more specific, conflicting provisions. *RadLAX,* 132 S. Ct. at 2070-71 ("[I]t is a commonplace of statutory construction that the specific governs the general.") (internal quotation omitted). *See also* Antonin Scalia & Bryan A. Garner, *Reading Law: Interpretation of Legal Texts* 183 (2012). The appellees were indicted under three provisions of 30 C.F.R. § 250.113, all of which are directed at "You," not at just any person, and § 250.146(c), which as previously addressed, does not impose criminal liability beyond the definition of "You." Because the applicable regulatory definitions unambiguously exclude contractors, more general liability provisions do not control.[11]

V.

Without actually conceding that its asserted OCSLA enforcement powers have never before been exercised against contractors and subcontractors, the government takes the position that the statute and regulations have *always* been broad enough to embrace such powers, and the lack of prior use demonstrates, at most, the exercise of prosecutorial discretion. Consequently, **[—18—]** contractors and subcontractors *always* had fair notice of their potential exposure to civil penalties up to $42,704/day[12] and criminal liability. But "where, as here, an agency's announcement of

[10] *But see* 30 C.F.R. § 550.105, BOEM regulations, which defines "You" exactly as in § 250.105—excluding contractors and subcontractors

[11] If the arguments on the application of the regulations to contractors were equally persuasive, the appellees argue the rule of lenity should break the tie. *See United States v. Santos,* 553 U.S. 507, 514, 128 S. Ct. 2020, 2025 (2008). But that "venerable rule," *id.,* is unnecessary to the resolution of this case. Properly read, the regulations are not ambiguous; they plainly do not subject contractors to criminal liability.

[12] This is the current maximum civil penalty for violating OCSLA per day per violation. 30 C.F.R. § 250.1403.

its interpretation is preceded by a very lengthy period of conspicuous inaction, the potential for unfair surprise is acute." *Christopher v. SmithKline Beecham Corp.*, 567 U.S. 142, 158, 132 S. Ct. 2156, 2168 (2012).

In fact, the government points only to events that preceded this incident by a few months as giving notice to the appellees and the industry. These include BSEE's announcement of its citations in connection with the Deepwater Horizon blowout; indirect references to section 250.146(c) when announcing other new regulations, *see* 77 Fed. Reg. 50,856, 50,879 (Aug. 22, 2012); and its publication in August 2012 of Interim Policy Document No. 12-07 (Aug. 15, 2012), which purports to elucidate principles for enforcing civil penalties only—not criminal enforcement—against contractors and subcontractors. The government, however, undercuts reliance on the Interim Policy Document as it disclaims that the policy statement, which was issued without notice and comment rulemaking, has any binding force so as to induce reliance by the regulated entities.

More revealing, in our view, is that when BSEE has promulgated recent regulations, it has gone out of its way to specifically include contractors and subcontractors within the regulatory purview. *See, e.g.*, BOEM's OCS alternative energy regulation, which expressly includes contractors. 30 C.F.R. § 585.112; 79 Fed. Reg. 21,617, 21,621 (Apr. 17, 2014).

If this case involved only civil sanctions against the appellees, the government would perhaps ask this court to apply *Auer* deference to its **[—19—]** interpretation of the regulations. *Auer v. Robbins*, 519 U.S. 452, 117 S. Ct. 905 (1997). The government would then have to defend its novel approach against a series of **{-315-}** Supreme Court decisions that have afforded "considerably less deference" when an agency interpretation conflicts with an earlier, consistently held view. *I.N.S. v. Cardoza-Fonseca,* 480 U.S. 421, 446 n.30, 107 S. Ct. 1207, 1221 n.30 (1987). The Court recently reiterated that deference may be "unwarranted" "when the agency's interpretation conflicts with a prior interpretation . . . ." *Christopher*, 567 U.S. at 155, 132 S. Ct. at 2166 (citation omitted). "[P]ersuasive weight" is due to an agency's contemporaneous construction of applicable law and subsequent consistent interpretation, *Watt v. Alaska,* 451 U.S. 259, 272-73, 101 S. Ct. 1673, 1681 (1981), whereas a "current interpretation, being in conflict with its initial position, is entitled to considerably less deference." *Id.* (citation omitted).

The Court summarized the relevant approach in an oft-cited decision where it concluded that "[w]e have declined to follow administrative guidelines in the past where they conflicted with earlier pronouncements of the agency." *General Elec. Co. v. Gilbert,* 429 U.S. 125, 143, 97 S. Ct. 401, 411 (1976) (citations omitted). The Court overturned an EEOC guideline that, having been promulgated eight years after the law passed, was "not a contemporaneous interpretation of Title VII," and "more importantly, the 1972 guideline flatly contradicts the position which the agency had enunciated at an earlier date, closer to the enactment of the governing statute." *Id.*

The analogy to the present case cannot be missed. BSEE and its predecessors enforced the regulations here at issue for over sixty years only against lessees, permittees and designated operators of offshore production rights. The agency placed responsibility, both civil and potentially criminal, on the named parties for ensuring compliance with the regulations by all of the many contractors, subcontractors and individual employees whose efforts are **[—20—]** necessary to develop the Outer Continental Shelf. The agency explicitly disclaimed imposing direct regulatory control on the subordinate parties. The agency's 2011 about-face "flatly contradicts" the agency's earlier, contemporaneous interpretation of the regulations. Its new position is hardly entitled to deference in the civil context. *See Island Operating Co., supra* n.8.[13]

---

[13] In the civil context, there are grave implications of the new policy for contractors, who heretofore have had no need to price their services according to the regulatory risk; no ability to engage insurance protection for regulatory violations; no need to personally review and apply

Worse, this is no civil enforcement proceeding where "only" money is at stake. "[D]ue process bars courts from applying a novel construction of a criminal statute to conduct that neither the statute nor any prior judicial decision has fairly disclosed to be within its scope . . . ." *United States v. Lanier,* 520 U.S. 259, 266, 117 S. Ct. 1219, 1225 (1997). It was novel for the government to indict these appellees for violating the welding regulations, the regulatory duty for which rested on "You," the lessees, permittees and designated operators of the West Delta Lease Block 32 facilities. No prior judicial decision countenanced this action, which is at odds with a half century of agency policy, and we will not do so now.

CONCLUSION

For the foregoing reasons, the judgment of the district court dismissing the OCSLA **{–316–}** counts of indictment against these appellees is **AFFIRMED**.

---

the exact regulations (because they followed the directives of the designated operator or lessee); and no incentive to impose themselves in the offshore workplace as self-protection against others' potential regulatory violations. *See generally,* John Cossa, *Liability of Owners, Contractors, and Non-operators*, 2016 No. 1 Rocky Mt. Min. L. Inst. Paper No. 6, 6-11 to -13.

United States Court of Appeals
for the Fifth Circuit

No. 16-31150

UNITED STATES
vs.
AMERICAN COMMERCIAL LINES, L.L.C.

Appeal from the United States District Court for the Eastern District of Louisiana

Decided: November 7, 2017

Citation: 875 F.3d 170, 5 Adm. R. 324 (5th Cir. 2017).

Before **SMITH**, **OWEN**, and **HIGGINSON**, Circuit Judges.

[—1—] {–171–} HIGGINSON, Circuit Judge:

On July 23, 2008, nearly 300,000 gallons of oil spilled into the Mississippi River **{–172–}** when a tugboat veered across the river, putting the oil-filled barge it towed into the path of an ocean-going tanker. The tugboat, the M/V MEL OLIVER, was owned by American Commercial Lines ("ACL") but operated by DRD Towing Company pursuant to a contractual agreement between the companies. As the statutorily-defined responsible party under the Oil Pollution Act ("OPA"), ACL incurred approximately $70 million in removal costs and damages. The United States also incurred approximately $20 million in removal costs and damages. **[—2—]**

The United States initiated this action in 2014, seeking a declaration that ACL is liable for all removal costs and damages resulting from the spill and to recover the costs that it incurred. The United States moved for partial summary judgment on its claims that ACL was not entitled to any defenses to liability under OPA. The district court granted that motion, and later entered final judgment ordering ACL to pay the United States $20 million. ACL appealed. We AFFIRM.

I

In 2007, ACL, a marine-transportation company that operates a fleet of barges and tugboats, contracted with DRD Towing, another marine-transportation company, to operate some of its tugboats. ACL and DRD entered into two charter agreements. Under the "Master Bareboat Charter," ACL chartered several tugboats, including the M/V MEL OLIVER, to DRD for one dollar per day.[1] Under the "Master Fully Found Charter," DRD agreed to crew the tugboats and charter its services back to ACL. Both agreements required compliance with "all applicable laws and regulations [with] respect to the registration, licensing, use, manning, maintenance, and operation of the Vessel(s)."

The MEL OLIVER's crew consisted of Captain Terry Carver, Steersman John Bavaret, and two deckhands. Captain Carver was the only crewmember with a valid United States Coast Guard Master of Towing Vessels license, which authorized him to lawfully operate tugboats on the lower Mississippi River. Steersman Bavaret held only an Apprentice Mate (Steersman) license, which authorized him to serve as an apprentice mate under the direct supervision of a properly licensed master. He was not authorized to operate **[—3—]** the vessel without continuous supervision. *See* 46 C.F.R. § 10.107(b) (requiring that Steersman "be under the direct supervision and in the continuous presence of a master"); 46 C.F.R. § 15.401 (prohibiting mariners from serving in any positions that exceed the limits of their credentials).

On July 20, 2008, Captain Carver left the MEL OLIVER to go on shore, leaving Steersman Baravet in control of the vessel. Two days later, while—unbeknownst to ACL—Captain Carver was still on shore, ACL directed the MEL OLIVER to tow an ACL barge, the DM-932, to pick up fuel from a facility in Gretna, Louisiana. At that time, Steersman Bavaret had worked for 36 hours with only short naps, in violation of Coast Guard regulations. *See* 46 U.S.C. § 8104(h) ("[A]n individual licensed to operate a towing

[1] The Master Bareboat Charter specified three vessels, M/V PAM D, M/V REGINA ANN, and M/V CELESTE MCKINNEY. When the PAM D suffered an engine failure, the MEL OLIVER was substituted in its place by amendment to the initial charter.

vessel may not work for more than 12 hours in a consecutive 24-hour period except in an emergency."); 46 C.F.R. § 15.705(d) (stating that "a master or mate (pilot)" may not work "more than 12 hours in a consecutive 24-hour period except in an emergency"). Still under Steersman Bavaret's control, the MEL **{–173–}** OLIVER arrived at the Gretna facility around 2:00 p.m. on July 22, 2008. The DM-932 was loaded with fuel, and the MEL OLIVER departed for its return trip, with the fuel-filled barge in tow, at about 12:30 a.m. on July 23, 2008.

As the MEL OLIVER pushed the DM-932 along the Mississippi River, it began travelling erratically. At about 1:30 a.m., it turned to cross the path of an ocean-going tanker, the TINTOMARA, owned by a third party. The TINTOMARA's pilot and the Coast Guard's New Orleans Vessel Traffic Service staff attempted to hail the MEL OLIVER by radio, but no one answered. The TINTOMARA also sounded its alarm whistle. Unable to change course, the TINTOMARA collided with the DM-932. The DM-932 broke away from the MEL OLIVER and sank downriver, spilling approximately 300,000 gallons of oil into the Mississippi River. Immediately after the collision, a crewmember **[—4—]** on the MEL OLIVER found Steersman Bavaret slumped over the steering sticks and non-responsive.

Following the spill, the government prosecuted DRD, Captain Carver, and Steersman Bavaret for criminal violations of federal environmental law. DRD and Steersman Bavaret each pleaded guilty to one count of violating the Ports and Waterways Safety Act, 33 U.S.C. § 1232(b)(1), and one count of violating the Clean Water Act ("CWA"), 33 U.S.C. § 1319(c)(1)(A). Captain Carver pleaded guilty to one count of violating the Ports and Waterways Safety Act.

In the course of the criminal investigation, DRD admitted that it knowingly allowed its crewmembers to work without appropriate licenses or qualifications and to work more hours than were permitted under Coast Guard safety regulations and that it failed to report those "manning deficiencies" to the Coast Guard, also in violation of Coast Guard regulations. Captain Carver and Steersman Bavaret admitted to knowing that Bavaret was not licensed to act as captain in Carver's absence.

In addition to the criminal prosecution, the government sued ACL and DRD under OPA to recover clean-up costs resulting from the spill.[2] DRD promptly declared bankruptcy and later dissolved its LLC. The government moved for summary judgment against ACL on the issue of liability under OPA. The district court granted summary judgment in favor of the government, and later issued a final judgment ordering ACL to pay the government $20 million. This appeal followed. **[—5—]**

II

We review a district court's grant of summary judgment de novo, applying the same legal standards as the district court. *Robinson v. Orient Marine Co.*, 505 F.3d 364, 365 (5th Cir. 2007). Summary judgment is appropriate only "if the movant shows that there is no genuine dispute as to any material fact and the movant is entitled to judgment as a matter of law." Fed. R. Civ. P. 56(a). Any reasonable inferences are to be drawn in favor of the non-moving party. *Robinson*, 505 F.3d at 366.

III

A

OPA was enacted in 1990 in response to the Exxon Valdez oil spill. It "was intended to streamline federal law so as to provide **{–174–}** quick and efficient cleanup of oil spills, compensate victims of such spills, and internalize the costs of spills within the petroleum industry." *Rice v. Harken Exploration Co.*, 250 F.3d 264, 266 (5th Cir. 2001) (citing S. Rep. No. 101-94, *reprinted in* 1990 U.S.C.C.A.N. 722, 723). OPA's cost-internalization measures, which increased the financial consequences of oil spills, were

[2] Related litigation came to this court in *United States v. Am. Commercial Lines, L.L.C.*, 759 F.3d 420, 2 Adm. R. 283 (5th Cir. 2014).

intended to "encourage greater industry efforts to prevent spills and develop effective techniques to contain them." S. REP. NO. 101-94 at 3. To that end, OPA redresses "gross inadequacies . . . in the CWA's provisions dealing with spiller responsibility for cleanup costs" by extending the CWA's regime of strict, joint, and several liability; limiting the available defenses to liability; increasing the applicable limits to liability; and eliminating the liability limits altogether under certain circumstances. *Id.* at 4–5, 12–14.

OPA holds statutorily-defined "responsible parties" strictly liable for pollution-removal costs and damages associated with oil spills. *See Buffalo Marine Servs. Inc. v. United States*, 663 F.3d 750, 752 (5th Cir. 2011) (stating that OPA "creates a strict-liability scheme for the costs of cleaning up oil **[—6—]** spills"). It provides that "each responsible party for a vessel or a facility from which oil is discharged . . . is liable for the removal costs and damages . . . that result from such incident." 33 U.S.C. § 2702(a). With respect to vessels, the "responsible party" is "any person owning, operating, or demise chartering the vessel." 33 U.S.C. § 2701(32)(A).

OPA generally limits the liability of a responsible party to a specified dollar amount based on the tonnage of the vessel from which oil was discharged. 33 U.S.C. § 2704(a). However, the limits on liability do not apply if:

> the incident was proximately caused by—(A) gross negligence or willful misconduct of, or (B) the violation of an applicable Federal safety, construction, or operating regulation by, the responsible party, an agent or employee of the responsible party, or a person acting pursuant to a contractual relationship with the responsible party . . . .

33 U.S.C. § 2704(c)(1). Accordingly, under those circumstances, there is no limit to the liability of the responsible party.

In addition to the general limits on liability, OPA provides for a complete defense to liability under four enumerated circumstances. It provides that:

> [a] responsible party is not liable for removal costs or damages . . . if [that] party establishes, by a preponderance of the evidence, that the discharge . . . of oil and the resulting damages or removal costs were caused solely by—(1) an act of God; (2) an act of war; (3) an act or omission of a third party, other than an employee or agent of the responsible party or a third party whose act or omission occurs in connection with any contractual relationship with the responsible party . . . or (4) any combination of paragraphs (1), (2), and (3).

33 U.S.C. § 2703(a). To be entitled to the third-party defense, a responsible party must also establish that it "exercised due care with respect to the oil **[—7—]** concerned" and that it "took precautions against foreseeable acts or omissions" of the third party. 33 U.S.C. § 2703(a)(3)(A)–(B).[3] **{-175-}**

ACL contends that it is entitled to the third-party defense under § 2703(a)(3) or, in the alternative, that it is entitled to limit its liability pursuant to § 2704(a). For the reasons stated below, we disagree.

B

ACL contends that it is entitled to a complete defense to liability under 33 U.S.C. § 2703(a)(3) on the ground that the conduct of DRD, a third party, caused the spill. The government responds that the third-party defense is not available because DRD's conduct occurred in connection with a contractual relationship with ACL. The parties agree that DRD's acts and omissions

[3] The district court concluded that ACL failed to present sufficient evidence to establish that it satisfied those two requirements. Because we hold that ACL is not entitled to the third-party defense on the ground that DRD's conduct occurred "in connection with" its contractual relationship with ACL, we do not reach the issues of whether ACL exercised due care and took the necessary precautionary measures.

were the sole cause of the spill and that ACL and DRD had a contractual relationship. They dispute only whether DRD's acts and omissions occurred in connection with that contractual relationship.

The meaning of § 2703(a)(3)'s "in connection with" language is a question of first impression. To determine whether DRD's conduct occurred "in connection with" its contractual relationship with ACL, we begin with the meaning of "connection." *See Taniguchi v. Kan Pac. Saipan, Ltd.*, 566 U.S. 560, 566 (2012). Because the term is not defined in the statute, we must give it its ordinary meaning. *See id.* ("When a term goes undefined in a statute, we give the term its ordinary meaning."). Webster's Third New International Dictionary defines "connection" as "relationship or association in thought (as of cause and effect, logical sequence, mutual dependence or involvement)." WEBSTER'S THIRD NEW INTERNATIONAL DICTIONARY 481 (2002). The Oxford **[—8—]** English Dictionary defines it as "[t]he condition of being related to something else by a bond of interdependence, causality, logical sequence, coherence, or the like; relation between things one of which is bound up with, or involved in, another." 3 OXFORD ENGLISH DICTIONARY 747 (2d ed. 1989).

"Connection" is therefore a capacious term, encompassing things that are logically or causally related or simply "bound up" with one another. It is, however, not so capacious as to be rendered meaningless. Conduct does not automatically occur "in connection with" a contractual relationship by the mere fact that such a relationship exists. *See Westwood Pharm., Inc. v. Nat'l Fuel Gas Distrib. Corp.*, 964 F.2d 85, 89 (2d Cir. 1992) (interpreting virtually identical language in the Comprehensive Environmental Response, Compensation and Liability Act ("CERCLA") and holding that "[t]he mere existence of a contractual relationship . . . does not foreclose the owner of and from escaping liability"). Rather, the conduct must be causally or logically related to the contractual relationship. Accordingly, the third party's acts or omissions that cause a spill occur "in connection with any contractual relationship" between the responsible party and the third party whenever the acts or omissions relate to the contractual relationship in the sense that the third party's acts and omissions would not have occurred but for that contractual relationship.

This reading of the ordinary meaning of "connection" is consistent with OPA's purpose. *See Buffalo Marine Servs.*, 663 F.3d at 757 ("To determine the meaning of a statute, 'we look not only to the particular statutory language, but to the design of the statute as a whole and to its object and policy.'" (quoting *Crandon v. United States*, 494 U.S. 152, 156–58 (1990))). The legislative history shows that, in enacting OPA, Congress wanted not only to quickly contain and clean up spills, but also to prevent spills from occurring in the first place by **{-176-}** using weighty financial consequences to encourage responsible parties **[—9—]** to take all available precautionary measures. S. REP. NO. 101-94 at 3. To give effect to that purpose, Congress intended to narrowly limit the third-party defense in order to "preclude defendants from avoiding liability by claiming a third party was responsible, when that third party had a contractual relationship with the defendant and was acting, in essence, as an extension of the defendant." *Id.* at 13. Accordingly, the third-party defense should not be available where a spill is caused by third-party acts or omissions that would not have occurred but for the contractual relationship between the third party and the responsible party.

ACL's proposed definition of "in connection with" is contrary to both the statute's text and its purpose. ACL contends that we should adopt the Second Circuit's interpretation of similar language CERCLA.[4] In *Westwood*, the Second Circuit held that the "in connection with" language in CERCLA's third-party defense requires that "the contract between

---

[4] CERCLA's third-party defense provides for a complete defense to liability where the release of a hazardous substance was caused solely by "an act or omission of a third party other than an employee or agent of the defendant, or than one whose act or omission occurs in connection with a contractual relationship, existing directly or indirectly, with the defendant." 42 U.S.C. § 9607(b)(3).

the landowner and the third party must either relate to the hazardous substances *or* allow the landowner to exert some element of control over the third party's activities." 964 F.2d at 91–92 (emphasis added). Even though that test is met here factually in light of the parties' contract to transport oil, we decline to adopt that approach because its additional requirements go beyond what is required by OPA's plain text. Section 2703(a)(3) requires only two things: (1) that a third party's act or omission caused the spill at issue and (2) that that act or omission did not "occur[] in connection with *any* contractual relationship with the responsible party." 33 U.S.C. § 2703(a)(3) (emphasis added). It does not condition the applicability or inapplicability of the exception on the nature of the contract **[—10—]** between the parties. Accordingly, the contract need not explicitly relate to hazardous substances (here, oil) or permit the responsible party to control the third party's activities.

ACL also contends that DRD's acts and omissions cannot be "in connection with" their contractual relationship because those acts and omissions directly violated the terms of their contracts. The charter agreements specifically required DRD to comply with all applicable laws and regulations, but the acts and omissions that caused the spill did not. But "in connection with" does not mean "in compliance with," and the meaning of "connection" is broad enough to encompass acts that are not specifically contemplated, or even acts that are specifically not contemplated, in a contract. A contrary reading would permit responsible parties to circumvent OPA by easily contracting out of liability, a result Congress specifically sought to avoid. *See* S. REP. NO. 101-94 at 13 (stating that the contractual-relationship exception from the third-party defense is intended to "preclude defendants from avoiding liability" through contractual relationships); *see also Buffalo Marine Servs.*, 663 F.3d at 757 & n.36 (citing to *United States v. LeBeouf Bros. Towing Co.*, 621 F.2d 787, 789 (5th Cir. 1980) and rejecting interpretation of "contractual relationship" that would enable defendants to easily avoid liability).

Given the broad meaning of "in connection with," ACL has failed to establish **{-177-}** that it is entitled to the third-party defense. The conduct that caused the spill—Captain Carver's leaving the MEL OLIVER under the control of an unlicensed Steersman and Bavaret's working more consecutive hours than permitted under Coast Guard regulations, becoming unconscious while in command of the vessel, and veering into the path of the TINTOMARA while transporting oil at ACL's direction—occurred "in connection with" DRD's contractual relationship with ACL. Pursuant to the charter agreements, DRD **[—11—]** agreed to crew the MEL OLIVER and charter DRD's services to ACL. But for those charter agreements, DRD would not have been operating the MEL OLIVER and transporting ACL's fuel-filled barge, and the spill would not have occurred.

C

ACL alternatively contends that it is entitled to OPA's general limit on liability. The government responds that DRD's conduct falls within the exception from limited liability for spills proximately caused by "gross negligence," "willful misconduct," or federal regulatory violations committed by "a person acting pursuant to a contractual relationship with the responsible party." *See* 33 U.S.C. § 2704(c)(1). We agree.

The parties dispute whether DRD was acting "pursuant to" its contractual relationship with ACL when it committed the regulatory and criminal violations that caused the spill. Once again, the meaning of § 2704(c)(1)'s "pursuant to" language, which is not defined in the statute, appears to be a matter of first impression. As before, we turn to the ordinary meaning of the words. Black's Law Dictionary defines "pursuant to" as "[i]n compliance with; in accordance with," "[a]s authorized by," or "[i]n carrying out." BLACK'S LAW DICTIONARY 1431 (10th ed. 2014). Webster's Third similarly defines "pursuant to" as "in the course of carrying out; in conformance to or agreement with; [or] according to." WEBSTER'S THIRD NEW INTERNATIONAL DICTIONARY 1848 (2002). *See also* OXFORD ENGLISH DICTIONARY 887 (2d ed.

1989) (defining "pursuant to" as "following upon, consequent and conformable to, [or] in accordance with"). Accordingly, and as ACL contends, "pursuant to" has a narrower meaning than "in connection with." While the latter encompasses any conduct that is logically related to the contractual relationships in the sense that it would not have occurred but **[—12—]** for the third party's contractual relationship with the responsible party, the former contemplates compliance or conformity.

However, ACL goes too far when it argues that the specific acts or omissions that cause the spill must be authorized by the contract. Section 2704(c)(1) requires only that the gross negligence, willful misconduct, or federal regulatory violations that cause the spill be committed by the responsible party, its agent or employee, or "a person acting pursuant to a contractual relationship with the responsible party." Accordingly, the "pursuant to" language is satisfied if the person who commits the gross negligence, willful misconduct, or regulatory violation does so in the course of carrying out the terms of the contractual relationship with the responsible party. Reading the statute to require that the negligent or wrongful act itself be "pursuant" to the contract would be nonsensical; it would be a rare contract indeed that specifically contemplated gross negligence, willful misconduct, or the violation of federal safety regulations. Exceptions to statutes are to be construed narrowly, but ACL's proposed construction would read the exception out of the statute altogether.

That the conduct that caused the spill here rose to the level of a criminal violation **{-178-}** does not take it out of § 2704(c)(1). ACL contends that because § 2704(c)(1) specifically mentions gross negligence, willful misconduct, and the violation of federal regulations, but says nothing of criminal violations, the exception from limited liability must not apply to the latter. But that draws a false distinction. As evidenced by the facts of this case, there is considerable overlap between gross negligence, willful misconduct, and violations of federal regulations, on the one hand, and criminal violations on the other. There is no principled basis on which to distinguish between the negligent acts that would lift the general limits on liability and the criminal acts that would not. Would the relevant conduct simply have to *be* a criminal violation? That would seem **[—13—]** to largely eviscerate the exception. Or would the responsible actors have to be actually charged with a criminal violation, or convicted, to take the conduct out of § 2704(c)(1) and reimpose the limits to liability?

Nor would such a distinction give effect to OPA's purpose. OPA increased the financial consequences of oil spills in order to encourage responsible parties to take precautionary measures to prevent such spills. Section 2704(c)(1), in particular, encourages compliance with the kinds of regulations that are themselves intended to prevent oil spills—like the manning requirements violated by DRD—by providing for unlimited liability where those regulations are flouted. *See* S. REP. NO. 101-94 at 14 (stating that "where compliance [with federal regulations] perhaps could have prevented or mitigated the effects of an oilspill [sic], no such limits [to liability] will apply"). There is no reason to think that Congress intended to lift the limits on liability for spills caused by conduct that is forbidden by federal regulation but to reimpose those limits for spills caused by conduct considered so dangerous or risky that it is also subject to criminal penalties. Such a distinction would run counter to OPA's purpose of encouraging compliance with the very rules and regulations intended to prevent oil spills in the first instance.

Finally, ACL's reliance on the doctrine of *respondeat superior* is inapposite. Under that doctrine, employers are not liable for the intentional torts or criminal acts of their employees if those acts are committed outside the scope of their employment. But that is of no help to ACL. First, employer liability under the doctrine of *respondeat superior* is a creature of the common law of agency. *See* RESTATEMENT (THIRD) OF AGENCY § 2.04 cmt. b (2006) (noting that the doctrine of *respondeat superior* "has long been classified as an element of agency doctrine"). The liability of a responsible party for oil spills caused by the negligence or misconduct of a third party under OPA is a creature of statute. Second, even if the doctrine of *respondeat superior* were **[—14—]** applicable here by analogy, it appears to support our reading of "pursuant to." Employers *are* liable for the intentional torts of their employees if committed by an employee "acting within the scope of their employment." *Id.* § 2.04. Conduct may be within the scope of employment, even if not authorized, if it occurs "while performing work assigned by the employer" and if it is "intended to further any purpose of the employer." *Id.* § 7.07 cmt. b. Accordingly, even if the doctrine of *respondeat superior* were relevant here, our reading of what it means to be "acting pursuant to a contractual relationship" appears to be consistent with the imposition of liability on employers for torts committed by employees in the course of their employment.

Here, there is no dispute that the July 23, 2008 spill was caused by DRD's wrongful conduct and regulatory violations, committed in the course of carrying **{–179–}** out its contractual obligation to transport ACL's fuel-filled barge. Accordingly, the spill was caused by the gross negligence, willful misconduct or regulatory violations of "a person acting pursuant to a contractual relationship with" ACL, and ACL is therefore not entitled to limited liability.

IV

For the foregoing reasons, we AFFIRM the district court's grant of summary judgment.

United States Court of Appeals for the Fifth Circuit

No. 17-30007

MANSON GULF, L.L.C.
vs.
MODERN AM. RECYCLING SERV., INC.

Appeal from the United States District Court for the Eastern District of Louisiana

Decided: December 18, 2017

Citation: 878 F.3d 130, 5 Adm. R. 331 (5th Cir. 2017).

Before **REAVLEY, ELROD,** and **SOUTHWICK,** Circuit Judges.

[—2—] {–132–} **REAVLEY,** Circuit Judge {–133–}:

Longshoreman James "J.J." LaFleur fell 50 feet to his death after stepping through a hole in a decommissioned oil platform. The platform sat atop a barge chartered by Manson Gulf, L.L.C., who ordered the hole's creation but did not cover the hole or warn J.J. of its existence.

J.J.'s spouse alleged negligence on the part of Manson and sought damages. The district court, however, granted summary judgment for Manson, finding no liability under any of the three *Scindia* duties—the duties a vessel owner owes to a longshoreman. Because we conclude a fact issue precluded summary judgment with respect to the duty to warn of hidden dangers, we reverse.

I. BACKGROUND

Manson Gulf, L.L.C. is in the business of decommissioning oil-drilling platforms in the Gulf of Mexico. In 2015, Manson acquired one such platform, the BA A-23-A, from Freeport-McMoRan Oil & Gas. Manson extracted the 50-foot-tall, four-leg platform and placed the structure on a chartered barge. To lift the structure, Manson ordered four holes cut in the platform's grating adjacent to each of the support legs. Rigging chains could then be passed through the holes and around the legs to take hold of the platform. Each hole was approximately two feet by two feet. Manson left the holes uncovered and unmarked. [—3—]

Modern American Recycling Service (MARS) is in the business of dismantling steel structures and selling the metal for scrap. MARS agreed to purchase and scrap the BA A-23-A platform, and Manson delivered the structure to MARS's dock, located on Bayou Black, Louisiana.

On the morning of June 16, 2015, a Manson project engineer, Dustin Clement, warned MARS of oil in the platform's pipes but not of the unmarked holes. Afterwards, Clement left MARS's dock and no Manson personnel remained. Jeff Smith, a MARS foreman in charge of riggers and cutters, then boarded the platform (still atop the barge) to locate the presence of oil. After Smith investigated for ten minutes, J.J. LaFleur joined Smith aboard the platform to lend a hand. J.J. was an independent contractor, employed by MARS to take inventories, do inspections, and perform other miscellaneous tasks.

As Smith and J.J. walked across the platform, they discussed the oil dilemma and looked at the pipes that ran overhead. While turning, J.J. stepped through an unmarked hole. Smith, then eight feet behind, attempted to intervene, but it was too late—J.J. fell 50 feet to the barge's deck and died from his injuries. Pictures of the structure and hole in the grating are attached. *See* Appendix, figs. 1–3.

Following J.J.'s death, Manson filed a complaint seeking exoneration or limitation from liability. MARS answered the complaint and asserted various claims and defenses. And Angie LaFleur, J.J.'s surviving spouse, filed claims for damages against Manson and MARS, alleging negligence under both maritime and Louisiana law. Manson and MARS then moved for summary judgment, and the district court granted both parties' motions, finding neither liable under § 905 of the Longshore and Harbor Workers' Compensation Act (LHWCA). The LaFleur claimants appealed only from the summary judgment with respect to Manson. **[—4—]** **{-134-}**

II. DISCUSSION

A. Standard of Review

We review a "district court's grant of summary judgment *de novo* applying the same standards as the district court." *DePree v. Saunders*, 588 F.3d 282, 286 (5th Cir. 2009). Summary judgment is appropriate if "the movant shows that there is no genuine dispute as to any material fact and the movant is entitled to judgment as a matter of law." FED. R. CIV. P. 56(a).

The decision-making process is tweaked slightly when the case is to be tried before the court and not a jury. *See Nunez v. Superior Oil Co.*, 572 F.2d 1119, 1123–24 (5th Cir. 1978). In that circumstance, "the court may conclude on the basis of the affidavits, depositions, and stipulations before it, that there are no genuine issues of material fact, even though [the] decision may depend on inferences to be drawn from what has been incontrovertibly proved." *Id.* However, the court may exercise this inference-drawing function only when "the evidentiary facts are not disputed" and "there are no issues of witness credibility." *Id.*

B. The *Scindia* Duties

Section 905(b) of the LHWCA governs the present suit and supplies the relevant tort-based duties owed by vessel owners to longshoremen. 33 U.S.C. § 905(b); *see also Kirksey v. Tonghai Mar.*, 535 F.3d 388, 391 (5th Cir. 2008). Decades ago, those duties were open-ended, premised in part on a nondelegable warranty of seaworthiness that required no proof of fault. *Scindia Steam Navigation Co. v. De Los Santos*, 451 U.S. 156, 164 (1981). But following the 1972 amendment to § 905(b), the Supreme Court clarified in *Scindia* that vessel-owner liability sounds only in negligence. *Id.* at 165. To that end, *Scindia* articulated three "narrow duties" owed by the vessel owner: "(1) a turnover duty, (2) a duty to exercise reasonable care in the areas of the ship **[—5—]** under the active control of the vessel, and (3) a duty to intervene." *Kirksey*, 535 F.3d at 391.

The turnover duty encompasses two distinct-but-related obligations. First, the vessel owner "owes a duty to exercise ordinary care under the circumstances to turn over the ship and its equipment in such condition that an expert stevedore can carry on stevedoring operations with reasonable safety." *Id.* at 392. And second, the vessel owner "owes a duty to warn the stevedore of latent or hidden dangers which are known to the vessel owner or should have been known to it." *Id.* However, a vessel owner need not warn of "dangers which are either: (1) open and obvious or (2) dangers a reasonably competent stevedore should anticipate encountering." *Id.*

The active control duty requires that the vessel owner "exercise due care to avoid exposing longshoremen to harm from hazards that they may encounter in areas, or from equipment, under the active control of the vessel during the stevedoring operation." *Scindia*, 451 U.S. at 167.

Finally, the duty to intervene imposes liability "if the vessel owner fails to intervene in the stevedore's operations when he has actual knowledge both of the hazards and that the stevedore, in the exercise of 'obviously improvident' judgment means to work on in the face of it and therefore cannot be relied on to remedy it." *Burchett v. Cargill, Inc.*, 48 F.3d 173, 178 (5th Cir. 1995) (quoting *Pimental v. LTD Canadian Pac. Bul*, 965 F.2d 13, 15 (5th Cir. 1992)).

C. The Active Control Duty and the Duty to Intervene

As a preliminary matter, we agree with the district court that neither the **{-135-}** active control duty nor the duty to intervene apply to this case. Both liability theories fail for the same reason: it is undisputed that all Manson personnel departed the barge prior to J.J.'s fall.

Though the mere presence of vessel employees is not necessarily indicative of active control, we have twice cited the complete *absence* of such **[—6—]** personnel as evidence of the opposite—a lack of vessel control. *See Fontenot v. United States*, 89 F.3d 205, 208 (5th Cir. 1996); *Burchett*, 48 F.3d at 179. The LaFleur claimants point to testimony that Manson had not yet transferred ownership of the platform when J.J. fell. But our cases speak in terms of control, not legal ownership.[1] Without evidence that Manson continued to exercise control over the platform, liability cannot rest on the second *Scindia* duty.

As for the duty to intervene, the absence of Manson personnel is similarly dispositive. Assuming Manson had actual knowledge of the hole, the LaFleur claimants still needed to prove Manson had actual knowledge of "obviously improvident judgment" on the part of MARS (the stevedore). *Burchett*, 48 F.3d at 178. Because no Manson personnel remained when Smith and J.J. boarded the platform, the LaFleur claimants offered no evidence that Manson observed MARS employees interacting with the hazard, let alone in an obviously improvident manner. *See id.* (affirming summary judgment on the duty-to-intervene issue because the vessel owner "had no personnel present at the job site who could have had knowledge of any peculiar dangers related to [the stevedore's] operations"). As a consequence, the duty to intervene is inapplicable.

D. The Turnover Duty

We disagree, however, with the district court's decision to grant summary judgment with respect to Manson's turnover duty. The parties frame the turnover duty in terms of the duty-to-warn component, several elements of which are undisputed. First, the hole was, needless to say, a "danger"—it was **[—7—]** at such a height to make death or grievous injury a near certainty for anyone who fell through it. Second, Manson had actual knowledge of the hole, or is at least charged with knowledge, because Manson orchestrated the cutting before delivering the platform. *See Hernandez v. M/V Rajaan*, 841 F.2d 582, 586 (5th Cir. 1988) ("If the condition existed from the outset, the shipowner is charged with actual knowledge of the dangerous condition . . . ."). And finally, Manson warned MARS only of explosive fluids, not holes.

Therefore, the validity of the LaFleur claimants' turnover-duty claim hinges on whether the hole was hidden or was instead (1) open and obvious or (2) a danger "a reasonably competent stevedore" should have anticipated. *Kirksey*, 535 F.3d at 392. The district court concluded the hole was both open and obvious and to be anticipated by a competent stevedore, and on that basis, granted summary judgment for Manson. Sure enough, some evidence in the record supports that finding. Jeff Smith testified that nothing would have obstructed J.J.'s view of the hole. Smith testified also that if J.J. had looked at the hole from four or eight feet away, he would have seen the hole. And Smith opined that, were he in J.J.'s shoes, he **{–136–}** would not have fallen because he "double-check[s] were [he] go[es]." On the general foreseeability of holes, Smith testified that he would expect a decommissioned structure (like the platform at issue) to contain holes. Dwight Caton, the owner of MARS, likewise stated that holes are a common occurrence on decommissioned platforms.

But so too did record evidence provide a contrasting account, supporting instead the notion that the hole was a hidden hazard, one a stevedore would not anticipate. Smith, the only witness to view the hole from J.J.'s vantage point,[2] provided the contradiction (indeed, a self-contradiction of the testimony

[1] Indeed, if mere ownership of a hazardous condition was sufficient to create control, would not every vessel owner automatically control hazards appurtenant to its vessel? Our cases say otherwise. *See, e.g., Fontenot*, 89 F.3d at 208 (a vessel's hatch cover was not under the vessel owner's control).

[2] A panel of this court once observed that an open-and-obvious inquiry should take place from the perspective of the injured longshoreman. *See McCuller v. Nautical Ventures, L.L.C.*, 434 F. App'x 408, 412 (5th Cir. 2011) (per curiam) (explaining that a defective ladder's **[—8—]** obviousness should not be gauged by what would be revealed if "the ladder was laid out flat and the rungs could be examined from several angles" but rather by what would be apparent "to a longshoreman climbing up and down the ladder"). We agree.

[—8—] cited above). On the visibility of the hole, Smith explained that the platform's "grating can play tricks on your eyes," the hole was not easily seen until one was right on top of it, and the hole "look[ed] like a solid floor." Moreover, Smith did not see the hole until J.J. began to fall through it. The hole's size (or lack thereof) is also relevant; Caton testified the hole was approximately the size of two legal pads and he "still [did not] know how a person fit through" it. Finally, we have reviewed the pictures of the hole and its surroundings, and those pictures cement further the conclusion that the hole's obviousness is subject to live dispute. True, the pictures taken directly over the hole, as one might expect, depict a visible opening. *See, e.g.*, Appendix, fig. 2. But the pictures taken from an angle—similar to the point of view of a person approaching the hole—depict the way in which the platform's grating, in Smith's words, can "play tricks on your eyes" and make the opening difficult to see. *See, e.g.*, Appendix, fig. 3. As for the hole's foreseeability, Smith clarified that, though he expected holes to be present, those holes are "typically covered" by replacing the grating or marked by "cables going all the way around." More pointedly, Smith explained that an uncovered, unmarked hole—the very danger that befell J.J.—was "just not common at all." And Caton echoed that sentiment: "usually everything is roped off."

The district court did not acknowledge this testimonial conflict in its summary-judgment opinion. Instead, the court appeared to place great weight on the procedural nuance we mentioned earlier—that of summary judgment in a bench-trial case—when it remarked, "proceeding to trial would not enhance the Court's ability to draw inferences and conclusions." The court was quite right that the *Nunez* rule allows a judge to sometimes draw inferences in **[—9—]** rendering summary judgment. *See* 572 F.2d at 1123–24. But neither *Nunez* nor any other case permits the court to do so when a factual dispute exists. *Id.* at 1124. Smith's divergent testimony created such a dispute here, and on the key issues no less. By adopting one side of Smith's story as "[t]he most convincing evidence" while neglecting Smith's contrary account, the court, in essence, found one version more credible than the other. And *Nunez* forbids credibility determinations on a cold summary-judgment record. *Id.* at 1123.

Judicial efficiency is a noble goal, to be sure. But when an evidentiary record contains a material factual dispute (as this one does), we simply cannot bypass the role of the fact-finder, whoever that may be. Summary judgment was improper. **{-137-}**

E. The *West* Caveat and Manson's Alternative Basis for Affirmance

We pause to consider Manson's final ground for affirmance, one premised on a little-explored exception to vessel-owner liability. In a pre-*Scindia* case, *West v. United States*, 361 U.S. 118, 119 (1959), the United States hired a contractor to overhaul a deactivated vessel. A shore-based employee of the contractor suffered a repair-related injury. *Id.* at 120. The Supreme Court denied recovery because, among other things, the defect was not hidden and the vessel owner was "under no duty to protect [the employee] from risks that were inherent in the carrying out of the contract." *Id.* at 123. This circuit has applied the *West* rationale under similar circumstances. *See Hess v. Upper Miss. Towing Corp.*, 559 F.2d 1030, 1035–36 (5th Cir. 1977) (no liability when gasoline was obvious and "the danger inherent in removing gasoline . . . from a barge was well known" to the independent contractor hired to do just that); *Hill v. Texaco, Inc.*, 674 F.2d 447, 451 (5th Cir. 1982) (no liability when rust on a tank's walls—the precise condition an independent contractor was retained to inspect—injured an employee of the contractor). Manson argues the *West* rule should apply here because J.J.'s role (vis-à-vis his stevedore) was to check **[—10—]** the platform for hazards, including holes. The LaFleur claimants reply that the record reveals J.J.'s responsibility was to investigate for oil, not holes.

Setting aside whether the evidence actually supports Manson's characterization of J.J.'s role, we decline Manson's request to affirm because we find no authority for extending the

West exception to situations beyond (1) an open and obvious defect that (2) an independent contractor is retained by the vessel owner to repair or inspect. *West* itself acknowledged the limits of its holding. *See* 361 U.S. at 124 ("[T]here might be instances of hidden or inherent defects, sometimes called 'latent,' that would make the owner guilty of negligence, even though he had no control of the repairs . . . .").

This case is different. When control of the structure was turned over, a warning was given about oil but not holes—and this is more than a hole in the grating. Unseen is a hole in the platform underneath, and if a man slips or steps over the edge of the hole, he will fall to a terribly painful death. Surely, this danger could be found to constitute a latent hazard. And, moreover, this case involves a stevedore retained by the vessel owner to remove a structure for scrap, not to repair or inspect for particular known dangers. It is thus outside *West*'s narrow liability bar.

III. CONCLUSION

The judgment is reversed and the case is remanded for proceedings consistent with this opinion. **[—11—]**

Appendix **{-138-}**

Fig. 1

Fig. 2 **{-139-}**

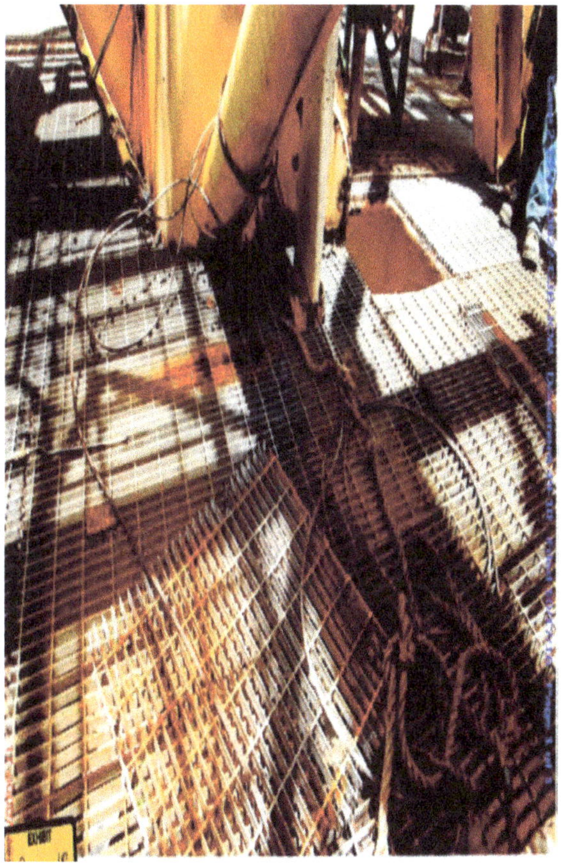

Fig. 3

This page intentionally left blank

United States Court of Appeals for the Sixth Circuit

United States Court of Appeals
for the Sixth Circuit

No. 16-2126

HERR
vs.
UNITED STATES FOREST SERV.

Appeal from the United States District Court for the Western District of Michigan at Marquette

Decided: July 26, 2017

Citation: 865 F.3d 351, 5 Adm. R. 338 (6th Cir. 2017).

Before **SUTTON** and **DONALD**, Circuit Judges, and **ZOUHARY**, District Judge.*

* The Honorable Jack Zouhary, United States District Judge for the Northern District of Ohio, sitting by designation.

[—2—] {-353-} **SUTTON**, Circuit Judge:

David and Pamela Herr bought lakefront property on Crooked Lake in the Upper Peninsula of Michigan, hoping to use the lake's waters for recreational boating and fishing. The United States Forest Service had other plans. Most of Crooked Lake lies in the federally owned Sylvania Wilderness yet some of it remains under private ownership. Congress gave the Forest Service authority to regulate any use of Crooked Lake and nearby lakes "subject to valid existing rights." The Forest Service promulgated two regulations, one prohibiting gas-powered motorboats, the other limiting electrically powered motorboats to no-wake speeds throughout the wilderness area. Both regulations exceed the Forest Service's power as applied to the Herrs and the other private property owners on the lake. Under Michigan riparian-rights law, in truth littoral-rights law, lakeside property owners may use all of a lake, making the Herrs' right to use all of the lake in reasonable ways the kind of "valid existing rights" that the Forest Service has no warrant to override.

I.

Crooked Lake stretches three miles from one end to the other connected by a series of meandering channels and bays. Nestled within an old growth forest, the **{-354-}** lake offers a variety of outdoor activities for public and private visitors from kayaking to bird watching to hiking along its shore. Fishing apparently attracts a lot of visitors as well, as the glacier lakes in the area contain "world-class smallmouth bass fisheries." *Herr v. U.S. Forest Serv.*, 803 F.3d 809, 813, 3 Adm. R. 461, 462 (6th Cir. 2015). Ninety-five percent of the land surrounding the lake belongs to the federally protected Sylvania Wilderness, a nature preserve open to the public. The remaining five percent, **[—3—]** positioned in the northern bay, belongs to approximately ten private landowners who own the property under state law.

The United States first purchased land in the area in 1966, about 14,000 acres surrounding the southern portion of Crooked Lake, to supplement the Ottawa National Forest. In 1987, Congress enacted the Michigan Wilderness Act, 101 Stat. 1274, dedicating these and other lands to the National Wilderness Preservation System as part of the Sylvania Wilderness, an area encompassing over 18,000 acres and 36 lakes.

"Subject to valid existing rights," the Michigan Wilderness Act directs the Forest Service to administer this area "in accordance with the provisions of the Wilderness Act of 1964." Pub. L. No. 100-184, § 5, 101 Stat. 1274, 1275–76 (1987). The Wilderness Act of 1964 provides that the Forest Service, a branch of the Department of Agriculture, "shall be responsible for preserving the wilderness character" of the land. 16 U.S.C. § 1133(b). It also addresses motorboat use, explaining that "subject to existing private rights . . . there shall be . . . no use of . . . motorboats" within any wilderness area. *Id.* § 1133(c). "[W]here these uses have already become established," the Act provides that they "may be permitted to continue subject to such restrictions as the [Forest Service] deems desirable." *Id.* § 1133(d)(1).

In 1992, the Forest Service amended the management plan for the Ottawa National Forest. Through what became known as Amendment No. 1, the Service prohibited the use of sailboats and houseboats on all portions of Crooked Lake within the Sylvania

Wilderness. In 1993, several landowners filed a lawsuit challenging the prohibitions, *see Stupak-Thrall v. United States*, 843 F. Supp. 327, 328–29 (W.D. Mich. 1994), ominously referred to as *Stupak-Thrall I*.

Stupak-Thrall I ended in a victory for the Forest Service but not for the law of this Circuit. By an equally divided vote, the en banc court affirmed the district court's decision to uphold Amendment No. 1, allowing the sailboat and houseboat restrictions to remain but leaving no controlling law in its wake. *Stupak-Thrall v. United States*, 89 F.3d 1269 (6th Cir. 1996) (en banc). Neither the concurring nor the dissenting opinions at the en banc stage, nor indeed the vacated panel decision in *Stupak-Thrall I*, agreed with the district court's rationale for upholding **[—4—]** these restrictions. *Compare Stupak-Thrall*, 89 F.3d at 1271 (Moore, J., concurring), *with id.* at 1290 (Boggs, J., dissenting); *Stupak-Thrall v. United States*, 70 F.3d 881, 889 (6th Cir. 1995) (vacated).

The Forest Service issued another amendment to its plans for Crooked Lake in 1995. Known as Amendment No. 5, it prohibited the use of "any motor or mechanical device capable of propelling a watercraft by any means" on the wilderness portion of Crooked Lake. R. 49-4 at 1. This amendment came with an exception: one electric motor no greater than 24 volts in size or 48 pounds of thrust. Amendment No. 5 also prohibited the operation of any watercraft "in excess of a 'slow-no wake speed,'" defined as a maximum of five **{–355–}** miles per hour. *Id.*; R. 50-8 at 23. The Forest Service eventually incorporated these restrictions into the 2006 Forest Plan and a subsequent 2007 Forest Order, which subjected violators of Amendment No. 5 to criminal liability.

Kathy Stupak-Thrall, once again joined by the Gajewskis, filed a second lawsuit. *See Stupak-Thrall v. Glickman*, 988 F. Supp. 1055 (W.D. Mich. 1997) (*Stupak-Thrall II*). The property owners won this round, securing an injunction prohibiting enforcement of Amendment No. 5. The district court held that the motorboat restrictions interfered with Thrall's "'valid existing right' to use gas motor boats on Crooked Lake" and thus fell outside the Forest Service's regulatory authority. *Id.* at 1062. It also held that Amendment No. 5, as applied to Thrall and the Gajewskis, effected a regulatory taking under the Fifth Amendment. *Id.* at 1064.

After this decision, the Forest Service "facilitate[d] the sale of the Gajewski property ... to a third-party conservation organization," The Conservation Fund, which agreed "to resell the property after encumbering it with a conservation easement" paid for by the Forest Service. R. 53-44 at 13. Because this development "substantially" reduced motorboat use on Crooked Lake, the Forest Service voluntarily dismissed its appeal. *Id.* That left the other piece of property involved in that case protected by the injunction. To this day, Kathy Stupak-Thrall (and her guests) remain the only people free to use motorboats, though not sailboats or houseboats, on all of Crooked Lake. **[—5—]**

When the Amendment No. 5 regulations first went into effect, David and Pamela Herr were occasional visitors to Crooked Lake. In 2010, they made a commitment to the place, purchasing two waterfront lots on the lake's northern bay. The Herrs bought the land with the intention of using gas-powered motorboats. The seller confirmed these intentions, telling the Herrs that he had used motorboats in the past "without hindrance by the Forest Service." R. 4 at 11.

That turned out to be true for the Herrs as well, at first. The Forest Service not only allowed such use at the time but facilitated it for them and others. It regularly sold boating permits to visitors and residents—allowing them access to the lake—and allowed motorboat use through its public boat landing, located in a federally-owned portion of the northern bay just outside the wilderness area.

The Forest Service changed course in 2013. It stopped offering motorboat access at the landing dock and sent a letter to the Herrs informing them that it planned to "fully enforce" the existing motorboat restrictions on the federal wilderness portion of the lake, though not the private portion of the lake. R.

4-5 at 2. The Herrs sued the Forest Service under the Administrative Procedure Act (APA), seeking to enjoin it from enforcing the motorboat restrictions against them. *See* 5 U.S.C. § 702. Two environmental-protection organizations and two property owners (Tim Schmidt and Sylvania Wilderness Cabins) intervened to support the Forest Service.

At the Forest Service's urging, the district court dismissed the case. It held that the federal courts lacked subject matter jurisdiction over the dispute because the statute of limitations had run on any APA challenges to the 2007 Forest Order. We reversed. The limitations period, we explained, amounted to a claims-processing rule and did not create a limit on our subject matter jurisdiction. The limitations period had not lapsed anyway, we added, because the Herrs never had an opportunity to challenge the validity of the rule's application to them until 2010, when they bought the land, and the Service had not **{–356–}** enforced Amendment No. 5 against them until 2013. *Herr*, 803 F.3d at 813, 819, 3 Adm. R. at 467. **[—6—]**

On remand, the district court ruled for the Forest Service again, this time on the merits. The court held that the Herrs' rights to use Crooked Lake did not "exist" at the time of the Michigan Wilderness Act's enactment, meaning that the reservation of "valid existing rights" did not apply to them. *Herr v. U.S. Forest Serv.*, 212 F. Supp. 3d 720, 727–28 (W.D. Mich. 2016).

Here we are. Again.

II.

After nearly a quarter century of litigation over the recreational uses of Crooked Lake, the parties share some common ground about the resolution of today's dispute. The parties agree with, or at least do not dispute, these features of the legal landscape.

One: The Property Clause of the United States Constitution enables Congress to "make all needful Rules and Regulations respecting the Territory or other Property belonging to the United States." U.S. Const. art. IV, § 3, cl. 2. Though Congress has broad discretion to determine what regulations it "needs" on its own property, *see Kleppe v. New Mexico*, 426 U.S. 529, 539–40 (1976), it does not have the same authority over private property, *see Camfield v. United States*, 167 U.S. 518 (1897). If private property affects public lands, the government may regulate the private property to the extent needed to "protect[]" the relevant "federal property." *Kleppe*, 426 U.S. at 538 (discussing *Camfield*); *see* Allison H. Eid, *The Property Clause and New Federalism*, 75 U. Colo. L. Rev. 1241, 1242 (2004). By way of example, Congress has authority to prevent an individual from leaving an unmonitored fire near any public "forest, timber, or [] inflammable material," even if the fire is on private property. *United States v. Alford*, 274 U.S. 264, 266–67 (1927). Congress likewise may prohibit private landowners from fencing in public property, though the fences remain on the private side of the property line. *Camfield*, 167 U.S. at 525.

Two: The national government exercised its Property Clause power here through the Michigan Wilderness Act, which granted the Forest Service authority over the Sylvania Wilderness. This specific grant of authority allowed the Forest Service to regulate the public's use of Crooked Lake for boating and related recreation, "subject to valid existing rights." **[—7—]**

Three: State-law riparian and littoral rights represent a form of protected rights under the Act. *See* Forest Service Manual § 2320.5(16), http://www.fs.fed.us/cgi-bin/Directives/get_dirs/fsm?2300; Forest Service Br. 25. Riparian rights give property owners authority to use rivers that run through or adjacent to their property. *Dyball v. Lennox*, 680 N.W.2d 522, 526 (Mich. Ct. App. 2004). Littoral rights give property owners authority to use lakes on or adjacent to their property. *Bott v. Comm'n of Nat. Res. of State of Mich. Dep't of Nat. Res.*, 327 N.W.2d 838, 841 (Mich. 1982). This case concerns littoral rights.

Under Michigan law, a littoral landowner owns the rights to the bed of any inland lake, like Crooked Lake, "to the thread or midpoint of the water." *Id.* at 841; *Lorman v. Benson*, 8 Mich. 18, 22 (1860). But littoral landowners also share a right to the reasonable use of the water's full surface. *Bott*, 327 N.W.2d at 842; *see* 78 Am. Jur. 2d, Waters § 35; *Holton v. Ward*, 847 N.W.2d 1, 4–6 (Mich. Ct. App. 2014). That means the surface of **{-357-}** Crooked Lake, even the part in the Sylvania Wilderness, does not belong exclusively to the federal government. So too of the surface of Crooked Lake outside the Sylvania Wilderness; it does not belong exclusively to the State or the private property owners. The surface belongs jointly to the federal government and the private owners of state land on Crooked Lake, *both* of which maintain a littoral right to "reasonable use" of the lake's surface. *See Tennant v. Recreation Dev. Corp.*, 249 N.W.2d 348, 349 (Mich. Ct. App. 1976); *Rice v. Naimish*, 155 N.W.2d 370, 372 (Mich. Ct. App. 1967); *see also Yates v. City of Milwaukee*, 77 U.S. 497, 499 (1870); *Hilt v. Weber*, 233 N.W. 159, 168 (Mich. 1930).

With these background principles in place, we can turn to the question at hand: Does the Forest Service's ban on using any motorboats or any other boat that exceeds five miles per hour violate the "[1] subject to [2] valid existing [3] rights" clause of the Michigan Wilderness Act? Yes, as an examination of each part of the clause confirms.

"Subject to." "[S]ubject to" means "subordinate" or "subservient." *Black's Law Dictionary* 1278 (5th ed. 1979). That means the Forest Service's regulations must respect the Herrs' littoral rights, as the Service's ability to regulate begins where the Herrs' "valid existing rights" end. To the extent the Herrs have the right to use a motorboat under Michigan law on Crooked Lake, the Forest Service must honor that right—must in short be "subject to" it. **[—8—]**

"Existing." But did these littoral rights exist at the time Congress passed the Michigan Wilderness Act in 1987? Yes. Littoral rights, like most property rights, run with the land. *Thompson v. Enz*, 154 N.W.2d 473, 483 (Mich. 1967) (opinion of Kavanagh, J.). The question is not whether the Herrs had littoral rights on Crooked Lake before Congress passed the Act. It is whether the prior property owners had those rights before Congress passed the Act. They did. And they sold those rights along with the rest of the property to the Herrs in 2010. In reaching a contrary conclusion, the district court erred, as the Forest Service concedes. The Act does not refer to "valid rights of existing owners"; it refers to "valid existing rights." Because littoral and riparian rights run with the land, the Herrs purchased those "existing" rights along with others when they bought the Crooked Lake property.

"Valid Rights." That brings us to the nub of the dispute. As the Forest Service sees it, littoral and riparian rights permit property owners to use the waters only in reasonable ways, and a ban on motorboat use and a five-mile-an-hour limit on other boat use amounts to a reasonable limit for a remote body of water like Crooked Lake. The premise is correct. State law may indeed impose reasonable limits on littoral and riparian rights. *See* Mich. Comp. Laws § 324.80108; *Miller v. Fabius Twp. Bd., St. Joseph Cty.*, 114 N.W.2d 205, 208 (Mich. 1962). But the conclusion is not. When the statute refers to "valid existing rights," it asks whether the property owners have such rights under state law, not federal law, and certainly not federal law as construed by a federal agency. The Herrs plainly have such rights under state law, as ample Michigan authorities confirm. Recreational boating, the Michigan courts have repeatedly indicated, amounts to a reasonable use. *See Burt v. Munger*, 23 N.W.2d 117, 119–20 (Mich. 1946); *Rice*, 155 N.W.2d at 372; *People v. Hulbert*, 91 N.W. 211, 211–12, 218 (Mich. 1902); *Pierce v. Riley*, 264 N.W.2d 110, 114 (Mich. Ct. App. 1978); *Tennant*, 249 N.W.2d at 349. **{-358-}**

Not just these legal authorities, but the facts as well, point in this direction. Landowners and visitors have used motorboats on Crooked Lake since the 1940s. *Stupak-Thrall II*, 988 F. Supp. at 1059. Longstanding prior use is one indicator that a co-riparian (a term used by Michigan courts to cover littoral and riparian landowners) acts reasonably relative to others. *Dumont v. Kellogg*, 29 Mich. 420, 425 (1874). **[—9—]**

No doubt, Michigan could have regulated motorboat use on Crooked Lake during this time. *See* Mich. Comp. Laws § 324.80108. And it may even be possible that it could have banned motorboats, though at the risk of imposing a regulatory taking under the State or Federal Constitutions. *See Difronzo v. Vill. of Port Sanilac*, 419 N.W.2d 756, 758 (Mich. Ct. App. 1988). But the key point is that it never did. All agree that Michigan law permits motorboat use on the northern bay of the lake, outside the Sylvania Wilderness. The best evidence of reasonable use under Michigan law is what Michigan law allows on *this* lake. To our knowledge, no co-riparian has challenged the Herrs' (or anyone else's) use of gas-powered motorboats on this part of Crooked Lake.

No less significantly, the Forest Service long allowed motorboat use on all of the lake after it obtained this regulatory authority. And it still does with respect to one property owner. Until 2013, the Service not only allowed motorboat use, but it also facilitated such use by selling boating permits and allowing the public to use a loading dock on federal land. It never appealed the injunction in *Stupak-Thrall II*, which means that one of the ten property owners on the lake (and her guests) currently may use motorboats on all of the lake. How odd to allow one property owner to operate motorboats on the lake, while trying to exclude the other nine. If motorboat use is objectively unreasonable for one, it is objectively unreasonable for all.

That does not mean the Herrs have a right to use any size boat at any speed on any part of the lake, as the district court worried. The Herrs have a right to *reasonable* use of the lake. That means a right to travel at reasonable speeds within the lake. But the Forest Service has not shown that it would be *unreasonable* under Michigan law to travel on 95% of the lake above a low-wake-zone speed. If you think otherwise, try being at one end of a three-mile lake with a five-mile-an-hour speed limit as an unexpected storm sets in.

A pre-existing use, we suppose, may not invariably amount to a right in all settings. But Michigan law tells us that boating is typically one stick in the bundle of littoral and riparian rights. Only if boating on this lake would be unreasonable under state law could we say otherwise. The long history of pre-existing use confirms that it is not unreasonable to use a gas-powered motorboat at speeds above five miles per hour on Crooked Lake. **[—10—]**

The Forest Service tries to ground its authority to ban gas-powered motorboats in state law and the Wilderness Act itself. Neither source delivers. The Forest Service tells us that it can regulate littoral and riparian rights under the Property Clause to the same extent that state regulators can regulate them. Maybe; maybe not. But we need not decide. For the Michigan Wilderness Act does not grant the Forest Service a power coextensive with Congress' plenary authority under the Property Clause. It instead delegates a power limited by existing rights—"subject to valid existing rights." For that reason, any "police power" the Forest Service may have must respect pre-existing property rights, not just the limits of state power. Unless or until the State permissibly says otherwise, littoral property rights include **{–359–}** the right to reasonable use of the water's surface for recreational motorboating. No matter how reasonable the Forest Service may think this regulation is, it has no power to nullify the Herrs' pre-existing right under Michigan law to use the lake for recreational motorboating.

That the Wilderness Act contemplates "desirable" regulation of pre-existing motorboat use ignores the fact that the Michigan Wilderness Act makes the Forest Service's authority to enforce the Wilderness Act subject to independent limitations. Though the Michigan Wilderness Act provides that the Forest Service is to manage this area "in accordance" with the Wilderness Act, it also provides that such management is "[s]ubject to valid existing rights." Pub. L. No. 100-184, § 5, 101 Stat. 1274, 1275–76 (1987). That limitation remains controlling.

All of this does not leave the Forest Service or the Herrs' neighbors without options. Fellow riparians may enjoin unreasonable uses under state law through the state and federal courts. They may petition the State of Michigan to change the boating rules on the surface of Crooked Lake. Or they may pay the Herrs for an easement on their property, which would limit motorboat use in the same way the Gajewskis' property became limited. Even the serenity of nature sometimes comes at a price.

For these reasons, we reverse.

(Reporter's Note: Dissenting opinion follows on p. 344).

[—11—] {-359-} **DONALD,** Circuit Judge, dissenting:

I agree with the majority that the Herrs have valid existing rights to which any regulation by the Forest Service must be subservient. I agree also that the district court erroneously concluded that the Herrs' rights were not "existing" because the Herrs purchased their land after the Forest Service passed Amendment No. 5. Where I disagree, however, is with the majority's conclusion that a federal agency, in the same manner as a state, may not impose reasonable restrictions on littoral and riparian rights, when expressly authorized by Congress to do so.

First, as the Supreme Court has held, "[t]he general government doubtless has a power over its own property analogous to the police power of the several states, and the extent to which it may go in the exercise of such power is measured by the exigencies of the particular case." *Kleppe v. New Mexico*, 426 U.S. 529, 540 (1976) (citing *Camfield v. United States*, 167 U.S. 518, 525 (1897)). This also "includes the power to regulate in a manner affecting non-federal property." *Burlison v. United States*, 533 F.3d 419, 432 (6th Cir. 2008). As such, the power of Congress to regulate under the Property Clause "may have some effect on private lands not otherwise under federal control." *Id.* (quoting *Kleppe*, 426 U.S. at 546). Second, as even the majority notes, Congress has authorized the Forest Service to regulate the Sylvania Wilderness. This authority, "subject to valid existing rights," is coextensive with Congress' own authority under the Property Clause when the Forest Service acts to preserve the wilderness character of the Sylvania Wilderness. It thus follows that the Forest Service possesses a power that is "analogous to the police power of the several states," and where the Forest Service does not exceed the scope of the permissible police power of the state, it may exercise this power.

It is important then that we first examine the scope of the state's power to regulate littoral and riparian rights. In Michigan, "[t]he rights associated with riparian {-360-} ownership generally include . . . the right to a reasonable use of the water for general purposes such as boating, domestic use, etc." *Tennant v. Recreation Dev. Corp.*, 249 N.W.2d 348, 349 (Mich. Ct. App. 1976). These rights, however, are not without limitation. To protect the public safety, Michigan [—12—] permits regulation of the operation of vessels on the waters of the state. Mich. Comp. Laws § 324.80108. To this end, Michigan courts have upheld restrictions from local governments as they relate to the riparian and littoral rights of citizens within their jurisdictions. *See, e.g., Square Lake Hills Condominium Ass'n v. Bloomfield Twp.*, 471 N.W.2d 321, 326 (Mich. 1991) (permitting Bloomfield Township to regulate boat docking and launching on inland lakes under the township's police power); *Miller v. Fabius Twp. Bd.*, 114 N.W.2d 205, 209 (Mich. 1962) (allowing time regulations on water skiing).

Recognizing that the state may impose such regulations, the majority nevertheless concludes that the Forest Service may not regulate Crooked Lake in this manner because Michigan has not imposed such restrictions itself. But Forest Service's powers, while restricted, do not depend on state action. Put another way, state law determines the scope of the Forest Service's authority to regulate the surface of Crooked Lake because Congress has placed the specific constraint of "subject to valid existing rights"; rights that are determined by state law. But state regulation is not a prerequisite to the Forest Service's ability to regulate. The determining factor, rather, is whether the regulation is a proper exercise of the state's police power. And, as previously mentioned, Michigan state law confirms that restrictions on kinds of vessels and speed of motorboats are permissible.

The next question is the reasonableness of the restriction. "The reasonableness of an ordinance . . . depends upon the particular facts of each case. The test for determining whether an ordinance is reasonable requires us to assess the existence of a rational relationship between the exercise of police power and the public health, safety, morals, or general welfare in a particular manner in a given case." *Square Lake Hills*, 471 N.W.2d at 324 (citation omitted). As the district court noted, Amendment No. 5's restrictions are rationally related to achieving the Michigan Wilderness Act's goal of preserving the wilderness character of Sylvania. Also, these restrictions are certainly reasonable. Amendment No. 5 does not ban the use of all motorboats on the surface of Crooked Lake; rather, it merely restricts the use of gas-powered motorboats, the size of the motor, and the speed at which a boat may travel on ninety-five percent of the lake.

The majority approaches the issue of reasonableness by looking at whether recreational boating constitutes reasonable use under Michigan law. I agree that the use of gas-powered **[—13—]** motorboats is generally not unreasonable under Michigan law; but this alone is not dispositive of whether the Forest Service's ban of such use on Crooked Lake is unreasonable. Neither is the fact that the Forest Service has previously allowed motorboat use on the entire surface of Crooked Lake. As the majority notes, a pre-existing use does not always amount to a right. Initially, what was reasonable in the past is not necessarily reasonable today. But more importantly, the Herrs' right to engage in recreational motorboating under Michigan law, which does not necessarily equate to a *right* to use gas-powered motorboats, is not immune from reasonable future regulation. "Congress chose to 'grandfather' private rights in the 'subject to valid existing rights' phrase, but in doing so, it never intended **{-361-}** that those rights be ossified against further regulation." *Stupak-Thrall v. United States*, 89 F.3d 1269, 1271 (6th Cir. 1996) (memo) (Moore, J., concurring in order affirming district court opinion by divided en banc vote).

Ultimately, I believe that Amendment No. 5 was squarely within the Forest Service's authority to enact, and that the restrictions do not infringe on the Herrs' "valid existing rights." For these reasons, I would affirm the district court. I respectfully dissent.

United States Court of Appeals
for the Sixth Circuit

No. 16-3408

KALAMA
vs.
MATSON NAVIGATION CO.

Appeal from the United States District Court for the Northern District of Ohio

Decided: September 13, 2017*

Citation: 875 F.3d 297, 5 Adm. R. 346 (6th Cir. 2017).

Before **ROGERS**, **COOK**, and **STRANCH**, Circuit Judges.

* This decision was originally filed as an unpublished opinion on September 13, 2017. The court has now designated the opinion for full-text publication.

[—2—] **{–299–}** **ROGERS**, Circuit Judge:

This case arose in the late 1980s, when merchant marine plaintiffs began filing asbestos-liability suits against ship-owner and manufacturer defendants in the Northern District of Ohio. At that time, the N.D. of Ohio ruled that it lacked personal jurisdiction over many of the defendants and indicated that it would transfer the relevant cases to scattered venues with proper jurisdiction. Eventually, the cases were consolidated into multidistrict litigation in the Eastern District of Pennsylvania. The E.D. of Pennsylvania held again **{–300–}** in 2013 that the N.D. of Ohio lacks personal jurisdiction over the relevant defendants and that those defendants had not waived or forfeited their personal-jurisdiction defense. The E.D. of Pennsylvania accordingly dismissed thousands of parties. Now, ten plaintiffs appeal the E.D. of Pennsylvania's decision as it relates to nineteen defendants. The E.D. of Pennsylvania did not abuse its discretion when it decided that the nineteen defendant–appellees did not waive or forfeit their personal-jurisdiction defense in the ten plaintiff–appellants' suits.

I.

Numerous merchant marine plaintiffs began suing various ship-owners and asbestos manufacturers and suppliers in the late 1980s in the N.D. of Ohio for injuries related to asbestos exposure on commercial vessels. *In re Asbestos Prods. Liab. Litig. (No. VI)* (*Bartel Opinion*), 965 F. Supp. 2d 612, 614–15 (E.D. Pa. 2013). These plaintiffs became known as the maritime docket ("MARDOC") plaintiffs, and Judge Thomas Lambros presided over their cases in the N.D. of Ohio at that time.[1] *Id.* at 615. Among the earliest filings in the N.D. of Ohio were ship-owner defendants' motions to dismiss for lack of personal jurisdiction. **[—3—]**

Judge Lambros held a hearing on these motions to dismiss on October 31, 1989, at which he ruled that a significant number of the defendants were not subject to personal jurisdiction in Ohio. It is undisputed that defendant–appellees are among the group of defendants who had no specific contacts with the state of Ohio and therefore were not subject to personal jurisdiction there under Judge Lambros's ruling. Instead of granting the defendants' motions to dismiss, however, Judge Lambros announced that the relevant cases should be transferred to a venue with proper jurisdiction. At a later hearing, on November 21, 1989, Judge Lambros indicated that, if a defendant did not wish to be transferred, it could "waive the in personam jurisdiction problem" by filing an answer with the court by January 5, 1990.

Judge Lambros formalized these rulings in two orders. Order No. 40, issued on November 22, 1989, incorporated the October 31 and November 21 rulings, instructed the MARDOC plaintiffs to "report the choice of forum as to those cases which are" subject to

[1] Ten of those original MARDOC plaintiffs, represented by The Jaques Admiralty Law Firm, are the appellants in this appeal. Throughout this opinion, "plaintiff–appellants" refers to this group of ten, while "MARDOC plaintiffs" refers to the broader group of merchant-marine plaintiffs who originally filed asbestos-liability lawsuits in the N.D. of Ohio. Nineteen of the original ship-owner defendants, or their successors in interest, represented by Thompson Hine, are the appellees in this appeal. "Defendant-appellees" refers to this group of nineteen, while "ship-owner defendants" refers to the larger group of entities that were originally sued in the N.D. of Ohio.

transfer for lack of personal jurisdiction, and stated that "[p]arties who, upon reconsideration of their motions to dismiss or transfer, wish to remain in this jurisdiction need only file answers to the complaints" by January 5, 1990. Order No. 41 followed on December 29, 1989. The order transferred numerous cases "as to defendant shipowners which were determined not to be subject to in personam jurisdiction" to various federal district courts with personal jurisdiction over those defendants. The order also states: "Shipowner defendants, not subject to this transfer order, shall file answers by January 5, 1990 in accordance with the Order issued at the November 21, 1989 MARDOC conference." Although Order No. 41 purported to transfer cases to scattered **{-301-}** courts across the country, those transfers never actually occurred.

The ship-owner defendants did two things on December 29, 1989, in response to Judge Lambros's orders. First, they moved the N.D. of Ohio to certify Order No. 40 for immediate interlocutory review. Second, they filed two master answers, both of which expressly preserved the defendants' personal-jurisdiction defense. Master Answer No. 2, the more detailed of the two, reads:

> In response to defendants' motion to dismiss for lack of personal jurisdiction, the Court has issued MARDOC Order Nos. 40 and 41 which transfer the numerous cases against defendant to multiple jurisdictions, up to and including thirteen separate districts around the nation. Each defendant maintains **[—4—]** that the transfers are contrary to law. A motion to certify the order of transfer for interlocutory appeal has been filed on behalf of defendant, and in order to preserve the status quo pending appellate review of such order, defendant files its answer to the complaints as directed by MARDOC Order Nos. 40 and 41 under protest, so that said cases will not be transferred automatically pursuant to MARDOC Order No. 40 prior to completion of appellate review. By filing its answer, defendant specifically does not waive its defense of lack of personal jurisdiction or waive its objections to the propriety of the transfers.

The court never ruled on the defendants' motion to certify Order No. 40 for interlocutory appeal.

The MARDOC plaintiffs were also unhappy with Judge Lambros's decision to transfer their claims across the country and on February 13, 1990, filed a motion to transfer all defendants to a single forum. All ship-owner defendants represented by Thompson Hine vehemently opposed the motion to transfer in toto. Their brief in opposition states:

> Several nonresident defendants, although not subject to the personal jurisdiction of this Court, nevertheless agreed to waive their personal jurisdiction defense as the quid pro quo to avoid the expense of litigating these cases in as many as 13 different jurisdictions simultaneously, and to take advantage of the consolidated handling available in this Court.
>
> . . .
>
> Furthermore, some nonresident defendants who are not subject to the personal jurisdiction of this Court elected to waive that valuable due process right and submit themselves to the Court's jurisdiction to take advantage of this Court's experience in the handling of mass tort litigation, the consolidated handling of cases available in this Court, and to avoid the inconvenience of litigating these cases simultaneously in 13 scattered jurisdictions. After having pressured those defendants into submitting to jurisdiction here, plaintiffs now seek to turn the tables on them and scatter the cases against them to the four winds on the basis that a court may transfer a case under Sec. 1404(a) where the court has jurisdiction over the defendant. The interests of justice do not favor such tactics.

Judge Lambros denied the motion to transfer in toto.

As the litigation continued in the N.D. of Ohio, a group of twenty cases was set to be tried together there. After four of the twenty had been tried, Judge Lambros held a hearing on January 8, 1991, to discuss the remaining sixteen. After deciding that a magistrate judge would oversee the remaining sixteen cases, Judge Lambros turned his attention at the hearing to two **[—5—]** groups of forty-four cases each, one **{-302-}** assigned to Ohio and one assigned to Michigan. In the ensuing discussion, a Thompson Hine attorney asserted:

> I had one point that I wanted to be sure that the Court understood; we did not agree or concede to trials of any of these cases in Detroit. We had put our objection on the record before, but trials of the Ohio cases in Detroit are something that our clients waived jurisdictional objections to proceed here in Cleveland.

One group of forty-four cases was eventually transferred to the Eastern District of Michigan. Once there, the defendants who had been transferred argued for retransfer to the N.D. of Ohio, and petitioned the Sixth Circuit for a writ of mandamus to halt proceedings in the E.D. of Michigan. Because the forty-four cases transferred to the E.D. of Michigan did not include any of plaintiff–appellants' cases, the statements made in opposition to the transfer in these filings have little relevance to this appeal.

Later in 1991, the Judicial Panel on Multidistrict Litigation (JPML) consolidated asbestos litigation from around the nation into MDL No. 875, located in the E.D. of Pennsylvania. *Bartel Opinion*, 965 F. Supp. 2d at 615. The ship-owner defendants represented by Thompson Hine in the MARDOC litigation in the N.D. of Ohio strongly opposed the consolidation and transfer. They argued to the JPML that, because a litigation plan was already in place in the N.D. of Ohio, the cases should remain there. The MARDOC cases were nevertheless transferred to the MDL court in the E.D. of Pennsylvania, where they were essentially inactive from 1996 to 2008, when they were reassigned to Judge Robreno and reactivated. *See id.*

The next important step came in 2013, when the E.D. of Pennsylvania, through the "Bartel Opinion," 965 F. Supp. 2d 612, granted 418 defendants' motions to dismiss for lack of personal jurisdiction. These motions to dismiss required the E.D. of Pennsylvania to decide whether the N.D. of Ohio—the transferor court that would eventually oversee trials in the MARDOC cases—could exercise personal jurisdiction over the ship-owner defendants. While deciding the motions to dismiss, the MDL court first recognized, as the N.D. of Ohio had in 1989, that the N.D. of Ohio lacks personal jurisdiction over those defendants who did not maintain any specific contacts with Ohio. *See id.* at 619–20. The MDL court then rejected the **[—6—]** MARDOC plaintiffs' argument that the ship-owner defendants had waived their personal-jurisdiction defense by filing answers in the N.D. of Ohio, explaining:

> [I]t is apparent from the record that despite filing answers, defendants did not intend to waive the defense. In addition to including standard language about the personal jurisdiction defense, the answers included prefaces that specifically stated that defendants were filing the answers "under protest" pending review by the Court of Appeals of Judge Lambros' decision to transfer rather than dismiss the cases. In seeking to comply with Judge Lambros' orders, the defendants faced a Hobson's choice: they could either have agreed to a transfer of the cases to another jurisdiction (and thus lost the ability to assert cross-claims against manufacturer defendants), or they could have chosen to remain in the Northern District of Ohio and lost the defense of lack of personal jurisdiction.
>
> By filing answers which clearly identified the defense, while at the same time seeking interlocutory review of Judge Lambros' order, defendants preserved and did not waive the defense.

Id. at 621–22 (footnote omitted) (citations omitted). **{–303–}**

The E.D. of Pennsylvania also denied the MARDOC plaintiffs' request to transfer the claims against the defendants over which there was no personal jurisdiction in Ohio to a venue with proper jurisdiction. *Id.* at 622–23. The court reasoned that, under *Lexecon Inc. v. Milberg Weiss Bershad Hynes & Lerach*, 523 U.S. 26 (1998), an MDL transferee court may not transfer a case under 28 U.S.C. § 1404(a) to another district court. *Bartel Opinion*, 965 F. Supp. 2d at 622. The court further reasoned that, even if *Lexecon* allowed it to directly transfer the MARDOC plaintiffs' cases to another district, no good cause for such transfer existed. *Id.* at 623. The court explained:

> Plaintiffs continued filing thousands of cases in the Northern District of Ohio after Judge Lambros stated in 1989 that the court did not have personal jurisdiction over the defendants. Being on notice that there was no personal jurisdiction over the defendants in the Northern District of Ohio, and having chosen to continue the litigation there, Plaintiffs cannot complain that it is now unjust for the motions to dismiss to be granted.

Id. (citation omitted).

The MDL court faced an additional 5,974 motions to dismiss in 2014 in the "Jacobs Opinion," *In re Asbestos Prods. Liab. Litig. (No. VI)* (*Jacobs Opinion*), MDL No. 875, 2014 WL **[—7—]** 944227 (E.D. Pa. Mar. 11, 2014). While arguing against these motions to dismiss, the MARDOC plaintiffs relied on additional evidence that the ship-owner defendants had abandoned their personal-jurisdiction defense. None of the evidence persuaded the E.D. of Pennsylvania. First, the MDL court rejected the MARDOC plaintiffs' attempt to rely on Thompson Hine's response in opposition to the motion to transfer in toto from February 1990, reasoning that the response "is not evidence that any specific defendant waived the defense of lack of personal jurisdiction." *Id.* at *3, *5. The court held the same for Thompson Hine's opposition to consolidation into MDL No. 875, reasoning that the evidence "merely shows that defendants resisted the idea of being included in a federal asbestos MDL." *Id.* at *3–5. Furthermore, the court construed the statements made in opposition to transfer to the E.D. of Michigan at the January 8, 1991 hearing as relevant "only [to] those sixteen specific cases" being tried in the N.D. of Ohio at the time. *Id.* at *3, *5. Because those sixteen cases were not before the E.D. of Pennsylvania, the court disregarded the evidence. *See id.* at *5. Finally, the court did not accord any weight to an affidavit from Hartley Martyn, who served as Special Master for the N.D. of Ohio MARDOC litigation from 1988 to 1991 and recalled that the defendants represented by Thompson Hine wished to waive their personal-jurisdiction defense at that time. *See id.* at *4, *6. The court questioned whether Martyn's declaration was even admissible, then reasoned that it was unhelpful anyway, because it "fails to show that defendants affirmatively waived the defense." *Id.* at *6.

The MDL court summed up its reasoning:

> Viewed together, the Court is not persuaded that these exhibits show by a preponderance of the evidence a universal waiver by all defendants, in all cases, in perpetuity. What the snippets from briefs and letters reflect, at best, is that some defendants in these cases either considered or would have been willing to accept a court order keeping their individual case in the Northern District of Ohio (as opposed to being transferred to various districts) in return for waiving the defense of personal jurisdiction.

Id. at *5 (footnote omitted).

In two orders from March 11 and April 14, 2014, the E.D. of Pennsylvania granted **{–304–}** thousands of motions to dismiss based on the Bartel and Jacobs Opinions. Each of the defendant–appellees was dismissed from plaintiff–appellants' cases through these orders. At **[—8—]** some point later in 2014 or early in 2015, the MDL court recommended that each of the plaintiff–appellants' cases be remanded back to the N.D. of Ohio, and the JPML remanded the cases accordingly. In most cases, only one defendant, John Crane Inc., remained by the time the JPML remanded to the N.D. of Ohio, although several plaintiff–appellants retained claims against Chesterton Co., Gatke Corp., and General Refractories—none of which are parties to this appeal. After remand, the N.D. of Ohio completely disposed of plaintiff–appellants' cases by dismissing these remaining defendants on March 15, 2016. Plaintiff–appellants timely appealed from the March 15, 2016 final judgment as well as from the E.D. of Pennsylvania's orders dismissing defendant–appellees for lack of personal jurisdiction.

II.

A.

As a preliminary matter, we have appellate jurisdiction to review the E.D. of Pennsylvania's orders. Although both parties argue that appellate jurisdiction is proper, the court has an independent obligation to examine its own jurisdiction. *Hitchcock v. Cumberland Univ. 403(B) DC Plan*, 851 F.3d 552, 557 (6th Cir. 2017). 28 U.S.C. § 1294(1) provides for appellate jurisdiction over "appeals from reviewable decisions" of a U.S. district court in the "court of appeals for the circuit embracing the district." Pursuant to § 1294(1), we are usually asked to review judgments arising entirely out of a district court within the Sixth Circuit's territorial jurisdiction. This case presents an odd scenario, which asks us to review non-final orders issued by the MDL transferee court in the E.D. of Pennsylvania, outside the Sixth Circuit's territorial jurisdiction. Because the MDL court's orders became reviewable only after plaintiff–appellants' cases reached a final judgment in the N.D. of Ohio, however, we have appellate jurisdiction over the orders.

EEOC v. Northwest Airlines, Inc., 188 F.3d 695 (6th Cir. 1999), compels this conclusion. In that case, the underlying lawsuit originated in the E.D. of Michigan. The E.D. of Michigan transferred the case for the parties' convenience under 28 U.S.C. § 1404(a) to the District of Minnesota, which then granted summary judgment to the defendants on several claims. The District of Minnesota next transferred the case back to the E.D. of Michigan, again under **[—9—]** § 1404(a), and the E.D. of Michigan granted summary judgment to the defendants on the remaining claims. The plaintiff appealed both summary-judgment orders to the Sixth Circuit. In response to the defendants' argument that the appeal of the District of Minnesota's order was untimely, we noted that the order did not become appealable until after the case had been retransferred to the E.D. of Michigan and that court had entered a final judgment. *See Nw. Airlines*, 188 F.3d at 700. We then held that we had appellate jurisdiction over the District of Minnesota's order: "We thus find ourselves in the position of reviewing a final judgment partially disposed of in a district court of another circuit. Although unusual, this case is properly before us." *Id.*

This case's procedural posture closely resembles that in *Northwest Airlines*. Plaintiff–appellants ask us to review a partial dismissal issued by a district court outside of the Sixth Circuit. Partial dismissals are not appealable final decisions under 28 U.S.C. § 1291 and ordinarily become reviewable only after an action reaches a final judgment. **{-305-}** *In re Refrigerant Compressors Antitrust Litig.*, 731 F.3d 586, 589 (6th Cir. 2013). Thus, the E.D. of Pennsylvania's partial dismissals became appealable only after the N.D. of Ohio, a district court within the Sixth Circuit's territorial jurisdiction, issued its final judgment on March 15, 2016. As we exercised jurisdiction to review a final judgment from the E.D. of Michigan that had been "partially disposed of" elsewhere in *Northwest Airlines*, we may now exercise appellate jurisdiction over the N.D. of Ohio's final judgment, which was partially disposed of in the E.D. of Pennsylvania.

This result also accords with § 1294, which limits our appellate jurisdiction to "reviewable decisions" of the district courts within our territorial jurisdiction. A partial dismissal is not "reviewable" until it can be appealed—

generally, when it "merges" into a final, appealable judgment.[2] *See Hill v. Henderson*, 195 F.3d 671, 675–76 (D.C. Cir. 1999); *see also Jones v. InfoCure Corp.*, 310 F.3d 529, 534 (7th Cir. 2002). Here, the E.D. of Pennsylvania's orders became appealable, and therefore "reviewable decisions," only through the N.D. of Ohio's final **[—10—]** judgment. Because that final judgment arose within our territorial jurisdiction, § 1294(1) required plaintiff–appellants to appeal to the Sixth Circuit.

B.

On the merits, the MDL court did not abuse its discretion when it decided that the Thompson Hine defendants, including defendant–appellees, did not waive or forfeit their personal-jurisdiction defense. Under the unusual circumstances of this case, the court reasonably concluded that the MARDOC plaintiffs failed to prove waiver or forfeiture, either through the ship-owner defendants' filing answers in response to Judge Lambros's directives, or through their conduct later in the litigation.

First, the MDL court correctly decided that the act of filing answers, alone, did not constitute waiver. Once Judge Lambros denied the ship-owner defendants' motions to dismiss for lack of personal jurisdiction and elected to transfer the cases instead, he instructed those defendants who wished to "waive the in personam jurisdiction problem" to file answers by January 5, 1990. Plaintiff–appellants frame Judge Lambros's order as an ultimatum—waive personal jurisdiction in the N.D. of Ohio by filing answers there, or be transferred out and argue that the only logical inference when the ship-owner defendants filed answers in response is that the defendants were consenting to personal jurisdiction. However, the defendants' express objection to personal jurisdiction in the N.D. of Ohio in their master answers, along with the motion requesting leave to immediately appeal Judge Lambros's transfer order, negates that inference. The ship-owner defendants' intent could not have been clearer from their assertion in Master Answer No. 2 that they were filing answers "under protest" to "preserve the status quo" while they continued to seek dismissal through an immediate appeal of Orders 40 and 41. Because the Federal Rules of Civil Procedure do not authorize a district court to strip a defendant of its right to assert an affirmative defense in an answer, it was not an abuse of discretion to determine that the ship-owner defendants could seek to preserve their personal-jurisdiction defense at that time.

Furthermore, even assuming that Judge Lambros considered defendant–appellees' **{-306-}** personal-jurisdiction defense waived—given that he moved forward with the MARDOC **[—11—]** litigation and ignored the defendants' motion to certify Orders 40 and 41 for interlocutory review—it was not an abuse of discretion for the district court to nevertheless reach the opposite conclusion. Perhaps the record supports an inference that the parties considered the defendants' personal-jurisdiction defense waived once the defendants filed answers, but that is not the only reasonable inference. Given the strength of the ship-owner defendants' statements in their answers that they did not intend to forgo their personal-jurisdiction defense, and in light of the full record at that juncture, it was within the MDL court's discretion to take the answers at face value and reject plaintiff–appellants' waiver argument.

Second, the MDL court did not abuse its discretion when it determined that the MARDOC plaintiffs' proffered supplemental evidence does not prove the ship-owner defendants forfeited their personal-jurisdiction defense. Such forfeiture occurs when a defendant's "submissions, appearances and filings [give] '[p]laintiff a reasonable expectation that [the defendant] will defend the suit on the merits or must cause the court to go to some effort that would be wasted if personal jurisdiction is later found lacking.'" *Gerber v. Riordan*, 649 F.3d 514, 519 (6th Cir. 2011) (quoting *Mobile Anesthesiologists Chi.,*

[2] Alternatively, a district court may enter a final judgment as to some, but not all, of the parties or claims in an action under Federal Rule of Civil Procedure 54(b), or certify a partial dismissal for an immediate interlocutory appeal under 28 U.S.C. § 1292(b).

LLC v. Anesthesia Assocs. of Hous. Metroplex, P.A., 623 F.3d 440, 443 (7th Cir. 2010)).

To start, the ship-owner defendants' objections against transfer of a group of forty-four cases to the E.D. of Michigan—raised before Judge Lambros at the January 8, 1991 hearing, in a motion for retransfer, and in a petition to the Sixth Circuit for a writ of mandamus—cannot prove forfeiture, because the forty-four transferred cases did not include plaintiff–appellants' cases. While the cases that were transferred to the E.D. of Michigan did include several of the named defendant–appellees, it was only in their capacity as defendants in lawsuits brought by MARDOC plaintiffs that are not party to this appeal. On this record, it would be improper to impute statements about waiver of personal jurisdiction made on behalf of a defendant in one lawsuit to the same defendant in a separate suit. Thus, this evidence does not govern whether the defendants in this appeal forfeited their personal-jurisdiction defense.

Moreover, the fact that the Third Circuit relied on this evidence in *In re Asbestos Products Liability Litigation (No. VI)*, 661 F. App'x 173 (3d Cir. 2016), to overturn the MDL court's decision to grant several ship-owner defendants' motions to dismiss is unpersuasive, **[—12—]** because unlike here, the Third Circuit's review involved cases that were actually transferred to the E.D. of Michigan. Three MARDOC plaintiffs, Wilson, Braun, and Guiden, appealed the MDL court's dismissal of their claims against two ship-owner defendants, Matson Navigation Co. and American President Line, to the Third Circuit. *Id.* at 174. The Third Circuit's reasoning in holding that the MDL court abused its discretion when it granted these defendants' motions to dismiss was specific to the particular actions being appealed; the Third Circuit noted that the ship-owner defendants before it "consented at [the January 8, 1991] hearing to proceed with 'these cases' in the Northern District of Ohio, and that phrase clearly refers to the clusters that Chief Judge Lambros intended to transfer to the Eastern District of Michigan, which included the lawsuits brought by Wilson, Braun, and Guiden." *Id.* at 177. The court later cabined its holding again by stating, "it was incorrect to dismiss *the cases before* **{-307-}** *us*." *Id.* at 179 (emphasis added). The Third Circuit neither relied on any evidence aside from the relevant ship-owner defendants' objections to transfer to the E.D. of Michigan nor ruled on the forfeiture issue aside from Matson's and American's waiver in Wilson's, Braun's, and Guiden's lawsuits. Thus, the Third Circuit's opinion has no relevance to this appeal.[3]

The MDL court also did not abuse its discretion by finding an insufficient showing of forfeiture in the remaining proffered evidence, including the Martyn affidavit and Thompson Hine's statements in opposition to transfer in toto and in opposition to consolidation into MDL No. 875. Under both Third Circuit and Sixth Circuit law, the burden was on the MARDOC plaintiffs to convince the MDL court that personal jurisdiction exists over the ship-owner defendants in the N.D. of Ohio. *See Control Screening LLC v. Tech. Application & Prod. Co.*, 687 F.3d 163, 167 (3d Cir. 2012); *MAG IAS Holdings, Inc. v. Schmückle*, 854 F.3d 894, 899 (6th **[—13—]** Cir. 2017). While the remaining evidence could reasonably support an inference that some ship-owner defendants represented by Thompson Hine, at some point,

[3] The Third Circuit correctly determined that the MDL court clearly erred when it found that the objection to transfer out of the N.D. of Ohio from the January 8, 1991, hearing pertains only to sixteen cases that were not before the MDL court in 2014. *See In re Asbestos Prods. Liab. Litig.*, 661 F. App'x at 177–78 (the Third Circuit's reasoning); *Jacobs Opinion*, 2014 WL 944227, at *5 (the MDL court's reasoning). Reading the hearing transcript as a whole, it is clear that the objection arose after Judge Lambros had switched the topic of conversation from the sixteen cases set for trial in the N.D. of Ohio to the group of cases destined for the E.D. of Michigan. 01/08/1991 Tr., Appellant App. 1 at 1029–1117 (PDF 1039–1127). Furthermore, it would not make sense for the defendants to object to a "transfer" of the sixteen cases set for trial in the N.D. of Ohio, because Judge Lambros was not considering transferring those cases. However, because the forty-four cases set for transfer to the E.D. of Michigan did not include any of the cases currently before us, the MDL court's error nevertheless does not render its decision an abuse of discretion as to the ten plaintiff–appellants' cases.

consented to personal jurisdiction in the N.D. of Ohio to avoid transfer to scattered venues, the evidence is too vague to render forfeiture the only reasonable conclusion. Faced with thousands of motions to dismiss for lack of personal jurisdiction, the MDL court was justifiably skeptical that statements about "several nonresident defendants" having waived their personal-jurisdiction defense, and general opposition to consolidation into multidistrict litigation, could prove that each of the ship-owner defendants forfeited its defense. On this record and absent concrete evidence that any specific ship-owner defendant had abandoned its personal-jurisdiction defense, it was not a clear error of judgment for the MDL court to reject the MARDOC plaintiffs' forfeiture argument.

C.

Furthermore, the MDL court did not violate the law-of-the-case doctrine by granting defendant–appellees' motions to dismiss for lack of personal jurisdiction, because the court's decision did not diverge from Judge Lambros's prior ruling. Although the parties dispute whether Judge Lambros "granted" or "denied" the ship-owner defendants' motions to dismiss in 1989, how Judge Lambros technically disposed of the motions is irrelevant, because the issues he decided at that time are clear. First, Judge Lambros ruled that the N.D. of Ohio lacked personal jurisdiction over those ship-owner defendants who had no specific contacts with Ohio. Second, he ruled that the cases involving defendants over which the N.D. of Ohio had no **{-308-}** personal jurisdiction should be transferred rather than dismissed. The law-of-the-case doctrine "comes into play only with respect to issues previously determined." *Holloway v. Brush*, 220 F.3d 767, 777 (6th Cir. 2000) (quoting *Quern v. Jordan*, 440 U.S. 332, 347 (1979)). Thus, the MDL court's decision implicates the doctrine only if it contradicted either issue previously decided by Judge Lambros, and it did not.

The MDL court agreed that the N.D. of Ohio lacks personal jurisdiction over those shipowner defendants without specific contacts to the state. *See Bartel Opinion*, 965 F. Supp. 2d at 620. Furthermore, the MDL court did not revisit Judge Lambros's initial decision to transfer the relevant cases out of the N.D. of Ohio. Finally, the remaining issues before the MDL court—whether the ship-owner defendants waived their personal-jurisdiction defense and whether **[—14—]** *Lexecon* permits an MDL transferee court to directly transfer a case to another district—had not been decided previously in the MARDOC litigation. Based on the entirety of the record, the law-of-the-case doctrine does not prohibit the MDL court from granting defendant–appellees' motions to dismiss for lack of personal jurisdiction.

D.

Finally, the MDL court did not err by dismissing, rather than transferring, the defendants over which the N.D. of Ohio lacks personal jurisdiction. Under *Lexecon*, the MDL court had no power to directly transfer plaintiff–appellants' cases to a venue with personal jurisdiction over defendant–appellees. In *Lexecon*, an MDL transferee court used 28 U.S.C. § 1404(a), which allows a district court, "[f]or the convenience of parties and witnesses, [and] in the interest of justice," to transfer "any civil action to any other district or division where it might have been brought," to transfer an MDL case to itself for trial. The Supreme Court held that such "self-transfer" was improper. *Lexecon*, 523 U.S. at 40. The Court relied on 28 U.S.C. § 1407(a), which requires that each transferred MDL action "be remanded by the [JPML] at or before the conclusion of . . . pretrial proceedings to the district from which it was transferred unless it shall have been previously terminated." This provision leaves two options for an MDL transferee court at the close of pretrial proceedings: terminate the case or allow the JPML to remand the case to the originating, transferor court. *See id.* at 34–37. To allow the transferee court to transfer a case to itself for trial under § 1404(a) would "conclusively thwart[] the Panel's capacity to obey the unconditional command of § 1407(a)" to remand cases at the close of pretrial proceedings. *Id.* at 36.

The Court's reasoning in *Lexecon* is not limited to self-transfer under § 1404(a). The Court specifically stated that its reasoning applies to *any* § 1404(a) transfer: "[W]e find that the statutory language of § 1407 precludes a transferee court from granting any § 1404(a) motion . . . ." *Id.* at 41 n.4. That § 1407 prohibits an MDL transferee court from directly transferring an action to another district court makes sense, because any direct transfer would thwart the JPML's ability to remand to the originating court at the end of pretrial proceedings. Thus, the E.D. of Pennsylvania correctly held that it had no authority to transfer plaintiff–appellants' claims to a district with proper jurisdiction. **[—15—]**

Furthermore, the MDL court did not abuse its discretion by refusing plaintiff–appellants' proposed alternative of requesting the JPML to remand to the N.D. of Ohio with instructions for the N.D. of **{-309-}** Ohio to transfer the cases to an appropriate venue. This approach is allowed but not mandated under *Lexecon*. *See id.* at 39. The MDL court correctly reasoned that yet another transfer after nearly thirty years of litigation would not serve the interest of justice, and there is no guarantee that, had the court recommended remand and subsequent transfer, the JPML would have adopted the recommendation.

Finally, the MDL court appropriately dismissed defendant–appellees after deciding that the N.D. of Ohio could not exercise personal jurisdiction over them. Plaintiff–appellants make a strange argument that § 1407(a) and *Lexecon* compelled the MDL court to recommend to the JPML that the defendants' cases be remanded to the N.D. of Ohio. Under plaintiff–appellants' argument: § 1407(a) requires remand unless an action was "previously terminated"; "previously terminated" means "previously terminated on the merits"; and dismissal for lack of personal jurisdiction is not "on the merits." Thus, according to plaintiff–appellants, once the MDL court dismissed the relevant defendants for lack of personal jurisdiction, the MARDOC plaintiffs' claims against those defendants were not "terminated," and the JPML was still required to remand claims against those particular defendants to the N.D. of Ohio. Following this logic would defeat the purpose of consolidated MDL litigation, which is for the MDL transferee court to weed out improper parties and claims before trial, including dismissing parties over which the transferor court could not exercise personal jurisdiction. That is what the E.D. of Pennsylvania did here, and neither § 1407 nor *Lexecon* demands a different result.

III.

The judgment of the district court is affirmed.[4]

(Reporter's Note: Concurring opinion follows on p. 355).

[4] Because the MDL court's orders dismissing defendant–appellees for a lack of personal jurisdiction stand, we need not address defendant–appellees' motion to dismiss this appeal as barred by res judicata.

[—16—] {-309-} STRANCH, Circuit Judge, concurring:

I write separately to note that though this case is part of a very large MDL group of cases, its result hinges on the unique circumstances surrounding the claims of ten individual plaintiffs against nineteen specific defendants. I concur because our result is based on the particulars of these cases and because the opinion accords with the understanding—and actual practice in this MDL—that § 1407 permits a transferee court to remand a case to the transferor court with a recommendation to send the case to an appropriate venue. *See, e.g.*, *Musselman v. Amphenol Corp.*, No. 10-cv-69486, 2011 WL 6415165, at *1 (E.D. Pa. Nov. 2, 2011) (remanding a MDL No. 875 case to the Delaware transferor court with a suggestion to transfer the case to Arkansas). Although the MDL court declined to elect that path for these ten plaintiff-appellants, other plaintiffs, including those participating in MDL No. 875, may still request that relief.

Also, although these ten plaintiff-appellants were unable to present specific evidence that the nineteen defendant-appellees waived personal jurisdiction in their individual cases, today's opinion confirms that other plaintiffs may prove waiver. *See supra* p. 14, note 3 (discussing *In re: Asbestos Prods. Liab. Litig.*, 661 F. App'x 173 (3d Cir. 2016)). The opinion notes that the Third Circuit "correctly" reversed dismissal because the January **{-310-}** 1991 statements made by counsel for two of the defendant-appellees confirmed that they had consented to proceeding in the N.D. of Ohio for the purposes of a cluster of twenty cases. Where such evidence of waiver exists, dismissal remains inappropriate.

This page intentionally left blank

United States Court of Appeals for the Seventh Circuit

United States Court of Appeals
for the Seventh Circuit

No. 15-3112

KRIK
vs.
EXXON MOBIL CORP.

Appeal from the United States District Court for the Northern District of Illinois, Eastern Division

Decided: August 31, 2017

Citation: 870 F.3d 669, 5 Adm. R. 358 (7th Cir. 2017).

Before **WOOD**, Chief Judge, and **ROVNER** and **SYKES**, Circuit Judges.

[—1—] {-671-} **ROVNER**, Circuit Judge:

Charles Krik has lung cancer. And like some people suffering from a devastating illness, he sought to know if someone or something was to blame. In his case, as in many, there are several sources at which to point a finger. Krik smoked a pack and a half of cigarettes every day for thirty years. From 1954 until 1960 Charles Krik also worked aboard navy vessels removing insulation produced **[—2—]** by Owens-Illinois, Inc., which he claimed exposed him to asbestos fibers. And for two weeks, he worked as an independent contractor at **{-672-}** Exxon Mobil's (Mobil) Joliet refinery replacing heaters that Krik claimed were insulated with asbestos. Mobil presented counter-evidence that the insulation at its refinery did not contain asbestos. Nevertheless, Krik's position was that Owens-Illinois and Mobil exposed him to asbestos which was a substantial cause of his lung cancer.[1] Before a district court and jury, the defendants maintained that cigarettes and not asbestos exposure caused Krik's lung cancer. After a seven-day trial, the jury found that cigarettes were the sole cause of Krik's cancer. Krik now claims that two rulings by the district court deprived him of a fair trial. First, he claims that the district court erred by excluding testimony about medical causation from his expert, Dr. Arthur Frank, and second, that he was denied a fair trial when Mobil, with the knowledge of Owens-Illinois, hired a private investigator to secretly conduct an interview of a sitting juror's acquaintance, to verify and investigate information revealed by the juror. Because we hold that neither issue was prejudicial and denied Krik a fair trial, we affirm the judgment of the district court in all respects.

A. Dr. Frank's expert witness testimony

The battle over the expert testimony began during pre-trial motions. Prior to trial, the defendants filed motions before Judge Lee of the Northern District of Illinois seeking to exclude Dr. Arthur Frank and other witnesses from testifying about a theory of causation often referred to as "each and **[—3—]** every exposure theory," "any exposure theory," "the single fiber theory," or "no safe level of exposure theory" among others.[2] These theories posit that any exposure to asbestos fibers whatsoever, regardless of the amount of fibers or length of exposure constitutes an underlying cause of injury to the exposed individual. At the conclusion of the presentation of these pre-trial motions, Judge Lee concluded that Krik had not established that the "any exposure" theory was sufficiently reliable to warrant admission under Rule 702 and the Supreme Court's seminal case on the admissibility of expert witness testimony, *Daubert v. Merrell Dow Pharmaceuticals, Inc.*, 509 U.S. 579 (1993). Judge Lee precluded Krik from offering any expert testimony espousing such a theory at trial. Krik does not challenge that ruling through this appeal.

[1] Krik initially sued many other corporations, but only these two defendants remain. *See* R. 1 (All references are to the record in the district court.)

[2] In the second part of the motion, Mobil sought to bar Dr. Frank "from offering any specific causation testimony regarding Mobil." R. 140 at 1, pageID 2618. Judge Lee held that "to the extent that Plaintiff will present facts at trial that he was exposed to asbestos at ExxonMobil facilities and Dr[s]. Frank and Parker will rely upon such facts at trial, the experts will be permitted to testify at trial regarding such exposure, subject to the Court's ruling precluding testimony as to the "Any Exposure" theory." *Krik v. Crane Co.*, 76 F. Supp. 3d 747, 756 (N.D. Ill. 2014).

Before trial, the case was transferred to Judge Manish Shah. Despite the earlier *Daubert* ruling, Krik called Dr. Frank at trial, hoping that a newly packaged "cumulative exposure theory" would skirt Judge Lee's earlier ruling on the motion in limine. During voir dire of Dr. Frank, however, Judge Shah concluded that Dr. Frank's testimony was still "not tied to the specific quantum of exposure attributable to the defendants, but was instead based on his medical and scientific opinion that every exposure is a substantial contributing factor to the cumulative exposure that causes cancer." **{–673–}** *Krik v. Owens-* **[—4—]** *Illinois, Inc.*, No. 10-CV-07435, 2015 WL 5050143, at *1 (N.D. Ill. Aug. 25, 2015) (hereinafter *Krik*, 2015 WL 5050143 (J. Shah)). He cited, as examples, the following statements of Dr. Frank: "... If there is exposure to a cancer causing agent, that becomes part of the totality of the exposure. Some may contribute more, some may contribute less, but they are all part of the exposure." *Id.* (citing R. 376 at 262, pageId 10135); and "If the exposure took place, it was part of the cumulative exposure that someone had." *Id.* Judge Shah indicated that he was following the pre-trial determination of Judge Lee and that the "cumulative exposure" testimony was no different than the testimony proffered in front of Judge Lee. *Krik*, 2015 WL 5050143, at *1 (J. Shah).

On appeal, we review a district court's decision to deny a motion for a new trial for an abuse of discretion. *United States v. Lawrence*, 788 F.3d 234, 244 (7th Cir. 2015). Whether the district court applied the *Daubert* framework properly is a question we review de novo but we review the decision to exclude or admit the expert witness testimony for an abuse of discretion only. *C.W. ex rel. Wood v. Textron, Inc.*, 807 F.3d 827, 835 (7th Cir. 2015). The party seeking to introduce the expert witness testimony bears the burden of demonstrating that the expert witness testimony satisfies the standard by a preponderance of the evidence. *Lewis v. CITGO Petroleum Corp.*, 561 F.3d 698, 705 (7th Cir. 2009).

Krik does not dispute that the district court identified and applied the appropriate *Daubert* framework, rather, he argues that Judge Shah made an errant factual determination that the cumulative exposure theory was the same as the "each and every exposure" theory that Judge Lee had barred. We there- **[—5—]** fore review this decision and the decision to exclude the cumulative exposure-based testimony for an abuse of discretion. Judge Shah found that the cumulative exposure theory was the same as the "each and every exposure" theory and prohibited testimony based on this theory and the reasoning of Judge Lee supplemented by his own analysis. We agree and therefore conclude that it was not an abuse of discretion to exclude the testimony nor to deny the motion for a new trial.

Subsumed within this question of the expert testimony are really four issues: First, whether the cumulative exposure theory was sufficiently similar to the "each and every exposure" theory such that Judge Lee's pre-trial ruling covered the former theory as well. Second, and relatedly, whether Judge Shah properly followed Judge Lee's ruling. Third, whether Judge Shah abused his discretion by refusing to allow Dr. Frank to testify about a cumulative exposure theory, and fourth, whether he abused his discretion when he refused to grant a new trial. Because these issues are intertwined and overlap, we address them wholesale as we review the propriety of excluding Dr. Frank's testimony.

Any assessment of the admissibility of expert witness testimony begins with Federal Rule of Evidence 702 and the Supreme Court's opinion in *Daubert*, as together they govern the admissibility of expert witness testimony. Rule 702 states:

> A witness who is qualified as an expert by knowledge, skill, experience, training, or education may testify in the form of an opinion or otherwise if: **[—6—]**
>
> (a) the expert's scientific, technical, or other specialized knowledge will help the trier of fact to understand the evidence or to determine a fact in issue;

(b) the testimony is based on sufficient facts or data; **{–674–}**

(c) the testimony is the product of reliable principles and methods; and

(d) the expert has reliably applied the principles and methods to the facts of the case.

Fed. R. Evid. 702. In addition, Federal Rule of Evidence 403 overlays all other evidentiary rules by stating that a court may "exclude relevant evidence if its probative value is substantially outweighed by the danger of ... unfair prejudice, confusing the issues, [or] misleading the jury." Fed. R. Evid. 403.

The Supreme Court has interpreted Rule 702 with a flexible standard that boils down to two over-arching requirements for expert witness testimony. The expert testimony must be "ground[ed] in the methods and procedures of science" and must "assist the trier of fact to understand or determine a fact in issue." *Daubert*, 509 U.S. at 590–91. *Daubert* requires the district court to act as an evidentiary gatekeeper, ensuring that an expert's testimony rests on a reliable foundation and is relevant to the task at hand. *Id.* at 589. To do this a trial judge must make a preliminary assessment that the testimony's underlying reasoning or methodology is scientifically valid and properly applied to the facts at issue. *Id.* at 592–93. The district court holds broad discretion in its gatekeeper function of determining the relevance and reliability of the expert opinion testimony. *Kumho Tire Co. v. Carmichael*, 526 U.S. **[—7—]** 137, 141 (1999). Our circuit has given courts the following guidance to determine the reliability of a qualified expert's testimony under *Daubert*, stating that they are to consider, among other things: "(1) whether the proffered theory can be and has been tested; (2) whether the theory has been subjected to peer review; (3) whether the theory has been evaluated in light of potential rates of error; and (4) whether the theory has been accepted in the relevant scientific community." *Baugh v. Cuprum S.A. de C.V.*, 845 F.3d 838, 844 (7th Cir. 2017); *see also Smith v. Ford Motor Co.*, 215 F.3d 713, 719 (7th Cir. 2000). Despite the list, we have repeatedly emphasized that "no single factor is either required in the analysis or dispositive as to its outcome." *Smith,* 215 F.3d at 719; *see also Kumho Tire Co.*, 526 U.S. at 151–52. The district court may apply these factors flexibly as the case requires. *United States v. Brumley*, 217 F.3d 905, 911 (2000). Indeed *Daubert* itself contemplated a flexible standard with broad discretion given to district court judges. *Daubert*, 509 U.S. at 593.

Judge Lee's pre-trial motion concluded that under both Illinois law and maritime law, a plaintiff must demonstrate that asbestos was a "substantial contributing factor" to his injury. *Krik v. Crane Co.*, 76 F. Supp. 3d 747, 753 (N.D. Ill. 2014) (hereinafter *Krik*, 76 F. Supp. 3d 747 (J. Lee)), *citing Lindstrom v. A-C Prod. Liab. Tr.*, 424 F.3d 488, 493 (6th Cir. 2005) (maritime law); *Thacker v. UNR Indus., Inc.*, 603 N.E.2d 449, 457 (Ill. 1992) (Illinois law). Judge Lee noted that asbestos-induced lung cancer is dosage dependent—that is, the risk of contracting lung cancer from asbestos depends on the length of time of exposure and the amount of exposure. To determine whether any exposure constitutes a substantial contributing factor, therefore, one would have to understand the timing and amount of exposure. But rather than testifying **[—8—]** that the particular dose of asbestos to which Krik had been exposed was a substantial contributing factor to his illness, Judge Lee explained, Dr. Frank's theory was based on a premise that each and every exposure to asbestos, including the first exposure, no matter how de minimis, **{–675–}** "is a substantial contribution to the cumulative total." *Krik*, 76 F. Supp. 3d at 753 (J. Lee). As Dr. Frank further explained: "Either it's zero or it's substantial; there is no such thing as not substantial." R. 66-3 at 23, pageID 923. Even one minute of exposure, he opined, would be a substantial contributing factor to a person's ultimate disease. R. 376 at 273–74, pageID 10146-47. Applying *Daubert*, the court concluded that the "any exposure" theory ignored fundamental principles of toxicology that illnesses like cancer are dose dependent. Krik's experts did not plan to offer any evidence about how much asbestos exposure Krik experienced and whether that dosage could have been a substantial contributing factor to lung cancer. In fact Krik's experts readily admitted in their depositions that they had not considered any information about amount of exposure in their analyses. Instead, Dr. Frank's asserted theory would be that any and all exposure to asbestos is a substantial contributing factor to lung cancer. The law of causation, however, required the plaintiff to prove that the *defendants'* acts or products were a "*substantial* contributing factor" to Krik's illness. De minimis exposure is not sufficient. *Krik*, 76 F. Supp. 2d at 753 (Lee) (citing maritime and Illinois law). And substantial exposure that cannot be attributed to a particular defendant is likewise insufficient. Moreover, the experts, as Judge Lee described, had not presented any individualized analysis of the level of asbestos exposure, had provided only generalized citations to scientific literature with no indication that they were **[—9—]** authorities upon which the experts would rely, did not identify any peer-reviewed scientific journal adopting this theory, did not cite any medical studies or discuss an error rate. *Id.* at 754. The experts used the theory with "little to no evaluation of the actual facts of this case." *Id.* In short, Krik failed to bear the burden of demonstrating that Dr. Frank's theory would satisfy the minimal requirements of Federal Rule of Evidence 702 and *Daubert*. Judge Lee thus precluded Krik from offering any expert testimony espousing such a theory at trial.

In light of Judge Lee's ruling barring the use of "each and every exposure" testimony, Krik attempted to repackage Dr. Frank's testimony as being based on a "cumulative exposure" theory. Under this theory, every minute of exposure adds to the cumulative exposure and thus becomes a substantial contributing factor. Judge Shah concluded, however, that the "cumulative exposure" theory was merely more of the same. He followed and then reiterated Judge Lee's finding by noting:

> To find a defendant liable, plaintiff must prove causation attributable to that defendant. It would be misleading and confusing for an expert to opine—particularly using the legal terminology of "substantial contributing factor"—that Krik's cancer was caused by defendants when the foundation for the opinion was that every exposure (without regard to dosage) contributes to cause cancer.

Krik, 2015 WL 5050143, at *1 (J. Shah). In other words, causation requires that an expert connect the nature of the asbestos exposure and pair it with a *Daubert*-approved methodology **[—10—]** that can be used to determine whether such an exposure was a substantial cause of the defendant's injury.

We agree that Dr. Frank's cumulative exposure theory was no different from the "each and every exposure" theory in all relevant ways. In fact, at the *Daubert* hearing, Krik's counsel explained how they were the same:

> THE COURT: Looking at the September 16, 2011 expert report … , which states: "The *cumulative* exposures he, meaning Krik, had to asbestos from any **{-676-}** and all products containing any and all fiber types would have contributed to his developing these two conditions." … So does he mean as part of this opinion that *any* exposure to asbestos should be considered a substantial factor to Mr. Krik's ailment?
>
> Mr. McCoy: Yes, Judge. That's right. That's how Dr. Frank would say, *any* exposure. All exposures contribute.

R. 295 at 29–30, pageID 7365-66 (emphasis added). Counsel went on to explain:

> … *the cumulative exposure* is considered the cause from the scientific and medical perspective. You don't open up scientific publications and read these articles, and the articles saying, well, this two days doing this is a cause, and this two days doing this is a cause of whatever person or group is being written about. What they always say is that *the cumulative exposure is the cause. So that's why Dr. Frank is saying, each expo-* **[—11—]** *sure*

> *is [sic] substantial contribution to that cumulative total.* That's what he's saying. And that's what—that's what his testimony will be.

Id. at 33, pageID7369 (emphasis added).

Dr. Frank's own testimony at his deposition about his theory conflated "each and every exposure" with a cumulative exposure theory as highlighted below. During the deposition, Krik's counsel asserted several positions one after another and asked his opinion on each one. He agreed with each of the following statements:

> - "Once the cancer has been attributed to asbestos, *each exposure* can be considered a substantial contributing cause of lung cancer."
> - "The *cumulative exposure to* asbestos from *each and every* product of any and all fiber types contributes to asbestos caused lung cancer."
> - It is virtually never possible to know the exact dose from any product, but it is recognized that *any exposure* above zero is a contributing factor to the *cumulative exposure*."
> - "Since the exposures are *cumulative*, individual exposures cannot be ruled out as a cause."
> - "No minimum duration is needed for an asbestos exposure to be a cause if the cancer is attributed to *cumulative exposure*."

R. 328-3, 167–68, pageID 8733 (emphasis added).

Based on Dr. Frank's own testimony and Krik's counsel's position, Judge Shah readily and correctly concluded that the **[—12—]** cumulative exposure theory was no different from the "each and every exposure" theory that had been excluded at the motion in limine:

> as became clear during a voir dire of the witness, his causation testimony was not tied to the specific quantum of exposure attributable to the defendants, but was instead based on his medical and scientific opinion that every exposure is a substantial contributing factor to the *cumulative* exposure that causes cancer. *See*, Trial Tr. at 262:13–16 ("... if there is exposure to a cancer-causing agent, that becomes part of the totality of the exposure. Some may contribute more, some may contribute less, but they are all part of the exposure."); *Id.* at 262:8–9 ("If the exposure took place, it was part of the *cumulative* exposure that someone had."). This "cumulative exposure" testimony was no different than the testimony proffered at the *Daubert* stage. *See Krik,* 76 F.Supp.3d at 752–53 (quoting plaintiff's counsel as describing the testimony as one based on cumulative exposure)

Krik, 2015 WL 5050143, at *1 (J. Shah) (emphasis added). **{-677-}**

Thus, Judge Shah made clear that he was following Judge Lee's previous ruling when he made a determination in line with that ruling—that is, that both theories are the same for purposes of determining causation:

> Judge Lee addressed the "cumulative exposure" testimony proposed by the plaintiff in his opinion. And at pages 7 to 8 of his opinion, he **[—13—]** quotes plaintiff's counsel as saying that cumulative exposure is the cause, and that what Dr. Frank is saying is that each exposure is a substantial contribution to the cumulative total. Judge Lee then held that, "This is not an acceptable approach for a causation expert to take."
>
> ***
>
> That is the "each and every exposure" theory that Judge Lee has barred, and so Dr. Frank cannot give a similar response to a hypothetical in this case.

> … So I am not expanding Judge Lee's ruling in any way. I am simply implementing it.

R. 336 at 4–6, pageID 9409-9411. *See also* R. 376 at 354, PageID 10227 ("As was clear when Judge Lee said that it is not an acceptable approach for a causation expert to take, namely … to take an approach based on cumulative exposure that's informed by an each-and-every exposure opinion, it remains clear to me in light of the factual proffer that Dr. Frank's cumulative exposure testimony is based on the each-and-every-exposure theory above … .")

To summarize, the principle behind the "each and every exposure" theory and the cumulative exposure theory is the same—that it is impossible to determine which particular exposure to carcinogens, if any, caused an illness. In other words, just like "each and every exposure," the cumulative exposure theory does not rely upon any particular dose or exposure to asbestos, but rather all exposures contribute to a cumulative dose. The ultimate burden of proof on the element of causation, however, remains with the plaintiff. *Shelton v.* **[—14—]** *Old Ben Coal Co.*, 933 F.2d 504, 508 (7th Cir. 1991); *Nolan v. Weil-McClain*, 233 Ill. 2d 416, 435 (Ill. 2009). Requiring a defendant to exclude a potential cause of the illness, therefore, improperly shifts the burden to the defendants to disprove causation and nullifies the requirements of the "substantial factor" test. The Sixth and Ninth Circuits have likewise excluded these cumulative and/or "each and every exposure" theories for similar reasons. As the Ninth Circuit explained:

> such a theory of liability would render the substantial-factor test essentially meaningless. Allowing causation to be established through testimony like [the expert's] would "permit imposition of liability on the manufacturer of any [asbestos-containing] product with which a worker had the briefest of encounters on a single occasion." This is precisely the sort of unbounded liability that the substantial factor test was developed to limit.

McIndoe v. Huntington Ingalls Inc., 817 F.3d 1170, 1177, 4 Adm. R. 380, 384 (9th Cir. 2016) (internal citations omitted). *Lindstrom v. A-C Prod. Liab. Tr.*, 424 F.3d 488, 493 (6th Cir. 2005) ("The requirement, however, is that the plaintiff make a showing with respect to *each* defendant that the defendant's product was a substantial factor in plaintiff's injury … . A holding to the contrary would permit imposition of liability on the manufacturer of any product with which a worker had the briefest of encounters on a single occasion.")

As Owens-Illinois points out in its brief, more than thirty other federal courts and state courts have held that this cumulative/" any exposure" theory is not reliable. **{-678-}** *See* Brief of Owens-Illinois at 46–47 (citing cases); Notice of Supplemental **[—15—]** Authorities, Appellate Court Record at 70. The district court did not err and certainly did not abuse its discretion by excluding this testimony.

The final piece of Krik's expert witness argument is that the district court errantly excluded a document entitled "the Helsinki document," which Krik's counsel sought to offer to support the "cumulative exposure" theory. As with the other evidentiary decisions, we review this decision for an abuse of discretion. *Chemetall GMBH v. ZR Energy, Inc.*, 320 F.3d 714, 722 (7th Cir. 2003). The Helsinki document is a statement developed at an international public policy conference in Helsinki in 1997 by consensus by a group of nineteen experts in the field of asbestos disease. R. 412-4 at 1, pageID . One proposition within the Helsinki document states that "[c]umulative exposure on a probability basis should thus be considered the main criteria for the attribution of a substantial contribution by asbestos to lung cancer risk." R. 412-4 at 4, pageID 13657. No party established that the Helsinki criteria came from a learned treatise or was the result of any scientific studies. As Dr. Frank himself testified, the document came from the consensus of a number of experts and, indeed, Dr. Frank disagreed with some of the statements in the document, particularly the document's probability-based methodology that concludes that the "likelihood that asbestos exposure has made a substantial contribution increases when the exposure increases." *Id.* Dr. Frank did not refer to the document, let alone rely on it. Judge Shah concluded that the generalness of the document would end up being unfairly prejudicial and would confuse the jury. Specifically, Judge Shah explained:

> As a set of consensus principles announced by an international public policy conference, these **[—16—]** criteria were not substantive evidence of causation; rather, they were materials that could be relied upon by an expert. In this case, the Helsinki Criteria provided a backdrop to the history of the study of asbestos and disease, and fodder for cross-examination of defendants' experts. But they were not admissible as independent exhibits of substantive evidence or as a foundation for inadmissible causation testimony. Moreover, based on the ruling excluding unreliable and non-case-specific causation testimony, *Krik,* 76 F. Supp. 3d at 753–54, it would have been confusing and unfairly prejudicial to allow the Helsinki Criteria to stand as evidence from which a jury could infer defendants' liability as to causation. Finally, because the criteria were discussed during testimony several times during the trial, the limitation on the use of one article during the direct examination of Frank did not render the entire trial unfair to the plaintiff.

Krik, 2015 WL 5050143, at *1, n.3 (J. Shah). Many other courts have rejected the Helsinki criteria for similar reasons. *See, e.g., Rockman v. Union Carbide Corp.*, No. CV RDB-16-1169, 2017 WL 3022969, at *5 (D. Md. July 17, 2017); *Bell v. Foster Wheeler Energy Corp.*, No. CV 15-6394, 2016 WL 5847124, at *3, n.3 (E.D. La. Oct. 6, 2016), *reconsideration denied,* No. CV 15-6394, 2017 WL 876983 (E.D. La. Mar. 6, 2017); *Watkins v. Affinia Grp.*, 2016-Ohio-2830, ¶ 37, 54 N.E.3d 174, 182; *Matter of James Wilson Assoc.*, 965 F.2d 160, 173 (7th Cir. 1992); *United States v. Dixon*, 413 F.3d 520, 524–25 (5th Cir. 2005); *Yates v. Ford Motor Co.*, 113 F. Supp. 3d 841, 862 (E.D.N.C. 2015); *Betz v. Pneumo* **[—17—]** *Abex, LLC*, 44 A.3d 27, 47, 55 n.35 (Pa. 2012); *Bostic v. Georgia-Pacific Corp.*, 439 S.W.3d 332, 356–57 (Tex. 2014). We cannot say that it was an **{–679–}** abuse of discretion for the district court to do likewise.

B. The juror investigation issue

During jury selection, the prospective jurors were asked both collectively and individually if they recognized anyone involved in the case, including the parties and potential witnesses. Juror McGregor reported that she did not know anyone on the list. The next day, however, McGregor delivered a note to the court in which she stated: "While I do not know Mr. Krik personally we might have been at a birthday party for a former pipefitter and a good friend of mine last year. His name is Bob Scamen. I just wanted you to be aware of this. I did not think about this until the ride home last night." R. 349 at 3, pageID 9547.

The court read the note to counsel for all parties. Krik's counsel responded, "From plaintiff's end, I don't see that poses any problem." R. 375 at 108, pageID 9980. Outside the presence of the jury, the Judge questioned both Krik and McGregor about the events set forth in the note. Krik told the court that he did not know Bob Scamen and that he did not think he was at the birthday party. McGregor stated that she was not sure whether she encountered Krik at Scamen's birthday party, that Scamen was her only pipefitter friend, and that her association with him would not improperly influence her. The defendants moved to remove McGregor from the jury, but the district court denied their motion as well as a subsequent motion for a mistrial. We review a district court's decision to deny the request for a new trial for an abuse of discretion. *United States v. Hilliard*, 851 F.3d 768, 778 (7th Cir. 2017). **[—18—]**

After the jury returned the verdict, Judge Shah met with the jurors to thank them for their service. During that conversation, McGregor revealed that she had learned that an investigator, whom she believed to be working for the defense, had contacted her friend Scamen to ask about his birthday party. No one had ever approached the court about such an investigation, and thus it came as a surprise to the district court judge. Consequently, several days later the court, sua sponte, scheduled an unusual post-trial status conference in which the judge advised all counsel of the information he had received from juror McGregor. Counsel for Mobil confessed to having sent out the investigator, admitting in the process that it researched the permissibility and found nothing directly on point, and that it had considered advising the court but opted against it. R. 399-11 at 3, pageID 12731. The defense counsel further admitted that it was aware of the risk that the investigation might have an impact on a sitting juror, that it might be deemed to be an invasion of her privacy, and that it was willing to take the risk nevertheless. *Id.* at 4-5, pageID 12732-33. Owens-Illinois was also aware of the investigation, but neither defense counsel informed Krik's counsel.

Krik argues that the investigation prejudiced the trial and filed a motion requesting a new trial. Krik's arguments can be summarized as follows: the questioning of Scamen could have influenced McGregor by intimidating her, by causing her to worry about her privacy and potential harassment, and by distracting her with details of a private investigation during the course of a trial.

To obtain a new trial based on improper contact with a juror, the complaining party must show prejudice. *United States v. Olano,* 507 U.S. 725, 739 (1993) (the ultimate inquiry is "Did **[—19—]** the intrusion affect the jury's deliberations and thereby its verdict?") The party seeking a new trial bears the burden of demonstrating the **{-680-}** likelihood of prejudice, and it is a heavy burden at that. *Aldridge v. Forest River, Inc.*, 635 F.3d 870, 876 (7th Cir. 2011).

In order to determine whether there was such prejudice, the Supreme Court dictates that in the face of allegations of juror influence, the court should hold a hearing in which the complainant has the opportunity to prove actual bias. *Smith v. Phillips*, 455 U.S. 209, 215 (1982). But the hearing must walk a fine line. Our system stringently protects the confidential deliberations of juries both for the sake of finality and lest jurors be chilled from frank discussion in their deliberations and subject to continual harassment by those wishing to set aside a verdict. *See, e.g. Tanner v. United States*, 483 U.S. 107, 119–20 (1987). This protection is embodied in Federal Rule of Evidence 606(b) which prohibits most testimony about what influenced a juror. The rule states:

> **(b) During an Inquiry Into the Validity of a Verdict or Indictment.**
>
> **(1) Prohibited Testimony or Other Evidence.** During an inquiry into the validity of a verdict or indictment, a juror may not testify about any statement made or incident that occurred during the jury's deliberations; the effect of anything on that juror's or another juror's vote; or any juror's mental processes concerning the verdict or indictment. The court may not receive a **[—20—]** juror's affidavit or evidence of a juror's statement on these matters.
>
> **(2) Exceptions.** A juror may testify about whether:
>
> **(A)** extraneous prejudicial information was improperly brought to the jury's attention;
>
> **(B)** an outside influence was improperly brought to bear on any juror; or
>
> **(C)** a mistake was made in entering the verdict on the verdict form.

Fed. R. Evid. 606.

To balance those competing interests between the required hearing and Rule 606(b)'s prohibitions, a court must

> limit the questions asked the jurors to whether the communication was made and what it contained, and then, having determined that communication took

> place and what exactly it said, to determine—without asking the jurors anything further and emphatically without asking them what role the communication played in their thoughts or discussion—whether there is a reasonable possibility that the communication altered their verdict.

Hall v. Zenk, 692 F.3d 793, 806 (7th Cir. 2012) (citing *Haugh v. Jones & Laughlin Steel Corp.*, 949 F.2d 914, 917 (7th Cir. 1991)).

The district court determined that no hearing was required in this case, both because Krik had not asked for one, and more importantly, there was no dispute as to the existence or content of the communication. *See United States v.* **[—21—]** *Sanders*, 962 F.2d 660, 673 (7th Cir. 1992) (no hearing required where questioning jurors would not have revealed additional information). The only question is one that cannot be helped by a hearing—whether there is a reasonable possibility that the jury's verdict was altered by the investigation in any manner. That question could only be answered by asking the jurors the quintessential forbidden question as to what role the communication played in their thoughts or discussion. *See Hall*, 692 F.3d at 806.

In this case, the district court determined that:

> There was no prejudice to Krik in Mobil's interview of Scamen. In this context, **{-681-}** prejudice is demonstrated through conduct that leads to a compelling inference of external pressure to return a verdict unfavorable to the movant. No such inference is reasonable here because defendants did not directly contact the juror and the subject of their interview with Scamen was entirely independent of the merits of the case.

Krik, 2015 WL 5050143 at *3 (J. Shah). The district court surveyed the types of contact that might be deemed prejudicial—attempted or perceived bribes, exposure to extraneous information directly concerning liability, threats, indirect communications suggesting a party's guilt, and external contact that forces a verdict. *See Id.* (citing cases). The court noted that conduct that has no obvious implication on the outcome of the trial is not prejudicial.

Despite our holding in this case, we note that in general investigating a sitting juror is fraught with danger—such an **[—22—]** investigation could be seen by the juror as intimidation or harassment. Such an investigation might lead a juror to be concerned that the continued investigations might reveal embarrassing or private details of her life, or worry that even a benign short investigation might be just the beginning of a much more thorough and invasive one. This could breed resentment, anxiousness, or distract a juror from the task at hand. *See Sinclair v. United States*, 279 U.S. 749, 765 (1929) ("The mere suspicion that he, his family, and friends are being subjected to surveillance by such persons is enough to destroy the equilibrium of the average juror and render impossible the exercise of calm judgment upon patient consideration.") It could also be viewed by a court as a bad faith attempt to purposely create prejudice and thus have an unwanted juror removed from the jury. In this case, just after McGregor sent her note, the defendants moved unsuccessfully to have her removed from the jury. A cynical court might view the investigation of the juror as a back-door attempt to create prejudice. Moreover, there is no reason why counsel for Mobil could not have asked the court for permission to conduct this limited investigation. From the discussion during the post-trial proceeding, it appears that Mobil's counsel was either hoping that its investigation would not be discovered or banking on the possibility that it could ask for forgiveness later rather than be denied permission up front. We do not condone such behavior and would encourage, as the district court proposed, that such a practice be evaluated by the court's rules committee or chief judge. We also do not think that, in the normal course of events, a judge's admonition that "anything that you have seen or heard outside the courtroom is not evidence and must **[—23—]** be entirely disregarded" cures this particular potential problem. The curative instruction is unlikely to remedy the ills of a distracted, unnerved, or embarrassed juror.

For this case, however, we need not rule about the propriety of such a practice because we have determined that there was no prejudice to Krik and that the investigation could not have altered the course or outcome of the trial. The investigator questioned McGregor's friend and not McGregor. McGregor herself notified the court about the birthday party, thus indicating that she recognized that it might be relevant, and decreasing the chance that its revelation would bring about any embarrassment or surprise for her. As the district court noted, the "nature of the investigation was relatively benign and there is no proof that prejudice was reasonably likely." *See Krik*, 2015 WL 5050413 at *4 (J. Shah). Moreover, the facts of this case are far from that of *Sinclair*, upon which Krik relies. In *Sinclair*, the jurors themselves were surveilled from the moment **{–682–}** they left the courtroom until they went to sleep. *Sinclair*, 279 U.S. at 758. In this case, an investigator approached a non-juror and asked a few benign questions that had no bearing on the substance of the case and there was no evidence that the juror was intimidated or pressured by the investigation.

In determining whether a party was prejudiced, a court also may consider the strength of the party's case. *See Hall*, 692 F.3d at 807 ("If, hypothetically, the legitimate evidence presented by the State in a habeas petitioner's case was overwhelming, and the trial judge in such a case gave a stern pre-verdict warning to the jurors to only consider facts that were presented during trial, concerns about the prejudicial impact **[—24—]** of extraneous information might be lessened."). As we concluded above, Krik's proffered expert testimony on causation did not meet the standards required under Federal Rule 702 and *Daubert* and without it his case was fatally weak. *Krik*, 2015 WL 5050413 at *4 (J. Shah). Krik was not prejudiced by Mobil's investigation because judgment in favor of the defendants was inevitable once it became clear that Krik could not prove causation.

The Appellee's Motions to Strike Appellant's Letter of Supplemental Authority is denied. The decision of the district court is affirmed in all respects, including the assignment of costs and fees.

United States Court of Appeals
for the Seventh Circuit

No. 16-4264

ALEXANDER
VS.
INGRAM BARGE CO.

Appeal from the United States District Court for the Northern District of Illinois, Eastern Division

Decided: November 21, 2017

Citation: 876 F.3d 269, 5 Adm. R. 368 (7th Cir. 2017).

Before **WOOD,** Chief Judge, and **BAUER** and **SYKES,** Circuit Judges.

[—1—] {-271-} **WOOD,** Chief Judge:

At 5:33 in the evening on April 18, 2013, a 14-barge tow pushed by the *M/V Dale A. Heller* was sucked into a powerful cross-current and broke up. Some of the barges crashed (or allided, as mariners would say) into the Marseilles Dam; some sank; some were saved. The accident happened during record-breaking rains and high water, and **[—2—]** a day later, the nearby town of Marseilles experienced significant flooding. This lawsuit, brought by a group who call themselves the Flood Claimants, represents an effort to fix blame for the allision and to recover for their flood damage. The Flood Claimants were stymied, however, when the district court ruled that the United States, which manages the Dam through its Army Corps of Engineers, was immune from suit for its role in the allision, and that the Corps was solely responsible for the accident. The Flood Claimants believe that Ingram Barge, the company that owns and operates the *Dale Heller*, shares some of the blame because of its failure to follow certain inland navigation rules and its more general negligence. We conclude, however, that the facts found by the district court were not clearly erroneous, and that those facts support the court's assignment of sole responsibility to the Corps.

I

We have no need or desire to replicate the district court's painstaking, minute-by-minute, account of the events leading up to the allision and its immediate aftermath. We commend that court's opinion to those who are interested in the details. *See In the Matter of the Complaint of Ingram Barge Co.*, 219 F. Supp. 3d 749 (N.D. Ill. 2016). We offer here only the highlights that pertain to the arguments on appeal.

Geographically, we are talking about a stretch of the Illinois River that runs from the upriver town of Channahon, Illinois, down to the Marseilles Lock and Dam, just downriver from the town of Marseilles. The Illinois River is a tributary of the Mississippi River, which it joins at Grafton, Illinois, a short distance northwest of St. Louis, Missouri. **[—3—]**

Downriver from Channahon, which is about 50 miles southwest of Chicago, several points on the river play a part in this story. Dresden Island lies six miles downstream; another 26 miles down, at River Mile 248.0, is Ballards Island. Next one comes to Gum Creek, and finally, at River Mile 247.1, is the Dam. The Lock is another 2.5 miles downriver. Vessels heading downstream must use the Marseilles Canal, which is on the left descending side of the river below the Dam. The area between the Dam and Dresden Island is **{-272-}** known as the Marseilles Pool. The Corps regulates its depth by opening and closing eight large gates, called tainter gates, at the Dam: higher openings correspond to a reduction in water level, and vice versa. The Dam's total opening is expressed in gate-feet, which is calculated by adding together the clearance between the bottom of each of the eight gates and the riverbed. The town of Marseilles is on the right descending bank of the river.

On April 16, 2013, in the evening, the *Dale Heller* began heading downriver from Channahon with a 14-barge tow. The weather forecast indicated that periods of heavy rainfall were expected in LaSalle County, where Marseilles is located. A hydrograph sent to Ingram's shoreside personnel, as well as to the Captain of the *Dale Heller*, Charles White, showed that the river was expected to rise on April 17 to a crest of 11.3 feet, well below flood level, and then recede. On the morning of April 17, Captain White had the *Dale Heller* hold up at Ballards Island, in the hope that conditions would improve before he had to navigate past the Dam.

At that point, another actor entered the picture: the *M/V Loyd Murphy*, under the command of Captain Anthony Ice. The *Loyd Murphy* had just traversed northbound through the **[—4—]** Marseilles Canal and was heading upriver. Because of the severe weather conditions, Captain Ice radioed Captain White and asked if he could tie up at Ballards Island alongside the *Dale Heller*. The two agreed that this made sense, and so the *Loyd Murphy* (with its tow of 15 barges) shoved in with the *Dale Heller*. The barges were lashed together with various head and stern lines. The resulting combination was huge: 29 barges, six across and five long, which measured 210 feet wide and 1,000 feet long.

Weather conditions, and thus river conditions, continued to deteriorate overnight. Around 10:00 p.m. the North Central River Forecast Center (a branch of the National Weather Service), which had been issuing increasingly gloomy forecasts, for the first time predicated that the river would reach flood stage at Marseilles. By the morning of April 18, Captains White and Ice were having trouble holding their position at Ballards Island, even though both towboats were using most of their power to stay in place. "Drift" (that is, floating debris of all sizes) was becoming a serious problem—one that potentially could take out a propeller, stop the engines of the towboat, and set the entire flotilla loose in the fast water. The forecast had worsened from moderate flooding to just below major flooding. The captains decided to try to reinforce their mooring by strengthening the ties linking the barges and by tying the combined tow to some trees on the island. Later that day, however, the strength of the current ripped the trees out of the ground and the tow slipped a short distance downriver. The captains also called for and received assistance from several other boats, including the *Nancy S.* and the *M/V City of Ottawa*. **[—5—]**

With conditions so bad, the River Industry Action Committee and the Illinois River Carriers Association (IRCA) scheduled an emergency conference call to discuss the rapidly rising Illinois and Mississippi River levels and to come up with a plan for, among others, the *Dale Heller*. The call took place at 2:00 p.m. on April 18; representatives from Ingram, the Corps, and the Coast Guard, among others, participated. Given the problems that Captains White and Ice were having staying in place at Ballards Island, the group decided that the best option was for the Dam's lockmaster, Corpsman Larry Rodriguez, to lower the tainter gates so that each of the eight gates would leave a clearance of two **{–273–}** feet between the river bottom and the bottom of the gate—in other words, 16 gate-feet—for a time just long enough to permit the *Dale Heller* safely to enter the Marseilles Canal. (There was some dispute in the district court over the question whether Rodriguez promised to lower the gates *by* 16 feet or *to* 16 feet, but the district court resolved this in favor of the latter, and the Flood Claimants do not contest that here.) Lowering the gates would have several effects: it would reduce the outdraft (that is, the cross-current pulling water toward the Dam) enough to permit safe passage; but at the same time, because the lower a setting is, the more water accumulates in the Marseilles Pool, the risk of flooding in the town would increase. At the time of the IRCA decision, the gate settings were quite high—70 feet—and so the Corps's commitment to lower them to 16 feet represented a significant undertaking.

Another aspect of the IRCA plan was that several vessels, including the *Loyd Murphy*, the *City of Ottawa*, and the *M/V Creve Coeur*, would help the *Dale Heller* flotilla hug the left descending bank of the river and guide it into the Marseilles Canal. Shortly after the IRCA call ended, the captains of **[—6—]** several of the affected vessels, including Captain White, met aboard the *City of Ottawa* to review their various roles in the maneuvers. By this time it was clear that they were facing record-breaking high waters. Captain White continued to believe, however, that if Lockmaster Rodriguez played his part and lowered the gates to 16 feet, he could get the tow into the canal.

At 5:02 p.m., Captain Ice relayed that the gates were "at 76 right now, ... going down to 55." Captain White understood this to be an interim report; no one said that the plan had changed. He set out a minute later, moving slowly because that was the only way the group of 4 vessels and 14 barges could stay coordinated. At 5:15 p.m., Captain Ice radioed that it was still possible to abort the plan (or, as he later put it, they were at the "whoa or go spot"), but that he saw no reason to do so. Two minutes later, there was a garbled transmission from Captain Ice. He radioed that he was telling Rodriguez to "open up a little more" because some flooding in the town was starting to occur. Somehow the wrong words came out of his mouth. As he later explained, he inadvertently had repeated something that an observer from the Corps stationed on the *Loyd Murphy*, Jeff Griffin, had said. While Captain Ice did not actually make the call, Griffin *did* call Rodriguez to tell him to open the gates. After receiving Griffin's call, Rodriguez chucked the entire plan out the window: he stopped lowering the gates and instead *raised* them all the way up to 88 feet. This action intensified the cross-current elevenfold, causing the *Dale Heller*'s tow to break up, some barges to allide with the Dam, and some to sink. A picture of the resulting mess tells the story: **[—7—] {-274-}**

Kenneth R. Olson & Lois Wright Morton, *Runaway Barges Damage Marseilles Lock and Dam during 2013 Flood on the Illinois River*, 69 J. SOIL & WATER CONSERVATION 104A, 105A (2014). The *Dale Heller* itself briefly went out of control and spun around 360 degrees, nearly capsizing. Captain White managed to recover, however, and successfully brought to safety both the *Dale Heller* itself and, with the help of the other towboats, several of the barges in the flotilla. Some time later, the town of Marseilles experienced severe flooding. Over two **[—8—]** hundred residents sustained damage to their property, as did an elementary school.

II

This suit began as a limitation action brought by Ingram under 46 U.S.C. §§ 30501, *et seq.*, but it became more complex over time. At one point, it involved claims, cross-claims, and counterclaims among the Flood Claimants, Ingram, the United States (on behalf of the Corps of Engineers), and Inland Marine Service (the owner of the *Loyd Murphy*). The United States and the Corps dropped out after the district court ruled that the United States was entitled to sovereign immunity under the discretionary function exception to the Federal Tort Claims Act, 28 U.S.C. § 2680(a). *See also* 33 U.S.C. § 702c, ¶ 2. Other controversies were settled, **{-275-}** leaving for trial only the Flood Claimants' claims against Ingram.

For purposes of case management, the district court divided the proceedings into three phases: (1) liability for the allision; (2) whether the allision caused the flooding in the town; and (3) damages. It held a ten-day bench trial on the first question—whether anything Ingram did or anything for which it was responsible caused the allision. In a 127-page opinion, it concluded that the answer was no, and that the *sole* proximate cause of the accident was the negligence of Lockmaster Rodriguez. It also held that Ingram was entitled to exoneration and limitation of liability under 46 U.S.C. § 30505. These findings rendered phases 2 and 3 unnecessary, and so the court entered final judgment in Ingram's favor.

On appeal, the Flood Claimants focus on Ingram's alleged violations of three Inland Navigation rules. If even one was violated, they argue, the district court should have applied **[—9—]** the *Pennsylvania* Rule (announced in *The Pennsylvania*, 86 U.S. 125 (1873)), which requires such a violator to show that its action *could not* have been a contributory cause of the accident. They also argue that Ingram knew enough about the allegedly negligent actions that it was not entitled to exoneration or limitation of liability. Although they say at the outset that they are largely satisfied with the district court's findings of fact, they argue that some are clearly erroneous, and that the court failed to apply the facts properly to the regulations.

III

The Inland Navigation rules on which the Flood Claimants rely are issued by the Department of Homeland Security (where the Coast Guard is now lodged). *See* 33 U.S.C. § 2071. The Claimants single out three rules that they contend Ingram violated: Rule 2, the Responsibility rule, 33 C.F.R. § 83.02; Rule 5, the Lookout rule, 33 C.F.R. § 83.05; and Rule 7, the Risk of Collision rule, 33 C.F.R. § 83.07. The district court examined each rule against the backdrop of its findings of fact and found no violation. The Flood Claimants assert that the court committed legal error in some of its interpretations of the rules, and clear error in its application of the law to the facts in other instances.

Rule 2, the Responsibility rule, reads as follows:

> (a) Nothing in these Rules shall exonerate any vessel, or the owner, master, or crew thereof, from the consequences of any neglect to comply with these Rules or of the neglect of any precaution which may be required by the ordinary practice of seamen, or by the special circumstances of the case. **[—10—]**
>
> (b) In construing and complying with these Rules due regard shall be had to all dangers of navigation and collision and to any special circumstances, including the limitations of the vessels involved, which may make a departure from these Rules necessary to avoid immediate danger.

33 C.F.R. § 83.02. The Claimants assert that the planning behind the *Dale Heller*'s ill-fated effort to reach the Marseilles Canal was "disjointed, poorly communicated, and poorly conceived." Indeed, they accuse Ingram of behaving in a cavalier fashion about the whole situation. They find the IRCA call confused and unclear, the transit planning inadequate, and the arrangements to keep lines of communication open defective. And the Captains' meeting did nothing, in their view, to correct these deficiencies.

In addition to these problems, the Flood Claimants argue that there was no process **{-276-}** to review or double-check the plan; that the pilot of the *Dale Heller*, Ron Shrader, objected to the plan; that the details of the plan were never committed to writing; and that no one ever nailed down the critical question of how long the gates were to remain at 16 feet. Taken together, they assert, these failings are so severe that the district court's conclusion that Rule 2 was not violated cannot stand.

As Ingram points out, however, Rule 2 calls for prudent action in the circumstances faced by the vessels. Those circumstances, as of the afternoon of April 18, were fraught with danger. The combined flotilla of the *Dale Heller* and the *Loyd Murphy* was slipping downriver despite the use of the full horsepower available to both vessels; the effort to secure the tows to Ballards Island had been thwarted when the force of **[—11—]** the current literally pulled the trees out of the ground; and none of the options was risk-free. The participants in the IRCA call considered the possibilities and opted for the best plan possible. If it was to work, every part of the plan had to be executed as well as possible.

The fact that the plan was not in writing meant nothing. As the district court found, "both maritime custom and private arrangement provided Ingram the right to rely on the lockmaster's representation that he would lower the gates to 16 feet to allow the *Dale Heller* safe harbor in the Marseilles Canal." Confirmation in writing made no sense in any event under the rapidly developing conditions the mariners faced. Nor was there time for a risk assessment any more formal than the one the IRCA group and then the captains undertook—the transit commenced only three hours after the IRCA call began. These were all experienced people, who were well aware of the risks from the outdraft, the lockmaster's ability to raise and lower the tainter gates, and his control over the entry to the Canal. These findings were all well supported in the record.

The court also found that the group made adequate arrangements for communications among the critical players—Captain White, the captains of the assist vessels, and the lockmaster. The Flood Claimants fault Captain White for not re-confirming the lowering of the gates with Lockmaster Rodriguez while the *Dale Heller* was proceeding toward the mouth of the Canal with its tow, but at the time he had no reason to think this was necessary. The burden was on Rodriguez to alert the others that he had decided to change the gate settings, and Captain White was entitled to rely on that understanding. Obviously, with 20-20 hindsight one can **[—12—]** say that additional checks might have helped. But Rule 2 does not punish failures to see into the future. And, depending on when they occurred, additional communications might not have helped. At some point—presumably the "whoa or go" moment Captain Ice mentioned—the *Dale Heller* and its tow of 14 barges would have been unable to do anything but continue downriver toward the Marseilles Canal.

We consider the question whether Inland Navigation Rule 2 was violated to be one of fact: were the measures Ingram's vessel took appropriate for purposes of this rule? The district court weighed the evidence and concluded that the Claimants failed to prove a violation of that rule. We see no clear error in that assessment.

Next we look at Rule 5, the Lookout rule, which reads as follows:

> Every vessel shall at all times maintain a proper look-out by sight and hearing as well as by all available means appropriate in the prevailing circumstances and conditions so as to make a full appraisal of the situation and of the risk of collision. **{-277-}**

33 C.F.R. § 83.05. This appears to be the Flood Claimants' principal argument, at least if number of pages in the brief is any measure. They assert that the district court committed legal error by finding (as they characterize it) that Rodriguez's verbal commitment to lower the tainter gates to 16 gate-feet "eliminated Ingram's obligation to maintain a proper lookout." If that were what the district court had said, we would indeed be concerned. But the court held no such thing. **[—13—]**

Rule 5 does not demand that a vessel have a separate person whose sole responsibility is to serve as a lookout. Instead, according to testimony at the trial, a vessel captain can serve as the required lookout if he has a

360-degree unobstructed view during transit. As the Flood Claimants admit, ample case law supports this proposition as well. *See Marport, Inc. v. Stabbert & Associates, Inc.*, 771 F.2d 1216, 1218 (9th Cir. 1985) (discussing the "well-settled" rule that the helmsman may "serve as lookout from the wheelhouse of a tug"). Captain White was aware of this rule and testified that he had the necessary unobstructed, 360-degree view from the bridge. If that were not enough, the court noted, Pilot Shrader was in a position to supplement Captain White's observations, as was Captain Ice in the *Loyd Murphy*, which was assisting in the transit operation.

The Flood Claimants respond that the record demonstrates that no one on the *Dale Heller*'s bridge had a truly unobstructed 360-degree view, because the barges it was pushing were covered, and so the water ahead of the tow (some 1,000 feet, it appears) was not visible. Only a person stationed at the front of the lead barge or on one of the assist boats could have alerted the captain to the moment when the tow hit the outdraft. Such a person, they argue, would also have seen how high the gates were after Rodriguez raised them to 88 feet; the Claimants assert that the gates were literally out of the water at that point and their height was unmistakable.

Once again, the Claimants' argument fails to take the entire record into account. Captain White, assisted by his pilot and the other vessels, was able to keep an adequate lookout. And he knew just where the greatest risk of outdraft was located—approximately 200 to 300 feet from the dam. Outdraft, **[—14—]** he explained, is ubiquitous on the Illinois River: it is present "[n]ot only just [at] this lock, but every lock." The critical fact had nothing to do with his lookout; it was instead that he was proceeding on the understanding that the outdraft would correspond to 16 gate-feet, whereas in reality he was moving into an outdraft at least 11 times stronger, associated with 88 gate-feet.

The district court rejected, as a matter of fact, the Claimants' hypothesis that a proper lookout would have seen that the gates were entirely out of the water. Testimony in the record indicated that upriver mariners cannot see the gate setting at the Marseilles Dam, at least with any precision. In broad terms, mariners can tell if the gates are wide open, or largely closed. Nevertheless, after reviewing the photographic evidence, the court concluded that the position of the gates was not plain. It also commented that

> [T]he visibility of an 88-foot gate setting by 5:27PM does not tell the Court that—with a proper lookout—a prudent mariner would have stopped the transit minutes before, having decided that the lockhouse could not get back to a 16-foot gate setting in time for the tow to avoid a powerful outdraft.

These findings are supported by the record and are not tainted by any legal error. We thus conclude that the district court's **{-278-}** analysis of Inland Navigation Rule 5 was sound.

Finally, we consider Rule 7, the Risk of Collision rule, which in pertinent part says:

> (a) Every vessel shall use all available means appropriate to the prevailing circumstances and **[—15—]** conditions to determine if risk of collision exists. If there is any doubt such risk shall be deemed to exist.
>
> * * *
>
> (c) Assumptions shall not be made on the basis of scanty information, especially scanty radar information.

33 C.F.R. § 83.07.

The Claimants' arguments with respect to Rule 7 largely repeat the points they make with respect to Rules 2 and 5. Once again, they contend that Captain White and Pilot Shrader violated the rule (this time Rule 7) by failing to speak up when they realized that the transit was not going as planned. The captain should have realized, they argue, that the plan to lower the gates to 16 feet had been scrapped or at least had run into trouble. They criticize Captain White for thinking, at 5:02

p.m., that Captain Ice's statement that the gates were "going down to 55" was a progress report, not a statement that 16 gate-feet was no longer the goal. Worse, at 5:16 p.m. when Captain Ice radioed that he was "telling [the lockmaster] to open up a little bit more gate because they're starting to flood up into them houses already," Captain White responded, "Okay." At that point, the Claimants insist, Captain White should have checked back with Lockmaster Rodriguez to find out what was happening. Rule 7 imposes a duty to take all steps to determine if a risk of collision exists. One easy such step, Claimants argue, would have been to check with the Lockmaster. Claimants conclude that his failure to do so was based on nothing more than an assumption, and such an action is forbidden by Rule 7. **[—16—]**

The Claimants point to three transmissions in support of this argument: one at 4:23 p.m., one at 5:02 p.m., and one at 5:17 p.m. The first of these, from Captain Slack of the *City of Ottawa,* informed Captain White that "it takes them 4 minutes to shut the gates and 4 minutes to open them. So, they, they're going to shut four on the, the uh, left side and that's all." Pilot Shrader heard this and understood it to be a statement about the time it would take to move the tainter gates to 16 gate-feet. In fact, this was wrong: the gates move at the rate of one foot per minute, but there is no evidence that any of the river mariners knew this. Under the circumstances, the court found nothing unreasonable about the *Dale Heller*'s lack of a reaction to this transmission.

We already have discussed the 5:02 p.m. transmission, known to the parties here as the "76-to-55" message. Although a stranger to the situation might see this as ambiguous, Captain White had no reason to think that the IRCA plan, as confirmed at the captains' meeting, was not in place. A change from a 16-foot gate to a 55-foot gate would have been enormous, and he had no reason to think that such a significant change would be made without anyone's informing him. Tellingly, Captain White was uncomfortable with a gate setting of only 23 feet, which first prompted him to hold at Ballards Island on April 17. The court found his reliance on the earlier plan to be reasonable. That finding is not clearly erroneous.

Finally, while the 5:17 p.m. "open more gate" transmission from Captain Ice to Captain White is certainly troublesome, the court discussed it in detail earlier in its opinion. Captain Ice explained it this way: **[—17—]**

> Prior to that transmission—that was actually a mix-up in my words—Captain **{-279-}** Charlie [White] had said to me, I'm starting to get aground or I'm starting to suck down, as he's trying to come ahead on it. And I was getting ready to tell him, I'm going to pull your stern out, and just as I grabbed the radio, Jeff [Griffin] [a crane operator for the Corps who was working as an observer] said, hey, they're flooding the houses; I'm telling them to open up dam. And I just instantly repeated what he said rather than finishing my transmission.

The district court credited this explanation. Importantly, it also found that neither a towboat operator such as Captain Ice, nor a crane operator for the Corps, had the authority to instruct the Lockmaster to take *any* actions. The Lockmaster had the exclusive authority and duty to operate the gates and to manage all traffic through the canal. 33 C.F.R. § 207.300(a). Just as Rodriguez's regulatory authority supports the district court's conclusion that his actions were the sole proximate cause of the allusion, it suggests that Captain White did not violate Rule 7 by continuing after the "open more gate" transmission. He reasonably—although erroneously, as it turned out—relied on Rodriguez prudently to exercise his sole authority over the gates and passage through the canal. In addition, the court's review of other evidence, including photographs, convinced it that there was no flooding at that point to be observed.

Taking all the facts into account, the district court concluded that the Claimants also failed to establish a violation **[—18—]** of Inland Navigation Rule 7. We find no clear error in the factual finding that Ingram, and its vessel the *Dale Heller*, were not at fault for failing to question, mid-transit, whether everyone was still following the IRCA plan.

The Flood Claimants' failure to demonstrate a violation of any Rule of Inland Navigation means that the *Pennsylvania* rule does not come into play. That rule, which the Claimants raised for the first time in their post-argument briefing at the district court, addresses the finding of fault when a regulatory violation has been shown:

> But when, as in this case, a ship at the time of a collision is in actual violation of a statutory rule intended to prevent collisions, it is no more than a reasonable presumption that the fault, if not the sole cause, was at least a contributory cause of the disaster. In such a case the burden rests upon the ship of showing not merely that her fault might not have been one of the causes, or that it probably was not, but that it could not have been.

The Pennsylvania, 86 U.S. at 136 (1873). This shifts the burden of proof from the claimant to the shipowner, and it requires the shipowner to rule out all possibility that the regulatory violation contributed to the accident. But that onerous burden does not arise unless the predicate violations are proven, and they were not in this case. The *Pennsylvania* rule is thus of no help to the Flood Claimants.

Our conclusions with respect to the Inland Navigation Rules make it unnecessary for us to address Ingram's entitlement to exoneration and limitation of liability under **[—19—]** the Limitation Act, 46 U.S.C. § 30501, *et seq*. We thus have no comment on this part of the district court's opinion.

IV

The flooding that struck Marseilles in April 2013 was terrible. It caused millions of dollars of damage to individual property owners, the City itself, and an elementary school. Whether the barge accident we have been discussing caused some or all of that flooding is an issue the district court **{-280-}** did not reach, because it found that the accident itself was solely caused by the Army Corps of Engineers' Lockmaster Rodriguez. Because of the discretionary function exception to the Federal Tort Claims Act, the Corps cannot be sued for Rodriguez's actions, however negligent or inexplicable they may have been. The court's finding that Rodriguez was solely responsible is, like its other findings of fact in this case, supported by the record and not clearly erroneous. We thus AFFIRM the judgment of the district court.

This page intentionally left blank

United States Court of Appeals for the Eighth Circuit

United States Court of Appeals
for the Eighth Circuit

No. 16-3687

ROYAL
vs.
MISSOURI & N. ARKANSAS R.R. CO.

Appeal from the United States District Court for the Western District of Arkansas - Texarkana

Decided: May 22, 2017

Citation: 857 F.3d 759, 5 Adm. R. 378 (8th Cir. 2017).

Before **GRUENDER, MURPHY,** and **KELLY,** Circuit Judges.

[—1—] {–761–} **GRUENDER,** Circuit Judge:

Shawn Royal, a North American Railway Services ("NARS") employee, and his wife, Regina Royal, sued Missouri & Northern Arkansas Railroad Company ("MNA") for injuries he sustained while working on MNA's railroad tracks. They sought relief pursuant to the Federal Employers' Liability Act ("FELA") and under **[—2—]** Arkansas negligence law. The district court[1] granted MNA's motion for summary judgment, and the Royals appealed. For the reasons discussed below, we affirm.

In February 2012, NARS entered into a Master Service Agreement with RailAmerica Transportation Corporation ("RailAmerica") to provide track-related services to RailAmerica's affiliated and subsidiary railroads. At the time, MNA was a wholly owned subsidiary of RailAmerica. The Agreement stipulated that NARS "is not an agent, representative, or employee of [RailAmerica] or any of its Railroads, but rather is an independent contractor." The Agreement also stated that NARS "shall be responsible for all actions of its employees, subcontractors, agents and representatives" while working at the railroad sites and that RailAmerica and its subsidiaries had the right to inspect and test NARS's work and direct NARS to make corrections as needed.

NARS employed Shawn Royal to operate a ballast regulator and sent him to perform maintenance work at several different **{–762–}** railroad locations. NARS provided Royal with safety training and equipment instruction, furnished his personal protective and service equipment, and was responsible for all of his compensation. Pursuant to his employment with NARS, Royal did maintenance work on MNA's railroad tracks, which involved operating a machine that picked up and spread ballast, the stone or material placed around railroad tracks that provides structural support, drainage, and erosion protection. While working as a NARS employee on MNA's railroad tracks, Royal was required to abide by RailAmerica-MNA safety guidelines. For example, the safety guidelines directed NARS employees to refrain from drug or alcohol use while on the job. Furthermore, for certain forms of railroad maintenance work, the safety guidelines mandated job briefings with MNA employees or for an MNA employee to be present. An MNA employee would also coordinate locations **[—3—]** and schedules for work assignments. Nonetheless, Royal's chain of command consisted only of NARS employees, and NARS maintained sole authority to discipline or fire Royal. While Royal testified that MNA often told him to "hurry up," he also stated that MNA did not rush him on the day of the incident and never directed or controlled how he was to perform his work.

On September 25, 2012, Royal was operating his ballast regulator on MNA's railroad tracks when his machine picked up and struck a piece of "rip-rap," a large rock mixed in with the smaller ballast. In certain areas around railroad tracks, rip-rap is commonly placed for structural integrity. However, rip-rap can also be dangerous because if it is pulled onto the railroad tracks, a ballast regulator may run over it, abruptly stopping the machine and injuring the driver. Royal often encountered rip-rap while working on his ballast regulator; was trained to spot it; and had struck a piece three weeks prior, bringing his machine to a sudden stop. This

[1] The Honorable Susan O. Hickey, United States District Judge for the Western District of Arkansas.

time, Royal struck the rip-rap and was thrown forward, causing back injuries.

The Royals sued MNA claiming that MNA supervised and controlled Shawn Royal's work, and as such, he was MNA's employee and entitled to hold MNA liable under FELA. Additionally, the Royals alleged that MNA was liable for negligently placing rip-rap in the ballast section near its railroad tracks. The district court granted MNA's motion for summary judgment, and the Royals now appeal.

We review a district court's grant of summary judgment *de novo*, viewing the facts in the light most favorable to the non-moving party and giving the non-moving party the benefit of reasonable inferences evident from the record. *Francisco v. Burlington N. R.R. Co.*, 204 F.3d 787, 789 (8th Cir. 2000). Summary judgment is proper "if the movant shows that there is no genuine dispute as to any material fact and the movant is entitled to judgment as a matter of law." Fed. R. Civ. P. 56(a). The Royals challenge the district court's grant of summary judgment on both the FELA and Arkansas negligence claims. **[—4—]**

FELA allows employees of interstate railroads to recover against railroads for injuries sustained in the course of employment. *Cowden v. BNSF Ry. Co.*, 690 F.3d 884, 889-90 (8th Cir. 2012). FELA states that "[e]very common carrier by railroad while engaging in commerce between any of the several States . . . shall be liable in damages to any person suffering injury while he is employed by such carrier in such commerce." 45 U.S.C. § 51. Thus, in order to maintain a FELA action against MNA, the Royals must demonstrate that Royal was employed by MNA. **{-763-}**

While the Royals concede that Royal was formally an employee of NARS, not MNA, they are correct that our inquiry does not end there. In *Kelley v. Southern Pacific Co.*, the Supreme Court noted that for FELA purposes, "employment" describes a master-servant relationship "determined by reference to common-law principles." 419 U.S. 318, 323 (1974). Under the common law, a plaintiff can establish employment with a railroad carrier even while nominally employed by another if he can show he is (1) a borrowed servant, (2) a dual servant, or (3) a subservant. *Id.* at 324. Determining whether a plaintiff constitutes a borrowed servant, dual servant, or subservant turns on whether the railroad controlled or had the right to control the plaintiff's performance of his job. *Vanskike v. ACF Indus., Inc.*, 665 F.2d 188, 198-99 (8th Cir. 1981) (citing *Kelley*, 419 U.S. at 322-26).

Royal does not qualify as MNA's employee because the evidence shows that NARS was the sole entity that had the right to control his work. Royal's chain of command consisted only of NARS employees. NARS hired him, trained him, and sent him to do maintenance work on railroads. NARS was responsible for all of Royal's compensation and maintained sole authority to discipline or fire him. Furthermore, NARS provided all safety training and equipment instruction to Royal and furnished all his personal protective and service equipment. Royal responds that MNA nonetheless controlled or had the right to control his work because MNA employees often told him to "hurry up," he was required to abide by RailAmerica-MNA safety guidelines, MNA employees inspected his work, and an onsite MNA **[—5—]** employee coordinated locations and schedules for work assignments. These facts, however, are immaterial because they would not allow a reasonable jury to find that MNA controlled or had the right to control Royal's work.

First, Royal's testimony that MNA employees told him to hurry up is not a material fact when examined against the backdrop of his entire testimony. Elsewhere, Royal testified that nobody rushed him on the day of the incident and that MNA never directed him on how to operate his ballast regulator. Thus, Royal's lone reference to being hurried is not enough to allow a reasonable jury to find that MNA controlled or had the right to control Royal's work. *See Brunsting v. Lutsen Mountains Corp.*, 601 F.3d 813, 820 (8th Cir. 2010) ("A mere 'scintilla of evidence' is insufficient to defeat summary judgment." (quoting *Anderson v. Liberty Lobby, Inc.*, 477 U.S. 242, 256 (1986))).

Second, the mere existence of safety guidelines does not suggest that MNA had the right to control Royal's work. The obligation to conform to safety requirements was a "mutually agreed upon practice[] that merely insured worker and premises safety." *Campbell v. BNSF Ry. Co.*, 600 F.3d 667, 669, 674 (6th Cir. 2010) (holding that adherence to a railroad's safety protocols is not enough to show a contractor's employees were railroad employees). The agreement to abide by certain safety regulations is a reasonable request necessary to safeguard against dangerous work and does not constitute control or supervision. *See id.* at 674.

Finally, MNA's inspection of NARS's and Royal's work and its coordination of locations and schedules for work assignments are likewise insufficient to indicate that MNA had the right to control Royal's work. "[M]inimum cooperation necessary to carry out a coordinated undertaking . . . cannot amount to control or **{-764-}** supervision," *Shenker v. Baltimore & Ohio R.R. Co.*, 374 U.S. 1, 6 (1963) (citation omitted), because evidence of contacts between a railroad's employees and a contractor's employees "may indicate, not direction or control, but rather the passing of **[—6—]** information and the accommodation that is obviously required in a large and necessarily coordinated operation," *Kelley*, 419 U.S. at 329. As a result, "[t]he mere fact that a railroad reserves the right to assure performance in accordance with the specifications of the contract does not render [the] contractor a railroad employee." *Morris v. Gulf Coast Rail Grp., Inc.*, 829 F. Supp. 2d 418, 424 (E.D. La. 2010). Accordingly, we conclude that no reasonable jury could find that MNA controlled or had the right to control Royal's work and therefore affirm the district court's grant of summary judgment on the Royals' FELA claim.

The Royals next assert that the district court erred in dismissing their claim that MNA negligently placed rip-rap in the ballast section near its railroad tracks. We apply Arkansas law and "are bound by decisions of the Arkansas Supreme Court." *See Chew v. Am. Greetings Corp.*, 754 F.3d 632, 635 (8th Cir. 2014) (quotation omitted). In order to establish a *prima facie* case of negligence under Arkansas law, "a plaintiff must show that damages were sustained, that the defendant breached the standard of care, and that the defendant's actions were the proximate cause of the damages." *Union Pac. R.R. Co. v. Sharp*, 952 S.W.2d 658, 661 (Ark. 1997). "The issue of whether a duty exists is always a question of law, not to be decided by a trier of fact. If no duty of care is owed, summary judgment is appropriate." *Lacy v. Flake & Kelley Mgmt., Inc.*, 235 S.W.3d 894, 896 (Ark. 2006) (citations omitted).

"[A]n employer of an independent contractor owes a common law duty to the contractor's employees to exercise ordinary care for their safety and to warn against any hidden dangers or unusually hazardous conditions." *Jackson v. Petit Jean Elec. Co-op.*, 606 S.W.2d 66, 68 (Ark. 1980). This duty, however, "does not contemplate a duty to warn of obvious dangers which are an integral part of the work the contractor was hired to perform." *D.B. Griffin Warehouse, Inc. v. Sanders*, 76 S.W.3d 254, 262 (Ark. 2002). The Royals do not disagree with these statements of law or even MNA's contention that rip-rap is an obvious danger in this line of work. The Royals do claim, however, that the dangers posed by rip-rap in this case are not **[—7—]** obvious because MNA negligently placed rip-rap in a section of the tracks where it did not belong. We are not persuaded by their argument.

In *Chew v. American Greetings Corp.*, we applied an Arkansas Supreme Court case, *D.B. Griffin Warehouse, Inc. v. Sanders*, 76 S.W.3d 254 (Ark. 2002), and found that an employer of independent-contractor electrical workers owed no duty to warn of the danger in approaching a transformer with improper equipment because the work necessarily implicated these obvious hazards. 754 F.3d at 639. The plaintiffs argued that the defendant failed to warn them of the "unique nature of its transformers, [which] caused [the plaintiff's] incorrect assumptions about the [transformer's voltage]." *Id.* at 635. We held that "though some details about [the] transformers may have been hidden, . . . the ultimate hazard the transformer posed was obvious, and the contractors retained the ultimate responsibility to assess these risks." *Id.* at 639 ("[The] duty to warn of latent or hidden dangers. . . . does not encompass an obligation to warn of the latent characteristics of an **{–765–}** obvious hazard that arises because of the nature of the contractor's work.").

This logic applies here with equal force. The dangers posed by rip-rap were obvious. Royal testified that he was trained to operate his machine in an area with rip-rap, that he had noticed there was rip-rap along the railroad in the area where he was operating, that it was a common occurrence to pull rip-rap from outside the rails to inside the rails, and that he had previously struck a piece of rip-rap on this same MNA railroad line. Thus, "[t]hough some details about [the rip-rap] may have been hidden, . . . the ultimate hazard [the rip-rap] posed was obvious, and [Royal] retained the ultimate responsibility to assess these risks." *See id.* at 639. We determine that MNA did not owe Royal a duty to warn of the well-known dangers of rip-rap and that the Royals' negligence claim therefore fails as a matter of law.

Accordingly, we affirm the district court's grant of summary judgment.

United States Court of Appeals
for the Eighth Circuit

No. 16-4000

TRAVELERS PROPERTY CAS. CO. OF AM.
vs.
KLICK

Appeal from the United States District Court for the District of Minnesota - Minneapolis

Decided: August 14, 2017

Citation: 867 F.3d 989, 5 Adm. R. 382 (8th Cir. 2017).

Before **SMITH**, Chief Judge, and **COLLOTON** and **KELLY**, Circuit Judges.

[—1—] {-990-} **COLLOTON**, Circuit Judge:

Christopher Klick was seriously injured after suffering carbon monoxide poisoning while aboard a friend's fishing boat. Klick sued the boat dealer in state court. The dealer had an insurance policy from Travelers Property Casualty Company of America that required Travelers to pay for liabilities resulting from bodily injury. The policy, however, had a pollution exclusion providing that the policy did not cover **[—2—]** liability for injuries arising out of the release, dispersal, or migration of certain pollutants. Travelers sued in federal court, seeking a declaration that the policy did not cover liability for Klick's injuries. The district court[1] granted summary judgment for Travelers. We conclude that the pollution exclusion applies, and we therefore affirm.

Klick and his two friends, Lonnie Norberg and Jeffrey Wheeler, were fishing aboard Norberg's 25-foot fishing boat on Lake of the Woods in northern Minnesota. According to Klick, Choice Financial Group and Rainy River Marina, Inc., sold Norberg the boat a few weeks earlier. Norberg was at the helm of the boat as the men returned to shore. The helm was near the front of the boat in the wheelhouse, a roofed area with walls or windows to the front, left, and right. The back of the wheelhouse was open. The boat's engine was housed in an enclosed compartment beneath the wheelhouse.

Norberg and Klick noticed that the engine was not operating properly. Klick took the helm and Norberg opened the hatch of the engine compartment to check the engine. Unbeknownst to Klick and Norberg, an exhaust pipe had broken off at the spot where it connected with the engine. As a result, the engine had been expelling carbon monoxide gas into the engine compartment rather than through the exhaust pipe and out behind the boat.

When Norberg opened the engine compartment hatch from within the wheelhouse, carbon monoxide flowed up into the wheelhouse. Klick quickly lost consciousness and fell into the engine compartment. He awoke there several hours later, severely burned from lying on the engine. He also suffered brain damage from the carbon monoxide. The gas killed Norberg and Wheeler, but Klick survived. **[—3—]**

Klick sued Rainy River and Choice in state court, seeking damages for injuries from the accident. Rainy River held a marine general liability insurance policy from Travelers at the time of the accident. The policy required Travelers to pay damages resulting from bodily injury. The policy, however, included a pollution exclusion stating that Travelers had no obligation to pay for "[a]ny liability . . . arising out of the actual . . . seepage, discharge, dispersal, disposal or dumping, release, migration, emission, spillage, escape, or leakage of 'pollutants' into . . . atmosphere."

Travelers then sued Klick, Rainy River, and Choice in the district court, seeking a declaration that the policy did not cover Klick's injuries because of the pollution exclusion. The district court granted summary **{-991-}** judgment for Travelers, concluding that Klick's injuries arose out of the release of a pollutant into atmosphere.

Our jurisdiction in this case is based on diversity of citizenship, and the parties agree that Minnesota law applies. Under Minnesota law, a provision in an insurance policy is "to

[1] The Honorable Donovan W. Frank, United States District Judge for the District of Minnesota.

be interpreted according to both plain, ordinary sense and what a reasonable person in the position of the insured would have understood the words to mean." *Farmers Home Mut. Ins. Co. v. Lill*, 332 N.W.2d 635, 637 (Minn. 1983) (internal quotations omitted). Because most insurance policies are preprinted forms drafted by insurance companies, Minnesota courts construe an insurance policy's words of inclusion broadly and words of exclusion narrowly. *Gen. Cas. Co. of Wis. v. Wozniak Travel, Inc.*, 762 N.W.2d 572, 575 (Minn. 2009). "An insurer has the burden of proving that a policy exclusion applies." *Henning Nelson Constr. Co. v. Fireman's Fund Am. Life Ins. Co.*, 383 N.W.2d 645, 652 (Minn. 1986).

The policy's pollution exclusion provides that Travelers does not cover liability for injuries "arising out of" the movement of pollutants into "atmosphere." The parties agree that carbon monoxide is a "pollutant" under the exclusion. *See Midwest Family Mut. Ins. Co. v. Wolters*, 831 N.W.2d 628, 637 (Minn. 2013). Klick argues, **[—4—]** however, that his injuries did not arise out of the release, dispersal, or migration of carbon monoxide into "atmosphere," and that the exclusion therefore does not apply.

Klick first posits that the engine compartment did not contain "atmosphere." He then reasons that his injuries arose out of the engine's initial "release" of carbon monoxide into the engine compartment, not the subsequent movement of the gas from the engine compartment into the wheelhouse.

Assuming for the sake of analysis that Klick is correct that the engine compartment did not contain "atmosphere," Klick's injuries did not arise only out of the release of carbon monoxide into the engine compartment. The movement of the carbon monoxide from the engine compartment into the wheelhouse was also a "release," "dispersal," or "migration" of a pollutant. The pollution exclusion is not limited to liability arising out of an *initial* "release" of pollutant or a "dispersal" or "migration" of the pollutant from an *original* source.

Klick argues next that the boat dealer's liability would not be "arising out of" a release, dispersal, or migration of a pollutant into the wheelhouse, because his injuries arose out of the release of carbon monoxide into the engine compartment. Under Minnesota insurance law, the phrase "arising out of" means "'causally connected with' and not 'proximately caused by.'" *Meadowbrook, Inc. v. Tower Ins. Co.*, 559 N.W.2d 411, 419 (Minn. 1997) (quoting *Faber v. Roelofs*, 250 N.W.2d 817, 822 (Minn. 1977)). The release of the carbon monoxide into the wheelhouse is causally connected to Klick's injuries: it caused him to lose consciousness and fall into the engine compartment, where Klick suffered most of his injuries. That the release of carbon monoxide from the engine into the engine compartment was also a cause of Klick's injuries does not make the exclusion inapplicable, for an injury can arise out of multiple causes with varying degrees of proximity to the injury. The pollution exclusion applies where, as here, a release, dispersal, or migration of a pollutant into atmosphere was causally connected with the injury. **[—5—]**

Klick contends finally that even if the boat dealer's liability would arise out of the release of carbon monoxide into the wheelhouse, the wheelhouse did not contain "atmosphere." **{-992-}** In *Board of Regents of the University of Minnesota v. Royal Insurance Co. of America*, 517 N.W.2d 888, 892-93 (Minn. 1994), the Minnesota Supreme Court concluded that the word "atmosphere," as used in a pollution exclusion, meant "ambient air." The court thus held that a pollution exclusion similar to the one at issue here did not exclude coverage for injuries resulting from asbestos fibers being released into the air within a building. *Id.* at 893. In reaching this conclusion, the court juxtaposed "ambient air" in its "natural setting" (atmosphere) with the air in the "controlled environment" of a building's interior (not atmosphere). *Id.*

The wheelhouse where Klick was exposed to a pollutant was not a "controlled environment." The back of the wheelhouse was wide open, and air readily flowed to and from the surrounding environment. A person standing in the wheelhouse was exposed to ambient air. A reasonable person in the position of the insured thus would have understood that a person in the wheelhouse is in "atmosphere."

The undisputed facts show that the insured boat dealer's liability for Klick's injuries would arise out of the release, dispersal, or migration of a pollutant into atmosphere. The pollution exclusion therefore applies, and Travelers is entitled to a declaratory judgment in its favor. The judgment of the district court is affirmed.

United States Court of Appeals
for the Eighth Circuit

No. 16-1958

WHITE
VS.
UNION PAC. R.R. CO.

Appeal from the United States District Court for the Southern District of Iowa - Des Moines

Decided: August 15, 2017

Citation: 867 F.3d 997, 5 Adm. R. 385 (8th Cir. 2017).

Before **SMITH,** Chief Judge, and **COLLOTON** and **KELLY,** Circuit Judges.

[—1—] {-999-} **SMITH,** Chief Judge:

Corey White sued Union Pacific Railroad Company ("Union Pacific") under the Federal Employers' Liability Act (FELA), 45 U.S.C. § 51 *et seq.*, alleging liability for a lower-back injury. The question we address is whether White's August 2012 suit is time-barred by the three-year FELA statute of limitations. More specifically, should White reasonably have known before August 2009—three years before filing suit—that Union Pacific's rough tracks were injuring his lower back? White, a **[—2—]** locomotive engineer for Union Pacific, testified that in 2007 and 2008 he experienced recurring lower-back pain that he attributed to potholes in the tracks, and that this was the same pain for which he later sought medical treatment. Because White should have known about his injury and its cause more than three years before filing suit, the suit is time-barred. We therefore affirm the district court's[1] judgment.

I. *Background*

White first injured his back in a work-related mishap in 1999. As White pulled a work implement for a concrete company, he felt burning and tingling down to his hands and his knees. The injury kept him from working for seven or eight months. His chiropractor "thought maybe there were some dis[c] issues." But White believes that he healed from that injury "[f]or the most part."

In 2001, White began working for the Iowa Missouri Rail Link (IMRL) as a switchman and conductor.[2] He passed a physical examination and had no back problems while with IMRL. In 2004, White went to work for Union Pacific. He passed a Union Pacific medical exam. He worked as a switchman and conductor from 2004–2006, mostly on the "road" but sometimes in the yard. During this time, White had no back problems.

In 2006, Union Pacific promoted White from conductor to engineer. Engineers receive better pay and have different responsibilities. As an engineer, White was responsible for the brake and the throttle—in White's words, "the movement of that **[—3—]** train." The nature of the engineer's job means that he pays close attention to the feel of the train. "[A]s an engineer," White said, "you feel these jarring dips and bumps," which White compared to "a pothole in the street." White noted that an engineer who was not prepared for a pothole would find the contents of his desk in his lap. And when the train would bottom out, "you would feel that through the bottom of the seat into your rump all the way up your back, just a jarring, tingling, sharp pain sensation."

Beginning in 2007, White worked frequently on the Clinton subdivision—a part of the railroad that runs from Boone, Iowa, to Chicago, Illinois. White's run began at Boone, in central Iowa, and ended at Clinton, on the Illinois border—about 200 miles away. On this run, several trains moved constantly back and forth over two **{-1000-}** sets of track, making this a high-density traffic section. White considered the Clinton subdivision track to be in the worst condition of any track that he traveled. White testified that during 2007 and

---

[1] The Honorable James E. Gritzner, United States District Judge for the Southern District of Iowa.

[2] White explained the difference between the positions: A switchman "[s]witches car in the yard as a switchman, builds trains, makes up trains. The conductor is more of a freight conductor, you're riding the trains. That's your responsibility is the train, everything that's located behind the locomotive."

2008, he regularly experienced bottoming-out situations caused by irregularities in the track. The worst ones—which occurred at least once a run—caused him to feel pain in his lower back.

In 2010, White first saw a doctor for his lower-back pain. After seeing other doctors for further treatment, White left Union Pacific in 2011. In August 2012, he sued Union Pacific under FELA, alleging that its work conditions caused his lower-back injury.

Union Pacific moved for summary judgment, arguing that White's claim was barred by FELA's three-year statute of limitations. *See* 45 U.S.C. § 56. Based on White's statement that his pain had gotten progressively worse from 2001 to 2011, Union Pacific argued that his claim accrued in 2001. The district court disagreed.[3] **[—4—]** The court noted that White's pain was "sufficiently minimal as late as 2004 that he was cleared by [Union Pacific]'s medical personnel" and that White "did not seek medical treatment until September 2009."[4] The court also noted that White's testimony about his injuries focused on what he knew as of summer 2009. Based on this evidence, the court concluded that a jury must determine, as a factual matter, when White's claim accrued.

At trial, White testified about his injury and its cause. He affirmed that beginning in 2007 and 2008, at least once every run his train would bottom out on the track. He affirmed that these situations would cause the type of lower-back pain for which he later sought medical treatment. Sometimes this "pretty bad pain" would run into his buttocks and down his leg as a sharp burning sensation. White attributed his pain to these bottoming-out situations—he said that he made this connection in his mind every run, day after day.

Based on that testimony, the district court granted judgment for Union Pacific as a matter of law, concluding that White's claim accrued before August 2009 and was therefore time-barred. The court noted that "both the record facts and the applicable law ha[d] evolved" since the court had earlier denied Union Pacific's summary judgment motion. White appeals, arguing that the district court should have allowed the jury to determine when his claim accrued.

II. *Discussion*

We review de novo whether the district court erred in granting judgment as a matter of law. *Tatum v. City of Berkeley*, 408 F.3d 543, 549 (8th Cir. 2005). Federal Rule of Civil Procedure 50 allows the trial court, after a party has been fully heard on an issue, to resolve the issue against that party and enter judgment accordingly if a **[—5—]** reasonable jury could not find in that party's favor. Fed. R. Civ. P. 50(a)(1). The inquiry is the same as on summary judgment: Does the evidence present "sufficient disagreement to require submission to a jury," or is it "so one-sided that one party must prevail as a matter of law"? *Tatum*, 408 F.3d at 549 (quoting *Kinserlow v. CMI Corp.*, 217 F.3d 1021, 1025 (8th Cir. 2000)). In making this decision, the court must draw all reasonable inferences in favor of the nonmoving party **{-1001-}** and must not judge credibility or weigh evidence. *Id.*

Here, the court decided as a matter of law that White's suit was untimely. "No action shall be maintained under [FELA] unless commenced within three years from the day the cause of action accrued." 45 U.S.C. § 56. When the injury is not a single traumatic one with immediate symptoms, but rather a latent one with symptoms appearing over time, "the cause of action does not accrue until the employee is aware or should be aware of his condition." *Fletcher v. Union Pac. R.R. Co.*, 621 F.2d 902, 906 (8th Cir. 1980) (citing *Urie v. Thompson*, 337 U.S. 163 (1949)). In addition to knowing of his condition, the employee must also know—or have reason to know—the condition's cause. *Courtney v. Union Pac. R.R. Co.*, 713 F. Supp. 305, 308 (E.D. Ark. 1989).

[3] The district judge who ruled on the summary judgment motion was not the district judge who later tried the case.

[4] White saw a doctor in September 2009 about shoulder pain; his first visit about lower-back pain was in October 2010.

"Both components require an objective inquiry into when the plaintiff knew or should have known, in the exercise of reasonable diligence, the essential facts of injury and cause." *Fries v. Chi. & Nw. Transp. Co.*, 909 F.2d 1092, 1095 (7th Cir. 1990); *see also Sweatt v. Union Pac. R.R. Co.*, 796 F.3d 701, 707, 3 Adm. R. 502, 506 (7th Cir. 2015).[5]

White contends that he was not on notice about the aggravation of his lower-back injury until he saw a doctor in October 2010. Citing *Fletcher*, he discerns a rule **[—6—]** in this circuit that a latent injury manifests itself "when a plaintiff first seeks medical treatment." This rule is necessary, according to White, because to hold that "garden variety aches and pains" trigger the statute of limitations would encourage laborers to rush to their doctors—and lawyers—with every minor ache. The premise is that such aches ordinarily would not cause a reasonable person to seek treatment, and thus are not serious enough to put someone on notice of an injury worth suing over.

While we have held that seeking medical treatment is a *sufficient* sign that a claim has accrued, we have never held that it is a *necessary* sign. Thus, in *Fletcher*, we held that the employee's cause of action accrued, at the latest, on the date that his back problem was medically diagnosed. *Fletcher*, 621 F.2d at 907. But we also noted that "[i]f his back bothered him constantly from [an earlier date], his cause of action accrued on that date." *Id.* at 907 n.7. Thus, a formal diagnosis is not required. *See also Sweatt*, 796 F.3d at 708, 3 Adm. R. at 506 ("[A] plaintiff cannot wait until he receives a medical diagnosis to begin pursuit of his claim." (discussing *Fries*, 909 F.2d at 1095)).

Fries, a Seventh Circuit case, is instructive. There, the court held that as a matter of law the plaintiff should reasonably have known about his hearing problems and their cause by 1981, four years before a diagnosis. *Fries*, 909 F.2d at 1095–97. The plaintiff had testified that in 1981 the frequency of the ringing in his ears would increase toward the end of the work day, worsen during the work week, and improve only on the weekend. *Id.* at 1094. He also said that the only cause he could think of was his work. *Id.* The court noted that even though the plaintiff lacked actual knowledge of his injury, and the injury had not reached maximum severity as of 1981, his symptoms as of that date imposed a duty to investigate. *Id.* at 1096. Otherwise, **{–1002–}** the court said, a plaintiff could "unilaterally postpone the running of the statute of limitations by negligently failing to investigate the fact of and cause of his injury." *Id.* (quoting district court opinion). The plaintiff's suit was therefore time-barred because if he had exercised reasonable diligence, he would have known both his injury and its cause many years before he first saw a doctor and filed suit. *Id.* at 1097. **[—7—]**

Sweatt is a similar case. 796 F.3d 701, 3 Adm. R. 502. It involved a plaintiff who noticed hand and shoulder pain in May or June 2009, saw a nurse practitioner for hand pain in mid-November 2009, and saw a doctor in late November 2009. *Id.* at 704, 3 Adm. R. at 506. His lawsuit—filed exactly three years after the doctor's visit—was held untimely. *Id.* at 708, 3 Adm. R. at 507. Despite the plaintiff's attempt to characterize his pain as the intermittent result of a minor injury and nothing more than muscle soreness, he had also testified that his pain was "unbearable" and had sought help from coworkers. *Id.*, 3 Adm. R. at 506. Relevant to our case, the court noted two things: (1) the plaintiff's failure to miss work was not controlling, because "his effort in working in the face of injury does not forestall the date of accrual"; and (2) the plaintiff's "plea of ignorance" about the seriousness of his injury was insufficient, because "a plaintiff cannot wait until he receives a medical diagnosis to begin pursuit of his claim." *Id.*, 3 Adm. R. at 506.

For one more example, in *Campbell v. Grand Trunk Western Railroad Co.*, the

[5] Because it is immaterial to the outcome of this case, we do not discuss the legal difference, if any, between a new yet latent injury and the aggravation of a preexisting injury. *See Aparicio v. Norfolk & W. Ry. Co.*, 84 F.3d 803, 815 (6th Cir. 1996), *overruled in part on other grounds by Reeves v. Sanderson Plumbing Prods., Inc.*, 530 U.S. 133 (2000).

plaintiff testified that beginning in 1993 or 1994, he experienced daily tingling and pain when working with power tools on the railroad and that the pain would subside when he stopped using the tools. 238 F.3d 772, 775 (6th Cir. 2001). Beginning in 1994 or 1995, he would wake up with numbness in his hands. *Id.* at 776. In 1998, when his symptoms worsened, he saw a doctor and was diagnosed with carpal tunnel syndrome. *Id.* His suit, filed six months later, was time-barred. *Id.* at 776–77. Notwithstanding his attempts to minimize or claim ignorance about his injuries, his daily symptoms triggered a duty to investigate. *Id.* at 777.

White contends that *Green v. CSX Transportation, Inc.* is the more factually similar precedent. 414 F.3d 758 (7th Cir. 2005). In that case, more than three years before filing a FELA claim, Green had mentioned shoulder pain and discomfort to her doctor three times and been treated with a mild anti-inflammatory for it once. *Id.* at 764. A coworker had also noted Green's shoulder discomfort in a letter to their employer. *Id.* The court determined that Green's pain complaints and symptoms were **[—8—]** not serious enough to put her on notice: "[H]er shoulder pain prior to [the statute-of-limitations period] may have been little more serious than a scratch, failing to put a reasonable person on notice that she had suffered a cognizable injury and must sue or risk losing her right to do so." *Id.* There was thus a fact issue on when Green's claim had accrued. *Id.* at 764–65.

As the district court recognized, White's case is more like *Fries*, *Sweatt*, and *Campbell* than it is like *Green*. At trial, White acknowledged that in 2007 and 2008 he experienced "pretty bad pain" in his lower back at least once a run; that this was the same pain for which he later saw several doctors; that this pain would sometimes run into his buttocks and down his legs as a "sharp burning sensation"; and that this pain was connected to irregularities in the railroad track. This information put White on notice to investigate "his known physical problem," i.e., his frequent, serious, track-induced pain. *See Campbell*, 238 F.3d at 777. This is true even if White did not actually think that he was injured before seeing a doctor in 2010. "Actual **{-1003-}** notice is not required for accrual. After a condition manifests itself, the question becomes whether the plaintiff knew or, through the exercise of reasonable diligence, *should have known* of the cause of his injury." *Sweatt*, 796 F.3d at 707, 3 Adm. R. at 506 (citation omitted). A medical diagnosis is certainly sufficient to put an injured party on notice, but it is not always required where, as here, the plaintiff acknowledges injury awareness before a medical diagnosis occurs. The better rule is that a claim accrues when one reasonably should know that his symptoms are fairly attributable to a workplace injury. The district court correctly concluded, as a matter of law, that White's symptoms were serious enough in 2007 and 2008 to raise a duty to investigate. Because White did not investigate and file suit within three years of the accrual of his claim, the claim is time-barred.

III. *Conclusion*

Accordingly, we affirm the district court's judgment.

United States Court of Appeals for the Ninth Circuit

United States Court of Appeals
for the Ninth Circuit

No. 15-55924

WILLIAMS
vs.
YAMAHA MOTOR CORP.

Appeal from the United States District Court for the Central District of California

Decided: March 24, 2017

Citation: 851 F.3d 1015, 5 Adm. R. 390 (9th Cir. 2017).

Before SMITH and OWENS, Circuit Judges, and HELLERSTEIN, District Judge.*

*The Honorable Alvin K. Hellerstein, United States Senior District Judge for the Southern District of New York, sitting by designation.

[—5—] {-1019-} SMITH, Circuit Judge:

This appeal challenges two separate rulings by the district court: the dismissal of Defendant-Appellee Yamaha Motor Co. Ltd. (YMC) for lack of personal jurisdiction, and the dismissal of Plaintiffs-Appellants' claims against Defendant-Appellee Yamaha Motor Corporation, U.S.A. (YMUS) pursuant to Federal Rule of Civil Procedure 12(b)(6). For the reasons set forth in this opinion, we affirm the district court on both accounts.

FACTUAL AND PROCEDURAL BACKGROUND

Appellants are a group of twenty named plaintiffs who purchased "first-generation . . . four stroke outboard motors" (the Class Motors) manufactured by YMC from 2000 to 2004. Appellants brought suit against YMC, which designed and manufactured the Class Motors in Japan, and YMC's wholly-owned subsidiary, YMUS, which imported and marketed them in California. Appellants allege that the Class Motors contained an inherent design defect that caused severe, premature corrosion in the motors' dry exhaust system. Appellants assert that this defect caused the motors to fail after between 500 to 700 hours of use, even when properly serviced and maintained, when absent this defect an outboard motor would have an expected useful life of at least 2000 hours. Although the alleged defect manifests early in an engine's expected lifespan, the average recreational boater only uses her engine an average of 100 hours per year. Accordingly, the defect typically will not manifest until the three-year warranty period has expired. Appellants assert on appeal that Appellees knew of the dry exhaust defect prior to the sales of the Class Motors to Appellants, and that the defect poses an unreasonable safety hazard. **[—6—]**

Appellant Williams filed the initial complaint on behalf of himself and all others similarly situated on July 15, 2013, naming YMC and YMUS as defendants. The complaint asserted claims for violations of federal and state warranty law; California's Consumer Legal Remedies Act, California Civil Code § 1750; and California's Unfair Competition Law, California Business and Professions Code § 17200.

Appellees filed a motion to dismiss, in response to which Appellants filed an amended complaint. YMUS then filed a second motion to dismiss for failure to **{-1020-}** state a claim, and YMC filed a motion to dismiss for lack of personal jurisdiction. While these motions were pending, the district court consolidated this matter with two similar cases and vacated all pending motions, after which Appellants filed a consolidated class action complaint. The consolidated complaint contained, in addition to the claims asserted in the initial complaint, ten new statutory claims from five different states, as well as claims for negligence and unjust enrichment.

YMUS subsequently filed a third motion to dismiss for failure to state a claim, and YMC filed a second motion to dismiss for lack of personal jurisdiction. On August 19, 2014, the district court granted in part YMUS's motion, dismissing Appellants' warranty and consumer fraud claims, and granting YMC's motion in its entirety. Appellants then filed their first amended complaint, to which YMUS responded with a fourth motion to dismiss. The district court granted YMUS's motion entirely, but granted Appellants leave to replead their consumer fraud claims.

Finally, on February 2, 2015, Appellants filed their second amended complaint (SAC), to which YMUS responded with its fifth motion to dismiss for failure to state a claim. On April 29, 2015, the district court granted **[—7—]** YMUS's motion and dismissed Appellants' only remaining claims with prejudice. Appellants now appeal the district court's grant of YMC's motion to dismiss for lack of personal jurisdiction, and its grant of YMUS's fifth motion to dismiss Appellants' consumer fraud claims.

JURISDICTION AND STANDARD OF REVIEW

We exercise jurisdiction over appeals from final decisions of the district court pursuant to 28 U.S.C. § 1291. We review *de novo* a district court's dismissal of a party for lack of personal jurisdiction pursuant to Federal Rule of Civil Procedure 12(b)(2). *Mavrix Photo, Inc. v. Brand Techs., Inc.*, 647 F.3d 1218, 1223 (9th Cir. 2011). We similarly conduct *de novo* review of "a district court's dismissal for failure to state a claim pursuant to Federal Rule of Civil Procedure 12(b)(6)." *Walker v. Beard*, 789 F.3d 1125, 1131 (9th Cir. 2015).

ANALYSIS

I. The District Court Lacked General Jurisdiction Over YMC

Federal courts apply state law to determine the bounds of their jurisdiction over a party. *See* Fed. R. Civ. P. 4(k)(1)(A). California's long-arm statute permits the exercise of jurisdiction to the full extent that such exercise comports with due process. Cal. Code Civ. P. § 410.10.

Under *Goodyear Dunlop Tires Operations, S.A. v. Brown*, 564 U.S. 915 (2011), courts have general jurisdiction over a foreign corporation only if the corporation's connections to the forum state "are so 'continuous and systematic' as to render [it] essentially at home in the forum State." *Id.* at 919. A corporation's "continuous activity of **[—8—]** some sorts within a state is [generally] not enough to support the demand that the corporation be amenable to suits unrelated to that activity." *Int'l Shoe Co. v. Washington*, 326 U.S. 310, 318 (1945). Rather, in the paradigmatic circumstance for exercising general jurisdiction, the corporate defendant is incorporated or has its principal place of business in the forum state. *Goodyear*, 564 U.S. at 924.

In *Daimler AG v. Bauman*, 134 S. Ct. 746 (2014), the Supreme Court considered for the first time "whether a foreign corporation may be subjected to a court's general **{–1021–}** jurisdiction based on the contacts of its in-state subsidiary." *Id.* at 759. The plaintiffs sought to sue Daimler, a German corporation, in California on the basis that Daimler's subsidiary's contacts could be attributed to Daimler under an agency theory, thereby establishing Daimler's "continuous and systematic" presence within California. *Id.* at 752. Daimler's subsidiary, MBUSA, served as Daimler's exclusive U.S. importer and distributor and had multiple California facilities. *Id.* We found general jurisdiction over Daimler under an agency theory, applying a test that asked whether MBUSA's services were "sufficiently important to the foreign corporation that if it did not have a representative to perform them, the corporation's own officials would undertake to perform substantially similar services." *Bauman v. DaimlerChrysler Corp.*, 644 F.3d 909, 921 (9th Cir. 2011) (quoting *Doe v. Unocal Corp.*, 248 F.3d 915, 928 (9th Cir. 2001) (emphasis omitted)).

The Supreme Court reversed our finding of general jurisdiction, emphasizing that the test for general jurisdiction asks whether a corporation is essentially "at home" in the forum state. *Daimler*, 134 S. Ct. at 754, 757. The Supreme Court assumed that MBUSA could be considered "at home" in California, and that its in-state contacts could be attributed **[—9—]** to Daimler, but it rejected a theory that would permit "the exercise of general jurisdiction in every State in which a corporation 'engages in a substantial, continuous, and systematic course of business.'" *Id.* at 760–61. In so doing, the

Court noted that while general jurisdiction is not strictly limited to a corporation's place of incorporation or principal place of business, those exemplars illustrate the need for predictability in jurisdiction and "afford plaintiffs recourse to at least one clear and certain forum in which a corporate defendant may be sued on any and all claims." *Id.* at 760.

Subsequently, in *Ranza v. Nike, Inc.*, 793 F.3d 1059 (9th Cir. 2015), we considered whether an in-state corporation's contacts could be attributed to its foreign subsidiary to establish general jurisdiction over the subsidiary. *See id.* at 1065. We stated that while *Daimler* invalidated our previous "agency" test, it "left intact" the alternative "alter ego test for 'imputed' general jurisdiction." *Id.* at 1071. We made clear, however, that the parent-subsidiary relationship does not on its own establish two entities as "alter egos," and thus does not indicate that general jurisdiction over one gives rise to general jurisdiction over the other. *Id.* at 1070 (citing *Dole Food Co. v. Patrickson*, 538 U.S. 468, 474 (2003); *United States v. Bestfoods*, 524 U.S. 51, 61 (1998)). Rather, we held that "the alter ego test may be used to extend personal jurisdiction to a foreign parent or subsidiary when, in actuality, the foreign entity is not really separate from its domestic affiliate." *Id.* at 1073 (emphasis omitted). To satisfy this test, "a plaintiff must make out a prima facie case (1) that there is such unity of interest and ownership that the separate personalities of the two entities no longer exist and (2) that failure to disregard their separate identities would result in fraud or injustice." *Id.* (quotation marks and alterations omitted). **[—10—]**

We first consider whether YMC itself has sufficient contacts with California for the exercise of general jurisdiction. We conclude that it does not.

YMC is incorporated and has its principal place of business in Japan, and has no offices or employees in California. Considering YMC's California sales, "the general jurisdiction inquiry examines a corporation's activities worldwide—not just the extent of its contacts in the forum **{-1022-}** state—to determine where it can be rightly considered at home." *Ranza*, 793 F.3d at 1071 (citing *Daimler*, 134 S. Ct. at 762 n.20). Appellants' own evidence indicates that YMC has 109 consolidated subsidiaries located in at least 26 different countries and spanning five continents. It further shows that in 2012, net sales in North America—a figure that includes sales in all 50 states and Canada, not merely in California—accounted for approximately 17% of YMC's total net sales. While the California market may be important for YMC, Appellants failed to submit evidence to support a finding that YMC is "at home" in California.[1]

Nevertheless, Appellants argue that YMUS's California contacts may be imputed to YMC for the purpose of establishing jurisdiction. Appellants fail, however, to plead facts sufficient to make out a prima facie case that YMC and YMUS are "alter egos." Appellants' complaint makes almost no factual allegations regarding the nature of the parent-subsidiary relationship, and the evidence Appellants **[—11—]** submitted in opposition to YMC's motion to dismiss did not provide any additional clarity.

Moreover, even assuming that YMUS's contacts could be imputed to YMC, this does not, on its own, suffice to establish general jurisdiction. In *Daimler*, the Court assumed that the subsidiary's in-state contacts could be imputed to the foreign parent, but nevertheless found the exercise of general jurisdiction inappropriate.[2] 134 S. Ct. at 760. **[—12—]**

---

[1] This is particularly so in light of the Supreme Court's rejection of the "stream of commerce" theory for general jurisdiction. *Goodyear*, 564 U.S. at 927–29.

[2] Appellants cite out-of-circuit district court cases, *Barriere v. Juluca*, No. 12-23510-CIV, 2014 WL 652831 (S.D. Fla. Feb. 19, 2014), and *Associated Energy Group, LLC v. Air Cargo Germany GMBH*, 24 F. Supp. 3d 602, 607 (S.D. Tex. 2014), to argue that the district court had general jurisdiction over YMC due to (1) YMUS's status as a codefendant in this case, (2) the allegation of in-state harm, and (3) YMC's status as a foreign corporation. These arguments lack merit. *Daimler*'s holding did not rest on whether the in-state entity was a party, and the location of the

In short, the district court correctly found that it lacked general jurisdiction over YMC.

II. The District Court Lacked Specific Jurisdiction Over YMC

The exercise of jurisdiction over a non-resident defendant requires that the defendant "have certain minimum contacts . . . such that the maintenance of the suit does not offend traditional notions of fair play and substantial justice." *Int'l Shoe*, 326 U.S. at 316 (internal quotation marks omitted). In order for a court to have specific jurisdiction over a defendant, "the defendant's suit-related **{–1023–}** conduct must create a substantial connection with the forum State." *Walden v. Fiore*, 134 S. Ct. 1115, 1121 (2014). The relationship between the defendant and the forum state "must arise out of contacts that the 'defendant [itself]' creates with the forum State." *Id.* at 1122 (quoting *Burger King Corp. v. Rudzewicz*, 471 U.S. 462, 475 (1985)). Additionally, the requisite "minimum contacts" must be "with the forum State itself, not . . . with persons who reside there." *Id.*

We will exercise specific jurisdiction over a non-resident defendant only when three requirements are satisfied: (1) the defendant either "purposefully direct[s]" its activities or "purposefully avails" itself of the benefits afforded by the forum's laws; (2) the claim "arises out of or relates to the defendant's forum-related activities; and (3) the exercise of jurisdiction [] comport[s] with fair play and substantial justice, i.e., it [is] reasonable." *Dole Food Co. v. Watts*, 303 F.3d 1104, 1111 (9th Cir. 2002).

Addressing the first prong of the specific jurisdiction analysis, Appellants do not allege any actions that YMC **[—13—]** "purposefully directed" at California.[3] Appellees submitted unrebutted evidence in support of their Rule 12(b)(2) motion that YMC does not conduct any activities within the state of California, nor does it target California via marketing or advertising. The only connection Appellants identify between YMC and California is via YMUS. Accordingly, we must ask whether YMUS's in-state connections may be attributed to YMC under an agency theory for the purpose of establishing specific jurisdiction.[4]

alleged harm has no role in the general jurisdiction analysis. Regarding YMC's status as a foreign corporation, *Daimler* and *Ranza* both also dealt with foreign corporations with no United States principal place of business.

Appellants further argue that YMUS's contacts with California render this case distinguishable from *Daimler*, because the subsidiary in *Daimler* was not a California corporation. Again, this is a distinction without a difference: The Supreme Court expressly assumed that the subsidiary in that matter was properly subject to general jurisdiction in California. *Daimler*, 134 S. Ct. at 760. Finally, Appellants point to numerous other lawsuits YMC has litigated in the United States. *See Yamaha Motor Corp., U.S.A. v. Calhoun*, 516 U.S. 199 (1996); *Rissew v. Yamaha Motor Co.*, 129 A.D.2d 94 (N.Y. App. Div. 1987); *Stephens v. Yamaha Motor Co.*, 627 P.2d 439 (Okla. 1981). But none of these cases found that California courts may exercise general jurisdiction over YMC. Accordingly, they have no relevance to the jurisdictional inquiry in this matter.

[3] Appellants' citation to *Sinatra v. National Enquirer, Inc.*, 854 F.2d 1191, 1197 (9th Cir. 1988), for the proposition that "a nonresident defendant may purposefully direct its conduct toward a forum state by marketing the product through a distributor who has agreed to act as the sales agent in the forum State" is unavailing. The *Sinatra* court specifically found that the plaintiff actively directed the advertising and sales efforts of its in-state agent, thereby justifying the exercise of specific jurisdiction. *Id.* It contrasted this conduct with that found insufficient to support specific jurisdiction in *Asahi Metal Industry Co. v. Superior Court of Solano County*, 107 S. Ct. 1026 (1987). The *Asahi* defendant knew that its products would be sold and used in California, and benefited economically from those sales, but "[t]he Court relied on the absence of any business solicitation or promotional conduct to determine that . . . the exertion of personal jurisdiction was unreasonable." *Sinatra*, 854 F.2d at 1197 (citing *Asahi*, 107 S. Ct. at 1033). The facts of the present matter bear far more similarity to those of *Asahi* than to those of *Sinatra*.

[4] As discussed *supra*, Appellants have failed to make a prima facie showing that YMC and YMUS are alter egos. YMUS's contacts can thus only be attributed to YMC if we find that the agency theory of imputed contacts applies.

While *Daimler* voided our agency approach for imputing contacts for the purpose of general jurisdiction, it left open the question of whether an agency relationship might justify the exercise of specific jurisdiction. *Daimler*, 134 S. Ct. at 759 n.13 ("Agency relationships, we have recognized, may **[—14—]** be relevant to the existence of *specific* jurisdiction"). Appellees point to *Walden*'s emphasis on the necessity of a relationship between the defendant *itself* and the forum state to suggest that YMUS's relationship to California cannot support specific jurisdiction over YMC. But *Walden* did not address an agency theory of jurisdiction. Rather, that case dealt with the scenario in which the connection between the defendant and the forum was provided only by the *plaintiff*, and could aptly be described as "random, **{-1024-}** fortuitous, or attenuated." 134 S. Ct. at 1123 (citation omitted). This contrasts sharply with the circumstance at hand, in which the relationship between the in-state entity and the defendant is that of a parent and a subsidiary purportedly acting as that parent's agent. If an agency theory of imputable contacts survives *Daimler* in the context of specific jurisdiction, then *Walden*'s directive that contacts must be directly between the defendant and the forum is inapposite, because imputing an in-state entity's contacts to the defendant would necessarily establish that direct connection.

Notwithstanding *Daimler*'s express reservation on the question of agency theory's application to specific jurisdiction, more than one district court within our circuit has expressed some uncertainty on that point post-*Daimler*, as "the rationale set forth in *Daimler* . . . would seem to undermine application of [our agency test] even in specific jurisdiction cases." *Corcoran v. CVS Health Corp.*, 169 F. Supp. 3d 970, 982 (N.D. Cal. 2016) (quoting *Los Gatos Mercantile, Inc. v. E.I. DuPont De Nemours & Co.*, No. 13-cv-01180-BLF, 2015 WL 4755335, at *5 (N.D. Cal. Aug. 11, 2015)).

As noted *supra*, our agency analysis asks whether the subsidiary "performs services that are sufficiently important to the foreign corporation that if it did not have a **[—15—]** representative to perform them, the corporation's own officials would undertake to perform substantially similar services." *Unocal*, 248 F.3d at 928 (internal quotation marks omitted). The Supreme Court found in *Daimler* that, "[f]ormulated this way, the inquiry into importance stacks the deck, for it will always yield a pro-jurisdiction answer: Anything a corporation does through an independent contractor, subsidiary, or distributor is presumably something that the corporation would do 'by other means' if the independent contractor, subsidiary, or distributor did not exist." 134 S. Ct. at 759 (internal quotation marks omitted). This criticism applies no less in the context of specific jurisdiction than in that of general jurisdiction. Accordingly, *Daimler*'s reasoning is clearly irreconcilable with the agency test set forth in *Unocal*. *See Miller v. Gammie*, 335 F.3d 889, 892–93 (9th Cir. 2003) (holding that where a prior decision in our circuit "is clearly irreconcilable with the reasoning or theory of intervening higher authority, a three-judge panel should consider itself bound by the later and controlling authority, and should reject the prior circuit opinion as having been effectively overruled."). The *Daimler* Court's express recognition of the potential viability of agency relationships for establishing specific jurisdiction does not alter our holding. While the Court reserved judgment on the viability of agency theory as a general concept, it did not suggest that our particular *formulation* for finding an agency relationship should survive in the context of specific jurisdiction. To the contrary, the *Daimler* Court's criticism of the *Unocal* standard found fault with the standard's own internal logic, and therefore applies with equal force regardless of whether the standard is used to establish general or specific jurisdiction.

Assuming, however, that some standard of agency continues to be "relevant to the existence of *specific* **[—16—]** jurisdiction," *Daimler*, 134 S. Ct. at 759 n.13, Appellants fail to make out a prima facie case for any such agency relationship. Fundamental tenets of agency theory require that an agent "act on the principal's behalf and subject to the principal's control." Restatement (Third) Of Agency § 1.01 (2006); *see also Batzel v. Smith*,

333 F.3d 1018, 1035 (9th Cir. 2003) ("Agency requires that the principal maintain control over the agent's actions"). Accordingly, under any **{–1025–}** standard for finding an agency relationship, the parent company must have the right to substantially control its subsidiary's activities. *See, e.g.*, *Unocal*, 248 F.3d at 926; *Murphy v. DirecTV, Inc.*, 724 F.3d 1218, 1232 (9th Cir. 2013). Appellants neither allege nor otherwise show that YMC had the right to control YMUS's activities in any manner at all.[5] Consequently, even assuming the validity of some formulation of agency analysis such that a subsidiary's contacts *could* be attributed to its parent, Appellants failed to establish specific jurisdiction over YMC.

III. Plaintiffs Failed to Plead a Prima Facie Case of Consumer Fraud

Federal Rule of Civil Procedure 8(a)(2) requires only that a plaintiff provide "a short and plain statement of the claim showing that the pleader is entitled to relief," such that the defendant receives "fair notice" of the claims against it. *Bell Atl. Corp. v. Twombly*, 550 U.S. 544, 555 (2007) **[—17—]** (citation omitted). A sufficiently pleaded cause of action "requires more than labels and conclusions, and a formulaic recitation of the elements of a cause of action will not do." *Id.* Rather, "[f]actual allegations must be enough to raise a right to relief above the speculative level." *Id.*; *see also Ashcroft v. Iqbal*, 556 U.S. 662, 678 (2009). The requirement that a plaintiff provide "plausible grounds" for her claim does not, however, "impose a probability requirement at the pleading stage." *Twombly*, 550 U.S. at 556. On the contrary, "a well-pleaded complaint may proceed even if it strikes a savvy judge that actual proof of those facts is improbable, and that a recovery is very remote and unlikely." *Id.* (internal quotation marks omitted).

Appellants' SAC asserts claims under a number of state consumer fraud statutes, each of which requires either an affirmative misrepresentation or an omission of material fact.[6] Appellants allege no affirmative misrepresentation. Rather, they rely entirely on YMUS's failure to notify consumers of the alleged dry exhaust defect. To state a claim for failing to disclose a defect, a party must allege "(1) the **[—18—]** existence of a design defect; (2) the existence of an unreasonable safety hazard; (3) a causal connection between the alleged defect and the alleged safety hazard; and that the manufacturer knew of the defect at the time a sale was made." **{–1026–}** *Apodaca v. Whirlpool Corp.*, No. 13-00725 JVS (ANx), 2013 WL 6477821, at *9 (C.D. Cal. Nov. 8, 2013); *see also Wilson v. Hewlett-Packard Co.*, 668 F.3d 1136, 1142–43 (9th Cir. 2012) (holding that where a defendant has not made an affirmative misrepresentation, a plaintiff must allege the existence of an unreasonable safety hazard and a causal connection between the defect and the hazard).

Contrary to the district court, we find that Appellants adequately pleaded Appellees' presale knowledge of the alleged dry exhaust

[5] Appellants do allege that "Defendants . . . were the agents or employees of each other and were acting at all times within the course and scope of such agency and employment . . . and are legally responsible because of their relationship with their co-Defendants." This is, however, a conclusory legal statement unsupported by any factual assertion regarding YMC's control over YMUS (or regarding any other aspect of the parent-subsidiary relationship), and we accordingly do not credit it. *Ashcroft v. Iqbal*, 556 U.S. 662, 678 (2009).

[6] Appellants have asserted claims under the California Consumers Legal Remedies Act, Cal. Civ. Code §§ 1750, *et seq.*; California Unfair Competition Law, Cal. Bus. & Prof. Code §§ 17200, *et seq.*; Massachusetts Consumer Protection Act, Mass. Gen. L., Ch. 93A, § 2; N.Y. Gen. Bus. L. § 349; North Carolina Unfair and Deceptive Trade Practices Act, N.C. Gen. Stat. §§ 75-1.1, *et seq.*; Washington Consumer Protection Act, Wash. Rev. Code §§ 19.86.010, *et seq.*; Florida Deceptive and Unfair Trade Practices Act, Fla. Stat. §§ 501.201, *et seq.*; Texas Deceptive Trade Practices Act, Tex. Bus. & Com. Code §§ 17.12, *et seq.*; Rhode Island Unfair Trade Practice and Consumer Protection Act, R.G.G.L. §§ 6-13.1.1, *et seq.*; Virginia Consumer Protection Act, Va. Code. Ann. §§ 59.1-200, *et seq.*; Maryland Consumer Protection Act, Md. Code, Com. L. §§ 13-301, *et seq.*; New Jersey Consumer Fraud Act, N.J. Stat. §§ 56:8-1, *et seq.*; and Connecticut Unfair Trade Practices Act, Conn. Gen. Stat. §§ 42-110a, *et seq.*

defect. However, we also find that Appellants failed to plausibly plead that the alleged defect constituted an unreasonable safety hazard. We therefore affirm the district court's dismissal of Appellants' consumer fraud claims pursuant to Rule 12(b)(6).

A. Appellants Adequately Pleaded Appellees' Presale Knowledge of the Alleged Dry Exhaust Defect

The SAC alleges that YMUS began receiving consumer complaints regarding dry exhaust corrosion as early as 2001. It states that "the complaints from owners regarding the dry exhaust corrosion in the First Generation Outboards were so frequent that individual Customer Relations supervisors personally handled as many as 40 or 50 different consumer complaints, or more, regarding the issue," which was an unusually high number of complaints for Yamaha to receive regarding corrosion "this soon in the life of the engines." The SAC goes on to explain that the high volume of calls led to the creation of "a marine-only customer relations service department in Kennesaw, Georgia, with approximately two **[—19—]** dozen customer service employees to assist in handling the complaints," and identifies Lindsey Foster as the Manager of Customer Relations who reviewed the complaints handled by the Kennesaw facility. Finally, the SAC explains how consumer complaints were recorded and transmitted by the Kennesaw facility so as to make YMUS management aware of the number and substance of the complaints, and states that Ms. Foster specifically reviewed the submitted complaints through YMUS's private Customer Relations Management (CRM) database.

The district court found that the alleged consumer complaints did not support a finding of YMUS's presale knowledge, and agreed with YMUS's characterization of Appellants' allegations of 2001 customer complaints as "inherently inconsistent with [their] over-arching theory of the defect" because Appellants had "consistently alleged that the defect does not manifest until 500–700 hours of use, 'which for a typical consumer using the boat 100 hours a year would take *five to seven years* to achieve.'" *Williams v. Yamaha Motor Corp., U.S.A.*, 106 F. Supp. 3d 1101, 1114 (C.D. Cal. 2015) (emphasis added by district court)). The district court ignored, however, Appellants' allegation that "the corrosion problem (which typically took 500 to 700 engine hours to manifest) had surfaced first primarily among heavy users who used their engines much more than typical recreational boat owners' usage." It was not "inherently inconsistent" to allege that a subset of "heavy users" encountered the defect much sooner than the typical user otherwise would.

The district court also cited multiple cases, from within this circuit and elsewhere, to illustrate the disfavored nature of customer complaints as a basis for establishing a party's presale knowledge. These cases are, however, **[—20—]** distinguishable. The district court particularly cited *Wilson v. Hewlett-Packard Co.*, 668 F.3d 1136 (9th Cir. 2012), for its observation that "[s]ome courts have expressed doubt that customer complaints in and of themselves **{-1027-}** adequately support an inference that a manufacturer was aware of a defect," because "complaints posted on a manufacturer's webpage 'merely establish the fact that some consumers were complaining.'" *Id.* at 1147 (quoting *Berenblat v. Apple, Inc.*, Nos. 08-4969 JF (PVT), 09-1649 JF (PVT), 2010 WL 1460297, at *9 (N.D. Cal. Apr. 9, 2010)). The facts of *Wilson*, however, differ significantly from those alleged here: *Wilson* concerned fourteen complaints, and the plaintiffs did not identify "where or how the complaints were made" and did not provide dates for twelve of the complaints. *Id.* at 1148. We found that absent dates to indicate that the complaints were made pre-sale, and some evidence that defendant actually *received* the complaints, it would be speculative at best to find that the defendant knew of the alleged defect. *See id.* at 1147. Here, by contrast, Appellants gave at least approximate timing for the complaints, and explained in detail how those complaints were lodged, how YMUS responded, and the mechanism through which information travelled from consumers to YMUS management.[7] [—21—]

Wilson did not hold that consumer complaints may never support an allegation of presale knowledge. On the contrary, it cited to—and distinguished—*Cirulli v. Hyundai Motor Co.*, No. SACV 08-0854 AG (MLGx), 2009 WL 5788762 (C.D. Cal. June 12, 2009), in which the plaintiff successfully alleged presale knowledge of a defect largely through its allegation that,

> Since 1999, [Defendant] has . . . constantly tracked the National Highway Traffic Safety Administration . . . database to track reports of defective Sonata sub-frames. From this source, [Defendant] knew that its 1999–2004 Sonatas were experiencing unusually high levels of sub-frame deterioration, steering control arm separation, steering loss, and highway accidents.

Wilson, 668 F.3d at 1146 (quoting *Cirulli*, 2009 WL 5788762, at *4). The facts alleged by the SAC are remarkably similar to those alleged in *Cirulli*, and provide an even stronger basis for finding presale knowledge because rather than tracking an outside database, YMUS is alleged to have set up its own proprietary complaint-tracking system to account for a similarly "unusually high level[]" of corrosion complaints. *Id.*[8] [—22—] {-1028-}

Importantly, Appellees have filed a motion to dismiss, not a motion for summary judgment. Discovery has not yet occurred. The district court faulted Appellants for failing to provide specific names and dates for consumer complaints, but in doing so it ignored the context of the particular consumer complaint system alleged by Appellants. Appellants specifically allege a private internal complaint system, and describe the manner in which it functions and the individual supervisor responsible for its management. In other words, Appellants do not know names and dates precisely because these complaints are not the sort of public internet posts that courts have previously found insufficient for providing notice to a company. Pre-discovery, when the court must take Appellants' factual allegations as true, Appellants' description of

Here, by contrast, Appellants allege that individual supervisors dealt with "40 or 50" consumer complaints, an "unusual volume," as early as 2001. While the numbers "40 or 50" lack context from which the court could determine whether or not that is truly a sizable volume, YMUS's alleged response to those complaints—the establishment of a dedicated customer care center—suggests that YMUS *itself* saw this number as significant and beyond the norm. Moreover, unlike cases in which complaints were posted to online forums, here Appellants allege not only that complaints were made directly with YMUS, but that YMUS affirmatively responded to this unusual volume of complaints by instituting a dedicated customer care center.

---

[7] At oral argument, counsel for Appellees emphasized that while YMUS may have known of the dry exhaust corrosion, it did not know of an *unreasonable safety hazard*. This argument elides two separate prongs of the test for consumer fraud: presale knowledge of a defect, and the status of that defect as an unreasonable safety hazard. *See Apodaca*, 2013 WL 6477821, at *9. In other words, counsel argued that the defect did not pose the safety risk necessary for a finding of consumer fraud. As discussed *infra*, we agree. That does not negate, however, YMUS's alleged presale knowledge of the premature corrosion itself.

[8] The district court cases cited by the court in this matter are similarly distinguishable from the case at hand. Each of those cases dealt with an insufficiently small number of complaints, complaints posted in forums unrelated to the defendant, complaints made after the sale dates, or some combination of these circumstances. *See, e.g.*, *Fisher v. Honda North Am., Inc.*, No. LA CV13-09285 JAK (PLAx), 2014 WL 2808188, at *5 (C.D. Cal. June 12, 2014) (finding a single consumer complaint predating the sale date did not plausibly suggest that defendant was on [—22—] notice of a defect); *Grodzitsky v. Am. Honda Motor Co.*, No. 2:12-cv-1142-SVW-PLA, 2013 WL 690822, at *7 (C.D. Cal. Feb. 19, 2013) (finding insufficient ten complaints submitted after sale to plaintiffs or posted to websites unrelated to defendant); *Baba v. Hewlett-Packard Co.*, No. C 09-05946 RS, 2011 WL 317650, at *3 (N.D. Cal. Jan. 28, 2011) ("Awareness of a few customer complaints . . . does not establish knowledge of an alleged defect."); *Oestriecher v. Alienware Corp.*, 544 F. Supp. 2d 964, 974 n.9 (N.D. Cal. 2008) ("Random anecdotal examples of disgruntled customers posting their views on websites at an unknown time is not enough to impute knowledge upon defendants.").

a separate consumer response **[—23—]** system dedicated to handling an unusually high volume of complaints specific to premature corrosion in F-Series motors supports a claim of presale knowledge.

B. Appellants Failed to Plead the Existence of an Unreasonable Safety Hazard

Appellants proffer two theories of unreasonable hazard resulting from the dry exhaust defect: (1) the potential for onboard fires, and (2) the risk of accident and associated injuries due to loss of steering power. However, Appellants' claim that the dry exhaust defect poses an unreasonable safety hazard fails due to Appellants' own characterization of the defect. According to Appellants' allegations, the purported defect merely accelerates the *normal and expected process* of corrosion in outboard motors. In other words, Appellants do not assert that the corrosion would not or should not occur absent the defect, they merely contend that the defect causes corrosion to occur earlier in a motor's lifetime than a consumer would otherwise expect. Were we to conclude that Appellants' allegations of premature but otherwise normal wear and tear plausibly establish an unreasonable safety hazard, we would effectively open the door to claims that *all* of Yamaha's outboard motors eventually pose an unreasonable safety hazard. The factual allegations here do not support either conclusion.

Additionally, the alleged safety risk is speculative and unsupported by factual allegations. Where a plaintiff alleges a sufficiently close nexus between the claimed defect and the alleged safety issue, the injury risk need not have come to fruition. *See Apodaca*, 2013 WL 6477821, at *9; *Ehrlich v. BMW of. N. Am., LLC*, 801 F. Supp. 2d 908, 918 (C.D. Cal. 2010). Nevertheless, a party's allegations of an unreasonable safety hazard must describe more than merely "conjectural and hypothetical" injuries. *Birdsong v. Apple,* **[—24—]** *Inc.*, 590 F.3d 955, 961 (9th Cir. 2009). Here, the SAC lacks any allegations indicating that any customer, much less any plaintiff, experienced such a fire—a notable omission **{-1029-}** if the alleged unreasonable safety hazard arises in *all* Yamaha outboard motors sooner or later.

We further note that the standard is one of an "unreasonable" safety risk. The loss of steering power, while plausibly hazardous, is a potential boating condition of which Yamaha expressly warns consumers. Moreover, the nature of the alleged defect as being primarily one of accelerated timing rather than the manifestation of a wholly abnormal condition weighs against its characterization as "unreasonable."

Finally, the fact that the alleged defect concerns premature, but usually post-warranty, onset of a natural condition raises concerns about the use of consumer fraud statutes to impermissibly extend a product's warranty period. *See Wilson*, 668 F.3d at 1141–42 (acknowledging that unless liability for failure to disclose a defect is limited to unreasonable safety risks, "the failure of a product to last forever would become a 'defect,' a manufacturer would no longer be able to issue limited warranties, and product defect litigation would become as widespread as manufacturing itself" (internal quotation marks and alteration omitted)).

CONCLUSION

The district court correctly found that it lacked either general or specific jurisdiction over YMC. Additionally, Appellants failed to state a claim for state-law consumer fraud, as they failed to adequately plead that the alleged dry exhaust defect constituted an unreasonable safety hazard. We therefore AFFIRM the district court's dismissal of YMC **[—25—]** as a party, and AFFIRM its dismissal of Appellants' claims against YMUS pursuant to Rule 12(b)(6).

United States Court of Appeals
for the Ninth Circuit

No. 14-71768

SANCHEZ
vs.
SESSIONS

On Petition for Review of an Order of the Board of Immigration Appeals

Decided: August 30, 2017

Citation: 870 F.3d 901, 5 Adm. R. 399 (9th Cir. 2017).

Before **PREGERSON, PAEZ,** and **CHRISTEN,** Circuit Judges.

[—4—] {-904-} PREGERSON, Circuit Judge:

INTRODUCTION

This case is about Luis Sanchez, a small boat owner, who took some friends on a fishing trip within United States territorial waters, and ended up in removal proceedings before an immigration judge ("IJ") under section 240 of the Immigration and Nationality Act, 8 U.S.C. § 1229a.

Here is what happened: Sanchez's small boat was dead in the water because of engine failure near Channel Islands Harbor in Oxnard, California. His friend issued a distress call, and responding United States Coast Guard officers towed Sanchez's boat into Channel Islands Harbor, a private recreational harbor. When they arrived at Channel Islands Harbor, eight Coast Guard officers were waiting for Sanchez and his companions. The Coast Guard officers immediately **[—5—]** detained, frisked, and arrested Sanchez and his companions. The Coast Guard officers contacted Customs and Border Protection because the officers suspected that Sanchez and his companions were "undocumented worker[] aliens." Sanchez was then placed in removal proceedings. The matter before us is limited to Sanchez's removal proceedings.

During removal proceedings before the IJ, the Government sought to establish **{-905-}** Sanchez's alienage and his entry into the United States without inspection by introducing: (1) a Form I-213 (Record of Deportable/Inadmissible Alien) that was prepared by a Customs and Border Protection officer after Sanchez's immigration arrest and (2) Sanchez's Family Unity Benefits and Employment Authorization applications.

At the removal hearing before the IJ, Sanchez moved to suppress the Form I-213 and the Family Unity Benefits and Employment Authorization applications as the fruits of an egregious Fourth Amendment violation. Sanchez argued that the Coast Guard officers egregiously violated his Fourth Amendment rights by detaining him based on his Latino ethnicity alone. The IJ denied Sanchez's motion to suppress and ordered Sanchez removed to Mexico. The Board of Immigration Appeals ("BIA") affirmed. This Petition for Review timely followed.

We grant Sanchez's Petition for Review. We conclude that the Coast Guard officers committed an egregious Fourth Amendment violation and violated an immigration regulation because they seized Sanchez based on his Latino ethnicity alone. Thus, we hold that the IJ erred in failing to suppress the Form I-213, but do not reach the question of the Family Unity Benefits and Employment Authorization applications. Additionally, because Sanchez has shown that **[—6—]** the Government violated its own regulation that is designed to benefit Sanchez, and that Sanchez was prejudiced by the violation, we hold that Sanchez's removal proceedings must be terminated.

FACTUAL BACKGROUND

Luis Enrique Sanchez's Immigration History

Luis Enrique Sanchez is forty-five years old. He was born in, and is a citizen of, Mexico. He entered the United States without inspection in March 1988 when he was seventeen years old. For the last three decades—most of his life—he has lived in Ventura County, California.

On May 11, 2004, Sanchez submitted Family Unity Benefits and Employment

Authorization applications to the United States Citizenship and Immigration Service ("USCIS"). USCIS granted Sanchez Family Unity Benefits, which granted him authorization to reside and work in the country, through his father.[1] Sanchez's Benefits expired on May 11, 2006. Sanchez applied for an extension of his Benefits on December 2, 2008. However, on May 28, 2009, USCIS denied Sanchez's applications because Sanchez had three misdemeanor convictions for violations of California's Vehicle Code, and was therefore ineligible for Family Unity Benefits.[2] 8 C.F.R. § 236.13(b). **[—7—]**

Fishing Trip and Immigration Arrest

On February 25, 2010, Sanchez, two adult Latino friends, and one of the friend's 14-month-old son took a fishing trip. Using Sanchez's small pleasure boat, they departed from the Channel Islands Harbor, a recreational harbor near Port **{-906-}** Hueneme in Oxnard, California. Sanchez declared that he and his companions did not travel outside United States territorial waters; indeed, that they did not travel more than two or three miles from the harbor. *See* Nat'l Oceanic & Atmospheric Admin., *U.S. Maritime Limits and Boundaries*, https://www.nauticalcharts.noaa.gov/csdl/mbound.htm (Sept. 13, 2013) (describing that territorial waters extend to 12 nautical miles).

About thirty minutes into the fishing trip, the small boat's engines lost power and the boat was dead in the water. One of Sanchez's friends on the boat called 911 to request a tow back to the recreational harbor. The U.S. Coast Guard (the "Coast Guard") responded. Upon reaching the boat, the Coast Guard officers towed Sanchez's boat back to Channel Islands Harbor.

Upon arriving at Channel Islands Harbor around 5:00 p.m., approximately eight Coast Guard officers were waiting onshore for Sanchez and his companions. Once Sanchez and his companions disembarked the boat, the Coast Guard officers immediately detained and frisked them. The Coast Guard officers demanded that Sanchez and his **[—8—]** companions hand over their identifications and belongings. Sanchez handed his driver's license to a Coast Guard officer.

The Coast Guard officers told Sanchez and his companions that they were not allowed to leave. When Sanchez asked why the group was not allowed to leave, a Coast Guard officer told Sanchez not to ask any questions and to wait for someone else to speak with him. Sanchez testified that the Coast Guard officers asked him only two questions, which he answered: (1) what is your name? and (2) where do you live?

A Coast Guard officer could not "establish positive identity or nationality" of Sanchez.[3] Without any other information, the Coast Guard officers notified U.S. Customs and Border Protection to report "the possibility of 4 undocumented worker[] aliens."[4]

About two hours later, Customs and Border Protection officers arrived at Channel Islands Harbor and detained the men for two more hours, during which time someone arrived to pick up the infant. Customs and Border Protection officers then transported Sanchez and the two adult Latino males to a Customs

[1] Sanchez qualified for Family Unity Benefits through his father because he was the unmarried child of his father, who had obtained lawful status as a Special Agricultural Worker. 8 C.F.R. § 236.12.

[2] On September 16, 1993, Sanchez was convicted of violating California Vehicle Code § 23109(c) (exhibition of speed on a highway), § 12500(a) (driving without a license), and § 40508(b) (failing to pay **[—7—]** court fine). On September 27, 1995, Sanchez was convicted of violating California Vehicle Code § 20002(a) (failing to stop after a vehicular accident). On February 8, 2008, Sanchez was convicted of violating California Vehicle Code § 12500(a) (driving without a license).

[3] According to the U.S. Customs and Border Protection Form I-213 prepared after Sanchez's arrest, the following Government computer databases were searched using Sanchez's information, and all of them returned "negative" results: the Automated Fingerprint Identification System; the Consular Consolidated Database; the National Crime Information Center; and the Treasury Enforcement Communications System.

[4] There is no indication that Coast Guard officers searched Sanchez's boat. It is undisputed that neither the boat nor the passengers carried contraband.

and Border Protection facility. The **[—9—]** Customs and Border Protection officers detained and interrogated Sanchez, strip searched him, and retained his identification and wallet. Through this questioning, Customs and Border Protection officers obtained information about Sanchez's alienage and entry into the United States. Customs and Border Protection released Sanchez later that night.

Customs and Border Protection Officer Carlos Rubio prepared a Form I-213 (Record of Deportable/Inadmissible Alien)[5] for **{-907-}** Sanchez. The Form I-213 included Sanchez's admission that he was undocumented and had entered the United States without inspection. The Form I-213 also stated that the Coast Guard officers suspected that Sanchez was an "undocumented worker[] alien[]," detained Sanchez, and thereafter contacted Customs and Border Protection.

PROCEDURAL BACKGROUND

Nine months after the fishing trip, on November 10, 2010, the United States Department of Homeland Security served Sanchez with a Notice to Appear for removal proceedings. The Government charged Sanchez as removable. On December 27, 2011, Sanchez appeared with counsel before an immigration judge ("IJ") and denied the charges of removability. **[—10—]**

At the removal hearing before the IJ, the Government established Sanchez's alienage and that he entered the country without inspection by submitting the following documents: (1) the Form I-213 prepared by Customs and Border Protection officer Rubio; and (2) Sanchez's Family Unity Benefits and Employment Authorization applications.

Sanchez filed a motion to suppress these documents and to terminate proceedings. He argued that the documents should be suppressed because the Government obtained and produced those documents in violation of his Fourth Amendment rights when they seized and detained him solely on the basis of his Latino appearance.[6] Sanchez argued that if his motion to suppress were granted, the IJ must terminate proceedings. The IJ denied Sanchez's motion to suppress and ordered Sanchez removed to Mexico.

Sanchez appealed the IJ's decision to the BIA. Sanchez again argued that the Coast Guard officers racially targeted him because of his Latino ethnicity. On May 27, 2014, the BIA affirmed the IJ's decision and further concluded that Sanchez's identity and "evidence of his alienage that is independently derived from a routine record search based on that identity is not suppressible."[7] This Petition for Review timely followed. **[—11—]**

JURISDICTION & STANDARD OF REVIEW

We have jurisdiction under 8 U.S.C. § 1252. Where, as here, the BIA adopts the IJ's decision while adding some of its own reasoning, we review both decisions. *Lopez-Cardona v. Holder*, 662 F.3d 1110, 1111 (9th Cir. 2011). We review constitutional claims and questions of law de novo. *Id.*

DISCUSSION

The central issue on appeal is a constitutional and legal question: whether the evidence establishing Sanchez's alienage and his entry without inspection (*i.e.*, the Form I-213) must be suppressed as the fruits of an egregious Fourth Amendment violation. *Lopez-Rodriguez v. Mukasey*, 536 F.3d 1012,

[5] A "Form I-213 is essentially a recorded recollection of a[n immigration official's] conversation with a [noncitizen]." *Bustos Torres v. I.N.S.*, 898 F.2d 1053, 1056 (5th Cir. 1990). It is created by an immigration official "with biographical information about a noncitizen. . . . It is generally created during the questioning of a noncitizen to obtain information to place him in removal proceedings." *Immigration Trial Handbook*, § 7:12: Form I-213 (July 2016 Update).

[6] Sanchez submitted a declaration in support of his motion to suppress. In the declaration, Sanchez recounted the events leading to his immigration arrest. Sanchez testified before the IJ in support of the motion to suppress. The IJ found Sanchez's testimony was consistent with his declaration.

[7] Here, the BIA was referring to Sanchez's Family Unity Benefits and Employment Authorization applications.

1016–19 (9th Cir. 2008). The exclusionary rule applies in civil removal proceedings where a noncitizen's Fourth **{-908-}** Amendment rights are egregiously violated. *Martinez-Medina v. Holder*, 673 F.3d 1029, 1033–34 (9th Cir. 2011).

For the exclusionary rule to apply in civil removal proceedings, a noncitizen must first establish (1) a prima facie case that law enforcement violated his or her Fourth Amendment rights; and (2) that the Fourth Amendment violation was egregious. *Lopez-Rodriguez*, 536 F.3d at 1016. Once a prima facie case and egregiousness are established, the burden shifts to the Government to defend the constitutionality of its actions. *Matter of Barcenas*, 19 I.&N. Dec. 609, 611 (BIA 1988). If the Government fails to adequately defend the constitutionality of its actions, the noncitizen's motion to suppress should be granted.

Thus, to resolve whether Sanchez can suppress the Government's evidence establishing his alienage and that he **[—12—]** entered the country without inspection (*i.e.*, the Form I-213), we must ask a series of questions: (1) whether Sanchez was seized at the border, where Fourth Amendment protections are lower; (2) whether Sanchez established a prima facie case that the Coast Guard officers violated his Fourth Amendment rights; and, if so, (3) whether that violation was egregious.

We answer these questions below and conclude that the Coast Guard officers committed an egregious Fourth Amendment violation and violated an immigration regulation when they seized Sanchez based on his Latino ethnicity alone. The exclusionary rule therefore applies, and we hold that the Form I-213 must be suppressed because it is tainted by the underlying egregious Fourth Amendment violation. We also hold that the immigration judge erred by failing to terminate Sanchez's removal proceedings based on the Coast Guard officers' violation of an immigration regulation. We do not reach the issue whether the Family Unity Benefits and Employment Authorization applications should have been suppressed.

I. Was Sanchez seized at the United States border?

The Government argues that the Coast Guard officers seized Sanchez at the United States border, where Fourth Amendment protections are lower. We disagree.

Generally, "[a] border search is by its very nature reasonable under the [F]ourth [A]mendment, and requires neither a warrant, probable cause, nor even articulable suspicion." *United States v. Dobson*, 781 F.2d 1374, 1376 (9th Cir. 1986). The Fourth Amendment still applies at the border, however, and searches or seizures that implicate a person's dignity "require some level of suspicion." *United States v. Flores-Montano*, 541 U.S. 149, 152 (2004). **[—13—]**

To determine whether the seizure was a "border stop," we must assess whether the seizure (1) occurred at a United States port of entry, *United States v. Villamonte-Marquez*, 462 U.S. 579, 589–92 (1983), or (2) took place on the high seas when reasonably certain facts suggested that the vessel sailed from international waters, *United States v. Tilton*, 534 F.2d 1363, 1366 (9th Cir. 1976).

First, Sanchez was not seized at a United States port of entry. Sanchez was seized at Channel Islands Harbor, which is not a port of entry as defined in 8 C.F.R. § 100.4 and 19 C.F.R. §§ 101.1, 101.3 (defining Port Hueneme as a United States port of entry). Rather, Channel Islands Harbor is a recreational harbor about one mile from the Port Hueneme port of entry. **{-909-}**

Second, there is no evidence that Sanchez's boat had entered United States territorial waters from international waters. The Coast Guard officers first encountered Sanchez's boat in United States territorial waters only two miles from a recreational fishing harbor. There is nothing in the record that shows whether Sanchez's small boat came from international waters, or whether the Coast Guard asked him whether it did, and the Government has not offered any "reasonably certain" facts that suggest that Sanchez's boat traveled from international waters. *Tilton*, 534 F.2d at 1366.

We conclude that the Coast Guard officers did not seize Sanchez at the United States border. Therefore, the lower Fourth Amendment standard does not apply. Accordingly, we must determine whether Sanchez established a prima facie case that the Coast Guard officers' actions were unreasonable under the ordinary Fourth Amendment standard. **[—14—]**

II. Did Sanchez establish a prima facie case that the Coast Guard officers violated his Fourth Amendment rights?

Under the ordinary Fourth Amendment standard, "[w]hen an encounter between a law [enforcement officer] and another person escalates to the point where it is considered a 'seizure,' the officer must have a reasonable, articulable basis for his actions." *Orhorhaghe v. I.N.S.*, 38 F.3d 488, 494 (9th Cir. 1994).

It is well-settled that it is unreasonable for a law enforcement officer to seize a person the officer presumes is undocumented based solely on the person's appearance or name. *See id.* at 497–98 ("[A]llowing INS agents to seize and interrogate an individual simply because of his foreign-sounding name *or* his foreign-looking appearance risks allowing race or national-origin to determine who will and who will not be investigated."); *see also United States v. Brignoni-Ponce*, 422 U.S. 873, 885–86 (1975) (holding that a person's proximity to the United States-Mexico border and apparent Mexican descent was not enough to constitute reasonable suspicion).

First, Sanchez argues that immediately after he disembarked his boat, the Coast Guard officers seized him based on his Latino ethnicity alone. An encounter with law enforcement becomes a seizure when a reasonable person, considering the totality of the circumstances, would not feel "free to decline the officers' requests or otherwise terminate the encounter." *Florida v. Bostick*, 501 U.S. 429, 438 (1991). It is undisputed that immediately upon being brought ashore, eight Coast Guard officers were waiting for Sanchez and his companions. It is further undisputed that the Coast Guard officers (1) immediately detained and frisked Sanchez, (2) demanded that Sanchez provide **[—15—]** identification, (3) told Sanchez that he was not free to leave until someone else questioned him, (4) instructed Sanchez not to ask questions, and (5) detained Sanchez for two hours.

Considering the totality of the circumstances, we conclude that Sanchez was seized immediately as he disembarked his boat at Channel Islands Harbor because a reasonable person in Sanchez's position would not have felt free to decline the Coast Guard officers' requests or otherwise terminate the encounter.

Second, Sanchez argues that the Coast Guard officers detained him based on his Latino ethnicity alone. When the Coast Guard officers seized Sanchez, they did not explicitly state that they seized him and his companions because they are Latinos. But the Government has not offered a **{–910–}** satisfactory alternative explanation for the warrantless seizure.

The Government's only evidence explaining the Coast Guard officers' conduct is the Form I-213 prepared by Customs and Border Protection Officer Rubio after Sanchez's arrest. According to the Form I-213, the Coast Guard officers reported Sanchez to Customs and Border Protection because the officers suspected that Sanchez and his companions were "undocumented worker[] aliens."

On the record before us, it appears that the Coast Guard officers seized and detained Sanchez based on his Latino ethnicity alone. Accordingly, the Coast Guard officers' conduct was unreasonable. We therefore conclude that Sanchez established a prima facie case that the Coast Guard officers violated his Fourth Amendment rights. **[—16—]**

III. Did the Coast Guard officers egregiously violate Sanchez's Fourth Amendment rights?

A Fourth Amendment violation alone does not trigger the exclusionary rule in civil removal proceedings: the exclusionary rule only applies if the Government's Fourth Amendment violation is egregious. *Lopez-Rodriguez,* 536 F.3d at 1016. Because we conclude that Sanchez established a prima facie case that the Coast Guard officers violated his Fourth Amendment rights, we must consider whether the Coast Guard officers' conduct was egregious.

A Fourth Amendment violation is egregious if "evidence is obtained by deliberate violations of the Fourth Amendment, or by conduct a *reasonable officer should have known* is in violation of the Constitution." *Gonzalez-Rivera v. I.N.S.*, 22 F.3d 1441, 1449 (9th Cir. 1994) (emphasis added and internal citations omitted). We have held that a reasonable officer should have known that his or her conduct violates the Constitution if the case law clearly established that such conduct was unconstitutional. *Id.* at 1450.

Sanchez argues that a reasonable Coast Guard officer would have known that the case law clearly established that it was unconstitutional to seize him based on his Latino ethnicity alone. We agree.

In 1975, the Supreme Court pronounced in *Brignoni-Ponce* that "[e]ven if [the authorities] saw enough to think that the occupants were of Mexican descent, this factor alone would justify neither a reasonable belief that they were [noncitizens], nor a reasonable belief that the car concealed other [noncitizens] who were illegally in the country." 422 U.S. at 886. **[—17—]**

In 1994, nineteen years later, this court in *Gonzalez-Rivera* held that it was an egregious constitutional violation when an officer detained an immigrant because of his ethnic appearance and other not credible reasons because case law had clearly established the unconstitutionality of seizing a person based solely on his race or ethnicity. 22 F.3d at 1449–50 ("[The stop] occurred long after the Supreme Court . . . made clear that the Constitution does not permit such stops."). By contrast, in *Martinez-Medina*, although the plaintiffs alleged that they were detained based on their ethnic appearance, this court held that there was not an egregious violation because the sheriff seized the plaintiffs *after* he knew that the plaintiffs were not legally present in the country. 673 F.3d at 1037.

As discussed, the Coast Guard officers did not have any information other than Sanchez's Latino ethnicity when they initially seized him on suspicion of being an "undocumented worker[] alien[]." At the time the Coast Guard officers seized Sanchez, **{–911–}** the principle from *Brignoni-Ponce* that a detention based solely on a person's race or ethnicity is unconstitutional was clearly established as it had been on the books for 35 years. Unlike the sheriff in *Martinez-Medina,* the Coast Guard officers did not know that Sanchez was not legally present in the country when they seized him. Because the case law clearly established that seizing a person solely based on ethnic appearance was unconstitutional, a reasonable Coast Guard officer should have known that he or she was violating the Fourth Amendment by seizing Sanchez based on his Latino ethnicity alone.

We therefore conclude that Sanchez satisfied his initial burden for suppressing the Form I-213 because he **[—18—]** established a prima facie that the Coast Guard officers egregiously violated his Fourth Amendment rights.

IV. Is the Form I-213 suppressible?

The Government introduced the Form I-213 at Sanchez's removal hearing to establish his alienage and that he entered the country without inspection. Sanchez argues that the Form I-213 should be suppressed because it is the product of the Coast Guard officers' egregious Fourth Amendment violation.

Because we conclude that Sanchez has established a prima facie case that the Coast Guard officers egregiously violated Sanchez's Fourth Amendment rights, the burden shifts to the Government to defend the constitutionality of the Coast Guard officers' actions. *Matter of Barcenas,* 19 I.&N. Dec. at 611. If the Government cannot defend the Coast Guard officers' actions, then the exclusionary rule applies to all direct products of the seizure, which here would be the Form I-213. We conclude that the Government's arguments in defense of the Coast Guard officers' unconstitutional actions lack merit.

First, the Government cites a number of cases to argue that Coast Guard officers may reasonably question persons on a vessel seeking to come ashore. But, in those cases, the Coast Guard officers' actions were constitutional because there were suspicious circumstances that justified the search or seizure. *See, e.g., United States v. Klimavicius-Viloria*, 144 F.3d 1249, 1263–64 (9th Cir. 1998) (finding that the Coast Guard officers' search of a fishing boat was reasonable under the Fourth Amendment because the occupants claimed to be on a fishing trip, but lacked any fishing equipment); *see also Villamonte-Marquez*, 462 U.S. at 589–92 (finding that the Coast Guard officers' **[—19—]** "suspiciousless" boarding of a sailboat was constitutional because the sailboat's markings indicated that it was from Switzerland and the officers inspected the sailboat's documents at a designated port of entry to establish that the sailboat was authorized to enter the country).

These cases are clearly distinguishable from Sanchez's case because here there was a complete lack of suspicious circumstances. Sanchez was not carrying contraband, the Coast Guard officers did not ask Sanchez what he was doing at sea, and there is no evidence in the record showing that the Coast Guard officers boarded Sanchez's boat to inspect the vessel's documents. There was no reason for the Coast Guard officers to suspect that Sanchez had done anything unlawful or traveled from international waters.

Second, the Government argues that Coast Guard regulations[8] authorized the **{-912-}** Coast Guard to seize Sanchez and board his boat. But, "no Act of Congress can authorize a violation of the Constitution." *Almeida-Sanchez v. United States*, 413 U.S. 266, 272 (1973), and the Government failed to adequately defend the constitutionality of its seizure.

We therefore hold that the Form I-213, which the Government introduced to establish Sanchez's alienage and **[—20—]** entry without inspection, must be suppressed. We do not reach whether Sanchez's Family Unity Benefits and Employment Authorization applications are indirect fruits of the poisonous tree because, as discussed below, Sanchez's removal proceedings should have been terminated because the Government violated immigration regulations.

V. Did the Coast Guard officers violate an immigration regulation that is meant to protect Sanchez? If so, was the violation prejudicial?

Sanchez argues that the Coast Guard officers violated an immigration regulation when they seized him without reasonable suspicion that he had violated any laws.[9] We agree.

8 C.F.R. § 287.8(b)(2) provides that an immigration officer may briefly detain an individual only if the officer "has a reasonable suspicion, based on specific articulable facts, that the person being questioned is, or is attempting to be, engaged in an offense against the United States or is an alien illegally in the United States."

It is clear that the Coast Guard officers violated 8 C.F.R. § 287.8(b)(2) because they detained Sanchez solely on the basis of his

[8] "The Coast Guard may make inquiries, examinations, inspections, searches, seizures, and arrests upon the high seas and waters over which the United States has jurisdiction, for the prevention, detection, and suppression of violations of laws of the United States." 14 U.S.C. § 89(a). An Executive Order also instructs the Coast Guard to "stop and board defined vessels, when there is reason to believe that such vessels are engaged in . . . violations of United States law or . . . [t]o make inquiries of those on board, examine documents and take such actions as are necessary to establish the registry, condition and destination of the vessel and the status of those on board the vessel." Exec. Order No. 12324, 46 Fed. Red. 48, 109 (Sept. 29, 1981).

[9] Because we find one regulatory violation, we need not consider whether the Coast Guard and Customs and Border Protection officers also violated the other regulations.

Latino ethnicity, with no reasonable suspicion that criminal activity was afoot.[10] **[—21—]**

When the Government violates its own immigration regulation, a noncitizen's deportation proceeding may be terminated, so long as (1) the regulation serves a "purpose of benefit to the [noncitizen]," and (2) the violation prejudiced the noncitizen's "interests in such a way as to affect potentially the outcome of the[] deportation proceeding." *Matter of Garcia-Flores,* 17 I. & N. Dec. 325, 328 (BIA 1980) (adopting *United States v. Calderon-Medina,* 591 F.2d 529 (9th Cir. 1979)); *see also Choyon Yon Hong v. Mukasey,* 518 F.3d 1030, 1036 (9th Cir. 2008) (applying *Garcia-Flores*'s two-prong test to evaluate whether the Government violated a regulation in an immigration case).

The immigration regulation that the Coast Guard violated here was meant to preserve Sanchez's privacy and protect him from racial profiling. *Matter of Garcia-Flores,* 17 I. & N. Dec. at 329. Requiring a warrant or reasonable suspicion, rather than allowing for detention solely **{-913-}** on the basis of race, protects against racial stereotypes influencing law enforcement's actions. *See Gonzalez-Rivera,* 22 F.3d at 1449–50. Sanchez's interest in being free from racial profiling and unjust detention clearly fall within the regulations' purposes.

The violation of this regulation also certainly prejudiced Sanchez. "Where compliance with the regulation is mandated by the Constitution, prejudice may be presumed." *Garcia-Flores,* 17 I.&N. Dec. at 328–29. Here, compliance with the regulation requiring reasonable suspicion for detention was mandated by the Fourth Amendment. **[—22—]**

Because the Government violated a regulation meant to benefit Sanchez, and because he was prejudiced by that violation, Sanchez's removal proceedings must be terminated. *See United States ex rel. Accardi v. Shaughnessy,* 347 U.S. 260, 268 (1954) (holding that when an agency violates its own regulations in making a given determination, that determination is invalidated); *Matter of Garcia-Flores,* 17 I. & N. Dec. at 328–29 (holding that deportation proceedings may be "invalidated" in the case of a qualifying regulatory violation); *see also Waldron v. INS,* 17 F.3d 511, 518 (2d Cir. 1994) ("[W]hen a regulation is promulgated to protect a fundamental right derived from the Constitution or a federal statute, and the INS fails to adhere to it, the challenged deportation proceeding is invalid and a remand to the agency is required.").

CONCLUSION

For the foregoing reasons, we GRANT Sanchez's Petition for Review and REMAND to the BIA with instructions to terminate Sanchez's removal proceedings.

PETITION FOR REVIEW GRANTED. REVERSED and REMANDED.

(Reporter's Note: Concurring opinion follows on p. 407).

---

[10] These immigration regulations apply to the Coast Guard officers here because Coast Guard officers enforcing any law of the United States shall "be deemed to be acting as agents of the particular executive **[—21—]** department or independent establishment charged with the administration of the particular law" and "subject to all the rules and regulations promulgated by such department." 14 U.S.C. § 89(b).

[—22—] **{-913-}** **PREGERSON,** Circuit Judge, concurring:

I write separately to explain why it is unfair for the Government to encourage noncitizens to apply for immigration relief, and at a later date use statements in those relief applications against noncitizens in removal proceedings. **[—23—]**

The Government should not be permitted to use noncitizens' applications for immigration relief to remove noncitizens from their homes and their families in our country. When the Government enacts immigration relief programs, it encourages noncitizens to apply because there are "significant social costs borne by our Nation when select groups are denied the means to absorb the values and skills upon which our social order rests." *Plyler v. Doe*, 457 U.S. 202, 220 (1982).

The Government asks noncitizens to provide personal information to receive benefits, such as driver's licenses, visas, deferred action, and work authorization. But because noncitizens are afraid that the Government could at a later date use that information against them, many are reluctant to apply. *See* Angélica Cházaro, *Challenging the "Criminal Alien" Paradigm*, 63 UCLA L. Rev. 594, 642–43 (2016) ("Coming out of the shadows to be counted and accounted for, however, while it may bring the benefits of work authorization and a social security number, involves stepping into the potential net of immigration enforcement.").

The Government's practice in this regard contradicts the principle of welcoming immigrants into our communities. This practice also contradicts President Kennedy's view that our nation's "[i]mmigration policy should be generous; it should be fair; it should be flexible." John Fitzgerald Kennedy, *A Nation of Immigrants* (1964). **{-914-}** We should encourage, not punish, noncitizens who come out of the shadows seeking avenues to lawful status.

I am also concerned about the Government's argument that the exclusionary rule does not apply to Sanchez's Family Unity Benefits and Employment Authorization applications because they predate the egregious **[—24—]** constitutional violation. *See United States v. Del Toro Gudino*, 376 F.3d 997 (9th Cir. 2004).

Categorically exempting applications that predate an egregious constitutional violation from the exclusionary rule allows immigration and other law enforcement agencies to prey on migrant and working-class communities. Law enforcement officers can unconstitutionally round up migrant-looking individuals, elicit their names, and then search through Government databases to discover incriminating information in pre-existing immigration records. *See* Eda Katharine Tinto, *Policing the Immigrant Identity*, 68 Fla. L. Rev. 819, 864 (2016).

Nothing prevents law enforcement from engaging in this unfair tactic if, as the Government contends, immigration records that predate an egregious constitutional violation can never be the fruit of the poisonous tree. *See Elkins v. United States*, 364 U.S. 206, 217 (1960) ("[The] purpose [of the exclusionary rule] is . . . to compel respect for the constitutional guaranty in the only effectively available way—by removing the incentive to disregard it."); *United States v. Olivares-Rangel*, 458 F.3d 1104, 1120 (10th Cir. 2006) ("[T]he deterrence purpose of the exclusionary rule would effectively be served only by excluding the very evidence sought to be obtained by the primary illegal behavior, not just the means used to obtain that evidence.").

This troubling end-around the exclusionary rule corrupts our justice system. The Government should not be allowed to flout the protections of the Fourth Amendment and then use a noncitizen's application for immigration relief against her or him. We should foster communication, not distrust, between migrant communities and law enforcement.

(Reporter's Note: Concurring opinion follows on p. 408).

[—25—] **{-914-}** CHRISTEN, Circuit Judge, concurring:

I agree with the panel that this was not a border stop. The Coast Guard did not seize Sanchez at a U.S. port of entry, nor did the evidence show that Sanchez's boat had sailed from international waters. *See United States v. Villamonte-Marquez*, 462 U.S. 579, 591–93 (1983); *United States v. Tilton*, 534 F.2d 1363, 1364–66 (9th Cir. 1976).

The record shows that Sanchez provided identification when he arrived back at the port. The record also shows that the Coast Guard ran several computer searches that yielded negative results. Despite the absence of hits in these various databases, the Coast Guard's Form I-213 reflects that the reason for detaining Sanchez was that the Coast Guard "was not able to establish positive identity or nationality." But Sanchez had provided proof of his identity and the Coast Guard did not put forth evidence that it had any concern that his identification was invalid. Nor did its computer searches give reason for detaining Sanchez. In response to Sanchez's prima facie showing, the government failed to offer "specific articulable facts" justifying his detention, *see* 8 C.F.R. § 287.8(b)(2), and therefore violated an immigration regulation intended to benefit Sanchez. Because the violation was clearly prejudicial to Sanchez, *see Matter of Garcia-Flores*, 17 I. & N. Dec. 325, 328 (BIA 1980), I agree that **{-915-}** his removal proceedings must be terminated.

United States Court of Appeals
for the Ninth Circuit

No. 14-36056

MURRAY
vs.
SOUTHERN ROUTE MARITIME SA

Appeal from the United States District Court for the Western District of Washington

Decided: August 31, 2017

Citation: 870 F.3d 915, 5 Adm. R. 409 (9th Cir. 2017).

Before **McKEOWN, BEA,** and **SMITH** Circuit Judges.

[—4—] {-918-} **McKEOWN,** Circuit Judge:

The events underlying this appeal center on Roger Murray, a longshoreman who experienced an electrical shock while working aboard the M/V APL IRELAND, a vessel owned by Southern Route Maritime SA and Synergy Maritime Pvt. Ltd. (collectively, the "vessel owner"). While Murray was descending a ladder and holding a piece of rebar, the rebar came into contact with a floodlight provided by the vessel owner which allowed electrical current to flow through his right arm, across his chest, and out through his left pinky, where it left a visible burn mark. Murray exhibited a range of ailments after the shock, including stuttering, balance and gait problems, and erectile dysfunction.

Murray sued under the Longshore and Harbor Workers' Compensation Act ("Longshore Act"), 33 U.S.C. § 901 *et seq.*, alleging that the vessel owner had been negligent in turning over the ship with a faulty floodlight. The jury awarded Murray over $3.3 million for his injuries and awarded his wife $270,000 for loss of consortium. The district court denied the vessel owner's motions for judgment as a matter of law, new trial, and remittitur.

Unwilling to go down with the ship, the vessel owner appeals, asserting three trial errors—a flawed jury instruction and two errors related to the admission of testimony by Murray's experts. We disagree on all counts. The district court properly instructed the jury that the vessel owner owes a duty to Murray as a longshoreman to turn over the ship and its equipment in a reasonably safe condition, which necessarily requires the vessel owner to take reasonable steps to inspect the ship and equipment before **[—5—]** turnover. Further, the court did not abuse its discretion in allowing Murray's key scientific expert to describe his theory of electrical injury because the court adequately assessed the reliability of his theory and fulfilled its gatekeeping function under Federal Rule of Evidence 702 and *Daubert v. Merrell Dow Pharmaceuticals, Inc.*, 509 U.S. 579 (1993). Likewise, there was no error in admitting the medical experts' testimony. We affirm.

Analysis

I. Jury Instruction Defining the Turnover Duty Under the Longshore Act

The Longshore Act provides a cause of action to longshoremen against the vessel **{-919-}** owner "[i]n the event of injury . . . caused by the negligence of a vessel." 33 U.S.C. § 905(b). Here, Murray claims that the vessel owner breached its duty to turn over the vessel and its equipment in a safe condition.

At issue is Instruction 14, in which the district court defined the vessel owner's turnover duty:

> One of the duties [vessel owners] owe to longshoremen is called "the turnover duty of safe condition." [The vessel owner] ha[s] the duty to use reasonable care to turn over the vessel and its equipment in such condition that an expert and experienced longshoreman would be able, by the exercise of reasonable care, to carry on his work on the vessel with reasonable safety to persons and property. In exercising such reasonable care, [the vessel owner] ha[s] a duty to take reasonable steps to inspect the vessel and its equipment. **[—6—]**

The first sentence is introductory. The second sentence captures almost word-for-word the Supreme Court's general description of the turnover duty:

> A vessel [owner] must exercise ordinary care under the circumstances to turn over the ship and its equipment and appliances in such condition that an expert and experienced stevedoring contractor, mindful of the dangers he should reasonably expect to encounter, arising from the hazards of the ship's service or otherwise, will be able by the exercise of ordinary care to carry on cargo operations with reasonable safety to persons and property.

Howlett v. Birkdale Shipping Co., S.A., 512 U.S. 92, 98 (1994) (citation and internal quotation marks omitted); *Scindia Steam Navigation Co. v. De Los Santos*, 451 U.S. 156, 166–67 (1981). The third sentence of the instruction gives practical meaning to the turnover duty by recognizing a duty to inspect the ship and equipment.

In the vessel owner's view, Instruction 14's formulation of the turnover duty is legally flawed because the instruction improperly expands the vessel owner's obligation to inspect the ship and equipment, states that the duty is to the longshoremen rather than the stevedoring company, and imposes an ongoing duty to inspect. Reviewing de novo, we conclude that the district court did not commit instructional error. *See Image Tech. Servs., Inc. v. Eastman Kodak Co.*, 125 F.3d 1195, 1208 (9th Cir. 1997). **[—7—]**

A. Turnover Duty Encompasses Duty to Inspect

The Supreme Court's first major exposition on the turnover duty under § 905(b) came in *Scindia Steam*, which contemplates a duty to inspect as part and parcel of the turnover duty. Although a duty to inspect is not mentioned explicitly, the Court defined the vessel owner's "duty with respect to the condition of the ship's gear, equipment, tools, and work space to be used in the stevedoring operations." *Scindia Steam*, 451 U.S. at 167. To that end, a vessel owner fulfills its responsibilities when it provides a reasonably safe workplace for the longshoremen. *Id.* at 166–67. The only way the vessel owner can do so is by checking the ship and equipment before turning them over in order to confirm that they are safe enough to be used in cargo operations. Otherwise, the turnover duty would be rendered nugatory, taking on a "see no evil" approach.

As one treatise puts it, *Scindia Steam* "implicate[s] the shipowner's duty to inspect the ship for hazards before turning the ship over . . . because inspection is integral to providing the stevedore with a **{-920-}** reasonably safe workplace." Robert Force & Martin J. Norris, The Law of Maritime Personal Injuries § 8:30 (5th ed. 2016). Justice Brennan's concurrence in *Scindia Steam* reads the majority opinion the same way, explaining that the law requires a vessel owner to "take reasonable steps to determine whether the ship's equipment is safe before turning that equipment over to the stevedore." 451 U.S. at 179 (Brennan, J., concurring).

The Court's later pronouncements on the turnover duty reinforce the inspection obligation. After reiterating a vessel owner's general turnover duty, the Court in *Howlett* examined the "corollary" duty to warn the stevedore of latent hazards that are known or should be known to the vessel owner. 512 U.S. at 98–99. The Court went on to conclude **[—8—]** that the duty to warn attaches where "the exercise of reasonable care would place upon the shipowner an obligation to inspect for, or discover, the hazard's existence." *Id.* at 100. In explaining the relationship between the duty to warn and the inspection duty, the Court cited a Third Circuit case for the proposition that "the shipowner's duty to warn the stevedore of hidden dangers necessarily implies a duty to inspect to discover those dangers." *Kirsch v. Plovidba*, 971 F.2d 1026, 1029 (3d Cir. 1992), *cited in Howlett*, 512 U.S. at 100. *Howlett* more than suggests that reasonable steps be taken to inspect the ship and equipment before turnover.

Our court has been even clearer on a vessel owner's duty to perform an inspection to fulfill its turnover duty. We have unequivocally held that "[w]here the shipowner itself supplies equipment, it has a duty to inspect the equipment before turning it over for use by the stevedore." *Hedrick v. Daiko Shoji Co.*, 715 F.2d 1355, 1357 (9th Cir. 1983); *see also Lincoln v. Reksten Mgmt.*, 354 F.3d 262, 268 (4th Cir. 2003) ("[T]he vessel might have been negligent in the maintenance, upkeep, and *especially the inspection* of the deck in question, so that, in the exercise of reasonable care, it might have discovered the defect . . . , enabling it to warn the stevedore of the defect." (emphasis added)); *Reed v. ULS Corp.*, 178 F.3d 988, 992 (8th Cir. 1999) (affirming summary judgment for vessel owner because "[t]he record reflects that the inspection of the gangway . . . was reasonable"); *Kirsch*, 971 F.2d at 1029 (noting "the shipowner's duty to inspect the ship for hazards *before* turning the ship over to the stevedore").

This formulation of the turnover duty produces doctrinal coherence because it logically fits the duty to inspect within the general turnover duty and its corollary duty to warn. The **[—9—]** turnover duty mandates exercising reasonable care to provide a ship and equipment that are reasonably safe for the stevedore to carry on cargo operations. Part of that duty is to examine the ship and equipment. When that inspection turns up latent hazards that would not be obvious to or anticipated by a competent stevedore, the vessel owner's duty to warn kicks in because the vessel owner is in the best position to detect and avoid harm and should be liable if it does not speak up. *See Howlett*, 512 U.S. at 101–03. The vessel owner's belated argument to limit the inspection to identifying latent hazards would dilute the turnover duty envisioned by the case law and would be unworkable in practice.

Recognizing a duty to inspect as part of the turnover duty does not expand shipowner liability. The inspection is constrained by what is reasonable under the circumstances, and the ultimate measure of whether the vessel owner has satisfied its turnover duty is whether the vessel owner has provided a reasonably safe environment **{-921-}** for the longshoremen to carry out their work. The limited nature of the duty undercuts the vessel owner's fear that it will be obligated to scour every inch of the vessel and tear apart all of the equipment. Because the inquiry turns on reasonableness, our rule also does not resurrect the strict-liability unseaworthiness regime that Congress dismantled by passing § 905(b). *See Scindia Steam*, 451 U.S. at 168–69. The duty to inspect falls comfortably within the turnover duty, and the district court's instructional clarifier was on the mark.

B. Turnover Duty Runs to the Longshoremen

The vessel owner's complaint that Instruction 14 improperly states that the turnover duty is "owe[d] to longshoremen" was not adequately raised in the district **[—10—]** court. Granted, the vessel owner's counsel objected to another instruction on this ground and proposed an instruction regarding the stevedoring company's duties to the longshoremen. However, those efforts did not raise the objection to Instruction 14 with sufficient specificity to "bring into focus the precise nature of the alleged error." *Palmer v. Hoffman*, 318 U.S. 109, 119 (1943); *see also* Fed. R. Civ. P. 51(c)(1). At a minimum, the vessel owner would have to demonstrate plain error in the instruction to warrant reversal. *See* Fed. R. Civ. P. 51(d)(2).

The vessel owner cannot make that showing because the law supports the proposition that vessel owners owe the turnover duty to the longshoremen. The relevant statute, § 905(b), speaks of "injury to a person covered under this chapter," which includes longshoremen. *See* 33 U.S.C. §§ 902(1), (3); 905(b). The two leading Supreme Court cases involve suits brought by longshoremen against vessel owners and say that "the vessel owes to the stevedore and his longshoremen employees the duty of exercising due care." *Scindia Steam*, 451 U.S. at 166; *see Howlett*, 512 U.S. at 98 (outlining the "three general duties shipowners owe to longshoremen"). We have framed the inquiry in the same way: "Although the turnover duty of safe condition is usually framed in terms of stevedores, it is clear that danger to *longshore workers* is an essential part of the inquiry." *Thomas v. Newton Int'l Enters.*, 42 F.3d 1266, 1270 n.4 (9th Cir. 1994).

The stevedoring company's separate obligation under 33 U.S.C. § 941(a) to provide a "reasonably safe" workplace for its longshoremen does not somehow override the vessel owner's duty to the longshoremen to turn over the ship and equipment in a safe condition. Those duties happily coexist, with the vessel owner ensuring a safe ship upon turnover and **[—11—]** the stevedoring company ensuring a safe work environment during cargo operations. *See Scindia Steam*, 451 U.S. at 170–72. The district court properly instructed the jury on the vessel owner's turnover duty to longshoremen.

C. Turnover Duty Is Not Continuing

The vessel owner also did not put the district court on notice about its complaint that Instruction 14 creates a temporally unrestricted duty to inspect and leaves the vessel owner open to a virtually unlimited obligation. *See Benigni v. City of Hemet*, 879 F.2d 473, 475–76 (9th Cir. 1988) (noting that "the record indicates that the trial court was not made aware of any specific concern with the proposed instructions"). In any event, regardless of the standard of review, the vessel owner's challenge cannot be sustained because Instruction 14 plainly refers to the moment of turnover and not to a perpetual duty, **{-922-}** and other instructions confirm that limitation.

Instruction 14 itself refers to the vessel owner's duty when it "*turn[s] over* the vessel and its equipment." Looking at the surrounding instructions, Instruction 12 summarizes Murray's theory of the case "that [the vessel owner was] negligent because the vessel and its equipment were not *turned over* in a [safe] condition." And Instruction 13, which sets forth the elements of Murray's negligence claim, states that liability cannot be found unless the vessel owner "*turned over* the [vessel] and its equipment in [an unsafe] condition." These related instructions make clear that the district court did not charge a continuing post-turnover duty. **[—12—]**

II. Reliability of Dr. Morse's Testimony Under *Daubert*

The district court admitted Murray's scientific expert, Dr. Michael Morse, who testified that low-voltage shock can cause bodily injuries far from the path of the electrical current. Following a hearing, the court issued an order detailing why Dr. Morse's diffuse electrical injury theory was reliable under Federal Rule of Evidence 702 and *Daubert*. We review for abuse of discretion and conclude that the court performed a sufficiently rigorous evaluation of Dr. Morse's theory and did not "reach[] a result that is illogical, implausible, or without support in inferences that may be drawn from the record." *United States v. Hinkson*, 585 F.3d 1247, 1262 (9th Cir. 2009) (en banc).

The starting point for our analysis is the Supreme Court's decision in *Daubert*, a case that effected a sea change in the way that courts consider admission of expert testimony. Before *Daubert*, courts generally followed the "general acceptance" test, which focused on recognition in the relevant field. 509 U.S. at 585–86. The Court in *Daubert* rejected that test as too rigid; drawing on Federal Rule of Evidence 702, the Court constructed a flexible test examining the "reliability" and "fit" of the offered expert testimony. *See id.* at 589–92.

The question of reliability probes "whether the reasoning or methodology underlying the testimony is scientifically valid." *Id.* at 592–93. To give shape to the inquiry, the Court identified four factors that may bear on the analysis: (1) whether the theory can be and has been tested, (2) whether the theory has been peer reviewed and published, (3) what the theory's known or potential error rate is, and (4) whether the theory enjoys general acceptance in the applicable scientific community. *See id.* at 593–94. But **[—13—]** the Court was quick to emphasize that the factors are not "a definitive checklist or test" and that the reliability analysis remains a malleable one tied to the facts of each case. *Id.* at 591, 593. Later cases have reiterated that the *Daubert* factors are exemplary, not constraining. *Kumho Tire Co. v. Carmichael*, 526 U.S. 137, 150 (1999); *id.* at 159 (Scalia, J., concurring) ("[T]he *Daubert* factors are not holy writ . . . .").

It is important to remember that the factors are not "equally applicable (or applicable at all) in every case." *Daubert v. Merrell Dow Pharm., Inc.*, 43 F.3d 1311, 1317 (9th Cir. 1995). Applicability "depend[s] on the nature of the issue, the expert's particular expertise, and the subject of his testimony." *Kumho Tire Co.*, 526 U.S. at 150 (citation omitted). A district court may permissibly choose not to examine factors that are not "reasonable measures of reliability in a particular case." *Id.* at 153. **{-923-}**

Because of the fluid and contextual nature of the inquiry, district courts are vested with "broad latitude" to "decid[e] *how* to test an expert's reliability" and "*whether or not* [an] expert's relevant testimony is reliable." *Id.* at 152–53. District judges play an active and important role as gatekeepers examining the full picture of the experts' methodology and preventing shoddy expert testimony and junk science from reaching the jury. *See Daubert*, 509 U.S. at 595–97. That is why we owe the court's ruling "the deference that is the hallmark of abuse-of-discretion review" and may not second-guess its sound judgments. *Gen. Elec. Co. v. Joiner*, 522 U.S. 136, 141–43 (1997).

The court did not abuse its discretion here because its reliability inquiry satisfies these standards and the court applied the correct legal framework to the facts in a manner that was neither illogical nor implausible nor contrary to the record. In its *Daubert* order, the court first explains that Dr. **[—14—]** Morse "has published his findings in peer-reviewed papers." "[S]ubmission to the scrutiny of the scientific community" can be a strong indicator of reliability "because it increases the likelihood that substantive flaws in methodology will be detected." *Daubert*, 509 U.S. at 593. Dr. Morse's theory has been peer-reviewed and published many times over: Murray's filings in the district court cite eight articles by Dr. Morse published in reputable scientific journals. More generally, Murray submitted a wealth of examples of other scientists publishing in peer-reviewed journals on the theory of low-voltage and diffuse electrical injury.

The court then discusses acceptance of Dr. Morse's theory by other professionals in the biomedical engineering field. The court was on solid ground in rejecting the vessel owner's contention that "the number of confirmed low-voltage cases is too small to draw scientifically valid conclusions and that the minimum voltage required to cause injury has not yet been established with any degree of certainty." Relying on the record, the court specifically credited Dr. Morse's response that "over the past two decades both the immediate and extended symptomology of low-voltage shock has been recognized," an observation grounded in his expertise in electrical injury and years of research in the field. Also, the record is replete with examples of articles that explicitly agree with Dr. Morse's theory and methodology as well as articles that cite to and expand on his conclusions. Even if the vessel owner presented medical sources disagreeing with Dr. Morse, the district court could properly give weight to the fact that Dr. Morse's theory has been acknowledged and credited by scientists in the community without determining the exact degree of acceptance. *See id.* at 594. **[—15—]**

The court's analysis does not end there. It evaluates the genesis of the expert opinion, a factor recognized in the advisory notes and our case law: Dr. Morse's theory "w[as] not developed for purposes of this litigation." *See* Fed. R. Evid. 702 advisory committee's note to the 2000 amendments; *Daubert*, 43 F.3d at 1317. Importantly, our cases call this consideration a "very significant fact" that "provides important, objective proof that the research comports with the dictates of good science." *Daubert*, 43 F.3d at 1317. The order also goes on to say that "[Dr. Morse's] conclusions are reasonable extrapolations from the patient files reviewed," tracking another known factor. *See Joiner*, 522 U.S. at 146 ("A court may conclude that there is simply too great an analytical gap between the data and the opinion proffered."); *see also* **{-924-}** Fed. R. Evid. 702 advisory committee's note to the 2000 amendments (listing "[w]hether the expert has unjustifiably extrapolated from an accepted premise to an unfounded conclusion"). Based on these multiple considerations, the district court concluded that Dr. Morse's theory was grounded in science, as demanded by *Daubert*. *See* 509 U.S. at 594 (explaining that the "overarching subject is the scientific validity").

The adequacy of the court's review and the soundness of its judgment are further underscored by its discretionary decision to convene a *Daubert* hearing to explore matters with the parties. *See United States v. Alatorre*, 222 F.3d 1098, 1102, 1105 (9th Cir. 2000). At the hearing, the district judge played a proactive role: he was eager to receive information from the parties, asking them to submit all relevant articles and stating that he would "look[] at the entire body of the case, every document that has been filed beforehand, and every document that's filed in this motion and response." He gave the attorneys the opportunity to debate the issues and actively questioned them about the **[—16—]** strengths and weaknesses of their positions. Only after this extensive back-and-forth and consideration of the parties' papers did the court issue its order admitting Dr. Morse's testimony.

It is true that the order does not scrutinize the testability and error rate factors. Although *Daubert* does not require a methodical walkthrough of each factor, the best practice may be for district courts to at least reference the four *Daubert* factors so as to avoid an appeal issue like the one here. *See Black v. Food Lion, Inc.*, 171 F.3d 308, 311–12 (5th Cir. 1999) ("In the vast majority of cases, the district court first should decide whether the factors mentioned in *Daubert* are appropriate. Once it considers the *Daubert* factors, the court then can consider . . . other factors . . . ."). That said, we emphasize that not every factor is relevant to reliability in every case and that the significance of each factor is case-dependent. District courts have broad range to structure the reliability inquiry and may choose not to comment on factors that would not inform the analysis.

The district court's silence about the testability and error rate factors falls within that broad discretion. The omission may be attributed in part to the parties' nearly exclusive concentration on the other two factors—peer review and general acceptance. Those issues were teased out at length in the parties' motions and at the *Daubert* hearing, and thus the court put them front and center in its order assessing Dr. Morse's testimony.

Even more forcefully, the district court's order highlighted that the subject of Dr. Morse's testimony was narrow: he would discuss his theory of low-voltage diffuse electrical injury, but he would not offer an opinion on whether Murray's particular injuries were caused by the low-voltage shock. That limited focus made many of the vessel **[—17—]** owner's critiques on testability misplaced and made the error rate a poor measure of reliability in this case. *See Kumho Tire Co.*, 526 U.S. at 153 (permitting district courts to discount factors that are not "reasonable measures of reliability in [the] particular case"). And to the extent that testability was raised before the district court, it was not forgotten or wholly ignored—the parties and district judge spent time at the *Daubert* hearing exploring whether Dr. Morse had followed a modified methodology drawn from one of his published papers. All of this convinces us that the district court fulfilled its gatekeeping role and did not jump to a conclusion that is unreasonable or unsupported by record evidence. **{-925-}**

Our view that the district court acted well within its discretion is in accord with how we have treated other *Daubert* challenges. On many occasions, we have found an abuse of discretion when a district court completely abdicates its gatekeeping role. *See, e.g., City of Pomona v. SQM N. Am. Corp.*, No. 15-56062, 2017 WL 3378770, at *7 (9th Cir. Aug. 7, 2017) (explaining that the district court's "failure to make any findings regarding the efficacy of [the] expert opinions constituted an abdication of the district court's gatekeeping role, and necessarily an abuse of discretion"); *Pyramid Techs., Inc. v. Hartford Cas. Ins. Co.*, 752 F.3d 807, 814 (9th Cir. 2014) (faulting the district court for "provid[ing] no explanation or analysis for rejecting [the expert's] qualifications"); *Estate of Barabin v.*

AstenJohnson, Inc., 740 F.3d 457, 464 (9th Cir. 2014) (en banc) ("[T]he district court failed to assume its role as gatekeeper with respect to [the expert's] testimony."); *United States v. Vallejo*, 237 F.3d 1008, 1019 (9th Cir. 2001) ("The district court never clearly articulated why it excluded this evidence."). Other times, the analytical error has been egregious, like when a court would not let a highly qualified **[—18—]** and experienced doctor comment that prosthetic elbows normally do not wear out in eight months. *See Primiano v. Cook*, 598 F.3d 558, 562–63, 566 (9th Cir. 2010). In rare instances, we have even faulted district courts for being too robotic in applying *Daubert*. *See Wendell v. GlaxoSmithKline LLC*, 858 F.3d 1227, 1233 (9th Cir. 2017) ("The district court looked too narrowly at each individual consideration, without taking into account the broader picture of the experts' overall methodology."). None of those circumstances is applicable here.

At the end of the day, the appropriate way to discredit Dr. Morse's theory was through competing evidence and incisive cross-examination. *See Primiano*, 598 F.3d at 564 ("Shaky but admissible evidence is to be attacked by cross examination, contrary evidence, and attention to the burden of proof, not exclusion."). Indeed, many of the vessel owner's complaints focus on statements made by Dr. Morse at trial. The best medicine was adversarial testing, not exclusion, and the vessel owner had abundant opportunity to undermine Dr. Morse's theory and advance its own position. We decline the invitation to severely curtail district courts' discretion to determine reliability under *Daubert* merely because the vessel owner's defense was unsuccessful.

III. Admission of Medical Experts

The district court had a proper basis to admit Murray's medical experts, who testified that Murray's symptoms were caused by the electrical shock. The vessel owner's claim that the experts did not testify on a more-probable-than-not basis is belied by the record. Before trial, Murray's experts confirmed their medical opinion to a reasonable degree of certainty on a more-probable-than-not basis. And, at trial, there were numerous instances in which the experts testified in the same fashion. For example, one of the experts **[—19—]** explicitly referenced the relevant standard in attesting that "[i]t's my opinion that on a *more probable than not* basis [Murray] suffered a brain injury in the accident" and "that [the brain injury] relate[d] directly to th[e] incident [where he was electrocuted]."

Similarly, Murray's experts properly followed the differential diagnosis framework. Differential diagnosis is appropriate to reject alternative causes where it is "grounded in significant clinical experience and examination of medical records and literature." **{-926-}** *Messick v. Novartis Pharm. Corp.*, 747 F.3d 1193, 1199 (9th Cir. 2014). Here, the experts who did not have experience with diffuse electrical injury reviewed the medical literature. The experts fully explained how Murray's symptoms fit with the literature or their experience and were not pre-existing or unrelated to the shock. The district court did not abuse its discretion in admitting the medical testimony.

AFFIRMED.

(Reporter's Note: Opinion dissenting in part follows on p. 416).

[—19—] **{-926-}** BEA, Circuit Judge, dissenting in part:

I concur in the panel majority opinion's conclusions and reasoning regarding the jury instructions, the scope of the defendants' turnover duty, and the admission of the statements by Murray's medical experts. I write separately to dissent on the issue of whether the district court properly admitted the testimony of Dr. Morse regarding the harms that can be caused by low voltage electric shocks. Put simply, the district court failed to exercise properly its gatekeeping function by permitting Dr. Morse's testimony without examining the methodologies by which Dr. Morse identified the injuries purportedly caused by low voltage **[—20—]** shocks, even though Dr. Morse could not explain the causal mechanism by which such injuries occur.

As explained in *Daubert v. Merrell Dow Pharmaceuticals, Inc.*, 509 U.S. 579, 591–93 (1993), which interpreted Federal Rule of Evidence 702, the touchstone for admissibility of testimony by scientific experts is "whether the reasoning or methodology underlying the testimony is scientifically valid." Given the many ways that scientific expertise is developed and applied, however, the Supreme Court and this court have recognized that the four factors articulated in *Daubert* do not constitute a mandatory checklist. *Id.* at 593–95. Rather, each factor should be addressed to the extent relevant to a particular expert's testimony. *Id.*; *see also Kumho Tire Co. v. Carmichael*, 526 U.S. 137, 153 (1999), *Daubert v. Merrell Dow Pharmaceuticals, Inc.*, 43 F.3d 1311, 1317 (9th Cir. 1995). While an appeals court may not second guess the sound judgment of the district court on the admissibility of expert testimony, *Gen. Elec. Co. v. Joiner*, 522 U.S. 136, 146 (1997), the unreasonable failure to consider a relevant *Daubert* factor is an abuse of discretion. *See Kumho Tire*, 526 U.S. at 152.

In this case, the district court evaluated only two of the relevant *Daubert* factors: whether the expert's research was peer reviewed and whether it was generally accepted by other scholars. The district court failed to consider whether Dr. Morse's theory can be and has been tested and the error rate associated with the methodologies he relied upon to render his opinion. The district court did not offer any reasons as to why it overlooked these two factors.

First, the relevance of Dr. Morse's testimony to Murray's injuries is unclear. Dr. Morse testified that Murray's symptoms were consistent with the low voltage shocks he **[—21—]** had studied, but Dr. Morse's expert report discusses low-voltage shocks as being those of 110 volts. This was roughly twice the voltage of the shock experienced by Murray, which was somewhere between 41 and 58 volts. Expert testimony should not be admitted if it is not relevant, which this court has defined as evidence that "logically advance[s] a material aspect of [a] party's case." *Estate of Barabin v. AstenJohnson, Inc.*, 740 F.3d 457, 463 (9th Cir. 2014) (citation omitted). In this case, the definition of "low voltage" relied upon by Dr. Morse (110 volts) differed significantly from the "low voltage" shock suffered by Murray (41–58 volts). Such a difference raises serious doubts **{-927-}** about the relevance to Murray's injuries of Dr. Morse's expertise, a doubt which the district court failed to address in its *Daubert* order. The district court failed to cite any record evidence that would allow Dr. Morse's findings regarding 110 volt shocks to be extrapolated to the lower voltage shock experienced by Murray.

Second, the district court does not explain why the *Daubert* factors of testability and error rate were not relevant to evaluating the admissibility of Dr. Morse's expert testimony. As Dr. Morse conceded, the mechanism by which the hypothesized injuries resulting from low voltage shocks occur is not understood. Such an admission should reasonably have led the district court to apply greater scrutiny to the methodology by which Dr. Morse arrived at his hypothesis about diffuse injury from low voltage shock. If the mechanism for an injury is not understood, it is that much more important to ensure the reliability of the methods by which a correlation between low voltage shocks and certain injuries was identified. Instead, the district court ignored the exact *Daubert* factors that evaluate the rigor of these methodologies. Namely, the district court failed to evaluate whether the theory or technique in question "can be **[—22—]** (and has been) tested." *Daubert*, 509 U.S. at 593. While Dr. Morse's hypothesis that low voltage shocks cause certain injuries can be tested, the record evidence does not establish that Dr. Morse's theory was tested either through animal testing or other controlled experiments. Even if Dr. Morse is correct that low voltage shocks cause injury, this record does not establish whether such injuries are commonplace or extremely rare results of low voltage shock. In addition, the error rate of the particular research methodologies employed by Dr. Morse to identify the relationship between low voltage shocks and certain injuries was not addressed by the district court. For example, Dr. Morse relies in part on self-reported internet surveys of people who purportedly suffered a low voltage shock. *See* Michael S. Morse et al., *Diffuse Electrical Injury: A Study of 89 Subjects Reporting Long-Term Symptomatology that Is Remote to the Theoretical Current Pathway*, 51 IEEE Transaction on Biomedical Engineering 1449 (2004). By not considering the error rate of such self-reported surveys, the district court ignored the degree to which the survey respondents may have made up or imagined their symptoms, may not have actually received a low voltage electric shock, may have exaggerated their symptoms, or may have misunderstood the questions posed in the survey.

Taken together, the fact that Dr. Morse could not explain the causal mechanism behind the hypothesized relationship between low voltage shocks and certain injuries means that the *Daubert* factors that address the reliability of the methods—such as error rate and testability—used to identify this correlation had special importance in this case. By ignoring these factors, without stating a reasonable basis for such omissions, the district court's *Daubert* analysis in fact merely evaluated the general acceptance of Dr. Morse's theories as demonstrated through certain peer reviewed **[—23—]** articles (functionally the same as the *Frye* test rejected in *Daubert*) and failed to evaluate the methodologies underlying Dr. Morse's opinion. This was an abuse of discretion in its gate-keeping function which the deference owed cannot overcome.

Finally, there are important problems with the analysis performed by the district court of *Daubert* factors of peer review and general acceptance. First, while the district court placed a great deal of weight on the fact that Dr. Morse's research on low voltage shocks had been subject to **{–928–}** peer review, the Supreme Court has explained that the peer review factor is not alone dispositive and even if an expert's research is peer reviewed, a district court must still ensure that the expert's opinion is based on a reliable methodology. *Daubert*, 509 U.S. at 594 ("[t]he fact of publication (or lack thereof) in a peer reviewed journal thus will be a relevant, though not dispositive, consideration"). Moreover, while the scientific literature in the record does establish that some experts accepted Dr. Morse's theories, the record makes clear that this acceptance did not rise to the level of general acceptance as a number of scientists criticized Dr. Morse's theory as controversial or not persuasive, in part because, as discussed above, the mechanism by which injuries from low voltage shocks purportedly occur is not understood. *See Daubert*, 509 U.S. at 594 ("a known technique which has been able to attract only minimal support within the community…may properly be viewed with skepticism" (citation omitted)).

Because the causal mechanism by which low voltage shocks purportedly cause certain injuries is not understood and because the district court did not evaluate the methodologies used by Dr. Morse to identify the posited correlation between low voltage shocks and certain injuries, **[—24—]** the district court failed to carry out its gatekeeping function. *Barabin*, 740 F.3d at 464 ("Just as the district court cannot abdicate its role as gatekeeper, so too must it avoid delegating that role to the jury."). For these reasons, I respectfully dissent.

United States Court of Appeals
for the Ninth Circuit

No. 13-36165

STURGEON
VS.
FROST

On Remand from the United States Supreme Court

Decided: October 2, 2017

Citation: 872 F.3d 927, 5 Adm. R. 418 (9th Cir. 2017).

Before **FARRIS, NELSON,** and **NGUYEN,** Circuit Judges.

[—5—] {-929-} **NGUYEN,** Circuit Judge:

John Sturgeon would like to use his hovercraft in a national preserve to reach moose hunting grounds. The State of Alaska is fine with that;[1] the federal government is not. Sturgeon's case turns on which entity—state or federal—gets to decide the matter. On remand from the Supreme Court, we again conclude that the federal government properly exercised its authority to regulate hovercraft use on the rivers within conservation system units in Alaska.

I.

A.

The Yukon-Charley Rivers National Preserve conservation system unit ("Yukon-Charley") is among the 104 million acres of land in Alaska set aside for preservation purposes by the Alaska National Interest Lands Conservation Act ("ANILCA"), 16 U.S.C. § 3101 *et seq.* (1980). Like other conservation system units created by **[—6—]** ANILCA, Yukon-Charley was drawn around a mix of federal, state, Native Corporation, and private owners.

Within the boundaries of the Yukon-Charley lies a stretch of the Nation River. Sturgeon would like to travel by hovercraft on this part of the river to get to moose hunting grounds located upstream from the preserve. Park Service regulations prohibit the use of hovercraft within "[w]aters subject to the jurisdiction of the United States located within the boundaries of the National Park System . . . without regard to the ownership of submerged lands, tidelands, or lowlands." 36 C.F.R. § 1.2(a)(3); *see id.* § 2.17(e). Alaska permits hovercraft on its waterways. Sturgeon contends that the Nation River belongs to Alaska and that the Park Service has no authority to regulate it. He seeks declaratory **{-930-}** and injunctive relief preventing the Park Service from enforcing its hovercraft ban.

B.

ANILCA balanced the need to protect "the national interest in the scenic, natural, cultural and environmental values on the public lands in Alaska" with the need to provide "adequate opportunity for satisfaction of the economic and social needs of the State of Alaska and its people." 16 U.S.C. § 3101(d). Thus, while ANILCA provided that conservation system units in Alaska generally "shall be administered . . . under the laws governing the administration of [National Park Service system unit] lands," *id.* § 410hh, it "specified that the Park Service could not prohibit on those lands certain activities of particular importance to Alaskans." *Sturgeon v. Frost*, 136 S. Ct. 1061, 1066, 4 Adm. R. 2, 3 (2016). For example, Park Service regulations applicable nationwide prohibit hunting and snowmobiling for the most part, *see* 36 C.F.R. §§ 2.2, 2.18, whereas ANILCA permits, subject to reasonable regulations, "the use **[—7—]** of snowmachines . . . for travel to and from villages and homesites," 16 U.S.C. § 3170(a),

[1] The State of Alaska was previously a party to the litigation in the district court and in this court. In our prior opinion, we held that Alaska lacked standing, vacated the district court's judgment as to the State, and remanded with instructions to dismiss the State for lack of jurisdiction. *Sturgeon v. Masica*, 768 F.3d 1066, 1075, 2 Adm. R. 503, 513 (9th Cir. 2014). Alaska did not seek Supreme Court review of that holding, and the district court amended its judgment to dismiss Alaska for lack of jurisdiction. That judgment being final, it is unaffected by the Supreme Court's vacatur of our prior opinion, *Sturgeon v. Frost*, 136 S. Ct. 1061, 4 Adm. R. 2 (2016). We have considered Alaska's supplemental briefing along with that submitted by the other amici curiae and the remaining parties.

and "the taking of . . . wildlife for sport purposes and subsistence uses," *id.* § 3201.

II.

"Section 103(c) of ANILCA . . . addresses the scope of the Park Service's authority over lands within the boundaries of conservation system units in Alaska." *Sturgeon*, 136 S. Ct. at 1067, 4 Adm. R. at 5. It provides as follows:

> Only those lands within the boundaries of any conservation system unit which are public lands (as such term is defined in this Act) shall be deemed to be included as a portion of such unit. *No lands which, before, on, or after December 2, 1980, are conveyed to the State, to any Native Corporation, or to any private party shall be subject to the regulations applicable solely to public lands within such units.* If the State, a Native Corporation, or other owner desires to convey any such lands, the Secretary may acquire such lands in accordance with applicable law (including this Act), and any such lands shall become part of the unit, and be administered accordingly.

16 U.S.C. § 3103(c) (emphasis added). The parties dispute the meaning of section 103(c) and in particular what it means to "be subject to the regulations applicable solely to public lands within such units."

The key to understanding section 103(c) is the difference between "Federal lands" and "public lands." ANILCA defines "public lands" as "land situated in Alaska which, **[—8—]** after December 2, 1980, are Federal lands" except for land selected by the State of Alaska or a Native Corporation the title to which has not yet been conveyed. *Id.* § 3102(3). Similarly, "Federal land" is defined as "lands the title to which is in the United States after December 2, 1980." *Id.* § 3102(2). Simply put, Federal lands include land selections made by Alaska and Native Corporations but not yet transferred to them. Public lands do not. These land selections, while still formally belonging to the federal government, are not to be regulated as part of conservation system units.

The first sentence of section 103(c) establishes that the land selections by Alaska and Native Corporations are not "deemed to be included as a portion of such unit[s]" because that distinction belongs "[o]nly" to "public lands." Both the first and third sentences refer to public lands as being "a portion of" or "part of" the conservation system units in Alaska. This is distinct from lands that are merely "within such units," a phrase used in the second sentence **{–931–}** as shorthand for lands "within the boundaries of" such units but not necessarily a part of them. Land "within such units" includes public lands, the land selections, and non-federal lands. *See, e.g.*, Solid Waste Sites in Units of the National Park System, 59 Fed. Reg. 65,948, 65,949 (Dec. 22, 1994) ("[T]he phrase 'within the boundaries' is commonly employed to refer to both Federal land and nonfederally owned land or interests in land within the outer boundaries [of] a [National Park System] unit.").

The confusion in the second sentence stems from the awkward placement of "within such units." The phrase is not modified by "solely." *See Sturgeon*, 136 S. Ct. at 1070, 4 Adm. R. at 7. Rather, it modifies "applicable." Thus, "regulations applicable solely to public lands within such units" means **[—9—]** regulations applicable within such units solely to *public* lands—as opposed to *Federal* lands. In other words: regulations that apply only to lands that are deemed part of the units themselves. Outside Alaska, all federally owned lands within conservation system units are deemed part of the unit. *See* 54 U.S.C. § 100501. "Alaska is different." *Sturgeon*, 136 S. Ct. at 1070, 4 Adm. R. at 7.

The import of the second sentence is that Federal lands within conservation system units that have been transferred to a non-federal party—like Federal lands that have been selected for state or tribal use—are not "subject to" regulations specific to the conservation system units.[2] Regulations applicable solely to public lands include Park Service regulations applicable nationwide and Alaska-specific regulations found in ANILCA.[3] These contrast with regulations of general applicability, such as the Clean Air **[—10—]** Act, that also affect non-public lands located within such units, such as the land selections and private lands.

Section 103(c) directly responds to the controversy that "Congress . . . stepped in to settle" when it enacted ANILCA. *Sturgeon*, 136 S. Ct. at 1066, 4 Adm. R. at 3. Many Alaskans "were concerned that . . . new monuments [designated by President Carter] would be subject to restrictive federal regulations." *Id.* at 1065–66, 4 Adm. R. at 3. By exempting Federal lands selected for state or tribal use from being regulated as a part of the unit, ANILCA serves one of its stated goals of providing "adequate opportunity for satisfaction of the economic and social needs of the State of Alaska and its people." 16 U.S.C. § 3101(d).

Of course, regulation by the Park Service serves ANILCA's other goal of providing "sufficient protection for the national interest in the scenic, natural, cultural and environmental values." *Id.* But that goal is expressly limited to "public lands" in Alaska. *Id.* Land that is transferred to or selected for non-federal entities is generally **{-932-}** not subject to the regulation of conservation system units. However, non-public land is still subject to such regulation if the United States retains an interest in it because the land is public to the extent of the interest.[4] That is clear from ANILCA's definition of "land" as "lands, waters, *and interests therein*." *Id.* § 3102(1) (emphasis added). **[—11—]**

ANILCA recognizes that the federal government retains an interest in at least some otherwise non-public lands. It directs the Secretary of the Interior to "develop and transmit to . . . Congress a conservation and management plan for each of the units of the National Park System established or [expanded] by [ANILCA]." *Id.* § 3191(a). One component of the plan is a description of any privately-owned areas within the unit, their purposes, the actual or anticipated activities in the privately-owned areas, the effects of such activities on the unit, and "methods (such as cooperative agreements and *issuance or enforcement of regulations*) of controlling the use of such activities to carry out the policies of [ANILCA] and the purposes for which such unit is established or expanded." *Id.* § 3191(b)(7)(E) (emphasis added). Congress plainly expected that the Park Service could issue regulations governing conservation system units that would affect privately-owned lands.

III.

The hovercraft ban "do[es] not apply on non-federally owned lands and waters . . . located within National Park System boundaries," 36 C.F.R. § 1.2(b), except, as relevant here, on "[w]aters subject to the jurisdiction of the United States," *id.*

---

[2] We previously upheld as reasonable an agency determination that certain regulations specific to Alaska units applied to land selections as well as Federal lands. *See John v. United States* (*Katie John III*), 720 F.3d 1214, 1244–45 (9th Cir. 2013) (construing 36 C.F.R. § 242.4(2)). The basis for this holding was the apparently "inconsistent" directive in section 906(o)(2) of ANILCA: "Until conveyed, all Federal lands within the boundaries of a conservation system unit . . . shall be administered in accordance with the laws applicable to such unit." 43 U.S.C. § 1635(o)(2). Subsection (o), however, concerns land withdrawals—not land selections—and it expressly does not apply to those subsections of § 1635 pertaining to land selections. *See id.* § 1635(o)(1). Regardless, *Katie John III* acknowledged that "[s]ection 102 of ANILCA expressly excludes selected-but-not-yet-conveyed lands from the definition of 'public lands.'" *Katie John III*, 720 F.3d at 1243.

[3] Of course, Park Service regulations applicable to conservation system units nationwide may be modified by Alaska-specific regulations. *See* 36 C.F.R. § 13.2(a).

[4] The parties disagree about the Park Service's authority to regulate lands to and in which the United States has no title or interest by enacting regulations that apply to public and non-public land alike. We need not decide whether such a regulation would be enforceable on non-public land on the ground that it is not "applicable solely to public lands." 16 U.S.C. § 3103(c).

§ 1.2(a)(3), and on "[o]ther . . . waters over which the United States holds a less-than-fee interest, to the extent necessary to fulfill the purpose of the National Park Service administered interest and compatible with the nonfederal interest," *id.* § 1.2(a)(5). The question is whether the Nation River is subject to the jurisdiction or an interest of the United States such that it is public land that the Park Service is authorized to regulate. **[—12—]**

A.

Before Alaska gained statehood, the Submerged Lands Act "release[d] and relinquishe[d] unto [the] States . . . all right, title, and interest of the United States" to "the lands beneath navigable waters within the boundaries of the respective States, and the natural resources within such lands and waters." 43 U.S.C. § 1311(a)–(b). The Alaska Statehood Act secured these rights for Alaska. Pub. L. No. 85-508, § 6(m), 72 Stat. 343 (1958). In addition, Alaska enjoys similar rights under the equal footing doctrine. *See United States v. Alaska*, 521 U.S. 1, 6 (1997). While "the United States can prevent lands beneath navigable waters from passing to a State upon admission to the Union by reserving those lands in federal ownership" for "an appropriate public purpose," *id.* at 33–34; *see also* 43 U.S.C. § 1313(a) (excepting from the Submerged Lands Act "lands expressly retained by . . . the United States when the State entered the Union"), we have held that the Nation River was navigable at statehood and that Alaska took title to the riverbed at that time. **{-933-}** *See Alaska v. United States*, 201 F.3d 1154, 1160, 1166 (9th Cir. 2000).

But lands submerged beneath inland waterways are distinct from the waterways 3themselves.[5] "Ownership [of **[—13—]** submerged lands] may not be necessary for federal regulation of navigable waters . . . ." *Alaska*, 521 U.S. at 42. Under the Submerged Lands Act, "[t]he United States retains all its navigational servitude and rights in and powers of regulation and control of [submerged] lands and navigable waters for the constitutional purposes of commerce, navigation, national defense, and international affairs." 43 U.S.C. § 1314(a).

We have held that the navigational servitude "is not 'public land' within the meaning of ANILCA" because "the United States does not hold title to the . . . servitude." *City of Angoon v. Hodel*, 803 F.2d 1016, 1027 n.6 (9th Cir. 1986) (per curiam) (citing *United States v. Va. Elec. & Power Co.*, 365 U.S. 624, 627–28 (1961)). We expanded that holding in *Alaska v. Babbitt* (*Katie John I*), deciding that Congress did not intend "to exercise its Commerce Clause powers over submerged lands and navigable Alaska waters" when it enacted ANILCA. 72 F.3d 698, 703 (9th Cir. 1995).

Katie John I analyzed the United States' interest in navigable waters in Alaska under the reserved water rights doctrine. Under this doctrine, when the federal government "withdraws its land from the public domain and reserves it for a federal purpose," the government impliedly "reserves appurtenant water then unappropriated to the extent needed to accomplish the purpose of the reservation." *Cappaert v. United States*, 426 U.S. 128, 138 (1976). The United States thus "acquires a reserved right in unappropriated water **[—14—]** which vests on the date of the reservation and is superior to the rights of future appropriators." *Id.*

---

[5] Sturgeon, suggesting otherwise, quotes the Supreme Court's statement that "the Submerged Lands Act transferred 'title to and ownership of' the submerged lands *and waters*." *United States v. California*, 436 U.S. 32, 40 (1978) (emphasis added) (quoting 43 U.S.C. § 1311(a)). We do not understand the Supreme Court to have breezily adopted an interpretation of the Submerged Lands Act at odds with the statute's plain meaning. In contrast to ANILCA, which includes "waters" within the definition of "lands," the Submerged Lands Act distinguishes "lands" from the various "waters" lying above them. 43 U.S.C. § 1301(a). *California* involved a dispute over the right to **[—13—]** license kelp harvesting, *see* 436 U.S. at 35 n.8; neither "ownership of" nor rights to the waters was at issue. Presumably, the Court used "submerged lands and waters" to refer to submerged lands and water *resources*. *See* 43 U.S.C. § 1301(e) ("The term 'natural resources' includes . . . kelp . . . .").

Whether a federally reserved water right is implicit in a federal reservation of public land depends on whether the government intended to reserve unappropriated water. *Id.* at 139. "Intent is inferred if the previously unappropriated waters are necessary to accomplish the purposes for which the reservation was created." *Id.*

In *Katie John I,* we concluded that "[t]he United States has reserved vast parcels of land in Alaska for federal purposes through a myriad of statutes," including ANILCA, and thereby has "implicitly reserved appurtenant waters, including appurtenant navigable waters, to the extent needed to accomplish the purposes of the reservations." 72 F.3d at 703 & n.10. This reservation of water rights gave the United States "interests in some navigable waters." *Id.* at 703. We held that ANILCA's "definition of public lands includes those **{-934-}** navigable waters in which the United States has an interest by virtue of the reserved water rights doctrine." *Id.* In *John v. United States* (*Katie John II*), we decided without discussion that *Katie John I*'s holding "should not be disturbed or altered." 247 F.3d 1032, 1033 (9th Cir. 2001) (en banc) (per curiam).

In *Katie John III,* we considered regulations implementing Title VIII of ANILCA pertaining to subsistence management on public lands, 36 C.F.R. pt. 242. These regulations "included within the definition of 'public lands'"—and thus applied to—"all navigable and non-navigable water within the outer boundaries of . . . 34 listed land units," including Yukon-Charley. *Katie John III,* 720 F.3d at 1232; *see* 36 C.F.R. § 242.3(c)(28). As here, it was argued that State- and privately-owned lands located within a conservation system unit, referred to as **[—15—]** "inholdings," were not public lands and thus not subject to regulation. *Id.* at 1233.

We upheld the agency's inclusion of waters that lie on inholdings in the definition of public lands. *Id.* We reasoned that water rights impliedly acquired by the United States are not forfeited or conveyed to third parties along with the inholdings. *Id.* Because the water bodies were "actually situated within the boundaries of federal reservations," it was "reasonable to conclude that the United States ha[d] an interest in such waters for the primary purposes of the reservations." *Id.*

B.

We are bound under our *Katie John* precedent to reach a similar conclusion here. To begin with, ANILCA's definition of "public lands" applies throughout the statute. It would be anomalous if we treated the regulation at issue in *Katie John III* regarding the geographic scope of regulations implementing Title VIII, 36 C.F.R. § 242.3, as employing a different construction of "public lands" than applicable elsewhere in ANILCA. The regulation does not define "public lands." By merely referencing the term,[6] which is defined globally in the statute, the regulation implies that there is but a single definition. **[—16—]**

While *Katie John III* involved ANILCA's rural subsistence priority, that was only one of the purposes for which ANILCA reserved lands as conservation system units. *Katie John III* recognized that "water rights may be essential to a purpose of the reservation other than subsistence." 720 F.3d at 1240. Just as important was ANILCA's purpose of "provid[ing] sufficient protection for the national interest in the scenic, natural, cultural and environmental values on the public lands in Alaska." 16 U.S.C. § 3101(d).

Three years before the statute's enactment, President Carter withdrew and reserved the land for Yukon-Charley "for the protection of . . . historical, archeological, biological, [and] geological . . . phenomena" including habitat for "isolated wild populations of Dall sheep, moose, bear, wolf, and other large mammals." Proclamation No. 4626, 43 Fed. Reg. 57,113

---

[6] The Title VIII regulations "apply on all public lands" within some conservation system units, *id.* § 242.3(b), but "exclud[e] marine waters" within others, *id.* § 242.3(c). Outside of the enumerated conservation system units, Title VIII regulations "apply on all other public lands, other than to the military, U.S. Coast Guard, and Federal Aviation Administration lands that are closed to access by the general public." *Id.* § 242.3(d).

(Dec. 5, 1978). In particular, he "reserved all water necessary to the proper care and management of those objects protected by [Yukon-Charley] and for [Yukon-Charley's] proper administration." *Id.* at 57,114. In that vein, Congress specified in section 201 of ANILCA that Yukon-Charley "shall **{-935-}** be managed for the following purposes, among others":

> To maintain the environmental integrity of the entire Charley River basin, including streams, lakes and other natural features, *in its undeveloped natural condition* for public benefit and scientific study; to protect habitat for, and populations of, fish and wildlife, including but not limited to the peregrine falcons and other raptorial birds, caribou, **[—17—]** moose, Dall sheep, grizzly bears, and wolves . . . .

16 U.S.C. § 410hh(10) (emphasis added).

Consistent with this intent, Congress has authorized the Secretary of the Interior to "prescribe regulations . . . concerning boating and other activities on or relating to water located within System units, including water subject to the jurisdiction of the United States." 54 U.S.C. § 100751(b). The Park Service's hovercraft ban, applicable to federally managed conservation areas nationwide, "was adopted pursuant to [§] 100751(b)." *Sturgeon*, 136 S. Ct. at 1067, 4 Adm. R. at 4. To be more precise, the hovercraft ban was adopted pursuant to § 100751(b)'s statutory predecessor, which similarly provided the Secretary of the Interior with the authority to "[p]romulgate and enforce regulations concerning boating and other activities on or relating to waters located within areas of the National Park System, including waters subject to the jurisdiction of the United States." 16 U.S.C. § 1a-2(h) (1982).[7] This earlier version was enacted four years before ANILCA. Act to Amend the Administration of the National Park System, Pub. L. No. 94-458, 90 Stat. 1939 (1976). ANILCA specified that it did not in any way affect "any law governing appropriation or use of, or Federal right to, water on lands within the State of Alaska," and did not supersede, modify, or repeal "existing laws applicable to the various Federal agencies which are **[—18—]** authorized to develop or participate in the development of water resources or to exercise licensing or regulatory functions in relation thereto." 16 U.S.C. § 3207(1), (3).

The hovercraft ban is also consistent with Congressional intent. Hovercraft were prohibited "because they provide virtually unlimited access to park areas and introduce a mechanical mode of transportation into locations where the intrusion of motorized equipment by sight or sound is generally inappropriate." General Regulations for Areas Administered by the National Park Service, 48 Fed. Reg. 30,252, 30,258 (June 30, 1983). The hovercraft ban thus serves the purpose of keeping waterways in their "undeveloped natural condition . . . to protect [wildlife] habitat." 16 U.S.C. § 410hh(10).

C.

Sturgeon argues that "[r]eserved water rights are not a 'title' interest." While that is true in a narrow, technical sense, *see Fed. Power Comm'n v. Niagara Mohawk Power Corp.*, 347 U.S. 239, 247 n.10 (1954) ("Neither sovereign nor subject can acquire anything more than a mere usufructuary right [in the water itself] . . . ."), by the same logic the State also lacks a "title" interest in the waters above its riverbeds. Water cannot be owned, *see, e.g.*, 2 Amy K. Kelley, *Waters and Water Rights* § 36.02 (3d ed. 2017) (observing the Supreme Court's impatience "with claims of absolute **{-936-}** 'ownership' by *either* [state or federal] government"), but "the right of [water's] use, as it flows along in a body, may become a property right." *Niagara Mohawk Power Corp.*, 347 U.S. at 247 n.10.

[7] The hovercraft ban was implemented in 1983. *See* General Regulations for Areas Administered by the National Park Service, 48 Fed. Reg. 30,252, 30,258 (June 30, 1983). Section 100751(b) took effect in 2014 when Congress added Title 54 to consolidate "provisions relating to the National Park Service and related programs" in "one distinct place." H.R. Rep. No. 113-44, at 2 (2013).

The word "title" has many meanings. Equitable title, for example, is a beneficial interest in property. *See, e.g.*, *R.T. Vanderbilt Co. v. Babbitt*, 113 F.3d 1061, 1067 n.6 (9th Cir. **[—19—]** 1997) (using the phrases "vested interest" and "equitable title" interchangeably). Thus, "title" to an "interest" in water almost certainly means a vested interest in the water, such as a reserved water right. But even if we were uncertain, *Katie John I* already decided the matter when it held that ANILCA's "definition of public lands includes those navigable waters in which the United States has an interest by virtue of the reserved water rights doctrine." 72 F.3d at 704. That could not be so unless title to an interest in Alaska's navigable waters is in the United States. *See* 16 U.S.C. § 3102(1)–(3).

Sturgeon also argues that "[t]he reserved water rights doctrine is premised on the need for actual use and withdrawal of water" and that the Park Service has shown no need for a specific quantity of water because the water in conservation system units is not scarce. *Katie John III* forecloses that argument. There was similarly "no suggestion that any federal reservation along any Alaskan waters risks being turned into a 'barren waste' . . . , or a substantially diminished pool . . . , or is in any way short of water." 720 F.3d at 1238. For that reason, in determining the geographic scope of the United States' reserved water rights, *Katie John III* "include[d] . . . all the bodies of water on which the United States' reserved rights *could at some point* be enforced—*i.e.*, those waters that are or *may become necessary* to fulfill the primary purposes of the federal reservation at issue." *Id.* at 1231 (emphasis added). Here, one of the reservation's primary purposes is to protect fish. The diminution of water in any of the navigable waters within Yukon-Charley's boundaries would necessarily impact this purpose, giving rise to a reserved water right.

Sturgeon points out that some 18 million acres within ANILCA-established conservation system units, **[—20—]** approximately one-sixth of the total, are land selections for Native Corporations. He worries that federal regulation of navigable waters within the units will result in "economic catastrophe" to native shareholders by "impeding any efforts . . . to productively utilize their lands." Even if true, that is not at issue in this case. Sturgeon lacks standing to assert hypothetical claims on the Native Corporations' behalf. In any event, "Congress clearly did not state in ANILCA that subsistence uses are always more important than . . . other uses of federal lands; rather, it expressly declared that preservation of subsistence resources is *a* public interest and established a framework for reconciliation, where possible, of competing public interests." *Amoco Prod. Co. v. Village of Gambell*, 480 U.S. 531, 545–46 (1987). Should Sturgeon's concerns materialize, they can be resolved in an appropriate case.

IV.

ANILCA section 103(c) does not limit the Park Service from applying the hovercraft ban on the Nation River in Yukon-Charley because, under our *Katie John* precedent, the United States has an implied reservation of water rights, rendering the river public lands. Therefore, the district court's order granting summary judgment to defendants is

AFFIRMED.

(Reporter's Note: Concurring opinion follows on p. 425).

[—20—] {-937-} **NGUYEN**, Circuit Judge, with whom Circuit Judge **NELSON** joins, concurring:

We are bound by our *Katie John* decisions to analyze this case under the reserved water doctrine. That is unfortunate. A reserved water right is the right to a sufficient *volume* of [—21—] water for use in an appropriate federal purpose. *See John v. United States* (*Katie John III*), 720 F.3d 1214, 1226 (9th Cir. 2013) ("[A]pplications of the federal reserved water rights doctrine have focused on the amount of water needed for a specific federal reservation, rather than the locations of water sources that might generally be needed . . . ."). This case has nothing to do with that. Rather, it is about the right to regulate navigation on navigable waters within an Alaska national preserve. That is a Commerce Clause interest and should be analyzed as such.

Alaska v. Babbitt (*Katie John I*), 72 F.3d 698 (9th Cir. 1995), expressed two concerns with analyzing regulatory issues under the navigational servitude or, more generally, the Commerce Clause. One concern was that by treating the federal government's power to regulate under the Commerce Clause as an interest in water, we render ANILCA's definition of Federal lands meaningless because the United States cannot have "title to" such an interest. 72 F.3d at 704. But that is no less true of the United States' ability to have "title to" a reserved water right. *See John v. United States* (*Katie John II*), 247 F.3d 1032, 1047 (9th Cir. 2001) (Kozinski, J., dissenting) ("[A] usufructuary right does not give the United States *title* to the waters or the lands beneath those waters."). And treating either interest—a navigational servitude or a reserved water right—as a property interest to which the United States holds title is a reasonable interpretation of the statute. The Supreme Court has referred to navigable waters as "the public property of the nation" insofar as "[t]he power to regulate commerce comprehends [federal] control for that purpose, and to the extent necessary." *United States v. Rands*, 389 U.S. 121, 123 (1967) (quoting *Gilman v. City of Philadelphia*, 70 U.S. 713, 724–25 (1865)). [—22—]

Katie John I's textual concern misses a larger point: even if the federal interest in navigable waters under the Commerce Clause is not a property right at all, it is a power "paramount to . . . proprietary rights of ownership, or the rights of management, administration, leasing, use, and development of the lands and natural resources [of] the respective States." 43 U.S.C. § 1314(a); *see also New Eng. Power Co. v. New Hampshire*, 455 U.S. 331, 338 n.6 (1982) ("Whatever the extent of the State's proprietary interest in the river, the pre-eminent authority to regulate . . . resides with the Federal Government."). The proper exercise of the Commerce Clause power is "not an invasion of any private property rights in the stream or the lands underlying it." *United States v. Cherokee Nation of Okla.*, 480 U.S. 700, 708 (1987) (quoting *Rands*, 389 U.S. at 123). Thus, whether the navigational servitude is "public land" or not is irrelevant. ANILCA expressly left in place federal jurisdiction to regulate the navigable waters. *See* 16 U.S.C. § 3207 ("Nothing in this Act shall be construed as limiting or restricting the power and authority of the United States or . . . as expanding or diminishing Federal or State jurisdiction, responsibility, interests, or rights in water resources development or control . . . .").

Katie John I's other concern was that reliance on the Commerce Clause would allow "a complete assertion of federal control" over "all [navigable] waters in Alaska." 72 F.3d at 704. But the United States' {-938-} power to regulate activity within the sphere of federal interests on navigable waters is not an exclusive right. States may regulate their waterways to the extent their regulations do not conflict with federal ones. *See Barber v. Hawai'i*, 42 F.3d 1185, 1191 (9th Cir. 1994) ("The purpose of [the Submerged Lands Act] was not for the Federal Government to retain exclusive jurisdiction over navigation of the waters above the [—23—] submerged lands, but for the Federal Government to retain concurrent jurisdiction over those waters."); *see also Courtney v. Goltz*, 736 F.3d 1152, 1160, 1 Adm. R. 428, 432 (9th Cir. 2013) (holding that states may regulate business franchises on navigable waters so long as they do not "encroach on the federal commerce power").

Although *Katie John I* purported to eschew the Commerce Clause as a source of federal regulatory power, it conceded that the reserved water rights doctrine originates in part in the Commerce Clause. 72 F.3d at 703 (citing *Cappaert v. United States*, 426 U.S. 128, 138 (1976)). In fact, the doctrine arises solely from the Commerce Clause insofar as Alaska's navigable waters are concerned. The doctrine's other source, the Property Clause, merely "permits federal regulation of federal lands." *Cappaert*, 426 U.S. at 138 (citing U.S. Const. art. IV, § 3). Alaska's navigable waters are not federal lands in the usual (non-ANILCA) sense because the riverbeds by default now belong to Alaska. It is the Commerce Clause that "permits federal regulation of navigable streams" regardless of who owns the land beneath. *Id.* (citing U.S. Const. art. I, § 8).

Katie John I described its own holding as "inherently unsatisfactory." 72 F.3d at 704. We have since criticized it as a "problematic solution to a complex problem, in that it sanctioned the use of a doctrine ill-fitted to determining which Alaskan waters are 'public lands.'" *Katie John III*, 720 F.3d at 1245. I could not agree more.

I would adopt the well-reasoned approach set forth in Judge Tallman's concurrence to *Katie John II.* Rather than continuing to shove a square peg into a hole we acknowledge is round, we should embrace a Commerce Clause rationale for federal regulation of Alaska's navigable waters.

United States Court of Appeals
for the Ninth Circuit

No. 15-35824

MAKAH INDIAN TRIBE
vs.
QUILEUTE INDIAN TRIBE

Appeal from the United States District Court for the Western District of Washington

Decided: October 23, 2017

Citation: 873 F.3d 1157, 5 Adm. R. 427 (9th Cir. 2017).

Before **HAWKINS** and **McKEOWN**, Circuit Judges, and **FOOTE**, District Judge.*

*The Honorable Elizabeth E. Foote, United States District Judge for the Western District of Louisiana, sitting by designation.

[—5—] {-1159-} McKEOWN, Circuit Judge:

Who would imagine that more than 150 years after the Treaty of Olympia (the "Treaty") was signed between the United States and the Quileute and Quinault tribes, we would be asked to determine whether the "right of taking fish" includes whales and seals? Although scientists tell us sea mammals are not fish,[1] these appeals ask us to go back to the 1855 treaty negotiation and signing and place ourselves in the shoes of two signatory tribes—the Quileute Indian Tribe (the "Quileute") and the Quinault Indian Nation (the "Quinault")—to determine what they intended the Treaty to cover. In light of the evidence presented during the 23-day trial, the district court did not clearly err in its finding that **[—6—]** the Quileute and Quinault understood that the Treaty's preservation of the "right of taking fish" includes whales and seals. The court's extensive factual findings supported its ultimate conclusion that "'fish' as used in the Treaty of Olympia encompasses sea mammals and that evidence of customary harvest of whales and seals at and before treaty time may be the basis for the determination of a tribe's [usual and accustomed fishing grounds]." We affirm the court's judgment on that score. However, we reverse the court's delineation of the fishing boundaries because the lines drawn far exceed the court's underlying factual findings.

Background

This appeal is one of many stemming from the long-running litigation over fishing rights in Western Washington. As we have noted, this litigation has a "lengthy background." *Tulalip Tribes v. Suquamish Indian Tribe*, 794 F.3d 1129, 1131, 3 Adm. R. 577, 577 (9th Cir. 2015). The story began in the mid-1850s, when Governor Isaac Stevens approached the tribes of Western Washington with a proposal that the tribes cede most of their land to the United States but without giving up certain vital rights. His endeavor was successful: from December 1854 to January 1856, the United States entered into a series of similarly-worded treaties with the Washington tribes. Crucial to this appeal, the tribes preserved their right to "tak[e] fish" at all "usual and accustomed grounds and stations." That right has engendered a number of disputes between and among tribes about where each tribe can and cannot fish.

Here we address the Treaty of Olympia, which the Quileute and Quinault (as well as the Hoh Indian Tribe) **[—7—]** signed in July 1855. As with the other Stevens Treaties,[2] the

[1] Modern popular culture recognizes that whales are mammals, not fish. An amusing exchange between two of the characters on *Seinfeld* provides one illustration:

> George: I'm such a huge whale fan. These marine biologists were showing how they communicate with each other with these squeaks and squeals, what a fish!
>
> Jerry: It's a mammal.
>
> George: Whatever.

Seinfeld: The Marine Biologist (NBC television broadcast Feb. 10, 1994).

[2] We refer to the Treaty of Olympia as a "Stevens Treaty," as it was one of the similarly-worded treaties entered into by Governor Stevens between December 1854 and January 1856. In February 1855, Stevens negotiated with the Quinault a draft that formed the basis for the Treaty negotiations. On July 1, 1855, Stevens sent

Treaty protects the tribes' "right of taking **{–1160–}** fish at all usual and accustomed grounds and stations" ("U&A"). Treaty of Olympia, art. III, July 1, 1855–Jan. 25, 1856, 12 Stat. 971, 972. In 1974, Judge Boldt of the Western District of Washington established standards and procedures for determining a tribe's U&A and made U&A determinations for several tribes. *United States v. Washington*, 384 F. Supp. 312 (W.D. Wash. 1974) (*Decision I*), *aff'd*, 520 F.2d 676 (9th Cir. 1975).

This case is one in the ongoing saga arising from Judge Boldt's original decision but presents a slight twist on the usual facts. Rather than asking whether the Quileute and Quinault have presented enough evidence to establish U&A in a particular location, the central issue here is whether evidence of hunting whales and seals can establish where the Quileute and Quinault were "taking fish" at and before treaty time.

Litigation on this issue began in 2009, when the Makah Indian Tribe (the "Makah") followed procedures to invoke the district court's continuing jurisdiction to determine "the location of any of a tribe's usual and accustomed fishing grounds not specifically determined" in *Decision I*. The Makah asked the district court to adjudicate the western boundary of the Quileute's U&A and the Quinault's U&A in the Pacific Ocean. The court held a 23-day trial—exceeding **[—8—]** the length of Judge Boldt's original trial leading to *Decision I*—and issued extensive findings.

Employing the Indian canon of construction, the court considered the Quileute and Quinault's understanding of the Treaty's ambiguous use of the word "fish" and found that, based on the historical and linguistic evidence, the tribes intended the term "fish" to encompass whales and seals. The court then looked at the evidence of pre-treaty Quileute and Quinault whaling and sealing and set the Quileute's U&A boundary at 40 miles offshore and the Quinault's U&A boundary at 30 miles offshore. Both the Makah and the State of Washington appeal.

Analysis

I. Evidence of Whaling and Sealing Is Appropriate to Establish U&A Under the Treaty of Olympia

A. *Makah* Is Not Law of the Case

The crux of this appeal is whether the term "fish" in the Treaty includes whales and seals. The Makah seeks to short-circuit the inquiry by reference to *United States v. Washington (Makah)*, 730 F.2d 1314 (9th Cir. 1984). In the Makah's view, we need not do much analytical heavy-lifting here because we already ruled in *Makah* that evidence of whaling and sealing cannot establish U&A. That reading of the case obscures what was actually decided and ignores a linchpin issue—in *Makah* we considered the Makah's Treaty of Neah Bay, not the Treaty of Olympia.

The two treaties have an important textual difference: unlike the Treaty of Olympia, the Treaty of Neah Bay secures "[t]he right of taking fish *and of whaling or sealing* at usual and accustomed grounds and stations." Treaty of **[—9—]** Neah Bay, art. IV, Jan. 31, 1855, U.S.–Makah, 12 Stat. 939, 940 (emphasis added). In addressing the Treaty of Neah Bay, we concluded that the Makah did not establish that its U&A extends 100 miles from the shore out to sea. *Makah*, 730 F.2d at 1318. Given the express protection of the right to whale and seal, we had no need in *Makah* to separate out fishing from whaling and sealing or to address the significance of different types of evidence. It should be obvious that *Makah* is neither controlling nor informative because the question whether the Treaty of Olympia's "right of taking fish" includes whales and seals was not "decided explicitly or by necessary implication." **{–1161–}** *United States v. Lummi Indian Tribe*, 235 F.3d 443, 452 (9th Cir. 2000). Just as obviously, we cannot simply transport analysis of the Treaty of Neah Bay to the Treaty of Olympia because the member tribes' intent is important to, if not dispositive of, the meaning of particular provisions. *See Choctaw Nation of Indians v.*

Colonel Michael Simmons in his stead to negotiate the Treaty, which Stevens signed on January 25, 1856.

United States, 318 U.S. 423, 432 (1943) (holding that treaties involving Indian tribes "are to be construed, so far as possible, in the sense in which the Indians understood them . . . .").

In *Makah* we described the question presented as "what . . . we find to be the Makahs' usual and accustomed fishing areas." 730 F.2d at 1316. Consistent with that narrow framing of the issue on appeal, in discussing whether the Makah had presented sufficient evidence to establish its U&A out to 100 miles from shore, we explained:

> Ocean fishing was essential to the Makahs at treaty time. The Makahs probably were capable of traveling to 100 miles from shore in 1855. They may have canoed that far for whale and seal or simply to explore. They did go that distance at the turn of the century, **[—10—]** although it is not clear how frequently. About 1900, they fished regularly at areas about 40 miles out, and probably did so in the 1850's.
>
> These facts do not show that their usual and accustomed fishing areas went out 100 miles in 1855. There is no basis for an inference that they customarily fished as far as 100 miles from shore at treaty time.
>
> On the contrary, Dr. Lane [an anthropologist] suggested that the Makahs would travel that distance only when the catch was insufficient closer to shore. The earliest evidence of insufficient catch was Oliver Ides' statement about disappearing halibut when he was young, some 50 years after the treaty. Even under the less stringent standards of proof of this case, we cannot conclude that the Makahs usually and customarily fished 100 miles from shore in 1855.

Id. at 1318.

The first paragraph hones in on the absence in the Makah's evidence of *regular* fishing at 100 miles from shore. Although members of the Makah *"were capable* of traveling to 100 miles from shore" and "[t]hey *may have* canoed that far for whale and seal or simply to explore," at the turn of the century it was *"not clear how frequently"* they fished at that distance. In contrast, we noted that "[a]bout 1900, they fished *regularly* at areas about 40 miles out, and probably did so in the 1850's." Based on those facts and inferences, we held that the Makah's U&A did not extend 100 miles into the ocean. **[—11—]**

The concluding paragraph builds on that analysis, citing to Dr. Lane's suggestion that "the Makahs would travel [100 miles from shore] only when the catch was insufficient closer to shore." Because "[t]he earliest evidence of insufficient catch" came "some 50 years after the treaty," there was no basis to say that the Makah often traveled to the 100-mile mark at or before treaty time. The disparity between the Makah's evidence with respect to 40 miles versus 100 miles drove our conclusion that the Makah did not *"usually and customarily* fish[] 100 miles from shore in 1855."

This is not the first time that we have characterized *Makah* as turning on the extent of the evidence presented. In an appeal involving the Tulalip Tribes, we noted that the "[e]vidence of frequent fishing in the disputed areas is stronger . . . than in the Makah case." *United States v. Lummi Indian Tribe*, 841 F.2d 317, 320 (9th Cir. 1988). While the Makah's evidence provided "no basis for an inference that [the Makah] customarily fished as far as 100 miles from shore at treaty time," **{–1162–}** the Tulalip Tribes' evidence "readily support[ed] an inference that the Tulalips frequently fished the disputed areas." *Id.* This later case reinforces that *Makah* did not explicitly or implicitly decide the question of what role whaling and sealing evidence plays in a U&A determination, let alone address the Treaty of Olympia.

B. The Treaty of Olympia Reserves the Quileute and Quinault's Right to Take Whales and Seals

Having put the *Makah* case in context, we turn to the interpretation of the Treaty of Olympia. The pertinent provision reads: **[—12—]**

> The *right of taking fish at all usual and accustomed grounds and stations* is secured to said Indians in common with all citizens of the Territory, and of erecting temporary houses for the purpose of curing the same; together with the privilege of hunting, gathering roots and berries, and pasturing their horses on all open and unclaimed lands. Provided, however, That they shall not take shell-fish from any beds staked or cultivated by citizens; and provided, also, that they shall alter all stallions not intended for breeding, and shall keep up and confine the stallions themselves.

Treaty of Olympia, *supra,* 12 Stat. at 972 (emphasis added). The parties dispute whether the term "fish"—and the corresponding right to "tak[e] fish"—embraces whales and seals.

1. Textual Ambiguity

The text of the Treaty of Olympia does not nail down whether the term "fish" was meant to include or exclude whales and seals. At the time of signing, "fish" had multiple connotations of varying breadth. For example, Webster's Dictionary simultaneously defined "fish" broadly as "[a]n animal that lives in water" (which would include whales and probably seals) and narrowly as a "name for a class of animals subsisting in water" that "breathe by means of gills, swim by the aid of fins, and are oviparous" (which would exclude whales and seals). *Webster's American Dictionary of the English Language* (1828). Other sources also acknowledged the popular understanding that the word "fish" could cover sea mammals; for example, the Supreme **[—13—]** Court wrote that "For all the purposes of common life, the whale is called a fish, though natural history tells us that he belongs to another order of animals." *In re Fossat*, 69 U.S. 649, 692 (1864).

The context in which the term "fish" is used does nothing to resolve the ambiguity. Although the Treaty preserves the "right of *taking* fish," the action of "taking" is far-reaching and offers no meaningful constraint. Tribes may "tak[e]" whales and seals just as they may "tak[e]" fish. The shellfish proviso—which prohibits the tribes from "tak[ing] shellfish from any beds staked or cultivated by citizens"—is similarly inconclusive, though it tends to point to a broader definition of fish. *See United States v. Washington* (*Shellfish*), 157 F.3d 630, 643 (9th Cir. 1998). We are left uncertain as to whether the Treaty employs the narrow or broad definition.

Nevertheless, the parties' decision to employ capacious language, and particularly the expansive word "fish," provides an indication of the provision's comprehended scope. As we have recognized, if "the Treaty parties intended to limit the harvestable species, the parties would not have chosen the word 'fish'" because that word has "perhaps the widest sweep of any word the drafters could have chosen." *Id.* (citation omitted). Notably, Judge Boldt's original determination of the Quileute's U&A relied on evidence of harvesting sea mammals. *See Decision I*, 384 F. Supp. at 372 (noting that "[a]long the adjacent Pacific Coast Quileutes caught . . . seal, sea lion, porpoise and whale"). **{-1163-}**

The Makah does not advance a competing interpretation of the actual words of the Treaty of Olympia. Instead, it jumps to language in its own Treaty of Neah Bay, which explicitly references the right of "whaling [and] sealing" in addition to the right of "taking fish." The Makah contends **[—14—]** that, to avoid the problem of surplusage, the right of "taking fish" must be construed so as to exclude "whaling [and] sealing." That argument is hard to swallow because we are not even talking about the same treaty.

As the district court observed, the Treaty of Neah Bay is of limited import because it "w[as] negotiated by different individuals and in [a] different context[]."[3] Indeed, the "argument that similar language in two Treaties involving different parties has precisely the same meaning reveals a fundamental misunderstanding of basic principles of treaty construction." *Minnesota v. Mille Lacs Band of Chippewa Indians*, 526 U.S. 172, 202 (1999). Rather than comparing and contrasting language and rights across treaties, courts "must interpret a treaty right in light of the particular tribe's understanding of that right at the time the treaty was made." *United States v. Smiskin*, 487 F.3d 1260, 1267 (9th Cir. 2007).

2. Indian Canon of Construction

Recognizing the ambiguity in the Treaty and underscoring that the Treaty of Neah Bay does not control interpretation of the Treaty of Olympia brings us to the Indian canon of construction. As a general rule, treaties "are to be construed, so far as possible, in the sense in which the Indians understood them," *Choctaw Nation*, 318 U.S. at 432, and "ambiguous provisions [should be] interpreted to their benefit," *Cty. of Oneida v. Oneida Indian Nation*, 470 U.S. 226, 247 (1985). That rule applies to "[t]reaty language **[—15—]** reserving hunting, fishing, and gathering rights." Cohen's Handbook of Federal Indian Law § 18.02, at 1157 (Nell Jessup Newton ed., 2012). The Makah, however, seeks to cut off the Quileute and Quinault's argument from the get-go, asserting that the Indian canon does not apply here because "expand[ing] [the Quileute's and Quinault's] traditional fishing grounds adversely affects Makah." The Makah's contraction of the Indian canon is unwarranted.

Implicit in the Indian canon is the recognition that this principle inures to the benefit of the tribes that are parties to the treaty. As the Supreme Court has explained, the ultimate question is "how the [Indian] *signatories* to the Treaty understood the agreement because we interpret Indian treaties to give effect to the terms as the Indians themselves would have understood them." *Mille Lacs*, 526 U.S. at 196 (emphasis added). The canon is "rooted in the unique trust relationship" between the United States and the sovereign tribes, who stood in an unequal bargaining position. *Cty. of Oneida*, 470 U.S. at 247; *Jones v. Meehan*, 175 U.S. 1, 11 (1899). As a non-signatory party, the Makah cannot usurp application of the Indian canon with respect to the Treaty of Olympia. Such an incursion would undermine tribal sovereignty and the signatory tribes' government-to-government relations. *See Tavares v. Whitehouse*, 851 F.3d 863, 877 (9th Cir. 2017); Cohen's, *supra*, § 2.02, at 117.

The Makah reads our precedent too broadly to advocate for its seemingly **{-1164-}** limitless rule that the Indian canon is inapplicable whenever another tribe would be disadvantaged. Not surprisingly, the Makah cites authority involving tribes claiming contradictory rights under the same statute or treaty; in those circumstances, the Indian canon is indeterminate because the government owes the same legal obligations to all interested tribes and "cannot **[—16—]** favor one tribe over another." *Rancheria v. Jewell*, 776 F.3d 706, 713 (9th Cir. 2015); *Confederated Tribes of Chehalis Indian Reservation v. Washington*, 96 F.3d 334, 340 (9th Cir. 1996).

Here, by contrast, we are faced with an interpretive choice that would favor the signatory tribes on the one hand and the United States on the other. *See Rancheria*, 776 F.3d at 713. That conceptualization of the Indian canon also fits with Judge Boldt's recognition that a tribe may establish U&A in an area "whether or not other tribes then also fished in the same waters." *Decision I*, 384 F. Supp. at 332. To the extent the Indian canon plays a part in understanding the Treaty, it is appropriate to invoke it here. We also note that we would reach the same conclusion without a beneficial preference, as the evidence alone supports a broad interpretation of the Treaty language.

[3] One difference was that Colonel Simmons, sent by Governor Stevens to negotiate the Treaty of Olympia in Stevens's stead, "lacked the authority to tailor provisions in the way that [] Stevens was able to do when negotiating the Treaty of Neah Bay."

3. Intent of Quileute and Quinault

To ascertain the tribes' understanding, courts "may look beyond the written words to the history of the treaty, the negotiations, and the practical construction adopted by the parties." *Water Splash, Inc. v. Menon,* 137 S. Ct. 1504, 1511 (2017) (quoting *Volkswagenwerk Aktiengesellschaft v. Schlunk,* 486 U.S. 694, 700 (1988)). After a 23-day bench trial, followed by 83 pages of Findings of Fact and Conclusions of Law, the district court undertook this task in a thoughtful and comprehensive manner.

Central to our review is the district court's ultimate determination "that the Quinault and Quileute's usual and accustomed fishing locations encompass those grounds and stations where they customarily harvested marine mammals—including whales and fur seals—at and before treaty time." This conclusion rested on the extensive factual **[—17—]** findings of the treaty negotiators' intent—including the finding that the Quileute and Quinault understood the term "fish" covered whales and seals—and the underlying findings of historical fact, which were not clearly erroneous. *See Shellfish,* 157 F.3d at 642.

The general context and tenor of the negotiations is a helpful starting point. Governor Stevens was appointed to negotiate with the tribes to extinguish their claims to Washington land and allow for peaceful cohabitation of Indians and non-Indians. During negotiations, the Indians' main concern was reserving their "freedom to move about to gather food at their usual and accustomed fishing places" because harvesting fish was necessary for survival. Stevens and the other treaty commissioners made assurances throughout the process that the Indians would be able to continue their fishing activities and nowhere indicated that the Indians' existing activities would be restricted or impaired by the treaties.

Stevens's first attempt to reach an agreement with the Quinault in February 1855 at Chehalis River failed for reasons unrelated to this dispute. But in July 1855, the Quileute and Quinault (as well as the Hoh Indian Tribe) entered into the Treaty of Olympia, which protects the tribes' "right of taking fish."

The minutes from the failed negotiations offer some insight into key negotiating points, as the draft treaty from Chehalis River formed the basis for the negotiations **{-1165-}** of the Treaty of Olympia.[4] Like Indians in other Stevens Treaty **[—18—]** negotiations, the Indians at Chehalis River sought to preserve their entire subsistence cycle and worried that they would not be able to feed themselves if they ceded too much land. The commissioners explained that the treaty would confine where the tribes would live but would "not call[] upon [them] to give up their old modes of living and places of seeking food." Stevens informed the tribes that the treaty "secures [their] fish" and permits them to "take fish where [they] have always done so and in common with the whites."

Multiple aspects of the Treaty of Olympia negotiations shed light on the Quileute and Quinault's understanding of the scope of "fish." Although minutes from the negotiations do not exist today, the district court relied on ethnology studies and expert reconstructions of what likely happened at the negotiations. Because the commissioners and tribes did not speak the same languages, they used a limited trade medium of communication called Chinook jargon for translation. Colonel Shaw, the treaty commission's official interpreter, translated provisions and remarks from English to Chinook jargon, then Indian interpreters translated the Chinook jargon into the tribes' native languages.

One linguistic clue provides powerful evidence that the Quileute and Quinault assigned a broad meaning to the use of "fish." The district court found, based on linguist Professor Hoard's testimony, that "[t]he negotiators most likely used the Chinook word 'pish,'" which translates into English as "fish."

[4] The value of the minutes is somewhat diminished because the Quileute was not officially represented at this council; the tribe did, however, send along members to watch.

The court credited Professor Hoard's explanation that the negotiators would have opted for a broad cover term because Chinook language had general terms referring to large groups (like "fish") and specific terms referring to individual species (like "whales," "seals," and "salmon") but no intermediate terms referring to taxonomies (like "finfish" and "sea mammals"). **[—19—]**

The Quileute's and Quinault's corresponding words for "pish" have even wider sweep. Like Chinook jargon, the Quileute and Quinault languages have no intermediate terms for taxonomies. As Professor Hoard explained, the Quileute would likely have used "?aàlita?," which translates as "fish, food, salmon." Similarly, the Quinault's term "Kémken" is defined alternatively as "salmon," "fish," and "food." Because the Quileute and Quinault traditionally harvested whales and seals for food at and before treaty time, these pieces of linguistic evidence strongly support the district court's finding that the tribes "would have understood that the treaty reserved to them the right to take aquatic animals, including . . . sea mammals, as they had customarily done."

The Makah counters that the Chinook, Quileute, and Quinault languages had separate words for "fish," "whales," and "seals" as well as for "fishing," "whaling," and "sealing." But the mere existence of different words does not preclude some overlap in meaning. Such reasoning is as faulty as concluding that "tennis" and "volleyball" are not "sports" because "tennis," "volleyball," and "sports" are different words. Nor does the Makah's identification of practical and cultural differences in the real-world occupations of fishing, whaling, and sealing bridge that gap. Additionally, that the tribes had distinct terms available does not undermine what terms were actually utilized and how the Quileute and Quinault would have translated them. Because the Makah does not dispute that "pish" was used during negotiations and that **{-1166-}** "pish" can mean something as broad as "food" in the Quileute and Quinault languages, it has not shown that the district court's findings were erroneous, let alone clearly erroneous.

The district court made extensive findings regarding fishing and subsistence activities at the time of the treaty. **[—20—]** For both the Quileute and the Quinault, "fishing constituted the principle economic and subsistence activity . . . at and before treaty time." As to the Quinault, "whale, seal, otter, deer, bear, elk, sea-gulls, ducks, geese," and "a variety of shellfish" were among the wide range of animals harvested. Among other witnesses, Dr. Ronald Olson, an ethnologist, described in detail offshore fishing, whaling, and fur sealing. As to the Quileute, Judge Boldt recognized the significant role of oceanic resources and found that before and at treaty time, the Quileute harvested diverse resources, specifically singling out seal, sea lion, porpoise, and whale, among others. Supporting the link between food and whales, the district court related testimony that "[t]he Indians did not want all fish or all whale but liked to get something of everything which they wanted to eat." Multiple witnesses contributed to the detailed findings on Quileute offshore fishing, whaling, and fur sealing.

Evidence of post-treaty activities further supports the view that the Quileute and Quinault (and possibly even the commissioners) understood the Treaty to protect whaling and sealing. No party contests the district court's finding that "[d]uring the post-treaty period, the[] tribes continued to harvest whales and seals from the Pacific Ocean" with active encouragement from government agents. Although the government's acquiescence does not definitively show that the parties believed the right was preserved by the Treaty, the district court rightly noted that this important fact tends to suggest that "both sides believed the right to harvest sea mammals to have been reserved to the tribes."

During the Chehalis River negotiations, neither the tribes nor the commissioners used the term "fish" in a manner inconsistent with its inclusion of whales and seals. The district court identified only two times where the tribes **[—21—]** mentioned sea mammals explicitly—in both instances, the Indians asked for beached whales. Stevens answered one request for beached whales by stating that the tribes "should have the right to fish in common with the whites, and get roots and berries." Stevens replied to the other request with: "[The tribes] of course were to fish etc. as usual. As to whales they were theirs, but wrecks belonged to the owners . . . ." Neither statement is clear as to whether Stevens understood fish and whales to be synonymous or overlapping, but we do not read his statements as drawing an incompatible distinction between the two. The broader understanding finds further support in a book by James Swan, who attended the negotiations and later wrote that "[t]he Indians, however, were not to be restricted to the reservation, but were to be allowed to procure their food as they had always done."

As a practical matter, interpreting "fish" to cover whales and seals also respects the reserved-rights doctrine, which recognizes that treaties reserving fishing rights on previously owned tribal lands do not constitute "a grant of rights to the Indians, but a grant of right from them—a reservation of those not granted." *United States v. Winans*, 198 U.S. 371, 381 (1905); Cohen's, *supra*, § 18.02, at 1156–57. In other words, absent a clear written indication, courts are reluctant to conclude that a tribe has forfeited previously held rights "because the United States treaty drafters had the sophistication and experience to use express **{-1167-}** language for the abrogation of treaty rights." *Mille Lacs*, 526 U.S. at 195. That doctrine favors reading the "right of taking fish" to include the Quileute's and Quinault's established historical whaling and sealing, particularly because there are independent indications that "fish" was understood that expansively. *See Shellfish*, 157 F.3d at 644 (employing the reserved-rights doctrine to assist in understanding the scope **[—22—]** of a treaty provision that could otherwise be read to encompass the right at issue). That practical point further solidifies that the Quileute and Quinault understood the "taking fish" provision to cover whales and seals.

Based on the considerable evidence submitted throughout the lengthy trial, the district court's finding that the Quileute and Quinault intended the Treaty's "right of taking fish" to include whales and seals was neither illogical, implausible, nor contrary to the record. We conclude that the district court properly looked to the tribes' evidence of taking whales and seals to establish the U&A for the Quileute and the Quinault and did not err in its interpretation of the Treaty of Olympia. We do not address or offer commentary on whether the same result would obtain for the "right of taking fish" in other Stevens Treaties.

II. The Quileute and Quinault Have Identified the "Grounds and Stations" Where They Engaged in Whaling and Sealing

The State of Washington raises a separate argument, not joined by the Makah, namely whether the Treaty of Olympia's "grounds and stations" language mandates that the Quileute and Quinault provide evidence of "*specific location[s]* that the[y] regularly and customarily hunted whales or seals." (Emphasis added). This argument falls into the sea.

The State's suggestion that the tribes must identify specific named locations directly conflicts with Judge Boldt's description of "grounds and stations." Judge Boldt defined "stations" as "fixed locations such as the site of a fish wier or a fishing platform or some other narrowly limited area" and "grounds" as "larger areas which may contain numerous stations and other unspecified locations **[—23—]** which . . . could not then have been determined with specific precision and cannot now be so determined." *Decision I*, 384 F. Supp. at 332.

While "stations" concerns particular locations and landmarks, "grounds" is not so limited. By definition, "grounds" includes "unspecified locations which . . . could not then have been determined," vitiating the State's assertion that the tribes must come forward with specific named locations. The State's claim also runs headlong into the practical reality that documentation of Indian fishing in 1855 is scarce, and requiring extensive and precise proof would be "extremely burdensome and perhaps impossible," especially deep in the ocean. *Shellfish*, 157 F.3d at 644. The district court appropriately examined the substantial evidence of ocean whaling and sealing proffered by the Quileute and Quinault to determine that their usual and accustomed "grounds and stations" respectively extend 40 miles offshore and 30 miles offshore.[5]

III. The Longitudinal Lines Do Not Match the District Court's Findings

Having made U&A determinations for the Quileute and Quinault, the district **{–1168–}** court endeavored to draw precise boundaries where the tribes could fish. The parties agreed as to the northern boundaries but "dispute how the parties believe the Western boundary for the Quileute and Quinault should be demarcated as the line proceeds south." The court **[—24—]** decided to use longitudinal lines because it had done so in a prior proceeding with respect to the Makah's boundaries. The court started at the northernmost point of the Quileute's U&A, drew a line 40 miles west, and used that longitudinal position as the western boundary for the entire area. The court did the same with 30 miles for the Quinault. The map below depicts the final result.

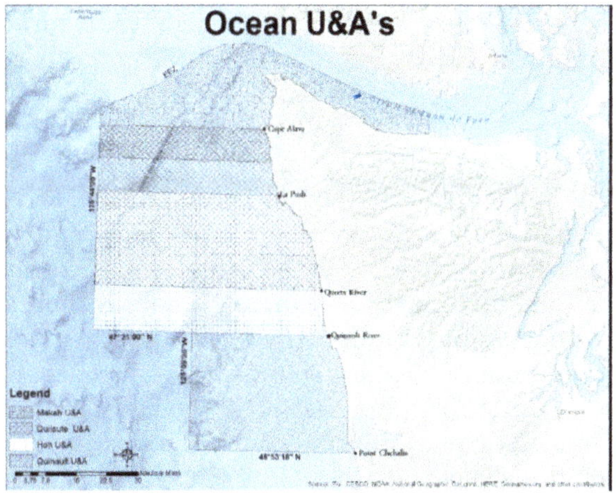

The Makah takes issue with the court's use of a straight vertical line because the coastline trends eastward as one moves south. The Makah calculates the coast-to-longitude distance at the southernmost point as 56 miles for the Quileute and 41 miles for the Quinault. In other words, the Quileute's and Quinault's southernmost boundaries respectively extend 16 miles and 11 miles beyond the court's finding of usual and accustomed fishing, and their total areas respectively sweep in an extra 413 square miles (16.9% of **[—25—]** the total 2,450 square miles) and 387 square miles (17.4% of the total 2,228 miles). The result would be different, for example, had the boundary lines been drawn parallel to the coastline.

These significant disparities underscore the deficiencies in the court's longitudinal boundaries. The language of the Treaty of Olympia and countless judicial opinions spell out that the proceedings are designed to evaluate where the tribes were engaged in usual and accustomed fishing in 1855. After the court made that determination here, it effectively nullified parts of that same determination by creating a boundary containing large swaths of ocean where the Quileute and Quinault did not present sufficient evidence to establish U&A. Of course, practical difficulties mean that courts need not achieve mathematical exactitude in fashioning the boundaries. Nevertheless, the error rate here is too high and sweeps in areas that extend beyond the court's factual findings. In our **{–1169–}** view, there are other

[5] Because no party challenges the adequacy of the submitted whaling and sealing evidence, there is no basis to overturn the district court's 40- and 30-mile findings. Nor do we need to reach the Makah's and the State's separate contention that the evidence was insufficient to establish that the Quileute's customary finfishing extended 20 miles offshore.

solutions that better approximate the court's findings.

The court's stated reason for invoking longitudinal lines was that the approach "is the status quo method of delineating U & A ocean boundaries by this Court" and "equity and fairness demand the same methodology for delineating the boundary at issue here." Although longitudinal lines were used to mark the Makah's western boundaries in a separate case, nothing in that case suggests that longitudinal lines are the required methodology. *See United States v. Washington*, 626 F. Supp. 1405, 1467 (W.D. Wash. 1985). Notably, the court drew longitudinal boundaries there "[o]n the basis of all evidence submitted and reasonable inferences drawn therefrom . . . ." *Id.* In denying a motion for reconsideration of the vertical boundaries, the court stated that the lines appropriately **[—26—]** reflected "with some certainty the extent of the area which the Court intends to encompass within its determination of a tribe's treaty-secured fishing area." *United States v. Washington*, No. 70-9213, Dkt. # 8763, Mem. Op. on Mot. for Recons., at 2 (W.D. Wash. Jan. 27, 1983). As shown in the map below, the lines tracked the coastline (and thus the court's findings) in a way that avoids the problem presented by this case.

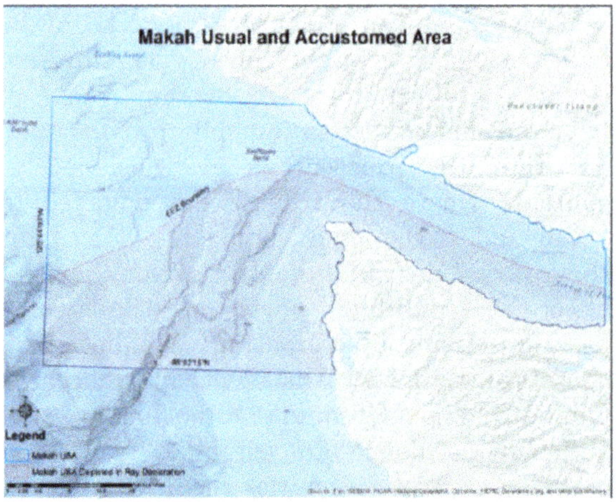

A different approach is warranted here to account for the dissimilarities between the cases. Although the Quileute and Quinault assert that the longitudinal lines also are appropriate because they are supported by the evidence, the boundaries do not reflect the district court's findings. The Quileute and Quinault cannot vastly expand their U&A determinations without accompanying findings by the district court. Nor is the evidentiary gap solved by the **[—27—]** court's general statement that "tribal fishermen did not only fish due west of their villages, but moved in all directions from the coastline."

Accordingly, we reverse the district court's order imposing longitudinal boundaries. Because the law does not dictate any particular approach or remedy that the court should institute, we leave it to the **{-1170-}** court on remand to draw boundaries that are fair and consistent with the court's findings.

AFFIRMED IN PART, REVERSED IN PART, AND REMANDED.

Each party shall bear its own costs on appeal.

United States Court of Appeals for the Ninth Circuit

No. 15-16881

YANG
VS.
DONGWON INDUS. CO.

Appeal from the United States District Court for the District of Guam

Decided: November 30, 2017

Citation: 876 F.3d 996, 5 Adm. R. 437 (9th Cir. 2017).

Before **FISHER, PAEZ,** and **NGUYEN,** Circuit Judges.

[—3—] {-997-} **NGUYEN,** Circuit Judge:

Chang Cheol Yang was a seaman who died when the fishing vessel he worked on sank because of inadequate repairs and an incompetent crew provided by Dongwon Industries Co. Ltd ("Dongwon"). His widow **{-998-}** commenced a wrongful death action against Dongwon on behalf of his three minor children, herself, and his estate. Dongwon moved to compel arbitration based on an employment **[—4—]** agreement between Mr. Yang and the vessel's owner, Majestic Blue Fisheries, LLC ("Majestic"). Because Dongwon is neither a signatory nor a party to the employment agreement, the district court denied Dongwon's motion. We affirm.

I.

In 2008, Dongwon sold the vessel, the F/V Majestic Blue, for $10 to Majestic, which is owned by the same family that owns Dongwon. *In re Majestic Blue Fisheries, LLC*, No. CV 11-00032, 2014 WL 3728556, at *10–11 (D. Guam July 25, 2014). Around that time, Majestic and Dongwon entered into contracts that required Dongwon both to supply the vessel's crew and to supervise its repairs and maintenance. *Id.* at *11. By then, the vessel was the oldest in Dongwon's fleet. *Id.*

On May 21, 2010, after undergoing repairs and despite a known rudder leak, the vessel set sail from Guam with Mr. Yang on board. *Id.* at *22, 32. Three weeks later, on June 14, 2010, the vessel sank in fair weather after being flooded with water. *Id.* at *29, *42. The crew failed to properly respond to the flooding, leaving Captain David Hill to execute critical abandon ship procedures on his own. *Id.* at *30, *48. Shortly after Mr. Yang re-boarded to look for Captain Hill, the vessel sank and both men died. *Id.* at *26.

Following this tragedy, the widows of Mr. Yang and Captain Hill filed separate wrongful death actions with overlapping claims and legal theories. Both widows contend that the vessel's inadequate repairs and incompetent crew rendered it unseaworthy and caused it to sink. The complaints in both actions assert the same four claims against Dongwon and Majestic: (1) a survival action based on negligence for pre-death pain and suffering under the **[—5—]** Jones Act, 46 U.S.C. § 30304; (2) a wrongful death action under general maritime law; (3) a wrongful death action under the Death on the High Seas Act, 46 U.S.C. § 30301 *et seq.*; ("DOHSA"); and (4) a wrongful death action under the Jones Act.

Unencumbered by an arbitration clause, Captain Hill's widow successfully litigated her claims, obtaining a $3.2 million judgment that we affirmed on appeal. *Hill v. Majestic Blue Fisheries, LLC,* 692 F. App'x 871 (9th Cir. 2017). In that case, the district court found that the vessel sank because it was unseaworthy due to shoddy repairs (which resulted in the rudder leak) and an incompetent and untrained crew (who failed to close watertight doors or properly abandon ship). *Majestic Blue*, 2014 WL 3728556 at *30–31, *37, *49. But while Captain Hill's widow accessed a judicial forum for her claims against Majestic and Dongwon without litigating the arbitration issue, Yang's litigation has been stalled by a motion to compel arbitration filed by Dongwon (and joined by Majestic). Dongwon's motion relies on a March 23, 2010 employment agreement in which Majestic agreed to hire Mr. Yang as a Chief Engineer aboard the vessel. The agreement, which contains an arbitration clause, is signed by Mr. Yang and by Dongwon "on behalf of MAJESTIC BLUE FISHERIES, LLC."

The district court compelled arbitration of the claims against Majestic, but denied the motion as to Dongwon. Dongwon now appeals. **[—6—]**

II.

A. The Convention Act Does Not Allow Non-Signatories or Non-Parties to Compel Arbitration

Dongwon seeks to compel arbitration under the Convention on the Recognition **{-999-}** and Enforcement of Foreign Arbitral Awards, 9 U.S.C. § 201 *et seq.* ("Convention Act"), which implements a treaty of the same name[1] ("Convention Treaty") regarding arbitration agreements entered into by foreign entities or individuals. *See Rogers v. Royal Caribbean Cruise Line*, 547 F.3d 1148, 1152–53 (9th Cir. 2008). A party seeking to compel arbitration under the Convention Act must prove the existence and validity of "an agreement in writing within the meaning of the Convention" Treaty. *Balen v. Holland Am. Line Inc.*, 583 F.3d 647, 654–55 (9th Cir. 2009) (citation omitted). The Convention Treaty in turn defines an "agreement in writing" to "include an arbitral clause in a contract or an arbitration agreement, *signed by the parties* or contained in an exchange of letters or telegrams." Convention Treaty, art. II(2) (emphasis added). Recognizing that it is neither a signatory nor a party to Mr. Yang's employment agreement, Dongwon seeks to compel arbitration under the theory that the "signed by the parties" requirement in Article II(2) applies only to "an **[—7—]** arbitration agreement" and not "an arbitral clause in a contract." We disagree.

We do not write on a blank slate. In *Kahn Lucas Lancaster, Inc. v. Lark International Ltd.*, the Second Circuit conducted the first reasoned analysis of Article II(2)'s text and legislative history to reverse an order compelling arbitration because, as here, the arbitration clause in the contract was not signed by one of the litigants. 186 F.3d 210, 215–18 (2d Cir. 1999) *abrogation on other grounds recognized by Sarhank Grp. v. Oracle Corp.*, 404 F.3d 657, 660 n.2 (2d Cir. 2005). Turning first to the text, the court concluded that the comma before the phrase "signed by the parties" signaled that it modified both "an arbitral clause in a contract" and "an arbitration agreement." *Id.* at 217. The court relied on two common canons of construction. First, it explained that, under the rule of punctuation, a modifying phrase that is set off from a series of antecedents by a comma applies to each of those antecedents. *Id.* at 216–17.[2] The court reasoned that interpreting the phrase "signed by the parties" to modify only an "arbitration agreement" rendered the comma superfluous, thereby violating the rule against surplusage. *Id.* at 217. Next, the court considered not only the final English text of the Convention Treaty but also the official French and Spanish texts, each of which used a plural form of the word "signed," consistent with the conclusion that the signature requirement applies not only to an "arbitration agreement" but also to an "arbitral clause in **[—8—]** a contract." *Id.* at 216, 217. Finally, cognizant of the Supreme Court's instruction that an "analysis based only on punctuation is necessarily incomplete," the court analyzed Article II(2)'s legislative history, which confirmed the drafters' intent to apply the signing requirement to both phrases. *Id.* at 216, 218 (quoting *U.S. Nat'l Bank of Or. v. Indep. Ins. Agents of Am., Inc.*, 508 U.S. 439, 454 (1993)). **{-1000-}**

Consistent with *Kahn Lucas*, both we and our sister circuits have recognized the punctuation canon, under which "a qualifying

---

[1] United Nations Convention on the Recognition and Enforcement of Foreign Arbitral Awards, June 10, 1958, 21 U.S.T. 2517, 330 U.N.T.S. 3 *available at* http://www.uncitral.org/pdf/english/texts/arbitration/NY-conv/New-York-Convention-E.pdf. While the Convention Treaty was executed in 1958, *id.*, the Convention Act was not enacted until 1970. *Rogers*, 547 F.3d at 1152.

[2] Under the last-antecedent rule, "the series 'A or B with respect to C' contains two items: (1) 'A' and (2) 'B with respect to C.' On the other hand, under the [punctuation canon] the series 'A or B, with respect to C' contains these two items: (1) 'A with respect to C' and (2) 'B with respect to C.'" *Stepnowski v. C.I.R.*, 456 F.3d 320, 324 n.7 (3d Cir. 2006) (citing *Kahn Lucas*, 186 F.3d at 216 n.1).

phrase is supposed to apply to all antecedents instead of only to the immediately preceding one [where the phrase] is separated from the antecedents by a comma." *Davis v. Devanlay Retail Grp., Inc.*, 785 F.3d 359, 364 n.2 (9th Cir. 2015) (applying California law) (citation omitted). In *Davis*, for example, we applied this rule when reasoning that the phrase "[r]equest, or require as a condition to accepting the credit card as payment" indicates that the payment clause would modify only "require," not "request."' *Id.* at 364–65; *see also Am. Int'l Grp., Inc. v. Bank of Am. Corp.*, 712 F.3d 775, 781–82 (2d Cir. 2013) ("When there is no comma, . . . the subsequent modifier is ordinarily understood to apply only to its last antecedent. When a comma is included, . . . the modifier is generally understood to apply to the entire series."); *Finisar Corp. v. DirecTV Grp., Inc.*, 523 F.3d 1323, 1336 (Fed. Cir. 2008) ("[W]hen a modifier is set off from a series of antecedents by a comma, the modifier should be read to apply to each of those antecedents.") (internal quotation marks omitted) (quoting *Kahn Lucas*, 186 F.3d at 215); *Stepnowski v. Comm'r*, 456 F.3d 320, 324 (3d Cir. 2006) ("[W]here there is a comma before a modifying phrase, that phrase modifies all of the items in a series and not just the immediately preceding item."); *Bingham, Ltd. v. United States*, 724 F.2d 921, 925–26 & n.3 (11th Cir. 1984) ("Where the modifier *is* **[—9—]** set off from two or more antecedents by a comma, . . . the comma indicates the drafter's intent that the modifier relate to more than the last antecedent.").[3]

The case relied upon by Dongwon—*Azure v. Morton*, 514 F.2d 897 (9th Cir. 1975)—is not to the contrary. There, we applied the last antecedent rule, not the punctuation rule. *See id.* at 900. Properly applying the punctuation rule here, the signature requirement applies not only to "an arbitration agreement" but also to "an arbitral clause in a contract."

We are persuaded by *Kahn Lucas*'s faithful adherence to the principles of treaty interpretation, which involve examining "the text of the treaty and the context in which the written words are used," as well as "the history of the treaty, the negotiations, and the practical construction adopted by the parties." *E. Airlines, Inc. v. Floyd*, 499 U.S. 530, 534–35 (1991) (internal quotation marks and citations omitted). Dongwon does not challenge *Kahn Lucas*'s detailed analysis of Article II(2)'s legislative history and negotiations. Instead, Dongwon urges us to consider a 2006 recommendation by a United Nations commission that only vaguely addresses Article II(2)'s application and dates more than three decades after the Convention Treaty's 1970 implementation.[4] While Dongwon argues that the **[—10—]** recommendation's **{-1001-}** musings are "persuasive," it then relies on a case that does not support that proposition. In *In re Condor Insurance Ltd.*, the court examined a model law drafted by a United Nations commission that was later implemented almost verbatim via a federal statute expressly instructing courts to "consider its international origin" when interpreting it. 601 F.3d 319, 321–22 (5th Cir. 2010) (quoting 11 U.S.C. § 1508). Here, in contrast, the Convention Treaty was not drafted by the United Nations commission that issued the 2006 recommendation, and its recommendation has never been implemented by Congress. *See Kahn Lucas*, 547 F.3d at 216 (noting that the United Nations Conference on International Commercial Arbitration drafted the Convention Treaty). While we have occasionally interpreted an ambiguous treaty

---

[3] As with the last antecedent rule, the punctuation canon is not absolute. *See U.S. Nat'l Bank of Or. v. Indep. Ins. Agents of Am., Inc.*, 508 U.S. 439, 454-55 (1993).

[4] *See* United Nations Commission on International Trade Law, Recommendation Regarding the Interpretation of Article II, Paragraph 2, and Article VII, Paragraph 1, of the Convention on the Recognition and Enforcement of Foreign Arbitral Awards, U.N. Doc. A/61/17 (July 7, 2006) (recommending that Article II(2) be "applied recognizing that the circumstances described therein are not exhaustive"), available at **[—10—]** http://www.uncitral.org/pdf/english/texts/arbitration/NY-conv/A2E.pdf. Dongwon argues that this 2006 recommendation and Article II(2)'s use of the word "include" show that an agreement in writing "can be formed in multiple ways." But even if that were so, it does not negate the requirement that the agreement—regardless of how it was formed—be "signed by the parties." Convention Treaty, art. II(2).

term in light of the signatory nations' post-ratification understanding, the 2006 recommendation is nothing like the kind of evidence we have found persuasive. *See, e.g., In re 840 140th Ave. NE, Bellevue, Wash.*, 634 F.3d 557, 568 (9th Cir. 2011) (examining decisions by signatory nations' courts).

Moreover, every circuit to consider *Kahn Lucas*'s cogent analysis has adhered to it. *See Standard Bent Glass Corp. v. Glassrobots Oy*, 333 F.3d 440, 449 (3d Cir. 2003) (following *Kahn Lucas* to hold that the Convention Treaty's "signed by the parties" requirement applied to "an arbitral clause within a contract or a separate arbitration agreement"); *Czarina, LLC v. W.F. Poe Syndicate*, 358 F.3d 1286, 1290–91 (11th **[—11—]** Cir. 2004) (following *Kahn Lucas* to affirm the district court's refusal to enforce an arbitration award based on an unsigned arbitration clause). Dongwon nonetheless urges us to follow an outlier decision from the Fifth Circuit, issued before *Kahn Lucas*, which deemed the "signed by the parties" requirement to be inapplicable to an arbitration clause agreed to by the parties. *Sphere Drake Ins. PLC v. Marine Towing, Inc.*, 16 F.3d 666, 669–70 (5th Cir. 1994). That decision cited no authority and provided no analysis, *id.*, and has therefore been rejected by our sister circuits. *See Kahn Lucas*, 186 F.3d at 214, 218; *Standard Bent*, 333 F.3d at 449–50. Moreover, the Fifth Circuit has since expressly adopted the punctuation canon that *Sphere Drake* omitted and *Kahn Lucas* applied. *See Sobranes Recovery Pool I, LLC v. Todd & Hughes Const. Corp.*, 509 F.3d 216, 223 (5th Cir. 2007) ("[W]hen there is a serial list followed by modifying language that is set off from the last item in the list by a comma, this suggests that the modification applies to the whole list and not only the last item.").

Regardless, we need not rely solely on *Kahn Lucas* or its progeny to hold that Dongwon cannot compel arbitration. The Convention Treaty contemplates that only a "party" or "parties to the agreement referred to in article II" may litigate its enforcement. Convention Treaty, art. IV(1), V(1)(a), VI. Indeed, Article II makes clear that arbitration is permissible only where there is "an agreement in writing under which the parties undertake to submit to arbitration all or any differences which have arisen or which may arise between *them*"—not disputes between a party and a non-party. *Id.* at art. II(1) (emphasis added). Dongwon has therefore failed to satisfy not only the "signed by the parties" requirement discussed in *Kahn Lucas* but also the more basic requirement that a litigant be a "party" to the agreement under which it moves to compel. Because the Convention Treaty does not **[—12—]** allow non-signatories or non-parties to compel arbitration, Dongwon cannot do so here.

B. Dongwon Cannot Compel Arbitration on Other Grounds

Nor can Dongwon compel arbitration on grounds other than the Convention **{–1002–}** Treaty. Federal arbitration law is codified in different chapters of Title 9 of the United States Code, and each chapter imposes unique requirements on a party seeking to compel arbitration. *See Rogers*, 547 F.3d at 1152–53. Dongwon moved to compel arbitration only under the second chapter—the Convention Act—but failed to satisfy its requirements. Dongwon did not and cannot seek to compel arbitration under the first chapter—the Federal Arbitration Act ("FAA"), 9 U.S.C. § 1 *et seq.*—because the FAA expressly exempts from its scope any "contracts of employment of seamen." 9 U.S.C. § 1; *Rogers*, 547 F.3d at 1152–53.

The failure to satisfy either the requirements of the Convention Act or the FAA should end the inquiry. But Dongwon urges us to circumvent the Convention Act's requirements by importing into our Convention Act analysis precedent permitting a "litigant who is not a party to an arbitration agreement to invoke arbitration *under the FAA* if the relevant state contract law allows the litigant to enforce the agreement." *Kramer v. Toyota Motor Corp.*, 705 F.3d 1122, 1128 (9th Cir. 2013) (emphasis added).

We reject this doctrinal sleight of hand because the Convention Act and the FAA impose conflicting requirements on a litigant seeking to compel arbitration. While the FAA permits arbitration where an arbitration agreement is enforceable under state law, *id.*, the Convention Act requires a litigant to satisfy additional prerequisites **[—13—]** established by the Convention Treaty. *See Balen*, 583 F.3d at 654–55. One such prerequisite is that the litigant prove the agreement is in writing and "signed by the parties." Convention Treaty, art. II(2). Another is that the dispute at issue be one between the "parties." Convention Treaty, art. II(1). To the extent the FAA provides for arbitration of disputes with non-signatories or non-parties, it conflicts with the Convention Treaty and therefore does not apply. 9 U.S.C. § 208. Accordingly, cases interpreting the FAA as allowing a non-signatory or non-party to compel arbitration where an arbitration agreement is enforceable under state law offer no guidance in interpreting the Convention Act's requirement that an agreement in writing be signed by the parties.

Even if we ignore the Convention Act's requirements and instead look to our precedent interpreting the FAA, Dongwon would still not be entitled to relief. Under that precedent, we first determine, as a threshold matter, which state's contract law governs the agreement at issue. *See Kramer*, 705 F.3d at 1128. Under the relevant California law, none of Dongwon's three theories—equitable estoppel, agency, and alter ego—provide a basis to compel arbitration.[5]

"Equitable estoppel 'precludes a party from claiming the benefits of a contract while simultaneously attempting to avoid the burdens that contract imposes.'" *Comer v. Micor, Inc.*, 436 F.3d 1098, 1101 (9th Cir. 2006) (quoting *Wash.* **[—14—]** *Mut. Fin. Grp., LLC v. Bailey*, 364 F.3d 260, 267 (5th Cir. 2004)). The doctrine does not apply where, as here, a plaintiff "would have a *claim* independent of the existence of the" agreement containing the arbitration provision. *Kramer*, 705 F.3d at 1131 (affirming denial of non-signatory's motion to compel arbitration). Dongwon's contrary argument "erroneously equates" the Complaint's allegation of an employment *relationship* between Mr. Yang and Dongwon **{–1003–}** with reliance upon the employment *agreement* between Mr. Yang and Majestic.[6] *Id.* at 1132. But Yang's DOHSA and general maritime law claims do not require proof of an employer agreement.[7] And, while the Jones Act claims require a finding that Dongwon was an employer, that finding does not require proof of a written employment agreement.[8] Because Yang's claims against Dongwon rely on its acts and omissions—furnishing an unseaworthy vessel and crew—and not on any obligations created by the employment agreement, Dongwon cannot compel arbitration under an equitable estoppel theory. *See Goldman v. KPMG LLP*, 92 Cal. Rptr. 3d 534, 550, 555 (Ct. **[—15—]** App. 2009) (affirming denial of non-signatory's motion to compel arbitration).

The authorities invoked by Dongwon do not suggest a different result. In *Metalcad*, the non-signatory defendant was able to compel arbitration under an equitable estoppel theory because the plaintiff's breach of contract and fraud claims alleged that defendant "caused" the signatory-defendant "to breach the underlying contract" with the plaintiff that contained the arbitration clause. *Metalclad*

[5] Given the absence of Guam cases on point, we follow the Guam Supreme Court's instruction to look to California law as persuasive authority regarding equitable estoppel. *Mobil Oil Guam, Inc. v. Young Ha Lee*, 2004 Guam 9, ¶ 24 n.2 (Guam 2004); *Limtiaco v. Guam Fire Dep't*, 2007 Guam 10, ¶ 58 (Guam 2007).

[6] The Complaint describes an "agent and alter ego" relationship between Dongwon and Majestic and alleges that both were employers for purposes of the Jones Act.

[7] *See Norfolk Shipbuilding & Drydock Corp. v. Garris*, 532 U.S. 811, 819–20 (2001) (recognizing a general "maritime cause of action" for wrongful death against an entity that had never "employed" decedent); *Davis v. Bender Shipbuilding & Repair Co.*, 27 F.3d 426, 428 (9th Cir. 1994) ("DOHSA claims may be pursued against defendants other than employers.").

[8] *See Glynn v. Roy Al Boat Mgmt. Corp.*, 57 F.3d 1495, 1498–99 (9th Cir. 1995) (explaining that employer status under the Jones Act claims may be established based on several factors, including whether the alleged employer hired and controlled the crew), *abrogated on other grounds by Atl. Sounding Co., Inc. v. Townsend*, 557 U.S. 404 (2009).

Corp. v. Ventana Envtl. Organizational P'ship, 1 Cal. Rptr. 3d 328, 337 (Ct. App. 2003). That is the quintessential example of a plaintiff "claiming the benefits of a contract while simultaneously attempting to avoid the burdens that contract imposes." *Kramer*, 705 F.3d at 1128. The other cases relied upon by Dongwon are also inapposite because they do not apply California law[9] and have been overruled or abrogated due to their failure to specify the applicable state law.[10]

Nor can Dongwon compel arbitration based on the Complaint's allegations of an agency or alter ego relationship between Dongwon and Majestic. Not only did **[—16—]** Dongwon waive arguments under these theories by failing to timely raise them in the district court, *see Hendricks & Lewis PLLC v. Clinton*, 766 F.3d 991, 998 (9th Cir. 2014), it affirmatively represented to the district court in related litigation that Dongwon and Majestic were "separate and distinct companies." Where, as here, an alter ego or agency relationship "was expressly disavowed," the non-signatory cannot **{-1004-}** compel arbitration under that theory. *Murphy v. DirecTV, Inc.*, 724 F.3d 1218, 1233 (9th Cir. 2013) (reversing order compelling arbitration). Moreover, Dongwon cannot invoke an alter ego theory to compel arbitration of the statutory claims at issue here because the alter ego rationale "applies only to" breach of contract claims. *Rowe v. Exline*, 63 Cal. Rptr. 3d 787, 794 (Ct. App. 2007) (rejecting non-signatory's argument to compel arbitration of statutory claims under alter ego theory).

Finally, we see no reason to depart from the general rule that the contractual right to compel arbitration "may not be invoked by one who is not a party to the agreement and does not otherwise possess the right to compel arbitration." *Britton v. Co-op Banking Grp.*, 4 F.3d 742, 744 (9th Cir. 1993). Dongwon argues that the state law exceptions to this general rule—equitable estoppel, agency, and alter ego—must be construed in Dongwon's favor given the federal policy in favor of arbitration. But the "public policy in favor of arbitration does not extend to those who are not parties to an arbitration agreement." *Comedy Club, Inc. v. Improv W. Assocs.*, 553 F.3d 1277, 1287 (9th Cir. 2009) (quoting *Buckner v. Tamarin*, 119 Cal. Rptr. 2d. 489, 490 (Ct. App. 2001). That is because the federal policy applies to "the scope of arbitrable issues" and "is inapposite when the question is whether a particular party is bound by the arbitration agreement." *Norcia v. Samsung Telecomm. Am., LLC*, 845 F.3d 1279, 1291 (9th Cir. 2017) (internal quotation **[—17—]** marks and citation omitted) (affirming denial of non-signatory's motion to compel arbitration); *accord Rajagopalan v. NoteWorld, LLC*, 718 F.3d 844, 847 (9th Cir. 2013) (same).

Accordingly, we affirm the district court's denial of Dongwon's motion to compel arbitration.

Costs shall be taxed against Dongwon.

AFFIRMED.

---

[9] *See, e.g., Ragone v. Atl. Video at Manhattan Ctr.*, 595 F.3d 115, 122, 128 (2d Cir. 2010) (citing New York and federal law); *Brown v. Pac. Life Ins.*, 462 F.3d 384, 389 (5th Cir. 2006) (citing Louisiana and federal law).

[10] *See, e.g., MS Dealer Serv. Corp. v. Franklin*, 177 F.3d 942, 948 (11th Cir. 1999) (failing to specify which law applied), abrogated by *Arthur Andersen LLP v. Carlisle*, 556 U.S. 624 (2009) as recognized in *Lawson v. Life of the S. Ins. Co.*, 648 F.3d 1166, 1170–71 (11th Cir. 2011) (rejecting non-signatory's equitable estoppel argument as a basis to compel arbitration because MS Dealer's failure to make "clear that the applicable state law provides the rule of decision" meant that MS Dealer was either overruled or abrogated).

United States Court of Appeals for the Ninth Circuit

No. 15-35661

LOWER ELWHA KLALLAM INDIAN TRIBE
VS.
LUMMI NATION

Appeal from the United States District Court for the Western District of Washington

Decided: December 1, 2017

Citation: 876 F.3d 1004, 5 Adm. R. 443 (9th Cir. 2017).

Before **HAWKINS** and **McKEOWN**, Circuit Judges, and **FOOTE**, District Judge.*

*The Honorable Elizabeth E. Foote, United States District Judge for the Western District of Louisiana, sitting by designation.

[—4—] {-1007-} **McKEOWN**, Circuit Judge:

This appeal asks whether the Treaty of Point Elliott (the "Treaty") reserves to the Lummi Nation (the "Lummi") the right to fish in the waters west of Whidbey Island, Washington. We previously concluded that the Treaty secures the Lummi's right to fish in Admiralty Inlet because the Lummi would have used the Inlet as a passage to travel from its home in the San Juan Islands to present-day Seattle. The same result holds here because the waters at issue are situated directly between the San Juan Islands and Admiralty Inlet and also would have served as a passage to Seattle. We reverse the district court's judgment to the contrary.

Background

The 1855 Treaty of Point Elliott secures the Lummi's "right of taking fish at usual and accustomed grounds and **[—5—]** stations" ("U&A"). Treaty of Point Elliott, art. V, Jan. 22, 1855, 12 Stat. 927, 928. Over 100 years later, Judge Boldt of the Western District of Washington developed a framework for determining U&As for Indian signatories to the Treaty and other similarly worded treaties. *See generally United States v. Washington*, 384 F. Supp. 312 (W.D. Wash. 1974) (*Decision I*), *aff'd*, 520 F.2d 676 (9th Cir. 1975). Litigation over the various tribes' U&As has been ongoing ever since.

Judge Boldt defined a U&A as "every fishing location where members of a tribe customarily fished from time to time at and before treaty times, however distant from the then usual habitat of the tribe, and whether or not other tribes then also fished in the same waters." *Decision I*, 384 F. Supp. at 332. Importantly, a U&A cannot be established by "occasional and incidental trolling" in marine waters "used as thoroughfares for travel." *Id.* at 353. As to the Lummi, Judge Boldt provided some general background on the tribe's fishing and techniques in Finding of Fact 45, and then made a U&A finding in Finding of Fact 46:

> 45. Prior to the Treaty of Point Elliott, the Lummi, Semiahmoo and Samish Indians had been engaged in trade in salmon, halibut and shellfish both with other Indians and with non-Indians. This trade continued after the treaty. At the time of the treaty they maintained prosperous communities by virtue of their ownership of lucrative saltwater fisheries. The single most valuable fish resource was undoubtedly the sockeye, which the Lummis were able to intercept in the Straits on the annual migration of the sockeye from the ocean to the Fraser River. *Lummi Indians developed a highly efficient* **[—6—]** *technique, known as reef netting, for taking large quantities of salmon in salt water.* Aboriginal Indian 'reef netting' differs from present methods and techniques described by the same term. *The Lummis had reef net sites on Orcas Island, San Juan Island, Lummi Island and Fidalgo Island, and near Point Roberts and Sandy Point.* When nature did not provide optimum reef conditions the Indians artificially created them. Reef netting was one of the two most important economic activities engaged in by these Indians, the other being the sale of dog fish oil. These Indians also took spring, silver and humpback salmon and steelhead by gill nets and harpoons near the mouth of the

> Nooksack River, and steelhead by harpoons and basketry traps on Whatcom Creek. They trolled the waters of the San Juan Islands for various species of salmon.
>
> 46. In addition to the reef net locations listed above, the usual and accustomed fishing places of the Lummi Indians at **{-1008-}** treaty times included the marine areas of Northern Puget Sound from the Fraser River south to the present environs of Seattle, and particularly Bellingham Bay. Fresh-water fisheries included the river drainage systems, especially the Nooksack, emptying into the bays from Boundary Bay south to Fidalgo Bay.

Id. at 360–61 (emphases added) (citations omitted). **[—7—]**

These findings formed the foundation of our earlier adjudication of parts of the Lummi's U&A. Notably, we held that Admiralty Inlet was included in the Lummi's U&A but the Strait of Juan de Fuca was excluded. *See United States v. Lummi Indian Tribe*, 235 F.3d 443, 445, 451–52 (9th Cir. 2000) (*Lummi I*). Admiralty Inlet is due south of the waters contested here—the waters west of Whidbey Island. The Strait of Juan de Fuca lies further west of both of those waters.

This dispute began in 2011. The Lower Elwha Klallam Tribe, the Jamestown S'Klallam Tribe, and the Port Gamble S'Klallam Tribe (collectively, the "Lower Elwha") invoked the district court's continuing jurisdiction under *Decision I* to determine whether the Lummi has the right to fish in the waters west of Whidbey Island. The district court granted summary judgment to the Lower Elwha, reasoning that *Lummi I* had determined that the waters west of Whidbey Island are excluded from the Lummi's U&A.

On appeal, we disagreed with the district court's conclusion that the law of the case doctrine applied. *United States v. Lummi Nation*, 763 F.3d 1180, 1185–88, 2 Adm. R. 489, 491–94 (9th Cir. 2014) (*Lummi II*). Examining the decision in *Lummi I*, we noted that while there were some indications that the contested waters were excluded from the Lummi's U&A, there were strong indications pointing the other way too. *Id.* at 1186–87, 2 Adm. R. at 492–94. In particular, *Lummi I*'s geography-based reasoning suggested that "the waters immediately west of northern Whidbey Island *are* a part of the Lummi's U & A." *Id.* at 1187, 2 Adm. R. at 494 (emphasis in original). Thus, we concluded that *Lummi I* had not yet decided the issue explicitly or by "necessary implication." *Id.* at 1187–88, 2 Adm. R. at 494. In other words, the law of the case was not the operative standard. Instead, we remanded for the district court to apply the usual U&A procedures. *Id.*, 2 Adm. R. at 494. **[—8—]**

On remand, the district court reached the same conclusion as it did before—that the disputed waters are not included in the Lummi's U&A—and again granted summary judgment to the Lower Elwha. The court explained that "neither logic nor linguistics would compel the conclusion that the waters to the west of northern Whidbey Island were intended by Judge Boldt to be included in the Lummi U&A."

The Lummi appealed. Reviewing de novo, we reverse. *See Tulalip Tribes v. Suquamish Indian Tribe*, 794 F.3d 1129, 1133, 3 Adm. R. 577, 579 (9th Cir. 2015).

Analysis

This is another chapter in the "ongoing saga" arising from Judge Boldt's original decision. *See Makah Indian Tribe v. Quileute Indian Tribe*, 873 F.3d 1157, 1160, 5 Adm. R. 427, 428 (9th Cir. 2017). In Finding of Fact 46, Judge Boldt stated that "the usual and accustomed fishing places of the Lummi Indians at treaty times included the marine areas of Northern Puget Sound from the Fraser River south to the present environs of Seattle." *Decision I*, 384 F. Supp. at 360. To determine whether the waters west of Whidbey Island are included in the Lummi's U&A, we follow a two-step procedure. At step one, we decide whether a particular finding of fact is ambiguous. *See Upper Skagit Indian*

Tribe v. Washington, 590 F.3d 1020, 1023 (9th Cir. 2010). All parties agree that Finding of **{-1009-}** Fact 46 is ambiguous because it does not clearly include or exclude the disputed waters. At step two, we examine the record before Judge Boldt to clarify his intent. *Id.* Given this standard and our prior case law concerning the Lummi, we conclude that the district court erred in excluding the waters west of Whidbey Island from the Lummi's U&A. **[—9—]**

We also highlight that the district court improperly imposed a heightened standard in holding that logic or linguistics need to "*compel the conclusion*" that contested waters be included in a U&A. (Emphasis added). We do not countenance such a standard because it imposes a nearly insurmountable burden on tribes in view of *Decision I*'s decades-long lookback approach. The better approach is to construe Judge Boldt's language in light of the available evidence.

Our analysis harkens back to *Lummi I*, where we examined whether Admiralty Inlet is part of the Lummi's U&A. We began by noting that Judge Boldt's *Decision I* does not mention Admiralty Inlet at all, so "there [we]re no linguistic clues to compare." 235 F.3d at 452. But we reasoned that, as a matter of geography, Admiralty Inlet fell within the "marine areas of Northern Puget Sound from the Fraser River south to the present environs of Seattle." *Id.* Because "Admiralty Inlet would likely be a passage through which the Lummi would have traveled from the San Juan Islands in the north to the 'present environs of Seattle,'" the disputed area was deemed part of the Lummi's U&A. *Id.*

This case is almost identical. As a linguistic matter, in *Decision I* Judge Boldt does not reference Whidbey Island with respect to the Lummi's or any other tribe's U&A. 384 F. Supp. at 348–82.[1] The only mention of "Whidbey **[—10—]** Island" in *Decision I* comes in a section labeled "DEPARTMENT OF GAME POLICIES AND PRACTICES" and says that "The Game Department permits fishing for steelhead in all marine areas within its regulatory jurisdiction. Saltwater steelhead fisheries are insignificant. Most are located on *Whidbey Island* at Bush Point and Lagoon Point." *Id.* at 393, 398 (emphasis added). That reference does not indicate whether the waters west of Whidbey Island are included in "the marine areas of Northern Puget Sound from the Fraser River south to the present environs of Seattle." *Id.* at 360. Like Admiralty Inlet in *Lummi I*, the disputed area here is "just as likely" to be included in "Northern Puget Sound" as it is to be excluded. 235 F.3d at 452.

Turning to the geographic indicators, as we did in *Lummi I*, there is no doubt that the waters west of Whidbey Island "would likely be a passage through which the Lummi would have traveled from the San Juan Islands in the north to the 'present environs of Seattle.'" *Id.* (quoting *Decision I*, 384 F. Supp. at 360). The nautical path that we traced in *Lummi I* from the San Juan Islands to Seattle cuts right **{-1010-}** through the waters at issue here. *See Lummi I*, 235 F.3d at 452. Indeed, the waters west of Whidbey Island are situated just north of Admiralty Inlet, which is included in the Lummi's U&A, and just south of the waters surrounding the San Juan Islands (such as Haro and Rosario Straits), which are also included in the Lummi's U&A. As we have already observed, "[*Lummi I*'s] reasoning suggests that the waters immediately to the west of northern Whidbey Island would **[—11—]** be included within the Lummi's U & A." *Lummi II*, 763 F.3d at 1187, 2 Adm. R. at 493.

[1] The fact that later U&A decisions for other tribes make explicit reference to "the waters off the west coast of Whidbey Island" does not change our view. *See United States v. Washington*, 626 F. Supp. 1405, 1442–43 (W.D. Wash. 1985); *United States v. Washington*, 459 F. Supp. 1020, 1056–57 (W.D. Wash. 1978), *aff'd*, 645 F.2d 749 (9th Cir. 1981) (describing fishing grounds "off of Whidbey Island's West Beach"). Just as we did not infer that Judge Boldt intended to exclude Admiralty Inlet from the Lummi's U&A simply because U&A decisions after *Decision* **[—10—]** *I* explicitly reference Admiralty Inlet, we decline to make such an inference here concerning the waters west of Whidbey Island. *See Lummi I*, 235 F.3d at 452; *Washington*, 459 F. Supp. at 1059 (stating that the U&A of the Tulalip Tribes includes Admiralty Inlet).

Importantly, expert anthropologist Dr. Barbara Lane tied travel in this corridor to fishing: "The deeper saltwater areas, the Sound, the straits, and the open sea, served as public thoroughfares, and as such, were used as fishing areas by anyone travelling [sic] through such waters." *Tulalip Tribes*, 794 F.3d at 1135, 3 Adm. R. at 581. Dr. Lane also reported that "Lummi fishermen were *accustomed* . . . to visit fisheries as distant as" the endpoints of the path we carved in *Lummi I*, and "utilized" other fisheries in between. (Emphasis added). Judge Boldt lauded Dr. Lane's work as "exceptionally well researched and reported"; Dr. Lane testified extensively at trial and Judge Boldt relied heavily on her report in Finding of Fact 46 and throughout *Decision I*. 384 F. Supp. at 350.

The Lower Elwha's most persuasive argument is that general evidence of travel cannot by itself establish U&As. Judge Boldt defined "usual and accustomed grounds and stations" as "every fishing location where members of a tribe customarily fished from time to time at and before treaty times, however distant from the then usual habitat of the tribe, and whether or not other tribes then also fished in the same waters." *Id.* at 332. He also specified what was not included: "Marine waters were also used as thoroughfares for travel by Indians who trolled en route. Such occasional and incidental trolling was not considered to make the marine waters traveled thereon the usual and accustomed fishing grounds of the transiting Indians." *Id.* at 353 (citations omitted). In the Lower Elwha's view, Judge Boldt's statements stand for the principle that transit through an area is insufficient for a U&A finding.

Although the Lower Elwha's general statement is accurate as far as it goes, in *Lummi II*, we already addressed **[—12—]** and rejected this argument in the specific context of the Lummi's U&A. We held that "the Lummi's use of 'the marine areas of Northern Puget Sound from the Fraser River south to the present environs of Seattle' was more than mere 'occasional and incidental trolling.'" *Lummi II*, 763 F.3d at 1187, 2 Adm. R. at 494. We explained further: "If to 'proceed through Admiralty Inlet' rendered Admiralty Inlet a part of the Lummi U & A, then to proceed from the southern portions of the San Juan Islands to Admiralty Inlet would have the same effect: to render the path a part of the Lummi U & A, just like Admiralty Inlet." *Id.*, 2 Adm. R. at 494. That explanation covers our exact situation and fits within our long-accepted framework, which requires looking at the evidence "before Judge Boldt that the [tribe] fished *or traveled* in the . . . contested waters." *Tulalip Tribes*, 794 F.3d at 1135, 3 Adm. R. at 581 (emphasis added) (citing *Upper Skagit*, 590 F.3d at 1023).[2] **{-1011-}**

We conclude that the waters west of Whidbey Island, which lie between the southern portion of the San Juan Islands and Admiralty Inlet, are encompassed in the Lummi's U&A. In coming to this conclusion, we need not **[—13—]** determine the outer reaches of the Strait of Juan de Fuca for purposes of the Lummi's U&A.

REVERSED AND REMANDED.

---

[2] It is true, as the Lower Elwha points out, that the evidence in *Tulalip Tribes* was more than general evidence of travel. For example, in addition to evidence that the Suquamish "would have passed through the waters west of Whidbey Island, and likely would have fished there while traveling," there was evidence from an expert report that the "Suquamish travelled [sic] to Whidbey Island to fish." 794 F.3d at 1135, 3 Adm. R. at 581. Nevertheless, *Tulalip Tribes* appears to indicate that the general evidence of travel was "some evidence" that was sufficient to satisfy the necessary standard. *See id.*, 3 Adm. R. at 581 ("This general evidence, too, constitutes some evidence before Judge Boldt . . . ."). And, in any event, the Lower Elwha cannot overcome the court's strong statements in *Lummi I* and *Lummi II* that counter its position.

United States Court of Appeals
for the Ninth Circuit

No. 15-72258

VORTEX MARINE CONSTR.
vs.
GRIMM

Appeal from the Benefits Review Board

Decided: December 22, 2017

Citation: 878 F.3d 709, 5 Adm. R. 447 (9th Cir. 2017).

Before **HAWKINS, BERZON,** and **HURWITZ,** Circuit Judges.

[—3—] {-709-} ORDER:

After Vortex Marine Construction and Signal Mutual Indemnity Association dismissed the petition for review, we granted Terry Grimm's motion for an award of attorneys' fees on review and referred the determination of an appropriate amount of fees on review to the Appellate Commissioner. *See* 9th Cir. R. 39-1.9. We also referred to the Appellate Commissioner for a report and recommendation Grimm's supplemental attorney's fees motion, including the issue of entitlement to fees for defending the fee application. The Appellate Commissioner awarded Grimm's attorneys' fees and costs for the petition for review in the amount of **[—4—]** $32,280, and recommended that we award Grimm's attorneys' fees for the fee litigation in the amount of $20,060.

The parties have not requested reconsideration of the Appellate Commissioner's order or objected to the Appellate Commissioner's report and recommendation. We agree with the Appellate Commissioner's determination that *Baker Botts L.L.P. v. ASARCO LLC,* 135 S. Ct. 2158, 2168 (2015), does not prevent an award of attorneys' fees for the fee litigation here under the Longshore and Harbor Workers' Compensation Act ("LHWCA"), 33 U.S.C. § 928(a). In *Baker Botts,* the court held that the text of § 330(a)(1) of the Bankruptcy Code does not shift the costs of adversarial litigation from one side to the other, and it does not **{-710-}** displace the American Rule with respect to fee-defense litigation. *See id.* at 2165–67; *see also Micha v. Sun Life Assurance of Canada, Inc.,* 874 F.3d 1052, 1062 n.2 (9th Cir. 2017) (Berzon, J., concurring). But § 928(a) of the LHWCA is a fee-shifting statute that departs from the American Rule and explicitly shifts to the employer or carrier the responsibility for payment of a reasonable fee for attorney services for the adversarial litigation if the claimant successfully prosecutes the claim. *See Shirrod v. Dir., OWCP,* 809 F.3d 1082, 1084, 1086 (9th Cir. 2015); *see also Baker Botts,* 135 S. Ct. at 2164–65, 2167–68. Under fee-shifting statutes like § 928(a), courts have uniformly declined to treat fee-application and fee-litigation work differently, and have consistently held that time spent establishing the entitlement to and amount of the fee is compensable. *See Baker Botts,* 135 S. Ct. at 2167–68 (citing *Comm'r, INS v. Jean,* 496 U.S. 154, 158, 162 (1990)); *Blixseth v. Yellowstone Mtn. Club,* 854 F.3d 626, 629, 631–32 (9th Cir. 2017) (citing *In re S. Cal. Sunbelt Developers, Inc.,* 608 F.3d 456, 462–64 & n.4 (9th Cir. 2010)). **[—5—]**

Thus, the Appellate Commissioner's order awarding attorneys' fees and costs for the petition for review in the amount of $32,280 in favor of Terry Grimm and against Vortex Marine Construction and Signal Mutual Indemnity Association, and amending the mandate, remains in effect. Accordingly, we hereby award attorneys' fees for the fee litigation in the amount of $20,060 in favor of Terry Grimm and against Vortex Marine Construction and Signal Mutual Indemnity Association. This order amends the court's mandate.

United States Court of Appeals
for the Ninth Circuit

No. 15-35859

CORVUS ENERGY LTD.
VS.
1169997 ONTARIO, LTD.

Appeal from the United States District Court for the Western District of Washington

Decided: December 27, 2017

Citation: 878 F.3d 1144, 5 Adm. R. 448 (9th Cir. 2017).

Before **TALLMAN** and **WATFORD,** Circuit Judges, and **BENITEZ,** District Judge.*

*The Honorable Roger T. Benitez, United States District Judge for the Southern District of California, sitting by designation.

[—3—] {-1144-} PER CURIAM:

Appellant Corvus Energy Ltd. ("Corvus") appeals from the district court's grant of summary judgment for 1169997 Ontario Ltd., d/b/a Aspin Kemp & Associates ("AKA") in its third-party contribution and indemnity action. We have jurisdiction under 28 U.S.C. § 1291, and we review the district court's grant of summary judgment *de novo*. *Colwell v. Bannister*, 763 F.3d 1060, 1065 (9th Cir. 2014).

In 2010, Foss Maritime Co. ("Foss") and Corvus entered into a contract for Corvus to design, build, and install a hybrid power **{-1145-}** system on Foss's vessel, the CAMPBELL FOSS. Foss contracted with AKA to integrate the Corvus hybrid power system into the existing diesel power system. On August 20, 2012, the CAMPBELL FOSS suffered a battery fire in one of the modules provided by Corvus. Corvus alleges that the fire occurred because AKA **[—4—]** disregarded Corvus's instruction regarding the proper charging algorithm. AKA counters that Corvus wrote a defective software algorithm for its battery system. An investigation by a team of representatives of Foss, Corvus, AKA, and the Coast Guard found both Corvus and AKA to be at fault for the fire.

In 2014, Foss brought tort and contract claims against Corvus for damage to its tugboat. After Corvus impleaded AKA, Foss amended its complaint to include AKA as a co-defendant. Foss and AKA thereafter settled with Foss explicitly releasing all claims against Corvus "for liabilities arising from the actions or inaction of [AKA]." Corvus then settled with Foss. AKA successfully moved for summary judgment seeking to dismiss Corvus's third-party contribution and indemnity action against AKA. We affirm.

On appeal, Corvus asserts that it should not be barred from seeking indemnity because (1) Corvus and AKA are not joint tortfeasors and AKA is wholly at fault; (2) Corvus could still be held liable under contract and strict liability theories regardless of fault; and (3) the equities lie with Corvus. We find these arguments unavailing.

In *McDermott, Inc. v. AmClyde*, the Supreme Court addressed the issue of whether non-settling defendants in admiralty cases may seek contribution from a settling defendant. 511 U.S. 202 (1994). Establishing that each co-defendant only bears its own proportionate share of liability, the Court held that "no suits for contribution from the settling defendants are permitted, nor are they necessary, because the nonsettling defendants pay no more than their share of the judgment." *Id.* at 209. In its decision, the Court found "three considerations . . . paramount: consistency with the proportionate fault approach of [earlier case law], promotion of settlement, and judicial economy." *Id.* at 211. **[—5—]**

We have not yet decided whether the *AmClyde* rule applies to suits for indemnity. Corvus argues that it has a right to tort indemnity, which is available if Corvus paid damages for which it and AKA were jointly liable but which were caused almost entirely by AKA, essentially rendering Corvus liable for AKA's actions. *See* Thomas J. Schoenbaum, Admiralty and Maritime Law § 5-19(2)(a) (5th ed. 2017); 2-1 Benedict on Admiralty § 13 (2017). Contractual indemnity is unavailable because the parties agree that there was no express indemnification agreement between Corvus and AKA. Implied contractual indemnity is generally unavailable outside of the context of personal injury, *see Knight v. Alaska Trawl Fisheries*, 154 F.3d 1042, 1046 (9th Cir. 1998); Admiralty and Maritime Law § 5-9, and this action involves only property damage.

Other courts have barred indemnity and contribution actions by co-defendants in contexts where the proportionate share approach governed the allocation of damages. *See Ondimar Transportes Maritimos v. Beatty St. Props., Inc.*, 555 F.3d 184, 187 (5th Cir. 2009) (holding that *AmClyde*'s proportionate liability scheme bars a settling tortfeasor from seeking contribution from a non-settling tortfeasor); *Lexington Ins. Co. v. S.H.R.M. Catering Servs., Inc.*, 567 F.3d 182, 185 (5th Cir. 2009) (holding that a settling tortfeasor may not seek recovery from a non-settling tortfeasor based on an assignment of the property damage claim by the plaintiff); **{–1146–}** *Murphy v. Fla. Keys Elec. Co-op. Ass'n, Inc.*, 329 F.3d 1311, 1315 (11th Cir. 2003) ("No suit for contribution will lie against a nonsettling defendant who is not released from liability, because that defendant remains liable for its proportionate share of damages regardless of the terms of the settlement the other defendant made."); *Koppers Co. v. Aetna Cas. & Sur. Co.*, 98 F.3d 1440, 1453 n.15 (3d Cir. 1996) ("[T]he apportioned share set-off rule is superior **[—6—]** to a rule permitting (or requiring) suits for contribution and indemnity because the former rule promotes both judicial economy and settlement—while also avoiding collusive settlement by placing the burden of a low settlement on the plaintiff.").

Here, the proportionate share approach governed the damages Foss sought from AKA and Corvus. Fault-based tort damages are apportioned by proportionate fault. *See AmClyde*, 511 U.S. at 207–08; *United States v. Reliable Transfer Co.*, 421 U.S. 397, 411 (1975). We have held that strict product liability damages are also apportioned by proportionate fault in the personal injury context, *see Pan-Alaska Fisheries v. Marine Const. & Design Co.*, 565 F.2d 1129, 1138 (9th Cir. 1977), and we see no reason why that rule should not extend to property damage. *See GIC Services v. Freightplus USA*, 866 F.3d 649, 663–64, 5 Adm. R. 287, 295–96 (5th Cir. 2017). Unlike in *Evanow v. M/V Neptune*, 163 F.3d 1108 (9th Cir. 1998), a case on which Corvus relies heavily, there was no salvage contract here that determined the division of damages and no judge- or jury-imposed damage award. *See id.* at 1119.

Therefore, Corvus's assertion that it is not at fault but still could have been held liable under contract or strict liability theories is not persuasive in the maritime context. *See Reliable Transfer Co.*, 421 U.S. at 411. Moreover, its failure to litigate against Foss, as plaintiff, precludes Corvus from disrupting AKA's settlement with Foss for *all* claims related to AKA's wrongdoings. To hold otherwise, would "discourage[] settlement and lead[] to unnecessary *ancillary* litigation." *AmClyde*, 511 U.S. at 211 (emphasis added).

Therefore, because (1) Corvus settled with Foss and no fact-finder made a determination of fault, (2) Foss explicitly released all claims against Corvus related to AKA's **[—7—]** wrongdoing, and (3) allowing Corvus's indemnity action would dissuade settlement, contrary to the Supreme Court's rationale in *AmClyde*, we will not disturb the district court's ruling.

Costs are awarded to Appellee.

AFFIRMED.

This page intentionally left blank

United States Court of Appeals for the Eleventh Circuit

United States Court of Appeals
for the Eleventh Circuit

No. 15-10713

GLOBAL QUEST, LLC
vs.
HORIZON YACHTS, INC.

Appeal from the United States District Court for the Southern District of Florida

Decided: February 24, 2017

Citation: 849 F.3d 1022, 5 Adm. R. 452 (11th Cir. 2017).

Before **MARCUS** and **FAY**, Circuit Judges, and **FRIEDMAN,*** District Judge.

*Honorable Paul L. Friedman, United States District Judge for the District of Columbia, sitting by designation.

[—2—] {-1024-} FRIEDMAN, District Judge:

Plaintiff Global Quest, LLC appeals from the district court's grant of summary judgment to defendants on all but one count of plaintiff's amended complaint and to defendant Horizon Yachts, Inc. on its counterclaim for foreclosure of a promissory note. Plaintiff appeals from the district court's entry of partial final judgment pursuant to Rule 54(b) of the Federal Rules of Civil Procedure.[1] We reverse the district **{-1025-}** court's grant of summary judgment to defendants on Counts I, III, IV, VII, and VIII of plaintiff's amended complaint and the grant of summary judgment to defendant Horizon Yachts, Inc. on its counterclaim.[2]

I. BACKGROUND

Plaintiff purchased a 105 foot luxury super-yacht, specifically a CC-105 Horizon Explorer named "Starlight," from defendant Horizon Yachts, Inc. ("Seller"). The yacht was manufactured by defendant Horizon Yacht Co., Ltd. ("Horizon") and its wholly-owned subsidiary Premier Yacht Co., Ltd. ("Premier") **[—3—]** in Taiwan. While both Horizon and Premier are Taiwanese companies, Seller is an independent U.S. Corporation based in Florida. It is undisputed, however, that the Seller is Horizon's agent and appears to be owned, at least in part, by Horizon and Premier's founder and CEO, John Lu. HORIZON YACHTS, INC., http://www.horizonyachtusa.com (last visited May 10, 2016) ("Horizon Yacht USA is the U.S. agent for Horizon Yachts").

Plaintiff purchased the Starlight for $6,835,000 after negotiating and executing a Purchase and Sale Agreement with Seller, along with an Addendum executed shortly thereafter. That contract, as modified by the Addendum, contains a seemingly self-contradictory provision. The "as is" clause in the original Agreement, paragraph 10, states that "upon closing, buyer will have accepted the vessel in its 'as is' condition. Seller and the brokers have given no warranty, either express or implied, and make no representation as to the condition of the vessel, its fitness for any particular purpose or merchantability, *all of which are disclaimed.*" The Addendum, however, modifies this clause—providing that before the word "Seller," "the following language is inserted: 'Other than the limited express warranty attached here as Exhibit A.'" With this alteration, paragraph 10 thus reads: "Other than the limited express warranty attached here as Exhibit A, Seller and the broker have given no warranty, either express or implied . . . ." Thus, while the original Agreement purported to disclaim all warranties, express or **[—4—]** implied, the Addendum inserted an express limited warranty into the contract. But the Addendum also contains a further provision stating that "[t]he terms of this Acceptance shall govern over any inconsistent terms in the Purchase Agreement which is

[1] "When an action presents more than one claim for relief . . . or when multiple parties are involved, the court may direct entry of a final judgment as to one or more, but fewer than all, claims or parties only if the court expressly determines that there is no just reason for delay." FED. R. CIV. P. 54(b); *see Lloyd Noland Found., Inc. v. Tenet Health Care Corp.*, 483 F.3d 773, 778-80 (11th Cir. 2007).

[2] Plaintiff does not challenge the district court's entry of summary judgment on Counts II, V, VI, IX, and X of the amended complaint. Counts VIII, IX, and X incorrectly are labeled in the amended complaint as IX, X, and XI respectively.

hereby ratified and declared to be in full force and effect."

As stated in the Addendum, Plaintiff was given a limited express warranty, the terms of which were negotiated by the parties as part of the sale. Issued on Seller's letterhead but purporting to be from "Horizon Group," a trade name for Horizon's companies, the limited warranty covers certain manufacturing and design defects for a period of one year from the contract date. It is limited, however, to "covered defects first discovered and reported to Horizon or the Original Selling Dealer." The limited warranty also disclaims "all other express and implied warranties (except title)," and states that "[n]o employee, representative, authorized dealer or agent of Horizon other than an executive officer of Horizon is authorized to **{-1026-}** alter or modify any provision of the Limited Warranty or to make any guaranty, warranty or representation, express or implied, orally or in writing which is contrary to the foregoing." The limited warranty also lists Premier and its contact details on the final page, without any explanation as to their relationship to the warranty.

Plaintiff contends that defendants made numerous false representations regarding the yacht's condition during the negotiation of the sale. Specifically, **[—5—]** plaintiff claims that the yacht was represented to be MCA LY2 compliant and built to DNV standards, both in statements made by Seller's sales representative and on Horizon's webpage advertising the Starlight.[3] Plaintiff claims that after it took possession it quickly discovered that the yacht was not MCA LY2 compliant nor was it built to DNV standards. The yacht had numerous problems that sharply limited the range of the vessel to short distances and also had electrical issues that rendered it unsafe. After defendants refused to repair or address the problems under the warranty, plaintiff filed suit against the three defendants, bringing ten claims under the amended complaint against each defendant: (1) fraud in the inducement; (2) revocation of acceptance under the Magnuson-Moss Warranty Act; (3) breach of the implied warranties of merchantability and usage of trade; (4) breach of the implied warranty of fitness for a particular purpose; (5) breach of a pre-purchase express oral warranty; (6) breach of a post-purchase express oral warranty; (7) breach of the implied warranty of workmanlike performance; (8) breach of the express written limited warranty; (9) rescission of the promissory note executed with the purchase; and (10) an injunction barring defendants from foreclosing on the promissory note or taking possession of the yacht for non-payment. Seller counterclaimed to foreclose on the promissory note. **[—6—]**

The district court entered summary judgment for defendants on all but two claims: the breach of express warranty claims against Horizon and Premier. The district court also entered summary judgment for Seller on its counterclaim to foreclose on the promissory note. Pursuant to Rule 54(b) of the Federal Rules of Civil Procedure, the district court certified the judgment as a partial final judgment for interlocutory review. Plaintiff appeals, challenging the district court's entry of summary judgment as to Counts I, III, IV, VII, and VIII and the counterclaim.

II. DISCUSSION

We review a district court's grant of summary judgment *de novo*. *Stephens v. Mid-Continent Cas. Co.*, 749 F.3d 1318, 1321 (11th Cir. 2014) (citing *Kragor v. Takeda Pharm. Am., Inc.*, 702 F.3d 1304, 1307 (11th Cir. 2012)). Summary judgment is appropriate when the evidence, viewed in the light most favorable to the nonmoving party, presents no genuine issue of material fact and compels judgment as a matter of law. *Id.*; see also FED R. CIV. P. 56(a); *Celotex Corp. v. Catrett*, 477 U.S. 317, 322-23 (1986).

[3] MCA is an acronym for the United Kingdom's Maritime and Coastguard Agency. The agency publishes, among other codes, the Large Commercial Yacht Code, abbreviated "LY2", which is a set of building standards for large yachts. DNV stands for "Det Norske Veritas" and it is the world's largest classification society. The organization sets safety, reliability, and environmental standards for maritime vessels.

Plaintiff challenges the entry of summary judgment as to: (1) the fraudulent inducement claims against all three defendants (Count I); (2) the breach of implied warranty claims against all three defendants **{-1027-}** (Counts III, IV, and VII); and (3) the breach of express warranty claim against Seller, Horizon Yachts, Inc. (Count VIII). Each is addressed in turn. **[—7—]**

A. Fraudulent Inducement: Count I

The district court granted summary judgment to all three defendants on plaintiff's fraudulent inducement claim, relying on Florida precedent holding that a plaintiff "cannot recover for fraudulent oral representations which are covered in or contradicted by a later written agreement." *Sherwin-Williams Co. v. Auto Body Tech. Inc.*, No. 12-23362, 2014 WL 2177961, at *4 (S.D. Fla. May 26, 2014) (citing *Giallo v. New Piper Aircraft, Inc.*, 855 So. 2d 1273, 1275 (Fla. Dist. Ct. App. 2003)). Relying on the "as is" and "entire agreement" clauses in the contract, the district court held that the claim is based on alleged pre-contractual misrepresentations that were expressly contradicted by the later written agreement, concluding that plaintiff could not have relied on the earlier statements as a matter of law due to the conflicting conditions in the agreement.

The district court expressly declined to follow *Oceanic Villas, Inc. v. Godson*, 4 So. 2d 689 (Fla. 1941), which, contrary to the district court's reasoning, held that an "as is" clause does not bar a plaintiff from bringing a fraud claim. Specifically, the Florida Supreme Court in *Oceanic Villas* held that where an agreement is procured by fraud or misrepresentation "every part of the [] contract" is vitiated because "[i]t is well settled that a party can not contract against liability for his own fraud." *Id.* at 690. The district court declined to follow *Oceanic Villas* because, in its view, (1) it "is distinguishable because it did not involve a warranty **[—8—]** disclaimer or address recent Florida law, stating that a party cannot recover in fraud for misrepresentations covered or expressly contradicted in a later written agreement;" (2) it was decided before the enactment of Florida's Uniform Commercial Code in 1965, which permits "as is" clauses and the exclusion of warranties; and (3) the Florida Supreme Court's holdings are "fact intensive and depend on a review of the conditions of the contract as a whole, not just one clause."

Plaintiff argues that the district court erred by refusing to follow *Oceanic Villas* and granting summary judgment to defendants on the fraudulent inducement claim. We agree.

"As a federal court sitting in diversity jurisdiction, we apply the substantive law of the forum state, in this case Florida, alongside federal procedural law." *Horowitch v. Diamond Aircraft Indus., Inc.*, 645 F.3d 1254, 1257 (11th Cir. 2011) (citing *Erie R.R. Co. v. Tompkins*, 304 U.S. 64, 58 (1938)). The Florida Supreme Court "does not intentionally overrule itself sub silentio." *Puryear v. Florida*, 810 So. 2d 901, 905 (Fla. 2002). "Where a court encounters an express holding from [the Florida Supreme] Court on a specific issue . . . , the court is to apply [the] express holding in the former decision until such time as [the Supreme] Court recedes from the express holding." *Id.*; *see also Hoffman v. Jones*, 280 So. 2d 431, 434 (Fla. 1973). The Florida Supreme Court has not overruled *Oceanic Villas*, **[—9—]** explicitly or implicitly. In fact, Florida's intermediate courts of appeal have continued to apply *Oceanic Villas* as recently as 2011. *See, e.g., Lower Fees, Inc. v. Bankrate, Inc.*, 74 So. 3d 517, 519 (Fla. Dist. Ct. App. 2011); *D & M Jupiter, Inc. v. Friedopfer*, 853 So. 2d 485, 488-89 (Fla. Dist. Ct. App. 2003); *Burton v. Linotype Co.*, 556 So. 2d 1126, 1127 (Fla. Dist. Ct. App. 1990); *see also* **{-1028-}** *Carolina Acquisition, LLC v. Double Billed, LLC*, No. 07-61738-CIV, 2009 WL 3190807, at *2 (S.D. Fla. 2009). *Oceanic Villas* therefore remains binding precedent on the law of fraudulent inducement in Florida, a fact unchanged by the more recent case law cited by the district court. And neither the district court nor this Court is "at liberty to disregard binding case law that is so closely on point," and has not been directly overruled by the Florida Supreme Court. *United States v. Clarke*, 780 F.3d 1131, 1133 (11th Cir. 2015) (second alteration in original) (quoting

United States v. Chubbuck, 252 F.3d 1300, 1305 n.7 (11th Cir. 2001)).

Oceanic Villas also is not distinguishable from this case. Nor was its holding "fact intensive" such that its reasoning must be limited to the precise contract provisions it considered. *Oceanic Villas* held that a contract provision, including an "as is" clause, cannot preclude a fraud claim, unless the contract expressly states that it is incontestable on the ground of fraud. 4 So. 2d at 690-91 ("We recognize the rule to be that fraud in the procurement of a contract is ground for rescission and cancellation of any contract unless for consideration or **[—10—]** expediency the parties agree that the contract may not be cancelled or rescinded for such cause."). This rule is directly contrary to the district court's holding that plaintiff's claim is barred by virtue of the provisions of the contract. That the contract at issue in *Oceanic Villas* did not contain a warranty disclaimer is a distinction without a difference. Nothing in *Oceanic Villas* suggests that the result would have been different with a warranty disclaimer, or any other contract provision save a specific disclaimer of liability for fraud. Absent such a disclaimer, no matter the context, "a party can not contract against liability for [its] own fraud." 4 So. 2d at 690.

The district court appears to have confused the threshold question of whether a claim is barred as a matter of law with the later question of whether the evidence is sufficient to survive summary judgment. The Sixth Circuit, applying *Oceanic Villas* in a diversity case, recently explained this distinction as follows:

> Attempting to overcome this conclusion [that its alleged reliance on statements was unreasonable], [Appellant] relies on two Florida cases—*Oceanic Villas, Inc. v. Godson*, 4 So. 2d 689, 690 (Fla. 1941); *Allen v. Stephan Co.*, 784 So. 2d 456 (Fla. Dist. Ct. App. 2000)—to show that a fraud claim can survive an integrated lease. But simply because [Appellant] is not *prohibited* from bringing a fraud claim does not mean [Appellant] can prove the *elements* of its fraud claim. Neither case suggests otherwise. In *Oceanic Villas*, the Florida Supreme Court held that an integration clause similar to the ones at issue here did not "estop[]" the lessee from alleging fraud or "make the contract incontestable because of fraud." *Oceanic Villas, Inc v. Godson*, 4 So. **[—11—]** 2d at 690-91. But the court went on to call an integration clause "evidence[]" that "neither party has relied upon the representation of the other party made prior to the execution of the contract." *Id.* at 691; *accord Cassara v. Bowman*, 186 So. 514, 514 (1939). Here, we have that precise "evidence" *and* [Appellant]s' actual knowledge that Best Buy Mobile would enter the relevant malls or already had done so before any final leases were signed [directly contradicting the alleged fraudulent misrepresentations]. . . . But again, no one here thinks [Appellant]'s claim is barred; the claim just lacks merit."

Beeper Vibes, Inc v. Simon Property Grp., Inc., 600 Fed. App'x 314, 318-19 (6th Cir. Dec. 12, 2014). The "as is" clause and the rest of the Purchase Agreement in this case may constitute evidence against plaintiff's fraud allegations, but plaintiff's **{-1029-}** claims are not precluded as a matter of law.

The confusion over this distinction appears to have led the district court to conclude that two Florida cases, *Faulk v. Weller K-F Cars, Inc.*, 70 So. 2d 578 (Fla. 1954), and *Lou Bachrodt Chevrolet, Inc. v. Savage*, 570 So. 2d 306 (Fla. Dist. Ct. App. 1990), are irreconcilable and that *Faulk* suggests an implicit rejection of *Oceanic Villas*. In *Faulk*, the Florida Supreme Court held that a written guarantee with a clear disclaimer of warranties and representations "negatives the idea of fraudulent misrepresentations" and that plaintiff's "allegations and the proof with reference to fraudulent misrepresentations were wholly insufficient." 70 So. 2d at 579. *Faulk* thus is an illustration of the above distinction—the court did not address whether the claim was barred as a matter of law; the claim just lacked **[—12—]** merit because the allegations and evidence "were wholly insufficient" and the clear contract provisions weighed in the other direction. Similarly, in *Lou*, the Florida District Court of Appeal did not consider whether a claim was barred as a matter of law by a contract provision, but instead found sufficient evidence to affirm a jury verdict because the plaintiff had "produced evidence as to all the elements of fraud in the inducement" despite the existence of an "as is" provision in the contract. 570 So. 2d at 308. Neither *Faulk* nor *Lou* applied the rule from *Oceanic Villas*, and they are irrelevant for our purposes here.

Lastly, the fact that *Oceanic Villas* was decided before Florida's enactment of the Uniform Commercial Code also is of no moment because, although the UCC permits "as is" clauses and warranty disclaimers, it is silent as to the impact, if any, that such contract provisions have on fraud claims. *See Hill v. Florida*, 711 So. 2d 1221, 1224 (Fla. Dist. Ct. App. 1998) ("In the absence of clear constitutional or statutory authority reflecting a change in established law, we do not possess the authority to disregard controlling precedent of the [Florida Supreme Court]."); *see also Hoffman v. Jones*, 280 So. 2d at 434. There is no indication that the Florida legislature intended to overrule *Oceanic Villas* by passing the UCC. *See also Tinker v. De Maria Porsche Audi, Inc.*, 459 So. 2d 487, 491 (Fla. Dist. Ct. App. 1984) (Florida's UCC "states that the pre-Code law with regard to fraud supplements the U.C.C. and is not displaced by the Code, unless a particular **[—13—]** provision specifically provides for such displacement.") (citing Fla. Stat. § 671.103).

Defendants suggest two alternatives bases on which we might affirm the district court. First, defendants maintain that they are entitled to summary judgment because there are no genuine issues of material fact. Specifically, defendants argue that plaintiff has failed to present "any record evidence of the required elements of knowledge and intentional deceit." In fraud cases, however, summary judgment "is rarely proper as the issue so frequently turns on the axis of the circumstances surrounding the complete transaction, including circumstantial evidence of intent and knowledge." *Coastal Investment Properties, Ltd. v. Weber Holdings, LLC*, 930 So. 2d 833, 834 (Fla. Dist. Ct. App. 2006) (quoting *Cohen v. Kravit Estate Buyers, Inc.*, 843 So. 2d 989, 991 (Fla. Dist. Ct. App. 2003)); *see also Burton*, 556 So. 2d at 1129-30 ("Fraud is ordinarily inappropriate for summary disposition; only after a full explanation of the facts and circumstances can the occurrence of fraud be determined."). To establish a claim of fraud in the inducement under Florida law, a plaintiff must establish that: (1) the representor made a false statement concerning a material fact; (2) the representor knew or should have known that **{–1030–}** the representation was false; (3) the representor intended to induce another party to act in reliance on the false statement; and (4) the party acted in justifiable reliance on the representation and was injured as a result. **[—14—]** *Butler v. Yusem*, 44 So. 3d 102, 105 (Fla. 2010) (citing *Johnson v. Davis*, 480 So. 2d 625, 627 (Fla. 1985)). Despite defendants' protestations that there is no direct evidence proving intent and knowledge, suffice it to say that the elements of fraud—particularly including intent and knowledge—may be, and often are, proven by circumstantial evidence. *See, e.g., Bacon & Bacon Mfg. Co. Inc. v. Bonsey Partners*, 62 So. 3d 1285 (Fla Dist. Ct. App. 2011); *Century Properties, Inc. v. Machtinger*, 448 So. 2d 570 (Fla. Dist. Ct. App. 1984). Viewed in the light most favorable to plaintiff, there is sufficient evidence on the elements of fraudulent inducement for this case to proceed to trial.

Internal emails of the defendants indicate knowledge of the yacht's very poor condition, and plaintiff's representative, Paul Queyrel, and its brokers testified in depositions that defendants and their representatives made representations to them during the sales pitch about the condition of the yacht and specifically that it met international standards, which allegedly proved false after delivery. In addition, plaintiff alleges that defendants advertised the yacht, both on the internet and in physical handouts, as being MCA LY2 compliant and built to DNV standards. Plaintiff's representative and its brokers also testified that they discussed these two standards at length with defendants and relied on defendants' written and oral representations, and that defendants were aware that these standards were "the selling point" of the sale. Plaintiff claims that these repeated **[—15—]** representations induced it to purchase the yacht. Plaintiff's representative and its brokers further testified that the yacht was represented to be new, not a used "dealer-demo" as defendants claim, and that when certain problems were discovered prior to the sale, defendants "represented that Horizon would 'take care of' and fix th[e] problem."

The CEO of the Seller, Roger Sowerbutts, denied under oath ever making representations that the yacht was MCA LY2 compliant, denied that defendants were aware of manufacturing defects and damage to the yacht, and claimed that defendants believed the yacht to have been built to DNV standards. Mr. Sowerbutts conceded, however, that defendants' website incorrectly described the yacht as MCA LY2 compliant, despite the fact that the yacht "never was inspected by MCA." There therefore are genuine issues of material fact and evidence sufficient to survive summary judgment as to all four elements of the claim of fraudulent inducement.

Second, defendants argue that the economic loss rule bars plaintiff's claim for fraudulent inducement. The "economic loss rule is a judicially created doctrine that sets forth the circumstances under which a tort action is prohibited if the only damages suffered are economic losses." *Tiara Condominium Assoc., Inc. v. Marsh & McLennan Companies*, 110 So. 3d 399, 401 (Fla. 2013). The rule was designed to prevent the application of tort remedies to traditional contract law damages. *Id.* **[—16—]** The economic loss rule "has its roots in the products liability arena," *id.*, and the Florida Supreme Court recently clarified in *Tiara* that under Florida law "the economic loss rule applies only in the products liability context." *Id.* at 407. The Florida Supreme Court thus "recede[d] from [its] prior rulings to the extent that they [] applied the economic loss rule to cases other than products liability." *Id.*; *see also* **{-1031-}** *Alpha Data Corp. v. HX5, L.L.C.*, 139 So. 3d 907, 910 (Fla. Dist. Ct. App. 2013) (citing *Tiara* and summarily reversing a district court's decision that the economic loss rule barred a fraudulent inducement claim).

Although a fraudulent inducement claim still must be independent of a breach of contract claim, that minimal requirement is readily met here—the fraud allegations are separate and distinct from defendants' performance under the contract. The fraud allegations concern representations about the yacht's condition and certain international building standards. The contract contains no statements about either the international standards or the yacht's condition. Such claims therefore could not form the basis of a breach of contract claim.[4]

B. Breach of Implied Warranties: Counts III, IV, and VII

The district court granted summary judgment to all three defendants—Horizon Yachts, Inc., Horizon Yacht Co., Ltd., and Premier Yacht Co., Ltd.—on **[—17—]** plaintiff's breach of implied warranty claims due to the contract's express disclaimer of all implied warranties. Plaintiff argues that Section 2308(a) of the Magnuson-Moss Warranty Act ("MMWA"), 15 U.S.C. § 2308(a), prohibits a seller from disclaiming implied warranties if an express warranty, including a limited warranty, is given. The district court rejected this argument because "limited warranties are not governed by MMWA." Not so.

The Magnuson-Moss Warranty Act *does* apply to limited warranties. As relevant, Section 2308(a) provides that:

> (a) No supplier may disclaim or modify (except as provided in subsection (b) of this section) any implied warranty to a consumer with respect to such consumer product if . . . such supplier makes any

[4] Because judgment in favor of plaintiff on the fraudulent inducement claim would "vitiate" the contract, we also reverse the grant of summary judgment to the Seller on its counterclaim to foreclose on the promissory note.

written warranty to the consumer with respect to such Consumer Product . . . ."

15 U.S.C. § 2308(a). As Section 2303 of the Act makes clear, the term "written warranty" encompasses both "full" warranties, written warranties that meet "the Federal minimum standards for warranty set forth in section 2304 of [the Act]," and "limited" warranties, written warranties that do not meet the Federal minimum standards. 15 U.S.C. § 2303(a). By its plain language, Section 2308 prohibits sellers from disclaiming implied warranties when either a full or a limited warranty is provided by the seller. *Accord Abraham v. Volkswagen of America, Inc.*, 795 F.2d 238, 248 (2d Cir. 1986) ("Implied warranties . . . may not be disclaimed if a written warranty, "full" or "limited," is given, 15 U.S.C. § 2308(a)."); *Boelens v.* **[—18—]** *Redman Homes, Inc.*, 748 F.2d 1058, 1063 (5th Cir. 1984) ("Although 'limited' warranties are not subject to [the standards of Section 2304], the Act does provide that the terms of a limited warranty may limit the duration of implied warranties only to the duration of the written warranty.") (quoting 15 U.S.C. § 2308). If a jury concludes that one or all of the defendants issued or agreed to be bound by the limited written warranty, the disclaimer of implied warranties therefore would be ineffective to bar plaintiff's claim.[5] **{-1032-}**

Defendants argue in the alternative that Horizon and Premier are entitled to summary judgment because they are not in privity of contract with plaintiff, that only the Seller—Horizon Yachts, Inc.—is. *See Kramer v. Piper Aircraft Corp.*, 520 So. 2d 37, 38 (Fla. 1988) (Florida law requires privity of contract for a breach of implied warranty claim). Because, as we discuss *infra* at 21-25, there is a genuine issue of material fact regarding who issued the limited express warranty (Horizon, Premier, Horizon Yachts, or some combination thereof), there also is a genuine issue of fact regarding privity of contract. Florida courts have found the **[—19—]** privity requirement to be satisfied when a manufacturer directly provides a warranty to, or otherwise has direct contact with, a buyer who purchases from a third party. *See ISK Biotech Corp. v. Douberly*, 640 So. 2d 85 (Fla. Dist. Ct. App. 1994) (finding privity where manufacturer's representative told third-party seller that seller could assure plaintiff that product would not destroy plaintiff's crop); *Cedars of Lebanon Hosp. Corp. v. European X-Ray Distribs. of America, Inc.*, 444 So. 2d 1068, 1072 n.4 (Fla. Dist. Ct. App. 1984) (finding privity where manufacturer's representative made express warranty through direct contacts with the purchaser who bought product from third-party distributor).

Here, a jury could find that Horizon and Premier directly issued to plaintiff a unique limited express warranty that was provided and specifically negotiated as part of the purchase of the yacht they manufactured. *See Cedars of Lebanon*, 444 So. 2d at 1072 ("It seems fundamentally unfair, and anomalous in the extreme, to allow the manufacturer to hide behind the doctrine of privity when the product, which it induced the purchaser to buy, turns out to be worthless."). There also is evidence that the founder and CEO of Horizon and Premier was directly involved in the negotiation of the purchase and limited warranty, it is undisputed that the Seller, Horizon Yachts, is an agent of Horizon. HORIZON YACHTS, INC., http://www.horizonyachtusa.com (last visited May 2, 2016) ("Horizon Yacht USA **[—20—]** is

[5] The district court's reliance on *Bailey v. Monaco Coach Co.*, 350 F. Supp. 2d 1036, 1042 (N.D. Ga. 2004), to reach the opposite conclusion was misplaced. In *Bailey*, the Northern District of Georgia correctly noted that the MMWA distinguishes between full and limited warranties and that "[o]nly full warranties are required to meet the minimum standards set forth in 15 U.S.C. § 2304." 250 F. Supp. 2d at 1042. The court then concluded that "because the law relating to limited warranties is not expressly modified, limited warranties . . . are not governed by Magnuson-Moss but by the Uniform Commercial Code" and went on to discuss relevant state law warranty standards. *Id.* This overly broad statement is correct as to Section 2304—the minimum standards of Section 2304, by definition, apply only to full warranties—but incorrect as to Section 2308, which, as discussed above, does apply to limited warranties.

the U.S. agent for Horizon Yachts").[6] Plaintiff therefore might well be able at trial to establish privity through the agency relationship. *See Ocana v. Ford Motor Co.*, 992 So. 2d 319, 324-25 (Fla. Dist. Ct. App. 2008) (an agency relationship can establish the requisite privity).

C. Breach of Express Limited Warranty: Count VIII

The district court granted summary judgment to the Seller, Horizon Yachts, Inc., on plaintiff's breach of express warranty claim, but not to Horizon Yacht Co., Ltd. or to Premier Yacht Co., Ltd. It held that the Seller did not issue or provide an express limited warranty to plaintiff. The district court concluded that the Addendum did not incorporate the limited express warranty into the contract because: (1) "it would be unreasonable to interpret paragraph ten of the agreement, indicating both that the [Seller] makes no warranties and sells the yacht "AS IS," and to thereafter include a limited warranty by the [Seller];" **{-1033-}** and (2) the Purchase Agreement, Addendum, and limited warranty "indicate[] that [Horizon Yachts] is not part of "Horizon" or "Horizon Group," the party that issued the limited warranty."

We disagree that it would be unreasonable to interpret the Purchase Agreement, as amended by the Addendum, to include both the limited warranty and an "as is" clause. The amended "as is" clause specifically demarcates the **[—21—]** limited warranty as an exception to the clause. And the Addendum states that "[t]he Terms of this Acceptance shall govern over any inconsistent terms in the Purchase Agreement." Thus, to the extent that the original "as is" clause conflicts with the Addendum or the added limited warranty, the Addendum and limited warranty would govern—assuming, of course, that they are a part of the contract—a question to which we now turn.

A collateral document, such as the limited warranty, is deemed to be incorporated by reference into a contract if the contract "(1) specifically provide[s] that it is subject to the incorporated [collateral] document and (2) the collateral document to be incorporated must be sufficiently described or referred to in the incorporating agreement so that the intent of the parties may be ascertained." *BGT Grp., Inc. v. Tradewinds Engine Servs., LLC*, 62 So. 3d 1192, 1194 (Fla. Dist. Ct. App. 2011) (quoting *Kantner v. Boutin*, 624 So. 2d 779, 781 (Fla. Dist. Ct. App. 1993)). The first requirement mandates that "there must be some expression in the incorporating document . . . of an intention to be bound by the collateral document." *Kantner*, 624 So. 2d at 781. As to the second requirement, "[i]t is a generally accepted rule of contract law that, where a writing expressly refers to and sufficiently describes another document, that other document, or so much of it as is referred to, is to be interpreted as part of the writing." *Id.* (quoting *OBS Co. v. Pace Constr. Corp.*, 558 So. 2d 404, 406 (Fla. 1990)). **[—22—]**

Viewing the evidence in the light most favorable to the plaintiff, as we must on summary judgment, we conclude—while it is a very close question—that there are genuine issues of material fact as to whether the limited warranty was incorporated into the contract or whether the Seller, Horizon Yachts, otherwise agreed to be bound by the warranty. Admittedly, the Purchase Agreement and the warranty appear to differentiate between "Buyer" and "Seller [Horizon Yachts]" on the one hand, and the "Horizon Group," on the other, an indication that the Seller, Horizon Yachts, is not a part of the Horizon Group, as the district court found. And paragraph 13 of the warranty suggests that it was not the Seller who issued the warranty and that the Seller did not agree to be bound by it. But this evidence, while strong, conflicts with three pieces of evidence that in our view raise genuine issues of material fact for a jury to resolve.

First, the Purchase Agreement, as amended by the Addendum, states that "[o]ther than the limited express warranty attached here as Exhibit A, Seller and the

[6] Horizon Yachts, Inc. also uses the name "Horizon Yacht USA."

brokers have given no warranty, either express or implied . . . ." This reasonably could be read to mean that the Seller, Horizon Yachts, itself, at least in part, issued the limited express warranty. The Purchase Agreement, together with the Addendum, specifically lists the limited warranty and states that it is attached "as Exhibit A." Moreover, the limited warranty was listed in the Closing Index, along with the Purchase Agreement and the Addendum, as a part of the parties' **[—23—]** agreement. Second, the limited warranty was issued on the Seller's letterhead, and it was negotiated alongside the Purchase Agreement and provided to plaintiff by the **{-1034-}** Seller prior to the execution of the Purchase Agreement. Finally, a jury also could reasonably conclude that the Seller is part of the "Horizon Group" mentioned in the limited warranty—its website states that it is the U.S. agent of Horizon and the Seller appears to be owned, at least in part, by Horizon's founder and CEO.

The Purchase Agreement as a whole thus contains conflicting provisions as to the Seller's relationship with the warranty, and it is bolstered by extrinsic evidence of the Seller's relationship with the other Horizon entities. While there is certainly strong evidence against finding that the Seller, Horizon Yachts, Inc., agreed to be bound by the limited warranty, we believe that there is also sufficient evidence in the record to create a genuine issue of material fact entitling the jury rather than the court to decide that question.

There is one final point to address with respect to the express limited warranty. As noted, the Purchase Agreement states that it is "attached here as Exhibit A," but it was not actually physically attached as an exhibit. Nevertheless, the limited warranty was negotiated by the parties in conjunction with the Purchase Agreement, provided to plaintiff well before the agreement was executed, and was listed in the Closing Index. *See Avatar Properties, Inc. v. Greetham*, 27 So. 3d **[—24—]** 764, 766 (Fla. Dist. Ct. App. 2010) (where a home warranty was not attached to any agreement, language that "the warranty was available for examination at [the seller's] offices and that upon request the warranty would be attached as an exhibit to the purchase and sale agreement" was sufficient to satisfy the second requirement for incorporation by reference). Reading the documents together, a jury could conclude that the parties intended for the Purchase Agreement, Addendum, and limited warranty all to be part of the same contract. *See Phoenix Motor Co. v. Desert Diamond Players Club, Inc.*, 144 So. 3d 694, 697-98 (Fla. Dist. Ct. App. 2014) (holding that documents "executed as part of the same transaction" are incorporated when "they indicate the parties' intent for the [incorporating document] and the [collateral document] to be part of the same contract"); *see also Collins v. Citrus Nat'l Bank*, 641 So. 2d 458, 459 (Fla. Dist. Ct. App. 1994) ("Where two or more documents are executed by the same parties, at or near the same time, in the course of the same transaction, and concern the same subject matter, they will be read and construed together.").

III. CONCLUSION

For the foregoing reasons, we vacate the district court's grant of summary judgment, as to Counts I, III, IV, VII, and VIII and remand for trial, but affirm the grant of summary judgment as to the remaining claims. We also reverse the district court's grant of summary judgment on defendants' counterclaim. **[—25—]**

AFFIRMED IN PART, VACATED IN PART, AND REMANDED.

United States Court of Appeals
for the Eleventh Circuit

No. 16-11246

SALVORS, INC.
vs.
UNIDENTIFIED WRECKED & ABANDONED VESSEL

Appeal from the United States District Court for the Southern District of Florida

Decided: July 5, 2017

Citation: 861 F.3d 1278, 5 Adm. R. 461 (11th Cir. 2017).

Before **MARCUS, PRYOR,** and **SILER,*** Circuit Judges.

*Honorable Eugene E. Siler, Jr., United States Circuit Judge for the Sixth Circuit, sitting by designation.

[—2—] {-1282-} MARCUS, Circuit Judge:

This *in rem* admiralty proceeding began in 1979, when Cobb Coin Company retrieved a cannon from wreckage discovered off the coast of Florida. That cannon was part of a shipwreck dating back to 1715, when eleven Spanish galleons carrying gold, silver, and precious jewels perished off the Florida coast in a hurricane. Over the next 264 years, the shifting tides spread and then buried the remains of these ships and their cargo along the coastline. In 1982, Cobb Coin was awarded exclusive salvaging rights to the shipwreck of one of those galleons, and the district court held (and continues to hold) a yearly distribution hearing to adjudicate title to the recovered artifacts and allow competing claimants to be heard. This process has been carried out faithfully since 1982.

Sometime in 2010, Cobb Coin's successor-in-interest assigned its exclusive salvaging rights to plaintiff-appellee 1715 Fleet-Queens Jewels, LLC ("Fleet-Queens"). By this time, the wreckage had spread out along forty-one miles of the **[—3—]** South Florida coastline. Fleet-Queens worked with subcontractors, including intervenor-appellant Gold Hound, LLC, to assist it in its salvaging operations. Gold Hound utilized allegedly proprietary maps, data, and software to salvage a specific area on behalf of Fleet-Queens. In 2013, Fleet-Queens sought to renegotiate its contract with Gold Hound and asked Gold Hound to relinquish ownership of this proprietary information; Gold Hound refused and the parties did not renew the contract.

During the 2015 salvage season, Fleet-Queens recovered approximately four hundred gold coins, among other treasures, from an area that Gold Hound had allegedly been salvaging while acting as a subcontractor for Fleet-Queens. Gold Hound claimed that this discovery was made using its proprietary maps and software, and accordingly it sought to intervene in the *in rem* action to assert a maritime lien over some of these artifacts and to assert several state-law claims. It also sought to contest Fleet-Queens's exclusive salvage rights because Fleet-Queens allegedly mishandled the artifacts in violation of the district court's 1982 order. The district court denied the motion to intervene. Gold Hound then filed a claim asserting a maritime lien and participated in the 2015 distribution hearing, but the district court concluded that it was not entitled to a maritime lien. Gold Hound now appeals these rulings and also challenges the district court's continued exercise of subject-matter jurisdiction over the entire dispute. **[—4—]**

After review, we conclude that the district court properly determined that it had and continues to have subject-matter jurisdiction over the *res*. However, Gold Hound should be granted leave to intervene in this proceeding to assert its *in rem* claims. On remand, we leave it to the district court's sound discretion to determine whether to exercise supplemental jurisdiction over Gold Hound's related state-law claims, including, *inter alia*, its claims for breach of contract, misappropriation of trade secrets, breach of fiduciary duty and constructive trust, and tortious interference. As for Gold Hound's claimed maritime lien, we cannot decide on this record whether Gold Hound may succeed because basic facts remain in dispute. We, therefore, vacate the district court's denial of Gold Hound's motion to intervene and its denial of Gold Hound's claim to a maritime lien and remand the case to the district court for further proceedings consistent with this opinion. **{-1283-}**

I.

This case began long ago as an *in rem* action brought by Cobb Coin Company against the "remains of what is believed to be the Almiranta of the New Spain Group of the 1715 Plate Fleet, known to the Spanish by two names: San Christo del Valle and Nuestra Senora de la Concepcion," which rests somewhere off the coast of Florida near Vero Beach ("the 1715 wreck"). *Cobb Coin Co. v. Unidentified, Wrecked & Abandoned Sailing Vessel*, 549 F. Supp. 540, 545 (S.D. Fla. 1982). The complex procedural history of this lawsuit began on August 17, **[—5—]** 1979, when Cobb Coin filed an in rem admiralty complaint against the vessel in the United States District Court for the Southern District of Florida to notify the district court and the U.S. Marshal that it intended to retrieve a cannon from the 1715 wreck; the cannon served as the basis for *in rem* jurisdiction. *Id.* at 547. Cobb Coin sought a declaration that it was the owner in possession of the wrecked vessel and sought exclusive salvage rights over the wreck. *Cobb Coin Co. v. Unidentified, Wrecked & Abandoned Sailing Vessel*, 525 F. Supp. 186, 190 (S.D. Fla. 1981). Because the area and cargo at issue lay within the territorial limits of the state of Florida, the State intervened, claiming ownership of the vessel and its cargo under the Florida Archives and History Act, Fla. Stat. ch. 267. *See Cobb Coin*, 525 F. Supp. at 197, 200.

Three days later, on August 20, 1979, Cobb Coin retrieved the cannon from the wreck site. *Id.* at 191. The district court concluded that it had subject-matter jurisdiction under 28 U.S.C. § 1333 and that Cobb Coin's possession of the cannon "constituted constructive possession of the wreck itself and everything that is a part thereof, wherever located, and whenever removed therefore, past, present or future." *Id.* (quotations omitted). Florida then sought injunctive relief designed to prevent Cobb Coin from continuing to salvage the site; the district court denied that request and Cobb Coin continued to salvage the 1715 wreck. *Id.* at 191–92. **[—6—]**

On July 7, 1981, the district court entered a temporary restraining order for Cobb Coin and enjoined the State from interfering with Cobb Coin's ongoing salvage operations. *Id.* at 192–93. The district court subsequently converted this order into a preliminary injunction. *Id.* at 220. And on August 31, 1982, after a two-day bench trial, the district court made the preliminary injunction permanent, concluding that "Cobb Coin ha[d] established a right to the protection of this Court to conduct further salvage activities, for as long as it demonstrates the requisite diligence and success in its efforts." *Cobb Coin*, 549 F. Supp. at 561.

The district court retained jurisdiction "[t]o protect the Plaintiff's valid salvage operations on the defendant wreck," "to adjudicate its rights vis-a-vis competing salvors who may assert a superior right to salve the defendant wreck," and "[t]o adjudicate the plaintiff's claim to a salvage award on a periodic basis." *Id.* The district court set a schedule accordingly: on February 1 of each year, Cobb Coin would be required to file a claim stating the value of the salvage services performed and cataloguing the artifacts salvaged in the previous calendar year. *Id.* Failure to file by that date would constitute prima facie evidence that Cobb Coin had abandoned the wreck, and it would have thirty days to rebut that presumption through appropriate pleadings. *Id.* The state of Florida, in turn, was "invited to intervene and seek certain artifacts to be exhibited throughout the State for the benefit of the People of Florida." *Id.* **[—7—]**

This injunction was never appealed or reversed and remains in effect today. In **{-1284-}** accordance with the district court's 1982 order, Cobb Coin and the state of Florida entered into a settlement agreement on June 3, 1983, adopting the order. On August 29, 1983, the district court issued a binding consent judgment approving the settlement. Salvage proceeded as dictated by the terms of the district court's 1982 order for the next twenty-seven years. Other parties would occasionally appear at the distribution hearings to assert claims over some of the recovered artifacts, and often the State would appear to reserve a portion of the recovered artifacts for display in museums.

Over the centuries, the wreckage had spread out along forty-one miles of the Florida coastline. Cobb Coin's successor-in-interest thus began working with various sub-contractors to assist in salvaging the wreck; Gold Hound, LLC, was one of them. In the spring of 2010, Gold Hound entered into an agreement with Cobb Coin's successor-in-interest under which it would perform salvage services as a subcontractor and would be entitled to 50 percent of the value of the treasure it recovered. A few months later, Cobb Coin's successor-in-interest assigned its exclusive salvaging rights to the plaintiff-appellee 1715 Fleet-Queens Jewels, LLC. That assignment was approved by the district court and by the state of Florida. Fleet-Queens then became a party to this action and continued the salvage operations in accordance with the district court's 1982 order. **[—8—]**

In 2011, Gold Hound and Fleet-Queens entered into a contract to engage in joint exploration of the 1715 wreck. Gold Hound acted as a subcontractor for Fleet-Queens and salvaged a specific area of the 1715 wreck on Fleet-Queens's behalf. Gold Hound purportedly used proprietary maps and computer software to conduct its salvaging work. On May 1, 2013, Fleet-Queens attempted to renegotiate its contract with Gold Hound to add new terms requiring that Gold Hound surrender ownership of its intellectual property. When Gold Hound refused, Fleet-Queens allegedly took a computer with the software on it, converted the data and maps to its own use, and barred Gold Hound from working as a subcontractor on the site. Some two years later, on June 30, 2015, gold treasure was discovered, allegedly in the area where Gold Hound had been working. Gold Hound now claims that the discovery was made based on the use of its proprietary software and trade secrets, which it claims were misappropriated by Fleet-Queens.

On September 15, 2015, the district court scheduled a distribution hearing for artifacts recovered during the 2014 salvage season for October 19, 2015. Fifteen days later, on September 30, 2015, Gold Hound moved to intervene in this suit, claiming a portion of the artifacts recovered during the 2014 and 2015 salvage seasons. Gold Hound also filed an intervening complaint in which it alleged breach of contract, various *in rem* claims, breach of fiduciary duty and constructive trust, tortious interference with a contractual relationship, civil remedies for certain **[—9—]** practices, misappropriation of trade secrets, and unfair competition. Finally, it claimed the district court acted without subject-matter jurisdiction over the *res*.

Gold Hound did not participate in or file a claim at the 2014 distribution hearing (held on October 19, 2015), but a hearing on its motion to intervene was conducted on November 17, 2015. The district court ultimately denied the motion on February 19, 2016, ruling that Gold Hound lacked standing, that it had been untimely in seeking intervention, and that it had failed to show either that its interests were properly cognizable in this admiralty action or that its interests weren't otherwise protected **{–1285–}** by the parties to the action. Gold Hound timely appealed.

Following the procedures that it had employed for many years, the district court scheduled the 2015 distribution hearing for March 16, 2016. Fleet-Queens and the district court gave notice that any potential claimants had to file their claims at least ten days before the hearing. Accordingly, Gold Hound timely filed a claim asserting a maritime lien over the 2015 artifacts on March 4, 2016, and it appeared at the hearing. On March 16, 2016, the district court issued its yearly order adjudicating title to the articles of salvage from the 2015 season. The district court concluded that there had been "continuous and on-going salvage activity" performed by Fleet-Queens during the 2015 salvage season and that Fleet-Queens had "continued to exercise such dominion and control over the various Defendant **[—10—]** vessels . . . so as to justify [its] exclusive right to continue the salvage activities herein." Gold Hound's claim was denied because "Gold Hound [did] not assert that it discovered or recovered any of the artifacts that [were] the subject of Plaintiff's Motion for Distribution." The district court's order denying Gold Hound's claim briefly mentioned Gold Hound's state-law claims and noted that those allegations "may be sufficient to support a new, separate action for damages, but they [were] insufficient to maintain a claim of a superior salvage right to the Defendant wreck than that which is possessed by [Fleet-Queens]." Gold Hound amended its notice of appeal to include the denial of its claim.

Gold Hound subsequently filed a motion to show cause regarding the alleged mishandling of artifacts, a motion to stay distribution of the *res*, and, finally, a motion for emergency consideration of the motion to stay distribution. All were denied by the district court. Gold Hound still again amended its notice of appeal, this time to include the denial of the motion to show cause.

Fleet-Queens, in turn, has cross-appealed for sanctions and has asked this Court to take judicial notice of a related, pending state-court action.

II.

We are obliged to review issues pertaining to a court's subject-matter jurisdiction *de novo*. *Peebles v. Merrill Lynch, Pierce, Fenner & Smith Inc.*, 431 F.3d 1320, 1324 (11th Cir. 2005). "Prior to making an adjudication on the merits, **[—11—]** we must assure ourselves that we have jurisdiction to hear the case before us." *Resnick v. AvMed, Inc.*, 693 F.3d 1317, 1323 (11th Cir. 2012). Thus, we begin our analysis by examining whether the district court properly exercised subject-matter jurisdiction over this admiralty proceeding in 1979 and whether it continues to have subject-matter jurisdiction over the ongoing proceedings. We hold that it had and continues to have jurisdiction over this basic admiralty claim.

A.

It is by now axiomatic that "[f]ederal courts exercise limited subject matter jurisdiction, empowered to hear only those cases within the judicial power of the United States as defined by Article III of the Constitution or otherwise authorized by Congress." *Taylor v. Appleton*, 30 F.3d 1365, 1367 (11th Cir. 1994). Article III of the United States Constitution extends the judicial power to "all Cases of admiralty and maritime Jurisdiction." U.S. Const. art. III, § 2, cl. 1. And Congress has specifically conferred on the federal district courts exclusive, original jurisdiction over "[a]ny civil case of admiralty or maritime jurisdiction," as well as over "[a]ny prize brought into the United States and all **{-1286-}** proceedings for the condemnation of property taken as prize." 28 U.S.C. § 1333.

It is also clear that "[a]n *in rem* suit against a vessel is . . . distinctively an admiralty proceeding, and is hence within the exclusive province of the federal courts." *Am. Dredging Co. v. Miller*, 510 U.S. 443, 446–47 (1994). But **[—12—]** "[a]lthough federal courts have the exclusive power to adjudicate *in rem* suits against a vessel, that power is dependent on the court's jurisdiction over the *res*, the property named as the defendant." *Odyssey Marine Expl., Inc. v. Unidentified Shipwrecked Vessel*, 657 F.3d 1159, 1171 (11th Cir. 2011). "Only if the court has exclusive custody and control over the property does it have jurisdiction over the property so as to be able to adjudicate rights in it that are binding against the world." *Id.* (quotations omitted). Thus, "when a party files an *in rem* complaint, the court issues a warrant for the arrest of the *res* and the *res* remains in the court's custody for the remainder of the proceedings." *Id.*

Admiralty jurisdiction in Cobb Coin's original case was based on a cannon recovered from the wreck site of an abandoned vessel believed to have been part of the Spanish 1715 fleet. *See Cobb Coin*, 525 F. Supp. at 191. The district court entered an arrest *in rem* for the cannon and directed the U.S. Marshal to take the cannon into custody. *See id.* at 190–91. In its 1981 order preliminarily enjoining Florida officials from interfering with Cobb Coin's salvaging activities, the district court concluded that actual possession of the cannon was tantamount to constructive possession of the wreck itself, which was enough to give the district court *in rem* jurisdiction "to dispose of all articles thereafter brought up" from the wreck site. *Id.* at 197. This conclusion was reaffirmed in the district court's 1982 **[—13—]**

order granting Cobb Coin a permanent injunction, and that order has never been appealed or modified. *See Cobb Coin*, 549 F. Supp. at 561.

Gold Hound now challenges the district court's exercise of subject-matter jurisdiction, arguing that the district court cannot exercise *in rem* jurisdiction over property that is not in the court's possession but is instead spread out over forty-one miles of the Florida coast. It also says that the district court erred by using the cannon as the foundation for exercising constructive *in rem* jurisdiction over the entire shipwreck. We are unpersuaded.

The theory of constructive *in rem* jurisdiction is well established in admiralty cases. The Supreme Court has long recognized that "[i]n order to institute and perfect proceedings *in rem*, it is necessary that the thing should be actually *or constructively* within the reach of the Court." *The Brig Ann*, 13 U.S. (9 Cranch) 289, 291 (1815) (emphasis added); *see also Republic Nat'l Bank of Miami v. United States*, 506 U.S. 80, 87 (1992) ("*The Brig Ann* simply restates the rule that the court must have actual *or constructive* control of the res when an *in rem* forfeiture suit is initiated.") (emphasis added). Federal appellate courts have followed suit. *See, e.g.*, *Dluhos v. Floating & Abandoned Vessel, Known as "New York"*, 162 F.3d 63, 69 (2d Cir. 1998) ("[I]n order to maintain an *in rem* action against a *res* where taking of actual possession is impracticable, a warrant of arrest must still issue from the court, but the possession of the *res* after the arrest may be **[—14—]** constructive as opposed to actual."); *R.M.S. Titanic, Inc. v. Haver*, 171 F.3d 943, 964 (4th Cir. 1999) ("While the *res* must be *in custodia legis* (in the court's possession), this possession may be actual or constructive."); **{-1287-}** *Treasure Salvors, Inc. v. Unidentified Wrecked & Abandoned Sailing Vessel*, 640 F.2d 560, 572 (5th Cir. 1981)[1] ("[A] finder need not always have manual possession of the thing. Rather, a finder may be protected by taking such constructive possession of the property as its nature and situation permit.") (quotations omitted); *Great Lakes Expl. Grp., LLC v. Unidentified Wrecked & (for Salvage-Right Purposes), Abandoned Sailing Vessel*, 522 F.3d 682, 694 (6th Cir. 2008) (noting that courts may "exercise constructive jurisdiction over [an] entire shipwreck").

The theory of constructive *in rem* jurisdiction also applies to cases in which a ship and her cargo are spread out on the ocean floor. Thus, for example, we have recognized that "a site where the remains of a vessel are strewn on the ocean floor is still a shipwreck even if an intact vessel no longer remains." *Odyssey Marine*, 657 F.3d at 1181 n.15; *see also id.* at 1174 (noting that even if "it is undisputed the shipwreck site does not contain an 'intact' vessel, this fact is not determinative"). So long as the court constructively possesses part of a scattered wreck, it may exercise constructive *in rem* jurisdiction over the entirety of that wreck just as the **[—15—]** court would exercise constructive *in rem* jurisdiction over the entirety of an intact vessel. *See R.M.S. Titanic*, 171 F.3d at 964 ("[E]xercising *in rem* jurisdiction over an entire ship wreck within the court's territorial jurisdiction when only part of that wreck is actually presented to a court rests upon the fiction that the *res* is not divided and that therefore possession of some of it is constructively possession of all."); *Great Lakes*, 522 F.3d at 694 ("To obtain possession over the *res*, district courts sitting in admiralty may issue a warrant of arrest for a physical part of a shipwreck (an 'artifact') and, based on this arrest, exercise constructive jurisdiction over the entire shipwreck."); *see also California v. Deep Sea Research, Inc.*, 523 U.S. 491, 496 (1998) (approving the exercise of *in rem* jurisdiction over a shipwreck when that jurisdiction was based on artifacts recovered from the wreck, including "china, a full bottle of champagne, and a brass spike from the ship's hull"). The plain meaning of the term "shipwreck" supports this idea: the term "covers not only a sunken intact vessel, but also a vessel that was 'dashed to pieces' or exploded at the surface and then sank to the ocean floor." *Odyssey Marine*, 657 F.3d at 1181 n.15; *see also id.* at 1180–81 (noting that the

[1] In *Bonner v. City of Prichard*, 661 F.2d 1206, 1209 (11th Cir. 1981) (en banc), this Court adopted as binding precedent all decisions of the former Fifth Circuit handed down prior to October 1, 1981.

Abandoned Shipwreck Act "defines 'shipwreck' as 'a vessel or wreck, its cargo and other contents'") (quoting 43 U.S.C. § 2102(d)).

Moreover, contrary to Gold Hound's assertion, this Court has not rejected the application of constructive *in rem* jurisdiction in cases like this one. Gold **[—16—]** Hound claims that this Court has rejected the theory of constructive *in rem* jurisdiction for cases in which "the debris field is isolated and not in geographical association with any shipwreck" (quotations omitted). Gold Hound relies on a single unpublished case, *Martin v. One Bronze Rod*, 581 F. App'x 744 (11th Cir. 2014), but even that case is readily distinguishable. In *Martin*, the plaintiff found and took possession of one bronze rod and also claimed that he had pinpointed the location of three buried chests that he had yet to retrieve. *Id.* at 745. The district court issued a warrant of arrest *in rem* as to the bronze rod but declined to issue a warrant for the three buried chests; a panel of this Court affirmed on appeal. *Id.* The panel concluded that "Martin ha[d] not sufficiently demonstrated **{-1288-}** that the rod and the chests [were] part of an undivided *res* so as to allow the court to exercise constructive *in rem* jurisdiction over the chests based on his salvage of the rod." *Id.* at 748–49. Indeed, the claimant himself asserted that "the chests were intentionally buried—as opposed to being scattered by the sinking of any ship." *Id.* at 749 n.6.

The Court went on to observe:

> Martin cites no case indicating that a theory of constructive possession, which courts have used to exercise constructive *in rem* jurisdiction over an entire shipwreck when only part of the wreck is presented to the court, extends to separate items of cargo that are isolated from one another and do not hail from any shipwreck. And we decline the opportunity to extend the theory in such a way under the circumstances of this case. **[—17—]**

Id. at 749 (footnote omitted). In this passage, the panel made it clear that constructive *in rem* jurisdiction *has* been exercised "over an entire shipwreck when only part of the wreck is presented to the court"—which exactly matches the facts of this case. *Id.*; *accord Treasure Salvors*, 640 F.2d at 572 ("[I]n order to acquire a legally cognizable interest in lost or abandoned property, a finder need not always have manual possession of the thing. Rather, a finder may be protected by taking such constructive possession of the property as its nature and situation permit.") (quotations omitted).

Critically, there was no indication in *Martin* that the salvaged items originated from the same wreck. While Martin's treasure chests may have come from an entirely different wreck than his bronze rod or, indeed, from no wreck at all, the 1715 wreck can fairly be seen as one undivided *res*, even if the *res* was no longer intact. The cannon that was recovered at the start of this case came from the 1715 wreck, and the cargo that was found does "hail from a[ ] shipwreck," *Martin*, 581 F. App'x at 749, even if that vessel is no longer intact. Indeed, in *Martin* we even noted that the facts of the case were "distinct from those in which courts have applied a theory of constructive *in rem* jurisdiction over an entire shipwreck based on actual possession of a part thereof." *Id.* at 749 n.6. Thus, even if it were binding, this Court's unpublished decision does not undermine the district court's **[—18—]** assertion of power over the ongoing proceedings in this case. The district court properly exercised subject-matter jurisdiction in 1979 and properly does so today.

B.

Gold Hound also argues that even if the district court had jurisdiction at the inception of the case, the Abandoned Shipwreck Act of 1987 (ASA), Pub. L. No. 100-298, 102 Stat. 432 (1988), codified at 43 U.S.C. § 2101–06, has denuded the court of jurisdiction and returned both title to the *res* and jurisdiction over the dispute to the state of Florida. Again, we disagree.

When this case was first filed, Florida intervened in the action and claimed ownership of the cannon under the Florida Archives and History Act, Fla. Stat. ch. 267.

See Cobb Coin, 549 F. Supp. at 544. Section 267.061(1)(b) says that "all treasure trove, artifacts, and such objects having intrinsic or historical and archaeological value which have been abandoned on state-owned lands or state-owned sovereignty submerged lands shall belong to the state" with the title to the property vested in the Division of Historical Resources of the Department of State. Fla. Stat. § 267.061(1)(b). The district court rejected the claim and instead found that the case was "governed by the federal maritime law of salvage, not the Florida Archives and {-1289-} History Act and the regulations promulgated thereunder." *Cobb Coin*, 549 F. Supp. at 548 (citation omitted). **[—19—]**

Some nine years later, Congress enacted the Abandoned Shipwreck Act. The ASA recognizes that "States have the responsibility for management of a broad range of living and nonliving resources in State waters and submerged lands." 43 U.S.C. § 2101(a). Included in that "range of resources are certain abandoned shipwrecks, which have been deserted and to which the owner has relinquished ownership rights with no retention." *Id.* at § 2101(b). Accordingly, the ASA provides that the United States has title to any abandoned shipwreck that is "(1) embedded in submerged lands of a State; (2) embedded in coralline formations protected by a State on submerged lands of a State; or (3) on submerged lands of a State and is included in or determined eligible for inclusion in the National Register." *Id.* at § 2105(a). Title to the shipwreck is then automatically "transferred to the State in or on whose submerged lands the shipwreck is located." *Id.* at § 2105(c). The ASA also states that "[t]he law of salvage and the law of finds shall not apply to abandoned shipwrecks to which section 2105 of this title applies." *Id.* at § 2106(a). Thus, as the Sixth Circuit has recognized, "[t]he ASA expressly rejects the application of the maritime laws of salvage and finds. If a diver now discovers a long-lost ship embedded in the submerged lands of a State, a finding of abandonment leaves the diver with neither title nor a salvage award (unless state law provides otherwise)." *Fairport Int'l* **[—20—]** *Expl., Inc. v. Shipwrecked Vessel*, 177 F.3d 491, 498 (6th Cir. 1999) (citation omitted).

Gold Hound argues that the codification of the ASA transferred title to the 1715 wreck to the state of Florida and thereby revoked the district court's subject-matter jurisdiction over the *res*. But this argument fails to account for the limiting language found in § 2106(c), which plainly says that the ASA "shall not affect any legal proceeding brought prior to April 28, 1988." As we have seen, this legal proceeding began on August 17, 1979. *See Cobb Coin*, 525 F. Supp. at 190. Thus, the ASA does not apply to this dispute, and the passage of that legislation did not deprive the district court of power over the *res*.

Gold Hound argues, nevertheless, that § 2106(c) does not apply because "the legal proceedings in *Cobb Coin* have been effectively terminated," "[t]he parties to the initial litigation are no longer in existence," and "the litigation has been artificially prolonged to benefit 1715 Fleet-Queens Jewels." But Gold Hound has not brought a new action against the *res*; rather, it has attempted to intervene in the same action initiated by Cobb Coin in 1979. The 1715 wreck still provides the basis for *in rem* jurisdiction because, as we have said, "a site where the remains of a vessel are strewn on the ocean floor is still a shipwreck even if an intact vessel no longer remains." *Odyssey Marine*, 657 F.3d at 1181 n.15. Finally, Florida's continued consent to the district court's arrangement and its participation in the **[—21—]** annual distribution and adjudication process cannot be reconciled with Gold Hound's claim that this dispute has been artificially prolonged to benefit Fleet-Queens. Whatever else may be unclear, the original 1979 dispute is alive and well, and because it predated the ASA, that Act does not affect the district court's jurisdiction.

III.

Gold Hound's central argument on appeal is that the district court erred in denying its motion to intervene. But before we can address the question whether intervention was proper, we must ensure that Gold Hound has standing to pursue this **{-1290-}** appeal. *See Dillard v. Chilton Cty. Comm'n*, 495 F.3d 1324, 1330 (11th Cir. 2007) ("Any party, whether original or intervening, that seeks relief from a federal court must have standing to pursue its claims.").

The Supreme Court recently answered whether a litigant must possess Article III standing in order to intervene of right under Federal Rule of Civil Procedure 24(a)(2). The Court first noted the "simple rule" that "[a]t least one plaintiff must have standing to seek each form of relief requested in the complaint." *Town of Chester, N.Y. v. Laroe Estates, Inc.*, No. 16-605, slip op. at 5–6 (U.S. June 5, 2017). This principle also extends to intervenors of right: "For all relief sought, there must be a litigant with standing, whether that litigant joins the lawsuit as a plaintiff, a coplaintiff, or an intervenor of right." *Id.* at 6. The **[—22—]** Court therefore held that "an intervenor of right must have Article III standing in order to pursue relief that is different from that which is sought by a party with standing." *Id.*

Here, Gold Hound's intervening complaint seeks a declaration that Fleet-Queens's salvage rights have been extinguished; that, alternatively, Fleet-Queens has abandoned the 1715 wreck, leaving the wreck open to salvage by others; and that the district court no longer has *in rem* jurisdiction over the 1715 wreck. This request does not overlap with the relief sought by any other party with standing in this case. Cobb Coin—the original plaintiff—sought title to the 1715 wreck as well as preliminary and permanent injunctive relief enjoining the State from interfering with its ongoing salvage operations. *See Cobb Coin*, 525 F. Supp. at 191. Cobb Coin's successor-in-interest, Fleet-Queens, annually seeks adjudication of title to each year's salvaged artifacts and now seeks to retain its exclusive salvage rights. And the state of Florida participates in the annual distribution hearings to reserve some of the recovered artifacts for display in its museums. Plainly, Gold Hound is "pursu[ing] relief that is different from that which is sought by" Cobb Coin, Fleet-Queens, and the State. *Laroe Estates*, slip op. at 6. Indeed, neither Fleet-Queens nor Florida is aligned in any way with Gold Hound in this dispute, and Gold Hound is the only party that has appealed. Thus, Gold Hound must demonstrate that it has Article III standing to continue this appeal. **[—23—]**

The well-settled test for establishing Article III standing includes three basic requirements. "First, the plaintiff must have suffered an injury in fact—an invasion of a legally protected interest which is (a) concrete and particularized, and (b) actual or imminent, not conjectural or hypothetical." *Lujan v. Defenders of Wildlife*, 504 U.S. 555, 560 (1992) (quotations, citations, and footnote omitted). "Second, the plaintiff must establish a causal connection between its injury and the defendant's conduct. Third, the plaintiff must show that it is likely—and not merely speculative—that a favorable decision by the court will redress the injury." *Duty Free Americas, Inc. v. Estée Lauder Cos.*, 797 F.3d 1248, 1271 (11th Cir. 2015) (citing *Lujan*, 504 U.S. at 560–61).

Gold Hound has sufficiently articulated Article III injury. Gold Hound claims that it suffered (and continues to suffer) an injury because Fleet-Queens unlawfully retains exclusive salvaging rights to a forty-one-mile stretch of Florida coastline, thereby preventing Gold Hound from conducting profitable salvage operations and causing Gold Hound to suffer a substantial loss of livelihood. Gold Hound also claims that Fleet-Queens has damaged **{-1291-}** or destroyed artifacts in violation of the district court's 1982 order, thereby forfeiting its salvage rights. Gold Hound claims continuous injury because it has not been afforded the opportunity to challenge Fleet-Queens's fitness to salvage and to argue that Gold Hound, instead, should be entitled to the salvaging rights. Finally, Gold Hound's **[—24—]** intervening complaint alleged a maritime lien over the recovered artifacts. From the face of the intervening complaint, these claimed injuries are concrete and particularized, actual rather than conjectural, and likely to be redressed by a favorable decision from the district court.

Gold Hound also asserts standing in this case because "an order awarding exclusive rights to conduct salvage is an order 'against the world' and [ ] anyone aggrieved by the order has standing to challenge it." The district court rejected this argument, distinguishing the case that Gold Hound cited for support—*R.M.S. Titanic, Inc. v. Wrecked & Abandoned Vessel*, 920 F. Supp. 96 (E.D. Va. 1996). In *R.M.S. Titanic*, a district court in the Eastern District of Virginia awarded "salvor-in-possession status of the *RMS Titanic* to RMS Titanic, Inc. (RMSTI) and grant[ed] it the exclusive rights over any items salvaged from the *RMS Titanic* while it remained the salvor in possession." *Id.* at 97. Just over a year and a half later, John A. Joslyn, a third party, filed a motion pursuant to Federal Rule of Civil Procedure 60(b)[2] asking the district court to rescind its order naming RMSTI the salvor in possession of the *Titanic*. *Id.* at 97–98. Although the district court recognized that Joslyn had not been a party to the original action, it concluded that **[—25—]** he did have standing to file a Rule 60(b) motion because "actions *in rem*, or 'against the thing,' are designed to adjudicate rights in specific property against *all of the world*, and judgments in such cases are binding to the same extent." *Id.* at 98 (quotations and alteration omitted). Thus, "[i]t logically follow[ed] that if the whole world are parties bound by the judgment, then the converse should also be true: the whole world are parties who may request relief from the judgment." *Id.*

In this case, the district court concluded that "the *RMS Titanic* case is readily distinguishable from the above-styled action because *Titanic* was not located in the territorial waters of any state, nor was any state a party to that action." The district court observed that in this case, Florida has "staunchly asserted the right of the people of the state of Florida to the artifacts recovered from the enjoined areas," and "Florida's appearance and participation as a party to this action has safeguarded the interests of the people of Florida since the very beginning." These facts were "more than sufficient to distinguish this action from the situation which confronted the court in the *RMS Titanic* case."

However, the district court cited no case law suggesting that those characteristics—the location of the wreck or the presence of a state as a party—have any legal significance. When the Supreme Court long ago discussed the principle that admiralty actions *in rem* are against the whole world in *The Mary*, 13 U.S. (9 Cranch) 126, 144 (1815), it did not reference the location of the vessel or **[—26—]** whether any state was involved in the action. Instead, it broadly proclaimed that "[t]he whole world, it is said, are parties in an admiralty **{-1292-}** cause . . . therefore, the whole world is bound by the decision"; as a result, "[e]very person may make himself a party, and appeal from the sentence." *Id.*

This Court has since recognized the against-the-world nature of orders in *in rem* admiralty proceedings, and we have not drawn any distinction based on where the *res* is located or on whether a state was a party to the action. *See, e.g., Thorsteinsson v. M/V Drangur*, 891 F.2d 1547, 1553 (11th Cir. 1990) (quoting *The Mary* and similar cases for the proposition that admiralty actions are against the whole world). The Second, Third, Fourth, Fifth, Sixth, and Ninth Circuits have said the same thing. *See In re Millennium Seacarriers, Inc.*, 419 F.3d 83, 93 (2d Cir. 2005) ("The *in rem* admiralty action, like the *in rem* adjudication of a bankruptcy estate, establishes title as against the whole world.") (quotations and alteration omitted); *Oil Shipping (Bunkering) B.V. v. Sonmez Denizcilik Ve Ticaret A.S.*, 10 F.3d 176, 179 (3d Cir. 1993); *Darlak v. Columbus-Am. Discovery Grp., Inc.*, 59 F.3d 20, 22–23 (4th Cir. 1995) (quoting *Thorsteinsson* and *The Mary* to hold that if a party has claims against the *res* that forms the subject of an *in rem* proceeding, he must participate in that proceeding to obtain relief); *Merchs. Nat'l Bank of Mobile v. Dredge Gen. G.L. Gillespie*,

[2] Rule 60(b) addresses grounds for relief from a final judgment, order, or proceeding and says that "[o]n motion and just terms, the court may relieve a party or its legal representative from a final judgment, order, or proceeding for" certain enumerated reasons or for "any other reason that justifies relief." Fed. R. Civ. P. 60(b).

663 F.2d 1338, 1350 (5th Cir. Unit A 1981) ("An action in admiralty to enforce a maritime lien is not an action against **[—27—]** any particular person to compel him to do or to forebear anything; it is an action *in rem* asserting against the world the claim of a plaintiff to an offending ship.") (quotations omitted); *Great Lakes*, 522 F.3d at 694 ("It is the court's exclusive custody and control over the property that gives an admiralty court jurisdiction to adjudicate the rights of the salvor against the world.") (quotations omitted); *DiGiovanni v. Kjessler*, 101 F.3d 76, 78–79 (9th Cir. 1996). These facts do not provide a basis for distinguishing between *R.M.S. Titanic* and this case. Gold Hound has Article III standing to intervene. The only remaining question is whether intervention was otherwise proper in this case.

IV.

"Our review of the denial of a motion for intervention as of right is *de novo.*" *Sierra Club, Inc. v. Leavitt*, 488 F.3d 904, 909–10 (11th Cir. 2007). Denial of a motion for permissive intervention is reviewed for an abuse of discretion. *Georgia v. U.S. Army Corps of Eng'rs*, 302 F.3d 1242, 1249 (11th Cir. 2002).

After the 1966 merger of the Federal Rules of Civil Procedure and the Federal Admiralty Rules, procedure in admiralty cases is governed by both the Federal Rules of Civil Procedure *and* the Supplemental Rules for Admiralty or Maritime Claims and Asset Forfeiture Actions. Notably, if there is a conflict between the Civil Rules and the Supplemental Rules, the Supplemental Rules control. *See* Supp. R. A(2) ("The Federal Rules of Civil Procedure also apply to **[—28—]** [admiralty or maritime claims] except to the extent that they are inconsistent with these Supplemental Rules."); 2 Am. Jur. 2d *Admiralty* § 115 (2017) ("The Supplemental Rules for Admiralty or Maritime Claims apply to procedure for admiralty and maritime claims, and the Federal Rules of Civil Procedure are specifically incorporated into [the Supplemental Rules] except to the extent that they are inconsistent therewith.") (footnote omitted); Thomas J. Schoenbaum, *Admiralty and Maritime Law* § 21-1 & n.6 (2016 ed.). Thus, "[a]s a result of the unification of admiralty and other civil actions, a district court judge, in considering admiralty claims, may apply all statutory powers, whether deriving **{-1293-}** from law, equity, or admiralty." 2 Am. Jur. 2d *Admiralty* § 115.

The Federal Rules of Civil Procedure are, in turn, supplemented by a district court's local admiralty rules, if any have been promulgated. *See* Supp. R. A, Advisory Committee Notes—1966 Adoption (noting that the Supplemental Rules do not "limit[ ] or impair[ ] the traditional power of a district court, exercising the admiralty and maritime jurisdiction, to adapt its procedures and its remedies in the individual case, consistently with these rules" and that "district courts retain the power to make local rules not inconsistent with these rules"); 2 C.J.S. *Admiralty* § 86 (2017) ("Each district court, acting by a majority of its district judges, may . . . make and amend rules governing its practice consistent with, but not duplicative of, federal statutes and other rules."). **[—29—]**

"Intervention in admiralty cases is governed by the Federal Rules of Civil Procedure"—specifically, Rule 24. 2 Am. Jur. 2d Admiralty § 170; *see also* Supp. R. C(6), Advisory Committee Notes—2000 Amendment ("[A] statement is filed only by a person claiming a right of possession or ownership. Other claims against the property are advanced by intervention under Civil Rule 24, as it may be supplemented by local admiralty rules."). The Supplemental Rules do not discuss intervention, but the Southern District of Florida has promulgated additional standards for intervention in *in rem* admiralty proceedings in its local admiralty rules. *See* S.D. Fla. Local Admiralty R. E(2).

In this case, then, Gold Hound's motion to intervene must be measured against both Federal Rule of Civil Procedure 24 and S.D. Fla. Local Admiralty Rule E(2). After careful review, we conclude Gold Hound has satisfied the requirements of each. The district court erroneously denied Gold Hound's motion to intervene.

A.

Intervention under Rule 24 can be either as of right or permissive.[3] If a party is seeking intervention as of right, the district court is required to allow intervention by anyone who files a timely motion and either: **[—30—]**

> (1) is given an unconditional right to intervene by a federal statute; or
>
> (2) claims an interest relating to the property or transaction that is the subject of the action, and is so situated that disposing of the action may as a practical matter impair or impede the movant's ability to protect its interest, unless existing parties adequately represent that interest.

Fed. R. Civ. P. 24(a); *see also Chiles v. Thornburgh*, 865 F.2d 1197, 1213 (11th Cir. 1989) (allowing intervention when (1) the "application to intervene is timely"; (2) there is "an interest relating to the property or transaction which is the subject of the action"; (3) "disposition of the action . . . may impede or impair [the intervenor's] ability to protect that interest"; and (4) that "interest is represented inadequately by the existing parties to the suit").

The district court concluded that Gold Hound's motion to intervene was untimely **{-1294-}** and otherwise failed to meet the requirements of Rule 24(a). The court determined that Gold Hound's interest in this action—a claim to a portion of the artifacts recovered during the 2015 season—did not require intervention in the case as a whole but rather an appearance at the annual distribution hearing. Moreover, the district court reasoned that "Gold Hound's interest as salvors and citizens of Florida [was] adequately represented since the state of Florida is a party to this suit."

"Although we generally review denial of intervention under rule 24(a) for error, with subsidiary factual findings subject to review for clear error, our review of the district court's determination of timeliness under both rule 24(a) and 24(b) is **[—31—]** conducted under the abuse of discretion standard." *Meek v. Metro. Dade Cty., Fla.*, 985 F.2d 1471, 1477 (11th Cir. 1993), *abrogated on other grounds by Dillard*, 495 F.3d at 1332–33. In considering whether a motion to intervene is timely, we consider several factors:

> 1. The length of time during which the would-be intervenor actually knew or reasonably should have known of his interest in the case before he petitioned for leave to intervene[;] 2. The extent of the prejudice that the existing parties to the litigation may suffer as a result of the would-be intervenor's failure to apply for intervention as soon as he actually knew or reasonably should have known of his interest in the case[;] 3. The extent of the prejudice that the would-be intervenor may suffer if his petition for leave to intervene is denied[;] and 4. The existence of unusual circumstances militating either for or against a determination that the application is timely.

Id. at 1478–79 (quotations and alterations omitted).

When measured against these standards, the district court abused its discretion in concluding that Gold Hound's motion to intervene was untimely. The length of time during which Gold Hound knew of its interest in the case before moving to intervene was short. Although the motion was filed thirty-three years after the district court's 1982 order, Gold Hound itself did not come into existence until approximately 2008. And while

[3] The parties did not argue, and the district court did not address, permissive intervention under Fed. R. Civ. P. 24(b); thus, only intervention as of right is at issue on appeal. Moreover, because we conclude that Gold Hound could intervene as of right, we need not address permissive intervention. If Gold Hound's motion was timely, then it could intervene either as a matter of right or permissively, because there is no dispute that Gold Hound alleged "a claim or defense that shares with the main action a common question of law or fact." Fed. R. Civ. P. 24(b)(1)(B).

the passage of seven years before a motion to intervene might be untimely, Gold Hound had no reason to intervene in the action while it was amicably performing salvage services as a subcontractor for Fleet-Queens. Even after the contract was terminated, Gold Hound had no knowledge of its need to intervene until it learned of the 2015 discoveries—which **[—32—]** it alleges were made due to its misappropriated intellectual property. The reason for Gold Hound's intervention—the September 15, 2015, order setting the date of the 2014 distribution hearing—arose only two weeks before it sought to intervene.

Moreover, and significantly, the original parties to the action have not claimed any prejudice stemming from Gold Hound's claimed delay, and we can discern none since the distribution hearings proceeded as scheduled without any delay. Gold Hound, however, would be prejudiced (and prejudiced substantially, at that) if intervention were denied because although it was permitted to appear at the 2015 distribution hearing, it was not allowed to raise claims challenging Fleet-Queens's continued rights to the *res* based on claims of misconduct while carrying out its salvage responsibilities. Intervention in the *in rem* proceeding would have been the best way for Gold Hound to raise these claims. *See Wilson v. Minor*, 220 F.3d 1297, 1301 (11th Cir. 2000) ("[I]ntervention pursuant to [Rule] 24 is the appropriate way for an outsider with an interest in an existing **{-1295-}** lawsuit to come in as a party. Intervention in the original action is also generally the proper mechanism for a nonparty to seek relief from an existing judgment.") (citation omitted), *abrogated on other grounds by Dillard*, 495 F.3d at 1332–33. As we see it, under these unusual circumstances, it was an abuse of discretion for the district court to conclude that Gold Hound's motion to intervene was untimely. **[—33—]**

Gold Hound has also satisfied the remaining requirements set forth in Rule 24(a)(2). Under circuit precedent, "[a]ll that is required under Rule 24(a)(2) is that the would-be intervener be practically disadvantaged by his exclusion from the proceedings." *Huff v. Comm'r of IRS*, 743 F.3d 790, 800 (11th Cir. 2014). As we have detailed, Gold Hound has asserted an interest in the property, having sought a maritime lien and levelled other *in rem* claims. Any disposition of this action without allowing intervention would deprive Gold Hound of the opportunity to be heard on those *in rem* claims. And while "[t]he proposed intervenor has the burden of showing that the existing parties cannot adequately represent its interest, [ ] this burden is treated as minimal." *U.S. Army Corps of Eng'rs*, 302 F.3d at 1255–56 (quotations omitted). Gold Hound has carried this minimal burden. Plainly, neither Fleet-Queens nor Florida adequately represents Gold Hound's interests: Fleet-Queens wants to retain its exclusive salvaging rights, while Florida represents the interests of its citizens by securing some artifacts for display in its museums. Thus, the district court erred in denying Gold Hound's motion to intervene under Rule 24(a)(2) of the Federal Rules.

B.

Rule 24 is supplemented by the Southern District of Florida's Local Admiralty Rules. *See* Supp. R. C(6), Advisory Committee Notes—2000 Amendment. These rules provide additional requirements for intervention beyond **[—34—]** the strictures of Rule 24. Local Admiralty Rule E(2) governs intervention in *in rem* admiralty proceedings, and it distinguishes between intervention as of right and permissive intervention based on whether a sale of the property is currently pending. If there is no sale pending, then intervention as of right is permitted "at any time before an order is entered by the Court scheduling the vessel or property for sale." S.D. Fla. Local Admiralty R. E(2)(a). If a sale is pending, a would-be intervenor is free to intervene more than twenty-one days before the sale. If the pending sale is within twenty-one days, the would-be intervenor must comply with additional procedural requirements, including filing a supplemental warrant of arrest, serving copies of the motion to intervene, and filing a certificate of service with the district court. S.D. Fla. Local Admiralty R. E(2)(b). So long as these requirements are satisfied, the district court may "permit intervention under such conditions and terms as are equitable to the interests of all parties." S.D. Fla. Local Admiralty R. E(2)(b).

Under Local Admiralty Rule E(2), the dispositive issue here is whether a sale was pending when Gold Hound filed its motion to intervene. While there was no order expressly mentioning a sale, the 2014 distribution hearing was scheduled for October 19, 2015, and Gold Hound moved to intervene on September 30, 2015—only nineteen days before the hearing. Thus, if an upcoming distribution hearing were equivalent to a pending sale, then Gold Hound could intervene only **[—35—]** permissively. Because it is undisputed that Gold Hound did not comply with the procedural requirements set out in Local Admiralty Rule E(2)(b), Gold Hound's motion would be untimely under the Local Admiralty **{–1296–}** Rules. But if no sale were pending, the twenty-one-day limitation would not apply and Gold Hound could, "as a matter of right, file an intervening complaint" at any time before a sale was scheduled. S.D. Fla. Local Admiralty R. E(2)(a).

No sale was pending in this case. While the district court had scheduled the 2014 distribution hearing, an order setting a distribution hearing is not the functional equivalent of a sale. Indeed, the district court never characterized the distribution as a sale, and it never observed Local Admiralty Rules E(16) and E(17)—governing "Notice of Sale" and "Sale of a Vessel or Property"—by advertising the sale as required and accepting bids for the artifacts. Instead, the notices referenced only "[a]djudication of [t]itle" and "potential claimants to the artifacts." The word "sale" and any equivalent terms were never mentioned in the notices. Rather than effect the sale of artifacts, the district court merely adjudicated title between the state of Florida and Fleet-Queens and distributed the artifacts in accordance with that adjudication. Thus, no sale was pending for the recovered artifacts and Gold Hound could intervene as of right under Local Admiralty Rule E(2)(a). **[—36—]**

Moreover, even if an order scheduling a distribution hearing were tantamount to a pending sale, this timeline would preclude claims pertaining to only the 2014 salvage season. At the time Gold Hound moved to intervene, Fleet-Queens's 2014 motion for distribution was pending and the 2014 distribution hearing was only nineteen days away. Treating an upcoming distribution hearing as a pending sale would thus make the 2014 claims untimely. But it is undisputed that the *2015* season's distribution process had not yet begun. The motion for distribution regarding the 2015 season was filed on February 12, 2016, which was well after Gold Hound's September 2015 motion to intervene. In compliance with its procedures, the district court issued a notice for the distribution hearing and advertised the hearing in the local newspaper. Both notices required that "[a]ny and [a]ll potential claimants to the artifacts must file their claim with the United States District Court at least ten (10) days prior to the date of the hearing." Gold Hound timely filed its claim to the 2015 artifacts on March 4, 2016—twelve days before the 2015 distribution hearing. Thus, Gold Hound's claim and motion to intervene were timely for the 2015 season.

In short, because Gold Hound fully satisfied the requirements for intervention found in the Federal Rules of Civil Procedure and in the Southern District of Florida's Local Admiralty Rules, the district court erred in denying Gold Hound's motion to intervene. **[—37—]**

C.

Gold Hound should have been allowed to intervene in this *in rem* proceeding. However, that a would-be intervenor has a sufficient interest for some issues in a case does not necessarily mean that it has an interest in all of the issues, so the district court "may limit intervention accordingly." *United States v. S. Fla. Water Mgmt. Dist.*, 922 F.2d 704, 707 (11th Cir. 1991). As we have explained, Gold Hound alleged several claims that go to the core of the *in rem* action. Gold Hound also levelled several supplemental state-law contract claims against Fleet-Queens. We express no opinion about whether these claims are more properly heard in the *in rem* proceeding or in an independent *in personam* action between Fleet-Queens and Gold Hound. We note, however, that these claims are now pending in a related action in Florida state court. *See* **{-1297-}** *1715 Fleet-Queens Jewels, LLC v. Gold Hound, LLC*, Case No. 31-2015-CA-828 (Fla. Cir. Ct. filed Oct. 21, 2015). We leave it for the district court to decide, on remand, whether and if so, how to exercise supplemental jurisdiction over Gold Hound's nonadmiralty claims.

V.

Gold Hound also contends that it has a maritime lien over the artifacts recovered during the 2015 salvage season because Fleet-Queens made those recoveries using Gold Hound's proprietary maps, software, and data. The district court rejected this claim, concluding that "Gold Hound's allegations may be **[—38—]** sufficient to support a new, separate action for damages, but they are insufficient to maintain a claim of a superior salvage right to the Defendant wreck than that which is possessed by [Fleet-Queens]." We think the district court was too quick to reject Gold Hound's claims. As we see it, basic factual issues must be resolved in order to make this determination, and, therefore, we remand to the district court for an examination of whether and to what extent Gold Hound provided salvage services that contributed to the recovery of the 2015 artifacts.

"We review the factual findings of a district court sitting without a jury in admiralty under the clearly erroneous standard, and its conclusions of law *de novo*." *Dresdner Bank AG v. M/V Olympia Voyager*, 463 F.3d 1210, 1214 (11th Cir. 2006). Whether a party's claims give rise to a maritime lien is a legal question that is reviewed *de novo*. *Myers v. Am. Triumph F/V*, 260 F.3d 1067, 1069 (9th Cir. 2001).

"A maritime lien is a special property right in a ship given to a creditor by law as security for a debt or claim, and it attaches the moment the debt arises." *Crimson Yachts v. Betty Lyn II Motor Yacht*, 603 F.3d 864, 868 (11th Cir. 2010) (quotations omitted). The Federal Maritime Lien Act, Pub. L. No. 100-710, 102 Stat. 4735, 4748–49 (1988), codified as amended at 46 U.S.C. § 31341–43, "grants maritime liens to particular persons based on their relationship to, or service of, a vessel." *Crimson Yachts*, 603 F.3d at 868. Significantly, "[t]he performance of **[—39—]** salvage services, like the furnishing of other services to a ship, gives rise to a maritime lien." *Treasure Salvors*, 640 F.2d at 567.

Maritime liens arising from salvage services presume that the claimant participated in the salvage of the property at issue. *See The Sabine*, 101 U.S. (11 Otto) 384, 386 (1879) ("Salvors, under the maritime law, have a lien *upon the property saved*, which enables them to maintain a suit *in rem* against the ship or cargo, or both where both are saved in whole or in part.") (emphasis added). This is due, in large part, to the risky nature of salvaging; salvage awards and salvage liens are intended to compensate salvors for undertaking those risks and to incentivize others to do the same. *See The Blackwall*, 77 U.S. (10 Wall.) 1, 14 (1869) (describing a salvage award as "a reward given for perilous services, voluntarily rendered, and as an inducement to seamen and others to embark in such undertakings to save life and property"); *Schiffaharts-gesellschaft Leonhardt & Co. v. A. Bottacchi S.A. De Navegacion*, 773 F.2d 1528, 1535 (11th Cir. 1985) ("[T]he principle of salvage rewards a salvor of property in peril with a maritime lien in that property in an attempt to induce rescue.").

However, a claimant need not actually salvage the property in order to be entitled to a maritime lien based on salvage services. As the Supreme Court long ago said, "all who engaged in the [salvage] enterprise and materially contributed to the saving of the property, are entitled to **{-1298-}** share in the reward which the law allows **[—40—]** for such meritorious service, and in proportion to the nature, duration, risk, and value of the service rendered." *The Blackwall*, 77 U.S. (10 Wall.) at 12. In this case, Gold Hound does not claim that it actually salvaged or recovered any of the artifacts at issue in the 2014 or 2015 distribution hearings. Instead, Gold Hound argues that it materially contributed to the salvage by creating proprietary maps and models that Fleet-Queens misappropriated and then used to salvage the artifacts at issue. Because Gold Hound contributed to the salvage by creating these maps, it argues it is entitled to a maritime lien over the recovered artifacts.

In support of this theory, Gold Hound relies on *Darlak v. Columbus-Am. Discovery Grp., Inc.*, 59 F.3d 20 (4th Cir. 1995). In *Darlak*, the plaintiff was a researcher who, along with a team of surveyors, took part in an expedition that was looking for the *S.S. Central America*. *Id.* at 21. When the *Central America* was later found by the Columbus-America Discovery Group, the surveyors intervened in the *in rem* proceeding and argued that they deserved a share of the salvage award because Columbus-America had relied on the surveyors' data. *Id.* Researcher Joseph W. Darlak was not part of that case, but he later brought a separate action arguing that he, too, was entitled to a portion of the salvaged *res* because Columbus-America relied on his coordinates. *Id.* at 22. The district court granted summary judgment for Columbus-America. *Id.* at 21. The Fourth Circuit affirmed, but it noted that "[i]f Columbus-America . . . had indeed availed [itself] **[—41—]** of information proprietary to Darlak to find the [wreck], Darlak would have undoubtedly deserved a salvage award. However, the time and place to present that claim was in the *in rem* proceeding, where all salvage awards are determined." *Id.* at 23.[4] Because Darlak did not participate in the *in rem* proceeding and instead brought his own separate suit, his claims failed. *Id.*

In this case, Gold Hound did appear in the *in rem* proceeding to assert a maritime lien based on its intellectual property. However, the district court treated Gold Hound's claim as a separate contract action against Fleet-Queens. The district court thus denied the claim without considering whether Gold Hound's services—creating proprietary maps and models for the purpose of salvaging the 1715 wreck—might have contributed to Fleet-Queens's recovery of the artifacts. If the maps did contribute to the recovery, then Gold Hound might have been entitled to a maritime lien. *See The Blackwall*, 77 U.S. (10 Wall.) at 12 ("*[A]ll* who engaged in the enterprise and *materially contributed to the saving of the property*, are entitled to share in the reward.") (emphasis added). And while *Darlak* is not binding on this Court, it is persuasive that the Fourth Circuit thought that Darlak "would have *undoubtedly* deserved a salvage award" had the salvors **[—42—]** availed themselves of his proprietary information—in that case, the search coordinates that he had researched and developed. *Darlak*, 59 F.3d at 21 (emphasis added).

Gold Hound's services and proprietary information may likewise have materially contributed to the recovery of the 2015 **{-1299-}** artifacts, and Gold Hound properly attempted to bring those claims in the *in rem* proceeding. Whether Fleet-Queens relied on Gold Hound's proprietary maps and models, and the extent to which those maps and models may have contributed to the recovery of the artifacts, are factual questions that profoundly affect whether Gold Hound is entitled to a maritime lien. We, therefore, remand this issue to the district court for a determination in the first instance.

VI.

On appeal, Fleet-Queens moved for sanctions against Gold Hound for filing frivolous appeals under Federal Rule of Appellate Procedure 38. We decline to impose sanctions on Gold Hound. For starters, Fleet-Queens's motion for sanctions is untimely. Eleventh Circuit Rule 38-1 says that "[m]otions for damages and costs pursuant to FRAP 38 must be filed no later than the filing

[4] In the earlier proceeding between the surveyors and Columbus-America, the district court concluded that Columbus-America had not relied on data from the original team of researchers, of which Darlak was a member. *Darlak*, 59 F.3d at 21 n.2. Darlak was not a party to that proceeding. Because the district court concluded that Darlak's absence from the *in rem* proceeding was fatal to his claims, the earlier factual finding had no bearing on his separate case. *Id.* at 23.

of appellee's brief." In this case, appellee's brief was filed on July 12, 2016. Appellee's motion for sanctions was filed on August 4, 2016. Thus, Fleet-Queens's motion was untimely. **[—43—]**

Moreover, even if the motion were timely, sanctions would not be appropriate. Appellate Rule 38 provides that "[i]f a court of appeals determines that an appeal is frivolous, it may, after a separately filed motion or notice from the court and reasonable opportunity to respond, award just damages and single or double costs to the appellee." In this Circuit, "Rule 38 sanctions have been imposed against appellants who raise clearly frivolous claims in the face of established law and clear facts." *Farese v. Scherer*, 342 F.3d 1223, 1232 (11th Cir. 2003) (quotations omitted). "For purposes of Rule 38, a claim is clearly frivolous if it is utterly devoid of merit." *Parker v. Am. Traffic Sols., Inc.*, 835 F.3d 1363, 1371 (11th Cir. 2016) (quotations omitted). But it was well within Gold Hound's right to appeal the denial of its motion to intervene. *See Fox v. Tyson Foods, Inc.*, 519 F.3d 1298, 1301 (11th Cir. 2008) ("Although orders denying a motion to intervene are not final orders, under the 'anomalous rule' we have provisional jurisdiction to determine whether the district court erroneously concluded that the appellants were not entitled to intervene as of right under [Rule 24(a)]."). The fact that Gold Hound has succeeded on some of its arguments strongly suggests that its appeal was not frivolous.

VII.

Finally, Fleet-Queens has filed a "notice of pendency" of a related action and informed the Court that we "may take judicial notice of the pendency in the **[—44—]** State Court of [a] related action." Fleet-Queens has provided notice but has not asked for any relief related to this notice. As of the date of this opinion, this action is pending without adjudication. *See 1715 Fleet-Queens Jewels, LLC v. Gold Hound, LLC*, Case No. 31-2015-CA-828 (Fla. Cir. Ct. filed Oct. 21, 2015). The district court may wish to consider the posture of the state court proceeding as it determines whether (and to what extent) it may exercise supplemental jurisdiction over Gold Hound's state-law claims.

We commend the district court for its dedication to the fair adjudication of title and the resolution of disputes arising from this centuries-old shipwreck. The district court properly determined that it had and continues to have subject-matter jurisdiction over the *res*. Under the circumstances of this case, however, we conclude that it was error to deny Gold Hound's motion to intervene, at least regarding Gold Hound's *in rem* claims. On remand, the district court should determine whether it will exercise supplemental jurisdiction over Gold **{-1300-}** Hound's remaining claims. As for Gold Hound's assertion of a maritime lien, we conclude that critical facts remain in dispute and, accordingly, we cannot reach a conclusion regarding the merits of this claim. We also deny Fleet-Queens's motion for sanctions. We, therefore, VACATE the denial of Gold Hound's motion to **[—45—]** intervene and REMAND this case to the district court for further proceedings consistent with this opinion.

VACATED and REMANDED.

United States Court of Appeals for the Eleventh Circuit

No. 15-10810

UNITED STATES
vs.
HERNANDEZ

Appeal from the United States District Court for the Southern District of Florida

Decided: July 28, 2017

Citation: 864 F.3d 1292, 5 Adm. R. 477 (11th Cir. 2017).

Before **HULL, MARCUS,** and **ROGERS*,** Circuit Judges.

*Honorable John M. Rogers, United States Circuit Judge for the Sixth Circuit, sitting by designation.

[—2—] {-1296-} ROGERS, Circuit Judge:

The United States prosecuted these four defendants—Lopez Hernandez, Hernandez Almaraz, Aguilar Lopez, and Savala Cisneros—under the Maritime Drug Law Enforcement Act (MDLEA), which criminalizes an individual's possessing with intent to distribute a controlled substance "[w]hile on board a covered vessel," which includes "a vessel subject to the jurisdiction of the United States," which in turn includes "a vessel without nationality." 46 U.S.C. §§ 70502(c)(1)(A), 70503(a)(1), (e)(1) (2012). The U.S. Coast Guard arrested the four defendants on board the *Cristiano Ronaldo*, which the defendants claimed was registered in Guatemala—and claimed so truthfully, as it later turned out. Shortly before the search of the ship, however, when asked by the Coast Guard, the Guatemalan government could neither confirm nor deny the ship's registry. The parties proceeded to trial. The Government presented evidence that the defendants threw **{-1297-}** overboard about 290 kilograms of cocaine shortly before arrest. The jury convicted all four defendants of every indicted crime.

On appeal, the defendants argue primarily that the *Cristiano Ronaldo* was not "a vessel without nationality" because the vessel was properly registered in Guatemala, as the U.S. Coast Guard should have been able to determine with the information that it had. But the *Cristiano Ronaldo* fit within the MDLEA's broad definition of a "vessel without nationality" because a designee of the U.S. Secretary of State has certified, and thereby "proved conclusively," that Guatemala **[—3—]** had not "affirmatively and unequivocally" asserted that the *Cristiano Ronaldo* was of Guatemalan nationality. Under the clear terms of the MDLEA, that certification put the crime within the territorial coverage of the statutory prohibition. The executive branch thereby effectively assumed responsibility for any diplomatic consequences of the criminal prosecution. The defendants' other arguments—insufficient evidence, prosecutorial misconduct, improper suppression or loss of evidence, erroneous admission of hearsay, and misapplication of two sentencing enhancements—are also without merit.

I.

On November 5, 2013, the U.S. Coast Guard identified a suspicious go-fast vessel in international waters, about 120 nautical miles southwest of the El Salvador/Guatemala border, in the Pacific Ocean. The vessel was not flying any national flag. When a Coast Guard helicopter approached it, the vessel sped off, despite radio-transmitted orders in English and in Spanish to halt, and despite several warning shots into the water. The Coast Guard fired at the *Cristiano Ronaldo*'s engines, immobilizing the vessel. Crewmen on the vessel then began dumping black packages overboard.

Officers of the Coast Guard boarded the *Cristiano Ronaldo* and ultimately arrested the four crewmen—the four defendants in this case. When the Coast Guard officers boarded the ship, Hernandez Almaraz said he was its captain. He **[—4—]** also said he was a Guatemalan citizen, as did the other three crewmen. He claimed that the *Cristiano Ronaldo* was registered in Guatemala. Soon thereafter, the Coast Guard contacted the Guatemalan government to confirm or deny the claim of registry. The Guatemalan government responded that it "could neither confirm nor deny." The Coast Guard proceeded to search the ship.

What happened during the intervening period—the period after Hernandez Almaraz claimed the ship's registry in Guatemala but before the Coast Guard contacted the Guatemalan government to check that claim—is unclear.

The Coast Guard states, "No registration documentation was provided to or located by United States law enforcement personnel." That may have been true when the Coast Guard asked the Guatemalan government about the ship's registry, but the Coast Guard later found registration documents on the ship, as the United States ultimately provided the documents to the defendants during discovery.

Some of the defendants claim, or at least suggest, that the Coast Guard had the registration documents before it asked Guatemala about the *Cristiano Ronaldo*'s registry. In support of the motion to dismiss the indictment, Aguilar Lopez wrote, "As soon as *Cristiano Ronaldo* was boarded by the U.S. Coast Guard, [Hernandez Almaraz] gave the Coast Guard a document, issued by the Guatemalan Navy, certifying that *Cristiano Ronaldo* is registered as a Guatemalan vessel." On appeal, Savala Cisneros states that "once the *Cristiano Ronaldo* was **[—5—]** boarded by the U.S. Coast Guard, [Hernandez Almaraz] **{-1298-}** gave the Coast Guard [the registration] document."

Later, the Coast Guard retrieved some packages where the defendants had thrown packages overboard. The retrieved packages contained about 290 kilograms of cocaine, valued contemporaneously on the streets at about $8.7 million.

Some of the evidence from the scene was lost. The *Cristiano Ronaldo* was accidentally sunk when Coast Guard officers, during a standard "At Sea Space Accountability" procedure, drilled holes in the *Cristiano Ronaldo* to check if there were hidden compartments; they used putty to cover the holes, but water nevertheless began pouring into the ship. The wet clothes that the defendants were wearing that day were discarded because of concerns of mold. Similarly, and out of the same concern, the burlap sacks that had covered the cocaine packages were discarded.

Before trial, the district court rejected the defendants' motion to dismiss for lack of jurisdiction, and granted the Government's motion to determine that the vessel was subject to the jurisdiction of the United States. The court relied on the certification from Commander Salvatore J. Fazio of the U.S. Coast Guard, as designee of Secretary of State John Kerry, which declared that Hernandez Almaraz claimed the *Cristiano Ronaldo*'s Guatemalan registry, and that the Guatemalan **[—6—]** government could neither confirm nor deny that claim. The district court specifically declined to inquire into "the factual underpinnings of the certificate" because the court reasoned that they were "neither relevant or appropriate" under the MDLEA. In the same order, the district court denied the motion to reconsider its previous order granting the Government's motion to quash the subpoena to Commander Fazio.

The parties proceeded to a four-day jury trial. The Government's trial evidence included the testimony of Officer Arambula of the U.S. Coast Guard about the actions and statements of his colleague Officer Ligsay. The closing arguments were somewhat heated, with the Government calling the defense attorneys "spin doctors," for example.

The jury convicted all four defendants of all indicted crimes.

The district court sentenced Lopez Hernandez, Savala Cisneros, and Aguilar Lopez to 188 months' imprisonment. The district court sentenced Hernandez Almaraz to 200 months' imprisonment, applying to him two sentencing enhancements related to his role as the captain of the *Cristiano Ronaldo*.

II.

The district court properly determined that the *Cristiano Ronaldo* was a vessel within the jurisdiction of the United States because it was a "vessel without **[—7—]** nationality" within the meaning of the plain text of the

MDLEA. Such a vessel is statutorily defined to include:

> [A] vessel aboard which the master or individual in charge makes a claim of registry and for which the claimed nation of registry does not affirmatively and unequivocally assert that the vessel is of its nationality.

46 U.S.C. § 70502(d)(1)(C). Defendants essentially challenge whether the terms of this provision have been met, but the Government has proved conclusively that they have. The Government produced the written certification of Commander Salvatore J. Fazio of the U.S. Coast Guard, in which Commander Fazio declared that: (i) the self-identified master of the *Cristiano Ronaldo* claimed that the ship was registered in Guatemala; (ii) the U.S. government asked the Guatemalan government to confirm or deny the vessel's registry; and (iii) **{-1299-}** the Guatemalan government responded that it "could neither confirm nor deny that the go-fast vessel was registered in Guatemala." As Commander Fazio further stated, "Accordingly, the Government of the United States determined the vessel was without nationality in accordance with 46 U.S.C. § 70502(d)(1)(C), rendering the vessel subject to the jurisdiction of the United States [under the MDLEA]." Commander Fazio's certification was accompanied by a certificate by Secretary of State John Kerry designating Commander Fazio to act on the part of the Department of State. The MDLEA specifies that "[t]he response of a foreign **[—8—]** nation to a claim of registry . . . is proved conclusively by certification of the Secretary of State or the Secretary's designee." *Id.* § 70502(d)(2). Because Commander Fazio is an appropriate designee of the U.S. Secretary of State, under the plain text of the MDLEA, his certification conclusively proves that the Guatemalan government responded that it "could neither confirm nor deny" the *Cristiano Ronaldo*'s registry. That response, in turn, unambiguously means that Guatemala did not at the time "affirmatively and unequivocally assert" the ship's registry. *Id.* § 70502(d)(1)(C). The absence of such an assertion rendered the *Cristiano Ronaldo* a "vessel without nationality," *id.* § 70502(d)(1), and thus a "vessel subject to the jurisdiction of the United States," *id.* § 70502(c)(1)(A), and therefore a "covered vessel," *id.* § 70503(e)(1), to which the MDLEA's criminal prohibition against possessing a controlled substance with distributary intent extends, *id.* § 70503(a)(1). The district court therefore properly exercised jurisdiction over the defendants under the MDLEA.

To avoid that outcome, the defendants primarily argue that the *Cristiano Ronaldo* was actually registered in Guatemala, that the Coast Guard possessed identifying information about the ship that would easily have confirmed its registry, and that the Coast Guard failed in bad faith to convey that information when it asked the Guatemalan government whether the ship was registered. The defendants' arguments based on actual registry and alleged bad faith fail, both as a **[—9—]** statutory argument about proof of the *Cristiano Ronaldo*'s lack of nationality under the MDLEA, and as an international-law argument about the U.S. government's failure to abide by its treaty promise to the Guatemalan government to convey all available identifying information when asking about a ship's registry.

Interpreted as a statutory jurisdictional argument, the defendants' argument cannot overcome the conclusive-proof provision of the MDLEA. The statute plainly states that the certification conclusively proves the foreign country's response. Here, because the certification conclusively proves that the Guatemalan government "could neither confirm nor deny" the *Cristiano Ronaldo*'s registry, the certification also establishes the fact that Guatemala did not "affirmatively and unequivocally assert" registry. The MDLEA does not state what information the United States must convey to the foreign government during its communication, and it does not state that actual registry overrides the certification's proof of statutory statelessness. MDLEA statelessness does not turn on actual statelessness, but rather on the response of the foreign government. Arguing actual registry against the certification therefore misses the mark.

This conclusion is supported by our decision in *United States v. Campbell*, 743 F.3d 802, 2 Adm. R. 543 (11th Cir. 2014). In that case, as in this case, the Commander of the U.S. Coast Guard (at the time, Commander Deptula) certified in writing that the ship's captain claimed foreign registry, that the Coast Guard asked the foreign **[—10—]** government whether the claim was true, and that **{-1300-}** the foreign government responded that it "could neither confirm nor deny" the claimed registry. *Id.* at 804, 2 Adm. R. at 543. The defendant, as in this case, nonetheless challenged the certification's conclusive proof of jurisdiction, arguing "that the certification . . . lacked details about the communications between the Coast Guard and Haiti and that the United States did not offer any testimony to corroborate the certification." *Id.* at 809, 2 Adm. R. at 548. We rejected that argument, explaining that the certification's statement "that Haiti responded that it could neither confirm nor deny the registry . . . provided conclusive proof that the vessel was within the jurisdiction of the United States." *Id.*, 2 Adm. R. at 548. Just as the certification's conclusive proof foreclosed any need for details or corroborations in that case, it also forecloses any inquiry into its veracity in this case.

While in *Campbell* the defendant "stipulated to . . . the representations by the Coast Guard in the certification," *Campbell*, 743 F.3d at 809, 2 Adm. R. at 548, and in this case the defendants specifically challenge the statement in the certification that "no registration document was provided to or located by United States law enforcement personnel," the difference triggers no distinction. The very concept of a conclusive proof entails not only that no detail or corroboration is needed, but also that any contrary evidence is futile. If a document states a proposition, a party introduces evidence that contradicts or undermines the proposition, and a court thereby inquires whether the proposition is true, then the court treats the document at most **[—11—]** as establishing a rebuttable presumption of the proposition's truth, but not as conclusively proving its truth. Congress instructs specifically that courts should treat the MDLEA certification as conclusive of the foreign nation's response.

It is true that in two cases relied upon by the defendants, we proceeded past a similar certification to examine whether the U.S. agents acted in good faith when communicating with the foreign government. *See United States v. Tinoco*, 304 F.3d 1088 (11th Cir. 2002); *United States v. Devila*, 216 F.3d 1009 (11th Cir. 2000). However, both of those cases are distinguishable because they applied prior versions of the MDLEA, versions without a conclusive-proof provision that applied to the determination in question. In *Devila*, the defendants were indicted in June 1996, 216 F. 3d at 1012, months before the amendment to the MDLEA on October 19, 1996, that added a conclusive-proof provision, Coast Guard Authorization Act of 1996, Pub. L. No. 104-324, § 1138, 110 Stat. 3901, 3988–89 (1996). We explicitly rejected a Government assertion that a Secretary of State certification was conclusive proof, applying what was then the law, that such a certification provided only rebuttable prima facie evidence. *Devila*, 216 F.3d at 1015 n.4. The applicable version of the MDLEA in *Devila* stated only that "[t]he denial of such claim of registry by the claimed flag nation *may be proved* by certification of the Secretary of State or the Secretary's designee." 46 U.S.C.A. App. § 1903(c)(2) (1996) (emphasis added). In *Tinoco*, the United States as in the **[—12—]** instant case had certified that Colombia "could neither confirm nor deny the verbal claim of Colombian registry," 304 F.3d at 1113, but this was at a time when the conclusive-proof provision applied only to the foreign state's "denial" of registry. 46 U.S.C.A. App. § 70502(d)(2) (2006) ("The denial of such a claim is proved conclusively by certification of the Secretary of State or the Secretary's designee."). The provision was amended in 2006, Coast Guard and Maritime Transportation Act of 2006, Pub. L. No. 109-241, § 303, 120 Stat. 516, 527 (2006), and codified in 2008, National Defense Authorization Act for Fiscal Year 2008, Pub. L. No. 110-181, § 3525(a)(6), **{-1301-}** 122 Stat. 3, 601 (2008), into its current form, which states that the certification conclusively proves "the response" of the foreign nation, no matter whether "the response" is a denial, a non-denial/non-confirmation, or a confirmation. *See generally United States v. Brant-Epigmelio*, 2010 WL 557283, at *5 n.6 (M.D. Fla. 2010) (outlining the two amendments that added the MDLEA's conclusive-proof language).

United States v. Wilchcombe, 838 F.3d 1179 (11th Cir. 2016), relied upon by defendants, is also not to the contrary, although it, too, proceeded to analyze good faith, and even though the current version on the MDLEA was in effect. That case arose from slightly different facts. There, the defendant claimed the ship's registry in the Bahamas and the Bahamian government confirmed the ship's registry. *Id.* at 1184. The issue with respect to jurisdiction was therefore whether the Bahamian **[—13—]** government thereafter consented to the United States' searching the ship. A separate provision of the MDLEA states that that "[c]onsent or waiver of objection by a foreign nation," too, "is proved conclusively by certification of the Secretary of State or the Secretary's designee." 46 U.S.C. § 70502(c)(2). The certification in that case stated that the Bahamian government so consented. 838 F.3d at 1187. The defendants there nevertheless argued that "the Coast Guard misled the Bahamian Government about the documentation of the registration status of [the boat in question] that was available to the Coast Guard when it was seeking the [statement of no objection]," and on that ground urged the court to look past the certification's conclusive proof of consent. *Id.* Without deciding whether doing so was required, we proceeded to do so and concluded that the argument did not defeat jurisdiction, listing "multiple reasons" why. *Id.* at 1188.[1] We did not hold that the law required looking past the certification's conclusive proof of consent upon evidence undermining the certification's veracity. Instead we ruled for the Government on one alternative basis (no evidence of bad faith or intentional misrepresentation) rather than on another (the conclusive proof provision). This hardly constitutes a holding that rejects the latter. **[—14—]**

Any remaining challenge to the way that the Coast Guard communicated with the Guatemalan government effectively asserts a violation of international law, which under the MDLEA is not a defense. Savala Cisneros relies on an agreement between the U.S. and Guatemalan governments which states that a request for verification of a ship's registry "shall contain the basis for the suspicion [of the ship's illicit activity], the geographic position of the vessel, and, if available the name of the suspect vessel, the registration number, home port, the port of origin and destination, and any other identifying information." Agreement Concerning Cooperation to Suppress Illicit Traffic in Narcotic Drugs and Psychotropic Substances by Sea and Air, U.S.-Guat., art. VII, § 2, June 19, 2003.[2] However, the MDLEA states that "[a] person charged with violating [the MDLEA] . . . does not have standing to raise a claim of failure to comply with international law as a basis for a defense," explains that that "claim of failure to comply with international law in the enforcement of [the MDLEA] may be made only by a foreign nation," and specifies **{-1302-}** that "[a] failure to comply with international law does not divest a court of jurisdiction and is not a defense." 46 U.S.C. § 70505. With that text, Congress has instructed: any battle over the United States' compliance with international law in obtaining MDLEA jurisdiction should be **[—15—]** resolved nation-to-nation in the international arena, not between criminal defendants and the United States in the U.S. criminal justice system. Assuming as true the defendants' suggestions that they provided the ship's registration document to the Coast Guard as soon as its officers boarded the ship,[3] assuming further that the Coast Guard

---

[1] While there is a statement in the *Wilchcombe* opinion that a district court "may take into account" evidence of bad faith or intentional misrepresentation, *id.* (citing *Tinoco*, 304 F.3d at 1114), the statement was based on *Tinoco*, a case which did not apply a conclusive-proof provision, as explained in the preceding paragraph.

[2] *Available at* <http://heinonline.org/HOL/Page?handle=hein.ustreaties/kav06486&start_page=&collection=ustreaties>.

[3] In his motion below to dismiss the indictment, Lopez Hernandez appeared to admit that the Coast

failed in bad faith to convey information in that document to the Guatemalan government, and assuming finally that that assumed failure violated the United States' obligation to Guatemala, still the defendants' international law argument does not touch the conclusion that the United States properly exercised statutory jurisdiction over this suit. If the United States hid information from Guatemala, then the Guatemalan government may complain in some form to the U.S. government; but Congress has instructed that these defendants may not litigate those complaints in an MDLEA prosecution. **[—16—]**

In his reply brief, Savala Cisneros insists that he "is not contesting the response of the foreign nation, but is instead contesting the facts alleged by the United States in the certification and jurisdiction."[4] Savala Cisneros may simply be insisting that we look beyond what the Guatemalan government is conclusively proven to have said, to the conduct of the U.S. Coast Guard that brought about that response. But the conclusive proof provision does not specify the requisite form of prior notice to the government of the claimed flag nation. To the extent that such prior notice may be required by international law, reliance on such a requirement is not warranted under the MDLEA. Congress explicitly stated: "A failure to comply with international law *does not divest a court of jurisdiction* and is not a defense." 46 U.S.C. § 70505 (emphasis added).

Savala Cisneros may also be arguing that even if the certification conclusively proves the Guatemalan government's response, i.e., that the certification could "neither confirm nor deny" the registry, it does not necessarily follow that the certification also conclusively proves the jurisdictional fact that Guatemala did not "affirmatively and unequivocally assert" registry under 46 U.S.C. § 70502(d)(1)(C). **{-1303-}** But a non-confirmation/non-denial of registry is necessarily the failure to "affirmatively and unequivocally assert" registry; the **[—17—]** wording of the Guatemalan response leaves no ambiguity that it was doing something other than "affirmatively and unequivocally assert[ing]" registry. This is particularly true given the certification's explicit reference to the relevant statutory language. To rule otherwise would be to impose an undue and burdensome formality on the content of the Secretary's certification. This conclusion is supported by our decision in *Wilchcombe*, which held that the certification in that case was not required to "precisely mirror" the statutory language. *Wilchcombe*, 838 F.3d at 1186–87.

Savala Cisneros presses two additional arguments related to jurisdiction. Both fail. First, the district court did not commit reversible error in quashing Aguilar Lopez's subpoena to Commander Fazio. Even though the district court granted the Government's motion to quash the subpoena before the defendants had the opportunity to respond to the motion, the error was harmless because the defendants later had the opportunity to respond in their motion to reconsider. In any event, the district court properly reasoned that Commander Fazio did not need to testify

---

Guard found the registration documents after it determined the ship to be stateless. But on that same motion, Aguilar Lopez wrote, "As soon as *Cristiano Ronaldo* was boarded by the U.S. Coast Guard, [Hernandez Almaraz] gave the Coast Guard a document, issued by the Guatemalan Navy, certifying that *Cristiano Ronaldo* is registered as a Guatemalan vessel." On appeal, Savala Cisneros states that "once the *Cristiano Ronaldo* was boarded by the U.S. Coast Guard, [Hernandez Almaraz] gave the Coast Guard [the registration] document," without specifying exactly how long after the boarding the tender occurred. Savala Cisneros also points out that the Coast Guard later produced the registration document to the defense during discovery and argues that that production of the document shows that the Coast Guard had obtained the registration document before it contacted the Guatemalan government for confirmation of registry. But this does not follow. The Coast Guard could have obtained the registration document after the communication with the Guatemalan government, during the following search of the vessel, and therefore before discovery.

[4] Elsewhere in the reply brief, Savala Cisneros claims that he is disputing jurisdiction in particular on the basis of "the false statements the United States government made to Guatemala," or as put elsewhere, "the United [States'] claims outlined in the certification."

because the MDLEA's conclusive-proof provision foreclosed any inquiry into the Commander's communications with the Guatemalan government in determining the *Cristiano Ronaldo*'s MDLEA statelessness. Second, Savala Cisnero's constitutional argument—that the MDLEA is an unconstitutional assertion of Congressional power because it reaches stateless vessels on the high **[—18—]** seas without a proven nexus to the United States—is foreclosed by our precedent. In *Campbell,* we held that the MDLEA was a constitutional exercise of Congressional authority under the Felonies Clause, and that the conduct proscribed by the MDLEA need not have a nexus to the United States. *Campbell,* 743 F.3d at 809–10, 2 Adm. R. at 548–49; *see also Wilchcombe,* 838 F.3d at 1186 (adhering to that conclusion).

III.

Finally, Aguilar Lopez makes what sounds like a plausible argument: How can defendants commit a crime on a vessel at a time when it is not yet determined to be a stateless vessel, only to have the vessel meet the statutory requirements for a stateless vessel after the crime has been committed? By the time the Coast Guard received word from the Guatemalan government that it could neither confirm nor deny the *Cristiano Ronaldo*'s registry, the crewmen had already thrown the packages overboard, and there were no longer any drugs on the ship. Aguilar Lopez therefore argues that, even under the Government's theory, when the response from the Guatemalan government "converted the Guatemalan vessel into a stateless one," Aguilar Lopez no longer possessed narcotics with intent to distribute, and that the Government has failed to prove that Aguilar Lopez was on board a stateless vessel subject to U.S. jurisdiction when he previously did allegedly possess narcotics with intent to distribute. **[—19—]**

Aguilar Lopez's insufficiency-of-the-evidence argument fails because whether the statutory requirements for MDLEA jurisdiction have been met is not an element of the crime that the Government must prove beyond a reasonable doubt. "[T]he [MDLEA's] jurisdictional requirement is not an essential ingredient or an essential element of the MDLEA substantive offense, and, as a result, it does not have to be submitted to the jury for proof beyond a reasonable doubt." *Tinoco,* 304 F.3d at 1109–10. Instead, the MDLEA's jurisdictional provisions allocate power between the courts and the executive as to which of the two will be responsible **{–1304–}** for complying with U.S. obligations under the international law of criminal jurisdiction.

Construed as a challenge to that allocation, Aguilar Lopez's argument fails because, by relying on the certification to exercise MDLEA jurisdiction over this case, we are not holding that the *Cristiano Ronaldo* was stateless under international law at the time of the criminal conduct. We are instead holding, as we need only hold, that the statutory requirements for MDLEA prosecution in U.S. courts have been met, while recognizing that any further jurisdictional complaint over that U.S. prosecution is to be handled by the executive branch, nation-to-nation, in the international arena. There is nothing anomalous about basing *that* decision on actions taken after the criminal activity. **[—20—]**

Some background helps explain why. Under international law, a nation may lack power to punish criminally the actions of a foreign citizen outside its territory, such that the nation whose national is tried may protest diplomatically. These limits are referred to as limits on a nation's jurisdiction to prescribe. *F.T.C. v. Compagnie De Saint-Gobain-Pont-a-Mousson,* 636 F.2d 1300, 1315 (D.C. Cir. 1980). In addition, under international law a nation may lack power to go on the territory of a foreign state without consent to seize a person, even a national of the seizing state, such that the state whose territory is violated may protest diplomatically. These limits fall under the rubric of a nation's jurisdiction to enforce. *Id.* at 1305–06. *See generally* Restatement (Second) of the Foreign Relations Law of the United States § 6 cmt. a (1965).

In the MDLEA, Congress has delineated between judicial and diplomatic compliance with international law limits on criminal jurisdiction over the actions of aliens on ships on the high seas, with respect to limits on both prescriptive and enforcement jurisdiction. To the extent that we determine a particular case to be on the diplomatic side of those lines, we are not necessarily saying that the United States could exercise territorial jurisdiction under international law limits, but only that Congress has determined that the question, if there is one, is to be dealt with diplomatically and not by the courts. On the protest of a foreign nation, for instance, the executive branch can decline to prosecute. So viewed, there is no **[—21—]** anomaly in finding jurisdiction under the MDLEA based on a Secretary of State certification of a vessel's state's post-crime non-assertion of registry.

IV.

The defendants' other arguments are also without merit. Despite arguments from Savala Cisneros and Aguilar Lopez to the contrary, sufficient evidence supported the defendants' convictions. Savala Cisneros argues, as he and his co-defendants argued at trial, that they had only been fishing that day and that the bales of cocaine that the Coast Guard recovered from the water had not been thrown from the *Cristiano Ronaldo*. The trial evidence included testimony, for example: (i) that the *Cristiano Ronaldo* was located more than 120 miles offshore, away from any fishing fleet, with essentially no fishing gear, but with a large amount of fuel; (ii) that the *Cristiano Ronaldo* sped off when the Coast Guard helicopter approached, despite the Coast Guard's radio-transmitted orders to halt, and despite several warning shots from the helicopter into the water; (iii) that the crew of the *Cristiano Ronaldo* threw overboard black packages from the boat when the Coast Guard immobilized the vessel; and (iv) that in that marked location the Coast Guard later recovered about ten bales containing about 290 kilograms of cocaine. Viewing the evidence in the light most favorable to the **{-1305-}** Government and accepting all reasonable inferences in favor of the verdict, *e.g.*, *United States v. Calhoon*, 97 F.3d 518, 523 (11th Cir. 1996), the presented evidence allowed a **[—22—]** reasonable trier of fact to find that the evidence established beyond a reasonable doubt that the four crewmen of the *Cristiano Ronaldo* were smuggling cocaine instead of fishing. Their intent to distribute the cocaine, moreover, reasonably could have been inferred from the large quantity. *See, e.g.*, *Tinoco*, 304 F.3d at 1123 (11th Cir. 2002).

V.

Contrary to the arguments of Savala Cisneros and Aguilar Lopez, the Government's statements made in closing argument and rebuttal did not constitute reversible prosecutorial misconduct, because they were not sufficiently prejudicial. Some of the challenged remarks do not reflect the high standards to which the Government should hold itself: instead of twice characterizing the defense attorneys as "spin doctor[s]," the Government could have cut to refuting the defense theory; instead of responding eye-for-eye to the defense counsel's statement that the Government's case was "insulting" by calling the defense theory "insulting," the Government could have cut to arguing on the merits why it had proven its case and why the defense had failed to plant a reasonable doubt in it; instead of referring to its witnesses as the "fine men and women of the Coast Guard [who] put their lives on the line every single day," the Government could have highlighted the facts adduced at trial from which the jury could have inferred **[—23—]** their credibility. Other challenged remarks do not appear improper at all.[5] In any event, to be reversible

[5] For example, this remark—"the Government submits to you that Lieutenant Hawn and Petty Officer Brown were extremely credible when they told you what are the priorities"—does not improperly bolster the witnesses' credibility, especially since it was followed directly by arguments why the testimony was credible. The Government's statement that Savala Cisneros's boarding the *Cristiano Ronaldo* sufficed to support conspiratorial agreement to distribute cocaine was not improper when viewed in the context, which was that, in order for there to be conspiratorial agreement, the members did not have to know every aspect of the plan regarding the cocaine and that the magnitude of any particular defendant's role was not relevant. The Government's closing remarks that characterized a witness's testimony, regardless of whether they were mischar-

error, prosecutorial misconduct must raise a reasonable probability that, but for the prejudicial remarks, the outcome at trial would have been different. *E.g.*, *United States v. Lopez*, 590 F.3d 1238, 1256 (11th Cir. 2009). The challenged remarks do not raise that probability both because they are not sufficiently substantive and because of the strength of the Government's evidence supporting the defendants' guilt.

VI.

Neither the Coast Guard's accidental destruction of the *Cristiano Ronaldo* on the day of arrest, nor the Government's discarding the defendants' clothes and the burlap sacks in which the bales of cocaine were found, violated Savala Cisneros's rights, either under *Brady v. Maryland*, 373 U.S. 83 (1963), or under *Arizona v. Youngblood*, 488 U.S. 51 (1988). These pieces of evidence were not **[—24—]** sufficiently exculpatory, particularly in light of the strength of the inculpatory evidence, for the following reasons.

Savala Cisneros first asserts that the *Cristiano Ronaldo* contained fishing equipment, that he was wearing fishing clothes, and that the equipment and his clothes **{-1306-}** would have shown that he was, in fact, fishing the day he was apprehended by law enforcement. But Savala Cisneros does not specifically allege what fishing equipment was on board the *Cristiano Ronaldo* when it sank, and does not argue how even with fishing equipment and even wearing fishing clothes one cannot also smuggle cocaine. Savala Cisneros next asserts that the precise dimensions of the *Cristiano Ronaldo*'s fish hold would have conclusively established that the large amount of cocaine recovered would not have fit in it. However, the Government introduced a photograph that depicted the four defendants standing in the fish hold, which made the jury aware of its relative size. The loss of the burlap sacks that had covered the bales did not prevent Savala Cisneros from arguing as follows: that the photographs of the bales that had been thrown from the *Cristiano Ronaldo* show yellow tape on the bales, but that the packages of cocaine recovered from the water did not have any yellow markings and therefore did not come from the *Cristiano Ronaldo*. In response, the Government introduced testimony from multiple Coast Guard witnesses that the packages jettisoned from the *Cristiano Ronaldo*, and subsequently recovered by the Coast Guard, were all black. **[—25—]** Furthermore, the witness familiar with the camera noted that the coloring could be distorted if the camera was not set up perfectly. Savala Cisneros finally asserts that the vessel would have shown that it did not have a radio, which could have explained why the defendants did not stop the vessel when the Coast Guard radio-transmitted orders to halt. But even putting aside the radio-transmitted orders, at trial, a Coast Guard lieutenant testified that the helicopter he flew in pursuit of the *Cristiano Ronaldo* had an insignia indicating that it was a Coast Guard helicopter. He also testified that one of the helicopter's crew members was waving to the defendants in an attempt to make them stop, and that warning shots were fired near the vessel to stop it.

For both a *Youngblood* claim that the Government failed to preserve potentially useful defense evidence and a *Brady* claim that the prosecution failed to disclose exculpatory evidence, there is a materiality requirement. To warrant reversal, the evidence that the prosecution suppresses under *Brady* must raise "a reasonable probability," i.e., "a probability sufficient to undermine confidence in the outcome," that "had the evidence been disclosed to the defense, the result of the proceeding would have been different." *United States v. Bagley*, 473 U.S. 667, 682 (1985); *id.* at 685 (White, J., concurring); *see Turner v. United States*, 137 S. Ct. 1885, 1893 (2017) (explaining that evidence is material under *Brady* "when there is a reasonable probability that, had the evidence been disclosed, the result of **[—26—]** the proceeding would have been different"). Similarly, to warrant reversal, the unpreserved evidence under *Youngblood* must be the sort of evidence "that might be expected

acterizations, did not amount to reversible impropriety, especially in light of the district court's reminder to the jury to recall the witness's testimony itself.

to play a significant role in the suspect's defense." *California v. Trombetta*, 467 U.S. 479, 488 (1984). None of the unavailable pieces of evidence that Savala Cisneros points to would have been expected to play a significant role in defense or raise the reasonable probability that the outcome could have been different, not just because the alleged unavailable evidence is insufficiently probative or sufficiently substituted, but also because the evidence of guilt is overwhelming.[6] **{–1307–}**

United States v. Revolorio-Ramo, 468 F.3d 771 (11th Cir. 2006), confirms this result. In that case, we affirmed MDLEA convictions and rejected the defendants' argument that their due process rights were violated when the Coast Guard destroyed their vessel after determining the vessel was not seaworthy and could not be towed safely. *Id.* at 774–75. There, as here, photographs and a video **[—27—]** had been taken of the boat, but they were poor in quality, and the parties disagreed about the quantity and condition of the fishing equipment on board. *Id.* at 773. We nevertheless determined that any exculpatory evidence aboard the vessel would have, at most, bolstered the arguments already presented to the jury, and would not have allowed the defense to present an otherwise unavailable argument. *Id.* at 774. We emphasized that the defendants had the opportunity to question law enforcement at trial to attempt to raise doubts for the jury. *Id.* at 774-75. Likewise, in this case, Savala Cisneros's claims about the lost evidence, at best, would have merely bolstered the arguments that he made at trial—that he was merely a fisherman, that the fish hold could not conceal such a large amount of cocaine, that the packages thrown from the vessel were not the ones later recovered, and that no radio was on board. Savala Cisneros was able to review photographs of the lost evidence and extensively question the Coast Guard personnel present the day the *Cristiano Ronaldo* was interdicted.

VII.

Despite Savala Cisneros's arguments to the contrary, the district court did not err in admitting Officer Arambula's testimony about the statements and actions of another Coast Guard crew member, Officer Ligsay.

First, the district court did not err in admitting Officer Arambula's testimony that he saw Officer Ligsay inspect the fish hold of the *Clara Luz*, the vessel that the **[—28—]** officers stopped before encountering the *Cristiano Ronaldo*, and that in his opinion Officer Ligsay did not appear concerned during and after the inspection. While Officer Arambula's testimony permitted the Government to argue that the *Clara Luz* did not contain anything suspicious and therefore could not have been the source of the cocaine found in the water, Savala Cisneros has not shown that Officer Ligsay's nonverbal conduct constituted a statement. Nonverbal conduct can constitute a statement where the person intended the conduct to communicate a message, but nothing in the record suggests that Officer Ligsay intended through his conduct to communicate any message to Officer Arambula. *See* Fed. R. Evid. 801(a). Officer Ligsay was just inspecting the *Clara Luz*'s fish hold; Officer Arambula just saw that Officer Ligsay did so and that he did not react in a way that displayed concern. That conduct and reaction are not hearsay because they are not statements. **{–1308–}**

Nor did the district err in admitting Officer Arambula's testimony about Officer Ligsay's

---

[6] Savala Cisneros's claims here might also fail for alternative reasons, which we note but do not reach. His *Brady* claim might fail also because the prosecution never had access to some of the lost evidence. *Brady* applies only to the suppressed evidence that was available to the prosecution. *United States v. Vallejo*, 297 F.3d 1154, 1164 (11th Cir. 2002). His *Youngblood* claim might fail also because he failed to prove the Government's bad faith in destroying the evidence. Unlike in a *Brady* claim, bad faith must be proven in a *Youngblood* claim. *Youngblood*, 488 U.S. at 58. Here, any argument that the Government acted in bad faith is speculative. Officer Arambula testified that the *Cristiano Ronaldo* was sunk accidentally despite attempts to prevent it; another agent testified that the clothes and the burlap sacks were wet and therefore discarded due to mold and sanitation concerns. Savala Cisneros offers no concrete argument that those reasons were pretextual.

joke. Officer Arambula testified that on the *Cristiano Ronaldo* there was "a box of chicken" with "some bones . . . and a few pieces of chicken," and that "Officer Ligsay asked [the four defendants] if they were using the chicken as bait and then we just all laughed." Officer Ligsay's question appears not to have been a statement offered to prove the truth of the matter asserted—indeed, it is unclear just what the question asserts. Savala Cisneros nevertheless argues that **[—29—]** Officer Ligsay's question allowed the jury to infer that no bait was on the boat. But even if it did, and even if Officer Ligsay intended his question to assert that there was no bait on the *Cristiano Ronaldo*, admitting Officer Arambula's testimony about the question did not prejudice Savala Cisneros, as improper admission of hearsay, to warrant reversal, must have had a "substantial influence on the outcome" of the case. *United States v. Fortenberry*, 971 F.2d 717, 722 (11th Cir. 1992). There was more than sufficient evidence establishing Savala Cisneros's guilt outside of the existence or non-existence of bait on the *Cristiano Ronaldo*.

Finally, the Government concedes the hearsay nature of Officer Arambula's testimony about Officer Ligsay's comment that the cocaine bales they pulled from the water were weighted down with cement. Savala Cisneros claims the Government used this hearsay testimony to support its theory of the case in closing, by arguing that the defendants had thrown the cocaine from the boat, hoping the concrete buckets would sink the cocaine and they would evade responsibility. But Savala Cisneros has here again failed to show that he was prejudiced by admission of the testimony. Regardless of whether the cocaine bales were weighted down with cement, strong evidence supported that the bales were **[—30—]** thrown overboard the *Cristiano Ronaldo* while the defendants were fleeing from the Coast Guard.[7]

VIII.

The district court properly applied the two sentencing enhancements that Hernandez Almaraz challenges: a two-level enhancement for "act[ing] as a . . . captain . . . aboard any craft or vessel carrying a controlled substance," U.S.S.G. § 2D1.1(b)(3)(C), and another two-level enhancement for "recklessly creat[ing] a substantial risk of death or serious bodily injury to another person in the course of fleeing from a law enforcement officer," U.S.S.G. § 3C1.2.

The district court properly determined that Hernandez Almaraz "acted" as the captain of the *Cristiano Ronaldo* under U.S.S.G. § 2D1.1(b)(3). Hernandez Almaraz identified himself as the captain when the Coast Guard boarded the vessel; he held a captain's license in Guatemala; and Lopez Hernandez later confirmed that Hernandez Almaraz was the ship's captain. **{-1309-}** Hernandez Almaraz **[—31—]** relies on cases like *United States v. Cartwright*, 413 F.3d 1295 (11th Cir. 2005), to argue that while that evidence may show that he was the ship's captain, it does not show that he "acted" as such. *Cartwright* did focus on whether the defendant "acted" as a captain by operating the vessel, but the case did so in the context of expanding the scope of § 2D1.1(b)(3) to apply to the defendant who was "a lifelong fisherman" and who was "driving the boat when the Coast Guard boarded it," even though he "was not officially named the captain." *Cartwright*, 413 F.3d at 1299. That case shows therefore that a non-captain can "act" as a captain under § 2D1.1(b)(3); it does not show that a captain does not "act" as a captain when he is not operating the boat. A captain generally acts as

[7] Savala Cisneros also cites the Confrontation Clause in his brief, but fails to develop the claim, only stating that "Savala Cisneros was deprived [of] his Sixth Amendment right to confront the witnesses against him, by the court's erroneous admission of hearsay testimony." The Confrontation Clause was not raised below. Before the district court, defense counsel objected to only one of the three statements Savala Cisneros now challenges, and even that objection challenged the testimony only on hearsay grounds. Plain error review therefore applies. *See United States v. Arbolaez*, 450 F.3d 1283, 1291 n.8 (11th Cir. 2006). Under plain error review, Savala Cisneros bears the burden of establishing that the district court erred. *See United States v. Aguilar-Ibarra*, 740 F.3d 587, 592 (11th Cir. 2014). Because Savala Cisneros has not developed the Confrontation Clause claim, he has not established that the district court plainly erred in admitting this testimony.

a captain as the ship's ultimate decisionmaker, even when the captain delegates aspects of the operation of the vessel. The district court properly determined that Hernandez Almarez "acted" as the *Cristiano Ronaldo*'s captain based on the evidence that he was the captain.

The district court also properly determined that Hernandez Almaraz "recklessly created a substantial risk of death or serious bodily injury to another person in the course of fleeing from a law enforcement officer," U.S.S.G. § 3C1.2, by overseeing as its captain the *Cristiano Ronaldo*'s aggressive maneuvers in response to the Coast Guard's approach and orders to halt. The trial testimony established that the boat maneuvered "aggressively" and refused to stop, requiring **[—32—]** the Coast Guard helicopter to move close to the vessel in order to follow it and fire warning shots. The district court did not clearly err in finding on that evidence that the aggressive maneuvers "recklessly created a substantial risk of death or serious bodily injury." The district court did not clearly err, either, in attributing the aggressive maneuvers to Hernandez Almaraz, since he was the ship's captain and the district court specifically found that Hernandez Almaraz actively caused the risk by controlling the actions of the boat. This met the requirement, restated in *United States v. Dougherty,* 754 F.3d 1353, 1360 (11th Cir. 2014), that the district court make "a specific finding [] that the defendant actively caused or procured the reckless behavior at issue." *Id.* (citing *United States v. Johnson,* 694 F.3d 1192, 1196–97 (11th Cir. 2012)).

IX.

The judgments of the district court are affirmed.

United States Court of Appeals
for the Eleventh Circuit

No. 15-15360

UNITED STATES
vs.
WILLIAMS

Appeal from the United States District Court for the Southern District of Florida

Decided: August 1, 2017

Citation: 865 F.3d 1328, 5 Adm. R. 489 (11th Cir. 2017).

Before **JORDAN** and **PRYOR,** Circuit Judges, and **PROCTOR,*** District Judge.

*Honorable R. David Proctor, United States District Judge for the Northern District of Alabama, sitting by designation.

[—2—] {-1333-} PRYOR, Circuit Judge:

In the waning hours of May 9, 2015, the crew of the Rasputin—defendants Vanston Venner Williams, Mario Alin Bent Barker, Carlos Clemente Henry Taylor, Edince Garcia Cardoza, and Hendrick Guillermo Linero Duffis—were traveling away from Colon, Panama when, much like their vessel's namesake, their luck ran out. A Coast Guard cutter approached the Rasputin, which sped away as four of the crew members swiftly threw dozens of packages overboard, none of which were recovered. Although the defendants successfully jettisoned their contraband, they could not elude the Coast Guard, who boarded the Rasputin and arrested its crew. After a trial, a jury concluded that the jettisoned packages contained cocaine, convicting each defendant of conspiracy to distribute at least five kilograms of a substance containing cocaine while on board a covered vessel, in violation of 46 U.S.C. §§ 70503(a)(1) and 70506(b) and 21 U.S.C. § 960(b)(1)(B), and possession with intent to distribute at least five kilograms of a substance containing cocaine, in violation of 46 U.S.C. §§ 70503(a)(1) and 70506(a) and 21 U.S.C. § 960(b)(1)(B). The jury also convicted Williams of failure to heave to, in violation of 18 U.S.C. § 2237(a)(1), and the remaining **[—3—]** defendants of aiding and abetting Williams's failure to heave to, in violation of 18 U.S.C. §§ 2237(a)(1) and (2). The defendants appeal their convictions, challenging several of the district court's evidentiary rulings as well as the sufficiency of the evidence supporting their convictions. After oral argument and thorough review of the record, we affirm each defendant's drug convictions and Williams's failure-to-heave-to conviction but reverse for lack of evidence the remaining defendants' aiding and abetting failure-to-heave-to convictions.

I. BACKGROUND

We present only the facts relevant to the issues on appeal, which are the defendants' challenges to the admission of the testimony of government expert Gustavo Tirado, the testimony of several Coast Guard officers that the objects they witnessed being jettisoned resembled cocaine bales seized in previous interdictions, and a document listing the Rasputin's next port of call, as well as the defendants' challenges to the sufficiency of the evidence as to each of their convictions.[1]

The United States Coast Guard cutter "Bear" was patrolling waters off the coast of Colombia and Panama—an area where drug trafficking is known to occur—searching for vessels that might be smuggling drugs. Around midnight, **[—4—]** crew member Petty Officer Turner Adair noticed that the Bear's radar was picking up a vessel approximately six to eight nautical miles away. The vessel was heading north-northwest away from Colon, Panama at eight to ten knots. As the Bear approached **{-1334-}** the vessel, Adair used a forward-looking infrared system (FLIR) to view it. The FLIR system could capture images of body heat miles away. Objects that were body temperature or warmer appeared as black, while objects cooler than body temperature appeared as white. Through the FLIR, Adair could see that the vessel was a fishing boat containing a driver and four other

[1] Because the defendants challenge the sufficiency of the evidence against them, we recite the facts relevant to their convictions in the light most favorable to the jury's verdict. *See United States v. Haile*, 685 F.3d 1211, 1219 (11th Cir. 2012).

individuals.[2] When the Bear's crew hailed the vessel on the radio, Adair observed that the four individuals who were not driving the vessel began to move about in a "worried manner." Trial Tr. 9/8/2015, Doc. 118 at 189-90, 201.[3] The four individuals began to place objects, each measuring approximately one foot high by three feet long, into a fishing net.

As the four men on the vessel gathered the objects, the vessel increased its speed to 12 to 14 knots and began zig zagging from left to right for no apparent reason. Adair testified that such maneuvers were dangerous given that the waves and swells that night were between six and eight feet. After the four men finished **[—5—]** placing at least ten bale-like objects into the fishing net, they tied the net up and threw it into the sea. Noticing that it took all four men to lift the net, Adair estimated (based on bales he had handled) that each bale weighed 65 to 75 pounds. After dumping the first net overboard, the four men loaded five more bales into another fishing net then threw that net overboard as well. The vessel changed direction, then heading south, and the four men dumped a third net full of bales.

Meanwhile, on board the Bear, Petty Officer Stephen Fleming and his team prepared to pursue the vessel. Fleming's team gave chase in a rigid hull inflatable boat, activating blue law enforcement lights and giving orders to stop in both English and Spanish via both a loudhailer and the radio tuned to Channel 16. The vessel failed to stop or slow down; instead it continued to change direction erratically at full speed. Only when Fleming's craft pulled within a few feet of the vessel did it finally stop.

Fleming observed that the vessel was a 34-foot fishing boat called the Rasputin and that it was flying an American flag. After Fleming and his team boarded the Rasputin, defendant Williams identified himself as the ship's master. He explained that the ship was a U.S. vessel and that he and the four other men aboard were Colombian nationals. According to Williams, the Rasputin had come from Colombia and was headed to Colon, Panama. But when the Rasputin was spotted, it was headed north-northwest away from Colon. **[—6—]**

Fleming discovered that the Rasputin's radio was turned to Channel 16—the channel that the Coast Guard had been using to attempt to communicate with the vessel—and the volume was turned all the way up. Fleming observed two empty fuel drums aboard the vessel and four empty 40-gallon gas containers. He recognized the strong smell of gasoline, noting that the fish hold had more than an inch of gasoline covering the floor. The Rasputin did not run on gasoline, however; it ran on diesel. The presence of gasoline suggested to the officers that it was being used as a masking agent to alter the chemical composition of contraband residue. And despite the fact that the Rasputin was registered in Florida as a commercial fishing vessel, there was no fishing gear, bait, ice, or fish aboard. Fleming and his crew seized three Global Positioning Systems (GPS) from the **{-1335-}** Rasputin and one $20 bill each from Williams and Cardoza. The officers also seized from the vessel a "zarpe"—a Colombian document including the names of the defendants and their ports of call. The zarpe listed Colon, Panama as the Rasputin's next port of call. The zarpe was admitted into evidence at trial over the defendants' objection that it was hearsay and unauthenticated.

No quantity of drugs was found aboard the Rasputin, nor were any of the jettisoned packages recovered, as they apparently sank. In an attempt to detect the presence of contraband aboard the vessel, Fleming's boarding team used an IonScan machine. IonScan technology is designed to detect trace amounts of illicit **[—7—]** materials—often amounts so small as to be imperceptible to the human eye. Samples, or "swipes," are taken of areas and objects thought to contain

---

[2] Although Adair recorded everything picked up by the FLIR that evening, recordings approximately 85 minutes in length, most of the footage was lost. All that remained was a 12 minute video—a highlight reel of sorts that Adair produced to send to higher command. The 12 minute video was played at trial.

[3] Citations to "Doc." refer to docket entries in the district court record in this case.

contraband. The samples are then run through the IonScan machine, which measures the amount of time it takes for ions from vaporized molecules to drift from one side of a tube into a collector. Because every substance has a unique, predictable drift time, the machine can identify a substance on a sample based on the amount of time it takes for the vaporized molecules to drift into the collector. Fleming collected 34 IonScan swipes aboard the Rasputin.

To protect against contamination and to ensure the boarding team introduced no contraband onto the Rasputin, the officers who boarded had their gear swiped for testing prior to boarding. Aboard the Rasputin, Fleming conducted IonScan swipes by putting on rubber gloves from sealed boxes and using small circular pads (also from sealed boxes) to swipe various surface areas of the Rasputin and its crew. Another member of Fleming's team kept a log of each swipe, assigning a number and description to each swipe. After each swipe, Fleming removed his gloves and placed them into a sealed bag, which was identified with a number corresponding to the number logged for each swipe. The sealed bags containing the IonScan pads were transported back to the Bear for analysis.

Petty Officer Richard Caruso was the IonScan operator aboard the Bear. Caruso had attended a three-day training course where he learned how the IonScan **[—8—]** machine worked and how to maintain the machine, calibrate it properly, run swipes through it, and read the results of its analysis. Caruso testified at trial that he had operated the machine more than five times in training and at least eight to ten times since, and that no scientific degree was required to operate it. The Bear's IonScan machine underwent a weekly preventative maintenance check and a daily parts check, and it was located in a secure area with limited access. While the Coast Guard pursued the Rasputin, Caruso turned on the IonScan machine and calibrated it, determining that it was operating correctly. He then swiped himself, the machine, and the area around the machine to ensure there was no contamination.

Caruso received the swipes Fleming had taken aboard the Rasputin. Of the 34 swipes, 13 tested positive for cocaine. After each positive hit, Caruso ran two blank swipes through the machine to clear it, again to prevent contamination. The IonScan analysis detected positive hits for cocaine in the Rasputin's fish hold, marine toilet, and sink, as well as on seat cushions and on a knife. The IonScan also revealed cocaine on the person of each occupant of the Rasputin except defendant Taylor. By contrast, the IonScan tests conducted on the Rasputin's fantail—the area of the ship from which the bales were jettisoned—were negative.

At trial, the government called Senior Chief Petty Officer Gustavo Tirado as its expert witness on IonScan technology. Tirado **{–1336–}** explained that he had trained as an IonScan machine operator and that he had operated IonScan machines hundreds **[—9—]** of times, running thousands of swipes. From 2006 to 2011 and from 2013 on, Tirado was an IonScan machine instructor, teaching others on hundreds of occasions how to use IonScan machines. Tirado was initially trained to operate IonScan machines at a four-day seminar in 1999, where he was taught both how to operate the machine and to interpret its results. In 2006, when Tirado first became an IonScan instructor, he participated in more in-depth training, where he learned in greater detail how to interpret the results of IonScan testing. He attended additional training almost every year from 2006 to 2015. The district court permitted him to testify as an expert on the IonScan process and the meaning of the results of IonScan testing, after a hearing to assess the admissibility of expert testimony under *Daubert v. Merrell Dow Pharmaceuticals*, 509 U.S. 579 (1993). Tirado explained at trial the scientific process used by the IonScan machine, including how it measures drift time. He noted that to avoid false positive results, the IonScan machine was programmed to identify the presence of cocaine only where certain other parameters were met. He further explained that when an IonScan machine yields a positive result, it will produce values for three variables—delta, maximum amplitude, and number of segments—that indicate whether the sample had a high or low concentration of a particular substance. Tirado applied those variables to Caruso's IonScan results, explaining that some of the positive hits showed greater concentrations of cocaine than others. He further **[—10—]** testified that according to the operator's manual the IonScan machine reported false positives of less than 1%.

Tirado was unable to tell from the IonScan results that any particular quantity of cocaine was ever aboard the Rasputin, however. He was also unable to say whether the positive samples resulted from direct contact with cocaine or indirect contact from traces of cocaine brought aboard the ship by a person or object that had had direct contact with cocaine. Nor did he say how long the cocaine traces detected by the IonScan machine had been aboard the Rasputin.

On cross examination, Tirado testified that Caruso deviated from standard Coast Guard protocol in conducting the IonScan testing in two ways. First, although Caruso properly ran two blanks through the machine in between positive results, he violated protocol by failing to note whether the blanks indicated for an illicit substance. It is unclear, therefore, from Caruso's log alone whether two blanks were run, and if so, whether the blanks indicated the presence of cocaine. Second, Tirado testified that Fleming violated protocol by wearing only one glove on one hand when conducting swipes, when Coast Guard protocol required gloves on both hands and multiple layers of gloves on the swiping hand.

Adair testified at trial that the jettisoned objects he saw on the FLIR resembled cocaine bales he had seen in prior drug interdictions. Other Coast Guard officers gave similar testimony, including Caruso, Fleming, and Petty **[—11—]** Officer William Coffey. The defense's objections—and the district court's handling of those objections—were inconsistent. The defense strenuously objected to Fleming's comparison between cocaine bales from prior drug interdictions on the grounds that such testimony was speculative, irrelevant, prejudicial, and unnoticed expert testimony, but let Adair[4] **{–1337–}** and Caruso[5] give similar testimony largely without objection. The district court sustained an objection to Coffey's testimony that the bales seen on the FLIR looked like bales found during previous cocaine interdictions.

Although several Coast Guard witnesses testified that the objects seen on the FLIR appeared similar in shape and size to cocaine bales from previous interdictions, they also testified that the size and shape were consistent with everyday objects. For example, when Adair was asked whether a "bale" was different from a package, he answered no and explained that a "bale" could be "the same size [and] same weight" as a package. Trial Tr. 9/8/2015, Doc. 118 at 230. Fleming explained that a bale is "slightly larger than a file box" and is "similar to **[—12—]** your suitcase or your briefcase." Trial Tr. 9/9/2015, Doc. 119 at 110. Coffey testified that a bale is approximately the size of a burlap sack or a briefcase.

The jury returned a guilty verdict as to all charges against all defendants. Each defendant was sentenced to 10 years' imprisonment on each drug conviction. Williams was sentenced to 5 years' imprisonment, to be served concurrently, on the failure-to-heave-to conviction, as were the remaining defendants for their aiding and abetting failure-to-heave-to convictions. The defendants timely appealed.

---

[4] The defense failed to object to Adair's testimony that the FLIR appeared to show bales, which "usually contain[] cocaine." Trial Tr. 9/8/2015, Doc. 118 at 190. The defense subsequently lodged a speculation objection—which the court overruled—to Adair's testimony that similar looking bales from previous interdictions contained cocaine.

[5] Although the defense failed to object when Caruso compared the packages seen on the FLIR to bales from previous cocaine interdictions, the district court sustained the defense's objection when Caruso was asked what he thought was in the jettisoned packages, on the ground that the question called for speculation.

II. LEGAL STANDARDS

"We review evidentiary rulings for an abuse of discretion." *United States v. Henderson*, 409 F.3d 1293, 1297 (11th Cir. 2005). Basing an evidentiary ruling on a legal error constitutes an abuse of discretion *per se. Id.*

We "review *de novo* the sufficiency of the evidence supporting a criminal conviction." *United States v. Walker*, 490 F.3d 1282, 1296 (11th Cir. 2007). In doing so, we consider the evidence in the light most favorable to the jury's verdict, here drawing all reasonable inferences and making all credibility choices in the government's favor. *United States v. Haile*, 685 F.3d 1211, 1219 (11th Cir. 2012). "We will reverse a conviction based on insufficient evidence only if no reasonable trier of fact could have found guilt beyond a reasonable doubt." *Walker*, 490 F.3d at 1296 (internal quotation marks omitted). **[—13—]**

III. DISCUSSION

On appeal, the defendants argue that the district court erred in admitting several key pieces of evidence, including Tirado's expert testimony concerning the IonScan results, the testimony of several Coast Guard witnesses that the jettisoned objects they saw on the FLIR resembled cocaine bales from prior drug interdictions, and the zarpe. They also challenge the sufficiency of the evidence as to each conviction. We address each argument in turn.[6]

A. Evidentiary Issues

The defendants argue that the district court abused its discretion in admitting **{-1338-}** three key pieces of evidence over their objections. First, they assert that the district court improperly admitted Tirado's testimony, challenging his qualifications as well as his testimony's relevance. Second, the defendants argue that the district court should have precluded—as expert testimony for which proper notice was not given—the statements of several Coast Guard witnesses that the objects they saw on the FLIR were similar in shape and size to cocaine bales from previous interdictions. Third, the defendants posit that the zarpe should have been excluded because it was unauthenticated and contained hearsay. Each of these arguments lacks merit. **[—14—]**

1. IonScan Evidence

The defendants lodge a number of attacks on Tirado's testimony introducing the results of the IonScan testing conducted on swipes taken from the Rasputin. The defendants challenge Tirado's qualifications to interpret IonScan test results, the relevance of his opinions to the issues in this case, and whether the nature of his testimony was overly prejudicial. We reject these arguments.

Federal Rule of Evidence 702, which governs expert testimony, permits a "witness who is qualified as an expert by knowledge, skill, experience, training, or education" to give an opinion or otherwise testify if "the expert's scientific, technical, or other specialized knowledge will help the trier of fact to understand the evidence or to determine a fact in issue," "the testimony is based on sufficient facts or data . . . [and] is the product of reliable principles and methods," and "the expert has reliably applied the principles and methods to the facts of the case." Fed R. Evid. 702.

No one disputes that Tirado delivered expert testimony, the admissibility of which is governed by Rule 702. In *Daubert*, the Supreme Court defined the contours of a proper Rule 702 inquiry, explaining that Rule 702's requirement that expert testimony "assist the trier of fact to understand the evidence or to determine a fact in issue . . . goes primarily to relevance." 509 U.S. at 591 (internal quotation marks omitted). Indeed, expert testimony unrelated to the issues in the case does **[—15—]** not assist the trier of fact. *Id.* This requirement "has been aptly described . . . as one of 'fit.'" *Id.* In essence, "Rule 702's helpfulness standard requires a valid scientific connection to the pertinent

6 On appeal, each defendant raises different issues, but each also adopts the arguments made by the others. We therefore treat each argument as though it were raised by all defendants.

inquiry as a precondition to admissibility." *Id.* at 591-92 (internal quotation marks omitted).

Moreover, the proponent of expert testimony bears the burden of demonstrating the expert's qualifications and competence to give his proposed testimony. *United States v. Frazier*, 387 F.3d 1244, 1260 (11th Cir. 2004) (en banc). Experts may be qualified by scientific training, education, or experience in the relevant field; they need not be formally educated to qualify as experts. *Id.* at 1260-61. But even if an expert is qualified, and his testimony is relevant and methodologically sound, Federal Rule of Evidence 403 permits the exclusion of all testimony—expert or otherwise—if "its probative value is substantially outweighed by a danger of . . . unfair prejudice, confusing the issues, misleading the jury, undue delay, wasting time, or needlessly presenting cumulative evidence." Fed. R. Evid. 403; *see also Daubert*, 509 U.S. at 595. Under this framework, we evaluate the district court's admission of Tirado's testimony.

i. Tirado's Qualifications and Reliability

The defendants lodge a narrow challenge to Tirado's qualifications. Conceding that Tirado is qualified as an expert **{-1339-}** in the operation of IonScan machines, they challenge his qualifications to interpret IonScan test results. **[—16—]** Importantly, the defendants concede that IonScan technology is, in general, a reliable tool for identifying the presence of narcotics—and cocaine specifically—in a given location.[7] They argue only that, assuming IonScan technology generally is reliable, Tirado was unqualified to testify to whether the IonScan results Caruso generated indicated that traces of cocaine were present in certain areas of the Rasputin. We find no merit in their argument.

Tirado was qualified by his training and experience to testify to the results of the IonScan testing aboard the Rasputin. *See Frazier*, 387 F.3d at 1260-61 (noting than an expert may be qualified by training or experience). At the *Daubert* hearing, Tirado testified that he was first trained on IonScan technology by the machine's manufacturer in 1999, which included instruction on how to interpret IonScan test results. At trial, Tirado elaborated that he was trained to interpret the variables generated by an IonScan test, including "maximum amplitude, delta, [and] number of segments." Trial Tr. 9/10/2015, Doc. 121 at 109. That training was reinforced in annual courses from 2006 to 2015, including more in-depth **[—17—]** training on "how to interpret the results of the machine" when he first became a certified IonScan instructor. *Id.* at 106. Tirado also testified at trial that between 1999 and 2015, he operated an IonScan machine hundreds of times as part of Coast Guard drug interdictions. In short, ample testimony supported the district court's conclusion that Tirado was qualified as an expert in the interpretation of IonScan test results.

In challenging Tirado's qualifications, the defendants argue that he has no background in science, that his work in the field has never been peer reviewed, and that he was unfamiliar with literature assessing the general reliability of IonScan testing. These concerns fail to establish that the district court abused its discretion in admitting the testimony.

First, the defendants identify no specific opinions that were beyond the scope of Tirado's expertise, instead vaguely referring to his "scientific opinions." At trial, Tirado's opinions essentially concerned compliance

[7] After the *Daubert* hearing, the district court asked the defendants if they challenged the reliability of IonScan technology in general. Counsel for defendant Cardoza responded, "in light of Your Honor's ruling, we think that it would also go to weight, not the admissibility" of the IonScan evidence. Hearing Tr. 8/21/2015, Doc. 63 at 43. No other defendant lodged a challenge to the general reliability of IonScan technology in the district court. So, to the extent the defendants argue that the district court should have rejected Tirado's testimony because he was unqualified to assess the general reliability of IonScan technology, they failed to preserve that argument for appeal. *See Goulah v. Ford Motor Co.*, 118 F.3d 1478, 1483 (11th Cir. 1997) ("An objection on one ground will not preserve an error for appeal on other grounds.").

with Coast Guard procedure and the meaning of the IonScan machine's outputs. For example, he explained whether and why the IonScan's outputs for the samples taken aboard the Rasputin—delta, maximum amplitude, and number of segments—indicated a relatively low or high concentration of cocaine in that particular sample. The defendants never explain how any gaps in Tirado's training or experience should **[—18—]** have precluded him from delivering these opinions. On the contrary, the opinions he delivered fell squarely within his training and experience.

Second, a witness need not have formal education as a scientist if his other training and experience otherwise qualifies him to testify as an expert. *See Frazier*, 387 F.3d at 1260-61; *see also* **{-1340-}** *United States v. Holt*, 777 F.3d 1234, 1265 (11th Cir. 2015) (noting that an expert was qualified based on "her extensive involvement in this particular investigation . . . as well as her training, experience in previous wiretaps, and general investigative experience during her six years as a DEA Agent"). Tirado unquestionably had such training and experience.

Third, that Tirado was unfamiliar with literature assessing the general reliability of IonScan technology does not matter because the defendants explicitly declined to challenge in the district court Tirado's opinions on the machine's reliability. *See supra* note 7.

The district court acted within its discretion in determining that, given Tirado's extensive training and experience, any quarrels with his qualifications were fodder for cross examination rather than reason to exclude his testimony altogether. "[The] district court's gatekeeper role under *Daubert* is not intended to supplant the adversary system or the role of the jury." *Quiet Tech. DC-8, Inc. v. Hurel-Dubois UK Ltd.*, 326 F.3d 1333, 1341 (11th Cir. 2003) (internal quotation marks omitted). "Quite the contrary, vigorous cross-examination, presentation of **[—19—]** contrary evidence, and careful instruction on the burden of proof are the traditional and appropriate means of attacking shaky but admissible evidence." *Id.* (internal quotation marks omitted). Although Tirado's qualifications may have been imperfect, the district court did not err in finding that any defects were slight enough that the defendants could explore them on cross examination. The district court did not abuse its discretion in finding Tirado qualified as an expert on the interpretation of IonScan testing.[8]

ii. *Daubert* "Fit" and Rule 403

The defendants next argue that Tirado's testimony does not "fit" for *Daubert* purposes and has insufficient probative value for Rule 403 purposes because it leaves several questions unanswered: for example, Tirado failed to address the quantity of cocaine aboard the Rasputin or how recently cocaine was present, and he was unable to account for a number of purported inconsistencies in the government's theory of the case. We disagree that these gaps required the district court to exclude Tirado's testimony. To be admissible, expert testimony need not answer every question. *See id.* at 1348 (affirming district court's admission of **[—20—]** expert testimony over a *Daubert* "fit" challenge where the testimony related to one, but not another, of the issues before the court). Indeed, at its core, the *Daubert* "fit" question is one of relevance, 509 U.S. at 591, and the positive IonScan tests have some "tendency" to make it "more . . . probable" that the jettisoned packages contained cocaine "than it would be without the [IonScan evidence]." Fed. R. Evid. 401 (defining relevant testimony). Tirado's testimony was helpful to the jury because the singular presence of traces of cocaine aboard the Rasputin made it more likely that the jettisoned packages contained cocaine. We

[8] The defendants also argue that Tirado failed to explain how his training and experience informed his opinions in this case. This argument is belied by the record, which reveals that Tirado provided a robust explanation of how the interpretive tools he learned in training and employed in practice over the past 17 years enabled him to form his opinions in this case. He discussed at length the meaning of the IonScan's outputs—part of his training in the interpretation of IonScan results—and applied those concepts to the facts of this case. We therefore reject the defendants' argument.

cannot say that the testimony wholly lacked relevance—such that the district court abused its discretion in admitting it—simply because the IonScan {-1341-} evidence was imperfect or could not definitively answer every question concerning the presence of cocaine aboard the Rasputin.

Nor can we say that the district court abused its discretion by admitting the IonScan evidence over the defendants' objection that it was unduly prejudicial. Federal Rule of Evidence 403 requires a showing that the prejudicial effect of relevant evidence *substantially* outweighs its probative value. Expert testimony creates a unique risk of prejudice as it "may be assigned talismanic significance in the eyes of lay jurors." *Frazier*, 387 F.3d at 1263. Here, though, the district court properly found that the IonScan evidence had probative value. And the defendant's explanation for why Tirado's testimony was prejudicial—it failed to **[—21—]** address time period or quantity, and it could have misled the jury into believing that the tests definitively proved that the jettisoned packages contained cocaine—easily could have been mitigated by thorough cross examination. *See Quiet Tech.*, 326 F.3d at 1341 (noting that "vigorous cross-examination" is a traditional tool for attacking weak, but admissible evidence). Recognizing that expert testimony poses a unique risk of prejudice, we cannot say that the risk of prejudice here so substantially outweighed the IonScan evidence's probative value as to require the district court to exclude it.[9]

2. Lay Opinion Testimony

Next, the defendants argue that the district court abused its discretion in admitting the testimony of Adair, Caruso, Coffey, and Fleming that the jettisoned objects they saw through the FLIR resembled cocaine bales found in previous drug interdictions. The defendants contend that the testimony was expert testimony that was improperly admitted because it failed to comply with Federal Rule of Evidence 702. We disagree.

Under Federal Rule of Evidence 701, lay witnesses are permitted to give opinions so long as they are "rationally based on the witness's perception," **[—22—]** "helpful to clearly understanding the witness's testimony or to determining a fact in issue," and "not based on scientific, technical, or other specialized knowledge within the scope of Rule 702." Fed. R. Evid. 701. The central question here is whether the Coast Guard witnesses' testimony was based on "scientific, technical, or other specialized knowledge," such that it was governed by Rule 702's expert testimony requirements rather than Rule 701's lay opinion standard. The district court acted within its discretion in admitting the testimony as lay opinion.

A witness is permitted to deliver a lay opinion testimony based on his professional experiences as long as the testimony is "rationally based on" those experiences, rather than on scientific or technical knowledge. *United States v. Toll*, 804 F.3d 1344, 1355 (11th Cir. 2015); *see also Tampa Bay Shipbuilding & Repair Co. v. Cedar Shipping Co.*, 320 F.3d 1213, 1223 (11th Cir. 2003) (affirming a district court's admission of lay opinion testimony where witnesses testified not using scientific or technical "knowledge subject to Rule 702," but only "knowledge garnered from years of experience within the field"). Here, the Coast Guard witnesses compared the packages they saw on the FLIR to packages they had seen in previous cocaine interdictions, {-1342-} an assessment of "the appearance" and "size" of objects that required no scientific or technical knowledge. *Tampa Bay Shipbuilding*, 320 F.3d at 1222 (explaining that opinion relating to "the appearance of persons or things, . . . size, weight, [and] distance" are "prototypical examples of **[—23—]** the type of evidence contemplated by . . . Rule 701" (alteration and internal quotation marks omitted)).

---

[9] In his reply brief, defendant Cardoza argues for the first time that Tirado's testimony should have been excluded because Tirado admitted that two Coast Guard officials involved in the IonScan testing deviated from Coast Guard procedures. Because Cardoza advances this argument only on reply, we decline to address it. *See Big Top Koolers, Inc. v. Circus-Man Snacks, Inc.*, 528 F.3d 839, 844 (11th Cir. 2008).

The defendants rely on *United States v. Jayyousi*, 657 F.3d 1085 (11th Cir. 2011), to argue that opinions based on prior law enforcement investigations necessarily are expert opinions governed by Rule 702. But *Jayyousi* does not support their position. In *Jayyousi*, we affirmed a district court's decision admitting a law enforcement agent's testimony that interpreted code language used by the defendant and his co-conspirators. We held that the agent's testimony was lay opinion because "[h]e limited his testimony to what he learned during this particular investigation, and he testified that he interpreted code words based on their context." *Id.* at 1103-04.

Nothing in *Jayyousi* indicates that the lay opinion of a law enforcement official automatically becomes an expert opinion simply because it involves knowledge that preexisted the investigation in the present case. The code language testimony at issue in *Jayyousi* would have required "scientific, technical, or other specialized knowledge" had the witness been speaking generally from prior experiences or training instead of using her knowledge of the code language used by the conspirators during the investigation of that very case. *See id.* at 1120 n.3 ("[T]his Circuit generally require[s] a law enforcement officer's testimony about the modus operandi of drug smugglers and the meaning of coded language in **[—24—]** conversations to qualify as expert and not lay opinion when derived from their years of experience."). The court concluded that an officer's investigation can provide sufficient foundation for an opinion that would otherwise require technical expertise. It never addressed the central question here, which is whether the opinions delivered by the Coast Guard witnesses were of the kind that *ever* require expert testimony.

They were not. The Coast Guard witnesses' assessments were well within the ken of the average layperson; they simply compared the size and shape of the objects they saw on the FLIR to bales they had seen previously in cocaine arrests. Because the Coast Guard witnesses' opinions were not based on any scientific or technical knowledge, but instead on their rationally based perceptions of the size and shape of objects, the district court acted within its discretion in admitting the testimony under Rule 701.[10] *See United States v. Tinoco*, 304 F.3d 1088, 1119 (11th Cir. 2002) (officer's characterization of vessel as a "go fast" boat was **[—25—]** permissible lay testimony under Rule 701); *see also Tampa Bay Shipbuilding*, 320 F.3d at 1222.

3. The Zarpe

The defendants argue that the district court improperly admitted the zarpe into **{-1343-}** evidence, asserting that it was unauthenticated and that it contained hearsay. Both of these arguments lack merit.

First, we easily reject the defendants' argument that the zarpe was not properly authenticated. Federal Rule of Evidence 901 "require[s] only enough evidence that a jury could have reasonably concluded that a document was authentic." *In re Int'l Mgmt. Assocs., LLC*, 781 F.3d 1262, 1267 (11th Cir. 2015) (internal quotation marks omitted). The defendants contend that the government had to demonstrate the zarpe's authenticity through the procedures outlined by Federal Rule of Evidence 902(3). But Rule 902(3) is inapplicable here: it defines the circumstances in which a foreign public document is *self-authenticating*, i.e., where a party need not provide any additional evidence to demonstrate that the document is authentic. There is no contention here—nor was there at

---

[10] Assuming that these arguments were properly preserved for appeal, we also reject as meritless the defendants' arguments that the district court abused its discretion in admitting each Coast Guard witness's testimony over the defendants' objections that the testimony was speculative, irrelevant, and more prejudicial than probative. The testimony was based directly on the witnesses' observations and tended to demonstrate that the jettisoned packages contained cocaine. And while the testimony may have had a prejudicial effect by linking the jettisoned packages to cocaine bales from interdictions with which the defendants had no involvement, we cannot say as a matter of law that such an effect improperly and substantially outweighed the testimony's probative value. The district court therefore committed no abuse of discretion in admitting the Coast Guard witnesses' testimony.

trial—that the zarpe was self-authenticating. Instead, under Rule 901, "[t]he government may authenticate a document solely through the use of circumstantial evidence, including the document's own distinctive characteristics and the circumstances **[—26—]** surrounding its discovery." *United States v. Smith*, 918 F.2d 1501, 1510 (11th Cir. 1990).

Here, the government introduced evidence indicating that the zarpe was authentic: Fleming testified that it contained the precise information typically found on a zarpe and that it was found aboard the Rasputin. This showing sufficed to satisfy Rule 901. *See Int'l Mgmt. Assocs.*, 781 F.3d at 1267 (upholding a bankruptcy court's decision that a document was authentic where a witness "testified that all of the underlying documents were found at [the debtor's] offices and that the information in those documents substantially matched the records kept by the financial institutions and clients with which [the debtor] had transacted").

Second, the zarpe was not hearsay because it was not offered "to prove the truth of the matter asserted" in it. Fed. R. Evid. 801(c)(2). At trial, the government explained that it intended to use the zarpe to demonstrate that when the Coast Guard approached Rasputin, it was heading away from its purported destination. The zarpe indicated—and Williams told the boarding team—that the Rasputin's next port of call was Colon, Panama, but when the Coast Guard encountered the Rasputin, it was traveling away from Colon. The zarpe was admitted not to show that Colon was actually the Rasputin's next port of call, but rather to demonstrate that the document, and Williams's story, was a ruse. When a statement is entered into evidence to show its falsity, the statement is not hearsay. **[—27—]** *See United States v. Costa*, 31 F.3d 1073, 1080 (11th Cir. 1994) (explaining that a statement is not hearsay where "[t]he government offered the statement not for its truth . . . but rather to show its falsity").

B. Sufficiency of the Evidence: Drug Convictions

All the defendants argue that their convictions for conspiracy to distribute and possession with intent to distribute five kilograms or more of a substance containing cocaine should be reversed because the government's evidence was insufficient to establish that the contraband jettisoned from the Rasputin was cocaine. Admittedly, this case is an unusual one—no visible amount of drugs was found on board the Rasputin and no drugs were recovered from the sea. Even so, we find sufficient evidence to support the drug conspiracy convictions.

We must affirm the district court if the evidence and any reasonable inferences from that evidence—taken in the light most favorable to the government— **{-1344-}** would permit a reasonable jury to find guilt beyond a reasonable doubt. *United States v. Harrell*, 737 F.2d 971, 979 (11th Cir. 1984). We do not ask whether *we* believe that the evidence established guilt beyond a reasonable doubt; the "relevant question is whether, after viewing the evidence in the light most favorable to the prosecution, *any* rational trier of fact could have found the essential elements of the crime beyond a reasonable doubt." *Jackson v. Virginia*, 443 U.S. 307, 319 (1979). We consider the evidence "with all inferences and **[—28—]** credibility choices drawn in the government's favor," and we "are bound by the jury's credibility choices, and by its rejection of the inferences raised by the defendant[s]." *United States v. Broughton*, 689 F.3d 1260, 1276-77 (11th Cir. 2012) (citation omitted). Importantly, the "evidence need not exclude every reasonable hypothesis of innocence or be wholly inconsistent with every conclusion except that of guilt." *Harrell*, 737 F.2d at 979; *see also Holland v. United States*, 348 U.S. 121, 139-40 (1954) (rejecting the argument that, where the government's evidence is circumstantial, "it must be such as to exclude every reasonable hypothesis other than that of guilt").

"To establish a conspiracy, the government must prove beyond a reasonable doubt that two or more persons entered into an unlawful agreement to commit an offense, that the defendant knew of the agreement, and that he voluntarily became a part of the conspiracy." *United States v. Cruickshank*, 837 F.3d 1182, 1188, 4 Adm. R. 472, 473 (11th Cir. 2016). "In order to convict a defendant for possession with intent to distribute a controlled substance, the government must prove knowing possession and an intent to distribute." *Id.* at 1189, 4 Adm. R. at 474 (internal quotation marks omitted). To convict a defendant for conspiracy to possess with intent to distribute a controlled substance or possession with intent to distribute a controlled substance, "the identity of [the drug] must be established beyond a reasonable doubt." *United States v. Sanchez*, 722 F.2d 1501, 1506 (11th Cir. 1984). **[—29—]**

The government may establish the identity of a drug using circumstantial evidence. *United States v. Clavis*, 956 F.2d 1079, 1088 (11th Cir. 1992). Generally, "identification of a controlled substance can be established by such circumstantial evidence as lay experience based on familiarity through prior use, trading, or law enforcement; a high sales price; on-the-scene remarks by a conspirator identifying the substance as a drug; and behavior characteristic of sales and use, such as testing, weighing, cutting and peculiar ingestion." *United States v. Baggett*, 954 F.2d 674, 677 (11th Cir. 1992) (internal quotation marks omitted). We have previously held that "[t]he uncorroborated testimony of a person who observed [the] defendant in possession of a controlled substance is sufficient if the person is familiar with the substance at issue." *United States v. Zielie*, 734 F.2d 1447, 1456 (11th Cir. 1984), *abrogated on other grounds by Bourjaily v. United States*, 483 U.S. 171, 177-79 (1987).

At trial, the government presented evidence more than sufficient to demonstrate that the defendants jettisoned contraband of some kind. The defendants were traveling at night, in rough waters, along a known drug trafficking route. When the Coast Guard encountered the Rasputin, the vessel was going in the opposite direction from where Williams initially stated it was headed and what was indicated on the vessel's manifesto (the zarpe). The defendants had no fish, bait, ice, or fishing equipment on board a registered fishing vessel, and the area **[—30—]** where the Rasputin was found is not known for fishing. Several Coast Guard witnesses testified **{-1345-}** that as the Bear pursued the Rasputin, they saw through the FLIR that the Rasputin's crew began to gather packages and throw them overboard. Coast Guard officers found gasoline—a known masking agent—on board the diesel-fueled vessel, including several near-empty 40-gallon gasoline containers and nearly an inch and a half of gasoline in the fish hold. In addition to these suspicious circumstances, the FLIR images showed that once the cutter attempted to hail the vessel, the Rasputin sped up and moved erratically for no discernible reason. Collectively, these circumstances provided compelling evidence that the Rasputin contained contraband that the defendants jettisoned as the Bear approached.

As for the identity of the contraband—the difficult issue in this case—four Coast Guard officers testified that they had made prior drug interdictions in that same area off the coast of Panama and that only cocaine was recovered on those occasions. Three Coast Guard witnesses also testified to the size and shape of the packages they saw (through the FLIR) being jettisoned by the defendants, and they compared those packages to cocaine bales they had personally recovered and handled during these past interdictions.

Tirado testified that the IonScan samples from the Rasputin and the defendants resulted in 13 hits positive for cocaine and no hits positive for any other **[—31—]** drugs—even though the IonScan machine could detect up to 40 substances.[11] These included positive

[11] The record reflects that the IonScan machine used aboard the Rasputin was optimized for cocaine, heroin, and methamphetamine. Although the defense's IonScan expert appeared to suggest that the machine would have to be specifically programmed to detect a substance besides cocaine, heroin, or methamphetamine, viewing the evidence in the light most favorable to the verdict, the jury could find that the IonScan machine was able to detect other substances, such as different drugs or explosives.

hits on the person of four of the five defendants. Tirado also explained that certain swipe results indicated high concentrations of cocaine. Certainly, Tirado's testimony concerning the IonScan results had imperfections. For example, defendant Taylor—one of the defendants alleged to have jettisoned packages off the back of the Rasputin—did not test positive for cocaine when swiped. And the back of the vessel, where the jettisoning occurred, did not test positive either. But the record contained an explanation for this, which we must accept in drawing all inferences in favor of the jury's verdict: several Coast Guard officers testified as to the rough conditions of the sea that night, including constant sea spray washing over the Rasputin. Fleming explained that it was difficult to swipe the back of the vessel because the swipes kept getting wet and deteriorating. Fleming and Tirado both testified that certain conditions aboard the Rasputin—including saltwater, wind, humidity, and gasoline—could erode the presence of cocaine and interfere with the successful sampling of an area.

Although the defendants theorize that the cocaine traces could have come aboard the Rasputin via contact with currency, the rigid hull boat, the boarding **[—32—]** team, a personal amount of cocaine carried by one of the crew members, or cocaine that pre-dated the defendants' involvement with the ship, the record contained little to no evidence supporting these propositions. Indeed, the record explicitly contradicted some of these hypotheses—for example, the team that boarded the Rasputin was swiped prior boarding and tested negative for cocaine, while the rigid hull boat was brand new and had never been used in a drug interdiction before. Even to the extent the defendants' hypotheses were supported by some modicum of evidence, the **{-1346-}** jury was not required to return a verdict of acquittal. *See Harrell*, 737 F.2d at 979 (noting that the evidence need not disprove "every reasonable hypothesis of innocence" to permit a guilty verdict). The jury was free to "choose between or among the reasonable conclusions to be drawn from the evidence presented at trial." *United States v. Molina*, 443 F.3d 824, 828 (11th Cir. 2006).

We conclude that sufficient evidence supported the jury's determination that the jettisoned packages contained cocaine. We recognize that this case is like no other in this circuit in that there was no witness who identified the jettisoned contraband as cocaine, nor was any cocaine recovered. While no single piece of evidence in this case, on its own, sufficed to permit a reasonable jury to conclude that the jettisoned packages contained cocaine, that is not the relevant question. Instead, the question is whether all of the evidence presented by the government, **[—33—]** taken together, permitted any reasonable jury to arrive at that conclusion. *See, e.g., United States v. Waymer*, 55 F.3d 564, 571 (11th Cir. 1995); *United States v. Draine*, 811 F.2d 1419, 1421 (11th Cir. 1987); *see also United States v. Vergara*, 687 F.2d 57, 61 (5th Cir. 1982) ("While each piece of evidence, standing alone, may have been susceptible of innocent interpretation, we are convinced that the jury reasonably could have concluded that the evidence, when examined in the aggregate, sufficed to establish that Vergara was a culpable member of the conspiracy as charged in the indictment."). In sum, the government presented evidence that: (1) the Coast Guard witnesses had been involved in previous drug interdictions in the area where the Rasputin was stopped, and only cocaine had been recovered; (2) the packages the Coast Guard witnesses saw through the FLIR had the same size and shape as cocaine bales seized in prior drug interdictions; (3) IonScan testing revealed traces of cocaine aboard the Rasputin, including on the person of four of the five defendants; and (4) some of the IonScan swipes reflected high concentrations of cocaine. The cumulative effect of this evidence was enough to permit a reasonable jury to determine, beyond a reasonable doubt, that the substance jettisoned from the vessel was cocaine, notwithstanding the fact that no visible amount of cocaine was recovered by the Coast Guard. *See also United States v. Cruz-Valdez*, 773 F.2d 1541, 1546-47 (11th Cir. 1985) (en banc) (explaining that juries and courts "frequently take into account matters of common **[—34—]** sense or general knowledge," such as the "almost ritualistic series of precautionary maneuvers that often characterize large controlled substance transactions").[12]

C. Sufficiency of the Evidence: Failure-to-Heave-To Convictions

1. Williams

The government presented evidence sufficient to permit a reasonable fact finder to convict Williams for failure to heave to. Under 18 U.S.C. § 2237(a)(1), "[i]t shall be unlawful for the master, operator, or person in charge of a vessel of the United States, or a vessel subject to the jurisdiction of the United States, to knowingly **{-1347-}** fail to obey an order by an authorized Federal law enforcement officer to heave to that vessel." "Heave to" means "to cause a vessel to slow, come to a stop, or adjust its course or speed to account for the weather conditions and sea state to facilitate a law enforcement boarding." 18 U.S.C. § 2237(e)(2).

The government presented evidence that Williams was the master of the Rasputin, the Rasputin sped up and made erratic movements after it was hailed by the Coast Guard, and such movements were inappropriate and dangerous given the sea conditions that night. Williams nonetheless contends that the record contains **[—35—]** no evidence that he heard or saw the Coast Guard's attempts to hail the Rasputin with a loudhailer. Coffey testified, however, that the Rasputin was hailed through both the loud hailer and the radio via Channel 16. Fleming testified that when he boarded the Rasputin, the radio was tuned to Channel 16 with the volume turned all the way up. Fleming also testified that when another officer gave the instruction to heave to over the loudhailer, the Rasputin responded by speeding up and beginning to move erratically. This testimony easily permits the inference that Williams attempted to evade the Coast Guard after hearing the loudhailer and/or the radio.

Williams argues in the alternative that the evidence adduced at trial compels the conclusion that it would have been unsafe for him to heave to faster than he did. But the government presented evidence indicating the opposite: that the Rasputin's movements after being hailed were dangerous given the marine conditions that night. Adair testified that after the Coast Guard hailed the Rasputin, the vessel started "going from left to right for no apparent reason, going through swells that a[] 24-foot [sic] vessel should not be going through." Trial Tr. 9/8/2015, Doc. 118 at 190. Fleming testified that the Rasputin "started operating erratically doing sudden course changes" just after the Coast Guard hailed the vessel, suggesting that Williams's maneuvers resulted from the presence of the Coast Guard rather than weather or sea conditions. Trial Tr. 9/9/2015, Doc. 119 at **[—36—]** 32-33. This testimony sufficed to permit the jury to find that Williams' erratic movements were an attempt to evade the Coast Guard, rather than an effort to stay safe in rough waters.

2. Barker, Cardoza, Duffis and Taylor

The remaining defendants' convictions for aiding and abetting Williams' failure to heave to must be reversed for insufficient evidence. "To prove guilt under a theory of aiding and abetting, the Government must prove: (1) the substantive offense was committed by someone; (2) the defendant committed an act which contributed to and furthered the offense; and (3) the defendant intended to aid in its commission." *United States v. Camacho*, 233 F.3d 1308, 1317 (11th Cir. 2000). At trial, the government presented no evidence of the third element—that Williams's codefendants intended to aid him in failing to heave to. On appeal, the government argues that the mere

[12] To the extent the defendants argue that the trial evidence was insufficient to establish that they jettisoned at least five kilograms of cocaine, we disagree. Adair testified that he initially witnessed, through the FLIR, four men gathering ten or so bales into a net. Adair then explained that it took all four men to throw the first net of bales overboard. Based on that observation and the size of the bales, Adair estimated that each bale weighed between 65 and 75 pounds. Adair further testified that the four men threw overboard two additional sets of bales. This testimony permitted a reasonable jury to conclude that the defendants jettisoned at least five kilograms of cocaine.

fact that the codefendants jettisoned packages from the Rasputin indicates that they intended to aid Williams by making the Rasputin lighter and therefore faster. But, to support its theory, the government points to nothing other than the fact that the codefendants jettisoned the packages. The government's proof is especially tenuous given that the defendants had an obvious alternative motive for their behavior—ridding the boat of contraband before law enforcement arrived. Without more, no reasonable jury could find beyond a reasonable doubt that Williams's codefendants intended to help him **[—37—]** evade the Coast Guard by jettisoning the packages. *See* **{-1348-}** *United States v. Hamblin*, 911 F.2d 551, 558 (11th Cir. 1990) (overturning a firearm conviction where the government failed to meet its "burden of proving that [the defendant] shared the criminal intent of his co-defendant with respect to the firearm charges"). We therefore reverse these defendants' convictions for aiding and abetting failure to heave to.

IV. CONCLUSION

For the foregoing reasons, we affirm the drug convictions of all defendants. We affirm Williams's failure-to-heave-to conviction and reverse the remaining defendants' aiding and abetting failure-to-heave-to convictions. We remand for resentencing of Barker, Cardoza, Duffis, and Taylor.

AFFIRMED IN PART, REVERSED IN PART, AND REMANDED.

United States Court of Appeals
for the Eleventh Circuit

No. 16-15105

THACKER
vs.
TENNESSEE VALLEY AUTH.

Appeal from the United States District Court for the Northern District of Alabama

Decided: August 22, 2017

Citation: 868 F.3d 979, 5 Adm. R. 503 (11th Cir. 2017).

Before **CARNES,** Chief Judge, and **ROSENBAUM** and **DUBINA,** Circuit Judges.

[—1—] {-980-} PER CURIAM: **[—2—]**

Gary and Venida Thacker sued the Tennessee Valley Authority ("TVA") for its alleged negligence involving a tragic accident on the Tennessee River. On July 30, 2013, while Gary Thacker and his friend Anthony Szozda were participating in a local fishing tournament, TVA was attempting to raise a downed power line that was partially submerged in the river. The power line, which crossed the river, had become lax earlier in the day when a pulling cable failed during a conductor-replacement project. At the same moment that TVA began lifting the conductor out of the water, the fishing partners' boat passed through the area at a high rate of speed, and the conductor struck both Thacker and Szozda. As a result, according to the complaint, Thacker suffered serious physical injuries, his wife suffered loss-of-consortium damages, and Szozda was killed instantly.

The district court dismissed the Thackers' complaint for lack of subject-matter jurisdiction. We now must affirm.

The Thackers assert that the district court erred in two ways: (1) in the Thackers' view, the discretionary-function exception to the government's sovereign-immunity waiver in the TVA Act cannot apply to TVA's activities at issue here; and (2) even if the exception applies, the challenged conduct does not fall within it. We address the Thackers' arguments in order. **[—3—] {-981-}**

I.

When we review a district court's decision to grant a motion to dismiss under Rule 12(b)(1), Fed. R. Civ. P., for lack of subject-matter jurisdiction, we review its legal conclusions, which are all that are at issue here, *de novo*. *McElmurray v. Consol. Gov't of Augusta-Richmond Cty.*, 501 F.3d 1244, 1250 (11th Cir. 2007).

II.

The United States enjoys sovereign immunity from suit unless it unequivocally waives it in statutory text. *Lane v. Pena*, 518 U.S. 187, 192 (1996) (citation omitted). When Congress waives sovereign immunity, we must strictly construe that waiver, in terms of its scope, in favor of the United States. *See id.* (citation omitted).

Yet we have recognized that the doctrine of sovereign immunity does not entirely bar suit against TVA, *Peoples Nat'l Bank of Huntsville, Ala. v. Meredith*, 812 F.2d 682, 684-85 (11th Cir. 1987) (citing 16 U.S.C. § 831c(b)), a corporate agency of the United States that is expressly authorized to engage in commercial, power-generating activities, among other functions, 16 U.S.C. §§ 831c(j), 831d(*l*), 831k; *Tenn. Elec. Power Co. v. Tenn. Valley Auth.*, 306 U.S. 118, 127 (1939) ("The [TVA] Act erects a corporation, an instrumentality of the United States, to develop by a series of dams on the Tennessee River and its tributaries a system of **[—4—]** navigation and flood control and to sell the power created by the dams." (footnote omitted)). Rather, the TVA Act expressly provides that TVA "[m]ay sue and be sued in its corporate name." 16 U.S.C. § 831c(b). Though "sue-and-be-sued" waivers are liberally construed, *Loeffler v. Frank*, 486 U.S. 589, 554 (1988) (quoting *Fed. Hous. Admin., Region No. 4 v. Burr*, 309 U.S. 242, 245 (1940)), courts have interpreted this language to mean that TVA is "liable to suit in tort, subject to certain exceptions." *United States v. Smith*, 499 U.S. 160, 168-69 (1991) (citing *Meredith*, 812 F.2d at 684-85; *Queen v. Tenn. Valley Auth.*, 689 F.2d 80, 85 (6th Cir. 1982), *cert. denied*, 460 U.S. 1082 (1983)).

As relevant here, we have held that TVA cannot be subject to liability when engaged in governmental functions that are discretionary in nature. *Meredith*, 812 F.2d at 685. And we have specifically applied the discretionary-function exception in cases arising out of TVA's commercial, power-generating activities. *See, e.g.*, *Johns v. Pettibone Corp.*, 843 F.2d 464, 466–67 (11th Cir. 1988) (negligence suit arising out of electrocution death caused by a TVA power transmission line).

We must do so here as well because TVA's challenged actions occurred in the context of its performance of a governmental function. Under the TVA Act, TVA has the "power to acquire real estate for the construction of . . . transmission lines, power houses, and other structures . . . , and in the event that the owner or owners of such property shall fail and refuse to sell to [TVA] at a price deemed fair **[—5—]** and reasonable . . . , then [TVA] *may . . . exercise the right of eminent domain* . . . ." 16 U.S.C. § 831c(i) (emphasis added); *see also id.* at § 831c(h) (TVA "[s]hall have power *in the name of the United States of America* to exercise the right of eminent domain . . . .") (emphasis added).

The power of eminent domain that TVA may exercise when it constructs power-transmission lines, of course, belongs solely to the United States, not to commercial entities. Since TVA can exercise that power **{-982-}** when it constructs power-transmission lines, we conclude that it acts as an agency of the United States when constructing power-transmission lines. *Cf. Lynn v. United States*, 110 F.2d 586, 590 (5th Cir. 1940) ("In the erection of dams [TVA] is only an agency of the United States.") (citing 16 U.S.C. § 831c(h), (i), (k)). Because the construction of power lines is a governmental activity, TVA cannot be sued for actions arising out of that activity if those actions fall within the discretionary-function exception. *See Meredith*, 812 F.2d at 685–86.

The Thackers' allegation that TVA negligently "failed to exercise reasonable care in the assembly and installation of power lines across the Tennessee River" is encompassed within TVA's construction of power-transmission lines. And their contention that TVA "failed to exercise reasonable care in warning boaters on the Tennessee River of the hazards the TVA created" allegedly occurred incident to **[—6—]** TVA's construction of power-transmission lines. As a result, we must determine whether TVA's challenged actions fall within the discretionary-function exception.

III.

To determine whether TVA is shielded from liability under the discretionary-function exception based on the challenged conduct, we use the same test that applies when the government invokes the discretionary-function exception to the Federal Tort Claims Act ("FTCA"). *See, e.g.*, *Bobo v. Tenn. Valley Auth.*, 855 F.3d 1294, 1310 (11th Cir. 2017) (relying on cases analyzing the FTCA's discretionary-function exception to evaluate the exception's applicability in a lawsuit against TVA).

Before applying the test, however, we must first identify "exactly what conduct is at issue." *Swafford v. United States*, 839 F.3d 1365, 1370 (11th Cir. 2016) (citation and quotation marks omitted). As we have noted, the Thackers allege that TVA negligently "(1) failed to exercise reasonable care in the assembly and installation of power lines across the Tennessee River, and (2) failed to exercise reasonable care in warning boaters on the Tennessee River of the hazards the TVA created."

Having identified the challenged actions, we apply a two-part test to that conduct to ascertain whether the conduct falls within the bounds of the discretionary-function exception. *Id.* At the first step, we evaluate whether the **[—7—]** conduct at issue "is a matter of choice for the acting employee." *Id.* (quoting *Berkovitz ex rel. Berkovitz v. United States*, 486 U.S. 531, 536 (1988) (internal quotation marks omitted)). An action is not a matter of choice—and therefore not discretionary—"when a federal statute, regulation, or policy specifically prescribes a course of action for an employee to follow." *Id.*

(quoting *Berkovitz*, 486 U.S. at 536 (internal quotation marks omitted)). Under those circumstances, an employee is required to follow the directive, meaning that the employee's actions are not discretionary and do not fall within the discretionary-function exception. *Id.*

Here, the Thackers point to no specific federal statute, regulation, or policy that sets forth a particular course of action for employees raising a power line from a river to follow, either in the construction of the line or in safety precautions to undertake to protect the public. Instead, for the first time in their reply brief, the Thackers cite generally 29 C.F.R. § 1926, a group of regulations that concerns safety and health regulations for construction. But arguments raised for the first time in a reply brief are not properly before this Court. **{-983-}** *Herring v. Sec'y, Dep't. of Corr.*, 397 F.3d 1338, 1342 (11th Cir. 2005) (citations omitted).

And even if we were to address the Thackers' argument, their general citation to § 1926 is inadequate. Section 1926 consists of multiple subparts governing items varying from fire protection and prevention (29 C.F.R. §§ 1926.150-1926.155) to fall protection (29 C.F.R. §§1926.500-1926.503) to **[—8—]** stairways and ladders (29 C.F.R. §§ 1926.1050-1926.1060) to toxic and hazardous substances (29 C.F.R. §§ 1926.1100-1926.1153). So even if we ignored the lateness of the Thackers' reliance on § 1926, they have not pointed to a specific regulation that TVA allegedly transgressed. This does not suffice. Under these circumstances, the first step of the discretionary-function test is satisfied.

At the second step, we consider whether the conduct at issue involves the kind of judgment designed to be shielded by the discretionary-function exception. *Swafford*, 839 F.3d at 1370. "[T]he purpose of the exception is to prevent judicial 'second-guessing' of . . . administrative decisions grounded in social, economic, and political policy through the medium of an action in tort." *United States v. Gaubert*, 499 U.S. 315, 322 (1991) (quoting *United States v. Varig Airlines*, 467 U.S. 797, 814 (1984)). For this reason, the discretionary-function exception applies to only that conduct "that involves the permissible exercise of policy judgment." *Berkovitz*, 486 U.S. at 539. This type of conduct, in turn, concerns "governmental actions and decisions based on considerations of public policy." *Id.* at 537 (citation omitted); *see also Gaubert*, 499 U.S. at 322-23.

In this case, the challenged actions plainly involved public-policy considerations. The challenged actions and decisions in this case could require TVA to consider, among other things, its allocation of resources (such as personnel and time), public safety, cost concerns, benefits, and environmental impact. *See* **[—9—]** *OSI, Inc. v. United States*, 285 F.3d 947, 950–51 (11th Cir. 2002) ("The exception does not require there to have been actual weighing of policy considerations.") (quotation marks omitted). As a result, the second step of the discretionary-function exception is also satisfied, and the exception applies.

IV.

For these reasons, we affirm the district court's dismissal for lack of subject-matter jurisdiction.

AFFIRMED.

United States Court of Appeals for the Eleventh Circuit

No. 16-15535

SCL BASILISK AG vs. AGRIBUSINESS UNITED SAVANNAH LOGISTICS LLC

Appeal from the United States District Court for the Southern District of Georgia

Decided: November 14, 2017

Citation: 875 F.3d 609, 5 Adm. R. 506 (11th Cir. 2017).

Before **PRYOR, JORDAN,** and **RIPPLE,*** Circuit Judges.

*Honorable Kenneth F. Ripple, United States Circuit Judge for the Seventh Circuit, sitting by designation.

[—2—] {-611-} RIPPLE, Circuit Judge:

Invoking the district court's maritime jurisdiction, the plaintiffs SCL Basilisk AG ("SCL Basilisk") and Thorco Shipping A/S ("Thorco") brought this action for an order requiring the posting of security by Agribusiness United Savannah Logistics LLC ("Agribusiness Savannah"), Agribusiness United Inc., Agribusiness United DMCC, Inc., and Sonada Agro Limited (UK) LLC ("Sonada"), in aid of a pending international arbitration in London, United Kingdom. After a hearing, the district court denied relief, and the plaintiffs timely appealed. We now affirm the district court's judgment. The relief sought by the plaintiffs is not authorized by Rule B of the Supplemental Rules for Admiralty or Maritime Claims and Asset Forfeiture Actions ("Supplemental Rules"), Georgia law, or principles of maritime law.

I

The underlying petition arose out of a commercial dispute between the plaintiffs, SCL Basilisk and Thorco, and defendants Agribusiness Savannah and Sonada,[1] over the performance of a charter agreement. On December 30, 2015, **[—3—]** SCL Basilisk executed a voyage charter party with Agribusiness Savannah for the carriage of grain from New Orleans to Portugal and Morocco. Agribusiness Savannah later requested that the charterer be changed to Sonada **{-612-}** for insurance coverage reasons.[2] On March 4, 2016, a letter of indemnity was issued by Sonada as charterer and Agribusiness Savannah as guarantor. The letter required the posting of security if the SCL Basilisk were arrested or detained, and provided for indemnification against liability, loss, and damage.

The M/V SCL BASILISK was detained pursuant to a writ of attachment issued in the Eastern District of Louisiana at the request of a nonparty on a claim unrelated to the present dispute. There was a delay by Sonada and Agribusiness Savannah in posting security, and, as a result, SCL Basilisk incurred damages in the amount of $452,528.86. In February 2016, SCL Basilisk instituted arbitration proceedings against Sonada and Agribusiness Savannah in a London arbitration as required by the charter agreement. **[—4—]**

On June 24, 2016, SCL Basilisk filed a "Petition and Application for an Order for Security in Aid of Foreign Arbitration Pursuant to O.C.G.A. § 9-9-30" in the federal district court in Savannah, Georgia.[3] In its petition, SCL Basilisk identified Sonada as a foreign entity having an office and registered agent in Savannah, Georgia, and a registered agent in Roswell, Georgia; Agribusiness United Inc. as a Georgia corporation with a principal office and registered agent in Savannah, Georgia; Agribusiness Savannah as a Florida corporation with a principal office address in Savannah, Georgia; and the other Agribusiness entities as foreign companies,

[1] In their petition, SCL Basilisk and Thorco identified the primary defendants as Agribusiness Savannah and Sonada; they alleged that the other named defendants, Agribusiness United Inc., **[—3—]** Agribusiness United DMCC Inc., and Agribusiness United DMCC (Dubai) LLC, were the primary defendants' "paying agents and/or alter egos." R.1, ¶ 3.

[2] SCL Basilisk discovered later that Sonada had been incorporated only two days before Agribusiness Savannah requested the change.

[3] *See* R.1 (capitalization removed).

but registered to do business, and with registered agents for service of process, in either Atlanta or Savannah, Georgia.[4] The petition sought $667,528.86[5] to secure a possible judgment in the pending arbitration in London. It asserted that the requested relief was authorized by section 9-9-30 of the Georgia Code.

The district court expedited the matter and held a hearing on July 11, 2016. One week later, it issued an order denying the requested relief. In its order, the **[—5—]** district court first noted that the relief that the plaintiffs sought was not available under maritime law. The court explained that Supplemental Rule B allows entities to sue in personam and attach property as security for a claim.[6] Supplemental Rule B requires, **{-613-}** however, that the plaintiff or the plaintiff's attorney sign and file an affidavit stating that the defendant cannot be found within the district. The plaintiffs could not meet this requirement because, "according to their filings, all **[—6—]** Defendants are present in some fashion in this district."[7] Rule C of the Supplemental Rules[8] also was not available to the plaintiffs. The district court explained that Supplemental Rule C allowed a party to sue a ship directly in rem. **[—7—]** Because the

---

[4] R.1, ¶¶ 6–10.

[5] This includes $200,000 for recoverable costs, including attorneys' fees, and for interest at the rate of 3.5% compounded quarterly. *Id.*, ¶ 43.

[6] Supplemental Rule B states in relevant part:

> **(1) When Available; Complaint, Affidavit, Judicial Authorization, and Process.** In an in personam action:
>
> **(a)** *If a defendant is not found within the district* when a verified complaint praying for attachment and the affidavit required by Rule B(1)(b) are filed, a verified complaint may contain a prayer for process to attach the defendant's tangible or intangible personal property—up to the amount sued for—in the hands of garnishees named in the process.
>
> **(b)** The plaintiff or the plaintiff's attorney must sign and file with the complaint an affidavit stating that, *to the affiant's knowledge, or on information and belief, the defendant cannot be found within the district.* The court must review the complaint and affidavit and, if the conditions of this Rule B appear to exist, enter an order so stating and authorizing process of attachment and garnishment. The clerk may issue supplemental process enforcing the court's order upon application without further court order.
>
> . . .
>
> **(e)** The plaintiff may invoke state-law remedies under Rule 64 for seizure of person or property for the purpose of securing satisfaction of the judgment.

Fed. R. Civ. P. Supp. B (emphasis added).

[7] R.30 at 5.

[8] Supplemental Rule C provides in relevant part:

> **(1) When Available.** An action in rem may be brought:
>
> **(a)** To enforce any maritime lien;
>
> **(b)** Whenever a statute of the United States provides for a maritime action in rem or a proceeding analogous thereto.
>
> Except as otherwise provided by law a party who may proceed in rem may also, or in the alternative, proceed in personam against any person who may be liable.
>
> Statutory provisions exempting vessels or other property owned or possessed by or operated by or for the United States from arrest or seizure are not affected by this rule. When a statute so provides, an action against the United States or an instrumentality thereof may proceed on in rem principles.
>
> **(2) Complaint.** In an action in rem the complaint must:
>
> **(a)** be verified;
>
> **(b)** describe with reasonable particularity the property that is the subject of the action; and
>
> **(c)** state that the property is within the district or will be within the district while the action is pending.

Fed. R. Civ. P. Supp. C.

plaintiffs are the owners of the M/V SCL BASILISK, pursuing attachment under Supplemental Rule C would result in a suit against themselves.

The district court then evaluated whether the plaintiffs could recover under section 9-9-30 of the Georgia Code. That provision states: "Before or during arbitral proceedings, a party may request from a court an interim measure of protection, and a court may grant such measure, and such request shall not be deemed to be incompatible with an arbitration agreement." Ga. Code Ann. § 9-9-30. According to the plaintiffs, section 9-9-30 grants courts the authority to award petitioners "a broad range of provisional or interim relief."[9] In evaluating this request, the district court noted that it could apply state law to supplement maritime law if the result did not "frustrate national interests in having uniformity in admiralty law."[10] The court looked to the test set forth in *Misener Marine Construction, Inc. v. Norfolk Dredging Co.*, 594 F.3d 832, 839 (11th Cir. 2010): "State law may be applied to issues of a maritime nature if: (1) there is not an act of Congress that speaks to the issue; (2) the state law does not contravene a characteristic feature of the general maritime law; and (3) the state law does not **[—8—]** interfere with the proper harmony and uniformity of maritime law." The district court then determined that, if section 9-9-30 had the broad scope that the plaintiffs imputed to it, the provision would run afoul of all three requirements.

First, the court observed that federal law already spoke to the intersection of maritime law, arbitration, and security pending arbitration. Section 8 of Title 9 of the United States Code allowed a party to begin a proceeding "hereunder by libel and seizure of the vessel or other property of the other party according to the usual course of admiralty proceedings," and still proceed to arbitration. "The usual course of admiralty proceedings," the court continued, involves "libel or seizure pursuant **{-614-}** to Rule B or Rule C."[11] "Because there is an act of Congress that speaks to the issue, and because the application of § 9-9-30 would contravene the application of this act," the court concluded that it could not "grant the relief Plaintiffs seek."[12]

The court further expressed the concern that the state statute "contravenes a characteristic feature of general maritime law and interferes with its harmony and **[—9—]** uniformity."[13] In its view, "[m]aritime attachment is by any test a characteristic feature of the general maritime law."[14] Plaintiffs, however, were seeking a remedy under state law because they were unable to meet the requirements of attachment under the Supplemental Rules. According to the district court, allowing plaintiffs to seek attachment outside of the rules would not only subject entities to varying security and attachment requirements, it also would allow them to bypass the procedural requirements of the Supplemental Rules.

Finally, the court observed, even if there were no impediments to invoking the state statute, it could not "discern what relief would be applicable."[15] In the district court's view, section 9-9-30 did not have the expansive scope that the plaintiffs attributed to it. Instead, it simply permitted the court to grant remedies otherwise available under federal and Georgia law. It did not create new remedies.

Accordingly, the district court denied the plaintiffs' request for an order of security. The plaintiffs timely appealed. **[—10—]**

II

"Maritime parties are peripatetic, and their assets are often transitory." *Aqua Stoli Shipping Ltd. v. Gardner Smith Party Ltd.*, 460 F.3d 434, 443 (2d Cir. 2006), *overruled on*

[9] R.1, ¶ 44.

[10] R.30 at 7 (quoting *Coastal Fuels Mktg., Inc. v. Fla. Express Shipping Co.*, 207 F.3d 1247, 1251 (11th Cir. 2000)).

[11] *Id.* at 8.

[12] *Id.*

[13] *Id.*

[14] *Id.* (quoting *ContiChem LPG v. Parsons Shipping Co.*, 229 F.3d 426, 433 (2d Cir. 2000)).

[15] *Id.* at 10.

other grounds by Shipping Corp. of India Ltd. v. Jaldhi Overseas Pte Ltd., 585 F.3d 58, 61 (2d Cir. 2009). Thus, "it is frequently, but not always, more difficult to find property of parties to a maritime dispute than of parties to a traditional civil action." *Id.* As plaintiffs acknowledge, "[t]he standard procedural mechanism . . . to address this problem is maritime attachment, which allows a plaintiff to secure its claim against a defendant's property found within a district and simultaneously to subject the defendant to the personal jurisdiction of the corresponding district court up to the value of the property attached."[16]

A.

"Typically actions for attachment are brought under Rule B(1)(a) [of the] Supplemental Rules . . . ." *Everspeed Enters. Ltd. v. Skaarup Shipping Int'l*, 754 F. Supp. 2d 395, 400 (D. Conn. 2010). Rule B states in relevant part:

> **(1) When Available; Complaint, Affidavit, Judicial Authorization, and Process.** In an in personam action: **[—11—]**
>
> **(a)** *If a defendant is not found within the district* when a verified complaint praying for attachment and the affidavit required by Rule B(1)(b) are filed, a verified complaint may contain a prayer for process to attach the defendant's tangible or intangible personal property—up to the amount sued for—in the **{-615-}** hands of garnishees named in the process.

Fed. R. Civ. P. Supp. B (emphasis added). "[T]here are two reasons for the procedure authorized in Supplemental Rule B: to assure a respondent's appearance, and to assure satisfaction in case the suit is successful." *Nehring v. Steamship M/V Point Vail*, 901 F.2d 1044, 1051 (11th Cir. 1990) (alteration in original) (quoting *Polar Shipping Ltd. v. Oriental Shipping Corp.*, 680 F.2d 627, 637 (9th Cir. 1982)). "Supplemental Rule B, however, cannot be used purely for the purpose of obtaining security: 'The two purposes may not be separated, however, for security cannot be obtained except as an adjunct to obtaining jurisdiction.'" *Id.* (quoting *Seawind Compania, S.A. v. Crescent Line, Inc.*, 320 F.2d 580, 582 (2d Cir. 1963)).

Here, SCL Basilisk and Thorco cannot meet the requirements for invoking Rule B(1)(a). Specifically, all of the defendants *can be found* in the district.[17] **[—12—]** Thus, at least in these circumstances, the plaintiffs' purpose in invoking Rule B is not "to gain jurisdiction over an absent defendant," *Aqua Stoli Shipping Ltd.*, 460 F.3d at 437, and Rule B(1)(a) is inapplicable. *See Everspeed Enters. Ltd.*, 754 F. Supp. 2d at 400 (holding that "Rule B(1)(a) is inapplicable" where each of the defendants resides or has a principal place of business in the district in which the action is brought). Indeed, the plaintiffs admit that such is the case: "When a defendant appears by registration within a district, attachment under Rule B(1)(a) is no longer available."[18]

---

[16] Appellants' Br. 10–11.

[17] The plaintiffs suggest for the first time in their reply brief that, depending on how the language of Rule B is interpreted, the defendants' registrations to do business in the district may not render them "found within the district" for purposes of Supplemental Rule B. Reply Br. 5 (internal quotation marks omitted). This is both contrary to the position they took in their opening brief, **[—12—]** *see* Appellants' Br. 22 ("When a defendant appears by registration within a district, attachment under Rule B(1)(a) is no longer available."), and in the district court, *see* R.35 (Tr. Hr'g July 11, 2016) at 15 ("Now, because the defendants know that Rule B was going to be employed against them, they took affirmative steps to avoid us from being able to use the Rule B remedy."); *see also id.* at 11, 13, 17 & 19. However, even if the plaintiffs had not conceded the point, we would not consider this argument because they failed to raise it before the district court, *see Norelus v. Denny's, Inc.*, 628 F.3d 1270, 1296 (11th Cir. 2010) ("[I]ssues not raised in the district court should not be considered on appeal."), and they failed to raise it in their opening brief, *see Conn. State Dental Ass'n v. Anthem Health Plans, Inc.*, 591 F.3d 1337, 1351 n.11 (11th Cir. 2009) ("Because they raised this argument for the first time in their reply brief, we treat this argument as waived.").

[18] Appellants' Br. 22.

B.

Rule B, however, also allows plaintiffs to employ state measures of protection. Supplemental Rule B(1)(e) provides that a "plaintiff may invoke **[—13—]** state-law remedies under Rule 64 for seizure of person or property for the purpose of securing satisfaction of the judgment." Fed. R. Civ. P. Supp. B(1)(e). For its part, Federal Rule of Civil Procedure 64 provides:

> **(a) Remedies Under State Law—In General.** At the commencement of and throughout an action, every remedy is available that, under the law of the state where the court is located, provides for seizing a person or property to secure satisfaction of the potential judgment. But a federal statute governs to the extent it applies.
>
> **(b) Specific Kinds of Remedies.** The remedies available under this rule include the following—however designated **{-616-}** and regardless of whether state procedure requires an independent action:
>
> - arrest;
> - attachment;
> - garnishment;
> - replevin;
> - sequestration; and
> - other corresponding or equivalent remedies.

Fed. R. Civ. P. 64.

Although at least some of these specifically enumerated remedies are available under Georgia law, *see* Ga. Code Ann. § 18-3-1 (identifying grounds of attachment); *id.* § 18-4-1 *et seq.* (setting forth garnishment procedures), the plaintiffs have not pursued them. Instead, they have petitioned for "an order **[—14—]** requiring the posting of security pursuant to Georgia Code . . . § 9-9-30."[19] According to the plaintiffs, section 9-9-30 provides a remedy that "correspond[s]" or is "equivalent" to those enumerated in Rule 64(b).[20] In their view, the provision is a grant of authority empowering courts to *create* interim measures of protection. We cannot accept this argument.

1. Language and history of section 9-9-30

Section 9-9-30 of the Georgia Code is a provision within Georgia's relatively recently enacted International Commercial Arbitration Code.[21] The provision states, "Before or during arbitral proceedings, a party may request from a court an interim measure of protection, and a court may grant such measure, and such request shall not be deemed to be incompatible with an arbitration agreement." Ga. Code Ann. § 9-9-30. On its face, the language of section 9-9-30 reflects the policy that a party's resort to a court for an order to preserve assets (in the event of arbitral victory) or to protect trade secrets (in the course of arbitral discovery) is compatible with having the merits of a dispute determined in an **[—15—]** arbitral forum. The provision therefore serves an important function in fostering a legal climate conducive to international arbitration[22]: it guarantees that a party's resort to a court for interim measures cannot be interpreted as a waiver of his or her right to arbitrate the merits of the underlying dispute.

This plain meaning is confirmed by the notes to the working drafts and the final report of the United Nations Commission on International Trade Law regarding the Model Law on International Commercial Arbitration ("UNCITRAL Model Law"), on which Georgia's International Commercial Arbi-

[19] R.1, ¶ 1.

[20] Appellants' Br. 14 (alteration in original) (quoting Fed. R. Civ. P. 64(b)).

[21] *See* Ga. Code Ann. § 9-9-20(a) ("This part shall be known and may be cited as the 'Georgia International Commercial Arbitration Code.'").

[22] *See* Ga. Code Ann. § 9-9-20(b) ("The purpose of [the Georgia International Commercial Arbitration Code] is to encourage international commercial arbitration in this state, to enforce arbitration agreements and arbitration awards, to facilitate prompt and efficient arbitration proceedings consistent with this part, and to provide a conducive environment for international business and trade.").

tration Code is based. *See* Stephen L. Wright & Shelby S. Guilbert Jr., *Recent Advances in International Arbitration in Georgia: Winning the Race to the Top*, 18 Ga. B.J., June 2013, at 18–19 ("The ICA Code itself is based primarily upon the 1985 UNCITRAL Model Law on International Commercial Arbitration . . . , as amended in 2006.").[23] In the notes to the Fourth Draft, the drafters observe: **[—16—] {-617-}**

> 20. Article 9 expresses the principle of compatibility of an arbitration agreement with a request to a court for an interim measure. There are two aspects of this principle.
>
> 21. One aspect is that it applies to courts of the State of the model law requested to grant an interim measure and provides that a court shall not refuse to grant such a measure on the ground that there is an arbitration agreement.
>
> 22. The other aspect is that the rule expresses the principle according to which a request by a party for an interim measure should not be construed as a waiver of the arbitration agreement. This principle should apply irrespective of whether such a request is made to a court in the State of the model law or to a court in any other State.

Howard M. Holtzmann & Joseph E. Neuhaus, *A Guide to the UNCITRAL Model Law on International Commercial Arbitration* 341 (1989) ("Holtzmann & Neuhaus") (quoting Fifth Secretariat Note Territorial Scope of Application and Related Issues A/CN.9/WG.II/WP.49 (21 December 1983)) (bracketed references omitted). Moreover, the Commission's final report confirms that Article 9 was not meant to expand the panoply of remedies available in the courts of states that may adopt the UNCITRAL Model Code: **[—17—]**

> It was understood that article 9 itself did not regulate which interim measures of protection were available to a party. It merely expressed the principle that a request for any court measure available under a given legal system and the granting of such measure by a court of "this State" was compatible with the fact that the parties had agreed to settle their dispute by arbitration.

Id. at 345–46 (quoting Commission Report A/40/17 (21 August 1985)). Thus, the official commentary to the UNCITRAL Model Law dispels any notion that the provision was intended to authorize new remedies. Instead, section 9-9-30 simply confirms that a party's request to have a court order an interim measure already within its legal arsenal is compatible with that party's desire to submit the merits of the dispute to arbitration.[24] **[—18—] {-618-}**

---

[23] Section 9-9-30 is based on Article 9 of the UNCITRAL Model Code which reads: "It is not incompatible with an arbitration agreement for a party to request, before or during arbitral proceedings, from a court an interim measure of protection and for a court to grant such measure." In their reply brief, the plaintiffs submit that, because the Georgia General Assembly **[—16—]** used the active, as opposed to the passive, voice in part of section 9-9-30, it must have intended a different—and broader—meaning. There is no support for this assertion.

As will be discussed in greater detail, *see infra* note 28, UNCITRAL amended the Model Code in 2006. The language that forms the basis of section 9-9-30, however, did not change.

[24] A number of other states have adopted a version of Article 9 of the UNCITRAL Model Code. *See* Cal. Civ. Code § 1297.91; Conn. Gen. Stat. Ann. § 50a-109; 710 Ill. Comp. Stat. Ann. § 30/5-15; La. Rev. Stat. Ann. § 9:4249. As with Georgia's version, courts in those jurisdictions have not had the opportunity to address definitively the meaning of those provisions. Two cases, however, shed some light on how these statutes are viewed. *See Stemcor USA Inc. v. CIA Siderurgica Do Para Cosipar*, 870 F.3d 370, 5 Adm. R. 306 (5th Cir. 2017); *Everspeed Enters. Ltd. v. Skaarup Shipping Int'l*, 754 F. Supp. 2d 395 (D. Conn. 2010). In *Stemcor USA*, the Fifth Circuit held that the Louisiana attachment statute could be used to secure an arbitral judgment prior to the prevailing party commencing a confirmation proceeding. 870 F.3d at 380, 5 Adm. R. at 312. In doing so, the court noted that "[r]eading Louisiana law to allow for pre-suit attachment in aid of arbitration makes sense of the statutory scheme as

2. Language and history of section 9-9-38

The plaintiffs also note that the term "interim measure" is employed in another part of the International Commercial Arbitration Code, section 9-9-38. They explain that "[t]he ICA Code expressly gives *an* arbitrator the authority, upon application of a party, to 'grant interim measures as [the arbitrator] deems appropriate' and to 'modify, suspend or terminate' such measures."[25] "With no indication to the contrary," the plaintiffs conclude, "it then follows that § 9-9-30, which employs the same phrase, 'interim measure,' is designed to extend a similar authority to the courts."[26] **[—19—]**

The fact that sections 9-9-30 and 9-9-38 both employ the term "interim measure" does not mean that the measures available to courts under section 9-9-30 are coextensive with those available to arbitrators under section 9-9-38. Read in its entirety, the language of the two provisions is not the same; section 9-9-38 expressly gives an arbitrator the authority to "grant interim measures *as it deems appropriate*." Ga. Code Ann. § 9-9-38(a) (emphasis added).[27] Courts are not granted the same leeway. **[—20—]**

That the Georgia General Assembly intended to provide arbitrators with greater flexibility than courts with respect to interim measures also finds support in section 9-9-39.

---

a whole because other provisions of Louisiana law *assume that some state-law preliminary remedies are available* to aid arbitration." *Id.* at 379 n.6, 5 Adm. R. at 311 n.6 (emphasis added). The court went on to observe that Louisiana had adopted the UNCITRAL Model Law and that "[i]t would be strange for Louisiana to have adopted the UNCITRAL Model Law without allowing for state law interim remedies in aid of arbitration." *Id.*, 5 Adm. R. at 311 n.6. Had the court believed that Louisiana's version of the UNCITRAL Model Law was an independent grant of substantive relief, it would not have had to consider if Louisiana's attachment statute provided a remedy. **[—18—]**

Similarly, in *Everspeed Enterprises*, the plaintiff had supplemented a previous application for prejudgment remedy "with an application for an order *pendente lite* in aid of the arbitration" under sections 50a-109 (Connecticut's version of Article 9) and 52-422 (Connecticut's *pendente lite* statute). *Id.* at 404. While recognizing that it had the "jurisdiction and authority to grant injunctions and provisional remedies in the context of pending arbitrations, including international arbitrations" under section 50a-109, the court questioned whether it had the authority to provide the plaintiff with the relief it sought because the specific statutory requirements for an order *pendente lite* had not been met. *Id.* at 405 (quoting *Bahrain Telecomm. Co. v. Discoverytel, Inc.*, 476 F. Supp. 2d 176, 180 (D. Conn. 2007)). As in *Stemcor USA*, if the court perceived section 50a-109 as an independent grant of substantive authority, as opposed to an enabling statute that authorized the use of existing state remedies in aid of international arbitration, it would not have undertaken this inquiry.

[25] Appellants' Br. 28 (second alteration in original) (emphasis added).

[26] *Id.*

[27] Section 9-9-38 reads in relevant part:

> (a) Unless otherwise agreed by the parties, the arbitration tribunal may, at the request of a party, grant interim measures as it deems appropriate.
>
> (b) The arbitration tribunal may modify, suspend, or terminate an interim measure it has granted, upon application of any party or, in exceptional circumstances and upon prior notice to the parties, on the arbitration tribunal's own initiative.
>
> (c) The arbitration tribunal may require the party requesting an interim measure to provide appropriate security in connection with the measure.
>
> . . .
>
> (g) The party who is seeking or has obtained recognition or enforcement of an interim measure shall promptly inform the court of any termination, suspension, or modification of that interim measure.
>
> (h) Where recognition or enforcement of an interim measure is sought in a court of this state, such court may order the requesting party to provide appropriate security if the arbitration tribunal has not already made a determination with respect to security or where such a decision is necessary to protect the rights of third parties.

Section 9-9-39, concerning enforcement of interim measures, recognizes that **{-619-}** an arbitral panel's authority to order interim measures of protection may extend beyond that of the courts. It provides that a court may refuse to recognize or enforce an interim measure ordered by an arbitrator if the court determines that the measure "is incompatible with the powers conferred upon the court, unless the court decides to reformulate the interim measure to the extent necessary to adapt it to its own powers and procedures." Ga. Code Ann. § 9-9-39(a), (a)(2)(A). If the power of arbitrators and courts to order interim measures were coextensive, this provision would be unnecessary.

The commentary to the UNCITRAL Model Code also supports the conclusion that the scope of 9-9-30 and 9-9-38 are very different. As originally drafted, Article 17 of the UNCITRAL Model Code, on which 9-9-38 is based, stated:

> Unless otherwise agreed by the parties, the arbitral tribunal may, at the request of a party, order any party to take such interim measure of protection as the arbitral tribunal may consider necessary in respect of the subject-matter of the dispute. The arbitral tribunal may require any party to provide appropriate security in connection with such measure. **[—21—]**

UNCITRAL Model Law Art. 17 (1985), *reprinted in* Holtzmann & Neuhaus at 1245. Commentators observed that Article 17 was "related to, but distinct from, Article 9, which states that it is not incompatible with the arbitration agreement for a party to request from a *court*—or for the court to grant—an interim measure of protection." Holtzmann & Neuhaus at 530. The articles differ in that, "[u]nlike Article 17, *Article 9 does not grant any authority* but only states the principle that certain action, if permitted under other law, is not inconsistent with arbitration." *Id.* (emphasis added). Although the 2006 Amendments to the UNCITRAL Model Law significantly expanded Article 17, those amendments did not blur the distinction between the powers of arbitrators and the powers of courts to grant interim measures of protection.[28] **[—22—]** **[—23—]** **{-620-}**

[28] Article 17 now reads:
Article 17. Power of arbitral tribunal to order interim measures

(1) Unless otherwise agreed by the parties, the arbitral tribunal may, at the request of a party, grant interim measures.

(2) An interim measure is any temporary measure, whether in the form of an award or in another form, by which, at any time prior to the issuance of the award by which the dispute is finally decided, the arbitral tribunal orders a party to: **[—22—]**

> (a) Maintain or restore the status quo pending determination of the dispute;
>
> (b) Take action that would prevent, or refrain from taking action that is likely to cause, current or imminent harm or prejudice to the arbitral process itself;
>
> (c) Provide a means of preserving assets out of which a subsequent award may be satisfied; or
>
> (d) Preserve evidence that may be relevant and material to the resolution of the dispute.

UNCITRAL Model Law on International Commercial Arbitration 1985 With amendments adopted in 2006 (2008), http://www.uncitral.org/pdf/english/texts/arbitration/ml-arb/ 07-86998_Ebook.pdf. The 2006 Amendments also expanded Article 17 in other ways, most notably by (1) the addition of Articles 17 B and 17 C, which set forth procedures for a different procedural tool, "preliminary orders"; and (2) the addition of Articles 17 H and 17 I, which address the recognition and enforcement of interim measures. *Id.*

Although the Georgia General Assembly incorporated much of the new recognition and enforcement language into its International Commercial Arbitration Code, *see* Ga. Code Ann. §§ 9-9-38, 9-9-39, it did *not* incorporate the 2006 Amendments' definition of interim measure.

Despite this fact, the plaintiffs urge that this definition should govern the court's consideration of their petition. The plaintiffs' argument proceeds as follows: The Georgia General Assembly modeled the International Commercial Arbitration Code on

In sum, none of the SCL Basilisk's arguments persuade us that section 9-9-30 grants a court authority to create new substantive remedies; rather it confirms that a court's grant of interim relief, utilizing existing state remedies, is not inconsistent with submitting a merits determination to an arbitrator.[29]

C.

The plaintiffs' final argument is that, even if the relief they seek is not specifically authorized by Supplemental Rule B or section 9-9-30, the district court nonetheless possesses equitable powers under maritime law to grant the security in aid of arbitration that they seek. In making this argument, the plaintiffs rely **[—24—]** primarily on *Schiffahartsgesellschaft Leonhardt & Co. v. A. Bottacchi S.A. de Navegacion*, 773 F.2d 1528 (11th Cir. 1985) (en banc).

In *Leonhardt*, Bottacchi's property had been attached pursuant to Supplemental Rule B. Bottacchi then moved to dismiss the complaint and quash the process of attachment. It "argued that Rule B(1)[30] violated due process in failing to provide adequate judicial supervision of the attachment process and that, because the rule constituted the sole authority for the court's issuance of the writ, the writ had to be dissolved." *Id.* at 1530. The district court held that Bottachi's due process rights had not been violated because it had been afforded preseizure notice and a timely hearing. *See id.* Nevertheless, the district court held Rule B(1) invalid under the Due Process Clause because it failed to provide "(1) procedural safeguards in place of preseizure notice and hearing; and (2) a prompt postattachment hearing." *Id.*

A panel of this court reversed, holding "that because Bottacchi was accorded due process in the particular case, the lower court erred in proceeding to determine the **{-621-}** facial constitutionality of Rule B(1)." *Id.* We took "the case en banc to **[—25—]** address the confusion that appears to have arisen in the district courts over the relationship between Rule B(1) and the courts' inherent admiralty powers." *Id.* at 1530–31.

Turning to the question of the courts' inherent admiralty powers, we determined that the district court did have "the power to

---

the UNCITRAL Model Code. UNCITRAL defined "interim measure" broadly in its Arbitration Rules. *See* Reply Br. 9. The plaintiffs therefore conclude that,

> [i]f the Assembly had meant to limit parties' relief to use of Georgia's attachment statute, the Assembly would not have adopted this broad language wholesale when a simple cross-reference to the attachment statute would have sufficed. Notably, the Assembly did not simply copy Article 9 of the Model Law; it rearranged the language as it saw fit, yet it retained "interim measure of protection." This suggests that the Assembly meant to incorporate the prevailing international meaning of the term "interim measure."

Id. at 10 (citations omitted). **[—23—]**

The plaintiffs are correct that the Georgia General Assembly did not adopt wholesale the UNCITRAL Model Code. However, the discretion the General Assembly exercised in determining which provisions to adopt and which to leave out cuts against the plaintiffs' argument. The UNCITRAL Model Code contains an expansive definition of interim measure (indeed, one that is materially indistinguishable from that incorporated into the UNCITRAL Model Arbitration Rules, *see id.* at 9); yet this definition was *not* incorporated into Georgia's International Commercial Arbitration Code. This intentional omission suggests that the General Assembly did not intend for courts to employ the UNCITRAL Model Law's definition of interim measure.

[29] Because section 9-9-30 is not a substantive grant of authority, it does not conflict, indeed it is consonant, with 9 U.S.C. § 8, which "permit[s] a party having an admiralty cause of action to commence a suit in admiralty, despite an agreement to arbitrate, so that 'the vessel or other property' may be seized and held as security until the arbitration is concluded." *Greenwich Marine, Inc. v. S.S. ALEXANDRA*, 225 F. Supp. 671, 674 (S.D.N.Y. 1964).

[30] At issue in *Schiffahartsgesellschaft Leonhardt & Co. v. A. Bottacchi S.A. de Navegacion*, 773 F.2d 1528 (11th Cir. 1985) (en banc), was the constitutionality of the former version of Supplemental Rule B.

issue the writ of attachment independent of its authority derived under Rule B(1)." *Id.* at 1531. We observed that, "[w]hen the Constitution was adopted, the existing maritime law became the law of the United States 'subject to power in Congress to alter, qualify or supplement it as experience or changing conditions might require.'" *Id.* at 1531–32 (quoting *Detroit Trust Co. v. The Thomas Barlum,* 293 U.S. 21, 43, 55 (1934)). Among the maritime procedures in place at the time of the Constitution was maritime attachment, according to which "the person injured may have his action *in personam*, and compel appearance by the process of attachment on the goods of the trespasser." *Id.* at 1532–33 (quoting *Manro v. Almeida,* 23 U.S. (10 Wheat.) 473, 495–96 (1825)).

We then turned to whether Congress had altered the concept of maritime attachment as it existed at the time of the Constitution's adoption. We observed that the Supplemental Rules, "promulgated by the Supreme Court and enacted by **[—26—]** Congress[,] constitute[d] the only statutory restrictions on maritime attachment placed on a federal district court's power to apply admiralty law and procedure." *Id.* at 1533. The advisory committee notes to those rules made clear, however, that the Supplemental Rules were "not to be construed as limiting or impairing the traditional power of a district court, exercising the admiralty and maritime jurisdiction, to adapt its procedures and its remedies in the individual case, *consistently* with these rules." *Id.* (quoting Fed. R. Civ. P. Supp. A advisory committee's note) (emphasis added). Evaluating the procedures that the district court had employed, we concluded that those procedures, which included a timely postattachment hearing, were "entirely consistent with Rule B(1)." *Id.* Because the court had exercised its inherent maritime powers—and had done so consistently with the Supplemental Rules—there was no occasion to consider the constitutionality of Rule B. The only remaining question was whether "the procedures utilized by the district court" comported with due process. *Id.* We concluded that "the concept of due process [was] sufficiently flexible and the realm of admiralty sufficiently distinct to uphold the constitutionality of the procedures afforded Bottacchi by the district court in the exercise of its inherent power to apply maritime law." *Id.* at 1539. **[—27—]**

Similar to their reading of section 9-9-30, the plaintiffs perceive *Leonhardt* as granting district courts *carte blanche* "to fashion appropriate prejudgment remedies" as justice so requires.[31] We do not **{-622-}** view *Leonhardt* as supporting such a broad proposition. In *Leonhardt,* we determined that district courts possess the inherent admiralty powers that existed at the time the Constitution was adopted. Congress, we acknowledged, had the power to alter those powers and had done so in the Supplemental Rules. Nevertheless, district courts still may apply and adapt their inherent admiralty powers as long as they do so consistently with the Supplemental Rules. **[—28—]**

Properly understood, therefore, it is clear that *Leonhardt* does not support the plaintiffs' claim for security in aid of arbitration. Although we recognized in *Leonhardt* that district courts have inherent admiralty

---

[31] Appellants' Br. 22. In their reply brief, the plaintiffs rely on *United Shipping Services Three, Inc. v. U.S. Express Lines, Ltd.,* No. CIV. A. 98-950, 1998 WL 770599 (E.D. Penn. Nov. 5, 1998), and *Trans Ocean v. Baltic Shipping Co.,* Civ.A. Nos. 95-2192 & 95-2635, 1995 WL 495908 (E.D. La. Aug. 18, 1995), for the proposition that *Leonhardt* "only required that a district court act 'consistently with [the] rules' holistically, and it did not specify any brightline requirements." Reply Br. 4 (quoting *Leonhardt,* 773 F.2d at 1533). Neither case, however, is persuasive. In *United Shipping Services Three,* the court mistakenly characterized our holding in *Leonhardt* accordingly: "even if Rule B does not apply because the defendant could be found within the district, a district court might attach property under its general inherent admiralty powers." 1998 WL 770599, at *1. The court went on to state that it did not agree with that holding and determined, instead, that "a maritime attachment of defendant's property must comply with Rule B." *Id. Trans Ocean,* as well, does not support plaintiffs' assertion. It merely summarizes the general principle from *Leonhardt* that "federal courts have inherent power to issue and maintain writs of maritime attachment quite apart from the requirements of Rule B." *Trans Ocean,* 1995 WL 495908, at *2 n.2.

powers, those powers are the ones that existed at the time the Constitution was adopted. At the time the Constitution was adopted, courts did possess the power to attach a vessel; however, then as now, one of the purposes of maritime attachment was to secure jurisdiction. *See id.* at 1532–33 ("[T]he person injured may have his action *in personam*, and compel appearance by the process of attachment on the goods of the trespasser . . . ." (quoting *Manro*, 23 U.S. (10 Wheat.) at 496). Thus, the plaintiffs are seeking a remedy different from any historical concept of maritime attachment. Moreover, *Leonhardt* confirmed that a district court must exercise its inherent admiralty powers consistent with the Supplemental Rules. As we have discussed at some length,[32] Supplemental B "cannot be used purely for the purpose of obtaining security: . . . security cannot be obtained except as an adjunct to obtaining jurisdiction." *Nehring*, 901 F.2d at 1051 (quoting *Seawind Compania, S.A.*, 320 F.2d at 582). A district court's order of attachment solely for the purpose **[—29—]** of obtaining security, therefore, would be contrary to the Supplemental Rules. However, this is exactly the relief that the plaintiffs are seeking.

Conclusion

We conclude that neither Rule B, section 9-9-30, nor principles of maritime law authorize the specific relief sought by the plaintiffs. We therefore affirm the district court's judgment.

AFFIRMED

(Reporter's Note: Concurring opinion follows on p. 517).

[32] *See supra* at 10–12.

[—30—] {-622-} **JORDAN,** Circuit Judge, concurring:

For me, this case ultimately comes down to how we interpret the phrase "interim measure of protection" in Ga. Code. Ann. § 9-9-30. Unfortunately, we do not have any guidance from the Georgia courts on the meaning of this language.

Admiralty courts may in appropriate cases apply equitable principles, *see, e.g., Schoenamsgruber v. Hamburg Am. Line*, 294 U.S. 454, 477 (1935), but the Supreme Court has not allowed federal courts to order the pre-judgment restraint of assets under their traditional equity powers. *See, e.g., Grupo Mexicano de Desarollo, S.A. v. Alliance Bond Fund, Inc.*, 527 U.S. 308, 332 (1999); *De Beers Consolidated Mines Ltd. v. United States*, 325 U.S. 212, 222–23 (1945). Against this backdrop, I would not read the phrase "interim measure of protection" as permitting an **{-623-}** order requiring the posting of pre-judgment security for a pending arbitral proceeding. With these thoughts, I join the court's opinion.

United States Court of Appeals
for the Eleventh Circuit

No. 16-17755

BARCLIFF, LLC
vs.
M/V DEEP BLUE

Appeal from the United States District Court for the Southern District of Alabama

Decided: November 30, 2017

Citation: 876 F.3d 1063, 5 Adm. R. 518 (11th Cir. 2017).

Before **CARNES,** Chief Judge, and **BLACK,** Circuit Judges, and **MAY,*** District Judge.

*Honorable Leigh Martin May, United States District Judge for the Northern District of Georgia, sitting by designation.

[—2—] {–1065–} **BLACK,** Circuit Judge:

The M/V Deep Blue is a pipe-laying vessel deployed in the Gulf of Mexico. In late 2014, the Deep Blue required a routine refueling. Its owner contacted a global marine fuel supplier. The supplier agreed to sell the fuel and deliver it to the Deep Blue at the Port of Mobile, Alabama. Rather than fulfill the order out of its own stocks, the supplier purchased the fuel from an affiliate. The affiliate, in turn, subcontracted with Plaintiff-Appellant Barcliff, LLC, d/b/a Radcliff/Economy Marine Services (Radcliff), a Mobile-based maritime fuel provider, to supply and deliver the fuel. Radcliff rendered performance and fueled the Deep Blue in November 2014.

This otherwise ordinary transaction ultimately became a problem for Radcliff because, before any money changed hands, the global marine fuel conglomerate collapsed into bankruptcy. Radcliff found itself in the position of **[—3—]** having supplied several hundred metric tons of fuel on the credit of a now-insolvent counterparty. Radcliff asserted a maritime lien on the Deep Blue in a bid to recover directly from the ship, giving rise to this litigation.

After a bench trial, the district court determined Radcliff did not have a lien on the Deep Blue. Instead, a lien had arisen in favor of the global fuel supplier, and was duly assigned to ING Bank N.V. (ING), an intervenor in the suit. Radcliff appeals, and we affirm.

I. BACKGROUND

The significance of the contractual structure of the sale outlined above will become clear in the course of our analysis. Accordingly, we begin by introducing the parties to the transaction in relation to their contractual counterparties.

A. The Sequence of Contracts

1. Technip purchases bunkers from O.W. UK

Technip UK Limited (Technip) is a U.K.-based company and the owner of the Deep Blue. Since 2001, Technip has used the Deep Blue to lay pipe for oil rigs in the Gulf. The Deep Blue requires periodic refueling. Each time, Technip's Scotland-based procurement team solicits bids from a handful of international fuel suppliers. The suppliers respond with price quotes, and Technip selects the most appropriate proposal. **[—4—]**

O.W. Bunkers (UK) Limited (O.W. UK), also a U.K. entity, is a member of the O.W. Bunker Group, a global fuel supply conglomerate. On October 22, 2014, Technip sent out a request for quotations to O.W. UK and two other suppliers, seeking bunker fuel[1] for the Deep Blue in the Port of Mobile, Alabama. After reviewing the bids, Technip awarded the supply contract to O.W. UK, whose offer, at $824 per metric **{–1066–}** ton, was the least expensive.[2] Payment was to be due within thirty days of delivery.

---

[1] Bunker fuel (or "bunkers") is synonymous with maritime fuel. *See Bunker fuel*, Webster's Third New International Dictionary, Unabridged, http://unabridged.merriam-webster.com/bunker%20fuel (last visited Nov. 13, 2017) (defining bunker fuel as "any of various fuel oils used especially on ships"). This opinion uses the terms interchangeably.

[2] O.W. UK agreed to sell fuel to Technip; it did not agree to become Technip's agent or broker to

2. O.W. UK purchases bunkers from O.W. USA

Now obligated to supply the Deep Blue in the Gulf of Mexico, O.W. UK entered into a second purchase and sale contract in order to procure the 850 metric tons of bunkers it had agreed to sell to Technip. This time, O.W. UK was the buyer of the fuel and O.W. Bunker USA, Inc. (O.W. USA) was the seller. O.W. USA, a Houston-based sibling company of O.W. UK, agreed to sell 850 metric **[—5—]** tons of bunker fuel to O.W. UK for $823.30 per ton, with delivery to be made to the Deep Blue in Mobile.

3. O.W. USA purchases bunkers from Radcliff

O.W. USA had agreed to sell O.W. UK 850 tons of fuel, but the fuel would not come from its own stocks. Rather, O.W. USA added a final link to the chain of contracts by retaining Radcliff to supply the bunkers. Radcliff agreed to sell the fuel to O.W. USA and deliver it to the Deep Blue at a price of $823 per ton, payment due within thirty days.

B. The Fueling

After the contractual arrangements were worked out, O.W. USA emailed Radcliff and put Radcliff in touch with the Chief Engineer of the Deep Blue, Ian Ladyka, to coordinate delivery. Radcliff communicated with Ladyka, rather than O.W. USA, from that point on with respect to the logistics of the fueling.

Radcliff fueled the Deep Blue outside the Port of Mobile on November 1, 2014. When the fueling was complete, Ladyka signed a bunker delivery certificate acknowledging that the 850 tons of fuel had been conveyed. Each seller sent an invoice to its respective buyer at their agreed prices: Radcliff to O.W. USA for the fuel sold to it and delivered to the Deep Blue; O.W. USA to O.W. UK; and O.W. UK to Technip. **[—6—]**

C. ING Bank and the Collapse of the O.W. Bunker Group

The ship now fueled and having recommenced its operations, all that remained was settlement. Had everything gone according to plan, Technip would have paid O.W. UK $700,400 for 850 tons of fuel at $824 per ton; O.W. UK would have paid O.W. USA $699,805; and O.W. USA would have paid Radcliff $699,550. But none of these sums was remitted because the O.W. Bunker Group, the global marine fuel conglomerate of which O.W. UK and O.W. USA were members, imploded. The Group's parent company filed for bankruptcy in its native Denmark on November 7, 2014, one week after the Deep Blue was fueled, and concurrent bankruptcy cases were opened for its subsidiaries, including O.W. UK and O.W. USA, in jurisdictions around the world. Relevant here, O.W. USA's proceeding commenced on November 13, 2014, in the District of Connecticut. *See* Chapter 11 Voluntary Petition, *In re* **{-1067-}** *O.W. Bunker USA Inc.*, No. 14-51722 (Bankr. D. Conn. Nov. 13, 2014). Thus, Radcliff remained unpaid.

An overview of the O.W. Bunker Group explains the involvement of ING in this case. The O.W. Bunker Group was founded in Denmark in 1980 and grew to be one of the world's largest maritime fuel providers. The Group's operations consisted of a physical supply division, which provided bunkers directly from the Group's onshore stocks using its own fleet of ships, and a trading and reselling division, which bought fuel from third parties and sold it at a markup. **[—7—]**

In December 2013, eleven months before the transaction at issue in this case, members of the O.W. Bunker Group, including O.W. UK and O.W. USA, entered into a $700 million

bind Technip to a fuel purchase agreement with a third party. The sales order confirmation listed O.W. UK as seller and was addressed to Technip as purchaser and it stated the price, date of delivery, and port of delivery, but there was no indication of any delegation of authority to purchase on Technip's behalf. Evidence presented at trial indicated that, consistent with their purchaser-seller relationship, if Technip had had any quality or quantity issues, they would have been addressed with O.W. UK, and not with any downstream local supplier-subcontractors retained by O.W. UK. This is also Radcliff's understanding, as its pretrial stipulations indicate.

revolving credit agreement with ING and a syndicate of other lenders to supply working capital. The credit was secured by O.W. Bunker Group's receivables due from customers around the world pursuant to a security agreement governed by English law (the Security Agreement).

Over the course of 2014, the Group drew down nearly the entire facility, which empowered ING to take its security, namely, payments that third parties owed to members of the Group. ING began to do so pursuant to a cooperation agreement between ING and the bankruptcy estate of O.W. UK, by which ING became entitled to collect on O.W. UK's outstanding receivables, with all recoveries to be paid into ING accounts. Among them was Technip's unpaid invoice for the fuel supplied to the Deep Blue.

D. This Suit

Having received no payment, and with its contractual counterparty, O.W. USA, in bankruptcy, Radcliff filed this suit in the Southern District of Alabama on December 19, 2014, seeking a lien on the Deep Blue so that it could collect from the ship. Notwithstanding the fact that its contractual obligation to supply the ship had been owed to O.W. USA, not to Technip, Radcliff contended that it had supplied the vessel and not been paid, so it was entitled to a lien. Technip made a **[—8—]** restricted appearance for the purpose of defending the claim against the vessel. Technip was willing to pay for the fuel supplied to its ship, but wanted to be sure it only paid once, since its contractual debt was to O.W. UK, not to Radcliff, with whom it had no contractual relationship at all. Consequently, Technip deposited $705,529.50 into the registry of the court, equal to the value of the invoice from O.W. UK for the fuel plus interest, to be distributed according to the court's ultimate determination.

In April 2015, ING intervened in the suit. ING alleged that O.W. UK supplied the fuel to the ship, albeit using subcontractors, and Technip had not yet paid O.W. UK, so O.W. UK, not Radcliff, had a lien on the Deep Blue. In addition, ING had taken title to O.W. UK's accounts receivable as a result of the credit arrangements. Thus, ING asserted that it, not Radcliff, was entitled to the money Technip paid into the court.

The parties consented to try the case before a magistrate judge.[3] Following a two-day bench trial, the court entered an order concluding that Radcliff did not possess a lien on the ship. O.W. UK, on the other hand, did have a lien, and had duly assigned it to ING. The court entered judgment against Radcliff and in favor of ING and directed that the full amount Technip paid into its registry be disbursed to ING. Radcliff appealed. **[—9—] {-1068-}**

II. STANDARD OF REVIEW

When a district court sitting in admiralty conducts a bench trial, we review the court's factual findings for clear error and its conclusions of law *de novo*. *Venus Lines Agency, Inc. v. CVG Int'l Am., Inc.*, 234 F.3d 1225, 1228 (11th Cir. 2000).

III. DISCUSSION

"A maritime lien is a special property right in a ship given to a creditor by law as security for a debt or claim, and it attaches the moment the debt arises." *Crimson Yachts v. Betty Lyn II Motor Yacht*, 603 F.3d 864, 868 (11th Cir. 2010) (quotations omitted). The Federal Maritime Lien Act (FMLA)[4] determines when a person is entitled to such a lien. It reads:

> [A] person providing necessaries to a vessel on the order of the owner or a person authorized by the owner . . . has a maritime lien on the vessel . . . .

---

[3] As such, we have appellate jurisdiction under 28 U.S.C. § 636(c)(3).

[4] In 1989, FMLA was recodified under the heading "Commercial Instruments and Maritime Liens." *See* Coast Guard Authorization Act of 1989, Pub. L. 101-225, 103 Stat 1908. The parties and the district court refer to the statute as "CIMLA," but this opinion will retain the act's original title. The amendments did not change the substance of the statute. *Crimson Yachts*, 603 F.3d at 872.

46 U.S.C. § 31342(a). We have held that under a plain reading of the statute, "to obtain a maritime lien, a person must: (1) provide necessaries; (2) to a vessel; **[—10—]** (3) on the order of the owner or agent."[5] *Galehead, Inc. v. M/V Anglia*, 183 F.3d 1242, 1244 (11th Cir. 1999).

In this case, the parties agree Radcliff satisfied the first and second elements of the statute when it provided 850 metric tons of bunker fuel to the Deep Blue in Mobile, Alabama. The subject of their dispute is whether Radcliff supplied the ship "on the order of the owner." If not, then Radcliff has no lien.

ING's asserted lien, on the other hand, requires us to answer two questions. First, did O.W. UK actually "provide necessaries" to the Deep Blue, even though it subcontracted the job to O.W. USA, and in turn to Radcliff? Second, even if a lien arose in O.W. UK's favor, did O.W. UK assign the lien to ING? If we answer both those questions in the affirmative, the district court was correct that ING has a lien on the Deep Blue.

We begin with Radcliff.

A. Whether Radcliff Has a Lien

1. The general rule: A subcontractor does not receive a lien

As noted above, the parties agree that neither O.W. UK nor O.W. USA was Technip's agent or broker.[6] Thus, Radcliff cannot aver that Technip authorized **[—11—]** those entities to establish an agreement between Radcliff and Technip. Rather, as we have discussed, each party entered into a separate contract—Technip with O.W. UK, O.W. UK with O.W. USA, and O.W. USA with Radcliff. Radcliff's case turns, then, on whether it can show that it acted "on the order of the owner," Technip, in some more indirect way.

To that end, we first address Radcliff's contention that the district court erred in refusing to follow *Marine Fuel Supply & Towing, Inc. v. M/V Ken Lucky*, 869 F.2d 473 (9th Cir. 1988). In Radcliff's view, this nearly three-decades-old Ninth Circuit case "applies with dispositive force" because of its ostensible factual similarity. **{-1069-}** Brief of Appellant at 15. In *Ken Lucky*, Bulkferts, a subcharterer of the ship the Ken Lucky, ordered its managing agent, Eurostem, to procure fuel for the ship.[7] *Ken Lucky*, 869 F.2d at 475. Eurostem contacted Brook which, in turn, instructed Gray to place an order with Marine Fuel. Marine Fuel supplied the ship, billed Gray, and sought payment from Brook, but Brook went bankrupt. Marine Fuel asserted a lien on the vessel. *Id.* The district court wanted to know whether Brook was also Bulkferts's agent, in which case Marine Fuel might be said to have performed the work on the order of "a person authorized by the owner." *Id.* at 476. The Ninth Circuit, however, concluded such a determination was unnecessary because the defendants had admitted that "Marine Fuel sold marine fuel and **[—12—]** bunkers to Bulkferts." *Id.* Because the parties had "agree[d] that the order originated from Bulkferts" and Bulkferts accepted the fuel when Marine Fuel delivered it, Marine Fuel obtained a lien on the ship. *See id.* at 477. In essence, the court decided that the appellees' admission satisfied the order-of-the-owner requirement.

Radcliff appears to read *Ken Lucky* as standing for the proposition that any time an owner orders fuel for its ship, and that fuel is accepted from the third-party supplier by a member of the crew, a maritime lien arises in favor of the supplier—even if the owner ordered the fuel from a different entity. That view of *Ken Lucky* is strained because of the appellees' admission noted above. *See id.* ("[W]e need not reach the question whether the district court's conclusion that Brook was not Bulkfert's [sic] agent is erroneous because appellees have already admitted that the fuel and bunkers were sold *to Bulkferts*." (emphasis in original)). We read the case as

[5] *Sweet Pea Marine, Ltd. v. APJ Marine, Inc.* adds an additional requirement that the necessaries be supplied "at a reasonable price," 411 F.3d 1242, 1249 (11th Cir. 2005), but that is not at issue in this case.

[6] *See supra* note 2.

[7] Full names of the entities are omitted for clarity.

highly dependent upon that particular factual stipulation, which is not present here. But more fundamentally, we have difficulty comprehending how the district court here could have committed an error of law in declining to follow *Ken Lucky*, as it is not binding law in this Circuit. *See United States v. Rosenthal*, 763 F.2d 1291, 1294 n.4 (11th Cir. 1985) ("[A]ny decision of another circuit, published or unpublished, is only of persuasive value."). **[—13—]**

Radcliff's rejoinder is that *Ken Lucky* "mirrors this Circuit's broad[ ] interpretation of 'order of the owner.'" Brief of Appellant at 14. That is, whereas the district court invoked the principle of *stricti juris*,[8] it should have construed the FMLA broadly, in which case it would have found *Ken Lucky* persuasive. Radcliff cites *Atlantic & Gulf Stevedores, Inc. v. M/V Grand Loyalty*, 608 F.2d 197, 202 (5th Cir. 1979),[9] for the proposition that FMLA is to be given a liberal application. Some of the Court's statements in that case might appear on their face to cast doubt on the time-honored principle that "[m]aritime liens are governed by the principle *stricti juris* and will not be extended by construction, analogy or inference."[10] **{-1070-}** *Inbesa Am., Inc. v. M/V Anglia*, 134 F.3d 1035, 1037 n.3 (11th Cir. 1998) **[—14—]** (quotations omitted). However, our subsequent decisions have clarified this Court's position. In *In re Container Applications International, Inc.*, we held that *Grand Loyalty*'s sweeping statement is confined to its facts. 233 F.3d 1361, 1366 (11th Cir. 2000) ("*Grand Loyalty* simply held that it was unnecessary to apply this rule of construction [*stricti juris*] because it was clear that Congress intended, through the 1971 amendments, to make it easier and more certain for stevedores performing traditional services to be protected."). Indeed, we expressly rejected the argument that *Grand Loyalty* "requires that we interpret all provisions of the FMLA liberally," stating that "[w]e do not find this to be the holding in *Grand Loyalty*." *Id.*; *cf. Crimson Yachts*, 603 F.3d at 872 ("Like its predecessors, Congress passed the current version of the Federal Maritime Lien Act to resolve misunderstandings that had developed about the meaning of the Act; Congress did not intend to effect any dramatic substantive change.").

Accordingly, we decline Radcliff's invitation to read "on the order of the owner" so broadly. Were we presented with an issue of first impression, we might also question the practical utility of Radcliff's desired interpretation. *Stricti juris* or not, however, we have already had occasion to construe "on the order of the owner," and the result we reached is inconsistent with Radcliff's position. *Galehead, Inc. v. M/V Anglia*, 183 F.3d 1242 (11th Cir. 1999), is our leading case in this area and it squarely controls this appeal. In light of *Galehead*, it cannot be **[—15—]** said that Technip ordered Radcliff to supply the fuel to the Deep Blue within the meaning of the FMLA.

---

[8] "Of strict right of law; according to the exact law, without extension or enhancement in interpretation." *Stricti juris*, Black's Law Dictionary (10th ed. 2014).

[9] In *Bonner v. City of Prichard*, 661 F.2d 1206, 1209 (11th Cir. 1981) (en banc), this Court adopted as binding precedent all decisions of the former Fifth Circuit handed down prior to close of business on September 30, 1981.

[10] Specifically, in *Grand Loyalty*, the Court opined that, in light of the legislative history of the 1971 amendments to the FMLA, the Act "is not to be viewed through the constricting glass of Stricti juris, or as some would suggest, Strictissimi juris." *Grand Loyalty*, 608 F.2d at 201. The case centered on the question of which individuals have authority to procure necessaries such that a maritime lien would attach. The Court cited legislative history indicating Congress was concerned with the problem of materialmen furnishing necessaries to a vessel without having the time or ability to check if the charterer and the owner had entered into a "no lien" clause, the effect of which would be to limit the agency of the charterer and specifically to prevent him from ordering necessaries that would result in a lien under the statute. *Id.* at 201–202 n.7 (citing 1971 U.S.C.C.A.N. 1364–65). From the perspective of the materialman, it would be impossible to know whether or not the charterer's authority was so limited. Congress enacted the 1971 amendments to provide a presumption in such situations, analogous to the apparent authority rule in agency law. *Id.* However, it is important to note that *Grand Loyalty* did not involve the meaning of "on the order of the owner," but only "a person authorized by the owner."

In *Galehead*, we considered three purported liens on the M/V Anglia arising from three occasions on which fuel was supplied to it. First, in August 1995, Genesis, the charterer, contacted Polygon to obtain bunkers.[11] *Id.* at 1244. Polygon subcontracted with Asamar, and Asamar found a supplier, which supplied and delivered the fuel to the ship. Asamar paid the supplier, but never received payment. It assigned its claim to Galehead, a collection agency. *Id.* The same sequence of events occurred again in September 1995, and Asamar assigned its second claim against the ship to Galehead as well. *Id.* In October 1995, Genesis once again sought fuel for the Anglia. This time, Polygon bypassed Asamar and subcontracted directly with the supplier. Once again, Genesis did not pay. Polygon assigned its claim to Galehead. *Id.*

Galehead brought suit seeking payment and asserted three liens on the ship, the first two assigned by Asamar and the third by Polygon. We held Asamar had no liens to assign to Galehead because it did not **{-1071-}** act "on the order of the owner;" rather, Asamar acted at Polygon's request. *Id.* at 1245 ("Asamar did not provide the bunkers on order of the owner or an authorized agent. Asamar provided the bunkers at Polygon's request, and Polygon is not [an agent of Genesis]."). **[—16—]** Polygon, however, was in direct privity with Genesis, and clearly acted on Genesis's orders. *Id.* Although Polygon subcontracted to a third party rather than supply the vessel with its own personnel, it nevertheless satisfied all three elements of the maritime lien statute: Polygon provided necessaries (the fuel) to the ship (the Anglia) on the order of the owner (Genesis). *Id.* Galehead was entitled to one lien on the Anglia, that assigned by the general contractor, Polygon, but it was not entitled to the liens ostensibly assigned by the subcontractor, Asamar.

Galehead stands for the rule in this Circuit: Where the owner directs a general contractor to provide necessaries to its vessel, a subcontractor retained by the general contractor to perform the work or provide the supplies is generally not entitled to a maritime lien. *Id.* at 1245; *accord Cianbro Corp. v. George H. Dean, Inc.*, 596 F.3d 10, 17 (1st Cir. 2010); *Lake Charles Stevedores, Inc. v. Professor Vladimir Popov MV*, 199 F.3d 220, 229 (5th Cir. 1999); *S.C. State Ports Auth. v. M/V Tyson Lykes*, 67 F.3d 59, 61 (4th Cir. 1995); *Port of Portland v. M/V Paralla*, 892 F.2d 825, 828 (9th Cir. 1989). This is because, absent facts indicating the owner has designated the general contractor as its agent to procure necessaries on its behalf, a general contractor does not have the authority to bind the ship.[12] *See* **[—17—]** *Port of Portland*, 892 F.2d at 828 ("It is the general rule that a general contractor does not have the authority to bind a vessel."). As such, the subcontractor is merely a contractual counterparty of the general contractor; it has no relationship with the owner. It is the general contractor that, on the order of the owner, provides the necessaries to the ship. Whether it does so with its own employees and supplies or by retaining a subcontractor is immaterial. Absent certain extraordinary circumstances as discussed below, a subcontractor cannot meet the third statutory element required to obtain a maritime lien. *Id.*; 46 U.S.C. § 31342(a).

Under the general rule as stated, Radcliff does not have a maritime lien on the Deep Blue. Radcliff acted on the order of O.W. USA, not Technip.

---

[11] Once again, full names of the entities are omitted for clarity.

[12] The statute does not list a general contractor as a party presumed to have authority to bind the ship. *See* 46 U.S.C. § 31341(a). It is, of course, entirely possible that the facts of a case would show that the general contractor was in an actual agency relationship with the vessel, in which case it would have authority to bind it. *See Galehead*, 183 F.3d at 1245 n.2. However, as noted above, *see supra* note 2, the parties stipulated in this case that neither O.W. UK nor O.W. **[—17—]** USA was an agent of Technip. To the extent Radcliff suggests otherwise, the district court did not clearly err in so finding.

2. The exception: Significant and ongoing involvement

However, *Galehead* recognizes an exception to the general rule. Even where the general contractor is not an agent of the owner, and the owner does not initially order the subcontractor to perform the work, it might still be said that the owner "somehow authorized" the work if it "was sufficiently aware of, and involved in, [the] work that it might be said that [the subcontractor] was working for [the owner]." *Galehead*, 183 F.3d at 1245. Specifically, we held that "[w]here **[—18—]** the level of involvement between the owner and the third-party provider was significant and ongoing during the pertinent transaction," a question **{-1072-}** of fact may arise as to whether the third-party provider (i.e., the subcontractor) in effect performed the work on the order of the owner. *Id.*

Galehead arrived at the significant-and-ongoing-involvement exception by looking to prior Eleventh Circuit cases on the subject. On the one hand, our Court has discerned certain circumstances in which a subcontractor could obtain a lien even though the general contractor was the one that took the official order from the owner. Those cases involved extensive maintenance, such as painting, coating, and cleaning, *Marine Coatings of Ala., Inc. v. United States*, 932 F.2d 1370 (11th Cir. 1991), or repair work, *Stevens Tech. Servs., Inc. v. United States*, 913 F.2d 1521 (11th Cir. 1990). Moreover, in those cases, although the initial order to do the work was given to the general contractor, the owner and the subcontractor developed a relationship over an extended period of time as the work progressed. In *Stevens*, for example, the owner was in contact almost exclusively with the subcontractor because the general contractor did not have the capability to perform the work. *Id.* at 1535. Instead, the owner dealt directly with the subcontractor and its employees directed, inspected, tested, and approved the subcontractor's work on a continuing basis. *Id.* at 1525–26, 1535. Thus, the owner's participation with the **[—19—]** subcontractor was so substantial that it could not seriously be argued the work was not done on the owner's orders. *Id.*

The *Galehead* panel juxtaposed *Marine Coatings* and *Stevens* with cases involving a one-off transaction, "where the degree of involvement with the owner is minimal or nonexistent." *Galehead*, 183 F.3d at 1246. One of those cases involved fuel provision. *Id.* (citing *Tramp Oil & Marine, Ltd. v. M/V Mermaid I*, 805 F.2d 42, 45 (1st Cir. 1986)). In those circumstances, the subcontractor would not receive a lien. *Id.*

In light of these precedents, the *Galehead* panel determined Asamar did not fall within the exception to the general rule that subcontractors do not receive liens. There was no genuine dispute as to whether Asamar "had the kind of relationship with Genesis that would establish that Genesis authorized Asamar's work on the vessel." 183 F.3d at 1246. Asamar's contact with Genesis was much more limited than the significant and ongoing involvement between the sub-contractors and the owners in *Marine Coatings* and *Stevens*.

Radcliff attempts to avail itself of the significant-and-ongoing-involvement exception in this case. The problem for Radcliff is that it does so for the first time on appeal.[13] It

[13] Radcliff contends that *Galehead* established a five-factor test for significant and ongoing involvement, consisting of the following elements: (1) whether the owner was aware of the subcontractor's performance before and during the performance; (2) the amount of work **[—20—]** performed by the subcontractor; (3) whether the owner inspected the subcontractor's work; (4) whether the owner gave provisional and final acceptance of the subcontractor's work; and (5) whether the work was fully accepted and compensated. *See Galehead*, 183 F.3d at 1245–46; Brief of Appellant at 18. While we are not required to address Radcliff's new reading of *Galehead* because it was not raised before the district court, we nonetheless are not persuaded by it. *Galehead*, rather than enshrining those factors into a legal test, merely listed them as some of the facts present in *Marine Coatings* that were relevant to the disposition of that case. *Id.* Though analogous facts could be relevant, they are not dispositive: the touchstone is significant and ongoing involvement. *See id.* at 1245 ("Where the level of involvement between the owner and the third-party provider was significant and ongoing during the pertinent transaction, the courts have found a triable issue of

offered the district court no occasion to consider the exception, so **[—20—]** the trial proceeded without any reference to it. Rather, Radcliff argued that, even if **{-1073-}** *Ken Lucky* did not control the case, the acceptance of the fuel by the Deep Blue's Chief Engineer constituted "ratification" of a contract between Technip and Radcliff directly. *See* Amended Brief in Support of Summary Judgment at 5; Trial Transcript at 216, 221–223, 245. This "ratification" argument is markedly different from *Galehead*'s significant-and-ongoing-involvement test. Radcliff's failure to present the district court with the possibility that it fell into the *Galehead* exception deprived the court of the opportunity to weigh the facts in light of it. Consequently, the argument is not properly before us.[14] *Access Now, Inc. v. Sw. Airlines Co.*, 385 F.3d 1324, 1331 (11th Cir. 2004) ("This Court has repeatedly **[—21—]** held that an issue not raised in the district court and raised for the first time in an appeal will not be considered by this court." (quotations omitted)); *accord Hurley v. Moore*, 233 F.3d 1295, 1297 (11th Cir. 2000) ("Arguments raised for the first time on appeal are not properly before this Court.").

As a result, the district court did not err in determining Radcliff does not have a lien on the Deep Blue.[15]

B. Whether ING Has a Lien

As previously stated, whether ING has a lien on the Deep Blue depends first on whether O.W. UK had a lien and second on whether that lien was assigned to ING under the Security Agreement. The district court answered both questions in the affirmative, and we find no error in its determination.

1. Whether O.W. UK Had a Lien

There is no dispute that O.W. UK acted "on the order" of Technip, the owner of the Deep Blue, when it agreed to sell 850 metric tons of bunker fuel to Technip for the ship's use. Whether O.W. UK had a lien on the ship comes down to whether it "provided" the fuel within the meaning of the statute. Radcliff contends O.W. UK did not. After all, Radcliff ultimately delivered it. **[—22—]**

The last time we considered this question was, once again, in *Galehead*. And under that case, the answer would appear to be straightforward: O.W. UK clearly "provided" the fuel, by delegating performance to Radcliff, who then delivered it. Basic contract principles provide that in general, a party meets its obligations under an agreement when the party's delegate renders performance. *See Galehead*, 183 F.3d at 1245 ("A contracts to deliver to **{-1074-}** B coal of specified kind and quality. A delegates the performance of this duty to C, who tenders to B coal of the specified kind and quality. The tender has the effect of a tender by A." (citing Restatement (Second) of Contracts § 318 cmt. a, illus. 2 (1979))). When we were presented with this question in *Galehead*, on materially identical facts, we held that the general contractor, Polygon, obtained a lien when its subcontractor delivered fuel on its behalf. *Id.* ("[A]lthough [general contractor] Polygon did not physically supply the bunkers, a party need not be the physical supplier or deliverer to have 'provided' necessaries under the

---

fact about whether the third-party deserved a lien.").

[14] Radcliff admitted at oral argument that it did not make this argument to the district court, but urged us to consider it nonetheless. Although we have the discretion to consider an argument that was not presented to the district court, we do so only when "special circumstances" exist. *Access Now, Inc. v. Sw. Airlines Co.*, 385 F.3d 1324, 1332 (11th Cir. 2004) (listing five instances when this Court may consider an argument raised for the first time on appeal). Radcliff does not show how any of those special circumstances are present here; it merely asserts that the record is sufficiently developed for this Court to apply the legal test it submits on appeal. We disagree and decline to consider the merits of Radcliff's argument.

[15] It is unfortunate that Radcliff supplied the fuel and was not paid. But by entering into a contractual relationship exclusively with O.W. USA, Radcliff became O.W. USA's creditor. It is assuredly not the only one. O.W. USA's other creditors are doubtless vying for repayment in bankruptcy court. Rather than pursue its claim there, Radcliff elected to go after Technip for the full amount by asserting a lien on the Deep Blue, even though Technip purchased the fuel from O.W. UK and was contractually obligated to pay O.W. UK for it. It was Radcliff's right to gamble, but its choice should elicit no sympathy.

statute."). We specifically stated that Polygon "provided" the necessaries within the meaning of § 31342(a) when it caused them to be delivered by contract. *Id.* ("[The agreement between Genesis and Polygon] caused, or provided for, the delivery of the fuel to the vessel. Therefore, Polygon 'provided' necessaries to the vessel under the contract irrespective of how, or by whom, the delivery was carried out."). **[—23—]**

Nevertheless, Radcliff contends that the general contractor bears an additional obligation not mentioned in *Galehead* before it can receive a lien: it must pay the subcontractor to whom it delegated performance. Radcliff acknowledges that no authority directly supports this proposition, but submits that it lies latent in the case law.

Radcliff's argument is meritless. First and foremost, it finds no support in the text of the statute. Section 31342(a) merely requires that the would-be lienor "provid[e] necessaries" to the vessel. It does not forbid the supplier from using a subcontractor to do so, or require that the parties be current on their accounts payable before a lien arises. We have consistently held that a maritime lien attaches the moment the necessaries are supplied; subsequent administrative matters such as tendering an invoice are irrelevant. *Dresdner Bank AG v. M/V OLYMPIA VOYAGER*, 465 F.3d 1267, 1276–77 (11th Cir. 2006); *see also Container Applications*, 233 F.3d at 1362 n.1 ("A maritime lien is [a] special property right in a ship given to a creditor by law as security for a debt or claim subsisting from the moment the debt arises." (internal quotation marks and citation omitted)). Likewise, payment by the general contractor to the subcontracted supplier is immaterial to the general contractor's lien—it arises at the moment the subcontractor renders performance on the general contractor's behalf. **[—24—]**

Accordingly, the district court did not err in determining that O.W. UK provided the bunkers to the vessel within the meaning of § 31342(a), and as a result that O.W. UK had a lien on the Deep Blue.

2. Whether O.W. UK Assigned the Lien to ING

The district court found that O.W. UK assigned its lien on the Deep Blue to ING pursuant to the Security Agreement. Radcliff contests that determination on appeal. Here too, we are unpersuaded.

To begin with, we note that maritime liens are assignable. Robert Force & Kris Markarian, Fed. Judicial Ctr., Admiralty and Maritime Law Second Edition, 2013 WL 6732869 ("Maritime liens are assignable; the assignee ordinarily assumes the rank of the assignor in determining lien priority."); Thomas J. Schoenbaum, 1 Admiralty and Maritime Law § 9-1 (5th ed.) ("A maritime lien may be assigned, and one who advances money for the discharge of a lien occupies the position of an assignee."). The question, then, is simply whether the Security Agreement in fact assigned O.W. UK's lien on the Deep Blue. The Security Agreement is, as the parties agree, governed by English law. Questions of contract interpretation and matters of **{-1075-}** foreign law are reviewed *de novo*. *Hegel v. First Liberty Ins. Corp.*, 778 F.3d 1214, 1219 (11th Cir. 2015); *Cooper v. Meridian Yachts, Ltd.*, 575 F.3d 1151, 1163 n.5 (11th Cir. 2009). **[—25—]**

Pursuant to § 2.3(a) of the Security Agreement, O.W. UK assigned all "rights, title and interest in respect of the Supply Receivables." "Supply Receivables" is defined to include the monetary sum Technip owed to O.W. UK for supplying the fuel.[16] Radcliff asserts that any maritime lien that arose in O.W. UK's favor was not a "right[ ], title [or] interest in respect of" Technip's obligation to pay O.W. UK for the fuel. That is, O.W. UK assigned the monetary debt but not the corresponding maritime lien. There is no merit to this contention.

[16] "Supply Receivables" means "any amount owing, or to be owed, to a Receivables Chargor under any Supply Contract," which would include the contract to fuel the Deep Blue between O.W. UK and Technip, because O.W. UK is a "Receivables Chargor" under the Agreement and the contract between Technip and O.W. UK was a "Supply Contract."

English principles of contract interpretation ring familiar to the American ear. A court "is concerned to identify the intention of the parties by reference to what a reasonable person having all the background knowledge which would have been available to the parties would have understood them to be using the language in the contract to mean." *Arnold v. Britton*, [2015] AC 1619, ¶ 15 (UKSC), https://www.supremecourt.uk/cases/docs/uksc-2013-0193-judgment.pdf (quotation omitted). That intention is discerned by looking to the words of the contract in their "documentary, factual and commercial context," considering, inter alia, "the natural and ordinary meaning of the clause" and "the overall purpose" of the contract. *Id.* **[—26—]**

The lien on the Deep Blue is, without a doubt, a "right" or "interest" under the agreement "in respect of"—in other words, "[a]s regards, as relates to; with reference to"[17]—Technip's obligation to pay O.W. UK for the fuel. Indeed, the whole purpose of the lien is to secure the debt. *See Galehead*, 183 F.3d at 1247 (noting that a maritime lien is "security for a debt" (citation omitted)). The debt was assigned; it is only reasonable that the security would be assigned as well. The documentary, factual, and commercial context confirm that it was the intention of the O.W. Bunker Group and ING to assign the lien to ING. As ING notes, the Security Agreement was executed in connection with a $700 million credit facility extended to the O.W. entities during their financial hardship. There is little reason to believe parties intended to exclude the lien, by which the bank could enforce the debts it had acquired to secure the loan to the O.W. Bunker entities.

The district court did not err in determining that O.W. UK had a lien on the Deep Blue and that O.W. UK assigned it to ING.

[17] *See In respect of*, Oxford English Dictionary Online, http://www.oed.com/view/Entry/163779?redirectedFrom=in+respect+of#eid177413195 (last visited Nov. 13, 2017).

IV. CONCLUSION

For the foregoing reasons, the district court did not err in finding that ING has a lien on the Deep Blue and Radcliff does not. Accordingly, its judgment is **AFFIRMED.**

This page intentionally left blank

United States Court of Appeals for the District of Columbia Circuit

United States Court of Appeals
for the District of Columbia Circuit

No. 15-7070

NANKO SHIPPING, USA
vs.
ALCOA, INC.

Appeal from the United States District Court for the District of Columbia

Decided: March 10, 2017

Citation: 850 F.3d 461, 5 Adm. R. 530 (D.C. Cir. 2017).

Before **ROGERS**, **BROWN**, and **PILLARD**, Circuit Judges.

[—2—] {-462-} **PILLARD**, Circuit Judge:

The Republic of Guinea is one of the world's principal sources of bauxite, an aluminum ore. After Guinea declared independence from France in the middle of the last century, it sought to ensure that the exploitation of its natural resources would not only provide business for multinational corporations based overseas that invested in the ore's extraction, but would also benefit the Guinean economy. Plaintiff Nanko Shipping Guineé (Nanko) claims to be the beneficiary of one of Guinea's legal undertakings to that end, and contends in this case that defendants (collectively, Alcoa) violated corresponding obligations. Other named plaintiffs—Nanko's owners, Nanko Shipping USA and Mori Diané, an American of Guinean descent—are not before us, having not appealed the district court's order dismissing them for lack of standing.

The district court granted Alcoa's motion to dismiss the complaint under Federal Rule of Civil Procedure 12(b)(7) for failure to join Guinea, which Alcoa asserts is a Rule 19 required party. The district court concluded that Guinea could not be joined because it is entitled to sovereign **{-463-}** immunity. But it is not apparent why Guinea is a required party and, if it is, whether Nanko's allegations bring Guinea within the commercial-activity exception to foreign sovereign immunity such that its joinder would be feasible. We accordingly reverse and remand for further proceedings.

I.

On review of the order granting the motion to dismiss, we assume—as did the district court—the truth of the facts alleged in Nanko's proposed Second Amended Complaint. According to that complaint, in 1963 the Republic of Guinea and the Harvey Aluminum Company of Delaware (now Halco) signed an agreement establishing the Compagnie des Bauxites de **[—3—]** Guinée (CBG) for the purpose of developing Guinea's rich bauxite mines.[1] CBG is a corporation of which Guinea owns a 49 per cent share and Halco 51 per cent. Nanko alleges that defendant Alcoa, in turn, is somehow both the minority owner and alter ego of Halco. Over the last half century, CBG has extracted and exported more than 600 million tons of Guinean bauxite.

Under Article 9 of the CBG Agreement, Guinea reserved the right to require that up to 50 per cent of the Republic's bauxite be shipped on vessels flying the Guinean flag or chartered by the Guinean government, provided that the freight rates those Guinean shippers offered are no higher than, and the services equal to, those otherwise available on the international shipping market. That clause presumably was designed to ensure that some of the business generated by the bauxite mines would go to qualified Guinean shipping firms and thereby benefit the Guinean economy.

Nanko alleges that, in August 2011, Guinea entered into a Technical Assistance Agreement (TAA) with Nanko. That document is neither quoted in nor attached to the pleadings, nor is it otherwise in the record. Pursuant to the TAA, Nanko alleges, it "assumed Guinea's rights" under Article 9 of the CBG Agreement "to manage, control and

[1] Nanko calls this agreement a "convention," *see* Appellant's Br. 2, but that term usually denotes an accord between states. The cover page of the agreement describes it as an "Agreement Between the Republic of Guinea and Harvey Aluminum Co. of Delaware."

ship" up to 50 per cent of Guinean-produced bauxite. Prop. Second Am. Compl. at 2.

Later in 2011, CBG's Board of Directors allegedly invited its constituent corporations, including Halco and Alcoa, to contact Nanko to make shipping arrangements. Nevertheless, **[—4—]** Halco and Alcoa refused to deal with Nanko, offering "only a few limited micro-tender shipping opportunities" that were "substantially less in value and volume than the shipping rights and contracts" to which Nanko claims it is entitled under the TAA. Prop. Second Am. Compl. ¶¶ 26, 46. Halco and Alcoa allegedly added insult to injury, posing questions about Nanko's "background and capacity" that were not asked of other shipping companies and then refusing to credit Nanko's responses. *Id.* at ¶¶ 42, 65. Guinea, for its part, "repeatedly urged" Halco and Alcoa to hire Nanko to ship their bauxite. *Id.* at ¶ 76.

In this action, Nanko initially brought two claims: one for breach of the CBG Agreement, asserting that it is a third-party beneficiary thereof, and another for racial discrimination in violation of 42 U.S.C. § 1981. Alcoa moved to dismiss on a variety of grounds, including lack of standing, failure to state a claim, and failure to join a required party. Nanko responded with a proposed Second Amended Complaint adding Halco as a defendant and asserting an additional claim against **{-464-}** Alcoa for tortious interference with contractual relations.

The district court dismissed the case under Rule 12(b)(7) for failure to join a Rule 19 party. Guinea was a required party under Rule 19(a), the court concluded, because resolving Nanko's claims would depend on defining Guinea's rights under its CBG Agreement with Halco, which might "impair or impede Guinea's right to protect its interests" under that Agreement. *Nanko Shipping, USA v. Alcoa, Inc.*, 107 F. Supp. 3d 174, 181 (D.D.C. 2015) ("*Nanko I*"). Proceeding to the Rule 19(b) inquiry, the court concluded Guinea could not be joined because it is entitled to sovereign immunity, and that the case could not "in equity and good conscience" proceed in Guinea's absence. *Id.* at 181-82. Although it considered the allegations of the proposed Second Amended Complaint in its analysis, the **[—5—]** district court denied leave to file that complaint on grounds of futility because it concluded that, even if it accepted the additional allegations, it would still conclude that the case cannot proceed without Guinea.

The district court alternatively noted that if Guinea could be joined the case "would have to be dismissed so that the parties could proceed to mandatory arbitration." *Nanko I*, 107 F.Supp. 3d at 182 n.7. Because it is not clear on the present record that Alcoa (as distinct from Halco and CBG) bound itself to the relevant arbitration agreement, and because the parties have not briefed the issue, we do not here address that ground.

Nanko timely appealed and simultaneously moved the district court to reconsider its dismissal of the discrimination claim. The district court denied the reconsideration motion in an order that postdates Nanko's notice of appeal. *See Nanko Shipping, USA v. Alcoa, Inc.*, 118 F. Supp. 3d 372 (D.D.C. 2015) ("*Nanko II*"). In that order, the district court said that it had dismissed the discrimination claim for failure to state a claim, though its original dismissal rested exclusively on Rule 19 grounds. We conclude that the district court's Rule 19 holding failed to fully grapple with Nanko's allegations and that those allegations, accepted as true, state a claim for racial discrimination under § 1981.

II.

Federal Rule of Civil Procedure 19 calls on a district court confronting a Rule 12(b)(7) motion to dismiss a case for failure to join an absent party to decide first (under Rule 19(a)) whether the absent party should be joined, and, if joinder is infeasible, to assess (under subsection (b)) whether the action among the existing parties should proceed or be dismissed in light of the missing party's absence. We have summed up the **[—6—]** Rule 19 inquiry as posing three questions: Should the absentee be joined, *i.e.*, is it necessary to the litigation? If so, can the absentee be joined? And finally, if the absentee should but cannot be joined, may the lawsuit nonetheless proceed "in equity and good conscience"? *W. Md. Ry. Co. v. Harbor Ins. Co.*, 910 F.2d 960, 961 (D.C. Cir. 1990); *see Kickapoo Tribe of Indians of Kickapoo Reservation in Kan. v. Babbitt*, 43 F.3d 1491, 1494 (D.C. Cir. 1995). Rule 19 promotes fair treatment of nonparties in certain circumstances where their interests, and particularly their due process rights, are at risk from litigation between others. It also seeks to avoid multiple and wasteful litigation, such as where the absence of a party would prevent the court from granting the relief sought or expose an existing party (typically the defendant) to a substantial risk of incurring double, multiple, or otherwise inconsistent obligations. Rule 19 does not apply merely because dispute resolution would be more efficient with the nonparty's **{-465-}** participation, nor because the pending case could yield precedent adverse to the absentee's interests. A decision under Rule 19 "*not* to decide" a case otherwise properly before the court is a power to be exercised only "[i]n rare instances." *Nat'l Ass'n of Chain Drug Stores v. New England Carpenters Health Benefits Fund*, 582 F.3d 30, 42 (1st Cir. 2009); *see also Fort Yates Pub. Sch. Dist. No. 4 v. Murphy ex rel. C.M.B.*, 786 F.3d 662, 671 (8th Cir. 2015).

We review the district court's application of Rule 19(b)'s "equity and good conscience" test for abuse of discretion, *Cloverleaf Standardbred Owners Ass'n, Inc. v. Nat'l Bank of Wash.*, 699 F.2d 1274, 1276 (D.C. Cir. 1983), but "[q]uestions of law that inform a district court's Rule 19 determination are reviewed *de novo*," *Am. Trucking Ass'n, Inc. v. N.Y. State Thruway Auth.*, 795 F.3d 351, 356 (2d Cir. 2015). Under Rule 12(b)(7), we accept Nanko's allegations as true and draw all reasonable inferences in its favor. *Paiute-Shoshone Indians* **[—7—]** *of the Bishop Cmty. of the Bishop Colony, Cal. v. City of Los Angeles*, 637 F.3d 993, 996 n.1 (9th Cir. 2011). We have not specifically addressed the standard of review of decisions whether an absent party is necessary and whether it cannot be joined—the first and second questions in the above triad—and we need not do so here. Under any standard of review, we cannot, on the current record, affirm the district court's conclusion that Alcoa has shown that Guinea is a necessary party to this litigation that cannot be joined, and that the case accordingly must be dismissed.

The district court determined that Guinea is a potential party required to be joined if feasible. Guinea is a necessary party under Rule 19, the district court held, simply because "[t]he Court's interpretation of the [CBG Agreement] may impair or impede Guinea's right to protect its interests" under that Agreement. *Nanko I*, 107 F. Supp. 3d at 181. But due process protects Guinea from being bound by any judgment rendered in its absence, and it is not obvious what interests Guinea would retain in the CBG Agreement if Nanko "assumed Guinea's rights" thereunder, as Nanko alleges. Prop. Second Am. Compl. at 2. *See SEC v. Bilzerian*, 378 F.3d 1100, 1108 (D.C. Cir. 2004) (absent party not required to be joined where it merely assigned rights to party). Alcoa expresses concern that the court might "construe the CBG [Agreement] in a manner inconsistent with or contrary to Guinea's own understandings or positions, without the opportunity for Guinea to be heard." Appellee Br. at 29. Rule 19 precedent is admittedly scant, but we agree with the Third Circuit that "the requirements of Rule 19(a) are not satisfied simply because a judgment against Defendants in this action might set a persuasive precedent in any potential future action." *Huber v. Taylor*, 532 F.3d 237, 250 (3d Cir. 2008). Insofar as the existing parties' interests are concerned, evidence of Guinea's actions, views, or prerogatives can be discovered and **[—8—]** introduced where relevant to the parties' claims and defenses even if Guinea remains a nonparty. At the current pleading stage, we do not believe the allegations can reasonably be read to show that Guinea is a necessary party.

The district court further held that Guinea could not be joined involuntarily on the ground that it is entitled to sovereign immunity under the Foreign Sovereign Immunities Act (FSIA), 28 U.S.C. § 1602 *et seq. See Nanko I*, 107 F. Supp. 3d at 181. The FSIA "renders a foreign government 'presumptively immune from the jurisdiction of United States courts unless one of the Act's express exceptions to sovereign immunity applies.'" **{-466-}** *Bank Markazi v. Peterson*, 136 S. Ct. 1310, 1317 n.1 (2016) (quoting *OBB Personenverkehr AG v. Sachs*, 136 S.Ct. 390, 394 (2015)). Under the FSIA, a foreign state is not immune from claims "based [1] upon a commercial activity carried on in the United States by the foreign state; or [2] upon an act performed in the United States in connection with a commercial activity of the foreign state elsewhere; or [3] upon an act outside the territory of the United States in connection with a commercial activity of the foreign state elsewhere and that act causes a direct effect in the United States." 28 U.S.C. § 1605(a)(2).

Nanko and Alcoa sparsely briefed the immunity issue before the district court. That court's immunity holding rested exclusively on Nanko's failure to "contest" Alcoa's bare assertion that the court lacked jurisdiction over Guinea. *See Nanko I*, 107 F. Supp. 3d at 181 n.6. But Nanko did contest the point. *See* Opp'n to Mot. to Dismiss at 24 (characterizing as "a red herring and meritless" Alcoa's argument that "because Guinea is a foreign sovereign this Court lacks jurisdiction"). And Nanko's motion for reconsideration argued that the court was "not in [a] position to resolve," absent discovery, what Nanko identified as the "fact question" whether Guinea "enjoys **[—9—]** sovereign immunity." Mot. for Recons. at 4. Nanko's assumption that Alcoa's assertion of Guinea's immunity "may be correct" is not, in context, fairly read to concede the matter. *See* Opp'n to Mot. to Dismiss at 25. Nor did Nanko give up the point in its motion for reconsideration by stating that the district court "properly acknowledged that it [has no] jurisdiction over ... Guinea *as a sovereign entity*." Mot. for Recons. at 6 (emphasis added). That statement leaves open a critical question for FSIA purposes: whether the district court has jurisdiction over Guinea *as a commercial actor*.

Before this Court, Alcoa argues in a footnote that Nanko "has utterly failed to allege any facts" establishing a FSIA exception, thus failing to overcome the "presumption of immunity." Appellee Br. at 35 n.54 (citing *Bell Helicopter Textron, Inc. v. Islamic Republic of Iran*, 734 F.3d 1175, 1183 (D.C. Cir. 2013)). That is not necessarily so. Most notably, Nanko alleges that the CBG Board—of which Guinea is a member—hosted a 2011 meeting in New York City at which Guinea "announced its authorization and contract award to [Nanko] regarding shipment of bauxite." Prop. Second Am. Compl. ¶ 22. That alleged authorization appears to be central to Nanko's theory of the case. For instance, it is that authorization on which Nanko rests its claim that defendants knew of but disregarded their contractual responsibility to deal with Nanko to ship bauxite out of Guinea. The facts as Nanko alleges them suggest that Guinea's participation in the shipping of bauxite falls within the FSIA's commercial-activity exception.

At this preliminary stage, based only on the pleadings, we see no adequate basis for the district court's dismissal of the complaint under Rule 12(b)(7). With the benefit of discovery and further briefing, as appropriate, the district court may wish to revisit the Rule 19 issues. Further proceedings may help to **[—10—]** clarify what interests of Guinea, if any, would be impaired in its absence, what role Guinea would play in this litigation if joined, and whether sovereign immunity prevents its involuntary joinder here. *See In re Papandreou*, 139 F.3d 247, 252 (D.C. Cir. 1998) (district courts often must "look beyond the pleadings" to decide whether an FSIA exception applies); *Ilan-Gat Eng'rs, Ltd. v. Antigua Int'l Bank*, 659 F.2d 234, 242 (D.C. Cir. 1981) ("[T]he court failed to consider whether more facts were needed before making the indispensable party determination **{-467-}** given the rather unusual situation before it.").

III.

Our dissenting colleague would hold that the complaint failed to state a section 1981 claim sufficient to withstand a motion to dismiss under Federal Rule of Civil Procedure 12(b)(6). We disagree.

Section 1981 protects the right "to make and enforce contracts" free from racial discrimination, 42 U.S.C. § 1981(a), and the pleading standards under section 1981 track those in the familiar *McDonnell Douglas* rubric for alleging a *prima facie* case of purposeful employment discrimination. *See Patterson v. McLean Credit Union*, 491 U.S. 164, 186 (1989) (citing *Tex. Dep't of Cmty. Affairs v. Burdine*, 450 U.S. 248 (1981), and *McDonnell Douglas Corp. v. Green*, 411 U.S. 792 (1973)); *Brown v. Sessoms*, 774 F.3d 1016, 1022-23 (D.C. Cir. 2014) (citing *McDonnell Douglas*, 411 U.S. at 802-04). The plaintiff's initial burden "is not onerous." *Patterson*, 491 U.S. at 186. Further, discrimination against a business based on the race of its owner violates section 1981. *See McClain v. Avis Rent A Car Sys., Inc.*, 648 F. App'x 218, 222 n.4 (3d Cir. 2016); *Gersman v. Group Health Ass'n, Inc.*, 931 F.2d 1565, 1567-70 (D.C. Cir. 1991), *vacated on other grounds*, 502 U.S. 1068, *reinstated*, 975 F.2d 886 (D.C. Cir. 1992). Nanko alleges that **[—11—]** Alcoa, aware of Diané's race, treated the company he owns and operates less favorably than similarly situated white-owned companies. *See, e.g.*, Prop. Second Am. Compl. ¶¶ 3, 17, 57-68. By alleging those basic elements of a *prima facie* case of intentional discrimination, Nanko raised its "right to relief above the speculative level." *Bell Atlantic Corp. v. Twombly*, 550 U.S. 544, 555 (2007); *see Brown*, 774 F.3d at 1023 (plaintiff stated section 1981 claim where she "identified a similarly-situated employee who is not in her protected class and explained why she has equivalent qualifications"). The burden at the summary judgment stage and at trial is different and substantially more onerous than the pleading burden. Allegations regarding comparators, racial comments, and pretext obviously strengthen a discrimination complaint, but the evidentiary requirements the dissent identifies are inapplicable at the pleading stage.

We do not reach any of the other grounds, such as the applicability of a mandatory arbitration clause in the CBG Agreement, on which Alcoa moved to dismiss. The absence of a putative required party is not a jurisdictional question. *Ilan-Gat Eng'rs, Ltd.*, 659 F.2d at 240. The district court accordingly may decide to address those other grounds on remand before or in tandem with further consideration of the Rule 19 issue.

* * *

For the foregoing reasons, we reverse the district court's dismissal of the complaint and remand for further proceedings.

So ordered.

(Reporter's Note: Dissenting opinion follows on p. 535).

[—1—] {–467–} **BROWN**, Circuit Judge, dissenting:

The Court finds the question whether the Foreign Sovereign Immunities Act ("FSIA") applies—and therefore whether jurisdictional discovery is necessary—was properly presented to the district court. Op. 8–9. Its opinion further holds the district court erred in deciding Nanko failed to state a claim upon which relief can be granted for violations of 28 U.S.C. §§ 1981 and 1985. Op. 10–11. I disagree on both points and respectfully dissent. **{–468–}**

I.

The district court specifically noted, "Plaintiffs do not contest the assertion that Guinea is protected from suit by sovereign immunity." *Nanko Shipping, USA v. Alcoa, Inc.*, 107 F. Supp. 3d 174, 181 n.6 (D.D.C. 2015) (citing Nanko's opposition to Alcoa's motion to dismiss). We, therefore, review Nanko's filings in the district court to determine whether the court abused its discretion in finding the argument forfeited. *See GSS Grp. Ltd. v. Nat'l Port Auth.*, 680 F.3d 805, 812 (D.C. Cir. 2012). It did not.

Nanko's brief opposing the motion to dismiss contains two relevant statements:

- "Defendants claim that Guinea is an indispensable party and further allege that because Guinea is a foreign sovereign this Court lacks jurisdiction under the Foreign Soverign [sic] Immunities Act, unless a specified exception applies. This argument is a red herring and meritless. Contrary to Defendants' contention, there is no basis for Guinea involvement given the Technical Assistance Agreement . . . ," and
- "[w]hile Defendants may be correct in its [sic] view that this Court lacks jurisdiction over Guinea, Defendants miss two critical facts; as plead, the CBG and the TAA are valid legal contracts." **[—2—]**

Nanko Opp'n to Alcoa Mot. to Dismiss at 24–25, *Nanko Shipping, USA v. Alcoa, Inc.*, No. 14-cv-1301 (D.D.C. Sept. 25, 2014), ECF No. 11. These statements, read together and in succession, discuss whether Guinea was an indispensable party, mentioning the applicability of the FSIA only in passing. Of course, reasonable minds may differ regarding the precise interpretation of these statements, *see* Op. 8, but the district court judge did not *abuse her discretion* in concluding the FSIA issue was not contested. *See Cement Kiln Recycling Coal. v. EPA*, 255 F.3d 855, 869 (D.C. Cir. 2001) ("A litigant does not properly raise an issue by addressing it in a cursory fashion with only bare-bones arguments.").

The majority points to Nanko's Motion for Reconsideration filed before the district court, Op. 8–9, which *does* appear to discuss the FSIA. Nonetheless, "[Federal] Rule [of Civil Procedure] 59(e) motions are aimed at reconsideration, not initial consideration." *GSS Grp.*, 680 F.3d at 812. Accordingly, a "Rule 59(e) motion may not be used to . . . raise arguments or present evidence that could have been raised prior to the entry of judgment." 11 CHARLES ALAN WRIGHT ET AL., FEDERAL PRACTICE & PROCEDURE § 2810.1, at 163–64 (3d ed. 2012). Since Nanko could have raised its FSIA argument earlier, but chose not to do so, the argument is forfeited. *See District of Columbia v. Doe*, 611 F.3d 888, 896 (D.C. Cir. 2010).

II.

The district court also properly dismissed Nanko's claims pursuant to 42 U.S.C. §§ 1981 and 1985 for failure to state a claim upon which relief could be granted.

I agree with the Court's starting premise: "Nanko alleges that Alcoa, aware of Diané's race, treated the company he **[—3—]** owns and operates less favorably than similarly situated white-owned companies." Op. 10–11. Indeed, Nanko's complaint recounts multiple incidents, over a three-year period, when Alcoa failed to award bids to Nanko and awarded contracts to white-owned companies instead.

But, as the majority also notes, a Section 1981 claim cannot "reach[] more than *purposeful* discrimination." **{–469–}** *Gen. Bldg. Contractors Ass'n v. Pennsylvania*, 458 U.S. 375, 388, 391 (1982) (emphasis added).

Accordingly, to plead a *prima facie* case, a plaintiff must show the defendant intended to discriminate against the plaintiff on the basis of race. *See Williams v. Lindenwood Univ.*, 288 F.3d 349, 355 (8th Cir. 2002); *Mian v. Donaldson, Lufkin & Jenrette Secs. Corp.*, 7 F.3d 1085, 1087 (2d Cir. 1993).

Nanko has failed to plead sufficient facts to carry that burden here. In fact, *no facts* presented in the complaint suggest Alcoa intentionally discriminated against Nanko on account of race. Rather, Nanko states it is an African-American owned company, *see* Prop. Second Am. Compl. ¶¶ 78–79, alleges Alcoa had done business with white-owned Klaveness, *id.* ¶¶ 17, 80, and asserts "[Alcoa] imposed certain unreasonable requirements, offered multiple limited shipping opportunities in 2012 after telling Nanko that all such bid opportunities had been contracted out and expressly stated that their decision making process would be arbitrary and subjective," *id.* ¶ 82. Further, Nanko claims it used the "same exact shipping companies" as Alcoa and also "attained equal or lower shipping prices and similar assurances regarding shipping security." *Id.* ¶ 87. Indeed, all of Nanko's factual allegations are consistent with an arbitrary, *but not racially discriminatory*, decision-making process. Everyone can be characterized by race, and many contracting parties are "harsh, unjust, and rude," but a failure to do business with a **[—4—]** particular African-American individual or company does not automatically constitute a federal civil rights claim. *See generally Alfano v. Costello*, 294 F.3d 365, 377 (2d Cir. 2002).

The inadequacy of Nanko's pleading is hardly surprising. Intentional discrimination may be relatively easy to plead via comparator evidence—as Nanko apparently attempts to do—in the employment discrimination context, where a plaintiff is keenly aware of his coworkers' performance and familiar with his employers' policies. *See Brown v. Sessoms*, 774 F.3d 1016, 1023 (D.C. Cir. 2014) (pleading the underlying facts necessary to rely on comparator evidence in an employment case). In the commercial context, however, it is often very difficult to plead facts raising an inference of racially discriminatory intent. *See Denny v. Elizabeth Arden Salons, Inc.*, 456 F.3d 427, 429–31, 435 (4th Cir. 2006) (finding a viable § 1981 claim where an individual purchased a salon gift card for her mother, but the salon refused service to the mother, stating it did not "do black people's hair"). This difficulty is systemic, but it is not for this Court to remedy policy deficiencies: "Trying to make [the statute] a cure-all not only goes beyond any expression of congressional intent but would produce satellite § 1981 litigation of immense scope." *Domino's Pizza, Inc. v. McDonald*, 546 U.S. 470, 479 (2006).

Accordingly, I would affirm the district court's dismissal of Nanko's claims pursuant to 42 U.S.C. §§ 1981 and 1985 for failure to state a claim upon which relief can be granted. *See Nanko Shipping, USA v. Alcoa, Inc.*, 118 F. Supp. 3d 372, 377 (D.D.C. 2015); *United Bhd. of Carpenters & Joiners v. Scott*, 463 U.S. 825, 833 (1983) (noting § 1985 "provides no substantial rights itself").

United States Court of Appeals
for the District of Columbia Circuit

No. 17-7023

SCHERMERHORN
VS.
STATE OF ISRAEL

Appeal from the United States District Court for the District of Columbia

Decided: December 1, 2017

Citation: 876 F.3d 351, 5 Adm. R. 537 (D.C. Cir. 2017).

Before **ROGERS** and **TATEL,** Circuit Judges, and **EDWARDS,** Senior Circuit Judge.

[—1—] {-353-} **TATEL,** Circuit Judge:

On May 29, 2010, Plaintiffs—three United States citizens and one foreign national—set sail aboard **[—2—]** the U.S.-flagged ship *Challenger I* as part of the "Gaza Freedom Flotilla." Compl. ¶ 31. The Flotilla's stated aim was to "draw international public attention to the situation in the Gaza Strip and the effect of the [Israeli] blockade." *Id.* ¶ 24. According to Plaintiffs, when the *Challenger I* was approximately seventy nautical miles from the Gaza Strip and still in international waters, Israeli Defense Forces attacked the vessel and detained them in violation of international law. *Id.* ¶¶ 7-11, 28, 40. Seeking to recover for these alleged torts, Plaintiffs filed suit against Israel and its ministries in the United States District Court for the District of Columbia. Israel moved to dismiss under Federal Rule of Civil Procedure 12(b)(1), arguing that it enjoyed immunity from suit under the Foreign Sovereign Immunities Act of 1976 (FSIA). Plaintiffs responded that the FSIA's "non-commercial torts" and "terrorism" exceptions allowed the district court to exercise jurisdiction. Finding neither exception applicable, the district court dismissed the case. *Schermerhorn v. Israel*, 235 F. Supp. 3d 249 (D.D.C. 2017). For the reasons set forth in this opinion, we affirm.

I.

The FSIA provides "the sole basis for obtaining jurisdiction over a foreign state in our courts." *Argentine Republic v. Amerada Hess Shipping Corp.*, 488 U.S. 428, 434 (1989). Under the FSIA, foreign sovereigns enjoy absolute immunity from suit unless the case falls within one of several specified exceptions, two of which—the "non-commercial torts" exception, 28 U.S.C. § 1605(a)(5), and the "terrorism" exception, *id.* § 1605A—are at issue in this case. We consider each in turn, "[r]eview[ing] the District Court's sovereign **[—3—]** immunity determination de novo." *Odhiambo v. Republic of Kenya*, 764 F.3d 31, 35 (D.C. Cir. 2014).

Non-Commercial Torts Exception

The FSIA's non-commercial torts exception confers jurisdiction in any case

> in which money damages are sought against a foreign state for personal injury or death, or damage to or loss of property, occurring in the United States and caused by the tortious act or omission of that foreign state or of any official or employee of that foreign state while acting within the scope of his office or employment.

28 U.S.C. § 1605(a)(5). In this case, the dispositive question is whether Israel's alleged torts—which took place aboard a U.S.-flagged vessel in international waters—"occur[ed] in the United States." *Id.*

Under the FSIA, the "'United States' includes all territory and waters, continental or insular, subject to the jurisdiction of the United States." *Id.* § 1603(c). Although this definition speaks primarily in geographic terms, Plaintiffs argue that it also includes U.S.-flagged ships on the high seas. **{-354-}**

Plaintiffs begin by noting that the definition of "United States" is introduced by the word "includes" rather than the word "means." Appellants' Br. 13-15. Invoking the rule of statutory interpretation that "[a] definition which declares what a term 'means'

. . . excludes any meaning that is not stated," *Colautti v. Franklin*, 439 U.S. 379, 393 n.10 (1979) (alterations in original) (quoting 2A C. Sands, Statutes and Statutory Construction § 47.07 (4th ed. Supp. 1978)), Plaintiffs contend that the use of "includes" permits us to adopt a broader interpretation of the term "United States." Appellants' Br. 14; **[—4—]** *see also National Wildlife Federation v. Gorsuch*, 693 F.2d 156, 171-72 (D.C. Cir. 1982) (contrasting the "restrictive phrasing" using the word "means" with "the looser phrase 'includes'").

Relying on this interpretative leeway, Plaintiffs contend that a U.S.-flagged ship in international waters is part of the "United States." The determinative test, Plaintiffs assert, is whether a U.S.-flagged ship and the territory and waters of the United States "share a comparable degree of U.S. sovereign control." Appellants' Br. 15. Arguing that they do, Plaintiffs invoke several non-FSIA cases that refer to a ship sailing under a particular country's flag in international waters as constructively part of the flag state's territory. Appellants' Br. 19-20; *see Patterson v. Eudora*, 190 U.S. 169, 176 (1903) ("A ship which bears a nation's flag is to be treated as a part of the territory of that nation." (quoting *Queen v. Anderson*, (1868) L. R. 1 C. C. 161 (U.K.)); *Ross v. McIntyre*, 140 U.S. 453, 464 (1891) ("The deck of a private American vessel, it is true, is considered, for many purposes, constructively as territory of the United States . . . ."). Plaintiffs also point out that a country's law may extend to vessels flying its flag. *See Lauritzen v. Larsen*, 345 U.S. 571, 585 (1953) (holding that Danish tort law extends to a Danish ship because it "is deemed to be a part of the territory of that sovereignty (whose flag it flies)" (quoting *United States v. Flores*, 289 U.S. 137, 155 (1933))).

Were we tasked with identifying the outer limits of the "United States" in general terms, Plaintiffs' arguments might have some merit. But this case requires that we interpret a particular term in a particular law. And, fatal to Plaintiffs' theory, the cases interpreting the FSIA—as opposed to the ones cited by Plaintiffs—not only "counsel[] that [section 1605(a)(5)] should be narrowly construed," *MacArthur Area* **[—5—]** *Citizens Ass'n v. Republic of Peru*, 809 F.2d 918, 921 (D.C. Cir. 1987), but also require that we read the term "United States" in the FSIA to include only the geographic territory of the United States.

Our starting point is the Supreme Court's discussion of the non-commercial torts exception in *Argentine Republic v. Amerada Hess Shipping Corp.*, 488 U.S. 428, 434 (1989). That case involved a Liberian-chartered oil tanker traveling from the Virgin Islands to Alaska around Cape Horn in South America during the Falklands War. *Id.* at 431. When the tanker was approximately 600 nautical miles from Argentina, it was attacked by the Argentine military. *Id.* at 431-32. The Liberian companies that owned and chartered the tanker brought suit against Argentina in the United States under the FSIA's non-commercial torts exception, arguing that because the high seas were within the admiralty jurisdiction of the United States, the tort occurred "in the United States." *Id.* at 440. Rejecting that view—and calling into question **{-355-}** how Plaintiffs in our case read the term "United States"—the Supreme Court explained that it "construe[s] the modifying phrase 'continental and insular' to restrict the definition of United States to the continental United States and those islands that are part of the United States or its possessions; any other reading would render this phrase nugatory." *Id.*

Of course, as Plaintiffs point out, *Amerada Hess* does not entirely foreclose their position because it primarily addresses whether the term "waters" includes the high seas, *see id.* at 441 ("Because respondents' injury unquestionably occurred well outside the 3-mile limit then in effect for the territorial waters of the United States, the exception for non-commercial torts cannot apply."), whereas they are concerned with whether the term "territory" is capacious enough to include U.S.-flagged vessels. Although the Supreme Court had no occasion to **[—6—]** resolve the question before us—the ship involved was a foreign vessel—it did instruct courts interpreting the term "United States" to give full effect to the "modifying phrase 'continental and insular'" and to "apply '[t]he canon of construction which teaches that legislation of Congress, unless contrary intent appears, is meant to apply only within the territorial jurisdiction of the United States.'" *Id.* at 440 (alteration in original) (quoting *Foley Brothers v. Filardo*, 336 U.S. 281, 285 (1949)).

But even if Plaintiffs' reading of "United States" survives *Amerada Hess*, it is defeated by our court's decision in *Persinger v. Islamic Republic of Iran*, 729 F.2d 835 (D.C. Cir. 1984). There, plaintiffs sought to invoke the non-commercial torts exception with respect to torts that allegedly occurred at the United States Embassy in Tehran, arguing that Congress has "power to exercise jurisdiction over certain activities at U.S. embassies." *Id.* at 839. Although the court acknowledged that "the United States has some jurisdiction over its Embassy in Iran," it rejected plaintiffs' invocation of the non-commercial torts exception because the embassy was not within the territorial United States. *Id.* As the court explained, the use of "the words 'continental or insular' to modify the scope of the phrase 'all territory and waters . . . subject to the jurisdiction of the United States'" is "clearly intended to restrict the definition of the United States to the continental United States and such islands as are part of the United States or are its possessions." *Id.* (alteration in original) (quoting 28 U.S.C. § 1603(c)). This unambiguous language makes plain that the "United States," at least for purposes of the FSIA, is limited to the geographic territories and waters of the United States.

Plaintiffs seek to distinguish *Persinger* on two grounds. First, they argue that unlike the plaintiffs in *Persinger*, they rely on "the unique status of ships" as part of the flag state's **[—7—]** territory "deriving from centuries of legal evolution," rather than the mere fact that the United States exercises "some form of jurisdiction" over U.S. embassies on foreign soil. Appellants' Br. 29. It is true, as Plaintiffs point out, that several cases recognize that "for the purposes of jurisdiction a ship, even on the high seas, is often said to be a part of the territory of the nation whose flag it flies." *Scharrenberg v. Dollar S. S. Co.*, 245 U.S. 122, 127 (1917). But not only are these non-FSIA cases, they caution that "in the physical sense this expression is obviously figurative." *Id.* (rejecting a claim that seamen employed on a ship are working "in the country of its registry" for purposes of a labor law); *see also Lauritzen*, 345 U.S. at 585 ("Some authorities reject, as a rather **{–356–}** mischievous fiction, the doctrine that a ship is constructively a floating part of the flagstate . . . ."). Thus, even outside the FSIA context, courts have sometimes rejected attempts to include U.S.-flagged vessels within the statutory definition of "United States," *see, e.g., Cunard S. S. Co. v. Mellon*, 262 U.S. 100, 122, 128 (1923) (holding that the Eighteenth Amendment and National Prohibition Act's restriction on the sale and transport of liquors within "the United States and all territory subject to the jurisdiction thereof" does not include U.S.-registered ships outside territorial waters), and we have no indication that the drafters of the FSIA intended a different result, *see Asociacion de Reclamantes v. United Mexican States*, 735 F.2d 1517, 1525 (D.C. Cir. 1984) (Scalia, J.) (explaining that the legislative history of section 1605(a)(5) indicates that the primary purpose of the exception "was to enable officials and employees of foreign sovereigns to be held liable for the traffic accidents which they cause in this country" (discussing H.R. Rep. No. 94-1487, at 20-21 (1976), *as reprinted in* 1976 U.S.C.C.A.N. 6605, 6619-20)).

Plaintiffs also seek to distinguish *Persinger* on the ground that the U.S. Embassy in Tehran was within the territory of **[—8—]** Iran, and thus necessarily could not be "in the United States." Appellants' Br. 30. *Persinger*'s discussion of what was "in the United States," Plaintiffs argue, is dicta. *Id.* But Plaintiffs misunderstand the court's holding in *Persinger*. Like this panel, the court in *Persinger* was asked to determine whether a particular location was "within the definition of 'United States'" under the FSIA. *Persinger*, 729 F.2d at 839. To resolve that issue, the court set forth a positive account of what the FSIA meant by "United States"—"the continental United States and such islands as are part of the United States or are its possessions"—and determined that U.S.

embassies on foreign soil did not fall within that definition. *Id.* Hardly dictum, this discussion was necessary to the court's holding. *See De Csepel v. Republic of Hungary*, 859 F.3d 1094, 1113 (D.C. Cir. 2017) (explaining that "it is not only the result but also those portions of the opinion necessary to that result by which we are bound" (quoting *Seminole Tribe of Florida v. Florida*, 517 U.S. 44, 67 (1996))). It would not have been enough, as Plaintiffs suggest, for the court to rely only on the fact that the U.S. Embassy in Tehran was on foreign soil, given that the *Persinger* plaintiffs argued for an interpretation of "United States" that included all areas—including those outside the territorial United States—where the U.S. exercised some jurisdiction.

Bound by *Persinger*'s strictly geographical interpretation of the "United States," we hold that U.S.-flagged ships on the high seas do not fall within the FSIA's non-commercial torts exception. Accordingly, this exception gives Plaintiffs no basis for invoking the district court's jurisdiction in this case.

Terrorism Exception

Congress first enacted the FSIA's terrorism exception as part of the Antiterrorism and Effective Death Penalty Act of 1996 (AEDPA), Pub. L. No. 104-132, 110 Stat. 1214 (codified **[—9—]** as amended in scattered sections of the U.S. Code). As initially drafted, the exception—then codified at 28 U.S.C. § 1605(a)(7)—abrogated a foreign sovereign's immunity in any case

> (7) . . . in which money damages are sought against a foreign state for personal injury or death that was caused by an act of torture, extrajudicial killing, aircraft sabotage, hostage taking, or the provision of material support or resources **{–357–}** . . . [if] engaged in by an official, employee, or agent of such foreign state while acting within the scope of his or her office, employment, or agency, except that the court shall decline to hear a claim under this paragraph—
>
> (A) if the foreign state was not designated as a state sponsor of terrorism under [certain statutes] at the time the act occurred, unless later so designated as a result of such act . . . .

Pub. L. No. 104-132, § 221, 110 Stat. at 1241-43 (codified at 28 U.S.C. § 1605(a)(7) (2006) (repealed 2008)).

Had this case been brought under section 1605(a)(7), Plaintiffs "readily concede that this action would be barred . . . because . . . Israel has never been designated a state sponsor of terrorism by the Government of the United States." Appellants' Br. 32. But Congress amended the FSIA's terrorism exception in 2008, and although the primary impetus for the amendment was to resolve a dispute over whether the exception provided a cause of action directly against a foreign state, *see Owens v. Republic of Sudan*, 864 F.3d 751, 763-65 (D.C. Cir. 2017) (discussing the history of FSIA amendments), Plaintiffs believe that it also eliminated the requirement that a state be designated a sponsor of terrorism for the exception to apply. **[—10—]**

As amended by section 1083 of the National Defense Authorization Act for Fiscal Year 2008 (NDAA), Pub. L. No. 110-181, § 1083, 122 Stat. 3, 338-44 (2008) (codified at 28 U.S.C. § 1605A), the revised terrorism exception, now codified at 28 U.S.C. § 1605A, provides in relevant part:

> (1) No Immunity.—A foreign state shall not be immune from the jurisdiction of courts of the United States or of the States in any case not otherwise covered by this chapter in which money damages are sought against a foreign state for personal injury or death that was caused by an act of torture, extrajudicial killing, aircraft sabotage, hostage taking, or the provision of material support or resources for such an act if such act or provision of material support or resources is engaged in by an official, employee, or agent of such foreign state while acting within the scope of his or her office, employment, or agency.

(2) Claim heard.—The court shall hear a claim under this section if—

(A)(i)(I) the foreign state was designated as a state sponsor of terrorism at the time the act described in paragraph (1) occurred . . . .

28 U.S.C. § 1605A(a) (2012).

Although section 1605A(a) and its predecessor section 1605(a)(7) are nearly identical, Plaintiffs emphasize the slight shift from the double negative construction of the old exception—"the court *shall decline* to hear a claim . . . if the foreign state *was not* designated as a state sponsor of terrorism"—to the affirmative, two-sentence construction of the new exception—"The court *shall* hear a claim . . . if . . . the **[—11—]** foreign state *was* designated as a state sponsor of terrorism." According to Plaintiffs, by so revising the exception, Congress established a two-tiered approach to jurisdiction. The first sentence, section 1605A(a)(1), strips all foreign states of immunity in cases involving "personal injury or death" caused by certain specified terroristic acts. And the second sentence, section 1605A(a)(2), provides that when certain other conditions are met, such as when the defendant state is designated a state sponsor of terrorism, a court has no choice but to hear the case. Read together, these sentences, Plaintiffs argue, mean that when a case is brought only under section 1605A(a)(1), a court still has discretion to dismiss the case on grounds such as political question, act of state, or forum non conveniens; by contrast, a court **{–358–}** must hear cases that fit the criteria of section 1605A(a)(2). And although Plaintiffs agree that their case does not qualify as one the district court must hear, they contend that the court should have considered whether it might nonetheless have jurisdiction under section 1605A(a)(1).

Plaintiffs' reading of the statute is intriguing. Treating each sentence in isolation, as Plaintiffs urge, we could read section 1605A(a)(1) as establishing a seemingly unqualified abrogation of sovereign immunity and section 1605A(a)(2) as providing only when cases *must* be heard.

But this construction of the statute simply cannot be correct. The FSIA is premised on "a presumption of foreign sovereign immunity" qualified only by a small number of "discrete and limited exceptions." *Price v. Socialist People's Libyan Arab Jamahiriya*, 294 F.3d 82, 87-88 (D.C. Cir. 2002) (collecting cases). As our court has explained, the terrorism exception, in particular, represents a "delicate legislative compromise" that rests in part on the fact that "only a defendant that has been specifically designated by the State Department **[—12—]** as a 'state sponsor of terrorism' is subject to the loss of its sovereign immunity." *Id.* at 89 (quoting 28 U.S.C. § 1605(a)(7)(A)) (discussing the historical evolution of the FSIA).

Yet under Plaintiff's view, Congress, without any acknowledgement whatsoever, abandoned this longstanding compromise and authorized victims of alleged terrorism to bring suit against any state without regard to its designation as a state sponsor of terrorism. Asked at oral argument whether they knew of any support in the legislative history for their reading, Plaintiffs' counsel conceded they knew of none. *See* Oral Arg. 12:27-33 ("There is nothing that we have been able to find in the legislative history that discusses this either way."). In fact, the only relevant legislative history discusses the terrorism exception as though the state-sponsor requirement remains a mandatory prerequisite to invoking jurisdiction. *See Ensuring Legal Redress for American Victims of State-Sponsored Terrorism: Hearing on Victims of State-Sponsored Terrorism Before the H. Comm. on the Judiciary*, 110th Cong. 6 (2008), *available at* 2008 WL 2441390 (statement of Rep. Bruce Braley) (explaining that under the proposed amendment Iraq faced "no threat of future claims since Iraq is no longer designated as a state sponsor of terrorism").

Plaintiffs' reading of section 1605A is all the more implausible given that it would require discarding not just the state-sponsor prerequisite, but also other longstanding prerequisites to invoking the terrorism exception. Although this case concerns only the state-sponsor prerequisite, former section 1605(a)(7)—now section 1605A(a)(2)—listed several other requirements for invoking the exception. For instance, section 1605(a)(7)(B) provided that, even if a foreign state was designated a sponsor of terrorism, "the court shall decline to **[—13—]** hear a claim . . . if . . . neither the claimant nor the victim was a national of the United States . . . when the act upon which the claim is based occurred." 28 U.S.C. § 1605(a)(7)(B)(ii) (2006). After eliminating the double negative, the NDAA amendment carried this language into section 1605A(a)(2) in the clause just after the state-sponsor requirement. *See id.* § 1605A(a)(2)(A)(ii)(I) ("The court shall hear a claim under this section if . . . the claimant or the victim was . . . a national of the United States . . . ."). Under Plaintiffs' interpretation of section 1605A(a)—which reads the provisions of section 1605A(a)(2) as establishing only when a court must hear a case but not limiting when a court may hear such a case—this requirement would also no longer be a **{–359–}** necessary prerequisite to invoking the court's jurisdiction.

The implications of Plaintiffs' reading of section 1605A(a)(1) are breathtaking. Without the state-sponsor and U.S.-national requirements, individuals with no connection at all to this country could bring suit here against any foreign sovereign, including a U.S. ally, for any injury or death caused by an "act of torture, extrajudicial killing, aircraft sabotage, hostage taking, or the provision of material support or resources for such an act." *Id.* § 1605A(a)(1). As counsel for Israel pointed out at oral argument—and Plaintiffs' counsel agreed—this would mean that "if a foreign national is concerned that someone has been killed in Iraq or Afghanistan by the British, that would be an extrajudicial killing and this court would have jurisdiction." *Compare* Oral Arg. 23:46-24:02 (raising hypothetical), *with id.* 30:54-31:21 ("Congress opened the door to that kind of suit.").

Although Congress may one day decide that the state-sponsor and U.S.-national requirements are no longer necessary, we cannot conclude from an unexplained editorial change that it has already done so. Such "[f]undamental **[—14—]** changes in the scope of a statute are not typically accomplished with so subtle a move." *Kellogg Brown & Root Services Inc. v. United States ex rel. Carter*, 135 S. Ct. 1970, 1977 (2015). Rather, the FSIA's terrorism exception continues to apply only to a foreign state "designated as a state sponsor of terrorism at the time the act . . . occurred, or was so designated as a result of such act." 28 U.S.C. § 1605A(a)(2)(A)(i)(I).

Given the consequences of Plaintiffs' interpretation, it is unsurprising that no court has countenanced such a reading of the terrorism exception after the NDAA amendment. Rather, cases in this circuit and elsewhere have continued to treat the state-sponsor requirement as a jurisdictional prerequisite to invoking the terrorism exception. *See, e.g.*, *Owens*, 864 F.3d at 777 ("§ 1605A strives to hold designated state sponsors of terrorism accountable for their sponsorship of terror . . . ."); *Mohammadi v. Islamic Republic of Iran*, 782 F.3d 9, 14 (D.C. Cir. 2015) ("The exception further requires that (i) the foreign country was designated a 'state sponsor of terrorism at the time [of] the act' . . . ." (quoting 28 U.S.C. § 1605A(a)(2))); *In re Terrorist Attacks on Sept. 11, 2001*, 714 F.3d 109, 115 n.7 (2d Cir. 2013) (explaining that section 1605A "is only available against a nation that has been designated by the United States government as a state sponsor of terrorism at the time of, or due to, a terrorist act"); *Doe v. Bin Laden*, 663 F.3d 64, 65 (2d Cir. 2011) (finding it undisputed that section 1605A "is not available against Afghanistan . . . because the State Department has not designated Afghanistan as a state sponsor of terrorism"). Although none of those cases squarely confronted the precise argument before us, they provide further support for the proposition that this slight revision to the terrorism exception did not bring about the dramatic departure from well-established FSIA practice that Plaintiffs seek. **[—15—]**

II.

For the foregoing reasons, the judgment of the district court is affirmed.

So ordered.

This page intentionally left blank

Tables of Authority

This page intentionally left blank

Table of Cases

This page intentionally left blank

TABLE OF CASES[1]

PAGE

[1] Cases named solely after ships, *see, e.g.*, *The Pennsylvania*, 86 U.S. (19 Wall.) 125 (1873), are alphabetized under the letter "T." Cases where the United States is the plaintiff are alphabetized by defendant under the letter "U."

B

C

D

E

F

G

H

I

J

K

L

M

N

O

P

Q

R

S

T

U

V

W

Y

This page intentionally left blank

Table of Statutes and Rules

This page intentionally left blank

TABLE OF STATUTES AND RULES[1]

PAGE

TREATIES/INTERNATIONAL

FEDERAL

CONSTITUTION

MISCELLANEOUS

[1] As cited in the opinions reported.

Statutes

RULES

Regulations

State

Index

This page intentionally left blank

INDEX

PAGE

A

B

C

D

E

F

G

H

I

J

L

M

N

O

P

R

S

T

U

V

W

Y

Z

www.ingramcontent.com/pod-product-compliance
Lightning Source LLC
LaVergne TN
LVHW060012210926
848481LV00013B/3690
* 9 7 8 0 9 9 8 3 8 5 3 8 9 *